TEXTBOOK OF BIOLOGICAL PSYCHIATRY

TEXTBOOK OF BIOLOGICAL PSYCHIATRY

Edited By

Jaak Panksepp, Ph.D.

J. P. Scott Center for Neuroscience, Mind and Behavior, Department of Psychology,
Bowling Green State University, Bowling Green, Ohio

and

Falk Center for Molecular Therapeutics, Department of Biomedical Engineering,
Northwestern University, Evanston, Illinois

and

Adjunct Professor of Psychiatry, Medical College of Ohio, Toledo

A JOHN WILEY & SONS, INC., PUBLICATION

Library of Congress Cataloging-in-Publication Data:

Textbook of biological psychiatry / edited by Jaak Panksepp.
     p. ; cm
Includes bibliographical references and index.
  ISBN 0-471-43478-7 (cloth : alk. paper)
  1. Biological psychiatry.
  [DNLM: 1. Biological Psychiatry. WM 102 T355 2004] I. Panksepp, Jaak, 1943-
  RC341.T438 2004
  616.89—dc21

                                         2003006225

CONTENTS

Part I   FOUNDATIONAL CONCEPTS   1

1   BIOLOGICAL PSYCHIATRY SKETCHED—PAST, PRESENT, AND FUTURE   3

Jaak Panksepp

2   IMAGING HUMAN EMOTIONS AND AFFECTIVE FEELINGS: IMPLICATIONS FOR BIOLOGICAL PSYCHIATRY   33

Mario Liotti and Jaak Panksepp

v

3 NEURAL SUBSTRATES OF CONSCIOUSNESS: IMPLICATIONS   75
FOR CLINICAL PSYCHIATRY

Douglas F. Watt and David I. Pincus

4 STRESS, SLEEP, AND SEXUALITY IN PSYCHIATRIC   111
DISORDERS

Terrence Deak and Jaak Panksepp

17 SOMATIC TREATMENTS IN PSYCHIATRY   521

Ziad Nahas, Jeffrey P. Lorberbaum, Frank A. Kozel, and Mark S. George

18 PSYCHOANALYSIS AND PSYCHOPHARMACOLOGY: ART AND SCIENCE OF COMBINING PARADIGMS   549

Marcia Kaplan

19 DEPTH PSYCHOLOGICAL CONSEQUENCES OF BRAIN DAMAGE   571

Oliver H. Turnbull and Mark Solms

20 SOCIOPHYSIOLOGY AND EVOLUTIONARY ASPECTS OF PSYCHIATRY

Russell Gardner, Jr. and Daniel R. Wilson

21 FUTURE OF NEUROPEPTIDES IN BIOLOGICAL PSYCHIATRY AND EMOTIONAL PSYCHOPHARMACOLOGY: GOALS AND STRATEGIES

Jaak Panksepp and Jaanus Harro

Appendix A PHARMACODYNAMICS AND PHARMACOKINETICS

Jaanus Harro

Index   683

FOREWORD

This is not the first attempt to integrate biology with human behavior and mental illness. The Bible attributes emotional and cognitive functions to heart, bowels, and kidneys. The ancients favored a humoral view of temperament (sanguine, phlegmatic, choleric, and melancholic). Over the ages the many attempts to treat mental illness have included physical and medicinal measures: purging, hydrotherapy, galvanic stimulation, and many other strange interventions, in the belief that doing something to the body would exorcise mental illness.

With the discovery of hormones, their effects on body, mind, and behavior—both normal and abnormal—were studied in the hope that they would be therapeutically useful. Early electroencephalographic investigation was expected to give us easy access to the functions of the brain and mind, but instead revealed disappointingly little information about mental illness and, in fact, about mental function in general. Only in the mid-20th century did Adolf Meyer promote a biological psychiatry that brought everything that was known to be relevant to mental health and illness to bear upon psychiatric diagnosis and treatment.

Sigmund Freud, who was best known for his original and perceptive insights into the psychology of mental illness, in fact maintained a consistent interest in biology. From the outset he argued that the same neural systems and functions that, in illness, give rise to the signs and symptoms of neurological disease, also bring about the signs and symptoms of mental illness. In 1891, Waldeyer gave final form to the neuron theory. Freud enthusiastically embraced it as a possible basis for what he called a "scientific psychology," resulting in an uncompleted work, later known as the Project for a Scientific Psychology. He abandoned that effort when he realized that it was a will o' the wisp, an illusory scheme, based on verbal constructs rather than neural mechanisms. Biological psychiatry, as it became fully biologized, has also abandoned many ambiguous mental constructs. Now a key challenge is how to bring those subtle attributes of the brain-mind, such as affects, into the neurobiological arena. One credible way is to try to link the visually observable instinctual apparatus of animals to affective processes.

Freud's concept of drive was closely aligned with the ethologic concept of instinct; he attributed qualities to the drive that resemble closely those commonly associated with instinct. He saw instinct as "a concept on the frontier between the mental and the somatic, . . . the psychical representative of the stimuli originating from within the organism and reaching the mind." (*Instinct and Their Vicissitudes*, 1915, p. 121–122, *Standard Edition*) Running like a red thread throughout his work was the concept of *energy*, which always remained poorly defined. That too was a border concept: On the one hand, it was psychic energy; on the other hand it anticipated that medications still to be discovered in 1939, the year of his final statement, would exert their therapeutic effect by influencing this psychic energy.

Early intimations of a direct relation between the brain and hallucinated images and emotions were disclosed by the studies of the effects of direct stimulation of the exposed human brain by Wilder Penfield and his disciples in the middle of the 20th century. Soon thereafter, psychedelic and other psychoactive drugs revealed a chemically based mental apparatus with which neither scientific psychiatry nor psychology has come to terms.

It was soon after World War II that modern neuroscientific studies were initiated and rapidly developed momentum. Applied neuroscience (i.e., psychopharmacology) exerted its initial impact on a clinical psychiatry that had yet to become fully biologized. Though they had been preceded by the barbiturates that, in their day, had proved very useful, the newer agents now exhibited antipsychotic and mood-correcting powers. When the possibility of affecting mental illness chemically became clear, the drug companies addressed the problem with their formidable resources and in rapid succession introduced new variants of the basic therapeutic agents. Although the psychiatric profession accepted and employed these medications enthusiastically, the early literature exhibited little interest in using psychopharmacologic experience as a point of entry for a neuroscience of mental illness. The amazing development of molecular neuropharmacology recently has catalyzed that coordination.

The present volume represents a landmark in this developing trend. Trained as a behavioral neuroscientist and psychologist, editor Jaak Panksepp is knowledgeable in the field of psychoanalysis and experienced in practical psychotherapy. He has actively pursued reliable knowledge about brain function in its relation to behavior through careful animal experiments. He proceeds from the assumption that affect is the central variable in human behavior, to which other features are secondary. His 1998 work, *Affective Neuroscience*, is becoming one of the scriptures of the third revolution in 21st-century psychiatry. I consider psychoanalytic psychiatry the first, psychopharmacologic psychiatry the second, and a functional neuroscientific psychiatry the third.

In *Affective Neuroscience*, Panksepp examined the several instinctual systems, their affective correlates, and the autonomic and physiologic systems that subserve them. The neurochemistries involved also provided points of correlation with established and potentially new pharmacologic strategies. His was a novel and original approach to human behavior that permitted clinicians like myself a view of the opportunities and the promise of the neuroscientific approach to psychiatry.

In this *Textbook of Biological Psychiatry*, Panksepp fulfills this promise. I draw the reader's attention especially to his introductory chapter in which he points the way to the elusive synthesis of studies of mind and brain, focusing on affect as the essential and functional link. This emphasis is both timely and ironic since affect had been remote from the central interest of both psychoanalysts and neuroscientists.

For this endeavor, he has assembled a group of scientists and clinicians and invited them to apply contemporary neuroscience to psychiatric issues. This coordination of Panksepp's persistence and brilliance along with the insights of his carefully selected collaborators will afford a new, practical understanding of biological psychiatry, at once imaginative and realistic.

Mortimer Ostow, M.D., Med. Sc. D.
President, Psychoanalytic Research and Development Fund

PREFACE

This work was initiated with the aim of bringing together the traditions that have helped create modern biological psychiatry. The hope was to craft a perspective that could help project our thinking fruitfully into the future. During the past few decades, we have learned to quantify normal and abnormal brain functions at a level of precision unimaginable just a generation ago. However, progress in biological psychiatry is also based on new theoretical perspectives, for it is only through theory that we can envision what may emerge on the horizon of knowledge. Of course, theory can also be a lens that distorts reality.

Our aim was to seek the middle ground—a balance of facts and theories, as well as consideration of both clinical and preclinical perspectives. My hope is that this text will be useful for students, teachers, and practitioners, as well as the scientists who harvest the basic knowledge from which future understanding must emerge. I owe a debt of gratitude to the many contributors who took precious time from their busy schedules to summarize the important themes covered in this book. The only regret I have is that space constraints made it impossible to treat all topics as fully as they deserve. Luna Han, the acquisition editor for this contribution, exhibited remarkable forebearance and did not outwardly waver in her faith that the project would reach completion in a reasonably timely manner. That proved to be a challenge for many.

A special word of gratitude goes to my wife Anesa who read and commented extensively on the entire text. Each of the chapters underwent at least one major revision to optimize style and coverage, and several underwent cycles of intellectual adventure for both the contributors and editors. But even where the needs of the book and the desires of authors briefly clashed, the middle road was eventually found. Jeff Burgdorf, Casey Cromwell, and Nikki Gordon also provided assistance at several critical phases of the project. I thank all for their contributions.

We wish to dedicate this text to the many pioneers, past and present, who have devoted their lives to understanding the normal and abnormal functions of the human mind. Many now appreciate that such a quest cannot be completed unless we also try to understand the brains and minds of other creatures. Indeed, some of the most interesting research on mind, brain, and behavioral relations has been emerging from animal research conducted in departments of psychiatry and neurology. This is a tradition in which all of the three giants—Emil Kraepelin, Adolf Meyer, and Sigmund Freud—to

XX

PREFACE

whom we dedicate this volume were immersed at some point in their illustrious careers. Their portraits are used with the permissions, respectively, of The University of Tartu Library, The Adolf Meyer Library of Medicine at Johns Hopkins University, and the Freud Archive, London.

Although each of these pioneers started with physiological and neurological interest, their intellectual paths eventually diverged. However, because of historical and intellectual circumstances that emerged during the 20th century (as summarized in Chapter 1), all hewed paths that made contributions to future efforts to blend mind, brain, and body perspectives to understanding mental disorders. The whole person is no less important that the dizzying arrays of parts of which he or she is composed. Below the surface features of mental phenomena are mechanisms with which we must become conversant in order to make progress, never forgetting that the emergent whole is greater than the parts. This book was constructed with such perspectives in mind, and thank everyone that contributed to this effort.

Jaak Panksepp
Falk Center for Molecular Therapeutics
J.P. Scott Center for Neuroscience, Mind and Behavior

Emil Kraepelin   Adolf Meyer   Sigmund Freud
(1856–1926)   (1866–1950)   (1856–1939)

Color images from this volume are available at ftp://ftp.wiley.com/public/sci_tech_med/biological_psychiatry/

CONTRIBUTORS

Fredric N. Busch, M.D., Department of Psychiatry, Weill Cornell Medical College, and Columbia University Center for Psychoanalytic Training and Research, New York, New York

Terrence Deak, Ph.D., Department of Psychology, SUNY–Binghamton, Binghamton, New York

Pedro L. Delgado, M.D., Department of Psychiatry, University Hospitals of Cleveland and Case Western Reserve University School of Medicine, Cleveland, Ohio

Russell Gardner, Jr., M.D., Department of Psychiatry, University of Wisconsin Medical School and Medical College of Wisconsin, Madison, Wisconsin; 214 DuRose Terrace, Madison, Wisconsin 53705

Mark S. George, M.D., Center for Advanced Imaging Research (CAIR), Radiology Department, Medical University of South Carolina, Charleston, South Carolina

Jaanus Harro, M.D., Ph.D., Department of Psychology, Center of Behavioral and Health Sciences, University of Tartu, Tartu, Estonia

Andreas Heinz, M.D., Clinic for Psychiatry and Psychotherapy, Humboldt University, Berlin, Germany

Michael D. Jibson, M.D., Ph.D., Department of Psychiatry, University of Michigan Medical Center, Ann Arbor, Michigan

Marcia Kaplan, M.D., Department of Clinical Psychiatry, University of Cincinnati College of Medicine, Cincinnati, Ohio

Shitij Kapur, M.D., FRCPC, Ph.D., Schizophrenia-PET Program, Center for Addiction and Mental Health, University of Toronto, Ontario, Canada

Amy Kieswetter, M.D., Department of Geriatric Psychiatry, Medical College of Ohio, Toledo, Ohio

Brian Kirkpatrick, Ph.D., Maryland Psychiatric Research Center, Department of Psychiatry, University of Maryland School of Medicine, Baltimore, Maryland

Nikolas Klein, M.D., Schizophrenia-PET Program, Center for Addiction and Mental Health, University of Toronto, Ontario, Canada

Brian Knutson, Ph.D., Department of Psychology, Stanford University, Stanford, California

Frank A. Kozel, M.D., Department of Psychiatry, Medical University of South Carolina, Charleston, South Carolina

Mario Liotti, Ph.D., Department of Psychiatry, University of Nottingham, Nottingham, United Kingdom

Jeffrey P. Lorberbaum, M.D., Department of Psychiatry and Behavioral Science, Medical University of South Carolina, Charleston, South Carolina

Helen S. Mayberg, M.D., Departments of Psychiatry and Medicine (Neurology), The Rotman Institute, University of Toronto, Ontario, Canada

A. John McSweeny, Ph.D., Department of Psychiatry, Medical College of Ohio, Toledo, Ohio

Barbara L. Milrod, M.D., Department of Psychiatry, Cornell University Medical College, New York, New York

Ziad Nahas, M.D., Brain Stimulation Laboratory, Medical University of South Carolina, Institute of Psychiatry, Charleston, South Carolina

Jaak Panksepp, Ph.D., Department of Psychology, Bowling Green State University, Bowling Green, Ohio and Falk Center of Molecular Therapeutics, Northwestern University, Evanston, Illinois

Christine Pesold, Ph.D., Department of Psychiatry, University of Illinois at Chicago, Chicago, Illinois

Bradley S. Peterson, M.D., Department of Psychiatry, Columbia College of Physicians and Surgeons and the New York State Psychiatric Institute, New York, New York

David I. Pincus, Ph.D., Department of Psychiatry, Case Western Reserve University School of Medicine, Cleveland, Ohio

Rosalinda C. Roberts, Ph.D., Maryland Psychiatric Research Center, Departments of Psychiatry, Anatomy, and Neurobiology, University of Maryland School of Medicine, Baltimore, Maryland

Lisa A. Snider, M.D., Pediatrics and Developmental Neuropsychiatry Branch, National Institute of Mental Health, Bethesda, Maryland

Mark Solms, Ph.D., Department of Psychology, University College of London, United Kingdom, and Department of Psychology, University of Cape Town, South Africa

Susan E. Swedo, M.D., Pediatrics and Developmental Neuropsychiatry Branch, National Institute of Mental Health, Bethesda, Maryland

Rajiv Tandon, M.D., Department of Psychiatry, University of Michigan Medical Center, Ann Arbor, Michigan

Johannes Tauscher, M.D., Department of General Psychiatry, University of Vienna, Austria

Oliver H. Turnbull, Ph.D., School of Psychology, University of Wales, Bangor, United Kingdom

Bessel A. van der Kolk, M.D., Department of Psychiatry, Boston University School of Medicine, Boston, Massachusetts

Douglas F. Watt, Ph.D., Department of Neuropsychology, Quincy Medical Center, Boston University School of Medicine, Quincy, Massachusetts

Daniel R. Wilson, M.D., Ph.D., Departments of Psychiatry and Anthropology, Creighton University School of Medicine, Omaha, Nebraska

Mark T. Wright, M.D., Department of Psychiatry, Medical College of Ohio, Toledo, Ohio

Paul Zarkowski, M.D., Department of Psychiatry, University Hospitals of Cleveland and Case Western Reserve University School of Medicine, Cleveland, Ohio

Part I

FOUNDATIONAL CONCEPTS

The background topics relevant to psychiatric disorders in biological terms is vast and typically includes neuroanatomy, neurophysiology, and neurochemistry. Since such approaches are remarkably well represented in various recent handbooks, and typically all substantive neuroscience courses, one more redundant effort in that direction would not be all that useful. Accordingly, we have used the limited space available to focus on topics that are more intimately related to psychological issues—the nature of emotionality, consciousness, stress, personality, and the brain imaging technologies that have changed the face of psychiatry in the past decade.

This decision was also fostered by the recognition that we have finally reached an era where the mind-brain barrier is beginning to dissolve. Although there are many ambiguities about what we may mean when we talk about "the mind," most generous scholars accept that the dynamics of mind ride upon the dynamics of the brain, and we now know that for any psychotherapy to work, it must influence brain functions (Cozolino, 2002). Empirical demonstrations of this concept are growing rapidly, ever since Baxter and colleagues (1989) demonstrated that cognitive behavioral therapy could reduce the frontal cortical overactivity in obsessive-compulsive disorders. A few years ago the *Archives of General Psychiatry* published two back-to-back lead articles on how interpersonal therapy modified brain activities of depressed individuals in ways resembling those of modern serotonin-specific antidepressants (Brody et al., 2001; Martin, 2001).

Textbook of Biological Psychiatry, Edited by Jaak Panksepp
ISBN 0-471-43478-7   Copyright © 2004 John Wiley & Sons, Inc.

Daniel J. Stern said it well in the foreword to Cozolino's (2002) treatise on the *Neuroscience of Psychotherapy*, as he indicated that clinicians immerse themselves "in the stories of individuals who come for help in feeling better.... Whatever the approach, lasting change in therapy occurs as a result of changes in the human mind... which involve changes in the functions of the brain. Exactly how the mind changes during the therapeutic process is the fundamental puzzle that the synthesis of neuroscience and psychotherapy seeks to solve" (p. ix). Stern emphasized the difficult but productive marriage between clinical and neuroscientific disciplines, highlighting how "psychotherapy emphasizes the importance of *subjective* experience and the power of relationships to transform the growing mind" while "neuroscience focuses on quantifiable, *objective* data and the scientific method to create models of mind and brain" (p. x). The interpenetration of neuroscientific knowledge and psychiatric practice is becoming much more than the impressive recitation of the great victories of the neuroscience revolution of the past half century. We are finally seeing, in many experimental domains, how subjective psychological processes are related to a demonstrable impact on the objective dynamics of the brain.

The first half dozen chapters of this text attempt to bridge between the clinical and scientific issues. To do this, we have to blend the fine and abundant evidence that is being derived from rather indirect studies of the human brain/mind and the detailed knowledge about brain functions we can cull from our fellow creatures, who also live emotional lives that deserve our close attention and sympathy. These subtle issues, such as the fundamental neural nature of affective experiences, need to be discussed not only in neural terms, but also in terms of the evolved substrates and qualities of consciousness. The logo of this book reflects this philosophy of recognizing that the multiple layers of brain/mind evolution are reflected in the evolutionary passages which serve as a foundation for the human mind.

REFERENCES

Baxter RL, Schwartz JM, Phelps ME, et al. (1989). Reduction of prefrontal cortex glucose metabolism common to three types of depression. *Arch Gen Psychiatry* 46:243–250.

Brody AL, Saxena S, Stoessel P (2001). Regional brain metabolic changes in patients with major depression treated with either paroxetine or interpersonal therapy. *Arch Gen Psychiatry* 58:631–640.

Cozolino L (2002). *The Neuroscience of Psychotherapy: Building and Rebuilding the Human Brain*. W.W. Norton: New York.

Martin SD (2001). Brain blood flow changes in depressed patients treated with interpersonal therapy or venlafaxine hydrochloride. *Arch Gen Psychiatry* 58:641–648.

BIOLOGICAL PSYCHIATRY SKETCHED—PAST, PRESENT, AND FUTURE

Jaak Panksepp

J.P. Scott Center for Neuroscience Mind & Behavior, Department of Psychology, Bowling Green State University, Bowling Green, Ohio

OVERTURE

It is a difficult task to capture the history of biological psychiatry in a brief essay. Let me frame this modest effort in a timeless humanistic perspective.

Psychiatry is the study and treatment of troubled mental lives. Its ultimate goal is to heal broken spirits. At its core, it is an attempt to better understand human thoughts and emotions and to allow this understanding to inform the healing arts. Despite our modern scientific hubris, we know rather little about how brains truly construct our minds and passions. Partly, this is because few scholars have come to terms with the need to understand the evolutionary neural dynamics that affective experiences are ultimately made of. It is all too easy to accept emotions as primitive "givens" and proceed toward a superficial understanding based on words, arbitrary definitions, and the quiddities of logic rather than biology. But the greater and more significant

Textbook of Biological Psychiatry, Edited by Jaak Panksepp
ISBN 0-471-43478-7 Copyright © 2004 John Wiley & Sons, Inc.

depths of this mystery have to be plumbed by an integrative neuroscience that has barely emerged.

It is surely not off the mark to claim that the single most important scientific question for biological psychiatry is the accurate decoding of the basic neural nature of affective values and related cognitive experiences. Emotions and moods guide most of our thinking processes and behavioral choices, whether well-arranged or deranged. Many psychopathologies arise from imbalances in these feeling systems that motivate us to think and act in certain ways. At a deep psychological level, that often goes unspoken, emotionally disturbed people have some insight into the weaknesses of their minds. They simply don't know how to manage their persistent psychic disequilibrium. They are certainly no more accustomed to thinking about these psychic forces in neural terms than are the counselors and psychotherapists from whom they seek assistance.

Taxonomic schemes that do not directly acknowledge the underlying emotional faculties of the human mind and brain must be deemed provisional approximations of the goals to which we should aspire. Brain sciences that do not acknowledge or attempt to explore how such processes motivate and guide thinking do no great service to psychiatric thought. Mind sciences that do not dwell on the complexity of the internal world, replete with all manner of feelings and cognitions, do not serve our understanding well. The cognitive, behavioral, and affective sciences must devote equal effort to understanding the embeddedness of mind in brain, body, environment, and culture; otherwise essential components will be overlooked. Only by blending these perspectives judiciously, without inflaming simple-minded polarities such as nurture versus nature, is psychiatric practice well served.

By the end of the 20th century neuroscience had advanced to a point where we now understand the brain rather well. Unfortunately, the discussion of equally important, but more slippery, mind matters continues to lag far behind. Credibly linking facts about the brain to mental functions is maddeningly difficult. There are few incentives in our current system for integrating the abundant peppercorns of brain data into an integrated psychobiological understanding. A prevailing positivistic hope has been that knowledge will emerge automatically from the raw facts like cream rising from freshly expelled milk. To an undesirable degree, theoretical views have been demoted to second-class citizenship. Accordingly, rich discussions of many key functional issues almost disappeared in neuroscience as it mastered how to milk our neural nature during the last third of the 20th century. Indeed, the very concept of productive hypothesizing came to be termed, scornfully, as "mere speculation," perhaps because too many students of the mind (and certainly too many science popularizers) forgot the difference between a "working hypothesis" and a "provisional conclusion." Major textbooks of biological psychiatry and neuropsychiatry no longer discuss emotions prominently. Some consider them needless frills that intervene between reliable diagnostic categories and descriptions of related brain changes. Often, there is little tolerance for such "middle-level" theorizing that seeks to meaningfully link brain functions with mind. One aim of this text is to reverse this trend.

Thus, I proceeded to this historical sketch with several common but oft-neglected preoccupations that continue to trouble modern psychiatric thought. How are the passions of the mind truly created? How do they become overwhelming? How can mere words help heal minds? What is the healing touch? Why are character traits so important in healers as well as patients? What is the proper role of placebos in the therapeutic enterprise? Are our diagnostic categories as sound as they could be? Such concerns led me to encourage all contributors to this book to consider the central role of thought and emotions in psychiatrically significant disturbances of the psyche. My own bias is that the next great frontier in biological psychiatry is the topic that has been most neglected by modern neuroscience—the deep neurobiological nature of affective experiences. Even though our understanding of such key issues remains woefully incomplete, we must continue to share the harvest of knowledge we already have, and thereby fertilize the field, once more, so that those who come after us are better prepared to contend with the perennial joys and difficulties of mental existence.

HISTORICAL OVERVIEW

Although human interest in the nature of the mind and its passions surely goes back to a time long before the beginning of recorded history, the systematic scientific search for the causes of psychological disorders did not begin in earnest until the latter part of the 19th century. Prior to that, the practice of psychiatry was characterized more by superstition and punishment, punctuated by occasional humane concerns. Although there were several sustained periods of enlightened care of the emotionally distraught, as in the ritual purification (i.e., "incubation" or rest therapy) approaches of the Grecian period, it is likely that one of the main functions of those whole-body, whole-mind efforts—which included athletics, baths, music, dance, and ritualized sexual encounters—was the alleviation of everyday stress and sexual inadequacy. The holistic cures of those healing temples, organized symbolically under the aegis of Asclepius, the god of health, thrived for well over a millennium, but surely the stigmatization and brutalization of serious mental ailments also remained abundant yet uncelebrated. While a humanistic tradition was sustained in many middle eastern countries, Europe succumbed to the flea-ridden plagues and narrow-mindedness of the Dark Ages for an extended period, in which harsh punishments and the demonizing of nonstandard human souls prevailed [for a more detailed historical coverage, see Andreasen (2001), Mora (1985) and Stone (1997)].

Most biological approaches to treating mental ailments during the past several thousand years have been based on unsubstantiated beliefs and wild logic rather than scientific substance. Beatings, bleedings, starvation, hot and cold water shock treatments, and restraints have all been time-tested therapeutic failures, at least in the long-term. However, various socially sustained and often effective placebo approaches have often flourished, including witch-doctoring, shamanism, and occasional trepanations of skulls to release evil spirits. Apparently our social brains respond quite well to the sympathetic concerns of others, which may be the foundation of all pervasive placebo effects in psychiatry (Harrington 1999; Moerman 2002; Shapiro and Shapiro 2001). Of course, we now know that placebo effects have real effects on the brain (Mayberg et al., 2002), perhaps brain opioid mediated (Petrovic et al., 2002), and the intervening prosocial feelings may be mediated, in part, by endogenous opioids (Panksepp, 1998).

A few revolutionaries also made substantive biomedical advances. Paracelsus (1493–1541) enthusiastically promoted one of the few effective medicines available in his time (e.g., opioids), and in *Diseases Which Deprive Man of His Reason* (1567), he described many alchemical concoctions, some of which contained heavy metals such as mercury. We now know that some of these toxic agents can help purge the body of certain psychopathological vectors, one of which was recognized as *Treponema pallidum* in 1906—the agent responsible for causing syphilis and its resulting schizophreniform mental deteriorations. Unfortunately, the safety margin between the effective doses and lethal doses was not auspicious. The eventual discovery that induction of fevers could sometimes halt syphilis-induced mental deterioration was honored with Nobel recognition (Laureate Julius Wagner-Jauregg, 1927) for the "discovery of the therapeutic value of malaria inoculation in the treatment of dementia paralytica" (Jasper, 1983).

With the emergence of the scientific tradition in the physical sciences, enlightened thinkers sought to approach human psychological problems with a new sensitivity. Benjamin Rush (1745–1813) in America, along with Phillipe Pinel (1745–1826) in France, and Vincenzo Chiarugi (1759–1820) in Italy, set in motion the "moral treatment" of the insane, even though some also advocated somatic treatments: Benjamin Rush promoted bloodletting, emetics, purges, special diets, and his agitation-constraining, straight-jacket "tranquilizing chair," while Benjamin Franklin promoted electrical therapy for various ailments. These revolutionaries helped establish havens for the mentally ill in small humanistic hospitals where they sought to create therapeutic environments that aimed to facilitate the reestablishment of emotional homeostasis. The movement was sustained and amplified by social activists such as Dorothea Dix (1802–1887). Sadly, by the end of the 19th century this model had devolved in America into the massive warehousing of cognitively and emotionally impaired individuals in large state-run institutions.

Meanwhile, with the growth of scientific physiology and biochemistry throughout the latter half of the 19th century, especially in German universities, neuropsychiatry became integrated into the standard biologically oriented medical curriculum. Indeed, modern psychiatry emerged from the successes of neurology, and the hybrid subdiscipline of neuropsychiatry still thrives (Yudofsky and Hales, 1997). However, a clear division of duties also developed—classical neurologists came to focus on standard brain abilities (i.e., sensations, perceptions, actions, and only more recently cognitive activities) while psychiatrists occupied themselves more with how people feel and how they impulsively react and choose to behave on the basis of their internal passions and other affectively experienced value systems.

Thus, the two sister disciplines, neurology and psychiatry, also commonly deal with different parts of the nervous system, the former with the somatic components and the other more with the visceral components. Theodore Meynert's 1884 textbook *Psychiatry: A Clinical Treatise on the Diseases of the Forebrain* was prescient in this regard. Since then, it has become increasingly clear that emotional regulation and psychiatric diseases are related more to frontal-limbic executive functions than to posterior cortico-thalamic, sensory-intellectual functions. Parenthetically, Meynert was one of Freud's esteemed teachers, and even after he abandoned brain approaches, Freud continued to acknowledge that his wide-ranging psychoanalytic theories eventually needed to be linked to neuroscience. He recognized that what might eventually grow from that potentially fertile hybridization could be spectacular. As Freud noted in *Beyond the Pleasure Principle* (1920, p. 60): "Biology is truly a land of unlimited possibilities. We may expect it to give us the most surprising information, and we cannot guess what answers it will return in a few dozen years.... They may be of a kind which will blow away the whole of our artificial structure of hypotheses." And by the end of the 20th century, his premonitions had come true to such a degree that his own conceptual ideas also seemed to be blown away, or so it seemed to many who had become disenchanted with the possibility of scientifically understanding the "mental apparatus." However, there are recent indications of resurgent interest in the relations between brain and depth psychological issues in the newly emerging neuropsychoanalytic movement (Solms and Turnbull, 2002), which seeks to build substantively on past and present discoveries.

THREE GIANTS OF THE FIRST HALF OF THE 20TH CENTURY

The three pioneers who set the stage for thinking throughout the modern phase of 20th-century psychiatry were Emil Kraepelin (1855–1926) in Germany, Sigmund Freud (1856–1939) in Austria, and Adolph Meyer (1866–1950) in America. The influence of Kraepelin's perspective, derived from the successes of German neurology, has been most pervasive, yielding a lasting influence on our conceptualization of what a comprehensive psychiatry should look like. Kraepelin, now widely regarded as the titular father of biological psychiatry, started his academic work at Dorpat University at the edge of the German empire of medical science (now the University of Tartu, Estonia), where he wrote the first edition of his seminal *Textbook of Psychiatry*, which went through nine editions between 1883 and 1927. That contribution propelled him to Heidelberg and ultimately to Munich as the implicit leader of German psychiatry. Recognition of his seminal diagnostic and pathophysiological thinking remained widespread from the latter half of the 19th century until World War I shattered the vigorous beginnings of biological psychiatry.

Still, Kraepelin had laid the essential foundations, and his approach continues to symbolically represent how scientific psychiatry should proceed [his influence is still especially clear in Axis I diagnostics of the *Diagnostic and Statistical Manual of Mental Disorders, Fourth Edition*, (DSM-IV)]. He recognized that progress had to be based on systematic cross-sectional and longitudinal clinical observations, leading to diagnostic systematics. He recruited all possible varieties of objective measures including behavioral and cognitive as well as neurological and biochemical, to achieve the most comprehensive understanding possible in his day. Through his desire to reach a full appreciation of the organic underpinnings of pathological processes, Kraepelin gathered around him a remarkable group of talented neuroscientists who also became luminaries, such as Alois Alzheimer, Korbinian Brodmann, and Franz Nissl.

Concurrently, Sigmund Freud was abandoning his early emphasis with neurological approaches to the mind, including experimentation with drugs such as cocaine for the treatment of opiate addiction, and was setting in motion a dynamic depth psychology that eventually captivated American psychiatry. Unfortunately, Freud's psychodynamic approach, which revolutionized our views of how the mind operates with many unconscious "instinctual" dimensions and urges, did not foster a robust scientific movement to properly evaluate his own blossoming ideas. That, of course, would have been impossible in his day. Initial theory was built upon rather limited clinical observations, and then theoretical constructs were built upon other theoretical constructs, with no clear empirical operationalization or organic foundations. In the opinion of many, the resulting structure ultimately resembled a Tower of Babel, where one could not readily sift the good ideas from the bad. Freud's thesis that most psychiatric problems arose simply from psychological causes has now been largely abandoned in psychiatry, even though it is accepted that childhood trauma is a powerful neurobiological factor in disrupting mental homeostasis (Chapter 4; Heim and Nemeroff, 1999). Pathogenesis is now more commonly discussed in strictly organic terms, or at the very least in terms of psychological factors that are linked to neural substrates (Chapters 6, 7, and 8).

A new chapter in modern psychiatry opened when Adolf Meyer came to America from Switzerland in 1894, moving to Johns Hopkins School of Medicine in 1910, where, under his leadership, the university became the leading psychiatric training center in the world. He established a utilitarian psychobiological tradition in American psychiatry, which consisted of a multidimensional and systematic confrontation with patient's lives. He helped revolutionize the careful documenting of life histories and acknowledged the many psychological and biological themes that must go into the treatment of each emotionally troubled person. He emphasized the fact that all patients are unique and that one should consider all aspects of their lives in a careful workup of the individual's psychological status. His analysis of case studies led to the recognition that the systematic harvesting of certain types of personal information could make a real difference in the care and prognosis of patients. He aspired to recruit all relevant aspects into multimodal treatment approaches that suited individuals' abilities and aspirations. This holistic approach set the stage for the emergence of a uniquely American psychiatry.

The intersecting ideas and approaches of these giants permeated 20th-century psychiatry, but their different viewpoints also led to cross currents that remain to be resolved in a satisfactory synthesis to the present day. Partly this is due to the discovery of potent and highly effective drug therapies that swept most other approaches from the scene. However, with the gradual recognition that these remarkable phar-macological advances are not the comprehensive, long-term panaceas they initially seemed to be, a consensus is once again emerging that complex systems such as the brain/mind require multiple avenues of study. One aim of this text is to promote that consensus and to help forge a greater recognition that a neuroscientific understanding of the fundamental nature of affect is an essential ingredient for future progress in psychotherapeutic practice and drug development. The brain does contain an evolved *mental apparatus*, and future progress will depend on how well we penetrate into the functional tangle of the nervous system (Chapter 20). We now know this will require a judicious blend of human and animal behavioral, brain, and mind sciences.

THREE GREAT PHASES OF 20TH-CENTURY AMERICAN PSYCHIATRY

Following the decline of German medical influence in 1914, the progression of 20th-century psychiatry emerged largely on the Anglo-American scene, at least until the most recent psychopharmacological era when new agents were discovered, around the world, to have more remarkable and specific effects on the psyche than anything discovered since morphine and cocaine. This history can be conveniently broken down into three phases of about three decades each, with the Kraepelinian approach to diagnostics and pathophysiology providing a sustained background theme for all. His systematics matured when effective medicines were discovered to treat most major disorders—with the advent of powerful medications for the treatment of schizophrenia, depression, mania, and anxiety in the 1950s. It remains controversial how much each phase advanced the field relative to the ones that preceded it. Nonetheless, each period was distinctive, reflecting, perhaps, an evolving progression of scientific understanding fraught with essential growing pains. Future progress will arise from a weaving of these strands into a whole cloth that does not yet exist.

ABOUT 1910–1940: THE MEYERIAN SYNTHESIS OF A HOLISTIC PSYCHOBIOLOGY

Adolf Meyer, from his base at Johns Hopkins, developed a well-organized "mental hygiene" approach to the treatment of the whole person. He recognized certain essen-tials of well-rounded psychiatric practice, centered on comprehensive life histories in which one could see the many factors contributing to psychiatric disorders. Each patient was seen as a unique individual who deserved to be treated in highly indi-vidualized ways. Pressure to pigeon-hole people into diagnostic categories was not as important as the humane multimodal facilitation of lives that had been derailed. This era could also be seen as the humanistic era of American psychiatry. Psychopathology was recognized as a response to serious life events: When terrible things happened to people, their resources to cope were compromised. Meyer's approach to a com-prehensive mental status examination is still emulated today. Even if such extensive information is no longer as coherently incorporated into the care and prognosis of troubled lives, it remains an important way of knowing patients as individuals.

The Meyerian approach also fostered research into basic biological processes related to self-regulation. One of the pioneers was Kurt Richter at Johns Hopkins who pursued superlative animal research on feeding behavior, sleep, and circadian cycles (Slavney and McHugh, 1998). The hope was that such research could shed light on human issues that needed to be understood in some causal detail in order to effectively modify the underlying biological substrates. The support of basic animal research in many modern psychiatry departments correctly continues to be regarded as a cornerstone for future progress. The recognition that there is abundant natural variability of such underlying homeostatic processes, has also fostered dimensional views of mental illness (now recognized in Axis II diagnostics of DSM-IV). The work of Meyer and others suggested that troubled people should not simply be placed in diagnostic categories; rather their various dimensions need to be viewed through the lens of qualitative life histories reflecting temperamental strengths and weaknesses. With the completion of the Human Genome Project, and the recognition of deep homologies in the brain systems of all mammals, the role of genes and evolution in the governance of personality and developmental disorders is increasingly recognized (Chapters 5, 14, and 21).

WORLD WAR II THROUGH THE 1970s: THE PSYCHOANALYTIC ERA

Although psychoanalytic ideas have been percolating in American psychology since Freud and Jung's visit to Clark University in 1909, the full impact of depth psychology on psychiatry had to await the massive exodus of psychoanalysts to England and America with the onslaught of World War II. As these energetic immigrants captivated American psychiatry with remarkable speed, there was a dramatic shift toward the psychodynamics of the mental apparatus, as well as the controversy that still surrounds "talking cures." The overconfidence of this revolution, especially in the often successful treatment of war-trauma-induced neuroses, allowed new approaches such as clinical psychology to become established as a distinct discipline, along with the resulting proliferation of new psychotherapeutic ideas. Although we now recognize that certain psychotherapies can modify the executive functions of the brain concentrated primarily in frontal lobe areas (Baxter et al., 1992; Schwartz et al., 1996), the precise factors that promote such changes remain ambiguous. It is increasingly realized that the personal emotional qualities of a therapist are commonly more important than the specific psychotherapeutic approaches he or she employs (Beutler et al., 1994). Despite the bleak overall results of scientifically rigorous outcome studies of psychoanalytic therapies (MacMillan) 1997, this era firmly established a respect for the internal dynamics of the human mind within psychiatric practice.

Indeed, Eric Kandel (Nobel Prize, 2000), a psychiatrist who devoted his professional life to the neuroscience of basic memory processes in sea slugs in the hope of deriving general principles that would translate to humans (Kandel 2001), noted that "psychoanalysis still represents the most coherent and intellectually satisfying view of the mind that we have" (Kandel, 1999, p. 505). This comment probably speaks as much to the sheer creative richness of psychoanalytic thought as to the difficulty of developing a modern psychiatry that is based on adequate neuroscientific conceptions of the mind.

This middle era, with its shift of focus from studying the whole person to the nature of the drives and libidinal states of the mind, failed scientifically because it did not promote a solid research agenda. Likewise, the lack of replicable clinical results led to the decline of this untested (and some say untestable) theory of the mind and its influence on mainstream psychiatry, especially as pharmacological approaches were beginning to yield robust and replicable therapeutic effects.

This may again change as a new generation of scholars begins to blend neuro-science and depth psychological studies (Solms and Turnbull, 2002; Chapter 19) where mental and neuroscientific issues can be judiciously blended. The new armamentarium of brain manipulations and objective measurement tools presently offers the possibil-ity of a renaissance for depth psychological approaches to the brain/mind (Panksepp, 1999). Whether a sustained era of penetrating "psychoethological" research will arise from the emerging neuropsychoanalytic synthesis remains to be seen, but if it does, it will only be because of the positivistic and pragmatic phase of neuroscientifically informed psychiatric research of the past 30 years.

Before turning to modern biological psychiatry, it is worth noting that the mid-dle, psychoanalytic era, with its neglect of robust research agendas, allowed mere ideas, often endlessly debatable, too much influence on psychiatric thought. In a sense, this was also a "magical fantasy" era. Dramatic new somatic therapies, based on marginal research findings, flourished. Perhaps the Reichian concept of libidinal "orgone energy" and the resulting "orgone box" (to concentrate that "energy") could be taken as symbolic of this era: Willhelm Reich (1897–1957), whose own mental sta-bility was eventually questioned, was convicted of fraudulent claims and died during his incarceration in a federal penitentiary. Others, like Bruno Bettelheim, generated needless guilt with concepts such as "refrigerator mothering," which allegedly was instrumental in causing early childhood autism. It took many years for that needless "guilt trip" to become an embarrassment to the discipline (e.g., Pollak, 1997).

This period also introduced radical manipulations such as metrazol and insulin-induced seizures for treatment of schizophrenia and depression. Occasional successes gradually led to the highly effective and standardized electroconvulsive shock treat-ment for depression (Chapters 8 and 17), but there were casualties along the way. This era of radical experimentation was capped by the most controversial treatment of all, psychosurgery (for critical overview, see Valenstein, 1973). With the wisdom of hindsight, it is all too easy to criticize these approaches, but perhaps they are under-standable from a historical perspective. We should acknowledge that they sprang from understandable motives, given the historical times they were advanced. That was an era when many groups routinely inflicted incomprehensible harm on their fellow human beings—from the fields of Siberia, the ovens of Auschwitz, and "labs" of Dachau to the infection of impoverished Americans with syphilis—all in the name of political and cultural dogma and undisciplined curiosity. It was also a time when there were few predictably effective treatments, with morphine still being very high on the list of short-term panaceas. The hospitals were full of desperately debilitated patients. Hence the field was grasping at straws, whether psychic or somatic, and the scalpels of the time were aimed directly for frontal lobes—the executive seats of human imagination, acquired valuations, and creativity (Valenstein, 1973).

Since such drastic interventions worked "adequately" in a sufficiently large number of people (at least for management purposes), it was recognized that something of importance was happening to the homeostatic imbalances of the deranged brain/mind. Indeed, the final restricted target of psychosurgical interventions, the ventromedial quadrant of the frontal lobes, is now recognized as a hotbed of emotion–cognition interactions (Rolls, 1999). What really happens in the brain/mind as a result of these powerful somatic interventions required the advent of modern neuroscience and a neurochemical understanding of the brain that eventually permeated psychiatry.

ULTRAPOSITIVISTIC PSYCHOPHARMACOLOGY ERA (1970–PRESENT)

Modern biological psychiatry started in 1952 when the French psychiatrists Jean Delay and Pierre Deniker first evaluated the efficacy of chlorpromazine (trade name Thorazine) in a variety of psychiatric disorders and found it to be highly effective for ameliorating schizophrenic symptoms. This breakthrough was based on the recent discovery of surgeon Henri Laborit that such drugs were effective presurgical sedatives, and also potentially effective in controlling the agitation of various psychiatric disorders including schizophrenia. The robust calming effects and specific reductions in the positive symptoms of schizophrenia (e.g., delusions, hallucinations, and inappropriate moods) were so impressive that the use of chlorpromazine swept through psychiatry. The number of schizophrenics that had to be chronically institutionalized diminished precipitously as soon as these agents came into widespread use.

With the recognition that one of the main targets of these agents were recently characterized dopamine systems of the brain (Arvid Carlsson, 2001, Nobel Prize in 2000), and the discovery of the various receptor molecules for dopamine transmitters, the specificity and potency of antipsychotics were honed by creative pharmacologists such as Paul Janssen in Belgium (discoverer of haloperidol, or Haldol, and also risperidone, or Risperdal). This led to our current array of atypical antipsychotics (Chapter 10), which can also alleviate some of the negative symptoms of schizophrenia (the anhedonic flattening of affect, the social isolation, and cognitive impairments often characterized as "formal thought disorders"). These newer drugs also have the advantage of few troublesome long-term side effects such as motor dyskinesias that consistently emerged after long-term treatment with the earlier, more potent anti-dopaminergic antipsychotics. Within a few years of the discovery of chlorpromazine, antidepressants were developed, on the heels of the serendipitous discovery that certain drugs for tuberculosis gave many patients extra enthusiasm and psychic energy [the monoamine oxidase (MAO) inhibitor isoniazid and iproniazid].

Other molecules (e.g., the tricyclic imipramine) were soon discovered to be effective in treating depressive disorders and eventually panic attacks (Klein and Rabkin,

1981). With advances in neurochemistry, the two types of antidepressant effects were narrowed to classes of molecules that could inhibit MAO or block reuptake of synaptically released biogenic amines, especially of norepinephrine and serotonin (Julius Axelrod, Nobel Prize in 1970 for "discoveries concerning the humoral transmitters in the nerve terminals and the mechanism for their storage, release, and inactivation"). This eventually led to increasingly specific agents, until we now have an abundance of selective serotonin reuptake inhibitors (SSRIs) that effectively stabilize a variety of Axis I as well as some Axis II disorders (Chapter 8), with few troublesome side effects (except for occasional emotional numbing and diminished pleasure responses such as anorgasmia). Still the long-term therapeutic mechanisms remain uncertain.

Various benzodiazepine antianxiety agents came into use in the 1960s, directly developed from preclinical animal studies that initially observed sedation and antiaggressive effects with chlordizepoxide (Librium). At this same time, the even earlier preclinical and clinical work on lithium by John Cade (1949) in Australia was gradually crafted into a treatment for manic-depressive disorders by Mogens Schou (1992) in Denmark.

These great passages of the psychopharmacology revolution have been retold many times, but never as comprehensively as in the excellent three-volume series entitled *The Psychopharmacologists* by David Healy (1996, 1998, 2000). The history of this fascinating era is detailed through a series of personal interviews with the main protagonists of the biological psychiatry revolution. In those first-person accounts, the reader can try to sort out the many controversies, linkages between lines of thought and battles over priority.

The clinical successes of the 1950s rapidly led to the characterization of various neurochemical systems in the brain [especially of acetylcholine, dopamine, norepinephrine, serotonin, and gamma-aminobutyric acid (GABA)] and the emergence of preclinical psychopharmacology disciplines that sought to characterize how these drugs operated (for summaries, see Charney et al., 1999; D'Haenen et al., 2002). It became routine to evaluate all new molecules in animals, often with classical behaviorist techniques that were not based on any theoretically coherent ideas about how psychobehavioral systems might be organized in the brain. Indeed, the behaviorists who became "opinion leaders" in pharmaceutical firms, had an active dislike of psychological theorizing and often of the brain itself. Inputs and outputs were deemed more important than the brain/mind matters that intervened.

Cranking out simple positivistic drug behavior relationships was deemed of sufficient predictive power to guide drug development. Eventually, when techniques for measuring receptor binding kinetics were developed, one could utilize test-tube assays to predict the efficacy of psychotropic agents (Snyder, 1980). Many researchers concluded it was unnecessary to worry much about psychological constructs in generating medications that could effectively treat mental disorders. An atheoretical study of input-output relations sufficed, and thus we still know little about how most of the psychiatric medicines in common use help create mental environments that are conducive to therapeutic change. This has been common in medicine where serendipitous practical advances often precede any substantive understanding.

Most of the successes of biological psychiatry have arisen from our ability to manipulate just a few neurochemical systems (Fig. 1.1). This is now understandable. There exist a limited number of "state-control" neurochemical systems that arise from discrete brainstem nuclei and ramify widely in the brain, affecting many mind functions in fairly predictable ways: catecholamines such as norepinephrine (NE) and dopamine (DA) facilitate information transmission and energize affective responses (both positive and negative), and serotonin systems generally diminish and narrow the lines of information transmission, thereby perhaps decreasing the acute effects of both negative and positive instinctual and cognitive urges. The GABA system operates through much more widely dispersed clusters of small interneurons (as well as a few long axoned pathways) to generally dampen the arousability of the brain. Hence facilitation of GABA can have striking effects on various types of overarousal ranging from anxiety to epilepsy. A brief synopsis of the biological psychiatry revolution would look approximately like this (adapted from Panksepp, 1998, p. 117):

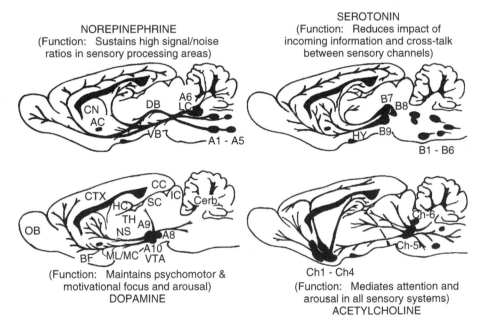

Figure 1.1. Parasagittal depiction of the dispersion of biogenic amine [dopamine (DA), norepinephrine (NE) and serotonin] and acetylcholine systems in the rat brain. LC, locus coeruleus; DB, dorsal NE bundle; VB, ventral NE bundle; CN, caudate nucleus; AC, anterior commissure; OB, olfactory bulb; CTX, cortex; BG, basal forebrain; HC, hippocampus; TH, thalamus; SC, superior colliculus; IC, inferior colliculus; NS, nigrostriatal DA pathway; ML/MC, mesolimbic and mesocortical DA pathways; HY, hypothalamus. "A" designations indicate major NE and DA cell groups; "B" designations indicate major serotonin/raphe cell groups; "CH" designations indicate major cholinergic cell groups. [This figure is reprinted from Panksepp (1998), *Affective Neuroscience*, with the permission of Oxford University Press.]

'Of the drugs currently used to alleviate depression, some prolong the synaptic availability of biogenic amine transmitters, while others slow degradation. In the former class are the many tricyclic antidepressants that can inhibit norepinephrine, serotonin, or dopamine reuptake at synapses. More recently, other specific reuptake inhibitors have been developed, perhaps the most famous being the SSRIs. Representatives of the other major class of drugs inhibit the enzyme monoamine oxidase (MAO) that normally helps degrade biogenic amines following release. MAO inhibitors are less commonly used than the reuptake inhibitors because they have more side effects, such as the increased toxicity of certain foods that are high in the amino acid tyramine. However, recent developments (e.g., discovery of several forms of MAO in the brain) have yielded some safer and more specific drugs of that class. Some of them, such as phenelzine, are also quite effective for other disorders, such as "social phobias," the strong discomfort that some people feel during social interactions.

The class of drugs known as antipsychotics generally dampens DA activity. Since there are several different DA receptors, modern work has sought to more specifically target the D_2 receptors, which are present in abnormally high quantities in the schizophrenic brain. Most antipsychotics are receptor blockers, which means that they prevent dopamine from having normal physiological interactions with its receptor. Other drugs that stimulate receptors are called agonists; such drugs can promote schizophrenic symptoms. For instance, the indirect agonists such as cocaine and amphetamines can induce sufficiently strong paranoid symptoms that psychiatrists have difficulty distinguishing them from the real thing.

Most modern antianxiety agents interact with their own receptor, a benzodiazepine receptor, which can facilitate GABA activity in the brain. More recently, some totally new types of antianxiety agents have been discovered, such as buspirone, which interact with serotonin receptors. With the revelation of the role of many other neuropeptides in the genesis of anxiety, perhaps specific anxieties, it is likely that even more specific antianxiety agents will be developed in the future.

Many investigators presently believe that functional psychiatric disorders result from neurochemical imbalances (i.e., lack of regulation) among many transmitter systems as opposed to a pathology in a single one, so there may be many ways to restore overall balance. The recent discovery of a large number of neuropeptide transmitter and receptor systems has opened the door to the development of a new generation of psychiatric medicines, which may modify discrete mood states and associated behavioral tendencies.'

It is also now widely recognized that the qualities of the therapist—his or her capacity for empathy—are as important for the efficacy of psychotherapy as any specific mode of treatment (Beutler et al., 1994). That is generally not thought to be the case for current biological interventions, where actions of drugs on specific chemical systems are believed to be the decisive factor in the efficacy of treatments, but many agents do work for several different diagnostic categories. For instance, SSRIs alleviate anxiety, panic attacks, and obsessive-compulsive disorders (Chapters 11, 12, 13, and 16). This may partly reflect the simple fact that broadly distributed neurochemical systems, such as the biogenic amines, are bound to influence practically all emotions and mental activities. Few emotion-specific therapies presently exist, but they may arise from the currently ongoing neuropeptide revolution (Chapter 21).

The systematic evaluation of all therapies is stymied by the existence of robust placebo effects that seem to emerge from our mysterious mental ability to improve when we simply perceive that we are being helped (Peters, 2001). In part, such effects are mediated by brain chemicals such as the endogenous opioids, which are influential in regulating pleasure and positive social feelings (Panksepp, 1998). Although some drugs and psychotherapies have effects on similar brain systems (e.g., Baxter et al., 1992), they are typically thought to access different aspects of the brain/mind. While the beneficial effects of psychotherapies are surely initiated through the higher functions of the mental apparatus (i.e., symbolically, through neocortical language functions that are uniquely human), drug therapies modulate tonic levels of arousability more directly within basic brain/mind operating systems that we share with the other animals. The convergence appears to be in the modulation of the neurodynamic tone of middle-level emotional systems of the "limbic brain."

The enormous success of the biological psychiatry revolution has led to a variety of practical socioeconomic dilemmas, related largely to the high efficacy of the available agents. They include the problems of managed care and profit-driven programs. Under such a system there are pressures to reduce type 1 errors as much as possible (i.e., the prescription of expensive therapies, when in fact they are not necessary). However, these same economic pressures tend to promote type 2 errors (i.e., claims that certain therapies are not effective, when in fact they are). Perhaps we should also be concerned about "type 3" errors (i.e., where certain high-priced drugs are aggressively pushed forward when equally effective low-priced drugs are available). When enormous economic factors come to bear on therapeutics, there is bound to be controversy about efficacy and optimal courses of action. If one can't demonstrate which treatment is unambiguously best, there is bound to be a heightened tendency by some (i.e., drug providers) to go for the more expensive options, while others (i.e., drug receivers) prefer to go for the cheaper alternatives. This makes the issue of psychiatric diagnostics and prognostics an increasingly contentious and politicized affair.

These concerns have filled the pages of important psychiatric journals for the past decade. The flagship journal in the Western Hemisphere remains the *American Journal of Psychiatry* (with its immediate predecessor, *The American Journal of Insanity*), which has now been summarizing psychiatric thought for almost a century and a half. The massive recent progress of the field can be dated by the appearance of increasingly biologized journals: first, the *Archives of General Psychiatry* in 1959 near the beginning of the psychopharmacology revolution, and then *Biological Psychiatry* in 1969, when the brain systems (e.g., biogenic amines and GABA) accounting for the initial wave of enthusiasm became well-recognized as major topics of neuroscientific inquiry. Many others have followed. We are presently at the threshold of the next great phase of the biological psychiatry revolution—with the harnessing of neuropeptidergic and molecular biological knowledge just around the corner. We can only imagine the new challenges that will need to be faced.

DILEMMA OF PSYCHIATRIC DIAGNOSTICS: DSMS AND BEYOND

Some mental disorders arise through stressful life circumstances. Others emerge more from constitutional infirmities. Nature-nurture arguments do not help us much in unraveling such intertwined complexities, unless discrete genetic differences can be discovered, as in fragile X and Williams syndrome (Chapter 14). Ultimately psychiatric thought must continue to be guided by a careful appreciation of the evolving stories of selves in action on the stage of life. Neither the "brainless" psychiatry of the middle of the 20th century, nor the "mindless" variety of the past 30 years should be taken to represent the most we can achieve. The future should yield a synthesis. However, since we have been unable to unambiguously link most mental functions to brain functions and have only been able to pinpoint biological causes for a few rare genetic disorders, we have been left no other option than to categorize mental disorders on the basis of outward symptoms. Hopefully brain imaging and new chemical measures will soon become more prominent tools in diagnostics. Meanwhile, problems of diagnostic specificity and individual sensitivity remain to be resolved (Chapter 6).

Kraepelin's original taxonomy described the outlines of major psychiatric categories still accepted today. His textbooks had clear descriptions of syndromes that we now recognize as schizophrenia, various phobias, depression, and anxiety disorders with their links to obsessions and compulsions. The modern standard classification schemes, ever since the DSM-1 of 1951, have clearly followed the Kraepelinian outline, although the early versions were well spiced with psychoanalytic perspectives on depth psychological issues.

This approach has been refined through three more cycles, with the current DSM-IV (APA, 1994) and its European counterpart, International classification of Diseases, Tenth Edition (ICD-10) (WHO, 1992), providing extensive descriptive guidance. Today's diagnostics are largely based on "what" symptoms constitute a disorder, with silence on the issues of "why" or "how" a disorder emerges from underlying psychobiological substrates. Still, the "multiaxial" approach of DSM-IV acknowledges psychological, (Axis I and II) as well as organic, psychosocial, and environmental concomitants (Axis III, IV, and V, respectively). While Axis I provides a Kraepelinian set of diagnostics of major psychiatric categories, Axis II offers a dimensional scheme for evaluating personality problems. This serves as a coherent way for clinicians to communicate pragmatically without worrying too much about unresolved etiological questions.

Although difficulties with previous versions of the DSM have been reduced, many still regard it as only a provisional scheme that needs substantial improvement (McHugh and Slavney, 1998). Several inconsistencies between DSM-IV and ICD-10 remain: for instance, in the way the two sets of guidelines handle somatoform and personality disorders, a discrepancy that contributes to international misunderstandings. The forces to construct a DSM-V are presently being marshaled, but it remains controversial whether this approach still reflects sustained progress toward a scientifically defensible solution or simply an essential stop-gap measure that is socially needed until the etiology of psychiatric disorders are revealed. If the scheme does not carve disturbed human nature at its joints, it may actively impede scientific progress, especially where only a "natural" subset of a presumably homogeneous disorder will respond well to the therapy being evaluated.

The extent to which diagnostic schemes are influenced by societal standards is highlighted by the disappearance of homosexuality as a psychiatric disorder in the more recent versions of the manual. Partly, this has arisen from the scientific evidence that to some degree homosexuality reflects a natural variation in the organization of gender-specific brain circuitries during the second trimester of gestation (Chapter 4). It also partly reflects the emergence of new human rights movements. Scientific advances and cultural tensions will continue to permeate diagnostic practices since some "disorders" are only extremes of normal human temperamental variability (especially among the Axis II disorders), while others, to put it metaphorically, are more likely to reflect "broken parts" in the brain (most abundantly in the severe Axis I disorders). The issue of attention deficit hyperactivity disorder (ADHD) is an especially poignant example since so many children are given medications that may have potent and less than desirable long-term effects on the nervous system (Moll et al., 2001).

All simple symptom-based approaches, such as the diagnosis of ADHD, are bound to remain controversial to some extent, for there are many useful ways to conceptualize every phenomenon. It is only possible to move forward substantively on biologically based diagnostic criteria if we can objectively monitor the relevant brain systems and resulting infirmities at an organic level (Castellanos and Tannock, 2002). Such work is now advancing on various diagnostic categories (Chapters 6, 7, 11, and 14). However, continuing ambiguities create a pressure to include more and more qualifiers. The emerging problem with the complexity of DSM-IV is evident in the proliferation of subcategories of mood disorders that can defy common sense. DSM-II had only 8 types, but by DSM-IIIR there were 97, and according to Paul McHugh (2001), if you consider all the subcategories and specifiers in DSM-IV, one could categorize 2665 subtypes. This problem may continue to be endemic to appearance-based classification systems, since small differences often compel notice. The "success" of DSM-IV may partially explain the current estimate that about 28 percent of the population in America fulfill one or another of the criteria for a bona fide psychiatric diagnosis (Regier et al., 1998).

A major goal is now to seek deeper levels of understanding, which confronts us with a series of interlocking dilemmas. Epistemologically, we must resolve what major disorders objectively exist, and we must be able to specify how we know they exist, above and beyond mere surface symptoms. This question—of how we go about measuring what actually exists at an ancient neuropsychological level—has gotten a spectacular boost in the past decade from molecular biological and modern brain imaging techniques. However, so far neither brain-based criteria nor core emotional processes of the evolved aspect of the mind appear prominently in psychiatric practice (Chapter 21).

A fuller recognition of basic emotional imbalances at the core of many psychiatric disorders may also help reverse a growing problem of modern psychiatry—the marginalization of patients by making them mere consumers of pills rather than agents in reconstructing meaningful human relationships and life insights. When the neu-ropeptides are finally harnessed for therapeutic purposes (Chapter 21), we may find that they work most effectively in social contexts comparable to those in which such neurochemistries first found their appointed roles in brain/mind evolution (Chapter 20). If so, some of the new medications may work optimally only when we help re-create those environments, perhaps through some type of Meyerian "sociopsychobiological" synthesis. Obviously, psychiatric disorders will continue to be permeated and modi-fied by hosts of meta-emotional factors—above all, individual capacities for affective self-regulation and thoughtfulness.

FUNCTIONS OF DIAGNOSTICS

It is generally accepted that medical diagnosis should be directly related to scientifically demonstrated underlying pathophysiological processes. Thus all medical diagnostics, including those in psychiatry, should eventually be assisted by biological measures. This has barely started to happen in modern psychiatry (Chapters 6 and 7).

We should recall that medical diagnostics have three major functions: (1) At the lowest level, they are designed to allow clinicians some assurance that they are talking about the same problems (DSM-IV fulfills that nicely). (2) They provide an efficient way to promote consistent therapeutic approaches (e.g., a short-hand path to prescrip-tion practices). (3) Also, they provide a rapid way to think about the etiology of disorders. Perhaps the take-home message of this last function should be that we must reach a better understanding of the basic emotional systems of the brain, especially as they contribute to both psychiatric disease and health. Of course, this is based on the assumption that most psychiatric disorders ultimately reflect disturbances of affect-generating processes of the brain, a position that remains controversial among both psychiatrists and psychologists. Indeed, for the cognitive disorders of schizophre-nia (Chapter 9) and some of the pervasive developmental disorders of childhood (Chapter 14), this may seem unlikely, even though changes in emotionality are surely contributory factors.

This third function of diagnostics relates directly to issues of pathophysiology and pathogenesis. With the emergence of an understanding of brain transmitter systems in the 1960s, there arose great hopes that imbalances in one or another system would map well onto psychiatric disorders. Schildkraut (1965) made the seminal suggestion that depression may arise from biogenic amine deficiencies, and norepinephrine depletion was suspected to be the major culprit. Unfortunately, the hope that different types of depression might be diagnosed by patterns of cerebrospinal amine metabolites never cashed out. However, at least one instance did bear fruit: The onset of manic episodes does correspond rather well to hyperarousal of brain norepinephrine systems (Garlow et al., 1999).

Likewise, there was optimism that certain forms of schizophrenia would ultimately reflect a variety of possible disruptions of metabolic pathways that would lead to the excessive synthesis of catechol- or indoleamine-like hallucinogens. The many fasci-nating hypotheses that were generated eventually led to no consensus concerning the role of such factors. Still, these ideas are open territory for further developments. A classic psychosis can be generated by imbalancing glutamate activity in the brain with the phencyclidine hallucinogens. Thus, it is still generally agreed that schizophrenia is closely linked to imbalanced activities of certain brain dopamine systems, in concert with various other neurochemistries (Carlsson et al., 2001) and that anxiety is intimately related to the activity of GABA along FEAR systems (Chapter 16).

As far as neuroscience is concerned, there have been spectacular advances in our knowledge of the molecules that will eventually be relevant for understanding psychiatric disorders (Charney et al., 1999) but much less enthusiasm for linking such entities to mental functions. Likewise ongoing attempts to link psychiatric disorders with specific brain systems has been criticized in recent years. Valenstein (1998) provides one provocative historical overview of the many attempts and failures. He emphasized how modest real progress has been and how, "in the absence of a coherent understanding of the pathological basis of a disease, only serendipity can provide effective drugs for its treatment. Nowhere is this more evident than in an examination of the history of psychotherapeutic drugs" (quote by Sneader, 1990, in Valenstein, 1998 p. 9). But his thesis has not gone unchallenged by leaders of the biological psychiatry community (for a debate, see Valenstein and Charney, 2000). It is now generally accepted that there is much more to psychiatric disorders than neurochemical imbalances, and with recent technological advances, the neurobiological search has shifted substantially to anatomical and genetic underpinnings.

FROM PATHOPHYSIOLOGY TO PATHOGENESIS

A clear description of pathophysiological processes is essential for the generation of insights into underlying pathogenic processes. At one time, there was the hope that psychiatric disorders would turn out to be as simple as gout, where elevated uric acid levels lead to buildup at susceptible joints causing inflamed tissues and excruciating pain. Elimination of uric acid buildup (whether by blockade of synthesis with allopurinol or reduced ingestion of purine precursors) eliminates the proximal causes and all the symptoms of gout. In a sense, the classic biogenic amine theories of psychopathologies were based on the expectation that such exquisitely linear logic might apply to certain mental disorders (e.g., Schildkraut, 1965). Unfortunately, they have not. Indeed, there has been movement to conceptualize psychiatric disorder more in terms of nonlinear dynamic perturbations (Tschacher et al., 1997), perhaps with basic emotional systems being strange attractors within such hypercomplex systems.

Without adequate pathophysiological foundations, the clarification of pathogenesis is bound to be limited. The tripartite cascade of analysis applies here as with any scientific question: First, one has to identify the correlates of the phenomena in which one is interested. Second, one has to determine whether or not the correlates actually have any relevant causal influences in the system. Finally, one has to develop a "mechanistic" theory of how the system operates. This has not been achieved for any of the classic psychiatric disorders, but the goal is being approximated for certain new degenerative disorders with psychotic implications (e.g., Chapters 14 and 15).

Alzheimer's disease and other dementias are classic neuropsychiatric examples of how a careful analysis of pathophysiology has gradually led the way to a deep molecular understanding of pathogenesis. From the initial description of the pathology of restricted cortical areas, the gradual revelation of underlying genetic factors that predispose one toward such degenerative processes has finally emerged (Chapter 15). This knowledge is now slowly being translated into new and more effective therapies.

Typically, schizophrenia has been the "gold standard" by which our understanding of psychiatric disorders will be judged. During much of the 20th century there were abundant reports of both neuroanatomical and biochemical correlates, but the patterns did not begin to gel until the past few decades. The most striking discovery was the enlargement of the ventricles, which suggests a neurodevelopmental disorder that may have multiple causes (see Chapter 9). The fact that among identical twins only the afflicted siblings exhibited the brain deficit suggests the contribution of nongenetic factors. The misarrangement of nerve cells also suggests that this type of brain impairment could have both genetic and gestational (perhaps viral) underpinnings. If misconnections in the brain are the critical causal feature, as opposed to dynamic neurochemical imbalances, then even the best medicines are bound to be simply beneficial for symptomatic control of the disorder with no realistic hope for a cure, as seems to be the case in pervasive developmental disorders (Chapter 14). For instance, the selective death of GABAergic cells in frontal areas may set in motion the disregulation of dopamine systems, which can be partly alleviated by antipsychotics. However, early interventions might still offer hope for better long-term management of the disease processes.

Most psychiatric disorders exhibit substantial genetic loadings, and for some childhood syndromes, such as Williams and Rett's syndromes, the details have been worked out (Chapter 14). Studies in molecular pathogenesis continue to promise remarkable riches in understanding many neuropsychiatric problems. The pervasive consequences of trinucleotide repeats in certain genes are now widely recognized. The most prominent ones for psychiatry are Huntington's disease and fragile X syndrome, in which a good protein is converted to a dysfunctional one by the addition of "junk" deoxyribonucleic acid (DNA) to a coding site. The resulting synthesis of poorly constructed proteins has cascading consequences in brain function. The fact that certain genetic influences such as trinucleotide repeats can expand generation by generation is now seen as a potential factor for the increasing incidence and severity of certain disorders (e.g., Huntington's disease). The identification of such disease vectors permits us to offer a definite diagnosis, usually leading to the designation of a distinct syndrome. For instance, the autistic-like mental impairment of fragile X children is now recognized as a separate medical entity (Chapter 14).

With the discovery of pathophysiological correlates that characterize specific disorders, the clarification of pathogenic causes is greatly facilitated. During the 20th century, some advances were made. Perhaps the most striking was the recognition of the devastating influences of early social loss (Bowlby, 1969) and other debilitating effects of stress (Chapter 4) that have many parallels in animal models (for a review, see Panksepp, 2001). Although the discovery of this relationship in humans came first, the cause will only be worked out by studies of other species. It is now generally recognized that the stress of social loss (whether it be in the form of separation distress or defeat in social encounters) may be a major factor in the precipitation of depressive disorders (Heim and Nemeroff, 1999). The emerging genetic data will be especially valuable in helping characterize the Axis II personality vulnerabilities that may increase susceptibility to certain emotional imbalances (Chapter 5).

The discovery of environmental vectors can rapidly lead to prophylactic maneuvers. The classic examples are the alleviation of mental retardation induced by phenylketonuria by the elimination of the toxic agent, phenylalanine, from the diet. Such a strategy, unfortunately, can currently be implemented in only a few metabolically induced disorders. For most organic disorders, the development of new therapies will require effective simulation of the disease processes in laboratory animals. To be effective, the animal models will have to be sufficiently homologous to critical aspects of a disease process so that effective translations can be made to the human condition. In the area of emotions, this remains a contentious issue that will only be resolved by the eventual achievement of practical success (Chapters 16 and 21).

Table 1.1 summarizes a highly simplified model of what a future brain-systems-based diagnostic scheme may look like. One reading of modern neuroscience (i.e., Panksepp, 1998) is that there is a limited but widely ramifying set of core emotional systems that regulate various instinctual urges critical for survival. These include systems that control appetitive-exploratory tendencies, anger-irritability, fear-anxiety, male and female eroticism, maternal nurturance, social bonding and separation distress, playful interactions, and a variety of bodily needs (thirst, hunger, and sleep). Another axis in this type of scheme would have to be based on an understanding of the status of the more general state-control systems (Fig. 1.1). Depression, for example, may reflect a global depletion of many of these neuroemotional resources (highlighted in Table 1.1 and Fig. 1.1), especially in those systems that facilitate positive emotions most prominently.

Of course, each core emotional system has complex neural substrates, with multiple interrelations among the various emotions, as well as diverse cortico-cognitive thinking structures they energize. Thus, even with such a "natural kind" of classificatory scheme, there is bound to be movement from the categorical description of major emotional disorders to the level of subspecies and mixed species. That seems inevitable as we focus on newly discovered details of the underlying processes. Still, the great challenge for the 21st century will be to coherently link the major psychiatric diseases to the basic evolved functions of the brain—to the activities of emotional systems, consciousness processes, as well as cognition and memory substrates (Chapters 2 and 3).

Such alternative conceptual schemes for the underpinnings of major psychiatric problems (Table 1.1) could also guide new drug developments and therapeutic programs in productive ways. Each emotional system is characterized by its own, at times unique, neuropeptidergic neuromodulators (Panksepp, 1998), which may become targets for novel therapeutic strategies (see Chapter 21). Viewing psychiatric disorder in this way, with reference to major emotional systems of the brain and their many general

T A B L E 1.1. Postulated Relationships Between Basic Emotional Systems, Common Emotional Processes, and Major Psychiatric Disorders[a,b]

Basic Emotional System[c]	Emergent Emotions	Related Emotional Disorders
SEEKING (+ and −)	Interest	Obsessive-compulsive
	Frustration	Paranoid schizophrenia
	Craving	Addictive personalities
RAGE (− and +)	Anger	Aggression
	Irritability	Psychopathic tendencies
	Contempt	Personality disorders
	Hatred	
FEAR (−)	Simple anxiety	Generalized anxiety disorders
	Worry	Phobias
	Psychic trauma	Post traumatic stress disorder variants
PANIC (−)	Separation distress	Panic attacks
	Sadness	Pathological grief
	Guilt/shame	Depression
	Shyness	Agoraphobia
	Embarrassment	Social phobias, autism
PLAY (+)	Joy and glee	Mania
	Happy playfulness	ADHD
LUST (+ and −)	Erotic feelings	Fetishes
	Jealousy	Sexual addictions
CARE (+)	Nurturance	Dependency disorders
	Love	Autistic aloofness
	Attraction	Attachment disorders

[a]The last two columns provide hypotheses of the major relationships. Obviously, multiple emotional influences contribute to each of the emergent emotions (e.g., jealousy is also tinged by separation distress and anger), and all the emotional disorders have multiple determinants. Plus and minus signs after each indicate major types of affective valence that each system can presumably generate (adapted from Panksepp, 2000)
[b]Capitalizations are used to designate the various emotional systems to highlight the fact that these are instantiated as distinct neural entities rather than simply psychological concepts. The essential neural components constitute command influences that coordinate the basic behavioral, physiological, and psychological aspects of each emotional response.
[c]From Panksepp (1998, 2000).

modulators such as the biogenic amines, may eventually help open a route past some of the conundrums of DSM-IV (McHugh, 2001).

An understanding of the basic emotional systems we share with other mammals is already shedding important new light on acquired behavior disorders such as substance abuse. Such tendencies are based upon natural psychobehavioral urges (mediated partly by mesolimbic dopamine systems) that motivate organisms to pursue resources needed for survival. This generalized appetitive SEEKING system of the brain energizes the instinctual apparatus for goal-directed behavior, but it can be commandeered and short-circuited "to run after its own tail," so to speak, as occurs when addictive drugs directly arouse this hedonically positive life-sustaining system. All the abused drugs from alcohol to nicotine release dopamine to some extent, leading organisms to perpetuate associated activities. As the arousal of this instinctual system becomes linked with the contingencies of drug acquisition and administration, free choice becomes constrained by the newly acquired conditional "drives." Thus this basic brain system that regulates the urge to pursue resources needed for survival becomes entrapped in a maladaptive vicious cycle. Similar processes may be operating in sexual addiction and various appetite control disorders.

This example highlights how the functional nature of certain brain systems can guide theorizing about underlying processes. However, our recognition of such systems is only the first step in the harvesting of psychiatrically useful knowledge. The actual details of how these systems operate will presumably provide insights on how they can be selectively modulated. Unfortunately, the recognition of such psychobiological constructs has been slow during this most recent molecular era of psychiatry because a widespread assumption has prevailed—one similar to that which characterized behavioristic psychology: that we could forego a deep psychological analysis of brain functions and move directly from DSM symptom-based diagnostics to underlying molecular causes. It now seems increasingly clear that this may not be possible. We do need psychological and psychoanalytic concepts to wrap our minds around what is happening to people in emotional distress. And it is not just cognitive concepts that are needed but sufficiently well-resolved affective ones as well (Ostow, 2003).

PERENNIAL PROBLEM: DISTINGUISHING AFFECTIVE AND COGNITIVE PROCESSES

Let us now briefly return to the key psychiatric issues of *affect* and *thought*: Brain imaging has finally given us an objective glimmer of the brain emotional systems in humans (Chapter 2), and the general neurogeography *is* that of the *limbic system* that Paul MacLean (1990) first brought to our attention 50 years ago. It is an everyday fact that during intense affective states, humans dwell obsessively on mood-congruent thoughts and strategies that readily flood their minds. One rotates these naturally aroused ideas persistently in the mind's eye as long as the affective states "insist," and if the ruminations (i.e., the "repetition compulsions"?) persist for too long, the resulting symptoms can become psychiatrically significant.

Although it is obvious that our thoughts can influence our feelings, for understanding psychopathology it may be more critical to fathom how our feelings channel and energize our thoughts. The prevailing assumption in cognitive science that cognitions trigger emotions, is the more obvious part of the interaction. The more psychiatrically relevant aspects may be the other way around—when perceptions enter the nervous system, they automatically get coded for affective significance, which normally coaxes the neocortical apparatus to cogitate, but which, in its more intense forms, also sets up the potential for life-long transference relationships. In psychiatry, it may be unwise to put the more recently evolved cortico-cognitive "cart" in front of the ancient evolved "horses" that create emotional and motivational urges. Thus there is as much need for an "affective neuroscience of cognitions" as a "cognitive neuroscience of emotions" (Lane and Nadel, 2000).

The classical distinction between rational and emotional processes, however actively the two may interconnect, must be recognized in order to understand how affective states emerge within the brain/mind. Thus, investigators should begin tackling the fundamental nature of affective processes more directly than has been common in neuroscience. It presently seems unlikely that the major *sources* of our basic affective capacities—to be happy, angry, sad, and fearful—will be found in the neocortex. Although our ignorance about such matters remains enormous, we can only provoke strong emotional feelings by manipulating brain areas below the cortex, in that extensive neural territory traditionally known as the limbic system.

It remains possible that affects fundamentally reflect the neurodynamics of instinctual emotional urges in action. In advancing such a position, it is worth recalling that much of Freud's thought about the mind was based on the then "unknowable" nature of the instincts. In this regard, we should consider that affective consciousness and cognitive consciousness are quite differently organized within the brain. While their interactions provide fascinating examples of the diversity of socially derived emotional experiences—such as shame, guilt, embarrassment, and empathy—it is from our understanding of the basic, evolutionarily derived affects rather than of experientially derived cognitions that major new insights into psychiatric therapies will emerge. World events are not as critical for the elaboration of the mind's basic affective potentials as they are for its cognitive ones. Affective functions appear to be genetically disposed in the underlying action systems of the brain, almost as if our basic pleasures and pains are the "affective voices of the genes."

In considering the affect-cognition distinction, we may be wise to consider Mesulam's (2000) perspective that major brain processes can be divided into "channel" and "state" functions, with the *channel functions* corresponding to the discrete, computable forms of information processing that have traditionally been recognized as cognitive capacities. On the other hand, *state functions* correspond to the noncomputable mass-action organic processes that are broadcast more widely and diffusely throughout the brain. The basic affects are examples of such global brain states, and most should be capable of being regulated quite well, and perhaps eventually quite precisely, neurochemically. This is not to deny that cognitive readjustments may also promote desired homeostatic changes, albeit more indirectly.

Although no credible working hypothesis has been advanced on how the affects penetrate (cathect) cognitive activities, this remains one of the foremost scientific problems for psychiatry. In general, we can advance three general frameworks: (1) Affects are read-outs of higher forms of cognitive consciousness that use activities of primitive emotional systems as tokens of information in their cognitive deliberations. (2) Affects are intrinsic aspects of the instinctual emotional systems in action. (3) Affects represent dynamic influences on quite primitive self-representational capacities that allow organisms a spontaneously active presence in the world (e.g., as developed in Panksepp, 1998). Although it is probably some complex combination of all three, I suspect we will eventually find that affects arise substantially from a very widespread paracrine broadcasting of neurochemical messages in the brain, as can be achieved by various neuropeptides (see Chapter 21).

To the extent that psychopathologies reflect such global state changes, the need for cognitive interventions may diminish and the need for organic, neuroemotional adjustments may increase. We should recognize that our neurobiological sciences are currently extremely well positioned to inform us about the nature of the general state principles that operate within the brain/mind continuum. Abundant pharmacological maneuvers already exist and will certainly improve for modulating these background *state* processes that provide a context for cognitive activities. This should be a clarion call for a new form of neuropsychoanalytic research that tries to systematically evaluate ongoing affective changes in individuals under a variety of conditions (Solms and Turnbull, 2002). Such strategies may give us a better image of the primal structure of the mental apparatus than preconceived paper-and-pencil questionnaires.

To the extent that channel functions are involved in mental disturbances, cognitive interventions will continue to be important. To readjust specific thoughts, there is no reasonable alternative but to continue to work with the details of individual lives. To understand the existential *meanings* of individual lives, we must become conversant with the patients' life stories and coping styles and identify the affectively charged associations that serve as impediments to growth. It may also be worth considering the degree to which critical aspects of individuality are lost, and any clear scientific analysis becomes problematic, when we group people into diagnostic categories that may not match brain/mind dynamics very well.

Despite the impressive advances and achievement in brain imaging (Chapters 2, 6, and 7), we should recognize and worry about how much neural complexity and individuality these pseudo-color clouds of arousal may contain. The distinct thoughts and schemes that can filter through these areas are enormous. Typically most individual-specific brain changes are discarded in generating group statistics. This brings us, again, to the managed-care issue of how important is it really for psychiatrists to understand and deal with the nuances of individual experiences? For mild depressions, the answer may be "very little," and neurochemical adjustments will tone down persistent and intrusive cognitions (Kramer, 1993). For specific phobias, obsessive-compulsive problems and perhaps panics, where cognitive behavioral and short-term psychoanalytic treatments are effective (Chapters 12 and 18), the proper answer must surely be "quite a bit."

Scientific psychiatry will need conceptualizations at various levels, ranging from "low-level" cellular and molecular models, to "middle-level" theories that focus on major functional systems of the brain, to "high-level" conceptualizations where the detailed mental events of individuals are considered. Because of the scientific successes of low-level molecular and cellular approaches, much of the field has shifted allegiances and forged commitments only to low-level theories, and hence major texts spend abundant time on the details of neuroanatomy, neurochemistry, neurophysiology, and molecular biology and comparatively little on the human mind.

The goal of the present text is not to compete with those archival treatments of the relevant biological substrates that are now detailed in several recent compendia (Charney et al., 1999; Yudofsky and Hales, 1997; D'Haenen et al., 2002). The aim is to provide a coverage closer to the middle level of analysis (also see Bittar and Bittar, 2000), where mental faculties can be related credibly to objective brain systems in ways that may be clinically productive. Unfortunately, there has been a widespread tendency in biological psychiatry to neglect evolutionary and emotional systems in considering how the brain/mind is organized (Chapter 20), and this may now be retarding new drug development (Chapter 21).

Without a clear understanding of emotional systems (e.g., Table 1.1), we can easily lose focus if we try to leap between molecular and global diagnostic issues. Might this be one reason that advances in the discovery of new types of drugs for psychiatric illness have been so modest? We should remember that most of the psychiatrically useful drugs—the antipsychotics, antidepressants, antianxiety, anticompulsive and antimanic agents—were discovered before the advent of modern neuroscience, often through little more than trial-and-error initiatives. At best, the neuroscience of the past quarter century has largely yielded variations on previously established themes. Practically no new and effective drugs, nor insightful brain organizational concepts, have emerged from the tsunami of research that has been conducted at the molecular level. Many of us have confidence that investments in the fine-grained molecular approaches will yield strikingly new concepts (e.g., the use of neuropeptide and neurotrophin modulators as discussed in Chapter 21). At the same time, some of us suspect that the implementation of middle-level affective and emotional systems concepts will help enormously in better framing our molecular inquiries (Chapters 2 and 16).

Middle-level analyses presently provide excellent opportunities for docking mind and brain issues meaningfully and help generate new ways to look at psychopathologies and pathophysiologies and to generate new ideas for therapeutics. For instance, the existence of a generalized mesolimbic dopamine-centered SEEKING system in the brain has only been recently recognized in biological approaches to the mind (Panksepp, 1998). The system was long misconceptualized as a simple pleasure, reward, or reinforcement system because of the pervasive failure to consider *all* the behavioral and psychological evidence (Panksepp and Moskal, 2003). However, even Aristotle recognized that the appetitive function of the "soul" permeated all other parts of the mental apparatus, and it may be quite informative to conceptualize the organization of affective processes in terms of distinct, albeit highly interactive, neuromental faculties once more. As already noted, this appetitive motivational SEEKING system contributes heavily to drug addictions and the psychic excesses of schizophrenia and other psychiatric problems.

In sum, we currently know a great deal about limbic system neuroanatomies and neurochemistries, but all too little about the functional subsystems of which the "emotional-visceral brain" is composed. However, animal research, especially if we are willing to accept the affective nature of animal life, should allow us to work out the general evolutionary principles, yielding useful concepts that should also apply to humans (Panksepp et al., 2002). Among such core neural processes, cross-species homologies do prevail. Of course, this work has no chance of clarifying the massive cognitive complexities that arise when these ancient systems interact with our expansive cortico-cognitive apparatus. To understand those interactions, a new *psychoethological* type of human mind research is needed (Panksepp, 1999). Still, a judicious blend of animal and human brain/mind research should eventually yield a new and coherent psychobiological view that is bound to be of penetrating psychiatric significance.

CODA: INTERSECTION OF 20TH-CENTURY FORCES LEADING TO A 21ST-CENTURY SYNTHESIS

There were periods during the 20th century (e.g., the Freudian era) when psychiatrists interested in the deep dynamics of the mind isolated themselves from a progressive understanding of the brain. More recently, with the neuroscience revolution and the striking molecular successes of biological psychiatry, the converse problem has emerged in some quarters—an excessive separation of psychiatric thinking from any coherent attempt to conceptualize the nature of the mind. Now that our mind inquiries can be supported by an impressive neuroscientific armamentarium, there is promise for ever more impressive docking of brain/mind issues.

Because of such advances, and only because of them, creative psychological approaches, such as those advanced by Freud, can now be tempered with neuroscience, allowing many neglected ideas to be tested rigorously for the first time. For instance, there are many neuroscientific ways to conceptualize repression, transference, projections, repetition compulsions, and various defense mechanisms. With the advent of modern brain imaging and psychopharmacology, revitalized depth psychological theories may point us toward subtle mind issues that can finally begin to be empirically resolved.

However, in cultivating diagnostic precision, we must avoid creating new disorders out of marginal differences. We must avoid constructing Kafkaesque nightmare documents similar to the *Malleus Maleficarum* that informed inquisitors of the Dark Ages, in great detail, how to identify and find witches. Without diagnostics that are linked to clear and measurable biological underpinnings, the classic tensions between the splitters and lumpers are bound to remain. There are no easy resolutions of the dilemmas such disparate views generate. With the one hand we must aspire to create a diagnostic precision that may be unattainable, and with the other we must help support the humanistic and deeply experienced affective needs of individuals in ways that are often beyond our reach. Only through a creative tension between such perspectives can a balanced synthesis emerge.

In the final accounting, we must invest in variants of the "Meyerian synthesis" by accepting the multidimensional psychobiological nature of individual therapeutic relationships. There is no substitute for the human touch. Psychological existence, of both doctor and patient, is built upon substantive emotional interactions. The life stories of individual patients should not be forsaken, even when managed care insists that simple medications should suffice. The individuality of each person is reflected within his or her unique life encounters, diverse dispositions, and vulnerabilities. Idiosyncratic individuality must continue to be cherished. Indeed, through an increasing understanding of genetic diversity, there may be personalized psychiatric medicines in the future. We may also be better able to identify individuals who can get by on lower doses of psychoactive agent than others, thereby minimizing side effects.

To achieve this, patients should be better educated so they can become more active participants in the evaluation of their holistic treatment plans. Indeed, if new and gentle neuropeptide-based therapies do eventually emerge, we may find that they do not operate well without appropriately supportive social contexts. Such issues will be difficult to analyze empirically, but we should remain open to the likelihood that there will eventually be medicines that facilitate opportunities for people to master the emotional subtleties of their lives. In addition, optimal therapeutic effects may only emerge when patients are encouraged, as in the ancient Greek "ritual purifications," to move their bodies in emotional ways, aided by dance, music, and the other bodily passions and arts.

As we increasingly recognize the actual emotional systems that evolution has built into the mammalian brain, we will better conceptualize the psychobiological nature of mental order as well as disorders. Our emerging knowledge about the biological sources of human nature, along with our traditional human tools to listen and to empathize, may eventually help us to regulate the passions of the mind with a precision that presently seems barely imaginable. Hopefully that will be achieved in the most humanistic way possible.

Acknowledgement

I thank Mortimer Ostow and Jaanus Harro for constructive comments on this chapter. This historical summary also owes a debt to Paul McHugh's state of the field presentation entitled "Beyond DSM IV: From Appearances to Essences" at the 2001 Annual Meeting of the American Psychiatric Association, themes that are also elaborated in his book with Phillip Slavney (McHugh and Slavney, 1998).

REFERENCES

American Psychiatric Association (APA) (1994). *Diagnostic and Statistical Manual of Mental Disorders* (Fourth Edition), American Psychiatric Association: Washington DC.

Andreasen NC (2001). *Brave New Brain: Conquering Mental Illness in the Era of the Genome.* Oxford University Press: New York.

Baxter LR, Jr., Schwartz JM, Bergman KS, et al. (1992). Caudate glucose metabolic rate changes with both drug and behavior therapy for obsessive-compulsive disorder. *Arch Gen Psychiatry* 49:681–689.

Beutler LE, Machado PPP, Neufeldt SA (1994). Therapist variables. In Bergin AE, Garfield SL (eds). *Handbook of Psychotherapy and Behavior Change.* Wiley: New York, pp. 229–269.

Bittar EE, Bittar N (2000). *Biological Psychiatry*, JAI: Stamford, CT.

Bowlby J (1969). Attachment and Loss, Vol. 1: *Attachment*. Basic Books: New York.

Cade J (1949). Lithium salts in the treatment of psychotic excitement. *Med J Australia* 36: 349–352.

Carlsson A (2001). A paradigm shift in brain research. *Science* 294:1021–1024.

Carlsson A, Waters N, Holm-Waters S, Tedroff J, Nilsson M, Carlsson ML (2001). Interactions between monoamines, glutamate, and GABA in schizophrenia: New evidence. *Ann Rev Pharmacol Toxicol* 41:237–260.

Castellanos FX, Tannock R (2002). Neuroscience of attention-deficit/hyperactivity disorder: The search for endophenotypes. *Nature Revs Neurosci* 3:617–628.

Charney DS, Nestler EJ, Bunney BS (eds) (1999). *Neurobiology of Mental Illness*. Oxford University Press: New York.

D'Haenen H, Den Boer JA, Willner P (2002). *Biological Psychiatry*. Wiley: New York.

Enserink M (1999). Can the placebo be the cure? *Science* 284:238–240.

Freud S (1920). *Beyond the Pleasure Principle*, Standard Edition, 18:1–64. Hogarth Press: London.

Garlow SJ, Muselman DL, Nemeroff CB (1999). The neurochemistry of mood disorders: Clinical studies. In Charney DS, Nestler EJ, Bunney BS (eds). *Neurobiology of Mental Illness*. Oxford University Press: New York, pp. 348–364.

Harrington A (ed) (1999). *The Placebo Effect: An Interdisciplinary Exploration*. Harvard University Press, Cambridge, MA.

Healy D (1996, 1998, 2000). *The Psychopharmacologists: Interviews*. Altman: London.

Healy D (1996). *The Psychopharmacologists I: Interviews*. Altman: London.

Healy D (1998). *The Psychopharmacologists II: Interviews*. Arnold: New York, co-published by Oxford University Press.

Healy D (2000). *The Psychopharmacologists III: Interviews*. Arnold: New York, co-published by Oxford University Press.

Heim C, Nemeroff CB (1999). The impact of early adverse experiences on brain systems involved in the pathophysiology of anxiety and affective disorders. *Biol Psychiatry* 46: 1509–1522.

Jasper HH (1983). Nobel Laureates in neuroscience: 1904–1981. *Ann Rev Neurosci* 6:1–42.

Kandel ER (1999). Biology and the future of psychoanalysis: A new intellectual framework for psychiatry revisited. *Am J Psychiatry* 156:505–524.

Kandel ER (2001). The molecular biology of memory storage: A dialogue between genes and synapses. *Science* 294:1030–1038.

Klein DF, Rabkin J (eds) (1981). *Anxiety: New Research and Changing Concepts*. Raven Press: New York.

Kramer PD (1993). *Listening to Prozac Viking*: New York.

Lane RD, Nadel L (eds) (2000). *Cognitive Neuroscience of Emotion*. Oxford University Press: New York.

MacLean PD (1990). *The Triune Brain in Evolution*. Plenum Press: New York.

MacMillan M (1997). *Freud Evaluated*. MIT Press: Cambridge, MA.

Mayberg HS, Silva JA, Brannan SK, et al. (2002). The functional neuroanatomy of the placebo effect. *Am J Psychiatry* 159:728–737.

McHugh PR (2001). *Plenary presentation "Beyond DSM IV: From Appearances to Essences"* at the 154th Annual Meeting of the American Psychiatric Association, May 5–10, New Orleans, LA.

McHugh PR, Slavney PR (1998). *The Perspectives of Psychiatry.* Johns Hopkins University Press: Baltimore MD.

Mesulam, M-M. (ed) (2000). *Principles of Cognitive and Behavioral Neurology.* Lawrence Erlbaum Associates: Philadelphia.

Moerman DE (2002). *Meaning, Medicine and the 'Placebo' Effect.* Cambridge University Press: New York.

Moll GH, Hause S, Ruther E, Rothenberger A, Huether G (2001). Early methylphenidate administration to young rats causes a persistent reduction in the density of striatal dopamine transporters. *J Child Adolesc Psychopharm* 11:15–24.

Mora G (1985). History of Psychiatry. In *Comprehensive Textbook of Psychiatry*, Vol. IV, Kaplan HI, Sadock BJ, (eds). Williams & Wilkins: Baltimore, pp. 2034–2054.

Ostow M (2003). Mood regulation, spontaneous, and pharmacologically assisted. *Neuro-Psychoanalysis*, in press.

Panksepp J (1998). *Affective Neuroscience: The Foundations of Human and Animal Emotions.* Oxford University Press: New York.

Panksepp J (1999). Emotions as viewed by psychoanalysis and neuroscience. An exercise in consilience. *Neuro-Psychoanalysis* 1:15–38.

Panksepp J (2000). The neuro-evolutionary cusp between emotions and cognitions, implications for understanding consciousness and the emergence of a unified mind science. *Consciousness Emotion* 1:17–56.

Panksepp J (2001). The long-term psychobiological consequences of infant emotions: Prescriptions for the twenty-first century. *Infant Mental Health* 22:132–173.

Panksepp J, Moskal J (2003). Dopamine, pleasure and appetitive eagerness: An emotional systems overview of the trans-hypothalamic "reward" system in the genesis of addictive urges. In Barch D (ed.) *Cognitive and Affective Neuroscience of Psychopathology*, in press.

Panksepp J, Moskal J, Panksepp JB, Kroes R (2002). Comparative approaches in evolutionary psychology: Molecular neuroscience meets the mind. *Neuroendocrinology Letters*, 23(Suppl. 4):105–115.

Peters D (2001). *Understanding the Placebo Effect in Complementary Medicine.* Churchill Livingstone: New York.

Petrovic P, Kalso E, Petersson KM, Ingvar M (2002). Placebo and opioid analgesia: Imaging a shared neuronal network. *Science* 295:1737–1740.

Pollak R (1997). *The Creation of Dr. B: A Biography of Bruno Bettelheim.* Simon & Schuster: New York.

Regier DA, Kaelber CT, Rae DS, et al. (1998). Limitations of diagnostic criteria and assessment instruments for mental disorders. *Arch Gen Psychiatry* 55:109–115.

Rolls ET (1999). The Brain and Emotion. Oxford University Press: Oxford, UK.

Schildkraut JJ (1965). The catecholamine hypothesis of affective disorders: A review of the supporting evidence. *Am J Psychiatry* 122:509–522.

Schou M (1992). Phases in the development of lithium treatment in psychiatry. In *The Neurosciences: Paths of Discovery II*, Samson F., Adelman G., (eds). Birkhauser: Boston, pp. 149–166.

Schwartz JM, Stoessel PW, Baxter LR, Jr., Martin KM, Phelps ME (1996). Systematic changes in cerebral glucose metabolic rate after successful behavior modification treatment of obsessive-compulsive disorder. *Arch Gen Psychiatry* 53:109–13.

Shapiro AK, Shapiro E (2001). *The Powerful Placebo: From Ancient Priest to Modern Physician.* Johns Hopkins University Press: Baltimore, MD.

Snyder SH (1980). *Biological Aspects of Mental Disorder.* Oxford University Press: New York.

Solms M, Turnbull O (2002). *The Brain and the Inner World.* Other Press: New York.

Stone MH (1997). *Healing the Mind: A History of Psychiatry from Antiquity to the Present.* W.W. Norton: New York.

Tschacher W, Scheier C, Hashimoto Y (1997). Dynamical analysis of schizophrenia courses. *Biol Psychiatry* 41:428–437.

Valenstein ES (1973). *Brain Control—A Critical Examination of Brain Stimulation and Psychosurgery.* Wiley: New York.

Valenstein ES (1998). *Blaming the Brain.* Free Press: New York.

Valenstein E, Charney D (2000). Are we "blaming" brain chemistry for mental illness. *Cerebrum* 2:87–114.

Yudofsky SC, Hales RE (eds) (1997). *The American Psychiatric Press Textbook of Neuropsychiatry.* American Psychiatric Press: Washington, DC.

2

IMAGING HUMAN EMOTIONS AND AFFECTIVE FEELINGS: IMPLICATIONS FOR BIOLOGICAL PSYCHIATRY

Mario Liotti[1] and Jaak Panksepp[2]

[1] Department of Psychiatry, University of Nottingham, Nottingham, United Kingdom NG7 2UH and [2] J.P. Scott Center for Neuroscience, Mind and Behavior, Department of Psychology, Bowling Green State University, Bowling Green, Ohio 43403 and [2] Falk Center for Molecular Therapeutics, Department of Biomedical Engineering, Northwestern University, Evanston, Illinois 60201

ON THE NATURE OF EMOTIONS

The complexity of emotions is vast, but during the past few decades, progress in clarifying the neurological substrates has been enormous. This knowledge will have increasing consequences for the reconceptualization of foundational issues in biological psychiatry. In deep subcortical regions of the mammalian brain, there exist a variety of genetically prescribed circuits that mediate basic (instinctual) emotional behaviors. As discussed in this chapter, and several others in this text, there are many reasons to believe that various basic affective experiences are dependent on the activities of such neural systems.

Textbook of Biological Psychiatry, Edited by Jaak Panksepp
ISBN 0-471-43478-7   Copyright © 2004 John Wiley & Sons, Inc.

Emotions have a variety of attributes, including autonomic-bodily, behavioral-expressive, cognitive-learned, and affective-experiential components. This last aspect—the subjective intensity and valence of our diverse emotional experiences—makes it a topic of foremost importance for psychiatry. Without affective feelings, it is hard to imagine that the concept of emotion would exist. People with psychiatric problems are commonly troubled by the chaotic, often misplaced and undesirable affective intensity of their lives. The success of most psychiatric interventions is premised on their ability to facilitate affect regulation.

Although there has now been enormous progress in imaging how the brain processes emotional information, until quite recently the fundamental neurobiological nature of affective experience remained totally mysterious. Substantial progress has now been made on imaging key brain areas that help elaborate affect in humans as well as neuroanatomical and neurochemical circuits that mediate core emotional responses in animals. Investigators are also learning how to blend information from the two sources. Most human brain imaging studies presently provide anatomical *correlates* that may or may not reflect causal processes. On the other hand, animal brain research can help decipher the details of the underlying causal issues in ways that ethical human research could never achieve. Through a balanced interplay of human and animal psychobiological research, a level of knowledge can be achieved that neither approach, alone, could achieve. The translation of knowledge among species will depend on the degree of evolutionary homology in the underlying substrates (Chapters 16, 20, and 21).

The assumption that animals also have affective experiences when they exhibit instinctual emotional behaviors can yield precise working hypotheses concerning the neural nature of basic affects that, after development and deployment of appropriate neuropharmacological tools, can be rigorously evaluated in the human species. For instance, various chemistries identified through preclinical animal research can already guide the selection of new pharmacological targets to be evaluated in humans (e.g., Chapter 21). Unfortunately, this level of evolutionary continuity is not yet widely accepted. Since the subjective-experiential aspects of emotions cannot be observed *directly* in either animals or humans, the study of emotional *feelings* has lagged behind the science of emotional *behaviors*. Indeed, some investigators have been eager to conceptually separate the two, but we doubt if that semantic maneuver is ontologically justified. Affective feelings may be closely linked to, indeed interpenetrant with, the neurodynamics of instinctual emotional systems in action.

In sum, a new neuroscience of emotions is emerging rapidly. Because of limited space, we shall not cover historical issues. Suffice it to say that the modern study of brain emotional systems qualifies and brings into question earlier peripheralist views that attributed emotions to visceral changes or cognitive-type propositional attitudes and appraisals that we acquire through life experiences. Even though it is still accepted that peripheral and cognitive factors modulate core emotional processes in many important ways, central brain mechanisms are taking center stage in modern analyses of emotions. While changes in the activity of the autonomic nervous system are important for the modulation of emotional intensity and specific types of bodily feelings that accompany emotions, the affective nature of our minds is not simply a result of the readout of bodily arousal by higher cortico-cognitive systems of the brain as has been long assumed in psychology (e.g., the classic James-Lange perspective). In fact, there are reasons to believe that brain emotional processes are very capable of modulating peripheral organ responses via direct neural as well as many hormonal routes, including direct secretions from the brain into the bloodstream (Kastin et al., 1999).

It is now generally recognized that specific brain circuits, highly interactive with the visceral and skeletal-muscular systems, are essential for emotions. The brain's emotional infrastructure is concentrated in midline, visceral regions of the brain (Papez, 1937) that were enshrined in the concept of the limbic system (MacLean, 1990). Although the utility of the limbic concept has been debated vigorously (e.g., Cory and Gardner, 2002; LeDoux, 1996), it is fair to say that most of the brain imaging work on affective processes (albeit not related cognitive information processing) affirms that the limbic concept correctly identifies the general neuronal territories where both the affects and emotional behaviors are elaborated in the mammalian brain.

The basic emotions come in various dynamic forms and certainly include core instinctual processes such as anger, fear, eager anticipation, joy, sadness, and playfulness (see Table 21.1, which also highlights the key neurochemistries identified so far). All of these complex brain functions can be linked to major psychiatric disorders in fairly straightforward, albeit speculative, ways (Table 1.1). These action–feeling systems allow all species of mammals to respond to the world in characteristic ways; and, to the best of our current knowledge, the underlying neurochemical controls have been evolutionarily conserved, in principle, across higher vertebrates. Within the higher limbic and neocortical reaches these systems interact with cognitive processes, considerably more variable among species, which yield layers of epigenetic complexities where cross-species comparisons will never be as robust.

The cortical-subcortical interactions create a special richness for human emotional life, as well as existential forms of emotional turmoil unknowable to other species. The various socially derived emotions include a vast number of variants—including shame, guilt, jealousy, envy, embarrassment, pride and many others—that provide a special subtlety to human emotional life. Although age-old debates continue over how our moods and emotions are best conceptualized (see Ekman and Davidson, 1994), the realization that neural criteria will be essential for defining such affective experiential states is now widely accepted, and increasingly so among even those mind sciences traditionally not accustomed to thinking in neural terms. The possibility of imaging such processes in the human brain, using positron emission tomography (PET) and functional magnetic resonance imaging (fMRI) technologies, has helped trigger the "affect revolution" that is currently sweeping across the mind sciences.

The aim of this chapter is to provide an overview of how emotions are generated within the brain. Since research on humans and research on animals presently provide rather distinct lines of evidence, they will be summarized separately. First we will summarize human data as derived from now classic studies of brain-damaged individuals, followed by a summary of evidence from modern brain-imaging approaches. Then we provide a synopsis of conclusions to be derived from animal brain research, and an attempt to blend these approaches into a coherent whole.

EMOTIONAL CHANGES FOLLOWING BRAIN DAMAGE

Cortical-Subcortical Factors in the Generation of Emotionality

Given that acquired brain lesions (such as strokes and tumors) are typically large and don't respect the boundaries of known cytoarchitectonic and functional areas (such as Brodmann areas; see Fig. 2.1), a main focus of lesion-behavior correlation studies in emotion studies has been hemispheric laterality. Studies in the sixties and early seventies found that lesions in the left hemisphere were associated with *catastrophic* emotional reactions (tears, depression, despair, anger), while damage to the right hemisphere was accompanied more by emotional *indifference* (lack of concern, emotional unawareness, and at times an unrealistic euphoria/hypomania). These early findings were explained by expressive difficulties in the patients with left-side damage, and by neglect and anosognosia in the right-damaged ones. However, at about the same time, a group of neurosurgeons in Italy reported similar emotional changes following unilateral hemispheric sedation with amobarbital sodium for the assessment of speech dominance (Rosadini and Rossi, 1967). Discounting cognitive or functional factors, they proposed that the left and right hemispheres exert opposite influences on emotional tone, with the left hemisphere subserving expressions of positive affect, and the right hemisphere organizing expressions of negative affect.

This view was further advanced by Gainotti (1972, 2001) and Sackheim et al. (1982), who reviewed the literature on pathological laughing and crying produced by nuclear brainstem (pseudo-bulbar) lesions. They confirmed a statistical association of pathological laughing with right hemisphere lesions and pathological crying with left hemispheric damage. In addition, they reviewed the literature on emotional outbursts as ictal components in epilepsy, leading to a significant association of ictal laughing with left-sided foci and ictal crying with right-sided foci. Thus, Sackheim et al. (1982) concluded that mood changes following unilateral lesions reflect disinhibition of contralateral regions and not ipsilateral subcortical release. More recently it has been proposed that lateralized hemispheric mood changes result from release of ipsilateral subcortical centers within a vertical hierarchy of emotional control rather than contralateral disinhibition (Liotti and Tucker, 1995). This issue remains empirically unresolved, although it has long been recognized that in animals certain types of bilateral cortical damage leads to the intensification of emotional behaviors (e.g., decorticate rage).

Cases of pseudo-bulbar palsy, a condition in which patients have uncontrollable episodes of laughter or crying without an apparent triggering stimulus and without associated feelings of happiness or sadness (reviewed in Poeck, 1969; Rinn, 1984), have been interpreted as reflecting damage to pathways that arise in the motor areas of the cerebral cortex, descend to the brainstem, and inhibit motor "output" systems for laughter and crying. In that view, the lesions placed mostly in subcortical structures (basal ganglia and the internal capsule), would *disinhibit* or *release* the laughter

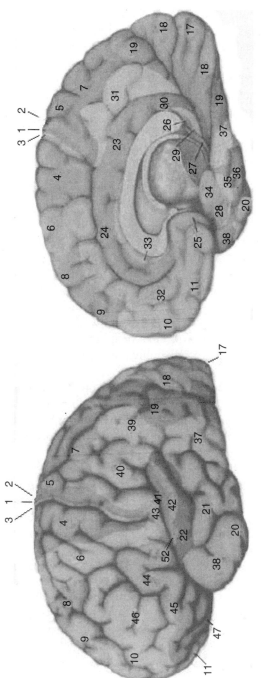

Figure 2.1. Representation of the Brodmann areas in the human brain: lateral surface (*left*); medial surface (*right*). See ftp site for color image.

and crying response systems (Poeck, 1969; Rinn, 1984). Recently, Parvizi et al. (2001) described a case of restricted damage to the cerebro-ponto-cerebellar pathways, highlighting a role for cerebellar structures in the automatic programming of crying and laughter. Although these studies emphasize the nonaffective subcortical motor output systems in such emotional responses, they should not be taken to indicate that subcortical systems have no role in the generation of affect. As discussed later, there is abundant evidence that parts of the subcortical instinctual action apparatus are critical for the generation of emotional feelings.

Other lesion-behavior correlations have emphasized different hemispheric contributions to the regulation of noncognitive emotional influences, such as arousal and emotional expression. Right hemisphere patients have been found to be underaroused, with reduced cortical and autonomic responsivity, particularly to emotionally charged stimuli (Heilman et al., 1978; Morrow et al., 1981; Caltagirone et al., 1989), with less avoidant eye movements to aversive stimuli (Caltagirone et al., 1989) and greater dysfunction in sexual arousal (see review in Tucker and Dawson, 1984). In addition, patients with right hemisphere damage are less facially expressive than patients with left hemisphere damage (Borod et al., 1985; Borod, 1992, 2000). Similarly, normal adults have been found to express emotions more intensely on the left side of the face, particularly during spontaneous displays, which is innervated predominantly by the contralateral right hemisphere (Borod et al., 1983). Interestingly, the left side of the face appears also to be more expressive in rhesus monkeys and in chimpanzees (Fernandez-Carriba et al., 2002), providing evidence for evolutionary continuity that argues for the ethological approach to the analysis of emotional behavior. On the other hand, voluntary emotional displays such as social smiling, are typically more intense on the right side of the face.

Another line of evidence on hemispheric asymmetry for emotion derives from half-field and dichotic studies in healthy volunteers and research on deficits of emotion recognition in brain-injured patients. Tachistoscopic studies in normal participants have shown that the right hemisphere is typically faster and more accurate than the left hemisphere in discriminating facial expressions of emotion, even when the effect of face identity is partialled out (e.g., Ley and Bryden, 1979; Strauss and Moscovitch, 1981). Similarly, patients with right hemisphere damage showed greater deficits in recognizing facial expressions of emotion (e.g., Bowers et al., 1985; Kolb and Taylor, 1981). Recently Adolphs et al. (2000) used an automated three-dimensional lesion reconstruction algorithm in a large group of right- and left-brain-damaged patients to identify a critical role for ventral primary and secondary somatosensory cortices (extending to the insular cortex), particularly on the right, in deficits of facial emotion recognition. These regions presumably contain neural maps of the bodily state associated with an emotion, in agreement with a theoretical framework emphasizing the role of somatic representation in feeling emotions (somatic marker hypothesis; Damasio, 1996).

Recognition of emotional prosody in speech has also been associated with predominantly right hemisphere lesion foci (Ross, 1981; Borod, 1992, 2000) and recently confirmed by neuroimaging studies in healthy participants (Morris et al., 1999; Buchanan et al., 2000; Rama et al., 2001).

Anterior-Posterior Factors in the Generation of Emotionality

The effect of precise lesion location was not taken into account by the early studies on lateralization of emotional behavior reviewed above. With improved anatomical specification of lesions (X-ray computed tomography and more recently MRI), it has become apparent that the anterior–posterior dimension is an important factor in predicting the occurrence of emotional changes following unilateral lesions. Robinson and colleagues (1984) found that poststroke depression was more frequent in the case of anterior lesions of the left hemisphere, and its severity correlated with the distance from the frontal pole (Robinson, 1996). In contrast, for the right hemisphere, poststroke mania was significantly associated with damage to right anterior regions (Starkstein and Robinson, 1988), while damage to right posterior lesions was more associated with depression (Robinson et al., 1984). Importantly, the relationship between poststroke depression and left anterior locus of lesion held when patients with aphasic symptoms were excluded or the effect of aphasia was partialled out (Starkstein and Robinson, 1988).

Another important variable not considered in early studies is the extent of damage to subcortical structures. The head of the caudate, particularly on the left, has been associated with poststroke depression (Robinson et al., 1984), while the right thalamus and right basal ganglia has been associated with mania (Starkstein et al., 1990).

NEUROIMAGING STUDIES OF EMOTION

As the topic of human emotions has been receiving greater scientific status in recent years, two methodologies, PET and fMRI, have contributed the most to our advancement of knowledge about the neural organization of emotions in humans. Before summarizing these results, let us briefly describe these technologies.

PET and fMRI Procedures

During the 1990s PET was the gold-standard of neuroimaging. In PET a small amount of a radiotracer is injected intravenously into the subject, and the concentration of tracer in brain tissue is measured by the scanner (see Fig. 2.2, top). While decaying, the radionucleotides emit positrons that, after traveling a short distance (3 to 5 mm) encounter electrons. The two types of particles annihilate each other, resulting in the emission of two gamma rays in opposite directions. The image acquisition is based on the detection in coincidence of the gamma rays in opposite directions by crystal detectors. Image reconstruction uses lines of response connecting the coincidence detectors through the brain (for more details on PET methods and a more comprehensive description of research uses of PET in psychiatry, see Chapter 6).

Once reconstructed, PET scans for (active and control conditions) are spatially normalized to stereotaxic atlas, and group averaged. Then a voxel-by-voxel parametric difference contrast is carried out, resulting in a difference image that is thresholded to a statistical cutoff, which is overlayed on the same subjects' MRI for registration and visualization (see Fig. 2.2, bottom). State-of-the-art PET scanners have a resolution of 6 mm, allowing precise localization of cortical and some subcortical structures.

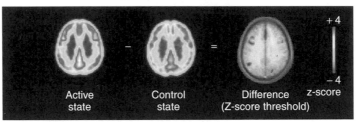

Figure 2.2. Positron emission tomography (PET). *Top*: A typical scanner. *Bottom*: Images in the control task are subtracted voxel-by-voxel from images in the active task. A statistical cutoff is applied to the difference image (*bottom right*). See ftp site for color image.

However, PET has no time resolution. ^{15}O-water, the radiotracer used for activation studies, has a half-life of 2 min. Due to the long integration time of each scan, only "block" designs are possible. Scans of active tasks and control tasks are separated by periods of no acquisition, lasting 10 min, to allow a complete return to baseline of the activations and a complete decay of the radiotracer. Typically 8 to 12 scans are acquired, with 2 to 4 repetitions of each task. The main limitation of PET is the radiation exposure, particularly for women of fertile age and children, which limits repeated testing, and the need of a cyclotron nearby, with a high cost.

In contrast to PET, fMRI is more user friendly and many more studies are available with the technology. It has rapidly replaced PET as the most popular form of neuroimaging. The MRI signal is induced with a strong magnet. When body tissues, rich in water, are placed in a strong magnetic field, all protons in the water molecules become systematically oriented. Radio-frequency pulses are then applied, producing spins in the protons. When they are no longer applied, the proton spins return to their original state releasing radio-frequency waves. Radio-frequency emissions vary with water density in different tissues and can be registered with detector coils (see Fig. 2.3, top).

The fMRI approach measures slight differences in radio frequencies produced by changes in local blood flow in activated regions during cognitive or motor tasks. An increase in oxygen accompanies increased local brain activity. Functional fMRI can measure the ratio of deoxygenated to oxygenated hemoglobin in order to obtain a measure of regional blood flow (yielding the BOLD, or blood oxygen level detection, method). For more details about the BOLD method and a more comprehensive description of research uses of fMRI in psychiatry, see Chapter 6.

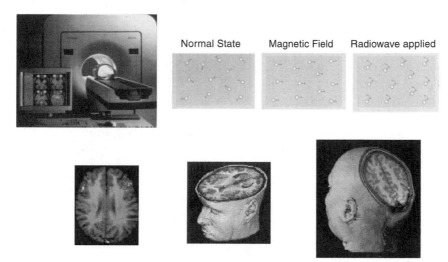

Figure 2.3. Functional magnetic resonance imaging (fMRI). *Top left*: Typical magnet. *Top right*: basic principles of proton density MRI, employed in fMRI: (a) protons systematically orient in a magnet; (b) radio-frequency pulses are applied, producing spins in the protons; (c) proton spins recover the original state releasing radio-frequency waves. *Bottom*: examples of fMRI data during cognitive tasks overlayed on three-dimensional renderings of the human head. See ftp site for color image.

Functional fMRI allows for higher spatial resolution [about 3 mm for 1.5-tesla (T) machines] and possesses better time resolution than PET. However, even if the specific imaging technique allows for superfast data acquisition (2 to 3 sec for an entire brain volume), temporal resolution is limited by the slowness of the hemodynamic response, which peaks at 5 sec from a discrete neural event, and decays slowly (in 12 to 15 sec), resulting in overlapping responses from temporally close events.

Most typically, fMRI studies utilize block designs (on-off), with alternations of tasks each typically lasting 30 to 60 sec. Since each volume is acquired in 2 to 3 sec, a large number of images can be included in task comparisons (typically 50 to 100). Voxel-by-voxel statistical comparisons are carried out with independent T tests and are then thresholded for statistical significance. Resulting differences can be overlayed on three-dimensional MRI renderings of the subject's head for impressive effects (see Fig. 2.3, bottom).

Unlike PET, fMRI is noninvasive, allowing for repeat studies in children and patients, and it can use clinical scanners with moderately priced hardware upgrades. The main limitations are claustrophobia, typically present in no more than 1 percent of the subjects, and less flexibility than PET with experimental situations because the intense magnetic fields disallow metal objects in the experimental field. Inhomogeneities in the fMRI signal are present in the ventral frontal areas and anterior temporal areas (due to nearby air cavities), making the study of emotion and memory more problematic (since these areas are implicated in those processes). One of the biggest problems is the very artificial and noisy environment in which subjects must be tested, which can easily reduce the ability of subjects to attain and sustain realistic emotional states. Thus PET may be considered better for monitoring affect (since radioactive and behavioral challenges can often be done outside the scanner, even though this is not possible for rapidly decaying tracers such as radioactive water), while fMRI, because of its temporal features, is often the better tool for monitoring cognitive processes than for affective ones.

Although functional neuroimaging methods have contributed greatly to our understanding of the neural correlates of human cognition and emotion (Posner and Raichle, 1994), a number of methodological hurdles make the study of emotion through these methodologies particularly challenging. To properly evaluate the rapidly increasing number of studies in the field, it is important to consider some of these difficulties.

Methodological Concerns

First, most neuroimaging studies use a contrast or subtraction method (see Sartori and Umilta, 2000), which critically relies on assumptions of linearity and additivity as well as on the critical choice of comparison control states. Experimental models in vogue in cognitive neuroscience have been applied to the study of emotion, but it is debatable whether this is legitimate, considering certain fundamental differences in the nature of cognitive and emotional processes (Panksepp, 1998a, 2000, 2003). Emotional affects impose *pervasive* influences on cognitions, in part as a consequence of different arousal states generated subcortically and broadcast widely via a variety of "state-control" pathways (e.g., acetylcholine, dopamine, norepinephrine, serotonin). To understand emotions, large-scale network properties and organic controls (neurohormonal effects) are as important as the flow of information through discrete neuronal pathways. There is no assurance that such brain changes are well reflected in blood flow dynamics. In contrast, cognitive processes may rely on more modular cortical representations that arise from more discrete informational "channel-control" functions of the brain. These brain changes may be more apparent under imaging procedures.

It is important to note that the statistical analysis of fMRI images using the most common method [statistical parametric mapping (SPM); Hammersmith, London] applies a general linear algorithm that assumes a typical time course of the hemodynamic function (peak at 5 sec, decay by 12 sec), but it has been shown that the time course of signal changes associated to emotional states generally starts later and has more protracted effects (over 30 sec) (Marcus Raichle, personal communications). In summary, methods perfected on the study of cognitive processes may not transfer automatically to the study of affective states and emotion/cognition interactions.

The choice of a control state is also of critical importance in evaluating most published functional imaging studies. Several studies have used as a baseline state an "eyes-closed rest" (ECR) condition. Others have adhered to the additive method tradition by proposing the use of a higher-level control state (e.g., nonemotional imagery) that matches more closely the active psychological condition (e.g., emotional imagery), thereby controlling, for example, basic sensory, motor, and attentional components of a complex psychological process. Use of the ECR condition has been criticized on the basis that the individual's mental state is typically not monitored, with random thoughts and feelings producing background "noise" (Andreasen et al., 1995). Greater interpretive leeway would emerge if all studies employed at least two control conditions (one being ECR and another a carefully selected "active" control), but that remains rare in the field.

Another limitation of early neuroimaging studies of emotion was the tendency to focus on selected anatomical regions of interest while ignoring many other areas of the brain. More recent studies tend to report more effects, due to the overall acceptance of a view of cognitive functions as represented in distributed networks of regions rather than discrete centers. Also, it used to be common to only report blood flow increases, while ignoring decreases or deactivations, which more recent studies highlight as important in emotional processing and emotion/cognition interactions (Drevets and Raichle, 1998; Mayberg et al., 1999).

Across existing studies, considerable variability in the regional findings derives from the variable choice of statistical thresholds employed in reporting effects (Liotti et al., 2000a). Another major source of variability arises from differences in data transformation steps and statistical processing software (e.g., AFNI [Analysis of Functional Neural Image], CDA [Change Distribution Analysis], etc.) used across laboratories. Most neuroimaging studies employ a considerable amount of filtering and smoothing of the data, resulting in large blobs with a final resolution of 12 to 20 mm (SPM, Hammersmith, London). While this may be an acceptable spatial resolution to localize cortical effects, it does not enable adequate identification of effects in smaller and more compact subcortical structures involved in triggering emotional reaction, especially critical hypothalamic, midbrain, and brainstem structures. Hence, many studies, especially those using fMRI, have found no participation of subcortical structures, long implicated by animal research, in the constitution of human emotions. Some PET and fMRI studies, particularly those with an *a priori* regional hypothesis, have employed less filtering of the image volumes, and thereby approach the actual resolution of the current state-of-the-art PET (6 to 7 mm) and MRI (2 to 3 mm) machines, which allows better localization of effects in subcortical structures (e.g., Liu et al., 2000; Tracey et al., 2002). The increasing use of high-field MRI scanners (3 to 7 T) and higher resolution PET cameras, combined with less filtering will improve spatial resolution of subcortical emotional effects.

Another important difficulty in the neuroimaging of human emotions arises from the wide discrepancy in experimental situations, mood induction paradigms, emotional tasks, and instructions employed. While some studies have been carefully designed to address a specific domain of emotional processing (emotion recognition, subjective feeling or affect, emotion expression), others have used a combination of these. Importantly, studies of affect (e.g., anxiety and sadness) have generally been biased toward cognitive processing of the emotion-inducing materials (perceptual, mnemonic, visual imagery tasks), resulting in widespread activations of cortical structures probably involved in the nonaffective components of the emotional task. Only a few studies have imaged the induced affect *after* the initial affect-induction phase, when the subjective experience had reached a desired intensity (see Damasio et al., 2000; Liotti et al., 2000a). A closely related problem reflects the timing of activation of critical brain structures participating in emotional processing. As an example, amygdala activations have been common in studies of facial expressions (particularly fear). However, it has been found that such activity: (1) habituates over multiple cycles of presentation (Breiter et al., 1996) and (2) shifts to a *deactivation* in the case of emotion categorization tasks (Hariri et al., 2000). In addition, (3) significant changes (increases or decreases) are typically absent in this brain territory in those studies that have taken pains to focus on the subjective affective feelings (Damasio et al., 2000; Liotti et al., 2000a). This suggests that the time courses of activity (both activation and deactivation) are critical variables, but all too commonly ignored, in studies of emotional processing.

Still, there is now an abundance of evidence that emotional stimuli can have regionally specific effects on the brain. Regional effects have been shown for both emotions generated externally by viewing films or emotional scenes, as well as internally generated, memory-driven emotional reminiscences. However, the two approaches often yield different results (Lane et al., 1997; Reiman et al., 1997; reviewed in Phan et al., 2002).

BRAIN CHANGES AS A FUNCTION OF EMOTIONAL STATES

In spite of the above limitations, neuroimaging studies of human emotion have now produced a wealth of data that have helped to promote a paradigm shift from a prevailing focus on cognitive issues in human neuroscience toward an affect revolution. As reviewed below, the available evidence points to discrete regional effects in limbic and neocortical regions for different affective states and different aspects of emotion processing. Important issues of affective homeostasis and regulation, including the nature of cortical–subcortical interactions during intense emotive states, and the exact interplay of limbic and neocortical areas in emotion-cognition interactions are also beginning to get substantive attention (Liotti and Mayberg, 2001; Drevets and Reichle, 1998).

The relationship of the human neuroimaging findings to the core midbrain and brainstem emotional circuits identified in animal research (e.g., Panksepp, 1998a,b) are beginning to emerge largely from studies that have focused on generating intense affective states (Damasio et al., 2000; Liotti et al., 2000a). Although there are abundant gaps in our cross-species knowledge concerning homologies in the underlying brain circuits, existing evidence permits a provocative new model of cortical–subcortical interactions (summarized at the end of this chapter) that may help bridge between animal and human emotion studies.

Neuroimaging of Sadness

A large number of imaging studies have reported neural correlates of the internal experience of sadness provoked in healthy individuals. This work has been largely motivated by its relevance for understanding clinical depression. Considerable variability in the findings can be explained by the use of widely different induction methods (externally driven or internally driven, Reiman et al., 1997) and the cognitive demands associated with the generation of the emotional state (Liotti et al., 2000a; Phan et al., 2002).

In a recent meta-analysis of 50 imaging studies of normal emotion, including 14 studies of sadness, Phan and colleagues identified the subgenual anterior cingulate (Brodmann area 25; see Fig. 2.1, right; Fig. 2.4, left) as the brain zone most consistently implicated in sadness, independent of induction method (Phan et al., 2002). This region has been identified as a brain area of functional and structural abnormality in familial depression (Drevets et al., 1997).

A series of studies have sought to pinpoint the neural correlates of sadness and dysphoria across health and disease, while controlling some of the confounds of previous imaging studies of sadness. Healthy subjects were scanned with ^{15}O-water PET only *after* they had achieved a desired intensity of sadness through retrieval and visualization of distressing autobiographic scripts, as contrasted to ECR (Mayberg et al., 1999) and neutral memory control conditions (Liotti et al., 2000a). The Mayberg et al. studies (also summarized in Chapter 7 from the perspective of depression) highlight subgenual anterior cingulate [Brodmann area 25 (BA25)] activation during transient

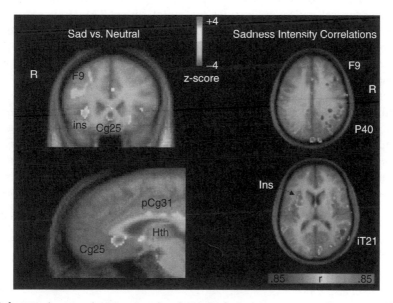

Figure 2.4. PET changes during normal sadness. *Left*: Sadness vs. neutral memory. *Right*: Yellow-red are blood flow increases, and green-blue, decreases. *Top*: coronal view; *bottom*: sagittal view. *Right*: images of correlation of sadness intensity scores with blood flow in the sad scans across subjects and repetitions. Note the striking negative correlations in right prefrontal and parietal cortex. [These data are adapted from Mayberg et al. (1999) and Liotti and Mayberg (2001).] See ftp site for color image.

sadness in the healthy subjects and during the chronic dysphoria of untreated depressed patients, while dorsolateral prefrontal cortex (DLPFC: BA9/46), predominantly in the right hemisphere, was deactivated in both (Mayberg et al., 1999). In addition, the activities of the two areas were inversely related. Healthy subjects induced to be anxious in the same manner showed no changes in these brain areas (Liotti et al., 2000a), confirming the specificity of those effects for feelings of sadness. The existence of reciprocal connections between the subgenual anterior cingulate and DLPFC in animals provides a mechanism whereby emotional and cognitive interactions could be accomplished, as recently highlighted by fMRI studies (Gray, et al., 2002).

Damasio et al. (2000) report activations in midbrain and hypothalamic areas during arousal of several emotions, including sadness, which is consistent with the animal evidence of the critical role of subcortex in generating basic emotions/affects (Panksepp, 1982, 1990, 1998a). However, such effects were not evident in Liotti et al.'s study using a similar memory-driven paradigm. These inconsistencies remain to be resolved but may be explained by the larger sample size (and hence higher statistical power) in the Damasio et al. study.

As mentioned above, early PET studies of induced sadness were carried out at the same time as the subject was involved in active cognitive processing of the emotion-inducing materials—either viewing sad film clips or sad faces or recalling sad memories (or a combination of these). Interestingly, the majority of these studies show neocortical *activation* in right prefrontal cortex BA9 (Reiman et al., 1997; George et al., 1995). This region has been associated with the cognitive evaluation of emotion (Phan et al., 2002), probably involving orienting attention to emotional stimuli and possibly retrieval of emotional memories as well. More importantly, this corresponds to the area deactivated during the maintenance phase of the subjective experience (Mayberg et al., 1999), effects not described in the earlier studies.

Another region associated with normal and abnormal dysphoria is the left ventral lateral prefrontal cortex (VLPC) BA47. Pardo et al. (1993) asked normal subjects to "think sad thoughts" or rest with their eyes closed. The only effect reported was an *activation* of left VLPC, an area previously associated with semantic fluency. Later studies have confirmed that it is the ruminative process that activates this region and not the sad mood per se, since the effect disappears when using a neutral memory control state instead of ECR (Liotti et al., 2000a). This region was also found to be activated during the emotional maintenance phase (Liotti et al., 2000a), perhaps as a result of spontaneous (or residual) ruminations. Of even greater interest is the fact that resting state PET studies in depressed patients with less severe, nonendogenous depression, show predominantly abnormal hypermetabolism in this region, which normalizes with treatment (Drevets, 2000).

Once again, this region appears to track down ruminative aspects of depression that dominate the picture in nonendogenous depression (see Liotti et al., 2002a, for a discussion). So, at variance with regions such as dorsal ACC, subgenual ACC 25 and right DLPFC, left VLPC appears to be activated both during verbal associations in cognitive tasks and ruminations accompanying sadness or dysphoria (see Drevets and Raichle, 1998).

Neuroimaging of Fear/Anxiety

The large majority of studies on fear processing have utilized recognition of frightening facial expressions and found activation of the amygdala (Phan et al., 2002). Such activations did not depend on the conscious, explicit processing of the expression, since they persisted in the absence of conscious registration of the stimuli, when visually "masked" faces were used (Morris et al., 1998; Whalen et al., 1998). However, amygdalar activations have also been observed to fear-associated words (Isenberg et al., 1999) and vocalizations (Phillips et al., 1998), as well as in response to aversive pictures (Garrett and Maddock, 2001), and in human adaptations of animal paradigms of conditioned fear (LaBar et al., 1995; Morris et al., 1998; Whalen et al., 1998), to aversive auditory, olfactory and gustatory stimuli (Zald, 2003), and to exposure to procaine and inhalation of CO_2 (Ketter et al., 1996; Brannan et al., 2001). These combined findings suggest a general role for the amygdala in the automatic, preconscious early detection of threat and danger in the environment, and possibly in triggering the experience of fear/anxiety. Interestingly, amygdalar responses to fearful faces are increased in childhood and adolescence (Killgore et al., 2001) and in childhood anxiety and in posttraumatic stress disorder (PTSD) patients (Thomas et al., 2001; Hull, 2002).

Temporal aspects of amygdala activity appear to have crucial importance. Amygdalar responses to fearful faces tend to habituate over multiple repetitions (Breiter et al., 1996). In addition, one study has shown that while passive presentations of fearful faces gave rise to amygdalar activations, explicit emotion categorization of the stimuli was accompanied by amygdalar deactivations and DLPFC activations (Hariri et al., 2000). There was also concomitant suppression of autonomic responses (Kapler et al., 2001), providing further evidence that processing of cognitive/explicit components of emotional stimuli is carried out by the prefrontal neocortex (see below). Further, this work highlights that DLPFC and amygdala, similar to DLPFC and subgenual cingulate, display opposite activities depending on the level of processing of the emotional task. Finally, no changes in amygdala activity appear to be present when subjects are *experiencing* fear/anxiety in the absence of external stimulation (Damasio et al., 2000; Liotti et al., 2000a).

Studies of fear/anxiety induction in healthy subjects appear to identify a different set of cortico-limbic effects than those present for sadness. In response to anxiety, there is a predominance of *ventral* cortical activations (orbitofrontal cortex, temporal poles, ventral insula) and a distinct set of ventral deactivations (posterior inferior temporal gyri BA37 and 20 and parahippocampal gyri; see Fig. 2.9; Liotti et al., 2000a), consistent with the established connectivities of the amygdala with more ventral cortical regions.

Neuroimaging of Anger

Fewer studies have reported brain responses associated with anger. Interestingly, in spite of the obvious threat content of angry faces, they do not consistently activate the amygdala, or they do so much less than fear. One possible explanation is that fear expressions serve the social communication function to alert and alarm conspecifics about an impending threat in the environment, the source of which has not yet been identified by the perceiver, while for angry expressions the source of threat is immediately apparent to the subject, being the portrayer itself.

One study reported activation of orbitofrontal cortex in response to angry facial expressions (Blair et al., 1999). Script-generated anger has been associated to activations in anterior temporal poles, orbitofrontal cortex (Dougherty et al., 1999; Kimbrell et al., 1999) and ventral anterior cingulate cortex (Dougherty et al., 1999), while one study has emphasized deactivation of medial prefrontal cortex possibly including the subgenual cingulate (Pietrini et al., 2000). The latter observations may be related to a recent study showing that transcranial magnetic stimulation (TMS) over the anterior midline frontal region selectively impairs recognition of anger (Harmer et al., 2001).

Neuroimaging of Happiness and Reward

The most consistent activation across several studies involving happiness induction is in the basal ganglia (ventral striate and putamen) (Phan et al., 2002). These include recognition of happy faces, pleasant pictures (including attractive faces), recall of happy memories, pleasant sexual arousal and competitive arousal of a successful nature (reviewed in Phan et al., 2002). In one study, transient happiness had no areas of significantly increased activity but was associated with significant and widespread reductions in cortical rCBF, especially in the right prefrontal and bilateral temporal-parietal regions (George et al., 1995).

Outcome of Reward

A number of recent neuroimaging studies have investigated reward mechanisms in humans. These studies have used monetary and nonmonetary rewards during planning and gambling tasks (Elliott et al., 2000; Breiter et al., 2001; Knutson et al., 2001a,b; Delgado et al., 2000), or primary taste rewards (e.g., fruit juice) (O'Doherty et al., 2002). Elliott and colleagues (2000) studied with ^{15}O-water PET the response to non-monetary feedback in planning and guessing tasks and found bilateral activation in the caudate nucleus (dorsal striatum) when feedback was given, as opposed to when it was absent. Delgado et al. (2000) used fMRI in a card game with monetary rewards or punishments. They found increases of activity in dorsal striatum (bilateral caudate nuclei) and left ventral striatum that were more sustained in cases of rewarding rather than punishing outcome. Similarly, Breiter et al. (2001) found that responses to rewarding outcomes increased with monetary value in the nucleus accumbens, sublenticular extended amygdala (SLEA) of the basal forebrain, and hypothalamus.

Anticipation of Reward

In their fMRI study, Breiter et al. (2001) found that the prospect of a monetary reward was associated with responses in SLEA and orbital gyrus. In a similar study, Knutson et al. (2001a,b) used fMRI and found that anticipation of increasing rewards elicited ventral striatal (nucleus accumbens) activation, along with increased self-reports of happiness. In contrast, anticipation of increasing punishment did not. Activity in dorsal striate (medial caudate) was present in anticipation of both rewards and punishments.

Using a primary reward (fruit juice) in an fMRI study, O'Doherty et al. (2002) found that expectation of a pleasant taste produced activation in dopaminergic midbrain, amygdala, striatum, and orbitofrontal cortex. Only the latter was activated by reward receipt.

A remarkable PET study by Koepp et al. (1998) examined in vivo dopaminergic activity during a videogame with monetary reward by measuring 11-C raclopride binding to striatal D_2 dopamine receptors. They found that binding was significantly reduced in the dorsal and ventral striatum during the video game compared with baseline levels, consistent with increased dopamine release. Importantly, the binding reduction in ventral striatum positively correlated with the performance level during the task. Thus, the anticipation and outcome of a reward (not separable in this study) activate the dorsal and ventral striatum, and this may be mediated by increased firing in dopaminergic mesolimbic neurons, and increased dopamine release. The more recent fMRI data are consistent with such a conclusion (e.g., Knutson et al., 2001a,b).

Neuroimaging of Disgust

Processing of facial expressions of disgust activates the basal ganglia and insula. Sprengelmeyer et al. (1996, 1997) found that patients with basal ganglia pathology, Huntington's disease, and obsessive-compulsive disorder show selective impairments in the recognition of disgust. Interestingly, recognition of disgust from prosody (Adolphs, 2002) is at chance levels in healthy subjects, suggesting that disgust may be an emotion largely conveyed through facial expression.

Neuroimaging of Primal Drives: Air Hunger

The arousal accompanying the primal drive of hunger for air or breathlessness is possibly one of the most powerful evolutionary subjective states. While there are well-defined medullary, mesencephalic, hypothalamic, and thalamic functions in the basic mechanisms of respiratory regulation, knowledge of cortical and affective control of breathing and the elements subserving the consciousness of breathlessness and air hunger is limited. A recent series of PET studies (Brannan et al., 2001; Liotti et al., 2001; Parsons et al., 2001) investigated such mechanisms in nine young adults, where air hunger was produced acutely by 8 percent CO_2 inhalation. Comparisons were made with inhalation of a N_2/O_2 gas mixture with the same apparatus, with paced breathing, and with ECR. Both respiratory parameters and subjective ratings were recorded for each condition. Independent of the control state (ECR, O_2 breathing, paced breathing), CO_2 stimulation activated a distributed network including pons, midbrain, hypothalamus, limbic and paralimbic areas (amygdala and periamygdalar region), ventral cingulate, parahippocampal and fusiform gyrus, caudate nuclei, and pulvinar. Strong deactivations were seen in dorsal cingulate, posterior cingulate, and prefrontal cortex (Brannan et al., 2001; see Fig. 2.5, left). In the same subjects, subjective breathlessness was manipulated while end-tidal CO_2 was held constant. Subjects experienced a significantly *greater* sense of air hunger breathing through a face mask

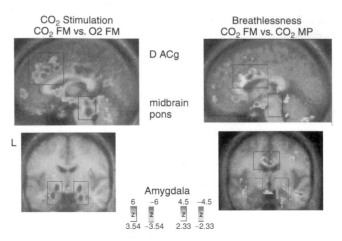

Figure 2.5. PET changes during CO_2 stimulation and air hunger. *Left*: CO_2 stimulation activates the amygdalae, pons-midbrain, cerebellum (*bottom*) and deactivates the dorsal anterior and posterior cingulate and prefrontal cortex (*top*). *Right*: Breathlessness is accompanied by increases in anterior and midcingulate cortex (*top*) and with minimal or no effects in amygdalae and pons/midbrain. [These data are adapted from Brannan et al. (2001) and Liotti et al. (2001).] See ftp site for color image.

than through a mouthpiece. The statistical contrast between the two CO_2 inhalation conditions delineated a distributed network of primarily limbic/paralimbic brain regions, including multiple foci in dorsal anterior and middle cingulate gyrus, insula/claustrum, lingual, and anterior temporal poles (see Fig. 2.5, right). This pattern of activations was confirmed by a correlational analysis with breathlessness ratings (Liotti et al., 2001).

RECIPROCITY OF HUMAN CORTICO-LIMBIC ACTIVITY

The studies reviewed above delineate potential mechanisms of limbic-cortical interactions that may be crucial to understand how the human brain accomplishes the business of normal and abnormal emotion regulation. Emotional arousal accompanying the experience of intense subjective feelings in healthy subjects (Liotti et al., 2000a; Damasio et al., 2000) or active episodes of major depression (Mayberg et al., 1999) as well the emotional arousal in the presence of basic drives such as air hunger, thirst, or pain (Liotti et al., 2001) give rise to activation of subcortical, paleocerebellum, and limbic structures, as well as paralimbic cortex, and the concomitant, inverse sign, namely deactivation of neocortical regions known to subserve cognitive functions (Liotti and Mayberg, 2001). Conversely, cognitive processing and recovery from an acute episode of depression are accompanied by increased activation in neocortical networks subserving attentional processing, such as the DLPFC, inferior parietal cortex, and dorsal ACC, and a concomitant deactivation of paralimbic cortex (subgenual ACC 25) and limbic structures (e.g., amygdala), all of which are well-known substrates of emotion (Drevets and Raichle, 1998; Liotti et al., 2000b).

In their study of the neural correlates of sadness and depression recovery, Mayberg et al. (1999) also carried out regional rCBF and rGlu correlations and found that subgenual ACC 25 and right DLPFC showed the most significant correlation (a negative one) among all regions studied (also see Chapter 7). They concluded that, since animal connectivity studies show definite reciprocal projections between subgenual cingulate cortex BA25 and DLPFC (BA9 and 46), the rCBF and metabolic interactions they observed in these regions during sadness and recovery from depression may reflect functional changes in obligatory, hard-wired circuits (Mayberg et al., 1999). A number of other neuroimaging studies have reported negative correlations between blood flow in prefrontal cortex and amygdala in depression (reviewed in Drevets and Raichle, 1998; Drevets, 2000).

Another line of evidence in favor of inverse-sign interactions between limbic and neocortical regions comes from evidence of modulations in fMRI amygdala response to fearful faces as a function of: (1) implicit (activation) versus explicit (deactivation) processing of emotion (Hariri et al., 2000), which may be mediated by the amygdala's inhibition by frontal cortex, and (2) development, with greater activation in preadolescence followed by a postadolescent shift from amygdala-mediated processing to frontal lobe-mediated processing (Killgore et al., 2001), as well as a later general decline of amygdala activation with increasing age (cited in Adolphs, 2002).

A third line comes from recent studies looking at voluntary suppression of emotion. Male sexual arousal has been found to produce a significant activation of the right amygdala, right anterior temporal pole (BA38), and hypothalamus, but when subjects voluntarily inhibited their sexual arousal, no significant loci of activation were noted in these structures. Instead, significant activations were present in the right medial DLPFC (BA10) and the right ACC BA32 (Beauregard et al., 2001). Similarly, healthy females induced into a sad state while watching sad film clips showed activation of subgenual cingulate, insula, amygdala, and midbrain. When instructed to suppress their sad feelings, subjects showed significant loci of activation in the right DLPFC (BA9) and the right orbitofrontal cortex (OFC) (BA11). This is consistent with the role of right DLPFC in negative mood, as pinpointed by Liotti and Mayberg (2001) as well as TMS methodologies in treating depression (see Chapter 19).

BASIC EMOTIONAL OPERATING SYSTEMS OF THE BRAIN: ANIMAL STUDIES

Let us now briefly consider emotions from the basic animal research side. The core of emotionality resides within the intrinsic subcortical systems of the brain that emerged in deep-time via evolutionary selection to provide organisms certain basic tools for survival. At least seven core emotional systems that course through subcortical regions of the mammalian brain have been provisionally identified (Panksepp, 1998a; the systems are capitalized to highlight that specific brain networks are the referents). They include (1) a dopamine-facilitated appetitive motivation SEEKING system that promotes energetic exploratory searching, foraging, and, with learning, specific goal-directed activities; (2) a FEAR network that mediates flight and freezing, with accompanying anxious feelings, which courses between the amygdala, bed nucleus of the stria terminalis and the periaqueductal gray (PAG) of the mesencephalon; (3) a RAGE (or defensive aggression) system, running approximately in parallel to FEAR circuitry, that promotes aggressive acts and feelings of anger and irritation; (4) a separation distress or PANIC system that triggers separation-induced crying (perhaps foundational for human grieving, sadness, and depressive moods related to loss) and elaborates bonding urges related to social attachments; (5) several LUST systems that contribute distinctly to female and male sexuality and associated erotic feelings; (6) a CARE system to promote maternal nurturance and presumably feelings of love and devotion; (7) a PLAY system that instigates youthful rough-and-tumble playfulness and other ludic activities (e.g., laughter) that may be primal brain ingredients for joyful affect.

Yet other emotional systems may exist, such as those that promote social dominance, but this tendency may reflect maturational effects of the childhood PLAY system, as they interact with FEAR and RAGE systems. In other words, many emergent emotions may arise epigenetically from core emotional systems that interact developmentally with each other and higher cognitive processes. Although these core systems may not be sufficient to evoke the designated affective states, they may be necessary for various distinct emotional affects to emerge in the brain. Although our understanding of these basic emotional networks is far from definitive, the existence of such circuits can focus our neurobiological research efforts in ways that can yield new psychiatric concepts as well as medicines (Chapter 21).

Before proceeding, we would only note that there are many other affective processes in the brain, including those related to specific motivational systems, such as thirst, hunger, and thermoregulation, as well as various sensory rewards associated with alleviation of these bodily imbalances. The general principle here is that negative affective states are generated when bodily states deviate from homeostatic equilibrium, and various forms of pleasure are experienced as organisms indulge in activities that restore bodily imbalances toward normal. Many of these sensory affects are conveyed, in part, by release of opioids in the brain (Panksepp, 1998a; Van Ree et al., 2000). We will not focus on those issues here, but rather upon the instinctual action apparatus that constitutes the basic emotional urges of the mammalian brain. There is space here only to portray these systems in broad strokes, with minimal referencing, but a detailed coverage is available elsewhere (Panksepp, 1998a, 2000, 2001), and how each of these systems may relate to drug development initiatives is outlined in Chapter 21.

Appetitive Motivation SEEKING System

Self-stimulation of circuitry that courses between the ventromedial mesencephalic area known as the ventral tegmental area (VTA) and the nucleus accumbens has long been recognized as the fundamental reinforcement or reward circuit of the brain (for overview, see Ikemoto and Panksepp, 1999). As we have come to appreciate the power and nature of instinctual systems of the brain, certain dubious ideas that came down to us from behavioral psychology have been recently recast into an ethological view of animal nature. This so-called reward circuitry is, in fact, more critical for arousing exploratory urges and energetic foraging as animals *seek* rewards (Panksepp, 1998a). The system is especially responsive when there is an element of unpredictability in forthcoming rewards (Schultz, 2000, 2002), for these are times when animals begin to exhibit especially vigorous curiosity and exploratory responses.

This system allows animals to search, find, and eventually eagerly anticipate the many things needed for survival. The system is not as concerned about the nature of specific rewards; it works equally well in seeking food, water, warmth as well as social goals, including sexual gratification, maternal engagement, and probably playful urges. In short, this system promotes interest, curiosity, and desire for engagement with a host of life activities, and in this capacity it helps animals learn about the reward contingencies in their environments (Berridge and Robinson, 1998; Ikemoto and Panksepp, 1999). This appetitive urge has now been imaged in humans (Breiter et al., 2001; Knutson et al., 2001a,b).

Underactivity in these circuits can promote depression and dysphoria—a generalized failure of "libido." As it facilitates the fulfillment of many goals, this system may be the closest we have yet come to envisioning neural underpinning for the generalized Freudian concept of drive. Overactivity is generally regarded to have important implications for understanding paranoid schizophrenia, as well as mania and various cravings, from food and drugs to sex and gambling. Every addictive drug converges on this system (Wise, 2002) and tends to amplify desire as a trait characteristic of an organism (Nocjar and Panksepp, 2002).

When this system is poorly regulated or overactive for extended periods, as indexed by elevated D_2 receptor populations, schizophrenic tendencies ensue—especially positive "functional" symptoms such as delusions and hyperemotionality (Kapur, 2003), which can be ameliorated with most existing antipsychotic medications (Chapter 10). Negative symptoms of social withdrawal and psychomotor retardation are promoted when this system is underactive. A key neurochemical in the SEEKING system is dopamine, especially the dopaminergic mesolimbic and mesocortical dopamine circuits arising from the VTA (see Fig. 1.1), but there are an enormous number of converging chemistries on this circuitry, and little is known about the specific types of information that are harvested. Nonetheless, we do know that this convergence does not simply yield "information" as an output but rather, an insistent urge to act in certain ways. We know this because all the dopamine neurons behave essentially in the same way, with no indication that they are parsing differences that reflect the many distinct aspects of the world. In other words, there appears to be a mass-action effect of this system that increases an organic pressure for action—a process that has often been called metaphorically "psychic energy."

A diversity of neuropeptide-containing circuits converge on the SEEKING system, including neurotensin, opioids, cholecystokinin (CCK), substance P, orexin, and others, allowing diverse neuropsychic influences to control exploration and anticipatory eagerness. Many of these chemistries are targets for antipsychotic drug development (Chapter 21). Psychostimulant drugs derive their affective appeal and potential to produce craving and psychosis by overarousing this emotional system. Other drugs of addiction, such as opiates, nicotine, and alcohol, also derive at least part of their addictive edge by interacting with this system (Wise, 2002). Among the interesting properties of this system are sensitization effects that emerge from stress as well as periodic experiences with neuropharmacological activators of the system such as amphetamines and cocaine (Robinson and Berridge, 2003). Sensitization reflects an elevated responsivity of the system to both internal and external stimuli.

Dopamine circuits tend to energize many basic appetitive behavioral tendencies as well as higher brain areas that mediate planning and foresight (such as the executive functions of the frontal cortex) promoting, presumably, psychic states of eagerness and hopefulness that help mold purposive behaviors by interacting with higher cortico-cognitive structures such as the working memory systems of frontal lobes. Only recently have we started to grasp the importance of such state-control systems of the brain, and many fit as well or better with the instinctive emotional conceptions of brain functions than currently popular theories of information processing. Indeed, we can generate a remarkable number of compelling working hypotheses when we consider this system from several different vantages:

1. Dopamine cells exhibit a rhythmic firing that resembles the second hand of a clock, and it has been found that this brain system elaborates behavioral eagerness on fixed-interval schedules of reinforcement (see Panksepp, 1981, 1998a), and they show bursting when animals are behaviorally excited and very regular firing when they are not, which is suggestive of some type of background clocking function (Hyland et al., 2002). When one gets tired and bored, subjective time is experienced as slowing down. This is especially evident during physical fatigue (e.g., presumably the internal clock is "ticking" very slowly, as at the end of an exhausting exercise program). Thus, a diminution in the rate of dopamine cell firing may contribute to feelings of fatigue. A related prediction would be that as we pharmacologically reduce dopamine firing, a psychological sense of fatigue would begin to emerge. If so, neuropeptides such as neurotensin and orexin, which facilitate dopamine activity (Chapter 21), might be developed into mild antifatigue agents.

2. The dopamine system seems to facilitate the transition from the perception of temporally correlated events to the conviction that there is causality among those events. There are many relevant examples from animal brain research, for instance, schedule-induced polydipsia and adjunctive (i.e., superstitious) behaviors that depend on dopamine systems (for reviews, see Panksepp, 1981, 1998a). Might delusions be facilitated by activity in this system? It is well known that paranoia tends to be increased by psychostimulants that promote dopamine transmission while being diminished by antidopaminergics (Kapur, 2003).

3. Remarkable relationships have been demonstrated between the psychic energy of the SEEKING system and the dreams of rapid eye movement (REM) sleep (see Chapters 7 and 8; Panksepp, 1998a). On the basis of such relationships, Solms (2000) has argued that dream "energies" can be disassociated from those that promote REM sleep, and that the former is more closely linked to dopamine arousal than to the pontine REM-sleep generators. On the basis of this, tight relations would be predicted between antipsychotic doses of dopamine receptor blocking agents and the vividness, and perhaps the frequency, of dreams. Predictions similar to these could be generated

for all of the basic emotional systems of the brain and thereby guide forward-looking thought in biological psychiatry and depth psychology.

Anger-Promoting RAGE System of the Brain

Operating in opposition to the anticipatory eagerness of the SEEKING system is an opponent process aroused by irritation and frustration that can instigate anger responses. This RAGE system facilitates defensive actions by inspiring fear in other animals. It also energizes anger responses that facilitate retention of valued resources when animals are irritated, frustrated, or restrained. Enraged attitudes and behavior can be provoked in both humans and other animals by stimulating neural circuits that extend from the medial amygdala to the PAG of the central mesencephalon (see Chapter 10, Panksepp 1998a). Human anger may derive much of its impulsive energy from this brain system. When brain tumors irritate this circuit, unpremeditated pathological aggression may ensue (e.g., Pontius, 2002), while damage or psychosurgery along this system has been observed to promote serenity (Panksepp, 1985). Some of the neurochemistries of this system are highlighted in Table 21.1, providing cogent pharmacological targets for diminishing the "heat of anger." Although no highly effective and specific antianger drugs have yet been created, a detailed analysis of the RAGE system may eventually yield such medications (Chapter 21).

A FEAR System in the Brain

Several distinct systems for anxious trepidation may exist in the brain. One FEAR circuit that courses parallel to the RAGE circuit has been extensively studied. When artificially aroused, this circuit promotes freezing and hiding at low levels of arousal and flight during more intense arousal. We can be confident that other animals experience negative affect when this circuit is aroused, since they avoid environmental contexts in which such brain stimulation has been experienced in the past. Humans stimulated at homologous brain sites are commonly engulfed by intense anxiety. If it turns out to be that there is much less variability across species in the subcortical FEAR systems of the brain that helps generate anxiety than in the cognitive structures that regulate such feelings, then it follows that the study of the FEAR system in animals constitutes an excellent strategy for coming to terms with the affective nature of fear in humans. This system as well as other variants of anxiety systems are more fully discussed in Chapter 16.

Separation Distress (PANIC) and Social Bonding (Affiliative-Love) Systems of the Brain

Every newborn mammal is socially dependent. Brain evolution has assured that parents (especially mothers) exhibit strong urges to take care of their offspring, which is suggestive of a basic affiliative-love system in the brain. Likewise, all infants have intrinsic emotional systems to facilitate care and attention when they are distressed.

One of the most distinct outputs of this care-soliciting system, quite easy to study in animal models, is crying or emission of separation calls when socially separated from caretakers. Based on the possibility that precipitous arousal of this circuitry, which courses between the PAG and more rostral brain areas (preoptic, septal, bed-nucleus of the stria terminalis, and anterior cingulate cortex) via medial thalamic corridors, may contribute to panic attacks, this system was originally designated the PANIC system (Panksepp, 1982). This and several other working hypotheses await empirical evaluation (Chapter 12).

A better neurobiological understanding of this circuitry is bound to have important implications for biological psychiatry. An enormous number of emotional disorders are related to feelings of social loss and deficits in the ability to relate socially (Schmidt and Schulkin, 1999). Indeed, the psychotherapeutic enterprise is a social process, and the sociophysiological aspects of brain organization are gradually being revealed (Carter et al., 1999, and Chapters 20 and 21).

The first neuroscience hypothesis concerning the neurochemical regulation of this system was based on the recognition that opioid-based social addictive processes may exist in the brain. Social dependence/bonding and persistent opiate use share three critical features: (1) an initial addiction, emotional attraction-euphoria, phase; (2) a spontaneously emerging tolerance-habituation process whereby the affective potency of narcotics diminishes, as does the power of certain social attractions, which may lead to weaning of the young and the breakup of established adult bonds (e.g., as in divorce); and (3) a robust withdrawal response arising from the severance of attachments. In short, opioids are very effective agents in reducing separation distress, partly by direct dampening of the emotional circuitry that promotes crying. Thus, one reason opiate addiction may be especially prevalent among emotionally distressed individuals is that they derive pleasure pharmacologically from brain systems that normally generate positive affect as a result of prosocial interactions.

It is now clear that brain oxytocin systems also promote the construction of social bonds (Carter et al., 1999; Insel, 1997; Nelson and Panksepp, 1998). Oxytocin is the most potent agent known to alleviate separation distress in animal models. Although this response is not dependent on opioid systems (as indicated by the fact that it is not naloxone reversible), oxytocin does tend to block the development of opiate tolerance (Kovacs et al., 1998). Thus, it remains possible that when oxytocin is released during social activities, as it is during nursing, a secondary benefit may be the maintenance of sensitivity in opioid-based social-reward activities within the brain.

One of the clearest neuropeptide facilitators of separation distress has been corticotrophin-releasing hormone (CRH). Whether such knowledge will lead to new drug development for the treatment of severe separation distress (e.g., CRH antagonists) remains to be seen (Chapter 21).

LUST (Sexual-Love) and Nurturant CARE Systems of the Brain

As described more fully in Chapter 4, the subcortical controls for hormonal control of female and male sexuality were identified decades ago, and they are concentrated in basal forebrain, septal, and anterior hypothalamic/preoptic areas of the brain, coursing medially down to the PAG (Pfaff, 1999). The gender specific LUST systems have distinct components as well as many overlapping ones. For instance, female sexuality has been linked more clearly to the dynamics of oxytocinergic brain systems, while male sexuality is more dependent on vasopressinergic components that uniquely energize male sexual eagerness. The orgasmic components for all genders have strong opioid and oxytocinergic aspects.

Considering the importance of peripherally secreted hormones such as oxytocin, endorphins, and prolactin in parturition and lactation, a satisfying discovery has been that in subcortical neuropeptide circuits these same chemistries promote maternal urges to exhibit care and nurturance. Thus, it would seem that both mother and child derive psychological pleasure and physical homeostasis from the release of such molecules during nursing and other prosocial activities. All of these systems figure heavily in the elaboration of social bonds and a working hypothesis is that they help generate positive feelings of social warmth and the various forms of love, from passionate to nurturant. It is most intriguing that the neurochemistries that regulate sexuality, maternal behavior, and separation distress overlap enormously. The evolutionary suggestion is that maternal feelings emerged from more ancient brain systems that once only mediated sexual ones, which adds a new dimension to the concept of infantile sexuality.

Rough-and-Tumble PLAY-Joy System

Among the genetically ingrained emotive systems of the mammalian brain, perhaps the most ignored has been the one that mediates playfulness. We can now be certain that certain mammals possess PLAY systems, largely subcortically situated, that encourage them to indulge in vigorous social engagements that probably promote socialization and the relevant forms of brain development (Panksepp, 1998a). It would be perplexing if the human brain did not contain psychobiological processes homologous to those found in other mammals that facilitate such joyful, emotionally positive behaviors and feelings of social exhilaration. Such systems are especially active in young animals, helping to weave them into their surrounding social structures, promoting many skills, including winning and losing gracefully. As animals mature, these systems may promote social competition and dominance urges, although the database on such developmental transitions remains modest.

Touch is essential for triggering normal play, and recent work suggests that animals besides humans also have "tickle skin," stimulation of which facilitates playful moods. A laughterlike process has been identified even in laboratory rats (Panksepp and Burgdorf, 2003). Although our understanding of these brain systems remains incomplete, the implications for psychiatry may be profound. For instance, if new, affectively positive neurochemicals are discovered, they may find a niche in the treatment of depression. Linkages to the etiology of attention deficit hyperactivity disorders (ADHD) have also been proposed and evaluated in animal models with promising results (Panksepp et al., 2002, 2003). One idea that now needs to be tested is that abundant access to rough-and-tumble play during early development may facilitate maturation of frontal cortical executive processes, perhaps by inducing genetic transcription of neuronal growth factors (Panksepp, 2001).

If that turns out to be the case, as preliminary data suggest (Gordon et al., 2003), it is possible that sustained access to vigorous, emotionally positive, social engagement during early childhood, from three to six, when rough and tumble is highest in our species (Scott and Panksepp, 2003), may help diminish ADHD-type symptomatology, which is steadily increasing in our culture (Panksepp et al., 2002, 2003). As Plato said In *The Republic* (Section IV) "our children from their earliest years must take part in all the more lawful forms of play, for if they are not surrounded with such an atmosphere they can never grow up to be well conducted and virtuous citizens."

Instinctual "Energies" and Affective States

It now seems evident that there is considerable chemical coding of basic affective processes, and one major way to decode those controls is to detail the neural underpinnings of instinctual-emotional processes in the brains of other mammals. This project is just beginning. An urgent question for biological psychiatry is how affect is actually generated in the brain. So far we only have biogenic amine theories of affect, especially dopamine, norepinephrine, and serotonin based hypotheses, but those very general state-control processes help regulate practically all emotions nonspecifically. The emergence of the idea that distinct affective states are created, in part through various neuropeptide modulators contained in emotional systems that may all have glutamatergic transmission at their core (Panksepp, 1993, 1998a), provides an abundance of novel therapeutic ideas (Chapter 21).

So far, the question of how affect is actually generated by neural activities has only been addressed in theoretical terms. As noted at the outset of this chapter, there is a prevailing notion that it is produced, in some manner, by higher cerebral activities that mediate cognitive consciousness, for instance, by brain areas that mediate working memory (e.g., LeDoux, 1996) or in those that allow us to resymbolize events in terms of language (Rolls, 1999). Damasio (1996), with his "somatic marker" hypothesis, has entertained the classic James-Lange view that emotional experience arises from inputs to the somatosensory processing areas of the cortex.

We would advance the view that affect is an intrinsic aspect of the neurodynamics of the subcortically situated emotional systems of the brain that generate characteristic instinctual actions in response to various situations (largely social) that promote survival as well as various archetypal threats to survival. This last perspective has envisioned that the primitive dynamics of affect operate, in substantial part, through a primal neural representation of a neurodynamically created virtual body schema—a "core self" concentrated in the paramedian brainstem areas, such as the PAG, that are richly interconnected with higher limbic areas (Panksepp, 1998b). This theme has also been advanced by Damasio (1999). In addition, there are also various *sensory affects* (e.g., the pleasure and aversion of various tastes) that arise from brain mechanisms that encode the value of simple external stimuli that have consistently enhanced or diminished survival in the history of the species (Berridge and Robinson, 1998; Panksepp,

1998a). Considering the complexity of this important topic, it may well be that all of the above views will contribute substantially to an ultimate solution of how affective experience is created within the brain. Indeed, it is possible to envision how cortico-cognitive systems of the brain, which transmit information from the cortex to basal ganglia via descending glutamatergic systems, would also have neuropeptide codes that increase the duration of arousal in subcortical systems (for an example of such descending anxiogenic and dopamine modulating effects of CCK, see You et al., 1998).

However, a disparity remains between the animal and human work. The animal data has tended to emphasize emotional circuits quite low in the neuroaxis, while the human data, as already summarized, has typically emphasized the functions of higher limbic areas that are well connected to these lower circuits. Although subcortical areas of the mammalian brain contain various genetically ingrained operating systems for certain basic emotional instinctual responses, to appreciate the full complexity of human emotions, we must obviously focus on the role of higher cognitive processes—those unique mental complexities that have arisen from a massive cortical evolution in hominids. The full spectrum of human affective experience clearly requires hierarchical interactions between lower and higher brain zones as highlighted throughout this chapter. However, it is also important to emphasize how much affect can still be elaborated in the human brain after most of the higher limbic reaches of the brain have been severely damaged (Adolphs et al., 2003).

GENERATING EMOTIONAL FEELINGS THROUGH UPPER BRAINSTEM–LIMBIC AND CORTICAL INTERACTIONS

The combined body of evidence reported above supports a complex hierarchical view of how emotions are elaborated in the brain. For instance, the reciprocal relations in limbic and cortical regions during the imaging of emotions and cognitions in the human brain has prompted the formulation of a model of emotional regulation in which activity in neocortical regions plays an important role in the regulation of emotional states, including emotion generation, maintenance, and suppression (see Figs. 2.6 to 2.8). Elaborating on the observations on decerebration and sham rage in cats and dogs, Reiman (1997) hypothesized that the cerebral cortex serves to "inhibit unbridled expressions of emotion."

This model proposes that cortical regions involved in specific aspects of conscious appraisal of emotion, including perception, evaluation, attention, and memory encoding/retrieval, such as the right prefrontal cortex BA9, right inferior parietal cortex BA40, right inferior temporal cortex BA20/37, and the parahippocampal cortex, can inhibit or "turn off" subcortical emotional responses through efferent connections to their specific limbic-paralimbic targets, such as the ventral cingulate BA25, insula, orbitofrontal cortex, anterior temporal cortex, amygdala, and structures all the way down to the PAG (Fig. 2.6). However, by engaging these cortico-limbic regions in emotional processing, the cortical regions can also participate in triggering the emotional responses that they normally suppress. As the expression of the

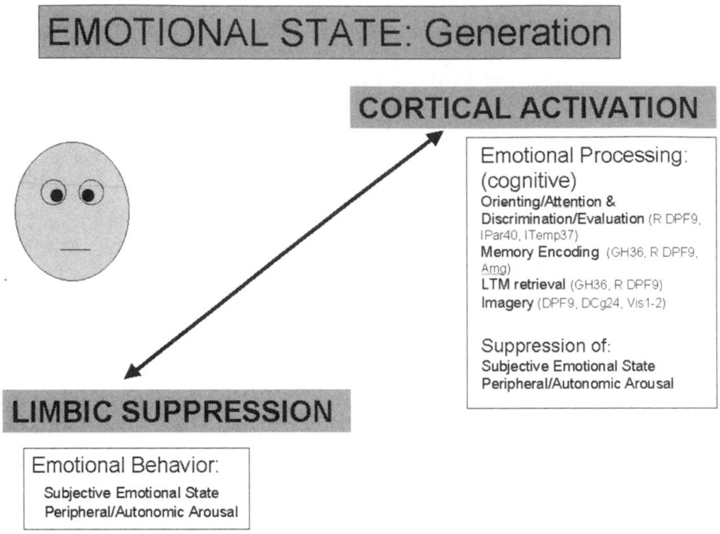

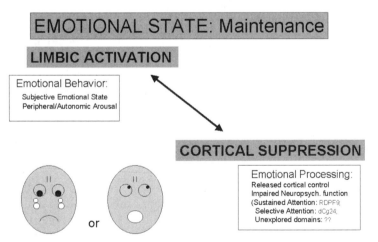

Figure 2.6. Schematic illustration of a model of limbic-cortical interactions: During the emotion generation phase, the neocortex is involved in conscious evaluation/processing of emotion, as well as in suppression of the connected limbic and subcortical targets involved in emotion expression. Abbreviations: DCg24 = dorsal anterior cingulate BA24, Vis1-2 = primary and secondary visual cortex. For all other abbreviations see legend of Fig. 2.9.

Figure 2.7. Schematic illustration of a model of limbic-cortical interactions: During the emotion maintenance phase, when a critical threshold in the engaged core emotional pathways is reached, the limbic and subcortical regions become activated (promoting subjective experience, emotional expression), and the neocortical regions switch off or release (resulting in cognitive impairments in attention). Abbreviations are the same as in Fig. 2.6.

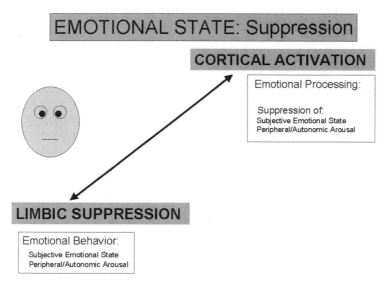

Figure 2.8. Schematic illustration of a model of limbic-cortical interactions: During the emotion suppression phase, when the subjective affective state wears off or is actively suppressed, the neocortex is activated again and the limbic-subcortical targets of emotion are switched off.

emotional response and the subjective state reach a critical threshold in the more subcortical regions of the engaged pathway, the limbic efferent targets become activated and the connected cortical regions become deactivated (Fig. 2.7), resulting in a "flip-flop" inversion of the functional relationship between cortical and subcortical systems (Mayberg et al., 1999; Reiman, 1997). State changes in emotion-cognition interactions would resemble those present during waking and dreaming sleep, where limbic system arousal is accompanied by sustained deactivation of certain frontal cortical zones (see Solms, 2002, for a review). During most waking activity, the cortex tends to suppress limbic activities (Fig. 2.8), helping create a dynamic "unconscious" that is always potentially conscious during environmental events that tend to arouse emotions.

This model of limbic-cortical function has the advantage of explaining both top-down influences (such as psychotherapy in affective disorders) and bottom-up influences (such as emotional arousal produced by CO_2 or pharmacological agents) on emotion regulation. Furthermore, it also provides a mechanism to explain neuropsychological deficits in affective disorders and other intense emotional states. During sad moods and depression, there is selective deactivation of the brain substrates of sustained attention/vigilance (right DLPFC, right inferior parietal), with reaction time performance improving with increased activity in right DLPFC during recovery from depression (Liotti and Mayberg, 2001). Also, sad mood selectively deactivates dorsal anterior cingulate, a substrate of selective attention (Liotti et al., 2000b). In other words, cortical deactivations during emotional states can provide clues into specific cognitive functions impaired during those states.

Segregated Limbic-Cortical Pathways

The available evidence suggests that limbic-cortical pathways are sufficiently segregated among different emotional systems, with some overlap in regions such as medial prefrontal cortex, insula, and cerebellar vermis (Phan et al., 2002; Damasio et al., 2000; Liotti et al., 2000a), possibly subserving common dimensions of emotion (such as arousal). The task of identifying such segregated pathways is complicated by the frequent coexistence of different basic emotions in both normal feelings and affective disorders, and by the fact that only a few studies report cortical deactivations (critical to an evaluation of such networks).

In a comparison to transient memory-script-induced sadness and anxiety in healthy subjects (Liotti et al., 2000a), it was found that the regions involved in emotion generation and suppression (neocortex) are distinct for sadness versus anxiety, with *dorsal* cortical regions—right dorsolateral BA9 and inferior parietal cortex BA40—more involved in the control/expression of sadness, and *ventral* regions, particularly the inferior temporal cortex and parahippocampal gyri, more involved in the control/expression of anxiety (Fig. 2.9).

This hypothesized model fits with reports of (1) prefrontal and inferior parietal abnormalities in clinical depression, but not with inferior temporal and parahippocampal ones (Bench et al., 1992; Mayberg, 1997); (2) prominent inferior and middle temporal but not inferior parietal deactivations in anxiety patients with PTSD (i.e., Bremner et al., 1999); and most strikingly, (3) consistent findings of right parahippocampal

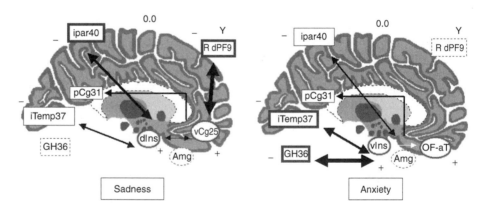

Figure 2.9. Segregated limbic-cortical pathways in sadness and anxiety. In sadness (*left*), cortical deactivations (thick blue and thick arrows) are chiefly dorsal, in right dorsolateral prefrontal BA9 (RDPF9) and inferior parietal BA40 (iPar40). Activations (thick red) are in ventral (subgenual) cingulate BA25 (vCg25), and dorsal insula (dIns). In anxiety, cortical deactivations (thick blue and thick arrows) are chiefly ventral, in inferior temporal gyrus BA37 (iTemp37) and parahippocampal gyrus BA36 (GH36), and activations (thick red) are in orbitofrontal cortex, anterior temporal poles (OF-aT), and ventral insula (vIns). Dashed lines indicate regions not showing significant signal change. Other abbreviations: Amygdala (Amg), posterior cingulate BA31 (pCg31). [These data are adapted from Liotti et al. (2000a).] See ftp site for color image.

deactivation associated with normal and pathologic panic attacks and anxiety provocation, highly suggestive of a role of this structure in the suppression of efferent emotional responses (Reiman, 1997; Reiman et al., 1989). The observation of greater dorsal cortical deactivations (right prefrontal BA9, posterior parietal BA40/7) during sadness as compared to anxiety, and greater ventral cortical deactivations (inferior temporal BA37/20, parahippocampal gyri BA35/36) during anxiety as compared to sadness, also fit with a previous theoretical model. Liotti and Tucker (1995) proposed that asymmetries in dorsal/ventral cortical streams are relevant not only to differences in cognitive processing but also to differences in motivational/emotional control, with the dorsal stream more involved in the regulation of emotional phasic arousal (from sadness/depression to happiness/mania) and the ventral stream more involved in the regulation of emotional tonic activation (from relaxation to anxiety and hostility; Liotti and Tucker, 1995).

Framework for Origin and Neural Elaboration of Human Consciousness

Another construct that benefits from such an integrated model of limbic-cortical function emphasizing vertical control is the problem of where basic conscious awareness is represented and how it may have originated. Several lines of evidence suggest that periconscious, affective processing of emotion takes place subcortically, in areas such as the brainstem, hypothalamus, and amygdala, while cognitive appraisal of emotions takes place in the prefrontal cortex and the anterior cingulate cortex.

To reemphasize some recent PET work, CO_2-induced air hunger has shown that when brain activity in all CO_2 trials were contrasted to low-level baseline tasks (room air, O_2 breathing, or paced hyperventilation), there were striking activations in the amygdalae, the hypothalamus, pons, and midbrain and cortical deactivations in dorsal anterior–midcingulate cortex, DLPFC, and orbitofrontal cortex, independent of the level of air hunger generated (Brannan et al., 2001, see Fig. 2.5, left). However, when CO_2 trials in which subjects experienced more air hunger (breathing through the nose, with a face mask) were contrasted to trials in which they experienced less air hunger (breathing through a mouth piece), the greatest activations were in dorsal ACC BA32, parahippocampal gyri, and anterior temporal poles, while little differential activity was present in the amygdalae and midbrain/pons (see Fig. 2.5, right; Liotti et al., 2001). The same results were obtained with a voxel-by-voxel correlation analysis of brain flow during the CO_2 trials with subjective breathlessness ratings; the greater the reported air hunger, the more active the dorsal ACC and other paralimbic cortical regions (Liotti et al., 2001).

The interpretation was that the amygdala constantly monitors the body milieu for changes in physiological functions triggered by chemoreceptors (such as changes in ventilation, blood pressure, glucose concentration, etc.), through bilateral projections from hypothalamus and brainstem nuclei, much in the same way that it signals threat in the external environment. Thereby, it may act like a thermostat, constantly readjusting its activity level independent of our awareness (even during sleep).

In contrast, the dorsal ACC and possibly other paralimbic structures (anterior temporal poles) would represent the alarm center, alerting the organism that immediate conscious action needs to be taken in order to remove the threat (Liotti et al., 2001). This interpretation fits nicely with Donald Klein's notion of an abnormal suffocation alarm center as central to the pathogenesis of panic disorder (Klein, 1993), a disease dominated by body-centered anxious feelings and anticipations, particularly respiratory. It also fits with the observation of Lane et al. (1998), who found the highest correlations between emotional awareness and cerebral blood flow to be situated in the anterior cingulate cortex.

A meta-analysis of neuroimaging studies involving basic drives and body-centered subjective states (thirst, air hunger, hunger, pain, impeded micturition) shows an overlap of activations in the region of the dorsal anterior and middle cingulate gyrus (BA24) (see Fig. 2.10; Liotti et al., 2001). All these basic and phylogenetically old behaviors share an affective appraisal of danger, likely signaling and prompting the rest of the brain onto a course of action that helps assure survival. Because such responses are present throughout phylogeny, subjective awareness of changes in internal states may represent the earliest glimmer of consciousness—a primitive affective form—that preceded any other form of consciousness. In other words, human consciousness may have been born as awareness of organic internal states and only gradually linked to processing of exteroceptive information. Consciousness is grounded on ancient brain systems that determine how the body is faring in the battle for survival. A concept such as "I feel therefore I am," is still quite revolutionary from the perspective of Cartesian thinking, which often dominates currently popular variants of cognitive psychologies,

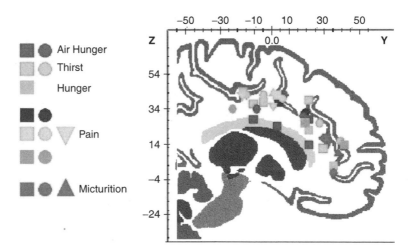

Figure 2.10. Meta-analysis of neuroimaging studies of basic drives: Including studies on pain, air hunger, hunger, thirst, and micturition. Coordinates of activations in anterior and middle cingulate gyrus. Brain map database, University of Texas, San Antonio. Note overlap of effects in these different manifestations of conscious appraisal of danger linked to body state. [These data are adapted from Liotti et al. (2001).] See ftp site for color image.

with its claim that consciousness is either computational or a mere local property of the highest brain systems, such as the neocortex. We believe that it is essential to parse consciousness in terms of evolutionary progressions, whereby higher cognitive functions are solidly based on more primitive forms such as affective consciousness.

The next chapter elaborates a vision of consciousness that is more consistent with the mass of neuroscientific evidence. It may be essential to recognize that the bodily forms of affective consciousness are grounded on the evolved organic processes of rather ancient regions of the mammalian brain. Without addressing the lower issues, we may have little chance of understanding the higher cortico-cognitive forms of consciousness that parse the infinitude of *differences* detected by our exteroceptive sensory-perceptual apparatus.

CONCLUSIONS AND SOME PSYCHIATRIC IMPLICATIONS

During the 20th century, the instinctual apparatus of the mammalian brain was marginalized in psychiatry as well as neuroscience, with only psychoanalysis attempting to grapple with such concepts as the "id" and the "dynamic unconscious." It should again become a foundational issue for all of psychiatry. Although affective consciousness has often been relegated to the unconscious aspects of the human mind, in many psychiatric disorders, this ancient form of consciousness has become so manifest that it overrides the dictates of rationality. Indeed, we must remain open to the possibility that quite often the cognitive aspects of mind are more unconscious than the affective dimensions, as is often demonstrated by conditioning experiments where visceral conditioning proceeds in the absence of any perceptual awareness of the conditional stimuli (e.g., Zald, 2003). Let us briefly consider a couple of examples where the weakness or strength of cognitive and affective coupling—in alexithymia and transference relationships—can cause emotional problems.

Consider the case of alexithymia, the inability to identify and communicate one's feelings. This is not necessarily a deficit in the brain's ability to detect the ancient affective processes elaborated by subcortical systems of the brain, but rather in the inability of higher cognitive-attributional brain regions to connect up well with the ancient autonomic forces of the instinctual emotional apparatus. It may be a partial disconnection syndrome between higher and lower brain functions. Alexithymia may represent a problem in affect regulation, whereby the linkages between subcortical and cortical systems are deviant. In a recent fMRI study that attempted to identify brain regions implicated in this personality trait, it was found that males who scored high on the Toronto Alexithymia Scale exhibited decreased cerebral activation in left mediofrontal-paracingulate cortices in response to highly negative visual images, but they showed more activation in the mediofrontal cortex, middle frontal gyrus, and anterior cingulate in response to highly positive pictures (Berthoz et al., 2002). The tendency of the brain to overrespond to positive emotional stimuli may be partly the cause of these same brains to underrespond to negative emotional provocations. In normal individuals, a tight interplay between cognitions and emotions leads to a balanced mental life. The decoupling of such processes, as in alexithymia, may promote various developmental problems.

Let us also briefly consider the phenomenon of *transference* whereby the emotional residues of early childhood relationships, especially the unconscious memories linked to disturbing affective interactions, continue to impinge on future interpersonal dynamics. Such emotional-cognitive habits are ubiquitous in human relationships and reflect how the stamp of early patterns of behavior often continues to distort how we respond to others. In extreme cases, emotional systems may have "kindled" so that they become excessive influences in people's lives (Chapter 11). One cardinal aim of psychoanalysis is to allow such transference relationships a psychosocial space to be elaborated in a therapeutic context, and thereby brought back into active cognitive consciousness. Through the refeeling and the redescribing of such affective-cognitive habits, it is hoped that people will derive new insights about their motivations and why they respond to other people in the way they do.

Thus, while the transference relationship starts with poorly understood, almost unconscious emotional habits, the ability of affect and analytic work to bring these dynamics back into a fuller consciousness gives people more options in the way they choose to live their lives. Many psychiatric medicines do the same by regulating the affective "energies" that seem to have a mind of their own. Affective states are so hard to regulate because they ultimately emerge from ancient brain areas that have a spontaneous *intentionality of action*, which serves as a foundation for our higher cognitive abilities. Clearly, certain popular targets of fine-grained neuroscientific inquiry, such as the amygdala, are only a fraction of the overall story, for that structure, which links certain external events to fear tendencies, is not essential for feelings of anxiety (Damasio et al., 2000; Zald, 2003).

Because of advances in neuroscience, we are now in a better position to understand the extensive neurobiological nature of this neuronal infrastructure—even the dynamic orchestra of genetic transcriptions that help sustain mental life, with potential new concepts in genetic medicine around the corner (Hannon, 2002). To do this effectively, we need to have new evolutionary perspectives concerning mental continuity among species. As Charles Darwin (1874/1917, p. 617) said, "the mental powers of the higher animals do not differ in kind, though greatly in degree, from the powers of man." If we do not seek to understand the emotions of other animals, we can only have a surface understanding of human emotions. The animal research allows us to work out the details of the subcortical sources of human emotional feelings that have now been well highlighted by brain imaging. That type of knowledge will allow us to modify the relevant brain systems with new and more specific pharmacological agents as well as psychotherapeutic interventions.

REFERENCES

Adolphs R (2002). Neural systems for recognizing emotion. *Curr Opin Neurobiol* 12:169–177.

Adolphs R, Damasio H, Tranel D, Cooper G, Damasio AR (2000). A role for somatosensory cortices in the visual recognition of emotion as revealed by three-dimensional lesion mapping. *J Neurosci* 20:2683–2690.

Adolphs R, Tranel D, Damasio AR (2003). Dissociable neural systems for recognizing emotions. *Brain Cogn*, 52:61–69.

Andreasen NC, O'Leary DS, Cizadlo T, et al. (1995). Remembering the past: Two facets of episodic memory explored with positron emission tomography. *Am J Psychiatry* 152: 1576–1585.

Beauregard M, Levesque J, Bourgouin P (2001). Neural correlates of conscious self-regulation of emotion. *J Neurosci* 21:RC165.

Bench CJ, Friston KJ, Brown RG, Scott LC, Frackowiak RS, Dolan RJ (1992). The anatomy of melancholia—focal abnormalities of cerebral blood flow in major depression. *Psychol Med* 22:607–615.

Berridge KC, Robinson TE (1998). What is the role of DA in reward: Hedonic impact, reward learning, or incentive salience? *Brain Res Revs*, 28:309–369.

Berthoz S, Artiges E, Van de Moortele P, Poline J, Rouquette S, Consoli SM, Martiinot J (2002). Effect of impaired recognition and expression of emotions on frontocingulate cortices: An fMRI study of men with alexithymia. *Am J Psychiatry* 159:961–967.

Blair RJ, Morris JS, Frith CD, Perrett DI, Dolan RJ (1999). Dissociable neural responses to facial expressions of sadness and anger. *Brain* 122:883–893.

Borod JC (1992). Interhemispheric and intrahemispheric control of emotion: A focus on unilateral brain damage. *J Consult Clin Psychol* 60:339–348.

Borod JC (2000). *Neuropsychology of Emotion*. Oxford University Press: Oxford, UK.

Borod JC, Koff E, White B (1983). Facial asymmetry in posed and spontaneous expressions of emotion. *Brain Cognit* 2:165–175.

Borod JC, Koff E, Lorch MP, Nicholas M (1985). Channels of emotional expression in patients with unilateral brain damage. *Arch Neurol* 42:345–348.

Bowers D, Bauer RM, Coslett HB, Heilman KM (1985). Processing of faces by patients with unilateral hemisphere lesions. I. Dissociation between judgments of facial affect and facial identity. *Brain Cognit* 4:258–272.

Brannan S, Liotti M, Egan G, Shade R, Madden L, Robillard R, Abplanalp B, Stofer K, Denton D, Fox PT (2001). Neuroimaging of cerebral activations and deactivations associated with hypercapnia and hunger for air. *Proc Natl Acad Sci USA* 98:2029–2034.

Breiter HC, Etcoff NL, Whalen PJ, Kennedy WA, Rauch SL, Buckner RL, Strauss MM, Hyman SE, Rosen BR. (1996). Response and habituation of the human amygdala during visual processing of facial expression. *Neuron* 17:875–887.

Breiter HC, Aharon I, Kahneman D, Dale A, Shizgal P (2001). Functional imaging of neural responses to expectancy and experience of monetary gains and losses. *Neuron* 30:619–639.

Bremner JD, Staib LH, Kaloupek D, Southwick SM, Soufer R, Charney DS (1999). Neural correlates of exposure to traumatic pictures and sound in Vietnam combat veterans with and without posttraumatic stress disorder: A positron emission tomography study. *Biol Psychiatry* 45:806–816.

Buchanan TW, Lutz K, Mirzazade S, Specht K, Shah NJ, Zilles K, Jancke L (2000). Recognition of emotional prosody and verbal components of spoken language: An fMRI study. *Brain Res Cogn Brain Res* 9:227–238.

Caltagirone C, Zoccolotti P, Originale G, Daniele A, Mammucari A (1989). Autonomic reactivity and facial expression of emotion in brain-damaged patients. In Gainotti G, Caltagirone C (eds). *Emotions and the Dual Brain*, Springer: Berlin, pp. 204–221.

Carter CS, Lederhendeler I, Kirkpatrick B (eds) (1999). *The Integrative Neurobiology of Affiliation*. MIT Press: Cambridge, MA.

Cory GA, Gardner R (eds) (2002). *The Evolutionary Neuroethology of Paul MacLean*. Praeger: Westport, CT.

Damasio AR (1996). The somatic marker hypothesis and the possible functions of the prefrontal cortex. *Philos Trans R Soc Lond B Biol Sci* 351:1413–1420.

Damasio AR (1999). *The Feeling of What Happens: Body and Emotion in the Making of Consciousness*. Harcourt Brace: New York.

Damasio AR, Grabowski TJ, Bechara A, Damasio H, Ponto LL, Parvizi J, Hichwa RD (2000). Subcortical and cortical brain activity during the feeling of self-generated emotions. *Nat Neurosci* 3:1049–1056.

Darwin C (1874/1917). *The Descent of Man and Selection in Relation to Sex*, Appleton: New York.

Delgado MR, Nystrom LE, Fissell C, Noll DC, Fiez JA (2000). Tracking the hemodynamic responses to reward and punishment in the striatum. *J Neurophysiol* 84:3072–3077.

Dougherty DD, Shin LM, Alpert NM, Pitman RK, Orr SP, Lasko M, Macklin ML, Fischman AJ, Rauch SL (1999). Anger in healthy men: A PET study using script-driven imagery. *Biol Psychiatry* 46:466–472.

Drevets WC (2000). Neuroimaging studies of mood disorders. *Biol Psychiatry* 48:813–829.

Drevets WC, Raichle ME (1998). Reciprocal suppression of regional cerebral blood flow during emotional versus higher cognitive processes: Implications for interactions between emotion and cognition. *Cognit Emot* 12:353–385.

Drevets WC, Price JL, Simpson JR Jr, Todd RD, Reich T, Vannier M, Raichle ME (1997). Subgenual prefrontal cortex abnormalities in mood disorders. *Nature* 386:824–827.

Ekman P, Davidson RJ (eds) (1994). *The Nature of Emotion: Fundamental Questions*, Oxford University Press: New York.

Elliott R, Friston KJ, Dolan RJ (2000). Dissociable neural responses in human reward systems. *J Neurosci* 20:6159–6165.

Fernandez-Carriba S, Loeches A, Morcillo A, Hopkins WD (2002). Asymmetry in facial expression of emotions by chimpanzees. *Neuropsychologia* 40:1523–1533.

Gainotti G (1972). Emotional behavior and hemispheric side of the lesion. *Cortex* 8:41–55.

Gainotti G (2001). Hemisphere asymmetries in representation and control of emotions: Evidence from unilateral brain damage. In Kaszniak A (ed). *Emotions, Qualia, and Consciousness*. World Scientific: Singapore, pp. 219–246.

Garrett AS, Maddock RJ (2001). Time course of the subjective emotional response to aversive pictures: Relevance to fMRI studies. *Psychiatry Res* 108:39–48.

George MS, Ketter TA, Parekh PI, Horwitz B, Herscovitch P, Post RM (1995). Brain activity during transient sadness and happiness in healthy women. *Am J Psychiatry* 152:341–51.

Gordon, NS, Burke S, Akil H, Watson SJ, Panksepp J (2003). Socially induced brain fertilization: Effects of play on brain derived neurotrophic factor. *Neurosci. Lett.* 341:17–20.

Gray JR, Braver TS, Raichle ME (2002). Integration of emotion and cognition in the lateral prefrontal cortex. *Proc Nat Acad Sci USA* 99:4115–4120.

George MS, Ketter TA, Parekh PI, Horwitz B, Herscovitch P, Post RM (1995). Brain activity during transient sadness and happiness in healthy women. *Am J Psychiatry* 152:341–351.

Hannon GJ (2002). RNA interference. *Nature* 418:244–251.

Hariri AR, Bookheimer SY, Mazziotta JC (2000). Modulating emotional responses: Effects of a neocortical network on the limbic system. *NeuroReport* 11:43–48.

Harmer CJ, Thilo KV, Rothwell JC, Goodwin GM (2001). Transcranial magnetic stimulation of medial-frontal cortex impairs the processing of angry facial expressions. *Nat Neurosci* 4:17–18.

Heilman KM, Schwartz HD, Watson RT (1978). Hypoarousal in patients with the neglect syndrome and emotional indifference. *Neurology* 28:229–232.

Hull AM (2002). Neuroimaging findings in post-traumatic stress disorder. Systematic review. *Br J Psychiatry* 181:102–110.

Hyland BI, Reynolds JNJ, Hay J, Perk CG, Miller R (2002). Firing modes of midbrain dopamine cells in freely moving rats. *Neuroscience* 114:475–492.

Ikemoto S, Panksepp J (1999). The role of nucleus accumbens DA in motivated behavior: A unifying interpretation with special reference to reward-seeking. *Brain Res Revs* 31:6–41.

Insel T (1997). A neurobiological basis of social attachment. *Am J Psychiatry* 154:726–735.

Isenberg N, Silbersweig D, Engelien A, Emmerich S, Malavade K, Beattie B, Leon AC, Stern E (1999). Linguistic threat activates the human amygdala. *Proc Natl Acad Sci USA* 96: 10456–10459.

Kapler ES, Hariri AR, Mattay VS, McClure RK, Weinberger DR (2001). Correlated attenuation of amygdala and autonomic responses: A simultaneous fMRI and SCR study. *Soc Neurosci Abstr* 645:3.

Kapur S (2003). Psychosis as a state of aberrant salience: A framework linking biology, phenomenology, and pharmacology in schizophrenia. *Am J Psychiatry* 160:13–23.

Kastin AJ, Pan W, Maness LM, Banks WA (1999). Peptides crossing the blood-brain barrier: Some unusual observations. *Brain Res* 848:96–1000.

Ketter TA, Andreason PJ, George MS, Lee C, Gill DS, Parekh PI, Willis MW, Herscovitch P, Post RM (1996). Anterior paralimbic mediation of procaine-induced emotional and psychosensory experiences. *Arch Gen Psychiatry* 53:59–69.

Killgore WD, Oki M, Yurgelun-Todd DA (2001). Sex-specific developmental changes in amygdala responses to affective faces. *NeuroReport* 12:427–433.

Kimbrell TA, George MS, Parekh PI, Ketter TA, Podell DM, Danielson AL, Repella JD, Benson BE, Willis MW, Herscovitch P, Post RM (1999). Regional brain activity during transient self-induced anxiety and anger in healthy adults. *Biol Psychiatry* 46:454–465.

Klein DF (1993). False suffocation alarms, spontaneous panics, and related conditions. An integrative hypothesis. *Arch Gen Psychiatry* 50:306–317.

Knutson B, Adams CM, Fong GW, Hommer D (2001a). Anticipation of increasing monetary reward selectively recruits nucleus accumbens. *J Neurosci* 21:1–5.

Knutson B, Fong GW, Adams CM, Varner JL, Hommer D (2001b). Dissociation of reward anticipation and outcome with event-related fMRI. *NeuroReport* 12:3683–3687.

Koepp MJ, Gunn RN, Lawrence AD, Cunningham VJ, Dagher A, Jones T, Brooks DJ, Bench CJ, Grasby PM (1998). Evidence for striatal dopamine release during a video game. *Nature* 393:266–268.

Kolb B, Taylor L (1981). Affective behavior in patients with localized cortical excisions: Role of lesion site and side. *Science* 214:89–91.

Kovacs GL, Sarnyai Z, Szabo G. (1998). Oxytocin and addiction: A review. *Psychoneuroendocrinology* 23:945–962.

LaBar KS, LeDoux JE, Spencer DD, Phelps EA (1995). Impaired fear conditioning following unilateral temporal lobectomy in humans. *J Neurosci* 15:6846–6855.

Lane RD, Reiman EM, Ahern GL, Schwartz GE, Davidson RJ (1997). Neuroanatomical correlates of happiness, sadness, and disgust. *Am J Psychiatry* 154:926–933.

Lane RD, Reiman EM, Axelord B, Lang-Sheng Y, Holmes A, Schwartz GE (1998). Neural correlates of levels of emotional awareness: Evidence of an interaction between emotional and attention in the anterior cingulate cortex. *J Cogn Neurosci* 10:525–535.

LeDoux JE (1996). *The Emotional Brain*. Simon and Schuster: New York.

Levesque J, Eugene F, Joanette Y, Paquette V, Mensour B, Beaudoin G, Leroux J-M, Bourgouin P, Beauregard M (2003). Neural circuitry underlying voluntary suppression of sadness. *Biol Psychiat*, 53:502–510.

Ley RG, Bryden MP (1979). Hemispheric differences in processing emotions and faces. *Brain Lang* 7:127–138.

Liotti M, Mayberg HS (2001). The role of functional neuroimaging in the neuropsychology of depression. *J Clin Exp Neuropsychol* 23:121–136.

Liotti M, Tucker DM (1995). Emotion in asymmetric cortico-limbic networks. In Davidson RJ, Hugdahl K (eds). *Brain Asymmetry*. MIT Press: Cambridge, MA, pp. 389–423.

Liotti M, Mayberg HS, Brannan SK, McGinnis S, Jerabek P, Fox PT. (2000a). Differential limbic-cortical correlates of sadness and anxiety in healthy subjects: Implications for affective disorders. *Biol Psychiatry* 48:30–42.

Liotti M, Mayberg HS, Jones VM, Agan LC, Cook CI, Woldorff MG, Jerabek PA, Fox PT (2000b). Interactive effects in the anterior cingulate of sadness and selective attention: A PET study (abstract). *Biol Psychiat* 47:125S54.

Liotti M, Brannan S, Egan G, Shade R, Madden L, Abplanalp B, Robillard R, Lancaster J, Zamarripa FE, Fox PT, Denton D (2001). Brain responses associated with consciousness of breathlessness (air hunger). *Proc Natl Acad Sci USA* 98:2035–2040.

Liotti M, Mayberg HS, McGinnis S, Brannan SL, Jerabek P (2002). Unmasking disease-specific cerebral blood flow abnormalities: Mood challenge in patients with remitted unipolar depression. *Am J Psychiatry* 159:1830–1840.

Liu Y, Pu Y, Gao JH, Parsons LM, Xiong J, Liotti M, Bower JM, Fo PT (2000). The human red nucleus and lateral cerebellum in supporting roles for sensory information processing. *Hum Brain Mapp* 10:147–159.

MacLean PD (1990). *The Triune Brain in Evolution*. Plenum Press: New York.

Mayberg HS (1997). Limbic-cortical dysregulation: A proposed model of depression. *J Neuropsychiatry Clin Neurosci* 9:471–481.

Mayberg HS, Liotti M, Brannan SK, McGinnis S, Mahurin RK, Jerabek PA, Silva JA, Tekell JL, Martin CC, Lancaster JL, Fox PT (1999). Reciprocal limbic-cortical function and negative mood: Converging PET findings in depression and normal sadness. *Am J Psychiatry* 156: 675–682.

Mesulam MM, Mufson EJ (1982). Insula of the old world monkey. I. Architectonics in the insulo-orbito-temporal component of the paralimbic brain. *J Comp Neurol* 212:1–22.

Morris JS, Ohman A, Dolan RJ (1998). Conscious and unconscious emotional learning in the human amygdala. *Nature* 393:467–470.

Morris JS, Scott SK, Dolan RJ (1999). Saying it with feeling: Neural responses to emotional vocalizations. *Neuropsychologia* 37:1155–1163.

Morrow L, Vrtunski PB, Kim Y, Boller F (1981). Arousal responses to emotional stimuli and laterality of lesion. *Neuropsychologia* 19:65–71.

Nelson EE, Panksepp J (1998). Brain substrates of infant-mother attachment: Contributions of opioids, oxytocin, and norepinephrine. *Neurosci Biobehav Revs* 22:437–452.

Nocjar C, Panksepp J (2002). Chronic intermittent amphetamine pretreatment enhances future appetitive behavior for drug- and natural-reward: Interaction with environmental variables. *Behav Brain Res* 128:189–203.

O'Doherty JP, Deichmann R, Critchley HD, Dolan RJ (2002). Neural responses during anticipation of a primary taste reward. *Neuron* 33:815–826.

Panksepp J (1981). Hypothalamic integration of behavior: Rewards, punishments, and related psychobiological process. In Morgane PJ, Panksepp J (eds). *Handbook of the Hypothalamus, Vol. 3, Part A. Behavioral Studies of the Hypothalamus*, Marcel Dekker: New York, pp. 289–487.

Panksepp J (1982). Toward a general psychobiological theory of emotions. *Behav Brain Sci* 5:407–467.

Panksepp J (1985). Mood changes. In Vinken PJ, Bruyn GW, Klawans HL (eds). *Handbook of Clinical Neurology. Clinical Neuropsychology. Vol. 1. (45)*, Elsevier Science: Amsterdam, pp. 271–285.

Panksepp J (1990). The psychoneurology of fear: Evolutionary perspectives and the role of animal models in understanding human anxiety. In Burrows GD, Roth M, Noyes R (eds). *Handbook of Anxiety, Vol. 3, The Neurobiology of Anxiety* Elsevier: Amsterdam, pp. 3–58.

Panksepp J (1993). Neurochemical control of moods and emotions: Amino acids to neuropeptides. In Lewis M, Haviland JM (eds). *Handbook of Emotions*, Guildford Press: New York, pp. 87–107.

Panksepp J (1998a). *Affective Neuroscience: The Foundations of Human and Animal Emotions*. Oxford University Press: New York.

Panksepp J (1998b). The periconscious substrates of consciousness: Affective states and the evolutionary origins of the SELF. *J Consciousness Studies*, 5:566–582.

Panksepp J (2000). The neuro-evolutionary cusp between emotions and cognitions. *Consciousness & Emotion*, 1:15–54.

Panksepp J (2001). The long-term psychobiological consequences of infant emotions: Prescriptions for the 21st century. *Infant Mental Health* 22:132–173.

Panksepp J (2003). At the interface of affective, behavioral and cognitive neurosciences. Decoding the emotional feelings of the brain. *Brain & Cognition*, 52:4–14.

Panksepp J, Burgdorf J, Gordon N, Turner C (2002). Treatment of ADHD with methylphenidate may sensitize brain substrates of desire. Implications for changes in drug abuse potential from an animal model. *Consciousness & Emotion*, 3:7–19.

Panksepp J, Burgdorf J, Turner C, Gordon N (2003). Modeling ADHD-type arousal with unilateral frontal cortex damage in rats and beneficial effects of play therapy. *Brain & Cognition*, 52:97–105.

Panksepp J, Burgdorf J (2003). "Laughing" rats and the evolutionary antecedents of human joy? *Physiol. Behav.* In press.

Papez JW (1937). A proposed mechanism of emotion, *Arch Neurol Psychiatry* 38:725–743.

Pardo JV, Pardo PJ, Raichle ME (1993). Neural correlates of self-induced dysphoria. *Am J Psychiatry* 150:713–719.

Parsons LM, Egan G, Liotti M, Brannan S, Denton D, Shade R, Robillard R, Madden L, Abplanalp B, Fox PT (2001). Neuroimaging evidence implicating cerebellum in the experience of hypercapnia and hunger for air. *Proc Natl Acad Sci USA* 98:2041–2046.

Parvizi J, Anderson SW, Martin CO, Damasio H, Damasio AR (2001). Pathological laughter and crying: A link to the cerebellum. *Brain* 124(Pt 9):1708–1719.

Pfaff DW (1999). *Drive: Neurobiological and Molecular Mechanisms of Sexual Motivation*. MIT Press: Cambridge, MA.

Phan KL, Wager T, Taylor SF, Liberzon I (2002). Functional neuroanatomy of emotion: A meta-analysis of emotion activation studies in PET and fMRI. *Neuroimage* 16:331–348.

Phillips ML, Young AW, Scott SK, Calder AJ, Andrew C, Giampietro V, Williams SC, Bullmore ET, Brammer M, Gray JA (1998). Neural responses to facial and vocal expressions of fear and disgust. *Proc R Soc Lond B Biol Sci* 265:1809–1817.

Pietrini P, Guazzelli M, Basso G, Jaffe K, Grafman J (2000). Neural correlates of imaginal aggressive behavior assessed by positron emission tomography in healthy subjects. *Am J Psychiatry* 157:1772–1781.

Poeck K (1969). Pathological laughing and weeping in patients with progressive bulbar palsy. *Ger Med Mon* 14:394–397.

Pontius AA (2002). Neuroethology, exemplified by limbic seizures with motiveless homicide in "limbic psychotic trigger reaction." In Cory GA, Gardner R (eds). *The Evolutionary Neuroethology of Paul MacLean*. Praeger: Westport, CT, pp. 167–192.

Posner MI, Petersen SE (1990). The attention system of the human brain. *Annu Rev Neurosci* 13:25–42.

Posner MI, Raichle ME (1994). *Images of Mind*. Scientific American Library: New York.

Rama P, Martinkauppi S, Linnankoski I, Koivisto J, Aronen HJ, Carlson S (2001). Working memory of identification of emotional vocal expressions: An fMRI study. *Neuroimage* 13:1090–10101.

Reiman EM (1997). The application of positron emission tomography to the study of normal and pathologic emotions. *J Clin Psychiatry* 58 Suppl 16:4–12.

Reiman EM, Raichle ME, Robins E, Mintun MA, Fusselman MJ, Fox PT, Price JL, Hackman KA (1989). Neuroanatomical correlates of a lactate-induced anxiety attack. *Arch Gen Psychiatry* 46:493–500.

Reiman EM, Lane RD, Ahern GL, Schwartz GE, Davidson RJ, Friston KJ, Yun LS, Chen K (1997). Neuroanatomical correlates of externally and internally generated human emotion. *Am J Psychiatry* 154:918–925.

Rinn WE (1984). The neuropsychology of facial expression: A review of the neurological and psychological mechanisms for producing facial expressions. *Psychol Bull* 95(1):52–77.

Rizzolatti G, Umilta C, Berlucchi G (1971). Opposite superiorities of the right and left cerebral hemispheres in discriminative reaction time to physiognomical and alphabetical material. *Brain* 94:431–442.

Robinson TE, Berridge KC (2000). The psychology and neurobiology of addiction: An incentive-sensitization view. *Addiction*, 95:S91–117.

Robinson TE, & Berridge KC (2003). Addiction. *Annual Review of Psychology*, 54:25–53.

Robinson RG (1996). Emotional and psychiatric disorders associated with brain damage. In Panksepp J (ed). *Advances in Biological Psychiatry, Vol. 2*, JAI Press: Greenwich, CT, pp. 27–62.

Rolls ET (1999). *The Brain and Emotion*. Oxford, UK: Oxford University Press.

Robinson RG, Kubos KL, Starr LB, Rao K, Price TR (1984). Mood disorders in stroke patients. Importance of location of lesion. *Brain* 107 (Pt 1):81–93.

Rosadini G, Rossi GF (1967). On the suggested cerebral dominance for consciousness. *Brain* 90:101–112.

Ross ED (1981). The aprosodias: Functional-anatomic organization of the affective components of language in the right hemisphere. *Arch Neurol* 38:561–569.

Sackheim HA, Greenberg MS, Weiman AL, Gur RC, Hungerbuhler JP, Geschwind N (1982). Hemispheric asymmetry in the expression of positive and negative emotions. Neurologic evidence. *Arch Neurol* 39:210–218.

Sartori G, Umilta C (2000). How to avoid the fallacies of cognitive subtraction in brain imaging. *Brain Lang* 74:191–212.

Schmidt LA, Schulkin J (eds) (1999). *Extreme Fear, Shyness, and Social Phobia*. Oxford University Press: New York.

Schultz W (2000). Multiple reward signals in the brain. *Nature Revs Neurosci* 1:199–207.

Schultz W (2002). Getting formal with DA reward. *Neuron* 36:241–263.

Scott E, Panksepp J (2003). Rough-and-tumble play in human children. *Aggressive Behavior*, in press.

Shulman GL, Corbetta M, Buckner RL, Raichle ME, Fiez JA, Miezin FM, Petersen SE (1997). Top-down modulation of early sensory cortex. *Cereb Cortex* 7:193–206.

Solms M (2000). Dreaming and REM sleep are controlled by different brain mechanisms. *Behav Brain Sci* 23:843–850.

Sprengelmeyer R, Young AW, Calder AJ, Karnat A, Lange H, Homberg V, Perrett DI, Rowland D (1996). Loss of disgust. Perception of faces and emotions in Huntington's disease. *Brain* 119:1647–1665.

Sprengelmeyer R, Young AW, Pundt I, Sprengelmeyer A, Calder AJ, Berrios G, Winkel R, Vollmoeller W, Kuhn W, Sartory G, Przuntek H (1997). Disgust implicated in obsessive-compulsive disorder. *Proc R Soc Lond B Biol Sci* 264:1767–1773.

Starkstein SE, Robinson RG (1988). Comparison of patients with and without poststroke major depression matched for size and location of lesion. *Arch Gen Psychiatry* 45:247–252.

Starkstein SE, Mayberg HS, Berthier ML, Fedoroff P, Price TR, Dannals RF, Wagner HN, Leiguarda R, Robinson RG (1990). Mania after brain injury: Neuroradiological and metabolic findings. *Ann Neurol* 27:652–659.

Strauss E, Moscovitch M (1981). Perception of facial expressions. *Brain Lang* 13:308–332.

Thomas KM, Drevets WC, Dahl RE, Ryan ND, Birmaher B, Eccard CH, Axelson D, Whalen PJ, Casey BJ (2001). Amygdala response to fearful faces in anxious and depressed children. *Arch Gen Psychiatry* 58:1057–1063.

Tracey I, Ploghaus A, Gati JS, Clare S, Smith S, Menon RS, Matthews PM (2002). Imaging attentional modulation of pain in the periaqueductal gray in humans. *J Neurosci* 22: 2748–2752.

Tucker DM, Dawson SL (1984). Asymmetric EEG changes as method actors generated emotions. *Biol Psychol* 19:63–75.

Tucker DM, Williamson PA (1984). Asymmetric neural control systems in human self-regulation. *Psychol Rev* 91:185–215.

Van Lancker D, Sidtis JJ (1992). The identification of affective-prosodic stimuli by left- and right-hemisphere-damaged subjects: All errors are not created equal. *J Speech Hear Res* 35:963–970.

Van Ree JM, Niesink RJM, Van Wolfswinkel L, et al. (2000). Endogenous opioids and reward. *Eur J Pharmacol* 405:89–101.

Whalen PJ, Rauch SL, Etcoff NL, McInerney SC, Lee MB, Jenike MA (1998). Masked presentations of emotional facial expressions modulate amygdala activity without explicit knowledge. *J Neurosci* 18:411–418.

Wise RA (2002). Brain reward circuitry: Insights from unsensed incentives. *Neuron*, 36:229–240.

You ZB, Tzschentke TM, Brodin E, Wise RA (1998). Electrical stimulation of the prefrontal cortex increases cholecystokinin, glutamate, and dopamine release in the nucleus accumbens: An *in vivo* microdialysis study in freely moving rats. *J Neurosci* 18:6492–6500.

Zald DH (2003). The human amygdala and the emotional evaluation of sensory stimuli. *Brain Res Revs* 41:88–123.

3

NEURAL SUBSTRATES OF CONSCIOUSNESS: IMPLICATIONS FOR CLINICAL PSYCHIATRY

Douglas F. Watt[1] and David I. Pincus[2]

[1] *Department of Neuropsychology, Quincy Medical Center, Boston University School of Medicine, Quincy, Massachusetts*
[2] *Department of Psychiatry, Case Western Reserve University School of Medicine, Cleveland, Ohio*

INTRODUCTION

What does consciousness have to do with psychiatry? It is certainly true that we diagnose, conduct a mental status exam, and complete a clinical interview, for example, only with patients who are conscious. While our understanding of consciousness is in its infancy and we have much to learn, it is doubtful that any clinician will ever be able to meaningfully provide a neuropsychiatric diagnosis of comatose or sleeping patients. We can imagine how new technologies, such as magnetoencephalography, or functional imaging while performing adaptive tasks, will enable us to observe some of the neural processes (though not the experienced mental contents) in states of dissociation, or mania, or even the excitement of an erotic dream. In each of these examples,

Textbook of Biological Psychiatry, Edited by Jaak Panksepp
ISBN 0-471-43478-7   Copyright © 2004 John Wiley & Sons, Inc.

such technologies will be drawing the outlines of a working mind. The functional relationship and intimacy between the field of psychiatry and the state of consciousness in the patient has often been taken for granted, but this represents a serious neglect. Psychiatry on the whole has paid little attention to just what consciousness might be, particularly in terms of its neural substrates. Yet the notion of consciousness must be acknowledged as the very epicenter of any concept of mind, such that any deep understanding of the disordering of mind, behavior, and emotion central to psychiatric and neuropsychiatric syndromes mandates a deeper understanding of consciousness. From these considerations, there can be little doubt that psychiatry will need to pay increasing systematic attention to consciousness as a foundational process for future progress. If we unravel the neurobiological bases for consciousness, we may discover many new psychiatric treatments, potentially even highly effective therapies we currently could barely imagine.

In the current climate of an exponentially expanding neuroscience, one of the most compelling questions still without a definitive answer is "What is consciousness really made of?" The nature of consciousness, like the nature of emotion, is a topic as old as culture, and yet still in its neuroscientific infancy (the word *conscious* did not enter the English vocabulary until the 17th century as before that time it was referred to as *conscience*). As scientific topics, both emotion and consciousness have just recently emerged from a scientific dark age in which behaviorism informed a systematic and deliberate neglect of both phenomena. Under the sway of behaviorism, consciousness was viewed as either impossible to understand or simply not an appropriate subject for serious scientific study. While these old prejudices are still active in some quarters, they are no longer scientifically justified, particularly in view of the growing empirical literature on consciousness emerging in both neuroscience and cognitive science. There has been a major renaissance of scientific interest in consciousness and its neural substrates over the past 10 years, and science no longer sleeps under the blanket assumption that subjectivity itself should, or even could, be neatly removed from the scientific equation. However, one might still wonder why a chapter on the topic of consciousness is included in a textbook of biological psychiatry. Some of the more obvious reasons are as follows:

1. There are a number of fundamental syndromes in clinical neuroscience best conceptualized as primary diseases or disorders of consciousness [schizophrenia, coma, persistent vegetative state (PVS), akinetic mutism, and delirium as just five of the more prominent]. Although several of these (coma, PVS, and to a lesser extent akinetic mutism) have traditionally been seen as the province of neurology, both disciplines are moving toward synthesis, and these syndromes also potentially inform basic issues in psychiatry.

2. Many other clinical syndromes in the *Diagnostic and Statistical Manual of Mental Disorders, Fourth Edition (DSM-IV)*, including anxiety disorders, affective disorders, autism, posttraumatic stress disorder (PTSD), and borderline and other personality disorders are probably best conceptualized as fundamental disorders of affect and affective regulation. While many psychiatric clinicians and

researchers tend to consider disorders of affect as distinct from disorders of consciousness, recent work suggests that affect and affective regulation may be foundational for "core" or primary consciousness, and therefore the understanding of affect and consciousness are deeply intertwined.

3. The monoamine systems [dopamine (DA), norepinephrine (NE), and serotonin or 5-hydroxytryptamine (5-HT)] and acetylcholine (ACh), almost exclusively the focus of classical clinical psychopharmacology, are key components of what is now conceptualized as an extended reticular activating system, comprising a multicomponent, distributed system for global state control foundational to consciousness. This suggests that most psychiatric therapies affect core aminergic components of these extended reticular activating systems (RAS) underpinning basic arousal mechanisms, and that the neural substrates of consciousness are more immediately relevant to psychiatry than generally appreciated.

For students relatively new to this topic, we would first acknowledge the intrinsic difficulty of the domains addressed in this chapter: (1) difficult philosophical issues about the ontological status of consciousness (what is it and how is it related to other phenomena); (2) terminological issues in the nosology of consciousness, including basic distinctions between a primary, core consciousness and its cognitive extensions ("extended consciousness"); (3) a new typology for diseases of consciousness and their complex lesion correlates; (4) a clinical case study section presenting two diseases of consciousness normally outside the domain of classical clinical psychiatry; (5) a complex and highly distributed neuroanatomy of consciousness; and (6) concepts from neurodynamic theory that attempt to explain how highly distributed neuronal systems might function in an integrated fashion to generate conscious states. Readers new to these subject matters may struggle with some of these concepts, but the three case studies provided should help anchor these complexities in the phenomenology and behavior of real clinical cases.

DUALISM VERSUS EMERGENT PROPERTIES

Most neuroscientifically oriented investigators support a *monistic* view of the mind and brain. Monism, as it applies to the mind-brain sciences, contends that mind and brain activity are of the same "stuff," the same order of things, although they *may* be different aspects of that "stuff" (known as *dual-aspect monism*). This position has largely prevailed over the older dualistic views that treated mind and brain as if they were two ontologically different orders of things. While dualism is philosophically out of fashion, it still pervades the assumptions and models of many neuroscientists, as it has been deeply ingrained in Western thinking for millennia. Still, it is far from intuitively obvious how we are to bridge conceptualizations in neurophysiology regarding the behavior of large-scale neural networks with the basic properties of sentience. Thus, the "mind-body" gap remains a vast chasm with only the beginnings of bridgework.

Spanning that chasm is a central challenge of contemporary neuroscience. The philosopher David Chalmers (1995) has called the building of this bridge the "hard problem" in consciousness studies.

In keeping with the monistic perspective, most brain-mind scientists believe that consciousness is a phenomenon that emerges from the complexity of central nervous system (CNS) development, arising from within the dynamics of the brain, and existing as an embodied and body-centered "subjective space," totally private to its owner. *Consciousness* is an intrinsically private process that has many components seamlessly integrated in normal experience: attention, intention, sensory input, affective states, including moods at the periphery of consciousness, and cognitive content. *Attention* is the selection of fields for potential conscious content; *intention* is defined here as voluntary, goal-directed, or purposeful activity; *sensory input* includes proprioceptive and any other sensory content from the five senses; and *affective states* of a wide range of intensities, including underlying *mood states* that often lie at the periphery of consciousness. In addition (in cortically intact humans and less apparently in animals without language as we understand it), consciousness contains a great deal of highly differentiated cognitive content as well, which correlates with the increasing complexity of sensory processing and the differentiation of sensory content. Central to consciousness is a body-centered frame of reference ("embodiment"), with fundamental properties of agency and "ownership," in which actions (outside of serious disturbances of brain function) are experienced as coming from the self. These properties of qualia, embodiment, agency, and ownership, and the seamless integration of all content in consciousness, have presented the most consistent signposts for consciousness researchers attempting to define and model the neural substrates, and also the field's most consistent and formidable scientific challenges.

NOSOLOGY: CORE VERSUS EXTENDED CONSCIOUSNESS

Four hundred years ago, Descartes concluded that consciousness was reserved for human beings. The weight of evidence now suggests at least primitive forms of sentience in creatures besides *Homo sapiens*. We share an enormous degree of subcortical architecture, paleocortex, aminergic and peptidergic neuromodulatory control systems, and basic affective-motivational systems with a wide variety of mammals. Considering the shared subcortical brain systems that mediate basic motivations and emotions, each with a characteristic feeling tone or subjective valence, how can we not conclude that evidence favors the assumption of phenomenal experience in other mammals, especially primates? Assuming otherwise would mean that these basic behavioral and neural system homologs do not generate an additional homology in terms of a basic sentience. Such a perspective is straightforwardly dualistic and therefore scientifically untenable.

Humans depart from other mammalian lines of evolution principally in terms of extended neocortical and prefrontal system development. These developments give humans vastly enhanced cognitive and conceptual abilities, including language, along with extended capacities for working memory (Baddeley, 1986), planning, and other highly cognitive aspects of executive functions and behavioral organization. The prefrontal and neocortical extensions offer potential cognitive extensions to more primitive executive functions provided by the brain's prototypic affective operating systems and by the basal ganglia.

A number of prominent neuroscience researchers (Damasio, 1999; Panksepp, 1998) have begun to argue that our higher cognitive processes rest on a primary or core form of consciousness. From this point of view, cognition is the latest evolutionary layer on the consciousness onion. This is explicitly different from most cognocentric notions advocating the reverse hypothesis, namely that consciousness depends on higher cognitive processes, including even a proposed dependence on language (Rolls, 1999). The preponderance of evidence favors the notion that these higher cognitive functions rest on foundations provided by the basic affective-homeostatic functions of the brain, as cognitive activity is directed and motivated by those affective systems although it is likely that these cortico-cognitive developments inform and perhaps even in some sense transform the more primitive aspects of core consciousness that we probably share with other mammals.

CLASSICAL WORK ON THE NEURAL SUBSTRATES OF CONSCIOUSNESS

The earliest contributions to a neurobiology of consciousness came from basic discoveries in electrophysiology made possible by the invention of the electroencephalogram (EEG) by Hans Berger (Millett, 2001). The EEG had the then-remarkable capacity of providing a graphical distinction between conscious and nonconscious states. Next, the classical cerveau isole and other modifications performed on animal brains provided initial insights into the brainstem's role in regulating consciousness. Beginning in 1930, Bremer's surgical procedures on animal brains provided key experimental foundations for a neurobiology of consciousness. In the encephale isole, where the spine is severed from the brain, consciousness was not found to be impaired but freedom of movement was devastated. A transection at the level of the high midbrain, termed the cerveau isole, left the animal in a coma for several weeks, with eventually some partial restoration of limited EEG desynchronization but with presumably permanent impairment of consciousness. In a lower transection, known as the midpontine pretrigeminal isole, a great deal of waking EEG activity was observed, suggesting that the space between the cerveau (midbrain) and the mid-pontine isoles contributed crucially to wakefulness. Additionally, because the midpontine isole provided no possibility of additional sensory input, wakefulness could only be due to contributions from the brainstem tissue between the cerveau and the midpontine isole, and not due to some quantitative or qualitative "threshold of sensory input" as the earliest concepts of consciousness and brain function emphasized.

First Articulation of the Concept of a Reticular Activating System

In 1949, building upon the work of Berger, Bremer, and others, Moruzzi and Magoun (1949), noted that electrical stimulation of the basal diencephalon and anterior midbrain resulted in physiological and behavioral activation in cats. This led to the hypothesis of the RAS as a group of structures and pathways necessary for "waking up," including the mental activity of dreaming during sleep. Moruzzi and Magoun noted Berger's observation that the transition from sleep to wakefulness correlated with a change in the EEG from high-voltage slow waves to lower voltage fast activity (*alpha blockade*). These EEG changes occurred with any afferent stimulation that produced increasing alertness. Several earlier investigators had stimulated various sites in the ventral diencephalon, midbrain (including periaqueductal gray (PAG)) and pons, leading to cortical activation, but until the articulation of the RAS concept, there was no integrated theory for how this transformation occurred, either physiologically or anatomically. Moruzzi and Magoun extended and integrated multiple findings around parameters of cortical activation and alertness and in so doing repudiated earlier assumptions that alpha blockade resulted from afferent stimulation directly to the cerebral cortex. In addition, Moruzzi and Magoun noted that when an activation pattern was induced in the cortex, the pattern was not constrained to the sensory cortex of appropriate modality, and the corresponding area of the sensory cortex was not the first to be activated. "Whether somatic, auditory, or, to a lesser extent, visual stimulation was employed, when an arousal reaction was evoked, it appeared simultaneously in all parts of the cortex, and often continued for considerable periods in it after afferent stimulation had ceased" (Moruzzi and Magoun, 1949, p. 469). Moruzzi and Magoun, through stimulating the RAS but avoiding any sensory afferents, achieved cortical activation. Data on brain lesioning studies from Lindsley et al. (1950), as well as their own barbiturate studies, led Moruzzi and Magoun to conclude that arousal begins with the RAS:

> The conception of sleep as a functional deafferentation of the cerebrum is not opposed by this evidence if the term "deafferentation" is broadened to include interruption of the ascending influence of the brain stem reticular activating system, the contribution of which to wakefulness now seems more important than that conducted to the cortex over classical sensory paths. (1949, p. 471)

RECENT WORK ON THE NEURAL SUBSTRATES OF CONSCIOUSNESS: BRIEF OVERVIEW OF ANATOMICAL, CONNECTIVITY, NEUROMODULATORY, AND NEURODYNAMIC ASPECTS

There has been much progress since early conceptions of a reticular activating system by Moruzzi and Magoun. Although there is still no universal agreement on many basic theoretical issues, a broad-based theoretical confluence is slowly emerging. Progress has been made in defining methods for rigorous empirical work; many studies now use a contrastive analysis methodology (first advocated by Baars 1994) in which consciousness becomes a dependent variable (i.e., studying conscious vs. unconscious forms of visual or emotional processing to map the difference). Many streams of research and theory about consciousness emphasize fundamental and intrinsic integrative processes that operate across widely distributed networks. Foundations for these integrative processes may be found in the structures comprising the extended reticular activating system (discussed shortly in detail), and in its thalamic extensions in "nonspecific" thalamic systems, such as the intralaminar nuclei and the counterposed inhibitory gating system organized by the nucleus reticularis thalami (nRt). This "expanded RAS" has been dubbed the *extended reticular thalamic activating system* (or ERTAS by Newman and Baars, 1993). These distributed structures are thought to facilitate *thalamocortical resonances and widespread thalamocortical communications that are likely informed and guided by brainstem and homeostatic mappings.* Although there are important differences in the details of various theories about consciousness by leading theorists and investigators, such as Frith (1989), Rees et al. (2002), Schiff and Plum (2000), Freeman (1999), Hobson & Pace-Schott (2002), Damasio (1999), Baars (1996, 2002), Llinas et al. (1999), Newman & Baars (1993), Ribary (1991, 2000), Edelman (1987, 1999), Tononi (1998, 2000), Taylor (1999), Singer (1998), and others, many theories support the assumption that consciousness reflects globally integrative processes derivative of neurodynamical interactions between multiple contributing brain systems, particularly communication between the critical triad of thalamus, brainstem, and cortex.

As an extension and modification of these ERTAS and thalamocortical theories, Damasio (1999) recently broadly proposed that consciousness reflects *second-order mappings* between structures that correlate ongoing changes in primary or *first-order mappings* emerging out of brainstem and other homeostasis-monitoring systems in conjunction with *object mappings* supported in various sensory systems. Structures contributing to body mapping in all of its many dimensions constitute *proto-self-systems*. This includes the extended set of reticular structures in the brainstem plus hypothalamus, parabrachial nucleus, periaqueductal gray, and several somatosensory systems, including the insula. *Proto-self* body-mapping systems at various levels of the neuroaxis include visceral, proprioceptive, musculoskeletal, and primary somatosensory systems and also structures in the brainstem responsible for maintaining homeostasis. In Damasio's theory, this broad group of body mapping proto-self-systems interact with object-mapping regions in secondary mapping systems located in thalamus, cingulate, and superior colliculi. In this formulation, consciousness emerges from correlational ongoing neurodynamic mappings of current objects in the world and the current state of body. These correlations facilitate enhanced mapping of the particular object, "popping it out" from the unconscious background, and are proposed to be the foundations for the "movie in the brain," the integrated multimodal sensory fields of conscious states.

Another basic principle broadly supported in the consciousness literature is that consciousness is a resource-intensive and "limited-bandwidth" system, and that the brain works endlessly to offload as much of its processing as possible to unconscious processes. Novel tasks that initially demand the resources of consciousness are quickly learned and become increasingly supported in basal ganglia and cerebellar systems that underwrite the consolidation of habits, procedural memories, and complex motor skills, thus allowing consciousness the luxury, so to speak, of focusing on the most essential and novel adaptive demands facing the organism.

Disorders of Consciousness: A Basic Typology

Recent work on diseases of consciousness suggests a basic taxonomy with a gradient from coma, to persistent vegetative state (PVS), then to akinetic mutism (AKM), hyperkinetic mutism (HKM, a rare and little studied disorder), and finally to delirium (Schiff and Plum, 2000). Table 3.1 outlines progressive impairment of functions that comprise essential components of primary or core consciousness and includes two basic components of more extended cognitive consciousness (short-term and working memory). As one can see from the table, arousal to wakefulness, attention, emotion, and intention are progressively impaired as one moves toward more severe disorders of consciousness. Conversely, in disorders of consciousness that are less severe, such as delirium, the disturbances of attention and intention are often more partial, while emotion is often disinhibited and arousal to wakefulness is preserved (outside of stuporous deliriums). The graded nature of these disorders of consciousness, with fuzzy borders and zones of transition between virtually all the syndromes, show increasing compromise of key mesodiencephalic regions as disorders become more severe. This suggests that consciousness is not an all-or-nothing phenomenon, and that it is built through organizational hierarchies in the brain that feed back and forward, integrating the processing performed by many systems. This is why we have not yet, and presumably will

T A B L E 3.1. Diseases of Consciousness

	Coma	PVS	AKM	HKM	Delirium
Arousal	−	+	+	+	+
Attention	−	−	$+/-^a$	+	$-/+$
Emotion	−	$-^b$	$-^c$	+	$++^d$
Intention	−	−	$-^c$	$-/+$	$-/+^e$
STM	−	−	$-^c$	−	$-/+^f$
WM	−	−	$-^c$	−	−

[a] Attentional tracking is preserved in classical vigilant AKM, and more disrupted in so-called slow or mixed AKM, which shares a border with PVS.

[b] Some PVS patients show occasional disconnected affective displays, probably a kind of sham emotion.

[c] Milder AKM states do appear to have some capacity for working memory and other cognitive content, probably in the context of preservation of some minimal degree of emotional activation and thus salience for stimuli (see Case Study 3.1).

[d] Typically, the agitated deliriums show affective disinhibition, while obtunded or stuporous deliriums (that sit on the border of coma) show flattening or attenuated affect.

[e] Intention, in the sense of organized, goal-directed behavior, is fragmented almost in direct proportion to the severity of the confusional state, but motivation and affect may be disinhibited in agitated deliriums and impaired in stuporous deliriums.

[f] Short-term memory is affected in uncomplicated delirium (without underlying or concomitant baseline dementia) by the disruption and disordering of encoding processes, and also by the disordering of retrieval as an executive operation dependent on an internally generated associative search. Confusional-state patients without a predisposing or underlying dementia can show ability for short-term memory when deficits in attentionally sensitive processes are compensated for [more typically delirium is associated with baseline dementias secondary to Alzheimer's disease (AD)].

not ever, find a specific "consciousness center." Consistent with this graded, recursive conceptualization of consciousness, modest lesions of mesodiencephalic or reticular components can generate deliriums, while massive lesions typically generate coma or persistent vegetative state. This notion of consciousness as graded is consistent with basic distinctions made recently (Damasio 1999; Panksepp, 1998) between primary, core, or affective consciousness and more cognitive, semantically informed, or extended consciousness.

Lesion Correlates for Major Disorders of Consciousness

These lesion correlates are best approached as strong general tendencies with clinical/predictive validity but not invariance, for there are exceptions.

Coma
1. Major lesions of mesodiencephalic areas or diffuse axonal injury.
2. Severe toxic-metabolic or neuromodulatory disturbances.

PVS
1. Initial stage of recovery from coma from brain injury, from above etiologies.
2. Lesser lesions of mesodiencephalic and reticular areas, typically sparing some pontine, midbrain, or other mesodiencephalic regions.

AKM
1. A secondary stage of recovery from Coma ⇒ PVS ⇒ AKM, especially from posterior intralaminar thalamic (ILN) lesions.
2. Bilateral cingulate lesions.
3. Extensive lesion of periaqueductal gray (PAG) or VTA lesions.
4. Extensive bilateral lesions of the basal ganglia (BG), especially nucleus accumbens and globus pallidus, more rarely bilateral caudate.
5. On rare occasions, medial forebrain bundle, other RAS areas.

HKM
1. Extensive bilateral lesions of posterior heteromodal cortical fields, typically from bilateral middle cerebralatery (MCA) infarctions.

Delirium
1. Serious toxic-metabolic disturbances or major disruption of neuromodulatory systems, particularly DA, ACh, but on occasion NE, very occasionally 5-HT.
2. Major lesions of right parietal or right prefrontal areas, right basal ganglia, thalamic, or reticular regions. Less frequently, left-hemisphere lesions of same regions.
3. Classically associated with Alzheimer's disease (AD) and superimposed but relatively more modest toxic metabolic or neuromodulatory disturbances. (AD, along with several other neurodegenerative disorders, appears to substantially lower thresholds for delirium from a host of factors—see chapter on neurodegenerative disorders).

In lesion studies, one must note that lesions necessary for serious impairment of consciousness in the adult may be somewhat different from lesions potentially interfering with the development of consciousness in the young, and neurodevelopmental dimensions of this problem are very poorly understood. Despite these complexities, lesion correlates suggest a fairly delimited, mostly midline set of structures that appear to be essential, with more dorsal and lateral structures enabling cognitive extensions of a core consciousness. This is consistent with other lines of evidence that midline and ventral structures in the brain provide the more primitive, affective, and integrative functions. Evidence from several lines of investigation suggests that the most critical components in descending order are:

1. The multicomponent distributed reticular systems previously outlined (the RAS broadly defined),
2. Several mesodiencephalic regions sitting above and in communication with those systems, including midbrain superior colliculus (SC) and cuneiform nucleus (CUN), the intralaminar thalamic nuclei, and the nRt (reticular nucleus of the thalamus), which jointly comprise the dorsal systems of the ERTAS or the extended reticular thalamic activating system (some schemes label both SC and CUN as "midbrain reticular formation" and therefore part of the ERTAS concept);
3. Regions of paleocortex, particularly anterior cingulate;
4. Heteromodal regions in posterior cortex, perhaps particularly right-hemisphere parietal regions, particularly inferior areas;

Regions for which there is incomplete evidence would include the cerebellum (particularly midline regions such as the vermis/fastigal nucleus that have largely reticular connectivities), primary somatosensory cortex, insula, and several other paralimbic regions. It seems likely that cerebellar vermis and paralimbic insula contribute more to core consciousness, while contributions of idiotypic somatosensory regions (S_1 and S_2) are more likely "extended" and cognitive. However, the matter is still largely undecided, with no conclusive empirical evidence yet available. Extensive bilateral damage to dorsolateral prefrontal cortices, essential for working memory and the executive aspects of attentional function and gaze control, produces a severely disorganized state, akin to a chronic delirium (see clinical case discussion). It is an open point whether this is a disorder of core or extended consciousness. Extensive bilateral lesions of these basic regions cause one of the disorders outlined in Table 3.1. Regions of other brain areas (particularly of widespread unimodal and idiotypic neocortical regions) can and do produce serious affective, behavioral, and cognitive changes but probably not disturbances of primary or core consciousness.

CASE STUDY 1: DELIRIUM—A COMMON DISORDER OF ATTENTIONAL FUNCTION AND WORKING MEMORY

A 58-year-old female with a history of coronary artery disease was found in a disoriented and mildly agitated state one morning, wandering outside her apartment after she failed to show up at work. All laboratory studies were negative. Head computed tomography (CT) revealed a relatively small right anterior pontine infarct just inferior to the fourth ventricle. Her confusional state cleared within a week, but for some time she continued to show significant disturbances in attentional function, in spatial relations, especially spatial synthesis, and in other forms of nonverbal or novel cognitive processing, along with quite poor and easily disrupted working memory. The attentional and working memory disturbance was significantly worse in the morning for uncertain reasons. She became depressed, though this was successfully treated with an antidepressant that possessed both serotonergic and noradrenergic properties. This type of antidepressant was chosen over a selective serotonin reuptake inhibitor (SSRI) with the hope that it would better improve right-hemisphere arousal presumably disrupted in the context of the right pontine reticular formation cerebrovascular accident (CVA).

Some 3 months later, the patient was brought to the hospital with congestive heart failure, with associated acute renal insufficiency blood urea nitrogen (BUN > 90). At this time she also showed a moderate confusional state, with marked disorientation to the environment, obvious disturbance in her ability to sustain coherent attentional processes or task frameworks, and mild agitation. This second delirium was clinically and phenomenologically virtually indistinguishable from the first, with the exception of some greater degree of fatigue. It is possible that the previous structural insult had left a residual disruption of right-hemisphere arousal, lowering the threshold for confusional states. In the context of toxic metabolic or neuromodulatory disturbances, this woman was likely more vulnerable to delirium. Unlike many patients with confusional states, this woman did not evidence any sign of baseline dementia, nor did she evidence significant prodromal stage cognitive declines from very early Alzheimer's disease (AD). Given her vascular history, however, she was deemed at risk for such a neurodegenerative process and followed at yearly intervals.

Delirium may be the most commonplace disturbance of consciousness encountered by psychiatric clinicians, as well as by other physicians, and is virtually ubiquitous on medical services in general hospitals. Its quite commonplace nature contrasts with a curious neglect within both clinical neuroscience and consciousness studies of the disorder, as relatively little attention has been paid to understanding the underlying neural and neurodynamic foundations for delirium and confusional states. Delirium is most classically associated with toxic-metabolic disturbances of a wide variety, or neuromodulatory disruptions secondary to psychotropic medicines, often superimposed upon and degrading a baseline dementia of the Alzheimer's type. In terms of neuromodulatory disruptions, it is most typically associated with the effect of anticholinergics, but it is also commonly seen in dopamine precursor loading, from the effects of opiates, and from gamma-aminobutyric acid (GABA) agonist effects of various medicines, including benzodiazepines and anticonvulsants. There is substantial clinical/anecdotal evidence that thresholds for anticholinergic deliriums (and deliriums from virtually all etiologies) are significantly lowered by preexisting AD, even very early stage AD, where there are only fairly modest cognitive deficits. This may possibly be due to early involvement in AD of the cholinergic basal forebrain, although this correlation between lowered thresholds for confusional states and cholinergic deprivation of the forebrain is also not empirically established in AD. As a wide variety of dementing disorders progress into their middle and late stages, the distinction between baseline dementia and confusional states gradually disappears, as patients progressively lose working memory integrity and task/behavioral organization. Diffuse Lewy body disease, more recently appreciated as a disorder distinct from classical Parkinson's disease, often produces a chronic confusional state after only 2 to 3 years of cognitive and behavioral declines, possibly due to its extensive disruption of numerous brainstem neuromodulatory systems, including ACh, DA, and NE (see chapter on neurodegenerative disorders).

Although older concepts of delirium emphasized sensory alterations, perceptual illusions and hallucinations (not unlike some descriptions of schizophrenia, contributing to the tendency to misconstrue delirium as a psychotic disorder), more recent concepts emphasize the core attentional derailment, and an associated collapse of the integrity of working memory. In delirium and confusional states, the normal segue of working memories collapses. Normally, working memories must in some sense "father their successors" and thus show a coherent trajectory. Instead, patients with delirium severely derail (losing task set) even when engaged in simple tasks, and working memory is highly vulnerable to interference. Patients with confusional states often become quite tangential, and language becomes increasingly fragmented (as confusional state worsens) due to the progressive failure of semantic working memory. Patients often fail to register simple information from the immediate environment, in direct proportion to the severity of the confusional state. They frequently cannot shift or maintain a focus of attention in an adaptive manner. Gross behavioral disorganization ensues, particularly as the degree of confusional state worsens, often accompanied by agitation (in nonobtunded confusional states). Confusional states sometimes show transient and disorganized paranoid ideation that can lead to misdiagnosis of the delirium as a psychosis. In misdiagnosed cases, subsequent treatment with neuroleptics (which often reduce the agitation), seem to confirm the psychosis, sometimes with unfortunate concomitant failures to identify reversible toxic-metabolic or neuromodulatory etiologies.

A major theoretical challenge remains for the clinical neurosciences to develop more heuristic concepts of delirium (like those of Mesulam, 2000), integrating the dozens of classical metabolic etiologies with less frequent structural lesion correlates. Case study 1 shows that structural insults to crucial reticular systems in the right hemisphere may generate a disorganized state virtually indistinguishable from classical toxic-metabolic encephalopathies. In this case, the structural insult was a right pontine CVA, leading to a disruption (possibly differentially although this is not known) of pontine noradrenergic, serotonergic, and cholinergic nuclei in the reticular portions of the anterior pons, and subsequently disrupting thalamocortical arousal and integration. However, the more classical structural correlates for CVAs in the right hemisphere would be the heteromodal portions of the parietal lobe, particularly the inferior parietal lobe, as well as dorsolateral prefrontal regions, the thalamus and basal ganglia, and the cingulate.

Thus, one must emphasize that there exist many pathways to the clinical presentation of delirium, and our case represents only one lesion and one metabolic correlate. Delirium also shows us that the coherent organization of working memory can be derailed by direct lesioning of the classical working memory systems in dorsolateral prefrontal cortex, closely related heteromodal systems in parietal lobe essential to attentional function, or by insults to thalamic, basal ganglia, and reticular support systems for these heteromodal cortical areas. Working memory in turn can be conceptualized as an important index of attentional function, the residue of what attentional mechanisms "capture" within a global workspace. The common toxic metabolic processes generating delirium do so presumably by disrupting the gamma band activity required to functionally instantiate these complex distributed networks, perhaps particularly their corticocortical aspects (see section on neurodynamics). Such gamma activity may be more physiologically demanding and thus more vulnerable to toxic-metabolic problems. Delirium also illustrates the close, intrinsic relationship of attentional processes to higher executive processes and organized purposeful behavior, as these two fundamental functional envelopes of consciousness are both affected in direct proportion to the severity of the confusional state. Indeed, the selection, maintenance and updating of working memories is a central executive task for the attentional systems of the brain.

Lastly, but not trivially, delirium presents a little appreciated comment on a very controversial point in consciousness studies, concerning the neuropsychological substrates for feeling states, the manifestation of emotion in consciousness. There are three basic arguments coming from behavioral neuroscience on how this might happen: (1) LeDoux (1996) argues that working memory comes to represent the otherwise unconscious changes associated with emotional activity, and this happens largely in dorsolateral prefrontal cortex; (2) Rolls (1999) suggests that language representation underpins feelings; (3) Panksepp and Damasio suggest that feelings emerge from largely subcortical dynamics, with Panksepp (1998) emphasizing the interactions between PAG, superior colliculus, and pontine motor systems, while Damasio (1999) emphasizes changes in the proto-self-systems, particularly somatosensory cortices remapping various changes in bodily state, generated by the interaction with an emotionally charged object or person. In the nonstuporous deliriums, emotion appears consistently disinhibited, despite the devastation of working memory, and in the severe deliriums, devastation of even coherent language. This argues for the subcortical view of emotion, suggesting that the collapse of working memory and higher cognitive functions does not prevent emotion from entering a very disorganized conscious state. Dysphoric emotion and highly agitated states appear particularly released and commonplace, although deliriums, from some ILN lesions, and other atypical deliriums, will sometimes show manic features. One might readily argue that most individuals would be expected to become dysphoric and agitated when faced with the collapse of basic cognitive functions including even perceptual integrity and stability, and that such a state is intrinsically frightening. Thus, any careful review of the clinical phenomenology of delirium does not support the notion that working memory or language are necessary for prototypical feeling states, and instead suggests that those states sit underneath cognition, underneath working memory, and other higher cortical functions.

Delirium remains very much a promising area for the neuroscientific study of consciousness. Yet, it is a curiously neglected "orphaned child" within clinical neuroscience, having achieved this status despite its virtually ubiquitous presence in general hospitals and nursing homes. Although the treatment of delirium has always emphasized the mitigation of the offending etiologies, research into interventions that might mitigate attentional and executive collapse in chronic confusional states or improve recovery has almost no initiative within the fields of psychiatry and neurology. Given that confusional states (particularly in their more serious forms) devastate capacities for independent functioning, the lack of any comprehensive theory or interest in ongoing empirical research is most puzzling.

NEUROANATOMICAL SYSTEMS AND CONSCIOUSNESS—BASIC LESION/FUNCTIONAL CORRELATES

Changing Concepts of the Reticular Activating System—Arousal Revisited

The concept of a reticular activating system has changed substantially since the original proposal by Moruzzi and Magoun. Although original concepts emphasized the brainstem and the notion of a primitive "nonspecific" architecture (a "reticulum" with diffuse projections), more recent concepts have emphasized a *highly distributed multicomponent system*, containing many structures with exquisite specificity and yet broad connectivities. Consistent with this, the brainstem in general has very complex and highly specific connectivities, containing at least 50 different nuclei running from medulla to ventral diencephalons, with enormously disparate functions that belie the unitary designation of "brainstem." It is not a coincidence, as Parvizi and Damasio (2001) emphasize, that the systems that regulate homeostasis, those that arouse the forebrain, and others that form the ventral foundations for attentional mechanisms are all closely contiguous in the brainstem. One might add that the brainstem also includes basic somatotopic motor maps, integrating these components of attentional function, forebrain arousal, and homeostasis with mechanisms for mapping (and activating) the body in basic motor coordinates. Recent work conceptualizes an "extended" RAS as containing several groups of structures, which for didactic purposes we will group into three functionally related systems (see Fig. 3.2):

1. The *classical reticular nuclei* include the midline raphe (5-HT) systems running from medulla up to the midbrain, and the lateral reticular nuclei. These lateral reticular nuclei (including the cuneiform nucleus, deep mesencephalic nucleus, noncholinergic portion of pedunculopontine tegmental nucleus, pontis oralis, magnocellullaris, and parvocellularis) send presumably mostly glutamatergic projections to basal ganglia (BG) and the more dorsal regions project to intralaminar nuclei (ILN). These lateral reticular nuclei located in the lower pons and medulla also project to ILN, but their brainstem afferents to ILN are most numerous in the upper brainstem, declining at lower levels of pons/medulla in a progressive gradient. Reticular nuclei in lower brainstem can modulate activity of upper brainstem nuclei, thus affecting the forebrain indirectly.

2. The *"autonomic" nuclei* include the parabrachial nucleus (PBN) and PAG in pons and midbrain. Clinicians are often surprised to discover that the PBN and PAG are thought to be reticular structures, though both systems have extensive

reciprocal connections with many other reticular components. There are projections from PBN and PAG to the lateral reticular nuclei, to basal forebrain, and also to various hypothalamic and monoamine nuclei. PAG has extensive projections to all the monoamine systems (particularly DA), and reentrant communication with the hypothalamus, as well as with the nonspecific intralaminar systems in thalamus, and the central (output) nucleus of the amygdala. PBN and PAG have long been known for involvement in control of autonomic/visceral functions, but they also modulate global activity of cerebral cortex, paleocortex, and amygdala. PAG is probably essential for affective arousal being an active, motoric process; full lesions of this structure generate a severe form of AKM (see later case discussions), underlining its poorly understood but probably essential role in all motivated behavior. Thus, PBN and the PAG can modulate the activity of the entire cerebral cortex, through either ILN or basal forebrain projections, and can also influence the lateral reticular nuclei, and monoaminergic/cholinergic nuclei as well. From these multiple connectivities, PBN and PAG can presumably tune the thalamocortical complex consonant with emotional needs and affective states.

3. The *monoamine and acetylcholine nuclei* are the classical neuromodulatory systems upon which psychiatry has focused much of its clinical intervention and research. They include three monoamine systems with differential projection targets and differential global modulatory functions. There are direct noradrenergic (NE) and serotonergic (5-HT) projections from the locus coeruleus/lateral tegmental area and rostral raphe systems, respectively, which spread to the cortical mantle. Dopaminergic (DA) projections are more targeted toward prefrontal and paralimbic systems, with projections from the substantia nigra to putamen, caudate nucleus, nucleus accumbens, along with DA projections from the midbrain VTA to many cortical areas, with strong predominance toward prefrontal, cingulate, insular, and other paleocortical regions. There are also projections from brainstem DA, NE, and 5-HT nuclei to the basal forebrain, regulating key cholinergic systems in the basal forebrain. Cholinergic systems in the pons, including the laterodorsal tegmental nucleus and cholinergic portions of the pedunculopontine tegmental nucleus, project to several midline and nonspecific thalamic nuclei, including particularly the nucleus reticularis and ILN systems, thus regulating thalamocortical function, and to also cholinergic basal forebrain regions essential to cortical regulation/modulation. In turn, the nucleus reticularis thalami (nRt) receives collaterals from all thalamocortical axons, inhibiting their activity via GABA interneurons, functioning as a competitive "global gate" for cortex that presumably allows the thalamocortical complex to settle in and out of various states.

This is a complex set of processes with parallel and overlapping systems in the brain stem that regulate the forebrain, thalamus, and cortex directly, and by influencing the cholinergic basal forebrain, thereby modulating the cortex indirectly. The monoamines themselves have differential global modulatory roles, underlining further that forebrain arousal is not a unitary process. Noradrenergic systems (NE) appear crucial to sensory tuning, to signal to noise in sensory systems, and for attentional sharpening of posterior cortical processing. DA systems from VTA mediate a non-specific seeking and motivational or affective arousal. ACh systems are central to thalamocortical and cognitive arousal, attention, and short-term memory. 5-HT, an indolamine, is relevant to behavioral inhibition, and may regulate "channelizing" of brain systems and some degree of inhibition of catecholamine systems. These differential roles are mirrored in their cortical projection targets (e.g., ACh tends to project to large pyramidal neurons critical to cortico-cortical communication, while 5-HT projections typically synapse onto inhibitory interneurons). As mentioned above, psychiatry has traditionally targeted the vast majority of its probes and therapies toward these systems. The basic topography of these aminergic regulatory systems for global state control can be summarized in terms of a few basic projection systems (see Fig. 3.1):

1. Largely glutamatergic projections from the dorsal portions of the lateral reticular nuclei into ILN, and continuing glutamatergic projections from ILN to cortex, as thalamic extensions of the RAS.

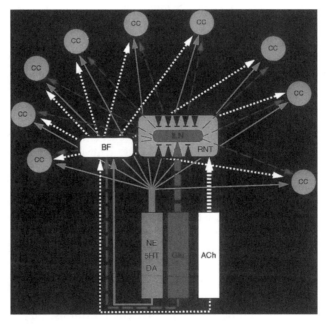

Figure 3.1. Graphic for the Extended Reticular Activating System. Glutamatergic projections from classical lateral reticular nuclei to thalamus, and from thalamic ILN systems to cortex. Dopaminergic, serotonergic and noradrenergic projections in midbrain and pons that bypass thalamus and project directly to cortex. DA, NE, 5-HT and lateral reticular glutamatergic projections regulating basal forebrain. Pontine and basal forebrain cholinergic systems projecting to thalamus and cortex respectively (from Parvizi and Damasio 2000, with permission from Elsevier Science). See ftp site for color image.

2. Projections from the cholinergic pontine nuclei into the thalamus, especially targeting nonspecific thalamic system; additional cholinergic projections from basal forebrain to cortex from four basal forebrain nuclei: nucleus basalis (substantia innominata in earlier terminology), medial septal nucleus, diagonal band of Broca, and magnocellular preoptic field.

3. Projections from the monoaminergic nuclei (serotonin, norepinephrine, and dopamine) bypassing the thalamus directly into forebrain and cortex, with differential projections to more anterior (dopaminergic) vs. somewhat more posterior (noradrenergic) cortical systems, consistent with the more executive or motivational as opposed to the sensory signal-to-noise function of those amine systems, respectively.

4. Projections from the lateral reticular nuclei, pontine cholinergic nuclei, and the NE, DA, and 5-HT aminergic nuclei (from locus ceruleus, VTA, serotonergic raphe, respectively) to basal forebrain regulating the cholinergic systems there.

5. There have been recent suggestions that hypothalamic histamine and orexin systems should be added to the RAS, given evidence that they are centrally involved in wakefulness.

Traditionally, the RAS has been seen as functionally synonymous with the concept of a nonspecific arousal system. There are large and generally unappreciated gaps in what this notion really explains. First of all, the notion of arousal as nonspecific is clearly mistaken from the standpoint of widely differential contributions from these many reticular structures. Additionally, the notion of "arousal" has been used in very different ways. Arousal has referred to: (1) any process that increases the likelihood of neuronal depolarization or that increases firing rates of distributed forebrain neurons, (2) affective arousal (as in states of anger), and (3) processes that mediate global state shifts, such as into wakefulness, dreaming, and the various stages of sleep. The first meaning of arousal (increased firing rates in forebrain) is not an adequate explanation at a neurodynamic level for either the achievement of arousal in behavioral/affective terms or for arousal to wakefulness, as consciousness cannot be meaningfully explained by the simple notion of increased firing of forebrain neurons under brainstem influence. The second and third meanings of the term are intrinsically related, as arousal to consciousness is fundamentally a "hot" (motivational) rather than "cool" process, gaining only the appearance of affective neutrality and cognitive calm in humans as we have a great deal of inhibitory neocortex. Lastly, arousal, as in simple arousal to wakefulness, is not an adequate functional correlate for the extended RAS systems, as wakefulness is preserved in PVS, where no consciousness is presumed present, often in the context of extensive RAS-mesodiencephalic lesions. Thus arousal to a conscious state cannot be conflated with simple wakefulness and requires other integrative functional "envelopes" (core elements) that we have emphasized: attention, intention, and emotion. Further, if arousal means that stimuli generate coherent behavioral responses, this notion simply begs many crucial questions about how these structures (and their modulators and connectivities) underpin consciousness.

These aminergic neuromodulatory systems sit in close communication with several more dorsal and equally critical mesodiencephalic structures: the thalamic intralaminar nuclei (ILN), the thalamic reticular nucleus (nRt), and the midbrain reticular formation [primarily the superior colliculus (SC) and cuneiform nucleus (CUN)]. ILN and nRt functional specialization are reviewed below in some detail. The functional roles of SC and CUN are incompletely mapped, particularly CUN. They may function as "gating" or "priming" systems, offering a kind of attentional "biasing" to higher resolution cortical systems. For example, SC projects to nRt, and also to various thalamic and cortical systems central to spatial mapping, and lesions of SC can cause hemispatial neglect (Mesulam, 2000). SC may offer a kind of low-resolution multimodal mapping of the total sensory envelope for the organism, with this basic biasing available to and essential for the higher resolution mappings the cortex is capable of making (Newman and Baars, 1993).

Evidence suggests that these distributed RAS and other closely situated mesodiencephalic systems underpin the brain's ability to instantiate global neurodynamics, providing for the functional integration of highly distributed systems running from top to bottom of the brain. In this sense, the notion of arousal cannot be neatly separated from the formidable process of widespread functional integration, and differential, task-variant, recruitment/inhibition. Modeling this neurodynamically, and thus illuminating the brain's functional integration in conscious states, is still the most difficult challenge facing the neuroscience of consciousness.

THALAMIC SYSTEMS

Intralaminar Nuclei (ILN)

The intralaminar nuclei are a group of midline systems that receive primarily glutamatergic projections from the classical lateral reticular systems in the brainstem (see summary of RAS) and also from pontine cholinergic systems. ILN in turn sends primarily glutamatergic connections to specific layers of cortex (typically layers I and II), to the basal ganglia, and to the basal forebrain. The ILN has traditionally been conceptualized as an extension of the RAS and, along with the nRt, part of the nonspecific thalamus. The ILN includes both anterior and posterior groups of nuclei. Because of the complex connectivities of the ILN, these nuclei play a central role in cortical arousal, attention, intention, working memory, and sensorimotor integration, including gaze control, with gaze control being virtually paradigmatic for attentional control in visual animals. Schiff and Plum (2000) propose that anterior ILN groups perhaps have a greater role in working memory/sensory integration, and that conversely, posterior ILN groups likely play a key role in motor integration/gating of voluntary motor processes, and emotion.

ILN lesions can generate (depending on their severity) relatively brief coma, vegetative states, akinetic mutism, delirium, and often various kinds of dementia as an end state (see case studies). Extensive bilateral lesions of the ILN systems (if other components of the extended reticular activating system are relatively undamaged) show a bizarre and fascinating clinical course, as we have seen in the second case. This is a rare syndrome, but it underlines major theoretical challenges to the neuroscience of consciousness, suggesting that the ILN systems may provide integrative functions that neurodynamically link the extended brainstem reticular components and the thalamo-cortical mantle. These linkages appear to be essential for core consciousness. However, unspecified collateral systems are able to progressively acquire these functions over time, in a fashion that is still poorly understood.

Bilateral lesions of the ILN discussed in cases study 2 may be one clinical syndrome that more dramatically than any other underlines the extent of our fundamental ignorance regarding the complex integrative reticular-thalamocortical mechanisms foundational for consciousness. This syndrome, which shows a walk-through of all the major disorders of consciousness, suggests that the fundamental integrative mechanisms for consciousness are "writ large" throughout the brain's connectivities and functional neurodynamics in a fashion still not well mapped. This walk-through syndrome suggests that these fundamental integrative mechanisms cannot be neatly localized to any particular brain system. Rather, they are likely to be heavily instantiated in the extended reticular thalamic activating system (ERTAS) and other anatomically closely related systems. Lesser (or greater) disturbance of integrative mesodiencephalic neurodynamics produces a lesser (or greater) disorder of consciousness, from coma all the way to confusional states, and even including transitions to dementia and milder cognitive deficits. The walk-through syndrome argues for a graded and recursive conceptualization of consciousness, and not the intuitively more appealing all-or-nothing concept of consciousness. It suggests that consciousness involves a progressive or epigenetic layering of poorly understood integrative mechanisms, from its core constitutive elements through to its more extended cognitive aspects. No existing theory of consciousness in the scientific literature adequately explains this walk-through syndrome, and most theorists and researchers are not even aware of its now reasonably well-validated existence.

Nucleus Reticularis Thalami (nRt)

nRt is a thin sheath of neurons on the entire lateral surface of the thalamus. It is a GABAergic inhibitory system that receives collateral projections from all thalamocortical axons passing through it. nRt provides a basis for adaptive gating and selective inhibition and activation of the highly distributed cortical systems, acting as a central pacemaker for thalamic oscillations. It receives projections from the pontine cholinergic nuclei and the midbrain portions of the reticular activating system, including the superior colliculus and cuneiform nucleus. Lesion correlates for nRt have not been well-established given that it is almost impossible for naturalistic lesions of the thalamus to be confined to nRt, but it presumably has a central role in attentional gating, and in underpinning mutual reciprocal inhibition of multiple cortical areas in the service of directed cognitive activity. Several theorists of thalamocortical function (Taylor, 1999; Scheibel, 1980; Baars and Newman, 1994) have jointly hypothesized that nRt functions as a "net" on which potential working memories and conscious content compete, proposing that material makes it into working memory by virtue of potentially widespread neurodynamic "alliances" established on its surface (in concert with activity in many other regions, particularly anterior and posterior heteromodal cortices and their thalamic counterparts). Cholinergic systems may play a role in the regulation of nRt, as it receives projections from the pontine cholinergic systems. One would predict from current models of nRt function that extensive damage to nRt, particularly on the right side of the cortex, could generate serious attentional disturbance and a delirium, as mechanisms for global thalamocortical selection and inhibition would be severely affected.

CORTICAL SYSTEMS

Paralimbic Cortex and Heteromodal Cortex

The role played by the neocortex in the generation of consciousness was long assumed essential. Recent work suggests that if one pays careful attention to a distinction between *conscious state versus conscious content*, the role of the cortex, particularly the neocortex, appears to be limited to its underpinning conscious cognitive contents, with these conceptualized as cognitive extensions of core consciousness. An exception to this general principle may be paleocortex, and possibly other heteromodal systems anteriorly and posteriorly, particularly parietal regions and prefrontal regions. The region of paralimbic cortex most consistently linked to consciousness is the anterior cingulate, long thought essential to attentional function, response arbitration, and motivational salience of virtually all stimuli.

The respective roles of heteromodal neocortex versus paleocortex in generating core or primary consciousness is incompletely understood, but research suggests that *some* paleocortex and heteromodal cortex is likely essential for the creation of phenomenal content ("the movie in the brain"). The ability to have coherent sensory content in ANY specific modality may require (counterintuitively) heteromodal systems. Functional imaging studies (see Rees et al., 2002, for summary) comparing conscious and unconscious visual stimuli demonstrate that conscious stimuli show activation of various heteromodal regions in prefrontal and parietal cortex, plus visual cortices, while unconscious stimuli only activate visual pathways. Lesion correlates of hyperkinetic mutism (associated with bilateral destruction of posterior temporal-parietal association cortex) also suggest that posterior heteromodal fields are likely essential for core consciousness. Hyperkinetic mutism resembles an extremely severe delirium, with severe fragmentation of intention, no evidence of working memory, and severe attentional collapse. (Perhaps the most puzzling aspect of the syndrome of hyperkinetic mutism is the question of why these patients are mute and do not produce Wernicke's aphasic speech output.) Interestingly, bilateral extensive damage to dorsolateral prefrontal heteromodal fields produces a very similar state, and also resembles a severe unremitting delirium, although without the puzzling mutism of hyperkinetic mutism if Broca's area is preserved.

This suggests that the posterior and anterior heteromodal fields and their reciprocal connectivities enable integrated action-perception linkages or cycles essential to coherent agency, and the meaningful organization of both behavior *and* perception in consciousness. A reasonable hypothesis from these lesion correlates is that extensive bilateral damage to posterior or anterior heteromodal cortical fields may prevent the organization of any kind of coherent perceptual object in any modality, or coherent working memory or task organization/procedural memory, respectively. Behavior is disorganized in either very extensive anterior or posterior bilateral heteromodal disease possibly because action-perception cycles (Fuster, 1991), linking behavioral organization to coherent perceptions of the world, are devastated in either instance.

The evidence argues though that consciousness is about "intrabrain relations and integrative communication." An ongoing dialog between paralimbic-heteromodal cortex and unimodal-idiotypic systems appears essential for normal sensory (and presumably motor content and the sense of agency also, although this has been much less closely studied). This communication between paralimbic-heteromodal and more unimodal-idiotypic systems seems to allow "category-specific". regions (e.g., those dedicated to faces, words, or objects) to get their processing into conscious workspace, possibly by virtue of critical gating and selective modulation performed by the heteromodal regions. Differential forms of gating and selective enhancement and modulation may also characterize the roles of many deep mesodiencephalic brainstem regions vis à vis the cortex. However, much in terms of the critical interactions between cortex and these multiple deep mesodiencephalic regions in constructing the core functional envelopes of intention, attention, emotion, and specific sensory content remains to be fully elucidated. Table 3.2 summarizes evidence for such a global workspace or global access theory, leaving many fundamental mechanisms still to be elucidated by future research.

Primary (or Idiotypic) and Unimodal (Early) Sensory Cortices

Unimodal and idiotypic systems in the cortex are not essential to sustain a primary consciousness but are clearly essential for normal cognitive and sensory contents. Early sensory cortices are essential for the generation of content in any particular modality, but the evidence suggests that, without "broadcasting" of the conjoint operations of the hierarchy of early and late sensory cortices into heteromodal systems, the content of those sensory operations do not make it into consciousness. Vision is clearly the best mapped of these sensory modalities. Evidence suggests that reentrant communications and various neural synchronies between a host of "early" sensory systems in V_1-V_4 and "late" ones in V_5 are essential to settle the distributed network into a stable "attractor state" that provides a discrete percept. These connectivities may allow "adaptive resonances" (Grossberg, 1980) between top-down conceptual predictions and bottom-up feature detectors, to enable the generation of whole perceptions. Deprived of all connection to early sensory cortices, the brain cannot even hallucinate in that modality. This suggests a conundrum with respect to specification of cortical anatomy and consciousness: We do not need early (primary and unimodal) sensory cortices for a conscious state, or probably for any aspect of core consciousness, but deprived of *all* early sensory cortices, consciousness would be empty indeed, except perhaps for our affective state (likely quite negative!) and perhaps some degree of proprioception.

T A B L E 3.2. Evidence for Global Access or Global Work Space Theories

Source	Method	Results of Non-Conscious Conditions (Not-Reportable)	Results of Conscious Conditions (Accurately Reportable)
Sensory Consciousness			
Logothetis et al. multiple studies (e.g.)	Binocular rivalry between diagonal contrast edges, color, motion, and objects. Multi-unit recording in visual cortex of the macaque.	In early visual cortex 12–20% of cells responded. In object recognition areas inferior temporal & superior temporal sulcus (IT/STS) no cells responded.	In early visual cortex 12–20% of cells responded. In object recognition areas (IT/STS) 90% of cells responded.
Tononi et al. 1999	MEG of flickering input with binocular rivalry in humans, allowing tracing of input signal with high signal-to-noise (S/N) ratio across large regions of cortex.	Widespread frequency-tagged activation in visual and nonvisual cortex.	50–80% higher intensity in many channels throughout cortex.
Srinivasan et al. 1999	As above.	Widespread frequency-tagged activation in visual and nonvisual cortex.	Higher intensity and coherence in visual and nonvisual cortex.
Dehaene et al. 2001	Functional MRI (fMRI) of visual backward masked vs. unmasked words in cortex.	Regional activation in early visual cortex only.	Higher intensity in visual cortex plus widespread activity in parietal and frontal cortex.
Rees et al. 1999	fMRI of unattended and attended words and pictures.	Less activation in word/picture areas of visual cortex.	More activation in word/picture areas of visual cortex.
Kjaer et al. 2001	Subliminal vs. supraliminal visual verbal stimuli using PET.	Activation in visual word areas only.	Activation in visual word areas plus parietal and prefrontal cortex.
Beck et al. 2002	Change blindness vs. change detection.	Activation of ventral visual regions including fusiform gyrus.	Enhanced activity in parietal and right dorsolateral prefrontal cortex as well as ventral visual regions.

TABLE 3.2 (*continued*)

Source	Method	Results of Non-Conscious Conditions (Not-Reportable)	Results of Conscious Conditions (Accurately Reportable)
Vuilleumier et al. 2001	Seen and unseen faces in visuospatial neglect, using fMRI and event related potentials (ERPs).	Activation of ventral visual regions.	Ventral visual activation plus parietal and prefrontal regions.
Driver and Vuilleumier 2001	Extinguished vs. conscious stimuli in unilateral neglect, fMRI, and ERPs.	Activation in ventral visual regions including fusiform gyrus.	Activation also in parietal and frontal areas of the intact left hemisphere.
Learning and Practice			
Haier et al. 1992	PET before and after learning computer game Tetris.	Drastic drop in cortical metabolic activity.	Widespread, intense cortical metabolic activity.
Raichle et al. 1999	Word association vs. simple noun repetition before and after training.	Trained word association indistinguishable from simple word repetition.	More intense activity in anterior cingulate, left prefrontal and left posterior temporal lobe and right cerebellar hemisphere.
Mental Effort			
Duncan and Owen 2000	Meta-analysis of 10 tasks comparing low and high mental effort (including perception, response selection, executive control, working memory, episodic memory and problem solving).	Low prefrontal activation.	High prefrontal activation, in middorsolateral, midventrolateral, and dorsal anterior cingulate cortex.
Waking vs. General Anesthesia			
John et al. 2001	Quantitative EEG (QEEG) for anesthesia vs. waking	Loss of gamma-band activity, loss of coherence across major quadrants of cortex.	Widespread gamma-band coherence across and within hemispheres.

Source: Baars (2002), used with permission of Elsevier.

TWO CASE STUDIES OF MESODIENCEPHALIC LESIONS

These case studies might traditionally fall under the province of behavioral neurology, but they provide important clues about the integrative functions necessary for conscious states supported in deep mesodiencephalic regions, in the midbrain structure of periaqueductal gray, and in the intralaminar thalamic nuclei. Case study 3.2 presents some of the most fascinating and little appreciated clinical data on disorders of consciousness stemming from ILN lesions. Both cases studies show akinetic mutism (AKM), one transitionally, one apparently more permanently. AKM is an important syndrome for both psychiatry and neurology, informing us about how consciousness is underpinned and driven at a most basic level by emotion. Stripped of motivation or emotion, consciousness appears to virtually empty out. AKM has obvious and important clinical parallels to common psychiatric problems of severely retarded depression, catatonia and schizophrenia, and other apathy states.

Case Study 3.2: Bilateral ILN Lesion—A Progressive Walk-Through of the Taxonomy of Disorders of Consciousness[1]

This patient was a male in his middle forties brought to the hospital after he could not be woken up normally in the morning. He was in a low-grade coma, with double incontinence, punctuated by brief periods of restlessness. His clinical and laboratory examinations were generally unremarkable with a blood pressure of 150/90, normal electrocardiogram, and normal metabolic studies. On neurological exam he had narrow pupils nonreactive to light, with the eyes remaining in midposition. Reactions to painful stimuli were predominantly extensor movements and some pained facial expression. Initial structural imaging with contrast enhancing revealed symmetrical bilateral paramedian thalamic lesions (see Fig. 3.2). The lesion was read as extending subthalamically somewhat into the ventral tegmental area. The EEG findings consisted of generalized slowing of background activity, loss of differentiation, and some delta bursting, frontotemporally and centrally. There were repeated bursts of generalized slowing, slow-wave and spike-and-wave discharges, at around 6 per second.

By the third day, there was some restoration of wakefulness and gaze, and the patient gradually transitioned out of the vegetative state. He began to pay more attention to his surroundings in terms of eye tracking but was totally akinetic and mute. One week after admission he remained in this condition. In week 2, he began to show more spontaneous movements, but there was still significant akinesia, with stereotypic movements, such as handling his guitar in a manner suggestive of some efforts to play, but without evidence of much conscious participation, since his movements continued when the guitar was removed. There were other aimless activities such as rubbing his abdomen for long periods of time without any evidence of discomfort. During the third week, the akinetic mute state changed into a more hypokinetic state with

---

[1]Case material and graphics from van Domburg, et al. (1996) with permission.

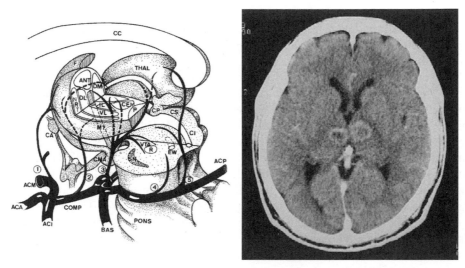

Figure 3.2. CT Scan of ILN patient and Schematic Graphic of Mesodiencephalic Regions. Key for Mesodiencephalic Graphic: CA = anterior commissure; CP = posterior commissure; ANT = anterior thalamus; IL = intralaminar region; CEM = centromedian ILN; VTA = ventral tegmental area; NRT = reticular thalamus; DL/VL = dorsolateral/ventrolateral thalamus; DM = dorsomedial thalamus; SN = substantia nigra; MT = mammillothalamic tract; EW = Edinger-Westphal nucleus; CS = superior colliculus; CI = inferior colliculus; F = fornix, P = pulvinar; BAS = basilar artery; ACA = anterior communicating artery; ACP = posterior communicating artery. (From van Domburg, P., ten Donkelaar, HJ, Notermans, SH 1996, with permission from Elsevier Science).

some signs of emotional expression. At the end of week 3, this hypokinesia gave way to excessive unintelligible talking, often slurred, with occasional delusional content, essentially a presentation of a delirium. During this period of confusional state, there was a growing lability (consistent with the resolution of the akinetic affectless state), and much disorganized behavior, including walking away from the ward.

During the fourth week he showed the beginning of the ability to meaningfully engage in neuropsychological assessment but with obvious global cognitive deficits, including a marked constructional apraxia and an obvious amnestic syndrome. Working memory and higher cognitive aspects of executive functions were still quite poor. By the fifth week, he still showed mild language pathology, including frequent semantic paraphasias and obvious dysnomia, along with a continued but improving amnestic syndrome, but improved attentional and executive functions. By this point the confusional state had largely resolved, and he continued to show gradual cognitive improvement over a protracted period of time. At one year out from bilateral paramedian thalamic infarction, a Wechsler Adult Intelligence Scale (WAIS) IQ score was calculated of 118 verbal and 94 performance IQ. By 15 months out, his verbal score had improved to 125 with little change in his performance IQ. There was still a selective downward gaze palsy, with continued incapacity for well-organized independent activity, some loss of initiative, mild forgetfulness, and slightly disturbed balance. Two years after the event there was only selective downward gaze palsy, a slight motivational inertia, and otherwise a virtually complete recovery of overall cognitive function, including short-term memory.

Follow-up EEGs done successively over a period of several weeks to months showed gradual restoration of normal background activity, gradual decline of the frontotemporal dysregulation, and no further signs of epileptiform activity or hypersynchronization. One might hypothesize that disruption of ILN participation in the process of ongoing thalamocortical feedback loops generates disinhibition of nRt-related spike wave and slow-wave discharges, as the nRt's inhibitory control over thalamocortical gating is disinhibited by the loss of ILN glutamatergic projections. During the earliest portion of this evolving syndrome, the EEG findings were similar to those found in absence seizures (and this is exactly how patients with PVS present).

Contrary to widespread clinical folklore on this issue, lesions restricted to the ILN virtually never generate a sustained coma. Several of these restricted paramedian thalamic vascular insults consistently show the fascinating syndrome of walking through the taxonomy of disorders of consciousness, beginning with the most severe and proceeding to the least severe. The clinical presentation begins with a brief period of initial coma lasting hours to days, followed by a restricted period of persistent vegetative state, oftentimes a more protracted period of akinetic mutism, and then typically a period of confusional lability, finally yielding various degrees of long-term baseline cognitive deficit. In some instances, the cases involve a nearly full recovery with only residual disorders of downward gaze, a finding presumed secondary to the disruption of intralaminar connections between brainstem ocular motor systems and the frontal eye fields. (See later discussion of intralaminar nuclei function for more details.) The initial period of akinetic mutism in this particular case may also have had some contributions from the partial disruption of the ventral tegmental area, as massive lesions of this tend to generate severe and largely unremitting AKM. However, other cases without VTA involvement show this progression, so it is unlikely that the VTA lesion played a major role in determining the clinical presentation.

Case Study 3.3: A Full Caudal-Rostral Periaqueductal Gray (PAG) Lesion: Akinetic Mutism and the Emptying Out of Consciousness[2]

This man in his early thirties was found unresponsive and in a deep stupor. Initial structural imaging with CT showed a large expanding mass lesion of the midbrain. The patient was treated with steroids to reduce swelling and had a marked, rapid regression of the lesion in the midbrain. After the lesion resolved, his stupor improved and he was then found to demonstrate a classic akinetic mute state: vigilant appearance, relatively intact ocular tracking, some quite limited spontaneous movements of the left arm with stimulation, but following no commands or showing any reliable signs of human social interaction, affect, speech output, higher cognitive

---

[2]Case materials from Schiff (personal communication).

functions, or any motivated behavior. An MRI (magnetic resonance imaging) then showed high signal abnormalities in the midbrain, pretectum around the aqueduct, and some involvement into the paramedian thalamus on the left, probably affecting various midline and intralaminar systems, but no other discernible structural pathology. A SPECT (single-photon emission computed tomography) scan showed diffuse hypometabolism widely affecting association cortices bilaterally, including frontal, parietal, and temporal association cortices, consistent with the supposition that higher cognitive and executive functions were all off-line. The patient died several months later secondary to pneumonia, but without any clinical change in his neurological or akinetic mute mental status. At autopsy, pathology confirmed a lymphoma that had regressed through and subsequently destroyed the paramedian tegmental mesencephalon, tracked through the aqueduct to the thalamus, extending partially into the anterior intralaminar region on left side, with the preservation of the right intralaminar region possibly allowing for some apparently purposeless movements of the left upper extremity.

As far as we know, no other case of full caudal-rostral PAG involvement (with relative sparing of the other mesodiencephalic areas) has been documented by this much structural imaging, functional imaging, and neuropathological data. This case is fully consistent with animal work in which extensive caudal-rostral lesions of PAG consistently produce a severe akinetic mute state with little progress toward any resolution or generation of visible affect or spontaneous motivated behavior. The PAG receives telencephalic projections restricted to limbic and paralimbic systems such as the central nucleus of amygdala and anterior paleocortices (cingulate and orbital frontal), and there is a close relationship between this structure and the largely DA-mediated seeking system (Panksepp, 1998). PAG has extensive reciprocal projections to these systems and also to the hypothalamus, multiple monoamine nuclei, and the thalamic ILN systems, the posterior ILN group in particular (centromedian/parafascicular).

Animal work suggests that PAG plays an essential role in making emotion an active motoric process, as most prototypic affective behaviors (fleeing, freezing, copulating, affective vocalizations, possibly many attachment behaviors, etc.) appear to be organized by PAG-hypothalamic-brainstem motor system networks. Its role in the complexity of more cognized human affective states is still poorly outlined empirically, but it may be responsible (by virtue of its extensive reticular and intralaminar connectivities) for widely influencing the thalamocortical system consonant with underlying affective states, thus being in a position to "gate" or restrict state space of the thalamocortical system (see Watt, 2000, for summary). This gating function might be an important substrate for basic aspects of prototype strong emotion, such as how playful behaviors are not available when we are angry.

Observation and discussion of AKM often begs the question "well, aren't these patients still conscious?" Lesser versions of the syndrome seen in more limited cases of bilateral cingulate disease typically show sufficient recovery that patients are later able to report experiencing events but lacking desire or intention. In some cases, bilateral cingulate patients will even respond to verbal inquiry, particularly if supplementary motor areas are spared. This leads to a deepening of the suspicion that AKM is not a "true" disease of consciousness. These milder versions of AKM *appear* to offer evidence of the independence of consciousness from an emotional bedrock, and that the former can exist without the latter. Our somewhat different conclusion is that lesser versions of AKM (classically associated with bilateral cingulate disease) may allow some phenomenal content, while the more severe versions (associated with very extensive lesions of PAG, or ventral tegmentum area (VTA), and some subcortical bilateral basal ganglia presentations) may show a virtual "emptying out" of consciousness. In these cases, events may be virtually meaningless and simply don't matter anymore. It may be an essential requirement that stimuli have at least some potential affective significance in order to gain access to the conscious workspace. In extensive PAG lesions, consciousness thus may be essentially "grayed out." This suggests that these more severe AKM patients live in a kind of strange, virtually unfathomable netherworld close to the border of a persistent vegetative state. With the patient discussed above, and in the few other closely studied cases with extensive PAG lesions, the clinical condition of akinetic mutism does not appear to resolve. In contrast, the akinetic mutism from an ILN lesion (Case study 3.2) is almost always temporary.

Our taxonomy of disorders of consciousness emphasizes their graded, progressive nature and eschews an all-or-nothing conceptualization. While intuitively appealing, an all-or-nothing picture of consciousness provides a limited basis for heuristic empirical study of the underpinnings of consciousness from a neural systems point of view, as compared to a graded or hierarchical one that emphasizes the core functional envelopes of emotion, intention, and attention. From this vantage point, akinetic mutism is a deeply informative syndrome, as it provides clues to the neural "minimums" for motivated behavior and emotion in the human brain. Additionally, it bears emphasis that the syndrome of akinetic mutism potentially provides clues to psychiatry about neural substrates of other related, but lesser, apathy states, such as those seen in severe retarded depression, schizophrenia, catatonia, and the like.

NEURODYNAMIC ASPECTS OF CONSCIOUSNESS

Hebb's visionary notion in 1949 of "reverberating cell assemblies" was an important beginning point for a neurodynamic emphasis. Neurodynamics is thus a relatively new discipline, addressing how brain activation changes over time. The neurodynamic perspective is complementary to traditional perspectives that emphasize structures, connectivities, and neuromodulators in that it seeks to understand the time-dependent changes that occur in neuronal populations (neural network models, by comparison, do not reference time). The behavior of these time-sensitive populations are typically measured by EEG, single unit recordings (inso far as these indirectly imply population behaviors), or magnetoencephalography (MEG) and also in dynamic neurochemical measures, such as in vivo dialysis. Neurodynamics attempts to correlate these signatures from various measurement modalities with behavioral and subjective measurements, focusing on the challenge of modeling context-dependent and sequential activation of these highly distributed transient neural ensembles on a moment-to-moment basis.

High levels of temporal resolution are necessary to investigate this, as the neurodynamic integrations that underpin specific "qualia" or subjective content happen quickly but not instantly [requiring, according to some researchers, approximately 300 msec (Libet, 1982)]. Most of the high temporal resolution technologies have poor spatial resolution past the surface of the brain, and even MEG cannot reconstruct neurodynamics in the brainstem.

Without a neurodynamic perspective, neuroscience cannot specify how any physical processes could satisfy the important criteria of *isomorphism* that many theorists feel is essential to bridging the hard problem: How is it that any aspect of the behavior of neurons can generate phenomenal experience? Most theorists assume that this bridge must be constructed by finding properties of large-scale neuronal ensembles that are *functionally isomorphic and temporally coincident with phenomenal experience*. Most theorists also agree that neurodynamics must model the integration of top-down and bottom-up processes, and this applies to both early (bottom-up) and late (top-down) sensory cortices, as well as to the larger issue of the relation between brainstem (bottom-up) and cortex (top-down). Neurodynamical models explicating the selectivity (attention), sensory integration, and sense of agency in consciousness would be important bridges indeed.

One of the most puzzling and yet essential properties of consciousness is its seamless integration and fundamental unity. Many investigators have suggested that populations of neurons are coordinated via the generation of coherent patterns or oscillatory envelopes that structure integrative communication between brain regions. Several investigators postulate that the synchronous firing behavior among these distributed populations could constitute the essential neurodynamic underpinnings for conscious states and their contents. Many if not most neurodynamic theories of consciousness are elaborations of basic neuroanatomical concepts that emphasize thalamocortical connectivities, and there is relatively little neurodynamic work looking closely at possible contributions of structures underneath the thalamus. These theories propose that essential features of functional integration are achieved thalamocortically, perhaps largely via the functioning and connectivities of the nonspecific thalamic systems (ILN/nRt). However, the lesion correlates that we have summarized in previous sections suggest that these nonspecific thalamic systems are highly dependent upon poorly understood processes in deeper mesodiencephalic regions, as the most severe disorders of consciousness are brought about by damage underneath the thalamus (see case study 3.2).

Singer and Gray et al. (1995) have proposed that neuronal synchronization is necessary for object representation, response selection, sensorimotor integration, and attention. They suggest that temporal synchronization of action potentials in a millisecond range underpins adaptive responses via recruitment of widespread neuronal groups. Corticotectal (not just corticocortical) synchronization has also been found to be crucial, underlining the importance of the various reticular structures just reviewed, with synchronization found to group superior collicular neurons into functionally coherent assemblies. These authors suggest that the stimulus need not come from external sensation, and they do not view the oscillatory activity as a passive response to external stimuli. Instead, they propose that synchronization results at least in part from internally generated goal states, and that external stimulation contributes to the selection of salient goals. Singer et al., argue that the binding that leads to consciousness is brought about by "phase locking" that occurs at single frequencies. From their point of view, the participating neurons sum their trains of action potentials after entrainment. Because the net effect is summed, this model would be considered a linear one, based on essentially proportional relationships. Non linear models do not have this proportion as a crucial feature, as in chaotic systems, where a tiny input can destabilize the system and have profound outcome. Freeman's work (discussed below), highlights the nonlinear, chaotic characteristics of neuronal population behavior.

Edelman's (1987) theory of neuronal group selection is not dissimilar. He has argued that representations arise from a Darwinian-like selection of neuronal groups, that these groups continually interact via "reentry" (reciprocal feedback) and that consciousness emerges from widespread neurodynamic coherences enabled by reentry. Using a 148-channel MEG and a binocular rivalry paradigm, Tononi and Edelman (2000) found that neuronal responses to visual stimuli occurred in a great number of cortical regions, both when the subjects consciously perceived the stimuli and when they did not. However, conscious perception resulted in highly significant differences: "neuromagnetic responses evoked by a stimulus were stronger by 50–85 percent when the subjects were conscious of the stimulus than when they were not conscious" (p. 394). This increase of coherence among various brain regions is consistent with the hypothesis that consciousness reflects rapid integration via reentry.

Both Singer's and Edelman's neurodynamic models advocate a selective and time-dependent coordination of neuronal ensembles that occurs on the order of milliseconds. Both agree upon a nonhierarchical model—that is, there is no reference to layers of binding at different ranges of organizational breadth or complexity. Singer and Edelman state that neuronal groups are selected and reentrantly reselected according to the evolving goals and needs of the organism. Damasio's model, by contrast, suggests that synchrony occurs via a hierarchical effect: convergence zones located in the association cortices create the binding of lower level neuronal groups.

Llinàs and Ribary (1991, 1993), and Joliot et al. (1994) have emphasized the importance of gamma-band 40-Hz oscillations and thalamocortical resonances as essential neurodynamic foundations for consciousness. Llinàs and Ribary (1993) studied gamma oscillation in rapid eye movement (REM) sleep and in wakefulness and found coherent 40-Hz activity was evident during REM sleep as well as during wakefulness using a 37-channel MEG. This was the first time that coherent gamma activity was found in REM sleep. No gamma activity was found during delta wave sleep, where consciousness is mostly presumed not to exist. There is evidence that pontine cholinergic projections into the thalamus are essential for the cortex to organize these fast 40+ Hz oscillatory states and that anticholinergics prevent this, outlining one possible mechanism for the induction of confusional states by anticholinergics (Steriade et al., 1991).

Walter Freeman, a pioneer in neurodynamics, has emphasized the nonlinear, chaotic characteristics of neuronal population behavior, suggesting that the essential neurodynamics of perception and consciousness are nonlinear. Freeman (1975) initially studied population activity via study of the olfactory system, utilizing a 64-lead microelectrode EEG. Freeman proposes that the cortex undergoes global transitions in reaction to meaningful stimuli, settling into a series of neural spatial patterns, a type of oscillatory envelope that is generated by chaotic dynamics of the population. Freeman, who along with Bressler (1980), first coined the term *gamma* activity to describe this extended synchronous activity, argues that this synchronized gamma activity arises from populations of excitatory and inhibitory neurons in negative feedback. Stimuli drive the system into a transiently more ordered state, in which neural activity can be modeled in terms of *mesoscopic wave packets*, neural spatial patterns that have time constants closely matching the temporal dynamics of perception and other contents in consciousness (300 to 500 msec). He cites evidence that synchronization is aperiodic and chaotic, spreading across the entire gamma band (40 to 70 Hz), and not reducible to a single frequency (e.g., 40 Hz). Consciousness, according to Freeman, emerges from how such spatially and temporally extended neural patterns across the gamma band underwrite widespread integration of brain activity. This kind of brain activity enables not a static set of representations but a highly plastic and evolving system of meanings for the organism.

SUMMARY HEURISTICS/QUESTIONS FOR FUTURE RESEARCH

1. *Evolutionary Perspectives.* From an evolutionary perspective, consciousness could only have been selected for its adaptive advantages in maintaining life and fostering procreation. Most agree that the conscious mind evolved from unconscious brain dynamics. Thus, basic evolutionary perspectives on both the adaptive functions and the neural interactions underlying consciousness seem a safe organizing assumption for theory building and hypothesis testing. This would include assuming Darwinian mechanisms for how neurons and neuronal groups are selected for the functional network integration(s) that subserve consciousness (Edelman, 1987). Thus, salience-related competition within attention, and competition between potential working memories and other content determines what potentially gains access to consciousness generating neuronal work spaces. Most empirical work and theory have emphasized the crucial roles played by multiple reticular systems, and/or by thalamocortical connectivities (and to a lesser extent, paralimbic/heteromodal cortices). However, more specific details regarding how these two major component systems (the highly distributed and extended reticular structures, reviewed in detail in this chapter, and the thalamocortical mantle) interact are still poorly mapped. How the brain segues effortlessly and seamlessly through a succession of these transient (and fraction-of-a-second) functional integrations of widespread regions from conscious moment to conscious moment also remains poorly understood (see item 2).

2. *Neurodynamic Perspectives and Functional Integration.* The clinical data suggest that consciousness must be conceptualized as a graded, recursive, and

hierarchically organized phenomenon, with various core aspects interacting with extended cognitive aspects. Core aspects include wakefulness, attentional functions, sensory content, salience, affective motivation, and agency. These core components permit cognitive extensions in extended working memories, language, and a host of higher cognitive-cortical functions that allow us an extraordinary richness and vast differentiation of conscious content. Although we have modeled consciousness in terms of these complex functional envelopes (attentional function, intention or directed activity, emotion, basic sensory content), these are clearly interdependent and seamlessly integrated aspects of consciousness, slices of the consciousness pie. Each of these functional domains represents a formidable neuroscientific problem in itself, and each requires widely distributed neural networks that are hard to study empirically. Global neurodynamical perspectives are essential to this task of mapping this functional integration, and neuroanatomy alone is certainly insufficient. An important focal point for future research and theory would be to explain neurodynamically how lesser lesions of multiple reticular activating system components can generate delirium or akinetic mutism, while more massive lesions of these very same systems yield coma or persistent vegetative state.

3. *Anatomical Perspectives and the Medioventral/Dorsolateral Distinction.* This is a perspective fully complementary to the neurodynamical. Neurodynamic perspectives uninformed by the functional neuroanatomy of consciousness run the risk of falling into a vague equipotentiality that does not adequately integrate the lesion correlate data summarized here. Indeed, understanding the organization of global neurodynamics will require untangling how the contributions of many distributed neuronal populations are hardly equal in consciousness (or that contributions from some populations are clearly *more equal* than others!). Global neurodynamic formulations have to incorporate evidence that virtually all the structures that appear essential to conscious states (with the exception of heteromodal systems in cortex) are *midline systems*. This finding is consistent with classical principles of functional neuroanatomy in which medial and ventral systems are earlier developing and more tied to homeostatic and emotional regulation, while anatomical systems situated more dorsolaterally are later developing and more tied to cognitive functions. Consistent with this midline-ventral hegemony for consciousness, even extensive lesions of the heteromodal systems in prefrontal and parietal lobes can only generate one of the lesser disorders of consciousness (HKM, or delirium, and *never* coma, PVS or AKM). Although we have emphasized that there are many disparate systems in these ventral mesodiencephalic regions, jointly they appear to provide the most crucial foundations for the functional integration of the brain in conscious states.

4. *Neurodevelopmental Perspectives.* The above considerations suggest that we will make considerably more progress if we can understand how consciousness unfolds from its earliest beginnings in a presumably primary affective form, in humans and in other mammals, and then develops into more complex,

cognitive-extended forms with the help of symbolic language acquisition. Neurodevelopmental research into the fundamental mechanisms of consciousness in infants is understandably modest for obvious epistemological/ethical reasons, as much of the current neuroscientific work focuses on neural correlates of higher conscious and cognitive activity in adult brains. This suggests that basic research will have to refocus attention on basic neural processes taking place in the first year of life, as core component processes must be brought on-line to operate in an integrated fashion very early in neurodevelopment. Such research into early development will also likely pay dividends clinically in terms of an increased ability to understand and treat disorders of consciousness, such as coma and persistent vegetative state, but also lesser forms of akinetic mutism, autism, and schizophrenia. We suspect that *the substrates for the early orienting/affective responses of the infant in its interactions with a caretaker potentially outline the most fundamental constituent neural processes for a primitive or core consciousness*. These considerations suggest that consciousness first develops within the milieu of a primary attachment to mother/parenting figures, and in the context of *affectively guided orienting toward and interacting with a primary caregiver*.

To more fully understand the nature of conscious processes would pay enormous dividends to all areas of psychiatry, illuminating many of the still well-hidden secrets within the mind-brain realms from where emotional distress arises. Such an understanding of functional neural integration in the brain would also no doubt open many new mysteries and questions. A special focus on early neurodevelopmental processes will also have crucially important implications for psychiatry (Schore, 2001), as the affective climate of early life must have a profound effect on the developing brain, substantially increasing or reducing an epigenetic vulnerability in later life to many psychiatric conditions. There is already abundant evidence from preclinical studies that positive social interactions have robust and life-long benefits for the neuroemotional resilience of young animals (Meaney, 2001). Such an understanding of early neurodevelopmental processes will eventually help clarify positive and negative risk factors for most if not virtually all Axis I and Axis II disorders. It may also herald many new ways to intervene positively in developmental programs that will help prevent future psychiatric problems while also giving us lasting insights into the nature of the emotional aspects of human consciousness. However, these fundamental neurodevelopmental questions are uncharted territories where an enormous amount of research remains to be done, and such neurodevelopmental-affective perspectives on investigating consciousness are certainly not the dominant heuristic in current consciousness studies.

REFERENCES

Baars BJ (1996). In *The Theater of Consciousness: The Workspace of the Mind*. Oxford University Press: New York.

Baars BJ (2002). The conscious access hypothesis. Origins and recent evidence. *Trends Cogn Sci* 1:47–51.

Baars B, Newman J (1994). A neurobiological interpretation of the global workspace theory of consciousness. In Revonsuo A, Kamppinen, M (eds). *Consciousness in Philosophy and Cognitive Neuroscience*. Lawrence Erlbaum: Philadelphia.

Baars BJ, Newman J, Taylor, JG (1998). Neuronal mechanisms of consciousness: A relational global workspace framework. In Hammeroff S, et al. (eds). *Towards a Science of Consciousness*. MIT Press: Cambridge, MA.

Baddeley A (1986). *Working Memory*. Oxford University Press: Oxford.

Barrie JM, Freeman WJ, Lenhart M (1996). Modulation by discriminative training of spatial patterns of gamma EEG amplitude and phase in neocortex of rabbits. *J Neurophysiology* 76:520–539.

Beck D, Rees G, Frith CD, Lavie N (2001). Neural correlates of change blindness and change awareness in humans. *Nature Neurosci* 4:645–650.

Bressler SL, Freeman WJ (1980). Frequency analysis of olfactory system EEG in cat, rabbit and rat. *Electroencephalog Clin Neurophysio* 50:19–24.

Chalmers D (1995). Facing up to the problem of consciousness. *Journal of Consciousness Studies* 2:200–219.

Damasio A (1999). *The Feeling of What Happens. Body and Emotion in the Making of Consciousness*. Harcourt Brace: New York.

Dehaene S, Naccache L, Cohen L, Bihan DL, Mangin JF, Poline JB, Riviere D (2001): Cerebral mechanisms of word masking and unconscious repetition priming. *Nature Neurosci* 4:752–758.

Driver J, Vuilleumier P (2001). Perceptual awareness and its loss in unilateral neglect and extinction. *Cognition* 79:39–88.

Duncan J, Owen AM (2000). Common regions of the human frontal lobe recruited by diverse cognitive demands. *Trends Neurosci* 23:475–483

Edelman, GM (1987). *Neural Darwinism: The Theory of Neuronal Group Selection*. Basic Books: New York.

Edelman GM (1999). Building a picture of the brain. *Ann NY Acad Sci* 882:68–89.

Engel, AK, Fries P, Singer W (2001). Dynamic predictions: Oscillations and synchrony in top-down processing. *Nat Rev Neurosci* 2:704–716.

Freeman WJ (1975). *Mass Action in the Nervous System*. Academic Press: New York.

Freeman WJ (1999). *How Brains Make Up Their Minds*. Weidenfeld and Nicolson: London.

Frith CD, Done DJ (1989). Experiences of alien control in schizophrenia reflect a disorder in the central monitoring of action. *Psychological Medicine* 19:359–363.

Frith CD, Blakemore SJ, Wolpert DM (2000). Explaining the symptoms of schizophrenia: Abnormalities in the awareness of action. *Brain Res Rev* 31:357–363.

Fuster JM (1991). The prefrontal cortex and its relation to behavior. *Progress in Brain Res* 87:201–211.

Grossberg S (1980). Direct perception or adaptive resonance? *Behav Brain Sci* 3:385.

Haier RJ, Siegel BV, MacLachlan A, Soderling E, Lottenberg S, Buchsbaum MS (1992). Regional glucose metabolic changes after learning a complex visuospatial/motor task: A positron emission tomographic study. *Brain Res* 570:134–143.

Hobson, JA, Pace-Schott, EF (2002). The cognitive neuroscience of sleep: Neuronal systems, consciousness, and learning *Nat Rev Neurosci* 3(9):679–693.

John, ER (2002). The neurophysics of consciousness *Brain. Res Rev* 39(1):1–13.

John ER, Prichep LS, Kox W, Valdes-Sosa P, Bosch-Bayard J, Aubert E, Tom M, di Michele F, Gugino LD (2001). Invariant reversible QEEG effects of anesthetics *Conscious Cogn* 10:165–183.

Joliot M, Ribary U, Llinás R (1994). Neuromagnetic coherent oscillatory activity in the vicinity of 40-Hz coexists with cognitive temporal binding in the human brain. *Proc Natl Acad Sci* 91:11748–11751.

Kjaer TW, Nowak M, Kjaer KW, Lou AR, Lou HC (2001). Precuneus–prefrontal activity during awareness of visual verbal stimuli. *Conscious Cogn* 10:356–365.

LeDoux JE (1996). *The Emotional Brain.* Simon & Schuster: New York.

Libet B (1982). Brain Stimulation in the study of neuronal functions for conscious sensory experience. *Human Neurobiol* 1:235–242.

Lindsley DB, Schreimer LH Knowles WB, Magoun MS, Magoun HW (1950). Behavioral and EEG changes following chronic brain stem lesions in cats. *Electroenceph Clin Neurophys* 2:483–498.

Llinás R, Ribary U (1993). Coherent 40-Hz oscillation characterizes dream state in humans. *Proc Natl Acad Sci* 90:2078–2081.

Magoun, HW (1952). Ascending reticular activating system in the brainstem. *Arch Neurol Psychiatry* 67:145–154.

Merker B (2003). The liabilities of mobility: A selection pressure for the transition to consciousness in animal evolution. *Conscious Cogn*, in press.

Mesulam MM (ed) (2000). *Principles of Cognitive and Behavioral Neurology.* Lawrence Erlbaum: New York.

Millett D (2001). Hans Berger: From psychic energy to the EEG. *Perspect Bio Med* 44:522–42.

Moruzzi G, Magoun HW (1949). Brain stem reticular formation and activation of the EEG. *Electroencephalog Clin Neurophys* 1:455–473.

Newman J, Baars BJ (1993). A neural attentional model for access to consciousness: A global workspace perspective. *Concepts Neurosci* 4:255–290.

Panksepp J (1998). *Affective Neuroscience: The Foundations of Human and Animal Emotions.* Oxford University Press: New York.

Parvizi J, Damasio A (2001). Consciousness and the brainstem. *Cognition* 79:135–160.

Purpura KP, Schiff ND (1997). The thalamic intralaminar nuclei: A role in visual awareness. *Neuroscientist* 3:8–14.

Raichle ME et al. (1994). Practice-related changes in human brain functional anatomy during nonmotor learning. *Cerebral Cortex* 4:8–26.

Rees G et al. (1999). Inattentional blindness versus inattentional amnesia for fixated but ignored words. *Science* 286:2504–2507.

Rees G Wojciulik E, Clarke K, Husain M, Frith CD, Driver J (2000). Unconscious activation of visual cortex in the damaged right hemisphere of a parietal patient with extinction. *Brain* 123:1624–1633.

Rees G, Kreiman G, Koch C (2002). Neural correlates of consciousness in humans. *Nat Rev Neuroscience* 3:261–270.

Ribary U, Ioannides AA, Singh KD, Hasson R, Llinás R (1991). Magnetic field tomography (MFT) of coherent thalamocortical 40-Hz oscillation in humans. *Proc Natl Acad Sci* 88:11037–11041.

Ribary U, Cappell J, Mogilner A, Hund M, Kronberg E, Llinas R (1999). Functional imaging of plastic changes in the human brain. *Adv Neurol* 81:49–56.

Rolls, ET (1999). *The Brain and Emotion.* Oxford University Press: Oxford, UK.

Scheibel AB (1980). Anatomical and physiological substrates of arousal. In Hobson, AH, Brazier, A. *The Reticular Formation Revisited*, Raven Press, New York.

Schiff ND, Plum F (2000). The role of arousal and gating systems in the neurology of impaired consciousness. *J Clin Neurophysiol* 17:438–452.

Schiff ND, Pulver, M (1999). Does vestibular stimulation activate thalamocortical mechanisms that reintegrate impaired cortical regions? *Proc R Soc Lond B* 266:421–423.

Schiff ND, Ribary U, Plum F, Llinas R (1999). Words without mind. *J Cog Neuro* 1:650–656.

Schore, AN (2001). Contributions for the decade of the brain to infant mental health. *Special Issue of Infant Mental health Journal* 22:1–269.

Sheinberg DL, Logothetis NK (1997). The role of temporal cortical areas in perceptual organization. *Proc Natl Acad Sci* 94:3408–3413.

Singer W (1998). Consciousness and the structure of neuronal representation. *Phil Trans R Soc B* 353:1829–1840.

Singer W, Gray CM (1995). Visual feature integration and the temporal correlation hypothesis. *Ann Rev Neurosci* 18:555–586.

Srinivasan, R et al. (1999). Increased synchronization of neuromagnetic responses during conscious perception. *J Neurosci* 19:5435–5448.

Steriade M, Curro Dossi R, Pare D, Oakson G (1991). Fast oscillations (20–40 Hz) in thalamocortical systems and their potentiation by mesopontine cholinergic nuclei in the cat. *Proc Natl Acad Sci* 88:4396–4400.

Taylor JG (1999). *The Race for Consciousness.* MIT Press: Cambridge, MA.

Tononi G, Edelman GM (1998). Consciousness and complexity. *Science* 282:1846–1851.

Tononi G, Edelman GE (2000). Schizophrenia and the mechanisms of conscious integration. *Brain Res Rev* 31:391–400.

van Domburg P, ten Donkelaar HJ, Notermans SH (1996). Akinetic mutism with bithalamic infarction. Neurophysiological correlates. *J Neurological Sci* 139:58–65.

Vuilleumier P. et al. (2001). Neural fate of seen and unseen faces in visuospatial neglect: A combined event-related functional MRI and event-related potential study. *Proc Natl Acad Sci* 98:3495–3500.

Watt DF (2000). The centrencephalon and thalamocortical integration: Neglected contributions of periaqueductal gray. *Emotion and Consciousness* 1:93–116.

4

STRESS, SLEEP, AND SEXUALITY IN PSYCHIATRIC DISORDERS

Terrence Deak[1] and Jaak Panksepp[2]

[1] *Department of Psychology, SUNY–Binghamton, Binghamton, New York*
[2] *Department of Psychology, Bowling Green State University, Bowling Green, Ohio and
Falk Center for Molecular Therapeutics, Department of Biomedical Engineering,
Northwestern University, Evanston, Illinois*

INTRODUCTION

Over the course of the past century, exposure to stressful life events has emerged as one of the most ubiquitous determinants of ultimate health outcomes for the individual. Stress is pervasive in human life, and it plays a prominent role in moderating both the onset and severity of many major psychiatric syndromes. Indeed, one of the primary issues that has driven stress research is the question of how a general construct such as "stress" can produce such a wide array of psychiatric and physiological ailments. This puzzle is further complicated by the observation that comparable life stressors produce widely discrepant effects across different individuals. It is clearly of interest for clinicians and researchers alike to develop a fundamental understanding of stress as a mitigating factor in disease susceptibility and progression. This chapter will provide an overview of the major stress responsive systems against a historical backdrop,

Textbook of Biological Psychiatry, Edited by Jaak Panksepp
ISBN 0-471-43478-7   Copyright © 2004 John Wiley & Sons, Inc.

delineate several important new areas of inquiry in the field of stress research, and demonstrate how these stress responsive systems can both propagate and exacerbate major psychiatric illnesses.

In addition to a coverage of stress, brief discussions of work on sleep and sexuality are included at the end. These may seem like odd bedfellows. Partly, this juxtaposition is a matter of expediency since those important topics could not be given separate chapters with the space constraints of this book. However, there are also good reasons to consider these foundational issues together. Individuals who have been exposed to stressors exhibit difficulty sleeping and are less likely to indulge in pleasurable activities such as sex, presumably because more pressing emotional and motivational concerns are monopolizing neuromental resources. However, even as we highlight such interrelations, we will treat these topics in series.

THEORETICAL FRAMEWORK FOR UNDERSTANDING STRESS RESPONSIVE SYSTEMS

On some level, we all have an intuitive understanding of *stress* as a psychological concept. Most people would define stress as a sense of internal pressure, nervous tension, anxiety, strain, or even a state of constant worry. While these terms are perfectly accurate and sufficient for communicating about stress in a colloquial setting, they are insufficient when we try to operationalize stress in a scientific manner. Indeed, scientists have argued for the better part of the last century about what would be an appropriate scientific definition for the term stress. In 1946, Hans Selye published a seminal paper describing a nonspecific biological response to physical stressors (Selye, 1946). His approach was based on the observation that the bodily consequences of physical trauma were independent of the nature of the precipitating insult. His ultimate synthesis was encapsulated as the general adaptation syndrome (GAS), which remains one of the guiding theories for stress research today. According to Selye, the GAS consisted of three successive stages of adaptation to insult: (1) the alarm reaction, (2) the stage of resistance, and (3) the stage of exhaustion. During the *alarm reaction*, or acute, phase of the GAS, the organism's general resistance to the stressor falls below normal. Then, as adaptation is acquired in the stage of resistance, the capacity to resist rises above normal. Small, repeated, or modest but continuous exposure to the precipitating stressor will be adequately handled by the organism during the stage of *resistance*. Eventually, continuous exposure to the stressor will lead to a state of exhaustion, in which organisms' defenses against further challenges systematically erode. This usually occurs when the agent or insult begins to overwhelm the capacity of the physiological systems to effectively respond. The *exhaustion* phase is where pathological processes begin to emerge.

While these stages have proven applicable to psychological stressors, it is important to note that Selye was trained as a physician. Thus, the basis of his original theory rested primarily within the bounds of physiological insult, such as pharmacological challenges, exposure to a cold environment, infections, and surgery. Nevertheless, the original framework provided by Selye continues to be a guiding light for stress researchers to this day and provides an effective springboard toward a more modern synthesis of stress as a psychological concept.

With this in mind, there are several key considerations regarding stress that must be conveyed from the outset. The first consideration is that of *stimulus* versus *state*. Irrespective of how we define stress, it is imperative that we distinguish between the stimulus that induces stress (referred to as the *stressor*) and the ultimate state that is produced in the individual by that stimulus (referred to as *stress*). Consider a deer meandering down to a stream for a drink of water, with a mountain lion poised ready to attack. Upon detection of the predator, the deer experiences an immediate rush of physiological, affective, and cognitive alterations that may be globally characterized as a heightened state of arousal. In this scenario, exposure to a predator is the precipitating stimulus, or stressor, that clearly elicits an internal state of stress in the host organism. This nomenclature, originally developed by Selye (1946, 1956), remains relevant for a proper discussion of the relationship between stress and major psychiatric illness.

In the above example, the presence of a predator is clearly identifiable as the environmental event that elicited the deer's stress reaction. Predator-prey interactions fit conveniently into the common parlance of stress terminology. However, if the deer had encountered a pathogen such as a virus or bacteria in the water rather than a mountain lion, a very similar complement of physiological, affective, and even cognitive alterations would likely ensue, although on a slightly delayed time course. Thus, the second consideration that we must take into account is that psychologically undetected physiological challenges representing threats to survival can elicit a stress reaction comparable to overt threats from the environment.

Perhaps the most important distinction between environmental and physiological stressors is that physiological stressors do not necessarily require cognitive appraisal, emotional evaluation, or conscious awareness to exert their effects. For instance, exposure to infectious agents (bacteria, viruses, toxins, etc.), hypoxia, hypoglycemia, and hypothermia are all examples of physiological stressors that elicit a stress reaction. Clearly, once the seriousness of the physiological challenge passes some identifiable threshold, the individual would normally develop a subjective experience of stress, which may then further activate stress responsive systems. Nevertheless, psychic stressors are qualitatively different than environmental ones and may activate stress responses via distinct pathways (Herman et al., 1996; Herman and Cullinan, 1997).

The final consideration is one of perception. It is common to view stress as a maladaptive, debilitating state that is best avoided. However, when we delve into the basics of stress physiology, it becomes clear that physiological responses to stress represent positive evolutionary adaptations. Most components of an organism's response to stress have evolved in such a manner as to promote an adaptive outcome (i.e., survival) under the given circumstances. However, this may not be the case when an organism is exposed to chronic stressors above and beyond those encountered in ancestral environments of evolutionary adaptation; repeated and sustained exposures to stressors eventually exhaust resources that are normally available for contending with more modest challenges, which in turn produce various adverse health outcomes [see McEwen (2000) for a superb review].

One conclusion that can be drawn from the discussion thus far is that regardless of the type of stressor an organism encounters (i.e., environmental, psychological, or physiological), there are several underlying characteristics that help us define a given event as a stressor: (i) It represents an immediate (real or perceived) threat to the individual, (ii) requires mobilization and coordination of multiple physiological systems (usually accompanied by increased metabolic demand), and (iii) necessitates behavioral adjustments that typically represent deviations from the prestressor agenda. Importantly, the successful implementation of these changes would normally promote survival, solidifying the adaptive nature of the organism's response to the stressor.

DIATHESIS-STRESS MODELS

Exposure to stressful life events has been recognized as an important promoter of major psychiatric illness for many years (i.e., the classic diathesis-stress model). This belief stems from observations that episodes of psychiatric illness are more frequently observed shortly after major life stressors and that clinical symptoms of many psychiatric illnesses worsen during times of stress (Mazure and Druss, 1995). Indeed, the role of life stressors as determinants for the onset and severity of many major psychiatric conditions has been common parlance in psychiatric settings for decades. Stress has been reported to promote symptomology in diverse psychiatric conditions ranging from personality disorders, to affective disorders, to dissociative disorders, and to somatic disorders. With such a wide range of conditions affected by exposure to stressors, it is clearly of interest to understand the organization and function of stress responsive systems in the brain that might serve as common threads for promoting mental health. With that in mind, it is not enough to simply state that stress exacerbates major psychiatric symptomology. Marked differences are observed across individuals in how the consequences of stress become manifest. Many individuals who experience adverse life events do not develop major psychiatric illness, and not everyone who develops a major psychiatric illness appears to have a precipitating life event. These findings have spurred research toward understanding (a) how exposure to qualitatively distinct stressors might differentially affect health outcomes, and (b) how individual subject's vulnerability may predispose or protect against the development of major psychiatric and psychosomatic illness.

For instance, exposure to stressors for some individuals produces gastrointestinal (GI) dysfunction (ulcers, colitis, etc.), while others may manifest immunological disturbances (frequent infection due to stress-induced immunosuppression, increased occurrence or worsening of autoimmune diseases, etc.). Such disparities in physiological outcomes of stressor exposure has led many researchers to postulate that individuals vary in the organs or brain systems that are constitutionally weakest and thus more susceptible to adverse health outcomes during times of stress. In this regard, one could attempt to explain the recurrence of chronic colitis in relation to stressor exposure by merging Selye's general adaptation syndrome with modern evolutionary principles. The interpretation would be that the GI tract was the least competent physiological system within that individual (or group of individuals), and thus reached the stage of exhaustion more rapidly than other systems. As a result, adverse symptoms (as in the case of colitis) repeatedly occur during times of stress (indeed Charles Darwin's own chronic health problems following his return to England may have had such an etiology).

Multiple models have been proposed to explain how similar life stressors can produce such highly variable health outcomes across different individuals. All of these models propose that adverse life events act as a triggering mechanism that activates some underlying predisposition toward the development of a specific disorder. The inherent differences in disease susceptibility are frequently cast in the light of genetic differences/predispositions. However, the availability of effective coping strategies and social support are also critical moderating variables that can be used as predictors for health outcomes following stressor exposure. Thus, the ultimate health outcome depends on a complex interaction between precipitating life stressors, individual differences in effective coping strategies, and underlying biological predispositions. See Dohrenwend and Dohrenwend (1981) for a thorough discussion of various permutations of diathesis-stress models that are applicable to biological psychiatry.

Given our understanding of diathesis-stress models and advances in molecular cloning and gene sequencing, a new generation of researchers are tracking down genetic markers that may point toward specific disease susceptibility. Likewise, clinicians have made similar progress in identifying specific coping strategies that, when absent in an individual, might promote the occurrence of major psychiatric illness following adverse life events. One recent breakthrough was the finding that disease-prone individuals often exhibit a higher propensity to seek out stressful life situations, thus further increasing the likelihood that psychiatric illness might develop (Mazure, 1998). Furthermore, clinical observations suggest that stress may be critical for initiating the first episode of psychiatric illness (e.g., depression) and much less important for subsequent episodes (e.g., Perris, 1984), suggesting sensitization/learning processes can occur in the system, although this issue is still far from resolved.

STRESS RESPONSIVE SYSTEMS

The theoretical construct provided by diathesis-stress models is a centerpiece of psychiatric thinking and a driving force behind diverse avenues of neurobiological and clinical research. Thus, it is likely that valuable insight into the etiology of psychiatric illness can be obtained through the identification and examination of biological responses to stress. For the sake of simplification, we have broken biological stress responses into four independent categories. The reader should note, however, that overall emotional, cognitive and behavioral responses to stress are more likely a result of synchronous activity among these systems. That is, none of these systems are singularly responsible for an individual's subjective experience of stress or the overall health consequences that might ensue. Nevertheless, the following categorical description of the four proposed systems is provided as a heuristic overview of both classical stress responsive systems (sympathetic nervous system and the hypothalamic-pituitary-adrenal axis) as well as more recently discovered systems implicated in stress [extrahypothalamic corticotropin-releasing hormone (CRH) systems and brain cytokines].

Sympathetic Nervous System

Perhaps one of the most widely documented of the stress responsive systems is the sympathetic nervous system. The impact of stress-induced catecholamine secretion for the maintenance of homeostatic processes was initially recognized by Walter Cannon in his seminal work during the first third of the 20th century (Cannon, 1935). In his original review, Cannon described the role of catecholamine secretion from the adrenal medulla as an essential element for (a) the mobilization of glucose to feed-heightened cellular activity during times of stress, and (b) effective physiological coping in the face of (diverse) challenges to homeostasis. Even at this early juncture, Cannon recognized that in the absence of a properly functioning sympathetic response to stress, the ability of the organism to survive the impending challenge was monumentally impaired.

Activation of the sympathetic nervous system produces an immediate and sustained increase in catecholamine secretion (i.e., epinephrine and norepinephrine; EPI/NE). Sympathetic nerve terminals secrete EPI/NE directly onto target tissues, which elicits an immediate postsynaptic response that clears and subsides within a very short time frame (i.e., within a few seconds). For instance, secretion of EPI/NE from sympathetic nerve terminals directly onto cardiac muscle potently increases heart rate and strengthens the force of contractions. Meanwhile, EPI/NE release within the eye dilates the pupil to boost visual acuity and responsivity. These are just two common examples of how direct sympathetic innervation can promote coordinated activity within different effector organs, and thus promote survival in a threatening context.

In addition to direct sympathetic input to target organs, the adrenal medulla also secretes EPI/NE into the general circulation during times of stress. Thus, EPI/NE release from the adrenal medulla has the ability to affect numerous target organs and cells distal to the site of origin, with a duration of action that persists 2 to 10 times as long as direct EPI/NE release from sympathetic nerve terminals (since the clearance rate in blood is much slower than that at synaptic clefts). Secretion of EPI/NE in this endocrine fashion augments the effects produced by EPI/NE released from sympathetic nerve terminals and serves as an avenue by which the functions of target cells that are not under direct sympathetic influence (such as immune cells) can also be modulated during times of stress. Irrespective of the source of catecholamine secretion, the importance of this response is clearly underwritten by the redundancy inherent in the system.

Catecholamines within the central nervous system also play a prominent role in coordinating an organism's response to stress. For instance, the locus coeruleus is a major catecholamine center in the brainstem that is responsible for coordinating stress responses via interactions with higher brain structures such as the hypothalamus, the amygdala, and the cortex (Svensson, 1987). Specifically, environmental stimuli that require perceptual organization, cognitive appraisal, or affective evaluation in order to be deemed "stressful" eventually activate peripheral sympathetics via descending autonomic output through the locus coeruleus. In this role, the locus coeruleus also serves as a final site of integration for the propagation of certain peripheral autonomic responses to stress.

On the other end of the spectrum would be physiological threats to homeostasis such as hypoxia, hypoglycemia, or hemorrhagic shock that are detected in brainstem structures such as the pons, medulla, and reticular formation. In cases such as these where threat is not necessarily detected by the cognitive or perceptual apparatus of the organism, but rather by alarm systems that continuously monitor peripheral physiological status, the locus coeruleus sends ascending catecholaminergic input to higher brain centers. Such information is then processed by higher cognitive structures in order to "encourage" behavioral strategies that will alleviate the threat to homeostasis. Thus, brainstem autonomic nuclei such as the locus coeruleus are critical sites of integration for threatening stimuli irrespective of whether the threat originates from higher brain centers or peripheral challenges to homeostasis [see Harro and Oreland (2001) for an excellent review].

Monoamine Systems

Since its neurons respond exquisitely to all attention-provoking and alarming external stimuli, the locus coeruleus is a primary gatekeeper of central nervous system (CNS) sympathetic nervous system responses to stress. However, this type of arousal occurs irrespective of whether the pervading stressful stimulus is of peripheral origin (such as with threatening physiological situations that require immune activation) or initiated centrally (as in the case of some perceptual or cognitive event). As a result, disturbances in locus coeruleus function have been implicated in a variety of psychiatric illnesses such as major depression. Specifically, it has been hypothesized that exposure to stressors can produce adaptations in locus coeruleus function that ultimately lead to depressivelike symptoms (Harro and Oreland, 2001). Along these same lines, adaptations in locus coeruleus function in response to stress would be expected to alter the individual's response to subsequent stressors (either hypo- or hyperresponsivity, depending on the nature of the stressor). Indeed, there is strong evidence to suggest that stress-induced alterations in locus coeruleus function and corresponding sympathetic output may play an etiological role in psychiatric illness, especially in the case of depression. Such a connection has long been suggested by the utility of monoamine modulating drugs to treat individuals suffering from this disorder. Clearly, the interaction of qualitatively different stressors and their corresponding effects on the ability of the locus coeruleus to integrate and coordinate sympathetic nervous system responses to subsequent challenge is a critical area of research in both basic and applied arenas today.

Indeed, one emerging animal model of depression relies on the interaction among multiple different stressors administered over 5 to 7 days to produce depressivelike symptoms. These models come in a variety of forms and are typically referred to as "chronic mild stress" paradigms (Willner, 1997). The real advantage of these models is that by employing different stressors on each day (foot shock on day 1 followed by social conflict on day 2, etc.), researchers can more appropriately model the cumulative nature of stress in human populations. Furthermore, using the sum consequence of exposure to multiple stressors helps eliminate experimental conclusions that might be a result of the contrived nature of some rodent stressor paradigms. (After all, what does a stressor such as foot shock in the rat really model in humans?) Nevertheless, evidence from chronic stress paradigms clearly demonstrate a role for sympathetic nervous system output and its governance by the locus coeruleus in psychiatric illness.

Neuroendocrine Responses to Stress

The hypothalamic-pituitary-adrenal (HPA) axis is one of the most widely studied of the stress responsive systems. This cascade begins with the release of CRH from the parvocellular neurons of the paraventricular nucleus of the hypothalamus into the external zone of the median eminence. From here CRH is carried through the portal blood system to the anterior lobe of the pituitary gland, where it acts as a secretagogue for adrenocorticotrophic hormone (ACTH). ACTH is then released into the systemic circulation and carried through the blood to the adrenal cortex, where it stimulates cells in the zona fasciculata to produce and release glucocorticoids. The glucocorticoid released in response to stress in the rat is corticosterone (CORT), while the human adrenal cortex secretes cortisol. Since corticosterone and cortisol vary only slightly in their chemical structure, both are classified as glucocorticoid hormones and bind to the same receptors in the body with comparable affinity. It is perhaps important to note that other species such as hamsters co-secrete corticosterone and cortisol during times of stress. As a result, it is necessary to measure cortisol and corticosterone in species that produce both of these glucocorticoid hormones during times of stress.

Although glucocorticoid secretion is the ultimate hormonal endpoint of the HPA axis, this is just the beginning of the most important physiological effects of HPA activation. Being highly lipophilic, glucocorticoids travel through the blood and passively diffuse across plasma membranes where they bind to cytosolic receptors (Drouin et al., 1992). When activated, the glucocorticoid-receptor complex translocates to the nucleus of the cell and has the ability to alter gene transcription. This in turn leads to glucose mobilization for the organism, alterations in immune function, and changes in CNS functioning [see Munck et al. (1984) for a classic review of glucocorticoid function]. Furthermore, glucocorticoids can bind to receptors in the hippocampus, hypothalamus, and the anterior pituitary and subsequently decrease the release of CRH and ACTH. This serves as a negative feedback mechanism that limits the amount of glucocorticoid secreted in response to subsequent stressors (e.g., Spencer et al., 1998).

As mentioned previously, the effects of CORT are mediated by two high-affinity intracellular receptors. These two receptors are referred to as mineralocorticoid receptors (MR; or type I receptors) and glucocorticoid receptors (GR; or type II receptors). The affinity of MR ($K_d = 0.5$ to 1 nM) for CORT is greater than that of GR ($K_d = 5$ to 10 nM), which leads to greater occupancy of MR under basal CORT conditions (Spencer et al., 1993). Both of these receptors are located in the cytoplasm until they become occupied by CORT. Receptor occupation leads to rapid receptor translocation to the nucleus where the receptor acts as a hormone-activated transcription factor (Drouin et al., 1992). Thus, the number of cytoplasmic CORT receptors reflects the number of unoccupied CORT receptors, while the number of nuclear CORT receptors reflects the number of occupied/activated CORT receptors. Indeed, the relative proportion of occupied receptors in the rat given different circulating levels of CORT has been well characterized (Spencer et al., 1993).

The magnitude and temporal dynamics of the CORT response varies markedly with the type and duration of the stressor. However, the time course of increases in plasma CORT levels in response to stress is slightly delayed relative to indices of sympathetic nervous system activity (as discussed in the previous section). For instance, observable increases in CORT can usually be detected within 3 to 5 min from the onset of the stressor, while a maximal CORT response is generally only observed if the stressor persists for at least 20 to 30 min. Finally, the stress-induced rise in CORT typically dissipates completely within 60 to 90 min following termination of the stressor (Jacobson et al., 1988). Thus, the unique temporal dynamics of the pituitary-adrenal response to stress must be taken into serious consideration when designing experiments to examine the potential role of glucocorticoids in mediating the ultimate health consequences of stressor exposure.

Implications for Biological Psychiatry. There are several facets of HPA activation that are particularly relevant for biological psychiatry. First and foremost, prolonged exposure to high circulating levels of CORT (such as with chronic stress) produce deleterious effects on normal CNS function. Since the hippocampus is extraordinarily rich in both MR and GR expression, it is not surprising that the hippocampal system has been the subject of intense scrutiny with regard to glucocorticoid action. Specifically, sustained high levels of CORT have been shown to produce dendritic atrophy (Galea et al., 1997), reduced neurogenesis (Cameron and McKay, 1999), and in extreme cases neurotoxicity (Reagan and McEwen, 1997) within the hippocampus. Such empirical findings have led to the belief that chronic stress throughout the life span—and the prolonged glucocorticoid exposure that ensues—may contribute to the development of multiple psychiatric conditions such as major depression, Cushings syndrome, posttraumatic stress disorder (PTSD), and age-related dementia [see Chapter 11 and Sapolsky (2000) for a recent review].

Extrahypothalamic CRH Systems

To reiterate a point made earlier, it is not simply exposure to aversive events that ultimately propagates stress in an individual, but also the anticipation of aversive events. The anticipation of aversive events may include learned associations that are formed across the life span as well as species-specific innate responses to biologically hard-wired threats. For instance, learned associations between fearful stimuli and the context where those stimuli are encountered are readily formed. Certain other fears appear to be unlearned such as the fear of open spaces in rodent species. Regardless of whether these fears are learned or innate, exposure to stimuli that elicit such fear will ultimately lead to activation of stress responsive systems. Common experimental paradigms used to examine the neural substrates of learned and innate fears (i.e., the anticipation of aversive events) include contextual and cue-elicited fear conditioning in the rat and exposure to predator cues such as fox feces and feline odors. The interesting point to be made here is that the anticipation of aversive events leads to mobilization of stress responsive systems. However, when sustained anticipation occurs over a prolonged period of time, the resources necessary for effective coping with such stressors eventually become depleted, and deleterious health consequences are likely to ensue. Indeed, the ultimate cost to the individual of prolonged negative anticipation has been conceptualized as "allostatic load" (McEwen, 2000; Schulkin et al., 1994). Thus, it is advantageous to look toward animal models of fear and anxiety for an understanding of the neuroanatomical and neurochemical basis of learned fears (see Chapter 16), which should in turn help elucidate how chronic anticipation of aversive events may predispose individuals toward psychiatric illness. Indeed, one of the most provocative advances in stress research over the past decade has been the demonstration that CRH in brain regions other than the paraventricular nucleus of hypothalamus that controls pituitary ACTH secretion (referred to as extrahypothalamic CRH systems) may play a critical role in stress-related disorders. Thus, we will now turn our discussion toward specific evidence supporting the important role for extrahypothalamic CRH.

Corticotropin-releasing hormone is a 41-amino-acid peptide initially identified as a hypothalamic factor responsible for stimulating ACTH from the anterior pituitary (Vale et al., 1981). As discussed in the previous section, stressors induce the synthesis and release of CRH from cells of the paraventricular nucleus into the portal blood, initiating the HPA response to stressors. CRH is also involved in mediation of the normal autonomic and behavioral consequences of exposure to stressors. For instance, the intracerebroventricular (icv) administration of CRH produces autonomic activation and many of the same behavioral (Koob and Britton, 1990), neurochemical (Dunn and Berridge, 1990), and electrophysiological (Valentino et al., 1983) alterations that are produced by stressors. Furthermore, the icv administration of CRH antagonists such as α-helical CRH_{9-41} and D-Phe CRH_{12-41} can blunt or block these stress-induced alterations in behavior and autonomic activity (e.g., Korte et al., 1994). Many of these effects can be obtained by infusing CRH or its antagonists into nonhypothalamic sites such as the locus coeruleus and amygdala (Butler et al., 1990), and persist in hypophysectomized and dexamethasone-treated subjects (Britton et al., 1986).

These facts together with the wide extrahypothalamic distribution of high-affinity CRH receptors and CRH-like immunoreactivity suggest that CRH functions as a neurotransmitter as well as a hormone, and that it mediates stress-related behavioral responses by action at extrahypothalamic sites (Dunn and Berridge, 1990; Koob, 1990). Given the widespread involvement of extrahypothalamic CRH in mediating the consequences of stressor exposure, these systems have been proposed as key mediators of anticipatory stress. Thus, a review of the relationship between extrahypothalamic CRH systems and learned fear as a model of anticipatory stress will provide further evidence to this end.

Brain CRH systems have been shown to be important in mediating the fear responses observed in fear conditioning experiments. Rats and other organisms freeze when placed in an environment in which they have previously received an aversive stimulus such as foot shock, and freezing has been shown to be a measure of fear conditioned to the environment by the aversive stimulus (Fanselow and Lester, 1988). The term *fear conditioning* refers to the fact that both discrete and contextual cues that are present during exposure to a stressor such as foot shock can elicit behavioral and physiological responses such as freezing, inhibited appetitive behavior, potentiated startle, increased autonomic and HPA activity, and the like (Davis, 1992). It is to be noted that freezing is not simply an absence of movement, but rather an active defensive response consisting of no movement beyond that required for respiration including the absence of vibrissae movement, typically accompanied by a hunched posture and muscular rigidity. Importantly, icv α-helical CRH reduces the freezing that occurred when rats were exposed to the environment in which they had received foot shock, and it also reduces the potentiation of startle produced by a light that had previously been paired with shock (Swerdlow et al., 1989). These data suggest that extrahypothalamic CRH is important for the normal expression of fear-related behavior.

The amygdala plays a key integrative role in both the induction of fear conditioning and the expression of fear-related behavior. Lesions in basolateral regions of the amygdala (Campeau and Davis, 1995) or microinjection of N-methyl-D-aspartate (NMDA) antagonists (Fanselow and Kim, 1994) in this region prevent the induction of fear conditioning. In contrast, infusions of NMDA antagonists into the central nucleus of the amygdala do not retard fear conditioning (Fanselow and Kim, 1994), even though electrolytic lesions of that structure are effective (Campeau and Davis, 1995). NMDA antagonists, injected either into the amygdala (Miserendino et al., 1990) or icv (Kim et al., 1992) have no effect on the expression of fear that has been previously conditioned. This pattern of data has led to the view that the association between the sensory cues that precede the stressor and the stressor itself are formed in basolateral regions of the amygdala and critically involves NMDA receptors. The information then flows to the central nucleus of the amygdala, which functions in the behavioral expressions of fear via a final common path that integrates the bodily manifestations of fear (Davis, 1992), and it is likely that unconditioned psychological (affective) fear responses are also so induced (Chapter 16). In sum, NMDA receptors that mediate learning of fear do not appear to be essential in the central nucleus expression mechanisms.

The amygdala contains CRH immunoreactive cells and fibers (Swanson et al., 1983), and both the type 1 and type 2 CRH receptor are widely distributed in both the basolateral region and central nucleus (Chalmers et al., 1995). Exposure to a stressor has been reported to increase CRH messenger ribonucleic acid (mRNA) in the amygdala (Kalin et al., 1994), and microinjection of α-helical CRH into the central nucleus decreases the expression of conditioned fear (Swiergiel et al., 1993) as well as other stressor-induced behavioral changes (Heinrichs et al., 1992). Thus previous research has implicated NMDA-related processes in the basolateral amygdala in the induction but not expression of fear conditioning, and CRH in the central nucleus in the expression of fear. The potential role of CRH in the induction of fear conditioning has only recently been explored, and the results suggest that CRH is important in both induction and expression of conditioned fear (Deak et al., 1999). Clearly, it would be of interest to determine whether the critical site of CRH action in the induction of fear is the basolateral amygdala.

Implications for Biological Psychiatry. The evidence described above clearly points to CRH transmission within discrete regions of the amygdala in the unconditional generation and learned maintenance of fear-related behavior. At the human level, extrahypothalamic CRH has been implicated in a number of human disorders such as major depression (Gold et al., 1996; Nemeroff, 1996), PTSD (Grillon et al., 1996), and bulimia (Krahn and Gosnell, 1989). As a result, the development of novel therapeutic agents that target specific CRH receptor subtypes has become a major thrust in recent years. However, one major problem associated with the use of anti-CRH drugs to treat human clinical populations has been that most of these agents do not pass through the blood-brain barrier efficiently and thus cannot bind to CRH receptors in the necessary neural substrates to effect therapeutic change. As a result, there has been a push in the past decade toward the development of nonpeptide CRH antagonists that cross the blood-brain barrier and can be used in treating human clinical populations. Several of these drugs are currently in clinical trials and have enjoyed moderate success in treating human clinical populations (Zobel et al., 2000).

INTEGRATIVE ROLE FOR BRAIN CYTOKINES

During an acute bout of stress, signs of behavioral activation are frequently displayed that presumably allow the organism to identify and escape the impending threat. However, after the acute threat has passed, it is common to observe delayed and sustained disruptions in normal behavior and reactivity. As a result, there has been the suggestion that behavioral alterations that occur during stressor exposure may be mediated by wholly separate neurobiological entities than the delayed and sustained behavioral alterations (Hennessy et al., 2001). Many of the immediate behavioral consequences of stressor exposure are mediated by the interaction of the sympathetic nervous system (including catecholaminergic cell groups in the brainstem) and extrahypothalamic CRH systems. In contrast, recent data suggest that long-term changes in behavior that are produced by stressor exposure (decreased food and water intake, decreased social and sexual interaction, reduced exploration of novel environments, etc.) may be mediated by factors that are more traditionally associated with the immune system (Maier and Watkins, 1998).

These immune factors are referred to as proinflammatory cytokines and are more commonly acknowledged for their role in coordinating the immune response during times of infection. Activation of the immune system also leads to a characteristic set of behavioral responses that are typically referred to as sickness behaviors (Hart, 1988). For example, immune activation can reduce food and water consumption, decrease sexual behavior, increase slow-wave sleep, decrease locomotor activity, reduce aggressive behavior, and decrease social interaction (see Kent et al., 1992). Interestingly, many of these same behavioral changes are also observed following stressor exposure (Short and Maier, 1993; Milligan et al., 1998). These similarities have led some investigators to postulate that the neural circuitry underlying the behavioral effects of stressor exposure and immune challenge may also be similar.

Many of these behavioral changes observed following immune stimulation are mediated by central production of the proinflammatory cytokine interleukin-1 (IL-1). Central administration of IL-1 produces fever, hyperalgesia (Watkins et al., 1994), induces slow-wave sleep (Opp and Krueger, 1991), reduces food and water intake (Kent et al., 1996), alters peripheral immune function (Sullivan et al., 1997), increases plasma ACTH and glucocorticoids (Dunn, 1995), reduces social interaction (Kent et al., 1992), and decreases some measures of anxiety (Montkowski et al., 1997). Many of the behavioral changes produced by icv administration of IL-1 can be blocked or attenuated by prior icv administration of IL-1 receptor antagonist (IL-1ra) (Opp and Krueger, 1991; Kent et al., 1996). Thus, central production of IL-1 appears to be a critical component of host defense against peripheral infection and subsequent recovery.

In addition to its role in mediating sickness behaviors, central production of IL-1 has also emerged as an important mediator of behavioral and neuroendocrine responses to stress. Shintani et al. (1995) have shown that central injection of IL-1 produced a robust activation of the HPA axis and increased hypothalamic monoamine turnover. These changes are typically considered the hallmarks of stressor exposure. Importantly, IL-1ra has been shown to block the HPA and monoamine response to immobilization stress (Shintani et al., 1995). Central IL-1 has also been implicated in mediating the behavioral consequences of inescapable tail shock since the enhancement of fear conditioning and interference with escape learning produced by this shock experience can also be blocked by icv administration of IL-1ra (Maier and Watkins, 1995). Likewise, α-MSH administered icv blocked all of the acute phaselike changes that have been observed following inescapable tail shock exposure (Milligan et al., 1998). When coupled with the demonstration that exposure to psychological stressors can increase IL-1 production in specific brain regions (Nguyen et al., 2000), it can be concluded that stress-induced production of IL-1 may be critically involved in long-term behavioral and physiological adjustments that are produced by stressor exposure.

This is *not* to say that all stressors induce central production of IL-1, or that IL-1 mediates all effects of stressors. Indeed, there are some stressors, such as exposure to predators, that do not affect brain cytokine levels at all (e.g., Plata-Salaman et al., 2000). As a result, the critical determinant(s) for the observation of stress-induced increases in brain IL-1 remains elusive and demands further study. These efforts must begin by determination of which stressors cause increases in central cytokine production, and the role that these cytokines play in mediating subsequent behavioral and physiological consequences of stressor exposure.

Implications for Biological Psychiatry. Traditionally, psychological stress and major depression have both been associated with impaired immune function and increased susceptibility to disease. In recent years, however, it has been recognized that exposure to psychological stressors and major depressive episodes are also associated with signs of immune activation [for an excellent review see Connor and Leonard (1998)]. One particularly interesting facet of this immune activation is that circulating levels of proinflammatory cytokines are elevated during times of stress and in clinically depressed populations. Since proinflammatory cytokines normally produce the behavioral and physiological adjustments that occur during sickness, it has been suggested that their release may mitigate some consequences of exposure to psychological stressors and major depressive episodes (Maier and Watkins, 1998). For instance, psychological stressors, depression, and sickness due to infection all produce disturbances in appetite, alterations in normal sleep patterns, reduced social interaction, impaired cognitive function, and psychomotor agitation or impairment (Connor and Leonard, 1998). Moreover, similarities have also been observed between the physiological responses to stressors and major depression. These physiological symptoms include changes in circulating lymphocytes, alterations in plasma levels of acute-phase proteins, persistent fever, elevated plasma cytokines, and hypercortisolemia (Deak et al., 1997; Maes, 1999). As a result of these findings, it has been suggested that activation of the immune system may be etiologically related to depressive illness in certain prone individuals.

The key element we are emphasizing here is that in some cases, exposure to psychological stressors alone (i.e., in the absence of any apparent tissue damage or pathogenic insult) is capable of inducing proinflammatory cytokine production. Furthermore, cytokine production in response to stress appears to be important for at least some of the long-term changes in behavior that are normally produced by that stressor, especially those that resemble depressive or despairlike behaviors (Hennessy et al., 2001). Thus, stressor-induced proinflammatory cytokine production may represent a novel mechanism underlying certain human psychiatric illnesses. This new conceptualization raises a whole host of empirical questions regarding the possible role of infection as a precipitating event in the onset of major psychiatric illness, especially if such a challenge were to occur during critical developmental periods.

In summary, while we have tried to emphasize the preeminent role of stress and its far-reaching implications for biological psychiatry, we have also tried to emphasize stress responsive systems are not restricted to a single neural pathway, a single neurochemical system, or even to the central nervous system itself. Rather, stress responsive systems—upon activation—have the ability to alter molecular, cellular, and systemic processes across the entire organism. Indeed, stress affects everything an organism does. In the following two sections, we will briefly focus on two systems that are especially stress responsive, sexuality and sleep. However, our aim is not simply to focus on the fact that both are greatly impaired by stress (that is true of all motivational systems) but to briefly discuss key aspects of the physiology of these systems.

SEXUALITY AND THE PASSIONS OF THE BRAIN

Introductory Remarks

Social stress is one of the prime vectors for quality-of-life issues in both humans and other animals (Sgoifo et al., 2001). This is especially evident in the capacity to sustain and enjoy sexual relationships. Sexual motivational systems lie at the root of some of the most intense human feelings, ranging from the eroticism and cravings of sexual arousal to the delights and disappointments of orgasm, not to mention social bondings and attachments, not to mention the ongoing dynamics of social relationships and dependencies. Sexual motivation and sexual performance are often dissociated (Everitt, 1990), as are social urges and commitments, especially in the presence of negative mood and emotional states. To better grasp how these relationships may permeate psychiatric concerns, the aim of this brief section is to provide an overview of the neural underpinnings of mammalian sexuality.

Reproductive fitness is the ultimate currency of evolution. *Sexual selection* and the sources of human *moral principles* were the topics Darwin struggled with in his second great book on evolution *Descent of Man* (1871, 1874, 1st and 2nd editions; for more on related evolutionary psychiatry issues, see Chapter 20). In laying the groundwork for modern sociobiology, Darwin made many provocative and often troublesome assertions, especially since human sexuality is politicized and regulated in most cultures. For instance, he asserted that "man is more courageous, pugnacious and energetic than woman, and has a more inventive genius" (1874, p. 552). We now know that this viewpoint reflects more cultural misconception than true biological fact. We now know that there are quite real gender differences in emotional/cognitive strengths/weaknesses at the population level, as well as at the level of brain structure and function (Kimura, 1999; Mealey, 2000), but it is exceedingly difficult to link the two. But one must proceed with caution since prejudicial attitudes incubate easily in human minds, perhaps in part due to our evolutionary heritage (Chapter 20).

To this day we struggle with our inability to distinguish biological fact from cultural fiction (Panksepp et al., 2002; Pinker, 2002). There was a time when diagnostic manuals placed homosexuality in the category of mental deviance, but now we recognize cross-gender psychological identities as a natural part of the way our brains are organized. At the social level we easily accept the dictum that "exotic is erotic" (Bem, 2000). At the same time it has been exceedingly difficult to accept that there are eroticism-promoting molecules in our brains, and that there may be many differences among the sexes and genders in the evolved mental aspects of sexuality. Still, during the past century we gradually came to accept sexual variety as the norm, with only two major remaining problem areas: the consequences of individual lives when people harm or offend each other, and the psychological difficulties that ensue when one cannot function sexually at the level one desires. When our complex sociosexual apparatus does not work properly, there can be a great deal of emotional distress.

Let us briefly consider these topics in reverse order: (1) What are the factors that impair sexual ability? (2) What is it about the organization of our brains that creates, at least at a statistical level, the neurophysiology of maleness and femaleness? (3) What leads us to have sexual urges? and (4) How can we minimize harm in sociosexual activities? Since there is not sufficient space to probe such issues in depth, we will restrict our discussion to those issues we feel are pertinent to treatment strategies in biological psychiatry.

Psychogenic Factors that Impair Sexual Ability

Through its pervasive influences on a diversity of mind-brain functions, stress can increase or diminish a variety of motivational urges, including sexuality. While mild stress can sometimes increase sexual urges, sustained stress diminishes erotic urges. Indeed, one of the primary stress hormones in the brain, CRH, dramatically reduces all prosocial and sexual activities, as well as all other appetites, when released within the brain (Chapter 21).

None of the major psychiatric drugs, aside from dopamine facilitators (Panksepp, 1998), consistently promote sexual urges, but many reduce them in ways that are often emotionally troublesome to people. The most widespread problems are associated with the anorgasmia and reductions in sexual motivation that result from the use of antidepressants, most recently the selective serotonin reuptake inhibitors (SSRIs) (Rosen et al., 1999). However, other agents are not without problems (Gitlin, 1994), and there are some drugs that can facilitate sexual abilities (Crenshaw and Goldberg, 1996). Mammalian sexual energy is dependent heavily on brain dopamine release, so it is not surprising that all antipsychotics tend to diminish sexual urges (Van Furth et al., 1995). There is no simple way around these problems except drug discontinuation. Despite the ability of sexual performance enhancers such as sildenafil (Viagra) to promote sexual capacity, they still need to be evaluated in interaction with the major psychiatric drugs as well as in terms of various psychological factors relevant to psychiatric practice.

Genetic and Epigenetic Creation of Maleness and Femaleness

We have a better understanding of the systems that control sexual urges in the brains of animals than of humans, but there are now abundant reasons to believe the principles, if not the details, will translate well across many mammalian species (Panksepp, 1998; Pfaus, 1996). However, since the variety of sexual strategies among species is so vast (Judson, 2002), the underlying brain details will also vary. Likewise, many complexities arise from the fact that sexual motivation and performance are distinguishable, albeit highly interactive, systems in the brain (Everitt, 1990). Although there has been resistance to the use of animal work to illuminate the human condition, here we will summarize the general principles, while not denying the abundant differences in details across species (Robbins, 1996).

To a remarkable degree, male and female sexuality are subservient to many distinct as well as several overlapping brain controls (summarized in Panksepp, 1998; Pfaff, 1999). The role of the testis-determining gene on the Y chromosome in elaborating male genital development and the resulting testosterone (T) based signaling of maleness to the brain has been worked out in considerable detail, at least in rats (Pfaff, 1999). If, during the critical *organizational* phase of gender determination, during the last few days before birth (in humans that happens in the second trimester of gestation, and a few days before birth in rats), the cascade of biochemical events goes according to the standard schedule, the brains of males become masculinized. To be effective in precipitating this developmental cascade, the pulsatile secretions of T in utero have to be converted to the metabolite estrogen via aromatization. If sufficient estrogen (E) does not bathe the male brain at the right time (e.g., because of a mistiming of T secretion, inadequate *aromatase,* or deficits of estrogen receptors in the right regions of the brain), the male brain remains organized in the primordial female-typical pattern. Parenthetically, since the mother's estrogen could promote masculinization of the female brain, female fetuses have "failsafe" prophylactic molecules, such as α-fetoprotein, that can sequester maternal estrogens.

Since male-typical body organization is elaborated more by a different metabolite of T, namely dihydrotestosterone (DHT), produced via the enzyme 5-α-reductase, one can a have male-typical brain in a female-typical body, and vice versa, depending on which hormones the fetus was exposed to during the critical organizational periods of sexual differentiation. Without denying the importance of psychosocial learning on many aspects of human development, the metabolic conversion of T into E and DHT may provide some insight into trans-sexual and homosexual tendencies. Although these issues cannot be analyzed readily in the human species, there is now substantial evidence, especially from work on rodents, that male bodies can contain female-typical brains, and female bodies can contain male-typical brains in rats. There is also suggestive evidence this can occur in humans (e.g., Imperato-McGinley, et al. 1979). These realignments of brain and body gender identities, no doubt produce substantial psychological consequences during adolescence as individuals reach sexual maturity (Kimura, 1999; LeVay, et al. 1993).

What does it mean to have a masculinized brain? In animals we know this is reflected in the fact that certain neuronal groups in the anterior hypothalamus [the sexually dimorphic nuclei of the preoptic area (SDN-POA)] grow larger than in most females. Partly this is due to the slowing of early neuronal "weeding" and partly to the neural growth-promoting effects of E. There is increasing data to show that the same type of effects are present in the human brain (LeVay, et al. 1993), especially in the intermediate nuclei of the anterior hypothalamus (INAH), but other brain areas as well (Zhou et al., 1995). These morphological differences participate in the elaboration of sex-typical psychological and behavioral differences. The failure to recognize that such neurobiological organizational processes do occur in humans has been a source of prolonged distress to those who have been treated according to culturally politicized psychosocial models of gender determination (Colapinto, 2000).

One of the remarkable aspects of these psychobiological findings, at least in rats, is that environmental events, such as maternal stress, can influence the brain organizational effects of early hormone secretions. The male fetuses of mother rats that have been stressed consistently exhibit a reduction in both neural and behavioral masculinization. This is partly due to the fact that the fetal secretions of T are too early, before adequate aromatization enzymes are present to convert T to E, and also before the receptive elements for estrogen have matured. Conversely, female offspring tend to exhibit some masculinization as a result of maternal stress, but the mechanisms for this phenomenon have not been worked out. There is a modest amount of evidence that similar effects can occur in our own species (Ellis and Ebertz, 1997).

Sexual Urges: Regrets and Remedies

The different gender identities of the brain, engraved during fetal development, are activated by maturing gonadal steroid secretions during puberty. To have a male brain means many things. The enlarged SDN-POA nuclei of males promotes male-typical sexual urges via the activational effects of T, and experimental damage to those brain areas diminishes male sexual behavior more than that of females. In contrast, female receptivity is dependent much more on circuits within the ventromedial hypothalamus, which are sensitized by E and progesterone (Pfaff, 1999), which are not essential for male sexuality. Of course, there are many other brain areas, including prominently the bed nucleus of the stria terminalis (BNST) and corticomedial amygdala, along with many neurochemistries, that contribute to the flow of sexual arousal. To some degree both males and females contain circuitry that is more typical of the other gender. For instance, administration of T into adult females can rapidly promote male-typical ways of thinking and feeling, while E can do the reverse for males (Van Goozen et al., 1995).

Under gender-typical hormone conditions, male and female sexual circuits have different neurochemical correlates (as summarized in Panksepp, 1998; Pfaff, 1999). One of the biggest differences is the higher prevalence of arginine-vasopressin (AVP) in the SDN-POA and associated sexual circuits of males as compared to females. AVP gene expression is under the tonic influence of T, and this neuropeptide diminishes dramatically following castration. This partly explains male sexual deficits, which emerge much more rapidly in male rats than humans following castration because human behavior is supported by more robust and subtle psychological abilities and habits. In any event, T restores sexual urgency in both, and in rats this can be achieved simply by replacing T in the SDN-POA.

The AVP intensifies male sexual arousal partly by promoting sexual persistence; in animals this is evident in sustained territorial marking behavior and elevations of sex-related aggression. In humans, plasma AVP levels surge during sexual arousal but decline sharply at orgasm (Murphy et al., 1990). Whether new drugs that can facilitate AVP activity in the brain might promote sexual desire remains a poorly developed line of inquiry that may have interesting therapeutic implications, as might AVP antagonists in the control of sexual aggression and jealousy (see Chapter 21).

On the other hand, various estrogen, progesterone, and oxytocin receptors are enriched in female brains, where they contribute to female-typical sexual receptivity (Pedersen et al., 1992; Pfaff, 1999). In this context, it is noteworthy that female sexual urges diminish dramatically when the male facilitator AVP is infused into the brain (Sodersten et al., 1983). On the other hand, oxytocin does contribute positively to male sexuality. It is one of the most effective ways to induce erections when placed directly into a variety of brain areas (Argiolas and Gessa, 1991), especially those where Paul MacLean originally mapped the erection circuits of the primate brain (MacLean and Ploog, 1962). In human males, plasma oxytocin levels remain low during sexual arousal but a large bolus is released at orgasm. Interestingly, the somatosensory pleasure of massage is able to increase peripheral oxytocin secretion (Uvnas-Moberg, 1998). If these changes also occur inside the brain, it would suggest that both males and females obtain an oxytocin-mediated affective reward not only at orgasm but also during pleasurable skin contact. However, these important neuropsychological events are surely not left to a single chemistry, for many neurochemicals, including opioids, contribute to the pleasure of sex as well as many other rewards (Van Ree et al., 2000). Another key player is the luteinizing hormone–releasing hormone, which can selectively increase female libido. Whether such manipulations could be deployed to facilitate human sexuality remains a poorly studied idea that is pregnant with possibilities (Chapter 21). There are some antiaging agents such as the monoamine oxidase (MAO) inhibitor, deprenyl, that can prolong sexual vitality in animals (Knoll, 1992), and hormone replacement therapies along with some pharmacological agents remain effective and ever popular (Crenshaw and Goldberg, 1996).

Sex-steroid control of sexual readiness operates partly through the ability of estrogen and testosterone to activate gene transcriptions in sexual readiness circuits (Pfaff, 1999). Estrogen priming (just like normal estrus) promotes oxytocin synthesis, oxytocin receptor proliferation in female sex circuits, especially in the medial hypothalamus, as well as promoting synaptogenesis within that system. After hormone priming, female sexual urges are markedly diminished by blocking oxytocinergic transmission at key points within this system—such as in the medial hypothalamus. Male sexual behavior is also diminished following central administration of these antagonists, suggesting there is a tonic level of oxytocin stimulation that provides a socioaffective background for sexual readiness (Carter, 1998). In this context, it is also noteworthy that oxytocin can prolong the sexual refractory period following ejaculation, suggesting it may participate in the affective "afterglow" following orgasm.

Finally, we would note that similar circuits and chemistries control sexuality in cold-blooded reptiles and that the location of maternal behavior circuits in mammals are closely intermeshed with those ancient sexuality systems, especially in preoptic and anterior regions of the hypothalamus (Panksepp, 1998). Thus, part of the gratification of nurturance may arise from circuits that originally evolved to mediate sexual attractions, urges, and pleasure, long before the "social-attachment bond" between mother and child had emerged in mammalian species. Now we know that a great deal of social bonding is mediated by chemistries such as oxytocin, vasopressin, and opioids (Carter, 1998; Insel, 1997; Nelson and Panksepp, 1998).

As already noted, environmental factors (e.g., stress) can strongly influence the course of psychosexual differentiation, and their influence does not diminish after birth. The number of long-term consequences on child development are enormous (Panksepp, 2001; Schore, 2003), and the list of long-term effects on adult competence resulting from modifications of socioenvironmental quality steadily grows. One of the most fascinating findings has been the effect of maternal quality care on promoting the emotional resilience of their offspring in species ranging from primates (Suomi, 1997) to rats (Meaney, 2001), with effects often lasting across generations (Fleming et al., 1999). The rat work indicates that the maternal care (partly in the form of anogenital licking) leads to life-long benefits for the mental and physical health of the offspring. In rats, mothers devote more of this type of nurturance toward male offspring, and if one experimentally offers the same levels of attention to females, they exhibit fewer differences in sexual behavior during adulthood than would otherwise be observed (Moore, 1995).

We now address the occurrence of the various aspects of sexual arousal in the human brain. The human brain has now been imaged during various types of sexual arousal. In males, visually induced sexual arousal, evaluated in a dose-response fashion with escalating doses of erotic materials, generates a dramatic increase in arousal just below the top of the skull, in the midcingulate region of the higher limbic system (Redoute et al., 2000). This is a key area where emotional and cognitive factors are intensely blended and represents the optimal brain region where sexual imagery provokes the cascade of lust. This, along with temporal lobe regions, especially the cortico-medial regions of the amygdala, appears to be where the neurochemistries of the subcortical systems are triggered into arousal by cognitive events.

And where is the epicenter for the experience of orgasm in this tangled skein? It has been imaged a few times, and initial single-photon emission computed tornography (SPECT) studies only saw arousal in the right frontal cortex (Tiihonen et al., 1994). More recently estimates of increased blood flow using positron emission tomography (PET) scanning indicate abundant arousal in many limbic cortical areas: the cerebellum, as well as the ventral tegmental area of the meso-dicencephalic junction (Georgiadis et al., 2002), where dopamine systems long implicated in animal sexual arousal and psychostimulant reward are situated (Pfaus, 1996; Van Ree, 2000). The female orgasmic response has regrettably not been visualized yet.

Although addictive processes are not specifically covered in this text, we would be amiss not to mention that there are strong relations between sexual urges and rewards and the pleasures derived from drugs of abuse, especially the psychostimulants and opioids. The role of opioids in elaborating social emotions has long been recognized (Panksepp, 1998), and the dopamine systems that figure heavily in the appetitive phase of sexuality (as well as every other reward) is aroused by sexual stimuli (Ikemoto and Panksepp, 1999; Pfaus, 1996). Indeed, the finding that animals sensitized to psychostimulants typically seek drugs and sex more vigorously than those that have not (Nocjar and Panksepp, 2002) is in accord with this conclusion.

SLEEP, STRESS, AND THE RESTORATION OF BRAIN AND MIND

Introductory Remarks

More research has been done on sleep mechanisms than any other state-control processes of the brain. We now know the locations of the major circuits that control slow-wave sleep (SWS) as well as those periodic arousals that are full of vivid emotional dreams and rapid eye movements (REM sleep). We know much about the neurophysiological changes that reflect these natural tides of the brain and the major neurochemistries that control these passages of consciousness, but rather little about the adaptive functions of sleep stages at a scientific level.

However, several everyday observations are important to keep in mind. Sleep, in proper amounts, alleviates tiredness that builds up during waking. Sleep also *knits up the raveled sleeve of care:* If one goes to sleep with a troubled mind, difficult as it often is to get to sleep, one usually wakes feeling emotionally less burdened. Was it simply due to the passage of time and ensuing forgetfulness, or was there an active emotional restoration process proceeding under the cover of our daily doses of unconsciousness during SWS and/or altered consciousness during REM sleep? No one knows for sure, but the number of intriguing, psychiatrically relevant findings that are emerging demonstrates the importance of sleep in the homeostasis of both cognitive and affective aspects of mind. Indeed, the possibility that the moods that accompany dreams may be a useful way to monitor the deep emotional status of psychiatric patients needs to be more fully examined (Domhoff, 2002). The aim of this short summary is neither to describe the patterns of sleep and the neurobiology of sleep stages nor to reiterate once more the well-established neuroscience findings in the field (for that see Kryger et al., 2000). The goal is to briefly highlight the most psychiatrically relevant themes that relate to emotional issues and also to delve into the emotional homeostatic functions of sleep.

Factors that Promote and Impair Sleep

It is well known that satisfying basic bodily needs, from hunger to sexual urgency, promote sleepiness. Conversely, all kinds of emotional distress tend to reduce sleep onset and quality. This effect is very prominent in the difficulty that depressed individuals commonly experience in falling asleep and sustaining sleep, and also in the disrupted sleep patterns found in various anxiety disorders, mania, and schizophrenia (Kryger et al., 2000). It is well known that physical exertion during the day tends to increase SWS, while mental and emotional exertions, as long as they are not too extreme, tend to increase REM (Panksepp, 1998).

Clearly there are several SWS generators in the brain, but one of the more prominent, highly localized, ones is in the lateral anterior lateral hypothalamus, which contains gamma-aminobutyric acid (GABA) as the main transmitter, which explains the utility of GABA facilitators (Table 4.1) to facilitate sleep (Kryger et al., 2000). The location of this generator helps explain one of the first findings in the neuroscience of sleep: von Economo's classic description of chronic insomnia in patients who had suffered damage to the anterior hypothalamus. On the other hand, the widely distributed waking generators, which are well represented by the acetylcholine and biogenic amine systems (including dopamine, norepinephrine, and histamine), are more concentrated in the posterior hypothalamus, where damage has long been known to produce somnolence (Panksepp, 1998).

The REM generator in the lower brain stem appears to be a remnant of an ancient waking/arousal system that may, at some point in premammalian evolution, have been one of the major regulators of waking activities, perhaps of the emotional subroutines of the limbic system (Panksepp, 1998). It has recently been effectively argued that dreaming mechanisms can be dissociated from REM mechanisms (Solms, 2000). Even though they are typically coordinated, it seems that while REM sleep is critically dependent on the pontine generators, dreaming is much more dependent on arousal of various

TABLE 4.1. Sleep Medications Currently in Use[a]

Traditional Benzodiazepine (BZ) Hypnotics

Triazolam: Common initial dose: 0.25 mg; FDA AMDD: 0.5 mg
Temazepam: Common initial dose: 15 mg; FDA AMDD: 30 mg
Flurazepam: Common initial dose: 15–30 mg; FDA AMDD: 30 mg

Nonbenzodiazepine, Selective BZ Receptor Agonist Hypnotics

Zaleplon: Common initial dose: 10 mg; FDA AMDD: 20 mg
Zolpidem: Common initial dose: 10 mg; FDA AMDD: 10 mg

Anxiolytic Benzodiazepines Used as Hypnotics (off-label)

Clonazepam: CID: 0.5 mg; FDA AMDD: 4 mg divided (for anxiety conditions)
Lorazepam: CID: 1 mg; FDA AMDD: 6 mg divided (for anxiety conditions)
Alprazolam: CID: 0.25 mg; FDA AMDD: 4 mg divided (for anxiety conditions)

Sedating Antidepressants Sometimes Used as Hypnotics (off-label)

Trazodone: CID: 50 mg; AMDD: FDA 400 mg divided (for depression)
Amitriptyline: CID: 50 mg; FDA AMDD: 300 mg divided (for depression)
Doxepin: CID: 50 mg; FDA AMDD: 300 mg divided (for depression)
Fluvoxamine: CID: 50 mg; FDA AMDD: 300 mg divided (for OCD)
Mirtazapine: CID: 15 mg; FDA AMDD: 45 mg (for depressions)
Nefazodone: CID: 100 mg; FDA AMDD: 600 mg divided (for depressions)

[a]Recommended CID—adult common initial doses; half-dose is generally recommended in elderly; FDA AMDD—Food and Drug Administration Approved Maximum Daily Dose. For nonhypnotic use, doses for FDA approved indications, such as obsessive–compulsive behaviors (OCD) are listed.

limbic emotional circuits, with perhaps especially strong influences through ascending dopamine-based appetitive-motivation SEEKING systems (Gottesmann, 2002; Solms, 2000). Thus, it would seem likely that REM sleep is especially important in regulating emotional/affective homeostasis.

The main evidence for this is as follows: REM-deprived animals are generally hyperactive and hyperemotional, suggesting that the neuropsychological activities promoted by REM (i.e., dreams) are able to dissipate excessive emotional "energies"—to keep the emotional and cognitive aspects of key mental urges and processes balanced in favor of the cognitive side. In other words, during dreaming, organisms may reprocess emotionally salient information in such a way as to reduce its affective impact during waking. Perhaps this is achieved, in part, by the ability of the brain, during REM, to extract useful cognitive relationships from waking activities (Domhoff, 2002). This may allow organisms to more effectively pursue long-term as opposed to short-term plans, especially those related to emotional stressors (Panksepp, 1998), which may partially explain why people are typically less emotionally stressed after waking from a good nights sleep.

Restorative Effects of Sleep

As mentioned above, sleep problems are common in psychiatric disorders. Again, the most prominent example is the tendency of depressed individuals to sustain sleep poorly and to wake in the middle of the night, partly because their pituitary adrenal stress waking/alarm system become active much earlier than normal (Kryger et al., 2000). Other features include an excessively rapid entry into the REM phase after sleep onset. Since sleep recruits endogenous antistress mechanisms and depression impairs quality sleep, the sleep problems of depression *may* tend to perpetuate ongoing problems. Although there is likely some truth to that hypothesis, such a problem would have to reside within the disruption of SWS rather than REM. A remarkable finding is that REM sleep deprivation is a fairly effective short-term antidepressant, and practically all of the pharmacological antidepressants are excellent REM sleep inhibitors (Kryger et al., 2000). One could construct a provisional explanation by supposing that the failure to dissipate emotional energies during REM might help make them available for waking activities, but no test of such an idea is available. An appropriate experiment would require some way of measuring these types of neuropsychological energies.

One way this has been done in animals is to see how specific emotional systems operate as a function of the REM sleep process. This has been achieved by surgically dampening REM atonia, which normally keeps animals recumbent during the supposed emotional episodes of their dreams. In such animals, the various instinctual-emotional action programs, which are presumably active in dreams, are now expressed physically—including predatory stalking, rage and fearful behaviors, and grooming. This informs us that emotional processes are, in fact, aroused in the dreams of other animals, which is consistent with the finding of high levels of emotionality in human dreams, as well as the fact that the limbic system tends to exhibit selective arousal during REM sleep (Nofzinger et al., 1997).

Another way to get at the relationship between REM and emotions would be to take one emotional system and study its dynamics as a function of REM deprivation. This has been done with self-stimulation of the lateral hypothalamus (the SEEKING system described in Chapter 1). This emotional substrate is more responsive in REM-deprived rats since they self-stimulate more. Even more remarkably, rats that are allowed to self-stimulate (i.e., to use up the energy in this system) during the course of the REM deprivation do not exhibit the type of compensatory REM sleep rebound (i.e., post-deprivation elevations in REM) that is normally seen in deprived animals. A similar absence of rebound following REM deprivation is also seen in schizophrenic patients, suggesting that their waking activities may be depleting the neuropsychological emotional energies that normally build up when organisms are not allowed to undergo REM sleep. One way to view these findings is that REM deprivation increases dopamine arousal in the brain, while REM sleep diminishes it. From this perspective, it is interesting that dopamine facilitators generally brighten mood, even to the point of euphoria, and some have found a place as antidepressants as well as anti craving medications for nicotine addiction (bupropion: Wellbutrin or Zyban, respectively).

Although there are many theories concerning the functions of dreaming, none has sufficient support to be well accepted (for summaries of controversies, see the special issue of *The Behavioral and Brain Sciences,* 2000, vol. 23(6), pp. 793–1121). In contrast, there are fewer theories about the functions of SWS, but the characteristic secretions of growth hormone that occur at the onset of SWS strongly suggest that at least part of the story is body restoration. Further, since one is truly unconscious during deep SWS, and cerebral metabolism is markedly reduced (Nofzinger et al., 1997), one would expect that there is abundant rejuvenation of brain functions during this phase of sleep. Attempts to characterize the changes in gene expression that accompany sleep indicate that about 0.5 percent of genes are expressed differentially in the cerebral cortex across phases of sleep, and those that are up-regulated during sleep tend to be presently unidentified genes (Tononi and Cirelli, 2001). This gives us very little leeway for any major interpretations, except to say that many important things are happening.

Sleep Problems and Remedies (from Ambien to Zolpidem)

The diagnosis of sleep problems is based on now standardized criteria summarized both in Diagnostic and statistical Manual of Mental Disorders, Fourth Edition (DSM-IV) and the more detailed classification of the ICSD (*International Classification of Sleep Disorders*) (Pressman and Orr, 1997). Unlike psychiatric diagnoses, which are typically obtained from a conversation with a psychiatrist through structured interview, sleep disorders have more "objective" criteria, consisting of electroencephalogram (EEG) measures of (i) sleep latency, (ii) REM latency (including "REM latency minus awake"), (iii) amount of SWS, (iv) amount of REM sleep, (v) eye movement density in REM sleep, and (vi) sleep efficiency (i.e., total number of minutes of sleep divided by the total time in bed). There is abundant data using these measures not only in standard nonpsychiatric sleep disorders, such as apnea, but also in many psychiatric disorders (Douglass, 1996).

Objectively measured sleep problems allow clinicians to provide pharmacological assistance that has been standardized in clinical populations (Kryger et al., 2000). The enormous amount of drug development in this area attests to the prevalence of sleep problems in our society. Although there is no space to detail this massive literature, the list of effective sleep aids now on the market is lengthy, and far exceeds the list of those agents approved by the Food and Drug Administration (FDA) (Table 4.1). This is because all the benzodiazepine (BZ) receptor agonists can serve as sleeping aids, but the approved ones are typically the shorter-acting agents such as triazolam (Halcion) for individuals simply having difficulty falling asleep. The longer-acting agents can sustain sleep, but are more likely to have sedative carryover effects into the morning (Mitler, 2000).

The problems with BZs, with regard to cognitive impairment, memory loss, and addictive potential (Chapter 19), are sufficiently large that a vigorous search was mounted for other effective agents that have no such problems. A new class of non-BZs that are stimulants for the BZ receptor, and hence GABA facilitators of SWS processes, has revolutionized the medication of sleep problems. The fast-acting, short-duration agent that has taken away a substantial market-share from triazolam (Halcion) is zolpidem (Ambien), which can be taken in the middle of the night to counteract early-morning wakenings. Of course there are also highly effective longer-acting agents, such as flurazepam, as well as a large number of BZs as well as sedating antidepressants that are still commonly used for sleep problems (Table 4.1). Also, there is vigorous research activity to develop slow-release forms of the fast-acting agents, as well as natural ingredients such as melatonin, to help sustain sleep through the night. Of course, chronic use of BZs is not advised because of strong withdrawal reactions when tolerance has developed to these agents (see Chapter 16). The one highly effective over-the-counter agent is the natural hormone melatonin, whose efficacy has long been known (Arendt, 1995) but which has not been promoted by the pharmaceutical or medical community since it has not been approved by government regulatory boards. Obviously, there is little incentive for conduct of necessary efficacy trials for agents that cannot be patented. Accordingly, the search continues to identify melatonin congeners that can be patented. Even though there is now a large number of such agents, there is yet no clear evidence that any of them will have a substantially better efficacy profile than the natural ingredient, except perhaps when they begin to market using slow-release forms that might better sustain somnolence.

Although there are no sleeping aids that are specific to the problems of any given psychiatric disorders, such as depression or schizophrenia, it is noteworthy that practically all the selective serotonin facilitating antidepressants can promote sleep and ameliorate sleep problems (Kryger et al., 2000). Among the earlier generation of drugs, Amitriptyline was especially sedating, but most of the modern SSRIs can improve sleep, especially as their antidepressant effects kick in, although none is approved for the treatment of insomnia.

Considering the antistress effects of a good night's sleep for all forms of mental distress, the search for more specific interventions will continue. Since CRH arousal in the brain provokes generalized stress and anxiety effects in the mammalian brain, antagonists for those receptors should be effective in promoting better sleep patterns. Preclinical data already suggest that such a beneficial profile is present in some of the available CRH receptor antagonists (Lancel et al., 2002).

Conclusions and Role of Positive Emotions in Regulating Stress

Our understanding of the stress processes of the brain has been impressive, especially since the emergence of brain CRH systems as a central regulator of the stress response. Not only is the CRH receptor now a prime target for drug development, but a host of other neuropeptide systems have been identified that participate in the stress response. This knowledge is percolating through all research areas interested in the etiology of stress-related psychiatric disorders as well as the nature of basic emotional and motivational systems (Chapter 21).

Considering the increasingly well-documented effects of stress on the body and the effects of chronic stress on a host of disease vectors (Booth et al., 2001; Mayer and Saper, 1999), there is an increasing acceptance of the interdependence of brain-mental and body-physical processes (Uchino et al., 1996). Social attachments are a powerful modulator of physiological stress responses (Feeney and Kirkpatrick, 1996; Hennessy, 1997), and our growing understanding of the brain mechanisms of social bonding (and hence mother-infant love) have implicated oxytocin, prolactin, and the endogenous opioids as prime movers of social attachments (Carter, 1998; Insel, 1997; Nelson and Panksepp, 1998). Females are generally more responsive to social support than males (Kirschbaum et al., 1995), as they are to the effects of prosocial hormones and stress (Cusing and Carter, 2000; DeVries et al., 1996). Couples who are better able to soothe each other's stress responses are more likely to remain married than those who tend to intensify each other's stress-related autonomic arousal (Gottman et al., 2002).

This recognition, as well as the "emotion revolution" that has been sweeping through psychology and other social science disciplines, has helped create a robust, scientifically based positive health movement that characterizes key factors that promote disease, while also identifying those that can facilitate a more positive spectrum of health. New composite measures of long-term bodily stress, such as the "allostatic load" and a variety of new concepts and hypotheses, are emerging (e.g., Ryff and Singer, 1998). The preliminary fruits of this movement have recently been harvested into a compendium of progress (Snyder and Lopez., 2002). When the aspirations of such mind-body initiatives are eventually established on a more solid empirical foundation, we may find that a host of new and milder psychotropic medicines could be developed (e.g., see Chapter 21).

The development of these medicines will require new types of research paradigms that are willing to evaluate the long-term effects of certain agents not only in traditional disease-targeted ways, but in the context of positive psychosocial support systems that may interact in beneficial ways with new medicinal agents that may only have rather modest effects on their own (Sachser et al., 1998; Taylor et al., 2000). For optimal efficacy, such agents may also require investments in new and more sophisticated views of depth psychology (e.g., Solms and Turnbull, 2002). In short, it is once again time in psychiatry to triangulate more completely between the molecular aspects of the brain, the behavioral symptoms of psychiatric disorders, and the intervening neuropsychological processes that comprise mental experience.

REFERENCES

Arendt J (1995). *Melatonin and the Mammalian Pineal Gland*. Chapman and Hill: London.

Argiolas AM, Gessa GL (1991). Central Functions of Oxytocin. *Neurosci Biobehav Revs* 15: 217–231.

Bem DJ (2000). Exotic becomes erotic: Interpreting the biological correlates of sexual orientation. *Arch Sex Behav* 29:531–548.

Booth RJ, Cohen S, Cunningham A, et al. (2002). The state of the science: The best evidence for the involvement of thoughts and feelings in physical health. *Adv Mind-Body Med* 17:2–59.

Britton KT, Lee G, Vale W, Rivier J, Koob F (1986). Corticotropin-releasing factor (CRF) receptor antagonist blocks activating and 'anxiogenic' actions of CRF in the rat. *Brain Res* 369:303–306.

Butler PD, Weiss JM, Stout JC, Nemeroff CB (1990). Corticotropin-releasing factor produces fear-enhancing and behavioral activating effects following infusion into the locus coeruleus. *J Neurosci* 10:176–183.

Cameron H, McKay R (1999). Restoring production of hippocampal neurons in old age. *Nature Neurosci* 2:894–897.

Campeau S, Davis M (1995). Involvement of subcortical and cortical afferents to the lateral nucleus and basolateral complex of the amygdala in fear conditioning measured with fear-potentiated startle in rats trained concurrently with auditory and visual conditioned stimuli. *J Neurosci* 15:2301–2311.

Cannon W (1935). Stresses and strains of homeostasis. *Am J Med Sci* 189:1–14.

Carter CS (1998): The neuroendocrinology of social attachment and love. *Psychoneuroendocrinology* 23:779–818.

Chalmers DT, Lovenberg TW, De Souza EB (1995). Localization of novel corticotropin-releasing factor receptor (CRF2) mRNA expression to specific subcortical nuclei in rat brain: Comparison with CRF1 receptor mRNA expression. *J Neurosci* 15:6340–6350.

Colapinto J (2000). *As Nature Made Him. HarperColins*:New York.

Connor T, Leonard B (1998). Depression, stress and immunological activation: The role of cytokines in depressive disorders. *Life Sci* 62:583–606.

Crenshaw T, Goldberg JP (1996). *Sexual Pharmacology: Drugs That Affect Sexual Functioning.* Norton:New York.

Cushing BS, Carter CS (2000). Peripheral pulses of oxytocin increase partner preferences in female, but not male, prairie voles. *Horm Behav* 37:49–56.

Darwin C (1871, 1874). *The Descent of Man: And Selection in Relation to Ssex.* Merrill and Baker:New York and London.

Davis M (1992). *A neural systems approach to the study of the amygdala, fear, and anxiety.* In Elliott JM, Marsden DJ Marsden CA (eds). Experimental Approaches to Anxiety and Depression. Wiley: Chichester, pp. 45–73.

Deak T, Meriwether JL, Fleshner M, Spencer RL, Abouhamze A, Moldawer LL, Grahn RE, Watkins LR, Maier SF (1997). Evidence that brief stress may induce the acute phase response in rats. *Am J Physiol* 273:R1998–R2004.

Deak T, Nguyen KT, Ehrlich AL, Watkins LR, Maier SF, Licinio J, Wong M-L, Chrousos GP, Webster E, Gold PW (1999). The impact of the nonpeptide Corticotropin-Releasing Hormone antagonist Antalarmin on behavioral and endocrine responses to stress. *Endocrinology* 140:79–86.

DeVries AC, DeVries MB, Taymans S, Carter CS (1996). The effects of stress on social preferences are sexually dimorphin in prairie voles. *Proc Natl Acad Sci* 93:11980–11984.

Dohrenwend B, Dohrenwend B (1981). *Stressful Life Events and Their Contexts.* Rutgers University Press: New Brunswick, NJ.

Domhoff GW (2002). *The Scientific Study of Dreams.* American Psychological Association, Washington DC.

Douglass AB (1996). *Sleep abnormalities in major psychiatric illness.* In Panksepp J (ed). Advances in Biological Psychiatry, Vol 2. JAI Press: Greenwich, CT, pp. 153–177.

Drouin J, Sun YL, Tremblay S, Lavender P, Schmidt TJ, deLean A, Nemer M (1992). Homodimer formation is rate limiting for high affinity binding by the glucocorticoid receptor. *Molec Endocrinol* 6:1299–1309.

Dunn AJ (1995): Interactions between the nervous system and the immune system: Implications for psychopharmacology. In Bloom FE, Kupfer DJ (eds). *Psychopharmacology: The fourth generation of progress.* Raven Press: New York, pp. 719–733.

Dunn AJ, Berridge CW (1990). Physiological and behavioral responses to corticotropin-releasing factor administration: Is CRF a mediator of anxiety of stress responses? *Brain Res Rev* 15:71–100.

Ellis L, Ebertz L (eds) (1997). *Sexual orientation: Toward biological understanding Praeger:* Westport, CT.

Everitt BJ (1990). Sexual motivation: A neural and behavioral analysis of the mechanisms underlying appetitive and copulatory responses of male rats. *Neurosci Biobehav Rev* 14:217–232.

Fanselow MS, Kim JJ (1994). Acquisition of contextual Pavlovian fear conditioning is blocked by application of an NMDA receptor antagonist D,L-2-amino-5-phosphonovaleric acid to the basolateral amygdala. *Behav Neurosci* 108:210–212.

Fanselow MS, Lester LS (1988). A functional behavioristic approach to aversively motivated behavior: Predatory imminence as a determinant of the topography of defensive behavior. In Bolles RC, Beecher MD (eds). *Evolution and Learning*. Erlbaum: Hillsdale, NJ, pp. 185–212.

Feeney BC, Kirkpatrick LA (1996). Effects of adult attachment and presence of romantic partners on physiological responses to stress. *J Person Soc Psych* 70:255–270.

Fleming AS, O'Day DH, Kraemer GW (1999). Neurobiology of mother-infant interactions: Experience and central nervous system plasticity across development and generations. *Neurosci Biobehav Rev* 23:673–685.

Galea L, McEwen B, Tanapat P, Deak T, Spencer R, Dhabhar F (1997). Sex differences in dendritic atrophy of CA3 pyramidal neurons in response to chronic restraint stress. *Neuroscience* 81:689–697.

Georgiadis JR, Reinders AATS, Paans AMJ, Meiners LC, van der Graaf FHCE, Holstege G (2002). Neural correlates of human male ejaculation. *Soc Neurosci Abstr* #681. 13.

Gitlin M (1994). Psychotropic medications and their effects on sexual function: Diagnosis, biology and treatment approaches. *J Clin Psychiatry* 55:406–413.

Gold PW, Wong J-L, Chrousos GP, Licinio J (1996). Stress system abnormalities in melancholic and atypical depression: Molecular, pathophysiological, and therapeutic implications. *Molec Psychiatry* 1:257–264.

Gottesmann C (2002). The neurochemistry of waking and sleeping mental activity: The disinhibition-dopamine hypothesis. *Psychiatry Clin Neurosci* 56:345–354.

Gottman JM, Murray JD, Swanson CC, Tyson R, Swanson KR (2002). *The Mathematics of Marriage*. MIT Press: Cambridge MA.

Grillon C, Southwick SM, Charney DS (1996). The psychobiological basis of posttraumatic stress disorder. *Molec Psychiatry* 1:278–297.

Harro J, Oreland L (2001). Depression as a spreading adjustment disorder of monoaminergic neurons: A case for primary implication of the locus coeruleus. *Brain Res Rev* 38:79–128.

Hart BL (1988). Biological basis of the behavior of sick animals. *Neurosci Biobehav Rev* 12:123–137.

Heinrichs SC, Pich EM, Miczek KA, Britton KT, Koob GF (1992). Corticotropin-releasing factor antagonist reduces emotionality in socially defeated rats via direct neurotropic action. *Brain Res* 531:190–197.

Hennessy MB (1997). Hypothalamic-pituitary-adrenal responses to brief social separation *Neurosci Biobehav Rev* 21:11–29.

Hennessy M, Deak T, Schiml-Webb P (2001). Stress-induced sickness behaviors: An alternative hypothesis for responses during maternal separation. *Devel Psychobiol* 39:76–83.

Herman J, Cullinan W (1997). Neurocircuitry of stress: Central control of the hypothalamo-pituitary-adrenocortical axis. *Trends Neurosci* 20:78–84.

Herman J, Prewitt C, Cullinan W (1996). Neuronal circuit regulation of the hypothalamo-pituitary-adrenocortical stress axis. *Critical Rev Neurobiol* 10:371–394.

Ikemoto S, Panksepp J (1999). The role of nucleus accumbens dopamine in motivated behavior: A unifying interpretation with special reference to reward seeking. *Brain Res Rev* 31:6–41.

Imperato-McGinley J, Peterson RE, Gautier T, Sturla E (1979). Androgens and the evolution of male gender identity among male pseudohermaphrodites with 5-alpha-reductase deficiency *N Engl J Med* 300:1233–1237.

Insel T (1997). A neurobiological basis of social attachment. *Am J Psychiatry* 154:726–735.

Jacobson L, Akana SF, Cascio CS, Shinsako J, Dallman MF (1988). Circadian variations in plasma corticosterone permit normal terminations of adrenocorticotropin responses to stress. *Endocrinology* 122:1343–1348.

Judson O (2002). *Dr. Tatiana's Sex Advice to All of Creation*. Henry Holt: New York.

Kalin NH, Takahashi LK, Chen FL (1994). Restraint stress increases corticotropin-releasing hormone mRNA content in the amygdala and paraventricular nucleus. *Brain Res* 656:182–186.

Kent S, Bluthe R-M, Kelley KW, Dantzer R (1992). Sickness behavior as a new target for drug development. *Trends Pharmacol Sci* 13:24–28.

Kent S, Bret-Dibat JL, Kelley KW, Dantzer R (1996). Mechanisms of sickness-induced decreases in food-motivated behavior. *Neurosci Biobehav Revs* 20:171–175.

Kim JJ, Fanselow MS, DeCola JP, Landeira-Fernandez J (1992). Selective impairment of long-term but not short-term conditional fear by the N-methyl-D-aspartate antagonist APV. *Behav Neurosci* 106:591–596.

Kimura D (1999). *Sex and Cognition*. MIT Press: Cambridge, MA.

Kirschbaum KM, Klauer T, Filipp SH, Hellahmmer DH (1995). Sex-specific effects of social support on cortisol and subjective responses to acute psychological stress. *Psychosom Med* 57:23–31.

Knoll J (1992). (−)Deprenyl-mediation: A strategy to modulate the age-related decline of the striatal dopaminergic system. *J. Am. Geriatr. Soc.* 409:839–847.

Koob GF (1990). Behavioral responses to stress-focus on corticotropin-releasing factor. In Brown MR, Rivier C, Koob G (eds). *Neurobiology and Neuroendocrinology of Stress*. Marcel Dekker: New York, pp. 255–271.

Koob GF, Britton KT (1990). Behavioral effects of corticotropin-releasing factor. Corticotropin-releasing factor: In De Souza EG, Nemeroff CB (eds). *Basic and Clinical Studies of a Neuropeptide*. CRC Press: Boca Raton, FL, pp. 253–266.

Korte SM, Korte-Bouws GA, Bohus B, Koob GF (1994). Effect of corticotropin-releasing factor antagonist on behavioral and neuroendocrine responses during exposure to defensive burying paradigm in rats. *Physiol Behav* 56:115–120.

Krahn DD, Gosnell BA (1989). CRH: Possible role in eating disorders. *Psychiatry and Medicine* 7:235–245.

Kryger MH, Roth T, Dement WC (eds) (2000). *Principles and Practice of Sleep Medicine*, 3rd ed. Saunders: Philadelphia.

Lancel M, Muller-Preuss P, Wigger A, Landgraf R, Holsboer F (2002). The CRH1 receptor antagonist R121919 attenuates stress-elicited sleep disturbances in rats, particularly in those with high innate anxiety. *J Psychiatric Res* 36:197–208.

MacLean PD, Ploog DW (1962). Cerebral representation of penile erection *J Neurophysiol* 25:29–55.

Maes M (1999). Major depression and activation of the inflammatory response system. *Adv Exp Med Biol* 461:25–46.

Maier SF, Watkins LR (1995). Intracerebroventricular interleukin-1 receptor antagonist blocks the enhancement of fear conditioning and interference with escape produced by inescapable shock. *Brain Res* 695:279–282.

Maier S Watkins L (1998). Cytokines for psychologists: implications of bidirectional immune-to-brain communication for understanding behavior, mood, and cognition. *Psych Rev* 105: 83–107.

Mayer EA, Saper CB (eds) (1999). *The Biological Basis for Mind Body Interactions.* Elsevier: Amsterdam.

Mazure C (1998). Life stressors as risk factors in depression. *Clinical Psychology: Science and Practice* 5:291–313.

Mazure C, Druss B (eds) (1995). *A Historical Perspective on Stress and Psychiatric Illness. Does Stress Cause Major Psychiatric Illness?* American Psychiatric Press: Washington, DC.

McEwen B (2000). The neurobiology of stress: From serendipity to clinical relevance. *Brain Res* 886:172–189.

Mealey L (2000). *Sex Differences: Development and Evolutionary Strategies.* Academic Press: San Diego.

Meaney MJ (2001). Maternal care, gene expression, and the transmission of individual differences in stress reactivity across generations. *Ann Rev Neurosci* 24:1161–1192.

Milligan E, Nguyen K, Deak T, Hinde J, Fleshner M, Watkins L, Maier S (1998). The long term acute phase-like responses that follow acute stressor exposure are blocked by alpha-melanocyte stimulating hormone. *Brain Res* 810:48–58.

Miserendino MJ, Sananes CB, Melia KR, Davis M (1990). Blocking of acquisition but not expression of conditioned fear-potentiated startle by NMDA antagonists in the amygdala. *Nature* 345:716–718.

Mitler MM (2000). Nonselective and selective benzodiazepine receptor agonists—where are we today? *Sleep* 23(Suppl 1):S39–47.

Montkowski A, Landgraf R, Yassouridis A, Holsboer F, Schobitz B (1997). Central administration of IL-1 reduces anxiety and induces sickness behaviour in rats. *Pharmacol Biochem Behav* 58:329–336.

Moore CL (1995). Maternal contributions to mammalian reproductive development and the divergence of males and females. *Adv Animal Behav* 24:47–118.

Munck A, Guyre PM, Holbrook NJ (1984). Physiological functions of glucocorticoids in stress and their relation to pharmacological actions. *Endocrine Revs* 5:25–44.

Murphy MR, Seckl JR, Burton S, Checkley SA, Lightman SL (1990). Changes in oxytocin and vasopressin secretion during sexual activity in men *J Clin Endocrinol Metab* 65:738–741.

Nelson EE, Panksepp J (1998). Brain substrates of infant-mother attachment: Contributions of opioids, oxytocin and norepinephrine. *Neurosci Biobehav Ref* 22:437–452.

Nemeroff CG (1996). The corticotropin-releasing factor (CRF) hypothesis of depression: New findings and new directions. *Molec Psychiatry* 1:336–342.

Nguyen K, Deak T, Will M, Hansen M, Hunsaker B, Fleshner M, Watkins L, Maier S (2000). Timecourse and corticosterone sensitivity of the brain, pituitary, and serum interleukin-1b protein response to acute stress. *Brain Res* 859:193–201.

Nocjar C, Panksepp J (2002). Chronic intermittent amphetamine pretreatment enhances future appetitive behavior for drug- and natural-reward: interaction with environmental variables. *Behav Brain Res* 128:189–203.

Nofzinger EA, Mintun MA, Wiseman MB, Kupfer DJ, Moore RY (1997). Forebrain activation in REM sleep: An FDG PET study. *Brain Res* 770:192–201.

Opp MR, Krueger JM (1991). Interleukin-1 receptor antagonist blocks interleukin-1-induced sleep and fever. *Am J. Physiol* 260:453–457.

Panksepp J (1998). *Affective Neuroscience*. Oxford University Press: New York.

Panksepp J (2001). The long-term psychobiological consequences of infant emotions: Prescriptions for the 21st century. *Infant Mental Health Journal* 22:132–173.

Panksepp J, Moskal J, Panksepp JB, Kroes R (2002). Comparative approaches in evolutionary psychology: Molecular neuroscience meets the mind. *Neuroendocrinol Let* 23(Suppl. 4):105–115.

Perris H (1984). Life events and depression. Part 2: Results in diagnostic subgroups, and in relation to the recurrence of depression. *J Affective Disorders* 7:25–36.

Pedersen CA, Caldwell JD, Jirikowski GF, Insel TR (eds) (1992). Oxytocin in Maternal, Sexual, and Social Behavior. Ann NY Acad Sci vol. 652, New York Academy of Sciences: New York.

Pfaff DW (1999). *Drive: Neurobiological and Molecular Mechanisms of Sexual Motivation*. MIT Press: Cambridge, MA.

Pfaus JG (1996). Homologies of animal and human sexual behaviors. *Horm Behav* 30:187–200.

Pinker S (2002). *The Blank Slate: The Modern Denial of Human Nature*, Viking: New York.

Plata-Salaman C, Ilyin S, Turrin N, Gayle D, Flynn M, Bedard T, Merali Z, Anisman H (2000). Neither acute nor chronic exposure to a naturalistic (predator) stressor influences the interleukin-1-beta system, tumor necrosis factor-alpha, transforming growth factor-beta-1, and neuropeptide mRNAs in specific brain regions. *Brain Res Bull* 51:187–193.

Pressman MR, Orr WC (1997). *Understanding Sleep: The Evaluation and Treatment of Sleep Disorders*. American Psychological Association: Washington DC.

Reagan L, McEwen B (1997). Controversies surrounding glucocorticoid-mediated cell death in the hippocampus. *J Chem Neuroanatomy* 13:149–158.

Redoute J, Soleru S, Gergoire MC, et al. (2000). Brain processing of visual sexual stimuli in human males. *Human Brain Imag* 11:162–177.

Robbins A (1996). Androgens and male sexual behavior: From mice to men. *Trends Endocrinol Metab* 7:345–350.

Rosen RC, Lane RM, Menza M (1999). Effects of SSRIs on sexual function: A Critical Review. *J Clin Psychopharm* 19:67–85.

Ryff CD, Singer B (1998). The contours of positive human health. *Psychol Inquiry* 9:1–28.

Sachser N, Durschlar M, Hirzel D (1998). Social relationships and the management of stress. *Psychoneuroendocrinology* 23:891–904.

Sapolsky RM (2000). Glucocorticoids and hippocampal atrophy in neuropsychiatric disorders. *Archives of general psychiatry* 57:925–935.

Schore A (2003). *Affect Regulation and the Repair of the Self*. W.W. Norton: New York.

Schulkin J, McEwen B, Gold P (1994). Allostasis, amygdala, and anticipatory angst. *Neurosci Biobehav Rev* 18:385–396.

Selye H (1946). The general adaptation syndrome and the diseases of adaptation. *J Clinical Endocrinol* 6:117–231.

Selye H (1956). *The Stress of Life*. McGraw-Hill: New York.

Sgoifo A, Koolhaas J, Alleva E, Musso E, Parmigiani S (eds) (2001). Social stress: Acute and long-term effects on physiology and behavior. *Physiol Behav* 73:253–449.

Shintani F, Nakaki T, Kanba S, Sato K, Yagi G, Shiozawa M, Aiso S, Kato R, Asai M (1995). Involvement of interleukin-1 in immobilization stress-induced increase in plasma adreno-corticotropic hormone and in release of hypothalamic monoamines in the rat. *J Neurosci* 15:1961–1970.

Short KR, Maier SF (1993). Stressor controllability, social interaction, and benzodiazepine systems. *Pharmacol Biochem Behav* 45:827–835.

Snyder CR, Lopez SJ (2002). *Handbook of Positive Psychology*. Oxford University Press: London.

Sodersten P, Henning M, Melin P, Ludin S (1983). Vasopressin alters female sexual behaviour by acting on the brain independently of alteration in blood pressure. *Nature* 301:608–610.

Solms M. (2000). Dreaming and REM sleep are controlled by different brain mechanisms. *Behav Brain Sci* 23:843–850.

Solms M, Turnbull O (2002). *The Brain and the Inner World*. Other Press: New York.

Spencer RL, Miller AH, Moday H, Stein M, McEwen BS (1993). Diurnal differences in basal and acute stress levels of Type I and Type II adrenal steroid receptor activation in neural and immune tissues. *Endocrinology* 133:1941–1950.

Spencer RL, Kim PJ, Kalman BA, Cole MA (1998). Evidence for mineralocorticoid receptor facilitation of glucocorticoid receptor-dependent regulation of hypothalamic-pituitary-adrenal axis activity. *Endocrinology* 139:2718–2726.

Sullivan GM, Canfield SM, Lederman S, Xiao E, Ferin M, Wardlaw SL (1997). Intracerebroventricular injection of interleukin-1 suppresses peripheral lymphocyte function in the primate. *Neuroimmunomodulation* 4:12–18.

Suomi SJ (1997). Early determinant of behaviour: Evidence from primate studies. *Br Med Bull* 53:170–184.

Svensson T (1987). Peripheral, autonomic regulation of locus coeruleus noradrenergic neurons in brain: Putative implications for psychiatry and psychopharmacology. *Psychopharmacology* 92:1–7.

Swanson LW, Sawchenko PE, Rivier J, Vale W (1983). The organization of ovine CRF-immuno-reactive cells and fibers in the rat brain: An immunohistochemical study. *Neuroendocrinology* 36:165–186.

Swerdlow NR, Britton KT, Koob GF (1989). Potentiation of acoustic startle by corticotropin-releasing factor (CRF) and by fear are both reversed by alpha-helical CRF (9–41). *Neuropsychopharmacology* 115:141–146.

Swiergiel AH, Takahashi LK, Kalin NH (1993). Attenuation of stress-induced behavior by antagonism of corticotropin-releasing factor receptors in the central amygdala in the rat. *Brain Res* 623:229–234.

Taylor SE, Dickerson SS, Klein LC (2002). Toward a biology of social support. In Snyder CR, Lopez SJ (eds). *Handbook of Positive Psychology*, Oxford University Press: London, pp. 556–569.

Tiihonen J, Kukka J, Kupila J, et al. (1994). Increase in cerebral blood flow of right prefrontal cortex in man during orgasm. *Neurosci Lett* 170:241–243.

Tononi G, Cirelli C (2001). Modulation of brain gene expression during sleep and wakefulness: A review of recent findings. *Neuropsychopharmacology* 25:S28–S35.

Uchino BN, Cacioppo JT, Kiecolt-Glser JC (1996). The relationship between social support and physiological processes: A review with emphasis on underlying mechanisms and implications for health. *Psych Bull* 119:488–531.

Uvnas-Moberg K (1998). Oxytocin may mediate the benefits of positive social interaction and emotions. *Psychoneuroendocrinology* 23:819–835.

Vale W, Spiess J, Rivier C, Rivier J (1981). Characterization of a 41-residue ovine hypothalamic peptide that stimulates secretion of corticotropin and b-endorphin. *Science* 231:1394–1397.

Valentino RJ, Foote SL, Aston-Jones G (1983). Corticotropin-releasing factor activates nora-drenergic neurons of the locus coeruleus. *Brain Res* 270:363–367.

Van Goozen SH, Cohen-Kettenis PT, Gooren LJ, Frijda NH, Van de Poll NH (1995). Gender differences in behaviour: Activating effects of cross-sex hormones. *Psychoneuroendocrinology* 20:343–363.

Van Furth WR, Wolterink G, Van Ree JM (1995). Regulation of masculine sexual behavior: Involvement of brain opioids and dopamine. *Brain Res Rev* 21:162–184.

Van Ree JM, Niesink RJM, Van Wolfswinkel L, et al. (2000). Endogenous opioids and reward. *Eur J Pharmacol* 405:89–101.

Watkins LR, Wiertelak EP, Goehler LE, Smith KP, Martin D, Maier SF (1994). Characteriza-tion of cytokine-induced hyperalgesia. *Brain Res* 654:15–26.

Willner P (1997). Validity, reliability, and utility of the chronic mild stress model of depression: A 10 year review and evaluation. *Psychopharmacology* 134:319–329.

Zhou JN, Hofman MA, Gooren LJ, Swabb DF (1995). A sex difference in the human brain and its relation to transsexuality. *Nature* 378:68–70.

Zobel, AW, Nickel, T, Kunzel, HE, Ackl, N, Sonntag, A, Ising M, Holsboer, F (2000). Effects of the high affinity corticotropin-releasing hormone receptor 1 antagonist R121919 in major depression: The first 20 patients treated. *J Psychiatric Res* 34:171–181.

5

PSYCHOBIOLOGY OF PERSONALITY DISORDERS

Brian Knutson[1] and Andreas Heinz[2]

[1] *Department of Psychology, Stanford University, Stanford, California*
[2] *Clinic for Psychiatry and Psychotherapy, Humboldt University, Berlin, Germany*

OVERVIEW

Historically, the definition and treatment of personality disorders has fallen under the rubric of psychodynamic theory (Reich, 1949). Initial empirical efforts to study personality disorders focused on clarifying connections between personality disorders and other psychiatric disorders (Akiskal, 1981). More recent efforts have focused on conceptualizing each personality disorder in terms of underlying dimensions or components (Silk, 1994). Findings from this literature are beginning to converge with a long tradition of psychometric work by psychologists on personality traits of healthy people (Costa and Widiger, 1994). In the first half of this chapter, we will review operational definitions of *personality disorders* and *personality* as well as points of convergence and divergence in their conceptualization and measurement.

In the second half of the chapter, we will review how recent developments in neuroscience and genetics relate to personality disorder symptoms and discuss some

Textbook of Biological Psychiatry, Edited by Jaak Panksepp
ISBN 0-471-43478-7   Copyright © 2004 John Wiley & Sons, Inc.

implications of these findings for treatment. Explosive advances in neuroscience and genetic techniques at the dawn of the 21st century have yielded findings that hold promise for the characterization and treatment of personality disorders. These new findings may help scientists to elucidate biological mechanisms and markers associated with different personality disorders, particularly when conceptualized from a dimensional perspective (Livesley, 2001).

WHAT ARE PERSONALITY DISORDERS?

The *Diagnostic and Statistical Manual of Mental Disorders* Fourth Edition (DSM-IV) describes several overarching aspects of personality disorders (Axis II) that theoretically distinguish them from other psychiatric disorders (Axis I). The personality disorders were originally placed on Axis II along with mental retardation because, in theory, they begin early in development and last a lifetime. However, recent research suggests that some personality disorder symptoms may respond to both pharmacotherapeutic and psychotherapeutic interventions (Sanislow and McGlashan, 1998). Personality disorders are additionally described by the DSM-IV as an enduring or chronic pattern of experience or behavior that deviates markedly from the expectations of an individual's culture involving cognition, affect, social function, or impulse control. Such a pattern:

1. is inflexible and pervasive across different domains of functioning;
2. leads to clinically significant distress or impairment;
3. is stable and begins early in life;
4. is not due to another mental disorder; and
5. is not due to the direct physiological effects of a substance or medical condition.

Detailed descriptions of each of the 10 personality disorder diagnoses can be found in the DSM-IV. However, because we believe that the clearest linkages between personality disorders and physiology may lie at the level of symptoms and their interrelationships rather than at the level of existing diagnoses, we will focus more on the symptoms that comprise the diagnoses rather than on the diagnoses themselves. The 10 personality disorders listed in the DSM-IV can be grouped into 3 clusters on the basis of similar symptoms. Specifically, people diagnosed with a personality disorder in cluster A (paranoid, schizoid, or schizotypal) tend to show odd and eccentric behavior. Interpersonally, they are often reclusive and suspicious. People diagnosed with a personality disorder in cluster B (histrionic, narcissistic, borderline, or antisocial) tend to show dramatic, emotional, and impulsive behavior. People diagnosed with a personality disorder in cluster C (avoidant, dependent, and obsessive-compulsive) tend to show anxious or fearful behavior (see Table 5.1).

Since personality disorders are difficult to diagnose reliably, incidence data are rare and variable. According to a recent review, current U.S. population estimates for any personality disorder (PD) based on DSM-III-R criteria ranged from 6.7 to 33.1 percent, with the authors concluding that lifetime prevalence of at least one personality

TABLE 5.1. Primary Symptoms of DSM-IV Personality Disorders

Cluster	Personality Disorder	Primary Symptoms
Odd/eccentric (A)	Paranoid	Distrust and suspiciousness
	Schizoid	Detachment from social relationships; restricted emotional expression
	Schizotypal	Discomfort in close relationships; cognitive/perceptual distortions; eccentric behavior
Impulsive/dramatic (B)	Antisocial	Disregard for and violation of the rights of others
	Borderline	Instability in interpersonal relationships, self-image, and affect; impulsive behavior
	Narcissistic	Grandiosity; need for admiration; lack of empathy
	Histrionic	Excessive emotionality; attention-seeking
Anxious/fearful (C)	Avoidant	Social inhibition; feeling of inadequacy; hypersensitivity to negative evaluation
	Dependent	Submissive and clinging behavior; excessive need to be taken care of
	Obsessive-compulsive	Preoccupation with orderliness, perfectionism, and control

disorder diagnosis appears to be approximately 10 to 15 percent. Estimates for the odd/eccentric cluster fell under 6 percent (with schizotypal PD being most prevalent), estimates for the impulsive/dramatic cluster fell under 8 percent (with histrionic PD being most prevalent), and estimates for the anxious/fearful cluster fell under 18 percent (with obsessive-compulsive PD being most prevalent) (Mattia and Zimmerman, 2001). However, these numbers surely overestimate the number of diagnoses actually made since most of the estimates were calculated from randomly sampled individuals that were recruited to receive a diagnostic psychiatric interview. Commonly, people with personality disorders lack awareness that they have a problem and so would be less likely to voluntarily submit themselves to such an interview.

Some research has hinted at demographic differences in the incidence of personality disorders. One of the better documented demographic differences involves gender specificity. People diagnosed with antisocial and obsessive-compulsive personality disorders are more likely to be male, whereas people diagnosed with dependent personality disorders are more likely to be female. Overall, people diagnosed with personality disorders also tend to be younger than the age of the general population, except in the case of schizotypal personality disorder (Zimmerman and Coryell, 1989).

Other differences may involve culture specificity. For instance, a lower incidence of antisocial personality disorder has been reported in some (e.g., China and Japan) but not all (e.g., Korea) Asian countries (Lee et al., 1987). Of course, these differences also raise the possibility that culturally biased value judgments influence the definition of personality disorder criteria.

Despite the heuristic and descriptive utility of DSM-IV personality disorder diagnoses in medical settings, researchers have noted several shortcomings of these categorical diagnostic schemes. First, although the DSM-IV places personality disorders on a separate axis from other psychiatric disorders (Axis I), personality disorders often co-occur with other psychiatric disorders, and often do so in predictable ways (Dolan-Sewell et al., 2001). For instance, people with antisocial personality disorder are more likely to also receive a diagnosis of substance dependence. Second, although the DSM describes personality disorders as belonging to a distinct category from normal personality, a preponderance of empirical evidence suggests that personality disorder symptoms are continuously distributed across both clinical and healthy samples (Livesley et al., 1994). This fact helps to explain why clinicians might have difficulty establishing stable "cutpoints" for distinguishing personality disorder diagnoses from normalcy. Third, personality disorder diagnoses are difficult to measure since they often show poor psychometric properties such as validity (i.e., diagnostic criteria index the targeted traits/symptoms but not other traits) and reliability (i.e., diagnostic criteria show stability across different measurement attempts) (Blais and Norman, 1997). Validity comes in many forms and can include either internal validity (i.e., criteria that index the same thing are more correlated with each other than with criteria that index something else) or external validity (i.e., criteria predict relevant external features such as etiology and prognosis). Studies of the internal validity of personality disorder criteria suggest that they show only modest convergent (O'Boyle and Self, 1990) and discriminant validity (Widiger et al., 1991). In other words, a criterion for a given diagnosis is as likely to correlate with criteria from different diagnoses as with criteria from the same diagnosis. Fourth, personality disorder diagnoses have limited clinical utility in that they do not typically help practitioners to choose between distinct pharmacological or psychotherapeutic interventions (Sanderson and Clarkin, 1994). Fifth, because they have been defined by the DSM-IV, the criteria for personality disorders have not been wholly empirically derived. Rather, they have emerged through a combination of historical precedence, clinical observations, legal necessity, and repeated deliberations by expert committees (Frances et al., 1994). As a result, the disorders and their criteria have changed somewhat with each new edition of the DSM. Together, these five shortcomings of the categorical diagnostic framework threaten to hinder investigators' abilities to define personality disorders in a quantitative and replicable way, and so might slow cumulative research on the occurrence and treatment of personality disorders.

In an attempt to circumvent these shortcomings, a number of theorists have proposed that personality disorders be defined dimensionally rather than categorically. An illustration of this distinction appears in the field of cognitive testing, where intelligence can be described either with a continuous measure such as the intelligence quotient (i.e.,

IQ) or according to a cutoff with a categorical label such as "normal" versus "retarded." In a similar manner, Siever and Davis (1991) proposed that four continuous behavioral dimensions may underlie both personality disorders at less severe levels (Axis II) and clinical psychiatric disorders at more severe levels (Axis I). These dimensions include cognitive/perceptual organization, impulse control, affect regulation, and anxiety modulation. According to their proposal, cognitive/perceptual aberrations should map onto the odd/eccentric cluster of personality disorders (i.e., cluster A of Axis II) as well as onto schizophrenia (Axis I). Poor impulse control and affect regulation should map onto some of the impulsive/dramatic cluster of personality disorders (i.e., cluster B, specifically, borderline and antisocial disorders of Axis II) as well as onto mood disorders (Axis I). Poor anxiety modulation should map onto the anxious/fearful cluster of personality disorders (i.e., cluster C of Axis II) as well as onto anxiety disorders (Axis I). These proposed dimensions suggest that several continua bridge Axis II and Axis I and can potentially account for the frequently observed co-occurrence of personality disorder and psychiatric diagnoses.

In support of this proposed continuity between Axis II and Axis I, research suggests that at least one disorder in the odd/eccentric cluster (schizotypal PD) lies on a continuum with schizophrenia (Oldham et al., 1995). This continuity particularly seems to hold in the case of negative symptoms such as affective blunting and a lack of social engagement (Chapman et al., 1994). However, research has generally not supported selective dimensional relationships between the impulsive/dramatic cluster of personality disorders and mood disorders, or between the anxious/fearful cluster of personality disorders and anxiety disorders. Instead, people with either impulsive/dramatic or anxious/fearful personality disorders have a higher risk for co-occurrence of all types of Axis I disorders (Dolan-Sewell et al., 2001). Some exceptions to this apparent lack of specificity include the findings that impulsive/dramatic cluster personality disorders uniquely co-occur with increased rates of substance abuse (Oldham et al., 1995) and that anxious/fearful cluster personality disorders preferentially co-occur with increased rates of somatoform disorders (Tyrer et al., 1997).

A second dimensional approach to assessing personality disorders has arisen from empirical data rather than from theory. Livesley and colleagues identified and culled a prototypical set of personality disorder symptoms (as judged by psychiatrists) spanning all Axis II diagnoses with minimal overlap. They then combined these items in order to construct a psychometric instrument called the Dimensional Assessment of Personality and Psychopathology (DAPP) (Livesley et al., 1992). Next, they administered the DAPP to patients with personality disorders as well as healthy volunteers. Finally, they conducted factor analyses (a mathematical method of examining the correlational structure between many items) on both patients' and healthy volunteers' responses. The investigators found that a similar factor structure described relations among symptoms in both patients and healthy volunteers, suggesting continuity across the groups, but also that the patients had more extreme scores than the healthy volunteers. While factor analysis with an oblique rotation (which allows dimensions to correlate with each other) yielded an underlying structure similar to the discrete personality disorders listed in the DSM-III-R (see column 2 of Table 5.1), factor analysis with an orthogonal rotation

T A B L E 5.2. Conceptual Translation Scheme for Personality Disorder Clusters and Personality Traits Measured by a Selection of Psychometric Inventories

DSM IV Cluster	DAPP-BQ[a]	IAS-R[b]	EPQ-R[c]	NEO-PIR[d]
Odd/ eccentric (A)	Introversion	Low dom/ low aff	Extraversion (−)	Extraversion (−)
Impulsive/ dramatic (B)	Disagreeableness	High dom/ low aff	Psychoticism	Agreeableness (−)
Fearful/ anxious (C)	Neuroticism	—	Neuroticism	Neuroticism
—	Compulsivity	—	—	Conscientiousness
—	—	—	—	Openness

[a]Livesley et al. (1992).
[b]Wiggins (1988).
[c]Eysenck and Eysenck (1992).
[d]Costa and McCrae (1992).

(which does not allow dimensions to correlate with each other) revealed four factors similar to those found in studies of healthy personality (i.e., neuroticism, introversion, disagreeableness, and compulsivity) (Livesley et al., 1993). Coincidentally, Clark and colleagues used a similar empirical strategy to construct a measure of personality disorder symptoms [called the Schedule for Nonadaptive and Adaptive Personality (SNAP)] and found similar results (Clark, 1993). Of greatest interest, the four orthogonal factors observed in both studies appear to comprise pathologically extreme versions of four of the "big 5" factors commonly observed in studies of normal personality (Clark and Harrison, 2001; Livesley et al., 1998) (see Table 5.2).

In sum, studies support some degree of continuity between Axis II and Axis I, given that the odd/eccentric cluster of Axis II may lie on a continuum with the Axis I diagnosis of schizophrenia. However, existing evidence even more strongly suggests that the impulsive/dramatic and anxious/fearful cluster disorders of Axis II lie on a continuum with symptoms shared not just by one but by several Axis I diagnoses (Angst and Ernst, 1993), as well as with traits that comprise "normal" personality. Thus, it may be that some personality disorder symptoms represent extreme variants of normal personality traits. Before addressing this possibility in greater detail, we briefly review how researchers operationally define and measure "normal" personality.

WHAT IS PERSONALITY?

Theories of human personality predate scientific methods. In the oldest documented examples, ancient Greek physicians at the time of Galen attributed individual differences in temperament to the balance of bodily fluids in a given individual (Siegel, 1968). Regardless of the mechanistic correctness of this explanatory framework, the

Greek physicians' observations intrigued and inspired many of the progenitors of modern experimental psychology, including Pavlov (1935) and Wundt (1896). Early in the 20th century, experimental psychologists turned their attention not only to describing individual differences in humans but also toward measuring them. While some focused on traits related to intelligence (Binet, 1905), others focused on traits related to emotional and social functioning.

Allport emphasized both the content and organization of these socioemotional traits when he defined personality as: "the dynamic organization within the individual of those psychophysical systems that determine characteristics of behavior and thought." Although traditionally, "temperament" referred to "immature" traits of biological origin while "character" referred to "mature" traits that have been sculpted by socialization, Allport included both types of traits under the rubric of "personality," due to concerns about moral or evaluative connotations of a distinction between temperament and character (Allport, 1961). His decision not to distinguish the two proved empirically prescient since recent studies suggest that both putatively "temperamental" and "characterological" traits share comparable degrees of heritability (Plomin et al., 1990), and indices purporting to measure each separately are often intercorrelated (Cloninger et al., 1993; Herbst et al., 2000).

Psychometric studies that followed Allport's early formulations (Allport and Odbert, 1936) helped to lay the foundation for current personality theory. Specifically, scientists began to employ factor analysis as a means of determining the underlying structure or dimensionality of peoples' personality descriptions of themselves and others. Some researchers randomly sampled descriptors from bodies of spoken or written language (e.g., dictionaries) while others selected descriptors on the basis of theory. Although resulting models of personality sometimes contained different numbers of factors, all of the models relevant to personality disorders tend to share a handful of common factors.

One such model was developed by Leary and colleagues and based on Sullivan's theory of interpersonal behavior (Freedman et al., 1951). This "interpersonal circumplex" model describes personality in terms of two independent dimensions: dominance and affiliation. An example of an instrument used to measure self-rated interpersonal descriptions is the Interpersonal Adjective Scales—Revised (Wiggins et al., 1988), and a second instrument that measures interpersonal problems is the Inventory of Interpersonal Problems (Horowitz et al., 1988). More recent extensions of this model that have been used to assess personality disorder symptomatology include the Structural Analysis of Social Behavior, developed by Benjamin and colleagues (Benjamin, 1996).

A second model that focused more on the individual than on his or her social interactions was proposed by Eysenck, who was inspired by Pavlov's observations of individual differences in the behavior of dogs as they learned to discriminate between different incentive cues (Eysenck, 1987). This "PEN" model described personality in terms of three dimensions: psychoticism, extraversion, and neuroticism. A modern extension of Eysenck's model (Costa and McCrae, 1992) also reflected the findings of extensive factor analytic studies of personality descriptors in the English language (Goldberg, 1990). This "five-factor model" (a.k.a. the "big 5") described personality in terms of five dimensions: extraversion, neuroticism, openness, agree-ableness, and conscientiousness. A currently popular instrument for measuring these five factors in healthy individuals is the NEO Personality Inventory, Revised (NEO-PIR; Neuroticism-Extraversion-Openness Personality Inventory, Revised) (Costa and McCrae, 1992). Investigators have also developed the Structured Interview for the Five-Factor Model of Personality (SIFFM) to assess these five factors in personality-disordered individuals (Trull and Widiger, 1997).

Subsequent research and analyses have verified that some factors from the five-factor model map both onto factors in the interpersonal circumplex and the PEN model in healthy individuals. Specifically, low extraversion corresponds with the low domi-nance/low affiliation quadrant of the interpersonal circumplex, while low agreeableness corresponds with the high dominance/low affiliation quadrant of the interpersonal circumplex (Costa and McCrae, 1989). Additionally, as one might predict based on the derivation of the NEO from Eysenck's PEN model, high NEO-PIR extraver-sion corresponds with high PEN extraversion, high NEO-PIR neuroticism corresponds with high PEN neuroticism, and low NEO-PIR agreeableness corresponds with high PEN psychoticism (see Table 5.2). Despite differences in the derivation and con-struction of these measures, this convergence suggests that decades of psychometric research have led to a remarkable consensus regarding the basic structure of personality traits (Digman, 1990). Four of the five factors (all but openness) have repeatedly been replicated in cross-cultural comparisons (De Raad et al., 1998), and each shows promi-nent heritable components in twin and adoption studies (30 to 50 percent) (Bouchard, 1994; Bouchard and Loehlin, 2001). Thus, these four traits probably reflect the oper-ation of integrated "psychophysical systems" (a la Allport), rather than culturally acquired semantic biases (Passini and Norman, 1966).

HOW ARE PERSONALITY DISORDERS AND PERSONALITY RELATED?

Thanks to the emergence of psychometrically reliable and valid measures of person-ality disorder symptoms and of personality traits, investigators have begun to map points of convergence between the two. As mentioned previously, the factor structure of personality disorder symptoms (as assessed by Livesley et al.'s DAPP-BQ or Clark et al.'s SNAP) shows broad similarity with the factor structure of normal personality traits (as assessed by Costa and McCrae's NEO-PI-R). Specifically, factor analyses of the DAPP-BQ yield common factors approximating neuroticism, extraversion (nega-tive), agreeableness (negative), and conscientiousness. Thus, the only NEO-PI-R factor not represented in measures of personality disorders appears to be openness to experi-ence (Clark et al., 1994; Schroeder et al., 1994). Together, this evidence suggests that personality disorders can be characterized in terms of the same types of dimensions that investigators use to characterize normal personality, even if these measures tap different ends of a severity spectrum running from health to psychopathology.

WHAT LEADS TO "DISORDERED PERSONALITY"?

The promise of measuring dimensions of personality disorder symptoms leads to the possibility of linking those measures to physiological substrates. As succinctly stated by Jang and Vernon (2001): "The definition of the phenotype remains the most important prerequisite for successful genetic studies" (p. 177). In other words, investigators can most easily link protein expression mechanisms to phenotypes that are internally coherent, distinct from other phenotypes, and stable across measurement attempts. Because some personality traits show desirable psychometric qualities of validity and reliability and describe key features of personality disorders, they may provide ideal "endophenotypes" for linkage to genetic and intermediate physiological mechanisms (Jang and Vernon, 2001). Investigations of the relationship between genetic polymorphisms and personality traits provide fertile ground for inquiry. For instance, mice genetically engineered to lack serotonin 1a receptors show increased anxious behavior, and this anxious behavior can be normalized by "knocking in" forebrain serotonin receptors through genetic induction in adulthood (Gross et al., 2002). These findings provide an exciting parallel to the recently observed association between a genetic polymorphism that regulates serotonin function and neuroticism (a personality trait that indexes the chronic experience of anxiety) in humans (Lesch et al., 1996).

Indeed, as in the case of "normal" personality traits, a large twin study has revealed substantial heritability of traits that index personality disorder symptoms (Jang et al., 2000). This heritable component implies a model in which gene expression leads to protein expression, which alters neurophysiological function, which manifests in behavioral tendencies, which over time manifest as a trait, which may confer vulnerability to an eventual personality disorder. Along with inheritance, environmental influences surely also influence gene expression. Either way, the simple causal model outlined above suggests that the physiological correlates of personality disorder symptoms should be more closely associated with behavioral traits than with specific diagnoses. We turn now to review evidence for physiological correlates of personality disorder symptoms.

Neurotransmitter Correlates

Perhaps because many psychiatric medications affect a class of neurotransmitters called the biogenic amines (i.e., serotonin, dopamine, and norepinephrine), associations between biogenic amine function and personality disorders have received the most extensive characterization. However, a limited number of studies also address links between acetylcholinergic as well as peptidergic function and personality disorder symptoms. We review those findings below.

Serotonin. The inverse relationship between brain serotonin activity and impulsive aggression represents one of the best replicated findings in biological psychiatry.

Valzelli first documented that decreased turnover of the neurotransmitter serotonin (induced by either selective breeding, pharmacological manipulations, or social isolation) reliably increased aggressive behavior in mice and rats (Valzelli, 1980). The fact that early social isolation can reduce brain serotonin in animal models and that cerebrospinal serotonergic indices show only moderate heritability ($\sim$30 percent) in humans suggests that serotonergic function responds both to genetic and environmental contingencies (Heinz et al., 2001). One indirect measure of brain serotonin function in humans involves administering a spinal tap and extracting a serotonin metabolite called 5-hydroxyindoleacetic acid from the cerebrospinal fluid (CSF 5-HIAA). An initial study that reported an association between low CSF 5-HIAA and history of violent suicides (Asberg et al., 1976) was followed by a string of reported associations between low CSF 5-HIAA with other impulsive aggressive behavioral correlates in personality-disordered patients. These behavioral correlates included a history of impulsive assault, murder, and arson (Virkkunen et al., 1987). However, these associations have proven more difficult to detect in noncriminal samples, possibly because CSF metabolite measures provide, at best, an indirect measure of brain serotonin function (Coccaro, 2001).

Another means of making inferences about brain serotonin in humans involves neuroendocrine challenges. For example, researchers have infused serotonin agonists such as fenfluramine into subjects' veins, which bind to serotonin receptors in the hypothalamus and cause release of the hormone prolactin from the pituitary gland into the peripheral circulation. Thus, the prolactin response to d,l-fenfluramine is thought to provide an index of brain serotonergic function. A number of studies conducted on this topic (but not all) have revealed inverse relationships between fenfluramine-induced prolactin release and indices of behavioral aggression and hostility in personality-disordered patients. Studies utilizing other serotonin agonists such as meta-chlorophenylpiperazine and ipsapirone have also revealed inverse associations with prolactin release and ratings of hostility in personality disordered subjects (Coccaro, 1998). Although comorbid alcoholism was a potential confounding factor in many of these clinical studies, fenfluramine-induced prolactin release was also negatively related to life history of aggression and NEO-PI-R neuroticism in a large sample of healthy men, but positively related to NEO-PI-R conscientiousness (Manuck et al., 1998). These relationships were also observed in postmenopausal but not premenopausal women. The authors raised the possibility that circulating estrogen may have obscured prolactin secretion in premenopausal woman.

In addition to examining the effects of serotonin agonists on neuroendocrine indices, a few studies have examined the effects of these agents on brain function. For instance, investigators have observed lower levels of resting prefrontal glucose metabolism in borderline personality-disordered subjects relative to healthy volunteers with positron emission tomography (PET). The magnitude of these reductions in prefrontal cortical activity was inversely correlated with life history of aggression (Goyer et al., 1994). The cause of these reductions is unclear since some evidence suggests that reduced frontal metabolism may result from prior trauma (e.g., due to physical abuse, accidental injury, or other insults), which has frequently been observed in murderers and other violent individuals (Brower and Price, 2001). While injection of serotonin agonists increased glucose utilization in prefrontal regions (i.e., orbitofrontal, mesial prefrontal, and anterior cingulate cortex) in healthy volunteers, this enhancement was blunted in patients with impulsive aggressive personality disorders (Siever et al., 1999; Soloff et al., 2000). Finally, recent PET studies of healthy volunteers utilizing serotonin ligands have reported negative correlations between basal serotonin binding in cortical regions and the anxiety subscale of NEO-PI-R neuroticism (Tauscher et al., 2001). Together, these findings suggest a possible link between brain serotonin function and traits characterized by impulsive aggressive behavior. In terms of personality traits, such a "low serotonin" phenotype might show increased neuroticism and disagreeableness (Knutson et al., 1998).

Dopamine. Cerebrospinal fluid measures of the dopamine (DA) metabolite homovanillic acid (CSF HVA) have revealed that patients with schizotypal personality disorder have increased CSF HVA relative to healthy volunteers. Further, the number of psychotic symptoms (e.g., suspiciousness, ideas of reference, magical thinking) shown by patients with schizotypal personality disorders correlated positively with CSF HVA levels (Siever et al., 1993).

Although no neuroendocrine challenge studies involving dopamine agonists have involved schizotypal patients, behavioral responses to injections of the dopamine releaser/reuptake blocker amphetamine have been examined. Specifically, patients with comorbid borderline and schizotypal personality disorders show psychotic symptoms in response to amphetamine injections, while patients with borderline personality disorder alone do not (Schulz et al., 1988). Thus, while there is less data regarding dopamine function in personality disorders than serotonin function, the existing data provide some evidence of dopaminergic dysregulation in schizotypal subjects, as has been reported in schizophrenics.

One neuroendocrine challenge study of healthy volunteers found a positive correlation between DA agonist (bromocryptine)-induced prolactin release and a trait variable called positive emotionality (Depue et al., 1994). Positive emotionality correlates with NEO-PI-R extraversion and so could be conceptualized as the inverse of DAPP introversion (see Table 5.2). PET studies suggest that dopamine ligand binding may be negatively related to psychometric indices of interpersonal detachment in the putamen (Farde et al., 1997) and positively related to psychometric indices of novelty-seeking in the insula (Suhara et al., 2001), suggesting links between basal dopamine function and traits similar to NEO-PI-R extraversion. Further, a recent study combining both PET and a challenge with the dopamine releaser/reuptake blocker amphetamine revealed a positive correlation between ventral striatal dopamine release and the personality trait of novelty seeking–exploratory excitability, which is conceptually similar to NEO-PI-R extraversion (Leyton et al., 2002). Together, this preliminary neurochemical evidence implies a positive relationship between extraversion in healthy volunteers and dopaminergic function, particularly in the ventral striatum.

Norepinephrine, Acetylcholine, and Peptides. Although CSF measures of the norepinephrine metabolite 3-methoxy-4-hydroxyphenylglycol (CSF MHPG) were reported to correlate with life history of aggression in a sample of personality-disordered subjects, covariance analyses revealed that most of this relationship could be statistically accounted for by reductions in CSF 5-HIAA (Brown et al., 1979). One study investigating the effects of the noradrenergic alpha-2 receptor agonist clonidine on the release of hypothalamic growth hormone release revealed a relationship with self-reported "irritability" in both personality-disordered patients and healthy volunteers (Coccaro et al., 1991), but this effect remains to be replicated.

Only one study has focused on the effects of an acetylcholinergic challenge in personality-disordered patients. The investigators reported that injections of physostigmine, which increases brain acetylcholine by inhibiting the enzyme acetylcholinesterase, increased self-reported depressive symptoms in borderline patients but not in healthy volunteers (Steinberg et al., 1997). In the only investigation of a neuropeptide in personality-disordered patients, Coccaro et al. (1998) found a significant positive correlation between CSF measures of vasopressin and life history of aggression and aggression against other people in particular. Notably, this association could not be accounted for by covarying out associations of serotonergic measures with life history of aggression (Coccaro et al., 1998)

Genetic Correlates

Research has also begun to focus on associations between genetic polymorphisms and personality traits. These polymorphisms may be either functional (i.e., they may encode for a specific protein) or not. Cloninger has developed a theory that explicitly links biogenic amine function with personality traits (Cloninger, 1987). In the first version of this theory, which included only putatively "temperamental" traits, Cloninger hypothesized that a trait called novelty seeking would be related to dopaminergic function, a trait called harm avoidance would be related to serotonergic function, and a trait called reward dependence would be related to noradrenergic function. Cloninger and colleagues also developed a questionnaire to measures these three constructs called the Tridimensional Personality Questionnaire (TPQ). An initial study reporting an association between a polymorphism of the dopamine 4 receptor gene (DRD4) and individual differences in a combination of high NEO-PIR extraversion and low conscientiousness (both purported to index aspects of TPQ novelty seeking) appeared to support this theory (Ebstein et al., 1996). While a meta-analysis of follow-up studies revealed a subsequent failure to replicate this particular association, it did suggest some evidence for an association of a different functional polymorphism in the upstream promoter region of the DRD4 gene (C-521T) with TPQ novelty seeking (Schinka et al., 2002).

Unfortunately, no studies have psychometrically related Cloninger's TPQ traits to those measured by either the NEO-PI-R or to the DAPP-BQ. This may be partially due to the fact that both Cloninger's theory and measures have since undergone at least two major revisions, expanding from three to four and then six traits in the process. However, accumulating evidence does appear to suggest a second set of relationships between NEO-PIR neuroticism as well as possibly disagreeableness and a functional polymorphism of a gene that regulates the expression of the serotonin reuptake mechanism (5-HTTLPR) (Lesch et al., 1996; Murphy et al., 2001).

While these initial findings are intriguing, biogenic amine function is complex and necessarily includes many physiological processes including gene expression, intracellular signaling, manufacture and release of neurotransmitters, changes in the number and affinity of postsynaptic receptors, and enzymatic breakdown or reuptake of released neurotransmitter. Different genetic polymorphisms could affect any or all of these steps, and many other polymorphisms remain to be examined. Additionally, currently popular statistical methods primarily deal with single-nucleotide polymorphisms (SNPs) or point mutations and are only beginning to address multivariate interactions such as multiple loci and gene-gene interactions, which must play important roles in generating complex phenotypes such as personality traits (Cloninger et al., 1998). Further, other neural systems besides the biogenic amines (e.g., amino acids, neuropeptides) undoubtedly play important roles in the expression of trait phenotypes. The present gap between heritability estimates for personality traits ($\sim$50 percent) and SNP effect sizes ($\sim$1 to 3 percent) may seem puzzling but may also indicate that exciting discoveries lie ahead.

HOW CAN "DISORDERED PERSONALITY" BE TREATED?

Studies of physiological correlates of personality disorder symptoms cannot establish causality. They leave open the question of whether the physiological correlate leads to symptoms, whether the symptoms perturb the physiological correlate, or both. Causal evidence for a physiological effect on personality disorder symptoms might come from double-blind studies in which neurotransmitter function is selectively manipulated and changes in specific symptoms are monitored. A few relevant studies have been conducted in humans. Based on the evidence presented above, one might hypothesize that serotonergic interventions should ameliorate symptoms related to impulsive aggression that are commonly observed in personality disorders such as borderline personality disorder, while dopaminergic interventions might reduce psychotic symptoms that sometimes accompany schizotypal personality disorders.

Four placebo-controlled double-blind studies have examined the effects of selective serotonin reuptake inhibitors (SSRIs) on personality disorder symptoms. In the first, fluoxetine treatment reduced the anger of 13 borderline patients, relative to 9 placebo-treated patients (Salzman et al., 1995). A second preliminary study reported general efficacy of fluoxetine in the treatment of borderline personality disorder in reducing a number of symptoms, including anger and aggression (Markovitz, 1995). In the third study, fluoxetine treatment reduced verbal aggression and aggression against objects in 20 personality disordered patients, relative to 20 placebo-treated patients (Coccaro and Kavoussi, 1997). In a fourth study, fluvoxamine treatment reduced neurotic symptoms (depression, irritability, and anxiety) but not impulsivity or aggression in 20 women with borderline disorder, relative to 18 placebo-treated patients (Rinne et al., 2002).

If traits that promote impulsive aggression in personality disorders are continuous with "normal" personality traits, then SSRI administration should also affect these traits in healthy individuals. Only two studies have examined the effects of chronic SSRI treatment in healthy volunteers with placebo-controlled double-blind designs. The first revealed that paroxetine treatment reduced indices of hostility (and more generally, negative activated mood), as well as enhanced a behavioral index of cooperation in 26 healthy volunteers, relative to 25 placebo-treated controls (Knutson et al., 1998). The second reported that citalopram treatment increased behavioral indices of both cooperation and dominance in 10 healthy volunteers, relative to 10 placebo-treated controls, although mood was not significantly affected (Tse and Bond, 2002). These studies provide some preliminary evidence that brain serotonin function may play a role in modulating personality traits related to neuroticism and/or agreeableness and so support the notion of continuity between healthy personality traits and those that contribute to some personality disorder symptoms.

In two large placebo-controlled double-blind studies, dopamine-blocking neuroleptics reduced psychotic symptoms (as well as anxiety) in patients with borderline and/or schizotypal personality disorder (Goldberg et al., 1986; Soloff et al., 1986). However, more recent studies have shown either modest or no efficacy for neuroleptic versus placebo treatment in personality-disordered patients (Cowdry and Gardner, 1988; Soloff et al., 1993). Administration of neuroleptics may be most efficacious in highly impaired schizotypal patients with preexisting psychotic symptoms. Further, studies that indicate a relationship between dopaminergic activity and extraversion in healthy volunteers raise the concern that dopamine blockade may have the unintended side effects of decreasing motivation and sociability in some patients.

Other psychoactive medications have proven effective in personality-disordered patients who do not respond to SSRIs or neuroleptics. For instance, lithium carbonate has been shown to reduce behavioral aggression in prison inmates with a probable diagnosis of antisocial personality disorder, relative to prisoners treated with placebo (Sheard et al., 1976). On the other hand, agents that increase dopaminergic or noradrenergic activity, in addition to anxiolytics, may increase "episodic dyscontrol" in patients with borderline personality disorder, and so are not recommended as treatment for this group (Cowdry and Gardner, 1988).

In summary, mounting evidence suggests that serotonin reuptake blockers modulate the expression of traits related to impulsive aggression in both patients with personality disorders and in healthy volunteers. The evidence for the utility of dopamine antagonists for treated patients with schizotypal personality disorder is more mixed. Regardless of the efficacy of a given pharmacotherapeutic intervention, neurotransmitter systems modulate and guide learning over the life span, so psychotherapy in conjunction with pharmacotherapy probably provides the optimum platform for patients to relearn more advantageous patterns of socioemotional behavior.

We should note here that personality disorders were placed on Axis II rather than Axis I because of their putative chronicity and inflexibility. Even clinicians who consider personality disorders to be malleable generally concur that they are among the most difficult of psychiatric diagnoses to treat. This is probably for good reason: in addition to their chronicity, inflexibility, and maladaptiveness, some personality disorders are marked by patients' inability to reflect on or acknowledge their complicity in their own dilemmas. Still, although only a few clinical controlled trials exist for either psychotherapy, pharmacotherapy, or combined treatment protocols of personality disorders, existing evidence does suggest that therapists can offer patients some relief from personality disorder symptoms (Sanislow and McGlashan, 1998). We contend here that better methods of assessing personality disorders and more precise physiological models of their symptoms may lead to better targeted and thus more effective treatments. Ultimately, we suspect that the most effective treatment will be multifaceted, including some combination of a supportive therapeutic alliance, pharmacotherapy as a short-term tool for forestalling affective or impulsive reactions, and cognitive-behavioral training as a long-term means of replacing maladaptive patterns of behaving and interacting.

SUMMARY

Although the scientific study of personality disorders is at an early phase, research provides some preliminary answers for a number of the questions raised in this chapter. First, in addition to diagnostic specification by the DSM-IV criteria, personality disorders can be parsimoniously characterized with a limited number of continuous trait dimensions using psychometrically sound instruments (Livesley et al., 1992). Second, healthy personality can also be characterized in terms of a limited number of continuous dimensions using psychometric instruments. Third, the content domain of personality disorder symptoms and personality traits overlaps and can be characterized in terms of four independent traits: introversion, neuroticism, disagreeableness, and compulsivity (but not necessarily openness). Fourth, preliminary research on physiological correlates of personality disorder symptoms suggests that low serotonergic function may be associated with neuroticism and/or disagreeableness, while low dopamine function may be associated with introversion. Fifth, serotonergic interventions appear to affect symptoms related to neuroticism and/or disagreeableness, while the effects of dopaminergic interventions on introversion have received less characterization, both in personality disordered and healthy samples.

While these answers provide some clarification, they also raise further questions. Instead of new theories or measures, perhaps what is needed most at the present is integration across different levels of analysis (Depue and Collins, 1999; Knutson et al., 1998). Despite the incompleteness of our knowledge regarding the description, causes, development, and treatment of personality disorders, the advent of psychometrically sound measures of personality disorder symptoms can provide an anchor for integrative analysis. These symptom-focused measures may also provide optimal endpoints for elucidating physiological mechanisms that can promote, perpetuate, and even prevent personality disorders.

POSTSCRIPT: A VIEW TO THE FUTURE

We began this chapter by noting advances in measurement and technology at the turn of the 21st century. Conceptual advances, too, are afoot. Both experimental psychologists and biological psychiatrists are turning from a strict focus on behavior and cognition to incorporate emotion. Spurred by comparative research, the idea of emotional operating systems in the brain offers fertile ground for generating hypotheses about mechanisms that might mediate connections between genes and traits (Panksepp, 1998).

Recurring basic emotional experiences may constitute key features of many of the traits common to both healthy personality and to personality disorders. For instance, in the rubric of the five-factor model of personality (see Table 5.2), fear might provide a core theme of neuroticism, playfulness of extraversion, and anger of disagreeableness. These connections can be verified not only psychometrically with measures designed to index emotional operating systems (Davis et al., in press) but also neurally with brain imaging methods that afford the necessary spatio-temporal resolution for visualizing the ongoing activity of emotional circuits (Canli et al., 2001; Knutson et al., 1999).

In the case of borderline and antisocial personality disorders, anger provides an especially relevant example. The chronic experience of anger constitutes a prominent feature of the personality traits neuroticism and disagreeableness. Accordingly, angry behavior may involve both negative emotion and lack of constraint. These phenomena may stem from a combination of hyperactivity in still vaguely defined threat processing regions of the subcortex (e.g., the amygdala and medial hypothalamus) and hypoactivity of inhibitory regions of the ventral prefrontal cortex (Davidson et al., 2000). Certainly, in both comparative and human research, frontal lobe damage can potentiate aggressive outbursts, while treatment with serotonergic agents, which enhances resting prefrontal metabolism, can diminish their frequency (Linnoila and Charney, 2000). In addition, peptides (e.g., substance P, vasopressin) and hormones (e.g., testosterone) may prime activity in subcortical circuits related to aggressive behavior in comparative models (Ferris et al., 1997; Siegel et al., 1999), and so may present promising pharmacotherapeutic targets for the future. An emotional systems perspective may thus inform both the diagnosis and treatment of personality disorders.

While applications of emotion theory may successfully generalize to the clinic, they may also inadvertently raise ethical issues (Farah, 2002). What if core features of personality disorders could be diagnosed with a brain scan? What if problematic behaviors could be selectively excised with pharmacological manipulations? At what point do people require treatment? Should effective treatments be administered to people who don't want to change? These emerging ethical questions underscore the continuing need for researchers and clinicians to work together toward a optimally combining of technological wisdom and human compassion in treating disorders of personality.

REFERENCES

Akiskal HS (1981). Subaffective disorders: Dysthymic, cyclothymic, and bipolar II disorders in the "borderline" realm. *Psychiatric Clin North Am* 4:25–46.

Allport GW (1961). *Pattern and Growth in Personality: A Psychological Interpretation*. Holt, Rinehart, & Winston: New York.

Allport GW, Odbert HS (1936). Trait-names: A psycho-lexical study. *Psychol Monographs* 47.

Angst J, Ernst C (1993). Current concepts of the classification of affective disorders. *Int Clin Psychopharmacol* 8:211–215.

Asberg M, Traskman L, Thoren P (1976). 5-HIAA in the cerebrospinal fluid: A biochemical suicide predictor? *Arch Gen Psychiatry* 33:1193–1197.

Benjamin LS (1996). *Interpersonal Diagnosis and Treatment of Personality Disorders*. Guilford Press: New York.

Binet A (1905). New methods for the diagnosis of the intellectual level of subnormals. *L'Annee Psychologique* 12:191–244.

Blais MA, Norman DK (1997). A psychometric evaluation of the DSM-IV personality disorder criteria. *J Pers Disorders* 11:168–176.

Bouchard TJ (1994). Genes, environment, and personality. *Science* 264:1700–1701.

Bouchard TJ, Loehlin JC (2001). Genes, evolution, and personality. *Behav Genetics* 31:243–273.

Brower MC, Price BH (2001). Neuropsychiatry of frontal lobe dysfunction in violent and criminal behaviour: A critical review. *J Neurol Neurosurg Psychiatry* 71:720–726.

Brown GL, Goodwin FK, Ballenger JC, Goyer PF, Major LF (1979). Aggression in humans correlates with cerebrospinal fluid amine metabolites. *Psychiatry Res* 1:131–139.

Canli T, Zhao Z, Desmond JE, Kang E, Gross JJ, Gabrieli JDE (2001). An FMRI study of personality influences on brain reactivity to emotional stimuli. *Behav Neurosci* 115:33–42.

Chapman LJ, Chapman JP, Kwapil TR, Eckblad M, Zinaer MC (1994). Putatively psychosis-prone subjects 10 years later. *J Abnormal Psychol* 103:171–183.

Clark LA (1993). *Manual for the Schedule for Nonadaptive and Adaptive Personality*. University of Minnesota Press: Minneapolis.

Clark LA, Harrison JA (2001). Assessment instruments. In Livesley WJ (ed). *Handbook of Personality Disorders: Theory, Research and Treatment*. Guilford, New York, pp. 277–306.

Clark LA, Vorhies L, McEwen JL (1994). Personality disorder symptomatology from the five-factor model perspective. In Costa PT, Widiger TA (eds). *Personality Disorders and the Five-Factor Model of Personality*. American Psychological Association, Washington, DC, pp. 1–12.

Cloninger CR (1987). A systematic method for clinical description and classification of personality variants. *Arch Gen Psychiatry* 44:579–588.

Cloninger CR, Svrakic DM, Przybeck TR (1993). A psychobiological model of temperament and character. *Arch Gen Psychiatry* 50:975–990.

Cloninger CR, Van Eerdewegh P, Goate A, Edenberg HJ, Blangero J, Hesselbrock V, et al. (1998). Anxiety proneness linked to epistatic loci in genome scan of human personality traits. *Am J Med Genet* 81:313–317.

Coccaro EF (1998). Central neurotransmitter function in human aggression and impulsivity. In Maes M, Coccaro EF (eds). *Neurobiology and Clinical Views on Aggression and Impulsivity*. Wiley: Chichester, UK, pp. 143–168.

Coccaro EF (2001). Biological and treatment correlates. In Livesley WJ (ed). *Handbook of Personality Disorders*. Guilford Press: New York: pp. 124–135.

Coccaro EF, Kavoussi RJ (1997). Fluoxetine and impulsive aggressive behavior in personality-disordered subjects. *Arch Gen Psychiatry* 54:1081–1088.

Coccaro EF, Lawrence T, Trestman R, Gabriel S, Klar HM, Siever LJ (1991). Growth hormone responses to intravenous clonidine challenge correlates with behavioral irritability in psychiatric patients and in healthy volunteers. *Psychiatry Res* 39:129–139.

Coccaro EF, Kavoussi RJ, Hauger RL, Cooper TB, Ferris CF (1998). Cerebrospinal fluid vaso-pressin levels: Correlates with aggression and serotonin function in personality-disordered subjects. *Arch Gen Psychiatry* 55:708–714.

Costa PT, McCrae RR (1989). Normal personality assessment in clinical practice: The NEO Personality Inventory. *Psychol Assess* 4:5–13.

Costa PT, McCrae RR (1992). *Revised NEO Personality Inventory (NEO-PI-R) and the NEO Five-Factor Inventory (NEO-FFI) Professional Manual.* Psychological Assessment Resources: Odessa, FL.

Costa PT, Widiger TA (1994). *Personality Disorders and the Five-Factor Model of Personality.* American Psychological Association: Washington, DC, p. 364.

Cowdry RW, Gardner DL (1988). Pharmacotherapy of borderline personality disorder: Alpra-zolam, carbamazepine, trifluroperazine, and tranylcypromine. *Arch Gen Psychiatry* 45:111–119.

Davidson RJ, Putnam KM, Larson CL (2000). Dysfunction in the neural circuitry of emotion regulation—a possible prelude to violence. *Science* 289:591–594.

Davis KL, Panksepp J, Normansell L (2003). The affective neuroscience personality scales: Normative data and implications. *Neuro-Psychoanalysis.* 5:57–69.

De Raad B, Perugini M, Hrebickova M, Szarota P (1998). Lingua franca of personality: Tax-onomies and structures based on the psycholexical approach. *J Cross Cult Psychol* 29:212–232.

Depue R, Collins F (1999). Neurobiology of the structure of personality: Dopamine, facilitation of incentive motivation, and extraversion. *Behav Brain Sci* 22:491–569.

Depue R, Luciana M, Arbisi P, Collins P, Leon A (1994). Dopamine and the structure of per-sonality: Relation of agonist-induced dopamine activity to positive emotionality. *J Pers Soc Psychol* 67:485–498.

Digman JM (1990). Personality structure: Emergence of the five-factor structure. *Ann Rev Psychol* 41:417–440.

Dolan-Sewell RT, Krueger RF, Shea MT (2001). Co-occurrence with syndrome disorders. In Livesley WJ (ed). *Handbook of Personality Disorders.* Guilford Press: New York, pp. 84–104.

Ebstein RP, Novick O, Umansky R, Priel B, Osher Y, Blaine D, et al. (1996). Dopamine D$_4$ receptor (DRD4) exon III polymorphism associated with the human personality trait of nov-elty seeking. *Nature Genet* 12:78–80.

Eysenck HJ (1987). The definition of personality disorders and the criteria appropriate to their definition. *J Pers Dis* 1:211–219.

Eysenc HJ, Eysenck S (1991). Eysenck Personality Questionnaire-Revised. Hodder, London.

Farah MJ (2002). Emerging ethical issues in neuroscience. *Nature Neurosci* 5:1123–1129.

Farde L, Gustavsson JP, Jonnsson E (1997). D$_2$ dopamine receptors and personality traits. *Nature* 385:590.

Ferris CF, Melloni RHJ, Koppel G, Perry KW, Fuller RW, Delville Y (1997). Vasopressin/serotonin interactions in the anterior hypothalamus control aggressive behavior in golden hamsters. *J Neurosci* 17:4331–4340.

Frances AJ, Mack AH, First MB, Widiger TA, Ross R, Forman L, et al. (1994). DSM-IV meets philosophy. *J Med Philos* 19:207–218.

Freedman MB, Leary TF, Ossorio AG, Coffey HS (1951). The interpersonal dimension of per-sonality. *J Pers* 20:143–161.

Goldberg LR (1990). An alternative "description of personality": The Big Five factor structure. *J Pers Soc Psychol* 59:1216–1229.

Goldberg SC, Schulz SC, Schulz PM, Resnick RJ, Hamer RM, Friedel RO (1986). Borderline and schizotypal personality disorders treated with low-dose thiothixene versus placebo. *Arch Gen Psychiatry* 43:680–686.

Goyer PF, Andreason PJ, Semple WE, Clayton AH, King AC, Compton-Toth BA, et al. (1994). Positron-emission tomography and personality disorders. *Neuropsychopharm* 10:21–28.

Gross C, Zhuang X, Stark K, Ramboz S, Oosting R, Kirby L, et al. (2002). Serotonin1A receptor acts during development to establish normal anxiety-like behaviour in the adult. *Nature* 416:396–400.

Heinz A, Mann K, Weinberger DR, Goldman D (2001). Serotonergic dysfunction, negative mood states, and response to alcohol. *Alc Clin Exp Res* 25:487–495.

Herbst JH, Zonderman AB, McCrae RR, Costa PT (2000). Do the dimensions of the Temperament and Character Inventory map a simple genetic architecture? *Am J Psychiatry* 157:1285–1290.

Horowitz LM, Rosenberg SE, Baer BA, Ureno G, Villasenor VS (1988). Inventory of interpersonal problems: Psychometric properties and clinical applications. *J Cons Clin Psychol* 56:885–892.

Jang KL, Vernon PA (2001). Genetics. In Livesley WJ (ed). *Handbook of Personality Disorders*. Guilford Press: New York, pp. 177–195.

Jang KL, Vernon PA, Livesley WJ (2000). Personality disorder traits, family environment, and alcohol misuse: A multivariate behavioural genetic analysis. *Addiction* 95:873–888.

Knutson B, Wolkowitz OM, Cole SW, Chan T, Moore EA, Johnson RC, et al. (1998). Selective alteration of personality and social behavior by serotonergic intervention. *Am J Psychiatry* 155:373–379.

Knutson B, Kaiser E, Westdorp A, Hommer D (1999). Personality predicts brain activation to incentives. *NeuroImage* 8:S360.

Lee KC, Kovac YS, Rhee H (1987). The national epidemiological study of mental disorders in Korea. *J Korean Med Sci* 2:19–34.

Lesch K-P, Bengel D, Heils A, Sabol SZ, Greenberg BD, Petri S, et al. (1996). Association of anxiety-related traits with a polymorphism in the serotonin transporter gene regulatory region. *Science* 274:1527–1531.

Leyton M, Boileau I, Benkelfat C, Diksic M, Baker G, Dagher A (2002). Amphetamine-induced increases in extracellular dopamine, drug wanting, and novelty seeking: A PET/[11C]raclopride study in healthy men. *Neuropsychopharmacology* 27:1027–1035.

Linnoila M, Charney DS (2000). The neurobiology of aggression. In Charney DS, Nestler EJ, Bunney BS (eds). *Neurobiology of Mental Illness*. Oxford University Press: New York, pp. 855–871.

Livesley WJ (2001). *Handbook of Personality Disorders*, Guilford Press: New York, pp. 626.

Livesley WJ, Jackson DN, Schroeder ML (1992). Factorial structure of traits delineating personality disorders in clinical and general population samples. *J Abnorm Psychol* 101:432–440.

Livesley WJ, Jang KL, Jackson DN, Vernon PA (1993). Genetic and environmental contributions to dimensions of personality disorder. *Am J Psychiatry* 50:1826–1831.

Livesley WJ, Schroeder ML, Jackson DN, Jang KL (1994). Categorical distinctions in the study of personality disorder: Implications for classification. *J Abnorm Psychol* 103:6–17.

Livesley WJ, Jang KL, Vernon PA (1998). Phenotypic and genetic structure of traits delineating personality disorder. *Arch Gen Psychiatry* 55:941–948.

Manuck SB, Flory JD, McCaffery JM, Matthews KA, Mann JJ, Muldoon MF (1998). Aggression, impulsivity, and central nervous system serotonergic responsivity in a nonpatient sample. *Neuropsychopharmacology* 19:287–299.

Markovitz PJ (1995). Pharmacotherapy of impulsivity, aggression, and related disorders. In Stein D, Hollander E (eds). *Impulsive Aggression and Disorders of Impulse Control.* Wiley: Sussex, UK, pp. 263–287.

Mattia JI, Zimmerman M (2001). Epidemiology. In Livesley WJ (ed). *Handbook of Personality Disorders: Theory, Research, and Treatment.* Guilford Press: New York, pp. 107–123.

Murphy DL, Li Q, Engel S, Wichems C, Andrews A, Lesch K-P, et al. (2001). Genetic perspectives on the serotonin transporter. *Brain Research Bulletin* 56:487–494.

O'Boyle M, Self P (1990). A comparison of two interviews for DSM-III personality disorders. *Psychiatric Res* 32:283–285.

Oldham JM, Skodol AE, Kellman HD, Hyler SE, Doidge N, Rosnick L, et al. (1995). Comorbidity of axis I and axis II disorders. *Am J Psychiatry* 152:571–578.

Panksepp J (1998). *Affective Neuroscience: The Foundations of Human and Animal Emotions.* Oxford University Press: New York.

Passini FT, Norman WT (1966). A universal conception of personality structure? *J Pers Soc Psychol* 4:44–49.

Pavlov IP (1935). *Physiology and Pathology of the Higher Nervous Functions.* Academy of Sciences: Leningrad.

Plomin R, Chipheur HM, Loehlin JC (1990). Behavior genetics and personality. In Pervin LA (ed). *Handbook of Personality: Theory and Research.* Guilford Press: New York, pp. 225–243.

Reich W (1949). *Character Analysis,* 3rd ed. Farrar, Straus, & Giroux: New York.

Rinne T, van den Brink W, Wouters L, van Dyck R (2002). SSRI treatment of borderline personality disorder: A randomized, placebo-controlled clinical trial for female patients with borderline personality disorder. *Am J Psychiatry* 159:2048–2054.

Salzman C, Wolfson AN, Schatzberg A, Looper J, Henke R, Albanese M, et al. (1995). Effect of fluoxetine on anger in symptomatic volunteers with borderline personality disorder. *J Clin Psychopharmacol* 15:23–29.

Sanderson C, Clarkin JF (1994). Use of the NEO-PI personality dimensions in differential treatment planning. In Costa PT, Widiger TA (eds). *Personality Disorders and the Five-Factor Model of Personality.* American Psychological Association Press: Washington, DC, pp. 219–236.

Sanislow CA, McGlashan TH (1998). Treatment outcome of personality disorders. *Can J Psychiatry* 43:237–250.

Schinka JA, Letsch EA, Crawford FC (2002). DRD4 and novelty seeking: Results of a meta-analysis. *Am J Med Genetics* 114:643–648.

Schroeder ML, Wormworth JA, Livesley WJ (1994). Dimensions of personality disorder and the five-factor model of personality. In Costa PT, Widiger TA (eds). *Personality Disorders and the Five-Factor Model of Personality.* American Psychological Association: Washington, DC, pp. 1–12.

Schulz SC, Cornelius J, Schulz PM, Soloff PH (1988). The amphetamine challenge test in patients with borderline personality disorder. *Am J Psychiatry* 145:809–814.

Sheard M, Marini J, Bridges C, Wapner A (1976). The effect of lithium on impulsive aggressive behavior in man. *Am J Psychiatry* 133:1409–1413.

Siegel RE (1968). *Galen's System of Physiology and Medicine*. Karger: Basel.

Siegel A, Roeling TA, Gregg TR, Kruk MR (1999). Neuropharmacology of brain-stimulation-evoked aggression. *Neurosci Biobehav Rev* 23:359–389.

Siever LJ, Davis KL (1991). A psychobiological perspective on the personality disorders. *Am J Psychiatry* 148:1647–1658.

Siever LJ, Amin F, Coccaro EF, Trestman R, Silverman T, Horath TB, et al. (1993). CSF homovanillic acid in schizotypal personality disorder. *Am J Psychiatry* 150:149–151.

Siever LJ, Buchsbaum MS, New AS, Spiegel-Cohen J, Wei T, Hazlett EA, et al. (1999). *d,l*-fenfluramine response in impulsive personality disorder assessed with [18F]fluorodeoxy-glucose positron emission tomography. *Neuropsychopharmacology* 20:413–423.

Silk KR (1994). From first- to second-generation biological studies of borderline personality disorder. In Silk K (ed). *Biological and Neurobehavioral Studies of Borderline Personality Disorder*. American Psychiatric Press: Washington, DC, pp. xvii–xxix.

Soloff PH, Cornelius J, George A, Nathan S, Perel JM, Ulrich RF (1993). Efficacy of phenelzine and haloperidol in borderline personality disorder. *Arch Gen Psychiatry* 50:377–385.

Soloff PH, George A, Nathan Rs, Schulz PM, Ulrich RF, Perel JM (1986). Progress in the pharmacotherapy of borderline disorders: A double-blind study of amitriptyline, haloperidol, and placebo. *Arch Gen Psychiatry* 43:691–697.

Soloff PH, Meltzer CC, Greer PJ, Constantine D, Kelly TM (2000). A fenfluramine-activated FDG-PET study of borderline personality disorder. *Biol Psychiatry* 47:540–547.

Steinberg BJ, Trestman R, Mitroupoulou V, Serby M Silverman J Collavo E, et al. (1997). Depressive response to physostigmine challenge in borderline personality disorder patients. *Neuropsychopharmacology* 17:264–273.

Suhara T, Yasuno F, Sudo Y, Yamamoto M, Inoue M, Yoshiro O, et al. (2001). Dopamine D_2 receptors in the insular cortex and the personality trait of novelty seeking. *NeuroImage* 13:891–895.

Tauscher J, Bagby RM, Javanmard M, Christensen BK, Kasper S, Kapur S (2001). Inverse relationship between serotonin 5-HT_{1A} receptor binding and anxiety: A [11C]WAY-100635 PET investigation in healthy volunteers. *Am J Psychiatry* 158:1326–1328.

Trull TJ, Widiger TA (1997). *Structured Interview for the Five-Factor Model*. Psychological Assessment Resources: Odessa, FL.

Tse WS, Bond AJ (2002). Serotonergic intervention affects both social dominance and affiliative behaviour. *Psychopharmacology (Berlin)* 161:324–330.

Tyrer P, Gunderson JG, Lyons M, Tohen M (1997). Special feature: Extent of comorbidity between mental state and personality disorders. *J Pers Dis* 11:242–259.

Valzelli L (1980). *Psychobiology of Aggression and Violence*. Raven: New York.

Virkkunen M, Nuutila A, Goodwin FK, Linnoila M (1987). Cerebrospinal fluid monoamine metabolite levels in male arsonists. *Arch Gen Psychiatry* 44:241–247.

Widiger TA, Frances AJ, Harris M, Jacobsberg L, Fyer M, Manning D (1991). Comorbidity among Axis II disorders. In Oldham J (ed). *Personality Disorders: New Perspectives on Diagnostic Validity*. American Psychiatric Press: Washington, DC, pp. 163–194.

Wiggins JS, Trapnell PD, Phillips N (1988). Psychometric and geometric characteristics of the revised Interpersonal Adjective Scales (IAS-R). 23:517–530.

Wundt W (1896). *Grundriss der Psychologie*. Wilhelm Engelmann: Leipzig.

Zimmerman M, Coryell W (1989). DSM-III personality disorder diagnoses in a nonpatient sample: Demographic correlates and comorbidity. *Arch Gen Psychiatry* 46:682–689.

6

FUNCTIONAL NEUROIMAGING IN PSYCHIATRY

Johannes Tauscher,[1] Nikolas Klein,[1] and Shitij Kapur[2]

[1] *Department of General Psychiatry, University of Vienna, Austria*
[2] *Schizophrenia-PET Program, Centre for Addiction and Mental Health,*
University of Toronto, Ont., Canada

INTRODUCTION

Historically, structural brain abnormalities have been of primary interest to researchers in the field of psychiatric diseases. However, the development of radioactive labeled compounds and appropriate detection devices has enabled researchers to study the underlying pathophysiology, in particular metabolic and neurochemical brain alterations of psychiatric diseases in vivo in humans. Isotopes can be incorporated into biological compounds to measure blood flow, glucose and amino acid metabolism, or to quantitatively analyze neurotransmitter receptors in psychiatric patients. Furthermore, both single-photon emission computed tomography (SPECT) and positron emission computed tomography (PET) allow in vivo assessment of psychotropic drug effects in animals and humans, providing a better understanding of drug effects. Thus, the introduction of functional neuroimaging with radioisotopes as well as functional

Textbook of Biological Psychiatry, Edited by Jaak Panksepp
ISBN 0-471-43478-7   Copyright © 2004 John Wiley & Sons, Inc.

magnetic resonance imaging (fMRI) has led to a remarkable increase in knowledge about brain function in psychiatric diseases.

This chapter provides an overview of major recent advances in the use of functional neuroimaging, with radioisotopes as well as with fMRI, while also pointing out how these findings impact (or don't) on clinical psychiatry at the "bedside."

MAGNETIC RESONANCE IMAGING

Since its inception in 1973, magnetic resonance imaging (MRI) has been a revolutionary development in its scope and utility. The range of parameters that may be mapped using nuclear magnetic resonance has continued to increase and currently spans such phenomena as proton density measurement, nuclear magnetic relaxation times T1 (longitudinal relaxation time) and T2 (transverse relaxation time), flow in large vessels, diffusion, perfusion, temperature, blood volume, and blood oxygenation. All of the above-mentioned parameters have applications of clinical relevance, and many of them are in routine use. Clinical MRI is likely to move on from its current role simply as a structural technique for visualizing pathology, since researchers have now developed methods used to measure dynamic or functional aspects of human physiology. One of the significant applications of dynamic/functional MRI is in the visualization of localized neuronal activity, inferred through its physiological correlates, such as accompanying changes in cerebral blood volume, cerebral blood perfusion, and cerebral blood oxygenation.

The investigation of neuronal activity via fMRI is based on three main principles: (1) blood volume imaging techniques, (2) blood flow imaging techniques, and (3) blood oxygenation imaging techniques—the last of these being the most commonly used.

Blood Volume Imaging Technique

For some years now, bolus injections of chelated contrast agents, in particular gadolinium diethylenetriamine pentaacetic acid, have been used to assess regional cerebral blood volume, and, when the mean transit time of the contrast agent through the brain is known, cerebral blood flow. The high paramagnetic nature of these contrast agents alters the relaxation processes of water molecules in their surrounding. Changes are evident as a shortening in the relaxation times, and it is this shortening that is used to obtain a qualitative map of regional cerebral blood volume. The major disadvantages of this technique are the necessity of repeated bolus injections of a contrast agent, the potential for subject motion between injections to mask any regional cerebral blood flow (rCBF) changes, and the limited number of neurological states that can be studied in a single session.

Blood Flow Imaging Technique

This second class of imaging sequence gains its contrast from the presence of moving spins, and in particular from water molecules in blood that have been magnetically labeled. When the perturbed water molecules pass through capillaries in the slice of interest, they diffuse into the brain tissue, where they exchange with extravascular tissue water molecules and cause an altering of the image signal intensity from that which would be seen had the arterial spins not been tagged. Though this effect is quite subtle, in a carefully designed experiment the signal change can be detected, and an rCBF map calculated. Such spin "tagging" sequences can theoretically yield a quantitative measure of rCBF, but are more often used to generate qualitative relative rCBF maps.

Blood Oxygenation Imaging Technique

Another method that provides images that may be used as indicators for neuronal activity is that of blood oxygenation dependent (BOLD) contrast. The underlying mechanism in BOLD contrast imaging is similar to that of blood volume mapping by intravascular paramagnetic contrast agents described above. The major difference is that blood itself is used as the intravascular contrast agent, or, more specifically, the change in the blood deoxyhemoglobin concentration provides the magnetic signal. Oxygenated hemoglobin has a magnetic susceptibility close to that of tissue, whereas deoxyhemoglobin has a susceptibility higher than that of oxygenated hemoglobin. The difference in the susceptibility is high enough to cause blood vessels to show a measurable signal when the basal oxygenation level falls. During neuronal stimulation it has been shown that blood flow increases substantially, whereas oxygen consumption is not increased as much. This leads to an increase in the concentration of oxygenated blood in capillaries and venules close to areas where neurons are active, relative to their resting state. Since the susceptibility of oxygenated hemoglobin is closer to that of brain tissue, a decrease in the strength of the microscopic gradients and a commensurate increase in MRI signal intensity is noted during neuronal activity. This is the basis of the postulated mechanism for BOLD image contrast.

PET AND SPECT

Both SPECT and PET use radioactive labeled ligands and radio detection devices to quantitatively analyze brain metabolism or neurotransmitter receptors. The major difference between the two is in terms of spatial resolution and the ability for absolute quantification. In PET the radiolabel is incorporated in naturally occurring elements (carbon, oxygen, nitrogen), giving it versatility. PET cameras provide higher spatial resolution ($\sim$3 mm), and with the use of arterial sampling it is possible to achieve absolute quantification of metabolic/pharmacologic parameters. However, this comes at a cost. Positron emitters have relatively brief half-lives, necessitating the use of an on-site cyclotron to produce short-lived isotopes ($\sim$2 min for [^{15}O] and $\sim$20 min for [^{11}C]), or sophisticated logistics in the case of longer acting ones ($\sim$109 min for [^{18}F]). Additionally, a PET center requires the capacity for incorporating these isotopes into the desired tracer compound quickly, and immediately applying the tracer to a test subject.

SPECT, on the other hand, uses much longer lived isotopes such as $[^{123}I]$ ($t_{1/2} \sim$ 13 hr), and for some purposes also $[^{99m}Tc]$, which although short-lived itself, may easily be obtained from a longer lived precursor. The latter can be produced off-site and shipped to the location of use, thereby posing much lesser technical demands than PET. However, SPECT isotopes are not biological constituents of most molecules desirable as tracers, thus restricting the availability of useful tracer substances. Also, compared to PET, SPECT applications allow less accurate, sometimes called "semiquantitative," estimation of labeled structures and are restricted by the relatively low resolution of the procedure. Thus, in practice, PET has largely been used as a research tool, whereas SPECT has established itself as a clinical diagnostic modality.

In principal, emission-based neuroimaging studies can be broadly divided into two categories. The first and more commonly used category is constituted by studies attempting to visualize blood flow, glucose, or amino acid metabolic processes thought to represent the "activation" of specific brain regions. The tracers commonly used for this purpose, such as $[^{99m}Tc]HMPAO$ for SPECT or $[^{15}O]H_2O$ and $[^{18}F]FDG$ for PET, represent cerebral blood flow ($[^{99m}Tc]HMPAO$, $[^{15}O]H_2O$), an indirect measure of cerebral metabolism, or, more directly, neuronal glucose uptake ($[^{18}F]FDG$). The second category, which may be termed "neurotransmitter imaging," employs receptor-specific ligands in order to investigate the concentration of available receptors (the "binding potential"), endogenous ligand concentration, or the pharmacodynamics and pharmacokinetics of psychotropic drugs.

Interpretation of Acquired Data

Both SPECT and PET images are generated to represent different signal intensities in diverse brain regions as variations in brightness or color. Because the acquired images are functional representations, their interpretation with respect to identification of specific active areas, requires a correlation with the underlying structural anatomy of the brain. There are several different approaches to overcoming the relatively poor structural resolution of these procedures. The first is to delineate a "region of interest" (ROI) around an area of predicted change on a composite PET image or on a co-registered MRI scan, allowing for comparisons of the previously defined, sometimes arbitrarily chosen, brain areas. Lately, this method has been further developed by superimposing MRI-based templates on PET scans to more reliably identify anatomical structures or regions (Meyer et al., 1999a; Resnick et al., 1993). In order to estimate specific tracer uptake, different tracer kinetic models can be applied: Either specific binding is compared to nonspecific and free radioligand in a reference region thought to be free of specific binding, which can be performed with a simplified reference tissue model (Lammertsma and Hume, 1996), or, less desirable for studies in psychiatric patients, a full arterial model measuring the arterial input function through arterial cannulation and time-consuming metabolite measurements. The parameter of interest for all models is the binding potential (BP), which is defined as the number of available binding sites ($B_{\max}$) over the dissociation constant (K_d), or affinity (Mintun et al., 1984).

Another approach aims at using a "voxel-wise" analysis of the brain. A voxel represents the smallest volume unit that can be reconstructed depending on the spatial resolution of a scanner. For a voxel-by-voxel comparison, parametric images representing the binding potential in any given voxel need to be generated. In addition, these parametric images need to be smoothed and normalized into a standardized three-dimensional coordinate system, such as one based on the Talairach brain atlas (Talairach and Tournoux, 1988) or the standard Montreal Neurologic Institute (MNI) brain space. This can be done using Statistical Parametric Mapping version 99 (Friston et al., 1995) (SPM99) and a ligand-specific template (Meyer et al., 1999a). Results can subsequently be displayed as probability maps, in which areas of significant difference or activation changes to baseline conditions (i.e., contrasts) are graphically displayed.

STUDIES OF CEREBRAL METABOLISM AND BLOOD FLOW

Since the introduction of emission-based neuroimaging techniques more than 20 years ago, a number of studies have attempted to improve our understanding of the underlying biology of mental processes in normal volunteers and humans suffering from psychiatric disorders through examining changes in cerebral metabolism and rCBF during activation paradigms as compared to a baseline condition. These activation patterns are thought to represent changes in the neuronal arousal of the corresponding brain regions, for instance, memory processing (Tulving et al., 1994). Studies of blood flow and metabolism depend on comparisons of relative changes. Studies of cerebral blood flow and metabolism have examined changes in global cerebral blood flow and hemispheric symmetry as well as in many specific cortical and subcortical regions such as the frontal lobe, temporal lobe, various limbic structures (i.e., the hippocampal formation, amygdala, and uncus), cingulate gyrus, parietal lobe, occipital lobe, basal ganglia, thalamus, and cerebellum. Although a variety of psychiatric entities have been examined in this fashion, by far the greatest body of literature has been accumulated on affective disorders and schizophrenia.

Studies of Cerebral Metabolism and Blood Flow in Depression

Because changes in rCBF and metabolism are thought to represent activation of the affected brain regions, neuroimaging enables researchers to study the involvement of specific brain regions in generating or modulating psychological phenomena such as mood and affect, drive, attention, and memory, which are the main psychological functions affected in the clinical presentation of mood disorders. For this reason, it has been the main focus of such studies to identify specific functional neuroanatomical circuits and pathological changes that may represent the biological basis of mood and related disorders. By now, a considerable body of evidence has accumulated that has led to the formulation of a neuroanatomical model of mood regulation comprising the prefrontal cortex, amygdala-hippocampus complex, thalamus, and basal ganglia as the main regions involved. In addition to the evidence provided by in vivo neuroimaging studies, these brain areas were found to have extensive interconnections in postmortem studies. It now appears that two main neuroanatomical circuits are responsible for the regulation of mood functions. The first is a limbic-thalamic-cortical circuit including the amygdala, mediodorsal nucleus of thalamus, and the medial and ventral prefrontal cortex. The second is a limbic-striatal-pallidal-thalamic-cortical circuit including the striatum, ventral pallidum, and a number of the regions also involved in the first circuit mentioned. The evidence from functional neuroimaging studies implicating the involvement of these two circuits has been summarized in several extensive reviews (e.g. Drevets, 2000; Soares and Mann, 1997).

The cingulate gyrus seems to play a central role among the findings of recent studies: Hypermetabolism in the rostral anterior cingulate cortex is predictive of good response to treatment with antidepressant drugs, while hypometabolism of the same region is predictive of malresponse (Mayberg, 1997). Another particularly interesting finding has been the demonstration of an inverse reciprocal relationship in the activation of subgenual cingulate cortex and the dorsolateral prefrontal cortex through changes from the depressed to euthymic mood state and vice versa. These two areas, both part of the above-cited functional circuits, have been shown to change dramatically in activation with changes in functional mood states. An increased activation of the first of these two regions, the subgenual cingulate cortex, has been found to represent a marker for sad or depressed mood that resolves upon remission, while increased activation of the other, the dorsolateral prefrontal cortex, has repeatedly been found to represent a marker of attentional processing (and, incidentally, metabolic normalization of this region has also been reported to be a marker of antidepressant treatment effects). These findings contribute to and support a comprehensive neurobiological model of the pathophysiology of depression, which so far has not been possible to replicate to the same extent for any other psychiatric condition. These findings may therefore also be seen as representative of the possibilities afforded by neuroimaging techniques toward advancing our understanding of the physiology and pathophysiology of mental functioning (also see Chapters 2 and 7).

Studies of Cerebral Metabolism and Blood Flow in Anxiety Disorders

Obsessive-Compulsive Disorder (OCD). A dysfunctional cortico-striato-thalamo-cortical circuitry may play an important role in this disorder (Rauch and Baxter, 1998; Rauch et al., 1998). According to this model, the primary pathology afflicts subcortical structures (striatum/thalamus), which leads to inefficient gating and results in hyperactivity within the orbito-frontal cortex and also within the anterior cingulate cortex. Compulsions are conceptualized as repetitive behaviors that are ultimately performed in order to recruit the inefficient striatum to achieve thalamic gating and hence to neutralize the unwanted thoughts and anxiety. PET and SPECT studies have consistently indicated that patients with OCD exhibit increased regional brain activity within orbitofrontal and anterior cingulate cortex, in comparison with normal control subjects (Baxter et al., 1988; Machlin et al., 1991; Nordahl et al., 1989; Rubin et al., 1992; Swedo et al., 1992). Observed differences in regional activity within the caudate nucleus have been less consistent (Baxter et al., 1988; Rubin et al., 1992). Pre- and posttreatment studies have reported treatment-associated attenuation of abnormal brain activity within orbito-frontal cortex, anterior cingulate cortex, and caudate nucleus (Baxter et al., 1992; Benkelfat et al., 1990; Schwartz et al., 1996; Swedo et al., 1992). In addition, both pharmacological and behavioral interventions appear to be associated with similar brain activity changes (Baxter et al., 1992; Schwartz et al., 1996). Symptom provocation studies using PET (McGuire et al., 1994) as well as fMRI (Breiter et al., 1996) have also most consistently shown increased brain activity within anterior-lateral orbitofrontal cortex, anterior cingulate cortex, and caudate nucleus during the OCD symptomatic state.

Cognitive activation studies using PET and fMRI have probed the functional integrity of the cortico-striato-thalamo-cortical circuitry in OCD. In these studies patients with OCD perform an implicit learning paradigm that has been shown to reliably recruit striatum in healthy individuals (Rauch et al., 1995b, 1997b). In both studies, patients with OCD failed to recruit striatum normally and instead activated medial temporal regions typically associated with conscious information processing. Taken together, these neuroimaging findings are consistent with dysfunctions of a cortico-striato-thalamo-cortical circuitry and support the view of a primary striatal pathology and striato-thalamic inefficiency, together with orbito-frontal hyperactivity in OCD.

Social and Specific Phobias. Relatively few imaging studies have investigated specific phobias. Most have employed PET imaging. While one study failed to demonstrate changes in rCBF (Mountz et al., 1989), results from others suggested activation of anterior-paralimbic regions (Rauch et al., 1995a) and sensory cortex (Fredrikson et al., 1995; Wik et al., 1993) corresponding to stimulus inflow associated with a symptomatic state. Although such results are consistent with a hypersensitive system for assessment of or response to specific threat-related cues, they do not provide clear anatomic substrates for the pathophysiology of specific phobia. Whereas one SPECT study of patients with social phobia and healthy control subjects found no significant between-group difference during resting conditions (Stein and Leslie, 1996), more recent cognitive activation neuroimaging studies revealed exaggerated responsivity of medial temporal lobe structures to human face stimuli (Birbaumer et al., 1998; Schneider et al., 1999). This hyperresponsivity may reflect a neural substrate for social anxiety.

The isotope [^{15}O] was used in one PET study to measure rCBF in 18 patients with social phobia and a nonphobic comparison group while they were speaking in front of an audience and in private (Tillfors et al., 2001). During public versus private speaking, subjective anxiety increased more in the social phobics, and their increased anxiety was accompanied by enhanced rCBF in the amygdala. Cortically, rCBF decreased in the social phobics and increased in the comparison subjects more during public than private speaking in the orbito-frontal and insular cortices, as well as in the temporal pole, and increased less in the social phobics than in the comparison group in the parietal and secondary visual cortices. In summary, rCBF patterns of relatively increased cortical rather than subcortical perfusions were observed in the nonphobic subjects, indicating that cortical evaluative processes were taxed by public performance. In contrast, the social phobia symptom profile was associated with increased subcortical activity. Thus, the authors proposed that the functional neuroanatomy of social phobia involves the activation of a phylogenetically older danger recognition system (Tillfors et al., 2001).

Another interesting PET study identified common changes in rCBF in patients with social phobia treated with citalopram or cognitive-behavioral therapy (Furmark et al., 2002). Within both groups, and in responders regardless of treatment approach, improvement was accompanied by a decreased rCBF response to public speaking bilaterally in the amygdala, hippocampus, and the periamygdaloid, rhinal, and parahippocampal cortices. The degree of amygdalar-limbic attenuation was associated with clinical improvement a year later. The authors proposed that common sites of action for citalopram and cognitive-behavioral treatment of social anxiety comprised the amygdala, hippocampus, and neighboring cortical areas, which are brain regions subserving bodily defense reactions to threat (Furmark et al., 2002).

Panic Disorder. Panic disorder (PD) may be characterized by fundamental amygdala hyperresponsivity to subtle environmental cues, triggering full-scale threat-related responses in the absence of conscious awareness. Resting-state neuroimaging studies have suggested abnormal hippocampal activity with abnormally low left/right ratios of parahippocampal blood flow and a rightward shift after treatment with imipramine (Nordahl et al., 1998). One study demonstrated a reduced blood flow in hippocampal area bilaterally (De Cristofaro et al., 1993). In contrast, others have observed elevated metabolism in the left hippocampus and parahippocampal area (Bisaga et al., 1998). Symptom provocation studies have revealed reduced activity in widespread cortical regions, including prefrontal cortex, during symptomatic states (Fischer et al., 1998; Reiman et al., 1989; Stewart et al., 1988; Woods et al., 1988).

In a [^{15}O] PET study, Meyer et al. (2000) found an increased left posterior parietal-temporal cortex activation after a challenge with D-fenfluramine in 17 women with panic disorder. In particular, they found hypoactivity in the precentral gyrus, the inferior frontal gyrus, the right amygdala, and the anterior insula during anticipatory anxiety in PD patients. Hyperactivity in patients compared to control subjects was observed in the parahippocampal gyrus, the superior temporal lobe, the hypothalamus, the anterior cingulate gyrus, and the midbrain. After the fenfluramine challenge, the patients showed decreases compared to the control subjects in the precentral gyrus, the inferior frontal gyrus, and the anterior insula. Regions of increased activity in the patients compared to the control subjects were the parahippocampal gyrus, the superior temporal lobe, the anterior cingulate gyrus, and the midbrain. Another [^{15}O] PET study described specific rCBF differences between panic disorder patients and control subjects during anticipatory anxiety and rest (Boshuisen et al., 2002): During anticipatory anxiety there was hypoactivity in the precentral gyrus, the inferior frontal gyrus, the right amygdala, and the anterior insula in the PD patients. Hyperactivity in patients compared to control subjects was observed in the parahippocampal gyrus, the superior temporal lobe, the hypothalamus, the anterior cingulate gyrus, and the midbrain. After a pentagastrin challenge, the patients showed decreases compared to the control subjects in the precentral gyrus, the inferior frontal gyrus, and the anterior insula. Regions of increased activity in the patients compared to the control subjects were the parahippocampal gyrus, the superior temporal lobe, the anterior cingulate gyrus, and the midbrain. The authors concluded that the pattern of rCBF activations and deactivations observed both before and after the pentagastrin challenge was the same, although different in intensity (Boshuisen et al., 2002).

Studies of Cerebral Metabolism and Blood Flow in Schizophrenia

The frontal lobes have played a prominent role in hypotheses of schizophrenia since the conceptualization of the illness. Early functional neuroimaging studies, beginning with Ingvar and Franzen's (1974) seminal finding that patients with schizophrenia had relatively lower blood flow to frontal regions, provided evidence for the involvement of the frontal lobes. Changes in blood flow in response to cognitive activation were also first observed in these early studies. A large number of activation studies were published over the past 15 years that report frontal lobe impairment in schizophrenia. The overwhelming majority of these investigations have detected abnormal prefrontal response to a variety of cognitive activities designed to access and/or control frontal neural circuitry, particularly working memory. The prefrontal site most commonly affected is the dorsolateral prefrontal cortex (DLPFC), and, until recently, the physiologic abnormality in this brain region was consistently seen as hyporesponsivity (Andreasen et al., 1992; Berman et al., 1992; Buchsbaum et al., 1992, 1990; Cantor-Graae et al., 1991; Daniel et al., 1991; Guich et al., 1989; Lewis et al., 1992; Rubin et al., 1991; Volkow et al., 1987; Weinberger et al., 1988). However, the relative universality with which the schizophrenic prefrontal cortex had been reported to be hypofunctional, in the past several years, has given way to the notion that the aberrant neural responses in prefrontal cortex are more complex, including hyperfunction under some circumstances (Callicott et al., 2000; Heckers et al., 1998; Manoach et al., 2000). Some studies reported no between-group differences (Braus et al., 2000; Buckley et al., 1997; Curtis et al., 1999; Frith et al., 1995; Spence et al., 1998). Studies finding an abnormally increased prefrontal response have been primarily carried out with fMRI, rather than PET, and mainly when the cognitive paradigms take advantage of the temporal properties of fMRI in order to employ shorter blocks of task performance, and/or require task switching. This fact suggests that the anatomical or chemical perturbations of the schizophrenic prefrontal cortex can be manifest by inappropriate overrecruitment of prefrontal neural circuitry during a relatively brief cognitive challenge with failure to sustain this recruitment over longer periods. However, regardless of the direction of prefrontal physiologic abnormality, the functional neuroimaging literature leaves little doubt that prefrontal pathology exists in schizophrenia.

A number of potential explanations for this pathology need to be considered. One potential confounding factor is antipsychotic medication, as the majority of studies was performed in neuroleptic treated patients. However, studies performed with first-degree relatives of patients with schizophrenia who have not been treated with antipsychotics have found similar frontal lobe functional abnormalities (Blackwood et al., 1999; Egan et al., 2001; O'Driscoll et al., 1999), and frontal lobe abnormalities during cognition have been found in a number of studies of young patients who have never received neuroleptics (Andreasen et al., 1992; Buchsbaum et al., 1992; Catafau et al., 1994; Rubin et al., 1994). Thus, there is limited evidence that neuroleptics generate the observed functional (pre)frontal abnormalities.

Most prominent among potential epiphenomena and confounds examined has been the effect of poor performance. Considerable controversy has arisen around the possibility that patients' poor performance on the given task somehow causes the frontal pathophysiology, rather than the neurobiologically plausible explanation that underlying pathology is responsible for the poor performance. Studies were carried out in patients who, like schizophrenics, perform poorly on frontal lobe tasks but have disorders other than schizophrenia (Esposito et al., 1999, 1996; Goldberg et al., 1990; Schapiro et al., 1999). Results of these studies indicated that poor performance per se does not necessarily produce the picture seen in schizophrenia.

The temporal lobe is of interest in schizophrenia for several reasons. Diseases of the medial temporal lobe can be associated with psychotic symptoms, and some neuropsychological aspects of schizophrenia implicate both lateral and medial temporal lobe structures. Although the data overall are less compelling than for the frontal lobe, and confounds and potential mechanisms are less well explored, a number of neuroimaging studies have reported functional abnormalities in both lateral and medial lobe structures (Zakzanis et al., 2000).

Studies of Cerebral Metabolism and Blood Flow in Dementia

Studies with FDG PET in Alzheimer's patients revealed a typical hypometabolism in neocortical structures, mainly the parietal, frontal, and posterior temporal association cortices, that is the same areas where neuronal as well as synaptic degenerations are most severe in postmortem studies. In addition to the regional abnormalities, these patients also exhibit a global reduction of cerebral glucose metabolism. Metabolic decrease in the parieto-temporal association cortex has been recognized as potentially diagnostic for Alzheimer's disease, and this recognition has facilitated the use of PET in clinical settings to evaluate patients with dementia. Also suggestive of dementia of Alzheimer's type (DAT) are: bilateral metabolic reduction in the parieto-temporal association cortex; glucose metabolism reduction in the frontal association cortex, mainly in advanced disease; relative preservation of primary neocortical structures, such as the sensorimotor and primary visual cortex, and also of subcortical structures, like basal ganglia, brainstem, and thalamus; and variable presentation of metabolic reduction in the mesial temporal cortex. A high diagnostic accuracy by FDG PET in the initial assessment of suspected DAT patients, and those who will subsequently be diagnosed with DAT, can be achieved by using such criteria as prefrontal and/or bilateral temporo-parietal hypometabolism. Longitudinal PET studies in DAT patients showed an expansion as well as an increased severity of hypometabolism in associated cortical areas and subcortical structures, and a close correlation between progressive metabolic reduction and impaired cognitive performance has been shown.

Recently, ligands were developed that bind to amyloid plaques, which are specific for DAT. 1-(1-{6-[(2-[18F]fluoroethyl)(methyl)amino]-2-[naphthyl}ethylidene)malononitrile ([^{18}F]FDDNP) in conjunction with PET allows for the determination of localization and load of neurofibrillary tangles (NFTs) and beta-amyloid senile plaques

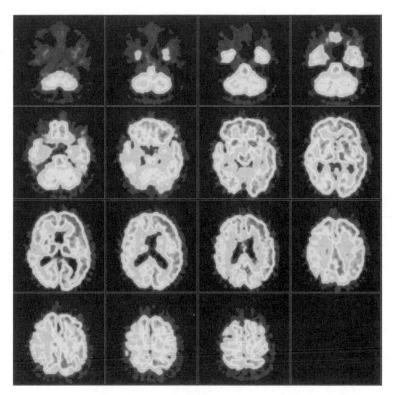

Figure 6.1. PET scan in this 74-year-old female patient with mild DAT (MMSE score 21/30) shows highest retention of the styrylbenzene [^{11}C]SB-13, a radiotracer for Aβ(1–40) amyloid aggregates in the left cerebral cortex, particularly in frontal and temporo-parietal association cortices. (Courtesy of Drs. Alan A. Wilson, N. Paul, L.G. Verhoeff, and Sylvain Houle, PET Centre, CAMH, Toronto, Ont.) See ftp site for color image.

anyloid plaques (AP) in the brains of living Alzheimser's disease patients. Similarly, the styrylbenzene [^{11}C]SB-13, is a promising radiotracer for Aβ(1–40) amyloid aggregates in the cerebral cortex of DAT patients (Fig. 6.1). This noninvasive technique for monitoring AP and NFT development is expected to facilitate diagnostic assessment of patients with Alzheimer's disease and assist in response-monitoring during experimental treatments.

NEUROTRANSMITTER IMAGING STUDIES

Neurotransmitter imaging studies employ receptor-specific ligands in a variety of different experimental protocols. For example, the two PET ligands [^{11}C]raclopride and [^{11}C]N-methylspiperone both bind to dopamine D_2 receptors, although [^{11}C]raclopride is thought to bind only to the monomeric form of the D_2 receptor whereas [^{11}C]N-methylspiperone is thought to bind to both the monomeric and the dimeric forms of the receptor. In addition, D_2 receptors, although usually localized to the cell membrane, may also be internalized in cell vesicles. While [^{11}C]raclopride is thought to bind only the membrane-bound receptors, [^{11}C]N-methylspiperone may also bind to internalized receptors because of its greater lipophilicity. As should be evident from this example, one ligand may be preferable to another depending on the specific question to be examined in a study. Data acquired using one ligand may not simply be extrapolated to another. Therefore, knowledge of both the ligands and the methodological approaches is necessary in order to avoid type I errors and interpretational mistakes. A brief overview of the ligands and methodological approaches used most frequently in psychiatric neuroimaging studies can be found in Tables 6.1 and 6.2.

T A B L E 6.1. Commonly Used Radiotracers for Neurotransmitter Imaging with PET and SPECT

SPECT-Ligand	Application	PET-Ligand
[^{123}I]β-CIT	DAT and 5-HTT	[^{11}C]cocaine [^{11}C]methylphenidate
[^{123}I]nor-β-CIT	5-HTT	—
[^{123}I]iodoketanserine	5-HT$_2$ receptors	[^{18}F]setoperone [^{18}F]altanserin
—	5-HT$_{1A}$ receptors	[^{11}C]WAY-100.635
[^{123}I]IBF [^{123}I]IBZM	Striatal D$_2$ receptors	[^{11}C]raclopride [^{11}C]N-methylspiperone
[^{123}I]epidepride	Extrastriatal D$_2$ receptors	[^{11}C]epidepride [^{11}C]FLB-457
[^{123}I]iomazenil [^{123}I]NNC13 - 8241	GABA$_A$ receptor	[^{11}C]flumazenil

T A B L E 6.2. Applications of Functional Neuroimaging in Neuropsychiatric Research

Method	Application
Radioligand	Distribution in brain and other organs
Radioligand in tracer dose application	Concentration of binding sites in brain and other tissue (= binding potential)
Competition of a tracer with a drug for binding sites	Relative receptor occupancy of the drug
Simultaneous use of a drug and a tracer with affinity to a different transmitter system	Effect of the drug on other neurotransmitter systems
[^{3}H]H$_2$O, [^{123}I]HMPAO, or [^{18}F]FDG	Regional cerebral blood flow or metabolism
Radiolabeled enzyme substrates	Indirect determination of enzyme activity or cerebral metabolism

The two best investigated neurotransmitter systems in psychiatry are the serotonin and dopamine systems, followed by the noradrenergic and cholinergic systems, and to a much lesser extent also the glutamatergic, GABAergic, and gycinergic systems. In addition, the opioid and endogenous cannabinoid systems are sometimes also of interest for psychiatric neuroimaging studies, primarily for investigations into the neurobiology of substance use and abuse.

Neurotransmitter Imaging of the Dopamine System

The classical psychiatric disorder primarily affecting the dopaminergic system is schizophrenia. Beyond that, dopamine is also thought to play a mayor role in substance abuse and the neurobiology of addiction, as well as in Tourette syndrome. A comprehensive review summarizing the state of knowledge on the involvement of dopamine in psychiatric and neurologic disorders was recently published (Verhoeff, 1999) and, although missing the more recently acquired knowledge, it is recommended to readers with special interest in the subject.

Dopamine and Schizophrenia. The dopamine hypothesis of schizophrenia (also see Chapter 9) was first formulated by Carlsson and Lindquist (1963). The central role for dopaminergic transmission in the pathogenetic model of schizophrenia has since been substantiated and developed by numerous later investigations, many of which were made possible by the new methodological possibilities afforded by the introduction of SPECT and PET into clinical research. Carlsson and Lindquist speculated that schizophrenia would be characterized by a hyperactivity of dopaminergic transmission. The correctness of this central idea has by now been well demonstrated in a number of PET investigations showing an increase in the level of both tonic and phasic subcortical dopaminergic transmission in schizophrenic patients (Abi-Dargham et al., 2000; Gjedde and Wong, 2001; Laruelle et al., 1996).

After more than 25 years of discussion about possible alterations of striatal D_2 receptors in schizophrenia, which were studied both postmortem and in vivo, there is now a consensus that specific alterations of the dopaminergic neurotransmission exist in schizophrenia. On the one hand, schizophrenic patients showed an increase in [^{18}F]fluorodopa binding with increased dopadecarboxylase activity (Reith et al., 1994), and on the other hand, schizophrenia was associated with an increased release of intrasynaptic dopamine after amphetamine challenge (Breier et al., 1997; Laruelle et al., 1996). It is still unclear whether the number of striatal D_2 receptors is altered in schizophrenia. The number of striatal D_2 receptors was not altered in antipsychotic naïve patients examined with [^{123}I]iodobenzamide (IBZM) or [^{11}C]raclopride (Farde et al., 1990). In contrast to studies with these benzamides, a PET study using [^{11}C]N-methylspiperone found an elevated number of D_2 receptors in schizophrenia (Wong et al., 1986). The discrepancy can be explained by the benzamides' sensitivity for intrasynaptic dopamine changes, whereas butyrophenones such as spiperone can undergo an agonist-mediated D_2 internalization. That schizophrenia indeed may be associated with an elevation of striatal D_2 receptors has recently been confirmed in another IBZM SPECT study after application of α-methylparatyrosine (AMPT). This led to an acute dopamine depletion in the synaptic cleft, which confirmed an elevated number of striatal D_2 receptors in schizophrenia (Abi-Dargham et al., 2000). Interestingly, in a similar study investigating the effect on both D_1 and D_2 receptors, AMPT-induced dopamine depletion uncovered D_2 receptors, but it did not do so for D_1 receptors (Verhoeff et al., 2002). It has been speculated that the relative up-regulation of D_2 receptors in schizophrenia may reflect constantly increased, basal dopamine levels (Gjedde and Wong, 2001). Besides a putative role for striatal D_2 receptors in the pathology of schizophrenia, there are reports of reduced D_1 receptor density in the prefrontal cortex, which were positively correlated with the severity of schizophrenic negative symptoms (Okubo et al., 1997), and of reduced extrastriatal D_2 receptors in the anterior cingulate cortex, which were inversely correlated with the severity of positive symptoms (Suhara et al., 2002). Recent studies point toward prefrontal D_1 receptor pathology being associated with negative symptoms (Okubo et al., 1997), and relatively reduced D_2 receptor number in the anterior cingulate cortex as one possible contributing factor in schizophrenic positive symptoms (Suhara et al., 2002). In summary, modern neuroimaging procedures provide strong evidence of a subcortical "hyperdopaminergic" system in the pathology of schizophrenia.

Dopamine and Antipsychotics. Even more important than their role in elucidating the primary pathology of schizophrenia, studies using SPECT and PET significantly advanced our knowledge of basic mechanisms of actions of antipsychotic drugs. The D_2 receptor is thought to be key for both the clinically desired "antipsychotic" effects and unwanted motor side effects. Using PET or SPECT to investigate the relative proportion of receptors occupied by a drug versus the available (i.e., drug-free) receptors, which is termed *receptor occupancy* of a given drug, it has been possible to establish a minimal threshold necessary for clinical antipsychotic effects with typical neuroleptics. Also established are upper thresholds with high risks for drug-induced extrapyramidal motor side effects (EPS) such as dystonic reactions, drug-induced parkinsonism, akathisia, tardive dyskinesia, or the consequences of increased prolactin secretion such as galactorrhea, amenorrhea, and impaired libido. Although these thresholds represent averages across a population and significant interindividual variations are possible, these findings represent a major advance in antipsychotic pharmacotherapy. From these studies, a minimal occupancy of approximately 65 percent D_2 receptors appears to be necessary for achieving antipsychotic effects clinically, while dopamine-dependent motor side effects begin to appear at occupancy levels from 78 to 80 percent upward (Farde et al., 1988; Kapur et al., 2000; Tauscher et al., 2002c). The importance of these findings can be underscored by the fact that one of the most frequently used classical neuroleptics, haloperidol, is commonly used in doses ranging from 10 to 20 mg/d, and more. This stands in stark contrast to results from PET and SPECT studies suggesting that the optimal dose of haloperidol lies between 2.5 and 5 mg/d, with complete saturation of D_2 receptors reached at around 7 mg in most patients (Kapur et al., 2000; Tauscher and Kapur, 2001). Findings from SPECT and PET as well as from clinical studies do not point to an advantage of the higher doses commonly used in clinical practice; rather such dosage may lead to a higher incidence of side effects. Most novel antipsychotics have been examined with either PET or SPECT to obtain dose/occupancy relationships. Results from these studies point to an optimal dose range of risperidone from 2 to 4 mg (Kapur et al., 1995) and of olanzapine from 10 to 20 mg (Kapur et al., 1998; Tauscher et al., 1999).

The use of neuroimaging techniques has also improved our understanding of the pharmacokinetics of antipsychotic drugs. The dosing of psychotropic drugs relies on their plasma kinetics (also see Appendix A). Consequently, drugs with shorter plasma elimination half-lives are dosed more frequently than longer-lasting drugs. However, it has recently been demonstrated that the kinetics in the brain differ substantially from the kinetics in plasma, with plasma half-lives for the atypical antipsychotic drugs risperidone and olanzapine being significantly shorter than the half-lives of these drugs in the brain (Tauscher et al., 2002a). The results of this study imply that for some antipsychotics dosing intervals of longer than once daily might be sufficient, whereas the current practice of dosing according to plasma kinetics may in fact lead to drug accumulation in the brain (Fig. 6.2). Furthermore, it may not even be necessary for

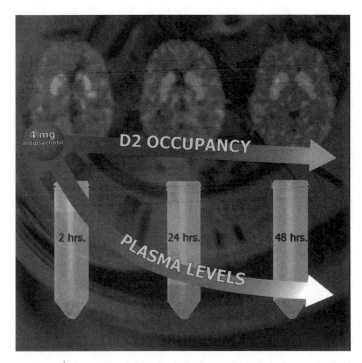

Figure 6.2. Significant dissociation of brain and plasma kinetics after a single dose of a novel antipsychotic questioning the current reliance on plasma elimination half-lives as a rational for developing dosing schedules with psychotropic medications. (With permission from Nature Publishing Group, this figure was first published on the cover of *Molecular Psychiatry*, vol. 7, no. 3, 2002.) See ftp site for color image.

antipsychotics to exert constant high D_2 blockade to achieve antipsychotic response. In a recent PET study with quetiapine, antipsychotic efficacy was demonstrated despite only transiently high D_2 receptor blockade with quetiapine administered once daily (Tauscher-Wisniewski et al., 2002).

Dopamine Neuroreceptor Imaging in Substance Abuse. Apart from schizophrenia and receptor-occupancy-imaging studies with antipsychotic drugs, SPECT and PET have also provided valuable information in other psychiatric illnesses thought to reflect abnormalities in dopaminergic function. The dopaminergic system in the nucleus accumbens (ventral striatum) is thought to be centrally involved in the regulation of the endogenous reward system. Some of the behaviorally most reinforcing psychoactive drugs, such as cocaine and methamphetamine, cause an increase in dopaminergic transmission by blocking the dopamine transporters (DAT) necessary for reuptake of dopamine. A number of PET studies investigating the pharmacological properties of these drugs, and the relationships of these to the symptoms of drug abuse and dependence have been performed. Much of this research has been performed on cocaine as this substance blocks DAT, an effect that is responsible for both the elicitation of euphoria and for the reinforcing effects of the drug. An interesting approach has been to correlate the subjective effects of cocaine with the extent of DAT blockade effected by the drug (Volkow et al., 1997). In this study, the minimal dose of cocaine able to elicit reinforcement was found to lie at less than 0.1 mg/kg, while the minimal dose needed to elicit euphoria was found to lie between 0.3 and 0.6 mg/kg. Correspondingly, the same study found that DAT occupancy rates from 47 percent upward were already sufficient to elicit reinforcement, while the doses commonly used by intravenous cocaine abusers, around 25 to 50 mg/kg, cause DAT occupancy rates between 65 and 80 percent. As evidenced by these findings, significantly lower doses than those needed to cause the euphoric effect sought by the abuser already appear to be sufficient for unleashing the reinforcing effects of the drug. Therefore, contrary to previous hypotheses, it appears possible that the neurobiologic basis of psychological drug addiction is not completely identical with that causing the subjective feeling of a "high." Another interesting finding from this line of research has been that a low density of central D_2 receptors may represent a susceptibility factor for some substance use disorders (Volkow et al., 1999). It has been found that a low density of central D_2 receptors correlates with a positive subjective experience with methylphenidate (a compound with similar pharmacologic actions to cocaine) use, while subjects with a high density of D_2 receptors have subjectively negative experiences with the same drug.

Neurotransmitter Imaging of the Serotoninergic System

The serotoninergic system is thought to be critically involved in a large number, if not the majority, of psychiatric illnesses. The most important and well studied of these is major depressive disorder (MDD). However, the serotonin system is also considered important in schizophrenia, anxiety and phobias, obsessive-compulsive disorder, eating disorders, sleep, and numerous other psychiatric conditions.

Serotonin and Depression. Several studies have found evidence for an increased availability of serotonin 5-HT$_{2A}$ receptors in the brains of unmedicated depressed patients and suicide victims (Cheetham et al., 1988; D'Haenen et al., 1992; Stanley and Mann, 1983). The extent to which these findings exist in depressed persons without recent suicide attempts remains controversial. A [^{18}F]setoperone PET study assessed the 5-HT$_2$ receptor binding potential in 14 depressed and 19 healthy subjects (Meyer et al., 1999b). Interestingly, the 5-HT$_2$ binding potential was not increased in untreated depressed subjects who have not made recent suicide attempts (Meyer et al., 1999b). However, the authors conclude that this negative finding does not rule out the possibility that there is a role for 5-HT$_2$ receptors in treatment or that 5-HT$_2$ receptors are increased in highly suicidal states.

In another study, the uptake of [^{11}C]-5-hydroxytryptophan was found to be decreased in the frontal cortex of unmedicated depressed patients, indicating an abnormality in the transport of the serotonin precursor substance 5-hydroxytryptophan across the blood-brain barrier (Agren et al., 1991; Hartvig et al., 1991). Finally, neuroimaging studies have also provided evidence for a blunted regional metabolism in response to oral *d,l*-fenfluramine induced serotonin release in 6 patients diagnosed with MDD (Mann et al., 1996). However, this could not be replicated in a larger sample of 13 depressed patients using [^{15}O]H$_2$O PET after intravenous *d*-fenfluramine administration, which revealed similar neuronal responsivity to *d*-fenfluramine in depressed and healthy subjects (Meyer et al., 1998).

In addition to the noted 5-HT$_2$ results, two PET studies recently reported a lower number of 5-HT$_{1A}$ receptors in untreated depression (Drevets et al., 1999; Sargent et al., 2000) and depression treated with SSRIs (Sargent et al., 2000). There is also evidence for altered serotonin transporter (5-HTT) density in depression. A SPECT study using β-CIT as a ligand for 5-HTT and DAT found significantly reduced 5-HTT availability in depression (Malison et al., 1998). This result was subsequently replicated in patients suffering from seasonal affective disorder (Willeit et al., 2000).

Taken together, these findings provide ample proof of the involvement of the serotonergic system in the pathophysiology of depression. This is further substantiated by a number of studies that have shown antidepressant drugs to bind to 5-HTT in vivo. For the majority of the substances, and similar to those described for antipsychotics above, curves representing the relationship of dosage to the percentage of inhibited 5-HTT may be calculated from the appropriate PET data. It is interesting to note, however, that while the clinically used dose of paroxetine is 20 to 60 mg a day, data from neuroimaging studies has shown 20 mg of paroxetine to effectively occupy around 80 percent of available 5-HTT in most patients (Meyer et al., 2001). Because of the exponential nature of the dose/occupancy relationships and the resulting hyperbolic shape of these curves, small increases in daily dosage may lead to significantly greater increases of 5-HTT occupancy within the low dose range, while at high doses great increases in daily dosage are necessary in order to effect even minor increases in 5-HTT occupancy. In this sense, the above-mentioned finding suggests that an escalation of the dose of paroxetine beyond the range of 20 mg per day would lead to only nonsignificant increases in 5-HTT occupancy (Meyer et al., 2001). Clinically, although many patients respond well to 20 mg of paroxetine, some only show a reasonable response once the dose is raised to 40 or even 60 mg a day. The clue to solving this apparent discrepancy may lie in the possibility that some antidepressants cause their clinical effects at least partially through mechanisms other than 5-HTT blockade.

Serotonin and Schizophrenia. Postmortem studies showed an elevation in cortical serotonin 5-HT$_{1A}$ receptor density in schizophrenia using [^{3}H]-8-OH-DPAT as a ligand (Hashimoto et al., 1993). The ligand WAY-100635 has been labeled at the [*carbonyl*-^{11}C] position (Farde et al., 1997) and can be used for the quantitative analysis of binding to 5-HT$_{1A}$ receptors in humans (Farde et al., 1998). Using PET and [^{11}C]WAY-100635, our group demonstrated an age-dependent decline of cortical 5-HT$_{1A}$ receptor BP (binding potential) in healthy volunteers (Tauscher et al., 2001b), consistent with postmortem studies that showed a decline in 5-HT$_{1A}$ receptor numbers with age (Dillon et al., 1991; Lowther et al., 1997; Matsubara et al., 1991).

Our group recently completed a PET study in 14 neuroleptic-naïve patients with a *Diagnostic and Statistical Manual of Mental Disorders*, Fourth Edition (DSM-IV) diagnosis of schizophrenia suffering from a first psychotic episode. On the basis of human postmortem studies, we hypothesized that the in vivo 5-HT$_{1A}$ receptor BP as measured with [*carbonyl*-^{11}C]WAY-100635 and PET will be higher in frontal and temporal cortex of schizophrenic patients, as compared to an age-matched control group of healthy volunteers. In a PET study comparing the 5-HT$_{1A}$ BP of 14 antipsychotic naïve patients to 14 age-matched healthy controls, we found a medio-temporal increase of cortical 5-HT$_{1A}$ receptor BP in patients suffering from a first episode of schizophrenia (Tauscher et al., 2002b) (Fig. 6.3).

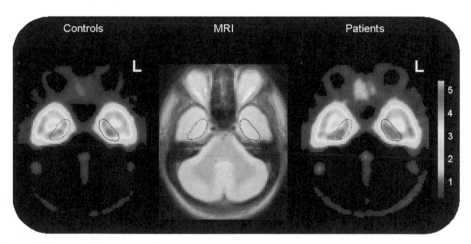

Figure 6.3. Composite mean 5-HT$_{1A}$ receptor binding potential images of 14 healthy controls and 14 age-matched patients with schizophrenia indicating higher 5-HT$_{1A}$ binding potential values in patients in the left and right mediotemporal regions of interest. (With permission from the Archives of General Psychiatry, this figure was first published in *Arch Gen Psychiatry* 59:514–520.) See ftp site for color image.

The published studies of 5-HT$_{2A}$ receptors in schizophrenic patients to date have mainly involved postmortem brain samples and produced conflicting results. While six studies found a reduction in 5-HT$_{2A}$ receptor density in the frontal cortex of schizophrenic patients, four others did not find significant differences compared to controls. Among numerous PET tracers developed for 5-HT$_{2A}$ receptors, only [^{18}F]altanserin, [^{18}F]setoperone, and [^{11}C]MDL 100,907 have demonstrated appropriate in vivo properties for a successful imaging agent in humans. In two recent [^{18}F]setoperone PET studies using ROI analysis, no decreases in 5-HT$_{2A}$ receptors were observed in neuroleptic-free or neuroleptic-naïve schizophrenic patients (Lewis et al., 1999; Trichard et al., 1998). However, localized differences may have been diluted in these ROIs, if either some areas were considerably smaller than the ROIs or if some areas were omitted or only partially included in the ROIs. Therefore, additional 5-HT$_{2A}$ PET studies have been performed using voxel-by-voxel analysis by the application of SPM. One study reanalyzed data from 13 schizophrenic patients obtained in a previous study (Lewis et al., 1999) but compared them with a larger group of 35 age-matched controls (Verhoeff et al., 2000). No substantial 5-HT$_{2A}$ receptor changes were observed in the schizophrenic patients. Another [^{18}F]setoperone PET study indicated significant 5-HT$_{2A}$ receptor decreases in the left and right prefrontal cortex in 6 schizophrenic patients versus 7 age-matched controls (Ngan et al., 2000). It is conceivable that the 5-HT$_{2A}$ receptor decreases observed in earlier postmortem studies in schizophrenic patients either on antipsychotic medication or withdrawn from antipsychotics before death was confounded by medication effects. The discrepant findings between the in vivo studies could, similar to the discrepancies between the postmortem studies, be due to heterogeneity in the populations of schizophrenic patients studied. An in vivo SPECT study investigating potential alterations of striatal DAT and brainstem 5-HTT density in schizophrenia did not find alterations of DAT in the striatum or 5-HTT in the brainstem (Laruelle et al., 2000), despite one postmortem study in schizophrenic patients that showed decreased 5-HTT in the prefrontal cortex.

Serotonin and Anxiety. Serotonin 5-HT$_{1A}$ receptors are thought to play a role in modulating anxiety. Lately, there has been a report of an inverse correlation between 5-HT$_{1A}$ receptor BP and anxiety in healthy subjects (Tauscher et al., 2001a), but thus far there are no published reports on in vivo 5-HT$_{1A}$ binding in anxiety disorders.

Imaging of Other Neurotransmitter Systems

The GABAergic system is thought to play a central role in mediating the effects of alcohol. This is substantiated by the finding that besides binding sites for gamma-aminobutyric acid (GABA) and benzodiazepines, the GABA$_A$ receptor also contains a binding site for alcohol. Direct measurements using PET and [^{11}C]flumazenil, an inverse agonist at the GABA$_A$ receptor, have found a reduction in the concentration of these receptors in the medial frontal lobes and cingulate gyrus of alcoholic subjects and the cerebellum of patients with alcoholic cerebellar degeneration (Gilman et al., 1996).

Similarly, a SPECT investigation also found decreased binding of [^{123}I]iomazenil to GABA$_A$ receptors in the anterior cingulate gyrus, frontal lobe, and cerebellum of alcoholic patients. However, based on these findings alone it is not possible to discern whether the described reduction in GABA$_A$ receptors represents a preexisting susceptibility factor or the result of chronic alcohol abuse.

FUTURE DIRECTIONS AND CHALLENGES

Currently, functional neuroimaging in psychiatry serves as a tool in basic research to understand the underlying pathophysiology of neuropsychiatric disorders and to elucidate basic principles of psychopharmacology at the synaptic/molecular level. In the coming years, one can expect better technology (i.e., better spatial and temporal resolution) and a better approach to methods, leading to more precise analysis. However, the main challenge for the field will be to deliver these basic science findings to the bedside. Whether the field can do that is a question to be answered over the next decade.

The current abundance of neuroimaging findings has been very useful in changing the theoretical conception of many psychiatric illnesses; prevalent concepts such as the "mood circuit" and the "occupancy threshold" are directly attributable to neuroimaging. However, this is not the same as a diagnostic test. The main challenge in turning these and other findings into clinical tools has been the small effect size. All the findings noted above have been ascertained using groups of approximately a dozen patients and comparing them to similar numbers of normal subjects. While these groups may differ, and this can be evaluated with appropriate statistical tests, such procedures do not solve the problems faced by the clinician. Clinicians are typically more interested in single individuals, and therefore they are especially interested in issues of sensitivity, specificity, and the positive predictive power of new data. Providing findings of high predictive power is the challenge for neuropsychiatric imaging.

There is hope on this front. In the field of geriatric psychiatry, fluorodeoxyglucose (FDG) PET (or similar SPECT) approaches are increasingly being incorporated into routine clinical use for the diagnosis or differential diagnosis of dementia and related illnesses (also see Chapter 15). It is conceivable that new specific ligands for neurofibrillary tangles and plaques in patients suffering from dementia of Alzheimer's type will provide major breakthroughs in the diagnostic assessment of this disorder, providing the first in vivo proof of these pathognomonic brain alterations. Another promising future clinical application of functional neuroimaging may be in predicting clinical response to specific pharmacological or nonpharmacological therapeutic interventions. And last but not least, functional neuroimaging can be combined with genetic studies with the aim of finding genotype-phenotype associations typical for specific neuropsychiatric disorders (also see Chapter 14). If the fast pace of developments in this field are any guide, there is every reason to be hopeful that clinical psychiatry may soon be transformed by these techniques in a manner comparable to their impact on basic psychiatric research.

REFERENCES

Abi-Dargham A, Rodenhiser J, Printz D, et al. (2000). From the cover: increased baseline occupancy of D_2 receptors by dopamine in schizophrenia. *Proc Natl Acad Sci USA* 97:8104–8109.

Agren H, Reibring L, Hartvig P, et al. (1991). Low brain uptake of L-[11C]5-hydroxytryptophan in major depression: a positron emission tomography study on patients and healthy Volunteers. *Acta Psychiatr Scand* 83:449–455.

Andreasen NC, Rezai K, Alliger R, et al. (1992). Hypofrontality in neuroleptic-naive patients and in patients with chronic schizophrenia. Assessment with xenon 133 single-photon emission computed tomography and the Tower of London. *Arch Gen Psychiatry* 49:943–958.

Baxter LR, Jr, Schwartz JM, Mazziotta JC, et al. (1988). Cerebral glucose metabolic rates in nondepressed patients with obsessive-compulsive disorder. *Am J Psychiatry* 145:1560–1563.

Baxter LR, Jr, Schwartz JM, Bergman KS, et al. (1992). Caudate glucose metabolic rate changes with both drug and behavior therapy for obsessive-compulsive disorder. *Arch Gen Psychiatry* 49:681–689.

Benkelfat C, Nordahl TE, Semple WE, King AC, Murphy DL, Cohen RM (1990). Local cerebral glucose metabolic rates in obsessive-compulsive disorder. Patients treated with clomipramine. *Arch Gen Psychiatry* 47:840–848.

Berman KF, Torrey EF, Daniel DG, Weinberger DR (1992). Regional cerebral blood flow in monozygotic twins discordant and concordant for schizophrenia. *Arch Gen Psychiatry* 49:927–934.

Birbaumer N, Grodd W, Diedrich O, et al. (1998). fMRI reveals amygdala activation to human faces in social phobics. *Neuroreport* 9:1223–1226.

Bisaga A, Katz JL, Antonini A, et al. (1998). Cerebral glucose metabolism in women with panic disorder. *Am J Psychiatry* 155:1178–1183.

Blackwood DH, Glabus MF, Dunan J, O'Carroll RE, Muir WJ, Ebmeier KP (1999). Altered cerebral perfusion measured by SPECT in relatives of patients with schizophrenia. Correlations with memory and P300. *Br J Psychiatry* 175:357–366.

Boshuisen ML, Ter Horst GJ, Paans AM, Reinders AA, den Boer JA (2002). rCBF differences between panic disorder patients and control subjects during anticipatory anxiety and rest. *Biol Psychiatry* 52:126–135.

Braus DF, Ende G, Hubrich-Ungureanu P, Henn FA (2000). Cortical response to motor stimulation in neuroleptic-naive first episode schizophrenics. *Psychiatry Res* 98:145–154.

Breier A, Su TP, Saunders R, et al. (1997). Schizophrenia is associated with elevated amphetamine-induced synaptic dopamine concentrations: Evidence from a novel positron emission tomography method. *Proc Natl Acad Sci USA* 94:2569–2574.

Breiter HC, Rauch SL, Kwong KK, et al. (1996). Functional magnetic resonance imaging of symptom provocation in obsessive-compulsive disorder. *Arch Gen Psychiatry* 53:595–606.

Buchsbaum MS, Haier RJ, Potkin SG, et al. (1992). Frontostriatal disorder of cerebral metabolism in never-medicated schizophrenics. *Arch Gen Psychiatry* 49:935–942.

Buckley PF, Friedman L, Wu D, et al. (1997). Functional magnetic resonance imaging in schizophrenia: Initial methodology and evaluation of the motor cortex. *Psychiatry Res* 74:13–23.

Callicott JH, Bertolino A, Mattay VS, et al. (2000). Physiological dysfunction of the dorsolateral prefrontal cortex in schizophrenia revisited. *Cereb Cortex* 10:1078–1092.

Cantor-Graae E, Warkentin S, Franzen G, Risberg J, Ingvar DH (1991). Aspects of stability of regional cerebral blood flow in chronic schizophrenia: An 18-year followup study. *Psychiatry Res* 40:253–266.

Carlsson A, Lindquist M (1963). Effect of chlorpromazine or haloperidol on the formation of 3-methoxytyramine and normetanephrine in mouse brain. *Acta Pharmacol Toxicol* 20:140–144.

Catafau AM, Parellada E, Lomena FJ, et al. (1994). Prefrontal and temporal blood flow in schizophrenia: Resting and activation technetium-99m-HMPAO SPECT patterns in young neuroleptic-naive patients with acute disease. *J Nucl Med* 35:935–941.

Cheetham SC, Crompton MR, Katona CL, Horton RW (1988). Brain 5-HT$_2$ receptor binding sites in depressed suicide victims. *Brain Res* 443:272–280.

Curtis VA, Bullmore ET, Morris RG, et al. (1999). Attenuated frontal activation in schizophrenia may be task dependent. *Schizophr Res* 37:35–44.

Daniel DG, Weinberger DR, Jones DW, et al. (1991). The effect of amphetamine on regional cerebral blood flow during cognitive activation in schizophrenia. *J Neurosci* 11:1907–1917.

De Cristofaro MT, Sessarego A, Pupi A, Biondi F, Faravelli C (1993). Brain perfusion abnormalities in drug-naive, lactate-sensitive panic patients: A SPECT study. *Biol Psychiatry* 33:505–512.

D'Haenen H, Bossuyt A, Mertens J, Bossuyt-Piron C, Gijsemans M, Kaufman L (1992). SPECT imaging of serotonin 2 receptors in depression. *Psychiatry Res* 45:227–237.

Dillon KA, Gross-Isseroff R, Israeli M, Biegon A (1991). Autoradiographic analysis of serotonin 5-HT$_{1A}$ receptor binding in the human brain postmortem: Effects of age and alcohol. *Brain Res* 554:56–64.

Drevets WC, Frank E, Price JC, et al. (1999). PET imaging of serotonin 1A receptor binding in degression. *Biol Psychiatry* 46:1375–1387.

Drevets WC (2000). Neuroimaging studies of mood disorders. *Biol Psychiatry* 48:813–829.

Egan MF, Goldberg TE, Kolachana BS, et al. (2001). Effect of COMT Val108/158 Met genotype on frontal lobe function and risk for schizophrenia. *Proc Natl Acad Sci USA* 98: 6917–6922.

Esposito G, Kirkby BS, Van Horn JL (1996). Impaired Wisconsin card sorting test performance in normal aging and in schizophrenia: PET evidence of different pathophysiological mechanisms for a common cognitive deficit. *Neuroimage* 3:3.

Esposito G, Kirkby BS, Van Horn JD, Ellmore TM, Berman KF (1999). Context-dependent, neural system-specific neurophysiological concomitants of ageing: Mapping PET correlates during cognitive activation. *Brain* 122:963–979.

Farde L, Wiesel FA, Stone-Elander S, et al. (1990). D$_2$ dopamine receptors in neuroleptic-naive schizophrenic patients. A positron emission tomography study with [11C]raclopride. *Arch Gen Psychiatry* 47:213–219.

Farde L, Ginovart N, Ito H, et al. (1997). PET-characterization of [carbonyl-11C]WAY-100635 binding to 5-HT$_{1A}$ receptors in the primate brain. *Psychopharmacology (Berl)* 133:196–202.

Farde L, Wiesel FA, Halldin C, Sedvall G (1988). Central D$_2$-dopamine receptor occupancy in solizophremic patients treated with antipsychotic drags. *Arch Gen Psychiatry* 45:71–6.

Farde L, Ito H, Swahn CG, Pike VW, Halldin C (1998). Quantitative analyses of carbonyl-carbon-11-WAY-100635 binding to central 5-hydroxytryptamine-1A receptors in man. *J Nucl Med* 39:1965–1971.

Fischer H, Andersson JL, Furmark T, Fredrikson M (1998). Brain correlates of an unexpected panic attack: A human positron emission tomographic study. *Neurosci Lett* 251:137–140.

Fredrikson M, Wik G, Annas P, Ericson K, Stone-Elander S (1995). Functional neuroanatomy of visually elicited simple phobic fear: Additional data and theoretical analysis. *Psychophysiology* 32:43–48.

Friston KJ, Holmes AP, Worsley KJ, Poline JP, Frith CD, Frackowiack RSJ (1995). Statistical parametric maps in functional imaging: A general linear approach. *Human Brain Mapping* 2:189–210.

Frith CD, Friston KJ, Herold S, et al. (1995). Regional brain activity in chronic schizophrenic patients during the performance of a verbal fluency task. *Br J Psychiatry* 167:343–349.

Furmark T, Tillfors M, Marteinsdottir I, et al. (2002). Common changes in cerebral blood flow in patients with social phobia treated with citalopram or cognitive-behavioral therapy. *Arch Gen Psychiatry* 59:425–333.

Gilman S, Adams KM, Johnson-Greene D, et al. (1996). Effects of disulfiram on positron emission tomography and neuropsychological studies in severe chronic alcoholism. *Alcohol Clin Exp Res* 20:1456–1461.

Gjedde A, Wong DF (2001). Quantification of neuroreceptors in living human brain. V. Endogenous neurotransmitter inhibition of haloperidol binding in psychosis. *J Cereb Blood Flow Metab* 21:982–994.

Goldberg TE, Berman KF, Mohr E, Weinberger DR (1990). Regional cerebral blood flow and cognitive function in Huntington's disease and schizophrenia. A comparison of patients matched for performance on a prefrontal-type task. *Arch Neurol* 47:418–422.

Guich SM, Buchsbaum MS, Burgwald L, et al. (1989). Effect of attention on frontal distribution of delta activity and cerebral metabolic rate in schizophrenia. *Schizophr Res* 2: 439–448.

Hartvig P, Agren H, Reibring L, et al. (1991). Positron emission tomography of [11C]5-hydroxytryptophan utilization in the brains of healthy volunteers and a patient with major depression. *Acta Radiol Suppl* 376:159–160.

Hashimoto T, Kitamura N, Kajimoto Y, et al. (1993). Differential changes in serotonin 5-HT$_{1A}$ and 5-HT$_2$ receptor binding in patients with chronic schizophrenia. *Psychopharmacology (Berl)* 112:S35–39.

Heckers S, Rauch SL, Goff D, et al. (1998). Impaired recruitment of the hippocampus during conscious recollection in schizophrenia. *Nat Neurosci* 1:318–323.

Ingvar DH, Franzen G (1974). Distribution of cerebral activity in chronic schizophrenia. *Lancet* 2:1484–1486.

Kapur S, Remington G, Zipursky RB, Wilson AA, Houle S (1995). The D$_2$ dopamine receptor occupancy of risperidone and its relationship to extrapyramidal symptoms: a PET study. *Life Sci* 57:L103–107.

Kapur S, Zipursky RB, Remington G, et al. (1998). 5-HT$_2$ and D$_2$ receptor occupancy of olanzapine in schizophrenia: A PET investigation. *Am J Psychiatry* 155:921–928.

Kapur S, Zipursky R, Jones C, Remington G, Houle S (2000). Relationship between dopamine D(2) occupancy, clinical response, and side effects: A double-blind PET study of first-episode schizophrenia. *Am J Psychiatry* 157:514–520.

Lammertsma AA, Hume SP (1996). Simplified reference tissue model for PET receptor studies. *Neuroimage* 4:153–158.

Laruelle M, Abi-Dargham A, van Dyck CH, et al. (1996). Single photon emission computerized tomography imaging of amphetamine-induced dopamine release in drug-free schizophrenic subjects. *Proc Natl Acad Sci USA* 93:9235–9240.

Laruelle M, Abi-Dargham A, van Dyck C, et al. (2000). Dopamine and serotonin transporters in patients with schizophrenia: An imaging study with [(123)I]beta-CIT. *Biol Psychiatry* 47:371–379.

Lewis SW, Ford RA, Syed GM, Reveley AM, Toone BK (1992). A controlled study of 99mTc-HMPAO single-photon emission imaging in chronic schizophrenia. *Psychol Med* 22:27–35.

Lewis R, Kapur S, Jones C, et al. (1999). Serotonin 5-HT$_2$ receptors in schizophrenia: A PET study using [18F]setoperone in neuroleptic-naive patients and normal subjects. *Am J Psychiatry* 156:72–78.

Lowther S, De Paermentier F, Cheetham SC, Crompton MR, Katona CL, Horton RW (1997). 5-HT$_{1A}$ receptor binding sites in post-mortem brain samples from depressed suicides and controls. *J Affect Disord* 42:199–207.

Machlin SR, Harris GJ, Pearlson GD, Hoehn-Saric R, Jeffery P, Camargo EE (1991). Elevated medial-frontal cerebral blood flow in obsessive-compulsive patients: A SPECT study. *Am J Psychiatry* 148:1240–1242.

Malison RT, Price LH, Berman R, et al. (1998). Reduced brain serotonin transporter availability in major depression as measured by [123I]-2 beta-carbomethoxy-3 beta-(4-iodophenyl)tropane and single photon emission computed tomography [see comments]. *Biol Psychiatry* 44: 1090–1098.

Mann JJ, Malone KM, Diehl DJ, Perel J, Cooper TB, Mintun MA (1996). Demonstration in vivo of reduced serotonin responsivity in the brain of untreated depressed patients. *Am J Psychiatry* 153:174–182.

Manoach DS, Gollub RL, Benson ES, et al. (2000). Schizophrenic subjects show aberrant fMRI activation of dorsolateral prefrontal cortex and basal ganglia during working memory performance. *Biol Psychiatry* 48:99–109.

Matsubara S, Arora RC, Meltzer HY (1991). Serotonergic measures in suicide brain: 5-HT$_{1A}$ binding sites in frontal cortex of suicide victims. *J Neural Transm Gen Sect* 85:181–194.

Mayberg HS (1997). Limbic-cortical dysregulation: A proposed model of depression. *J Neuropsychiatry Clin Neurosci* 9:471–481.

McGuire PK, Bench CJ, Frith CD, Marks IM, Frackowiak RS, Dolan RJ (1994). Functional anatomy of obsessive-compulsive phenomena. *Br J Psychiatry* 164:459–468.

Meyer JH, Kennedy SH, Brown GM (1998). No effect of depression on [(15)O]H$_2$O PET response to *d*-fenfluramine. *Am J Psychiatry* 155:1241–1246.

Meyer JH, Gunn RN, Myers R, Grasby PM (1999a). Assessment of spatial normalization of PET ligand images using ligand-specific templates. *Neuroimage* 9:545–553.

Meyer JH, Kapur S, Houle S, et al. (1999b). Prefrontal cortex 5-HT$_2$ receptors in depression: An [18F]setoperone PET imaging study. *Am J Psychiatry* 156:1029–1034.

Meyer JH, Swinson R, Kennedy SH, Houle S, Brown GM (2000). Increased left posterior parietal-temporal cortex activation after D-fenfluramine in women with panic disorder. *Psychiatry Res* 98:133–143.

Meyer JH, Wilson AA, Ginovart N, et al. (2001). Occupancy of serotonin transporters by paroxetine and citalopram during treatment of depression: a [(11)C]DASB PET imaging study. *Am J Psychiatry* 158:1843–1849.

Mintun MA, Raichle ME, Kilbourn MR, Wooten GF, Welch MJ (1984). A quantitative model for the in vivo assessment of drug binding sites with positron emission tomography. *Ann Neurol* 15:217–227.

Mountz JM, Modell JG, Wilson MW, et al. (1989). Positron emission tomographic evaluation of cerebral blood flow during state anxiety in simple phobia. *Arch Gen Psychiatry* 46:501–504.

Ngan ET, Yatham LN, Ruth TJ, Liddle PF (2000). Decreased serotonin 2A receptor densities in neuroleptic-naive patients with schizophrenia: A PET study using [(18)F]setoperone. *Am J Psychiatry* 157:1016–1018.

Nordahl TE, Benkelfat C, Semple WE, Gross M, King AC, Cohen RM (1989). Cerebral glucose metabolic rates in obsessive compulsive disorder. *Neuropsychopharmacology* 2:23–28.

O'Driscoll GA, Benkelfat C, Florencio PS, et al. (1999). Neural correlates of eye tracking deficits in first-degree relatives of schizophrenic patients: A positron emission tomography study. *Arch Gen Psychiatry* 56:1127–1134.

Okubo Y, Suhara T, Suzuki K, et al. (1997). Decreased prefrontal dopamine D_1 receptors in schizophrenia revealed by PET. *Nature* 385:634–636.

Rauch SL, Baxter LR, Jr (1998): *Neuroimaging of OCD and Related Disorders*. CV Mosby: Boston.

Rauch SL, Savage CR, Alpert NM, et al. (1995a). A positron emission tomographic study of simple phobic symptom provocation. *Arch Gen Psychiatry* 52:20–28.

Rauch SL, Savage CR, Brown HD (1995b). A PET investigation of implicit and explicit sequence learning. *Human Brain Mapping* 3:271–286.

Rauch SL, Whalen P, Dougherty D (1998). *Neurobiological Models of Obsessive Compulsive Disorders*. CV Mosby: Boston.

Reiman EM, Raichle ME, Robins E, et al. (1989). Neuroanatomical correlates of a lactate-induced anxiety attack. *Arch Gen Psychiatry* 46:493–500.

Reith J, Benkelfat C, Sherwin A, et al. (1994). Elevated dopa decarboxylase activity in living brain of patients with psychosis. *Proc Natl Acad Sci USA* 91:11651–11654.

Resnick SM, Karp JS, Turetsky B, Gur RE (1993). Comparison of anatomically-defined versus physiologically-based regional localization: Effects on PET-FDG quantitation. *J Nucl Med* 34:2201–2207.

Rubin RT, Villanueva-Meyer J, Ananth J, Trajmar PG, Mena I (1992). Regional xenon 133 cerebral blood flow and cerebral technetium 99m HMPAO uptake in unmedicated patients with obsessive-compulsive disorder and matched normal control subjects. Determination by high-resolution single-photon emission computed tomography. *Arch Gen Psychiatry* 49:695–702.

Rubin P, Holm S, Madsen PL, et al. (1994). Regional cerebral blood flow distribution in newly diagnosed schizophrenia and schizophreniform disorder. *Psychiatry Res* 53:57–75.

Sargent PA, Kjaer KH, Bench CJ, et al. (2000). Brain serotonin 1A receptor binding measured by positron emission tomography with [11C]WAY-100635: Effects of depression and antidepressant treatment. *Arch Gen Psychiatry* 57:174–180.

Schapiro MB, Berman KF, Alexander GE, Weinberger DR, Rapoport SI (1999). Regional cerebral blood flow in Down syndrome adults during the Wisconsin Card Sorting Test: Exploring cognitive activation in the context of poor performance. *Biol Psychiatry* 45:1190–1196.

Schneider F, Weiss U, Kessler C, et al. (1999). Subcortical correlates of differential classical conditioning of aversive emotional reactions in social phobia. *Biol Psychiatry* 45:863–871.

Schwartz JM, Stoessel PW, Baxter LR, Jr, Martin KM, Phelps ME (1996). Systematic changes in cerebral glucose metabolic rate after successful behavior modification treatment of obsessive-compulsive disorder. *Arch Gen Psychiatry* 53:109–113.

Soares JC, Mann JJ (1997). The functional neuroanatomy of mood disorders. *J Psychiatr Res* 31:393–432.

Spence SA, Hirsch SR, Brooks DJ, Grasby PM (1998). Prefrontal cortex activity in people with schizophrenia and control subjects. Evidence from positron emission tomography for remission of "hypofrontality" with recovery from acute schizophrenia. *Br J Psychiatry* 172: 316–323.

Stanley M, Mann JJ (1983). Increased serotonin-2 binding sites in frontal cortex of suicide victims. *Lancet* 1:214–216.

Stein MB, Leslie WD (1996). A brain single photon-emission computed tomography (SPECT) study of generalized social phobia. *Biol Psychiatry* 39:825–828.

Stewart RS, Devous MD, Sr, Rush AJ, Lane L, Bonte FJ (1988). Cerebral blood flow changes during sodium-lactate-induced panic attacks. *Am J Psychiatry* 145:442–449.

Suhara T, Okubo Y, Yasuno F, et al. (2002). Decreased dopamine D_2 receptor binding in the anterior cingulate cortex in schizophrenia. *Arch Gen Psychiatry* 59:25–30.

Swedo SE, Pietrini P, Leonard HL, et al. (1992). Cerebral glucose metabolism in childhood-onset obsessive-compulsive disorder. Revisualization during pharmacotherapy. *Arch Gen Psychiatry* 49:690–694.

Talairach J, Tournoux P (1988). *Coplanar Stereotaxic Atlas of the Human Brain*. Thieme Medical: New York.

Tauscher J, Kapur S (2001). Choosing the right dose of antipsychotics in schizophrenia: Lessons from neuroimaging studies. *CNS Drugs* 15:671–678.

Tauscher J, Kufferle B, Asenbaum S, et al. (1999). in vivo 123I IBZM SPECT imaging of striatal dopamine-2 receptor occupancy in schizophrenic patients treated with olanzapine in comparison to clozapine and haloperidol. *Psychopharmacology (Berl)* 141:175–181.

Tauscher J, Bagby RM, Javanmard M, Christensen BK, Kasper S, Kapur S (2001a). Inverse relationship between serotonin 5-HT_{1A} receptor binding and anxiety: A [(11)C]WAY-100635 PET investigation in healthy volunteers. *Am J Psychiatry* 158:1326–1328.

Tauscher J, Verhoeff NP, Christensen BK, et al. (2001b). Serotonin 5-HT_{1A} receptor binding potential declines with age as measured by [11C]WAY-100635 and PET. *Neuropsychopharmacology* 24:522–530.

Tauscher J, Kufferle B, Asenbaum S, Tauscher-Wisniewski S, Kasper S (2002c). Striatal dopamine-2 receptor occupancy as measured with [(123)I]Iodobenzamide and SPECT predicted the occurrence of EPS in patients treated with atypical antipsychotics and haloperidol. *Psychopharmacology (Berl)* 162:42–49.

Tauscher J, Jones C, Remington G, Zipursky RB, Kapur S (2002a). Significant dissociation of brain and plasma kinetics with antipsychotics. *Mol Psychiatry* 7:317–321.

Tauscher J, Kapur S, Verhoeff NP, et al. (2002b). Brain serotonin 5-HT_{1A} receptor binding in schizophrenia measured by positron emission tomography and [11C]WAY-100635. *Arch Gen Psychiatry* 59:514–520.

Tauscher-Wisniewski S, Kapur S, Tauscher J, et al. (2002). Quetiapine: An effective antipsychotic in first-episode schizophrenia despite only transiently high dopamine-2 receptor blockade. *J Clin Psychiatry* 63:992–997.

Tillfors M, Furmark T, Marteinsdottir I, et al. (2001). Cerebral blood flow in subjects with social phobia during stressful speaking tasks: A PET study. *Am J Psychiatry* 158:1220–1226.

Trichard C, Paillere-Martinot ML, Attar-Levy D, Blin J, Feline A, Martinot JL (1998). No serotonin 5-HT$_{2A}$ receptor density abnormality in the cortex of schizophrenic patients studied with PET. *Schizophr Res* 31:13–17.

Tulving E, Markowitsch HJ, Kapur S, Habib R, Houle S (1994). Novelty encoding networks in the human brain: Positron emission tomography data. *Neuroreport* 5:2525–2528.

Verhoeff NP (1999). Radiotracer imaging of dopaminergic transmission in neuropsychiatric disorders. *Psychopharmacology (Berl)* 147:217–249.

Verhoeff NP, Meyer JH, Kecojevic A, et al. (2000). A voxel-by-voxel analysis of [18F]setoperone PET data shows no substantial serotonin 5-HT$_{2A}$ receptor changes in schizophrenia. *Psychiatry Res* 99:123–135.

Verhoeff NP, Hussey D, Lee M, et al. (2002). Dopamine depletion results in increased neostriatal D(2), but not D(1), receptor binding in humans. *Mol Psychiatry* 7:322–328.

Volkow ND, Wang GJ, Fischman MW, et al. (1997). Relationship between subjective effects of cocaine and dopamine transporter occupancy. *Nature* 386:827–830.

Volkow ND, Wang GJ, Fowler JS, et al. (1999). Prediction of reinforcing responses to psychostimulants in humans by brain dopamine D$_2$ receptor levels. *Am J Psychiatry* 156:1440–1443.

Weinberger DR, Berman KF, Illowsky BP (1988). Physiological dysfunction of dorsolateral prefrontal cortex in schizophrenia. III. A new cohort and evidence for a monoaminergic mechanism. *Arch Gen Psychiatry* 45:609–615.

Wik G, Fredrikson M, Ericson K, Eriksson L, Stone-Elander S, Greitz T (1993). A functional cerebral response to frightening visual stimulation. *Psychiatry Res* 50:15–24.

Willeit M, Praschak-Rieder N, Neumeister A, et al. (2000). [123I]-beta-CIT SPECT imaging shows reduced brain serotonin transporter availability in drug-free depressed patients with seasonal affective disorder. *Biol Psychiatry* 47:482–489.

Wong DF, Wagner HN, Tune LE, et al. (1986). Positron emission tomography reveals elevated D$_2$ dopamine receptors in drug-naive schizophrenics. *Science* 234:1558–1563.

Woods SW, Koster K, Krystal JK, et al. (1988). Yohimbine alters regional cerebral blood flow in panic disorder. *Lancet* 2:678.

Zakzanis KK, Poulin P, Hansen KT, Jolic D (2000). Searching the schizophrenic brain for temporal lobe deficits: A systematic review and meta-analysis. *Psychol Med* 30:491–504.

Part II

CORE PSYCHIATRIC CHALLENGES

Conceptual categories reflect one of the crowning capacities of the human mind—the ability to see, and to create, finer and finer distinctions among the things we perceive. Indeed, one could argue that this is the main function of our cortico-cognitive apparatus. This function allows us to see deeply into the nature of things and also to make distinctions that serve no function other than endlessly detailing minor differences, both real and imaginary.

Modern psychiatric diagnostic categories have long been open to such criticisms. From a pragmatic, utilitarian perspective, the critical issue is at what point do our distinctions provide useful new understanding as opposed to weighing us down with irrelevant details. This has always been the diagnostic dilemma, and even though we have yet to create diagnostics that tell us much about the etiologies of the major psychiatric disorders, there is substantial agreement that distinctions of lasting importance have been envisioned.

There are characteristic disturbances of the mental apparatus that have sufficiently robust class similarities, to offer substantial confidence that we have now recognized, with considerable agreement, some of the major emotional difficulties of mental life. The schizophrenias, the depressions, manias, and varieties of anxiety disorders will remain with us as fundamental concepts for as long as humanity will survive. We know that various symptom clusters often go together, and we can utilize such diagnostics as heuristics for prescription practices. The major adult psychiatric problems will be the focus of discussion in this section (Chapters 7–13). Chapter 14 will be devoted to the many childhood

Textbook of Biological Psychiatry, Edited by Jaak Panksepp
ISBN 0-471-43478-7   Copyright © 2004 John Wiley & Sons, Inc.

syndromes that are now provisionally understood at the genetic level, and Chapter 15 is devoted to aging problems that have to be discussed in terms of the gradual dissolution of the nervous system.

There were many other topics that deserved to be covered, from addictions, to various sexual and other appetite problems, to disturbances of body image. Unfortunately, space did not permit any comprehensive coverage of such issues. Some of those topics are touched upon in various nooks and crannies of this text. However, our larger goal for this middle section of the text was to cover most of the main-line topics of biological psychiatry. In carefully crafted chapters, we cover the major syndromes from basic science and therapeutic perspectives. We must also hope that as the neuroscience revolution continues, and our understanding of the mental apparatus matures, that our capacity to use biological interventions in supportive humanistic frameworks, whereby patients can help create new and positive meanings for their lives, will increase rather than diminish.

7

DEPRESSION: A NEUROPSYCHIATRIC PERSPECTIVE

Helen S. Mayberg

Departments of Psychiatry and Medicine (Neurology) and The Rotman Research Institute, University of Toronto, Toronto, Canada

DIAGNOSTIC AND CLINICAL FEATURES

Clinical Nosology

Feeling "depressed" is a common human experience, occurring most often as a normal response to external events or personal loss. A major depressive episode, on the other hand, whether idiopathic or occurring as a part of a defined neurological disorder is a pathological condition, diagnosed not only by the presence of persistent negative mood or anhedonia but also by associated changes in (1) sleep pattern, (2) body weight, and (3) motor and mental speed, with (4) fatigue or loss of energy, (5) poor concentration and apathy, (6) feelings of worthlessness or inappropriate guilt, and (7) recurrent thoughts of death with suicidal ideations or suicide attempts (APA, 1994).

Symptom Dimensions. While these criteria provide a standardized method for ensuring reliable depression diagnoses, they offer little neurobiological context. Toward

Textbook of Biological Psychiatry, Edited by Jaak Panksepp
ISBN 0-471-43478-7   Copyright © 2004 John Wiley & Sons, Inc.

this goal, correlative studies examining relationships between behavioral features and specific neurochemical or anatomical systems provide an important perspective. For example, behavioral pharmacology studies have linked disturbances in energy, drive, and impulsivity to general dysfunction of the norepinephrine (NE), dopamine (DA), and serotonin or 5-hydroxytryptamine (5-HT) systems, respectively. In this context, core symptoms of depression would appear to involve multiple and interactive neurochemical systems: decreased motivation as a combined NE and DA disturbance (energy + drive), and anxiety and irritability as a change in NE/5-HT (energy + impulsivity). While not all depression symptoms are accommodated by such a biochemical construct, nor are known variations in illness presentation easily explained, this approach has nevertheless, provided an important framework for antidepressant drug development and general treatment strategies (Charney, 1998; Thase et al., 2001).

Alternatively, syndromal features can first be grouped categorically, based on general neurological principles of behavioral localization, with neurochemical dysfunction considered secondarily in context of specific regions and neural pathways (Mesulam, 1985). From this perspective, four behavioral domains appear to capture the principal components of depression: mood, circadian-somatic, cognitive and motor (Fig. 7.1). While this categorical approach is a gross oversimplification, it provides a conceptual framework to examine heterogeneity in clinical presentation as well as targets of antidepressant treatment from an anatomical, physiological, and biochemical perspective. For example, a depressed patient with motor slowness, executive dysfunction, apathy, and inattention is as classic a presentation as one with motor agitation, anxiety, and ruminative guilt. Similarly, typical and atypical patterns of sleep and appetite disturbances (anorexia with insomnia; excessive sleep with overeating) are both common. Despite these apparent contradictions, symptoms can nonetheless be categorized into motor, cognitive, and vegetative/circadian subsystems where mechanisms mediating

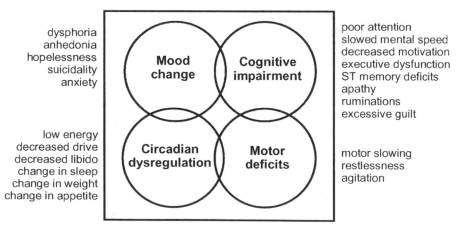

Figure 7.1. Depression: Clinical dimensions. DSM-IV diagnostic criteria are reorganized into four principal behavioral domains—mood, cognitive, circadian, and motor—of relevance to a putative neural systems model of the depression syndrome.

variations within a behavior domain might be more easily evaluated. This approach is in many ways analogous to that taken with hyperkinetic and hypokinetic movement disorders where variable presentations of motor functioning (e.g., dyskinesias versus bradykinesia) have been linked to different functional states of common neural pathways within the extrapyramidal motor system (Lange and Lozano, 1998). Such an approach has not been systematically applied to the study of depression subtypes using current or previous classification schemas despite experimental evidence that endogenomorphic/melancholic and neurotic-reactive/atypical depressions appear to be clinically and possibly etiologically distinct (Klein, 1974). The potential utility of this approach will be developed throughout this chapter.

Differential Diagnosis

While depression is generally thought of as a primary psychiatric disorder, it is also commonly seen with a variety of neurological and medical illnesses (Starkstein and Robinson, 1993; Glassman and Shapiro, 1998; Meyers and Scheibel, 1990). Recognition of these comorbid conditions is critical since different treatment strategies may be necessary for optimal clinical response in different populations. In evaluating a newly depressed patient, drug-induced mood changes, comorbid general medical illnesses, and substance abuse should always be considered, particularly in patients whose symptoms are atypical or of uncharacteristic onset. A related problem is the recognition of depression in patients with certain neurological disorders such as dementia or Parkinson's disease, where the diagnosis of depression may be obscured by neurological findings such as inattention, memory loss, apathy, motor slowing, or bradyphrenia (Marin, 1990; Starkstein et al., 1990a). Similarly, the presence of these cognitive symptoms in the absence of a true mood disturbance must also be considered, to avoid delaying more appropriate diagnostic or treatment interventions.

Epidemiology

Major depressive disorder has an average lifetime prevalence of about 15 percent, with a twofold greater prevalence in women than men. Age of onset is generally after age 20 and before age 50. Onset after age 50 is associated with a higher incidence of structural brain lesions, including strokes and subcortical white-matter changes (Coffey et al., 1993). While single episodes are not rare, depression is generally considered a chronic, relapsing, and remitting illness. While periods of clinical normality are seen throughout the natural course of the disorder, recurrences occur with higher frequently and with greater intensity if episodes are not treated (Frank and Thase, 1999).

Etiological Risk Factors

Family history, female gender, neurotic temperament, gene polymorphisms as well as developmental and early life insults, environmental stress, biochemical abnormalities

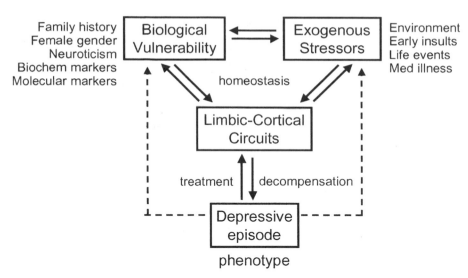

Figure 7.2. Depression pathogenesis. Schematic representation of the ongoing interactions between biological risk factors, exogenous environmental stressors and critical limbic-cortical circuits responsible for maintaining normal responses to ongoing emotionally salient stimuli. Decompensation of this system precipitated by unknown factors leads to a disequilibrium state otherwise know as a major depressive disorder. Adapted & modified from Akiskal & Mckinney (1973).

and certain brain lesions have all been linked to increased depression vulnerability (Fig. 7.2).

Genetics. Converging evidence from adoption, twin, and family studies point to a significant genetic contribution, although specific markers have yet to be identified (Johansson et al., 2001). Meta-analytic studies of twins identify an overall heritability of 37 percent with no effect of a shared environment and a 63 percent effect of the unique environment suggesting complex interactions between genes and environment (Sullivan et al., 2000). Linkage studies, however, have yet to define candidate genes, in contrast to the many linked thus far to bipolar disorder. Association studies examining polymorphisms in genes related to monoamine function, on the other hand, have identified several potential targets. One of the most promising is the insertion/deletion polymorphism in the promoter region of the serotonin transporter 5-HTT (Murphy et al., 2001). While the homozygous short allele version of this gene (s/s *5-HTTLPR*) has been linked to depression, the association is not disease specific; correlations with anxiety, alcoholism, aggression, and suicidality are also described (Lesch et al., 1996). Furthermore, these findings are extremely variable with many published nonreplications, perhaps reflecting complex interaction of this gene with other functional polymorphisms (i.e., monoamine oxidase-A, catechol-*o*-methyltransferase). Notable is a postmortem study demonstrating no correlation of the s/s

5-HTTLPR allele with either a depression diagnosis or the degree of reduced transporter binding in the brainstem and prefrontal cortex of deceased depressed patients (Mann et al., 2000).

Biochemical. Primary dysregulation of specific neurochemicals and neuropeptides is also theorized, supported by abnormalities in platelets, spinal fluid, and postmortem brain samples (Bauer and Frazer, 1994) (see discussion of biochemical biomarkers later in this chapter). Definitive links, however, have not been made to disease pathogenesis, nor are there clear preclinical biochemical markers identifying individuals at risk.

Exogenous Stressors. The influence of environmental factors is equally complex. While no correlations between depression and socioeconomic status, education, cultural background, or specific lifestyle have been demonstrated, stress is a common precipitant (Kendler et al., 2002). Recent studies in both human and animals provide further evidence that early life trauma and abuse, as well as prenatal and perinatal maternal stress may also contribute to an increased vulnerability to develop various types of affective disorders in later life (Heim et al., 2000; Lyons et al., 2000; Sanchez et al., 2001), but causal relationships between stress, disease vulnerability, and precipitation of an acute depressive episode are far from clear. The association of stress-provoking life events with the onset of a major depressive episode does, however, appear to be strongest for the first such episode than for subsequent recurrences. This association continues to hold true over time only for those patients without a positive family history, suggesting a more fundamental brain diathesis in those with genetic risk factors (Kendler et al., 2002). Neuroticism, a personality trait reflecting temperamental hypersensitivity to negative stimuli or the tendency to experience exaggerated negative mood states in situations of emotional instability or dissonance (Costa and McCrae, 1997) appears to be a significant independent risk factor (Roberts and Kendler, 1999). While links between neuroticism and the 5-HTT gene were initially considered quite promising, findings have been difficult to replicate across a number of samples worldwide, possibly due in part to use of different neuroticism scales as well as inconsistent control for gender and family history of depression (Flory et al., 1999; Neumeister et al., 2002). Additional studies are ongoing.

TREATMENT OPTIONS

Clinical Management

An untreated major depressive episode generally lasts 6 to 13 months. Treatment, whether with pharmacological or nonpharmacological strategies (APA, 2000), can significantly reduce this period. Empirically, it is well recognized that patients with a poor or incomplete response to one form of treatment often respond well to another. Others will respond to treatment augmentation or combination strategies using drugs with complementary pharmacological actions, combined drug and cognitive behavioral therapy, or in medication-resistant patients electroconvulsive therapy. Such resistance to treatment is reported to occur in 20 to 40 percent of cases. Newer strategies for more severe patients now also include repetitive transcranial magnetic and vagal nerve stimulation, although these are still considered experimental (George et al., 1999; Rush et al., 2000). More rarely, refractory patients are treated neurosurgically with selective lesions in the cingulum bundle, anterior internal capsule, or subcaudate tract (Cosgrove and Rauch, 1995). For patients with mild to moderate as well as more severe depressions, medication and cognitive therapies have been shown to be equal in their efficacy to treat depressive symptoms (DeRubeis et al., 1999). There are, however, no clinical, neurochemical, or imaging biomarkers that can either identify which patients are likely (or unlikely) to respond to a given intervention or predict which patients are vulnerable to relapse during maintenance treatment (Frank and Thase, 1999). While patient subtyping for the purpose of treatment selection has been attempted, there are at present, no clinical algorithms that can reliably determine the necessary and sufficient treatment of individual patients, as is the case for many medical conditions, such as diabetes and ischemic heart disease.

Postulated Mechanisms

Pharmacological. Preclinical studies of antidepressant drugs (serotonin and norepinephrine reuptake inhibitors, monamine oxidase inhibitors, tricyclics) demonstrate a chain of events including acute aminergic reuptake or degradation enzyme inhibition and more chronic presynaptic autoregulatory desensitization, up and down-regulation of multiple postsynaptic receptor sites, adaptation of intracellular signal transduction pathways, and neurotrophic effects (Bauer and Frazer, 1994; Vaidya and Duman, 2001). Requisite brain regions mediating actual response effects are unknown, although putative primary sites of action in the dorsal raphe, locus ceruleus, hippocampus, and hypothalamus, with secondary changes in frontal cortex are demonstrated (Blier and de Montigny, 1999; Freo et al., 2000).

Somatic. Changes in many of these same systems are seen with electroconvulsive therapy, with an emerging focus on common changes in intracellular signal transduction pathways. Axonal sprouting indicative of neurotrophic effects has also been identified in the dendate gyrus in animal electroconvulsive shock models (Nibuya et al., 1997). Other somatic treatments such as vagal nerve stimulation and repetitive transcranial magnetic stimulation are in early stages of investigation with an emphasis on studies of requisite neural pathways rather than specific biochemical or molecular effects. Preliminary imaging studies suggest modulation of selective limbic-cortical pathways, although results are quite variable (Lomarev et al., 2002; Teneback et al., 1999). Similar mechanisms are postulated for surgical ablation where three distinct lesions, anterior capsulotomy, cingulotomy, and subcaudate tractotomy—all show comparable clinical antidepressant efficacy but disrupt different white matter targets (Cosgrove and Rauch, 1995). Both top-down (corticothalamic, cortico-limbic) and bottom-up (thalamo-cortical, limbic-cortical) mechanisms have been proposed, although the precise limbic, subcortical, and cortical targets or pathways necessary for amelioration of depressive symptoms are not yet characterized. Chronic chemical changes associated with these ablative lesions have not been studied.

Cognitive. Nonpharmacological antidepressant treatments such as cognitive behavioral therapy and interpersonal psychotherapy aim to facilitate changes in depression-relevant cognitions, affective bias, and maladaptive information processing, modifying specific but alternative neural processes to those likely targeted by medication and somatic treatments (Beck et al., 1979; Derubeis et al., 1990). The time course of symptom changes with cognitive behavioral therapy, for example, suggests primary cortical sites of action with top-down neural effects, as improvement in hopelessness and views of self and mood precede changes in vegetative and motivational symptoms—a timeline not seen in patients treated with pharmacotherapy (Rush et al., 1982). Brain correlates of these phenomena are in early stages of investigation (see neuroimaging section below).

SYNDROMAL MARKERS

Circadian Dysregulation

Sleep Disturbances. Abnormal sleep is a core symptom of major depressive disorder, with sleep disruption seen at all stages in the sleep cycle (Benca, 1994). Symptoms include difficulty falling asleep, or staying asleep, as well as early-morning awakening. Hypersomnia is also described. Electroencephalography (EEG) abnormalities in depressed patients include prolonged sleep latency, decreased slow-wave sleep, and reduced rapid eye movement (REM) latency with disturbances in the relative time spent in both REM (increased) and non-REM sleep (decreased slow-wave sleep).

Reduced REM latency probably is the best studied and most reproducible sleep-related EEG finding in depressed patients, and this abnormality is reversed by most antidepressants. Sleep deprivation, particularly if instituted in the second half of the night, has a similar effect, although the rapid, dramatic improvement in depressive symptoms is short lived (Wu et al., 1999). Changes in nocturnal body temperature and attenuation of the normal fluctuations in core body temperature during sleep further suggest a more generalized dysregulation of normal circadian rhythms in patients with depression. To date, however, none of these markers have proven to be specific to depression.

Endocrine Disturbances. Dysregulation of the hypothalamic-pituitary-adrenal (HPA) axis is one of the most reproducible biomarkers of major depressive disorder (reviewed in Holsboer, 2000). Increases in urinary cortisol production, levels of corticotropin-releasing hormone (CRH) in spinal fluid (Nemeroff, 1996), and a general disturbance in the normal pattern of cortisol secretion have been identified (Carroll et al., 1981). Blunted suppression of morning cortisol levels following oral dexamethasone administration, the so-called dexamethasone suppression test (DST), was previously considered a specific marker of depressive illness. It is now recognized as an abnormality in only some subsets of depressed patients, notably psychotic depressives. Also reported is blunted adrenocorticotrophic hormone (ACTH) response to exogenous CRH. More sensitive to detect HPA dysregulation is the combined use of the DST and the CRH stimulation test. In the setting of an abnormal HPA axis test, clinical response appears to best correlate with normalization of the neuroendocrine abnormality. Elevated plasma cortisol following dexamethasone (DEX) predicts a protracted clinical course. The combined DEX/CRH test appears to be a useful predictor of increased relapse risk. Recent reports of alterations in cortisol regulation in women with a history of early life trauma or abuse further suggest that HPA axis dysregulation may be an important marker of vulnerability to various types of affective disorders in later life, paralleling studies in rodents and primates (Heim et al., 2000).

Thyroid markers have also been examined in patients with affective disorder (Nemeroff, 1989). Even with normal levels of circulating thyroid hormone, elevated levels of thyroid antibodies have been demonstrated in patients with depression but without overt thyroid dysfunction. A blunted response of thyroid-stimulating hormone to exogenous thyroid-releasing hormone (thyroid stimulation test) has also been described.

Motor Performance Deficits

Motor and psychomotor deficits in depression involve a range of behaviors including changes in motility, mental activity, and speech (Caligiuri and Ellwanger, 2000; Lemke et al., 1999). Depressed patients often perceive these signs as motor slowness, difficulty translating thought to action, and lack of interest or fatigue. These motor signs appear to be well correlated with both the severity of depression and treatment outcome. Spontaneous motor activity is significantly lower when patients are depressed compared to the euthymic, or nondepressed, state with a progressive increase in activity levels as other clinical features improve.

Cognitive Deficits

Neuropsychological Findings. Cognitive impairments in depressed patients are common (Elliott, 1998). Most often affected are the domains of attention, memory, and psychomotor speed; specific impairments in language, perception, and spatial abilities do not normally occur except as a secondary consequence of poor attention, motivation, or organizational abilities. Deficits are usually of moderate intensity but can become severe in prolonged or intractable depressions, adding to everyday functional disability. Anxiety symptoms may further impair cognitive performance. Age, in general, is an influential factor (Lyness et al., 1994). Patients over 40 generally demonstrate more focal deficits in tests of attention, information-processing speed, and executive function, while those over 50 often show more widespread abnormalities in memory and executive function. First onset of depression over age 70 is associated with an increased risk of subsequent dementia (van Reekum et al., 1999).

Mechanisms. Two mechanisms have been postulated for these cognitive behavioral findings: a generalized "energetic" deficit and domain-specific, localized brain dysfunction. The first hypothesizes reduced cognitive capacity or decreased efficiency in the allocation of cognitive resources to meet specific task demands (Roy-Byrne et al., 1986). Patients are unable to increase the "gain" of the system sufficiently to handle complex cognitive material and also show an inability to sustain cognitive effort across various task types. A differential impairment in effortful versus automatic tasks is demonstrated in depressed subjects when presented with concurrent tasks competing for limited attentional resources. Depressed subjects also perform disproportionately worse on recall of unstructured than structured verbal material, the former presumably requiring more effortful cognitive processing (Watts et al., 1990). Similarly, there is evidence of worsening cognitive performance with increased complexity and degree of encoding required by specific task demands. Decreased task motivation, intrusion of depressive thought content, and secondary effects of fatigue or restlessness are also proposed mechanisms for these generalized cognitive deficits.

In support of more regionally localized, domain-specific cognitive abnormalities is the observation that the pattern of deficits seen in patients with major depression shares many features with those seen in subcortical disorders typified by Parkinson's disease and Huntington's disease. These disorders selectively affect concentration, working memory, psychomotor speed, planning, strategic searching, and flexibility of goal-directed mental activity associated with frontal-striatal pathway dysfunction (Rogers et al., 1987; Starkstein et al., 1990b). Selective deficits on tasks targeting reward and motivation have also been demonstrated. In these paradigms, depressed patients fail to use negative feedback as a motivational stimulus to improve subsequent performance, implicating orbital frontal and ventral striatal pathways previously identified in both primate electrophysiology studies and with focal lesions in humans (Elliott et al., 1997b; Tremblay and Shultz, 1999). State-trait factors contributing to these findings are not yet defined; however, studies of negative cognitive bias suggest persistent deficits even in remitted patients (Segal et al., 1999). Relationships between deficits in verbal memory, cortisol dysregulation, and hippocampal atrophy is another area of active research (McEwen, 2000; Bremner et al., 1998).

Depressive Dementia. *Depressive dementia*, also known as *pseudodementia*, is seen in a subset of depressed patients, generally the elderly (Stoudemire et al., 1989). Estimates of the occurrence of depressive dementia range up to 15 percent in this clinical population. The differentiation of depressive dementia from primary dementia is generally straightforward. Most elderly patients with depression perform better overall on neuropsychologic tests than do age-matched subjects with primary dementia. Elderly depressed patients also show a pattern of cognitive deficits (e.g., poor memory and attention but intact language and visual-spatial abilities) that is different from that seen in subjects with dementia, as well as a number of clinical features that are specific to depression (e.g., sadness, poor self-esteem, somatic symptoms) (Jones et al., 1992). Nevertheless, occasionally a clinician may encounter a depressed patient with cognitive decline that is difficult to distinguish from early dementia. In these cases, a trial of antidepressant medication is often warranted. The general finding is a return to normal levels of cognitive function in patients with depression, in contrast to those with dementia, after an adequate course of treatment. However, more recent studies more strongly suggest that comorbid depression and cognitive impairment may be an early sign of Alzheimer's disease (van Reekum et al., 1999).

Cognitive Bias. While not a cognitive *deficit* in the classical sense, exaggerated sensitivity to negative emotional stimuli, or neuroticism, also influences the cognitive processing of emotional stimuli. Cognitive models of depression in fact focus on the development of maladaptive and highly reinforced learned associations that produce depressive ruminations, negative self-schemas, and impaired decision making in patients with vulnerable temperaments of this type (Beck et al., 1979). Neuroticism, as measured by the NEO personality inventory has been shown to correlate with measures of depression severity (Bagby et al., 1995). More significant, neuroticism scores remain elevated and stable above normative values even in the clinically remitted state. This neuroticism "trait," has long been postulated to increase vulnerability to a major depressive episode, a hypothesis now supported by large-scale multivariate analyses of depressed women (Fanous et al., 2002).

Consistent with these observations, depressed patients in general show better recall for negative words when presented with a list of words varying in emotional tone and are faster than nondepressed individuals at identifying negative adjectives as self-descriptive (Murphy et al., 1999). Depressed patients also produce higher probability estimates for future negative events and make more pessimistic predictions for themselves and others. Like depressed patients, normal individuals scoring high on neuroticism also respond faster to and recall more negative cue words, make more pessimistic predictions for self and others, and demonstrate a susceptibility to retrieving more negative personal memories. Activity in ventral medial frontal cortex, an area previously implicated in negative feedback and response performance in patients (Elliott et al., 1997b), is also highly correlated with negative temperament in healthy volunteers (Keightley et al., 2002; Zald et al., 2002), suggesting a potential brain biomarker for future illness vulnerability.

BIOCHEMICAL MARKERS

No single neurotransmitter abnormality has been identified that fully explains the pathophysiology of the depressive disorders or the associated constellation of mood, motor, cognitive, and somatic symptoms. Changes in norepinephrine, serotonin, dopamine, acetylcholine, opiates, and gamma-aminobutyric acid (Bauer and Frazer, 1994) have all been reported with new studies additionally focused on dysregulation of second messenger systems, gene transcription, neurotrophic factors, and cell turnover (Vaidya and Duman, 2001).

Serotonin and Norepinephrine. Disturbances in the serotonergic 5-HT and noradrenergic (NE) systems have dominated the neurochemical literature on depression for more than 30 years, based in large part on the consistent observations that most antidepressant drugs affect synaptic concentrations of these two transmitters via either presynaptic uptake transporters [tricyclics, selective serotonin, or noradrenergic uptake inhibitors, i.e., selective serotonium reuptake inhibitors (SSRIs), noradrenergic reuptake inhibitor (NRIs)] or degradation enzymes [monoamine oxidase inhibitors (MAOIs)] (Schildkraut, 1965; Charney, 1998; Ressler and Nemeroff, 1999). Consistent with these mechanisms, serotonergic and noradrenergic metabolite abnormalities have been identified in spinal fluid, blood, and urine in subsets of depressed patients. Decreased cerebrospinal fluid (CSF), 5-hydroxyindoleacetic acid (5-HIAA), and urinary 3-methoxy-4hydroxy-phenylglycol (MHPG) are the best replicated findings, as is the decrease of platelet transporter binding sites. The relationship of these measures to changes in brain stem nuclei or their cortical projections are unknown. In further support of a biogenic amine etiology, dietary restriction of tryptophan, resulting in an acute decrease in brain serotonin (the tryptophan depletion challenge), and catecholamines (the alpha-methyl-para-tyrosine challenge) are selectively associated with an abrupt transient relapse in remitted depressed patients (Moreno et al., 2000).

Postmortem studies of deceased depressed patients and suicide victims report changes in a number of additional serotonin and norepinephrine markers including regional transporter binding, postsynaptic receptor density, and second messenger and transcription proteins (Arango et al., 1997; Klimek et al., 1997). Recent work examining the serotonin transporter 5-HTT has identified brainstem and widespread ventral prefrontal binding decreases with prominent involvement of the rostral and subgenual segments of the anterior cingulate, overlapping functional imaging findings, discussed below. Changes associated with suicide without depression demonstrate more restricted orbital frontal decreases consistent with studies of impulsivity with acquired orbital frontal lesions. Correlative relationships between prefrontal 5-HTT binding and dorsal raphe 5-HT$_{1A}$ receptor messenger ribonucleic acid (mRNA) suggest ongoing compensatory modulation of serotonergic neurotransmission via these cortical binding sites (targets of many common antidepressant drugs) (Arango et al., 2001), a conclusion further supported by known afferent projections from subgenual cingulate to the dorsal raphe (Freedman et al., 2000).

Dopamine. While a primary dopaminergic mechanism for depression is generally considered unlikely, a role for dopamine in some aspects of the depressive syndrome is supported by several experimental observations (Rogers et al., 1987; Zacharko and Anisman, 1991). The mood and drive-enhancing properties and clinical utility of methylphenidate in treating some depressed patients is well documented, although dopaminergic stimulation alone does not generally alleviate all depressive symptoms. Dopaminergic projections from the ventral tegmental area (VTA) show regional specificity for the orbital/ventral prefrontal cortex, striatum, and anterior cingulate, overlapping areas of high 5-HTT transporter density. These are also areas repeatedly identified in functional imaging studies of primary and secondary depression (Mayberg, 1994). Degeneration of neurons or their projections from the ventral tegmental area, however, has not been demonstrated in patients with primary unipolar depression.

Central Corticosteroid Receptors. Consistent with evidence of HPA axis dysregulation, there is also a growing interest in the role of the central corticosteroid receptor (CR) in the pathogenesis of major depression (Nemeroff, 1996; Holsboer, 2000). Increased CRH has been measured in the CSF of actively depressed patients. Also described in postmortem samples are increases in the number of CRH-secreting neurons in the hypothalamus and decreased CRH-binding sites in frontal cortex, presumably a compensatory response to increased CRH secretion. These brain findings are complemented by neuroendocrine function tests described previously and supported by a number of rodent and primate studies of psychological stress (Lopez et al., 1999; Sanchez et al., 2001). Central CRH-1 and CRH-2 receptors are the focus of ongoing pharmacological studies, with CRH-1 antagonists seen as potential novel antidepressants or antianxiety medications.

ANIMAL MODELS

A variety of animal models of depression have been proposed (Willner and Mitchell, 2002). Many focus on reproducing the behavioral, biochemical, and physiological changes seen in depressed patients using various forms of chronic stress. Models include maternal separation, social subordination, forced swim, learned helplessness and exogenous glucocorticoids, among others (Harlow and Suomi, 1974; McEwen, 2000; Panksepp, 1998; Petty et al., 1997; Sanchez et al., 2001; Shively et al., 1997). Behavioral observations of animals exposed to these conditions generally confirm the face validity of such models with changes in posture and motor activity, disinterest in previously rewarding stimuli, and alterations in basic drives and circadian behaviors (feeding, mating behaviors, sleep, endocrine) all readily apparent. Despite clear chronic behavioral changes, there are no good transient or short-term stimulus-response models to reliably study parallels of disease vulnerability seen in humans. Rodent strains with particular "depressive" traits and genetic knockouts are a growing area of research (Overstreet, 1993), as are stress-induced neural apoptosis models where decreased hippocampal neurogenesis may provide plausible mechanisms mediating the hippocampal atrophy described in subsets of depressed humans (McEwen, 2000) (see imaging section below).

REGIONAL BRAIN MARKERS

Brain Localization

Historical Perspective. Modern theories regarding the neural localization of depressive illness date back to the 1930s, around the time of the first descriptions of functional neurosurgery for refractory melancholia (reviewed in Fulton, 1951). Kleist's early observations of mood and emotional sensations following direct stimulation of the ventral frontal lobes (Brodmann areas 47 and 11) focused attention on paralimbic brain regions. Building on early studies by Broca, Papez, Fulton, and MacLean, among others, elaborated many of the anatomical details of these cytoarchitecturally primitive regions of cortex, as well as adjacent limbic structures including the cingulate, amygdala, hippocampus, and hypothalamus; thus providing the first anatomical template for "emotions". Comparative cytoarchitectural, connectivity, and neurochemical studies have since delineated reciprocal pathways linking various "limbic" structures with widely distributed brainstem, striatal, paralimbic, and neocortical sites (Carmichael and Price, 1996; Haber et al., 2000; Vogt and Pandya, 1987; among others). Associations of specific regions and pathways with various aspects of motivational, affective, and emotional behaviors in animals have also been described (Barbas, 1995; Panksepp, 1998; Rolls, 2000; Tremblay and Schultz, 1999). Additional clinical observations in depressed patients have similarly identified a prominent role for the frontal and temporal lobes and the striatum in regulation of mood and emotions (Starkstein and Robinson, 1993), complemented by parallel experiments of specific affective behaviors mapped in healthy volunteers. Together these converging findings suggest that depression is likely best characterized as a systems-level disorder, affecting discrete but functionally linked pathways involving specific cortical, subcortical, and limbic sites and their associated neurotransmitter and peptide mediators (Mayberg, 1997).

Structural Abnormalities

Neurological Depressions. Lesion deficit correlation studies demonstrate that certain disorders are more likely to be associated with a major depression than others: (a) discrete brain lesions, as seen with trauma, surgery, stroke, tumors, and certain types of epilepsy; (b) neurodegenerative diseases with regionally confined pathologies such as Parkinson's, Huntington's, and Alzheimer's diseases; (c) disorders affecting diffuse or multiple random locations such as multiple sclerosis; and (d) system illness with known central nervous system effects such as thyroid disease, cancer, and acquired immunodeficiency syndrome (AIDS) (Table 7.1).

Computed tomography (CT) and magnetic resonance imagining (MRI) studies in stroke patients have demonstrated a high association of mood changes with infarctions of the frontal lobe and basal ganglia, particularly those occurring in close proximity to the frontal pole or involving the caudate nucleus (Robinson et al., 1984; Starkstein et al., 1987). Studies of patients with head trauma or brain tumors or who have undergone neurosurgery (Grafman et al., 1986) further suggest that dorsolateral rather than ventral-frontal lesions are more commonly associated with depression and depressive-like symptoms such as apathy and psychomotor slowing. As might be expected, more precise localization of "depression-specific regions" is hampered by the heterogeneity of these types of lesions.

These limitations shifted focus to those diseases in which the neurochemical or neurodegenerative changes are reasonably well localized, as in many of the basal ganglia disorders. Notable is the high association of depression with Parkinson's disease (Mayberg and Solomon, 1995), Huntington's disease (Folstein et al., 1983), and others. These observations directly complement the findings described in studies of discrete brain lesions and further suggest the potential importance of functional circuits linking these regions (Alexander et al., 1990; Haber, 2000).

T A B L E 7.1. Disorders Associated with Depressive Symptoms

Primary Psychiatric	Primary Neurological	Systemic Disorders
Mood/anxiety	Focal lesions	Endocrine
Major depressive disorder	Stroke/tumor	Hypothyroidism,
Bipolar disorder	Trauma/surgical ablation	hyperthyroidism
Schizoaffective disorder	Complex partial seizures	Adrenal disease
Dysthymia/cyclothymia	Multiple sclerosis	(Cushing's, Addison's)
Panic disorder	Degenerative diseases	Parathyroid disorders
Generalized anxiety	Parkinson's disease	Premenstrual,
Posttraumatic stress	Huntington's disease	perimenopausal,
disorder	Diffuse Lewy body disease	postpartum
Obsessive-compulsive	Progressive supranuclear	Metabolic
disorder	palsy	Uremia
Eating disorders	Fahr's disease, Wilson's	Porphyria
Anorexia nervosa	disease	Vitamin deficiencies
Bulimia nervosa	Alzheimer's disease	Inflammatory/infectious
Substance abuse	Frontal-temporal dementia	Systemic lupus
Alcohol and	Pick's disease	erythematosus
sedative/hypnotics	Other CNS	Sjogren's syndrome
Cocaine, amphetamines,	Neurosyphilis	Tuberculosis,
other stimulants	AIDS (limbic involvement)	mononucleosis
	Carbon monoxide exposure	AIDS (also medication
	Paraneoplastic (limbic	side effects)
	encephalitis)	Other
	Migraine, chronic pain	Cancer
		Ischemic heart disease
		Medication side effects
		Chronic fatigue syndrome
		Obstructive sleep apnea

Studies of systemic disorders, such as lupus erythematosus, Sjogren's syndrome, thyroid and adrenal disease, AIDS, and cancer, describe mood symptoms in subsets of patients. As with the more diffuse neurodegenerative diseases, such as Alzheimer's disease (Cummings and Victoroff, 1990), a classic lesion-deficit approach is generally difficult because consistent focal abnormalities are uncommon. Studies of plaque loci in patients with multiple sclerosis suggest an association of depression with lesions in the temporal lobes, although it is not yet clear whether this effect is lateralized (Honer et al., 1987).

Despite these apparent patterns, certain paradoxes remain. First, despite comparable underlying pathologies, not all patients with a given disorder develop depressive symptoms. For instance, in Parkinson's disease and Huntington's disease, the reported rate is about 50 percent. As postulated for primary affective disorders, mechanisms for this discordance focus on genetic and temperament markers. In Huntington's disease, a genetic disorder by definition, is associated with consistent affective symptoms in some but not all families, suggesting a more complex interaction at the molecular level (Folstein et al., 1983). Furthermore, in this population, depression and mania are both recognized. Unlike stroke, no localizing or regional differences can be offered to explain this phenomenon. In general, there is also no consensus as to whether the left or the right hemisphere is dominant in the expression of depressive symptoms in any neurological disorder. Reports of patients with traumatic frontal lobe injury indicate a high correlation between affective disturbances and right-hemisphere pathology (Grafman et al., 1986). Secondary mania, although rare, is most consistently seen with right-sided basal frontal-temporal or subcortical damage (Starkstein et al., 1990c). On the other hand, students of stroke patients suggest that left-sided lesions of both the frontal cortex and the basal ganglia are more likely to result in depressive symptoms than are right-sided lesions, where displays of euphoria or indifference predominate (Robinson et al., 1984). There is, however, considerable debate on this issue (Carson et al., 2000). Similar contradictions are seen in studies of patients with temporal lobe epilepsy where an association between affective symptoms (both mania and depression) and left, right, and nonlateralized foci have been described (Altshuler et al., 1990). Anatomic studies have yet to define the critical sites within the temporal lobe most closely associated with mood changes.

Lastly, and in some ways counterintuitive, is the absence of reported depressive symptoms with primary injury to limbic structures such as the amygdala, hippocampus, and hypothalamus, despite their fundamental involvement in critical aspects of motivational and emotional processes. This apparent contradiction would suggest that these key regions have a much more complex organizational structure than that revealed by classic lesion-deficit correlation methods.

Primary Unipolar Depression. Macroscopic anatomical findings in patients with primary affective disorders have been less consistent than those of depressed patients with neurological disorders (reviewed in Harrison, 2002; Soars and Mann, 1997). Brain anatomy is grossly normal, and focal neocortical abnormalities have not been identified using standard structural neuroimaging methods. Focal volume loss has been described using MRI in subgenual medial frontal cortex (Drevets et al., 1997). Also described are small hippocampi in patients with recurrent major depression (Sheline et al., 1999), with a postulated mechanism of glucocorticoid neurotoxicity, consistent with both animal models and studies of patients with posttraumatic stress disorder (Bremner and Narayan, 1998). Nonspecific changes in ventricular size, and T_2-weighted MRI changes in subcortical gray and periventricular white matter have also been reported in some patient subgroups, most notably, elderly depressed patients (Coffey et al., 1993). The parallels, if any, of these observations with the regional abnormalities described in lesion and neurological patients with depression are unclear. Further studies of new-onset patients, or preclinical at-risk subjects, are needed to clarify whether these changes reflect disease pathophysiology or are the consequence of chronic illness or treatment.

Neuropathology Studies. In vivo structural abnormalities identified using MRI, have provided a foundation for the systematic examination of histological and cellular correlates in postmortem brain (reviewed in Harrison, 2002; Rajkowska, 2000). To this end, morphometric and immunocytochemical changes in neurons and glia as well as synaptic and dendritic markers have been reported, with studies targeting some but not all subdivisions of the frontal cortex, anterior cingulate, hippocampus, and brainstem. A loss of glia is the best replicated and most robust finding, affecting orbital frontal (ventral prefrontal) and prefrontal cortex (BA9), as well as the cingulate (subgenual, pregenual). Glial abnormalities are seen in both bipolar and unipolar disorder, and are most consistent in patients with a positive family history of mood disorder. Neuronal abnormalities are less consistently identified and generally involve a decrease in size, not number. Synaptic terminal and dendritic abnormalities, in support of aberrant cellular plasticity or impaired neurodevelopment, are also reported but appear to be a more selective marker of bipolar disorder. Despite repeated demonstration of hippocampal atrophy on MRI, there are no consistent cellular correlates to support the hypothesis of stress-induced hippocampal vulnerability. Neither are there clear correlates of the stress-induced apoptosis and decreased hippocampal neurogenesis demonstrated in animal stress models.

Functional Abnormalities

Functional imaging further complements structural imaging findings in that the consequences of lesions for global and regional brain function in putative functional neurocircuits can also be assessed. In addition, one can test how similar mood symptoms occur with anatomically or neurochemically distinct disease states as well as why comparable lesions do not always result in comparable behavioral phenomena. Specific cohorts such as healthy family members or sib-pairs, presence or absence of specific risk factors (high and low neuroticism, presence and absence of specific genetic polymorphisms, family history, early abuse, etc.) can be systematically targeted. Parallel studies of primary affective disorder and patients with neurological depressions similarly provide complementary perspectives.

Brain Imaging. Positron emission tomography (PET) and single-photon emission tomography (SPECT) studies of both primary depression (unipolar, bipolar) and depression associated with specific neurological conditions (focal lesions, degenerative diseases, epilepsy, multiple sclerosis) identify many common regional abnormalities (reviewed in Mayberg, 1994; Ketter et al., 1996). For example, in depressed patients with one of three prototypical basal ganglia disorders—Parkinson's disease, Huntington's disease, and left caudate stroke—resting-state paralimbic hypometabolism (ventral prefrontal cortex, anterior cingulate, anterior temporal cortex) was found to differentiate depressed from nondepressed patients within each group, as well as depressed from nondepressed patients, independent of disease etiology (Mayberg, 1994). These regional findings, replicated in other neurological disorders (Bromfield et al., 1992; Hirono et al., 1998; Starkstein et al., 1990c), suggests involvement of critical common pathways for the expression of depression in distinct neurological populations, findings of potential relevance to studies of primary mood disorders (Fig. 7.3).

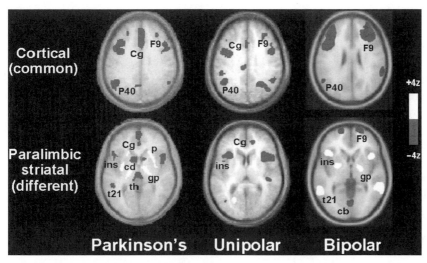

Figure 7.3. Metabolic profiles in depression of varying etiologies. Metabolic abnormalities identified with fluorodeoxyglucose (FDG) PET scanning in patients with unipolar depression (UP),
bipolar depression (BP), and depression with Parkinson's disease (PD) are illustrated. The top
row demonstrates a common pattern of symmetric dorsal and ventral prefrontal (F9), inferior
parietal (P40), and anterior cingulate (Cg) hypometabolism across the three patient groups.
The bottom row demonstrates disease-specific abnormalities, most notably in subcortical and
limbic structures such as the anterior insula and striatum. Striatal hypermetabolism, common
to BP and PD may contribute to mood lability, characteristic of BP but also seen in many PD
patients including acute changes in mood state with deep-brain stimulation in this region.
Abbreviations. F = frontal, cd = caudate, gp = globus pallidus, th = thalamus, ins = anterior
insula, T = temporal, P = parietal, Cg = anterior cingulate; numbers are Brodmann designations metabolic increases decreases. (Data from Mayberg et al., 1997, and Stefurak et al., 2001b).
See ftp site for color image.

Studies of blood flow and glucose metabolism in patients with primary depression also report frontal abnormalities, in general agreement with the pattern seen in
neurological depressions (Baxter et al., 1989; others reviewed in Ketter et al., 1996).
The most robust and consistent finding is decreased frontal lobe function, although
normal frontal as well as hyperfrontal activity has also been reported (Drevets et al.,
1992). Localization within the frontal lobe includes dorsolateral and ventral lateral prefrontal cortex (Brodmann areas 9, 46, 10, 47), as well as orbital frontal cortices (BA
10, 11). Findings are generally bilateral, although asymmetries are described. Cingulate
changes are also commonly seen and consistently involve anterior dorsal sectors (Ebert
and Ebmeier 1996; Mayberg et al., 1997). Other limbic-paralimbic (amygdala, anterior temporal, insula) and subcortical (basal ganglia, thalamus) abnormalities have
also been identified, but the findings are more variable (reviewed in Mayberg, 1997).
Use of different analytic strategies (voxel-wise versus regions of interest) has been
considered an important factor in explaining these apparent inconsistencies. Differences

among patient subgroups (familial versus sporatic; bipolar versus unipolar, primary versus neurological), as well as heterogeneous expression of clinical symptoms is also thought to significantly contribute to this variance, but there is not yet a consensus.

Biochemical Imaging. Several neurochemical markers have also been examined in depressed patients using imaging, but findings are quite variable. Decreases in serotonin transporter 5-HTT binding has been reported in brainstem (Malison et al., 1998) but not in any of the other regions identified in post-mortem studies of depressed suicides, such as ventral prefrontal cortex or anterior cingulate. $5\text{-}HT_{1A}$ and $5\text{-}HT_{2A}$ receptor densities have also been examined but with inconsistent findings in the drug-free state (Sargent et al., 2000; Meyer et al., 1999). Relationships between receptor and transporter markers or between neurochemical and regional metabolic changes have not yet been systematically explored, as has been a growing trend in postmortem examinations. Studies of other markers of interest are limited by the lack of suitable radioligands.

Clinical Correlates. The best replicated behavioral correlate of a resting-state abnormality in depression is that of an inverse relationship between prefrontal activity and depression severity (reviewed by Ketter et al., 1996). Prefrontal activity has also been linked to psychomotor speed and executive functions (Bench et al., 1993), parietal and parahippocampal activity with anxiety (Osuch et al., 2000), medial frontal and cingulate activity with cognitive performance (Bench et al., 1993), and that of amygdala with cortisol status (Drevets et al., 2002). A more complex ventral-dorsal segregation of frontal lobe functions has also been described with anxiety/tension positively correlated with ventral prefrontal activity and psychomotor and cognitive slowing negatively correlated with dorsolateral activity (Brody et al., 2001a). The prefrontal cortex overactivity seen in patients with a more ruminative/anxious clinical presentation is consistent with findings described in primary anxiety and obsessional disorders, memory-evoked anxiety and fear in healthy subjects, and even normal variations in individual response to the testing environment due to novelty or state anxiety (Liotti et al., 2000).

Correlative Mapping Studies. Direct mapping of specific behavioral features is an alternative approach, allowing head-to-head comparisons of patients and healthy controls (Dolan et al., 1993). With this type of design, one can both quantify the neural correlates of the performance decrement as well as identify potential disease-specific sites of task reorganization. These types of studies can be performed with any of the available functional methods, including PET, functional MRI (fMRI), and event related potentials (ERP). Using this strategy, for example, George et al. (1997) demonstrated blunting of an expected left anterior cingulate blood flow increase during performance of a Stroop task. A shift to the left dorsolateral prefrontal cortex, a region not normally recruited for this task in healthy subjects, was also observed. Elliot et al. (1997a), using the Tower of London test, described similar attenuation of an expected blood flow increase in dorsolateral prefrontal cortex and failure to activate anterior cingulate and caudate regions recruited in controls.

Treatment Studies

Regional Effects. Studies of regional metabolism and blood flow with recovery from a major depressive episode consistently report normalization of many regional abnormalities identified in the pretreatment state. Changes in cortical (prefrontal, parietal), limbic-paralimbic (cingulate, amygdala, insula), and subcortical (caudate/pallidum, thalamus, brainstem) areas have been described following various treatments including medication, psychotherapy, sleep deprivation, electroconvulsive therapy (ECT), repetitive transcranial magnetic stimulation (rTMS), and ablative surgery (Bench et al., 1995; Buchsbaum et al., 1997, Brody et al., 2001b; Nobler et al., 2001; Tenenback et al., 1999). Normalization of frontal hypometabolism is the best replicated finding, seen with all classes of medication, although normalization of frontal hypermetabolism is also reported. Changes in limbic-paralimbic and subcortical regions are also seen, often involving changes in previously "normal" functioning regions (Fig. 7.4a and b). Requisite changes mediating clinical recovery have not been determined, nor have clear distinctions been made between different modes of treatment.

Receptor Changes with Treatment. Treatment studies using SSRIs or tricyclic antidepressants report down-regulation of 5-HT$_{2A}$ receptors consistent with pharmacological studies in animals (Yatham et al., 1999; Meyer et al., 2001). Like the abnormalities identified in the pretreated depressed state, the reported changes are generally global rather than focal. 5-HT$_{1A}$ receptors show no change with treatment, suggesting the pretreatment abnormalities may be a compensatory rather than a primary etiological finding (Sargent et al., 2000), as postulated in recent postmortem studies of these markers. While there are no direct comparisons of SSRI and NRI action on serotonin binding, the areas with the greatest magnitude change with desipramine treatment are medial frontal regions—overlapping sites of the most robust metabolic decreases with more selective SSRIs such as fluoxetine and areas of highest concentration of the serotonin transporter. While striatal D$_2$-dopamine changes have been reported, extrastriatal binding is unreliable with currently available tracers.

Time Course of Brain Changes. Examination of the time course of changes and differences between responders and nonresponders to a given treatment provides additional localizing clues (Mayberg et al., 2000). Responders and nonresponders to 6 weeks of fluoxetine, for example, show similar regional metabolic changes after 1 week of treatment (brainstem, hippocampus increases; posterior cingulate, striatal, thalamic decreases), which is concordant with absence of clinical change in both groups. In contrast, the 6-week metabolic change pattern discriminates them, with clinical improvement uniquely associated with limbic-paralimbic and striatal decreases (subgenual cingulate, hippocampus, pallidum, insula) and brainstem and dorsal cortical increases (prefrontal, anterior cingulate, posterior cingulate, parietal). Failed response to fluoxetine was associated with a persistent 1-week pattern (hippocampal increases; striatal, posterior cingulate decreases) and absence of either subgenual cingulate or prefrontal changes.

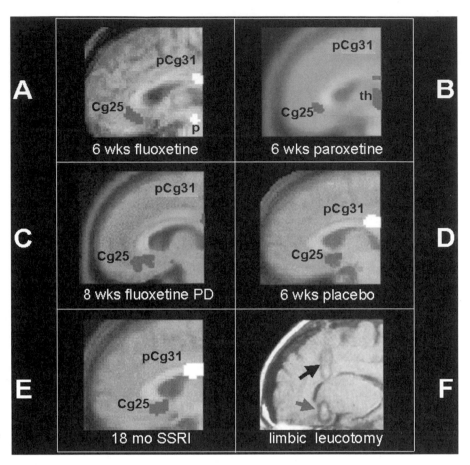

Figure 7.4. Common changes in subgenual cingulate (Cg25) with different treatments. Decreases in subgenual cingulate, relative to patient baseline pretreatment scans are seen with clinical response to both 6 weeks of fluoxetine in unipolar depressed (A) and Parkinson's depressed patients (C). A similar pattern is seen with response to 6 weeks of paroxetine (B) and placebo (D). Persistence of this pattern is seen in a separate group of patients in full remission on maintenance medication (E). Limbic leucotomy (F), a surgical procedure that combines subcaudate tractotomy (lower arrow) and cingulotomy (upper arrow), disrupts both afferent and efferent subgenual cingulate pathways as well as intercingulate connections, demonstrating additional anatomical concordance. Abbreviations: fluox, fluoxetine; SSRI, selective serotonin reuptake inhibitor. (Data from Cosgrove and Rauch, 1995; Kennedy et al., 2001; Liotti et al., 2002; Mayberg et al., 2000, 2002; Stefurak et al., 2001b). See ftp site for color image.

This same combination of reciprocal dorsal cortical and ventral limbic changes has also been demonstrated with response to paroxetine (Kennedy et al., 2001), in Parkinson's depression treated with fluoxetine (Stefurak et al., 2001b), as well as with placebo responders treated as such as part of the fluoxetine study just described (Mayberg et al.,

2002) (Fig. 7.4*b*–*d*). It is, however, the unique subcortical changes with active medication (brainstem, hippocampal, caudate), which are not seen with placebo-treated responders, that provides the best initial support for the hypothesis that both treatment-specific and response-specific effects can be identified.

Since improvement in depressive symptoms best correlates with increases in the activity of prefrontal cortex (F9/46) and decreases in subgenual cingulate (Cg25), it is additionally postulated that these changes may be most critical for illness remission. This hypothesis is further refined by preliminary evidence of persistent Cg25 hypometabolism and posterior cingulate hypermetabolism in a new group of fully recovered patients on maintenance SSRI treatment (Liotti et al., 2002) (Fig. 7.4*e*). These findings might suggest that persistent limbic changes in remitted patients are the adaptive homeostatic response necessary to maintain a recovered state. In this context, it is interesting to note that the limbic leukotomy procedure performed to treat severe refractory depression disrupts afferent and efferent subgenual cingulate pathways (subcaudate tractotomy component, Fig. 7.4*f*, bottom arrow), as well as intercingulate connections (cingulotomy component, top arrow) (Haber et al., 2000; Vogt and Pandya, 1987).

Despite this convergence of findings, a further demonstration of comparable changes with a formal nonpharmacological therapy is needed. At issue is whether remission mediated by cognitive or psychotherapies involve similar or unique brain changes as compared to those seen with medication. The few published studies thus far show no common patterns. A new preliminary analysis comparing remission achieved through cognitive behavioral therapy (CBT) on the one hand and through paroxetine on the other, studied in two separate outpatient cohorts revealing some interesting differences (Goldapple et al., 2002; Kennedy et al., 2001). Remission with paroxetine treatment, as seen with fluoxetine, was associated with metabolic increases in prefrontal cortex and decreases in subgenual cingulate and hippocampus. In contrast, CBT response was associated with a completely different set of changes: lateral prefrontal decreases, similar to those seen with interpersonal psychotherapy (Brody et al., 2001b), as well as medial frontal decreases and hippocampal and rostral cingulate increases, not previously described. These CBT-specific changes are particularly interesting given current cognitive models (Beck et al., 1979; Segal et al., 1999) and the known roles of rostral cingulate and hippocampus in emotional monitoring and memory and lateral and medial frontal cortices in perception, action, and self-reference (reviewed in Grady, 1999).

The differences in change effects between the two interventions thus provide new support for treatment-specific effects rather than a common response-effect pattern, as posited by previous studies. However, the similarity in change pattern seen with fluoxetine and paroxetine despite differences in baseline frontal activity further suggests a more complex interaction between pretreatment abnormalities, attempted compensatory responses, and actual treatment effects. Testing of this hypothesis likely requires the use of a multivariate statistical approach, where relationships between independent and dependent variables can be simultaneously observed (McIntosh, 1999).

Prognostic Markers

Response Predictors. In light of the described differences between responders and nonresponders with treatment, an obvious related question is whether baseline findings predict eventual treatment outcomes. Several studies have found that pretreatment metabolic activity in the rostral (pregenual) cingulate uniquely distinguishes medication responders from nonresponders (Mayberg et al., 1997), a pattern replicated in Parkinson's disease and other unipolar depressed cohorts (Kennedy et al., 2001; Stefurak et al., 2001b). A similar finding also predicts good response to one night of sleep deprivation (Wu et al., 1999). While additional studies are needed, these data suggest physiological differences among patient subgroups that may be critical to understanding brain plasticity and adaptation to illness, including propensity to respond to treatment. Additional evidence of persistent hypermetabolism in patients in full remission on maintenance SSRI treatment for more than a year further suggests a critical compensatory or adaptive role for rostral cingulate in facilitating and maintaining long-term clinical responses (Liotti et al., 2002).

Relapse Risk and Illness Vulnerability. A further goal concerns identification of patients at risk for illness relapse as well as those vulnerable to illness onset. Challenge or stress tests might be seen as a possible avenue toward this goal. As such, mood induction experiments initially conducted in healthy subjects to define brain regions mediating modulation of acute changes in mood state relevant to depressive dysphoria have been similarly performed in acutely depressed and remitted depressed subjects, and have identified disease-specific modifications of these pathways (Liotti et al., 2002). Specifically, with acute sad mood induction in healthy volunteers, ventral and subgenual cingulate blood flow increases are consistently described (Damasio et al., 2000; Mayberg et al., 1999). These cingulate increases are not found in depressed patients comparably provoked, where unique dorsal cingulate increases and medial and orbital frontal decreases are instead seen. Similar findings in both euthymic-remitted and acutely depressed patients suggest that these differences may be depression trait markers. In addition, the pattern seen with memory-provoked sadness shows striking similarities to resting state studies of refractory unipolar and neurologically depressed patients (Mayberg, 1994), as well as the changes seen following acute tryptophan depletion during the early phase of SSRI treatment (Bremner et al., 1997). This brain change pattern has also been described using fMRI in a recent case of iatrogenic mood symptoms induced by high-frequency deep-brain stimulation of the right subthalamic nucleus for treatment of intractable Parkinson's disease in a patient with a remote history of major depression (Stefurak et al., 2001a; see also Bejjani et al., 1999). Consistent with recent clinical studies demonstrating increased relapse risk in those remitted depressed patients with persistent hypersensitivity to negative emotional stimuli (Segal et al., 1999), the converging imaging evidence suggests strategies for future studies of potential neural mechanisms of relapse vulnerability.

Challenge experiments of this type may additionally identify presyndromal subjects with high illness risk as suggested by preliminary studies demonstrating differential rest and stress-induced patterns of change in healthy control subjects selected for high and low neurotic temperaments (Keightley et al., 2002; Zald et al., 2002). Partial but not complete overlap between the change patterns with sad-stress seen in high neurotic never depressed subjects and in remitted depressed patients suggests a potential marker of illness vulnerability, unmasked only with emotional stress. Further development of these types of paradigms may have future potential for preclinical testing of unaffected family members of genetically defined cohorts. Directly testing this hypothesis is the demonstration that sensitivity to the tryptophan depletion challenge among healthy volunteers with and without a family history of depression is most critically linked to the presence of the s/s homozygous form of the *5HTTLPR* gene (Neumeister et al., 2002). This question revisits the interesting but complex interactions between neuroticism, mood stress sensitivity, gene polymorphisms, and depression vulnerability.

Limbic-Cortical Dysregulation Model of Depression

In an attempt to synthesize the findings described in the previous sections, regions with known anatomical interconnections that also show consistent changes across studies are summarized in a simplified schematic model illustrated in Fig. 7.5 (updated from Mayberg, 1997). Failure of this regional network is hypothesized to explain

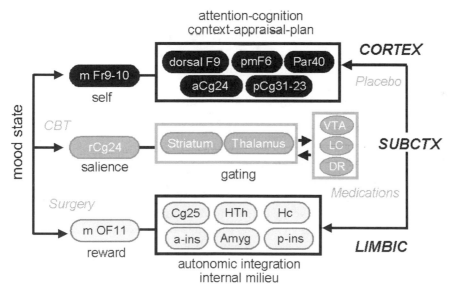

Figure 7.5. Limbic-cortical dysregulation model. Cortical compartment: limbic compartment: subcortical compartment: Arrows: relevant anatomical connections. Numbers: Brodmann designations. Abbreviations: CBT, cognitive behavioral therapy; mFr, medial prefrontal; dFr, prefrontal; pm, premotor; par, parietal; aCg, dorsal anterior cingulate; pCg, posterior cingulate; rCg, rostral cingulate; VTA, ventral tegmental area; LC, locus ceruleus; DR, dorsal raphe; mOF, medial orbital frontal; Cg25, subgenual cingulate; Hth, hypothalamus; Hc, hippocampus; a-ins, anterior insula; amyg, amygdala; p-ins, posterior insula. (Updated from Mayberg, 1997.)

the combination of clinical symptoms seen in depressed patients (i.e., mood, motor, cognitive, vegetative-circadian). Regions are grouped into three main "compartments" or levels: cortical, subcortical, and limbic. The frontal-limbic (dorsal-ventral) segregation additionally identifies those brain regions where an inverse relationship is seen across the different PET paradigms. Sadness and depressive illness are both associated with decreases in cortical regions and relative increases in limbic areas. The model, in turn, proposes that illness remission occurs when there is appropriate modulation of dysfunctional limbic-cortical interactions (solid black arrows)—an effect facilitated by various forms of treatment. It is further postulated that initial modulation of unique subcortical targets by specific treatments facilitates adaptive changes in particular pathways necessary for network homeostasis and resulting clinical recovery. Medial frontal, rostral cingulate, and orbital frontal regions are separated from their respective compartments in the model to highlight their primary role in self-referencing the salience of exogenous emotional events—a phenomenon that differentiates healthy from depressed states.

This working neural systems model can also be used in context of the multi-dimensional construct illustrated in Figure 7.1. Namely, the functional state of the depressed brain reflects both the initial insult or "functional lesion" and the ongoing process of attempted self-correction or adaptation influenced by such factors as heredity, temperament, early-life experiences, and previous depressive episodes. From this perspective, the net regional activity or sum total of various synergistic and competing inputs is what accounts for the observed clinical symptoms. For instance, if frontal hyperactivity is seen, it might be interpreted as an exaggerated and maladaptive compensatory process, manifesting clinically as psychomotor agitation and rumination, whose purpose is to override, at the cortical level, a persistent negative mood generated by abnormal chronic activity of limbic-subcortical structures. In contrast, frontal hypometabolism would be seen as the failure to initiate or maintain such a compensatory state, with resulting apathy, psychomotor slowness and impaired executive functioning as is common in melancholic patients. In this context, different interventions with varying primary mechanisms of action should be equally effective if the functional integrity of pathways is preserved within the depression circuit overall, perhaps offering a neurobiological explanation for the comparable clinical efficacy of pharmacological and cognitive treatments in randomized controlled trials. Similarly, progressively more aggressive treatments needed to relieve symptoms in some patients may reflect poor adaptive capacity or an actual disintegration of network connections in these patient subgroups. Lastly, unmasking of aberrant adaptive responses within these critical systems with properly targeted provocations might identify preclinical vulnerability or relapse risk. While such a network approach is a deliberate oversimplification, it provides a flexible platform to systematically test these hypotheses, as well as consider the relative contribution of additional genetic and environmental variables in disease pathogenesis and treatment response. Continued development of imaging and multivariate statistical strategies that optimally integrate these factors will be a critical next step in fully characterizing the depression phenotype at the neural systems level.

Acknowledgments. Research by the author described in this chapter was supported by grants from the National Institute of Mental Health, Canada Institute for Health Research, the National Alliance for Research on Schizophrenia and Depression (NARSAD), the Charles A. Dana Foundation, the Theodore and Vada Stanley Foundation, and Eli Lilly.

REFERENCES

Akiskal HS, Mckinney WT (1973). Depressure Disorders. Toward a unified hypothesis. *Science* 182:20–29.

Alexander GE, Crutcher MD, De Long MR (1990). Basal ganglia-thalamocortical circuits: Parallel substrates for motor, oculomotor, "prefrontal" and "limbic" functions. *Progr Brain Res* 85:119–146.

Altshuler LL, Devinsky O, Post RM, Theodore W (1990). Depression, anxiety, and temporal lobe epilepsy: Laterality of focus and symptoms. *Arch Neurol* 47:284–288.

American Psychiatric Association (APA) (1994). *Diagnostic and Statistical Manual of Mental Disorders* (Fourth Edition), American Psychiatric Association: Washington DC.

American Psychiatric Association (APA) (2000). Practice guideline for the treatment of patients with major depressive disorder (revision). *Am J Psychiatry* 157:1–45.

Arango V, Underwood MD, Mann JJ (1997). Postmortem findings in suicide victims. Implications for in vivo imaging studies. *Ann NY Acad Sci* 836:269–287.

Arango V, Underwood MD, Boldrini M, Tamir H, Kassir SA, Hsiung S, Chen JJ, Mann JJ (2001). Serotonin 1A receptors, serotonin transporter binding and serotonin transporter mRNA expression in the brainstem of depressed suicide victims. *Neuropsychopharmacology* 25:892–903.

Bagby RM, Joffe RT, Parker JDA, Kalemba V, Harkness KL (1995). Major depression and the five-factor model of personality. *J Personality Disorders* 9:224–234.

Barbas H (1995). Anatomical basis of cognitive-emotional interactions in the primate prefrontal cortex. *Neurosci Biobehavioral Rev* 19:499–510.

Bauer M, Frazer A (1994). Mood disorders, In Frazer A, Molinoff P, Winokur A (eds). *Biological Bases of Brain Function and Disease*, 2nd ed. Raven: New York, pp. 303–323.

Baxter LR, Schwartz JM, Phelps ME, Mazziotta JC, Guze BH, Selin CE, Gerner RH, Sumida RM (1989). Reduction of prefrontal cortex glucose metabolism common to three types of depression. *Arch General Psychiatry* 46:243–250.

Beck AT, Rush AJ, Shaw BF, Emery G (1979). *Cognitive Therapy of Depression*. Guilford Press: New York.

Bejjani BP, Damier P, Arnulf I, Thivard L, Bonnet A-M, Dormont D, Cornu P, Pidoux B, Samson Y, Agid Y (1999). Transient acute depression induced by high-frequency deep-brain stimulation. *N Eng J Med* 340:1476–1478.

Benca RM (1994). Mood disorders, In Kryger MH, Roth T, Dement WC (eds). *Principles and Practice of Sleep Medicine*. WB Saunders: Philadelphia, pp. 899–913.

Bench CJ, Friston KJ, Brown RG, Frackowiak RS, Dolan RJ (1993). Regional cerebral blood flow in depression measured by positron emission tomography: The relationship with clinical dimensions. *Psychological Medicine* 23:579–590.

Bench CJ, Frackowiak RSJ, Dolan RJ (1995). Changes in regional cerebral blood flow on recovery from depression. *Psychological Medicine* 25:247–251.

Blier P, de Montigny C (1999). Serotonin and drug-induced therapeutic responses in major depression, obsessive compulsive & panic disorders. *Neuropsychopharmacology* 21: 170–178.

Bremner JD, Narayan M (1998). The effects of stress on memory and the hippocampus throughout the life cycle: Implications for childhood development and aging. *Developmental Psychopathol* 10:871–885.

Bremner JD, Innis RB, Salomon RM, Staib LH, Ng CK, Miller HL, Bronen RA, Krystal JH, Duncan J, Rich D, Price LH, Malison R, Dey H, Soufer R, Charney DS (1997). Positron emission tomography measurement of cerebral metabolic correlates of tryptophan depletion-induced depressive relapse. *Arch General Psychiatry* 54:364–374.

Brody AL, Saxena S, Mandelkern MA, Fairbanks LA, Ho ML, Baxter LR (2001a). Brain metabolic changes associated with symptom factor improvement in major depressive disorder. *Biological Psychiatry* 50:171–178.

Brody AL, Saxena S, Stoessel P, Gillies LA, Fairbanks LA, Alborzian S, Phelps ME, Huang SC, Wu HM, Ho ML, Ho MK, Au SC, Maidment K, Baxter LR, Jr (2001b). Regional brain metabolic changes in patients with major depression treated with either paroxetine or interpersonal therapy: Preliminary findings. *Arch General Psychiatry* 58:631–640.

Bromfield EB, Altshuler L, Leiderman DB, Balish M, Ketter TA, Devinsky O, Post RM, Theodore WH (1992). Cerebral metabolism and depression in patients with complex partial seizures. *Arch Neurol* 49:617–623.

Buchsbaum MS, Wu J, Siegel BV, Hackett E, Trenary M, Abel L, Reynolds C (1997). Effect of sertraline on regional metabolic rate in patients with affective disorder. *Biological Psychiatry* 41:15–22.

Caligiuri MP, Ellwanger J (2000). Motor and cognitive aspects of motor retardation in depression. *J Affective Disorders* 57:83–93.

Carmichael ST, Price JL (1996). Connectional networks within the orbital and medial prefrontal cortex of macaque monkeys. *J Comp Neurol* 371:179–207.

Carroll BJ, Feinberg M, Greden J (1981). The dexamethasone suppression test, a specific laboratory test for the diagnosis of melancholia: Standardization, validation and clinical utility. *Arch General Psychiatry* 38:15–22.

Carson AJ, MacHale S, Allen K, Lawrie SM, Dennis M, House A, Sharpe M (2000). Depression after stroke and lesion location: A systematic review. *Lancet* 8:356:122–126.

Charney DS (1998). Monamine dysfunction and the pathophysiology and treatment of depression. *J Clin Psychiatry* 59(supp 14):11–14.

Coffey CE, Wilkinson WE, Weiner RD, Parashos LA, Djang WT, Webb MC, Figiel GS, Spritzer CE (1993). Quantitative cerebral anatomy in depression: A controlled magnetic resonance imaging study. *Arch General Psychiatry* 50:7–16.

Cosgrove GR, Rauch SL (1995). Psychosurgery. *Neurosurgery Clinic North Am* 6:167–176.

Costa PT, Jr, McCrae RR (1997). Stability and change in personality assessment: The revised NEO Personality Inventory in the year 2000. *J Personality Assessment* 68:86–94.

Cummings JL, Victoroff JI (1990). Noncognitive neuropsychiatric syndromes in Alzheimer's Disease. *Neuropsychiatry, Neuropsychol and Behavioral Neurol* 2:140–158.

Damasio AR, Grabowsky TJ, Bechara A, Damasio H, Ponto LLB, Parvizi J, Hichwa RD (2000). Subcortical and cortical brain activity during the feeling of self generated emotions. *Nature Neurosci* 3:1049–1056.

Derubeis JR, Evans MD, Hollon SD, Garvey MJ, Grove WM, Tuason VB (1990). How does cognitive therapy work? *J Consulting Clin Psychol* 58:862–869.

DeRubeis RJ, Gelfand LA, Tang TZ, Simons AD (1999). Medications versus cognitive behavioral therapy for severely depressed outpatients: Mega-analysis of four randomized comparisons. *Am J Psychiatry* 156:1007–1013.

Dolan RJ, Bench CJ, Liddle PF, Friston KJ, Frith CD, Grasby PM, Frackowiak RS (1993). Dorsolateral prefrontal cortex dysfunction in the major psychoses: Symptom or disease specificity? *J Neurol, Neurosurgery Psychiatry* 56:1290–1294.

Drevets WC, Videen TO, Price JL, Preskorn SH, Carmichael ST, Raichle ME (1992). A functional anatomical study of unipolar depression. *J Neurosci* 12:3628–3641.

Drevets WC, Price JL, Simpson JR, Jr, Todd RD, Reich T, Vannier M, Raichle ME (1997). Subgenual prefrontal cortex abnormalities in mood disorders. *Nature* 386:824–827.

Drevets WC, Price JL, Bardgett ME, Reich T, Todd RD, Raichle ME (2002). Glucose metabolism in the amygdala in depression: Relationship to diagnostic subtype and plasma cortisol levels. *Pharmacol, Bio Behav* 71:431–447.

Ebert D, Ebmeier K (1996). Role of the cingulate gyrus in depression: From functional anatomy to depression. *Biological Psychiatry* 39:1044–1050.

Elliott R (1998). The neuropsychological profile in unipolar depression. *Trends Cognitive Sci* 2:449–454.

Elliott R, Baker SC, Rogers RD, O'Leary DA, Paykel ES, Frith CD, Dolan RJ, Sahakian BJ (1997a). Prefrontal dysfunction in depressed patients performing a complex planning task: A study using positron emission tomography. *Psychological Med* 27:931–942.

Elliott R, Sahakian BJ, Herrod JJ, Robbins TW, Paykel ES (1997b). Abnormal response to negative feedback in unipolar depression: Evidence for a diagnosis specific impairment. *J Neurol, Neurosurgery Psychiatry* 63:74–82.

Fanous A, Gardner CO, Prescott CA, Cancro R, Kendler KS (2002). Neuroticism, major depression and gender: A population based twin study. *Psychological Med* 3:719–728.

Flory JD, Manuck SB, Ferrell RE, Dent KM, Peters DG, Muldoon MF (1999). Neuroticism is not associated with the serotonin transporter polymorphism. *Molec Psychiatry* 4:93–96.

Folstein SE, Abbott MH, Chase GA, Jensen BA, Folstein MF (1983). The association of affective disorder with Huntington's disease in a case series and in families. *Psychological Med* 13:537–542.

Frank E, Thase ME (1999). Natural history and preventative treatment of recurrent mood disorders. *Ann Rev Med* 50:453–468.

Freedman LJ, Insel TR, Smith Y (2000). Subcortical projections of area 25 (subgenual cortex) of the macaque monkey. *J Comp Neurol* 421:172–188.

Freo U, Ori C, Dam M, Merico A, Pizzolato G (2000). Effects of acute and chronic treatment with fluoxetine on regional glucose cerebral metabolism in rats: Implications for clinical therapies. *Brain Res* 854:35–41.

Fulton JF (1951). *Frontal Lobotomy and Affective behavior. A Neurophysiological Analysis.* Chapman and Hall: London.

George MS, Ketter TA, Parekh PI, Rosinsky N, Ring HA, Pazzaglia PJ, Marangell LB, Callahan AM, Post RM (1997). Blunted left cingulate activation in mood disorder subjects during a response interference task (the Stroop). *J Neuropsychiatry Clin Neurosci* 9:55–63.

George MS, Lisanby SH, Sackeim HA (1999). Transcranial magnetic stimulation: Applications in neuropsychiatry. *Arch General Psychiatry* 56:300–311.

Glassman AH, Shapiro PA (1998). Depression and the course of coronary artery disease. *Am J Psychiatry* 155:4–11.

Goldapple K, Segal Z, Garson C, Lau M, Bieling P, Kennedy SH, Mayberg HS (2002). Effects of cognitive behavioral therapy on brain glucose metabolism in patients with major depression. *Biological Psychiatry*. 57th Annual Meeting Abstracts, 51, 66S (#195).

Grady C (1999). Neuroimaging and activation of the frontal lobes. In Miller BL, Cummings JL (eds). *The Human Frontal Lobes, Functions and Disorders*. Guilford: Baltimore, pp. 196–230.

Grafman J, Vance SC, Weingartner H, Salazar AM, Amin D (1986). The effects of lateralized frontal lesions on mood regulation. *Brain* 109:1127–1148.

Haber SN, Fudge JL, McFarland NR (2000). Striatonigrostriatal pathways in primates form an ascending spiral from the shell to the dorsolateral striatum. *J Neurosci* 20:2369–2382.

Harlow HF, Suomi SJ (1974). Induced depression in Monkeys. *Behav Biol* 12:273–296.

Harrison PJ (2002). The neuropathology of primary mood disorder. *Brain* 125:1428–1449.

Heim C, Newport DJ, Heit S (2000). Pituitary-adrenal and autonomic responses to stress in women after sexual and physical abuse in childhood. *J Am Med Assoc* 284:592–597.

Hirono N, Mori E, Ishii K, Ikejiri Y, Imamura T, Shimomura T, Hashimoto M, Yamashita H, Sasaki M (1998). Frontal lobe hypometabolism and depression in Alzheimer's disease. *Neurology* 5:380–383.

Holsboer F (2000). The corticosteroid receptor hypothesis of depression. *Neuropsychopharmacology* 23:477–501.

Honer WG, Hurwitz T, Li DKB, Palmer M, Paty DW (1987). Temporal lobe involvement in multiple sclerosis patients with psychiatric disorders. *Arch Neurol* 44:187–190.

Johansson C, Jansson M, Linner L, Yuan QP, Pedersen NL, Blackwood D, Barden N, Kelsoe J, Schalling M (2001). Genetics of affective disorders. *European Neuropsychopharmacology* 11:385–394.

Jones RD, Tranel D, Benton A, Paulsen J (1992). Differentiating dementia from "pseudodementia" early in the clinical course: Utility of neuropsychological tests. *Neuropsychology* 6:13–21.

Keightley ML, Bagby RM, Seminowicz DA, Costa PT, Mayberg HS (2003). The influence of neuroticism on limbic-cortical pathways mediating transient sadness. *Brain and Cognition*, in press 51:181–183.

Kendler KS, Gardner CO, Prescott CA (2002). Toward a comprehensive developmental model for major depression in women. *Am J Psychiatry* 159:1133–1145.

Kennedy SH, Evans K, Kruger S, Mayberg HS, Meyer JH, McCann S, Arufuzzman A, Houle S, Vaccarino FJ (2001). Changes in regional glucose metabolism with PET following paroxetine treatment for major depression. *Am J Psychiatry* 158:899–905.

Ketter TA, George MS, Kimbrell TA, Benson BE, Post RM (1996). Functional brain imaging, limbic function, and affective disorders. *Neuroscientist* 2:55–65.

Klein DF (1974). Endogenomorphic depression. A conceptual and terminological revision. *Arch General Psychiatry* 31:447–454.

Klimek V, Stockmeier C, Overholser J, Meltzer HY, Kalka S, Dilley G, Ordway GA (1997). Reduced levels of NE transporters in the LC in major depression. *J Neurosci* 17:8451–8458.

Lang AE, Lozano AM (1998). Parkinson's disease. Part 2. *N Engl J Med* 339:1131–1143.

Lemke MR, Puhl P, Koethe N, Winkler T (1999). Psychomotor retardation and anhedonia in depression. *Acta Psych Scand* 99:252–256.

Lesch KP, Bengel D, Heils A, Sabol SK, Greenberg BD, Petri S, Benjamin J, Muller CR, Hamer DH, Murphy DL (1996). Association of anxiety-related traits with a polymorphism in the serotonin transporter gene regulatory region. *Science* 274:1527–1531.

Liotti M, Mayberg HS, Brannan SK, McGinnis S, Jerabek PA, Martin CC, Fox PT (2000). Differential neural correlates of sadness and fear in healthy subjects: Implications for affective disorders. *Biological Psychiatry* 48:30–42.

Liotti M, Mayberg HS, McGinnis S, et al. (2002). Mood challenge in remitted unipolar depression unmasks disease-specific CBF abnormalities. *Am J Psychiatry* 159:1830–1840.

Lomarev M, Denslow S, Nahas Z, Chae J, George M, Bohning D (2002). Vagus nerve stimulation (VNS) synchronized BOLD fMRI suggests that VNS in depressed adults has frequency/dose dependent effects. *J Psychiatric Res* 36:219.

Lopez JF, Akil H, Watson SJ (1999). Neural circuits mediating stress. *Biological Psychiatry* 46:1461–1471.

Lyness SA, Eaton EM, Schneider LS (1994). Cognitive performance in older and middle-aged depressed outpatients and controls. *J Gerontol* 49:P129–136.

Lyons DM, Yang C, Mobley BW, Nickerson JT, Schatzberg AF (2000). Early environmental regulation of glucocorticoid feedback sensitivity in young adult monkeys. *J Neuroendocrinol* 12:723–728.

Malison RT, Price LH, Berman RM, van Dyck CH, Pelton GH, Carpenter L, Sanacora G, Owens MJ, Nemeroff CB, Rajeevan N, Baldwin RM, Seibyl JP, Innis RB, Charney DS (1998). Reduced midbrain serotonin transporter binding in depressed vs healthy subjects as measured by 123b-CIT SPECT. *Biological Psychiatry* 44:1090–1098.

Mann JJ, Huang Y, Underwood MD, Kassir SA, Oppenheim S, Kelly TM, Dwork AJ, Arango V (2000). A serotonin transporter gene promoter polymorphism (5-HTTLPR) and prefrontal cortical binding in major depression and suicide. *Arch General Psychiatry* 57:729–738.

Marin RS (1990). Differential diagnosis and classification of apathy. *Am J Psychiatry* 147:22–30.

Mayberg HS (1994). Frontal lobe dysfunction in secondary depression. *J Neuropsychiatry Clin Neurosci* 6:428–442.

Mayberg HS (1997). Limbic-cortical dysregulation: A proposed model of depression. *J Neuropsychiatry Clin Neurosci* 9:471–481.

Mayberg HS, Solomon DH (1995). Depression in PD: A biochemical and organic viewpoint, In Weiner WJ, Lang AE (eds). *Behavioral Neurology of Movement Disorders: Advances in Neurology*, Vol. 65, Raven: New York, pp. 49–60.

Mayberg HS, Brannan SK, Mahurin RK, Jerabek PA, Brickman JS, Tekell JL, Silva JA, McGinnis S, Glass TG, Martin CC, Fox PT (1997). Cingulate function in depression: A potential predictor of treatment response. *NeuroReport* 8:1057–1061.

Mayberg HS, Liotti M, Brannan SK, McGinnis S, Mahurin RK, Jerabek PA, Silva JA, Tekell JL, Martin CC, Lancaster JL, Fox PT (1999). Reciprocal limbic-cortical function and negative mood: Converging PET findings in depression and normal sadness, *Am J Psychiatry* 156:675–682.

Mayberg HS, Brannan SK, Mahurin RK, McGinnis S, Silva JA, Tekell JL, Jerabek PA, Martin CC, Fox PT (2000). Regional metabolic effects of fluoxetine in major depression: Serial changes and relationship to clinical response. *Biological Psychiatry* 48:830–843.

Mayberg HS, Silva JA, Brannan SK, Tekell J, Mahurin RK, McGinnis S, Jerabek PA (2002). The functional neuroanatomy of the placebo effect, *Am J Psychiatry* 159:728–737.

McEwen BS (2000). Effects of adverse experiences for brain structure and function. *Biological Psychiatry* 48:721–731.

McIntosh AR (1999). Mapping cognition to the brain through neural interactions. *Memory* 7:523–548.

Mesulam MM (1985). Patterns in behavioral neuroanatomy: Association areas, the limbic system, and hemispheric specialization. In Mesulam MM (ed). *Principles of Behavioral Neurology*. FA Davis: Philadelphia, pp. 1–70.

Meyer J, Kapur S, Houle S, DaSilva J, Owczarek B, Brown G, Wilson A, Kennedy S (1999). Prefrontal cortex 5-HT$_2$ receptors in depression: A [18F] setoperone PET imaging study. *Am J Psychiatry* 156:1029–1034.

Meyer JH, Kapur S, Eisfeld B, Brown GM, Houle S, DaSilva J, Wilson AA, Rafi-Tari S, Mayberg HS, Kennedy SH (2001). The effect of paroxetine upon 5-Ht$_{2a}$ receptors in depression: An [^{18}F] setoperone PET imaging study. *Am J Psychiatry* 158:78–85.

Meyers CA, Scheibel RS (1990). Early detection and diagnosis of neurobehavioral disorders associated with cancer and its treatment. *Oncology (Huntington)* 4:115–130.

Moreno FA, Heninger GR, McGahuey CA, Delgado PL (2000). Tryptophan depletion and risk of depression relapse: A prospective study of tryptophan depletion as a potential predictor of depressive episodes. *Biological Psychiatry* 48:327–329.

Murphy FC, Sahakina BJ, Rubinsztein JS, Michael A, Rogers RD, Robbins TW, Paykel ES (1999). Emotional bias and inhibitory control processes in mania and depression. *Psychological Med* 29:1307–1321.

Murphy DL, Li Q, Engel S, Wichems C, Andrews A, Lesch KP, Uhl G (2001). Genetic perspectives on the serotonin transporter. *Brain Res Bull* 15:487–494.

Nemeroff CB (1989). Clinical significance of psychoneuroendocrinology in psychiatry: Focus on the thyroid and adrenal. *J Clin Psychiatry* 50(suppl):13–22.

Nemeroff CB (1996). The corticotropin-releasing factor (CRF) hypothesis of depression: New findings and new directions. *Molec Psychiatry* 1:336–342.

Neumeister A, Konstantinidis A, Stastny J, Schwarz MJ, Vitouch O, Willeit M, Praschak-Rieder N, Zach J, de Zwaan M, Bondy B, Ackenheil M, Kasper S (2002). Association between serotonin transporter gene promoter polymorphism (5HTTLPR) and behavioral responses to tryptophan depletion in healthy women with and without family history of depression. *Arch General Psychiatry* 59:613–620.

Nibuya M, Mornobu S, Duman RS (1997). Regulation of BDNF and trkB mRNA in rat brain by chronic electroconvulsive seizure and antidepressant drug treatments. *J Neurosci* 15:7539–7547.

Nobler MS, Oquendo M, Kegeles LS, Malone KM, Campbell CC, Sackeim HA, Mann JM (2001). Decreased regional brain metabolism after ECT. *Am J Psychiatry*, 158:305–308.

Osuch EA, Ketter TA, Kimbrell TA, George MS, Benson BE, Herscovitch MW, Post RM (2000). Regional cerebral metabolism associated with anxiety symptoms in affective disorder patients. *Biological Psychiatry* 48:1020–1023.

Overstreet DH (1993). The finders sensitive line rats: A genetic animal model of depression. *Neurosci Biobehav Rev* 17:51–68.

Panksepp J (1998). *Affective Neuroscience: The Foundations of Human and Animal Emotions*. Oxford University Press: New York.

Petty F, Kramer GL, Wu J, Davis LL (1997). Posttraumatic stress and depression. A neurochemical anatomy of the learned helplessness animal model. *Ann NY Acad Sci* 821:529–532.

Rajkowska G (2000). Postmortem studies in mood disorders indicate altered number of neurons and glial cell. *Biol Psychiatry* 48:766–777.

Ressler KJ, Nemeroff CB (1999). Role of norepinephrine in the pathophysiology and treatment of mood disorders. *Biological Psychiatry* 46:1219–1233.

Roberts SB, Kendler KS (1999). Neuroticism and self-esteem as indices of the vulnerability to major depression in women. *Psychological Med* 29:1101–1109.

Robinson RG, Kubos KL, Starr LB, Rao K, Price TR (1984). Mood disorders in stroke patients: Importance of location of lesion. *Brain* 107:81–93.

Rogers D, Lees AJ, Smith E, Trimble M, Stern GM (1987). Bradyphrenia in Parkinson's disease and psychomotor retardation in depressive illness: An experimental study. *Brain* 110:761–776.

Rolls ET (2000). The orbitofrontal cortex and reward. *Cerebral Cortex* 10:284–294.

Roy-Byrne PP, Weingartner H, Bierer LM, Thompson K, Post RM (1986). Effortful and automatic cognitive processes in depression. *Arch General Psychiatry* 43:265–267.

Rush AJ, Beck AT, Kovacs M, Weissenburger J, Hollon SD (1982). Comparison of the effects of cognitive therapy and pharmacotherapy on hopelessness and self concept. *Am J Psychiatry* 139:862–886.

Rush AJ, George MS, Sackeim HA, Marangell LB, Husain MM, Giller C, Nahas Z, Haines S, Simpson RK, Jr, Goodman R (2000). Vagus nerve stimulation (VNS) for treatment-resistant depressions: A multicenter study. *Biological Psychiatry* 47:276–286.

Sanchez MM, Ladd CO, Plotsky PM (2001). Early adverse experience as a developmental risk factor for later psychopathology: Evidence from rodent and primate models. *Develop Psychopathol* 13:419–449.

Sargent PA, Kjaer KH, Bench CJ, Rabiner EA, Messa C, Meyer J, Gunn RN, Grasby PM, Cowen PJ (2000). Brain serotonin-1A receptor binding measured by PET with 11C-Way-100635. *Arch General Psychiatry* 57:174–180.

Schildkraut JJ (1965). The catecholamine hypothesis of affective disorders: A review of supporting evidence. *Am J Psychiatry* 122:509–522.

Segal ZV, Gemar M, Williams S (1999). Differential cognitive response to a mood challenge following successful cognitive therapy or pharmacotherapy for unipolar depression. *J Abnormal Psychol* 108:3–10.

Sheline YI, Sanghavi M, Mintun MA, Gado MH (1999). Depression duration but not age predicts hippocampal volume loss in medically healthy women with recurrent major depression. *J Neurosci* 19:5034–5043.

Shively CA, Laber-Laird K, Anton RF (1997). Behavior and physiology of social stress and depression in female cynomolgus monkeys. *Biological Psychiatry* 41:871–882.

Soars JC, Mann JJ (1997). The anatomy of mood disorders—review of structural neuroimaging studies. *Biological Psychiatry* 41:86–106.

Starkstein SE, Robinson RG (eds) (1993). *Depression in Neurologic Diseases.* Johns Hopkins University Press: Baltimore.

Starkstein SE, Robinson RG, Price TR (1987). Comparison of cortical and subcortical lesions in the production of post-stroke mood disorders. *Brain* 110:1045–1059.

Starkstein SE, Preziosi TJ, Forrester AW, Robinson RG (1990a). Specificity of affective and autonomic symptoms of depression in Parkinson's disease. *J Neurol, Neurosurgery and Psychiatry* 53:869–873.

Starkstein SE, Bolduc PL, Mayberg HS, Preziosi TJ, Robinson RG (1990b). Cognitive impairments and depression in Parkinson's disease: A follow-up study. *J Neurol, Neurosurgery Psychiatry* 53:597–602.

Starkstein SE, Mayberg HS, Berthier ML, Fedoroff P, Price TR, Dannals RF, Wagner HN, Leiguarda R, Robinson RG (1990c). Mania after brain injury: Neuroradiological and metabolic findings. *Ann Neurol* 27:652–659.

Stefurak T, Mikulis DJ, Mayberg HS, Lang AE, Pahapill P, Lozano AM, Saint-Cyr JA (2001a). Deep brain stimulation associated with dysphoria and cortico-limbic changes detected by fMRI. *Movement Disorders* 16(suppl 1):S54.

Stefurak T, Mahurin R, Soloman D, Brannan TG, Mayberg HS (2001b). Response specific regional metabolism changes with fluoxetine treatment in depressed Parkinson's patients. *Movement Disorders* 16(suppl 1):S39.

Stoudemire A, Hill CD, Gulley LR (1989). Neuropsychological and biomedical assessment of depression-dementia syndromes. *J Neuropsychiatry Clin Neurosci* 1:347–361.

Sullivan PF, Neale MC, Kendler KS (2000). Genetic epidemiology of major depression: Review and meta-analysis. *Am J Psychiatry* 157:1552–1562.

Teneback CC, Nahas Z, Speer AM, Molloy M, Stallings LE, Spicer KM, Risch SC, George MS (1999). Changes in prefrontal cortex and paralimbic activity in depression following two weeks of daily left prefrontal TMS. *J Neuropsychiatry Clin Neurosci* 11:426–435.

Thase ME, Entsuah AR, Rudolph RL (2001). Remission rates during treatment with venlafaxine or selective serotonin reuptake inhibitors. *Br J Psychiatry* 178:234–241.

Tremblay L, Schultz W (1999). Relative reward preference in primate orbitofrontal cortex. *Nature* 398:704–708.

Vaidya VA, Duman RS (2001). Depression-emerging insights from neurobiology. *Br Med Bull* 57:61–79.

van Reekum R, Simard M, Clarke D, Binns MA, Conn D (1999). Late-life depression as a possible predictor of dementia: Cross-sectional and short-term follow-up results. *Am J Geriatric Psychiatry* 7:151–159.

Vogt BA, Pandya DN (1987). Cingulate cortex of the rhesus monkey II: Cortical afferents. *J Comp Neurol* 262:271–289.

Watts FN, Dalgleish T, Bourke P, Healy D (1990). Memory deficit in clinical depression: Processing resources and the structure of materials. *Psychological Med* 20:345–349.

Willner P, Mitchell PJ (2002). The validity of animal models of predisposition to depression. *Behav Pharmacol* 13:169–188.

Wu J, Buchsbaum MS, Gillin JC, Tang C, Cadwell S, Wiegand M, Najafi A, Klein E, Hazen K, Bunney WE, Jr, Fallon JH Keator D (1999). Prediction of antidepressant effects of sleep deprivation on metabolic rates in ventral ant cingulate & medial prefrontal cortex. *Am J Psychiatry* 156:1149–1158.

Yatham LN, Liddle PF, Dennis J, Shiah I-S, Adam MJ, Lane CJ, Lam RW, Ruth TJ (1999). Decrease in brain serotonin 2 receptor binding in patients with major depression following desipramine treatment. *Arch General Psychiatry* 56:705–711.

Zacharko RM, Anisman H (1991). Stressor-induced anhedonia in the mesocorticolimbic system. *Neurosci Biobehav Rev* 15:391–405.

Zald DH, Mattson DL, Pardo JV (2002). Brain activity in ventromedial prefrontal cortex correlates with individual differences in negative affect. *Proc Nat Acad Sci US Am* 99:2450–2454.

8

TREATMENT OF MOOD DISORDERS

Pedro L. Delgado and Paul Zarkowski

Department of Psychiatry, University Hospitals of Cleveland and Case Western Reserve University School of Medicine, Cleveland, Ohio

OVERVIEW

The fact that severe depressive states are not simply normal reactions to distressing life events has been recognized since the time of the ancient Greeks. However, it was not until the latter half of the 20th century that the diagnoses of major depression and bipolar disorder came to be fully defined and accepted as the two most important forms of mood disorders. Most of what is known about these conditions and their treatment has been learned in the past 50 years. An increasing body of clinical research has advanced our understanding of the theoretical basis and underlying causes of these illnesses and refined our knowledge of brain function and the mechanism of action of antidepressant and antimanic medications. The treatments discovered in the past 50 years have had a tremendously beneficial impact on millions of people suffering from these devastating conditions. Further, as our knowledge continues to grow, new treatments are being explored every day. As the rapid pace of discovery continues, the future for the development of more effective and rapidly acting treatment seems bright.

However, several key questions remain as the current focus of research and will have to be answered before we can significantly improve on the best of the

Textbook of Biological Psychiatry, Edited by Jaak Panksepp
ISBN 0-471-43478-7   Copyright © 2004 John Wiley & Sons, Inc.

currently available treatments. We only have a rudimentary knowledge of the genetic or biochemical factors that predispose to or cause depression or bipolar disorder. We are not sure if these different diagnostic categories represent biologically distinct entities or a spectrum of severity. We do not yet fully understand the mechanism of action of antidepressant or antimanic agents, the reason for time lag in therapeutic effects, or the reason some patients seem to respond to some treatments but not others. This chapter will provide an overview of mood disorders and the currently available medication and physical treatments for them.

CLASSIFICATION

The modern conception of mood disorders emerged in the 19th and 20th centuries. As the scientific method began to influence the methodological approaches used to understand mental disorders, anecdotal and impressionistic work began to be replaced by more observational and longitudinal approaches. The work of Emil Kraepelin is one of the most notable in this regard (Kraepelin, 1921). Through meticulous longitudinal observation, Kraepelin proposed that recurrent affective illnesses were distinct from other mental disorders and could be conceptualized as "manic-depressive insanity," now referred to as bipolar disorder. In part due to the influence of psychoanalytic theories, in the 1950s and 1960s depressions were grouped based on whether they were thought to have been caused by a stressful life event as opposed to having emerged spontaneously, presumably due to a chemical imbalance. The shift from a "brainless" view of mental illness in the 1950s to a "mindless" view of mental illness in the 1980s was stimulated by the advent of effective pharmacological treatments. As new research from studies of early social deprivation and studies of psychotherapeutic treatments began to accumulate, it became clear that more complex models for mental illness were needed. In the late 1990s, a more integrative perspective began to take hold, recognizing that brain structure and function can be modified by learning and life events. The abandonment of the concept of biological versus psychological types of depression has been important because it reflects our understanding that depressions do not exclusively have either environmental or biological causes, and these distinctions do not help us decide which patients will respond to medication treatment and/or psychotherapy (Goodwin and Jamison, 1990).

It is currently believed that mood disorders are caused by a complex interaction between many genetic and acquired factors, including but not limited to genetic differences, stressful life events and traumatic life experiences, inherent and acquired coping abilities, and general health and medical status. The most likely person to develop depression is someone with a family history of severe depression who is living with severe stress and has had many traumatic life experiences as well as a chronic general medical illness (such as diabetes) and also has poor coping strategies (e.g., tends to makes things worse for themselves when under stress). Add in substance abuse and the risk is even higher. Therefore, most people with depression have both stressful life events and genetic predispositions as causes for depression. A corollary is that all biological vulnerabilities are not necessarily genetic in origin. The brain's biological nature is altered by non-physical forms of stress and learning. It is likely that these nongenetic, psychosocially acquired biological differences can also predispose to depression (Hyman and Nestler, 1996; Duman et al., 1997, 1999; Stahl, 1998; Keller et al., 2001).

The most widely used classification system for mental disorders is the *Diagnostic and Statistical Manuel of Mental Disorders*, Fourth Edition (DSM-IV; American Psychiatric Association, 1994). The DSM-IV takes an agnostic and phenomenological approach to diagnostic classification, attempting to establish diagnostic categories when symptoms seem to cluster into longitudinally stable groupings. In regard to mood disorders, DSM-IV builds clinical diagnoses based on the presence of "episodes." DSM-IV divides mood disorders into unipolar and bipolar based on whether the person just has episodes of depression or episodes of both depression and mania or hypomania. Table 8.1 shows the criteria for a major depressive episode (MDE) and Table 8.2 shows the criteria for a manic episode. A hypomanic episode is qualitatively similar to mania but less severe.

TABLE 8.1. DSM-IV Criteria for Major Depressive Episode

A. Five (or more) of the following symptoms have been present during the same 2-week period and represent a change from previous functioning; at least one of the symptoms is either (1) depressed mood or (2) loss of interest or pleasure.
 1. Depressed mood most of the day, nearly every day, as indicated by either subjective report or observation made by others.
 2. Markedly diminished interest or pleasure in all, or almost all, activities most of the day, nearly every day (as indicated either by subjective account or observation made by others).
 3. Significant weight loss or weight gain when not dieting, or decrease or increase in appetite nearly every day.
 4. Insomnia or hypersomnia nearly every day.
 5. Psychomotor agitation or retardation nearly every day (observable by others, not merely subjective feelings of restlessness or being slowed down).
 6. Fatigue or loss of energy nearly every day.
 7. Feelings of worthlessness or excessive or inappropriate guilt (which may be delusional) nearly every day (not merely self-reproach or guilt about being sick).
 8. Diminished ability to think or concentrate, or indecisiveness, nearly every day (either by subjective account or as observed by others).
 9. Recurrent thoughts of death (not just fear of dying), recurrent suicidal ideation without a specific plan, or a suicide attempt or a specific plan for committing suicide.
B. Symptoms do not meet the criteria for a mixed episode.
C. Symptoms cause clinically significant distress or impairment in social, occupational, or other important areas of functioning.
D. Symptoms are not due to the direct physiological effects of a substance (e.g., a drug of abuse, a medication) or a general medical condition (e.g., hypothyroidism).
E. Symptoms are not better accounted for by bereavement, i.e., after the loss of a loved one, the symptoms persist for longer than 2 months or are characterized by marked functional impairment, morbid preoccupation with worthlessness, suicidal ideation, psychotic symptoms, or psychomotor retardation.

TABLE 8.2. DSM-IV Criteria for Manic Episode

A. Distinct period of abnormally and persistently elevated, expansive, or irritable mood lasting at least 1 week (or any duration if hospitalization is necessary).
B. During the period of mood disturbance, three (or more) of the following symptoms have persisted (four if the mood is only irritable) and have been present to a significant degree:
   1. Inflated self-esteem or grandiosity
   2. Decreased need for sleep (e.g., feels rested after only 3 hours of sleep)
   3. More talkative than usual or pressure to keep talking
   4. Flight of ideas or subjective experience that thoughts are racing
   5. Distractibility (i.e., attention too easily drawn to unimportant or irrelevant external stimuli)
   6. Increase in goal-directed activity (either socially, at work or school, or sexually) or psychomotor agitation
   7. Excessive involvement in pleasurable activities that have a high potential for painful consequences (e.g., engaging in unrestrained buying sprees, sexual indiscretions, or foolish business investments)
C. Symptoms do not meet criteria for a mixed episode.
D. Mood disturbance is sufficiently severe to cause marked impairment in occupational functioning or in usual social activities or relationships with others, or to necessitate hospitalization to prevent harm to self or others, or there are psychotic features.
E. Symptoms are not due to the direct physiological effects of a substance (e.g., a drug of abuse, a medication, or other treatment) or a general medical condition.

In depressive disorders (unipolar) people have MDEs but never have episodes of mania or hypomania. Depressive disorders include major depressive disorder and a less severe and more chronic form of depression called dysthymic disorder. Bipolar disorders include bipolar I disorder (episodes of full-blown mania with or without depression), bipolar II disorder (full-blown MDE and hypomania), and cyclothymia (mild depression and hypomania). Table 8.3 lists DSM-IV mood disorders. Major depressive episodes can further be described in regard to whether the person also has symptoms of psychosis, seasonal pattern, and atypical or melancholic features. Psychosis refers to a complete loss of touch with reality. This can include frank delusions and/or auditory or visual hallucinations. Psychosis can be present in many other mental disorders and does not help in establishing the diagnosis, although when psychosis occurs in a depressed individual, the psychotic symptoms usually involve markedly pessimistic, nihilistic, or guilty themes. When psychosis is present in people with mania, the delusions or hallucinations most often have a grandiose or paranoid content. Recognizing psychosis as a part of a severe mood disorder is very important because it is one of the few symptoms that is associated with preferential response to certain treatment combinations or electroconvulsive therapy and is more often associated with potentially dangerous behavior, including homicide or suicide.

TABLE 8.3. DSM-IV Mood Disorders

Depressive disorders (unipolar)
Major depressive disorder
    Major depressive episode (s) (MDE)
Dysthymia
    Chronic or recurrent depressive symptoms without
        full MDE
Depressive disorder not otherwise specified

Bipolar disorders
Bipolar I disorder
    Manic episode with or without MDE
Bipolar II disorder
    Hypomanic episode (s) with MDE (s)
Cyclothymic disorder
    Recurrent hypomanic episodes without full MDE
Bipolar disorder not otherwise specified

GENERAL TREATMENT PRINCIPLES

With the growth in knowledge and the availability of newer drugs has come an increase in the number of factors that should be taken into account in appropriately selecting antidepressant medications. This section will provide an overview of the decision-making process involved in using available medications for depression, including known benefits, potential side effects, and proper usage.

It is important to note the limitations in our current concepts of antidepressant, mood stabilizer, and antimanic. *Antidepressant* implies selectivity and specificity for depression. This is inaccurate. Antidepressant drugs are effective in the acute treatment of milder mood disorders such as dysthymia as well as other mental disorders such as generalized anxiety, panic disorder, social phobia, obsessive-compulsive disorder (OCD), bulimia and anorexia nervosa, and posttraumatic stress disorder (PTSD). Similarly, antimanic and mood stabilizer drugs can be used to enhance antidepressant effects as well as being useful in agitation.

Antidepressant, antimanic and mood stabilizer drugs affect the core brain systems involved in modulating stress. Not surprisingly, the conditions in which antidepressant drugs are indicated are exacerbated by stress, suggesting that antidepressants may simply restore function by reversing the adverse effects of stress or buffering the brain from stressful life events. Antidepressants do not "cure" depression or any other condition (Hyman & Nestler, 1996; Duman et al., 1997, 1999; Stahl, 1998). This is most evident through the high rates of recurrence on discontinuation of successful treatment, even after long periods of medication-induced remission (Keller, 2001).

The limitations of concepts such as 'antidepressant', 'antimanic', and 'mood stabilizer' argue for us to think about these drugs in a different way than we have in the past. Previously, we conceptualized the treatment of mental disorders as being analogous to insulin treatment of diabetes. However, this implies that antidepressants are providing some missing natural substance that leads to a cure. We know that this is not the case. It may be more accurate to use a different model. For example, the model of corticosteroids and inflammatory illnesses may be closer to what is actually happening. Corticosteroids do not restore a missing substance when they help someone with arthritis or someone else with a rash. Corticosteroids can reduce inflammation, no matter what the cause is. Corticosteroids work whether inflammation is caused by cancer, a genetic disease, or simply overuse. Corticosteroids also do not cure any disease or condition; they just slow down or reduce one of the consequences of disease (inflammation). Therefore, antidepressant drugs may be much more than antidepressant, they may be antistress and seem to have beneficial effects in many different mental conditions associated with stress (Duman et al., 1999; Delgado et al., 1997).

Decision to Initiate Medication Treatment

Treatment should follow a careful assessment of symptoms and course, a review of general health status, a formal diagnosis, and in some cases physical examination and laboratory testing (Depression Guideline Panel, 1993). This can usually be accomplished in one visit, especially if medically relevant history and past psychiatric and substance abuse history are available. Once a diagnosis of major depression or bipolar disorder has been made, medication treatment is usually indicated. Medication treatment should be initiated with the understanding that the choice of agent may be significantly affected by presenting symptoms and concurrent psychiatric, medical, or substance abuse diagnoses. Concomitant supportive, educational, and/or cognitive psychotherapy is usually indicated, although in severe depression or mania significant modifications in the methodology and goals of psychotherapy are usually required, and these will change over time depending on the extent and rate of clinical improvement and capacity to participate (also see, Chapter 18).

Hospitalization, once an expectation for most patients being treated for a major mood disorder, is now reserved for those situations where there is imminent risk of harm to self or others or an inability to maintain nutritional status. With the exception of mania or psychotic depression, treatment for most mood disorders can be accomplished entirely on an outpatient basis. Mania, severe psychosis, and/or suicidal intent are the most common situations in which hospitalization is usually required. Over the past 20 years, the purpose of hospitalization has undergone a major shift from a focus on definitive diagnostic evaluation and treatment to rapid stabilization and triage to an appropriate outpatient-based treatment setting.

Several situations call for initiation of medication treatment as soon as possible. These include conditions where improvement is unlikely without medication treatment, where possible harmful consequences may arise if the depression is untreated (e.g., loss of job or risk of suicide), or where relapse and recurrence are highly likely outcomes.

Medication treatment should be postponed if other treatable conditions may be responsible for the symptoms, the symptoms are very mild, the risk of harmful consequences minimal, or if the patient is strongly averse to the use of medication treatment. The most common of these situations occur when a recent life stress raises the possibility that the presenting symptoms represent a moderate to severe form of an adjustment disorder or that the depression may be secondary to medical illness, due to a side effect of medication treatment for another condition, or substance abuse. The decision to initiate medication treatment in these cases should follow one or two further evaluation meetings. Careful assessment for one of the many known causes of mania such hyperthyroidism, stimulant or decongestant abuse, or right-sided brain lesions (Goodwin and Jamison, 1990) is particularly important in patients with a first episode of acute mania, in a patient with a unusual symptom profile, or in mania or psychotic depression with a first onset after age 40 (Depression Guideline Panel, 1993; Schulberg et al., 1998; American Psychiatric Association, 2000).

Disease Management

Mood disorders are chronic disorders, with high rates of relapse on discontinuation of drug therapy, making it important that treatment be conceptualized as a long-term process (Kraepelin, 1921; Angst et al., 1973; Keller et al., 1982; Kupfer et al., 1992). Medications restore function but the disease process is not cured.

Most patients with a mood disorder will have more than one episode. Recurrence rates for depression are estimated to be at least 50 percent for patients with one episode of major depression and 80 to 90 percent if the person has had two episodes (Angst, 1990; Kupfer, 1991). Seventy to 90 percent of patients with a successfully treated major depression will experience a recurrence of illness when placebo is substituted for active medication during a 3-year maintenance phase, as opposed to only 15 to 20 percent taking a full dose of imipramine (Frank et al., 1990).

Three phases of treatment have been proposed: acute, continuation, and maintenance treatment phases (Kupfer, 1991). The stages are defined in relation to the status of symptoms and involve the concepts of treatment response, relapse, remission, recurrence, and recovery (Frank et al., 1991). Response refers to a partial diminution in symptoms following initiation of drug treatment (usually 50 percent reduction). Relapse involves the return of some symptoms of a disease during or on cessation of treatment. Remission refers to a diminution of the symptoms of a disease and implies that there has been a clinically meaningful decrease of same (usually 70 percent or greater reduction). Recurrence describes the return of symptoms after a remission. Recovery describes a more complete remission, implying the absence or near absence of symptoms.

The acute treatment phase begins with a clinical interview, diagnostic assessment, physical and neurological examination, and clinical and laboratory studies as appropriate (Schulberg et al., 1998; American Psychiatric Association, 2000). The goals of this phase include establishing a diagnosis, defining a short-term and long-term multidisciplinary treatment plan, selecting the most appropriate medication, titrating the dose to a therapeutic range, monitoring of side effects, compliance, and determining the magnitude and quality of response. This phase lasts from 6 to 12 weeks and patients are usually seen every 1 to 2 weeks during this phase.

If a response is obtained, then the continuation phase ensues and consists of monitoring for completeness of response and side effects. Discontinuation of medication during or before this phase is complete is associated with a high rate of relapse (Prien and Kupfer, 1986; Kupfer, 1991). Continuation treatment lasts 4 to 9 months and can be thought of as a consolidation phase. A recent World Health Organization (WHO) consensus meeting suggests that the minimum period of time for continuation treatment is 6 months (WHO Mental Health Collaborating Centers, 1989; Kupfer et al., 1992; Altamura and Percudani, 1993).

Maintenance is in general thought to be prophylactic, although it is increasingly clear that for many patients this phase is essential, not simply to prevent new episodes but to maintain the response since the illness persists. Newer data suggest that medication dosing during the maintenance phase should continue at the same level as during the acute phase and that supportive psychotherapy can help to reduce the rate of relapse and recurrence (Frank et al., 1990; Kupfer et al., 1992).

Patients should be seen every 4 to 12 weeks for the first year of maintenance treatment and at 6-month to yearly intervals thereafter. The frequency of visits during this phase should be individualized based on psychosocial factors, compliance, and presence of symptoms and side effects. Rates of depressive relapse appear to be higher when antidepressant drugs are discontinued rapidly compared to a slow (3 to 4 weeks) taper (Robinson et al., 1991; Kupfer, 1991). Therefore, if an antidepressant is discontinued, it should be tapered over at least a 4-week period.

Choosing a Drug

A large number of clinical and pharmacological factors can influence the selection of antidepressant drug, and therefore the choice should be made on an individual basis. Choosing the safest and most efficacious drug with the side effect profile most compatible with the patients' specific symptoms is the most pragmatic approach.

The clinical factors that can influence choice of drug include: primary diagnosis, subdiagnoses (e.g., presence of psychosis or atypical features), concomitant disorders, general health status, age, prior treatment history, and prior nonresponse to specific antidepressants, current severity of illness, and symptom profile. While certain subtypes of major depression have been suggested to have a greater likelihood of responding to specific antidepressant drugs or to specific combinations, the only subtype of depression that has consistently been found to selectively respond to a particular treatment is depression with psychotic features. When psychosis is present, either electroconvulsive treatment alone or combination treatment with antidepressant and antipsychotic medications is required.

It is important to understand the pharmacological effects of antidepressant medications that are most likely to relate to therapeutic action and those effects that primarily contribute to side effects. A growing body of data now suggests that the most important pharmacological effects of antidepressants that lead to their efficacy in major depression are their ability to increase neurotransmission through serotonin [5-hydroxytryptamine (5-HT)], norepinephrine (NE), and/or dopamine (DA) releasing neurons in the brain. Alternatively, side effects seem most related to adrenergic, cholinergic, and histaminergic receptor blocking properties. More detail on side effects and therapeutic mechanisms will be provided in the following sections.

ANTIDEPRESSANTS

Antidepressant drugs have been categorized in a variety of ways. The traditional classification scheme has been the distinction between monoamine oxidase inhibitors (MAOIs), tricyclic antidepressants (TCAs), and selective serotonin reuptake inhibitors (SSRIs). This system used pharmacological effects (what the drug actually does) for one group and chemical structure (the drug's molecular type) for the others. As we've learned more about the effects of antidepressant drugs that are essential for their beneficial effects, their classification of antidepressants has shifted to a focus on pharmacological properties.

Pharmacological Mechanisms of Antidepressant Drug Action

Most antidepressants have potent pharmacological effects that cause increased synaptic levels of the monoamine neurotransmitters NE and/or 5-HT and in some cases DA. Levels of monoamines can be increased by blocking their reuptake as well as by inhibition of their metabolism by the enzyme MAO. However, while levels of monoamines increase within hours of ingestion of the first dose of an antidepressant, the therapeutic response does not begin until 2 to 4 weeks later. This lack of temporal relationship between increased synaptic levels of monoamines and clinical response has led to a search for other effects of these medications that correlate more closely with therapeutic response.

Perhaps the most well-documented, noteworthy data concerning the pharmacological mechanisms underlying antidepressant action has been generated from neurotransmitter depletion studies conducted throughout the past 15 years (Delgado et al., 1997). The controlled depletion of 5-HT or NE in living people allows a more direct method for investigating the role of monoamines.

The methodology for neurotransmitter depletion in humans is relatively straightforward. 5-HT can be reduced in humans by rapid depletion of tryptophan, the precursor amino acid for 5-HT (Delgado et al., 1990). Brain NE can be reduced by administering alpha-methyl-para-tryosine (AMPT), an agent that blocks the rate-limiting step in the conversion of tyrosine to NE (Delgado et al., 1993). Prior research explored the effects of 5-HT or NE depletion in four sample populations: patients whose depression was being treated with SSRIs, patients whose depression was being treated with desipramine, patients whose depression remained untreated, and healthy control subjects who had no personal or family history of depression. When the depletion procedure is administered, changes in mood—if any—occur rapidly, often within a matter of hours. Conversely, when mood changes occurred, they lasted from 4 to 36 h (Delgado et al., 1997). Since these experiments began in the late 1980s, no person studied by the author has had to be hospitalized nor has a subject required a change in treatment due to adverse effects of depletion testing.

Composite results from multiple studies are presented in Figure 8.1. One of the most striking findings is that antidepressant responses can be rapidly but transiently reversed, with the response being dependent on the class of antidepressant. About 80 percent of patients who were taking an SSRI for depression experienced a transient return of depressive symptoms when 5-HT was depleted, and for about 80 percent of patients who were taking NE reuptake inhibitors depressive symptoms transiently reappeared when NE was depleted. Conversely, most patients who had been taking SSRIs for depression tended not to experience depressive symptoms with depletion of NE, and those who had been taking NE reuptake inhibitors did not experience depression with depletion of 5-HT. In healthy controls and patients whose depression was not being treated, depletion of 5-HT or NE did not worsen or lead to the onset of new depressive symptoms. The ability to selectively deplete and selectively reverse the antidepressant effects in people taking single-acting agents suggests that, at least in those patients, only one particular neurotransmitter had a role in the mechanism of action of that medication. The fact that the type and severity of depressive symptoms did not change in unmedicated, currently depressed patients—and did not surface in healthy patients—seems to imply that more than a simple disruption of monoamine synthesis is responsible for depression. In other words, drugs that increase either NE or 5-HT neurotransmission can help treat depression through parallel and partially independent pathways, but a deficiency of neither NE or 5-HT is sufficient to cause the symptoms of clinical depression.

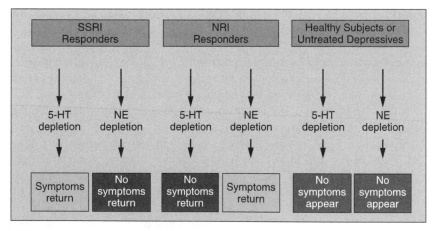

Figure 8.1. Summary of neurotransmitter depletion studies. SSRI, selective serotonin reuptake inhibitor; NRI, norepinephrine reuptake inhibitor; 5-HT, serotonin; NE, norepinephrine (Delgado et al., 1990, 1993, 1994, 1997, 1999). See ftp site for color image.

While the findings presented above are not conclusive, neurotransmitter depletion studies do provide important information from which further studies can be generated. Results are consistent with a model in which depression is caused not by an insufficiency in monoamines but by altered functioning in the areas of the brain that are regulated by monoamines (Delgado et al., 1994). Understanding whether antidepressants work through a final common pathway or through parallel pathways is critical to the development of new antidepressants and for optimal clinical use of existing medications.

Treatment Studies

Since the early 1950s, when MAOIs and imipramine were serendipitously discovered to have therapeutic effects in the treatment of depression (Loomer et al., 1957), a steady stream of new medications for depression have become available for clinical use. The first of these drugs were simple modifications of the original tricyclic antidepressant TCA or MAO inhibitor compounds. However, as our understanding of the pharmacology of these compounds has evolved, newer drugs have been tailored to have specific neurochemical effects. The vast majority of newer compounds have been designed to potently enhance NE and/or 5-HT neurotransmission without anticholinergic, antihistaminergic, or antiadrenergic properties. It was hoped that this would lead to drugs with fewer side effects and/or greater efficacy and faster onset of action.

The following sections provide a selected review of data from clinical studies investigating the efficacy of several drugs with potent effects of NE and/or 5-HT for treatment of major depression and several anxiety disorders. Table 8.4 lists currently available antidepressant drugs (and selected nonpharmacological treatments), grouping them based on the pharmacological effects of the parent compound that most likely underlie the therapeutic effects. The sections that follow describe important characteristics of medications in each category.

Monoamine Reuptake Inhibitors

Monoamine reuptake inhibition is the most common mechanism by which antidepressant drugs work. Drugs with this pharmacological action include the old TCAs, the selective 5-HT reuptake inhibitors (SSRIs), and several newer drugs such as venlafaxine, duloxetine, and reboxetine. The older drugs in this group (such as imipramine, desipramine, and amitriptyline) tend to be relatively nonselective and frequently have many active metabolites. The newer drugs tend to be highly selective for reuptake blockade with less receptor blocking properties and because of this have fewer side effects (e.g., venlafaxine). Table 8.5 shows the relative affinity of selected antidepressants for binding to the 5-HT and NE transporters.

NE Reuptake Inhibitors (NRIs). Desipramine is one of the classical NRIs, and there are extensive data available regarding its clinical efficacy profile. It is well established as effective in the acute treatment of major depressive episodes in 45 to 63 percent of outpatients and 48 to 63 percent in inpatients (Depression Guideline Panel,

TABLE 8.4. Antidepressant Treatments

NE reuptake inhibitors	5-HT/NE reuptake inhibitors	5-HT reuptake inhibitors
Desipramine (Norpramin and others)	Imipramine (Tofranil and others)	Fluoxetine (Prozac)
Nortriptyline (Pamelor)	Doxepin (Sinequan)	Sertraline (Zoloft)
Protriptyline (Vivactil)	Amitriptyline (Elavil and others)	Paroxetine (Paxil)
Maprotiline (Ludiomil)	Trimipramine (Surmontil)	Fluvoxamine (Luvox)
Atomoxetine (Strattera)	Venlafaxine (Effexor)	Citalopram (Celexa)
Reboxetine	Duloxetine (Cymbalta)	S-Citalopram (Lexapro)
	Milnacepram	
Drugs with mixed actions	**NE/DA reuptake inhibitors**	**Receptor antagonists**
Chlorimipramine (Anafranil)	Bupropion (Wellbutrin)	Nefazodone (Serzone)
Trazodone (Deseryl)		Mirtazapine (Remeron)
Amoxapine (Asendin)		Risperidone (Risperdal)
		Olanzepine (Zyprexa)
		Quetiapine (Seroquel)
Irreversible MAO inhibitors	**Monoamine releasing agents**	**5-HT$_{1A}$ partial agonists**
Isocarboxazid (Marplan)	d-Amphetamine (Dexedrine)	Buspirone (Buspar)
Phenelzine (Nardil)	Methylphenidate (Ritalin)	Gepirone
Tranylcypromine (Parnate)	Pemoline (Cylert)	
Somatic treatments	**Novel pharmacological targets**	**Psychotherapy treatments**
Electroconvulsive therapy	Neurokinin-1 receptor antagonists	Cognitive behavioral therapy
Full spectrum light therapy	CRF antagonists	Interpersonal therapy
Vagal nerve stimulation	Glucocorticoid antagonists	
Transcranial magnetic stimulation	Glutamate receptor antagonists	
Exercise		

MAO, monoamine oxidase; NE, norepinephrine; DA, dopamine; 5-HT, serotonin; CRF, corticotrophin releasing factor.

1993). Like other tricyclic antidepressants, it has a host of pharmacological properties that contribute to its side effect burden. These include anticholinergic, antihistaminergic, and antiadrenergic effects (Depression Guideline Panel, 1993).

Bupropion is a very weak DA reuptake blockade inhibitor; its behavioral profile in laboratory animals and humans is that of a central nervous system (CNS) stimulant and indirect DA agonist (Bolden-Watson and Richelson, 1993). It has no significant effects at blocking reuptake of 5-HT or NE, although its primary metabolite (hydroxybupropion) is a potent NE reuptake inhibitor (Ferris and Cooper, 1993). Hydroxybupropion

TABLE 8.5. Affinity of Selected Antidepressants for
Binding to NE and 5-HT Transporters

Drug	NE (nM/L)	5-HT (nM/L)	NE/5-HT
Reboxetine[a]	11.0	440.0	0.03
Atomoxetine[a]	5.0	77.0	0.06
Desipramine[b]	13.7	75.5	0.18
Amitriptyline[b]	13.8	9.4	1.47
Nefazodone[b]	586.5	339.5	1.73
Imipramine[b]	15.5	5.0	3.10
Duloxetine[c]	5.6	0.7	8.00
Venlafaxine[b]	1668.0	13.5	123.56
Fluoxetine[d]	599.0	1.1	544.55
Paroxetine[d]	45.0	0.1	450.00
Fluvoxamine[d]	1427.0	2.3	620.43
Sertraline[d]	714.0	0.3	2380.00
Citalopram[d]	6190.0	1.6	3868.75
Escitalopram[d]	7841.0	1.1	7128.18
Bupropion[a]	>10,000	>10,000	

[a]Bymaster et al. (2002).
[b]Roth B, (2003); NIH Psychoactive Drug Screening Program,
   http://pdsp.cwru.edu/stest.asp.
[c]Bymaster et al. (2001).
[d]Owens et al. (2001).

is produced rapidly in humans, with peak plasma levels of up to 3 times those of bupropion and a half-life of 24 hr. Therefore, orally administered bupropion is likely to lead to significant NE reuptake inhibition and relatively less DA reuptake inhibition. Bupropion increases locomotor activity and causes stereotyped behaviors in laboratory animals. In humans, it can cause restlessness, insomnia, anorexia, and psychosis. Bupropion is structurally related to phenylethylamines and unrelated to the TCAs, SSRIs, or MAOIs. It has no significant potency at binding to any known neurotransmitter receptors. Clinical studies have demonstrated that bupropion is effective in the treatment of major depressive episodes (Depression Guideline Panel, 1993). While early studies suggested that bupropion might be less likely to cause hypomania or mania in bipolar patients, subsequent studies suggested that it can cause mania and psychosis in bipolar patients, especially those with high pretreatment levels of the DA metabolite, homovanillic acid (HVA) (Golden et al., 1988). In a recent open-label study, bupropion was not effective for treatment of PTSD (Canive et al., 1998). However, contrary to commonly held clinical impressions, bupropion was reported to have therapeutic effects in a patient with social phobia (Emmanuel et al., 1991). Additionally, a recent review contrasting the relative efficacy of bupropion and sertraline in treatment of anxiety symptoms in patients with major depression showed that a baseline Hamilton Anxiety Scale (Ham-A) score did not predict response to either drug (Rush et al., 2001), and both drugs equally reduced Ham-A total score (Trivedi et al., 2001).

Reboxetine was approved for use as an antidepressant in much of western Europe, South America, and Mexico in 1998. Reboxetine is the only truly selective NRI being marketed as an antidepressant, although U.S. Food and Drug Administration (FDA) approval has recently been granted to atomoxetine, a selective NRI (Bymaster et al., 2002) approved for the treatment of attention deficit disorder. Reboxetine potently inhibits the reuptake of NE without having significant effects on the reuptake of 5-HT or DA. It does not inhibit MAO, nor does it bind to 5-HT_{1A} or 5-HT_{2A}, DA_1 or DA_2, α- or β-adrenergic, muscarinic cholinergic, gamma-aminobutyric acid (GABA), benzodiazepine, or histamine H_1 receptors. Reboxetine has primarily been studied in European trials involving about 665 nonelderly and 56 elderly (age >65 years) depressed patients (Burrows et al., 1998). It is administered twice per day at doses ranging from 4 to 12 mg/day. The European data show that reboxetine is more effective than placebo and comparable to imipramine, desipramine, and fluoxetine for the treatment of major depression. Reboxetine has also been found to be equally effective as imipramine in severely ill depressed patients and melancholic depressed patients. One study found that while reboxetine restored normal function as measured on a social adjustment scale, fluoxetine did not (Dubini et al., 1997). The finding of improved social adjustment was interpreted to support the specific involvement of the NE system in "sustaining drive" (Dubini et al., 1997). A recent study showed reboxetine to be highly effective in treatment of panic disorder (Versiani et al., 2002).

SSRIs. The five drugs in this class are fluoxetine, sertraline, paroxetine, fluvoxamine, and citalopram (and escitalopram). All are relatively new and were developed because they are potent and selective 5-HT reuptake inhibitors (Leonard, 1992). They share similar side effects and therapeutic spectrum of action, being effective in the treatment of MDE, OCD and panic disorder.

Early clinical experience suggests that while these drugs are more similar than they are different, variations are found in their side effect profiles that are unexplained by current knowledge. These include sedation/asthenia vs. activation and the propensity to cause nausea. In general fluvoxamine and paroxetine are more frequently associated with nausea and a sedation-like feeling referred to as "asthenia," whereas fluoxetine and sertraline are more "activating." Interesting differences that may have clinical relevance include the potency of sertraline in blocking DA reuptake (Bolden-Watson & Richelson, 1993) and in binding to sigma receptors (Tulloch & Johnson, 1992), and of paroxetine for inhibition of NE reuptake (Owens et al., 2000). These data suggest that sertraline may be problematic in psychotic depression and that in high doses paroxetine may be a dual 5-HT/NE reuptake inhibitor, although this is probably only seen at doses higher than the maximum recommended daily dose of 40 mg. Paroxetine is also an inhibitor of the enzyme nitric oxide synthetase (Finkel et al., 2002), possibly contributing to a slightly higher rate of sexual dysfunction compared with other SSRIs (Montejo et al., 2001).

Citalopram is intermediate in most side effects compared to other SSRIs, probably accounting for its popularity in Europe and the United States. Escitalopram, the l-stereoisomer of citalopram, improves on the selectivity of the racemic drug by increasing potency for the 5-HT transporter (Owens et al., 2001). Studies comparing it with citalopram suggest that it has equal efficacy and a similar side effect profile (Gorman et al., 2002).

Clinical Differences between SSRIs and NRIs in Depression Studies. Nelson (1999) recently published a comprehensive review of prior studies comparing an NRI to an SSRI in patients with major depression. Sixteen studies were reviewed (Nelson, 1999). The NE selective agents included desipramine, nortriptyline, reboxetine, lofepramine, and maprotiline, and SSRIs included fluoxetine, paroxetine, sertraline, fluvoxamine, zimelidine, and citalopram. A total of 1563 patients were included in these studies. Response rates were similar, 65 and 60 percent, for the SSRIs and NRIs. When baseline symptoms that predict response were examined, there were no consistent findings across studies, although some studies have found baseline anxiety to predict preferential response to SSRIs versus NRIs (Tyrer et al., 1980; Aberg-Wistedt, 1982). The topic of whether NRIs are as effective for anxiety symptoms/disorders as SSRIs continues to be an important focus of debate. In part, this debate is fueled by the lack of efficacy of NRIs for OCD (Goodman et al., 1990; Leonard et al., 1991; Lelliott and Montiero, 1986) and PTSD (Reist et al., 1989; Dow and Kline, 1997; Canive et al., 1998), as well as a generally held perception that SSRIs are more effective in depressed patients with moderate to severe anxiety symptoms (Blackwell, 1987). Arguing against a significant class difference in efficacy in patients with comorbid major depression and anxiety symptoms are the studies showing NRIs to be effective in panic disorder (Kalus et al., 1991; Lydiard et al., 1993; Villarreal, 1995; Rudolph and Feiger, 1999; Versiani et al., 2002) as well as a recent study showing that a baseline Ham-A score did not predict response to either sertraline or bupropion during treatment of depression (Rush et al., 2001).

Dual NE/5-HT Reuptake Inhibitors. Approved by the FDA for the treatment of major depression in 1994, venlafaxine is the oldest of the newer antidepressants and stands out from most of the others in having minimal effects on blocking neurotransmitter receptors. It is as potent at blocking 5-HT reuptake as imipramine, but is weaker at blocking NE reuptake, making it slightly more selective for 5-HT than NE, especially at lower doses. It does not inhibit MAO and does not significantly bind to 5-HT, NE, DA, muscarinic cholinergic, α_1-, α_2-adrenergic, or histamine H_1 receptors (Muth et al., 1991).

Venlafaxine has fared well in placebo-controlled studies and has shown efficacy in inpatients and outpatients with major depression and in patients with major depression with melancholia (Feighner, 1993; Rudolph and Feiger, 1999). In contrast to SSRIs, there is evidence for a dose-response relationship, with higher doses being more likely to lead to successful antidepressant responses than lower doses. This has been hypothesized to be due to the likelihood that at lower doses (less than 150 mg/day) venlafaxine is predominantly an SSRI and at higher doses the NE reuptake inhibition begins to contribute to its action (Nirenberg et al., 1994; Benkert et al., 1996).

Several studies suggest that venlafaxine may lead to higher rates of response and a more "robust" profile of response (when more stringent response criteria are used) when compared to fluoxetine, imipramine, or paroxetine (Thase et al., 2001). This is especially true in severely ill or melancholic depressed patients (Clerk et al., 1994).

Venlafaxine may have as broad (or broader) an efficacy profile as SSRIs. Small open-label studies have suggested efficacy in obsessive-compulsive disorder (OCD) (Zajecka et al., 1990; Rauch et al., 1996; Taryura-Tobias & Neziroglu, 1996; Grossman & Hollander, 1996), panic disorder (Geracioti, 1995; Papp et al., 1998), attention deficit hyperactivity disorder (Wilens et al., 1995; Pleak & Gormly 1995), and social phobia (Kelsey, 1995).

Duloxetine was approved by the FDA for the treatment of major depression in 2003. Like venlafaxine, it selectively and potently blocks reuptake of both 5-HT and NE. Unlike venlafaxine, the binding affinity of duloxetine for 5-HT and NE transporters suggests that it is likely to cause significant reuptake inhibition of both monoamines at the usual clinical doses, therefore requiring less titration to achieve "dual action." It does not inhibit MAO and does not significantly bind to most 5-HT, NE, DA, muscarinic cholinergic, α_1-, α_2-adrenergic, or histamine H_1 receptors (Bymaster et al., 2001). It has weak $5\text{-}HT_{2A}$ and $5\text{-}HT_6$ receptor binding affinities and weakly inhibits DA reuptake (Bymaster et al., 2001), although it is unlikely that these effects are clinically significant at the usual doses.

Duloxetine had a better than average rate of success in the Phase II and III clinical efficacy trials required for FDA approval (Detke et al., 2002; Goldstein et al., 2002). In Phase II and III trials it showed superiority over both placebo and comparator drugs (fluoxetine and paroxetine), reinforcing the message that dual 5-HT/NE antidepressants may have a more robust efficacy profile than selective 5-HT or NE reuptake inhibitors (Thase et al., 2001).

Duloxetine is dosed once daily with a usual initial daily dose of 60 mg. It shows a benign side effect profile, similar to SSRIs, with most patients tolerating the drug extremely well. When side effects occur, the most common include insomnia and asthenia (Goldstein et al., 2002; Detke et al., 2002). There were no significant cardiovascular or genitourinary side effects, no weight gain, and sexual side effects as measured by the Arizona Sexual Experiences Scale did not differ from placebo (Goldstein et al., 2002).

Duloxetine has been shown to be effective in reducing physical symptoms (back pain, shoulder pain, headache) in depressed patients as well as the core depressive symptoms (Detke et al., 2002), possibly due to its dual action on 5-HT and NE systems (Stahl, 2002). These findings have stimulated a renewed interest in reevaluating the diagnostic criteria for major depression given the relative underrepresentation of physical symptoms in the DSM-IV criteria (Fava, 1996).

NE Receptor Antagonist

Mirtazapine. FDA approved for the treatment of depression in the summer of 1998, mirtazapine is unique among antidepressants by virtue of the fact that it does not inhibit the reuptake 5-HT, NE, or DA. Its primary mechanism of action relates to its potent antagonism of α_2-adrenergic receptors and $5\text{-}HT_2$ receptors. It is also a potent antagonist of $5\text{-}HT_3$ and histamine H_1 receptors, effects that influence its side effect profile. Mirtazapine has no effects on DA, cholinergic, or α_1-adrenergic receptors (De Boer, 1996). By blocking α_2- but not the α_1-adrenergic receptors, mirtazapine leads to an increase in firing rate and release of both NE and 5-HT. This is because α_2-adrenergic receptors are localized on both NE and 5-HT neurons. On NE neurons, presynaptic α_2 receptors function as autoreceptors, inhibiting the release of NE. Blocking these receptors leads to an increase firing rate and release of NE in most brain regions. NE released near the cell bodies of 5-HT neurons activate α_1-adrenergic receptors located on 5-HT cell bodies, and since these receptors act in an excitatory fashion, the firing rate of 5-HT neurons is increased. 5-HT neurons also have α_2-adrenergic receptors, but in this case, the receptors are localized on 5-HT terminals and function to inhibit the release of 5-HT. Blocking these α_2-adrenergic receptors enhances the amount of 5-HT released each time the neurons fire.

Mirtazapine has been shown to be more effective than placebo in both hospitalized patients and outpatients, and patients with "severe" depression (17-item Hamilton Depression Scale score >25). It has comparable efficacy with amitriptyline (Bremner, 1995), doxepin (Marttila et al., 1995), and chlorimipramine (Richou et al., 1995) and has been shown to be more efficacious than trazodone (Van Moffaert et al., 1995) and fluoxetine (Wheatley et al., 1998) in severely ill depressed patients.

Monoamine Releasing Agents

These drugs are also categorized as stimulants and primarily include amphetamine, methylphenidate, and pemoline. They cause the release and weakly block the reuptake of NE, DA, and 5-HT. Amphetamine was available on an over-the-counter basis until the FDA reclassified it as a prescription drug in 1938 and further restricted its availability in 1951 due to widespread misuse and abuse (Grinspoon and Hedbloom, 1975).

The literature on the use of monoamine releasing agents in the treatment of depression is surprisingly large and disappointingly poorly controlled given the beneficial effects usually reported (Garvey et al., 1990). Almost all large, controlled trials were conducted before 1970, and different studies used different dosing strategies, diagnostic methods, and outcome measures. No long-term trials have been conducted. More recent studies have focused on medically ill or geriatric patients with MDE (Katon and Raskind, 1980; Woods et al., 1986; Fisch, 1985; Kaufmann et al., 1982).

Monoamine releasing agents are rapidly metabolized into inactive compounds and generally have relatively short half lives (4 to 8 hr). The most common side effects are insomnia, drowsiness, restlessness, nausea, weight loss, weight gain, and hypertension. At high doses these agents can cause a characteristic paranoid psychosis. These drugs are generally well tolerated in the clinical dose range (5 to 30 mg d-amphetamine/day), with most patients experiencing no side effects and insomnia being the most common side effect reported.

Hypericum and Other Alternatives

In the mid-1990s there was considerable interest in the possible use of *Hypericum perforatum* (St. John's Wort) as a new treatment for major depression. Numerous

European studies had suggested that *Hypericum* had equal efficacy to standard antide-pressant drugs but was safer and more tolerable (Whiskey et al., 2001). Unfortunately, two well-designed large placebo-controlled U.S. studies failed to support the efficacy of *Hypericum* for the treatment of major depression (Shelton et al., 2001; Hypericum Depression Trial Study Group, 2002).

Several other alternative treatments are currently under investigation. Acupuncture is currently being studied as a potential treatment for depression. Initial reports from a controlled clinical trial have been encouraging (Schnyer and Allen, 2001). Exercise treatment has also shown promise (Babyak et al., 2000; Mather et al., 2002), although accomplishing a truly placebo-controlled trial is difficult.

Side Effects of Antidepressants

The pharmacological properties that underlie the side effects of antidepressants have been better characterized than the properties responsible for the therapeutic effects. While newer antidepressants have provided little additional therapeutic efficacy com-pared to older drugs, they are unequivocally safer and much better tolerated. In general, side effects can be divided into those that occur early in the course of treatment and those that emerge gradually over continuous use.

Frequently Occurring Initial Side Effects (first 1 to 4 weeks). The majority of initial side effects of antidepressant and antimanic drugs relate in a dose-dependent way to muscarinic cholinergic, histamine H_1 and H_2, and α_1-adrenergic antagonist properties. Some initial side effects are also caused by increasing levels of 5-HT or NE (see Bolden-Watson and Richelson, 1993, for reviews). Most early side effects diminish in intensity over time, although cardiovascular side effects may not. Side effects due to receptor antagonist properties are seen almost exclusively in the older TCA and MAOI antidepressants, while side effects seen with the newer agents tend to be related to reuptake inhibition. Idiosyncratic and allergic responses also usually occur during the first 4 weeks of therapy and can occur with drugs in any of the classes.

Some of the most limiting side effects of antidepressant drugs are caused by α_1-adrenergic antagonist properties and include orthostatic hypotension, sedation, and reflex tachycardia. The most common drugs to cause these effects are TCAs, MAOIs, and trazodone.

Some medications, especially the TCAs, mirtazapine, and olanzapine, have potent antihistamine H_1 properties. This effect can cause sedation, weight gain, and in some instances hypotension. Most newer antidepressants such as the SSRIs, bupropion, ven-lafaxine, and duloxetine have no antihistamine effects.

Antimuscarinic cholinergic properties cause dry mouth, dental caries (due to dry mouth), blurred vision, constipation, sinus tachycardia, urinary retention, and memory loss and confusion. The most serious of these effects is the possibility of an anticholin-ergic delirium (atropine psychosis). This is usually associated with elevated plasma levels of TCA drugs but can be seen at therapeutic blood levels. Typical symptoms include impaired short-term memory, confusion, and peripheral signs of anticholiner-gic activity such as dry mouth, enlarged pupils, and dry skin. Older patients seem to be at much increased risk for this side effect and other anticholinergic side effects. The newer agents do not cause these effects. Antimuscarinic effects enhance pupillary dilatation, which can precipitate significant increases in intraocular pressure in patients with preexisting narrow-angle glaucoma.

Norepinephrine reuptake blockade can cause tremor, tachycardia, and erectile and ejaculatory dysfunction; 5-HT reuptake inhibition causes nausea and anxiety or sedation. DA reuptake inhibition causes activation and can exacerbate psychosis.

The causes of some side effects of antidepressant drugs are less understood and are probably related to combinations of pharmacological effects. These include most cardiovascular side effects, perspiration, tremor, speech blockage, sexual dysfunction, akathisia, insomnia, and seizures. Cardiovascular effects are potentially the most serious and are most often seen with TCA and MAOI antidepressants (see Roose and Glassman, 1989). These include dose-related increases in heart rate and prolongation of ventricular conduction (increased PR, QRS, and QTc), orthostatic hypotension, and quinidinelike antiarrhythmic effects. Trazodone may lead to increased ventricular irritability and ectopy.

5-HT Syndrome. Potent 5-HT reuptake inhibitors are the most likely to cause nausea, anorgasmia, and sometimes myoclonus. When these drugs are used in combination with MAOIs, a hypermetabolic syndrome can occur consisting of gastrointestinal distress, headache, agitation, hyperpyrexia, increase heart rate, increased respiratory rate, hypotension or hypertension, muscular rigidity, myoclonus, convulsions, coma, and often death (Sternbach, 1991) The hypermetabolic symptoms reported with this syndrome closely resemble the symptoms of malignant hyperthermia and neuroleptic malignant syndrome, raising questions as to whether these may be manifestations of a common mechanism. Many preclinical and clinical studies have shown that 5-HT reuptake inhibitors have effects on the DA system, and it has been suggested that changes in DA function may be a common element to these conditions (see Beasley et al., 1993, for comprehensive review).

Because of the potential lethality of this reaction, it is recommended that MAOIs be discontinued for at least 2 weeks prior to using an SSRI, and SSRIs should be discontinued for at least 2 weeks prior to initiation of a MAOI. The exception to this is fluoxetine. Because of its long half life and accumulation it should be discontinued for at least 6 weeks prior to using an MAOI.

Frequent Side Effects Occurring after Prolonged Treatment (>4 weeks). Late occurring side effects with antidepressant and antimanic drugs include weight gain, myoclonus, and sexual dysfunction. Weight gain is most common with tertiary TCAs, MAOIs, mirtazapine, and olanzapine but can also be seen with SSRIs after long-term treatment. Myoclonus can occur with any of these medications but may be relatively more common with MAOIs, SSRIs, and lithium.

While sexual side effects can appear at any time, they are more often reported later in the course of treatment, possibly because they are not noticed until the patient has begun to resume more normal function in other spheres of life. SSRIs are the most likely to cause these side effects but TCAs, MAOIs, venlafaxine, lithium, and carbamazepine can also cause them. SSRIs, MAOIs, and venlafaxine are more prone to causing anorgasmia and decreased libido while TCAs are the most likely to cause difficulty maintaining erection.

Withdrawal Reactions. Several types of withdrawal reactions have been reported to occur within hours to days following discontinuation of antidepressant drugs. Symptoms can include gastrointestinal disturbances, sleep disturbances, behavioral activation, agitation, and/or acute depressive reactions. Black et al. (1993) reported dizziness/incoordination, headaches, nausea, and irritability following acute discontinuation of SSRIs. The mechanisms underlying antidepressant withdrawal reactions are not known. Withdrawal is more likely after discontinuation of drugs with short-half lives.

SOMATIC TREATMENTS FOR MAJOR DEPRESSION

Electroconvulsive Therapy (ECT)

Convulsive therapy for psychiatric illness was first demonstrated by Ladislas Meduna in 1934 via camphor injections. In 1938, Cerletti and Bini demonstrated that electrical induction of seizures was more immediate and better tolerated by the patients. Today clinicians have a choice of either right (nondominant) unilateral or bilateral placement of electrodes. In right unilateral placement the highest concentration of current is across the motor cortex, and seizures are elicited at lower energies than with bilateral placement in which the greatest current is induced in the brain's midline structures including the hypothalamus and pituitary gland (Fink, 2001). Since a right-handed patient will usually have memory function localized to the left side, it was proposed that right unilateral placement would result in less memory loss. However, for right unilateral placement to approach the greater efficacy of bilateral placement, energies of up to five times the seizure threshold must be used (Sackeim et al., 2000). At these high energies, the memory effects of right unilateral placement increase dramatically (McCall et al., 2000).

There is no widespread agreement on the underlying mechanism of action of ECT. Electrophysiological studies (Ishihara and Sasa, 1999) have shown that ECT increases the sensitivity of 5-HT$_3$ receptors in the hippocampus, resulting in an increased release of glutamate and GABA. However, tryptophan depletion failed to reverse the improvement in mood seen in depressed patients after ECT (Cassidy et al., 1997) and does not support a primarily 5-HT-dependent mechanism. ECT has been shown to decrease the sensitivity of the noradrenergic and DA autoreceptors in the locus coeruleus and substantia nigra, resulting in an increased release of NE and DA (Ishihara and Sasa, 1999). Support for a noradrenergic mechanism also arises from a study showing a normalization of platelet alpha-2 receptors after a course of ECT (Werstiuk et al., 1996). However, the fact that ECT has efficacy in patients that fail treatment with medications argues against ECT having a similar mechanism of action (Persad, 1990). One of the most interesting hypotheses regarding ECT's mechanism of action relates to its potent effects on increasing levels of brain-derived neurotrophic factor and neuronal sprouting (Duman et al., 1997, 1999).

The effectiveness of ECT in depression is proven in multiple studies and usually ranges between 80 and 90 percent for nonrefractory cases (Persad, 1990). ECT was shown to be more effective than all currently available classes of antidepressant medication (Parker 2001).

Transcranial Magnetic Stimulation

Magnetic stimulators became commercially available in Sheffield (United Kingdom) in 1985. Transcranial magnetic stimulation (TMS) is currently an experimental technique and does not have an approved psychiatric indication. TMS is achieved by conducting a large current through a coil that is placed on the patient's scalp. A magnetic field is induced that passes freely though the skull and induces an electrical field in the cerebral cortex underlying the stimulating coil. TMS has been shown to preferentially activate the cortical interneurons, as opposed to the motor neurons of the cortical-spinal tract, due to the interneurons' orientation parallel to the scalp.

Activation or inhibition of the cortex has been shown to vary with the frequency of the magnetic pulses. A 20-Hz stimulation at the motor threshold (MT) over the left prefrontal cortex of depressed patients was shown to increase the perfusion of the prefrontal cortex (L > R) as well as the cingulate gyrus and left amygdala. A 1-Hz stimulation was only associated with decreases in rCBF (Speer, 2000). The intensity of the magnetic stimulation has also been shown to affect the pattern of activation. Repetitive TMS at 120 percent MT over the left prefrontal cortex produced greater local and contralateral activation than stimulation at 80 percent MT (Nahas, 2001). A negative correlation between the severity of negative symptoms in major depression and rCBF to the left dorsal-lateral prefrontal cortex has been reported (Galynker et al., 1998). Both converging lines of evidence support a hypofunction in the left prefrontal cortex in major depression that may be modified by rTMS and tentatively explain part of its antidepressant effect.

Repetitive TMS was first shown to be beneficial in the treatment of depression in a study with daily stimulation over the left prefrontal cortex at 20 Hz and 80 percent MT (George et al., 1995). Five meta-analyses of rTMS provide evidence for a beneficial acute antidepressant effect compared to placebo (see Chapter 17 for details). Attention to the stimulus parameters of frequency, intensity, and duration is indicated to avoid inducing seizures during rTMS (Wasserman, 1997).

Vagus Nerve Stimulation

Vagus nerve stimulation (VNS) has been commercially available in the United States with an indication for treatment-resistant partial onset seizures in epilepsy since 1997. VNS is achieved in the NCP system (Cyberonics, Houston) by coiling an electrode around the left vagus nerve in the neck near the carotid artery. A subcutaneous line connects the stimulating electrode to a bipolar pulse generator implanted in the left chest wall. The vagus nerve is composed of 80 percent afferent sensory fibers. These sensory fibers terminate in the nucleus tractus solitarus (NTS). The NTS sends information to the forebrain, hypothalamus, and thalamus through the LC and parabrachial nucleus (George et al., 2000). Animal studies have demonstrated that the LC must be intact for VNS to achieve an anticonvulsant effect (Krahl et al., 1998). The role of the LC in the treatment of depression with medications has been noted above. Brain imaging studies in epilepsy patients have shown VNS to cause an initial increase in the perfusion of the rostral medulla, hypothalamus, and thalamus bilaterally and a decrease at the hippocampus, amygdala, and posterior cingulate gyri bilaterally (Henry et al., 1998). The decrease in perfusion of the hippocampus and amygdala has been shown to be present after 6 months with chronic VNS (Van Laere et al., 2002). The decrease in perfusion to the hippocampus has been reported to differentiate a response to an active drug in the treatment of depression from a placebo response (Mayberg et al., 2002).

The first observations of the positive effect of VNS on mood were in epilepsy patients. Improvements in overall well-being were reported by the patients that were not entirely explained by improvements in seizure frequency (Handforth et al., 1998). In a study of 30 nonepileptic patients with treatment-resistant depression, a response rate of 40 percent was obtained with 10 weeks of VNS (Rush et al., 2000). These improvements were shown to be stable over a 1-year period on the same 30 patients with 91 percent of the original responders continuing to show a response with continued VNS. Of the 18 original nonresponders 41 percent showed a response at 6 months of VNS (Marangell et al., 2002). The most frequent side effect was voice alteration in 21 percent of the patients. No patient discontinued due to clear adverse effects, even though one patient elected to be explanted after failure to respond following 1 year of therapy, which may have been due to VNS-induced dysphoric hypomania.

ANTIMANIC AND MOOD STABILIZERS

In comparison to the data available for the use of antidepressant drugs, research with antimanic drugs is more limited. In part this is because alternatives to lithium and antipsychotics have only recently become widely available and in part because clinical research involving people afflicted with bipolar disorder is inherently difficult, especially long-term studies. While there is general agreement that the monoamine systems are involved in antidepressant responses, the neural systems involved in the mechanism of antimanic drugs are poorly defined.

Drugs with established antimanic and mood-stabilizing properties have a wide variety of pharmacological properties. Attention has been focused mostly on the intracellular properties of antimanic drugs, in part because very few significant changes in neurotransmitter levels have been identified. The systems being most intensively investigated in relation to possible mechanism of action are the adenylate cyclase and phosphotidylinositol second-messenger systems and the G protein coupling proteins (Avissar and Schreiber, 1992; Manji et al., 2001). Table 8.6 lists common antimanic drugs and describes important clinical parameters.

TABLE 8.6. Common Antimanic and Mood Stabilizers

Drug	Dose Range (mg/day)	Plasma Level	Half Life (hr)
Lithium	600–2100	0.5–1.5 mEq/L	14–30
Carbamazepine	400–1200	4–12 µg/mL	13–17
Valproic Acid	500–1500	50–100 µg/mL	6–16
Lamotrigine	50–200	—	15–70
Gabapentin	300–2400	—	6–7
Topiramate	50–400	—	18–23

TABLE 8.7. Treatment Recommendations for Patients with Bipolar Disorder by the American Psychiatric Association (2002)

Acute Treatment

Mania or mixed episodes	• Lithium plus an antipsychotic • Valproic acid plus an antipsychotic • Electroconvulsive therapy
Depressive episodes	• Lithium • Lamotrigine • Psychotherapy • Combinations • Electroconvulsive therapy
Rapid cycling	• Lithium • Valproic acid • Lamotrigine • Combinations

Maintenance Treatment

• Lithium
• Valproic acid
• Electroconvulsive therapy

A comprehensive review of the diagnosis and treatment of bipolar disorder has recently been published by the American Psychiatric Association (2002). Treatment recommendations are listed in Table 8.7.

Lithium

Lithium was used medically as a treatment for gout, diabetes, and epilepsy in the early 1800s. It was first used to treat mood disorders in the 1870s because it was theorized that these conditions were the result of uric acid deposits in the brain. The first reported use in mania was in 1949 when Cade reported that it was effective. Lithium began to be widely used in the United States in the mid to late 1960s and remains the only drug currently approved by the FDA for both the acute and maintenance treatment of mania. Because of side effects it is usually not initiated as the first treatment option.

Lithium is more effective in the acute treatment of mania than placebo or typical antipsychotic drugs (Prien et al., 1973). Response rates range from 60 to 80 percent. It may be less effective than divalproic acid in patients with dysphoric mania (mania with prominent anxiety or depressive symptoms) or rapid cycling (Post, 1992).

As with antidepressant treatments, there is a time lag in the onset of the therapeutic action of lithium, with the full effects often taking from 1 to 4 weeks to occur. This time lag is especially important with lithium because manic patients are difficult to manage and have extremely poor judgment, making the risk of self-injury or injury to others very real. For this reason, antipsychotic medications or benzodiazepines are usually required until the therapeutic effects occur.

Lithium is rapidly and completely absorbed, is not protein bound, and does not undergo metabolism. Peak plasma levels are achieved within 2 to 4 hr and the mean half-life is 18 hr (range 14 to 30 hr) in young patients (Gelenberg and Schoonover, 1991). Because lithium is filtered through the proximal tubules, changes in glomerular filtration rate will alter lithium clearance. Sodium is also filtered through the proximal tubule; therefore a decrease in plasma sodium can increase lithium reabsorption in the proximal tubule and cause an increase in plasma lithium levels. Conversely, an increase in plasma lithium levels can cause an increase in sodium excretion, dangerously depleting plasma sodium.

Therapeutic doses of lithium are quite variable, ranging from 600 mg/day to as high as 2100 mg/day. Because of the potential for serious toxicity, plasma levels of lithium are routinely used to establish a therapeutic dose. The usual therapeutic range is between 0.5 and 1.5 mEq/L. In the acute treatment phase, plasma lithium levels between 0.8 and 1.1 mEq/L are recommended in order to maximize therapeutic effect. Lithium levels above 0.8 mEq/L are associated with fewer relapses into mania or depression but greater noncompliance due to side effects than levels between 0.4 and 0.6 mEq/L (Gelenberg et al., 1989).

Lithium can cause short-term side effects including tremor, gastric irritation, nausea, abdominal cramping, diarrhea, vomiting, increased white blood cell count (up to 15,000 cells/mm^3), polyuria and polydipsia, dermatitis, extrapyramidal reactions, fatigue and muscle weakness, and flattening of T waves, T-wave inversion, or U-waves on an electrocardiogram. Long-term side effects include weight gain, hypothyroidism (5 to 30 percent), diabetes insipidus, potential kidney damage, and hence decreased glomerular filtration rate, hyperthyroidism, and hyperparathyroidism (Gelenberg and Schoonover, 1991). Lithium has been reported to cause fetal heart anomalies but recent data suggests the incidence is low, so risks must be weighed versus benefits. Because lithium is excreted in breast milk in significant quantities, breastfeeding should be approached with caution.

Carbamazepine

Carbamazepine is an anticonvulsant drug structurally related to the TCAs. Like TCAs, its absorption and metabolism is variable. It is rapidly absorbed, with peak plasma levels occurring within 4 to 6 hr. Eighty percent of plasma carbamazepine is protein bound and the half-life ranges from 13 to 17 hr. Carbamazepine is metabolized by the hepatic P450IID6 system. It induces the P450 enzymes, causing an increase in the rate of its own metabolism over time as well as that of other drugs metabolized by the P450 system. This often results in having to raise the dose within 2 to 4 months of treatment initiation.

Concomitant administration of carbamazepine with oral contraceptives, warfarin, theophylline, doxycycline, haloperidol, TCAs, or valproic acid leads to decreased plasma levels of these other drugs. Concomitant administration of drugs that inhibit the P450 system will increase plasma levels of carbamazepine. This includes fluoxetine, cimetidine, erythromycin, isoniazid, calcium channel blockers, and propoxyphene. Concomitant administration of phenobarbitol, phenytoin, and primidone causes a decrease in carbamazepine levels through induction of the P450 enzymes.

Since 1978 more than 19 studies (almost all small case series or open trials) have been published evaluating the effectiveness of carbamazepine in the treatment of mania. The majority of these trials have shown carbamazepine to be equal in efficacy to lithium and neuroleptics and more effective than placebo. However, the number of patients in each study has been small, the diagnoses heterogeneous or unspecified, concomitant medications have been used, and study designs have been unclear. Usual therapeutic doses of carbamazepine range from 400 to 1200 mg/day and therapeutic plasma levels range from 4 to 12 μg/mL.

Carbamazepine frequently causes lethargy, sedation, nausea, tremor, ataxia, and visual disturbances during the acute treatment phase (Zajecka, 1993). Some patients can develop mild leukopenia or thrombocytopenia during this phase and usually do not progress. Carbamazepine has been reported to cause a severe form of aplastic anemia or agranulocytosis that is estimated to occur with an incidence of about 2 to 5/100,000. This is 11 times more likely than in the general population. While more than 80 percent of these reactions occur during the first 3 months of therapy, some cases have been reported as late as 5 years following initiation of therapy treatment. If white blood cell count drops below 3000 cells/mm^3, the medication should be discontinued.

Carbamazepine has also been associated with fetal anomalies including a risk of spina bifida (1 percent), low birth weight, or small head circumference. It has also been shown to have effects on cardiac conduction, slowing AV conduction. Other reported side effects include inappropriate secretion of antidiuretic hormone (SIADH) with concomitant hyponatremia, decreased thyroid hormone levels without change in thyroid-stimulating hormone, severe dermatologic reactions such as the Stevens-Johnson syndrome, and hepatitis.

Carbamazepine is associated with more side effects and potential toxicity than most other mood stabilizers. Because of the cardiac, hematological, endocrine, and renal side effects associated with carbamazepine, patients should have had a recent physical examination, complete blood count (CBC) with platelet count, liver function, thyroid function, and renal indices prior to initiation of treatment. The CBC and liver function should be monitored every 4 to 8 weeks during the initial 3 to 4 months of treatment, and all baseline tests should be repeated at a minimum of yearly intervals thereafter. Any change in the above tests should warrant closer evaluation and follow-up. Carbamazepine shares with the TCAs the risk of hypertensive crisis when coadministered with MAOIs, and so this combination should not be routinely used. If it has a role, it is more likely as an adjunct in rapid cyclers and dysphoric mania and mixed states.

Valproic Acid

Valproic acid (dipropylacetic acid) is currently approved by the FDA for acute treatment of manic episodes associated with bipolar disorder. While it does not have FDA approval for maintenance treatment, it has become the most widely used medication in both acute and maintenance treatment of bipolar disorder in the United States. In a large multisite study, valproic acid did not differ from placebo in the length of time to recurrence of mania or depression in patients with bipolar disorder undergoing maintenance treatment (lithium also failed in this study) (Bowden et al., 2002). It is widely believed that this was a result of the high drop-out and noncompliance rate for all treatments in this study rather than a true reflection of lack of maintenance efficacy. Several open-label studies have shown efficacy for valproic acid in the maintenance therapy of bipolar disorder (American Psychiatric Association, 2002), as discussed below.

Valproic acid is produced in various preparations including syrup, sprinkles, capsules, enteric coated capsules, and tablets. One of the more commonly used preparations is divalproex sodium, a compound of sodium valproate and valproic acid in a 1 : 1 molar ratio. Absorption is different across the different preparations and is delayed by food. However, since anticonvulsant efficacy is not related to peak levels but rather related to total daily bioavailable dose, this variability is thought to be clinically irrelevant. Peak plasma levels are achieved between 2 and 4 hr of ingestion and the half-life ranges from 6 to 16 hr. More than 90 percent of plasma valproic acid is protein bound. The time of dosing is determined by possible side effects and, if tolerated, a once/day dosing could be employed. The therapeutic plasma levels used for the treatment of mania are the same as those used for anticonvulsant therapy (50 to 100 μg/mL) and the daily dose required to achieve these levels ranges from 500 to 1500 mg.

Valproic acid is metabolized by the hepatic P450IID6 system, but unlike carbamazepine it does not autoinduce its own metabolism. Concomitant administration of carbamazepine will decrease plasma levels of valproic acid, and drugs that inhibit the P450 system (SSRIs) can cause an increase in valproic acid levels.

At least 16 uncontrolled open-label and six controlled studies have been published investigating the efficacy of valproic acid in the treatment of mania. These studies demonstrate considerable efficacy for valproic acid. The first placebo-controlled comparison of divalproex sodium with lithium in 179 inpatients afflicted with mania demonstrates equal efficacy to lithium and greater efficacy than placebo for both lithium and divalproex sodium. The rate of early termination because of side effects was significantly greater for lithium than placebo or divalproex sodium (Bowden et al., 2002).

Valproic acid appears to have the most favorable side effect profile of all available antimanic drugs. Dose-related and common initial side effects include nausea, tremor, and lethargy. Gastric irritation and nausea can be reduced by dividing the dose or using enteric coated preparations. Valproic acid has been associated with potentially fatal hepatic failure, usually occurring within the first 6 months of treatment and most frequently occurring in children under age 2 and individuals with preexisting liver disease. Transient, dose-related elevations in liver enzymes can occur in up to 44 percent of patients. Any change in hepatic function should be followed closely and patients should be warned to report symptoms of hepatic failure such as malaise, weakness, lethargy, edema, anorexia, or vomiting. Valproic acid may produce teratogenic effects including spina bifida (1 percent) and other neural tube defects. Other potential side effects include weight gain, inhibition of platelet aggregation, hair loss, and severe dermatologic reactions such as the Stevens-Johnson's syndrome.

Antipsychotic and Atypical Antipsychotic Drugs

Antipsychotic drugs were some of the first drugs used to treat acute mania and are highly effective (Prien et al., 1973). While onset of action is often more rapid than lithium, carbamazepine, or valproic acid, antipsychotics can cause serious potential side effects.

A major concern with typical antipsychotics is the potential for tardive dyskinesia. Tardive dyskinesia may occur more frequently in patients with mood disorders than those with schizophrenia and also in those with intermittent exposure rather than continuous use, placing bipolar patients at higher risk (Casey, 1987). Because of this and the availability of safer and better tolerated drugs, antipsychotic medications should only be used in the management of acute agitation, excitement, or psychosis in manic patients or in those few patients who clearly relapse on gradual discontinuation of maintenance antipsychotics.

While only approved by the FDA for the treatment of drug-resistant schizophrenia, the atypical antipsychotic drug clozapine has been shown to be effective in the treatment of mania and dysphoric mania (McElroy et al., 1991; Alphs and Campbell, 2002). Eighty-six percent of 14 bipolar patients with psychotic features showed significant improvement, and 7 of these patients were followed for an additional 3- to 5-year period with no further hospitalizations (Suppes et al., 1992). Other studies suggest clozapine is also effective in maintenance treatment of patients with bipolar disorder (Alphs and Campbell, 2002). Because of the risk of potentially fatal agranulocytosis, clozapine should not be used unless other first-line agents or traditional antipsychotic drugs have failed.

Newer atypical antipsychotics that do not have a risk of agranulocytosis are now widely available. These drugs are being intensively studied for the treatment of bipolar and unipolar mood disorders because they appear to have a lower risk of tardive dyskinesia and are associated with a lower overall side effect profile compared with older antipsychotics. Olanzepine, risperidone, and quetiapine are all being studied as both monotherapy and as an adjunctive therapy for treatment of acute mania. Of the three, olanzapine is the best studied, with double-blind comparator trials as well as double-blind placebo-controlled trials showing significant efficacy (Tohen et al., 1999) in acute mania. All atypical antipsychotic drugs are being widely used in the United States for the treatment of agitation and psychosis in manic or psychotically depressed patients, in spite of the absence of controlled data. Interestingly, olanzapine and risperidone have both been reported to cause mania in some patients with schizophrenia, schizoaffective, or bipolar disorder. At this point, none of these drugs should be used for long-term monotherapy of bipolar disorder in patients who have been tried on other available agents since no long-term studies have been completed.

Newer Anticonvulsants

Several drugs that have been approved by the FDA as anticonvulsants have been studied as possible mood stabilizers or antimanic drugs (lamotrigine, gabapentin, and topiramate). In spite of extremely limited data on short- or long-term efficacy, their use for the treatment of bipolar disorder and refractory depression in the United States has become widespread.

Lamotrigine is the best studied of the newer anticonvulsants. While showing efficacy for treatment of depression and for maintenance treatment in bipolar patients, it may be less efficacious in the treatment of acute mania (Leadbetter et al., 2002; American Psychiatric Association, 2002). Along with many open-label studies, there is one large multisite placebo-controlled trial of lamotrigine monotherapy for treatment of depression in outpatients with bipolar disorder (Calabrese et al., 1999). In this study, 200 mg/day of lamotrigine demonstrated significant antidepressant effects in over 50 percent of these patients without inducing mania or rash. Lamotrigine inhibits voltage-gated sodium channels and reduces glutamate. It is absorbed within 1 to 3 hr and has a half-life of 25 hr. Rash can occur in up to 8 percent of adults, and serious rash requiring hospitalization can be seen in up to 0.5 percent of patients. Because of the possibility of Stevens-Johnson syndrome, toxic epidermal necrolysis, or angioedema, all rashes should be regarded as potentially serious and monitored closely. Low starting doses (25 mg/day) and slow titration may help reduce the occurrence of rash.

Gabapentin has been studied as both a monotherapy and adjunctive treatment for mania and bipolar depression (Cabras et al., 1999), and while the initial results were generally favorable, subsequent trials failed to show efficacy. Because of this, gabapentin is not recommended for use in mood disorders (American Psychiatric Association, 2002).

Topiramate inhibits rapid firing at voltage-dependent sodium channels, antagonizes kainate binding to the AMPA receptor, and potentiates the effects of GABA at the GABA-A receptor. In a small number of cases, topiramate addition to ongoing treatment with other drugs has been reported to be effective in reducing acute mania or refractory depression (Yatham et al., 2002). It has a half-life of 20 hr and is usually dosed twice daily. Eighty percent of the drug is excreted unchanged in the urine.

In the presence of metabolism-enhancing drugs, it is more extensively metabolized by the liver, causing the plasma levels and half-life to decrease by up to 50 percent. Topiramate can interfere with the efficacy of oral contraceptives, therefore women of child-bearing potential should be counseled and alternative sources of birth control should be considered. The most common side effects of topiramate include somnolence, dizziness, ataxia, speech and cognitive disorders, fatigue, and weight loss. Up to 20 percent of patients experience weight loss, a side effect that has led to the use of topiramate in psychiatric patients solely for this property (Yatham et al., 2002).

SUMMARY AND CONCLUSIONS

In the past 50 years a multitude of effective and safe treatments for mood disorders have been successfully introduced into the clinic. Conditions that once required long-term hospitalization for many patients are now routinely treated on an outpatient basis, and people suffering from mood disorders are more often than not able to lead relatively normal lives. Given the economic and social impact of these conditions, it is essential to improve diagnosis and provide consistent access to treatment.

During this period, the focus of psychiatric research was on understanding the role of monoamine systems in the pathophysiology of mental illnesses. These efforts were greatly influenced by the discovery of the CNS DA deficiency in patients suffering from Parkinson's disease (Ehringer and Hornykiewicz, 1960) and the remarkable therapeutic effects of L-DOPA treatment (Cotzias et al., 1967). The discovery of a DA deficiency in Parkinson's disease led psychiatric investigators to hope that the pathophysiology of mental disorders would be discovered by understanding the pharmacology of our treatments. The research of the past 30 years suggests that new, more complex models are in order. We have begun to understand that mood disorders are not simply the result of a deficiency on monoamine neurotransmitters and that we have to better understand the anatomy and function of brain circuits regulating emotion and cognition as well as the molecular events that modulate the function and viability of these circuits. As the pathophysiology of mood disorders becomes elucidated, future efforts will target disease pathophysiology, leading to more rapidly acting and effective treatments.

REFERENCES

Aberg-Wistedt A (1982). A double-blind study of zimelidine, a selective serotonin uptake inhibitor, and desipramine, a noradrenaline uptake inhibitor, in endogenous depression: I. Clinical findings. *Acta Psych Scand* 66:50–65.

Alphs LD, Campbell B.J (2002). Clozapine: Treatment of mood symptoms. *Psychiatric Ann* 32:722–729.

Altamura AC, Percudani M (1993). The use of antidepressants for long-term treatment of recurrent depression: Rationale, current methodologies, and future directions. *J Clin Psychiatry* 54(suppl 8):29–37.

American Psychiatric Association (1994). *Diagnostic and Statistical Manual of Mental Disorders*, Fourth Edition. American Psychiatric Association: Washington DC.

American Psychiatric Association (2000). Practice guideline for the treatment of patients with major depressive disorder (revision). *Am J Psychiatry* 157(Suppl 4).

American Psychiatric Association (2002). Practice Guideline for the Treatment of Patients with Bipolar Disorder (Revision). *Am J Psychiatry* 159(Suppl 4):1–50.

Angst J (1990). Natural history and epidemiology of depression: Results of community studies. In Cobb J, Goeting N (eds). *Prediction and Treatment of Recurrent Depression*. Duphar Medical Relations: Southampton, England, pp. 1–9.

Angst J, Baastrup P, Grof P, et al. (1973). The course of monopolar depression and bipolar psychoses. *Psychiatr Neurol Neurochir* 76:489–500.

Avissar S, Schreiber G (1992). Interaction of antibipolar and antidepressant treatments with receptor-coupled G proteins. *Pharmacopsychiatry* 25:44–50.

Babyak M, Blumenthal JA, Herman S, Khatri P, Doraiswamy M, Moore K, Craighead WE, Baldewicz TT, Krishnan KR (2000). Exercise treatment for major depression: Maintenance of therapeutic benefit at 10 months. *Psychosomatic Med* 62:633–638.

Beasley CM, Masica DN, Heiligenstein JH, Wheadon DE, Zerbe RL (1993). Possible monoamine oxidase inhibitor-serotonin uptake inhibitor interaction: Fluoxetine clinical data and preclinical findings. *J Clin Psychopharmacol* 13:312–320.

Black DW, Wesner R, Gabel J (1993). The abrupt discontinuation of fluvoxamine in patients with panic disorder. *J Clin Psychiatry* 54(4):146–149.

Blackwell B (1987). Side effects of antidepressant drugs. In Hales RE, Frances AJ (eds). *Psychiatry Update: The American Psychiatric Association Annual Review*. American Psychiatric Press: Washington, DC, pp. 724–745.

Bolden-Watson C, Richelson E (1993). Blockade by newly-developed antidepressants of biogenic amine uptake into rat brain synaptosomes. *Life Sci* 52:1023–1029.

Bowden CL, Lawson DM, Cunningham M, Owen JR, Tracy KA (2002). The role of divalproex in the treatment of bipolar disorder. *Psychiatric Annals* 32:742–750.

Bremner JD (1995). A double-blind comparison of Org 3770, amitriptyline, and placebo in major depression. *J Clin Psychiatry* 56:519–525.

Burrows GD, Maguire KP, Norman TR (1998). Antidepressant efficacy and tolerability of the selective norepinephrine reuptake inhibitor reboxetine: A review. *J Clin Psychiatry* 59(suppl 14):4–7.

Bymaster FP, Drechfield-Ahmad LJ, Threlkeld PG, Shaw JL, Thompson L, Nelson DL, Hemrick-Luecke SK, Wong DT (2001). Comparative affinity of duloxetine and venlafaxine for serotonin and norepinephrine transporters in vitro and in vivo, human serotonin receptor subtypes, and other neuronal receptors. *Neuropsychopharmacology* 25:871–880.

Bymaster FP, Katner JS, Nelson DL, Hemrick-Luecke SK, Threlkeld PG, Heiligenstein JH, Morin SM, Gehlert DR, Perry KW (2002). Atomoxetine increases extracellular levels of norepinephrine and dopamine in prefrontal cortex of rat: A potential mechanism for efficacy in attention deficit/hyperactivity disorder. *Neuropsychopharmacology* 27:699–711.

Cade JFJ (1949). Lithium salts in the treatment of psychotic excitement. *Medical Journal of Australia* 2:349–352.

Cabras PL, Hardoy MJ, Hardoy MC, Carta MG (1999). Clinical experience with gabapentin in patients with bipolar or schizoaffective disorder: Results of an open-label study. *J Clin Psychiatry* 60:245–248.

Calabrese JR, Bowden CL, Sachs GS, Ascher JA, Monaghan E, Rudd GD (1999). A double-blind placebo-controlled study of lamotrigine monotherapy in outpatients with bipolar I depression. *Clinical Psychiatry* 60:79–78.

Cassidy F, Murray E, Weiner RD, Carrol BJ (1997). Lack of relapse with tryptophan depletion following successful treatment with ECT. *Am J Psychiatry* 154:1151–1152.

Canive JM, Clark RD, Calais LA, Qualls C, Tuason VB (1998). Bupropion treatment in veterans with posttraumatic stress disorder: An open study. *J Clin Psychopharmacol* 18:379–383.

Casey DE (1987). Tardive dyskinesia. In Meltzer HY (ed). *Psychopharmacology: The Third Generation of Progress.* Raven Press: New York, pp. 1411–1419.

Cotzias GC, Van Woert MH, Schiffer LM (1967). Aromatic amino acids and modification of Parkinsonism. *N Engl J Med* 276(7):374–379.

De Boer Th (1996). The pharmacologic profile of mirtazapine. *J Clin Psychiatry* 57(suppl 4):19–25.

Delgado PL, Charney DS, Price LH, Aghajanian GK, Landis H, Heninger GR (1990). Serotonin function and the mechanism of antidepressant action: Reversal of antidepressant induced remission by rapid depletion of plasma tryptophan. *Arch Gen Psychiatry* 47:411–418.

Delgado PL, Miller HM, Salomon RM, Licinio J, Gelenberg AJ, Charney DS (1993). Monoamines and the mechanism of antidepressant action: Effects of catecholamine depletion on mood in patients treated with antidepressants. *Psychopharmacol Bull* 29:389–396.

Delgado PL, Miller HM, Salomon RM, Licinio J, Krystal JH, Heninger GR, Charney DS (1999). Tryptophan depletion challenge in depressed patients treated with desipramine or fluoxetine: Implications for the role of serotonin in the mechanism of antidepressant action. *Biol Psychiatry* 46:212–220.

Delgado PL, Price LH, Aghajanian, GK, Miller, HM, Salomon, RM, Heninger GR, Charney DS (1994). Serotonin and the neurobiology of depression: Effects of tryptophan depletion in drug-free depressed patients. *Arch Gen Psychiatry* 51:865–874.

Delgado PL, Moreno FA, Potter R, et al. (1997). Norepinephrine and serotonin in antidepressant action: Evidence from neurotransmitter depletion studies. In Briley M, Montgomery SA (eds). *Antidepressant Therapy at the Dawn of the Third Millennium.* Martin Dunitz: London, pp. 141–163.

Depression Guideline Panel (1993). Depression in primary care: Volume 2: Treatment of major depression. Technical Report Number 5. US Department of Health and Human Resources, Public Health Service: Rockville, M.D.

Detke MJ, Lu Y, Goldstein DJ, Hayes JR, Demitrack MA (2002). Duloxetine, 60 mg once daily, for major depressive disorder: A randomized double-blind placebo-controlled trial. *J Clin Psychiatry* 63:308–315.

Duman RS, Heninger GR, Nestler EJ (1997). A molecular and cellular theory of depression. *Arch Gen Psychiatry* 54:597–606.

Duman RS, Malberg J, Thome J (1999). Neural plasticity to stress and antidepressant treatment. *Biol Psychiatry* 46:1181–1191.

Ehringer E, Hornykiewicz O (1960). Verteilung von Noradrenalin and Dopamin (3-Hydroxytyramin): im Gehirn des Menschen und ihr Verhalten bei Erkrankungen des estrapyramidalen Systems. *Klin Wschr* 38:1236–1239.

Emmanuel NP, Lydiard BR, Ballenger JC (1991). Treatment of social phobia with bupropion. *J Clin Psychopharmacol* 11:276–277.

Fava M (1996). Somatic symptoms, depression, and antidepressant treatment. *J Clin Psychiatry* 63:305–307.

Feighner J (1993). The efficacy of venlafaxine in major depression and preliminary findings in the treatment of refractory depression. *J Clin Psychiatry* 54:123–124.

Ferris RM, Cooper BR (1993). Mechanism of antidepressant activity of bupropion. *J Clin Psychiatry Monograph* 11:2–14.

Fink M (2001). Convulsive therapy: a review of the first 55 years. *J Affective Disord* 63:1–15.

Finkel MS, Laghrissi-Thode F, Pollock BG, Rong J (2002). Paroxetine is a novel nitric oxide synthase inhibitor. *Psychopharmacol Bull* 32:653–658.

Fisch RZ (1985). Methylphenidate for medical inpatients. *Int J Psychiatry Med* 15:75–79.

Frank E, Kupfer DJ, Perel JM, Cornes C, Jarrett DB, Malinger AG, Thase ME, McEachran AB, Grocinski VJ (1990). Three-year outcomes for maintenance therapies in recurrent depression. *Arch Gen Psychiatry* 47:1093–1099.

Frank E, Prien RF, Jarrett DB, Keller MB, Kupfer DJ, Lavori P, Rush AJ, Weissman MM (1991). Conceptualization and rationale for consensus definitions of terms in major depressive disorder: Response, remission, recovery, relapse, and recurrence. *Arch Gen Psychiatry* 48:851–855.

Garvey M, Noyes R Jr, Cook B (1990). Use of psychostimulants in affective disorders. In Amsterdam JD (ed). *Pharmacotherapy of Depression. Applications for the Outpatient Practitioner.* Marcel Dekker: New York, pp. 159–183.

Galynker CJ II, Ongseng F, Finestone H, Dutta E, Serseni D (1998). Hypofrontality and negative symptoms in major depressive disorder. *J Nucl Med* 39:608–612.

Gelenberg, AJ, Schoonover SC (1991). Bipolar disorder. In Gelenberg AJ, Bassuk EL, Schoonover SC (eds). *The Practitioner's Guide to Psychoactive Drugs*, Third Edition. Plenum Medical: New York, pp. 91–123.

Gelenberg AJ, Kane JM, Keller MB, Lavori P, Rosenbaum JF, Cole K, Lavelle J (1989). Comparison of standard and low serum levels of lithium for maintenance treatment of bipolar disorder. *N Eng J Med* 321:1489–1493.

George MS, Sackeim HA, Rush AJ, Marangell LB, Nahas Z, Husain MM, Lisanby S, Burt T, Goldman J, Ballenger JC (2000). Vagus nerve stimulation: A new tool for brain research and therapy. *Biol Psychiatry* 47:287–295.

George MS, Wasserman EM, Williams WA, Callahan A, Ketter TA, Basser P, Hallett M, Post RM (1995). Daily repetitive transcranial magnetic stimulation (rTMS) improves mood in depression. Neuroreport 6:1853–1856.

Golden RN, Rudorfer MV, Sherer MA, Linnoila M, Potter WZ (1988). Bupropion in depression. *Arch Gen Psychiatry* 45:139–149.

Goldstein DJ, Mallinckrodt C, Lu Y, Demitrack MA (2002). Duloxetine in the treatment of major depressive disorder: A double-blind clinical trial. *J Clin Psychiatry* 63:225–231.

Goodman WK, Price LH, Delgado PL, Palumbo J, Krystal J, Rasmussen SA, Heninger GR, Charney DS (1990). Specificity of serotonin reuptake inhibitors in the treatment of obsessive compulsive disorder: Comparison of fluvoxamine and desipramine. *Arch Gen Psychiatry* 47:577–585.

Goodwin FK, Jamison, KR (1990). *Manic-Depressive Illness.* Oxford University Press: New York.

Gorman JM, Korotzer A, Su G (2002). Efficacy comparison of escitalopram and citalopram in the treatment of major depressive disorder: pooled analysis of placebo-controlled trials. *CNS Spectrums* 7(suppl 1):40–44.

Grinspoon L, Hedbloom P (1975). *The Speed Culture: Amphetamine Use and Abuse in America.* Harvard University Press: Cambridge, MA.

Handforth A, DeGiorgio CM, Schachter SC, Uthman BM, Naritoku DK, Tecoma ES, Henry TR, Collins SD, Vaughn BV, Gilmartin RC, Labar DR, Morris GL 3rd, Salinsky MC, Osorio I, Ristanovic RK, Labiner DM, Jones JC, Murphy JV, Ney GC, Wheliss JW (1998). Vagus nerve stimulation therapy for partial-onset seizures: A randomized active-control trial. *Neurology* 51:48–55.

Henry TR, Bakay RAE, Votaw JR, Pennell PB, Epstein CM, Faber TL, Grafton ST, Hoffman JM (1998). Brain blood flow alterations induced by therapeutic vagus nerve stimulation in partial epilepsy: I. *Acute effects at high and low levels of stimulation. Epilepsia* 39:983–990.

Hyman SE, Nestler EJ (1996). Initiation and adaptation: A paradigm for understanding psychotropic drug action. *Am J Psychiatry* 153:151–162.

Hypericum Depression Trial Study Group (2002). Effect of Hypericum perforatum (St John's wort): In major depressive disorder: A randomized controlled trial. *JAMA* 287:1807–1814.

Ishihara K, Sasa M (1999). Mechanism underlying the therapeutic effects of electroconvulsive therapy (ECT) on depression. *Jpn J Pharmacol* 80:185–189.

Kalus O, Asnis GM, Robinson E, Kahn R et al. (1991). Desipramine treatment in panic disorder. *J Aff Dis* 21:239–244.

Katon W, Raskind M (1980). Treatment of depression in the medically ill elderly with methylphenidate. *Am J Psychiatry* 137:963–965.

Kaufmann MW, Murray GB, Cassem NH (1982). Use of psychostimulants in medically ill depressed patients. *Psychosomatics* 23:817–819.

Keller MB (2001). Long-term treatment of recurrent and chronic depression. *J Clin Psychiatry* 62(Suppl 24):3–5.

Keller MB, Shapiro RW, Lavori PW, et al. (1982). Recovery in major depressive disorder: Analysis with the life table and regression models. *Arch Gen Psychiatry* 39:905–910.

Kraepelin E (1921). *Manic-Depressive Insanity and Paranoia.* Barclay RM (trans), Robertson GM (ed). Livingstone: Edinburgh, reprinted Arno Press: New York, 1976.

Krahl SE, Clark KB, Smith DC, Browning RA (1998). Locus coeruleus lesions suppress the seizure attenuating effects of vagus nerve stimulation. *Epilepsia* 39:709–714.

Kupfer DJ (1991). Long-term treatment of depression. *J Clin Psychiatry* 52(Suppl 5):28–34.

Kupfer DJ, Frank E, Perel JM, Cornes C, Jarrett DB, Malinger AG, Thase ME, McEachran AB, Grocinski VJ (1992). Five-year outcome for maintenance therapies in recurrent depression. *Arch Gen Psychiatry* 49:769–773.

Leadbetter R, Messenheimer J, Bentley B, Greene P, Huffman R, Spaulding T (2002). Mood-stabilizing properties of lamotrigine: A review of data from controlled clinical trials. *Psychiatric Annals* 32:766–772.

Lelliott PT, WO Montiero WO (1986). Drug treatment of obsessive compulsive disorder. *Drugs* 31:75–80.

Leonard HL, Swedo SE, Lenane MC, Rettew DC, et al. (1991). A double-blind desipramine substitution during long-term clomipramine treatment in children and adolescents with obsessive-compulsive disorder. *Arch Gen Psychiatry* 48:922–927.

Loomer HP, Saunders JC, Kline NS (1957). A clinical and pharmacodynamic evaluation of iproniazid as a psychic energizer. *Psychiatric Res Rep* 8:129–141.

Lydiard BR, Morton WA, Emmanuel NP, Zealberg JJ, et al. (1993). Preliminary report: Placebo-controlled, double-blind study of the clinical and metabolic effects of desipramine in panic disorder. *Psychopharmacol Bull* 29:183–188.

Manji HK, Moore GJ, Chen G. (2001). Bipolar disorder: Leads from the molecular and cellular mechanisms of action of mood stabilisers. *Br J Psychiatry* 178(Suppl 41):s107–s119.

Marangell LB, Rush AJ, George MS, Sackeim HA, Johnson CR, Husain MM, Nahas Z, Lisanby SH (2002). Vagus nerve stimulation (VNS) for major depressive episodes: One year outcomes. *Biol Psychiatry* 51:280–287.

Marttila M, Jaaskelainen J, Jarvi R, Romanov M, Miettinen E, Sorri P, Ahlfors U (1995). A double-blind study comparing the efficacy and tolerability of mirtazapine and doxepin in patients with major depression. *Eur Neuropsychopharmacol* 5:441–446.

Mather AS, Rodriguez C, Guthrie MF, McHarg AM, Reid IC, McMurdo MET (2002). Effects of exercise on depressive symptoms in older adults with poorly responsive depressive disorder: Randomised controlled trial. *Br J Psychiatry* 180:411–415.

Mayberg HS, Silva JA, Brannan SK, Tekell JL, Mahurin RK, McGinnis S, Jerabek PA (2002). The functional neuroanatomy of the placebo effect. *Am J Psychiatry* 159:728–37.

McCall WV, Reboussin DM, Weiner RD, Sackeim HA (2000). Titrated moderately suprathreshold vs fixed high-dose right unilateral electroconvulsive therapy: acute antidepressant and cognitive effects. *Arch Gen Psychiatry* 57:438–444.

McElroy SL, Dessain EC, Pope HG, Cole JO, Keck PE, Frankenberg FR, Aizley HG, O'Brien S (1991). Clozapine in the treatment of psychotic mood disorders, schizoaffective disorder, and schizophrenia. *J Clin Psychiatry* 52:411–414.

Montejo AL, Llorca G, Izquierdo JA, Rico-Villademoros F (2001). Incidence or sexual dysfunction associated with antidepressant agents: A prospective multicenter study of 1022 outpatients. *J Clin Psychiatry* 62(Suppl 3):10–21.

Muth EA, Moyer JA, Haskins JT, Andree TH, Husbands GEM (1991). Biochemical, neurophysiological, and behavioral effects of Wy-45,233 and other identified metabolites of the antidepressant venlafaxine. *Drug Dev Res* 23:191–199.

Nahas Z, Lomarev M, Roberts DR, Shastri A, Lorberbaum JP, Teneback C, McConnell K, Vincent DJ, Li X, George MS, Bohning DE (2001). Unilateral left prefrontal transcranial magnetic stimulation (TMS) produces intensity-dependent bilateral effects as measured by interleaved BOLD fMRI. *Biol Psychiatry* 50:712–720.

Nelson JC (1999). A review of the efficacy of serotonergic and noradrenergic reuptake inhibitors for treatment of major depression. *Biol Psychiatry* 46:2301–1308.

Owens MJ, Knight DL, Nemeroff CB (2000). Paroxetine binding to the rat norepinephrine transporter in vivo. *Biol Psychiatry* 47:842–845.

Owens MJ, Knight DL, Nemeroff CB (2001). Second-generation SSRIs: Human monoamine transporter binding profile of escitalopram and R-fluoxetine. *Biol Psychiatry* 50:345–350.

Parker G, Roy K, Wilhelm K, Mitchell P (2001). Assessing the comparative effectiveness of antidepressant therapies: a prospective clinical practice study. *J Clin Psychiatry* 62:117–125.

Persad E (1990). Electroconvulsive therapy in depression. *Can J Psychiatry* 35:175–182.

Post RM (1992). Anticonvulsants and novel drugs. In Paykel ES (ed). *Handbook of Affective Disorders*, Second Edition. Churchill Livingstone: Edinburgh, pp. 387–417.

Prien RF, Kupfer DJ (1986). Continuation therapy for major depressive episodes: How long should it be maintained? *Am Psychiatry* 143:18–23.

Prien RF, Caffey EM, Klett CJ (1973). Comparison of lithium carbonate and chlorpromazine in the treatment of mania. *Arch Gen Psychiatry* 26:146–153.

Reist C, Kauffmann CD, Haier RJ, Sangdahl C, et al. (1989). A controlled trial of desipramine in 18 men with posttraumatic stress disorder. *Am J Psychiatry* 146:513–516.

Richou H, Ruimy P, Charbaut J, Delisle JP, Brunner H, Patris M, Zivkov M (1995). A multicenter, double-blind, clomipramine-controlled efficacy and safety study of Org 3770. *Human Psychopharmacol* 10:263–271.

Robinson DS, Lerfald SC, Bennett B, Laux D, Devereaux E, Kayser A, Corcella J, Albright D (1991). Continuation and maintenance treatment of major depression with the monoamine oxidase inhibitor phenelzine: A double-blind placebo-controlled discontinuation study. *Psychopharmacol Bull* 27:31–39.

Roose SP, Glassman A (1989). Cardiovascular effects of tricyclic antidepressants in depressed patients. *J Clin Psychiatry Monograph Series* 7:1–13.

Rudolph RL, Feiger AD (1999). A double-blind, randomized, placebo-controlled trial of once-daily venlafaxine extended release (XR) and fluoxetine for the treatment of major depression. *J Aff Dis* 56:171–181.

Rush AJ, Batey SR, Donahue RMJ, Ascher JA, Carmody TJ, Metz A (2001). Does pretreatment anxiety predict response to either bupropion SR or sertraline? *J Aff Dis* 64:81–87.

Rush AJ, George MS, Sackeim HA, Marangell LB, Husain, MM, Giller C, Hahas Z, Haines S, Simpson RK Jr, Goodman R (2000). Vagus nerve stimulation (VNS) for treatment-resistant depression: a multicenter study. *Biol Psychiatry* 47:276–86.

Schnyer RN, Allen JJB (2001). *Acupuncture in the Treatment of Depression: A Manual for Practice and Research*, Churchill Livingstone: Edinburgh and New York.

Schulberg HC, Katon W, Simon GE, Rush JT (1998). Treating major depression in primary care practice: An update of the Agency for Health Care Policy and Research practice guidelines. *Arch Gen Psychiatry* 55:1121–1127.

Shelton RC, Keller MB, Gelenberg A, Dunner DL, Hirschfeld R, Thase ME, Russell J, Lydiard RB, Crits-Christoph P, Gallop R, Todd L, Hellerstein D, Goodnick P, Keitner G, Stahl SM, Halbreich U (2001). Effectiveness of St John's wort in major depression: A randomized controlled trial. *JAMA* 285:1978–1986.

Speer AM, Kimbrell TA, Wassermann EM, Repella JD, Willis MW, Herscovitch P, Post RM (2000). Opposite effects of high and low frequency rTMS on regional brain activity in depressed patients. *Biol Psychiatry* 48:1133–1141.

Stahl SM (1998). Basic psychopharmacology of antidepressants: Part 1. Antidepressants have seven distinct mechanisms of action. *J Clin Psychiatry* 59(Suppl 4):5–14.

Stahl SM (2002). Does depression hurt? *J Clin Psychiatry* 63:273–274.

Sternbach H (1991). The serotonin syndrome. *Am J Psychiatry* 148:705–713.

Suppes T, McElroy SL, Gilbert J, Dessain EC, Cole JO (1992). Clozapine in the treatment of dysphoric mania. *Biol Psychiatry* 32:270–280.

Thase ME, Entsuah AR, Rudolph RL (2001). Remission rates during treatment with venlafaxine or selective serotonin reuptake inhibitors. *Brit J Psychiatry* 178:234–241.

Tohen M, Sanger TM, McElroy SL, Tollefson GD, Chengappa KNR, Daniel DG, Petty F, Franca C, Wang R, Grundy SL, Greaney MG, Jacobs TG, David SR, Toma V (1999). Olanzapine versus placebo in the treatment of acute mania. *Am J Psychiatry* 156:702–709.

Trivedi MH, Rush AJ, Carmody TJ, Donahue RMJ, Bolden-Watson C, House TL, Metz A (2001). Do bupropion SR and sertraline differ in their effects on anxiety in depressed patients? *J Clin Psychiatry* 62:776–781.

Tyrer PJ, Lee I, Edwards JG, Steinberg B, Elliot EJ, Nightingale JH (1980). Prognostic factors determining response to antidepressant drugs in psychiatric out-patients and general practice. *J Aff Dis* 2:149–156.

Van Laere K, Vonck K, Boon P, Versijpt J, Dierckx R (2002). Perfusion SPECT changes after acute and chronic vagus nerve stimulation in relation to prestimulus condition and long term clinical efficacy. *J Nucl Med* 43:733–744.

Van Moffaert M, de Wilde J, Vereecken A, Dierick M, Evrard JL, Wilmotte J, Mendelwicz J (1995). Mirtazapine is more effective than trazodone: A double-blind controlled study in hospitalized patients with major depression. *Int Clin Psychopharmacol* 5:441–446.

Versiani M, Cassano G, Perugi G, Benedetti A, Mastalli L, Nardi A, Savino M (2002). Reboxetine, a selective norepinephrine reuptake inhibitor, is an effective and well-tolerated treatment for panic disorder. *J Clin Psychiatry* 63:31–37.

Villarreal G (1995). Desipramine plasma levels and treatment response in panic disorder. *Can J Psychiatry* 40:110–111.

Wassermann EM (1997). Risk and safety of repetitive transcranial magnetic stimulation: Report and suggested guidelines from the International Workshop on the Safety of Repetitive Transcranial Magnetic Stimulation, June 5–7, 1996. *Electroencephalogr Clin Neurophysiol* 108:1–16.

Werstiuk ES, Coote M, Griffith L, Shannon H, Steiner M (1996). Effects of electroconvulsive therapy on peripheral adrenoceptors, plasma, noradrenaline, MHPG and cortisol in depressed patients. *Br J Psychiatry* 169:758–765.

Wheatley DP, van Moffaert M, Timmerman L, Kremer CME, Mirtazapine Study Group. (1998). Mirtazapine: Efficacy and tolerability in comparison with fluoxetine in patients with moderate to severe major depressive disorder. *J Clin Psychiatry* 59:306–312.

Whiskey E, Werneke U, Taylor D (2001). A systematic review and meta-analysis of *Hypericum perforatum* in depression: A comprehensive clinical review. *Int Clin Psychopharmacol* 16:239–252.

WHO Mental Health Collaborating Centers (1989). Pharmacotherapy of depressive disorders: A consensus statement. *J Aff Dis* 17:197–198.

Woods SW, Tesar GE, Murray GB, Cassem NH (1986). Psychostimulant treatment of depressive disorders secondary to medical illness. *J Clin Psychiatry* 47:12–15.

Yatham LN, Kusumakar V, Calabrese JR, Rao R, Scarrow G, Kroeker G (2002). Third generation anticonvulsants in bipolar disorder: A review of efficacy and summary of clinical recommendations. *J Clin Psychiatry* 63:275–283.

Zajecka JM (1993). Pharmacology, pharmacokinetics, and safety issues of mood stabilizing agents. *Psychiatric Annals* 23:79–85.

9

NEUROSCIENCE OF SCHIZOPHRENIA

Christine Pesold,[1] Rosalinda C. Roberts,[2] and Brian Kirkpatrick[2]

[1] *Department of Psychiatry, University of Illinois at Chicago, Chicago, Illinois*
[2] *Maryland Psychiatric Research Centre,*
University of Maryland School of Medicine, Baltimore, Maryland

INTRODUCTION

Schizophrenia is a debilitating psychiatric disorder that affects about 1 percent of the world's population. In 1990, the World Health Organization ranked schizophrenia as one of the 10 leading causes of disability with an annual direct cost of 19 billion US dollars and an additional annual indirect cost of 46 billion US dollars from lost productivity. Two-thirds of people with schizophrenia will require public assistance from government social security systems within a few years after onset. While patients with schizophrenia occupy one-third of the nation's mental hospital beds, many are homeless, and 10 to 15 percent of them will commit suicide.

Despite more than 50,000 published articles and hundreds of symposia, schizophrenia still remains an elusive disease. In this chapter, we will review our present understanding of the disease and the current technology being used to advance this understanding. We will present evidence that schizophrenia is a heterogeneous disease of developmental origin, with problems that arise early in development and span the entire lifetime of the

Textbook of Biological Psychiatry, Edited by Jaak Panksepp
ISBN 0-471-43478-7   Copyright © 2004 John Wiley & Sons, Inc.

affected individual. The pharmacological treatment of schizophrenia will be discussed in the next chapter.

DIAGNOSIS AND CLASSIFICATION OF SCHIZOPHRENIA

Although schizophrenia is a developmental disorder with many neuropsychiatric manifestations, psychotic symptoms—hallucinations, delusions, and disorganized thought and behavior—have historically been the basis of diagnostic criteria. In the Fourth Edition, Revised, of the *Diagnostic and Statistical Manual* of the American Psychiatric Association (DSM IV), negative symptoms, duration of illness, and the temporal relationship to any depressive or manic syndrome are also part of the criteria but psychotic symptoms remain central (see Table 9.1).

These diagnostic criteria may leave a misimpression that people with schizophrenia have a uniform illness. In fact, they vary greatly relative to their symptoms, course of illness, treatment response, and other features. Statistical studies of the symptoms of schizophrenia have consistently identified four factors or groups of symptoms: (1) hallucinations + delusions, (2) disorganization, (3) negative symptoms, and (4) affective symptoms (manic symptoms, depressive symptoms, and anxiety). The multiple symptoms within a given cluster tend to show comparable severity but may differ in severity with symptoms outside the cluster. For instance, severe hallucinations are often found with severe delusions, but the severity of hallucinations + delusions does not correlate with the severity of disorganized speech.

Hallucinations are sensory experiences that occur without being caused by external stimuli. An example of a hallucination is the experience of hearing a voice when no one is speaking. Hallucinations can occur in any sensory modality, that is, they can be heard, seen, smelled, tasted, or felt. Auditory hallucinations are the most common form and usually take the form of distinct voices that only the patient can hear. These voices can be critical or hostile and may consist of commands to the patient or a dialog between two or more voices talking about the patient.

T A B L E 9.1. Summary of the DSM-IV (Revised) Diagnostic Criteria for Schizophrenia

1. Characteristic symptoms (at least two):
   a. Delusions
   b. Hallucinations
   c. Disorganized speech
   d. Disorganized or catatonic behavior
   e. Negative symptoms (blunted affect, poverty of speech, or avolition)
2. Marked social or occupational dysfunction
3. Six months duration
4. Mood disorder: no major affective syndrome during active phase of illness, or the duration of active phase affective syndromes is brief compared to the total duration of the illness.
5. Symptoms are not directly due to substance abuse or another medical illness.
6. If patient has a diagnosis of autism, must have prominent delusions or hallucinations.

Delusions are false beliefs that are not shared by the patient's culture. The false beliefs can relate to things that do happen but have not actually happened in the patient's life—such as infidelity by a romantic partner, or being the object of ridicule—or to things that are completely unrealistic, such as being controlled by a radio transmitter placed in the patient's tooth.

Like hallucinations and delusions, disorganized thought and behavior can be terribly impairing. The most common aspect of disorganization is called *thought disorder* and refers to speech that is either vague, rambling, or so disorganized that the patient cannot be understood. The behavior of some patients with schizophrenia is also very disorganized and can be so severe that the patient represents an unintended threat to him/herself or others.

Distinguishing schizophrenia from some other disorders with psychotic symptoms can often be difficult. The most common problem is distinguishing schizophrenia from an affective disorder (mania or depression) with psychotic symptoms. What adds to the uncertainty in diagnosis is that some forms of schizophrenia—especially the so-called paranoid form—and psychotic affective disorder share some risk factors and other clinical and neurobiological correlates.

In terms of symptoms, people with schizophrenia vary so greatly that researchers have often suggested that groups of patients with similar symptoms may have a different disorder than that found in others diagnosed with the same disease. A number of subtyping systems have been suggested, but most of these subtypes haven't proven to be stable over time; that is, a patient may belong to one subtype at one stage of the illness, then belong to another subtype a year later. Most systems for subtyping patients have also been very poor at predicting such things as treatment response. However, some systems have been more successful. The system of categorizing patients into deficit versus nondeficit schizophrenia, which built on previous attempts at devising subtypes, has been the most successful (Kirkpatrick et al., 2001).

Research on the deficit versus nondeficit categories suggests schizophrenia consists of at least two separate diseases. Patients with deficit schizophrenia meet diagnostic criteria for schizophrenia and, of course, have psychotic symptoms, but also have other symptoms that have long been noted in descriptions of the pathophysiology of this disease:

1. Blunted affect: a decrease in "body language" and a relative absence of normal variations in the pitch, speed, and volume of speech

2. Diminished emotional range: a decrease in the experience of emotion—depression, anxiety, joy, etc.

3. Poverty of speech: a decrease in the number of words and amount of information conveyed in speech

4. Diminished sense of purpose: a failure to pursue goals due to a loss of motivation

5. Diminished interests: a loss of curiosity and interests

6. Diminished social drive: a loss of interest in relationships

These symptoms (and some others) are often called negative symptoms. However, people with schizophrenia and many other disorders can exhibit negative symptoms, sometimes transiently, for a variety of reasons. In contrast, people with deficit schizophrenia have persistent negative symptoms that are a direct result of their disease. Nondeficit schizophrenia does not comprise a homogeneous group and is defined simply by an absence, in people with schizophrenia, of those features that define deficit schizophrenia. Other groups with important neurobiological differences may prove to exist within the nondeficit group.

ETIOLOGY

Genetic

Humans have 46 chromosomes: 22 pairs of autosomes and 1 pair of sex chromosomes (two X chromosomes in females, and one X and one Y chromosome in males). The approximately 80,000 genes in the human genome are arranged in a precise order along the chromosomes. Each gene is located at a precise position (locus) on a specific chromosome and has two alleles, one donated from the mother and the other from the father. These two alleles may be identical, or more commonly, they may have several variations in their sequences called polymorphisms.

The following is a summary of the research that has attempted to understand the genetic component of schizophrenia by studying its heritability, as well as chromosomes, their genes, and allelic variations in patients with schizophrenia and their families.

Heritability. While the rate of schizophrenia in the general population is approximately 1 percent, the incidence of schizophrenia in families is at least 10-fold greater, strong evidence that the disease runs in families. However, if schizophrenia was purely caused by a genetic abnormality, identical twins, who share 100 percent of their genes, should theoretically have a 100 percent concordance rate for the disease. In fact, the concordance rate for monozygotic twins is only about 45 percent, and dizygotic twins who share 50 percent of their genes, only have a concordance rate of 15 percent. The more genes a biological relative shares with a patient, the higher the incidence of schizophrenia (see Fig. 9.1). For instance, first-degree relatives such as parents, siblings, and children who share 50 percent of their genes, had a greater incidence of schizophrenia than second- or third-degree relatives, which only share 25 percent and 12.5 percent of their genes, respectively (Gottesman, 1991).

However, closer family members not only have more genes in common but generally also share social environments. To better understand the contribution of nature and nurture, several studies examined the incidence of schizophrenia among adoptees (Kringlen, 1991). The finding of higher rates of schizophrenia among the biological relatives of schizophrenia adoptees than normal adoptees is clear support for a genetic component. However, unlike primarily genetic diseases, such as Huntington's or cystic fibrosis in which the mutation of a single allele of the gene is sufficient

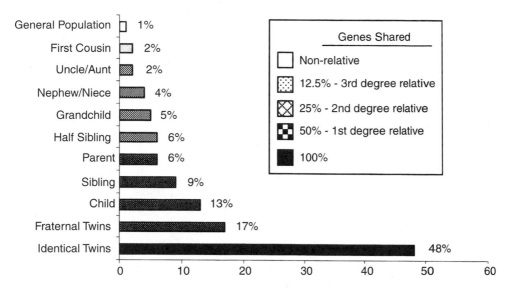

Figure 9.1. Relatives of schizophrenics' lifetime risk of developing the disease as a function of degree of genetic relatedness, compiled from all family and twin studies conducted in European samples between 1920 and 1987 [Adapted from Gottesman (1991), Figure 1 (p. 96). © 1991 by Irving I. Gottesman. Reprinted by permission of Henry Holt and Company, LLC.]

to express the disorder, or recessive diseases such as phenylketonuria in which a mutation of both alleles of the gene are required to produce the disorder, the transmission of schizophrenia is more complex. The most likely explanation for the unusual genetic transmission of schizophrenia is that there are several genes that may contribute to the risk of schizophrenia, or more precisely, several alleles of genes involved; and what is inherited may not be the certainty of the disease accompanying a particular genotype, but rather the susceptibility or predisposition to develop the disease.

Linkage Studies. In linkage analysis, entire genomes are screened for the presence of allelic variations in regions of the chromosome to identify susceptibility loci or "hot spots" that may be co-transmitted with the disease in families containing two or more affected individuals. Linkage studies thus far have failed to identify any locus of large effect size, that is, where mutation of a gene(s) is common to most patients. This is consistent with the idea that schizophrenia is in fact a heterogeneous disease and that different susceptibility loci or combinations of susceptibility loci are necessary to predispose an individual to the disease, and that these loci vary among families. Linkage studies have revealed at least 15 susceptibility loci that have weak to moderate linkage to schizophrenia on several chromosomes[1] (DeLisi and Crow, 1999; Berrettini, 2001).

[1] Susceptibility loci that have been linked with schizophrenia: 1q21-22, 2q, 3p26-24, 4q, 5p13, 5q, 6q, 6p24-22, 8p22-21, 9p23, 9q, 13q32, 15q13-14, 18p11.2, 20p12, 22q11–12, Xp.

Linkage studies therefore have been valuable in identifying chromosomal hot spots where diseased genes can be found, without any prior knowledge of disease etiology. However, each of these chromosomal regions contains numerous genes, and in some cases, these regions contain susceptibility genes that overlap with other disorders. An excellent example of this is the deletion of chromosome 22q11 (Murphy and Owen, 2001). Deletions on this chromosome represent one of the highest known risk factors for the development of schizophrenia. They are also known to be associated with velo-cardial-facial-syndrome (VCFS), a syndrome characterized by heart, limb, and craniofacial anomalies. Interestingly, these individuals also have high rates of psychotic disorders with 10 to 40 percent of affected individuals developing symptoms of schizophrenia. It is not clear, however, which of the approximately 30 genes found in this region are implicated in either or both diseases. In addition, linkage studies have revealed a number of susceptibility loci that are common to both schizophrenia and bipolar disorder, a neuropsychiatric disease clinically and pathologically very similar to schizophrenia.

Association Studies. In a normal population, any gene at any locus can be present in a number of different forms called alleles. In association studies, the frequency of alleles is compared in samples of unrelated patients and controls to identify allelic variations that are associated with the disease more often than would be predicted by chance alone. Since studying such polymorphisms in entire genomes would be prohibitively large, susceptibility loci identified in linkage studies, or candidate genes stimulated by known pharmacological or neurochemical abnormalities are selected for study. This approach has identified potential allelic association between schizophrenia and polymorphisms in a subtype of serotonin receptors (5-HTR$_{2A}$), and the D$_3$ subtype of dopamine receptors (Owen, 2000). While these findings are interesting in that these receptor subtypes may be involved in the therapeutic effects of many antipsychotics, they have not yet been replicated.

Chromosomal Studies. Evidence about the contribution of particular genes to the etiology of schizophrenia also comes from direct studies of chromosomal abnormalities. These are changes in the structure of chromosomes (as opposed to specific genes) that can be seen, using appropriate techniques, at the light microscopic level. Usually these are chromosomal translocations in which there is a break in a chromosome, and the fragment that has broken off becomes attached to another chromosome. Because it is possible to identify the point at which the break takes place, it is possible to identify the gene or genes that straddle the break point. If such a translocation is associated with a disease, this means that it is possible to identify a gene that increases the risk of the disease. Chromosomal translocations have been found that increase the risk of schizophrenia. Although in one case (DISC1 and DISC2) the genes are known, to date the role of these proteins in normal brains is not understood, much less the role of the gene(s) in causing schizophrenia (Millar et al., 2000).

Trinucleotide Repeats. Genes are made up of long sequences of nucleotides. Trinucleotide repeats are triplets of nucleotides that are repeated in an unusually high number in the coding region of a gene. To date, more than 12 neurological disorders, including Huntington's disease and fragile X syndrome, have been shown to be caused by trinucleotide repeat expansions, most of which involve the CAG triplet (Margolis et al., 1997). CAG triplet repeats are thought to interfere with the normal function of the protein thereby mediating the disease process. These expansions have the propensity to increase in size over generations. One phenomenon of this type of dynamic mutation, called "anticipation," is an increased severity of the disease or a decreased age of onset in subsequent generations. Studies of CAG triplets in schizophrenia have found evidence of expanded repeats. Furthermore, anticipation has also been reported in families with schizophrenia (Vaswani and Kapur, 2001). In addition, a recent study found evidence of seven or eight CAG triplet repeats in two alleles of chromosome 22, the loci associated with schizophrenia and VCFS (Saleem et al., 2001). While more research on trinucleotide repeats is needed, it seems possible that an abnormally high number of such repeats may play a role in some cases of schizophrenia.

Epigenetic. There is substantial evidence that schizophrenia is heritable and likely involves mutations in the nucleotide sequence of several genes, leading to abnormal messenger ribonucleic acid (mRNA) (transcription) and hence abnormal protein (translation). However, nongenetic factors such as stress, learning, hormones, social environment, and development can also modify the expression of a protein by altering the transcription of perfectly normal genes. This epigenetic regulation may therefore contribute to the nonheritable component of schizophrenia. The search for genetic mutations may therefore be only part of the story since it is proteins that ultimately define the functioning of brain cells, and protein expression can be regulated by genetic as well as epigenetic mechanisms. Measuring proteins or the transcripts that encode them may therefore be fruitful in fully understanding the pathology of schizophrenia.

Microarray analysis simultaneously can compare relative levels of thousands of gene transcripts in postmortem tissue from patients with schizophrenia and matched controls. This technology is fairly new and has only been applied by a few teams to the study of postmortem brains from people with schizophrenia. These studies have revealed changes in the expression of gene transcripts with developmental relevance including transcription factors, receptors, genes important for myelination, as well as a host of proteins involved in synaptic functioning and neurotransmission (Mirnics et al., 2001). While there is good correspondence between the findings of microarray and linkage studies, this technology has also revealed many new candidates for the study of schizophrenia. More microarray studies are emerging that should rapidly advance our knowledge of the biological pathology underlying schizophrenia.

ENVIRONMENTAL RISKS

Obstetric Complications

There are numerous studies suggesting that complications during pregnancy, birth, or within the first month after birth are important risk factors for at least some types of schizophrenia. Those that have been significantly associated with schizophrenia include preeclampsia, bleeding during pregnancy, umbilical cord complications, premature rupture of amniotic membranes, prematurity, prolonged labor, use of resuscitation, incubator, forcep or suction delivery, abnormal fetal presentation at delivery, low birth weight, small head circumference, and low Apgar scores (McNeil et al., 2000; Lobato et al., 2001). Perinatal abnormalities in particular, collectively called obstetric complications, have been reported in 21 to 40 percent of patients with schizophrenia. In sum, there are several obstetric complications that appear to be risk factors for schizophrenia.

Maternal Stressors

A recent review of the literature suggests there is some evidence that prenatal nutritional deficits may be risk factors for the development of schizophrenia (Brown et al., 1996). One study found an increased incidence of schizophrenia 20 years after a wartime famine hit a large Dutch population in 1944–1945. While these findings suggest that food deprivation during the first trimester of pregnancy increased the risk of developing schizophrenia, it is possible that maternal stress also played a role. In fact, increased risk of schizophrenia has also been significantly associated with extreme maternal stressors such as wartime conditions, death of a spouse, unwanted pregnancy, maternal depression during midpregnancy, and natural disasters (Lobato et al., 2001). Other stressors during gestation that have also been associated with increased risk of schizophrenia include maternal alcohol and substance abuse and parental Rh incompatibility. Increased paternal age also appears to be associated with increased risk for schizophrenia. While the precise mechanism(s) remains unclear, it is believed that these stressors increase the risk for schizophrenia by causing adverse neurodevelopmental effects (Koenig et al., 2002).

Viral Infection

Numerous studies have shown that in utero exposure to viruses during the second trimester of gestation is associated with increased risk of developing schizophrenia (O'Reilly, 1994). Precisely which virus(es) may be risk factors is unknown since it is impossible to do antibody titers from a gestational exposure that occurred 20 or 30 years before. Studies that have examined the incidence of schizophrenia following influenza epidemics of 1954, 1957, and 1959 in Australia and Japan have revealed positive associations between gestational exposure to this virus and development of schizophrenia. Reports of viral diseases from 1920 to 1955 in Connecticut and Massachusetts found associations between the development of schizophrenia and gestational exposure to the measles, varicella-zoster, and polio viruses (Torrey et al., 1988). Studies have also found that individuals exposed to rubella in utero, during the 1964 rubella epidemic, had a substantially greater risk of developing nonaffective psychosis than nonexposed subjects (Brown et al., 2000).

There are several other risk factors for schizophrenia that may also be related to viral infections. For instance, there is an increased prevalence of schizophrenia among individuals born in late winter–early spring. Many viral infections peak at certain times of the year, and it is likely, as in the case of other seasonal diseases such as anencephaly and mental retardation, that this can explain the seasonality of schizophrenia. Being born or raised in an urban area also increases one's chance of developing schizophrenia, which may be explained by greater exposure to infectious agents in densely populated areas (Lobato et al., 2001).

Recently, endogenous retroviruses have also been suggested as a possible etiological factor in schizophrenia. Retrovirus can infect brain cells, integrate into their cellular deoxyribonucleic acid (DNA), and cause long-term alterations in brain function. Possible transcripts of these viruses have been found in higher levels in the brains of schizophrenia patients than unaffected individuals (Yolken et al., 2000).

Understanding the causes of schizophrenia is made more difficult by several factors: our relative lack of knowledge about how the abnormal genes and environmental factors function in brain development; the likelihood that schizophrenia is more than one disease—that is, more than one underlying biological abnormality may cause similar symptoms; the fact that studies of genes and studies of environmental factors are rarely done in the same people; and the evidence that what is inherited is not just schizophrenia but a range of behavioral, physical, and cognitive abnormalities (the schizophrenia spectrum). There may be more than one "causal pathway" to schizophrenia, that is, different people may have the disorder due to different causes. Because the causes of schizophrenia are poorly understood, it remains possible that all of the following causal pathways lead to schizophrenia:

1. Everyone who has both genes *A* and *B* will have a schizophrenia spectrum disorder.
2. People with gene *A* have a schizophrenia spectrum disorder only if their mothers have a severe stress at a critical period during pregnancy.
3. If a mother has a sufficiently severe stress at the right time during gestation, anyone will have a schizophrenia spectrum disorder.

Other possibilities exist, and it is possible that each particular form of schizophrenia may have one or more of these causal pathways.

COURSE OF ILLNESS

Premorbid Period

Schizophrenia typically has its clinical onset in late adolescence to early adulthood. However, schizophrenia is a lifelong disorder, with numerous signs of abnormal development prior to its clinical onset.

Minor Physical Anomalies. Minor physical anomalies are structural deviations with little functional consequence that have been extensively studied because brain and skin are derived from the same ectodermal tissue. Thus minor physical anomalies are considered markers of early neurodevelopmental abnormalities (Lobato et al., 2001). Physical abnormalities are typical of neurodevelopmental disorders such as Down syndrome and epilepsy. Individuals with schizophrenia have a significantly greater number of anomalies than normal individuals. These include low-set ears, high arched palate, curved fifth finger, abnormal nail beds in the hands, excess branching of motor nerve endings, hypertelorism, small head circumference, and narrowing and elongation of the mid and lower facial region with widening of the skull base. The configuration of skin ridges (dermatoglyphics) has also been found to be abnormal or asymmetric in many patients with schizophrenia, including single simian crease and abnormal finger ridge counts. The pattern of minor physical and dermatoglyphic anomalies observed in patients with schizophrenia are indicative of prenatal insult around the second trimester of pregnancy, which may also affect the neuronal migration occurring at that time.

Functional Impairments. Generally, individuals who later go on to be diagnosed with schizophrenia suffer many functional impairments throughout their lives. Numerous studies using many different approaches have been used to try to identify premorbid precursors of schizophrenia. For example, researchers studied home movies of children who later went on to develop schizophrenia. Their motor and social behaviors were different enough from other children that following careful study, "blind" clinicians were able to identify the preschizophrenic children (Walker et al., 1994).

In some countries, large databases of neurocognitive and psychomotor performance are meticulously kept on children at various developmental time points. "Follow-back" studies of these databases revealed numerous socioemotional, cognitive, and motor abnormalities in children that were later diagnosed with schizophrenia. For instance, during infancy, many preschizophrenics were delayed in achieving milestones such as sitting up, standing, walking, talking, and continence (Isohanni et al., 2001). Throughout childhood, many have problems with speech, attention, sensory integration, and motor coordination, often being labeled clumsy. Preschizophrenic children are also more socially anxious and withdrawn and some studies reported a tendency to have poor scores on educational tests in school (Davies et al., 1998). Overall, these studies provide evidence that long before the clinical diagnosis of schizophrenia, these individuals have functional impairments.

Early Adulthood

It is the conventional wisdom that schizophrenia "begins" in early adulthood, but this is an oversimplification. The average age for the onset of the first clear-cut psychotic episode is usually in late adolescence or early adulthood. However, as noted above, adults with schizophrenia have cognitive and behavioral difficulties from early life, which can precede their first psychotic episode. The onset of psychosis is also variable and can come on gradually, over a period of months or relatively suddenly.

Early adulthood is when psychotic symptoms are most prominent, and patients typically have more hospitalizations during this period than at any other time in their lives. The severity of their symptoms, and the impairment of function that they suffer, usually plateaus within the first 5 to 10 years after onset. However, a small percentage of patients has severe and unremitting psychosis, and many are never able to return to independent function (Green, 1996).

Late Adulthood

On average, patients with schizophrenia have an improvement in both the severity of psychotic symptoms and their overall functioning in middle age (Harding et al., 1992). This improvement has led to speculation that the concentrations of testosterone and estrogen, which change with aging, play a role in the severity of symptoms, and in fact estrogen may augment the effect of antipsychotics in women.

Although there is an average improvement in function, the cognitive impairment found in schizophrenia does not appear to improve. There may also be a small percentage of patients who develop a dementia in later life that is due to schizophrenia and is not caused by other factors such as stroke, Alzheimer's disease, or the like. The distinctive features of deficit schizophrenia also fail to improve in later life, and their function remains poor. Some nondeficit subjects also have very severe psychotic symptoms that do not improve.

People with schizophrenia, on average, have a shortened life span. This is due to a number of factors, especially suicide and accidents (Siris, 2001). Patients with schizophrenia also have immunological changes as well as an increased prevalence of the *metabolic syndrome*, that is Type II diabetes, hypertension, other cardiovascular disease, and obesity. Antipsychotic medications certainly contribute to this problem, but it is possible that this is also a consequence of the abnormal development that causes psychotic symptoms.

NEUROPATHOLOGICAL ABNORMALITIES

One of the challenges of postmortem neuroanatomical observations in schizophrenia is that the changes that are seen are widespread and usually subtle (Harrison, 1999; Powers, 1999). There is no gross lesion that is typical of a schizophrenia brain such as that seen in Huntington's disease or Parkinson's disease. Moreover, many of the abnormalities that are detected in the brains of patients with schizophrenia are not selective and are associated with other psychiatric conditions as well. Finally, there are many unreplicated findings due in part to the problems of the heterogeneity of the disease, the course of the illness, and medication effects.

The neuroscience of schizophrenia has also been historically limited by long postmortem intervals, poor preservation, or harsh fixation of the tissue, which are incompatible with the application of sophisticated histochemical techniques. Nevertheless, the neuropathology of schizophrenia has been studied since the late 1800s, and reports exist of some abnormality in nearly every brain region.

Cerebral Ventricular Enlargement

One of the best replicated neuropathological findings in schizophrenia is that of enlargement of the fluid-filled spaces in the brain (cerebral ventricles), specifically the lateral ventricles and the third ventricle. Ventricular enlargements have been identified in postmortem studies, as well as in scanning studies of live patients using computerized tomography (CT) and magnetic resonance imaging (MRI). In a review of MRI studies, the ventricular size in schizophrenia patients is 40 percent larger than in controls (Lawrie and Abukmeil, 1998). It is important to note that the ventricular enlargement in patients with schizophrenia is present for the group as a whole and that there is some overlap in the range of ventricular size between schizophrenia patients and controls. Nonetheless, one recent study (Staal et al., 2001) showed a relationship between ventricular enlargement and schizophrenia outcome in that patients with poor outcomes have on average larger ventricles than patients with good outcomes (Fig. 9.2A–C). In studies of monozygotic twins discordant for schizophrenia, the affected twin usually has bigger ventricles (Stabenau and Pollin, 1993). The twin studies are important because they control for both genetic predisposition and environmental factors and show that this particular neuropathological abnormality is associated with the expression of the disease rather then being associated with the underlying genotype. However, people's genes do have an impact on the size of the ventricles such that the discordant twin who does not have schizophrenia will have larger ventricles than will other members of the family, and unaffected relatives have larger

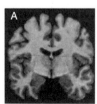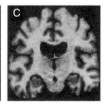

Figure 9.2. Magnetic resonance imaging of coronal sections of the brains of a healthy comparison subject (A), a patient with schizophrenia with good outcome (B) and a patient with schizophrenia with poor outcome (C). Note that patients that have schizophrenia with bad outcome have larger ventricles than either patients with good outcome or healthy controls. Schizophrenia patients with good outcome did not differ significantly from healthy controls [Adapted from Staal, *Am J Psychiatry* 2001, 158(7):1140–1142. Copyright 2001, the American Psychiatric Association, http://ajp.psychiatryonline.org. Reprinted by permission.]

ventricles than that of the control population. Ventricular enlargement does not appear to be due to a neurodegenerative process since there are no obvious signs of neuronal loss and no increase in gliotic cells, which would normally invade to remove any degenerating cells (Selemon and Goldman-Rakic, 1999). Rather, ventricular enlargement is likely related to changes in other brain structures, including thinning of the surrounding cortex.

Decreased Synaptic Connectivity

The cerebral cortex consists of six layers of neurons that have dense connections to each other, as well as to other neurons in different cortical and subcortical structures. The area between neurons (neuropil) consists of a dense network of dendrites, dendritic spines, axons, and axon terminals, which make connections between the neurons. In patients with schizophrenia, there are several lines of evidence indicating that there are fewer connections in the neocortex as well as the hippocampus.

Cerebral Cortex. In the cerebral cortex of patients with schizophrenia, concomitant with the increased cerebral ventricular space, there is a decrease in the thickness of the gray matter (Selemon et al., 1995; Selemon and Goldman-Rakic, 1999). Stereological studies of the density of neurons in the prefrontal cortex have found that while the total number of neurons is not changed (Selemon, 2001), they are packed closer together (increased neuronal packing density). This indicates that the thinning of gray matter is due to a loss of neuropil, that is, the area between neurons that make up all the synaptic connections (see Fig. 9.3A and B).

As mentioned above, microarray studies have also revealed decreased expression of many genes involved in synaptic function (Mirnics et al., 2001). In addition, there is considerable evidence from scanning studies in live patients and histological studies in postmortem brains of schizophrenia patients consistent with this view. Measures of regional cerebral blood flow using positron emission tomography (PET) with fluorodeoxyglucose (FDG), which are in part measures of synaptic activity, reveal decreased metabolism in cortical areas as well as subcortical areas such as the striatum. Phosphorous magnetic resonance spectroscopy indicates a decrease in synaptogenesis markers and an increase in markers of synaptic pruning. Immunocytochemical studies using markers of axon terminals [e.g., synaptophysin, γ-aminobutyric acid (GABA), and GABA transporter (GAT)] found reductions in axon terminal density in the dorsal lateral prefrontal cortex (Glantz and Lewis, 1997; McGlashan and Hoffman, 2000; Selemon, 2001). Studies of Golgi-impregnated pyramidal neurons in the prefrontal cortex (Garey et al., 1998; Glantz and Lewis, 2000) reveal a reduction in the number of dendritic spines (see Fig. 9.3C–E). Dendritic spines are protrusions on dendrites that consequently provide more surface area to the dendrite, allowing for more synaptic contacts to be made. The striatum, a brain structure that receives substantial dopaminergic projections, a neurotransmitter heavily implicated in schizophrenia, also manifests smaller dendritic spines (see Fig. 9.3F and G) and alterations in synaptic density consistent with changes in several different pathways (Roberts et al., 1996; Kung et al., 1998).

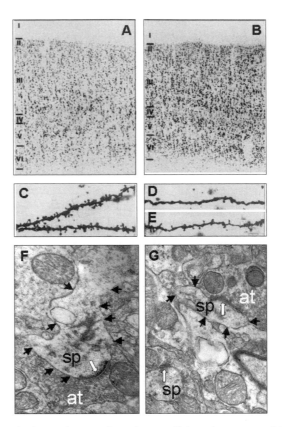

Figure 9.3. *Top panel:* Photomicrographs taken at light microscopy of Nissl-stained coronal sections from the prefrontal cortex (area 9) of a normal brain (A) and the brain of a person with schizophrenia (B). Note that the cortex of the person with schizophrenia is thinner and has less intraneuronal neuropil than the normal control [Modified from Selemon et al. (1995). Reprinted by permission.] *Middle panel:* Photomicrographs taken at light microscopy of Golgi impregnated pyramidal neurons from layer III of the prefrontal cortex from the postmortem brains of a normal control subject (C) and two patients with schizophrenia (D and E). Note the decreased number of spines on the dendrites of pyramidal neurons in the schizophrenic patients [Modified from: Glantz and Lewis (2000). Reprinted with permission.] *Bottom panel:* Electron micrographs showing dendritic spines (sp) from the striatum of a normal control (F) and a person with schizophrenia (G). Note that spines are smaller in the striatum of the individual with schizophrenia (Roberts et al., 1995). For illustrative purposes, the difference in size is very pronounced. Synapses (white arrows), axon terminals (at), black arrows outline the spines.

Synaptic density is highest in childhood, with a 30 to 40 percent decline in adolescence following extensive pruning, settling in a relatively stable level in adulthood. It is noteworthy that the typical clinical onset of schizophrenia and the appearance of psychotic symptoms are coincident with the completion of the intense pruning that occurs in adolescence. Consistent with this, although highly speculative, computer simulation that models normal cognitive development and pruning, including the elimination of synaptic connections in the cortex, indicates that excessive pruning may lead to hallucinations, that is, speech perceptions that occur in the absence of stimulation (McGlashan and Hoffman, 2000).

Hippocampus. The hippocampus is a complex limbic structure that plays a role in emotion, cognition, memory, and inhibitory gating. Numerous studies from postmortem work to imaging of live patients implicate the hippocampus in schizophrenia. Postmortem findings indicate that the hippocampus is modestly reduced in size bilaterally. Reports of cell density in the hippocampus using classical counting techniques have shown a reduction in the density of neurons, but thus far these findings have yet to be replicated using more modern stereological techniques. Markers of axon terminals, such as synaptophysin, synapsin, and SNAP-25 are decreased in the hippocampus. Moreover, markers of dendrites such as MAP2 and MAP5 show decreased staining (Selemon, 2001). Taken together, these results suggest that reduced hippocampal size, like cortical thickness, may partially be the result of diminished neuropil volume, and hence a decrease in synaptic connectivity.

Changes in Cortical and Subcortical Activity

Consistent with a decrease in synaptic connectivity is a decrease in synaptic activity. PET studies of regional cerebral blood flow (rCBF) using fluorodeoxyglucose (FDG) and functional MRI (fMRI) studies have revealed that abnormalities in numerous mental functions in patients with schizophrenia are associated with alterations in the normal activation of various cortical and subcortical areas.

Most consistently, PET and fMRI studies have shown that working memory and attention deficits in schizophrenia subjects are associated with decreased activity in the prefrontal cortex, particularly the dorsal lateral prefrontal cortex (DLPFC) (Velakoulis and Pantelis, 1996). In addition, several studies (Heckers et al., 1999; Lahti et al., 2001) have shown that patients with deficit schizophrenia have greater "hypofrontality" than patients with nondeficit schizophrenia, further supporting the concept of schizophrenia as a heterogeneous disease. Holcomb and colleagues (2000) showed that the anterior cingulate cortex is less activated in patients with schizophrenia than in normal volunteers during performance of a difficult cognitive task (see Fig. 9.4). In PET studies, patients with schizophrenia also exhibited abnormal activation of cortical areas such as the frontal eye fields. This occurred during other functions that are known to be abnormal in this patient population, including smooth pursuit and saccadic eye movements (Ross et al., 1995; O'Driscoll et al., 1998).

Changes in brain activity have also been reported in subcortical areas including the hippocampus, thalamus, and basal ganglia. For instance, patients with schizophrenia have reduced hippocampal activation during episodic memory retrieval (Heckers et al., 1998). In PET/FDG studies, floridly psychotic schizophrenia patients show increased activation in the hippocampus and parahippocampal gyrus, which correlate significantly with the severity of their positive psychotic symptoms (Tamminga et al., 1992). PET

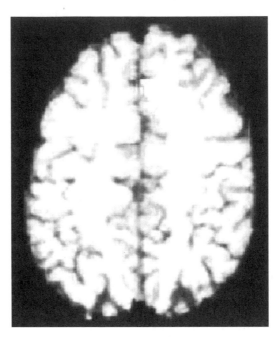

Figure 9.4. Subtraction analysis of PET scan showing lesser activation (yellow) of the anterior cingulate cortex in schizophrenic persons compared to normal volunteers during performance of a difficult cognitive task. [Adapted from: *Am J Psychiatry*, 2000 157(10):1634–1645. Copyright 2000, the American Psychiatric Association, http://ajp.psychiatryonline.org. Reprinted by permission.] See ftp site for color image.

revealed a reduced glucose metabolism in the thalamus of schizophrenia patients during an olfactory identification test (Clark et al., 2001). fMRI reveals lower metabolism in the striatum of schizophrenia subjects, and this is normalized by antipsychotic medication in subjects that respond to medication (Velakoulis and Pantelis, 1996). In addition, electron microscopic studies of postmortem striatum from patients with schizophrenia show a 20 percent decrease in the number of mitochondria, subcellular organelles that generate energy (Kung and Roberts, 1999). Fewer mitochondrial profiles suggest decreased energy demands or diminished capacity to respond to energy requirements. These data are consistent with in vivo imaging that show decreased striatal metabolism in people with schizophrenia (Buchsbaum et al., 1992).

The decreased metabolism in cortical and subcortical areas observed in PET and FDG studies is consistent with perturbations in synaptic activity. While these abnormalities appear to be widespread, it is likely that specific symptoms of schizophrenia are related to the dysfunction of particular brain regions that act in concert. These groups of functionally related brain regions, or circuits, normally perform such functions such as movement and vision (Alexander et al., 1986). There is evidence that abnormalities in one such circuit (the anterior cingulate or limbic circuit), which includes the hippocampus, some neocortical regions, and associated subcortical areas, underlie psychotic symptoms such as hallucinations, delusions, and formal thought disorders. In contrast, blunted affect, poverty of speech, and other features typical of deficit schizophrenia appear to be due to abnormalities in another circuit that includes the dorsolateral prefrontal cortex, inferior parietal cortex, and associated subcortical regions (Carpenter et al., 1993).

Loss of Asymmetry

Many structures are normally lateralized in the human brain with area or volume being consistently larger in one hemisphere or the other. Some asymmetries are related to lateralized functions such as language. Abnormal cerebral asymmetry in schizophrenia has been studied since its first observation in 1879 by Crichton-Browne. Many studies of schizophrenia have shown an absence or reversal of the normal cerebral asymmetries found in controls. These disruptions in normal asymmetry are thought to reflect abnormalities during development. The main regions where this asymmetry has been noted in neuropathological studies are the left superior temporal gyrus, a reversal of the normally larger left planum temporali, and loss of the normally larger left Sylvian fissure. Moreover, certain abnormalities in the brains of patients with schizophrenia are restricted to or worse in one hemisphere (usually the left) over the other. To site a few examples, schizophrenia subjects show thinning of the left parahippocampal gyrus, left temporal horn enlargement, reduction in size of the left medial temporal lobe, and loss of synaptic proteins from the left thalamus (Selemon, 2001).

Abnormal Cytoarchitecture

Investigations into the cellular organization or structure (cytoarchitecture) of the brain of schizophrenia patients have reported various abnormal arrangements of neurons in several structures, although some of these studies suffer from a lack of replicability. The pyramidal cells of the hippocampus, which normally lie in an orderly layer, have been found to be disoriented in some postmortem brains of patients with schizophrenia. Several studies have also reported cytoarchitectural disturbances in the entorhinal cortex of schizophrenia patients, including bizarre invaginations of the normally smooth surface, irregularities in the normal pattern of pre-alpha-cell clustering in layer 2, and misplacement of these layer 2 neurons into deeper cortical layers (Bunney et al., 1997; Arnold and Rioux, 2001).

There is also evidence for a mis-migration of neurons in the prefrontal, parietal, and temporal cortex (Bunney et al., 1997). During embryogenesis, cortical neurons are born in the ventricular zone and migrate to the cortical subplate, where they wait before migrating into the cortical plate to form the six layers of the cortex. This neuronal migration into the cortex is thought to be complete by the end of the second trimester in primates. With the use of several markers (MAP2, MAP5, SMI32), a number of studies found an abnormal density of cells in the subcortical white matter of postmortem schizophrenia patients. These cells are thought to be remnants of subplate neurons and therefore may indicate an incomplete migration of neurons into the cortex. Investigators also used NADPH-diaphorase as a marker of these subplate remnants. Normally, these neurons are found in high levels in the superficial white matter, with a smaller population found dispersed throughout the cortical layers. In postmortem studies of the prefrontal and temporal cortices, the majority of these neurons are found in the deeper white matter with very few located in the cortical mantle. This apparent "shift" in the distribution of this subpopulation of neurons is interpreted as representing an altered migration of neurons into the cortex. These findings are consistent with a neurodevelopmental disturbance occurring around the second trimester of gestation.

Altered Expression of Developmental and Other Proteins

The migration of neurons from the ventricular zone to their proper positioning in the cortex is well orchestrated and requires a multitude of neural events including start signals, cell-cell recognition, cell adhesion, motility, and stop signals. Since schizophrenia appears to involve disturbances in cortical migration, researchers have focused their attention on some of the molecules thought to play a role in this process. One such candidate is a protein called reelin. Reelin is thought to help guide newly arriving migrating neurons to their proper destination, though the precise mechanism is presently unknown. A recent study (Impagnatiello et al., 1998) revealed that patients with schizophrenia only have about half of the normal levels of reelin and its transcript in all of the brain areas examined (prefrontal and temporal cortex, hippocampus, caudate nucleus, and cerebellum). Interestingly, while reelin levels are normal in patients with other psychiatric disorders such as unipolar depression, reelin levels are also decreased in patients with bipolar disorder, a psychiatric disease characterized in part by psychotic symptoms (Guidotti et al., 2000).

Neural cell adhesion molecules (N-CAMs), which are important for the motility of neurons during migration, have also been found to be changed in postmortem studies. N-CAM levels are found to be increased in the brain of people with schizophrenia, however, more N-CAMs are found in their polysialylated form, rendering neurons less mobile. Schizophrenia has also been associated with changes in the expression of neurotrophic factors that regulate growth, survival, and plasticity such as brain-derived nerve growth factor (BDNF), which have their maximum expression during early neuronal differentiation and migration. GAP-43, a protein important for axon growth, targeting, and synaptogenesis, is also found to be altered in schizophrenia, although these results are still somewhat controversial (Selemon, 2001).

In summary, the neuropathological evidence clearly supports disturbances in early neurodevelopment. However, neurodevelopment is not limited to perinatal life. In fact, there are many "developmental" changes that occur at different stages of postnatal life, including neurite pruning, neurogenesis, apoptosis, neurite proliferation, axonal myelination, and structural brain changes. Many of the neuropathological abnormalities observed in schizophrenia may therefore be the result of neurodevelopmental lesions or insults that leave the brain more vulnerable to any number of further changes that may coincide with the "clinical onset" of schizophrenia, or acute relapses.

NEUROCOGNITIVE PROBLEMS

Patients with schizophrenia suffer from a range of cognitive deficits, which are common but vary in severity among patients. Cognitive impairments that have been extensively studied include deficits in working memory, attention, gating, executive function, abstraction, and language.

Working Memory Deficits

Working memory is the process of retaining recent information in order to perform a behavioral response after the informational cue is removed. Patients with schizophrenia have medication-resistant deficits in working memory that are thought to arise from dysfunction in the DLPFC or from disregulation of this region by other cortical or subcortical structures (Levy and Goldman-Rakic, 2000). During the Wisconsin Card Sorting Test, a neuropsychological measure of cognitive function, normal controls exhibit an increase in regional cerebral blood flow in the prefrontal cortex, while schizophrenia patients fail to do so. Patients with schizophrenia also show numerous deficits in executive function, including poor processing of cognitive information, decreased problem-solving skills as measured by the Tower of London test, and increases in perseverative errors.

Attention Deficits

Some people with schizophrenia are easily distracted and have difficulty remaining vigilant. Latent inhibition (LI) is a measure of selective attention in which the noncontingent presentation of a stimulus attenuates its ability to enter into subsequent associations. This latent inhibition occurs because following repeated nonconsequential presentations of a stimulus, one normally learns to ignore the stimulus, making it harder to then pair it with another stimulus. This measure of selective attention is disrupted in patients with schizophrenia (Gray, 1998). In addition to selective attention, immediate and sustained attention skills are also impaired. Thus, patients with schizophrenia also perform poorly on measures of sustained attention, such as the Continuous Performance Test.

Gating Deficits

In a world where we are simultaneously bombarded with a great deal of stimulation, we learn to focus our attention on important stimuli, while filtering out (gating) less relevant simulation. Patients with schizophrenia not only have difficulties focusing their attention on important stimuli, they also have difficulties filtering out irrelevant stimuli, rendering them continually overwhelmed by their environment.

Pre-Pulse Inhibition (PPI) is a paradigm commonly used to measure these gating deficits in schizophrenia patients. In this paradigm, a person's excitatory responses to loud stimuli are measured. Exposure to a loud stimulus will elicit a large excitatory response. Exposure to a soft stimulus (pre-pulse) immediately before the loud stimulus will cause a much smaller excitatory response to the loud stimulus. A ratio of the size of the second response to the first is inversely proportional to the strength of the inhibition. By placing a number of electrodes at distinct locations on the scalp, an electrically positive evoked potential (P50) can be recorded 50 msec after the presentation of the loud stimulus. This P50 response to the loud auditory stimulus is normally diminished when the loud stimulus is immediately (500 m sec) preceded by the soft stimulus in the pre-pulse condition. In patients with schizophrenia, the amplitude of the P50 auditory-evoked response is not diminished in the pre-pulse condition, indicating an inability to gate sensory information (Light and Braff, 1999). These gating deficits are thought to be due, at least in part, to disruptions in the hippocampus since the P50-evoked potential is thought to originate from this brain region.

Interestingly, many family members of patients with schizophrenia also show gating deficits without having any clinical signs of the disease. It seems therefore that gating deficits may be genetically inherited as one of the symptoms of schizophrenia that alone may be no more than a subtle cognitive abnormality.

Oculomotor Dysfunctions

At the turn of the century, two researchers working in a psychiatric hospital in New England made the observation that patients with dementia praecox (now termed schizophrenia) had difficulty following an oscillating pendulum with their eyes. The investigation of eye movement dysfunction in schizophrenia, which was revived in the 1970s, focuses on smooth pursuit and saccadic eye movement systems.

Smooth eye pursuit, which is evoked by slow-moving objects such as a swinging pendulum, is significantly impaired in schizophrenia patients. As mentioned above, PET scans show that schizophrenia patients with smooth eye pursuit impairments do not activate the frontal eye fields, the cortical region involved in initiating these eye movements (Ross et al., 1995; O'Driscoll et al., 1998). Patients with schizophrenia are also deficient in their ability to inhibit reflexive saccadic eye movements, which are high-velocity movements that shift the eyes from one position to the other. Interestingly, eye movement dysfunctions are also present in the clinically unaffected relatives of patients with schizophrenia (Calkins and Iacono, 2000). These findings suggest that eye movement dysfunction is clearly an inheritable vulnerability trait that is not sufficient to cause schizophrenia but may be important in the search for schizophrenia susceptibility genes.

Olfactory Deficits

Many patients with schizophrenia exhibit olfactory dysfunctions. They are impaired in their ability to detect odors due to an increased sensitivity threshold for detection. Their ability to identify odors, to discriminate between odors, and their olfactory memory are also significantly impaired. While the basis for this dysfunction is unclear, olfactory processing is mediated by limbic structures that have been implicated in the pathophysiology of schizophrenia, including the prefrontal cortex, ventromedial temporal lobe, basal forebrain, and diencephalon. The few studies that have examined the neurobiology of the olfactory system in schizophrenia patients have revealed a reduced evoked potential response to olfactory stimuli, a 23 percent decrease in size of the olfactory bulb, and a decrease in synaptophysin expression in the glomerulus of the olfactory bulb, indicating a reduction in synaptic functioning of this structure (Moberg et al., 1999). Neurodevelopment continues throughout life in the olfactory system, rendering it a good site for examining active neurodevelopmental processes in schizophrenia.

NEUROPSYCHIATRIC SYNDROMES

Most of the nongenetic risk factors of schizophrenia consist of problems during pregnancy and may have as a common thread the mother's stress response. It therefore shouldn't be surprising that the behavioral and anatomical effects of these problems (plus genetic vulnerability) are very widespread and include both neuropsychiatric syndromes other than psychosis and abnormalities outside of the brain.

The relationship between psychotic bipolar disorder and schizophrenia is unclear, but certainly within schizophrenia, full-fledged manic syndromes occur and serious depressive episodes are common. These can occur either during psychotic episodes or when psychotic symptoms are either absent or stable. The lifetime risk for major depression is very high, with perhaps a third to a half of patients experiencing at least one such episode. This problem contributes to the very high risk of suicide in schizophrenia; approximately 10 percent of patients may kill themselves.

Obsessive-compulsive symptoms such as excessive checking or excessive hand washing also appear to have an increased prevalence in schizophrenia (perhaps as much as 20 percent) and are sometimes difficult to distinguish from delusions.

Drug abuse is also much more common in schizophrenia than in the general population. Population-based estimates suggest that about a third of those with schizophrenia abuse alcohol at some point in their lives, while nearly half abuse alcohol or some other drug.

Other neuropsychiatric problems are also found in schizophrenia. With chronic use, the older antipsychotic drugs such as haloperidol and chlorpromazine cause abnormal, involuntary movements in some patients. These extra, purposeless movements are usually subtle but can be so frequent and severe that they are disfiguring and interfere with the patient's function. However, similar movements also occur in some patients with schizophrenia before they take such medications. Patients with deficit schizophrenia may exhibit these spontaneous movements more frequently than nondeficit patients.

NEUROCHEMICAL ABNORMALITIES

While schizophrenia is no longer thought to be strictly due to a chemical imbalance, the vast neuroanatomical defects will necessarily lead to alterations in many neurochemical systems. Pharmacotreatment of schizophrenia has been aimed at correcting these neuro-chemical disturbances, and this will be discussed in detail in Chapter 10. The following is a very brief overview of the neurochemical disturbances in schizophrenia.

Dopamine Disregulation

The efficacy of antipsychotic drugs, which traditionally worked through the dopamin-ergic system, has been the major stimulus driving the "dopamine hypothesis" of schizophrenia (Willner, 1997). The evidence that antipsychotic drugs all share the abil-ity to block dopamine receptors led to the concept that overactivity in some subcortical dopamine cells causes psychotic symptoms such as hallucinations, delusions, and dis-organized thought and behavior. A more recent modification of this theory suggests that hypofunction of dopamine in the mesocortical dopamine neurons is responsible for negative symptoms such as blunted affect and poverty of speech.

The formidable evidence that antipsychotic drugs work at least in large part because they block dopamine receptors does not necessarily mean that people with schizophre-nia have abnormal dopamine transmission. However, other evidence also suggests there is an abnormality in the dopamine system. For instance, dopamine agonists such as amphetamines and methylphenidate worsen the psychotic symptoms of schizophrenia, and some studies of dopamine function in living patients (using such methods as PET) have also revealed an abnormality in dopamine transmission.

Nonetheless, there are important limitations to the dopamine theory. First, block-ing dopamine receptors does not resolve all psychotic symptoms; despite taking high doses of such medications, some patients' psychotic symptoms improve little. More-over, these drugs do not improve other aspects of schizophrenia, such as the cognitive impairment or the blunted affect and poverty of speech. No one neurotransmitter can explain the widespread problems found in schizophrenia, and there is a great deal of evidence that other neurotransmitters are also abnormal in this disorder.

Glutamatergic Hypofunction

The suggestion that a glutamatergic dysfunction may be involved in the pathophysi-ology of schizophrenia was derived from the observation that when individuals came into the hospital under the influence of PCP (also known as angel dust), it was very difficult for clinicians to distinguish them from schizophrenia patients. Drugs such as PCP and ketamine function by blocking the N-methyl-D-aspartate (NMDA) subtype of glutamate receptors. Not only can these drugs mimic schizophrenia in a normal individual, they can exacerbate symptoms in patients with schizophrenia. Studies of glutamate receptors in postmortem tissue have generally found decreased binding to the kainate subtype of glutamate receptors in the hippocampus and limbic cortex, and increased binding to the alpha-amino-3-hydroxy-5-methyl-4-isoxazolepropionic acid (AMPA) and NMDA subtypes of glutamate receptors in the prefrontal cortex (Coyle, 1996). These changes in AMPA and kainate receptor subtypes have been reproduced in microarray studies (Mirnics et al., 2001).

GABAergic Hypofunction

Gamma-aminobutyric acid is the principal inhibitory neurotransmitter of the brain. There is considerable evidence for a decreased activity of the GABAergic system in patients with schizophrenia (Bunney et al., 1997; Selemon, 2001). Various studies have reported a decrease in GABA content, a decrease in GABA uptake sites, a decrease in the synthesizing enzyme for GABA (the 67 kd isoform of glutamic acid decarboxylase—GAD_{67}), a decrease in the GABA transporter (GAT), and a concomitant up-regulation of $GABA_A$ receptors. A down-regulation of GABAergic activity may have wide-ranging effects since the columnar firing pattern of cortical neurons is determined by a fine balance of glutamatergic excitation and GABAergic inhibition. Cortical malfunction is one of the hallmarks of schizophrenia.

Nicotinic Hypofunction

Patients with schizophrenia are notoriously heavy smokers, which lead researchers to examine the cholinergic system of the brain. Smoking may be a form of self-medication since gating deficits are temporarily restored by stimulation of the nicotine receptor, specifically the α_7-nicotinic receptor (Adler et al., 1998). There is an abnormal expression of α_7-nicotinic receptors in the hippocampus of postmortem brain from schizophrenia patients. While this was originally believed to be simply a consequence of heavy smoking, it is now being revisited as an inherited vulnerability factor since linkage studies have found a dinucleotide polymorphism at chromosome 15q13-14, the site of the α_7-nicotinic receptor (Freedman et al., 1997).

ANIMAL MODELS

The field of schizophrenia has only been marginally impacted by the study of animal models due to the lack of our understanding of the causes and mechanisms of the disease. In addition, since schizophrenia is largely a disease of higher cognitive functioning, it is difficult to conceive that schizophrenia can be simulated in an animal of lower phylogenetic origin than primates.

While some of the proposed paradigms are not themselves models of schizophrenia, they are nonetheless valuable tools to measure precise aspects of impaired cognition or behavior, including sensory gating and attention deficits, in pharmacological, surgical, genetic, and other models of schizophrenia. They are also useful for the development of new antipsychotic medications. The following will be a brief overview of these psychophysiological construct models, as well as animal models that have been used in the study of schizophrenia etiology, pathology, neurochemistry, and genetics.

Psychophysiological Construct Models

Sensory Gating. Pre-Pulse inhibition (PPI) is a paradigm in which the construct of gating can be studied in laboratory animals, usually rodents (Light and Braff, 1999; Kilts, 2001). Similar to the human paradigm, PPI measures the response to a loud auditory stimulus (120-dB click) when it is presented alone, as compared to when it is preceded by a soft click (15-dB pre-pulse). Animals will startle less to the loud click when it is preceded (100 m sec) by a soft click than when it is presented alone. This model is very similar to the paradigm used in humans except that in humans, an evoked potential (P50) is measured 50 msec after the presentation of the loud stimulus through electrodes placed on the scalp, whereas in rodents it is measured 40 msec after the presentation of the stimulus (N40) through electrodes placed in the skull, or in the CA3 region of the hippocampus. More commonly in the rodent, sensory gating is measured in the same paradigm as the amplitude of startle (pre-pulse inhibition of startle) as a flinch in the neck musculature, or in the whole body.

Latent Inhibition. The latent inhibition paradigm is used to measure selective attention in animals. Similar to the human paradigm, the noncontingent presentation of a stimulus attenuates its ability to enter into subsequent associations. In the animal paradigm water licks are paired with foot shock, whereas in the human paradigm non-sense syllables are paired with white noise (Gray, 1998; Kilts, 2001). Latent inhibition has face value in that it is facilitated by typical and atypical antipsychotic agents and disrupted by drugs that worsen symptoms of schizophrenia (Moser et al., 2000).

Pharmacological Models

Dopamine-Based Models. Amphetamines, which elevate extracellular levels of monoamines including dopamine, have numerous effects in humans and animals including effects on motor activity, sensory motor function, attention, learning, and memory. In addition, low doses of amphetamine in nonhuman primates can produce long-lasting psychomimetic effects (Lipska and Weinberger, 2000; Gainetdinov et al., 2001; Kilts, 2001).

Glutamate-Based Models. As in humans, moderate doses of NMDA receptor antagonists produce symptoms of schizophrenia in rodents and monkeys including increased locomotion and stereotypies, deficits in sensory gating and cognition, as well as impairments in social interaction. Furthermore, many of the abnormal behaviors induced by NMDA receptor antagonists (e.g., PCP, ketamine) are ameliorated by atypical antipsychotic drugs (Lipska and Weinberger, 2000; Gainetdinov et al., 2001; Kilts, 2001).

Models of Experimental Risk Factors

A number of factors have been identified that appear to be associated with an increased risk of developing schizophrenia. Such factors as obstetric complications, viral infections, and early stressful experiences have been mimicked in animals in an attempt to understand their relationship to schizophrenia etiology (Lipska and Weinberger, 2000).

As in humans, gestational malnutrition (or prenatal protein deprivation) in rats results in severe and permanent changes in the development of the brain, as well as deficits in cognitive functioning and learning and abnormalities in neurotransmitter systems; some of these resemble changes found in schizophrenia.

Viruses have gained considerable attention as etiological factors in schizophrenia. A variety of viruses with the potential to infect the developing brain have been found to produce abnormalities in infected offspring similar to those observed in schizophrenia, long after the virus has cleared. For instance, prenatal exposure to the influenza virus has been shown to produce several neuroanatomical abnormalities including pyramidal cell disarray, reduced thickness of the neocortex and hippocampus, enlarged ventricles, as well as a significant reduction in cortical reelin expression. In utero infections in rats and mice with the lymphocytic choriomeningitis virus (LCMV) cause impairment of GABAergic neurons as well as excitatory amino acid neurotransmission. Exposure to the Borna disease virus produces abnormalities in the development of the hippocampus and neocortex. Prenatal infection with influenza appears to alter reelin in the brain.

Perinatal complications such as Cesarean birth and anoxia during birth in rats have been reported to produce changes in limbic dopamine function. However, these studies are difficult to interpret since C-sections alone seemed to produce more debilitating effects than C-sections with anoxia.

Lesion Models

The functional and structural integrity of the DLPFC is critical for working memory. Alterations in dopamine input to, or turnover within, the DLPFC disrupt normal working memory. In experimental animals, lesions of the dopamine cells innervate the DLPFC, and lesions of the DLPFC increase dopamine turnover and impair working memory in ways similar to pharmacological manipulations of the dopamine system (Funahashi et al., 1993; Murphy et al., 1996). In both rats and monkeys the cognitive deficits induced by increased dopamine turnover in the DLPFC can be prevented by treatment with haloperidol and clozapine. Thus, these researchers concluded that dysfunction of the DLPFC may relate to some of the cognitive deficits present in people with schizophrenia.

Lesions of the developing ventral hippocampus in animals have been found to produce a variety of schizophrenia-like abnormalities that change over the life span of the animal (Lipska and Weinberger, 2000). For instance, excitotoxic lesions of the ventral hippocampus initially produce social deficits, followed by motor deficits reminiscent of dopamine hyperactivity, deficits of latent inhibition and PPI, and problems in working memory. Furthermore, many of these lesion-induced behaviors are normalized by antipsychotic agents. Lesions of the ventral hippocampus also produce many neurochemical and electrophysiological changes that are consistent with schizophrenia pathology.

Other lesion models that have been less extensively characterized at this point include excitotoxic lesions of the prefrontal cortex, neonatal intracerebroventricular infusions of kainic acid, and neonatal depletion of serotonin.

Genetic-Based Models

Generated. Although not straightforward in polygenic diseases such as schizophrenia, transgenic animals are being created to study possible candidate susceptibility genes. This approach can involve making knockouts (or knockdowns) of genes based on linkage analysis (Gainetdinov et al., 2001; Kilts, 2001). For instance, three separate genetic strains have been generated that delete the mouse equivalent (on chromosome 16) of the human 22q11 deletion that produces VCFS, which closely resembles the schizophrenia phenotype. These mice show some cardiovascular morphology and behavior that resembles their human counterpart; however, there is tremendous variability observed in these animal models.

Models can also be generated based on their function. For example, knockouts have been generated for candidate molecules such as N-CAM. These mice have abnormal neuronal migration, altered cytoarchitecture in several brain regions, enlarged ventricles, and deficits in PPI. Knockouts have also been generated for dopamine-related molecules such as dopamine receptors, the dopamine transporter, and catechol-O-methyltransferase (COMT), the major enzyme involved in the extraneuronal degradation of dopamine. These mice are hyperactive, stereotypic, and have reproduced some of the cognitive and gating impairments seen in patients with schizophrenia. Knockdown mice have also been produced for the NR1 and NR2A subtype of NMDA glutamate receptors. These transgenic mice show behavioral abnormalities that are similar to those treated with NMDA receptor antagonists such as PCP, which are attenuated by antipsychotic drugs.

Spontaneous. Since schizophrenia may result in part from mutations present in nature, an animal with a spontaneous mutation that shares some resemblance to schizophrenia would be of interest. The reeler mouse is a spontaneous mutant that has been around for over 30 years and has been extensively studied to understand the role of reelin in development. The heterozygous reeler mouse, which like patients with schizophrenia only expresses half of the normal levels of reelin, has recently emerged as a possible model of schizophrenia vulnerability. These mice have many neuroanatomical abnormalities that resemble those found in the brains of patients with schizophrenia, including decreased neuropil volume, increased cell packing density, decreased dendritic spine density, mis-migration of NADPH-diaphorase cells, and decreased GAD$_{67}$ mRNA and protein expression. These mice also show similar behavioral abnormalities including gating deficits (PPI), cognitive deficits (slow acquisition rate in radial maze task), increased anxiety in the elevated plus-maze test, and olfactory discrimination deficits (Costa et al., 2002). Further study of these mice may identify them as a good model to develop new therapeutic agents for the treatment of this disease.

CONCLUSION

In popular culture, "insanity" or "madness" often has a romantic aura. The reality is quite different. Few of us would want to experience schizophrenia, the most common disorder with psychotic symptoms. Auditory hallucinations are often accusatory, insulting, or threatening, and most delusions involve a painful experience, such as being spied on or persecuted. The anxiety and depression that are so common among people who suffer from schizophrenia are often severe, while deficit schizophrenia patients are unable to enjoy interests or relationships with other people. Aside from these more dramatic problems, there is the grinding burden of the cognitive difficulties associated with schizophrenia, which make it difficult to work or manage the problems of daily life.

Although the treatment of schizophrenia has improved with the advent of a second generation of antipsychotic drugs, not all patients respond to these medications, and the psychotic symptoms of many respond only in part. In addition, antipsychotic drugs carry the risk of a wide range of side effects, from stiffness and restlessness to a form of diabetes. Many patients find these side effects so uncomfortable that they stop taking their medications, despite the risk of the reappearance or worsening of their psychotic symptoms. Other patients do not understand that their thinking is impaired and refuse to take medications for that reason. Even among those for whom antipsychotic medications are effective, these drugs do little or nothing for the cognitive impairment that accounts for so much of the difficulty in functioning that patients face.

The severity of the disease and the limitations in current treatments underline the importance of furthering our understanding of this debilitating disorder. Fortunately, there is reason for hope for improvements. New treatments for psychotic symptoms and effective treatments for cognitive impairment are on the horizon. Advanced genetic screening technology, structural and functional brain imaging, sophisticated histological techniques, and other methods will be instrumental in identifying particular features of the disease. The combination of these approaches, coupled with a recognition of the heterogeneity of the disorder, will lead to greater understanding, better treatments, and eventually, prevention of schizophrenia.

REFERENCES

Adler LE, Olincy A, Waldo M, et al. (1998). Schizophrenia, sensory gating, and nicotinic receptors. *Schizophr Bull* 24:189–202.

Alexander GE, DeLong MR, Strick PL (1986). Parallel organization of functionally segregated circuits linking basal ganglia and cortex. *Annu Rev Neurosci* 9:357–381.

Arnold SE, Rioux L (2001). Challenges, status, and opportunities for studying developmental neuropathology in adult schizophrenia. *Schizophr Bull* 27:395–416.

Berrettini WH (2001). The human genome: susceptibility loci. *Am J Psychiatry* 158:865.

Brown AS, Susser ES, Butler PD, Richardson Andrews R, Kaufmann CA, Gorman JM (1996). Neurobiological plausibility of prenatal nutritional deprivation as a risk factor for schizophrenia. *J Nerv Ment Dis* 184:71–85.

Brown AS, Cohen P, Greenwald S, Susser E (2000). Nonaffective psychosis after prenatal exposure to rubella. *Am J Psychiatry* 157:438–443.

Buchsbaum MS, Potkin SG, Siegel BV Jr, et al. (1992). Striatal metabolic rate and clinical response to neuroleptics in schizophrenia. *Arch Gen Psychiatry* 49:966–974.

Bunney BG, Potkin SG, Bunney WE (1997). Neuropathological studies of brain tissue in schizophrenia. *J Psychiatr Res* 31:159–173.

Calkins ME, Iacono WG (2000). Eye movement dysfunction in schizophrenia: A heritable characteristic for enhancing phenotype definition. *Am J Med Genet* 97:72–76.

Carpenter WT, Buchanan RW, Kirkpatrick B, Tamminga CA, Wood F (1993). Strong infer-ence, theory falsification, and the neuroanatomy of schizophrenia. *Arch Gen Psychiatry* 50:825–831.

Clark C, Kopala L, Li DK, Hurwitz T (2001). Regional cerebral glucose metabolism in never-medicated patients with schizophrenia. *Can J Psychiatry* 46:340–345.

Costa E, Davis J, Pesold C, Tueting P, Guidotti A (2002). The heterozygote reeler mouse as a model for the development of a new generation of antipsychotics. *Curr Opin Pharmacol* 2:56–62.

Coyle JT (1996). The glutamatergic dysfunction hypothesis for schizophrenia. *Harv Rev Psychiatry* 3:241–253.

Crichton-Browne J (1879). On the weight of the brain and its component parts in the insane. *Brain* 2:42–67.

Davies N, Russell A, Jones P, Murray RM (1998). Which characteristics of schizophrenia predate psychosis? *J Psychiatr Res* 32:121–131.

DeLisi LE, Crow TJ (1999). Chromosome Workshops 1998: Current state of psychiatric linkage. *Am J Med Genet* 88:215–218.

Diagnostic and Statistical Manual of Mental Disorders DSM-IV-TR (Text Revision) (2000). American Psychiatric Press: Washington, DC.

Freedman R, Coon H, Myles-Worsley M, et al. (1997). Linkage of a neurophysiological deficit in schizophrenia to a chromosome 15 locus. *Proc Natl Acad Sci USA* 94:587–592.

Funahashi S, Bruce CJ, Goldman-Rakic PS (1993). Dorsolateral prefrontal lesions and oculomotor delayed-response performance: Evidence for mnemonic "scotomas." *J Neurosci* 13:1479–1497.

Gainetdinov RR, Mohn AR, Caron MG (2001). Genetic animal models: Focus on schizophrenia. *Trends Neurosci* 24:527–533.

Garey LJ, Ong WY, Patel TS, et al. (1998). Reduced dendritic spine density on cerebral cortical pyramidal neurons in schizophrenia. *J Neurol Neurosurg Psychiatry* 65:446–453.

Glantz LA, Lewis DA (1997). Reduction of synaptophysin immunoreactivity in the prefrontal cortex of subjects with schizophrenia. Regional and diagnostic specificity [corrected and republished article originally appeared in *Arch Gen Psychiatry* (1997), 54:660–669] *Arch Gen Psychiatry* 54:943–952.

Glantz LA, Lewis DA (2000). Decreased dendritic spine density on prefrontal cortical pyramidal neurons in schizophrenia. *Arch Gen Psychiatry* 57:65–73.

Gottesman II (1991). *Schizophrenia Genesis: The Origins of Madness.* Freeman: New York.

Gray JA (1998). Integrating schizophrenia. *Schizophr Bull* 24:249–266.

Green MF (1996). What are the functional consequences of neurocognitive deficits in schizophrenia? *Am J Psychiatry* 153:321–330.

Guidotti A, Auta J, Davis JM, et al. (2000). Decrease in reelin and glutamic acid decarboxylase67 (GAD67) expression in schizophrenia and bipolar disorder: A postmortem brain study. *Arch Gen Psychiatry* 57:1061–1069.

Harding CM, Zubin J, Strauss JS (1992). Chronicity in schizophrenia: Revisited. *Br J Psychiatry Suppl* 18:27–37.

Harrison PJ (1999). The neuropathology of schizophrenia. A critical review of the data and their interpretation. *Brain* 122:593–624.

Heckers S, Goff D, Schacter DL, et al. (1999). Functional imaging of memory retrieval in deficit vs nondeficit schizophrenia. *Arch Gen Psych* 56:1117–1123.

Heckers S, Rauch SL, Goff D, et al. (1998). Impaired recruitment of the hippocampus during conscious recollection in schizophrenia. *Nat Neurosci* 1:318–323.

Holcomb HH, Lahti AC, Medoff DR, Weiler M, Dannals RF, Tamminga CA (2000). Brain activation patterns in schizophrenic and comparison volunteers during a matched-performance auditory recognition task. *Am J Psychiatry* 157:1634–1645.

Impagnatiello F, Guidotti AR, Pesold C, et al. (1998). A decrease of reelin expression as a putative vulnerability factor in schizophrenia. *Proc Natl Acad Sci U S A* 95:15718–15723.

Isohanni M, Jones PB, Moilanen K, et al. (2001). Early developmental milestones in adult schizophrenia and other psychoses. A 31-year follow-up of the Northern Finland 1966 Birth Cohort. *Schizophr Res* 52:1–19.

Kilts CD (2001). The changing roles and targets for animal models of schizophrenia. *Biol Psychiatry* 50:845–855.

Kirkpatrick B, Buchanan RW, Ross DE, Carpenter WT Jr (2001). A separate disease within the syndrome of schizophrenia. *Arch Gen Psychiatry* 58:165–171.

Koenig JI, Kirkpatrick B, Lee P (2002). Glucocorticoid hormones and early brain development in schizophrenia. *Neuropsychopharmacology* 27:309–318.

Kringlen E (1991). Adoption studies in functional psychosis. *Eur Arch Psychiatry Clin Neurosci* 240:307–313.

Kung L, Roberts RC (1999). Mitochondrial pathology in human schizophrenic striatum: A postmortem ultrastructural study. *Synapse* 31:67–75.

Kung L, Conley R, Chute DJ, Smialek J, Roberts RC (1998). Synaptic changes in the striatum of schizophrenic cases: A controlled postmortem ultrastructural study. *Synapse* 28:125–139.

Lahti AC, Holcomb HH, Medoff DR, Weiler MA, Tamminga CA, Carpenter WT Jr (2001). Abnormal patterns of regional cerebral blood flow in schizophrenia with primary negative symptoms during an effortful auditory recognition task. *Am J Psychiatry* 158:1797–1808.

Lawrie SM, Abukmeil SS (1998). Brain abnormality in schizophrenia. A systematic and quantitative review of volumetric magnetic resonance imaging studies. *Br J Psychiatry* 172:110–120.

Levy R, Goldman-Rakic PS (2000). Segregation of working memory functions within the dorsolateral prefrontal cortex. *Exp Brain Res* 133:23–32.

Light GA, Braff DL (1999). Human and animal studies of schizophrenia-related gating deficits. *Curr Psychiatry Rep* 1:31–40.

Lipska BK, Weinberger DR (2000). To model a psychiatric disorder in animals: Schizophrenia as a reality test. *Neuropsychopharmacology* 23:223–239.

Lobato MI, Belmonte-de-Abreu P, Knijnik D, Teruchkin B, Ghisolfi E, Henriques A (2001). Neurodevelopmental risk factors in schizophrenia. *Braz J Med Biol Res* 34:155–163.

Margolis RL, Abraham MR, Gatchell SB, et al. (1997). cDNAs with long CAG trinucleotide repeats from human brain. *Hum Genet* 100:114–122.

McGlashan TH, Hoffman RE (2000). Schizophrenia as a disorder of developmentally reduced synaptic connectivity. *Arch Gen Psychiatry* 57:637–648.

McNeil TF, Cantor-Graae E, Ismail B (2000). Obstetric complications and congenital malformation in schizophrenia. *Brain Res Brain Res Rev* 31:166–178.

Millar JK, Wilson-Annan JC, Anderson S, et al. (2000). Disruption of two novel genes by a translocation co-segregating with schizophrenia. *Hum Mol Genet* 9:1415–1423.

Mirnics K, Middleton FA, Lewis DA, Levitt P (2001). Analysis of complex brain disorders with gene expression microarrays: Schizophrenia as a disease of the synapse. *Trends Neurosci* 24:479–486.

Moberg PJ, Agrin R, Gur RE, Gur RC, Turetsky BI, Doty RL (1999). Olfactory dysfunction in schizophrenia: A qualitative and quantitative review. *Neuropsychopharmacology* 21:325–340.

Moser PC, Hitchcock JM, Lister S, Moran PM (2000). The pharmacology of latent inhibition as an animal model of schizophrenia. *Brain Res Brain Res Rev* 33:275–307.

Murphy KC, Owen MJ (2001). Velo-cardio-facial syndrome: A model for understanding the genetics and pathogenesis of schizophrenia. *Br J Psychiatry* 179:397–402.

Murphy BL, Arnsten AF, Goldman-Rakic PS, Roth RH (1996). Increased dopamine turnover in the prefrontal cortex impairs spatial working memory performance in rats and monkeys. *Proc Natl Acad Sci U S A* 93:1325–1329.

O'Driscoll GA, Strakowski SM, Alpert NM, et al. (1998). Differences in cerebral activation during smooth pursuit and saccadic eye movements using positron-emission tomography. *Biol Psychiatry* 44:685–689.

O'Reilly RL (1994). Viruses and schizophrenia. *Aust N Z J Psychiatry* 28:222–228.

Owen MJ (2000). Molecular genetic studies of schizophrenia. *Brain Res Brain Res Rev* 31:179–186.

Powers RE (1999). The neuropathology of schizophrenia. *J Neuropathol Exp Neurol* 58:679–690.

Roberts RC, Conley R, Kung L, Peretti FJ, Chute DJ (1996). Reduced striatal spine size in schizophrenia: A postmortem ultrastructural study. *Neuroreport* 7:1214–1218.

Ross DE, Thaker GK, Holcomb HH, Cascella NG, Medoff DR, Tamminga CA (1995). Abnormal smooth pursuit eye movements in schizophrenic patients are associated with cerebral glucose metabolism in oculomotor regions. *Psychiatry Res* 58:53–67.

Saleem Q, Dash D, Gandhi C, et al. (2001). Association of CAG repeat loci on chromosome 22 with schizophrenia and bipolar disorder. *Mol Psychiatry* 6:694–700.

Selemon LD (2001). Regionally diverse cortical pathology in schizophrenia: Clues to the etiology of the disease. *Schizophr Bull* 27:349–377.

Selemon LD, Goldman-Rakic PS (1999). The reduced neuropil hypothesis: A circuit based model of schizophrenia. *Biol Psychiatry* 45:17–25.

Selemon LD, Rajkowska G, Goldman-Rakic PS (1995). Abnormally high neuronal density in the schizophrenic cortex. A morphometric analysis of prefrontal area 9 and occipital area 17. *Arch Gen Psychiatry* 52:805–818.

Siris SG (2001). Suicide and schizophrenia. *J Psychopharmacol* 15:127–135.

Staal WG, Hulshoff Pol HE, Schnack HG, van Haren NE, Seifert N, Kahn RS (2001). Structural brain abnormalities in chronic schizophrenia at the extremes of the outcome spectrum. *Am J Psychiatry* 158:1140–1142.

Stabenau JR, Pollin W (1993). Heredity and environment in schizophrenia, revisited. The contribution of twin and high-risk studies. *J Nerv Ment Dis* 181:290–297.

Tamminga CA, Thaker GK, Buchanan R, et al. (1992). Limbic system abnormalities identified in schizophrenia using positron emission tomography with fluorodeoxyglucose and neocortical alterations with deficit syndrome. *Arch Gen Psychiatry* 49:522–530.

Torrey EF, Rawlings R, Waldman IN (1988). Schizophrenic births and viral diseases in two states. *Schizophr Res* 1:73–77.

Vaswani M, Kapur S (2001). Genetic basis of schizophrenia: Trinucleotide repeats. An update. *Prog Neuropsychopharmacol Biol Psychiatry* 25:1187–1201.

Velakoulis D, Pantelis C (1996). What have we learned from functional imaging studies in schizophrenia? The role of frontal, striatal and temporal areas. *Aust N Z J Psychiatry* 30: 195–209.

Walker EF, Savoie T, Davis D (1994). Neuromotor precursors of schizophrenia. *Schizophr Bull* 20:441–451.

Willner P (1997). The dopamine hypothesis of schizophrenia: Current status, future prospects. *Int Clin Psychopharmacol* 12:297–308.

Yolken RH, Karlsson H, Yee F, Johnston-Wilson NL, Torrey EF (2000). Endogenous retroviruses and schizophrenia. *Brain Res Brain Res Rev* 31:193–199.

10

PHARMACOLOGICAL TREATMENT OF SCHIZOPHRENIA

Rajiv Tandon and Michael D. Jibson

Department of Psychiatry University of Michigan Medical Center Ann Arbor, Michigan

INTRODUCTION

Schizophrenia is a chronic, frequently life-time, remitting, and relapsing psychotic disorder with prominent symptoms and deficits even during phases of remission (Cancro and Lehman, 2000). Although there is a history of poor childhood and adolescent function in many patients, the illness is usually diagnosed in late adolescence or early adulthood when florid psychotic symptoms first appear. Periodic psychotic exacerbation (*relapse*) occurs throughout the course of the illness. Schizophrenia has devastating effects on several aspects of the patient's life and has been associated with a high risk of suicide (about 10 percent of patients die from suicide) and significant impairment in function (less than 10 percent of patients are fully employed and live independently). Its treatment requires a multimodal approach, including medication and psychosocial interventions, such as assistance with such routine demands of life as housing, financial sustenance, and personal relationships. The broad objective of treatment is to reduce

Textbook of Biological Psychiatry, Edited by Jaak Panksepp
ISBN 0-471-43478-7   Copyright © 2004 John Wiley & Sons, Inc.

the overall morbidity and mortality of the disorder, decrease the frequency and severity of episodes of psychotic exacerbation, and improve the functional capacity and quality of lives of the individuals afflicted with the illness. Most patients require comprehensive and continuous care over the course of their lives. This review focuses on the pharmacological aspects of schizophrenia. The clinical and neurobiological substrates on which those treatments work are briefly reviewed.

TARGETS OF PHARMACOLOGICAL TREATMENT

Clinical Substrate

Schizophrenia is characterized by a wide range of symptoms, accompanied by significant deficits in function and marked diminution in the quality of life. Since no cure currently exists, pharmacological treatment is directed at inducing and maintaining remission of various symptom dimensions. Treatment-relevant domains of pathology include *positive symptoms* (delusions, hallucinations, suspiciousness, disorganized thinking), *negative symptoms* (impoverished speech and thinking, lack of social drive, flatness of emotional expression, apathy), *cognitive and neuropsychological dysfunction* [average intelligence quotient (IQ) in schizophrenia is 80 to 84, with prominent memory and learning difficulties], and *mood symptoms* (depression, anxiety). Schizophrenia presents a unique set of symptoms in each individual affected, creating considerable diversity of clinical presentation. To a large extent, the unique features of each case are defined by the relative contribution of various domains to the overall picture of symptoms. The relative severity of symptoms within these domains varies across individuals, as also in the same individual over the course of illness. The diagnosis of schizophrenia is typically made at the time of development of frank psychotic symptoms.

These symptom domains contribute differentially to impairments in function, with the severity of negative and cognitive symptoms most strongly correlated with degree of functional impairment. Pharmacological treatment is directed at the different symptom domains with the objective of reducing the severity of these symptoms and thereby improving function and quality of life. While pharmacological treatment of schizophrenia does improve each of the different psychopathological domains to varying extents, side effects associated with such treatment can worsen some symptom domains and can also independently have an adverse impact on function and quality of life. Additionally, side effects [particularly extrapyramidal symptoms (EPS)] contribute to treatment noncompliance, leading in turn to a worse course of illness; medication-free patients are three times as likely to relapse as adequately medicated patients. Consequently, the optimal pharmacotherapy of schizophrenia is one that provides the best possible control of the various symptoms while minimizing side effects from such treatment.

Active psychosis is the most common cause of hospital admission and as such is evidence of poor symptom control and relapse. A primary goal of pharmacologic treatment in schizophrenia is the elimination or reduction of positive symptoms.

Control of these symptoms is remarkably effective in reducing the need for inpatient treatment, thereby allowing patients to remain in community settings. All antipsychotics are effective in the treatment of positive symptoms. Negative symptoms can improve or worsen (because of parkinsonian side effects) with antipsychotic treatment (Miller and Tandon, 2000). Even with optimal antipsychotic treatment, negative symptoms tend to be present throughout the course of schizophrenia, including the premorbid and remission phases of the illness. This combination of pervasiveness, modest response to treatment, and enormous impact on quality of life make them a major challenge in the treatment of schizophrenia. Similarly, impaired cognition may be a primary symptom of the illness or may be a consequence of pharmacological treatment. The anticholinergic properties that are a prominent feature of many antipsychotics contribute directly to cognitive impairment, as do parkinsonian side effects (*bradyphrenia*) (Casey, 1995; Bilder, 1997; Harvey and Keefe, 1997). The frequent use of adjunctive anticholinergic agents to treat or prevent parkinsonian side effects further exacerbates secondary cognitive impairment, especially difficulties with memory (Tandon, 1999).

Neuropathological Substrate

Schizophrenia is clearly a brain disease, and numerous abnormalities in structure, function, and neurochemistry have been reported (Chapter 9). Nevertheless, although certain areas of abnormality and dysfunction have emerged as especially suspect, no clear pathologic basis for the disease or any of its component symptoms has been identified. It appears likely that the abnormalities in schizophrenia arise from an early lesion (genetic, acquired, or both), interacting with altered postnatal developmental processes to produce the symptoms of the illness.

From the perspective of neurochemistry, the dopamine hypothesis has dominated biochemical and pharmacological research on schizophrenia for four decades. In its simplest form, the hypothesis states that schizophrenia is related to a relative excess of dopamine-dependent neuronal activity (Haase and Janssen, 1958). The major support for this hypothesis derives from the efficacy of the dopamine-blocking antipsychotics in treating psychotic symptomatology and the ability of dopamine-enhancing agents such as amphetamine to exacerbate the symptoms of schizophrenia. No drugs without dopamine-blocking activity have any proven efficacy in the treatment of schizophrenia. In fact, the clinical potency of various antipsychotic drugs is directly related to their in vitro ability to bind to dopamine D_2 receptors (Creese et al., 1976; Seeman et al., 1976).

Despite this body of pharmacological data supporting the dopamine hypothesis, there is little direct evidence of altered dopamine functioning in schizophrenic patients. Furthermore, while pharmacological data implicate increased dopamine activity in the pathogenesis of positive symptoms of schizophrenia, there is minimal association with negative or cognitive/neuropsychological symptoms. These observations have encouraged a reappraisal of the role of the dopamine system in schizophrenia. A "modified dopamine model" postulates a decrease in cortical dopamine activity, and a reciprocal increase in subcortical dopamine activity, these changes being linked to negative and positive symptoms, respectively. The other approach emphasizes interactions between dopamine and other neurotransmitters, with models of dopamine interactions with serotonin, glutamate, acetylcholine, and gamma-amino butyric acid (GABA) proposed.

PHARMACOLOGICAL TREATMENT

The class of antipsychotic drugs represents the primary pharmacological treatment of schizophrenia. There are approximately 40 antipsychotics available in the world; of these, 20 are available in the United States. From 1950 to 1990, first-generation antipsychotics (neuroleptics) were available; over the past decade, several second-generation or "atypical" antipsychotics have been introduced into clinical practice. Currently, 15 of the antipsychotics available in the United States are first-generation antipsychotics, while 5 are second-generation agents (Fig. 10.1).

First-Generation Antipsychotic Agents

When Emil Kraepelin first described the concept of schizophrenia over a century ago, he asserted: "The treatment of dementia praecox offers few points for intervention." The introduction of electroconvulsive therapy in 1938 provided the first somewhat efficacious somatic treatment of schizophrenia; prior to that time, good treatment consisted of providing the afflicted patient with a safe and supportive environment in the form of a long-term psychiatric hospitalization. Chlorpromazine was the first neuroleptic to be introduced into clinical practice. Discovery of its "tranquilizing" effects in 1952 (Delay and Deniker, 1952) led to the development of the first generation of antipsychotic medications, which constituted the primary pharmacological treatment of schizophrenia for the next 40 years. Approximately 30 such "typical" or "conventional" antipsychotics have been developed; 15 such agents are approved as antipsychotics in the United States. These medications have been very effective in establishing and maintaining remission of acute episodes of the illness, primarily by controlling positive symptoms;

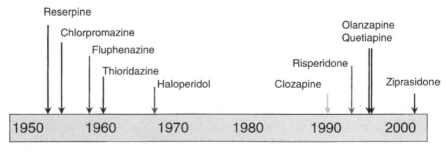

Figure 10.1. Antipsychotic therapy.

they are relatively ineffective, however, in treating the negative, cognitive, and mood symptom domains of schizophrenia. Furthermore, even with regard to positive symptoms, conventional antipsychotics are only partially effective in about 40 percent of patients, and completely ineffective in another 20 percent. While these medications [chlorpromazine (Thorazine), trifluoperazine (Stelazine), thioridazine (Mellaril), thiothixene (Navane), haloperidol (Haldol), etc.] differ from one another in potency and side effect profile, they have similar overall efficacy, and all cause significant EPS and tardive dyskinesia. EPS have a pervasive negative impact on treatment, contributing to dysphoria and poor compliance, worsening of negative symptoms and cognitive function, and increased risk of tardive dyskinesia. While appropriate use of lower doses of these agents can reduce these adverse effects, EPS and its consequences constitute the major limitation of first-generation antipsychotics (Casey, 1995; Jibson and Tandon, 1998).

Second-Generation Antipsychotic Agents

Until the past decade, acute EPS (and its pervasive adverse consequences) and tardive dyskinesia were considered unavoidable by-products of schizophrenia treatment—in fact, it was believed that there could be no antipsychotic efficacy without EPS. Over the past decade, five "atypical" or novel antipsychotic agents have been introduced into clinical practice in the United States; in chronological order of introduction, these include clozapine (Clozaril), risperidone (Risperdal), olanzapine (Zyprexa), quetiapine (Seroquel), and ziprasidone (Geodon). What principally distinguishes these newer antipsychotic agents from the older conventional agents is their ability to achieve an antipsychotic effect at least as good as that achieved by conventional agents with a much lower risk of EPS (Meltzer, 1995). In fact, this second generation of antipsychotics is called "atypical" because of its better ability to *separate antipsychotic effect from extrapyramidal side effect* (Fig. 10.2). The newer generation of antipsychotic agents thus clearly demonstrate important advantages over conventional agents in the area of EPS and tardive dyskinesia (Tandon et al., 1999a).

In addition to possessing at least equivalent efficacy to first-generation antipsychotics in treating positive symptoms, the newer generation of agents appears to provide greater efficacy in the other domains—notably negative symptoms, cognition, and mood. Much of the greater efficacy in these domains appears to be related to their ability to achieve an antipsychotic effect in the absence of EPS (Fig. 10.3). Consequently, it is essential that atypical agents be dosed in such a manner that they produce an antipsychotic effect in the absence of EPS, without the need for any anticholinergic or other antiparkinsonian medication, thereby preserving the broader efficacy and lower risk of tardive dyskinesia associated with their use (Kane et al., 1993; Jibson and Tandon, 2000).

Finally, in addition to their broader spectrum of efficacy and lower risk of neurological adverse effects, the newer generation of antipsychotics has greater efficacy than conventional antipsychotics in otherwise treatment-refractory patients (Kane et al., 1988). Among the five atypical agents, clozapine has the best proven track record in this regard (Chakos et al., 2001).

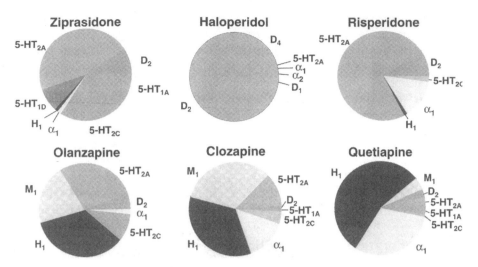

Figure 10.2. Comparative pharmacology of atypical antipsychotic drugs. [Adapted from Schmidt et al. (1998). *Soc Neurosci Abstr* 24(2): 2177.] See ftp site for color image.

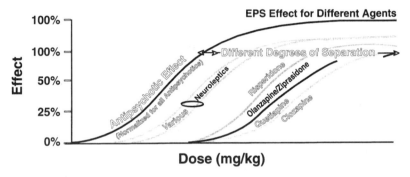

Figure 10.3. Dose-response curve: Antipsychotic effect vs. EPS. (Adapted from Jibson and Tandon, 1998.)

While the second generation of antipsychotics possesses several advantages over the first generation of conventional antipsychotics, and their introduction into clinical practice represents a significant advance in the pharmacotherapy of schizophrenia, they also have several limitations both with regard to safety/tolerability and to efficacy. Differences in the pharmacological profiles of these second-generation antipsychotics (Fig. 10.4 and Table 10.1) translate into differences in their side effect profiles (Table 10.2 and 10.3). Each available novel antipsychotic agent has a distinctive adverse effect profile; a comparison between them and two representative conventional agents (thioridazine and haloperidol) with regard to key side effects is provided in Table 10.4.

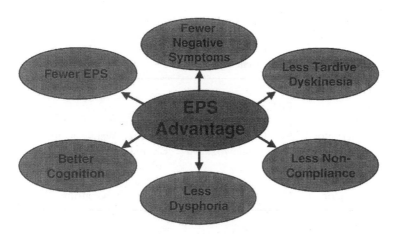

Figure 10.4. Essence of atypicality. (Adapted from Jibson and Tandon, 1998.)

TABLE 10.1. Pharmacological Profile of Atypical Antipsychotics

Receptor Blockade

All dopamine D_2 receptor blockade deliberately add serotonin 5-HT_{2A} receptor blockade that
  is more potent then D_2 blockade. What else they add differs?
Clozapine: several properties (D_1, D_2, D_3, D_4, 5-HT_{2A}, 5-HT_3, ACh, H_1, NE)
Risperidone: D_2 + 5-HT_{2A} + alpha-1 NE
Olanzapine: D_2 + 5-HT_{2A} + alpha-1 NE + M_1 + H_1
Quetiapine: D_2 + 5-HT_{2A} + alpha-1 NE + H_1
Ziprasidone: D_2 + 5-HT_{2A} + (increased NE, 5-HT, 5-HT_{1A})
Aripiprazole: D_2 partial agonist + 5-HT_{2A}

TABLE 10.2. Clinical Implications of Blockade of Various Receptors

Receptors	Possible Benefits	Possible Side Effects

Dopamine D_2 receptor	Antipsychotic effect
	Efficacy on positive
	  symptoms
	Efficacy on agitation
		Extrapyramidal movement disorders
		  (EPS), (dystonia, tremor, akathisia,
		  tardive dyskinesia)
		Endocrine changes (prolactin elevation
		  causing galactorrhea, gynecomastia,
		  menstrual changes, sexual dysfunction)

T A B L E 10.3. Clinical Implications of Blockade of Various Receptors

Receptors	Established Benefits	Likely Side Effects
Serotonin 5-HT receptors		
5-HT$_{2A}$ receptor	Reduced EPS	??
5-HT$_{2A}$ receptor	Not definitely known	Weight gain
Histamine H$_1$ receptor	Not definitely known	Sedation, Weight gain
Muscarinia receptor	Not definitely known	Blurred vision, dry mouth, constipation, urinary retention, sinus tachcardia, memory dysfunction
α_1-Adrenergic receptor	Not definitely known	Postural hypotension, dizziness

T A B L E 10.4. Conventional vs. Atypicals: Side Effect Profiles

	ZIP	THZ	HAL	CLZ	RIS	OLZ	QTP
EPS	0 to ±	+	+++	0 to ±	0 to ±	0 to ±	0 to ±
Dose-related EPS	+	++	+++	0	++	+	0
TD (tardive dyskinesia)	±	+++	+++	0	±	±	±
Prolactin elevation	±	++	+++	0	++	±	±
Agranulocytosis	±	±	±	++	±	±	±
Anticholinergic	±	+++	±	+++	±	±	±
AST/ALT elevation	±	+	+	+	±	+	±
Hypotension	+	+++	+	+++	++	+	++
Sedation	+	+++	+	+++	+	++	++
QTc prolongation	+	++	±	+	±	±	±
Weight gain	±	+	+	+++	++	+++	++

Key: 0 = absent; ± = minmal; + = mild; ++ = moderate; +++ = severe.
Source: Tandon et al. (1991a).

COURSE OF TREATMENT

It has been suggested that the pharmacologic treatment of schizophrenia be conceptualized as occurring in three distinct phases. First, active psychotic symptoms must be brought under control. Second, there must be a period in which normal functions are reconstituted. Third is a maintenance phase in which the gains of the first two stages are continued, and relapse prevention becomes the predominant objective. Although there is considerable overlap in treatments offered in each stage, there are also significant differences in the goals and methods of each step. It is essential that tactical decisions that facilitate treatment in the initial stage not be allowed to compromise the strategic goals of later phases.

Phase One (Acute Treatment)

The first phase of treatment begins with the recognition of acute psychotic symptoms. By definition, these symptoms include some combination of delusions, hallucinations, and thought disorganization. Positive symptoms can be accompanied by agitation, behavioral dyscontrol, and aggressive behavior. The primary goal of treatment in this phase of illness is the rapid resolution of these symptoms. Prompt control of psychosis will reduce the patient's and family's subjective distress, minimize disruption in functional activities such as work or school, and avoid possible danger to the patient or others. Although dosage requirements and time course of response can vary considerably among different patients, there is usually little to be gained by use of megadoses of antipsychotic drugs. Appropriate dosing of both conventional and atypical antipsychotics is critical to optimize the ratio of efficacy to adverse effects (Maixner et al., 1999). Excessively conservative doses will not reach optimal efficacy, and may lead to unnecessary augmentation or polypharmacy, whereas overly aggressive dosing leads to an unnecessary side effect burden and increased risk of noncompliance. The initial suggested dose and optimal dose range of various atypical antipsychotics and haloperidol for young, otherwise healthy, patients is summarized in Table 10.5. In first-episode patients, the low end of the suggested dose range is best utilized, whereas in more chronic patients, the upper part of the range is often more appropriate. In elderly patients, one-fourth to half of the recommended young adult dose is often optimal.

Few data are available to suggest that one agent works more rapidly than the others, although this has recently been the subject of clinical study. Similarly, clinical studies have not demonstrated any differences in speed of response among these atypical antipsychotics and conventional neuroleptics. Agitation, aggressive behavior, and motoric hyperactivity tend to respond to treatment within hours to days. Hallucinations and delusions typically take somewhat longer, and although these symptoms may begin to improve within a few days, a full response may require 4 to 8 weeks.

Phase Two (Transition and Consolidation of Improvement)

Once the psychotic symptoms have come under control, the second goal of treatment is to restore as much of the patient's premorbid function as possible. In general, this

TABLE 10.5. Recommended Dosing of First-Line Atypicals in Schizophrenia

	Daily Dose in Acute Phase (Refined after Clinical Experience)
Risperidone:	2–6 mg/days
Olanzapine:	10–20 mg/days
Quetiapine:	300–800 mg/days
Ziprasidone:	80–160 mg/days
Aripiprazole:	10–30 mg/days

phase of treatment involves resolution of acute-phase negative symptoms and cognitive impairments, and consolidation of improvement in positive symptoms. Negative symptoms typically improve slowly, over a period of 6 to 12 weeks, while cognitive and neuropsychological dysfunction show improvement for as much as 6 months to 1 year (Keefe et al., 1999). Critical elements of this phase of treatment are maintenance of compliance, optimization of medication dosage, solidification of a treatment alliance, and aggressive treatment of side effects. Obstacles to patient compliance include unacceptable side effects, denial of illness, lack of family and social support for treatment, and perceived social stigma associated with psychotropic medications. As noted in phase one, medications with superior side effect profiles are preferred. This is generally a period in which patients encounter significant changes or transitions in several aspects of their treatment: inpatient or partial hospitalization to outpatient, change in living situation, possible withdrawal of one or more acute-phase medications. Transitions are "dangerous times" in treatment, with a high risk of relapse, and hence should be as gradual as possible, with appropriate support provided as available.

At this stage of treatment, there may be a rational basis for selection of one atypical antipsychotic over another. As noted previously, the first-line atypicals differ primarily in side effect profile. The astute clinician will have identified the side effects of greatest concern to the particular patient by this stage of treatment and can then select the agent most favorable to the individual. A second issue to consider in this regard is the potential of antipsychotics (especially conventional agents) to contribute to negative symptoms, and for anticholinergic medications to worsen cognitive impairments. Balance must be achieved in maintaining resolution of psychotic symptoms, and in facilitating the progressive improvement of cognitive and negative symptoms. In general, atypical antipsychotics have substantial advantages over conventional neuroleptics in this phase of treatment. Gradual cross titration (over 6 to 12 weeks) from one antipsychotic to another is the preferred strategy if patients are to be switched from one antipsychotic to another (Fig. 10.5). Psychosocial interventions are an integral part of treatment at this time. Patient and family education regarding the illness and its treatment are essential to ensure compliance, promote a return to social and

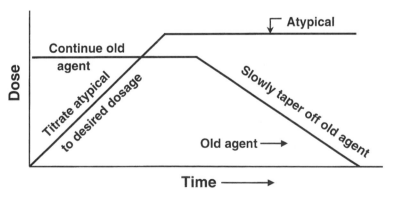

Figure 10.5. Switching antipsychotics: Recommended strategy.

occupational function, and permit reasonable planning for future activities. This is also the most effective time to assess the patient's functional ability and make recommendations for social and vocational rehabilitation. Psychosocial treatment and pharmacologic interventions are interdependent for their success (Mojtabai et al., 1998).

Phase Three (Maintenance Treatment)

The natural course of psychotic symptoms in schizophrenia includes a high rate of relapse, even when symptoms have been brought under good control. Maintenance antipsychotic treatment is essential for relapse prevention (Gilbert et al., 1995; Greden and Tandon, 1995). Furthermore, since much worsening of negative symptoms appears related to acute psychotic episodes, the most effective intervention to prevent the functional deterioration associated with these symptoms is to avoid further episodes of active psychosis. Although no treatment at present appears capable of reversing or correcting the premorbid component of dysfunction, effective antipsychotic treatment may prevent or at least limit the abnormalities associated with the deterioration phase. Finally, since the most severe deterioration occurs during the first few episodes of illness, aggressive maintenance therapy should be initiated early in the course of illness. Early, effective antipsychotic treatment can significantly limit deterioration and improve outcome in schizophrenia. Relapse prevention is a critical task in this phase of treatment; the risk of psychotic relapse in stabilized patients is about 75 percent within one year following drug discontinuation, in contrast to 15 to 20 percent if patients continue their prescribed antipsychotic treatment (DeQuardo and Tandon, 1998).

Long-term patient compliance is a major issue. As with other phases of treatment, unacceptable side effects, denial of illness, and inadequate social support are obstacles to treatment. Selection of an antipsychotic with a favorable side effect profile is essential. Long-standing or late-emergent side effects should be addressed with the patient. Patient education is essential during this phase of treatment. A patient with no active symptoms and no appreciation of the risk of relapse is unlikely to continue treatment. In patients whose compliance cannot otherwise be ensured, a depot antipsychotic is the treatment of choice (Kane, 1999).

COMBINING SEVERAL MEDICATIONS

Antipsychotic Polypharmacy

Combinations of antipsychotics are widely used clinically (about 15 to 20 percent of patients, with a clear trend toward increasing popularity), though no studies of their efficacy or safety are available. Thus, although combinations such as clozapine plus a high-potency conventional drug or clozapine plus an atypical agent have been suggested, their utility remains unclear. Despite these concerns, some situations may lend themselves to the concurrent use of more than one antipsychotic. A common dilemma faced in the clinic is the patient who responds well to clozapine but is consistently noncompliant and thus risks relapse. A combination of clozapine plus a depot neu-roleptic (as a "safety net") may prove superior to either agent alone, by offering the patient the benefit of clozapine, yet providing some degree of protection from relapse by the presence of the depot medication. Another common clinical situation is the patient being tapered off one antipsychotic and simultaneously titrated onto another who shows dramatic improvement midway through the process on moderate doses of the two medications. There is no clear basis to decide whether to continue the cross titration to monotherapy with the new agent or maintain the patient on lower doses of the two medications together. At this time, however, it is recommended that all patients receive a trial of monotherapy on the new antipsychotic agent with the precaution of slow cross titration (over 6 to 12 weeks), and optimal dosing with the newer agent. As we await controlled studies of this practice, it is important to systematically docu-ment the specific reasons for the use of multiple antipsychotics in a particular patient, describe the response of defined target symptoms, and assess adverse effects on an ongoing basis.

Adjunctive Medication

Judicious use of additional medications may be appropriate in selected schizophrenic patients and is very frequently utilized. The basis for the use of adjunctive medication may be treatment of side effects, refractory psychotic symptoms, comorbid conditions, or specific nonpsychotic symptoms such as agitation, anxiety, depression, or mood elevation. Careful consideration of potential side effects, additive effects, and drug interactions is essential.

Anticholinergics. Anticholinergic agents effectively treat the EPS associated with first-generation 'conventional' neuroleptics. The justification for the use of anticholiner-gics with atypical antipsychotics is more limited. As noted previously, anticholinergics may contribute to cognitive deficits, as well as to peripheral side effects such as constipation, dry mouth, urinary retention, and blurred vision. Indications for use of anticholinergics with atypical antipsychotics include akathisia, rare EPS, and excessive salivation with clozapine.

Mood Stabilizers. Mood stabilizers have long been used in conjunction with antipsychotic medications to address concurrent mood symptoms or treatment refrac-tory psychosis (Casey et al., 2001). Data in support of this practice are, however, sparse. Lithium has mood-stabilizing properties and can sometimes be useful for reducing excitement in patients suffering from schizophrenia. Valproate and other anti-convulsants are often employed (despite modest evidence of utility); they are beneficial in cases of mood elevation and may sometimes be helpful for persistent agitation. Adverse effects and impact on antipsychotic levels need to be monitored.

Benzodiazepines. Benzodiazepines are relatively benign agents useful in the treatment of agitation, insomnia, anxiety, and akathisia, all common concomitants of schizophrenia. Some evidence suggests that in agitated psychotic patients, lower total doses of antipsychotic may be used in the presence of benzodiazepines. The primary disadvantage of these drugs is the risk of abuse and dependency. They may also have a direct adverse effect on cognitive function.

Beta Blockers. Low doses of beta blockers can be useful in treating akathisia, which occurs in up to 20 percent of patients treated with conventional antipsychotics, and somewhat less commonly in patients treated with atypical antipsychotics.

Electroconvulsive Therapy (ECT). Electroconvulsive therapy should be considered in actively psychotic patients not responsive to other treatments. ECT is of clear, though short-term, benefit to many patients (Fink and Sackeim, 1996; Kales et al., 1999). Its safety in the presence of antipsychotic medications, including clozapine, is fairly well established.

FUTURE TRENDS

The advent of the second-generation atypical antipsychotics has revolutionized pharmacological treatment of schizophrenia and other psychotic disorders. In contrast to the first-generation conventional neuroleptics, these second-generation antipsychotic agents possess a broader spectrum of efficacy and cause fewer motor side effects, such as extrapyramidal symptoms (EPS) and tardive dyskinesia. Despite their substantial advantages, however, these second-generation agents also have significant limitations both in terms of efficacy and adverse effects. Adverse effects contribute to the major problem of medication noncompliance in schizophrenia; whereas injectable formulations of antipsychotics help with regard to this problem, no atypical agent is currently available in an injectable form (acute or depot). While possessing a broader spectrum of efficacy than conventional agents, even atypical antipsychotics are generally unable to completely normalize cognitive function or eliminate negative and mood symptoms. In fact, significant cognitive deficits and negative symptoms remain in schizophrenic patients treated with atypical agents. Although clozapine (and other novel agents to a less substantiated extent) may be effective in patients partially or completely refractory to treatment with conventional antipsychotics, these agents do not work in a significant proportion of patients. There is significant variation in the way patients respond to different antipsychotic medications, and currently there is no way of predicting which antipsychotic will work best for a particular patient and at what dose.

Finally, although our current pharmacological armamentarium has obvious limitations, it is also clear that "usual treatment" generally falls far short of the "best possible." Despite the publication of several treatment guidelines, there is significant variation in pharmacological treatment practice that cannot be explained away by "patient heterogeneity"; attempts to promote evidence-based "best possible" pharmacotherapy of schizophrenia have hitherto been unsuccessful. Efforts to address each of the above shortcomings are currently underway. While it is difficult to predict precisely when each of the following tools will become available to the clinician, some of these strategies are at very advanced stages of study, whereas others are at a very preliminary stage.

New Formulations of Currently available Second-Generation Antipsychotics

Currently, none of newer generation antipsychotic agents (clozapine, risperidone, olanzapine, quetiapine, or ziprasidone) is available in an injectable form in most countries (clozapine is licensed for parenteral administration in some countries). Injectable formulations are important because they have rapid onset of action, can be given when oral administration is precluded, and avoid some problems of patient resistance and noncompliance. Consequently, there are several clinical situations where first-generation antipsychotics have to be employed despite their many disadvantages.

Efforts to develop injectable formulations of atypical drugs are at different stages for the different agents. With regard to rapid-acting formulations for parenteral use, intramuscular olanzapine and ziprasidone have been developed and tested (Swift et al., 1998; Jones et al., 2001). Both these agents are currently being reviewed by the Food and Drug Administration (FDA) and are likely to become available within the next year. In patients whose compliance cannot otherwise be ensured, a depot antipsychotic is the treatment of choice. Currently, haloperidol decanoate and fluphenazine decanoate are the only agents available for such use in the United States. A long-acting formulation of risperidone is at a fairly advanced stage of evaluation and appears likely to become available by the year 2003/2004.

New Antipsychotic Agents

While several potential antipsychotic agents are at various stages of development, two agents have gone through extensive testing, and new drug applications for these agents will likely soon be submitted to the FDA for approval. While one of these agents (iloperidone) has significant similarities to currently available second-generation antipsychotic agents, the other (aripiprazole) is the first agent of its type likely to become available. Other agents with distinct mechanisms of action are at earlier stages of assessment of antipsychotic efficacy.

Iloperidone. Iloperidone has gone through several clinical trials in a variety of conditions. In addition to the D_2 and $5HT_{2A}$ antagonism characteristic of currently available atypical agents, it is also a potent antagonist at the alpha-1 and alpha-2 noradrenergic receptors; the magnitude of this effect is comparable to that of clozapine. While its precise clinical profile needs further elucidation, studies thus far suggest that it is an "atypical" agent with potent antipsychotic activity and a low EPS liability (Jain, 2000).

Aripiprazole. Aripiprazole is a partial agonist at the dopamine D_2 receptor, in contrast to existing antipsychotic agents, which are all full antagonists at the D_2 receptor, albeit with different degrees of affinity for the receptor. In vivo, aripiprazole has been shown to exhibit antagonistic properties in animal models of dopaminergic hyperactivity and agonist activity in an animal model of dopamine hypoactivity. Aripiprazole has undergone extensive clinical testing, including studies comparing it to haloperidol and risperidone. It appears to be a potent antipsychotic with a low EPS liability (Carson et al., 2001). Although several D_2 partial agonists have previously been evaluated for antipsychotic efficacy, none has reached the stage of development of aripiprazole, which is now available in the U.S.A.

Specific Targeting of Symptom Domains Other Than Positive Symptoms

Until now, efforts to identify an effective antischizophrenia medication have been directed toward development of a broad-spectrum, disease-specific panacea that would target all relevant symptom domains. Despite the broader spectrum of activity of the second-generation antipsychotic agents in comparison to first-generation drugs, they share the quality of being more effective in reducing positive symptoms than negative or cognitive symptoms. Specific pharmacological strategies directed at each of these other symptom domains are currently under investigation. It is, however, likely to be several years before any of the following strategies (assuming they are effective and safe) will become part of mainstream practice. At this stage, these nonpsychotic domain-specific treatments are conceived as add-on or adjunctive treatments to existing antipsychotic agents.

Specific Treatments for Negative Symptoms. Persistent negative symptoms are a major reason for the significant debilitation associated with schizophrenia; current treatments have only limited efficacy. Several pharmacological strategies to specifically treat negative symptoms have been evaluated with limited success thus far. Over the past decade, agents that stimulate the N-methyl-D-aspartate (NMDA) glutamate receptor have shown promise in this regard (Goff and Coyle, 2001). Partial and full agonists at the glycine site have also been used in conjunction with antipsychotics with some success in reducing negative symptoms. Large-scale studies are ongoing.

Specific Treatments for Cognitive Deficits. Perhaps, to an even greater extent than negative symptoms, cognitive dysfunction is correlated with functional impairment in schizophrenia. While novel antipsychotics are generally more effective than conventional agents in ameliorating cognitive symptoms, their efficacy is only modest. While there is some suggestion that different second-generation drugs may differentially improve various aspects of cognitive dysfunction in schizophrenia (and presumably could be matched to the specific cognitive deficits exhibited by a given patient), definitive data in this regard are lacking.

While several neuropharmacological mechanisms have been proposed to explain the cognitive advantages of the newer antipsychotic agents, none is considered definitive at present. In any event, three specific pharmacological targets to ameliorate cognitive impairments in schizophrenia are currently under study. The first target is the

NMDA receptor, with both partial (D-cycloserine) and full (serine and glycine) agonists at the glycine site being studied; modulators of the glutamatergic AMPA receptor are also being assessed for efficacy in treatment of cognitive deficits. Cholinergic augmentation strategies (Tandon and Greden, 1989; Tandon et al., 1999b) and 5-HT$_{1A}$ agonist strategies (Sumiyoshi et al., 2001) are also currently being investigated in this regard.

Other Pharmacological Targets. In addition to glutamatergic, cholinergic, and other serotonergic targets discussed above, several neuropeptidergic treatment strategies are also being pursued in the treatment of schizophrenia. While many types of agents are being studied, cholecystokinin agonists and neurotensin antagonists currently show greatest promise.

Matching Drug and Dose to Individual Patient

The significant recent advances in genetics and molecular neurobiology have led to considerable enthusiasm about the potential application of these strategies to improve schizophrenia treatment. Given the significant interindividual variation in response to antipsychotic drug treatment, a variety of pharmacogenetic studies are being conducted (Otani and Aoshima, 2000). While many such studies have focused on prediction of response to clozapine and other treatments, other molecular genetic investigations are directed at predicting side effects of antipsychotic treatment, such as tardive dyskinesia. Efforts to predict the optimal dose of different antipsychotics based on such studies are increasingly common.

Genomic advances also provide a powerful technique to dissect the heterogeneity of schizophrenia. Most experts believe that schizophrenia is not one disease but many distinct diseases with overlapping symptomatology. Advances in genomics will facilitate the identification of gene products involved in the pathophysiology of schizophrenia and thereby enable the development of specific therapeutic agents directed at such "disease-specific" targets. While these techniques have great potential, their specific application toward improving treatment of schizophrenia is still at a preliminary stage, and it appears unlikely that any major mainstream clinical application based on this approach is likely to become available for a decade.

Evidence-Based Pharmacological Treatment

There is marked variation in pharmacological treatment practices in schizophrenia, and it is also clear that the "usual treatment" generally falls far short of the best possible (Geddes and Harrison, 1997; Lehman and Steinwachs, 1998). Despite the publication of several treatment guidelines, efforts to promote evidence-based best possible pharmacotherapy of schizophrenia have hitherto been unsuccessful (Mellman et al., 2001). Critics of pharmacological treatment algorithms for schizophrenia suggest that existing algorithms are not empirically based and/or clinically applicable and relevant; furthermore, it is suggested that these treatment guidelines go much beyond existing data, thereby reducing their clinical utility (Slade and Priebe, 2001; Tandon et al., 2001).

CONCLUSION

Treatment of schizophrenia involves the judicious use of multiple treatment modalities, of which pharmacology is among the most important. Second-generation atypical antipsychotics provide substantial advantages over first-generation generation conventional agents. To maximize the benefits of atypical antipsychotics, the dose of medication should be carefully adjusted to achieve as complete a remission of psychotic symptoms as possible, without accompanying EPS. The major advantage of atypicals is lost if EPS occur; the occurrence of EPS should be considered an adequate justification for a downward adjustment in dose or change in medication. Since each pharmacological treatment regimen has its own unique range of likely benefits and side effects and these, in turn, are of very different relevance and importance to each individual patient, treatment obviously must be individualized. Optimal pharmacotherapy of schizophrenia requires a careful balance between the efficacy benefits and the side effect costs customized for each individual patient. Nonpharmacological treatments and mental health system issues (continuity of care, reimbursement, access to effective treatments, etc.) also warrant attention as one strives to improve the quality of life of individuals afflicted with schizophrenia.

REFERENCES

Bilder RM (1997). Neurocognitive impairment in schizophrenia and how it affects treatment options. *Can J Psychiatry* 42:255–264.

Cancro R, Lehmann HE (2000). Schizophrenia: Clinical features. In Sadock BJ, Sadock VA (eds). Kaplan and Sadock's *Comprehensive Textbook of Psychiatry*, 7th ed. Lippincott, Williams, and Wilkins: Philadelphia, pp. 1169–1199.

Carson WH, Ali M, Saha GC, Dunbar GC, Ingenito G (2001). A double-blind, placebo-controlled trial of aripiprazole and haloperidol. Presented at the annual meeting of the American Psychiatric Association, May 7–12, 2001, New Orleans.

Casey DE (1995). Motor and mental aspects of EPS. *Int Clin Psychopharmacol*, 10:105–114.

Casey DE, Daniel D, Tracy K, Wozniak P, Sommerville K (2001). Improved antipsychotic effect of divalproex combined with risperidone or olanzapine for schizophrenia. Presented at the World Assembly of Mental Health, Vancouver, July 22–27, 2001.

Chakos M, Lieberman J, Hoffman E, Bradford D, Sheitman B (2001). Effectiveness of second-generation antipsychotics in patients with treatment-resistant schizophrenia. *Am J Psychiatry* 158:518–526.

Creese I, Burt DR, Snyder SH (1976). Dopamine receptor binding predicts clinical and pharmacological potencies of antischizophrenic drugs. *Science* 192:481–485.

Delay J, Deniker P (1952). Le traitement des psychoses par une methode neurolyque derivee de l'hibernotherapie. Congres des Medicins Alienistes et Neurologistes de France. Masson Editeurs Libraires de France: Paris, pp. 497–502.

DeQuardo JR, Tandon R (1998). Do atypical antipsychotic medications favorably alter the long-term course of schizophrenia? *J Psychiatr Res* 32:229–242.

Fink M, Sackeim HA (1996). Convulsive therapy in schizophrenia? *Schizophr Bull* 22:27–42.

Geddes JR, Harrison PJ (1997). Closing the gap between research and practice. *Br J Psychiatry* 171:220–225.

Gilbert PL, Harris MJ, McAdams LA, et al. (1995). Neuroleptic withdrawal in schizophrenic patients: A review of the literature. *Arch Gen Psychiatry* 52:173–181.

Goff DC, Coyle JT (2001). The emerging role of glutamate in the pathophysiology and treatment of schizophrenia. *Am J Psychiatry* 158:1367–1377.

Greden JF, Tandon R (1995). Long-term treatment for lifetime disorders. *Arch Gen Psychiatry* 52:197–200.

Haase HJ, Janssen PAJ (1958). *The Action of Neuroleptic Drugs: A Psychiatric, Neurologic, and Pharmacological Investigation*. Year Book Medical Publishers, Chicago Amsterdam.

Harvey PD, Keefe RSE (1997). Cognitive impairment in schizophrenia and implications of atypical neuroleptic treatment. *CNS Spectrums* 2:41–55.

Jain KK (2000). An assessment of iloperidone in the treatment of schizophrenia. *Expert Opin Investigat Drugs* 9:2935–2943.

Jibson MD, Tandon R (1998). New atypical antipsychotic medications. *J Psychiatr Res*, 32:215–228.

Jibson MD, Tandon R (2000). Treatment of schizophrenia. *Psychiatr Clin North Am, Annual of Drug Therapy* 7:83–113.

Jones B, Taylor CC, Meehan K (2001). The efficacy of a rapid-acting intramuscular formulation of olanzapine for positive symptoms. *J Clin Psychiatry* (Suppl 2):22–24.

Kales HC, DeQuardo JR, Tandon R (1999). Combined electroconvulsive therapy and clozapine in treatment-resistant schizophrenia. *Prog Neuro-Psychopharmacol Biol Psychiatry* 23:547–555.

Kane JM (1999). Pharmacologic treatment of schizophrenia. *Biol Psychiatry* 46:1396–1408.

Kane J, Honigfeld G, Singer J, Meltzer H (1988). Clozapine for the treatment-resistant schizophrenic: A double-blind comparison with chlorpromazine. *Arch Gen Psychiatry* 45:789–796.

Kane JM, Woerner MG, Pollack S, Safferman AZ, Lieberman JA (1993). Does clozapine cause tardive dyskinesia? *J Clin Psychiatry* 54:327–330.

Keefe RSE, Silva SG, Perkins DO, Lieberman JA (1999). The effects of atypical antipsychotic drugs on neurocognitive impairment in schizophrenia: A review and meta-analysis. *Schizophr Bull* 25:201–222.

Kraepelin E (1919). Dementia Praecox and Paraphrenia. Translated by Barclay RM and Robertson GM. Edinburgh, E and S Livingstone.

Lehman AF, Steinwachs DM (1998). Translating research into practice: The Schizophrenia Patient Outcomes Research Team (PORT) treatment recommendations. *Schizophr Bull* 24:1–10.

Maixner SM, Mellow AM, Tandon R (1999). The efficacy, safety, and tolerability of antipsychotics in the elderly. *J Clin Psychiatry* 60(Suppl 8):29–43.

Mellman TA, Miller AL, Weissman EM, Crismon ML, Essock SM, Marder SR (2001). Evidence-based pharmacological treatment for people with severe mental illness: A focus on guidelines and algorithms. *Psychiatric Services* 52:619–625.

Meltzer HY (1995). The concept of atypical antipsychotics. In den Boer JA, Westenberg HGM, van Praag HM (eds). *Advances in the Neurobiology of Schizophrenia*. Wiley: Chichester, pp. 265–273.

Miller DD, Tandon R (2000). The biology and pathophysiology of negative symptoms. In Keefe R, McEvoy J (eds). *Negative Symptoms of Schizophrenia*. American Psychiatric Press: Washington DC.

Mojtabai R, Nicholson RA, Carpenter BN (1998). Role of psychosocial treatments in management of schizophrenia: A meta-analytic review of controlled outcome studies. *Schizophr Bull* 24:569–587.

Otani K, Aoshima T (2000). Pharmacogenetics of classical and new antipsychotic drugs. *Ther Drug Monitoring* 22:118–121.

Seeman P, Lee M, Chau-Wong M, et al. (1976). Antipsychotic drug doses and neuroleptic/dopamine receptors. *Nature* 261:717–720.

Slade M, Priebe S (2001). Are randomized controlled trials the only gold that glitters. *Br J Psychiatry* 179:286–287.

Sumiyoshi T, Matsui M, Yamashita I (2001). The effect of tandospirone, a serotonin (1A) agonist, on memory function in schizophrenia. *Biol Psychiatry* 49:861–868.

Swift RH, Harrigan EP, van Kammen DP (1998). A comparison of intramuscular ziprasidone and intramuscular haloperidol. 9th Congress of the Association of European Psychiatrists, Copenhagen, 20–24 September.

Tandon R (1999). Cholinergic aspects of schizophrenia. *Br J Psychiatry* 174(suppl 37):7–11.

Tandon R, Greden JF (1989). Cholinergic hyperactivity and negative schizophrenic symptoms: A model of dopaminergic/cholinergic interactions in schizophrenia. *Arch Gen Psychiatry* 46:745–753.

Tandon R, Milner K, Jibson MD (1999a). Antipsychotics from theory to practice: Integrating clinical and basic data. *J Clin Psychiatry* 60(Suppl 8):20–28.

Tandon R, Taylor SF, DeQuardo JR, Eiser A, Jibson MD, Goldman M (1999b). The cholinergic system in schizophrenia reconsidered. *Neuropsychopharmacology* 22:S189–202.

Tandon R, Glick I, Goldman M, Jibson MD, Marder SR, Mellman T (2001). *Managing Schizophrenia: A Comprehensive Primer*. McMahon: New York.

11

PSYCHOBIOLOGY OF POSTTRAUMATIC STRESS DISORDER

Bessel A. van der Kolk

The Trauma Center and Boston University School of Medicine, Boston, Massachusetts

INTRODUCTION

The human response to psychological trauma is one of the most important public health problems in the world. Traumatic events such as family and social violence, rapes and assaults, disasters, wars, accidents, and predatory violence may temporarily or permanently alter the organism's response to its environment. While people have evolved to be enormously resourceful and capable of surviving and overcoming extreme experiences, certain events, particularly if they occur early in the life cycle, can overwhelm the capacity of the organism to cope with stress and permanently alter the perception of danger and the regulation of internal homeostasis.

Historical Perspectives

Awareness of the role of psychological trauma as a contributory factor in psychiatric disturbances has off and on been a subject of serious study since the latter part of the 19th century. At the Hôpital du Salpêtrière in Paris Jean Martin Charcot first suggested

Textbook of Biological Psychiatry, Edited by Jaak Panksepp
ISBN 0-471-43478-7   Copyright © 2004 John Wiley & Sons, Inc.

that the symptoms of (what was then called) "hysterical" patients had their origins in histories of trauma. His colleague Pierre Janet proposed that posttraumatic reactions are caused by "vehement emotions" that interfere with coping capacities, that is, the incapacity to "process" the experience. As a result, sensory or affective aspects of the traumatic events are split off (dissociated) from everyday consciousness and from voluntary control (Janet, 1889, 1919/1925; van der Kolk and van der Hart, 1989). The imprints of these traumas tended to intrude in patients' lives, not primarily as memories of what had happened but as intense emotional reactions, aggressive behavior, physical pain, and bodily states in response to sensory or emotional reminders, reactions that could best be understood as elements of the original trauma response.

After two clinical rotations at the Salpêtrière, Sigmund Freud, with Joseph Breuer, noted that in case of traumatic stress: "The ... memory of the trauma ... acts like a foreign body which long after its entry must be regarded as an agent that is still at work. ... If a [motor] reaction is suppressed [the affect] stays attached to the memory. *It may therefore be said that the ideas which have become pathological have persisted with such freshness and affective strength because they have been denied the normal wearing-away processes by means of abreaction and reproduction in states of unhibited association*" (italicized in original) (Breuer and Freud, 1893, pp. 7–11).

Contemporary studies of traumatic memories have corroborated Janet and Freud's initial observations that traumatic memories persist primarily as implicit, behavioral, and somatic memories and secondarily as vague, overgeneral, fragmented, incomplete, and disorganized narratives. Previous work by Foa (1995) and ourselves (Hopper and van der Kolk, 2001) suggest that these memories change and become more like a coherent story as people recover from their posttraumatic stress disorder (PTSD).

In *The Traumatic Neuroses of War* Kardiner (1941) proposed that sufferers from "traumatic neuroses" develop an enduring vigilance for and sensitivity to environmental threat, and stated. "The nucleus of the neurosis is a physioneurosis. This is present... during the entire process of organization; it outlives every intermediary accommodative device, and persists in the chronic forms." He described extreme physiological arousal in these patients: They suffered from sensitivity to temperature, pain, and sudden tactile stimuli. "These patients cannot stand being slapped on the back abruptly; they cannot tolerate a misstep or a stumble. From a physiologic point of view there exists a lowering of the threshold of stimulation; and, from a psychological point of view a state of readiness for fright reactions" (p. 95). Kardiner articulated the central issue of PTSD: "The subject acts as if the original traumatic situation were still in existence and engages in protective devices which failed on the original occasion. This means in effect that his conception of the outer world and his conception of himself have been permanently altered" (p. 82).

In 1980 the American Psychiatric Association, faced with the necessity to create a diagnosis to capture the essence of the posttraumatic problems in Vietnam veterans, created a diagnosis, posttraumatic stress disorder (PTSD) that was predicated on the notion that overwhelming experiences leave a memory imprint that may become a central organizing principle in the victim's life. While this definition (detailed later) highlighted how a particular event, or series of events, can alter a person's response to subsequent stimuli, it largely ignores the recurrent observation that following exposure to traumatic life events, the organism may reorganize the way it regulates a large array of biological and psychological functions, not only in response to particular triggers but in its basic orientation to its environment. These problems include difficulty distinguishing relevant from irrelevant stimuli; problems with arousal modulation and attention, impairment in the capacity to plan and execute actions relevant to the present, difficulties peacefully negotiating interpersonal needs, and problems experiencing playfulness and pleasure.

Background Issues

The biology of routine stress responses and the biology of trauma are fundamentally different: Stress causes a cascade of biological and physiological changes that return to normal after the stress is gone or after the organism has established a new homeostasis. In contrast, in PTSD, the biological alterations persist well after the stressor itself has disappeared. The fundamental problem in PTSD is a "fixation of the trauma" (Janet, 1889; van der Kolk, 1985; Yehuda, 2002). Thus, the critical issue in understanding PTSD is: What keeps the organism from maintaining its homeostasis and returning to a nontraumatic state, and what causes these regulatory processes to break down?

Exposure to events that overwhelm the organism's coping mechanisms can damage the self-regulatory systems necessary to restore the organism to its previous state because of alterations in a variety of "filtering" systems in the central nervous system (CNS) that help distinguish relevant from irrelevant stimuli. As a result, traumatized individuals have difficulty engaging fully in current exigencies and distinguishing between what is threatening and what is safe. Traumatization produces the symptoms described in the Diagnostic and Statistical Manual of Mental Disorders, Fourth Edition (DSM-IV) definition of PTSD: intrusive reliving, numbing and hyperarousal, increased uncontrolled aggression against self and others, drug and alcohol abuse, depression, and chronic physical illnesses. Severe and prolonged childhood trauma has particularly dire consequences: Compared with normals, people with histories of severe child maltreatment showed a 4 to 12 times greater risk to develop alcoholism, depression, drug abuse, and suicide attempts, a 2 to 4 times greater risk for smoking, having had ≥ 50 sex partners, leading to increased incidence of sexually transmitted disease; a 1.4 to 1.6 times greater risk for physical inactivity and obesity; and a 1.6 to 2.9 times greater risk for ischemic heart disease, cancer, chronic lung disease, skeletal fractures, hepatitis, stroke, diabetes, and liver disease (Felitti et al., 1998).

Prevalence

Traumatic events are very common in most societies, though prevalence has been best studied in industrialized societies, particularly in the United States. Kessler et al. (1995) found that in the United States at least 15 percent of the population reports having been molested, physically attacked, raped, or been involved in combat. Each year, about 3 million children in the United States are reported for neglect and/or abuse to child protective services, with more than half of these cases later substantiated. The vast majority of the abuse and neglect found in children occurs at the hands of their primary caregivers and people they know: Four out of five assaults on children are at the hands of their own parents. For women and children, but not for men, trauma that results from violence within intimate relationships is a much more serious problem than traumatic events inflicted by strangers or accidents. Half of all victims of violence in the United States are under age 25; 29 percent of all forcible rapes occur before the age of 11. Among U.S. adolescents aged 12 to 17, 8 percent are estimated to have been victims of serious sexual assault; 17 percent are victims of serious physical assault; and 40 percent have witnessed serious violence (Kilpatrick et al., 1998). Over a third of the victims of domestic assault experienced serious injury, compared with a quarter of victims of stranger assault (van der Kolk, 2000).

Posttraumatic stress disorder now is a common diagnosis for patients in psychiatric hospitals. An examination of the records of the 384,000 Medicaid recipients in Massachusetts in 1997/98 (Macy et al., 2002) revealed that PTSD had the same prevalence as depression—generally considered the most common psychiatric diagnoses. However, patients with PTSD spent 10 times more days in the hospital than patients with the diagnosis of depression only. There is no evidence that the 22,800 Medicaid recipients in Massachusetts who were diagnosed as suffering from PTSD suffered only from a one-time traumatic incident, such as a rape or motor vehicle accident. Most suffer from a complex constellation of symptoms that include those of PTSD. However, currently the long-term psychiatric impact of chronic, multiple traumas receives the same diagnosis (PTSD) as do the effects of a one-time incident. The inevitable multiplicity of problems seen after chronic and repeated exposure are currently described oversimply as seemingly random "comorbid" conditions. PTSD, as a diagnosis, commonly fails to capture how convoluted the clinical presentation of many traumatized individuals is and how complex their treatment can be.

Symptomatology

When people are faced with a life-threatening experience, they focus on survival and self-protection. When their usual coping systems fail, they tend to turn to their environment to supply the resources they lack themselves. The quantity and quality of coping resources available depends on the maturity of the nervous system, as well as prior experience and training. Children and exhausted adults are more prone to develop lasting trauma symptomatology than youngsters who live in a protective family, or adults who are well prepared (such as physicians, fire fighters or police personnel). In the immediate aftermath of a traumatic event, victims may respond with a mixture of numbness, withdrawal, confusion, shock, and speechless terror. Some cope by taking action, while others dissociate. Neither response predictably *prevents* or *fosters* the subsequent development of PTSD, though being able to maintain an internal locus of control, and utilizing problem-focused coping significantly reduces the chance of developing PTSD. In contrast, dissociation, losing track of what is going on, and losing affective and cognitive engagement with the environment is an important predictor for the development of subsequent PTSD (Shalev et al., 1996). The longer the traumatic experience lasts, the more likely the victim is to react with dissociation.

The formal diagnosis of PTSD is characterized by three major elements:

1. The repeated reliving of memories of the traumatic experience. These tend to involve intense sensory and visual memories of the event that often are accompanied by extreme physiological and psychological distress, and sometimes by a feeling of emotional numbing, during which there usually is no physiological arousal. These intrusive memories may occur spontaneously or can be triggered by a range of real and symbolic stimuli.

2. Avoidance of reminders of the trauma, as well as of emotional numbing. Detachment and emotional blunting often coexist with intrusive recollections. This is associated with an inability to experience joy and pleasure, and with a general withdrawal from engagement with one's surroundings. Over time, these features may become the dominant symptoms of PTSD.

3. The third element of PTSD consists of a pattern of increased arousal, as expressed by hypervigilance, irritability, memory and concentration problems, sleep disturbances, and an exaggerated startle response. In the more chronic forms of the disorder, this pattern of hyperarousal and avoidance may be the dominant clinical features. Hyperarousal causes traumatized people to become easily distressed by unexpected stimuli. Their tendency to be triggered into reliving traumatic memories illustrates how their perceptions become excessively focused on the involuntary seeking out of the similarities between the present and their traumatic past. As a consequence, many neutral experiences become reinterpreted as being associated with the traumatic past.

Complexity of Adaptation

Once people develop PTSD, the recurrent unbidden reliving of the trauma in visual images, emotional states, or in nightmares produces a recurrent reliving of states of terror. In contrast to the actual trauma, which had a beginning, middle, and end, the symptoms of PTSD take on a timeless character. The traumatic intrusions themselves are horrifying: They interfere with "getting over" the past, while distracting the individual from attending to the present. The unpredictable exposure to unbidden feelings, physical experiences, images, or other imprints of the traumatic event leads to a variety of (usually maladaptive) avoidance maneuvers, ranging from avoidance of people or actions that serve as reminders to drug and alcohol abuse and emotional withdrawal from friends or activities that used to be potential sources of solace. Problems with attention and concentration keep them from being engaged with their surroundings with zest and energy. Uncomplicated activities like reading, conversing, and watching television require extra effort. The loss of ability to focus, in turn, often leads to problems with taking one thing at a time and interferes with readjusting their lives in response to the trauma (van der Kolk et al., 1996a).

Trauma early in the life cycle, particularly when it is recurrent and when it occurs in the context of an inadequate caregiving system, has pervasive effects on cognition, socialization, and the capacity for affect regulation (Cicchetti and Beeghly, 1996; Putnam and Trickett, 1993; van der Kolk and Fisler, 1995). Children exposed to abuse and neglect are at increased risk to develop depression and anxiety disorders. They have a high incidence of aggression against self and others, are vulnerable to develop disturbances in food intake, as in anorexia and bulimia, and suffer from a high incidence of drug and alcohol addiction (van der Kolk et al., 1996b; Felitti et al., 1998). It is thought that early and persistent sensitization of CNS circuits involved in the regulation of stress and emotion produces an increased vulnerability to subsequent stress by means of persistent hyper(re)activity of neurotransmitter systems, including corticotropin-releasing factor (CRF) (Heim and Nemeroff, 2001). Promising animal models for such chronic brain and behavior changes exist and provide opportunities for working out some of the essential neurological details (Adamec, 1997; Panksepp, 2001).

PSYCHOBIOLOGY

Background Neuroscience Issues

In order to understand how trauma affects psychobiological activity, it is useful to briefly revisit some basic tenets of neurobiology. Paul McLean (1990) defined the brain as a detecting, amplifying, and analyzing device for the maintenance of the internal and external environment. These functions range from the visceral regulation of oxygen intake and temperature balance to the categorization of incoming information necessary for making complex, long-term decisions affecting both individual and social systems. He proposed that, in the course of evolution, the human brain has developed roughly three interdependent subanalyzers, each with different anatomical and neurochemical substrates: (1) the brainstem and hypothalamus, which are primarily associated with the regulation of internal homeostasis, (2) the limbic system, which maintains the balance between the internal world and external reality, and (3) the neocortex, which is responsible for analyzing and interacting with the external world (McLean, 1990).

The circuitry of the brainstem and hypothalamus is most innate and stable, while the limbic system contains both innate circuitry and circuitry modifiable by experience, while the neocortex is most affected by environmental input (Damasio, 1995). It therefore would be expected that trauma would most profoundly affect neocortical functions, and have least effect on structures related to basic regulatory functions. However, while this seems to be true for the ordinary stress response, trauma (stress that overwhelms the organism) seems to affect core self-regulatory functions.

Interrelation between Regulatory Functions

One of the functions of the CNS is to take in new sensory information, categorize its importance, and integrate it with previously stored knowledge. Then, the organism needs to determine what is personally relevant and filter out irrelevant information. The brain networks that monitor relations with the outside world and assess what is new, dangerous, or gratifying involve the brainstem, hypothalamus, limbic system, and neocortex operating together in interdependent but also hierarchical ways (Panksepp, 1998). Together, these structures need to "formulate" an appropriate plan of action following the meaningful categorization of an incoming signal. As the CNS does this, it needs to attend to both short-term and long-term consequences of the anticipated action, which is clearly a cortical function (Damasio, 1999). After initiating an appropriate response and the challenge is gone, the organism needs to shift its attention. Finally, people need to be able to engage in sustained activities without being distracted by irrelevant stimuli.

A century ago William James noted that the power of the intellect is determined by people's perceptual processing style. The ability to comprehend (grasp, hold together, take hold of—from the Latin *cum-prendere*) depends on stimulus sampling and the formation of schematic representations of reality (Pribram, 1991). The organism needs to learn from experience and entertain a range of alternatives without becoming disorganized or without having to act on them. In order to do this, it needs to learn to discriminate relevant from irrelevant stimuli and only select what is appropriate for achieving its goals. Much of the evolution of the human brain has centered on developing the capacity to form highly complex mental images and collaborative social relationships that allow complex organization of social systems. In order to participate in this large collaborative social system, the organism needs to integrate its own immediate self-interest with a capacity to appreciate and to adhere to complex social rules (Donald, 1991).

People with PTSD have serious problems in carrying out all of these functions. There are qualitatively significant differences between the ways people with PTSD sample and categorize experience and the ways in which nontraumatized people do (van der Kolk and Ducey, 1989; McFarlane et al., 1993). Failure to *comprehend* the traumatizing experience (i.e., to dissociate) plays a critical role in making a stressful experience traumatic (van der Kolk et al., 1996a). People with PTSD tend to overinterpret danger, have trouble experiencing pleasure engaging in ordinary tasks, have difficulty staying focused until a job is finished; they often find it difficult collaborating with others in situations that require maintaining multiple perspectives.

PSYCHOPHYSIOLOGICAL EFFECTS OF TRAUMA

Posttraumatic stress disorder is not an inevitable outcome of stress: Only about 25 percent of individuals who have been exposed to a potential traumatic stressor develop PTSD (Yehuda and McFarlane, 1995). Hence, the central question regarding the biology of PTSD is how to account for the failure of the organism to reestablish its homeostasis and return to its pretraumatic state. Yehuda (2002) has pointed out that understanding the biological response that occurred during the traumatic event does not necessarily address the biology of PTSD. Rather, the central issue appears to be why some people recover and others do not.

It also has become clear that PTSD is not an issue of simple conditioning. Many people who have been exposed to an extreme stressor, but who do not suffer from PTSD, become distressed when they are once again confronted with the memory of the tragedy. The critical issue in PTSD is that the stimuli that cause people to overreact may not be conditional enough: A variety of triggers not directly related to the traumatic experience may come to precipitate extreme reactions. (Pitman et al., 1991).

Abnormal psychophysiological reactions in PTSD occur on two very different levels: (1) in response to specific reminders of the trauma and (2) in response to intense, but neutral, stimuli, such as loud noises, signifying a loss of stimulus discrimination.

Conditional Responses to Specific Stimuli

Most PTSD sufferers have heightened physiological arousal in response to sounds, images, and thoughts related to specific traumatic incidents, while others have decreased arousal. Initial research on acute trauma victims found that people with PTSD, but not controls, respond to reminders with significant increases in heart rate, skin conductance, and blood pressure (Pitman et al., 1987). The elevated sympathetic responses to reminders of traumatic experiences that happened years, and sometimes decades, ago illustrate the intensity and timelessness with which these trauma imprints continue to affect current experience (Pitman et al., 1987). Post and his colleagues (1992) have shown that life events play a critical role in the first episodes of major affective disorders but become less pertinent in precipitating subsequent occurrences. This capacity of triggers with diminishing strength to produce the same response over time is called *kindling*. About one third of chronically traumatized people respond to reminders of their past with decreased arousal: They appear to respond primarily with a parasympathetic reaction. This population has received little scientific scrutiny.

Medications that decrease autonomic arousal, such a β-adrenergic blockers, clonidine and benzodiazepines, tend to decrease traumatic intrusions, while drugs that stimulate autonomic arousal may precipitate visual images and affect states associated with prior traumatic experiences in people with PTSD, but not in controls. For example, in patients with PTSD the injection of drugs such as lactate (Rainey et al., 1987) and yohimbine (Southwick et al., 1993) tend to precipitate panic attacks, flashbacks (exact reliving experiences) of earlier trauma, or both. In our own laboratory, approximately 20 percent of PTSD subjects responded with a flashback of a traumatic experience when they were presented with acoustic startle stimuli.

Hyperarousal to Nontraumatic Stimuli; Loss of Stimulus Discrimination

Trauma may result in permanent neuronal changes that have a negative effect on learning, habituation, and stimulus discrimination. The effects of some of these neuronal changes do not depend on actual exposure to reminders of the trauma for expression. The abnormal startle response (ASR) characteristic of PTSD is one example of this phenomenon. Several studies have demonstrated abnormalities in habituation to the

ASR in PTSD (e.g., Ornitz and Pynoos, 1989). Interestingly, people who previously met the criteria for PTSD, but no longer do so now, continue to show failure of habituation of the ASR (van der Kolk et al., unpublished data; Pitman et al., unpublished data).

The failure to habituate to acoustic startle suggests that traumatized people have difficulty evaluating sensory stimuli and mobilizing appropriate levels of physiological arousal. Thus, the problems that people with PTSD have with properly integrating memories of the trauma, tending to get mired in a continuous reliving of the past, is mirrored physiologically in the misinterpretation of innocuous stimuli as potential threats. To compensate, they tend to shut down. However, the price for shutting down is decreased involvement in ordinary, everyday life.

Loss of Arousal Regulation

Elementary self-regulation involves an interconnected collection of neural patterns that maintain bodily processes and that represent, moment by moment, the state of the organism (Damasio, 1999). The immediate response to a traumatic experience involves dysregulation of arousal, with (a) exaggerated startle response, (b) over- or under-aroused physiological and emotional responses, (c) difficulty falling or staying asleep, and (d) dysregulation of eating, with lack of attention to needs for food and liquid. In people who develop PTSD, this pattern of disordered arousal persists.

Once people develop PTSD, they suffer from a fundamental dysregulation at the brain stem level (Sahar et al., 2001). The regulatory processes of the brainstem involve the reticular activating system, the origin of the sympathetic nervous system, as well as two branches of the parasympathetic system, innervated by the vagus nerve: the dorsal vagal system and the ventral vagus (Porges et al., 1996). Activation of the ascending reticular activating system stimulates attentional systems, the thalamus and cerebral cortex. The hyper- and hypoarousal seen in traumatized individuals likely involve excesses of sympathetic and parasympathetic activity, leading to a breakdown of attentional systems commonly seen in traumatized people who develop PTSD. Peritraumatic dissociation, that is, a breakdown of the capacity for focus and attention, at the time of the trauma has been found to be a powerful predictor for the long-term development of PTSD (Shalev, 1996).

Currently, power spectral analysis (PSA) of heart rate variability (HRV) provides the best available means of measuring the interaction of sympathetic and parasympathetic tone, that is, of brainstem regulatory integrity. Standardized heart rate analysis of PTSD patients at rest has demonstrated a baseline autonomic hyperarousal state in these patients: They have lower resting HRV, compared to controls, which suggests increased sympathetic and decreased parasympathetic tone (Cohen et al., 2000b). Individuals with PTSD have less vagal control over their heart rate in response to a mental arithmetic challenge, compared with controls. While about two thirds of PTSD patients respond to personalized trauma scripts with increased heart rates (Pitman et al., 1987), at least one study found that PTSD patients, unlike panic disorder patients and controls, failed to respond to reminders of their trauma with increases in heart rate and low-frequency components of HRV (Cohen et al., 2000a). In one study, traumatized subjects who did not develop PTSD exhibited significant autonomic responses to a reminder of their trauma, while PTSD patients showed almost no autonomic response to the recounting of the triggering stressful event. Interestingly, the PTSD patients demonstrated a comparable degree of autonomic dysregulation at rest as the control subjects' reaction to a personal stressor: They reacted to ordinary stimuli the way others reacted to reminders of traumatic incidents. One possible explanation for this phenomenon is that PTSD patients experience so great a degree of autonomic hyper-activation at rest that they are unable to marshal a further stress response to reminders of their trauma (Cohen et al., 1998). A recent study found that the HRV parameters that indicate autonomic dysregulation, which characterize PTSD patients at rest, are normalized in responding patients by use of selective serotonin reuptake inhibitors (SSRIs) (Cohen et al., 2000a).

Hormonal Response in Posttraumatic Stress Disorder

In a well-functioning person, stress produces rapid and pronounced hormonal responses. However, chronic and persistent stress inhibits the effectiveness of the stress response and induces desensitization. PTSD develops following exposure to events that over-whelm the individual's capacity to reestablish homeostasis. Instead of returning to baseline, there is a progressive kindling of the individual's stress response. Initially only intense stress is accompanied by the release of endogenous, stress-responsive neu-rohormones, such as cortisol, epinephrine, norepinephrine (NE), vasopressin, oxytocin, and endogenous opioids. In PTSD even minor reminders of the trauma may precipitate a full-blown neuroendocrine stress reaction: It permanently alters how an organism deals with its environment on a day-to-day basis, and it interferes with how it copes with subsequent acute stress.

Early stress can alter the development of the hypothalamic-pituitary-adrenal (HPA) axis, hypothalamic and extrahypothalamic corticotropin-releasing hormone, monoamin-ergic, and gamma-aminobutyric acid/benzodiazepine systems. Stress has also been shown to promote structural and functional alterations in brain regions similar to those seen in adults with depression. Emerging data suggest, however, that the long-term effects of early stress can be moderated by genetic factors and the quality of the subsequent caregiving environment (Kaufman et al., 2000).

A review of the neuroendocrine findings in PTSD to date shows very specific abnormalities in this disorder, compared with other psychiatric problems. The most prominent of these abnormalities appear to be in the HPA axis. PTSD patients show evidence of an enhanced negative feedback inhibition characterized by an exaggerated cortisol response to dexamethasone, an increased number of glucocorticoid receptors, and lower basal cortisol levels (Yehuda, 1998). These findings contrast with the blunted cortisol response to dexamethasone, the decreased number of glucocorticoid receptors, and the increased basal cortisol levels described in major depression. Women with a history of childhood abuse and a current major depression diagnosis exhibited a more than six-fold greater adrenocorticotrophic hormone (ACTH) response to stress than age-matched controls (Heim et al., 2000). These results show that cortisol basically functions as an "antistress" hormone: Through negative feedback inhibition, cortisol acts on the pituitary, hypothalamus, hippocampus, and amygdala sites initially responsible for the stimulation of cortisol release. Once the acute stress is over the HPA axis activates negative feedback inhibition, leading to the restoration of basal hormone levels (Yehuda, 2002). Simultaneous activation of catecholamines and glucocorticoids stimulates active coping behaviors, while increased arousal in the presence of low glucocorticoid levels may provoke undifferentiated fight-or-flight reactions.

Two prospective, longitudinal biological studies of trauma survivors confirm the notion that individuals with a low initial cortisol response to stress are most vulnerable to develop PTSD. Both studies examined the cortisol response to trauma within hours after the trauma occurred. In the first (McFarlane et al., 1993) the cortisol response to motor vehicle accidents was measured in persons appearing in the emergency room in the immediate aftermath (usually within 1 or 2 h) of the trauma. Six months later, subjects were evaluated for the presence or absence of psychiatric disorder. In subjects who had developed PTSD the cortisol response right after the motor vehicle accident was significantly lower than the cortisol response of those who subsequently developed major depression. Resnick et al. (1997) collected blood samples from 20 acute rape victims and measured their cortisol response in the emergency room. Three months later, a prior trauma history was taken, and the subjects were evaluated for the presence of PTSD. Victims with a prior history of sexual abuse were significantly more likely to have developed PTSD by 3 months following the rape than were rape victims who had not developed PTSD. Cortisol levels shortly after the rapes were correlated with histories of prior assaults: The mean initial cortisol level of individuals with a prior assault history was 15 μg/dL compared to 30 μg/dL in individuals without. These findings can be interpreted to mean either that prior exposure to traumatic events results in a blunted cortisol response to subsequent trauma or in a quicker return of cortisol to baseline following stress.

Most studies of catecholamine function in PTSD suggest chronic increased activation. There is also evidence for distinct changes in the hypothalamic-pituitary-thyroid and the hypothalamic-pituitary-gonadal systems (Yehuda, 1998), as well as in the endogenous opioid response to reminders of personal trauma (van der Kolk et al., 1989; Pitman et al., 1990). Finally, there is considerable evidence for a host of somatic problems in the wake of PTSD, including alterations in immune function (Wilson et al., 1999).

Intergenerational Transmission

In a study of risk factors for the development of PTSD, Yehuda and her colleagues examined the association between cortisol and PTSD in children of holocaust survivors. Low cortisol levels were significantly associated with both PTSD in parents and lifetime PTSD in subjects, whereas having a current psychiatric diagnosis other than PTSD was relatively, but nonsignificantly, associated with higher cortisol levels. Offspring with both parental PTSD and lifetime PTSD had the lowest cortisol levels of all study groups. They concluded that parental PTSD is associated with low cortisol levels in offspring, even in the absence of lifetime PTSD in the offspring. They suggested that low cortisol levels in PTSD may constitute a vulnerability marker related to parental PTSD as well as a state-related characteristic associated with acute or chronic PTSD symptoms (Yehuda et al., 2000).

Disintegration of Experience Accompanying PTSD

In a series of studies we demonstrated that memories of trauma initially tend to have few autobiographical elements: When PTSD patients have their flashbacks, the trauma is relived as isolated sensory, emotional, and motoric imprints, without much of a storyline. We have shown this in victims of childhood abuse (van der Kolk and Fisler, 1995), assaults, and accidents in adulthood (van der Kolk et al., 1997) and in patients who gained awareness during surgical procedures (van der Kolk et al., 2000). These studies support the notion that traumatic memories result from a failure of the CNS to synthesize the sensations related to the event into an integrated semantic memory. While most patients with PTSD construct a narrative of their trauma over time, it is characteristic of PTSD that sensory elements of the trauma itself continue to intrude as flashbacks and nightmares, in states of consciousness where the trauma is relived, unintegrated with an overall sense of current time, place, and sense of self. Because traumatic memories are so fragmented, it seems reasonable to postulate that extreme emotional arousal leads to a failure of the CNS to synthesize the sensations related to the trauma into an integrated whole.

These observations suggest that in PTSD the brain's natural ability to integrate experience breaks down. A large variety of CNS structures have been implicated in such integrative processes: (1) the parietal lobes integrate information between different cortical association areas (Damasio, 1999), (2) the hippocampus creates a cognitive map that allows for the categorization of experience, connecting it with other autobiographical information (O'Keefe and Nadel, 1978), (3) the corpus callosum allows for the transfer of information by both hemispheres (Joseph, 1988), integrating emotional and cognitive aspects of the experience, (4) the cingulate gyrus, which is thought to play a role both as amplifier and filter, helps integrate the emotional and cognitive components of the mind (Devinsky et al., 1995), and (5) various prefrontal areas, where sensations and impulses are "held in mind" and compared with previous information to plan appropriate actions. Recent neuroimaging studies of patients with PTSD have suggested a role for all of these structures in the neurobiology of PTSD, though, at this point, many of the findings are quite variable and at times contradictory.

LESSONS FROM NEUROIMAGING

Symptom Provocation Studies

Rapidly evolving brain neuroimaging techniques such as magnetic resonance imaging (MRI) and positron emission tomography (PET) have proven useful instruments to explore the pathogenesis and pathophysiology of PTSD. Structural abnormalities in PTSD found with MRI include nonspecific white matter lesions and decreased hippocampal volume. These abnormalities may reflect pretrauma vulnerability to develop PTSD or they may be a consequence of traumatic exposure, PTSD, and/or PTSD sequelae. Rauch, van der Kolk, and colleagues conducted the first PET scan study of patients with PTSD (Rauch et al., 1996). When PTSD subjects were exposed to vivid, detailed narratives of their own traumatic experiences, they demonstrated *increased* metabolic activity only in the right hemisphere, specifically, in the areas that are most associated with emotional appraisal: the amygdala, insula, and the medial temporal lobe. During exposure to their traumatic scripts, there was a significant *decrease* in activation of the left inferior frontal area—Broca's area, which is responsible for motor speech. Most neuroimaging studies have found activation of the cingulate cortex (which possibly plays an inhibitory role) in response to trauma-related stimuli in individuals with PTSD, but others have found decreases, even while using similar activation paradigms.

Amygdala Effects

It is hardly surprising that many (though not all) neuroimaging studies of PTSD find increased amygdala activation in response to traumatic reminders. A large body of animal research, mostly in rodents, has established the importance of the amygdala for emotional processes (Cahill and McGaugh, 1998; LeDoux, 1996). The amygdala establishes the initial interpretation of the nature of a particular stress and initiates the process of activating neurochemical and neuroanatomical fear circuitries (LeDoux, 1992). The time frame for this response is several milliseconds. In this very short time, projections from the amygdala to the reticularis pontis caudalis potentiate the startle responses and initiate defensive behaviors that do not require direct action of the sympathetic nervous system. Projections from the amygdala to the lateral hypothalamus and then to the rostral ventral medulla initiate sympathetic nervous system (and catecholamine) responses. One of the most immediate responses to stress is the coordinated sympathetic discharge that causes increases in heart rate and blood pressure, initially described by Walter Cannon as the fight-or-flight reaction. Exposure to traumatic reminders provokes autonomic activation in about two-thirds of patients with PTSD (e.g., Pitman et al., 1987), and this is likely mediated by activation of the amygdala and related structures.

Projections from the amygdala to the solitary tract initiate the parasympathetic responses that constrain autonomic arousal but operate independently of the sympathetic nervous system. Projections from the central amygdala to the bed nucleus of the stria terminalis initiate the HPA axis response. By way of these various connections, the amygdala transforms sensory stimuli into emotional and hormonal signals, thereby initiating and controlling emotional responses.

Numerous studies have reported activation of the amygdala during early phases of aversive conditions, showing that the amygdala is necessary for the establishment of conditioned fear (e.g., LaBar et al., 1998). Most of these studies have focused on fear perception, demonstrating that the amygdala is important for the recognition of cues of threat or danger. For example, the amygdala is activated in response to facial expressions of fear, compared with neutral, happy, or other control faces, even when people are exposed to masked-fear faces that were not consciously perceived (Whalen et al., 1998). Whether the amygdala is necessary for the *expression* of fear and whether the amygdala is the actual focus of where the learned information is stored are still unclear (see Packard and Cahill, 2001; Fanselow and LeDoux, 1999). Since Breiter et al. (1996) observed rapid habituation of the amygdala response, and since some neuroimaging studies of PTSD subjects fail to find amygdala activation during symptom provocation paradigms, it is likely that the amygdala has a time-limited function in the stream of affective information processing.

Hippocampus in PTSD

The hippocampus plays a significant role in the capacity to consciously recall a previous life event, that is, in declarative memory. Its role in emotion and affective style has only recently started to be explored. The hippocampus plays a significant role in context-dependent memory (O'Keefe and Nadel; Fanselow, 2000). When an animal is exposed to a cue-conditioning procedure, where a discrete cue is paired with an aversive outcome, the animal also learns to associate the context in which the learning occurs with the aversive outcome. Lesions to the hippocampus abolish this context-dependent form of memory but have no effect on learning cue-punishment contingencies (Davidson, 2001). The high density of glucocorticoid receptors in this structure supports the idea that the hippocampus may play an important role in emotion regulation. Glucocorticoids have been shown to have a powerful impact on hippocampal neurons (Cahill and McGaugh, 1998; McEwen, 1998). Exogenous administration of large doses of hydrocortisone to humans impairs explicit memory, while more moderate amounts of cortisol may facilitate memory (e.g., Kirschbaum et al., 1996).

A number of PTSD studies have reported significantly decreased hippocampal volume in patients with PTSD (e.g., Bremner 1997, 1999; Gurvits et al., 1998) and depression. For example, Bremner et al. (1997) compared hippocampal volume in adult survivors of childhood abuse to matched controls. PTSD patients had a 12 percent smaller left hippocampal volume relative to the matched controls ($p < .05$), without smaller volumes of comparison regions (amygdala, caudate, and temporal lobe), while Gurvits and her colleagues found both significantly smaller left and right hippocampi in combat veterans with PTSD compared to combat controls without PTSD and normal controls. However, several well-controlled studies have failed to replicate these findings (e.g., DeBellis et al., 1999; Bonne et al., 2001). In the studies in which hippocampal atrophy has been found, investigators have proposed that excessively high levels of cortisol caused hippocampal cell death, resulting in hippocampal atrophy.

At this time it appears that smaller hippocampal volume is not a necessary risk factor for developing PTSD and does not occur within 6 months of expressing the disorder. However, it is likely that subjects with long-standing PTSD and particularly those with histories of severe childhood trauma may have smaller hippocampi. These subjects also exhibit neuropsychological abnormalities that can be associated with impaired hippocampal functioning, such as difficulty learning from negative experiences, despite extreme emotional and biological reactivity to reminders of their traumas.

Davidson et al. (2000) have proposed that the impact of hippocampal involvement in psychopathology may be most apparent in the processing of emotional information and that, in individuals with compromised hippocampal function, the normal context-regulatory role of this brain region would be impaired. Consequently, individuals with hippocampal damage would be prone to display emotional behavior in inappropriate contexts. Indeed, PTSD does not involve the display of abnormal emotions per se, but the presentation of normal emotions in inappropriate contexts. Patients with PTSD behave in ways that are reminiscent of animals with hippocampal lesions, in being unable to modulate emotional responses in a context-appropriate manner.

Role of the Anterior Cingulate Cortex (ACC)

Numerous studies that have used neuroimaging methods to probe patterns of brain activation during the arousal of emotion have reported that the ACC activates in response to emotion. Recent work (e.g., Bush et al., 2000; Whalen et al., 1998) has started to distinguish between cognitive and affective subdivisions of the ACC, based on the location of activation in response to cognitive versus emotional tasks. For example, dorsal ACC activation is consistently found in response to the classical Stroop task, compared to the more anterior activation to an emotional Stroop task.

Every activation study of PTSD subjects finds involvement of the cingulate. However, in some studies there is increased (Bremner, 1999b, 1999a; Shin et al., 2001; Lanius et al., 2001) and in others decreased (Sachinvala, 2000) activations. The very process of activating emotion in the unfamiliar context of a laboratory environment might activate the anterior cingulate, including exposure to the stressful laboratory environment itself. Carter et al. (1999) have suggested that ACC activation results in a call for further processing by other brain circuits to address the conflict that has been detected. In most people, automatic mechanisms of emotion regulation are likely invoked to dampen strong emotion that may be activated in the laboratory. The PTSD neuroimaging studies suggest that many traumatized subjects are less capable of activating the ACC in response to emotionally arousing stimuli. In our treatment outcome study of PTSD (Levin et al., 1999), we found increased ACC activation after effective treatment.

Frontal Cortex

In recent years, neuropsychological investigations of PTSD have begun to shed light on cognitive control deficits in PTSD, and cognitive neuroscience studies have suggested the neural bases of these deficits. For example, using an array of attention and memory tests, Vasterling (1998) found a pattern of *generalized disinhibition* in cognitive and behavioral domains among combat veterans with PTSD compared to combat veterans without PTSD. Work in rats and monkeys in a variety of neuroscience laboratories indicates that stress exposure impairs cognitive functions dependent on prefrontal structures. Arnsten et al. (1991) used repetitive transcranial magnetic stimulation (rTMS) of the dorsolateral prefrontal cortex (DLPFC) to produce temporary functional lesions that resulted in worsened performance on a working memory task; these researchers simultaneously used PET to demonstrate that performance decrements caused by rTMS were associated with decreased regional cerebral blood flow in the DLPFC.

The prefrontal structures implicated in PTSD include the left inferior prefrontal cortex, or Broca's area, and the dorsolateral prefrontal cortex. Decreased activation in Broca's area in response to script-driven imagery or remembering was found in the first neuroimaging study of PTSD (Rauch et al., 1996) and has been replicated in two subsequent PET studies by Shin and colleagues (1997, 1999). Decreased activation in the dorsolateral prefrontal cortex (DLPFC; Brodmann's areas 9/46) has been found in a functional MRI study of subjects with PTSD (Lanius et al., 2002).

Recently Shaw et al. (2002) investigated distributed brain systems in PTSD patients and matched controls during performance of a working memory task. They found that the patient group was characterized by relatively more activation in the bilateral inferior parietal lobes and the left precentral gyrus than the control group, and less activation in the inferior medial frontal lobe, bilateral middle frontal gyri, and right inferior temporal gyrus. Their procedure provided direct evidence that working memory updating was abnormal in PTSD patients relative to matched controls.

Lanius et al. (2001) found that PTSD subjects showed significantly less activation of the thalamus, and the medial frontal gyrus (Brodmann's area 10/11), than did the comparison subjects upon trauma exposure. In women with child abuse histories Bremner et al. (1999a) found increases in blood flow in portions of anterior prefrontal cortex (superior and middle frontal gyri—areas 6 and 9).

Decreased dorsolateral frontal cortex activation in response to trauma scripts provides yet another level of understanding why people with PTSD plunge into reexperiencing their trauma with limited consciousness that they are simply remembering elements of experiences belonging to the past. In our treatment outcome study, subjects showed increased activation of the dorsolateral prefrontal cortex following effective treatment (Levin et al., 1999).

A study by Carter et al. (1999) demonstrated that, consistent with a role in cognitive control, the DLPFC is more active on trials requiring inhibition of an automatic (word-reading) response. Breakdowns of cognitive control in PTSD often occur in the context of "competition"—between processing external information and responses appropriate to the situation, on the one hand, and processing internally generated posttraumatic information and automatic but maladaptive posttraumatic responses. More generally, the DLPFC has been implicated in capacities for deliberate reflection, problem-solving, planning, and response selection. Thus impaired DLPFC function in the presence of posttraumatic "triggers" may cause traumatized people to experience situations and respond to them as if they were "back there" in the trauma.

Davidson and his colleagues have proposed that one of the key components of affective style is the capacity to regulate negative emotion and, specifically to decrease the duration of negative affect once it arises (Davidson, 1998; Davidson and Irwin, 1999). Their studies suggest that the connections between the PFC and amygdala play an important role in this regulatory process. They found that subjects with greater base-line levels of left prefrontal activation are better able to voluntarily suppress negative affect (Jackson et al., 2000). When subjects voluntarily regulate negative emotions this is reflected in changes in amygdala recorded signal intensity.

Hemispheric Lateralization in PTSD

Both Rauch et al. (1996) and Teicher and his group (2002) found marked hemispheric lateralization in PTSD subjects who were exposed either to a negative memory or to a personalized trauma script. This suggests that there is differential hemispheric involvement in the processing of traumatic memories. The right hemisphere, which developmentally comes "on-line' earlier than the left hemisphere (Schore, 1994), is involved in the expression and comprehension of global nonverbal emotional commu-nication (tone of voice, facial expression, visual/spatial communication), and allows for a dynamic and holistic integration across sensory modalities (Davidson, 1989). This hemisphere is particularly integrated with the amygdala, which assigns emotional sig-nificance to incoming stimuli and helps regulate the autonomic and hormonal responses to that information. While the right hemisphere is specialized in detecting emotional nuances, it has only a rudimentary capacity to communicate analytically, to employ syntax, or to reason (Schore, 2003).

In contrast, the left hemisphere, which mediates verbal communication and orga-nizes problem-solving tasks into a well-ordered set of operations and process infor-mation in a sequential fashion (Davidson, 1998), seems to be less active in PTSD. It is in the area of categorization and labeling of internal states that people with PTSD seem to have particular problems (van der Kolk and McFarlane, 1996). The failure of left-hemisphere function during states of extreme arousal may contribute to the dere-alization and depersonalization reported in acute PTSD (Marmar et al., 1999; Shalev et al., 1996).

IMPLICATIONS FOR TREATMENT

For over a century it has been understood that traumatic experiences can leave indeli-ble emotional memories. Contemporary studies of how the amygdala is activated by extreme experiences dovetail with the laboratory observation that "emotional memory may be forever" (LeDoux et al., 1991). The accumulated body of research suggests that patients with PTSD suffer from impaired cortical control over subcortical areas respon-sible for learning, habituation, and stimulus discrimination. Hence, current thinking is that indelible subcortical emotional responses are held in check to varying degrees by cortical and hippocampal activity, and that delayed onset PTSD is the expression of subcortically mediated emotional responses that escape cortical, and possibly hip-pocampal, inhibitory control (van der Kolk and van der Hart, 1991; Pitman et al., 1990; Shalev et al., 1992).

The early neuroimaging studies of PTSD showed that, during exposure to a trau-matic script, there was decreased Broca's area functioning and increased activation of the right hemisphere (Rauch et al., 1996). This means that it is difficult for a traumatized individual to verbalize precisely what he or she is experiencing, particularly when he or she becomes emotionally aroused. It is likely that excessive physiological arousal plays a role in the failure to "process" the trauma, causing fragments of memories to be activated in response to traumatic reminders. These activate neural networks that contain the "memory" of the traumatic event, that is, the sensations and emotions related to the trauma, often without much verbal or symbolic representation of the event: When a traumatic memory is activated, the brain is "having" its experience, rather than recollecting it.

A relative decrease in left-hemispheric activation during the reliving of the trauma (Rauch et al., 1996; Teicher et al., 2002) explains why traumatic memories often are experienced as timeless and ego-alien: The part of the brain necessary for generating sequences and for the cognitive analysis of experience (the dorsolateral prefrontal cortex) is not properly activated (Lanius et al., 2001). An individual may feel, see, or hear the sensory elements of the traumatic experience, but he or she may be physiologically prevented from being able to translate this experience into communicable language. During flashbacks, victims may suffer from speechless terror in which they may be literally "out of touch with their feelings." Physiologically, they may respond as if they are being traumatized again. Particularly when victims experience depersonalization and derealization, they cannot "own" what is happening and thus cannot take steps to do anything about it.

In order to help traumatized individuals process their traumatic memories, it is critical that they gain enough distance from their sensory imprints and trauma-related emotions so that they can observe and analyze these sensations and emotions without becoming hyperaroused or engaging in avoidance maneuvers. The serotonin reuptake blockers seem to be able to accomplish exactly that. Studies in our laboratory have shown that SSRIs can help PTSD patients gain emotional distance from traumatic stimuli and make sense of their traumatic intrusions (van der Kolk et al., 1995).

The apparently relative decrease in left-hemisphere activation while reexperiencing the trauma suggests that it is important to help people with PTSD find a language in which they can come to understand and communicate their experiences. It is possible that some of the newer body-oriented therapies, dialectical behavior therapy, or EMDR (Chemtob et al., 2000; van der Kolk, 2002) may yield benefits that traditional verbally based therapies may lack because they do not require that the victim be able to verbally communicate the details of his or her experience.

Research has shown that making meaning—by simply talking about the traumatic experiences—is usually not enough to help people put their emotional responses behind them. Traumatized individuals need to have experiences that directly contradict the emotional helplessness and physical paralysis that accompany traumatic experiences

Phase-Oriented Treatment

All treatment of traumatized individuals needs to be paced according to the degree of involuntary intrusion of the trauma and the individual's capacities to deal with intense emotions. For over a century, clinicians have advocated the application of phase-oriented treatment consisting of (1) establishing a diagnosis, including prioritizing the range of problems suffered by the individual, and (2) designing a realistic phase-oriented treatment plan, consisting of:

1. Stabilization, including identification of feelings by gaining mastery over trauma-related somatic states of hyper- and hypoarousal.
2. Deconditioning of traumatic memories and responses.
3. Integration of traumatic personal schemes.

In the treatment of single-incident trauma, it is often possible to move quickly from one phase to the next; in complex cases of chronic interpersonal abuse clinicians often need to refocus on stabilization (van der Kolk et al., 1996).

In order to overcome the effects of physical hyperarousal and numbing, it is critical for traumatized people to find words to identify bodily sensations and to name emotional states. Knowing what one feels and allowing oneself to experience uncomfortable sensations and emotions is essential in planning how to cope with them. Being able to name and tolerate sensations, feelings, and experiences gives people the capacity to "own" what they feel. Being "in touch' with oneself (a function of an active medial frontal and dorsolateral prefrontal cortex?) seems to be indispensable for mastery and for having the mental flexibility to contrast and compare, and to imagine a range of alternative outcomes (not only a recurrence of the trauma).

This capacity needs to be present before people are ready to be exposed to their traumatic memories. Desensitization, or association of the traumatic imprints to autobiographical memory, is not possible as long as intense emotions overwhelm the victim, just as they did at the time of the original trauma. When traumatized individuals feel out of control and unable to modulate their distress, they are vulnerable to pathological self-soothing behaviors, such as substance abuse, binge eating, self-injury, or clinging to potentially dangerous partners (van der Kolk et al., 1996).

With the advent of effective medications, such as the serotonin reuptake blockers (e.g., van der Kolk et al., 1995), medications increasingly have taken the place of teaching people skills to deal with uncomfortable physical sensations. As long as the trauma is experienced with conditioned physiological responses and "speechless terror," victims tend to continue to react to conditional stimuli as a return of the trauma, without the capacity to define alternative courses of action. However, when the triggers are identified and the individual gains the capacity to attach words to somatic experiences, these lose some of their terror (Harber and Pennebaker, 1992). Thus, the task of therapy is to both create a capacity to be mindful of current experience, and to create symbolic representations of past traumatic experiences with the goal of uncoupling physical sensations from trauma-based emotional responses, thereby taming the associated terror.

Affective hyperarousal can effectively be treated with the judicious use of serotonin reuptake blockers and emotion regulation training, which consists of identifying, labeling, and altering emotional states. Gradually, patients learn to observe, rather than avoiding, the way they feel, and to plan alternative coping strategies. For traumatic reminders to lose their emotional valence, patients must be able to experience new information that contradicts the rigid traumatic memory, such as feeling physically safe, while thinking about the event, not feeling they are to blame, and feeling able to cope with similar events in the future. The critical issue in treatment is reexposure to traumatic imprints, and at the same time experiencing sensations (of mastery, safety, etc.) that are incompatible with the fear and terror associated with the trauma.

Flooding and exposure are by no means harmless treatment techniques: Exposure to information consistent with a traumatic memory can be expected to strengthen anxiety (i.e., sensitize and thereby aggravating PTSD symptomatology). Excessive arousal may make the PTSD patient worse by interfering with the acquisition of new information. When that occurs, the traumatic memories will not be corrected, but merely confirmed: Instead of promoting habituation, it may accidentally foster sensitization.

CONCLUSIONS

The modern rediscovery of trauma as an etiological factor in mental disorders goes back only to about 1980. During this time there has been an explosion of knowledge about how experience shapes the central nervous system and the formation of the self. Developments in the neurosciences have started to make significant contributions to our understanding of how the brain is shaped by experience, and how life itself continues to transform the ways biology is organized. The study of trauma has been one of the most fertile areas within the disciplines of psychiatry and psychology in helping to develop a deeper understanding of the interrelationship between emotional, cognitive, social, and biological forces that shape human development. Starting with posttraumatic stress disorder (PTSD) in adults, but expanding into early attachment and coping with overwhelming experiences in childhood, our field has discovered how certain experiences can "set" psychological expectations and biological selectivity. Research in these areas has opened up entirely new insights in how extreme experiences throughout the life cycle can have profound effects on memory, affect regulation, biological stress modulation, and interpersonal relatedness. These findings, in the context of the development of a range of new therapy approaches, are beginning to open up entirely new perspectives on how traumatized individuals can be helped to overcome their past.

REFERENCES

Adamec RE (1997). Transmitter systems involved in neural plasticity underlying increased anxiety and defense—Implications for understanding anxiety following traumatic stress. *Neurosci Biobehav Rev* 21:755–765.

American Psychiatric Association (1980). *Diagnostic and Statistical Manual of Mental Disorders*, 3rd ed. Author: Washington, DC.

Arnsten A, Matthew R, Ubriani R, Taylor J, Li B (1991). alpha-1 Noradrenergic receptor stimulation impairs prefrontal cortical cognitive function. *Biological Psychiatry* 45:26–31.

Bonne O, Brandes D, Gilboa A, Gomori J, Shenton M, Pitman R, Shalev A (2001). Longitudinal MRI study of hippocampal volume in trauma survivors with PTSD. *Am J Psychiatry* 158:1248–1251.

Bremner JD, Randall PK, Vermetten E, Staib L, Bronen R, McCarthy G, Innis R, Charney D (1997). Magnetic resonance imaging based measurement of hippocampal volume in posttraumatic stress disorder related childhood physical and sexual abuse: A preliminary report. *Biological Psychiatry* 41:23–32.

Bremner JD, Narayan M, Staib LH, Southwick SM, McGlashan TH, Charney DS (1999a). Neural correlates of memories of childhood sexual abuse in women with and without posttraumatic stress disorder. *Am J Psychiatry* 156:1787–1795.

Bremner JD, Staib LH, Kaloupek DG, Southwick SM, Soufer R, Charney DS (1999b). Neural correlates of exposure to traumatic pictures and sound in Vietnam combat veterans with and without posttraumatic stress disorder: A positron emission tomography study. *Biological Psychiatry* 45:806–816.

Breuer J, Freud S (1893). The physical mechanisms of hysterical phenomena. In *The Standard Edition of the Complete Psychological Works of Sigmund Freud*. Hogarth Press: London.

Breiter H et al. (1996). *Neuron Cell Press* 17:875–887.

Bush G, Luu, P, Posner, MI (2000). Cognitive and emotional influences in anterior cingulate cortex. *Trends Cognitive Sci* 4:215–222.

Cahill L, McGaugh, IL (1998). Mechanisms of emotional arousal and lasting declarative memory. *Trends Neurosci* 21:273–231.

Carter CS, Botvinick MM, Cohen JD (1999). The contribution of the anterior cingulate cortex to executive functioning. *Cur Opin Neurol* 12:771–821.

Chemtob CM, Tolin DF, van der Kolk BA, Pitman RK (2000). Eye movement desensitization and reprocessing. In Foa EB, Keane TM, Friedman MJ (eds). *Effective Treatments for PTSD: Practice Guidelines from the International Society for Traumatic Stress Studies*. Guilford Press: New York, pp. 139–155, 333–335.

Cicchetti D, Beeghly M (1996). Child maltreatment, attachment, and the self system: Emergence of an internal state lexicon in toddlers at high social risk. In Hertzig Farber (eds). *Annual Progress in Child Psychiatry and Child Development*. Brunner/Mazel: Philadelphia, pp. 127–166.

Cicchetti D, Lynch M (1995): Failures in the expectable environment and the impact on individual development: The case of the child maltreatment. In: Cicchetti D, Cohen D (eds). *Developmental Psychopathology*. John Wiley New York 1995; Vol. II, 32–71.

Cohen H, Kotler M, Matar M, Kaplan Z, Loewenthal U, Miodownik H, Cassuto Y (1998). Analysis of heart rate variability in posttraumatic stress disorder patients in response to a trauma-related reminder. *Biological Psychiatry* 44:1054–1059.

Cohen H, Benjamin J, Geva AB, Matar M, Kaplan Z, Kotler M (2000a). Autonomic dysregulation in panic disorder and in post-traumatic stress disorder: Application of power spectrum analysis of heart rate variability at rest and in response to recollection of trauma or panic attacks. *Psychiatry Research* 96:1–13.

Damasio A (1995). On some functions of the human prefrontal cortex. In Grafman J, Holyoak KJ (eds). *Structure and Functions of the Human Prefrontal Cortex. Ann NY Acad Sci*: New York, pp. 241–251.

Damasio A (1999). The feeling of what happens. Harcourt, Brace: New York.

Davidson RJ, Irwin W (1999). The functional neuroanatomy of emotion and affective style. *Trends in Cognitive Science* 3:11–21.

Davidson J (2001). Recognition and treatment of posttraumatic stress disorder. *JAMA* 286: 584–588.

Davidson J, Tupler L, Wilson W, Connor K (1998). A family study of chronic post-traumatic stress disorder following rape trauma. *J Psychiatric Res* 32:301–309.

Davidson R (2000). Pharmacotherapy of posttraumatic stress disorder: Treatment options, long-term follow-up, and predictors of outcome. *J Clin Psychiatry* 61:52–59.

Devinsky O, Morrell MJ, Vogt BA (1995). Contributions of anterior cingulate cortex to behavior. *Brain* 118:279–306.

Donald M (1991). *Origins of the Modern Mind.* Harvard University Press: Cambridge, MA.

Fanselow MS (2000). Contextual fear, gestalt memories and the hippocampus. *Behav Brain Res,* 110:73–81.

Fanselow MS, LeDoux, JE (1999). Why we think plasticity underlying Pavlovian fear conditioning occurs: The basolateral amygdala. *Neuron* 23:229–232.

Felitti VJ, Anda RF, Nordernberg D, Willimason DF, Spitz AM, Edwards V, Koss MP, Marks JS (1998). Relationship of childhood abuse to many of the leading causes of death in adults: The adverse childhood experiences (ACE) study. *Am J Preventative Med* 14:245–258.

Foa EB, Riggs DS, Massie ED, Yarczower M (1995). The impact of fear activation and anger on the efficacy of exposure treatment for posttraumatic stress disorder. *Behavior Therapy* 26:487–499.

Gurvits T, Shenton M, Hokama H, Ohta H, Lasko N, Gilbertson M, Orr S, Kikinis R, Jolesz F, McCarley R, Pitman R (1998). Magnetic resonance imaging (MRI) study of hippocampal volume in chronic combat related posttraumatic stress disorder. *Biol Psychiatry* 40:1091–1099.

Harber KD, Pennebaker JW (1992). Memory emotion and response to trauma. In Christianson S-A (ed). *The Handbook of Emotion and Memory: Research and Theory.* New Jersey, Lawrence Erlbaum and Associates.

Heim C, Nemeroff CB (2001). The role of childhood trauma in the neurobiology of mood and anxiety disorders: Preclinical and clinical studies. *Biological Psychiatry,* 49:1023–1039.

Heim C, Newport DJ, Heit S, Graham YP, Wilcox M, Bonsall R, Miller AH, Nemeroff CB (2000). Pituitary-adrenal and autonomic responses to stress in women after sexual and physical abuse in childhood. *J Am Med Assoc* 284:592–597.

Hopper J, van der Kolk B (2001). Retrieving, assessing, and classifying traumatic memories: A preliminary report on three case studies of a new standardized method. *J Aggression, Maltreatment Trauma* 4:33–71.

Jackson J, Malmstadt M, Larson R, Davidson R (2000). Suppression and enhancement of emotional responses to unpleasant pictures. *Psychophysiology* 37:515–522.

Janet P (1889). *L'automatisme psychologique: essai de psychologie experimentale sur les formes inferieures de l'activité humaine.* Paris: Felix Alcan, 1973. Societé Pierre Janet/Payot: Paris.

Janet P (1919/1925). *Les medications psychologiques.* Felix Alcan: Paris (original work published in 1919).

Joseph R (1988). Dual mental functioning in a split-brain patient. *J Clin Psychol* 44:770–779.

Kardiner A (1941). *The Traumatic Neuroses of War.* Hoeber: New York.

Kaufman J, Plotsky PM, Nemeroff CB, Charney DS (2000). Effects of early adverse experiences on brain structure and function: Clinical implications *Biological Psychiatry* 48:778–790.

Kessler RC, Sonnega A, Bromet EJ, Hughes M, Nelson CB (1995). Posttraumatic stress disorder in the National Comorbidity Survey. *Arch Gen Psychiatry* 52:1048–1060.

Kilpatrick DG, Resnick HS, Saunders BE, Best CL (1998). Rape, other violence against women, and posttraumatic stress disorder. In Dohrenwend BP (ed). *Adversity, Stress, and Psychopathology*. Oxford University Press: London, pp. 161–176.

Kirschbaum C, Wolf 0T, May M, Wippich W, Hellhammer DH (1996). Stress- and treatment-induced elevations of cortisol levels associated with impaired declarative memory in healthy adults. *Life Sci* 58:1475–1483.

Kulka RA, Schlenger WE, Fairbank JA, et al. (1990). *Trauma and the Vietnam War Generation*. Brunner/Mazel: New York.

LaBar KS, Gatenby JC, LeDoux JE, Phelps EA (1998). Human amygdala activation during conditioned fear acquisition and extinction—A mixed-trial tMRI study. *Neuron* 20:937–945.

Lanius RA, Williamson PC, Densmore M, Boksman K, Gupta MA, Neufeld RW, Gati JS, Menon RS (2001). Neural correlates of traumatic memories in posttraumatic stress disorder: A functional MRI investigation. *Am J Psychiatry* 158:1920–1922.

Lanius R, Williamson P, Boksman K, Densmore M, et al. (2002). Brain activation during script-driven imagery induced dissociative responses in PTSD: A functional magnetic resonance imaging investigation. *Biological Psychiatry* 52:305–311.

LeDoux JE (1992). Emotion as memory: Anatomical systems underlying indelible neural traces. In Christianson SA (ed). *The Handbook of Emotion and Memory*. Lawrence Erlbaum: Hillsdale, NJ, pp. 269–288.

LeDoux J (1996). *The Emotional Brain*. Simon and Schuster: New York.

LeDoux JE, Romanski L, Xagoraris A (1991). Indelibility of subcortical emotional memories. *J Cogn Neurosci* 1:238–243.

Levin P, Lazrove S, van der Kolk B (1999). What psychological testing and neuroimaging tell us about the treatment of posttraumatic stress disorder by Eye Movement Desensitization and Reprocessing. *J Anxiety Disorders* 13:159–172.

Macy RD (2002). Prevalence rates for PTSD and utilization rates of behavioral health services for an adult Medicaid population. (Ph.D. Dissertating); Union College, Ohio.

Marmar C, Weiss DS, Metzler TJ, Delucchi K, Wentworth K (1999). Longitudinal course and predictors of continuing distress following critical incident exposure in emergency services personnel. *J Nervous Mental Disease* 187:15–22.

McEwen BS (1998). Protective and damaging effects of stress mediators. *N Engl J Med* 338:171–179.

McFarlane AC, Weber DL, Clark CR (1993). Abnormal stimulus processing in PTSD. *Biological Psychiatry* 34:311–320.

McLean P (1990). *The Triune Brain*. Oxford University Press: New York.

O'Keefe J, Nadel L (1978). *The Hippocampus as a Cognitive Map*. Clarendon Press: Oxford.

Ornitz EM, Pynoos RS (1989). Startle modulation in children with post-traumatic stress disorder. *Am J Psychiatry* 147:866–870.

Packard MG Cahill L (2001) Affective modulation of multiple memory systems. *Current Opinion in Neurobiology* 11:752–756.

Panksepp J (1998). *Affective Neuroscience: The Foundations of Human and Animal Emotions*. Oxford University Press: Oxford.

Panksepp J (2001). The long-term psychobiological consequences of infant emotions: Prescriptions for the twenty-first century. *Infant Mental Health J* 22:132–173.

Parvizi J, Damasio A (2001). Consciousness and the brainstem. *Cognition* 79:135–159.

Pennebaker J, Harber K (1993). A social stage model of collective coping: The Loma Prieta Earthquake and the Persian Gulf War. *Journal of Social Issues* 49 (4):125–145.

Pitman RK, Orr SP, Forgue DF, de Jong J, Claiborn JM (1987). Psychophysiologic assessment of posttraumatic stress disorder imagery in Vietnam combat veterans. *Arch Gen Psychiatry* 44:970–975.

Pitman RK, van der Kolk BA, Orr S, Greenberg MS (1990). Naloxone reversible stress induced analgesia in post traumatic stress disorder. *Arch Gen Psychiat* 47:541–547.

Porges S, Doussard-Roosevelt J, Portales A, Greenspan S (1996). Infant regulation of the vagal "brake" predicts child behavior problems: A psychobiological model of social behavior. *Developmental Psychobiol* 29:697–712.

Post RM (1992). Transduction of psychosocial stress into the neurobiology of recurrent affective disorder. *Am J Psychiatry* 149:999–1010.

Pribram KH (1991). *Brain and Perception: Holonomy and Structure in Figural Processing.* Lawrence Erlbaum: Hillsdale, NJ.

Putnam F, Trickett P (1993). Child sexual abuse: A model of chronic trauma. *Psychiatry: Interpersonal and Biological Processes* 56:82–95.

Rainey JM, Aleem A, Ortiz A, Yaragani V, Pohl R, Berchow R (1987). Laboratory procedure for the inducement of flashbacks. *Am J Psychiatry* 144:1317–1319.

Rauch SL, van der Kolk BA, Fisler RE, Alpert NM, Orr SP, Savage CR, Fischman AJ, Jenike MA, Pitman RK (1996). A symptom provocation study of posttraumatic stress disorder using positron emission tomography and script-driven imagery. *Arch Gen Psychiatry* 53:380–387.

Sachinvala N, Kling A, Suffin S, Lake R, Cohen M (2000). Increased regional cerebral perfusion by 99mTc hexamethyl propylene amine oxime single photon emission computed tomography in post-traumatic stress disorder. *Military Med* 165:473–479.

Sahar T, Shalev A, Porges S (2001). Vagal modulation of responses to mental challenge in posttraumatic stress disorder. *Biological Psychiatry* 49:637–643.

Schore A (1994). *Affect regulation and the Origin of the Self: The Neurobiology of Emotional Development.* Lawrence Erlbaum: Hillsdale, NJ.

Schore A (2003). *Affect Regulation and the Repair of the Self.* W.W. Norton: New York.

Shalev AY, Orr SP, Peri T, Schreiber S, Pitman RK (1992). Physiologic responses to loud tones in Israeli patients with post-traumatic stress disorder. *Arch Gen Psychiatry* 49:870–875.

Shalev AY, Peri T, Caneti L, Schreiber S (1996). Predictors of PTSD in injured trauma survivors: A prospective study. *Am J Psychiatry* 153:219–225.

Shaw ME, Strother SC, McFarlane AC, Morris PLP, Anderson J, Clark C, Egan GF (2002). Abnormal functional connectivity in posttraumatic stress disorder. *NeuroImage* 15:661–674.

Shin L, Kosslyn S, McNally R, Alpert N, et al. (1997). Visual imagery and perception in post-traumatic stress disorder: A positron emission tomographic investigation. *Arch Gen Psychiatry* 54:233–241.

Shin L, McNally R, Kosslyn S, Thompson WL, Rauch SL, et al. (1999). Regional cerebral blood flow during script-driven imagery in childhood sexual abuse-related PTSD: A PET investigation. *Am J Psychiatry* 156:575–584.

Shin LM, Whalen PJ, Pitman RK, Bush G, Macklin ML, Lasko NB, Orr SP, McInerney SC, Rauch, SL (2001). An fMRI study of anterior cingulate function in posttraumatic stress disorder. *Biological Psychiatry* 50:932–942.

Southwick SM, Krystal JH, Morgan A, Johnson D, Nagy L, Nicolaou A, Henninger GR, Charney DS (1993). Abnormal noradrenergic function in post traumatic stress disorder. *Arch Gen Psychiatry* 50:266–274.

Teicher M, Anderson S, Polcari A (2002). Developmental neurobiology of childhood stress and trauma. *Psychiatric Clin N Am* 25:397–426.

van der Kolk BA, Greenberg M, Boyd H, Kristal J (1985). Inescapable shock, neurotransmitters and addiction to trauma: Toward a psychobiology of post-traumatic stress. *Biol Psychiatry* 20:314–325.

van der Kolk BA, van der Hart O (1991). The intrusive past: The flexibility of memory and the engraving of trauma. *American Imago* 48:425–454.

van der Kolk BA (2000). Adult sequelae of assault. In Friedman, Kaplan, Sadock (eds). *Comprehensive Textbook of Psychiatry*, Williams and Wilkins: Baltimore.

van der Kolk BA, Ducey, CP (1989). The psychological processing of traumatic experience: Rorschach patterns in PTSD. *J Traumatic Stress* 2:259–274.

van der Kolk BA, van der Hart O (1989). Pierre Janet and the breakdown of adaptation in psychological trauma. *Am J Psychiatry* 146:1530–1540.

van der Kolk BA, Fisler RE (1995). Dissociation and the fragmentary nature of traumatic memories: Overview and exploratory study. *J Traumatic Stress* 8:505–525.

van der Kolk BA, Greenberg MS, Orr S, Pitman RK (1989). Pain perception and endogenous opioids in post traumatic stress disorder. *Psychopharm Bull* 25:117–121.

van der Kolk BA, McFarlane AC, Weisaeth L (eds) (1996a). *Traumatic Stress: The Effects of Overwhelming Experience on Mind, Body and Society*. Guilford Press: New York.

van der Kolk BA, Pelcovitz D, Roth S, Mandel F, McFarlane AC, Herman JL (1996b). Dissociation, somatization, and affect dysregulation: The complexity of adaptation to trauma. *Am J Psychiatry* 153:83–93.

van der Kolk B, Burbridge JA, Suzuki J (1997). The psychobiology of traumatic memory: clinical implications of neuroimaging studies. *Ann NY Acad Sci* 821:99–113.

van der Kolk BA, Hopper J, Osterman J (2000). Exploring the nature of traumatic memory: Combining clinical knowledge and laboratory methods. *J Aggression, Maltreatment, and Trauma* 4:9–31.

van der Kolk BA (2002). Beyond the Talking Cure: Somatic experience and the subcortical imprints in the treatment of trauma. In EMPR as an integrative Psychotherapy approached (Shapiro f) APA 2002.

Vasterling (1998). Attention and memory dysfunction in posttraumatic stress disorder. *Neuropsychology* 12:125–133.

Whalen P, Bush G, McNally RI, Wilhelm S, McInemey SC, Ienike MA, Rauch SL (1998). The emotional counting Stroop paradigm: A functional magnetic resonance imaging probe of the anterior cingulate affective division. *Biological Psychiatry* 44:1219–1228.

Wilson SN, van der Kolk BA, Burbridge JA, Fisler RE, Kradin R (1999). Phenotype of blood lymphocytes in PTSD suggests chronic immune activation. *Psychosomatics* 40:222–225.

Yehuda R, Haligan, Grossman, Golier, Wong (2002). The cortisol and glucocorticoid receptor response to low dose dexamethasone administration in aging combat veterans and Holocaust survivors with and without posttraumatic stress disorder. *Biological Psychiatry* 52:393–403.

Yehuda R, (1998). Psychoneuroendocrinology of post-traumatic stress disorder. *Psychiatric Clinics of North America* 21:359–379.

Yehuda R, Bierer LM, Schmeidler J, Aferiat DH, Breslau I, Dolan S (2000). Low cortisol and risk for PTSD in adult offspring of Holocaust survivors. *Am J Psychiatry* 157:1252–1259.

Yehuda R, McFarlane AC (1995). Conflict between current knowledge about posttraumatic stress disorder and its original conceptual basis *Am J Psychiatry* 152(12):1705–1713.

12

NATURE AND TREATMENT
OF PANIC DISORDER

Fredric N. Busch[1] and Barbara L. Milrod[2]

[1] *Department of Psychiatry, Weill Cornell Medical College and Columbia University Center for Psychoanalytic Training and Research, New York, New York*
[2] *Department of Psychiatry, Cornell University Medical College and New York Psychoanalytic Institute, New York, New York*

DEFINING THE SYNDROME OF PANIC DISORDER

The syndrome now called panic disorder was first described in the medical literature in 1895, by Sigmund Freud (1895a), under the term anxiety neurosis. His description differed from the currently accepted one in *Diagnostic and Statistical Manual of Mental Disorders* (DSM IV-TR) (APA, 2000), in that he included features of the illness other than panic attacks, including general irritability, anxious expectation, rudimentary anxiety attacks (which bear a similarity to our current conceptualization of limited symptom attacks), vertigo, phobias and agoraphobia, nausea and other gastrointestinal symptoms, and paresthesias.

In the DSM IV-TR description of panic disorder, recurrent and unexpected panic attacks are the central feature, along with persistent anxiety about having another attack or the consequences of the attacks, or a change in behavior in reaction to the attacks. Panic attacks are carefully defined with regard to time (abrupt development, reaching a

Textbook of Biological Psychiatry, Edited by Jaak Panksepp
ISBN 0-471-43478-7 Copyright © 2004 John Wiley & Sons, Inc.

peak within 10 min, discrete periods) and emotional quality (intense fear or discomfort). At least four of the following typical panic symptoms must be present: pounding heart or accelerated heart rate, sweating, trembling or shaking, sensations of shortness of breath or smothering, feeling of choking, chest pain or discomfort, nausea or abdominal distress, feeling dizzy, lightheaded, unsteady or faint, derealization (feelings of unreality) or depersonalization (feeling detached from oneself), fear of losing control or going crazy, fear of dying, paresthesias (numbness or tingling sensations), and chills or hot flushes. Panic disorder should be classified as either with or without agoraphobia, defined as fear of situations from which escape may be difficult or embarrassing or in which help may not be available in the event of a panic attack. The individual either avoids these situations, endures them with anxiety about having another panic attack, or can tolerate them only if a companion is present.

Many clinicians have expressed concerns about limitations of the DSM system of classification, including difficulty assessing early onset, atypical, and diminished but persistent symptoms of the disorder. In addition, symptoms that are at a subthreshold level for the disorder have been difficult to classify and appear to affect treatment outcome while causing ongoing functional impairment. A group of researchers and clinicians (Cassano et al., 1997, 1998) have proposed an alternate diagnostic system for panic spectrum disorder that allows assessment of these various symptoms. The classification system is similar to the description of anxiety neurosis by Freud described above. These symptoms are described in terms of: panic symptoms, anxious expectation, phobic and avoidant features, need for reassurance, substance sensitivity, stress sensitivity, and separation sensitivity and anxiety.

Panic symptoms in this classification include not just full-blown panic attacks but also limited symptom panic attacks and isolated panic symptoms that can lead to significant clinical impairment in the absence of panic attacks. Also included are less common symptoms that can be associated with anxiety, such as numbness and disorientation. Anxious expectation includes anticipatory anxiety about the occurrence of panic attacks and a general state of alertness, including a sense of insecurity about one's physical and psychological integrity. Phobias and avoidant behavior may occur secondary to panic attacks or may precede the onset of panic disorder. Avoidance represents an effort to cope with panic symptoms or to reduce anticipatory anxiety. Avoidant behavior includes agoraphobia as well as a variety of phobias, including claustrophobia when associated with threats to breathing, and social avoidance to avert fears of humiliation from panic symptoms.

Patients with panic disorder require a significant amount of reassurance due to their fears. In the view of Cassano et al. (1997, 1998), the significant relief of anxiety provided by such reassurance can lead to increasing interpersonal dependency. The patient can develop manipulative and dramatic behaviors in an effort to coerce reassurance from others. Other aspects of the panic spectrum include patients' high degree of sensitivity to panic attacks being triggered by substances, including medications, antidepressants, caffeine, thyroid hormones, drugs of abuse, as well as to a variety of homeopathic agents (Pitts and McClure, 1967; Charney et al., 1983; Dager et al., 1987; McCann and Ricaurte, 1992; Nutt and Lawson 1992). They also have a sensitivity to withdrawal of substances. Stress sensitivity refers to patients' vulnerability to the impact of stressful events (Roth et al., 1992; Last et al., 1984; Wade et al., 1993). In such sensitive patients, normal daily stresses may trigger panic symptoms. Patients may ask others to help them avoid negative information to reduce their panic risk. Finally, as has been frequently noted in the panic literature, but is not specifically incorporated in the DSM IV-TR criteria for panic disorder, patients often demonstrate sensitivity to separation (Gittelman and Klein, 1984; Deltito et al., 1986). Separation anxiety in adulthood can aggravate the dependency on others for reassurance described above.

COURSE OF PANIC DISORDER

Panic disorder has been generally found to have a chronic, recurring course (Pollack and Otto, 1997; Pollack and Marzol, 2000; Faravelli et al., 1995). There is often a persistence of subthreshold symptoms even in the absence of a DSM IV-TR diagnosable disorder. In a naturalistic, 5-year study following 99 patients with panic disorder without any psychiatric comorbidity (Faravelli et al., 1995), even transitory full remission was achieved by only 37.5 percent of patients, while full remission, sustained at 5 years only, occurred for 12 percent. Seventy-three percent of patients in this study experienced some improvement, but only 41 percent of those were still well at 5-year follow-up. On the other hand, many treatment outcome studies, particularly of cognitive–behavioral therapy, cite high rates of remission (Craske et al., 1991; Clark et al., 1994; Fava et al., 1995). It was the varying definitions of "remission" of panic disorder, ranging from a narrower view in which elimination of panic attacks signified remission, to a wider definition of panic disorder that included anxiety sensitivity, hypochondriacal and phobic concerns, and impairments in quality of life, that ultimately led to the National Institute of Mental Health (NIMH) Consensus Conference on Panic Disorder (Shear and Maser, 1994), in which the range of illness necessary to be monitored by panic disorder outcome studies was defined.

In addition to a spectrum of anxiety symptoms, patients with panic disorder have a high rate of comorbid psychiatric disorders, many of which have been shown to negatively influence outcome, including degree of impairment and suicidality (Roy-Byrne et al., 2000). Comorbid depression has been cited as increasing the likelihood of a chronic, disabling illness (Roy-Byrne et al., 2000; Hollifield et al., 1997). There is some data indicating that preexisting panic disorder increases the subsequent risk for the development of major depression in both men and women, and that controlling for prior anxiety disorders accounts for 50 percent of the observed twofold increased incidence of major depression in women over men (Breslau et al., 1995). The effect of comorbid personality disorders on the course of panic disorder has yet to be adequately studied.

Panic patients experience tremendous distress and have been shown to have a high level of functional impairment as a result of this (Roy-Byrne et al., 2000). They report poor physical health, poor emotional health, a higher incidence of alcohol and drug abuse than normals, and a higher incidence of attempted suicide (Rosenbaum, 1997). Medical costs are high for patients with panic disorder, with half of all primary care visits being precipitated by physical sensations associated with panic disorder, such as dizziness, heart palpitations, chest pain, dyspnea, and abdominal pain, as demonstrated by both epidemiological and retrospective studies (Katon, 1996). Patients with panic disorder account for 20 to 29 percent of all emergency room visits (Swenson et al., 1992; Weissman et al., 1989) and are 12.6 times more likely to visit emergency rooms than the general population (Markowitz et al., 1989).

Additionally, panic disorder has been found to co-occur with a variety of medical conditions, including mitral valve prolapse, cardiomyopathy, hypertension, irritable bowel syndrome, chronic obstructive pulmonary disease, and migraines (Zauber and Katon, 1996). Coryell et al. (1982) found that the death rate in patients with panic disorder exceeded that of the general population. In their study, 20 percent of deaths in 113 former psychiatric inpatients with panic disorder followed up 35 years later were the result of suicide. Also in this study, men with panic disorder were found to have twice the risk of death due to cardiovascular disease than men in the general population.

The high morbidity level in patients with panic disorder points to the importance of developing appropriate, broad-based treatments. As noted in the panic spectrum section, even lower levels of persistent symptoms can cause significant functional impairment and poor prognosis. Thus, strategies for treatment of panic disorder should aim for remission rather than simply symptom reduction.

BASIC MODELS OF THE ETIOLOGY OF PANIC DISORDER

Neurophysiological Models

Several lines of evidence suggest a neurophysiological basis for panic disorder, including genetic studies. The illness's medication responsiveness (discussed in the treatment section below) has been interpreted to imply a neurophysiological etiology. Evidence for a genetic basis for panic disorder has also been derived from studies of twins that demonstrate a higher rate of concordance for panic in monozygotic than dizygotic twins (Torgersen, 1983, Kendler et al., 1993; Skre et al., 1993).

Neurophysiological models of the etiology of panic disorder have developed primarily from animal models of brain functioning and studies of substances that provoke panic. The interpretation of these data by different theorists in developing models for panic will be described below. Neuroimaging studies are expected to be an increasingly important source of data.

An Oversensitive Fear Network. Gorman et al. (2000) hypothesize that panic originates in an abnormally sensitive fear network, which includes the prefrontal cortex, insula, thalamus, amygdala, and amygdalar projections to brainstem and hypothalamus (Fig. 12.1). The central nucleus of the amygdala is thought to be the center of this network. Amygdalar projections to various sites appear to coordinate physiological and behavioral responses to danger, including the parabrachial nucleus (increased respiratory rate), hypothalamus (activation of the sympathetic nervous system, release of corticosteroids), locus coeruleus (release of norepinephrine, increases in blood pressure

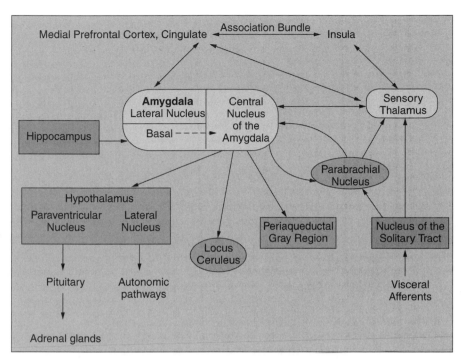

Figure 12.1. Neuroanatomical pathways of the fear network. [Reprinted from Gorman et al. (2000); by permission of the American Psychiatric Association.]

and heart rate), and periaqueductal gray region (defensive behaviors). In fact, data from animal models suggest that stimulation of the amygdala produces a fear response that has significant similarities to a panic attack (Ledoux et al., 1988; Davis, 1992). Medications effective in treating panic disorder diminish activity of the brainstem centers that receive input from the central nucleus of the amygdala.

The amygdala receives afferent input from brainstem structures and the sensory thalamus, which allow a more immediate response to danger, and from cortical regions involved in processing and evaluating sensory information. Neurocognitive deficits in cortical processing could result in misinterpretation of sensory information (bodily cues), and inappropriate activation of the fear network via misguided excitatory input to the amygdala. Gorman et al. (2000) and Ledoux (1996) postulate that psychotherapy may work by strengthening the ability of these cortical projections to assert reason over automatic behavioral and physical responses.

Gorman et al. (2000) interpret the data derived from substances that provoke panic attacks in patients with panic disorder at a much greater rate than in healthy controls or in patients with other psychiatric disorders, as being consistent with the sensitive fear network model. Rather than focusing on the specific biochemical impact of the various substances (sodium lactate, yohimbine, noradrenaline, adrenaline, and others), they emphasize the biological disparity of the various mechanisms of action. They therefore postulate that these agents trigger panic by causing precipitous somatic discomfort, nonspecifically triggering the fear network.

An abnormally sensitive fear network may result from an inherited tendency to fearfulness, perhaps a neurocognitive deficit, resulting in abnormal response to or modulation of the fear network. Disruptions of early attachment and traumatic events in childhood and adulthood may lead to persistent changes in the stress system and fear network. Gorman et al. (2000) speculate that a genetically based abnormality in the brain fear network may make the individual more susceptible to the emotional effects of trauma.

False Suffocation Alarm Model. Klein (1993) suggests an alternate model of a biological basis for panic disorder, a false suffocation alarm hypothesis. In this model, the brain is postulated to have an evolved suffocation alarm system that can be hypersensitive and can misfire in the absence of an actual suffocation risk. In Klein's view this misfire leads to an urge to flee, the onset of hyperventilation, shortness of breath, and panic. Panic, both spontaneous and carbon dioxide (CO_2) and lactate-induced, differs from a typical emergency fear response in that it includes shortness of breath as a symptom and does not activate the hypothalamic-pituitary-adrenal (HPA) axis. Klein is therefore critical of cognitive theory and other literature that equate fear with panic, including Gorman's fear circuit model.

This debate recently focused on the interpretation of an experiment on susceptibility to CO_2-induced panic in patients with various psychiatric diagnoses. Studies have shown that during inhalation of carbon dioxide, patients with panic and premenstrual dysphoric disorder (PMDD) are more likely to experience panic than healthy volunteers or patients with other psychiatric disorders (see Gorman et al., 2001). This susceptibility appears to decline after successful treatment of the panic disorder. The origins of this vulnerability could be secondary to specific abnormalities in the afferent neural pathways that respond to increased levels of CO_2 (Klein's suffocation monitor hypothesis) or to nonspecific somatic distress from CO_2 inhalation, including air hunger and breathlessness reminiscent of panic, triggering a central neural fear circuit.

Gorman et al. (2001) hoped to generate evidence with regard to these hypotheses by looking at ventilatory responses to CO_2 to see if an increase was specific to patients with panic disorder or was found in any patient experiencing panic attacks, regardless of diagnosis. Panic disorder and PMDD were found to have increased rates of panic attacks compared to controls and to patients with MDD. Measures of ventilatory response to 5 percent CO_2, however, varied more with respect to whether a panic attack occurred than with diagnosis.

Thus, Gorman et al. (2001) conclude that there is nothing fundamentally abnormal about the ventilatory physiology of panic patients. This finding, in the view of these authors, suggests the importance of central brain circuits in panic disorder, rather than simply abnormalities in the pulmonary, peripheral, or medullary chemoreceptors. CO_2 stimulation triggers the fear circuit, including activation of the amygdala and its projection sites, in patients with panic disorder or in subjects who experience panic attacks.

In response to Gorman's study, Klein (2002) argues against Gorman et al.'s (2001) suggestion that CO_2 and lactate produce panic via nonspecific distress that induces fear, noting that other substances that trigger distress do not trigger panic. In Klein's (1993, 2002) view, carbon dioxide sensitivity is due to a deranged suffocation alarm monitor. Thus, Klein believes that panic attacks represent a hyperreactivity of a common human adaptive mechanism, a view that is more specific than the conception of panic attacks as conditioned fear. He reemphasizes his view that panic attacks are not simply equivalent to fear, noting the lack of dyspneic air hunger in the fear response, the lack of HPA activation in panic, and the fact that imipramine and other antipanic antidepressants block panic attacks but not ordinary fear. He suggests that "vital requirements such as air, food and water require distinctive perceptual/emotional/motivational brain circuits that should not be subsumed under a fear circuit that, by conditioning, serves all purposes" (Klein, 2002, p. 568).

Separation Distress System. Panksepp (1998) suggests an alternate theory for the interrelationship of fear, panic, and neurophysiology. He differentiates a PANIC system in the brain, which he primarily views as related to separation distress, from a FEAR system associated with other types of fear, including anticipatory anxiety. The separation distress system is the origin of distress vocalizations (DVs), or isolation calls, which are primitive forms of communication by which an infant signals distress to elicit parental care. These communications are shared by all mammals and probably have a similar brain physiology. The PANIC system originates in the midbrain periaqueductal gray matter and continues in the medial diencephalon, the ventral septal area, the preoptic area, the bed nucleus of the stria terminalis, and in higher mammals the anterior part of the cingulate gyrus, the amygdala, and the hypothalamus.

Panksepp suggests that panic attacks may arise from sudden arousal of the separation distress system, thus the derivation of the term PANIC. This hypothesis was based in part on the link between a history of separation anxiety and panic disorder. In addition, tricyclics, which effectively treat panic, were found to diminish DVs. Panksepp also refers to Klein's (1964, 1981) early work on treatment of panic, in which he found that benzodiazepines, such as chlordiazepoxide and diazepam, had little impact on panic, whereas tricyclics affected panic but not anticipatory anxiety, again attesting to a separation between these two systems.

More recent clinical studies, however, cast doubt on the pharmacological discrepancy between these systems. Benzodiazepines, such as alprazolam and clonazepam, have been found to effectively treat panic. In addition, antidepressants, such as venlafaxine and paroxetine, have been found to effectively treat other forms of anxiety, such as generalized anxiety disorder. The impact of these agents on anticipatory anxiety has not been well studied.

The fear circuit network, the suffocation monitor alarm system, and the separation distress system may play a role in the onset and development of panic disorder or may play varying roles in the different forms or aspects of the panic syndrome. Further neurophysiological studies should help to clarify these factors.

Neuroimaging may provide another means of assessing neurobiological factors in panic disorder. An early study by Reiman et al. (1984), using positron emission topography (PET), suggested a focal asymmetry in cerebral blood flow in the region of the parahippocampal gyrus in panic patients responsive to lactate infusion, which was not present in normals or panic patients not responsive to lactate. However, the difficulty differentiating small brain structures, such as the amygdala, and capturing an image during a panic episode have limited the utility of imaging approaches (Gorman et al., 2000). In addition, hypocapnia-induced vasoconstriction caused by hyperventilation during a panic attack can obscure assessments of cerebral blood flow.

Further improvements in neuroimaging technology, including the use of functional magnetic resonance imaging (fMRI), may aid in further clarifying the brain structures involved in panic disorder. A recent study (Bystritsky et al., 2001) comparing fMRI in six patients with panic disorder in varying levels of anxiety-provoking situations to six normal controls found increased activity in the inferior frontal cortex, hippocampus, and the anterior and posterior cingulate, extending into the orbitofrontal cortex and to both hemispheres. The authors suggest that this is an important neural circuit in panic, related to retrieval of strong emotional events, facilitating recapitulation of traumatic experiences. There is limited overlap in this neural circuit with the various models described above.

Cognitive-Behavioral Model

The central feature of the cognitive-behavioral model of panic disorder is the patient's catastrophic misinterpretation of events and/or somatic sensations leading to feelings of imminent danger associated with panic attacks (Craske, 1988). Patients develop a fear of the somatic sensations associated with panic attacks, considered part of the body's fight-or-flight alarm response. Catastrophic misinterpretations of these sensations include fears of dying (e.g., having a heart attack or suffocating) and fears of losing control or "going crazy." Somatic sensations associated with panic attacks come to serve as cues of danger and potential panic via classical conditioning. Thus, increasing anxiety leads to increased fear of somatic sensations, which leads to increasing anxiety in a vicious cycle. Patients become vigilant to the presence of these sensations, increasing the likelihood that experienced somatic sensations will trigger the escalating cycle and panic attacks. These panic reactions may come to be directly triggered by somatic sensations, not requiring the presence of catastrophic cognitions. In addition to somatic sensation, cues can also be associated with particular situations. This can lead to agoraphobic avoidance to avoid panic triggers. As Freud (1895a) stated: "In the case of agoraphobia, etc., we often find the recollection of an anxiety attack; and what the patient actually fears is the occurrence of such an attack under the special conditions in which he believes he cannot escape it" (p. 81).

Psychodynamic Model of Panic Disorder

In the psychodynamic model of panic disorder, anxiety symptoms are believed to be triggered by unconscious fantasies and impulses that are experienced by the individual as unacceptable, and threaten to break through into consciousness. The anxiety also represents the failure of defense mechanisms to adequately protect against the emergence of these wishes in undisguised form. In addition, the physical symptoms of panic, as well as many other aspects of life, are a result of "compromise formations" (Freud, 1895b) between wishes that are unacceptable and defenses against these very wishes. As described below, unconscious fears of loss, separation, and conflicts about autonomy are important elements underlying panic attacks. Angry fantasies triggered by fantasies of being controlled by others, or unprotected by loved ones, represent an additional threat to attachment that can trigger panic. Panic attacks in part represent partial expressions of these wishes by easing the danger of separation, averting conscious expressions of anger, and expressing anger covertly by coercing others to respond to severe somatic complaints.

Busch et al. (1991) and Shear et al. (1993) developed a psychodynamic formulation for panic disorder based on psychological, clinical, and temperamental observations and studies about panic patients. Beginning with the studies of temperament of Kagan et al. (1990) and Biederman et al. (1990), the authors postulated that panic patients are constitutionally predisposed to fearfulness of unfamiliar situations early in life. This is based in part on Rosenbaum et al.'s (1988) finding that children of patients with panic disorder, who are likely to develop panic, are found to have a high rate of behavioral inhibition. Behaviorally inhibited children "manifested long latencies to interact when exposed to novelty, retreated from the unfamiliar, and ceased play and vocalizations while clinging to their mothers" (Biederman et al., 1990, p. 21). In addition, children with behavioral inhibition demonstrated higher rates of childhood anxiety disorders (Biederman et al., 1990). Rosenbaum et al. (1993) reported that 75 percent of children with separation anxiety at age 21 months had agoraphobia at 7 years, while only 7 percent of 21-month olds without separation anxiety developed agoraphobia. Additional evidence of early life fearfulness comes from retrospective assessments by panic patients. This predisposition leads individuals at risk to experience a sense of fearful dependency on parents to provide a sense of safety. Because these children experience narcissistic humiliation due to their fearfulness, they tend to blame their difficulties on parents, who are perceived as unreliable. Alternatively, such individuals may develop a fearful dependency through actual traumatic or frightening experiences in childhood. Patients with panic have been found in clinical observations and systematic assessments to perceive their parents as controlling, overprotective, temperamental, and frightening (Tucker, 1956; Parker et al., 1979; Arrindell et al., 1983).

In addition to struggling with separation fears, these fearful children feel threatened by the anger they experience toward their parents, whom they view as critical or unreliable. They fear that their anger will drive away their needed parents, increasing their sense of fearful dependency. Thus, a vicious cycle develops: anger leads to anxiety and guilt, adding to fearful dependency, eventually spiraling to panic levels of anxiety (see Fig. 12.2). Panic attacks diminish conscious anger, facilitate increased attachment, punish the self for guilt about angry feelings, and tend to punish others via coercing them to respond to patients' dire needs. Life events that involve actual or perceived separation, that have been found to occur at a high rate prior to panic onset, tend to trigger this vicious cycle in adulthood. In addition, aggressive, competitive wishes can

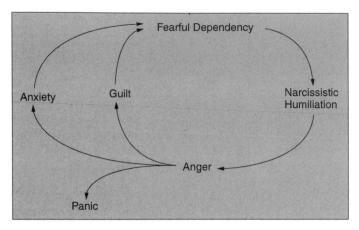

Figure 12.2. Vicious cycle of emotions in panic disorder.

be unconsciously experienced as threats to important attachments. Thus, life events that involve success or an increase in responsibilities may also trigger panic. Approaches to working with these dynamics psychotherapeutically have been developed and will be described below.

TREATMENT OF PANIC DISORDER

Medications, including tricyclic antidepressants, selective serotonin reuptake inhibitors, monoamine oxidase inhibitors, and benzodiazepines, as well as cognitive-behavioral therapy (CBT) have demonstrated efficacy for treatment of panic disorder in multiple double-blind, placebo-controlled studies. Common concerns have also surfaced in some of these studies (Nagy et al., 1989; Noyes et al., 1989; 1991; Pollack et al., 1993; Barlow et al., 2000). Because of the narrower definition of panic disorder that was used prior to 1994 (Shear and Maser, 1994), very few panic studies to date have assessed broader quality of life aspects of treatment response. Many patients have persistent, though frequently less intense, symptoms that may cause persistent morbidity and functional impairment following completion of treatment (Nagy et al., 1989; Noyes et al., 1991; Pollack et al., 1993). For example, in the most recent large-scale, multicenter, highly controlled outcome study of patients with panic disorder, patients treated with imipramine demonstrated only a 45.8 percent full remission rate while those treated with CBT had a remission rate of 48.7 percent (Barlow et al., 2000).

Combination treatments of antipanic medications and psychotherapy have shown mixed results. In the multicenter panic study referred to above, CBT imparted little additional benefit to imipramine treatment of panic disorder (Barlow et al., 2000). Other studies have found benefits from adding CBT to pharmacotherapy, but this has not yet been demonstrated in a randomized trial (Otto et al., 1999). Marks et al. (1993), in a study of benzodiazepines and CBT for treatment of panic, found that patients receiving the combination treatment did less well than those treated with CBT alone.

There is also evidence that CBT can aid in withdrawal from other medications (Otto et al., 1993).

Psychodynamic psychotherapy has undergone very little in the way of systematic study. However, in a randomized, controlled trial, Wiborg and Dahl (1996), employing a manualized form of psychodynamic psychotherapy, demonstrated that 3-month, weekly psychodynamic psychotherapy in addition to clomipramine (CMI) significantly reduced relapse rate at 18-month follow-up (9 percent 18 month relapse rate-combined cell), in comparison with patients treated with CMI alone (91 percent). This study unfortunately did not control for frequency of therapist contact.

Psychopharmacological Treatments

Several antidepressant medications and benzodiazepines have been found to be efficacious for panic treatment. Currently, selective serotonin reuptake inhibitors (SSRI's) are considered first-line treatment with regard to issues of safety and tolerability (APA, 1998). Paroxitene (Lydiard et al., 1998), fluvoxamine (Hoehn-Saric et al., 1993), fluoxitene (Michelson et al., 1998), sertraline (Rappaport et al., 1998), and citalopram (Wade et al., 1997) have all been found to be effective in placebo-controlled trials. Of these agents, paroxitene and sertraline are approved by the Food and Drug Administration (FDA) for the treatment of panic disorder. SSRIs were originally thought to have superior efficacy to tricyclic antidepressants, but treatment trials with larger numbers of subjects have suggested they are equivalent (Otto et al., 2001). Despite their overall tolerability, SSRIs may still have troubling side effects. These include sexual dysfunction, gastrointestinal symptoms (although these typically resolve), insomnia, and weight gain over time. Venlafaxine also shows promise for treatment of panic disorder (Pollack et al., 1996; Geracioti, 1995) but requires monitoring for blood pressure increases. Particularly important for panic patients, these medications can cause an initial increase in anxiety or agitation. Therefore, it is usually advisable to start these medications at lower doses than in major depression and to increase as tolerated. Benzodiazepines can aid in diminishing this agitation, which usually resolves within 1 to 2 weeks. Finally, following discontinuation of the medication, patients can struggle with a withdrawal syndrome, which includes dizziness, irritability, headache, nausea, and sometimes anxiety (Lejoyeux and Ades, 1997). This typically resolves within 2 weeks and can usually be eased with a slower taper of medication.

Although clomipramine, imipramine, and desipramine have shown efficacy in comparison with placebo (Lydiard, 1987; Uhlenhuth et al., 1989; Mavissakalian and Perel, 1995; Lecrubier et al., 1997; Fallon and Klein, 1997), they all have significant side effects, high rates of intolerance, and safety concerns (Noyes et al., 1989; Papp et al., 1997). These include anticholinergic side effects (dry mouth, constipation, difficulty urinating, blurred vision), sedation, orthostatic hypotension, weight gain, and sexual dysfunction. These agents can prolong cardiac conduction and in overdose or in patients with preexisting cardiac conduction defects, a fatal arrhythmia may occur. Clinical experience suggests that although monoamine oxidase inhibitors (MAOIs) are effective in treating panic, the dietary restrictions and the risks of serious side effects (potential hypertensive reaction, along with weight gain and orthostasis), greatly limit the usefulness of these agents. Some clinicians believe that MAOI's are superior to tricyclics for panic, but there is limited systematic data to support this notion, particularly given that most MAOI studies were done before the DSM III criteria for panic disorder were developed (Sheehan et al., 1980).

Benzodiazepines remain an important class of medications for treatment of panic disorder, despite their replacement as first-line agents by antidepressants. In clinical practice, these medications can provide rapid relief of panic attacks, allowing symptom reduction while other treatments, such as antidepressants or psychotherapy, are being introduced. An important limitation to the use of benzodiazepines is their lack of impact on depression or other commonly coexisting psychiatric conditions, such as agoraphobia, specific phobias, or obsessive-compulsive disorder. Side effects include sedation, fatigue, and memory impairment. Although these medications carry a potential risk of abuse, the risk is felt to be overestimated in patients with anxiety disorders (Uhlenhuth, et al., 1989). Avoidance of these medications out of fear of abuse may be more problematic than the risk of abuse. If benzodiazepines are employed over an extended period of time, patients are at risk for recurrence of symptoms when they are tapered. A more rapid taper or abrupt discontinuation or tapering of a shorter acting benzodiazepine increases the risk of symptom resurgence. Thus, a taper is best accomplished over 3 to 6 months, with a reduction in the rate of taper after the dose has reached half its original level.

More recent data suggests that some of the anticonvulsants may be effective in treating panic disorder. The potential efficacy of valproate has been indicated in two studies (Lum et al., 1990; Woodman and Noyes, 1994). Valproate is generally a well-tolerated agent but requires monitoring of hepatic enzymes, and there are rare reports of pancreatitis. Weight gain is also a potential side effect.

Cognitive-Behavioral Treatment Studies

Cognitive-behavioral treatments for panic disorder have been subjected to extensive clinical trials and have been found to be efficacious treatments for treating this condition (Lydiard et al., 2001, APA, 1998). The cognitive-behavioral approach to panic disorder generally involves components of interoceptive exposure and cognitive restructuring. Therapy consists of restructuring of cognitions, exposure, and training in arousal reduction. Patients are educated about the cognitive-behavioral model as a means for helping them to understand their illness. Therapists also work with patients to reappraise catastrophic beliefs by examining them as hypotheses and noting the distortions of the risk of catastrophic outcome. Using interoceptive exposure, somatic sensations similar to panic are induced in patients with a variety of techniques. Repeated exposure to these cues in a safe setting reduces patients' catastrophic experience of them. Patients are also taught skills for coping with these sensations. Finally, patients are taught arousal reduction skills, such as diaphragmatic breathing and relaxation techniques. Some CBT approaches to panic also include in vivo exposure to phobic situations and cue-controlled relaxation exercises.

Despite its consistently demonstrated efficacy for panic disorder, not all patients respond to CBT, nor does it provide total symptom relief for all patients who respond to it. Many long-term outcome studies of CBT for panic disorder report impressive response rates (Marks et al., 1993; Craske et al., 1991; Clark et al., 1994; Fava et al., 1995). Nonetheless, even in the most closely controlled sample that reports the highest response rate (Marks et al., 1993), 38 percent of patients remained symptomatic after completing their CBT trial. Despite the research success of CBT, in clinical practice many panic patients are unable or unwilling to comply with behavioral treatment (APA, 1998; Fava et al., 1995). As many of the groundbreaking CBT studies were performed before the articulation of the NIMH collaborative study on panic disorder that provided specific recommendations about domains of illness that should be monitored during panic disorder treatment trials (Shear and Maser, 1994), few CBT studies have assessed broader quality of life aspects in response to treatment. Additionally, many of the earlier CBT studies suffered from lack of systematic assessment and/or tracking of concomitant nonstudy antipanic medication use that likely contributed to measured outcome. The effects of these untracked medications became particularly important in studies that followed patients over long periods of time (Milrod and Busch, 1996).

In a novel study design using ideographic response, that assessed panic patients who had been treated with CBT over 24 months (assessing longer time periods than are usually evaluated cross sectionally), Brown and Barlow (1995) found that many patients experienced a fluctuating course of panic symptomatology after their CBT trial. Twenty-seven percent of these 63 patients sought further antipanic treatment during the 24-month follow-up interval because of continuing symptoms, but the additional treatment was not helpful. In this study, pretreatment panic severity was the most accurate predictor of poor response. This implies that further research on sicker patients needs to be accomplished.

Very few studies have assessed the efficacy of CBT in addition to antipanic medication. Marks et al. (1993) evaluated the comparative efficacy of alprazolam and CBT, both alone, and in combination in patients with panic and agoraphobia, and found that alprazolam dampened patients' response to CBT. In the recent multicenter treatment trial that extended over 7 years, CBT alone was compared with placebo, imipramine alone, the combination of both CBT and imipramine, and CBT plus placebo for panic disorder (Barlow et al., 2000). In this study, all active treatments produced responses superior to placebo, but the combined treatment cell was not significantly superior to either CBT or imipramine alone after the active treatment phase. However, the combination of CBT and imipramine conferred more substantial advantage than either treatment alone by the end of the 6-month maintenance phase of the study. The major limitation of this important multicenter study is that the patients studied had only mild to moderate agoraphobia with panic, leaving the question open as to how sicker patients with panic disorder would respond to these interventions. CBT has not been extensively studied in populations with combined panic and major depression, but some reports exist that indicate that it may be useful for these patients as well (Lydiard et al., 2001; Barlow et al., 2000).

Psychodynamic Psychotherapy for Panic Disorder

Systematic Psychodynamic Research. Systematic study of psychodynamic treatment*s* for panic disorder is in its infancy. As described above, a significant minority of patients fail to respond to the more extensively empirically tested treatments, and many patients experience residual symptoms after pharmacological and cognitive-behavior treatments (Nagy et al., 1989; Noyes et al., 1989, 1991; Pollack et al., 1993; Barlow et al., 2000). Thus, attention to psychodynamic issues may potentially provide further improvement for some patients.

Milrod and Shear (1991) found 35 cases in the literature with DSM-III-R panic disorder who were successfully treated with psychodynamic psychotherapy or psychoanalysis alone. Since then, other successful psychodynamic treatments for patients with panic disorder have been reported (Milrod, 1995; Stern, 1995; Renik, 1995; Busch et al., 1996; Milrod et al., 1996). Clinical reports cannot substitute for controlled clinical trials. Nonetheless, these reports suggest that psychodynamic treatment alone can bring symptomatic relief, as rapidly as psychopharmacologic or cognitive-behavioral interventions. This approach therefore deserves systematic study. As mentioned above, Wiborg and Dahl (1996) randomized controlled trial of psychodynamic psychotherapy in combination with clomipramine suggests the value of psychodynamic psychotherapy in reducing relapse in panic patients treated with clomipramine.

To further study a psychodynamic approach to panic disorder treatment in a systematic manner, other authors have developed clearly defined, panic-specific psychodynamic treatments in order to facilitate outcome research. One such approach shall be described below.

Panic-Focused Psychodynamic Psychotherapy (PFPP). PFPP is a modified form of psychodynamic psychotherapy that maintains central psychodynamic principles (Milrod et al., 1997). These include the core idea that unconscious mental dynamisms are responsible for biopsychological symptoms, such as panic attacks. The treatment makes use of fantasies, free association, and the centrality of the transference in effecting therapeutic change. The therapist focuses attention on all of these processes as they connect to the patient's experience of panic. Principles that have been observed to be common psychological dynamisms for panic patients, such as their difficulty with separation, inform interpretive efforts. Common factors with other psychodynamic psychotherapies include techniques of clarification, confrontation, and interpretation in and outside of the transference.

An open trial of PFPP has been completed (Milrod et al., 2001, 2000). In this study, PFPP followed a 24-session, psychodynamic psychotherapy program, delivered twice weekly in 45 to 50 min sessions, over 12 weeks. Twenty-one patients with primary DSM-IV panic disorder entered the treatment trial. Four patients dropped out. Sixteen of 21 patients experienced remission of panic and agoraphobia. Treatment completers with major depression ($N = 8$) also experienced remission of their depression. Symptomatic and quality of life improvements were substantial and consistent across all measured areas. Symptomatic gains were maintained over 6 months. While the sample size in this study was too small to draw firm conclusions, as a result of this pilot research, the authors concluded that psychodynamic psychotherapy appears to be a promising nonpharmacological treatment for panic disorder. A randomized controlled trial of PFPP conducted by the same group of researchers is currently underway. The clinical utility of this treatment approach for subpopulations of patients with panic disorder has yet to be tested. Empirical investigation must confirm these encouraging initial findings.

In summary, little attention has been paid to the intrapsychic aspects of panic disorder until recently. Based on reports in the literature, clinical experience, and some promising systematic research, there is encouraging evidence that a psychodynamic approach (that emphasizes unconscious mental processes, fantasy, free association, and interpretation of transference developed within psychotherapy) may be an important tool for optimal treatment of some patients with panic disorder. Psychodynamic psychotherapy may also be useful for residual symptoms, possibly linked to early life experiences, that continue to interfere with optimal emotional well-being and interpersonal functioning.

LONG-TERM OUTCOME OF TREATMENT TRIALS FOR PANIC DISORDER

Patients with panic disorder are a highly symptomatic, help-seeking group who tend toward recurrent exacerbations of symptoms (Pollack and Otto 1997; Pollack and Marzol, 2000; Faravelli et al., 1995). It is therefore important to gauge not only the effectiveness of treatments over the short term but to ascertain their effectiveness over longer follow-up intervals. Useful data with regard to long-term outcome, however, has been limited thus far in the literature. In a review of follow-up studies to date, Milrod et al. (1996) found that most did not monitor concurrent nonstudy treatments (e.g., untracked medication use in CBT studies or ongoing psychotherapies in medication studies) either during study treatment or during follow-up intervals. The authors concluded that there was limited evidence that patients responding to short-term treatments maintained their gains if they did not receive further treatment. Bakker et al. (1998) conducted a meta-analysis of studies that had information on long-term follow-up of treatments of panic disorder. Their analysis indicated that treatments of panic disorder show effectiveness acutely and at follow-up, finding an advantage to antidepressants plus in vivo exposure over cognitive behavioral treatments. Nevertheless, the authors note that an important limitation of their findings was "the studies presented surprisingly little information on the type of additional treatment received, frequency of visits to therapists, and kind and amount of medication during the follow-up period" (p. 417).

Barlow et al.'s (2000) study makes a strong case for the importance of monitoring both acute and longer-term response to treatments in determining the treatment efficacy for panic disorder. Patients in this study received either imipramine, up to 300 mg/d, CBT, CBT plus imipramine, CBT plus placebo, or placebo for a 3-month period. Patients who responded to treatment were seen monthly in a maintenance schedule that provided treatment similar to what they received in the acute phase for an additional 6 months. They were then followed for 6 months after all treatment was discontinued.

After the acute phase, while all active treatments were superior to placebo, CBT plus imipramine showed limited superiority over CBT alone, but not CBT plus placebo. However, CBT plus imipramine was superior to both CBT alone and CBT plus placebo after the maintenance phase. In responders to the treatment, the level of response to imipramine was found to be superior to that of CBT after the acute phase, and this trend continued after the maintenance phase. However, in the follow-up period, responders to imipramine, with or without CBT, had much higher rates of relapse than those who received CBT without medication. At follow-up, CBT alone and CBT plus placebo were superior to placebo, but imipramine and imipramine plus CBT were not. The study suggests that while medication may be a more effective initial intervention, CBT may have a more durable effectiveness, and medication may lead to a greater potential for relapse at drug discontinuation.

More recent studies are being designed more carefully to assess the nature of specific interventions the patients may receive in the follow-up period (Milrod et al., 2001; de Beurs et al., 1999; Mavissakalian and Perel, 1999). De Beurs et al. (1999), for example, in a naturalistic follow-up at 2 years of panic patients treated in four treatment conditions, more carefully assessed and reported interim treatment. Patients had received either fluvoxamine combined with exposure, placebo plus exposure, psychological panic management plus exposure, or exposure alone. Fluvoxamine plus exposure was found to be superior after acute treatment, but there were no significant differences between treatments at 2-year follow-up. Seventy-seven percent of patients received additional treatment during the follow-up period, which the authors attributed to the incomplete impact of the acute treatment. Patients were found to have had additional benefit from the follow-up treatment.

Mavissakalian and Perel (1999) treated 110 patients with panic disorder for 6 months with imipramine at 2.25 mg/kg/day. Thirty patients dropped out during this period due to typical imipramine side effects. Fifty-six patients who remitted and consented were placed into a double-blind maintenance condition ($n = 29$) or a placebo ($n = 27$) and followed for 12 months. The patients were not permitted to obtain treatment interventions outside the study. Within the study, they could obtain 1 or 2 crisis intervention sessions, but not panic-focused cognitive or behavioral treatment. Relapse in the maintenance treatment ($n = 1$) was significantly lower than in placebo ($n = 10$). However, the authors also note that 8 patients dropped out of the imipramine group and 7 out of the placebo group, although these dropouts were clinically stable at their last assessment. Eleven patients required supportive sessions unrelated to panic (total of 13 visits).

In summary, then, both specific medications and cognitive-behavioral treatments have demonstrated efficacy in the short-term treatment of panic disorder. The chronic and recurrent nature of panic symptoms in many patients, however, may require the ongoing use of medication with its attendant side effects. Cognitive-behavioral treatments may aid in the reduction of vulnerability to panic recurrence, although this has yet to be clearly demonstrated. Psychodynamic treatments show promise but have not yet been subjected to efficacy studies. Current and future efforts should focus on which factors, neurophysiological and psychological, predispose to panic relapse, and to determine which interventions, or sequence of interventions, reduce vulnerability to panic recurrence.

REFERENCES

APA (American Psychiatric Association). (2000). *Diagnostic and Statistical Manual of Mental Disorders*, 4th Ed., Text Revision. American Psychiatric Association: Washington, DC.

APA (American Psychiatric Association) (1998). *Practice Guideline for the Treatment of Patients with Panic Disorder. Am J Psychiatry* 155:(May suppl.).

Arrindell W, Emmelkamp PMG, Monsma A, Brilman E (1983). The role of perceived parental rearing practices in the etiology of phobic disorders: A controlled study. *Br J Psychiatry* 143:183–187.

Bakker A, van Blakom AJLM, Spinhoven P, Blaauw BMJW, van Dyck R (1998). Follow-up on the treatment of panic disorder with or without agoraphobia. *J Nerv Ment Dis* 186:414–419.

Barlow DH, Gorman JM, Shear MK, Woods SW (2000). Cognitive-behavioral therapy, imipramine, or their combination for panic disorder. *JAMA* 283:2529–2536.

Biederman J, Rosenbaum JF, Hirshfeld DR et al. (1990). Psychiatric correlated of behavioral inhibition in young children of parents with and without psychiatric disorders. *Arch Gen Psychiatry* 47:21–26.

Breslau, N, Schultz L, Peterson E (1995). Sex differences in depression: A role for preexisting anxiety. *Psychiatry Res* 58:1–12.

Brown TA, Barlow DH (1995). Long-term outcome in cognitive-behavioral treatment of panic disorder: Clinical predictors and alternative strategies for assessment. *J Consult Clin Psychol* 63:754–765.

Busch FN, Cooper AM, Klerman GL, Penzer RJ, Shapiro T, Shear MK (1991). Neurophysiological, cognitive-behavioral, and psychoanalytic approaches to panic disorder. *Psychoanal Inquiry* 3:316–332.

Busch F, Milrod B, Cooper A, Shapiro T (1996). Grand rounds: Panic-focused psychodynamic psychotherapy. *J Psychother Pract Res* 5:72–83.

Bystritsky A, Pontillo D, Powers M, Sabb FW, Craske MG, Bookheimer SY (2001). Functional MRI changes during panic anticipation and imagery exposure (in process citation). *Neuroreport*; 12(18):3953–3957.

Cassano GB, Michelini S, Shear MK, Coli E, Maser JD, Frank E (1997). The panic-agoraphobic spectrum: A descriptive approach to the assessment and treatment of subtle symptoms. *Am J Psychiatry* 54:27–38.

Cassano GB, Rotondo A, Maser JD, et al. (1998). The panic agoraphobic spectrum: Rationale, assessment, and clinical usefulness. *CNS Spectrums* 3:35–48.

Charney DS, Heninger GR, Redmond DE Jr (1983). Yohimbine induced anxiety and increase noradrenergic function in humans: Effects of diazepam and clonidine. *Life Sci* 33:19–29.

Clark DM, Salkovskis PM, Hackman A, Middleton H, Anastasiades P, Gelder M (1994). A comparison of cognitive therapy, applied relaxation, and imipramine in the treatment of panic disorder. *Br J Psychiatry* 164:759–769.

Coryell W, Noyes R, Clancy J (1982). Excess mortality in panic disorder: A comparison with primary unipolar depression. *Arch Gen Psychiatry* 39:701–703.

Craske MG (1988). Cognitive behavioral treatment of panic. In Frances AJ, Hales RB (eds). Review of Psychiatry, Vol. 7. American Psychiatric Press: Washington DC, pp. 121–137.

Craske MG, Brown TA, Barlow DH (1991). Behavioral treatment of panic disorder: A two-year follow-up. *Behav Ther* 22:289–304.

Dager SR, Holland JP, Cowley DS, Dunner DL (1987). Panic disorder precipitated by exposure to organic solvents in the work place. *Am J Psychiatry* 144:1056–1058.

Davis M (1992): The role of the amygdala in fear and anxiety. *Annu Rev Neurosci* 15:353–375.

de Beurs E, van Blakom AJLM, Vand Dyck R, Lange A (1999). Long-term outcome of pharmacological and psychological treatment for panic disorder with agoraphobia: A 2-year naturalistic study. *Acta Psychiatr Scand* 99:59–67.

Deltito JA, Perugi G, Maremmani I, Mignani V, Cassano GB (1986). The importance of separation anxiety in the differentiation of panic disorder from agoraphobia. *Psychiatr Dev* 4:227–236.

Fallon BA, Klein DF (1997). Clomipramine treatment of panic disorder. *J Clin Psychiatry* 58:423–425.

Faravelli C, Paterniti S, Scarpato A (1995). 5-year prospective, naturalistic follow-up study of panic disorder. *Compr Psychiatry* 36:271–277.

Fava GA, Zielezny M, Savron G, Grandi S (1995). Long-term effects of behavioral treatment for panic disorder with agoraphobia. *Br J Psychiatry* 166:87–92.

Freud S (1895a). On the grounds of detaching a particular syndrome from neurasthenia under the description "anxiety neurosis." In Strachey J (ed and trans). *The Standard Edition of the Complete Psychological Works of Sigmund Freud*, Vol. 3. Hogarth Press: London, pp. 87–120.

Freud S (1895b): Studies on hysteria. In Strachey J (ed and trans). *The Standard Edition of the Complete Psychological Works of Sigmund Freud*, Vol. 2. Hogarth Press: London, pp. 1–183.

Geracioti JD (1995). Venlafaxine treatment of panic disorder: A case series. *J Clin Psychiatry* 56:408–410.

Gittelman R, Klein DF (1984). Relationship between separation anxiety and panic and agoraphobic disorders. *Psychopathology* 17(suppl 1):56–65.

Gorman JM, Kent JM, Sullivan GM, Coplan JD (2000). Neuroanatomical hypothesis of panic disorder, revised. *Am J Psychiatry* 157:493–505.

Gorman JM, Kent J, Martinez J, Browne S, Coplan JD, Papp LA (2001). Physiological changes during carbon dioxide inhalation in patients with panic disorder, major depression, and premenstrual dysphoric disorder. *Arch Gen Psychiatry* 58:125–131.

Hoehn-Saric R, Mcleod DR, Hipsley PA (1993). Effect of fluvoxamine on panic disorder. *J Clin Psychopharmacol* 13:321–326.

Hollifield M, Katon W, Skipper B et al. (1997). Panic disorder and quality of life: Variables predictive of functional impairment. *Am J Psychiatry* 154:766–772.

Kagan J, Reznick JS, Snidman N et al. (1990). Origins of panic disorder. In Ballenger J (ed). *Neurobiology of Panic Disorder*. Wiley: New York, pp. 71–87.

Katon W (1996). Panic disorder: Relationship to high medical utilization, unexplained physical symptoms, and medical costs. *J Clin Psychiatry* 57(Suppl 10):11–18.

Kendler KS, Neale MC, Kessler RC, Heath AC, Eaves LJ (1993). Panic disorder in women: A population-based twin study. *Psychol Med* 23:397–406.

Klein DF (1964). Delineation of two drug-responsive anxiety syndromes. *Psychopharmacology* 5:397–408.

Klein DF (1981). Anxiety reconceptualized. In Klein DF, Rabkin J (eds). *Anxiety: New Research and Changing Concepts*. Raven Press: New York, pp. 235–264.

Klein DF (1993). False suffocation alarms, spontaneous panics, and related conditions; An integrative hypothesis. *Arch Gen Psychiatry* 50:306–317.

Klein DF (2002). Response differences of spontaneous panic and fear. *Arch Gen Psychiatry* 59:567–569. (Letter in response to Gorman et al.: Physiological changes during carbon dioxide inhalation in patients with panic disorder, major depression, and premenstrual dysphoric disorder. *Arch Gen Psychiatry* 58:125–131, 2001.)

Last CG, Barlow DH, O'Brien GT (1984). Precipitants of agoraphobia: Role of stressful life events. *Psychol Rep* 54:567–570.

Lecrubier Y, Bakker A, Dunbar G, Judge R (1997). A comparison of paroxitene, clomipramine and placebo in the treatment of panic disorder, Collaborative Paroxitene Panic Study Investigators. *Acta Psychiatr Scand* 95:145–152.

LeDoux JE (1996). *The Emotional Brain: The Mysterious Underpinnings of Emotional Life*. Simon and Schuster: New York.

LeDoux JE, Iwata J, Ciccheti, Reis DJ (1988). Different projections of the central amygdaloid nucleus mediate autonomic and behavioral correlates of conditioned fear. *J Neurosci* 8: 2517–2519.

Lejoyeux M, Ades J (1997). Antidepressant discontinuation: A review of the literature. *J Clin Psychiatry* 58(July suppl):11–16.

Lum M, Fontaine R, Elie R Ontiveros A (1990). Divalproex sodium's antipanic effect in panic disorder: A placebo-controlled study. *Biol Psychiatry* 27:164A–165A.

Lydiard RB (1987). Desipramine in agoraphobia with panic attacks: An open, fixed-dose study. *J Clin Psychopharmacol* 7:258–260.

Lydiard RB, Steiner M, Burnham D, Gergel I (1998). Efficacy studies of paroxitene in panic disorder. *Psychopharmacol Bull* 34:175–182.

Lydiard RB, Otto MW, Milrod B (2001). Panic disorder. In Gabbard GO (ed). *Treatments of Psychiatric Disorders*, 3rd ed. American Psychiatric Press: Washington, DC.

Markowitz JS, Weissman MM, Ouellette R, Lish JD, Klerman GL (1989). Quality of life in panic disorder. *Arch Gen Psychiatry* 46:984–992.

Marks IM, Swenson RP, Basoglu M et al. (1993). Alprasolam and exposure alone and combined in panic disorder with agoraphobia. *Br J Psychiatry* 162:776–787.

Mavissakalian MR, Perel JM (1995). Imipramine treatment of panic disorder with agoraphobia: Dose ranging and plasma level-response relationships. *Am J Psychiatry* 152: 673–682.

Mavissakalian MR, Perel JM (1999). Long-term maintenance and discontinuation of imipramine therapy in panic disorder with agoraphobia. *Arch Gen Psychiatry* 56:821–827.

McCann UD, Ricaurte GA (1992). MDMA ("ecstasy") and panic disorder: Induction by a single dose. *Biol Psychiatry* 32:950–953.

Michelson D, Lydiard RB, Pollack MH et al. (1998). Outcome assessment and clinical improvement in panic disorder: Evidence from a randomized controlled trial of fluoxitene and placebo. *Am J Psychiatry* 155:1570–1577.

Milrod B (1995). The continued usefulness of psychoanalysis in the therapeutic armamentarium for the treatment of panic disorder. *J Am Psychoanal Assoc* 43:151–162.

Milrod B, Busch F (1996). The long-term outcome of treatments for panic disorder: A review of the literature. *J Nerv Ment Dis* 184:723–730.

Milrod B, Shear MK (1991). Dynamic treatment of panic disorder: A review. *J Nerv Ment Dis* 179:741–743.

Milrod B, Busch F, Hollander E, Aronson A, Siever L (1996). A twenty-three year old woman with panic disorder treated with psychodynamic psychotherapy. *Am J Psychiatry* 153: 698–703.

Milrod B, Busch F, Cooper A, Shapiro T (1997). *Manual of Panic—Focused Psychodynamic Psychotherapy*. American Psychiatric Press: Washington, DC.

Milrod B, Busch F, Leon AC et al. (2000). An open trial of psychodynamic psychotherapy for panic disorder—a pilot study. *Am J Psychiatry* 157:1878–1880.

Milrod B, Busch F, Leon AC et al. (2001). A pilot open trial of brief psychodynamic psychotherapy for panic disorder. *J Psychother Pract Res* 10:239–245.

Nagy LM, Krystal JH, Woods SW, Charney DS (1989). Clinical and medication outcome after short-term alprasolam and behavioral group treatment in panic disorder: 2.5 year naturalistic follow-up study. *Arch Gen Psychiatry* 46:993–999.

Noyes R, Garvey MJ, Cook BL, Samuelson L (1989). Problems with tricyclic antidepressant use in patients with panic disorder or agoraphobia: Results of a naturalistic follow-up study. *J Clin Psychiatry* 50:163–169.

Noyes R Jr, Garvey MJ, Cook B, Suelzer M (1991). Controlled discontinuation of benzodiazepine treatment for patients with panic disorder. *Am J Psychiatry* 148:517–523.

Nutt D, Lawson C (1992). Panic attacks: A neurochemical overview of model and mechanism. *Br J Psychiatry* 160:165–178.

Otto MW, Pollack MH, Sachs GS, Reiter SR, Meltzer-Brody S, Rosenbaum JF (1993). Discontinuation of benzodiazepine treatment: Efficacy of cognitive-behavioral therapy for patients with panic disorder. *Am J Psychiatry* 150:1485–1490.

Otto MW, Pollack MH, Penaba SJ, Zucker BG (1999). Group cognitive-behavior therapy for patients failing to respond to pharmacotherapy for panic disorder: A clinical case series. *Behav Res Ther* 37:763–770.

Otto MW, Tuby KS, Gould RA, McLean RYS, Pollack MH (2001). An effect-size analysis of the relative efficacy and tolerability of serotonin selective reuptake inhibitors for panic disorder. *Am J Psychiatry* 158:1989–1992.

Panksepp J (1998). *Affective Neuroscience*. Oxford University Press: New York. (1997).

Papp LA, Schneier FR, Fyer AJ et al. (1979). Reported parental characteristics of agoraphobics and social phobics. *J Clin Psychiatry* 58:423–425.

Parker G (1979). Reported parental characteristics of agoraphobics and social phobics. *J Clin Psychiatry* 135:555–560.

Pitts FM, McClure JN (1967). Lactate metabolism in anxiety neurosis. *N Engl J Med* 277: 1329–1336.

Pollack MH, Marzol PC (2000). Panic: Course, complications, and treatment of panic disorder. *J Psychopharmacol* 14(2 Suppl 1):25–30.

Pollack MH, Otto MW (1997). Long-term course and outcome of panic disorder. *J Clin Psychiatry* 58(suppl 2):57–60.

Pollack MH, Otto MW, Tesar GE, Cohen LS, Meltzer-Brody S, Rosenbaum JF (1993). Long-term outcome after acute treatment with alprasolam and clonazepam for panic disorder. *J Clin Psychopharmacol* 13:257–263.

Pollack MH, Worthington JJ, Otto MW et al. (1996). Venlafaxine for panic disorder: Results from a double-blind, placebo controlled study. *Psychopharmacol Bull* 32:667–670.

Rappaport MH, Wolkow RM, Clary CM (1998). Methodologies and outcomes from the sertraline multicenter flexible-dose trials. *Psychopharmacol Bull* 34:183–189.

Reiman EM, Raichle ME, Butler FK, Herscovitch P, Robins E (1984). A focal brain abnormality in panic disorder, a severe form of anxiety. *Nature* 310:683–685.

Renik O (1995). The patient's anxiety, the therapist's anxiety, and the therapeutic process. In Roose S, Glick RA (eds). *Anxiety as Symptom and Signal*. Analytic Press: Hillsdale, NJ, pp. 121–130.

Rosenbaum JF (1997). Panic disorder: Making clinical sense of the latest research. *J Clin. Psychiatry* 58:127–134.

Rosenbaum JF, Biederman J, Bolduc-Murphy EA et al. (1993). Behavioral inhibition in childhood: A risk factor for anxiety disorders. *Harvard Rev. Psychiatry* 1:2–16.

Rosenbaum JF, Biederman J, Gersten M et al. (1988). Behavioral inhibition in children of parents with panic disorder and agoraphobia. *Arch Gen Psychiatry* 45:463–470.

Roth WT, Margraf J, Ehlers A et al. (1992). Stress test reactivity in panic disorder. *Arch Gen Psychiatry* 49:301–310.

Roy-Byrne PP, Stang P, Wittchen HU, Ustun B, Walters EE, Kessler RC (2000). Lifetime panic-depression comorbidity in the National Comorbidity Survey. Association with symptoms, impairment, course, and help-seeking. *Br J Psychiatry* 176:229–235.

Shear MK, Maser JD (1994). Standardized assessment for panic disorder research: A conference report. *Arch Gen Psychiatry* 51:346–354.

Shear MK, Cooper AM, Klerman GL, Busch FN, Shapiro T (1993). A psychodynamic model of panic disorder. *Am J Psychiatry* 150:859–866.

Sheehan DV, Ballenger J, Jacobsen G (1980). Treatment of endogenous anxiety with phobic, hysterical, and hypochondriacal symptoms. *Arch Gen Psychiatry* 37:51–59.

Skre I, Onsted S, Torgersen S, Lygren S, Kringlen E (1993). A twin study of DSM III-R anxiety disorders. *Acta Psychiatr Scand* 88:85–92.

Stern G (1995). Anxiety and resistance to changes in self-concept. In Roose S, Glick RA (eds). *Anxiety as Symptom and Signal*. Analytic Press: Hillsdale, NJ, pp. 105–119.

Swenson RP, Cox BJ, Woszezy CB (1992). Use of medical services and treatment for panic disorder with agoraphobia and for social phobia. *Can Med Assoc J* 147:878–883.

Torgersen S (1983). Genetic factors in anxiety disorders. *Arch Gen Psychiatry* 40:1085–1089.

Tucker WI (1956). Diagnosis and treatment of the phobic reaction. *Am J Psychiatry* 112:825–830.

Uhlenhuth EH, Matuzas W, Glass RM, Easton C (1989). Response of panic disorder to fixed doses of alprazolam or imipramine. *J Affect Disord* 17:261–270.

Wade AG, Lepola U, Koponen HJ, Pedersen V, Pedersen T (1997). The effect of citalopram in panic disorder. *Br J Psychiatry* 170:549–553.

Wade SL, Monroe SM, Michelson LK (1993). Chronic life stress and treatment outcome in agoraphobia with panic attacks. *Am J Psychiatry* 150:1491–1495.

Weissman MM, Klerman GL, Urankowitz J (1989). Suicidal ideation and suicide attempts in panic disorder and attacks. *NEJM* 321:1209–1216.

Wiborg IM, Dahl AA (1996). Does brief dynamic psychotherapy reduce the relapse rate of panic disorder? *Arch Gen Psychiatry* 53:689–694.

Woodman CL, Noyes R (1994). Panic disorder: Treatment with valproate. *J Clin Psychiatry* 55:134–136.

Zauber TS, Katon W (1996). Panic disorder and medical comorbidity: A review of the medical and psychiatric literature. *Bull Menninger Clinic* (2 Suppl A):12–38.

13

NATURE AND TREATMENT OF OBSESSIVE-COMPULSIVE DISORDER

Lisa A. Snider and Susan E. Swedo

Pediatrics and Developmental Neuropsychiatry Branch, National Institute of Mental Health, Department of Health and Human Services, Bethesda, Maryland

INTRODUCTION

Obsessive-compulsive disorder (OCD) is a complex brain disorder that affects the lives of 1 to 3 percent of children and adults worldwide without respect to cultural differences or geography. The onset of this illness can be as young as ages 2 to 4 years with approximately one-half of adults having experienced symptom onset during childhood or adolescence (Karno and Golding, 1990). The World Health Organization's 1996 summary of the global burden of disease found OCD to be the eighth leading cause of disease burden for adults ages 15 to 44 years in developed countries, and the fourth leading cause for women in this group. Almost one-third (28 percent) of the disease burden for all adults in this age group was attributed to mental illness, with 5 of the 10 leading causes including unipolar major depression (1), schizophrenia (4), self-inflicted injuries (5), bipolar disorder (6), and OCD (8) (Murray and Lopez, 1996).

Textbook of Biological Psychiatry, Edited by Jaak Panksepp
ISBN 0-471-43478-7   Copyright © 2004 John Wiley & Sons, Inc.

The symptoms of OCD are not new to our society and have been present and documented in many forms throughout written history. In medieval times, individuals who displayed sexual or blasphemous thoughts were considered to be possessed and would have been "treated" with an attempt to remove the offending spirit through various forms of torture often leading to death. One of the most well-recognized literary descriptions of OCD is Shakespeare's Lady MacBeth with her obsessive guilt and ritualistic hand-washing. Scrupulosity is a religious form of OCD documented for almost 500 years throughout the writings of members of the Roman Catholic Church. The described symptoms of this condition mirror our current definition of OCD (O'Flaherty, 1966). The Roman Catholic Church conducted the first systematic survey of scrupulosity in 1927 on 400 girls in a Catholic high school and found 17 of the girls to have behaviors and/or thoughts regarding religious preoccupations and cleaning and washing habits that were considered excessive (Mullen, 1927).

Obsessive-compulsive disorder was first described in the psychiatric literature in adults by Esquirol in 1839 and in children by Janet in 1903. Early reports in the literature contained descriptions of repetitive, unwanted thoughts or rituals often characterized by magical thinking. As the disorder came to be better defined, it was classified as one of the neuroses rather than a symptom of melancholy. By the early 20th century the description of OCD shifted to include psychodynamic features. Freud's writings conceptualized obsessions as resulting from unconscious conflicts and emotional antecedents (Freud, 1909; 1913). He also speculated on the similarities between the symptoms of OCD and children's games and religious rituals. However, even Freud questioned whether psychodynamic theory was sufficient to explain the symptoms of OCD.

Observations of the association between certain neurological disorders and OCD have lead to the current view of OCD as a neurobiologic illness. Clinical research has demonstrated an increase in obsessive-compulsive symptomatology in patients with neurologic diseases known to involve basal ganglia structures, including Sydenham chorea (Swedo et al., 1993), Tourette syndrome (Leckman et al., 1997), and Huntington's chorea (Cummings and Cunningham, 1992). Current neurobiological research has focused on the possible localization of brain circuits mediating obsessive-compulsive behaviors and possible mechanisms for behavioral encoding. This research has directly led to advancements in the diagnosis and treatment of OCD improving the quality of life and clinical outcomes for many people suffering with this illness.

EPIDEMIOLOGY

Although OCD was once considered rare in both the adult and pediatric populations, improvements in the recognition of this disorder have shown this illness to be a major worldwide heath problem. The first large-scale epidemiological study to include OCD as a separate category and to provide information about its incidence and prevalence was the U.S. Epidemiological Catchment Area (ECA) study (Robbins et al., 1981). This study was conducted on 18,500 adults using the Diagnostic Interview Schedule

(DIS) at five separate sites across the United States. The lifetime prevalence for OCD in this study ranged from 1.9 to 3.3 cases per 100 across the five sites. These rates were 25 to 60 times higher than had been estimated on the basis of clinical populations (Karno et al., 1988).

The most comprehensive study on cross-national epidemiology of OCD combined data from seven international epidemiologic studies done in the United States (the ECA study), Canada, Puerto Rico, Germany, Taiwan, Korea, and New Zeland (Weissman et al., 1994). The lifetime prevalence was remarkably similar among the different countries ranging from 1.9 per 100 in Korea to 2.5 per 100 in Puerto Rico, with the exception of 0.7 cases per 100 in Taiwan. It should be noted that the Taiwanese study reported lower rates for other psychiatric disorders as well (Hwu et al., 1989). The lifetime prevalence of OCD was found to be higher in women than men, with the exception of the German study, which had large standard errors in a smaller sample. In the New Zealand sample the female-male ratio was 3.8, while in Germany it was found to be 0.8. The samples from the other countries found OCD to be 1.2 to 1.8 times more likely in women than in men. The mean age at onset was found to be between 21.9 and 35.5 years across the studies (Weissman et al., 1994).

The rates of OCD in a younger population were assessed by (Flament et al., 1998) and colleagues, using trained mental health professionals and previously validated instruments to assess obsessive-compulsive symptomatology in an adolescent population. As part of a two-stage study of 5596 adolescents (Whitaker et al., 1990), the Leyton Obsessional Inventory was administered (along with other questionnaires on general mental health, anxiety, and eating disorders) to the entire high school population of a county 80 miles from New York City (Flament et al., 1988). Adolescents scoring above the clinical cut-off were interviewed by child psychiatrists with extensive clinical experience with OCD. A total of 20 subjects received a lifetime diagnosis of OCD (18 current and 2 with past illness). The weighted prevalence figure (without exclusion) for OCD was 1.9 percent, a figure that is in close agreement with the ECA estimates for adults. A 2-year follow-up demonstrated that the obsessive-compulsive symptoms were clinically significant, as the majority of subjects remained symptomatic (Berg et al., 1989).

In recent years, several additional epidemiological studies have been conducted in children and adolescents in the United States as well as abroad. In virtually all of these reports, the rates ascertained from direct child reports were higher than those derived from parent reports, supporting clinical data that children with OCD often hide their illness. Secrecy and difficulties of utilizing lay interviewers may have contributed to the low (0.5 percent) prevalence of OCD found by Wittchen and colleagues (1998) in a sample of 3021 adolescent subjects in Munich, Germany. Other investigators, such as Valleni-Basile et al. (1996) in the southeastern United States, Douglass et al. (1995) in New Zealand, and Zohar et al. (1992, 1999) in Israel, used mental health interviewers and semistructured clinical interviews and found more comparable rates of 2.9, 4.0, and 2.3 percent, respectively. A 2-year follow-up evaluation of the Israeli study found that the children who met the diagnostic criteria for OCD remained symptomatic (Zohar et al., 1992).

CLINICAL PRESENTATION

Obsessive-compulsive disorder is characterized by recurring obsessions or compulsions that cause significant distress or interference with normal routine, occupation, academics, or social activities. Obsessions can involve preoccupations with contamination, symmetry, pathologic doubting or uncertainty, harm to self and others, as well as preoccupations with sexual or violent thoughts, or a sense that something unpleasant may happen if a particular ritual is not performed. Compulsions include both repetitive physical behaviors and mental rituals such as repeating specific prayers or "protective" thoughts. Physical compulsions consist of ritualized behaviors such as washing, cleaning, counting, checking, repeating, arranging, or hoarding. Mental compulsions are less common but can be more problematic as they can cause significant interference and will be missed if not specifically asked about during a clinical evaluation. The majority of people with OCD have multiple obsessions and compulsions. The symptoms frequently change over time. A specific obsession or compulsion may be present 1 week and then disappear and be replaced by another, only to return after a period of 3 months or so. The obsessions and compulsions found in childhood-onset OCD have very similar content to those seen in adult-onset OCD (Table 13.1).

There is some controversy as to whether or not a compulsion can be present without an underlying obsession. The *Diagnostic and Statistical Manual of Mental Disorders*, Fourth Edition (DSM-IV) defines compulsions as repetitive behaviors that a person feels driven to perform in response to an obsession, although the current diagnostic criteria allow a diagnosis of OCD to be made with compulsions alone. In fact 35 percent of adults and about 40 percent of children deny that their compulsions are driven by an obsessive thought (Karno and Golding, 1990; Swedo, 1989). Some compulsions have been described as more ticlike in character. These behaviors require repetition until a feeling of anxiety or disquiet is alleviated. Frequently, these ticlike compulsions are not preceded by a specific obsessive thought.

The occasional experience of "obsessive" thoughts and the performance of repetitive or ritualistic behaviors are common among both children and adults. In order to meet the criteria for OCD, these symptoms must be of a sufficient intensity and/or frequency to cause marked distress or impairment in function. For many people with OCD, impairment is minimized by their families' efforts to allow them to remain functional in their environments. These family members may not be consciously aware that their loved one is suffering from an illness that would benefit from diagnosis and treatment. A parent or spouse might wash their child's or partner's clothing every night or prepare and package food that is "safe" in order to allow the child to attend school or their spouse to continue to work outside the home.

Distress related to the intrusive nature of obsessions and compulsions is compounded by the fact that most patients retain an intact sense of insight. People with OCD are acutely aware that their thoughts and behaviors are extreme and nonsensical, yet they are unable to stop them. There is a great deal of shame and embarrassment surrounding the obsessive thoughts. Patients are aware that their thoughts and behaviors are "not acceptable," or violate social taboos, and attempt to hide the symptoms

TABLE 13.1. DSM-IV Diagnostic Criteria for Obsessive-Compulsive Disorder

A. Either obsessions or compulsions:

Obsessions as defined by (1), (2), (3), and (4):

(1) Recurrent and persistent thoughts, impulses, or images that are experienced, at some time during the disturbance, as intrusive and inappropriate and that cause marked anxiety or distress.

(2) The thought, impulses, or images are not simply excessive worries about real-life problems.

(3) The person attempts to ignore or suppress such thoughts, impulses, or images or to neutralize them with some other thought or action.

(4) The person recognizes that the obsessional thoughts, impulses, or images are a product of his or her own mind (not imposed from without as in thought insertion.)

Compulsions as defined by (1) and (2):

(1) Repetitive behaviors (e.g., hand washing, ordering, checking) or mental acts (e.g., praying, counting, repeating words silently) that the person feels driven to perform in response to an obsession or according to rules that must be applied rigidly.

(2) The behaviors or mental acts are aimed at preventing or reducing distress or preventing some dreaded event or situation; however, these behaviors or mental acts either are not connected in a realistic way with what they are designed to neutralize or prevent or are clearly excessive.

B. At some point during the course of the disorder, the person has recognized that the obsessions or compulsions are excessive or unreasonable. Note: This does not apply to children.

C. The obsessions or compulsions cause marked distress, are time consuming (take more than 1 hour a day), or significantly interfere with the person's normal routine, occupational (or academic) functioning, or usual social activities or relationships.

D. If another Axis I disorder is present, the content of the obsessions or compulsions is not restricted to it (e.g., preoccupation with food in the presence of an eating disorder; hair pulling in the presence of trichotillomania; concern with appearance in the presence of body dysmorphic disorder; preoccupation with drugs in the presence of a substance use disorder; preoccupation with having a serious illness in the presence of hypochondriasis; preoccupation with sexual urges or fantasies in the presence of a paraphilia; or guilty ruminations in the presence of major depressive disorder.)

E. The disturbance is not due to the direct physiologic effects of a substance (e.g., a drug of abuse, a medication) or a general medical condition.

Source: American Psychiatric Association (2000).

from their families, friends, and co-workers. This need for secrecy also contributes to the fact that many people suffering from significant symptoms do not seek treatment for months or even years. A recent report found that there was a 10-year delay between the onset of symptoms during adolescence and the seeking of professional help during adulthood (Hollander et al., 1996).

Current diagnostic criteria require recognition of the irrationality of obsessive-compulsive symptoms. However, this criterion has been the subject of some debate.

Young children are exempt from this DSM-IV criterion for a diagnosis of OCD, as they often have not achieved the cognitive development required to have insight. When adults with OCD are systematically assessed on the degree of insight they have into their obsessions, limited insight was found up to 30 percent of the time (Eisen et al., 1998). In several studies of adults with OCD, it has been found that a subset of patients "believe" their obsessions at some point during the course of their illness (Insel and Akiskal, 1986; Kozak and Foa, 1994).

The differential diagnosis of OCD includes other psychiatric disorders that are characterized by repetitive behaviors and thoughts. To appropriately diagnose OCD, the content of the obsessions and/or compulsions cannot be completely attributed to another psychiatric illness. For example, a diagnosis of anorexia nervosa should be made if a person has only obsessive worries about gaining weight and compulsions that are centered on not allowing the consumption of calorie-containing foods. By the same token, all obsessions or compulsions revolve around a fear of a specific animal, situation, or object, a simple phobia should be diagnosed. The obsessions of OCD must be distinguished from the ruminations of major depression, racing thoughts of mania, and psychotic symptoms of schizophrenia. The compulsions of OCD must be distinguished from the stereotypic movements found in individuals with mental retardation or autism, the tics of Tourette syndrome, the stereotypies of complex partial seizures, and the ritualized self-injurious behaviors of borderline personality disorder.

COMORBIDITY

Comorbid psychopathology is common among patients with OCD. In a recently published study of a large health maintenance organization (HMO) population in northern California, 75 percent of adults with OCD were found to have at least one comorbid psychiatric diagnosis. Major depression affected 56 percent, other anxiety disorders affected 26 percent, including panic disorder and generalized anxiety disorder, and adjustment disorder affected 12 percent of the adult patients sampled (Fireman et al., 2001). The cross-national epidemiological study done by Weissman and colleagues also found that adults with OCD were at a substantially higher risk for having comorbid major depression or another anxiety disorder than persons without OCD at all seven sites in the study. Unlike the California HMO study, the risk of a comorbid anxiety disorder was found to be greater than the risk for a major depression. The overall proportion of persons with OCD who had a comorbid anxiety disorder (range 24.5 to 69.6 percent) was greater than those who had a comorbid major depression (range 12.4 to 60.3 percent). In the sample taken from the United States within this study, major depression affected 27 percent and another anxiety disorder affected 49 percent of adults with OCD (Weissman et al., 1994).

The patterns of comorbidity among childhood-onset cases are generally comparable to those for adult samples, with tic disorders and specific developmental disorders appearing more frequently in the pediatric populations. The California HMO study found that attention deficit hyperactivity disorder (ADHD) occurred most commonly

(34 percent), closely followed by major depression (33 percent), Tourette disorder (18 percent), oppositional defiant disorder (17 percent), and overanxious disorder (16 percent) (Fireman et al., 2001). The pattern of comorbidity found in this study was similar to that previously observed in the National Institute of Mental Health (NIMH) pediatric OCD cohort, where only 26 percent of the pediatric subjects had OCD as a single diagnosis. Tic disorders (30 percent), major depression (26 percent), and specific developmental disabilities (24 percent) were the most common comorbidities found. Rates were also increased for simple phobias (17 percent), overanxious disorder (16 percent), adjustment disorder with depressed mood (13 percent), oppositional disorder (11 percent), attention deficit disorder (10 percent), conduct disorder (7 percent), separation anxiety disorder (7 percent), and enuresis/encopresis (4 percent) (Swedo et al., 1989).

THE OCD SPECTRUM

In the past 10 years, research has begun to focus on a group of illnesses that have been labeled obsessive-compulsive spectrum (OC spectrum) disorders. People affected by these disorders have in common the symptoms of obsessive thoughts and compulsive behaviors and share a similar family history of mental illness and response to treatment. The current literature generally includes OCD, body dysmorphic disorder, hypochondriasis, and Tourette syndrome in the OC spectrum (Yaryura-Tobias and Neziroglu, 1997a, 1997b). Trichotillomania, eating disorders, and self-mutilation also have overlapping symptoms and some argue that they should be included in this group. Some authors also have included pathologic gambling and sexual impulse control problems within the spectrum (Hollander et al., 1996). All these conditions share a similar core in that a person performs an action or has repetitive thoughts that reduce their anxiety. This performance of a ritualistic behavior to alleviate anxiety is what maintains their disorder. Further research is needed to determine whether or not these phenomenologic similarities define a true "spectrum" of disorders or merely overlapping clinical features of several distinct disease entities.

Body Dysmorphic Disorder

Body dysmorphic disorder (BDD) was not recognized as a unique diagnosis until 1987. Since that time, there has been a marked increase in systematic research into the characterization, comorbidities, and treatment of BDD. The essential feature of BDD is preoccupation with an imagined defect in appearance in a normal-appearing person or a markedly excessive concern about a slight imperfection (Allen and Hollander, 2000). The preoccupation must cause significant distress or impairment in functioning and must not be confined to another disorder, for example, preoccupation with obesity in anorexia nervosa. BDD is relatively common and has been reported to affect 1.9 percent of nonclinical samples (Rich et al., 1992) and 12 percent of psychiatric outpatients (Zimmerman et al., 1998). Similar to OCD, serotonin reuptake inhibitors

(SRIs) (such as clomipramine, fluoxetine, and fluvoxamine) demonstrate specific efficacy in the treatment of BDD (Hollander et al., 1989; Phillips et al., 1998). Although only a few controlled studies on psychotherapy for patients with BDD have been done, cognitive-behavioral therapy has been found to be effective (Grant and Cash, 1995; Neziroglu et al., 1996).

Hypochondriasis

Hypochondriasis is characterized by the fear or belief that one has a serious illness with actual or perceived physical signs or symptoms. This fear or belief is not eliminated by appropriate reassurance from medical professionals or negative diagnostic evaluations. Occasionally the anxiety will be reduced for a short period of time after a negative medical workup, but it inevitably recurs when another symptom is noted. Many people who suffer from this disorder experience a cycle of intrusive thoughts about illness and disease followed by compulsive checking for possible signs of illness in themselves (Fallon et al., 2000). The characteristics that separate hypochondriasis from OCD are the single preoccupation with disease (rather than a shifting symptom content in OCD), the presence of somatic sensations, and the limited insight into the irrationality of the hypochondriacal concerns (Barsky, 1992). In hypochondriasis, the irrational fears are viewed as a rational concern about various signs and symptoms, while obsessive concerns about illness frequently occur in the absence of actual somatic sensations and are viewed as unrealistic (Fallon et al., 1991). The literature suggests that a chronic and an acute transient form of hypochondriasis exist. Acute onset has been associated with a good outcome among of 48 patients studied prospectively; greater improvement was associated with a shorter duration of illness and less depression at baseline (Noyes et al., 1994). Small case reports and clinical trials suggest that patients with hypochondriasis may be helped by treatment with one of the SRIs (Fallon et al., 1993, 1996).

Trichotillomania

Trichotillomania (TTM) is a complex, secretive condition of distressed hair pulling (O'Sullivan et al., 2000). There are limited data on the phenomenology of this disorder, but it appears to share many features with the other OCD spectrum disorders (Swedo and Leonard, 1992). TTM is characterized by the recurrent pulling out of one's hair resulting in noticeable hair loss. There is increased tension immediately before pulling or when attempting to resist the urge to pull and a sense of gratification or relief after the "right" hair has been plucked. This cycle must cause significant distress or impairment in order for the diagnosis of TTM to be made (American Psychiatric Association, 2000). Many people who suffer from problematic hair pulling do not meet the strict DSM-IV criteria, as they may not experience anxiety preceding the hair pulling and/or conscious relief after completing the behavior. The prevalence rate for TTM based on DSM-IIIR criteria in college students was found to be 0.6 percent, but when subthreshold hair pulling was included, this rose to 1.5 percent for males and 3.4

percent for females (Christenson et al., 1991a). Hair pulling is often comorbid with other psychiatric conditions, most commonly mood and anxiety disorders (Christenson et al., 1991b). Effective treatment of TTM involves a combination of behavioral psychotherapy, psychoeducation, peer support, and/or pharmacotherapy (Keuthen et al., 1998; Minichiello et al., 1994). Although the Food and Drug Administration (FDA) has not currently approved any medications for the treatment of TTM, several classes of medications, including the SRIs, have been reported to be of benefit (O'Sullivan et al., 1999).

NEUROBIOLOGY

Basal Ganglia Dysfunction

Systematic research over the past two decades has demonstrated that OCD is associated with dysfunction of the corticostriato-thalamocortical circuitry, particularly in the orbitofrontal cortex and caudate nucleus (see Saxena and Rauch, 2000, for review). The postulated models of pathogenesis is shown in Figures 13.1 and 13.2 demonstrates that dysfunction at several different points in the corticostriato-thalamocortical circuit might produce similar neuropsychiatric symptoms.

Evidence for basal ganglia dysfunction is provided by neuroimaging studies and the association of OCD with neurologic disorders known to involve basal ganglia structures, including Tourette syndrome, Sydenham chorea, and Huntington's chorea (Cummings and Cunningham, 1992). The first description of neurologically based OCD comes from Constantin von Economo's 1931 treatise on postencephalitic Parkinson's disease, wherein patients suffered basal ganglia destruction as a result of severe

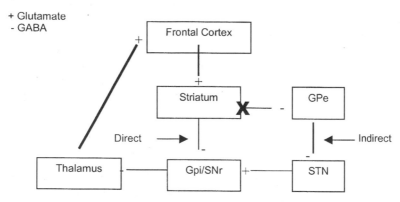

Figure 13.1. In this model, the primary area of dysfunction is in the striatum, reducing its inhibition of the globus pallidus externa (GPe; indirect pathway), which causes the GPe to increase its inhibition of the subthalamic nucleus, thus reducing the subthalamic nucleus' [STN's] stimulation of the globus pallidus interna/substantia nigra (pars reticulata) (GPi/SNr). This causes a reduction in GPi/SNr inhibition of the thalamus, which then can increase its stimulation of the frontal cortex (t, glutamate; −, GABA).

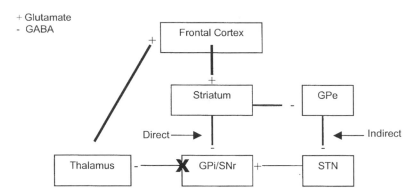

Figure 13.2. In this alternative construct, the globus pallidus interna (GPi) is the primary site of pathology. Without the GPi's inhibition, the thalamus increases its stimulation of the frontal cortex, which could produce symptoms directly, or through increased stimulation of the striatum (+ glutamate; −, GABA).

influenza infections. He noted the "compulsory nature" of the motor tics and ritualized behaviors that his patients exhibited. These patients, like OCD patients, described "having to" act, while not "wanting to"—that is, they experienced a neurologically based loss of volitional control (Von Economo, 1931).

Motor and vocal tics, including Tourette syndrome, occur frequently in association with OCD. The relationship between tics and OCD is complex, as motor tics often have a behavioral component suggestive of compulsive rituals, while OCD compulsions may lack accompanying obsessive thoughts, making them look like tics if the rituals are simple, repetitive behaviors like touching or tapping. The overlap between tics and OCD is most apparent in pediatric patient populations, where up to two-thirds of children with OCD are observed to have comorbid tics (Leonard et al., 1992) and 20 to 80 percent of children with Tourette disorder report obsessive-compulsive symptoms (Leckman et al., 1997). It is unknown just how the pattern and severity of obsessive-compulsive symptoms differ between patients with Tourette syndrome and those with primary OCD, but preliminary impressions suggest that the compulsions associated with Tourette syndrome may be less severe than in nontic OCD and more likely to involve symmetry, rubbing, touching, staring, or blinking rituals, rather than washing and cleaning (Leckman et al., 1997).

Indirect evidence for basal ganglia involvement in OCD is provided by the efficacy of psychosurgical lesions that disconnect the basal ganglia from the frontal cortex, particularly capsulotomy (Mindus, 1991) and cingulectomy (Dougherty et al., 2002). In capsulotomy, bilateral basal lesions are made in the anterior limb of the internal capsule in order to interrupt frontal-cingulate projections; however, the surgical target lies within the striatum, near the caudate nuclei. In order to perform a cingulectomy, the anterior portion of the cingulate gyrus is lesioned, interrupting tracks between the cingulate gyrus and the frontal lobes and destroying all of the efferent projections of the anterior cingulate cortex. Both procedures result in significant reduction of obsessions and compulsions. The success of psychosurgery is, of course, not conclusive evidence of a basal ganglia defect in OCD, as the lesions could be anywhere "upstream" from the site of surgical intervention (see Fig. 13.1), but it does focus interest on frontal-striatal tracts (for review, see Greenberg et al., 2000).

Neurotransmitter Abnormalities

Serotonin. The serotonergic hypothesis of OCD is based on, among other pieces of evidence, the selective efficacy of drugs with specific serotonergic activity (Ananth et al., 1981; Insel et al., 1985) and challenge tests with serotonergic agonists. Challenges with sumatriptin (Bastani et al., 1990) and mCPP metacholorophenyl-piperazine (Zohar et al., 1987, 1988; Pigott et al., 1991) show that OCD symptoms are exacerbated by these serotonin agonists. In contrast, metergoline, a serotonin antagonist, has been shown to protect against mCPP's behavioral effects (Pigott et al., 1991). Medications that block serotonin reuptake, such as clomipramine and the selective serotonin reuptake inhibitors (SSRIs), fluoxetine, fluvoxamine, sertraline, paroxetine, and citalopram, have been shown to be the most effective pharmacologic treatments for OCD. Clomipramine is a tricyclic antidepressant that is a *relatively* selective and potent inhibitor of active serotonin uptake in the brain (it also blocks histamine H_2 receptors, cholinergic, and adrenergic receptors and has antidopaminergic properties). Its metabolite, desmethylclomipramine, is also effective in blocking serotonin reuptake (and reuptake of noradrenaline) (Vythilingum et al., 2000). The response of OCD symptoms to clomipramine but not to the equally effective antidepressant desipramine (Ananth et al., 1981; Insel et al., 1985; Leonard et al., 1989) indicates a remarkable specificity of effect for the serotonin uptake inhibitors for OCD. No unselected group of depressed patients, for example, would show such a differential response.

Additional evidence for the serotonergic hypothesis is provided by several studies in children and adolescents with OCD. The first demonstrated that response to clomipramine correlated with pretreatment platelet serotonin concentration (Flament et al., 1985, 1987). A high pretreatment level of serotonin was a strong predictor of clinical response, and within this sample platelet serotonin concentrations were lower in the more severely ill patients. However, there were no differences in serotonin concentration from age-/sex-matched controls. A study of cerebrospinal fluid monoamines in 43 children and adolescents with OCD revealed that 5-hydroxyindole acetic acid (5-HIAA), the major metabolite of serotonin, correlated most strongly with response to clomipramine therapy; that is, the most successful responders had the highest levels of 5-HIAA in the cerebrospinal fluid (Swedo et al., 1992). A more recent study, employing positron emission tomography (PET) and serotonergic ligands, found evidence for decreased serotonin synthesis in the ventral prefrontal cortex and caudate nucleus in treatment naive OCD patients 8 to 13 years of age (Rosenberg et al., 1998). The latter study provides support for both the serotonergic hypothesis of OCD and also for dysfunction within the basal ganglia-frontal cortex circuitry.

The serotonergic hypothesis is undoubtedly too simplistic to account for the complexity of OCD. If the defect were limited to serotonergic dysfunction, clomipramine and the SSRIs should be effective in eliminating symptoms in all patients; unfortunately, this is not the case. Partial treatment response to SSRIs is common in OCD, but up to 40 percent of patients will fail to have any significant improvement with SSRI administration (Hollander et al., 2000). Individual patients also have variable patterns of response to the different SSRIs, suggesting that the nonserotonergic properties of the medications may also play key roles and that the antiobsessional effect may actually result from an alteration in the balance of serotonin and other monoamines and/or changes in receptor functions (Murphy et al., 1989). Support for this hypothesis is provided by the results of meta-analyses demonstrating that clomipramine (a neurochemically relatively nonspecific or "dirty" drug) is significantly more effective than the SSRIs, fluoxetine, fluvoxamine, and sertraline, in the treatment of OCD (Greist et al., 1995).

Dopamine and Other Neurotransmitters. Dopaminergic dysfunction in OCD is suggested not only by the obsessive-compulsive symptoms in patients with basal ganglia disorders but also by the increase in obsessive-compulsive symptoms following high-dose stimulant administration (Frye and Arnold, 1981) and occasional amelioration of symptoms following dopamine blocking agents (Goodman et al., 1990; McDougle 1997). High-dose stimulant administration has been thought to produce simple stereotypies, rather than more complex compulsive or obsessive behavior; however, "compulsive" symptoms have been observed in children with attention deficit disorder and hyperactivity during treatment with high-dose amphetamines (1 mg/kg *d*-amphetamine or 2 mg/kg methylphenidate) (Borcherding et al., 1990). For example, a 7-year-old boy spent several hours each evening vacuuming the carpet in his home, and another played with Lego blocks for 2 days, stopping only to eat and sleep. As in OCD, the children also became overly concerned with details and erased holes in their papers trying to get a single letter perfectly shaped. However, no psychological distress accompanied the obsessive-compulsive behaviors in the stimulant-induced cases, leading to speculation that repetitive thoughts and behaviors (obsessions and compulsions) may result from dopaminergic overactivity but that serotonin dysregulation is required for ego-dystonicity error. Observations in Tourette disorder appear to provide support for this hypothesis. In Tourette, motor and vocal tics are not reported to be ego-dystonic (although they may become physically uncomfortable) and appear to result from dopaminergic overactivity overcoming serotonergic inhibition. In contrast, if OCD is primarily a serotonergic defect, the disorder might arise from an inability to inhibit normal dopaminergic activity and the inappropriate release of dopaminergic-derived fixed action patterns (obsessions and compulsions). Ego-dystonicity could then be related to the primary serotonin defect, or secondary to the loss of volitional control (Swedo and Rapoport, 1990).

Neuroendocrine Dysfunction

Although most OCD investigations concentrate on hormonal aberrations as secondary rather than primary to the disorder, case reports and anecdotal experience suggest that hormonal dysfunction and OCD may be etiologically related (Swedo, 1989). OCD symptoms often begin during early puberty, and some female patients experience an increase in obsessive thoughts and rituals immediately before their menses. Other hints at an influence of gonadal steroid on obsessive-compulsive symptomatology include the increased frequency of OCD during the postpartum period (Rasmussen and Eisen, 1992) and reports of successful antiandrogen therapy for obsessive-compulsive symptoms (Casas et al., 1986). In the latter study, 5 out of 5 patients with OCD experienced a remission in their symptoms following treatment with cyproterone acetate, a potent antiandrogen. At the NIMH, two boys (ages 8 and 15) and a 14-year-old girl were treated with spironolactone, a peripheral antiandrogen (particularly antitestosterone) agent, and testolactone, a peripheral antiestrogen medication. All experienced a temporary reduction of obsessions and compulsions but relapsed within 3 to 4 months (Salzberg and Swedo, 1992).

Leckman and colleagues (1994) have suggested that oxytocin abnormalities may be involved in OCD. The investigators cite oxytocin-mediated mating behaviors in animals as a possible model for some OCD symptoms (Leckman and Mayes, 1999) and found abnormal concentrations of cerebrospinal fluid (CSF) oxytocin among a small group of children with OCD and tic disorders. In a larger group of 43 children and adolescents studied at the NIMH, CSF oxytocin levels were not significantly correlated with OCD severity but were correlated with depressive symptoms (Swedo et al., 1992). Interestingly, arginine vasopressin (AVP) concentrations decreased following treatment with clomipramine (Altemus et al., 1994), although baseline concentrations had shown a negative correlation with symptom severity (Swedo et al., 1992). In adult patients with OCD, significantly increased CSF AVP concentrations at baseline were found, and it was noted that patients secreted significantly more AVP into plasma in response to hypertonic saline than did controls (Altemus et al., 1992). The latter results are in keeping with Barton's (1987) observations of OCD among patients with diabetes insipidus, a disorder with elevated central AVP concentrations.

At present, there is not sufficient evidence to implicate hormonal dysfunction as a direct cause of OCD. However, some intriguing data build a circumstantial case for an association between OCD and growth hormone abnormalities, perhaps through the serotonergic system. In the epidemiological study of OCD among high school students, described earlier, males with OCD were noted to be smaller and lighter than the community of normal controls (Flament et al., 1988). This was also shown to be true of males with other anxiety disorders (Hamburger et al., 1989). There were no reductions in the height or weight of the adolescent girls with OCD. The small size of the OCD males could be due to an effective lack of growth hormone, or to a delay in the pubertal growth spurt, although, of course, no causality is demonstrated by the relationship. To address the issue of causality, future research might employ direct assays, hormonal challenges, or therapeutic interventions.

Genetics

Obsessive-compulsive disorder had been viewed as an inherited disorder long before recent advances in molecular biology allowed clinical researchers to isolate the genetic mechanisms of illness (for additional information, see Chapter 14). Genetic factors associated with OCD have been demonstrated in a number of twin, family genetic, segregation, and gene association studies (Wolff et al., 2000). Twin studies are often the best indicator of a genetic diathesis, and the concordance rate for OCD among monozygotic twins has been reported to be as high as 65 percent (Rasmussen and Tsuang, 1986). A familial study compares the risk for OCD in the relatives of a proband with OCD to that of the general population or a control group; if this risk is found to be significantly higher in the relatives, the illness is considered to be familial. The familial rates of OCD and subclinical OCD have been found to be 15 times higher than expected (Pauls et al., 1995; Nicolini et al., 1993), although this demonstration is not in itself sufficient to determine genetic transmission. Segregation analyses use the pattern of illness within a sample of families to ascertain if this pattern could have been predicted from basic Mendelian genetic principles. Evidence of this nature for OCD suggests that some genes contributing major effects are associated with the manifestation of this disorder (Nicolini et al., 1991; Alsobrook et al., 1999). Both linkage analyses and association studies have isolated genetic markers and candidate genes that appear promising in isolating persons with OCD. The next step in understanding the genetics of OCD is the replication of these studies and the localization and characterization of the genes that confer susceptibility. As with other psychiatric disorders, multiple genes are expected to play an etiologic role.

Neuroimmune Dysfunction

Parallels between Sydenham chorea (SC), the neurologic manifestation of rheumatic fever, and childhood-onset OCD suggest that the two disorders may have a shared etiopathogenesis (Garvey et al., 1998). The disorders have similar regional localization, with evidence of dysfunction of the orbitofrontal-striatal circuitry in both OCD and SC. Further, over 70 percent of children with SC report that they have experienced an abrupt onset of repetitive, unwanted thoughts and behaviors 2 to 4 weeks prior to the onset of their chorea (Swedo et al., 1993). The obsessions and compulsions peak in intensity concomitantly with the chorea and wane away slowly over the ensuing months. A subgroup of patients error with childhood-onset OCD was noted to have a similar symptom course. The OCD exacerbations occurred following Group A beta-hemolytic streptococcal (GABHS) infections, accompanied by a cluster of comorbid symptoms, including emotional lability, separation anxiety, and attentional difficulties (Swedo et al., 1998). The children were young (6 to 7 years old at symptom onset), predominantly male, and often had comorbid tics. To indicate their shared clinical features (and presumed etiopathogenesis), the subgroup was identified by the acronym PANDAS—pediatric autoimmune neuropsychiatric disorders associated with streptococcal infections (Swedo et al., 1998).

The major distinguishing feature of the PANDAS subgroup is the temporal association between neuropsychiatric symptom exacerbations and GABHS infections—that is, positive (or rising) antistreptococcal antibody titers or a positive throat culture during neuropsychiatric symptom relapses and evidence of GABHS negativity during periods of remission (Perlmutter et al., 1998). This one-to-one correlation is necessary to distinguish GABHS-triggered exacerbations of the PANDAS subgroup from the more typical waxing and waning course seen in Tourette disorder and some cases of childhood-onset OCD. The temporal association between GABHS infections and neuropsychiatric symptom exacerbations suggests that prevention of the infections might result in decreased severity of the obsessive-compulsive symptoms. An 8-month long placebo-controlled crossover trial of penicillin prophylaxis was undertaken (4 months of penicillin followed by 4 months of placebo, or the reverse) (Garvey et al., 1999). The penicillin prophylaxis failed to achieve the primary objective of significantly reducing GABHS infections (14 of 35 infections occurred during the penicillin phase), so it was not surprising that there were no between-phase differences in OCD or tic severity. However, poor compliance appeared to contribute to penicillin's lack of effectiveness, as missed doses were frequent.

The role of the immune system in the etiology of OCD and tic disorders is unclear, but clinical observations suggest that symptoms result from a combination of local, regional, and systemic abnormalities (Hamilton et al., 2001). Magnetic resonance imaging (MRI) scans reveal enlargements of the caudate, putamen, and globus pallidus, which points to regional inflammatory changes (Giedd et al., 1996, 2000), while local autoimmune reactions are suggested by the presence of serum antibodies that cross-react with neurons of these same brain regions (Kiessling et al., 1994). Husby and colleagues were the first to describe cross-reactive antibodies in Sydenham chorea. Although the antibodies were labeled "antineuronal," the investigators postulated that the antibodies must have been raised against epitopes on the GABHS bacteria and then cross-reacted with cells of the caudate nucleus and subthalamus. It was the cross-reactivity that distinguished the antibodies found in the SC patients from antineuronal antibodies found in patients with systemic lupus erythematosus and other neurologic disorders (Husby et al., 1976). Several groups have subsequently reported the presence of antineuronal antibodies in patients with childhood-onset OCD and/or tic disorders (Singer et al., 1998; Morshed et al., 2001).

The striking effectiveness of immunomodulatory therapies, such as therapeutic plasma exchange and intravenous immunoglobulin (IVIG) suggests that there is systemic involvement, at least among severely affected individuals. A randomized, placebo-controlled trial of IVIG and plasma exchange was conducted on 29 children in the PANDAS subgroup at the NIMH (Perlmutter et al., 1999). Both of these immunomodulatory therapies produced significant improvements in neuropsychiatric symptom severity—placebo administration had no demonstrable effect on obsessive-compulsive symptoms at 1-month follow-up, while IVIG and plasma exchange treatments had produced mean symptom reductions of 45 and 58 percent (respectively). One-year follow-up revealed that 14 of 17 children (82 percent) continued to be "much" or "very much" improved from baseline (Perlmutter et al., 1999). The effectiveness of the immunomodulatory therapies suggests that circulating immune factors play a role in the pathophysiology of the symptoms, but no specific hypotheses can be formulated on the basis of the treatment response because of the broad spectrum of action of both IVIG and plasma exchange.

TREATMENT

Recent therapeutic advances have stimulated a considerable increase in research on OCD. Much of this research has focused on the serotonergic system and the neurobiology of the corticostriato-thalamocortical circuitry. Not only have changes in regional brain function been demonstrated among OCD patients responding to pharmacologic treatment but also among those with a good response to cognitive behavior therapy (Baxter et al., 1992; Schwartz et al., 1996). The finding that both behavior therapy and pharmacotherapy are able to alter biologic systems is further evidence that OCD is a "brain-based" disorder.

The treatment of OCD requires an integrated approach, as it is unusual for patients to respond fully to either cognitive-behavior therapy (CBT) or medications. A combination of behavioral and pharmacological approaches provides the maximum benefit for most patients. Obsessive-compulsive disorder is a chronic condition, and long-term therapy is often required, although lower medication doses may suffice during the latter stages of treatment (Ravizza et al., 1998). Discontinuation studies have shown that 80 percent of cases have relapsed by 2-year follow-up (Dolberg et al., 1996), although the rate is somewhat lower among patients receiving concomitant CBT (Stanley and Turner, 1995). When discontinuation is attempted, tapering should be gradual, usually over several weeks. Long-term or lifetime drug maintenance is suggested after 2 to 4 relapses.

Cognitive-Behavioral Therapy

Cognitive-behavioral therapy for OCD encompasses three treatment types: (1) exposure and response prevention (ERP), (2) cognitive therapy, and (3) relaxation training. Of the three, only ERP has been shown to be consistently effective in reducing OCD symptom severity (Shafron, 1998; Baer and Greist, 1997; Marks, 1997). Cognitive therapy is the changing of false beliefs regarding risk and responsibility, thereby challenging the reality of obsessions and the necessity for compulsions (Emmelkamp and Beens, 1991). It is generally viewed as ineffective if used as the sole treatment for OCD (Neziroglu et al., 2000) but may be helpful in facilitating participation in ERP (Shafron and Somers, 1998). Relaxation therapy is used mainly to manage anxiety during exposure but has not been shown to have direct benefits for the obsessive-compulsive symptoms (March, 1995).

Exposure and response prevention for OCD involves (1) daily exposure to cues avoided because of their inducing discomfort and compulsive rituals and (2) maintaining exposure and not ritualizing for at least an hour or until the discomfort slowly subsides (Greist, 1996; March, 1995). A minimal trial of ERP consists of 10 to 20 hours of treatment with both exposure and response prevention (Baer and Greist, 1997), with in vivo exposure being preferred over imaginal exposure (Foa et al., 1985). The strategies employed must be tailored to the patient's specific symptoms. Contamination fears, symmetry rituals, counting/repeating, hoarding, and aggressive urges are amenable to ERP, but the technique is not generally appropriate for pathological doubting, or pure obsessions, such as scrupulosity or violent images. Of note, obsessional slowness and hoarding symptoms are difficult to treat with either behavioral therapy or medications (Wolff and Rapoport, 1988). Exposure with response prevention has been reported to produce long-lasting benefits, particularly when booster sessions are utilized to address migration of symptoms and relapses brought on by stress (Greist, 1996).

Therapist-directed ERP has been shown to be the most effective means of treating OCD (Abramowitz, 1998). However, the shortage of trained therapists and expense of therapist-directed ERP mandated the development of alternative strategies. Several self-help programs for behavior therapy have been developed, including computer- and telephone-administered programs (Baer and Greist, 1997; Clark et al., 1998). Self-administered workbooks have also proven successful for both adults (Van Noppen et al., 1997) and pediatric patients (March et al., 1994; March and Mulle, 1998). In general, ERP appears to confer similar benefits in the pediatric population as it does for adults (March et al., 2001). The child must be old enough to understand fully the goals and requirements of treatment and to tolerate the discomforts inherent to exposure.

Pharmacotherapy

Serotonin reuptake inhibitors have been shown to be the most effective pharmacologic treatment for OCD. If there is insufficient response to an SRI at 10 to 12 weeks, another SRI may be tried. Although only 50 to 60 percent of patients respond to initial SRI treatment, approximately 70 to 80 percent will have at least a partial response to at least one of the SRIs. To date, no baseline predictors of treatment response have been identified. Augmentation with other agents may be helpful for partial responders, particularly when comorbid tics are present (McDougle, 1997).

Serotonin Reuptake Inhibitors. Clomipramine (CMI) was the first SRI to be shown to be effective for OCD (Clomipramine Collaborative Study Group, 1991), with subsequent controlled trials documenting antiobsessional effects of the selective SRIs (SSRIs): fluoxetine, fluvoxamine, sertraline, paroxetine, and citalopram (in order of increasing selectivity). All have been shown to be effective in multicenter double-blind trials (see Vythilingum et al., 2000, for review of adult studies; Rapoport and Inoff-Germain, 2000, for review of pediatric studies).

Table 13.2 gives the dosage ranges of the SRIs for treatment of adult and pediatric patients, as well as the half-life of the compounds. To avoid difficulties with adverse effects, it is advisable to initiate therapy with low dosages and titrate upward slowly over a period of a few weeks. Patients should be warned that the medications take time to work and that an adequate trial is usually at least 10 weeks in duration (at maximally tolerated dosage). Patients should also be told that trials of more than one agent or use of augmenting agents may be required to achieve an optimum result.

Recent research in adults, including one placebo-controlled study, indicates that intravenous administration of CMI both speeds initial response and increases response rates even among previously nonresponsive patients (Fallon et al., 1998; Sallee et al., 1998). The hypothesized mechanism of effect for intravenous CMI involves the greater bioavailability of the more serotonergic parent compound versus the more noradrenergic metabolite desmethylclomipramine, as a result of bypassing first-pass hepatoenteric

TABLE 13.2. Serotonin Reuptake Inhibitor (SRI) Treatment of OCD [Metabolite of Fluoxetine Pharmacologic activity

Drug	Adult Dosage	Child/Adolescent Dosage	Half-life
Clomipramine	Up to 250 mg/day	Controlled trials ages >6 yr, 3 mg/kg (max. 4 mg/kg)	12–24 h
Fluoxetine	Up to 80 mg/day	Controlled trials ages >8 yr, 2.5–80 mg	48–96 h Norfluoxetine [metabolite of Fluoxetine pharmacologic activity] (Nor FLX = 7–10 days)
Fluvoxamine	Up to 300 mg/day	Indicated for ages >8 yr, 50–200 mg/day	12–24 h
Sertraline	Up to 200 mg/day	Indicated for ages >6 yr, 25–200 mg/day	24 h
Paroxetine	Up to 60 mg/day	Open trial in 8–17 yr, no pediatric indications	24 h
Citalopram	Up to 80 mg/day (indicated for treatment of depression, not OCD)	Open trial in 9–18 yr, no pediatric indications	35 h

metabolism. Following the initial intravenous (IV) infusion, clomipramine therapy is maintained orally. Experience in pediatric patients is limited, but two open trials and two placebo-controlled cases suggest that IV clomipramine may offer therapeutic benefits to children, as well (Sallee et al., 1998).

Other Medications. Clonazepam is a benzodiazepine with anxiolytic properties and serotonergic effects (Park et al., 1997). This medication has also been found to significantly improve symptom ratings of OCD severity when 3 to 4 mg/day was added to ongoing fluoxetine or clomipramine therapy (Pigott et al., 1992a). A case report of pediatric efficacy has also been published (Leonard et al., 1994).

Buspirone is a partial agonist of the 5-HT_{1A} serotonin receptor and appears to enhance serotonergic neurotransmission. Open trials had suggested benefit of buspirone augmentation of SSRIs, but placebo-controlled trials failed to demonstrate significant benefits when buspirone was added to clomipramine (Pigott et al., 1992b), fluvoxamine (McDougle et al., 1993), or fluoxetine therapy (Grady et al., 1993).

Neuroleptics, such as haloperidol, have been shown to be useful as augmenting agents, particularly in cases with comorbid tic disorders. Haloperidol (mean dose 6.2 ± 3.2 mg/day) demonstrated significant improvements when given in conjunction with fluvoxamine therapy. Eleven of 17 (65 percent) patients randomized to receive haloperidol responded to therapy, while none of the 17 patients receiving placebo had significant treatment gains. Further, 8 out of 8 patients with comorbid tics had a significant reduction in OCD symptom severity (McDougle et al., 1994). Pediatric experience with haloperidol has been limited in OCD, although it is used frequently in children and adolescents with tic disorders (Leckman et al., 1997). Pimozide was noted to be of significant benefit among 9 of 17 patients previously nonresponsive to fluvoxamine therapy (McDougle et al., 1990). Because of the long-term risks of tardive dyskinesias occurring with neuroleptics administration, these should only be considered if atypical antipsychotics are ineffective.

Risperidone is an atypical antipsychotic medication with demonstrated benefits as an augmenting agent in OCD. Out of 16 patients with treatment refractory obsessive-compulsive disorder maintained on an SRI, 14 (87 percent) had a significant reduction in OCD severity within 3 weeks after the addition of risperidone (Saxena et al., 1996). Of particular interest, given the treatment-refractory nature of violent obsessive images, patients with this symptom were most likely to respond and to demonstrate significant benefits after only a few days of augmentation (Saxena et al., 1996). Augmentation with risperidone to paroxetine or sertraline treatment was also found to be effective for pediatric patients with comorbid OCD and tic disorders (Lombroso et al., 1995).

SUMMARY

Great progress has been made in the recognition and treatment of OCD. Selective serotonin reuptake inhibitors and behavior therapy techniques (particularly exposure with response prevention) provide relief from both compulsive rituals and obsessional anxiety. Advances in neuroimaging and neurophysiologic technologies have opened new vistas for understanding the biologic basis of OCD, while increased knowledge of the genetics of the disorder and novel pathophysiologic models hold promise for the development of better strategies for treatment and prevention of OCD. Until that time, it is important to maximize the recognition and treatment of this troublesome disorder by educating parents and primary care physicians about the symptoms of OCD and mental health professionals about the wide range of effective therapies

REFERENCES

Abramowitz JS (1998). Does cognitive-behavioral therapy cure obsessive-compulsive disorder? A meta-analytic evaluation of clinical significance. *Behav Ther* 29:339–355.

Allen A, Hollander E (2000). Body dysmorphic disorder. *Psychiatr Clin North Am* 23:617–628.

Alsobrook JP, Leckman JF, Goodman WK, et al. (1999). Segregation analysis of obsessive-compulsive disorder using symptom-based factor scores. *Am J Med Genet* 15:669–675.

Altemus M, Pigott T, Kalogeras KT, et al. (1992). Abnormalities in the regulation of vasopressin and corticotropin releasing factor secretion in obsessive-compulsive disorder. *Arch Gen Psychiatry* 49:9–20.

Altemus M, Swedo SE, Leonard HL, et al. (1994). Changes in cerebrospinal fluid neurochemistry during treatment of obsessive-compulsive disorder with clomipramine. *Arch Gen Psychiatry* 51:794–803.

American Psychiatric Association (2000). *Diagnostic and Statistical Manual of Mental Disorders*, 4th ed., Text Revision. American Psychiatric Press: Washington, DC.

Ananth J, Pecknold J, van Den Steen N, Engelsmann F (1981). Double-blind comparative study of clomipramine and amitriptyline in obsessive neurosis. *Prog Neuropsychopharmacol Biol Psychiatry* 5:257–262.

Baer L, Greist JH (1997). An interactive computer-administered self-assessment and self-help program for behavior therapy. *J Clin Psychiatry* 58(Suppl.12):23–28.

Barsky AJ (1992). Hypochondriasis and obsessive-compulsive disorder. *Psychiatr Clin North Am* 15:791–801.

Barton R (1987). Diabetes insipidus and obsessional neurosis. *Adv Biochem Psychopharmacol* 43:347–349.

Bastani B, Nash JF, Meltzer HY (1990). Prolactin and cortisol responses to MK-212, a serotonin agonist, in obsessive-compulsive disorder. *Arch Gen Psychiatry* 47:833–839.

Baxter LR, Schwartz JM, Bergman KS, et al. (1992). Caudate glucose metabolic rate changes with both drug and behavior therapy for obsessive-compulsive disorder. *Arch Gen Psychiatry* 49:681–689.

Berg CZ, Rapoport JL, Whitaker A, et al. (1989). Childhood obsessive compulsive disorder: A two-year prospective follow-up of a community sample. *J Am Acad Child and Adolesc Psychiatry* 28:528–533.

Borcherding B, Keysor C, Rapoport JL, et al. (1990). Motor vocal tics and compulsive behaviors on stimulant drugs: Is there a common vulnerability? *Psychiatry Res*, 33:83–94.

Casas ME, Alvarez P, Duro C, et al. (1986). Antiandrogenic treatment of obsessive compulsive disorder neurosis. *Acta Psychiatrica Scand* 73:221–222.

Christenson GA, Mackenzie TB, Mitchell JE (1991a). Characteristics of 60 adult chronic hair pullers. *AM J Psychiatry* 148:365–370.

Christenson GA, Pyle RL, Mitchell JE (1991b). Estimated lifetime prevalence of trichotillomania in college students. *J Clin Psychiatry* 52:415–417.

Clark A, Kirby KC, Daniels BA, Marks IM (1998). A pilot study of computer-aided vicarious exposure for obsessive-compulsive disorder. *Austral New Zealand J Psychiatry* 32:268–275.

Clomipramine Collaborative Study Group (1991). Clomipramine in the treatment of patients with obsessive-compulsive disorder. *Arch Gen Psychiatry* 43:730–738.

Cummings JL, Cunningham K (1992). Obsessive-compulsive disorder in Huntington's disease. *Biol Psychiatry* 31:263–270.

Dolberg OT, Iancu I, Zohar J (1996). Treatment duration of obsessive compulsive disorder. *European Psychiatry* 11:403–406.

Dougherty DD, Baer L, Cosgrove GR et al. (2002). Prospective long-term follow-up of 44 patients who received cingulotomy for treatment-refractory obsessive-compulsive disorder. *Am J Psychiatry* 159(2):269–275.

Douglass HM, Moffitt TE, Dar R et al. (1995). Obsessive-compulsive disorder in a birth cohort of 18 year olds: Prevalence and predictors. *J Am Acad Child Adolesc Psychiatry* 34:1424–1431.

Eisen JL, Phillips KA, Rasmussen SA et al. (1998). The Brown Assessment of Beliefs Scale (BABS): Reliability and validity. *Am J Psychiatry* 155:102–108.

Emmelkamp PM, Beens H (1991). Cognitive therapy with obsessive-compulsive disorder: A comparative evaluation. *Behav Res Therapy* 29:293–300.

Fallon BA, Javitch JA, Hollander E et al. (1991). Hypochondriasis and obsessive compulsive disorder: Overlaps in diagnosis and treatment. *J Clin Psychiatry* 52:547–460.

Fallon BA, Liebowitz MR, Salman E et al. (1993). Fluoxetine for hypochondriacal patients without major depression. *J Clin Psychopharmacol* 13:438–441.

Fallon BA, Schneier FR, Marshall R et al. (1996). The pharmacotherapy of hypochondriasis. *Psychopharmacol Bull* 32:607–611.

Fallon BA, Liebowitz MR, Campeas R et al. (1998). Intravenous clomipramine for obsessive-compulsive disorder refractory to oral clomipramine. A placebo controlled study. *Arch Gen Psychiatry* 55:918–924.

Fallon BA, Qureshi AI, Laje G, Klein B (2000). Hypochondriasis and its relationship to obsessive-compulsive disorder. *Psychiatr Clin North Am* 23:605–616.

Fireman B, Koran LM, Leventhal JL, Jacobson A (2001). The prevalence of clinically recognized obsessive-compulsive disorder in a large health maintenance organization. *Am J Psychiatry* 158:1904–1910.

Flament MF, Rapoport JL, Berg CJ et al. (1985). Clomipramine treatment of childhood compulsive disorder: A double-blind controlled study. *Arch Gen Psychiatry* 42:977–983.

Flament MF, Rapoport JL, Murphy DL et al. (1987). Biochemical changes during clomipramine treatment of childhood obsessive compulsive disorder. *Arch Gen Psychiatry* 44:219–225.

Flament MF, Whitaker A, Rapoport J et al. (1988). Obsessive-compulsive disorder in adolescence: An epidemiological study. *J Am Acad Child Adolesc Psychiatry* 27:764–771.

Foa EB, Steketee GS, Grayson JB (1985). Imaginal and in vivo exposure: A comparison with obsessive-compulsive checkers. *Behav Therapy* 16:292–303.

Freud S (1909). Notes on a case of obsessional neurosis. In Strachey J (ed). *The Standard Edition of the Complete Psychological Works of Sigmund Freud*, Vol. 10 (1957), Hogarth Press: London, pp. 153–318.

Freud S (1913). The predisposition of obsessional neurosis. In Strachey J (ed). *The Standard Edition of the Complete Psychological Works of Sigmund Freud*, Vol. 12 (1957), Hogarth Press: London, pp. 311–326.

Frye P, Arnold L (1981). Persistent amphetamine-induced compulsive rituals: Response to pyridoxine (B_6). *Biol Psychiatry* 16:583–587.

Garvey MA, Giedd J, Swedo SE (1998). PANDAS: The search for environmental triggers of pediatric neuropsychiatric disorders. Lessons from rheumatic fever. *J Child Neurol* 13(9):413–423.

Garvey MA, Perlmutter SJ, Allen AJ et al. (1999). A pilot study of penicillin prophylaxis for neuropsychiatric exacerbations triggered by streptococcal infections. *Biol Psychiatry* 45:1564–1571.

Giedd JN, Rapoport JL, Leonard HL et al. (1996). Case study: Acute basal ganglia enlargement and obsessive-compulsive symptoms in an adolescent boy. *J Am Acad Child Adolesc Psychiatry* 35:913–915.

Giedd JN, Rapoport JL, Garvey MA et al. (2000). MRI assessment of children with obsessive-compulsive disorder or tics associated with streptococcal infection. *Am J Psychiatry* 157:281–283.

Goodman WK, McDougle CJ, Price LH et al. (1990). Beyond the serotonin hypothesis: A role for dopamine in some forms of obsessive compulsive disorder? *J Clin Psychiatry* 51(suppl):36–43.

Grady TA, Pigott TA, L'Heureux F et al. (1993). Double-blind study of adjuvant buspirone for fluoxetine-treated patients with obsessive-compulsive disorder. *Am J Psychiatry* 150:819–821.

Grant JR, Cash TF (1995). Cognitive-behavioral body-image therapy: Comparative efficacy of group and modest-contact treatments. *J Behav Ther Exp Psychiatry* 26:69–84.

Greenberg BD, Murphy DL, Rasmussen SA (2000). Neuroanatomically based approaches to obsessive-compulsive disorder. *Psychiatr Clin N Am* 23(3):671–686.

Greist JH (1996). New developments in behavior therapy for obsessive-compulsive disorder. *Intl Clin Psychopharmacol* 11(Suppl 5):63–73.

Greist JH, Jefferson JW, Kobak KA et al. (1995). Efficacy and tolerability of serotonin transport inhibitors in obsessive-compulsive disorder: A meta-analysis. *Arch Gen Psychiatry* 52:53–60.

Hamburger SD, Swedo S, Whitaker A et al. (1989). Growth rate in adolescents with obsessive-compulsive disorder. *Am J Psychiatry* 146:652–655.

Hamilton CS, Garvey MA, Swedo SE (2001). Therapeutic implications of immunology for tics and obsessive-compulsive disorder. In Cohen DJ, Goetz CG (eds). *Tourette Syndrome*. Lippincott, Williams & Wilkins: Philadelphia, pp. 311–318.

Hollander E, Liebowitz MR, Winchel R et al. (1989). Treatment of body dysmorphic disorder with serotonin reuptake blockers. *Am J Psychiatry* 146:768.

Hollander E, Kwon JH, Stein DJ et al. (1996). Obsessive-compulsive and spectrum disorders: Overview and quality of life issues. *J Clin Psychiatry* 57(suppl 8):3–6.

Hollander E, Kaplan A, Allen A, Cartwright C (2000). Pharmacotherapy for obsessive-compulsive disorder. *Psychiatr Clin N Am* 23(3):643–656.

Husby G, Van de Rijn I, Zabriskie JB et al. (1976). Antibodies reacting with cytoplasm of subthalamic and caudate nuclei neurons in chorea and acute rheumatic fever. *J Exp Med* 144:1094–1110.

Hwu HG, Yeh EK, Chang LY (1989). Prevalence of psychiatric disorders in Taiwan defined by the Chinese Diagnostic Interview Schedule. *Acta Psychiatr Scand* 79:136–147.

Insel TR, Akiskal HS (1986). Obsessive-compulsive disorder with psychotic features: A phenomenologic analysis. *Am J Psychiatry* 143:1527–1533.

Insel TR, Mueller EA, Alterman I et al. (1985). Obsessive-compulsive disorder and serotonin: Is there a connection? *Biol Psychiatry* 20:1174–1188.

Janet P. *Les Obsessions et la Psychiatrie*. Paris, France: Felix Alan; 1903.

Karno M, Golding J (1990). Obsessive compulsive disorder. In Robins L, Regrer DA (eds). *Psychiatric Disorders in America: The Epidemiological Catchment Area Study*. Free Press: New York.

Karno M, Golding J, Sorenson S, Burnam A (1988). The epidemiology of obsessive compulsive disorder in five US communities. *Arch Gen Psychiatry* 45:1094–1099.

Keuthen NJ, O'Sullivan RL, Goodchild P et al. (1998). Behavior therapy and pharmacotherapy for trichotillomania: Choice of treatment, patient acceptance, and long-term outcome. *CNS Spectrums* 3:72–78.

Kiessling LS, Marcotte AC, Culpepper L (1994). Antineuronal antibodies: Tics and obsessive-compulsive symptoms. *J Devel Behav Pediatrics* 15:421–425.

Kozak MJ, Foa EB (1994). Obsessions, overvalued ideas and delusions in obsessive-compulsive disorder. *Behav Res Ther* 32:343–353.

Leckman JF, Mayes LC (1999). Preoccupations and behaviors associated with romantic and parental love: Perspectives on the origin of obsessive-compulsive disorder. *Child Adolesc Psychiatric Clin Am* 8(3):635–665.

Leckman JF, Goodman WK, North WG et al. (1994). The role of central oxytocin in obsessive-compulsive disorder and related normal behavior. *Psychoneuroendocrinology* 19:723–749.

Leckman JF, Grice DE, Boardman J et al. (1997). Symptoms of obsessive-compulsive disorder. *Am J Psychiatry* 154(7):911–917.

Leonard HL, Swedo S, Rapoport J et al. (1989). Treatment of childhood obsessive compulsive disorder with clomipramine and desmethylimipramine: A double-blind crossover comparison. *Arch Gen Psychiatry* 46:1088–1092.

Leonard HL, Lenane MC, Swedo SE et al. (1992). Tics and Tourette's disorder: A 2- to 7-year follow-up of 54 obsessive-compulsive children. *Am J Psychiatry* 149:1244–1251.

Leonard HL, Topol D, Bukstein O et al. (1994). Clonazepam as an augmenting agent in the treatment of childhood-onset obsessive-compulsive disorder. *J Am Acad Child Adolesc Psychiatry* 33:792–794.

Lombroso PJ, Scahill L, King RA et al. (1995). Risperidone treatment of children and adolescents with chronic tic disorders: A preliminary report. *J Am Acad Child Adolesc Psychiatry* 34:1147–1152.

March JS (1995). Cognitive-behavioral psychotherapy for children and adolescents with OCD: A review and recommendations for treatment *J Am Acad Child Adolesc Psychiatry* 34:7–18.

March JS, Mulle K. (1998). *OCD in Children and Adolescents. A Cognitive-Behavioral Treatment Manual*. Guilford Press: New York.

March JS, Mulle K, Herbel B (1994). Behavioral psychotherapy for children and adolescents with obsessive-compulsive disorder: An open trial of a new protocol-driven treatment package. *J Am Acad Child Adoles Psychiatry* 33:333–341.

March JS, Franklin M, Nelson A, Foa E (2001). Cognitive-behavioral psychotherapy for pediatric obsessive-compulsive disorder. *J Clin Child Psychol* 30(1):8–18.

Marks I. (1997). Behavior therapy for obsessive-compulsive disorder. A decade of progress. *Canad J Psychiatry* 42:1021–1026.

McDougle CJ (1997). Update on pharmacologic management of OCD: Agents and augmentation. *J Clin Psychiatry* 58(Suppl 12):11–17.

McDougle CJ, Goodman WK, Price LH et al. (1990). Neuroleptic addition in fluvoxamine-refractory obsessive-compulsive disorder. *Am J Psychiatry* 147:652–654.

McDougle CJ, Goodman WK, Leckman JF et al. (1993). Limited therapeutic effect of addition of buspirone to fluvoxamine-refractory obsessive compulsive disorder. *Am J Psychiatry* 150:647–649.

McDougle CJ, Goodman WK, Leckman JF et al. (1994). Haloperidol addition in fluvoxamine-refractory obsessive-compulsive disorder—A double-blind, placebo-controlled study in patients with and without tics. *Arch Gen Psychiatry* 51:302–308.

Mindus P (1991). *Capsulotomy in Anxiety Disorders: A Multidisciplinary Study*. Karolinska Institute Press: Stockholm.

Minichiello WE, O'Sullivan RL, Osgood-Hayes D et al. (1994). Trichotillomania: Clinical aspects and treatment strategies. *Harv Rev Psychiatry* 1:336–344.

Morshed SA, Parveen S, Leckman JF et al. (2001). Antibodies against neural, nuclear, cytoskeletal, and streptococcal epitopes in children and adults with Tourette's syndrome, Sydenham's chorea, and autoimmune disorders. *Biol Psychiatry* 50(8):566–577.

Mullen J (1927). *Psychological Factors in the Pastoral Treatment of Scruples: Studies in Psychology and Psychiatry*. Catholic University of America Publishers: Washington, DC.

Murphy D, Zohar J, Pato M et al. (1989). Obsessive compulsive disorder as a 5-HT subsystem behavioral disorder. *Br J Psychiatry* 155(suppl):15–24.

Murray CJ, Lopez AD (1996). *The Global Burden of Disease.* Harvard University Press, Cambridge, MA.

Neziroglu F, McKay D, Todaro J et al. (1996). Effect of cognitive behavior therapy on persons with body dysmorphic disorder and comorbid axis II diagnosis. *J Behav Ther Exp Psychiatry* 27:67.

Neziroglu F, Hsia C, Yaryura-Tobias JA (2000). Behavioral, cognitive, and family therapy for obsessive-compulsive and related disorders. *Psychiatr Clin N Am* 23(3):657–670.

Nicolini H, Hanna G, Baxter L et al. (1991). Segregation analysis of obsessive-compulsive and associated disorders: Preliminary results. *Ursus Medicus J* 1:25–28.

Nicolini H, Weissbecker K, Mejia JM et al. (1993). Family study of obsessive-compulsive disorder in a Mexican population. *Arch Med Res* 24:193–198.

Noyes R, Kathol RG, Fisher MM et al. (1994). One-year follow-up of medical outpatients with hypochondriasis. *Psychosomatics* 35:533–545.

O'Flaherty VM (1966). *How to Cure Scruples.* Bruce Publishing: Milwaukee, WI.

O'Sullivan RL, Christenson GA, Stein D (1999). Pharmacotherapy of trichotillomania. In *Trichotillomania.* DJ Stein, GA Christenson, E Hollander (eds). American Psychiatric Press: Washington, DC.

O'Sullivan RL, Mansueto Lerner EA et al. (2000). Characterization of trichotillomania. *Psychiatr Clin North Am* 23:587–604.

Park LT, Jefferson JW, & Greist JH (1997). Obsessive-compulsive disorder. Treatment options. *CNS Drugs* 7:187–202.

Pauls DL, Alsobrook JP, Goodman W et al. (1995). A family study of obsessive-compulsive disorder. *Am J Psychiatry* 152:76–84.

Perlmutter SJ, Garvey MA, Castellanos X et al. (1998). A Case of pediatric autoimmune neuropsychiatric disorders associated with streptococcal infections (PANDAS). *Am J Psychiatry* 155(11):1592–1598.

Perlmutter SJ, Leitman SF, Garvey MA et al. (1999). Therapeutic plasma exchange and intravenous immunoglobulin for obsessive-compulsive disorder and tic disorders in childhood. *Lancet* 354:1153–1158.

Phillips KA, Dwight MM, McElroy SL. (1998). Efficacy and safety of fluvoxamine in body dysmorphic disorder. *J Clin Psychiatry* 59:165.

Pigott TA, Zohar J, Hill JL et al. (1991). Metergoline blocks the behavioral and neuroendocrine effects of orally administered m-CPP in patients with OCD. *Biological Psychiatry* 29:418–426.

Pigott TA, L'Heureux F, Rubenstein CS et al. (1992a). A controlled trial of clonazepam augmentation in OCD patients tested with clomipramine or fluoxetine [Abstract no.144]. In *New Research Program and Abstracts of the 145th Annual Meeting of the American Psychiatric Association.* APA: Washington, DC, p. 82.

Pigott TA, L'Heureux F, Hill JL et al. (1992b). A double-blind study of adjuvant buspirone hydrochloride in clomipramine-treated patients with obsessive-compulsive disorder. *J Clin Psychopharmacol* 12:11–18.

Rapoport JL Inoff-Germain G (2000) Treatment of obsessive-compulsive disorder in children and adolescents. *J Chil Psychol Psychiatry* 41(4):419–431.

Rasmussen SA, Eisen JL (1992). The epidemiology and differential diagnosis of obsessive-compulsive disorder. *J Clin Psychiatry* 53 (Suppl):4–10.

Rasmussen SA, Tsuang MT (1986). Clinical characteristics and family history in DSM-III obsessive-compulsive disorder. *Am J Psychiatry* 143:317–322.

Ravizza L, Maina G, Bogetto F et al. (1998). Long term treatment of obsessive-compulsive disorder. *CNS Drugs* 10:247–255.

Rich N, Rosen JC, Orosan PG et al. (1992). Prevalence of body dysmorphic disorder in non-clinical populations. Presented at the Annual Meeting for the Association for the Advancement of Behavior Therapy. Boston.

Robins L, Helzer J, Crougham J, Ratcliffe K (1981). The NIMH epidemiological catchment area study. *Arch Gen Psychiatry* 38:381–389.

Rosenberg DR, Chugani DC, Muzik O et al. (1998). Altered serotonin synthesis in fronto-striatal circuitry in pediatric obsessive-compulsive disorder. *Biological Psychiatry* 43:24S.

Sallee FR, Koran LM, Pallanti S et al. (1998). Intravenous clomipramine challenge in obsessive-compulsive disorder: Predicting response to oral therapy at eight weeks. *Biological Psychiatry* 44:220–227.

Salzberg A, Swedo SE (1992). Oxytocin and vasopressin in obsessive-compulsive disorder. *Am J Psychiatry* 149:713–714.

Saxena S, Rauch SL (2000). Functional neuroimaging and the neuroanatomy of obsessive-compulsive disorder. *Psychiatr Clin N Am* 23(3):563–586.

Saxena S, Wang D, Bystritsky A, Baxter LR, Jr (1996). Risperidone augmentation of SRI treatment for refractory obsessive-compulsive disorder. *J Clin Psychiatry* 57:303–306.

Schwartz JM, Stoessel PW, Baxter LR et al. (1996). Systematic changes in cerebral glucose metabolic rate after successful behavior modification treatment of obsessive-compulsive disorder. *Arch Gen Psychiatry* 53:109–113.

Shafron R (1998). Childhood obsessive-compulsive disorder. In Graham P (ed). *Cognitive Behavior Therapy for Children And Families*. pp. 45–73. University Press: Cambridge, pp. 45–73.

Shafron NA, Somers J (1998). Treating adolescent obsessive-compulsive disorder: Applications of the cognitive theory. *Behav Res Therapy* 36:93–97.

Singer HS, Giuliano JD, Hansen BH et al. (1998). Antibodies against human putamen in children with Tourette syndrome. *Neurology* 50:1618–1624.

Stanley MA, Turner SM (1995). Current status of pharmacological and behavioral treatment of obsessive-compulsive disorder. *Behavior Therapy* 26:163–186.

Swedo SE (1989). Rituals and releasers: An ethological model of OCD. In RapoportJL (ed). *Obsessive Compulsive Disorder in Children and Adolescents*. American Psychiatric Press: Washington, DC, pp. 269–288.

Swedo SE, Leonard HL (1992). Trichotillomania: An obsessive compulsive spectrum disorder? *Psychiatr Clin North Am* 15:777–790.

Swedo S, Rapoport JL. (1990). Neurochemical and neuroendocrine consideration of obsessive-compulsive disorders in childhood. In (Deutsch SI, Weizman A, Weizman R) (eds). Plenum Medical Books: New York, pp. 275–284.

Swedo S, Rapoport JL, Leonard HL et al. (1989). Obsessive-compulsive disorder in children and adolescents: clinical phenomenology of 70 consecutive cases. *Arch Gen Psychiatry* 46:335–341.

Swedo S, Leonard HL, Kruesi MJP et al. (1992). Cerebrospinal fluid neurochemistry of children and adolescents with obsessive compulsive disorder. *Arch Gen Psychiatry* 49:29–36.

Swedo SE, Leonard HL, Schapiro MB et al. (1993). Sydenham's chorea: Physical and psychological symptoms of St. Vitus dance. *Pediatrics* 91:706–713.

Swedo SE, Leonard HL, Garvey M et al. (1998). Pediatric autoimmune neuropsychiatric disorders associated with streptococcal infections (PANDAS): Clinical description of the first 50 cases. *Am J Psychiatry* 155:264–271.

Valleni-Basile LA, Garrison CZ, Waller JL et al. (1996). Incidence of obsessive-compulsive disorder in a community sample of young adolescents. *J Am Acad Child Adolesc Psychiatry* 35:898–906.

Van Noppen B, Skeketee G, McCorkle B, et al. (1997) Group and multifamily behavioral treatment for obsessive-compulsive disorder: A Pilot study. *J Anxiety Disord* 11:431–446.

Von Economo C (1931). *Encephalitis Lethargica: Its Sequelae and Treatment*. Oxford University Press: London.

Vythilingum B, Cartwright C, Hollander E (2000). Pharmacotherapy of obsessive- compulsive disorder: Experience with the selective serotonin reuptake inhibitors. *Intl Clin Psychopharm* 15(suppl 2):S7–S13.

Weissman MM, Bland RC, Canino GJ et al. (1994). The cross-national epidemiology of obsessive-compulsive disorder. *J Clin Psychiatry* 55(3, Suppl.):5–10.

Whitaker A, Johnson J, Schaffer D et al. (1990). Uncommon troubles in young people: prevalence estimates of selected psychiatric disorders in a non-referred adolescent population. *Arch Gen Psychiatry* 47:487–496.

Wittchen HU, Nelson CB, Lachner G (1998). Prevalence of mental disorders and psychosocial impairments in adolescents and young adults. *Psychological Medicine* 28:109–126.

Wolff R, Rapoport JL (1988). Behavioral treatment of childhood obsessive compulsive disorder. *Behavioral Modification* 12:252–256.

Wolff M, Alsobrook JP, Pauls DL (2000). Genetic aspects of obsessive-compulsive disorder. *Psychiatr Clin North Am* 23:535–544.

Yaryura-Tobias JA, Neziroglu F (1997a). *Biobehavioral Treatment of Obsessive-Compulsive Spectrum Disorders*. Norton: New York.

Yaryura-Tobias JA, Neziroglu F. (1997b). *Obsessive-Compulsive Disorder Spectrum*. American Psychiatric Press: Washington, DC.

Zimmerman M, Mattia JI. (1998) *Body dysmorphic disorder in an outpatient*: recognition, prevalence, comorbidity, demographic, and clinical correlates. *Compr Psychiatry.* 39(5):265–70

Zohar AH (1999). The epidemiology of obsessive-compulsive disorder in children and adolescents. *Child Adolesc Psychiatric Clinics N Am* 8(3):445–460.

Zohar J, Mueller EA, Insel TR et al. (1987). Serotonergic responsivity in obsessive- compulsive disorder: comparison with patients and healthy controls. *Arch Gen Psychiatry* 44:946–951.

Zohar J, Insel T, Zohar-Kadouch R (1988). Serotonergic responsivity in obsessive-compulsive effects of chronic clomipramine treatment. *Arch Gen Psychiatry* 45:167–172.

Zohar AH, Ratzoni G, Pauls DL et al.. (1992): An epidemiological study of obsessive- compulsive disorder and related disorders in Israeli adolescents. *J Am Acad Child Adolesc Psychiatry* 31:1057–1061.

14

BIOLOGICAL BASIS OF CHILDHOOD NEUROPSYCHIATRIC DISORDERS

Bradley S. Peterson[1] and Jaak Panksepp[2]

[1] *Department of Psychiatry, Columbia College of Physicians & Surgeons and New York State Psychiatric Institute, New York, New York*
[2] *Department of Psychology, Bowling Green State University, Bowling Green, Ohio*

INTRODUCTION

Our understanding of the biological basis of childhood neuropsychiatric disorders has improved dramatically over the past two decades. Some would argue that the advances made in understanding the biological basis of childhood disorders have outstripped those for adult-onset disorders. This improved understanding has been made possible primarily by technological advances in the fields of genetics, molecular biology, and neuroimaging. Many childhood neuropsychiatric illnesses have a strong genetic basis, and the application of the methodologies for family and genetic studies have begun to identify the precise genetic determinants for several of these conditions. In addition, the introduction of magnetic resonance imaging (MRI) as a research tool in the 1980s has allowed the safe study of brain tissue in living children over time, and this has helped immensely to identify the neuroanatomical and functional correlates of disease throughout development in the majority of childhood illnesses. Findings from

Textbook of Biological Psychiatry, Edited by Jaak Panksepp
ISBN 0-471-43478-7   Copyright © 2004 John Wiley & Sons, Inc.

genetic, molecular biological, and brain imaging studies have helped to refine clinical phenotypes that have helped guide and improve studies that employ these biologically based methodologies in the study of brain disorders in children.

No single review can cover adequately the entire range of biological findings for all childhood neuropsychiatric disorders, nor the range of therapies for these many conditions. Our aim here is therefore to provide an overview of many of the most dramatic and important advances in our understanding of the biology of these illnesses. Those advances, and the research strategies that made them possible, will likely serve as models or paradigms for future biologically based research of disorders in which recent advances have not been as dramatic. Thus the conditions considered herein will be those within the broad domains of pervasive developmental disorder and specific genetic conditions (autism, Rett syndrome, fragile X, Williams syndrome, Angelman and Prader-Willi syndromes), childhood-onset schizophrenia, and disorders of impulse control (especially Tourette syndrome, obsessive-compulsive disorder, and attention deficit hyperactivity disorder). Wherever possible, discussion will include a review of the clinical phenotype, genetics, neurochemistry, and neurobiological substrate for each disorder. We will suggest ways in which findings in each of these domains relate to one another, so as to provide a coherent understanding of the pathophysiology of the condition. Many more references exist for the numerous findings that are cited herein; because of space constraints, only the most recent have been included.

PERVASIVE DEVELOPMENTAL DISORDERS AND SPECIFIC GENETIC SYNDROMES

Autism

Autism is a pervasive developmental disorder. This means that autism is characterized by specific delays and deviance in social, communicative, and cognitive development that are typically manifested within the first few years of life. Although often associated with mental retardation, the disturbances in these domains are both qualitatively distinct from and quantitatively disproportionate to the mental age [intelligence quotient (IQ)] of the individual who exhibits them. The diagnostic criteria for autism currently emphasize disturbances in three broad areas of developmental dysfunction. These include: (1) qualitative disturbances in social interaction, such as impaired use of nonverbal behaviors, failure to develop peer relationships, and poor social reciprocity; (2) qualitative disturbances in communication, such as a significant delay in the development of spoken language, an inability to sustain a spoken conversation, stereotyped use of language, or paucity of symbolic or imitative play; and (3) restricted, repetitive behaviors and interests, such as motor stereotypies and rigid adherence to specific, nonfunctional routines or rituals. Symptoms must manifest clearly by the third year of life. The majority of outcome studies of autism suggest that its defining symptoms continue into adulthood, although some individuals can improve substantially in their overall level of functioning. Low IQ (especially IQs below 50), poor language functioning, and the degree of deficits in socialization are the best predictors of continuing major disability into adulthood. A substantial minority will, moreover, develop seizure disorders in late childhood, adolescence, or early adulthood that continue into late life.

Autism is a brain-based illness of unknown etiology. Prevalence estimates range from 0.7 to 21 in 10,000, with increasing prevalences reported over the past 20 years (Fombonne, 1999). Although the rising prevalence could be caused by an increasing exposure to environmental pathogens, experts generally concur that it can be attributed to improved case recognition and more inclusive diagnostic criteria. Males are roughly 4 times more likely than females to be affected.

Approximately 3 to 9 percent of individuals with autism are also diagnosed with tuberous sclerosis, and, concomitantly, 20 to 40 percent of tuberous sclerosis patients have autism. Seizures affect 20 to 30 percent, and 75 percent of autistic individuals are mentally retarded (Bailey et al., 1996). Many will have physical anomalies, neurological soft signs, primitive reflexes, or nonspecific abnormalities on electroencephalography (EEG). Autism is not infrequently diagnosed in association with various specific medical conditions, such as phenylketonuria, chromosomal deletion syndromes, Prader-Willi syndrome, Angelman's syndrome, or fragile X syndrome. It can also be a consequence of prenatal or postnatal infections, such as congenital rubella (Ritvo et al., 1990). Environmental toxins, vaccinations, and immunological disturbances have been suggested in the etiology of autism, although evidence for these as pathogens is weak (Stromland et al., 1994; Taylor et al., 2002).

Some investigators have hypothesized the presence of a single, unitary neuropsychological deficit in the etiology of autism. Proposed candidates for this deficit range from poor sensory gating, impaired attachment, and social-emotional disturbances, to higher order cognitive deficits involved in "theory of mind" and "central coherence" (Sigman and Mundy, 1989; Baron-Cohen, 1991; Happe et al., 2001). If a unitary neuropsychological deficit does cause autistic symptoms, then it probably functions as a final common pathway to illness because the etiology of autism is almost certainly heterogeneous and multifactorial, not unitary. Indeed, autism is increasingly viewed as a spectrum of illnesses that include Asperger syndrome and other syndromal variants that have disturbances in socialization as their core feature, although the neurobiological causes of the socialization deficits are multiple and unknown. Some conditions, such as fragile X and Rett syndromes, can present with autistic features, although they are now recognized as clinically distinct and genetically specific diagnostic entities. No doubt other genetically specified subtypes of autism will emerge in the future from the use of powerful new molecular biological techniques.

Genetics. Twin and family studies suggest that autism is one of the most strongly genetic of all the multifactorial, neuropsychiatric disorders affecting children. Same-sex twin studies in autism have shown a pairwise concordance rate of 90 percent in monozygotic twins and near 0 percent in dizygotic twins (Folstein and Rutter, 1977; Steffenburg et al., 1989). Concordance in monozygotic twins is even higher if milder autistic spectrum conditions are considered in the concordance assessments (Bailey et al., 1995). Family studies indicate that the risk of developing autism in a sibling of an affected individual is 50- to 250-fold higher than in the general population, although the actual risk for any individual sibling, at 2 to 8 percent, is still small (August et al., 1981). Family studies have not yet yielded convincing models for a single mode of genetic transmission.

Several full genome scans have failed to identify susceptibility loci with certainty, although regions of chromosomes 7 and 15 have yielded promising leads (Maestrini et al., 2000; Boyar et al., 2001; Badner and Gershon, 2002). The regions on 7q are near sites already identified in the production of the protein reelin (at 7q22) (see Chapter 9), and the regions on 15q overlap with genes involved in the encoding of various gamma-aminobutyric acid A (GABA-A) receptor subunits. Other promising leads include loci on chromosomes 3, 5, 8, and 19 (Liu et al., 2001; Auranen et al., 2002).

An additional strategy in the search for genes involved in autism has been to focus on candidate genes known to modulate social processes in animals. Thus, the promoter regions for the endogenous opioid, vasopressin, and oxytocin genes are currently being investigated (Insel et al., 1999). Other candidate genes being studied intensively include those related to serotonergic and GABAergic neurotransmitter pathways (Anderson and Cook, 2000). Of the various genetic factors that contribute to the emergence of autistic symptoms, many may be susceptibility factors that interact with nongenetic influences, such as perinatal problems, obstetrical complications, or environmental toxins (Bolton et al., 1997).

Neurochemistry. Neurochemical systems have been studied extensively in autistic children. The majority of studies of the dopaminergic neurotransmitter system in individuals with autism have yielded either negative or contradictory findings. Homovanillic acid (HVA, a dopamine metabolite) measurements in cerebrospinal fluid (CSF) and urine have been especially contradictory, whereas urinary measures of dopamine and plasma prolactin (a hormone under strong inhibitory control from central dopamine systems) have been normal (Martineau et al., 1992; Narayan et al., 1993).

Measures of the basal functioning of adrenergic and noradrenergic systems in plasma, serum, urine, and CSF have been consistently normal in autistic children (Barthelemy et al., 1988; Minderaa et al., 1994), whereas most studies have reported exaggerated responses of these systems and of the hypothalamic-pituitary-adrenal axis to acute stress among autistic subjects (Cook, 1990; Tordjman et al., 1997). These neurochemical findings are consistent with the hyperarousal, motoric hyperactivity, and anxiety often noted clinically in autistic children in response to novel experiences.

The most consistent neurochemical findings in autistic individuals have been those suggestive of hyperserotonemia. Platelet serotonin [5-hydroxytryptamine (5-HT)], thought to be a good peripheral indicator of central 5-HT, is consistently and robustly elevated (by nearly a standard deviation). The behavioral significance and cause of this well-replicated finding, however, is still unclear. It appears not to be caused by altered 5-HT metabolism or by increased basal levels of 5-HT in plasma; thus the platelet's handling of 5-HT seems the most likely locus of the 5-HT disturbance. Despite intensive research on the issue, no clear abnormality in platelet uptake or efflux of 5-HT has yet been demonstrated (Croonenberghs et al., 2000; Anderson et al., 2002).

Excess activity of the endogenous opioid system has been postulated in autism, based on observations in both humans and animals that administration of opioids can produce social withdrawal, self-injurious behaviors, stereotypies, and diminished pain sensitivity (Panksepp et al., 1979). Although this hypothesis suggested that opioid antagonists could be therapeutic in autism, double-blind, placebo-controlled trials of the antagonist naltrexone have yielded either marginally positive, negative, or contradictory findings (Campbell et al., 1993; Bouvard et al., 1995; Kolmen et al., 1995; Willemsen-Swinkels et al., 1995; Willemsen-Swinkels et al., 1996; Kolmen et al., 1997). Plasma levels of the opioid peptide beta-endorphin may not be relevant to levels in the central nervous system (CNS), and findings for CSF endorphins have been inconsistent in autistic individuals (Nagamitsu et al., 1997). Thus, more research is needed before the role of the endogenous opioid system in the etiology of autism is fully clarified (see Chapter 21).

Neurobiological Substrate. Several animal models have been suggested for autism. One model involves bilateral lesions of the amygdala of monkey neonates. These lesions can produce social isolation, poor eye contact, reduced facial expressivity, and motor stereotypies that emerge gradually during later development, reminiscent of the natural history of autistic symptoms (Bachevalier, 1994). These monkeys, when imaged in adulthood, have abnormalities in the concentrations of neurotransmitter metabolites within frontal cortex and altered dopaminergic activity in both frontal and basal ganglia regions (Bertolino et al., 1997; Saunders et al., 1998). Amygdala damage in adults does not produce these kinds of behavioral or metabolic disturbances. Findings from this animal model suggest that early developmental disturbances in the limbic system are capable of generating behavioral abnormalities in animals that have at least superficial similarities to the symptoms of autism.

Another animal model for autistic behaviors comes from nonhuman primate studies of social deprivation early in postnatal life. Total isolation of monkeys as neonates produces self-directed oral and clasping behaviors, fearfulness, social isolation from peers, and a profound inability to nurture offspring in adulthood (Harlow et al., 1965). These isolates to some extent can be "rehabilitated" when exposed to "therapist" monkeys who promote nonaggressive physical contact (Suomi, 1973). Although the neural systems that are developmentally disrupted by early social deprivation are unknown, this model has received increasing attention in recent studies of autism, as profound disturbances in social relatedness have come to light in children raised in relative social isolation within Eastern European orphanages. Neurobiological studies of those children, some of whom have autistic-like symptoms, are underway (Bailey et al., 1996; Gunnar, 2001).

Although postmortem studies of autistic individuals have yielded variable or conflicting results, reported abnormalities include abnormal size, density, and dendritic arborization of neurons in the amygdala, hippocampus, and entorhinal cortices (Bauman and Kemper, 1994, 1996). Also noted was a decrease in size of the cerebellum, which was attributable in part to decreases in the number of Purkinje cells and variable reductions in the number of granule cells throughout the cerebellar hemispheres (Bauman and Kemper, (1994, 1996)).

In vivo human studies have provided an increasing body of evidence that overall brain size is increased in autistic individuals, measured both as exterior head circumference (Lainhart et al., 1997) and as overall brain volume in neuroimaging studies (Piven et al., 1996). The brain regions that contribute most to this overall increase in brain size include temporal, parietal, and occipital cortices (Piven et al., 1996). Although the functional significance of the cerebral volume expansion and the timing of its origins are unknown, prenatal origins of disordered brain development have been suggested by case reports of polymicrogyria, macrogyria, and schizencephaly—morphological abnormalities that are believed to originate from abnormal neuronal migration during fetal life (Bailey et al., 1998). Volume expansion of the cerebrum could be a consequence of any number of disturbances in cellular growth, differentiation, and development, including abnormal neuronal or glial cell proliferation, neuronal migration, apoptosis, axonal or dendritic arborization, or myelination.

Clinicopathological investigations in autism have focused intensively on the morphology and function of the limbic system within the temporal lobe as the source of the profound social and emotional disturbances in the illness. Case studies have reported autistic behaviors associated with temporal lobe lesions (Gillberg, 1991; Hoon and Reiss, 1992). Tubers from tuberous sclerosis, if located within the temporal lobe, are believed to be especially likely to produce autism, probably by disrupting electrophysiological function in the temporal lobe (Bolton and Griffiths, 1997). Reduced functional activity in the temporal lobes has been reported in single-photon emission computed tomography (SPECT) study of autistic subjects (Mountz et al., 1995). Within anatomical subregions of the temporal lobe, the possible role of the amygdala in autism has received particular emphasis, as it plays a central role in assigning significance to environmental stimuli and mediating emotional learning (LeDoux, 1996). Anatomical imaging studies of the amygdala have been small and they have employed vastly different methodologies. Their findings, not surprisingly, have been inconsistent, with both smaller and larger volumes reported (Abell et al., 1999; Aylward et al., 1999).

Other temporolimbic regions have been implicated in the pathophysiology of autism. Functional MRI (fMRI) studies, for example, have reported that the fusiform gyrus, a specific region on the ventral surface of the temporal cortex, fails to respond fully in autistic adults to the human face during perceptual tasks (Critchley et al., 2000; Schultz et al., 2000). These studies may help to clarify the neural correlates of the cognitive deficits in facial recognition, memory, and imitation that have been demonstrated repeatedly in autistic individuals (Hobson, 1986; Boucher and Lewis, 1992; Klin et al., 1999).

Other brain regions, particularly frontal lobes, have been implicated by imaging studies in the etiology of autism. MRI-based measures of phospholipid metabolism, for example, have suggested the presence of excessive membrane degradation in the dorsal prefrontal cortices of autistic individuals (Minshew et al., 1993). Blood flow and metabolism in the frontal lobe is reportedly reduced (Haznedar et al., 1997), as is dopaminergic activity, in medial prefrontal cortices (Ernst et al., 1997). These dorsomedial regions of the prefrontal cortex are thought to subserve cognitive processes involved in socialization, including the ability to think about the thoughts, feelings, and intentions of other people (Baron-Cohen et al., 1994; Goel et al., 1995). These cognitive capacities, termed *metarepresentational thinking*, or *theory of mind*, are regarded by many as the core processes that are disrupted in the mental life of autistic people. Other recent imaging studies have suggested abnormalities in markers for neuronal numbers, metabolism, and second messenger systems that are widespread throughout the brains of young autistic children (Friedman et al., 2003).

One brain region that has long been the center of controversy in autism research is the cerebellum. A report of reduced volumes of vermian lobules VI and VII initially generated much excitement (Courchesne et al., 1988). Subsequent studies, however, did not replicate the findings, particularly when controlling for subject characteristics such as age, sex, and IQ (Kleiman et al., 1992; Piven et al., 1992). A subsequent reanalysis of data from previous work suggested that volumes of lobules VI and VII might be bimodally distributed in autistic subjects and unimodally distributed in control subjects (Courchesne et al., 1994). This bimodal distribution, if real, would argue for the existence of both hypoplastic and hyperplastic subtypes, but the matter is not yet resolved. Reported brainstem abnormalities include absent or abnormal nuclei of the cranial nerves or the superior olivary nucleus (Rodier et al., 1996).

Rett Syndrome

Rett syndrome (RS) has a prevalence of 1 in 10,000. Although first accepted as a distinct clinical entity only in 1983, progress in understanding the pathophysiology of RS has been spectacular. The phenotype of RS falls within the autism spectrum. Unlike autism, however, the symptoms of RS typically emerge only after a period of normal development, and they affect females almost exclusively. One of the most common first symptoms is the loss of purposeful hand movements, which are often replaced by incessant hand-wringing. Other symptoms and signs soon emerge. An arrest of language development and profound cognitive delays are seen in the majority. Play and motor skills are lost in more than half the cases. Regression most commonly occurs between 12 and 18 months of age, but it can be noted as early as 6 months or as late as 36 months (Charman et al., 2002). Growth retardation, microcephaly, ataxia, gait disturbance, and seizures are also common (Hagberg, 2002). The EEG in RS children is invariably abnormal, showing focal, multifocal, or generalized epileptiform abnormalities and rhythmic slow-wave (theta) activity, primarily in frontocentral regions (Glaze, 2002).

Genetics. The genetic deficit for RS has been narrowed to a region of the X chromosome (Xq27.3-Xqter). Being a dominant gene, the mutation for RS is thought to be lethal to males before birth. Females who have a spare X chromosome are spared death during fetal development and later life because one of the two X chromosomes in each of the postmitotic cells is randomly inactivated, leaving a significant subset of cells with normally functioning X chromosomes (Armstrong, 2002). All known mutations thus far associated with RS in this region have been shown to affect the *MeCP2* gene, which encodes methyl-CpG binding protein 2, a ubiquitous deoxyribonucleic acid (DNA)-binding protein. *MeCP2* has high affinity for binding to methylated CpG dinucleotides. When the MeCP2 protein binds to these dinucleotides within the pro-motor region of a gene, a complex is formed that contains the CpG dinucleotide, the

MeCP2 protein, a co-repressor (Sin3A), and certain enzymes (histone deacetylases). This complex then deacetylates histones associated with the chromatin, making the chromatin more compact and thereby repressing transcription of downstream genes (Van den Veyver and Zoghbi, 2002).

More than 200 mutations to the *MeCP2* gene have been reported. Nonsense, missense, or frameshift mutations are detected in more than 80 percent of affected girls. More than 60 percent of the mutations cause recurrent cytosine-to-thymine substitutions in a codon for arginine (CGA) at one of 8 different mutation hot spots containing CpG dinucleotides. In 10 percent of cases, recurrent multinucleotide deletions have been noted in the C-terminal region of the gene (Van den Veyver and Zoghbi, 2002). MeCP2 is normally abundantly present in most neurons and in many body tissues, especially lung and spleen, and it tends to be expressed increasingly as cells mature. Most of the known mutations of the *MeCP2* gene are predicted to produce total or partial loss of function of the MeCP2 protein.

The normal developmental function of the *MeCP2* gene seems to be to assist maturational programs in many body tissues by silencing numerous other genes that are expressed earlier in development (Shahbazian et al., 2002b). The failure of this global transcriptional repressor may allow biochemical processes active early in development to proceed with little regulation. This failure of gene "silencing" is thought in most cases to trigger the emergence of RS symptoms. The phenotypic variability in RS symptoms is presumably related to the many alternative ways in which the gene can be spliced, which would produce variable patterns and degrees of disruption in normal brain development. The degree of X-chromosome inactivation within the brain is also thought to be a major determinant of the clinical phenotype and disease severity (Van den Veyver and Zoghbi, 2002).

An alternative theory relating the *MeCP2* mutation and the timing of emergence of symptoms is that compounds expressed early in brain development are not repressed as they normally would be. These compounds may actually be toxic when present in excess, and it takes time for them to accumulate postnatally. When their concentration reaches a certain threshold, they might damage neurons and disrupt normal brain function. It is at this time that the symptoms of RS would then emerge, after a period of relatively normal brain development and the attainment of normal early maturational milestones. The recent development of an *MeCP2* knockout mouse that has neurological symptoms similar to those of RS should be helpful for evaluating the merits of these competing, though not necessarily mutually exclusive theories, and it may offer promise for developing genetically based therapeutic interventions (Shahbazian et al., 2002a).

Neurobiological Substrate. Consistent with the hypothesized role of *MeCP2* in repressing the expression of early developmental genes, histology of cortex from individuals with RS suggests the presence of a developmental immaturity (Belichenko et al., 1994; Cornford et al., 1994), including reductions of neurotransmitter metabolites and nerve growth factor (Lekman et al., 1989; Lipani et al., 2000). Histological immaturity is similarly seen in many body tissues of individuals who have RS (Armstrong, 2002).

The regions of the brain that are most dysfunctional and responsible for the generation of symptoms in RS are unknown. Imaging studies have reported higher levels of choline and lower levels of N-acetylaspartate (NAA, a putative marker of neuronal viability) in RS (Horska et al., 2000; Khong et al., 2002). Regional glucose metabolism, assessed with positron emission tomography (PET), shows reduced occipital cortical and increased cerebellar activity (Villemagne et al., 2002). Benzodiazepine (BZ) receptor binding as measured with SPECT seems reduced in front temporal cortices (Yamashita et al., 1998).

Taken together, extant imaging studies suggest the presence of neuronal pathology and reduced metabolism primarily in frontal cortices, although additional disturbances have been reported in parietal, temporal, and cerebellar tissues. These heteromodal association cortices are involved in higher level cognitive processes that develop later than primary sensory, sensory association, and motor cortices. Such deficits are consistent with the theories of maturational arrest and toxicity caused by deficient production of MeCP2 protein early in development.

Fragile X

Fragile X, a relatively common form of mental retardation caused by a single mutation in the long arm of the X chromosome, occurs once in every 2000 to 4000 live births. Approximately 20 percent of such children exhibit autistic symptoms. Conversely, 8 percent of males and 6 percent of females diagnosed with autism carry the fragile X abnormality. The mutation alters brain development and produces a distinctive physical, cognitive, and neuropsychiatric phenotype. Clinical symptoms are insufficient to make the fragile X diagnosis. Instead, specific genetic abnormality must be evident using molecular diagnostic techniques (Hagerman, 1999).

Because it is an X-linked disorder, fragile X affects males and females differently. In boys, fragile X is associated with variable presentations of mental retardation, difficulties with visuospatial and memory functioning, gaze avoidance, stereotypic behaviors, hyperactivity, and abnormal speech patterns, including echolalia, high-pitched speech, poor articulation, and dysfluency. Aggression and self-injurious behaviors are prominent in some individuals. Persons with fragile X commonly have a characteristic appearance that includes an elongated face, a large protruding jaw, large ears, enlarged testicles, and accentuated secondary sexual characteristics. In girls who are heterozygous for the fragile X full mutation, the syndrome is associated with a normal physical appearance, variable cognitive functioning that ranges from normal to mildly mentally retarded, and difficulties with mathematics, attention, social communication, and the regulation of anxiety (Reiss et al., 2000a). Because carrier females on average have milder symptoms, they are more likely to reproduce and transmit the fragile X gene (Nelson, 1995; Oostra and Halley, 1995).

Genetics. Some proportion of human cells, when grown in the absence of folic acid, display a break point on one of the X chromosomes. Fragile X co-segregates with this "fragile" site. Progression of disease severity over generations, referred to as *anticipation*, was noted before the gene was identified. In 1991, the molecular basis for anticipation was discerned when the *FMR-1* gene (i.e., the "first fragile X, mental retardation" gene) was identified. The mutation consists of the transgenerational expansion of a so-called DNA triplet repeat, a sequence of three successive bases [specifically, cytosine-guanine-guanine (CGG), a sequence encoding the amino acid arginine] repeated many times (O'Donnell and Warren, 2002). It is situated within a segment of the long arm of the X-chromosome, at Xq27.3.

Healthy individuals have between 6 and 50 repeats of these bases in their *FMR-1* gene. In affected individuals, the number of repeats typically ranges from 200 to 1000. Repeats numbering between 50 and 200, termed *premutations*, are typically present in the mothers of affected probands and yield milder symptoms. Individuals with permutations have a high risk for expanding the number of repeats in subsequent generations.

The CGG trinucleotide repeat of *FMR-1* is located in the promoter region of this gene. All regions rich in C+G nucleotides ("CpG islands") are prone to methylation, and therefore a greater expansion of the triplet repeat is accompanied by greater methylation of the promoter region, which increasingly represses expression of the *FMR-1* gene product, a protein termed fragile X mental retardation protein (FMRP). In addition to this primary cause of fragile X, a minority of children have microdeletions of the *FMR-1* gene. Thus, different mutations in different parts of the *FMR-1* gene can produce the same clinical phenotype, a phenomenon termed *allelic heterogeneity*.

Neurobiological Substrate. FMRP is a binding protein for ribonucleic acid (RNA) that associates with polyribosomes in the cytosol to form a large messenger ribonucleoprotein (mRNP) complex (Feng et al., 1997). FMRP is thought to modulate the translation of the RNA ligands that this mRNP polyribosomal complex processes. FMRP is located at the synapse, where it apparently modulates synaptic plasticity (Weiler et al., 1997). The brains of individuals with fragile X as well as *FMR-1* knockout mice have abnormal morphology of dendritic spines (Comery et al., 1997). Repression of the FMRP production in fragile X is thought to disrupt synapse formation and plasticity, cellular processes important for development of normal learning and memory. FMRP is widely distributed throughout the mammalian brain (Hinds et al., 1993), and in humans, the *FMR-1* gene is expressed most abundantly during early development in neurons of the hippocampus, nucleus basalis, and cerebellum (Abitbol et al., 1993), brain areas that subserve learning and memory.

This pattern of normal expression of FMRP prompted initial neuroimaging studies of individuals with fragile X to focus on these regions (Reiss et al., 1991a, b, 1994, 1995). MRI studies have found diminished sizes of lobules VI and VII of the cerebellar vermis and enlarged fourth ventricles in fragile X males but not other developmentally delayed individuals. Females with fragile X had similar, albeit smaller, reductions in the same brain areas (Reiss et al., 1991b). This suggests the presence of an "intermediate gene dosage effect" of the *FMR-1* mutation in heterozygote females. In girls, cerebellum volumes correlated inversely with ratings of social communication and stereotypic behaviors (Mazzocco et al., 1997), and with IQ and measures of executive functioning (Mostofsky et al., 1998). Volumes of the hippocampus, a structure important in learning and memory, have been reported to be larger in individuals with fragile X (Reiss et al., 1994), although this finding has not been replicated (Jakala et al., 1997). These studies suggest that the abnormal expression of FMRP observed in animal studies contributes to disturbances of brain development in fragile X and its associated cognitive and behavioral deficits.

Functional MRI studies have tried to elucidate the consequences of the *FMR-1* mutation for human brain function. Reduced activity in frontal-subcortical circuits, important for the regulation of impulses and attention, has been reported in individuals with fragile X (Hjalgrim et al., 1999), and FMRP levels in females with fragile X have been reported to correlate significantly with the magnitude of brain activation in the frontal and parietal cortices during a working memory task (Menon et al., 2000). These findings suggest that deficient production of FMRP may contribute to the hyperactivity, inattention, and perseveration that are important features of the fragile X clinical phenotype.

Williams Syndrome

With a prevalence of 1 in 20,000, Williams syndrome (WS) is a rare clinical diagnosis. Nevertheless, it is of considerable interest to clinicians and researchers because of its unique phenotype and the genetic mechanisms that produce it. The phenotype of WS is almost a mirror image of the phenotype of autism. These children are often outgoing, social, and communicative, and many have a special propensity for music, dance, and simple but highly embellished forms of storytelling. Children with WS are typically small, and they often have pixyish facial features, including a broad forehead, prominent ears, full lips, an upturned nose, and a small chin. IQ averages about 50, but the range is considerable and in some children IQ can be within the normal range. The cognitive profile in WS children is distinctive and includes prominent deficits in visuospatial skills. Relative strengths are seen in more verbal domains, including vocabulary, the social use of language, auditory memory, as well as recognizing and remembering faces (Bellugi et al., 1999). They have a variety of cardiovascular problems.

Genetics. Most children with WS have a large deletion of a segment on the long arm of chromosome 7 (1 to 2 Mb in the 7q11.23 region). The deletion typically occurs as a spontaneous new mutation, a consequence of an unequal crossover event during meiosis in the gametes of one of the parents (Urban et al., 1996). Historically, the cardiovascular problems associated with WS were noted to co-segregate with a gene in the deleted region that produces elastin, an important component of blood vessels, skin, and lung tissues. The absence of elastin is thought to cause the various cardiovascular and kidney problems of WS, as well as diminished joint flexibility. Deficient elastin production probably also causes the characteristic faces of these children. Because elastin is not present in fetal or adult brain tissue, however, deficient elastin production is unlikely to cause the cognitive impairments associated with WS.

A second gene was soon reported in this same deleted region, and its sequence was observed to be nearly identical to a previously identified gene, *LIM kinase 1*. This second gene is expressed in the brain in high concentrations, and many believe that disturbances in its protein product will prove to be responsible for the cognitive deficits associated with WS. At least 16 contiguous genes, however, are now known to reside in the deleted region. They include *CLIP-115*, replication factor C subunit, syntaxin 1A, Frizzled 9, and transcription factor 21. Although the role of these genes in WS is unknown, it seems likely that the specific deletion present in any one child will produce a particular constellation of symptoms and a specific clinical phenotype.

Neurobiological Substrate. The regions of the brain where expression of the protein product encoded by the WS gene are altered are thus far unknown, although it is an area of intense investigation. The relative specificity of the cognitive abnormalities in WS suggests, however, that the regions of altered expression will also be relatively specific. A number of imaging studies have suggested that the visuospatial deficits in these children are mediated by anatomical abnormalities in posterior brain systems.

The largest neuroanatomical imaging study of WS has come from a single cohort of young adults studied in a single laboratory. This investigation demonstrated a reduction in overall brain volume in the WS group. Volumes of the cerebellum and superior temporal gyrus are relatively preserved, whereas those of the brainstem are disproportionately reduced; also an increased ratio of volumes of frontal to posterior tissues was noted, and volumes of white matter were reduced to a greater degree than gray matter in the WS group, with the greatest reduction in gray matter observed in the right occipital lobe (Reiss et al., 2000b). Posterior portions of the corpus callosum were disproportionately small, consistent with the overall white matter findings, and the size of the posterior cerebellar vermis was larger in the WS subjects, but only when corrected for the reduction in overall brain size (Schmitt et al., 2001a, b). Subjects with WS also exhibited significantly increased gyrification of the cerebral cortex globally, especially in the right parietal, right occipital, and left frontal cortices (Schmitt et al., 2002). Taken together, this series of imaging studies suggests the presence of anatomical disturbances in dorsal and posterior brain regions of individuals with WS that may account for their relatively specific deficits in visuospatial processing.

The first anatomical MRI study of young children with WS (mean age 21 months) (Jones et al., 2002) reported enlarged cerebellums in the WS group, consistent with the findings in older children and adults. Finally, a magnetic resonance spectroscopy (MRS) study of children and adults with WS detected reduced phosphomonoesters in a frontoparietal region of interest (ROI) and reduced NAA (a marker for the number of viable neurons) in the cerebellum (Rae et al., 1998). Cerebellar NAA levels correlated with measures of verbal and performance IQ. Whether these findings would be detected in other regions of the brain, or whether they are specific to the cerebellum, is unknown.

Prader-Willi and Angelman Syndromes

Prader-Willi syndrome (PWS), with a prevalence of 1 in 10,000, is a rare condition. Children become symptomatic soon after birth. Infants are initially hypotonic and sometimes then fail to thrive. Subsequently, within the first 2 years of life, they become hyperphagic and, eventually, obese. Often they are mildly to moderately mentally retarded. They may be of short stature, with small hands, feet, and gonads. Behavioral problems are common and include obsessive-compulsive symptoms, compulsive food-related behaviors, temper tantrums, and aggression.

Angelman syndrome (AS), also rare, has a prevalence similar to that of PWS. Infants with AS are often hypotonic. They then develop motor delays, ataxia, and moderate to severe mental retardation. Only rarely do they develop speech. They often have characteristic facial features, including a wide mouth, large mandible, pointed chin, prominent tongue, wide spaced teeth, and blue eyes. Some develop the remarkable symptoms of excessive laughter or of puppetlike limb movements. Seizures usually develop soon after birth, and all with AS have abnormal EEGs.

Genetics. Both PWS and AS were known by the mid-1980s to be caused by deletions in the same span of chromosome 15 (15q11-13). How the same deletion could cause two syndromes with such differing phenotypes was at first perplexing. Subsequent investigation then demonstrated that the resulting phenotype depended on which parent donated the chromosome with this particular deletion. PWS resulted in most instances when the deleted chromosome originated from the father, and AS resulted when it originated from the mother.

Although all people had long been known to inherit half their genes from their mother and half from their father, maternally and paternally derived genes were also erroneously thought to be expressed equally in offspring. We now know, however, that the expression of genes in a child is influenced by their passage through the mother's egg and father's sperm. This epigenetic phenomenon, called *genetic imprinting*, occurs when certain genes become methylated within a gamete of one of the parent's gonads (Davies et al., 2001). Genetic imprinting influences the expression of more than 40 genes, including the genes on chromosome 15 that cause AS and PWS.

The PWS region on chromosome 15 resides immediately upstream from the AS region. Under normal circumstances, the PWS region on the chromosome from the father is active and the AS region is inactive. In the chromosome from the mother, in contrast, the PWS region is inactive and the AS region is active. All of the known genetic defects that produce PWS or AS have in common the abnormal inactivation of one of these normally active regions (Fig. 14.1).

Three different genetic defects can produce PWS (Cassidy et al., 2000; Nicholls and Knepper, 2001). The first, a deletion of both the PWS and AS regions within 15q11-13 on the paternally derived chromosome, occurs in 70 percent of individuals with PWS. This deletion leaves the AS region of the maternally derived chromosome normally functioning, whereas maternal imprinting renders the PWS region on this chromosome inactive. Production of the PWS protein product is therefore deficient. The second genetic defect occurs in 28 percent of children with PWS. In this instance, the child receives two copies of chromosome 15 from the mother, referred to as *uniparental disomy* (UPD). UPD occurs when two chromosomes from one parent and a single copy of the same chromosome from the other parent are inappropriately passed to the offspring, resulting in a total of three chromosomes instead of the usual two. One of

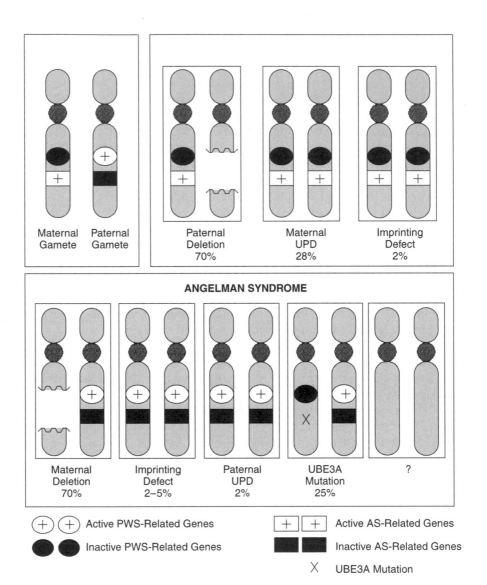

Figure 14.1. Genetic mechanisms in Prader-Willi and Angelman syndromes. *Upper left*: Under normal circumstances on the maternally derived chromosome, the Prader-Willi-related genes are inactive and the Angelman syndrome genes are active. On the paternally derived chromosome, the reverse is true—the Prader-Willi-related genes are active and the Angelman syndrome genes are inactive. *Upper right*: Paternal deletion, maternal uniparental disomy (UPD), and imprinting defects that cause Prader-Willi syndrome are represented in each of the chromosomes derived from the mother and the father. *Bottom*: Maternal deletion, paternal UPD, imprinting defects, and the *UBE3A* deletions that cause Angelman syndrome are shown. The percentages represent the approximate percentage of individuals affected by each of these syndromes who have the specified genetic defect.

the three chromosomes is then lost during fertilization. An extra chromosome from the mother and the loss of the chromosome from the father results in maternal UPD. Maternal UPD provides the child with two active AS regions and two inactive PWS regions, because of maternal imprinting of both chromosomes, and thus no production of the PWS protein product is possible. The third genetic defect, in 2 percent of individuals with PWS, results from a mutation in the imprinting center. This is a region of DNA that controls imprinting by regulating the extent of methylation and compaction of adjacent chromatin. A mutation in the imprinting center of the paternal chromosome causes an imprinting defect that inactivates the PWS region of the paternally derived chromosome, leaving no active PWS genes.

Similar genetic mechanisms produce AS. The first defect, occurring in approximately 70 percent of individuals with AS, is a deletion of 15q11-13 on the maternally derived chromosome. This deletion leaves only an active PWS region and inactive AS region (due to paternal imprinting) on the paternally derived chromosome, and thus no AS protein product. The second defect, affecting 2 percent of individuals with AS, is paternal UPD (both copies of chromosome 15 derive from the father). Paternal imprinting of both chromosomes leaves the child with two active PWS and two inactive AS regions, and no AS protein product. The third defect occurs in another 5 percent of individuals with AS. It is a mutation of the imprinting center of the maternally derived chromosome, thus inactivating the AS region of that chromosome. Because the AS region of the paternally derived chromosome is normal and inactive, the AS regions of both chromosomes are inactive and no AS protein product is possible.

Finally, a fourth genetic mechanism causes AS in another 25 percent of children. It is a mutation of a single gene, called *UBE3A*, that lies within the AS region. It encodes a protein that helps to regulate the action of ubiquitin in degrading recycled or damaged cellular proteins. UBE3A and other proteins attach to ubiquitin, which then is able to target proteins for degradation by cellular proteases. The deletion of *UBE3A* is therefore thought to lead to the accumulation of inappropriate cellular proteins that disrupt cellular functions. Incidentally, one of the genes within the AS region encodes for a subunit of the GABA-A receptor. Loss of this subunit and the subsequent disturbances in GABAergic transmission causes the seizures seen in children who have AS. Those children with the single gene deletion of *UBE3A* do not lose the GABA-A receptor subunit and therefore do not have a seizure disorder.

All of the mutations described above, except the single-gene mutation of AS, can be detected with methylation-sensitive DNA probes, because DNA methylation of the imprinting center is the mechanism by which the genes for these disorders are imprinted. The induction of imprinting by methylation in specific areas of DNA offers hope for the development of new genetic treatments of these disorders. Methylation possibly could be removed or reversed on the imprinting center that resides on the normal copy of chromosome 15 in these individuals, for example, thus activating the PWS or AS regions that imprinting otherwise normally inactivates.

Neurobiological Substrate. Although knockout mouse models for PWS and AS now exist, the regions of altered gene expression have not yet been identified. Isolated imaging case studies have not helped to identify anatomical or functional abnormalities in the brains of individuals affected with PWS or AS. Thus, the neurobiological substrate for these disorders is unknown.

CHILDHOOD-ONSET SCHIZOPHRENIA

Childhood-onset schizophrenia (COS) is a rare psychotic disorder that in certain ways resembles a pervasive developmental disorder. Information on its prevalence is limited, in part because diagnostic criteria have changed considerably over the last decade (Volkmar and Tsatsanis, 2002). COS is almost certainly less prevalent than autism, however, and it is often diagnosed in the presence of an autistic spectrum disorder. Males and females seem equally likely to be affected. Premorbidly, COS is associated with a number of developmental delays, including disturbances in motor, general cognitive, linguistic, and social development (Jacobsen and Rapoport, 1998; Nicolson et al., 2000). Some evidence suggests that the premorbid and clinical courses of COS are more severe than those of later onset schizophrenia (Alaghband-Rad et al., 1995). Episodes are more acute, and on average are of longer duration, in younger compared with older children (Werry, 1996). The course of illness is highly variable.

Neurobiological Substrate. Knowledge of the neural systems involved in COS comes mostly from MRI studies in a small number of cohorts. These children have been consistently reported to have smaller brains and enlarged ventricles (Hendren et al., 2000; Sowell et al., 2000). One longitudinal study has reported a fourfold greater decrement in volume of the cortical gray matter during adolescence compared to healthy controls, most prominently in frontal and temporal regions (Rapoport et al., 1999). This reduction in cortical gray matter may contribute to a more rapid decrease in volumes of the total brain and hippocampus and a more rapid increase in ventricular volumes during adolescence. These age-related changes in the COS group slow by early adulthood (Jacobsen et al., 1998; Giedd et al., 1999). Reductions in volume of the right posterior superior temporal gyrus during this time have been reported to predict the severity of positive psychotic symptoms at follow-up (Jacobsen et al., 1998). Children with COS also have smaller thalamic and basal ganglia volumes when receiving typical but not atypical antipsychotic medications (Frazier et al., 1996; Hendren et al., 2000).

Other imaging modalities have detected lower levels of NAA (an index of neuronal viability) in the frontal lobes and hippocampus of children with COS (Bertolino et al., 1998; Sowell et al., 2000). The few existing PET studies have reported reduced frontal blood flow (Chabrol et al., 1986), reduced metabolism in middle and superior frontal regions, and increased inferior frontal metabolism in adolescents with COS (Jacobsen and Rapoport, 1997).

DISORDERS OF IMPULSE CONTROL

Tourette Syndrome

Tourette syndrome (TS) is a disorder of motor and vocal tics. Motor tics are usually simple, nonpurposeful, and rapid movements affecting muscles of the face, neck, and shoulders, with less frequent involvement of the trunk and extremities. Vocal tics usually involve frequent and excessively forceful throat clearing, sniffing, snorting, humming, and explosive, monosyllabic, and nonsensical utterances. Less commonly, motor and vocal tics are more complex, in that they are more sustained and semipurposeful in quality. Tics are usually preceded by a vague discomfort or urge to move the body region affected by the tic. This "premonitory urge" relentlessly builds in intensity until the individual capitulates to the urge and performs the tic. This typically brings immediate but temporary relief from the urge, only to have it build quickly again and reinitiate the cycle of tension, capitulation, and relief. Tics can be suppressed voluntarily, but not indefinitely (Peterson et al., 1998).

The modal age of onset of tics is 6 years. Tics affect 10 to 20 percent of children at some time in their life, with a ratio of boys to girls of approximately 3 or 4:1 (Costello et al., 1996; Peterson et al., 2001a). Tics most commonly begin at a low frequency and with minimal forcefulness, and parents often attribute the behaviors to their child's "habit." In the majority of children, tics disappear of their own accord in a matter of weeks to months. Roughly 1 percent of all children will have tics that endure for more than a year, at which time they are arbitrarily designated "chronic." By definition, children who have the combination of chronic motor and vocal tics are said to have TS, although no phenomenological, natural history, or neurobiological evidence exists to suggest that transient tics, chronic tics, or TS differ from each other in any way other than their duration (Peterson et al., 2001a). Family-genetic and twin studies, in fact, suggest that TS and chronic tic disorders represent continua of the same underlying genetic diathesis (Price et al., 1985; Pauls and Leckman, 1986).

Tics that persist through later childhood and into adolescence have a characteristic natural history. Follow-up studies indicate that tics on average increase gradually through the grade school years before peaking at age 11 (Leckman et al., 1998). Tics then gradually decline in average severity through adolescence until stabilizing at relatively low levels by young adulthood. Superimposed on this gradual rise, plateau, and decline in average tic severity is a fluctuation, or "waxing and waning," of baseline tic severity. Although this fluctuation is nonrandom (Peterson and Leckman, 1998), the biological determinants of the fluctuations remain poorly characterized. Clinical experience has repeatedly shown that emotional stress, physical fatigue, and excitement can reliably exacerbate tics. Neuroendocrine studies provide supportive evidence for an important role of stress in modulating the severity of tic symptoms (Chappell et al., 1994).

Genetics. Tourette syndrome, obsessive-compulsive disorder (OCD), and attention deficit hyperactivity disorder (ADHD) commonly co-occur in clinical populations (Shapiro et al., 1988; Pauls et al., 1991; Leonard et al., 1992), supporting speculation that the conditions may share a common etiology (Peterson and Klein, 1997). The strongest evidence for a shared etiology comes from family studies of clinic patients. Those studies have shown that OCD is present in the families of probands who have TS more often than it is present in control families, whether or not the proband has comorbid OCD (Eapen et al., 1993). Conversely, tics are present in the family members of probands who have OCD more often than they are present in control families, whether or not the proband has a comorbid tic disorder (Grados et al., 2001).

These findings suggest that a particular genetic vulnerability may be variably expressed as tics, as OCD, or as both disorders in combination. Although the familial transmission of ADHD in persons who have either tics or OCD is less clear (Pauls et al., 1993), some investigators regard ADHD as an additional variable manifestation of putative TS vulnerability genes (Comings and Comings, 1987). These three disorders were significantly associated with one another both within and across time points, from early childhood to young adulthood, in an epidemiological sample (Peterson et al., 2001a), suggesting that the aggregation of comorbid illnesses in families of clinically identified probands were not likely to have been the consequence of biases associated with clinical ascertainment that could potentially affect familial aggregation (Peterson et al., 1995). Thus, family-genetic and epidemiological studies agree that tic disorders and OCD, and possibly some forms of ADHD, are etiologically related, and segregation analyses of their familial transmission suggest that this shared etiology has a genetic basis.

The genetic relatedness of these conditions is remarkable, given that, superficially at least, the phenotypes of TS, OCD, and ADHD differ dramatically. The genetic relatedness of these disorders raises the question of whether the phenotypes might be more intimately related than their surface phenomena would suggest. The resemblance between OCD symptoms and complex tics suggest, for example, that the symptoms of TS and OCD might lie on a spectrum of "compulsory" behaviors. Those symptoms that have a prominent ideational component may belong to OCD on the one end, those with little or no ideational component may belong to the simple tics of TS on the other, and complex tics might be positioned somewhere between these two extremes. Similarly, the symptoms of ADHD share certain phenomenological features with tics. Tics, for example, can be thought of as a "hyperkinesia," and motoric hyperactivity is a prominent feature of ADHD. Furthermore, TS patients can inhibit their tics for only brief periods of time, and the impaired inhibition of impulses is a hallmark of ADHD (Barkley, 1997). Thus both ADHD and TS children have excessive motor activity and difficulty inhibiting specific behaviors. Given the genetic relatedness and phenomenological similarities of these conditions, it seems likely that their vulnerability genes produce not three behaviorally unrelated disorders, but instead an entire spectrum of related semi-involuntary behaviors.

Despite intensive efforts and initial promising leads, genetic studies of TS have not yet yielded strong or replicable findings (Pauls, 2001). These include studies employing a variety of genetic techniques and experimental paradigms, including genetic linkage and haplotype relative risk analyses, transmission disequilibrium tests, and sib-pair analyses. Although early segregation analyses of family data were consistent with the hypothesis of an autosomal dominant mode of genetic transmission, recent studies suggest that the mode of inheritance is likely to be considerably more complex, with the expression of genes of major effect being modified by other genes. Several completed genome scans have identified several regions of interest, but the findings thus far are neither robust nor replicated. The strongest linkage finding to date was reported in a large Canadian kindred, in which a log of the odds ratio (LOD) score of 3.24 was reported for chromosome 11 (11q23) (Merette et al., 2000).

Neurochemistry. The most compelling evidence for the presence of abnormal neurochemical systems in TS has been the superior clinical efficacy of dopamine antagonists in the treatment of tic disorders (Peterson and Cohen, 1998). Measurements of dopamine metabolites in the CSF, postmortem brain tissue, and urine of patients with TS, however, have yielded either inconsistent or negative results (Anderson et al., 1999). Ligand studies of the dopamine D_2 receptor (Wong et al., 1997), the dopamine transporter (Stamenkovic et al., 2001), and dopamine decarboxylase (Ernst et al., 1999) have yielded mostly negative results, and the rare positive findings have failed to replicate (Peterson and Thomas, 2000). Apparently the central synthesis and metabolism of dopamine in persons with TS is largely unaltered.

Evidence for altered noradrenergic systems in persons with TS includes the modest benefits that clonidine, an $alpha_2$ agonist, confers on tic symptoms (Leckman et al., 1991). The largest neurochemical studies of the CSF in individuals with TS have shown normal 3-methoxy-4-hydroxyphenylglycol (MHPG) levels but nearly twofold elevations of norepinephrine (Leckman et al., 1995). In addition, stress hormones in CSF, urine, and plasma indicate an exaggerated stress response in some TS individuals (Chappell et al., 1994). These findings suggest normal functioning of basal stress systems and increased responsivity to acute stressors in some persons with TS.

Other neurotransmitter studies suggest the possibility that serotonergic systems, believed to be dysfunctional in OCD, could also be dysfunctional in TS. Reductions in 5-HT, its precursor tryptophan, and its major metabolite 5-hydroxyindoleacetic acid (5-HIAA) have been reported in a postmortem brain study (Anderson et al., 1992a). A postmortem study has also suggested disturbances in glutamatergic systems, with reduced levels of glutamate reported in the three major projection areas of the subthalamic nucleus—the medial and lateral segments of the globus pallidus and the reticular portion of the substantia nigra (Anderson et al., 1992a). Because the subthalamic nucleus is important in motor control, a glutamatergic dysfunction in this system could contribute to the motor disturbances of TS.

Neurobiological Substrate. The neural basis for TS is thought to consist of anatomical and functional disturbances in cortico-striato-thalamo-cortical (CSTC) circuits. These circuits loop between cortical and subcortical brain regions. They are composed of multiple, partially overlapping but largely "parallel" pathways that direct information from the cerebral cortex to the subcortex, and then back again to specific regions of the cortex. Although multiple anatomically and functionally related cortical regions provide input into a particular circuit, each circuit refocuses its projections back onto only a subset of the cortical regions contributing to the input of that circuit. Although the number of anatomically and functionally discrete pathways is still controversial (Parent and Hazrati, 1995), current consensus holds that CSTC circuitry has at least four components—those initiating from and projecting back to sensorimotor cortex, orbitofrontal cortex (OFC), limbic and associated anterior cingulate cortices, or association cortices. The etiologies of OCD and ADHD are also thought to involve disturbances in CSTC circuits, and it may be that the common involvement of these circuits across these disorders may account in part for the common co-occurrence with TS in clinical populations (Peterson and Klein, 1997).

The basal ganglia portions of CSTC circuits appear to be centrally involved in the pathophysiology of TS. Reduced volumes of the putamen and globus pallidus (the lenticular nucleus) were initially found in adults (Peterson et al., 1993a, b) but not in children (Singer et al., 1993). Then among identical twin pairs, the more severely affected twin was found to have smaller caudate volumes (Hyde et al., 1995). Because the twins were genetically identical, smaller caudates were presumably caused by nonshared environmental determinants, rather than by the effects of TS vulnerability genes. A large imaging study of 154 children and adults with TS and 130 healthy controls helped to reconcile these various basal ganglia findings (Peterson et al., in press). Smaller caudate volumes were detected in both children and adults with TS, consistent with the previous twin study. Lenticular nucleus volumes also were smaller in TS adults, consistent with the prior adult study, but not in children, consistent with the previous study of children. Detection of smaller caudate volumes across age groups suggests that smaller caudate nuclei may be a good candidate marker for a trait abnormality in TS subjects. Furthermore, smaller lenticular nucleus volumes may be a marker for the persistence of tic symptoms into adulthood. Consistent with these anatomical findings, PET and SPECT studies have repeatedly demonstrated reduced metabolism and blood flow to the basal ganglia (Braun et al., 1993; Moriarty et al., 1995).

One fMRI study has helped define the neural systems subserving the control of tic symptoms. Twenty-two adults with TS alternated periods of allowing themselves to tic freely with periods of suppressing their tics completely (Peterson et al., 1998). Tic suppression was associated with increased activity of the ventral portion of the right caudate nucleus and numerous cortical regions, especially prefrontal and temporal cortices. Tic suppression was also associated with decreased activity of the ventral globus pallidus, putamen, and thalamus bilaterally. The severity of tic symptoms correlated with the change in activity of the basal ganglia and thalamus regions, indicating that as symptom severity increased, the changes in subcortical activity during tic suppression decreased. These findings suggest that the changes in neural activity of subcortical regions—increases in the right caudate and decreases in the rest of the subcortex—participate in the suppression of tics. When these frontostriatal braking mechanisms fail, tics are progressively more likely to escape the inhibitory influences that these circuits have on motor behavior.

The hypothesized role of prefrontal regions in helping to suppress or regulate unwanted urges to tic was supported by a direct analysis of cortical volumes in which increases in volume of prefrontal cortices were detected in the TS group bilaterally (Peterson et al., 2001b). Frontal volumes were largest in younger children with TS, less prominent in older children, and then smaller by adulthood in subjects with TS. Smaller prefrontal volumes in symptomatic TS adults were suspected to be responsible for the relatively unusual persistence of tic symptoms into adulthood. Consistent with this interpretation was the finding that orbitofrontal volumes correlated significantly with the severity of tic symptoms, suggesting that smaller volumes in these regions may provide insufficient inhibitory activity to suppress tics. The larger prefrontal volumes detected in the children with TS were suspected to represent an activity-dependent, structural plasticity that helps to suppress tics. This interpretation is consistent with numerous preclinical and clinical studies suggesting that the orbitofrontal region plays an important role in inhibitory control (Fuster, 1997). It is also consistent with the fMRI finding that prefrontal activation is required by TS subjects to suppress their tics (Peterson et al., 1998). Presumably, the chronic need to suppress tics activates and then hypertrophies prefrontal cortices in children who have TS (Fig. 14.2).

The finding of a significant inverse association of tic severity with prefrontal volumes stands in stark contrast to the absence of association of basal ganglia volumes with the severity of tic symptoms. These differing associations of symptom severity with basal ganglia or cortical volumes implies that if a predisposition to having tics is indeed represented within the basal ganglia, then prefrontal volumes are likely to be relatively more important than basal ganglia volumes in determining whether that predisposition is manifested within a given individual. Moreover, if that predisposition to tic is manifested, the cortical volumes seem to be more important than the basal

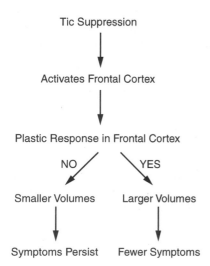

Figure 14.2. Theory of compensatory effects in Tourette syndrome. The voluntary suppression of tics activates frontal cortices. The need to suppress tics chronically is thought to induce hypertrophy of the frontal cortex in children, which in turn reduces the severity of tic symptoms. Failure to induce this plastic response of the frontal cortices is thought to yield smaller volumes, more severe symptoms, and the persistence of tics into adulthood.

ganglia in determining how severe the tic symptoms are likely to be. In other words, the morphological and functional integrity of cortical neuroregulatory systems may be clinically more salient for these patients than is the caudate hypoplasia that has been identified.

Obsessive-Compulsive Disorder

Adult OCD has been summarized in Chapter 13 of this volume. Herein we will address the childhood variant as an expression of vulnerability genes for TS and relevant brain imaging findings for this condition.

All forms of OCD are characterized by recurrent, distressing, and intrusive thoughts, images, or urges to action, together with their repetitive behavioral counterparts. Usually, performance of the compulsion brings some degree of relief from the urge to action and from the anxiety associated with the imagined consequences of failing to perform the compulsion.

Several large factor analytic studies have confirmed the presence of at least four main components to OCD symptoms: (1) aggressive, sexual, religious, and somatic obsessions, and checking compulsions; (2) symmetry and ordering; (3) cleanliness and washing; and (4) hoarding (Baer, 1994; Leckman et al., 1997). The age of onset of OCD in the general community is probably bimodal, with one mode of onset at 10 to 12 years of age and the other in early adulthood (Rasmussen and Tsuang, 1986; Berg et al., 1989; Valleni-Basile et al., 1996; Geller et al., 1998). The childhood-onset form of OCD most commonly occurs in the context of a personal history of a tic disorder, and it occurs even more commonly in the context of a personal or family history of tic disorder (this is the so-called tic-related form of OCD). The adult-onset form of OCD, in contrast, is much less likely to occur in the context of a personal or family history of tics, while the early onset form appears to be more strongly familial (Pauls et al., 1995).

The symptoms of the tic-related form of OCD are significantly more likely to be those of the first or third of the factor-based groupings listed previously, whereas the non-tic-related form is more likely to involve symmetry and ordering (Leckman et al., 1997). When present together, the severities of OCD and tic symptoms have been shown to covary with one another, suggesting an underlying common modulator of severity over the short term (Lin et al., in press). In contrast to tics, childhood-onset OCD symptoms over the long term tend more often to persist into late adolescence and adulthood, and they are usually more functionally debilitating than are tics alone (Swedo et al., 1989a; Leonard et al., 1990).

Genetics. Segregation analyses suggest the presence of genes of major effect, although the mode of transmission is likely to be complex (Alsobrook et al., 2002). Linkage and association studies of childhood-onset OCD have been initiated, but few findings have been reported thus far. Candidate genes related to the serotonin system have received the greatest attention, with few significant findings reported. The strongest evidence for linkage in a preliminary study of 7 families with childhood-onset

OCD was on chromosome 9 (9p, LOD $=$ 1.97), with weaker evidence for linkage on 19q (Hanna et al., 2002). In addition, an analysis of 77 sib-pairs with TS suggested significant joint effects of specific loci on 4q and 5q for developing the obsessive-compulsive symptom of hoarding (Zhang et al., 2002).

Neurochemistry. Virtually no studies of norepinephrine or dopaminergic systems have been reported in children with OCD. Data relevant to serotonin systems derives from the efficacy of serotonergic medications in the treatment of children with OCD (March et al., 1998; Liebowitz et al., 2002). Studies of glutamate and glutamine have been more extensive. An MRS study has reported elevated GLX (combined glutamate and glutamine) concentrations in the caudate nuclei of treatment-naive children who have OCD but no tics, and these caudate GLX concentrations normalized after a 12-week course of antiobsessional treatment with paroxetine (Rosenberg et al., 2000b) but not behavioral therapy (Benazon et al., 2002). Changes in GLX concentrations in the caudate correlated positively with changes in OCD symptom severity during paroxetine treatment, suggesting that elevated pretreatment GLX concentrations in the caudate may predict treatment response to serotonergic medications.

Cerebrospinal fluid studies of children have suggested that arginine vasopressin may be inversely associated with the severity of OCD symptoms (Swedo et al., 1992a). A subsequent study of adults (many with childhood-onset illness) failed to find group differences in vasopressin but did report elevated CSF levels of a related peptide, oxytocin, in individuals with OCD (Leckman et al., 1994). Yet another study failed to find group differences in oxytocin in the CSF associated with a diagnosis of OCD (Altemus et al., 1994). Finally, intranasal administration of oxytocin in adults with OCD in a placebo-controlled crossover study did not affect OCD symptoms (Epperson et al., 1996). Clearly, disturbances in these neuropeptide systems have not proved to be reproducible, leaving unclear the role of these compounds in the etiology of OCD.

Neurobiological Substrate. Structural and functional imaging studies implicate orbitofrontal portions of CSTC circuits in the pathophysiology of OCD. Hypermetabolism and elevated blood flow in prefrontal cortices are probably the most consistent findings in subjects with OCD. Furthermore, the severity of OCD symptoms correlates positively with resting prefrontal and orbitofrontal metabolism in adults (Swedo et al., 1992b). In response to successful antiobsessional therapies, hypermetabolism normalizes (Rubin et al., 1995), and the improvement in symptoms correlates with the decrement in blood flow or metabolism in most (Hoehn-Saric et al., 1991; Swedo et al., 1992b) but not all studies (Baxter et al., 1992; Schwartz et al., 1996). Conversely, symptom provocation increases blood flow in orbitofrontal regions (Rauch et al., 1994; Breiter et al., 1996). Despite these functional abnormalities in orbitofrontal cortices, prefrontal volumes seem to be normal in subjects with OCD (Robinson et al., 1995), although increased volumes of the anterior cingulate cortex have been reported in children (Rosenberg and Keshavan, 1998).

In the basal ganglia, the most consistent functional abnormalities reported in OCD have been elevated metabolism and blood flow in the right caudate nucleus both at rest (Baxter et al., 1988) and during symptom provocation (Rauch et al., 1994; Breiter et al., 1996). Caudate nucleus hypermetabolism appears to normalize in response to successful antiobsessional treatment (Baxter et al., 1992; Schwartz et al., 1996). Volumetric findings in the caudate nucleus are inconsistent, but the largest and most rigorous studies report volume reductions bilaterally (Luxenberg et al., 1988; Robinson et al., 1995), and they correlate inversely with the severity of OCD symptoms. In adults performing an attentional task, factor-based scores for OCD symptoms associated with tics (described previously) correlated only with blood flow to the striatum (Rauch et al., 1998), whereas non-tic-related OCD symptoms correlated significantly with flow in a variety of prefrontal regions, most strongly in the prefrontal cortex. Tic-related symptoms, in other words, were associated with basal ganglia functioning, whereas non-tic-related symptoms were associated with prefrontal functioning.

Increased volumes of the thalamus, another key structure in CSTC circuitry, have been reported at pretreatment baseline in OCD children (Gilbert et al., 2000). These volumes normalized after 12 weeks of treatment with paroxetine but not behavioral therapy (Rosenberg et al., 2000a). Abnormal levels of N-acetylaspartate (NAA, a measure of neuronal viability) (Birken and Oldendorf, 1989) were localized to the medial portion of the thalamus in these same children (Fitzgerald et al., 2000).

Attention Deficit Hyperactivity Disorder

The validity of ADHD as a clinical diagnosis has long excited debate and controversy in both lay and scientific circles. An expert panel convened and sponsored by the National Institutes of Health recently reviewed and documented extensively within a Consensus Statement the validity of ADHD as a clinical disorder, its public health importance for children and families, and the effectiveness of its treatments (NIH, 2000). Among their many conclusions, the conference panelists concurred that ADHD meets or exceeds the standards for validity established by most other disorders defined in the *Diagnostic and Statistical Manual of Mental Disorders*, Fourth Edition (DSM-IV). Still unclear, however, is whether the disorder represents a behavioral syndrome that is qualitatively and etiologically distinct from the range of ADHD-like symptoms present in children within the general population.

Attention deficit hyperactivity disorder comprises the symptomatic triad of inattentiveness, hyperactivity, and impulsivity, although predominantly inattentive (i.e., without prominent hyperactivity or impulsivity) and predominantly hyperactive/impulsive subtypes are recognized. Symptoms usually begin early in childhood, decrease gradually in adolescence (particularly symptoms of hyperactivity), and then reach some stable level by early adulthood (Biederman et al., 2000). ADHD affects approximately 3 to 9 percent of children in the general population (Szatmari et al., 1989; Taylor et al., 1991), with boys being 2 to 8 times more likely to be diagnosed than girls. Clinical, epidemiological, and family-genetic studies have shown ADHD to be a strong predictor of conduct disorder, depression, anxiety disorders, and substance abuse both in temporal cross section and in later life (McArdle et al., 1995; Peterson et al., 2001a). ADHD is widely believed to be a heterogeneous condition having multiple biological subtypes. This heterogeneity has probably helped to dilute the specificity of findings in biological studies.

Genetics. Family studies suggest that ADHD is highly familial (Biederman et al., 1992). A parent with ADHD has a 57 percent chance of having a child who also has ADHD (Biederman et al., 1995a). Adoption studies suggest that genetic factors contribute importantly to this familial predisposition (Morrison and Stewart, 1973; Cantwell, 1975), and twin studies indicate that genetic variance accounts for 70 to 90 percent of the phenotypic variance (Levy et al., 1997; Sherman et al., 1997). Quantitative analyses of family data sets have suggested a single gene mode of transmission (Faraone et al., 1992). Several candidate genes have been associated with ADHD, with varying degrees of reproducibility. These include the genes for the D_2 dopamine receptor (*DRD2*), the dopamine transporter (*DAT1*) (Cook et al., 1995; Gill et al., 1997), the seven repeat allele of the D_4 dopamine receptor (*DRD4*) (Faraone et al., 2001; Roman et al., 2001), and recently studies of other dopamine receptors and other neurotransmitter systems (Fisher et al., 2002; Roman et al., 2002). Even if the association of these genes with ADHD is indisputably established, the evidence suggests that the overall effects of these genes coding for transmitter systems in ADHD are likely to be modest at best.

Despite the demonstrated importance of genetic determinants in ADHD, nongenetic influences also contribute to its pathophysiology. Premature birth, other obstetrical complications, maternal smoking during pregnancy, pediatric head trauma, and chaotic family environments in particular are all thought to predispose to the later development of ADHD (Hinshaw et al., 2000; Roy et al., 2000).

Neurochemistry. Many studies of neurotransmitter metabolite levels in the blood and urine of ADHD children have been reported, both at baseline and after pharmacological treatments or challenges. Dopamine metabolite levels have been most extensively studied, but their variable and often contradictory findings have not yielded conclusive evidence for or against the involvement of dopamine in the pathophysiology of ADHD (Zametkin and Rapoport, 1987). Baseline measures of norepinephrine in serum, as well as MHPG (a norepinephrine metabolite) in plasma and 5-HIAA in platelets do not differ in ADHD children compared with controls. Findings for the levels of these compounds in urine have been inconsistent, and responses of these levels to pharmacological agents do not seem to differ across diagnostic groups. CSF studies in ADHD are relatively rare, but likewise do not clearly indicate the presence of disturbances in these neurotransmitter systems.

Neurobiological Substrate. Animal models, human in vivo imaging studies, and electrophysiological studies all suggest that anatomical and functional disturbances of frontostriatal components of CSTC circuits subserve the symptoms of ADHD. These circuits, moreover, are the primary sites of action for the dopaminergic properties of stimulant medication, the most robustly effective pharmacotherapy for ADHD.

Several animal models for ADHD have been proposed. One particularly attractive model is the spontaneously hypertensive rat (SHR). SHRs are hyperactive, and they exhibit inattention on certain behavioral tasks. They have lower metabolism of their medial and lateral frontal cortices (Papa et al., 1998), and lower basal levels of transcription factors in their nucleus accumbens (Papa et al., 1997), a region within the ventral striatum subserving learning and reward. Dopaminergic activity is reduced and noradrenergic activity is increased in the frontal cortices of SHRs (Russell, 2002), and catecholamine innervation of frontal cortices depends on perinatal androgen levels, possibly accounting for the higher prevalence of ADHD in males (King et al., 2000). Methylphenidate attenuates hyperactivity and inattention in these animals (Ueno et al., 2002).

Consistent with findings in this animal model, human imaging studies have most consistently reported abnormalities in the dorsal prefrontal cortex and basal ganglia of subjects with ADHD. Smaller volumes of the right prefrontal cortex have been reported in children with ADHD compared with normal controls (Castellanos et al., 1996a), a finding that has generally been replicated, although not always with regard to laterality (Aylward et al., 1996; Filipek et al., 1997). In an anatomical imaging study of 152 children with ADHD and 139 controls, cortical volume reductions were not specific to frontal regions, but were instead generalized to all cortical regions (Castellanos and Tannock, 2002). Additionally, smaller right globus pallidus nuclei have been detected in a subset of these children (Castellanos et al., 1996).

Positron emission tomography studies have reported reduced metabolic rates in, among other regions, the left anterior frontal area, where metabolism correlated inversely with measures of symptom severity (Zametkin et al., 1993). Functional MRI studies have reported abnormal activation of the striatum (Vaidya et al., 1998; Rubia et al., 1999), prefrontal cortex (Rubia et al., 1999), and anterior cingulate cortex (Bush et al., 1999). SPECT studies of ADHD adults have reported marked elevations of dopamine transporter levels in the basal ganglia (Dougherty et al., 1999; Krause et al., 2000), which, after a month of daily methylphenidate treatment, decreased to control levels (Krause et al., 2000). Additional findings in ADHD imaging studies include a smaller cerebellum (Castellanos and Tonnock, 2002), a region thought to be important in attentional processing (Middleton and Strick, 1994).

Electrophysiological studies support these findings from other brain imaging modalities. Event-related potential recordings during attentional tasks produces smaller P300s over parietal cortices, suggesting that parietal dysfunction may contribute to inattentive symptoms in ADHD (Overtoom et al., 1998). Quantitative EEG studies of large samples of ADHD children suggest abnormal activity of the frontal cortices (Chabot and Serfontein, 1996). Disordered brainstem involvement in ADHD is suggested by delayed latencies in components of the brainstem auditory evoked response (Lahat et al., 1995).

Psychostimulants. Countless studies have demonstrated that psychostimulants, methylphenidate and amphetamine in particular, improve ADHD symptoms (Greenhill et al., 2002). Indeed, such agents improve attentional functioning even in normal children and animals. A large and definitive multisite clinical trial has shown that stimulant medications generally are far superior to behavioral management alone, and that behavioral management added to treatment with stimulant medications provides little additional benefit (Group 1999a). Nonmedical treatments are most helpful for ADHD children who also have clinically significant anxiety symptoms (Group, 1999b). Many clinicians continue to believe that consistently and appropriately implemented parent management training alone can be effective for some children with ADHD, especially for younger children. Suggestions for early psychosocial interventions, including increased play, remain to be evaluated, although preliminary data from animal models are encouraging (Panksepp et al., 2002; Panksepp et al., 2003).

Stimulant medications are usually well tolerated. The most common side effects include impaired sleep, poor appetite, headaches, or irritability. Although several preliminary animal studies of these medications suggest the possibility of neurotoxic effects (Moll et al., 2001) or potential longer-term behavioral effects (Nocjar and Panksepp, 2002; Panksepp et al., 2002), long-term neuroimaging studies of children with ADHD have thus far not provided evidence of anatomical changes associated with chronic stimulant use (Castellanos and Tannock 2002). Moreover, behavioral studies in humans suggest that psychostimulants may reduce the long-term risks of substance abuse associated with the presence of ADHD earlier in life (Biederman et al., 1999; Barkley et al., 2003; Wilens et al., 2003). Stimulants also seem to improve peer, parent, and teacher ratings of the child's social skills (Group, 1999a, b). These longer-term benefits of stimulant medications for children with ADHD would seem likely to have important and enduring positive effects on self-esteem and adaptive functioning.

CONCLUSIONS

What we have learned over the past two decades about the pathophysiology of childhood neuropsychiatric disorders is astounding. Each of the conditions reviewed is known to have a strong genetic basis, which clearly has helped to track their pathophysiological pathways to illness, particularly in disorders caused by single genes. Continuing elucidation of the pathophysiology of these specific genetic disorders will improve our understanding of the normal biology of neural systems within the developing CNS, and it will provide experimental and disease models by which we can better understand the pathogenesis of genetically more heterogeneous conditions.

The genetic liability underlying each of these conditions seems uniquely to affect particular neural systems in each of the disorders. Mesial temporal lobe structures that subserve socialization functions seem to be especially important in autism; arrest of development of the association cortices caused by the *MeCP2* deletion may generate the symptoms of Rett syndrome; the hippocampus and other regions involved in learning and memory are important in fragile X; and disturbances in parietal cortices likely subserve visuospatial deficits affecting children with Williams syndrome. Abnormalities in frontal, temporal, and possibly parietal lobes likely subserve the psychotic symptoms and cognitive disturbances observed in childhood-onset schizophrenia. Disturbances in the structure and function of particular portions of CSTC circuits seem to underlie the symptoms of Tourette syndrome, obsessive-compulsive disorder, and attention deficit hyperactivity disorder; the portions of the circuits affected, together with the genetic relatedness of these conditions, may account for their common clinical co-occurrence.

Future studies will undoubtedly continue to unravel the pathophysiology of these and other childhood neuropsychiatric disorders. They will help us to understand how underlying genetic vulnerabilities contribute to disordered protein expression and abnormal cellular functions in particular neural systems, which then produce particular clinical phenotypes. Defining these pathways to illness will in turn help to define genetic and neurobiological subtypes of these illnesses, similar to the ways in which some specific genetic syndromes have been found to produce autistic symptoms. The most important future advances will likely come from combining genetic analyses, molecular techniques, imaging studies, and careful clinical phenotyping to help refine further our nosological classifications and to improve our understanding of gene-brain-behavior correlates across the many stages of CNS development, in both health and illness.

REFERENCES

Abell F, Krams M, Ashburner J, Passingham R, Friston K, Frackowiak R, Happe F, Frith C, Frith U (1999). The neuroanatomy of autism: A voxel based whole brain analysis of structural scans. *Neuroreport* 10:1647–1651.

Abitbol M, Menini C, Delezoide AL, Rhyner T, Vekemans M, Mallet J (1993). Nucleus basalis magnocellularis and hippocampus are the major sites of FMR-1 expression in the human fetal brain. *Nat Genet* 4:147–153.

Alaghband-Rad J, McKenna K, Gordon CT, Albus KE, Hamburger SD, Rumsey JM, Frazier JA, Lenane MC, Rapoport JL (1995). Childhood-onset schizophrenia: The severity of premorbid course. *J Am Acad Child Adolesc Psychiatry* 34:1273–1283.

Alsobrook JP, Grigorenko E, Pauls DL (2002). Genetic influences on child psychiatric conditions. In Lewis M (ed). *Child and Adolescent Psychiatry. A Comprehensive Textbook.* Lippincott Williams & Wilkins: Philadelphia, pp. 415–431.

Altemus M, Jacobson KR, Debellis M, Kling M, Pigott T, Murphy DL, Gold PW (1994). Normal CSF oxytocin and NPY levels in OCD. *Biol Psychiatry* 45:931–933.

Anderson GM, Cook EH (2000). Pharmacogenetics. Promise and potential in child and adolescent psychiatry. *Child Adolesc Psychiatr Clin N Am* 9:23–42, viii.

Anderson GM, Pollak ES, Chatterjee D, Leckman JF, Riddle MA, Cohen DJ (1992). Postmortem analysis of subcortical monoamines and amino acids in Tourette syndrome. *Adv Neurol* 58:123–133.

Anderson GM, Leckman JF, Cohen DJ (1999). Neurochemical and neuropeptide systems. In Leckman JF, Cohen DJ (eds). *Tourette's Syndrome: Tics, Obsessions, Compulsions. Developmental Psychopathology and Clinical Care.* Wiley: New York, pp. 261–280.

Anderson GM, Gutknecht L, Cohen DJ, Brailly-Tabard S, Cohen JH, Ferrari P, Roubertoux PL, Tordjman S (2002). Serotonin transporter promoter variants in autism: Functional effects and relationship to platelet hyperserotonemia. *Mol Psychiatry* 7:831–836.

Armstrong DD (2002). Neuropathology of Rett syndrome. *Ment Retard Dev Disabil Res Rev* 8:72–76.

August GJ, Stewart MA, Tsai L (1981). The incidence of cognitive disabilities in the siblings of autistic children. *Br J Psychiatry* 138:416–422.

Auranen M, Vanhala R, Varilo T, Ayers K, Kempas E, Ylisaukko-Oja T, Sinsheimer JS, Pelto-
nen L, Jarvela I (2002). A genomewide screen for autism-spectrum disorders: Evidence for
a major susceptibility locus on chromosome 3q25-27. *Am J Hum Genet* 71:777–790.

Aylward EH, Reiss AL, Reader MJ, Singer HS, Brown JE, Denckla MB (1996). Basal ganglia
volumes in children with attention-deficit hyperactivity disorder. *J Child Neurol* 11:112–115.

Aylward EH, Minshew NJ, Goldstein G, Honeycutt NA, Augustine AM, Yates KO, Barta PE,
Pearlson GD (1999). MRI volumes of amygdala and hippocampus in nonmentally retarded
autistic adolescents and adults. *Neurology* 53:2145–2150.

Bachevalier J (1994). Medial temporal lobe structures and autism: A review of clinical and
experimental findings. *Neuropsychologia* 32:627–648.

Badner JA, Gershon ES (2002). Regional meta-analysis of published data supports linkage of
autism with markers on chromosome 7. *Mol Psychiatry* 7:56–66.

Baer L (1994). Factor analysis of symptom subtypes of obsessive compulsive disorder and their
relation to personality and tic disorders. *J Clin Psychiatry* 55:18–23.

Bailey A, Le Couteur A, Gottesman I, Bolton P, Simonoff E, Yuzda E, Rutter M (1995). Autism
as a strongly genetic disorder: Evidence from a British twin study. *Psychol Med* 25:63–77.

Bailey A, Phillips W, Rutter M (1996). Autism: Towards an integration of clinical, genetic,
neuropsychological, and neurobiological perspectives. *J Child Psychol Psychiatry* 37:89–126.

Bailey A, Luthert P, Dean A, Harding B, Janota I, Montgomery M, Rutter M, Lantos P (1998).
A clinicopathological study of autism. *Brain* 121:889–905.

Barkley RA (1997). *ADHD and the Nature of Self-Control.* Guilfor Press, New York.

Barkley RA, Fischer M, Smallish L, Fletcher K (2003). Does the treatment of Attention-
Deficit/Hyperactivity Disorder with stimulants contribute to drug use/abuse? A 13-year
prospective study. *Pediatrics* 111:97–109.

Baron-Cohen S (1991). The development of a theory of mind in autism: Deviance and delay?
Psychiatr Clin North Am 14:33–51.

Baron-Cohen S, Ring H, Moriarty J, Schmidt B, Costa D, Ell P (1994). Recognition of mental
state terms: Clinical findings in children with autism and a functional neuroimaging study of
normal adults. *Brit J Psychiatry* 165:640–649.

Barthelemy C, Bruneau N, Cottet-Eymard JM, Domenech-Jouve J, Garreau B, Lelord G,
Muh JP, Peyrin L (1988). Urinary free and conjugated catecholamines and metabolites in
autistic children. *J Autism Dev Disord* 18:583–591.

Bauman ML, Kemper TL (1994). Neuroanatomic observations of the brain in autism. In Bauman ML, Kemper TL (eds). *The Neurobiology of Autism.* Johns Hopkins University Press:
Baltimore, pp. 119–145.

Bauman ML, Kemper TL (1996). Observations on the Purkinje cells in the cerebellar vermis in
autism. *J Neuropath Exp Neurol* 55:613.

Baxter L, Schwartz J, Mazziotta J, Phelps ME, Pahl JJ, Buze BE, Fairbanks L (1988). Cerebral
glucose metabolic rates in nondepressed patients with obsessive-compulsive disorder. *Am J
Psychiatry* 145:1560–1563.

Baxter L, Jr, Schwartz JM, Bergman KS, Szuba MP, Guze BH, Mazziotta JC, Alazraki A, Selin
CE, Ferng HK, Munford P, Phelps ME (1992). Caudate glucose metabolic rate changes with
both drug and behavior therapy for obsessive-compulsive disorder. *Arch Gen Psychiatry*
49:681–689.

Belichenko PV, Oldfors A, Hagberg B, Dahlstrom A (1994). Rett syndrome: 3-D confocal microscopy of cortical pyramidal dendrites and afferents. *Neuroreport* 5:1509–1513.

Bellugi U, Lichtenberger L, Mills D, Galaburda A, Korenberg JR (1999). Bridging cognition, the brain and molecular genetics: evidence from Williams syndrome. *TINS* 22:197–207.

Benazon NR, Moore GJ, Rosenberg DR. (2002). Cognitive behavior therapy in treatment-naive children and adolescents with obsessive-compulsive disorder: An open trial. *Behav Res Ther* 40:529–539.

Berg CZ, Rapoport JL, Whitaker A, Davies M, Leonard H, Swedo SE, Braiman S, Lenane M (1989). Childhood obsessive compulsive disorder: A two-year prospective follow-up of a community sample. *J Am Acad Child Adolesc Psychiatry* 28:528–533.

Bertolino A, Saunders RC, Mattay VS, Bachevalier J, Frank JA, Weinberger DR (1997). Altered development of prefrontal neurons in rhesus monkeys with neonatal mesial temporo-limbic lesions: A proton magnetic resonance spectroscopic imaging study. *Cereb Cortex* 7: 740–748.

Bertolino A, Kumra S, Callicott JH, Mattay VS, Lestz RM, Jacobsen L, Barnett IS, Duyn JH, Frank JA, Rapoport JL, Weinberger DR (1998). Common pattern of cortical pathology in childhood-onset and adult-onset schizophrenia as identified by proton magnetic resonance spectroscopic imaging. *Am J Psychiatry* 155:1376–1383.

Biederman J, Faraone SV, Keenan K, Benjamin J, Krifcher B, Moore C, Sprich-Buckminster S, Ugaglia K, Jellinek MS, Steingard R (1992). Further evidence for family genetic risk factors in ADHD: Patterns of comorbidity in probands and relatives in psychiatrically and pediatrically referred samples. *Arch Gen Psychiatry* 49:728–738.

Biederman J, Faraone SV, Mick E, Spencer T, Wilens T, Kiely K, Guite J, Ablon JS, Reed E, Warburton R (1995). High risk for attention deficit hyperactivity disorder among children of parents with childhood onset of the disorder: A pilot study. *Am J Psychiatry* 152: 431–435.

Biederman J, Wilens T, Mick E, Spencer T, Faraone SV (1999). Pharmacotherapy of attention-deficit/hyperactivity disorder reduces risk for substance use disorder. *Pediatrics* 104:e20.

Biederman J, Mick E, Faraone SV (2000). Age-dependent decline of symptoms of attention deficit hyperactivity disorder: Impact of remission definition and symptom type. *Am J Psychiatry* 157:816–818.

Birken DL, Oldendorf WH (1989). *N*-acetyl-ʟ-aspartic acid: A literature review of a compound prominent in ^{1}H-NMR spectroscopic studies of brain. *Neurosci Biobehavior Rev* 13: 23–31.

Bolton PF, Griffiths PD (1997). Association of tuberous sclerosis of temporal lobes with autism and atypical autism. *Lancet* 349:392–395.

Bolton PF, Murphy M, Macdonald H, Whitlock B, Pickles A, Rutter M (1997). Obstetric complications in autism: Consequences or causes of the condition? *J Am Acad Child Adolesc Psychiatry* 36:272–281.

Boucher J, Lewis V (1992). Unfamiliar face recognition in relatively able autistic children. *J Child Psychol Psychiatry* 33:843–859.

Bouvard MP, Leboyer M, Launay JM, Recasens C, Plumet MH, Waller-Perotte D, Tibuteau F, Bondoux D, Dugas M, Lensing P, Panksepp J. (1995). Low-dose naltrexone effects on plasma chemistries and clinical symptoms in autism: A double-blind, placebo-controlled study. *Psychiatry Res* 58:191–201.

Boyar FZ, Whitney MM, Lossie AC, Gray BA, Keller KL, Stalker HJ, Zori RT, Geffken G, Mutch J, Edge PJ, Voeller KS, Williams CA, Driscoll DJ (2001). A family with a grand-maternally derived interstitial duplication of proximal 15q. *Clin Genet* 60:421–430.

Braun AR, Stoetter B, Randolph C, Hsiao JK, Vladar K, Gernert J, Carson RE, Herscovitch P, Chase TN (1993). The functional neuroanatomy of Tourette's syndrome: An FDG-PET study. I. Regional changes in cerebral glucose metabolism differentiating patients and controls. *Neuropsychopharmacology* 9:277–291.

Breiter HC, Rauch SL, Kwong KK, Baker JR, Weisskoff RM, Kennedy DN, Kendrick AD, Davis TL, Jiang A, Cohen MS, Stern CE, Belliveau JW, Baer L, O'Sullivan RL, Savage CR, Jenike MA, Rosen BR (1996). Functional magnetic resonance imaging of symptom provocation in obsessive-compulsive disorder. *Arch Gen Psychiatry* 53:595–606.

Bush G, Frazier JA, Rauch SL, Seidman LJ, Whalen PJ, Jenike MA, Rosen BR, Biederman J (1999). Anterior cingulate cortex dysfunction in attention-deficit/hyperactivity disorder revealed by fMRI and the Counting Stroop. *Biol Psychiatry* 45:1542–1552.

Campbell M, Anderson LT, Small AM, Adams P, Gonzalez NM, Ernst M (1993). Naltrexone in autistic children: Behavioral symptoms and attentional learning. *J Am Acad Child Adolesc Psychiatry* 32:1283–1291.

Cantwell D (1975). Genetic studies on hyperactive children: Psychiatric illness in biologic and adoptive parents. In Fieve R, Rosenthal D, Brill H (eds). *Genetic Research in Psychiatry*. Johns Hopkins University Press: Baltimore,

Cassidy SB, Dykens E, Williams CA (2000). Prader-Willi and Angelman syndromes: Sister imprinted disorders. *Am J Med Genet* 97:136–146.

Castellanos FX, Tannock R, (2002). Neuroscience of attention-deficit/hyperactivity disorder. The search for endophenotypes. *Nature Revs Neurosci* 3:617–628.

Castellanos FX, Giedd JN, Hamburger SD, Marsh WL, Rapoport JL (1996a). Brain morphometry in Tourette's syndrome: The influence of comorbid attention-deficit/hyperactivity disorder. *Neurology* 47:1581–1583.

Chabot RJ, Serfontein G (1996). Quantitative electroencephalographic profiles of children with Attention Deficit Disorder. *Biol Psychiatry* 40:951–963.

Chabrol H, Guell A, Bes A, Moron P (1986). Cerebral blood flow in schizophrenic adolescents [letter]. *Am J Psychiatry* 143:130.

Chappell P, Riddle M, Anderson G, Scahill L, Hardin M, Walker D, Cohen D, Leckman J (1994). Enhanced stress responsivity of Tourette syndrome patients undergoing lumbar puncture. *Biol Psychiatry* 36:35–43.

Charman T, Cass H, Owen L, Wigram T, Slonims V, Weeks L, Wisbeach A, Reilly S (2002). Regression in individuals with Rett syndrome. *Brain Dev* 24:281–283.

Comery TA, Harris JB, Willems PJ, Oostra BA, Irwin SA, Weiler IJ, Greenough WT (1997). Abnormal dendritic spines in fragile X knockout mice: Maturation and pruning deficits. *Proc Natl Acad Sci USA* 94:5401–5404.

Comings DE, Comings BG (1987). A controlled study of Tourette syndrome. I. Attention-deficit disorder, learning disorders, and school problems. *Am J Hum Genetics* 41:701–741.

Cook EH (1990). Autism: Review of neurochemical investigation. *Synapse* 6:292–308.

Cook EH, Jr, Stein MA, Krasowski MD, Cox NJ, Olkon DM, Kieffer JE, Leventhal BL (1995). Association of attention-deficit disorder and the dopamine transporter gene. *Am J Hum Genet* 56:993–998.

Cornford ME, Philippart M, Jacobs B, Scheibel AB, Vinters HV (1994). Neuropathology of Rett syndrome: Case report with neuronal and mitochondrial abnormalities in the brain. *J Child Neurol* 9:424–431.

Costello EJ, Angold A, Burns BJ, Stangl DK, Tweed DL, Erkanli A, Worthman CM (1996). The Great Smoky Mountains study of youth. Goals, design, methods, and the prevalence of DSM-III-R disorders. *Arch Gen Psychiatry* 53:1129–1136.

Courchesne E, Yeung-Courchesne R, Press GA, Hesselink JR, Jernigan TL (1988). Hypoplasia of cerebellar vermal lobules VI and VII in autism. *New Eng L Med* 318:1349–1354.

Courchesne E, Townsend J, Saitoh O (1994). The brain in infantile autism: Posterior fossa structures are abnormal. *Neurology* 44:214–223.

Croonenberghs J, Delmeire L, Verkerk R, Lin AH, Meskal A, Neels H, Van der Planken M, Scharpe S, Deboutte D, Pison G, Maes M (2000). Peripheral markers of serotonergic and noradrenergic function in post-pubertal, caucasian males with autistic disorder. *Neuropsychopharmacology* 22:275–283.

Davies W, Isles AR, Wilkinson LS (2001). Imprinted genes and mental dysfunction. *Ann Med* 33:428–436.

Dougherty DD, Bonab AA, Spencer TJ, Rauch SL, Madras BK, Fischman JJ (1999). Dopamine transporter density is elevated in patients with attention deficit hyperactivity disorder. *Lancet* 354:2132–2133.

Eapen V, Pauls DL, Robertson MM (1993). Evidence for autosomal dominant transmission in Tourette's syndrome. United Kingdom cohort study. *Br J Psychiatry* 162:593–596.

Epperson CN, McDougle CJ, Price LH (1996). Intranasal oxytocin in Obsessive-Compulsive Disorder. *Biol Psychiatry* 40:547–549.

Ernst M, Zametkin AJ, Matochik JA, Pascualvaca D, Cohen RM (1997). Reduced medial prefrontal dopaminergic activity in autistic children. *Lancet* 350:638.

Ernst M, Zametkin AJ, Jons PH, Matochik JA, Pascualvaca D, Cohen RM (1999). High presynaptic dopaminergic activity in children with Tourette's disorder. *J Am Acad Child Adolesc Psychiatry* 38:86–94.

Faraone SV, Biederman J, Chen WJ, Krifcher B, Keenan K, Moore C, Sprich S, Tsuang M (1992). Segregation analysis of attention deficit hyperactivity disorder: Evidence for single gene transmission. *Psychiatr Genetics* 2:257–275.

Faraone SV, Doyle AE, Mick E, Biederman J (2001). Meta-analysis of the association between the 7-repeat allele of the dopamine D(4) receptor gene and attention deficit hyperactivity disorder. *Am J Psychiatry* 158:1052–1057.

Feng Y, Gutekunst CA, Eberhart DE, Yi H, Warren ST, Hersch SM (1997). Fragile X mental retardation protein: Nucleocytoplasmic shuttling and association with somatodendritic ribosomes. *J Neurosci* 17:1539–1547.

Filipek PA, Semrud-Clikeman M, Steingard RJ, Renshaw PF, Kennedy DN, Biederman J (1997). Volumetric MRI analysis comparing attention-deficit hyperactivity disorder and normal controls. *Neurology* 48:589–601.

Fisher SE, Francks C, McCracken JT, McGough JJ, Marlow AJ, MacPhie IL, Newbury DF, Crawford LR, Palmer CG, Woodward JA, Del'Homme M, Cantwell DP, Nelson SF, Monaco AP, Smalley SL (2002). A genomewide scan for loci involved in attention-deficit/hyperactivity disorder. *Am J Hum Genet* 70:1183–1196.

Fitzgerald KD, Moore GJ, Paulson LA, Stewart CM, Rosenberg DR (2000). Proton spectroscopic imaging of the thalamus in treatment-naive pediatric obsessive-compulsive disorder. *Biol Psychiatry* 47:174–182.

Folstein S, Rutter M (1977). Infantile autism: A genetic study of 21 twin pairs. *J Child Psychol Psychiatry* 18:297–321.

Fombonne E (1999). The epidemiology of autism: A review. *Psychol Med* 29:769–786.

Frazier JA, Giedd JN, Kaysen D, Albus K, Hamburger S, Alaghband-Rad J, Lenane MC, McKenna K, Breier A, Rapoport JL (1996). Childhood-onset schizophrenia: Brain MRI rescan after 2 years of clozapine maintenance treatment. *Am J Psychiatry* 153:564–566.

Friedman SD, Shaw DW, Artru AA, Richards TL, Gardner J, Dawson G, Posse S, Dager SR (2003). Regional brain chemical alterations in young children with autism spectrum disorder. *Neurology* 60:100–107.

Fuster JM (1997). *The Prefrontal Cortex: Anatomy, Physiology, and Neuropsychology of the Frontal Lobe*, 3rd ed. Lippincott-Raven: Philadelphia.

Geller D, Biederman J, Jones J, Park K, Schwartz S, Shapiro S, Coffey B (1998). Is juvenile Obsessive-Compulsive Disorder a developmental subtype of the disorder: A review of the pediatric literature. *J Am Acad Child Adolesc Psychiatry* 37:420–427.

Giedd JN, Jeffries NO, Blumenthal J, Castellanos FX, Vaituzis AC, Fernandez T, Hamburger SD, Liu H, Nelson J, Bedwell J, Tran L, Lenane M, Nicolson R, Rapoport JL (1999). Childhood-onset schizophrenia: Progressive brain changes during adolescence. *Biol Psychiatry* 46:892–898.

Gilbert AR, Moore GJ, Keshavan MS, Paulson LA, Narula V, Mac Master FP, Stewart CM, Rosenberg DR (2000). Decrease in thalamic volumes of pediatric patients with obsessive-compulsive disorder who are taking paroxetine. *Arch Gen Psychiatry* 57:449–456.

Gill M, Daly G, Heron S, Hawi Z, Fitzgerald M (1997). Confirmation of association between attention deficit hyperactivity disorder and a dopamine transporter polymorphism. *Mol Psychiatry* 2:311–313.

Gillberg IC (1991). Autistic syndrome with onset at age 31 years: Herpes encephalitis as a possible model for childhood autism. *Dev Med Child Neurol* 33:912–929.

Glaze DG (2002). Neurophysiology of Rett syndrome. *Ment Retard Dev Disabil Res Rev* 8:66–71.

Goel V, Grafman J, Sadato N, Hallett M (1995). Modeling other minds. *Neuroreport* 6: 1741–1746.

Grados MA, Riddle MA, Samuels JF, Liang KY, Hoehn-Saric R, Bienvenu OJ, Walkup JT, Song D, Nestadt G (2001). The familial phenotype of obsessive-compulsive disorder in relation to tic disorders: The Hopkins OCD family study. *Biol Psychiatry* 50:559–565.

Greenhill LL, Pliszka S, Dulcan MK, Bernet W, Arnold V, Beitchman J, Benson RS, Bukstein O, Kinlan J, McClellan J, Rue D, Shaw JA, Stock S (2002). Practice parameter for the use of stimulant medications in the treatment of children, adolescents, and adults. *J Am Acad Child Adolesc Psychiatry* 41:26S–49S.

Group MC (1999a). A 14-month randomized clinical trial of treatment strategies for attention-deficit/hyperactivity disorder. *Arch Gen Psychiatry* 56:1073–1086.

Group MC (1999b). Moderator and mediator challenges to the MTA study: Effects of comorbid anxiety disorder, family poverty, session attendance, and community medication on treatment outcome. *Arch Gen Psychiatry* 56:1088–1096.

Gunnar MR (2001). Effects of early deprivation: Findings from orphanage-reared infants and children. In Nelson CA, Luciana M (eds). *Handbook of Developmental Cognitive Neuroscience*. Massachusetts Institute of Technology: Cambridge MA, pp. 617–629.

Hagberg B (2002). Clinical manifestations and stages of Rett syndrome. *Ment Retard Dev Disabil Res Rev* 8:61–65.

Hagerman RJ (1999). Fragile X Syndrome. In *Neurodevelopmental Disorders: Diagnosis and Treatment*. Oxford University Press: New York, pp. 61–132.

Hanna GL, Veenstra-VanderWeele J, Cox NJ, Boehnke M, Himle JA, Curtis GC, Leventhal BL, Cook EH, Jr (2002). Genome-wide linkage analysis of families with obsessive-compulsive disorder ascertained through pediatric probands. *Am J Med Genet* 114:541–552.

Happe F, Briskman J, Frith U (2001). Exploring the cognitive phenotype of autism: Weak "central coherence" in parents and siblings of children with autism: I. Experimental tests. *J Child Psychol Psychiatry* 42:299–307.

Harlow HF, Dodsworth RO, Harlow MK (1965). Total social isolation in monkeys. *Proc Natl Acad Sci U S A* 54:90–97.

Haznedar MM, Buchsbaum MS, Metzger M, Solimando A, Spiegel-Cohen J, Hollander E (1997). Anterior cingulate gyrus volume and glucose metabolism in autistic disorder. *Am J Psychiatry* 154:1047–1050.

Hendren RL, De Backer I, Pandina GJ (2000). Review of neuroimaging studies of child and adolescent psychiatric disorders from the past 10 years. *J Am Acad Child Adolesc Psychiatry* 39:815–828.

Hinds HL, Ashley CT, Sutcliffe JS, Nelson DL, Warren ST, Housman DE, Schalling M (1993). Tissue specific expression of FMR-1 provides evidence for a functional role in fragile X syndrome. *Nat Genet* 3:36–43.

Hinshaw SP, Owens EB, Wells KC, Kraemer HC, Abikoff HB, Arnold LE, Conners CK, Elliott G, Greenhill LL, Hechtman L, Hoza B, Jensen PS, March JS, Newcorn JH, Pelham WE, Swanson JM, Vitiello B, Wigal T (2000). Family processes and treatment outcome in the MTA: Negative/ineffective parenting practices in relation to multimodal treatment. *J Abnorm Child Psychol* 28:555–568.

Hjalgrim H, Jacobsen TB, Norgaard K, Lou HC, Brondum-Nielsen K, Jonassen O (1999). Frontal-subcortical hypofunction in the fragile X syndrome. *Am J Med Genet* 83:140–141.

Hobson RP (1986). The autistic child's appraisal of expressions of emotion: A further study. *J Child Psychol Psychiatry* 2:671–680.

Hoehn-Saric R, Pearlson G, Harris G, Machlin S, Camargo E (1991). Effects of fluoxetine on regional cerebral blood flow in obsessive-compulsive patients. *Am J Psychiatry* 148:1243–1245.

Hoon AH, Reiss AL (1992). The mesial-temporal lobe and autism: Case report and review. *Dev Med Child Neurol* 34:252–259.

Horska A, Naidu S, Herskovits EH, Wang PY, Kaufmann WE, Barker PB (2000). Quantitative ^{1}H MR spectroscopic imaging in early Rett syndrome. *Neurology* 54:715–722.

Hyde TM, Aaronson BA, Randolph C, Weinberger DR (1995). Cerebral morphometric abnormalities in Tourette's syndrome: A quantitative MRI study of monozygotic twins. *Neurology* 45:1176–1182.

Insel TR, O'Brien DJ, Leckman JF (1999). Oxytocin, vasopressin, and autism: Is there a connection? *Biol Psychiatry* 45:145–157.

Jacobsen LK, Rapoport JL (1998). Research update: Childhood-onset schizophrenia: Implications of clinical and neurobiological research. *J Child Psychol Psychiatry* 39:101–113.

Jakala P, Hanninen T, Ryynanen M, et al. (1997). Fragile-X: Neuropsychological test performance, CGG triplet repeat lengths, and hippocampal volumes. *J Clin Invest* 100:331–338.

Jones W, Hesselink J, Courchesne E, Duncan T, Matsuda K, Bellugi U (2002). Cerebellar abnormalities in infants and toddlers with Williams syndrome. *Dev Med Child Neurol* 44:688–694.

Khong PL, Lam CW, Ooi CG, Ko CH, Wong VC (2002). Magnetic resonance spectroscopy and analysis of MECP2 in Rett syndrome. *Pediatr Neurol* 26:205–209.

King JA, Barkley RA, Delville Y, Ferris CF (2000). Early androgen treatment decreases cognitive function and catecholamine innervation in an animal model of ADHD. *Behav Brain Res* 107:35–43.

Kleiman MD, Neff S, Rosman NP (1992). The brain in infantile autism: Are posterior fossa structures abnormal? *Neurology* 42:753–760.

Klin A, Sparrow SS, de Bildt A, Cicchetti DV, Cohen DJ, Volkmar FR (1999). A normed study of face recognition in autism and related disorders. *J Autism Devel Dis* 29:499–508.

Kolmen BK, Feldman HM, Handen BL, Janosky JE (1997). Naltrexone in young autistic children: Replication study and learning measures. *J Am Acad Child Adolesc Psychiatry* 36: 1570–1578.

Krause KH, Dresel SH, Krause J, Kung HF, Tatsch K (2000). Increased striatal dopamine transporter in adult patients with attention deficit hyperactivity disorder: Effects of methylphenidate as measured by single photon emission computed tomography. *Neurosci Lett* 285:107–110.

Lahat E, Avital E, Barr J, Berkovitch M, Arlazoroff A, Aladjem M (1995). BAEP studies in children with attention deficit disorder. *Devel Med Child Neurol* 37:119–123.

Lainhart JE, Piven J, Wzorek M, Landa R, Santangelo SL, Coon H, Folstein SE (1997). Macrocephaly in children and adults with autism. *J Am Acad Child Adolesc Psychiatry* 36:282–290.

Leckman JF, Hardin MT, Riddle MA, Stevenson J, Ort SI, Cohen DJ (1991). Clonidine treatment of Gilles de la Tourette's syndrome. *Arch Gen Psychiatry* 48:324–328.

Leckman JF, Goodman WK, North WG, Chappell PB, Price LH, Pauls DL, Anderson GM, Riddle MA, McSwiggan-Hardin M, McDougle CJ (1994). Elevated cerebrospinal fluid levels of oxytocin in obsessive-compulsive disorder. Comparison with Tourette's syndrome and healthy controls. *Arch Gen Psychiatry* 51:782–792.

Leckman JF, Goodman WK, Anderson GM, Riddle MA, Chappell PB, McSwiggan-Hardin MT, Walker DE, Scahill LD, Ort SI, Pauls DL, Cohen DJ, Price LH (1995). Cerebrospinal fluid biogenic amines in obsessive compulsive disorder, Tourette's syndrome, and healthy controls. *Neuropsychopharmacology* 12:73–86.

Leckman JF, Grice DE, Boardman J, Zhang H, Vitale A, Bondi C, Alsobrook J, Peterson BS, Cohen DJ, Rasmussen SA, Goodman WK, McDougle CJ, Pauls DL (1997). Symptoms of Obsessive-Compulsive Disorder. *Am J Psychiatry* 154:911–917.

Leckman JF, Zhang H, Vitale A, Lahnin F, Lynch K, Bondi C, Kim Y-S, Peterson BS (1998). Course of tic severity in Tourette's syndrome: The first two decades. *Pediatrics* 102:14–19.

LeDoux JE (1996). *The Emotional Brain: The Mysterious Underpinnings of Emotional Life.* Simon & Schuster: New York.

Lekman A, Witt-Engerstrom I, Gottfries J, Hagberg BA, Percy AK, Svennerholm L (1989). Rett syndrome: Biogenic amines and metabolites in postmortem brain. *Pediatr Neurol* 5:357–62.

Leonard HL, Goldberger EL, Rapoport JL, Cheslow DL, Swedo SE (1990). Childhood rituals: Normal development or obsessive-compulsive symptoms? *J Am Acad Child Adolesc Psychiatry* 29:17–23.

Leonard HL, Lenane MC, Swedo SE, Rettew DC, Gershon ES, Rapoport JL (1992). Tics and Tourette's disorder: A 2- to 7-year follow-up of 54 obsessive-compulsive children. *Am J Psychiatry* 149:1244–1251.

Levy F, Hay DA, McStephen M, Wood C, Waldman I (1997). Attention-deficit hyperactivity disorder: A category or a continuum? Genetic analysis of a large-scale twin study. *J Am Acad Child Adolesc Psychiatry* 36:737–744.

Liebowitz MR, Turner SM, Piacentini J, Beidel DC, Clarvit SR, Davies SO, Graae F, Jaffer M, Lin SH, Sallee FR, Schmidt AB, Simpson HB (2002). Fluoxetine in children and adolescents with OCD: A placebo-controlled trial. *J Am Acad Child Adolesc Psychiatry* 41: 1431–1438.

Lin H, Yeh C-B, Peterson BS, Scahill L, Grantz H, Findley DB, Katsovich L, Okta J, Lombroso PJ, King RA, Leckman JF (2002). Assessment of symptom exacerbations in a longitudinal study of children with Tourette syndrome or obsessive-compulsive disorder. *J Am Acad Child Adolesc Psychiatry* 41:1070–1077.

Lipani JD, Bhattacharjee MB, Corey DM, Lee DA (2000). Reduced nerve growth factor in Rett syndrome postmortem brain tissue. *J Neuropathol Exp Neurol* 59:889–895.

Liu J, Nyholt DR, Magnussen P, Parano E, Pavone P, Geschwind D, Lord C, Iversen P, Hoh J, Ott J, Gilliam TC (2001). A genomewide screen for autism susceptibility loci. *Am J Hum Genet* 69:327–340.

Luxenberg JS, Swedo SE, Flament MF, Friedland RP, Rapoport J, Rapoport SI (1988). Neuroanatomical abnormalities in obsessive-compulsive disorder detected with quantitative X-ray computed tomography. *Am J Psychiatry* 145:1089–1093.

Maestrini E, Paul A, Monaco AP, Bailey A (2000). Identifying autism susceptibility genes. *Neuron* 28:19–24.

March JS, Biederman J, Wolkow R, Safferman A, Mardekian J, Cook EH, Cutler NR, Dominguez R, Ferguson J, Muller B, Riesenberg R, Rosenthal M, Sallee FR, Wagner KD, Steiner H (1998). Sertraline in children and adolescents with obsessive-compulsive disorder: a multicenter randomized controlled trial. *JAMA* 280:1752–1756.

Martineau J, Barthelemy C, Jouve J, Muh JP, Lelord G (1992). Monoamines (serotonin and catecholamines) and their derivatives in infantile autism: age-related changes and drug effects. *Dev Med Child Neurol* 34:593–603.

Mazzocco MM, Kates WR, Baumgardner TL, Freund LS, Reiss AL (1997). Autistic behaviors among girls with fragile X syndrome. *J Autism Dev Disord* 27:415–435.

McArdle P, O'Brien G, Kolvin I (1995). Hyperactivity: Prevalence and relationship with conduct disorder. *J Child Psychol Psychiatry* 36:279–303.

Menon V, Kwon H, Eliez S, Taylor AK, Reiss AL (2000). Functional brain activation during cognition is related to FMR1 gene expression. *Brain Res* 877:367–370.

Merette C, Brassard A, Potvin A, Bouvier H, Rousseau F, Emond C, Bissonnette L, Roy MA, Maziade M, Ott J, Caron C (2000). Significant linkage for Tourette syndrome in a large French Canadian family. *Am J Hum Genet* 67:1008–1013.

Middleton FA, Strick PL (1994). Anatomical evidence for cerebellar and basal ganglia involvement in higher cognitive function. *Science* 266:458–461.

Minderaa RB, Anderson GM, Volkmar FR, Akkerhuis GW, Cohen DJ (1994). Noradrenergic and adrenergic functioning in autism. *Biol Psychiatry* 36:237–241.

Minshew NJ, Goldstein G, Dombrowski SM, Panchalingam K, Pettegrew JW (1993). A preliminary 31P MRS study of autism: evidence for undersynthesis and increased degradation of brain membranes. *Biol Psychiatry* 33:762–773.

Moll GH, Hause S, Ruther E, Rothenberger A, Huether G (2001). Early methylphenidate administration to young rats causes a persistent reduction in the density of striatal dopamine transporters. *J Child Adoles Psychopharmacology* 11:15–24.

Moriarty J, Campos Costa D, Schmitz B, Trimble MR, Ell PJ, Robertson MM (1995). Brain perfusion abnormalities in Gilles de la Tourette's syndrome. *Br J Psychiatry* 167:249–254.

Morrison JR, Stewart M (1973). The psychiatric status of the legal families of adopted hyperactive children. *Arch Gen Psychiatry* 28:888–891.

Mostofsky SH, Mazzocco MM, Aakalu G, Warsofsky IS, Denckla MB, Reiss AL (1998a). Decreased cerebellar posterior vermis size in fragile X syndrome: correlation with neurocognitive performance. *Neurology* 50:121–130.

Mostofsky SH, Reiss AL, Lockhart P, Denckla MB (1998b). Evaluation of cerebellar size in attention-deficit hyperactivity disorder. *J Child Neurol* 13:434–439.

Mountz JM, Lelland CT, Lill DW, Katholi CR, Liu H (1995). Functional deficits in autistic disorder: Characterization by Technetium-99m-HMPAO and SPECT. *J Nucl Med* 36:1156–1162.

Nagamitsu S, Matsuishi T, Kisa T, Komori H, Miyazaki M, Hashimoto T, Yamashita Y, Ohtaki E, Kato H (1997). CSF beta-endorphin levels in patients with infantile autism. *J Autism Dev Disord* 27:155–163.

Narayan M, Srinath S, Anderson GM, Meundi DB (1993). Cerebrospinal fluid levels of homovanillic acid and 5-hydroxyindoleacetic acid in autism. *Biol Psychiatry* 33:630–635.

Nelson DL (1995). The fragile X syndromes. *Sem Cell Biol* 6:5–11.

Nicholls RD, Knepper JL (2001). Genome organization, function, and imprinting in Prader-Willi and Angelman syndromes. *Annu Rev Genomics Hum Genet* 2:153–175.

Nicolson R, Lenane M, Hamburger SD, Fernandez T, Bedwell J, Rapoport JL (2000). Lessons from childhood-onset schizophrenia. *Brain Res Brain Res Rev* 31:147–156.

NIH (2000). National Institutes of Health Consensus Development Conference Statement: diagnosis and treatment of attention-deficit/hyperactivity disorder (ADHD). *J Am Acad Child Adolesc Psychiatry* 39:182–193.

Nocjar C, Panksepp J (2002). Chronic intermittent amphetamine pretreatment enhances future appetitive behavior for drug- and natural-reward: Interaction with environmental variables. *Behav Brain Res* 128:189–203.

O'Donnell WT, Warren ST (2002). A decade of molecular studies of fragile X syndrome. *Annu Rev Neurosci* 25:315–338.

Oostra BA, Halley DJJ (1995). Complex behavior of simple repeats: the fragile X syndrome. *Pediatric Res* 38:629–637.

Overtoom CCE, Verbaten MN, Kemner C, Kenemans JL, van Engeland H, Buitelaar JK, Camfferman G, Koelega HS (1998). Associations between event-related potentials and measures of attention and inhibition in the continuous performance task in children with ADHD and normal controls. *J Am Acad Child Adolesc Psychiatry* 37:977–985.

Panksepp J (1979). A neurochemical theory of autism. *Trends Neurosci* 2:174–177.

Panksepp J, Burgdorf J, Gordon N, Turner C (2002). Treatment of ADHD with methylphenidate may sensitize brain substrates of desire. Implications for changes in drug abuse potential from an animal model. *Consciousness & Emotion* 3:7–19.

Panksepp J, Burgdorf J, Turner C, Gordon N (2003). Modeling ADHD-type arousal with unilateral frontal cortex damage in rats and beneficial effects of play therapy. *Brain Cognit.* 52:97–105.

Papa M, Sergeant JA, Sadile AG (1997). Differential expression of transcription factors in the accumbens of an animal model of ADHD. *Neuroreport* 8:1607–1612.

Papa M, Berger DF, Sagvolden T, Sergeant JA, Sadile AG (1998). A quantitative cytochrome oxidase mapping study, cross-regional and neurobehavioural correlations in the anterior forebrain of an animal model of Attention Deficit Hyperactivity Disorder. *Behav Brain Res* 94:197–211.

Parent A, Hazrati L (1995). Functional anatomy of the basal ganglia. I. The cortico-basal ganglia-thalamo-cortical loop. *Brain Res Rev* 20:91–127.

Pauls DL (2001). Update on the genetics of Tourette syndrome. *Adv Neurol* 85:281–293.

Pauls DL, Alsobrook JN, Goodman W, Rasmussen S, Leckman JF (1995). A family study of obsessive-compulsive disorder. *Am J Psychiatry* 152:76–84.

Pauls DL, Raymond CL, Stevenson JM, Leckman JF (1991). A family study of Gilles de la Tourette syndrome. *Am J Hum Genetics* 48:154–163.

Pauls DL, Leckman JF, Cohen DJ (1993). Familial relationship between Gilles de la Tourette's syndrome, attention deficit disorder, learning disabilities, speech disorders, and stuttering. *J Am Acad Child Adolesc Psychiatry* 32:1044–1050.

Pauls DL, Leckman JF (1986). The inheritance of Gilles de la Tourette's syndrome and associated behaviors. Evidence for autosomal dominant transmission. *NEJM* 315:993–997.

Peterson BS, Cohen DJ (1998). The treatment of Tourette's syndrome: A multimodal developmental intervention. *J Clin Psychiatry* 59(Suppl 1). 62–72.

Peterson B, Klein J (1997). Neuroimaging of Tourette's syndrome neurobiologic substrate. In Peterson BS (ed). *Child Psychiatry Clinics of North America: Neuroimaging*, vol. 6 (April). WB. Saunders: Philadelphia, pp. 343–364.

Peterson BS, Leckman JF (1998). The temporal characteristics of tics in Gilles de la Tourette syndrome. *Biol Psychiatry* 44:1337–1348.

Peterson BS, Thomas P (2000). Functional brain imaging in Tourette's syndrome: What are we really imaging? In Ernst M, Rumsey J (eds). *Functional Neuroimaging in Child Psychiatry*. Cambridge University Press: Cambridge, pp. 242–265.

Peterson BS, Riddle MA, Cohen DJ, Katz L, Smith JC, Leckman JF (1993a). Human basal ganglia volume asymmetries on magnetic resonance images. *Mag Reson Imaging* 11:493–498.

Peterson BS, Leckman JF, Cohen DJ (1995). Tourette's syndrome: A genetically predisposed and an environmentally specified developmental psychopathology. In Cicchetti D, Cohen DJ (eds). *Developmental Psychopathology, Vol. 2: Risk, Disorder, and Adaptation*. Wiley: New York, pp. 213–242.

Peterson BS, Skudlarski P, Anderson AW, Zhang H, Gatenby JC, Lacadie CM, Leckman JF, Gore JC (1998). A functional magnetic resonance imaging study of tic suppression in Tourette syndrome. *Arch Gen Psychiatry* 55:326–333.

Peterson BS, Pine DS, Cohen P, Brook J (2001a). A prospective, longitudinal study of tic, obsessive-compulsive, and attention deficit-hyperactivity disorders in an epidemiological sample. *J Am Acad Child Adolesc Psychiatry* 40:685–695.

Peterson BS, Staib L, Scahill L, Zhang H, Anderson C, Leckman JF, Cohen DJ, Gore JC, Albert J, Webster R (2001b). Regional brain and ventricular volumes in Tourette syndrome. *Arch Gen Psychiatry* 58:427–440.

Peterson BS, Thomas P, Kane MJ, Scahill L, Zhang Z, Bronen R, King R, Leckman JF, Staib L (2003). Basal ganglia volumes in patients with Gilles de la Tourette syndrome. *Arch Gen Psychiatry* 60:415–424.

Piven J, Nehme E, Simon J, Barta P, Pearlson G, Folstein SE (1992). Magnetic resonance imaging in autism: Measurement of the cerebellum, pons, and fourth ventricle. *Biol Psychiatry* 31:491–504.

Piven J, Arndt S, Bailey J, Andreasen N (1996). Regional brain enlargement in autism: A magnetic resonance imaging study. *J Am Acad Child Adolesc Psychiatry* 35:530–536.

Price RA, Kidd KK, Cohen DJ, Pauls DL, Leckman JF (1985). A twin study of Tourette syndrome. *Arch Gen Psychiatry* 42:815–820.

Rae C, Karmiloff-Smith A, Lee MA, Dixon RM, Grant J, Blamire AM, Thompson CH, Styles P, Radda GK (1998). Brain biochemistry in Williams syndrome: Evidence for a role of the cerebellum in cognition? *Neurology* 51:33–40.

Rapoport JL, Giedd JN, Blumenthal J, Hamburger S, Jeffries N, Fernandez T, Nicolson R, Bedwell J, Lenane M, Zijdenbos A, Paus T, Evans A (1999). Progressive cortical change during adolescence in childhood-onset schizophrenia. A longitudinal magnetic resonance imaging study. *Arch Gen Psychiatry* 56:649–654.

Rasmussen SA, Tsuang MT (1986). Clinical characteristics and family history in DSM-III Obsessive-Compulsive Disorder. *Am J Psychiatry* 143:317–322.

Rauch SL, Jenike MA, Alpert NM, Baer L, Breiter HC, Savage CR, Fischman AJ (1994). Regional cerebral blood flow measured during symptom provocation in obsessive-compulsive disorder using oxygen 15-labeled carbon dioxide and positron emission tomography. *Arch Gen Psychiatry* 51:62–70.

Rauch SL, Dougherty DD, Shin LM, Alpert NM, Manzo P, Leahy L, Fischman AJ, Jenike MA, Baer L (1998). Neural correlates of factor-analyzed OCD symptom dimensions: A PET study. *CNS Spectrums* 3:37–43.

Reiss AL, Aylward E, Freund LS, Joshi PK, Bryan RN (1991a). Neuroanatomy of fragile X syndrome: The posterior fossa. *Ann Neurology* 29:26–32.

Reiss AL, Freund L, Tseng JE, Joshi PK (1991b). Neuroanatomy in fragile X females: The posterior fossa. *Am J Hum Genetics* 49:279–288.

Reiss AL, Lee J, Freund L (1994). Neuroanatomy of fragile X syndrome: the temporal lobe. [Review] *Neurology* 44:1317–1324.

Reiss AL, Freund LS, Baumgardner TL, Abrams MT, Denckla MB (1995). Contribution of the FMR1 gene mutation to human intellectual dysfunction. *Nat Genet* 11:331–334.

Reiss AL, Eliez S, Schmitt JE, Patwardhan A, Haberecht M (2000). Brain imaging in neurogenetic conditions: Realizing the potential of behavioral neurogenetics research. *Mental Retardation & Developmental Disabilities Research Reviews* 6:186–197.

Ritvo ER, Mason-Brothers A, Freeman BJ, Pingree C, Jenson WR, McMahon WM, Petersen PB, Jorde LB, Mo A, Ritvo A (1990). The UCLA-University of Utah epidemiologic survey of autism: the etiologic role of rare diseases. *Am J Psychiatry* 147:1614–1621.

Robinson D, Wu H, Munne RA, Ashtari M, Alvir JMJ, Lerner G, Koreen A, Cole K, Bogerts B (1995). Reduced caudate nucleus volume in obsessive-compulsive disorder. *Arch Gen Psychiatry* 52:393–398.

Rodier PM, Ingram JL, Tisdale B, Nelson SF, Romano J (1996). Embryological origin for autism: Developmental anomalies of the cranial nerve motor nuclei. *J Comp Neurol* 370:247–261.

Roman T, Schmitz M, Polanczyk G, Eizirik M, Rohde LA, Hutz MH (2001). Attention-deficit hyperactivity disorder: A study of association with both the dopamine transporter gene and the dopamine D_4 receptor gene. *Am J Med Genet* 105:471–478.

Roman T, Schmitz M, Polanczyk GV, Eizirik M, Rohde LA, Hutz MH (2002). Further evidence for the association between attention-deficit/hyperactivity disorder and the dopamine-beta-hydroxylase gene. *Am J Med Genet* 114:154–158.

Rosenberg DR, Keshavan MS (1998). Toward a neurodevelopmental model of obsessive–compulsive disorder. *Biol Psychiatry* 43:623–640.

Rosenberg DR, Benazon NR, Gilbert A, Sullivan A, Moore GJ (2000a). Thalamic volume in pediatric obsessive-compulsive disorder patients before and after cognitive behavioral therapy. *Biol Psychiatry* 48:294–300.

Rosenberg DR, MacMaster FP, Keshavan MS, Fitzgerald KD, Stewart CM, Moore GJ (2000b). Decrease in caudate glutamatergic concentrations in pediatric obsessive-compulsive disorder patients taking paroxetine. *J Am Acad Child Adolesc Psychiatry* 39:1096–1103.

Roy P, Rutter M, Pickles A (2000). Institutional care: Risk from family background or pattern of rearing? *J Child Psychol Psychiatry* 41:139–149.

Rubin RT, Ananth J, Villanueva-Meyer J, Trajmar PG, Mena I (1995). Regional [133]Xenon cerebral blood flow and cerebral ^{99m}Tc-HMPAO uptake in patients with obsessive-compulsive disorder before and during treatment. *Biol Psychiatry* 38:429–437.

Russell VA (2002). Hypodopaminergic and hypernoradrenergic activity in prefrontal cortex slices of an animal model for attention-deficit hyperactivity disorder—the spontaneously hypertensive rat. *Behav Brain Res* 130:191–196.

Saunders RC, Kolachana BS, Bachevalier J, Weinberger DR (1998). Neonatal lesions of the medial temporal lobe disrupt prefrontal cortical regulation of striatal dopamine. *Nature* 393:169–171.

Schmitt JE, Eliez S, Warsofsky IS, Bellugi U, Reiss AL (2001a). Corpus callosum morphology of Williams syndrome: Relation to genetics and behavior. *Dev Med Child Neurol* 43: 155–159.

Schmitt JE, Eliez S, Warsofsky IS, Bellugi U, Reiss AL (2001b). Enlarged cerebellar vermis in Williams syndrome. *J Psychiatr Res* 35:225–229.

Schmitt JE, Watts K, Eliez S, Bellugi U, Galaburda AM, Reiss AL (2002). Increased gyrification in Williams syndrome: Evidence using 3D MRI methods. *Dev Med Child Neurol* 44:292–295.

Schultz RT, Gauthier I, Klin A, Fulbright R, Anderson A, Volkmar F, Skudlarski P, Lacadie C, Cohen DJ, Gore JC (2000). Abnormal ventral temporal cortical activity during face discrimination among individuals with autism and Asperger syndrome. *Arch Gen Psychiatry* 57:331–340.

Schwartz JM, Stoessel PW, Baxter LR, Martin KM, Phelps ME (1996). Systematic changes in cerebral glucose metabolic rate after successful behavior modification treatment of obsessive-compulsive disorder. *Arch Gen Psychiatry* 53:109–113.

Shahbazian M, Young J, Yuva-Paylor L, Spencer C, Antalffy B, Noebels J, Armstrong D, Paylor R, Zoghbi H (2002a). Mice with truncated MeCP2 recapitulate many Rett syndrome features and display hyperacetylation of histone H3. *Neuron* 35:243–254.

Shahbazian MD, Antalffy B, Armstrong DL, Zoghbi HY (2002b). Insight into Rett syndrome: MeCP2 levels display tissue- and cell-specific differences and correlate with neuronal maturation. *Hum Mol Genet* 11:115–124.

Shapiro AK, Shapiro ES, Young JG, Feinberg TE (1988). Signs, symptoms, and clinical course. In Shapiro AK, Shapiro ES, Young JG, Feinberg TE (eds). *Gilles de la Tourette Syndrome*. Raven Press: New York, pp. 127–193.

Sherman DK, McGue MK, Iacono WG (1997). Twin concordance for attention deficit hyperactivity disorder: A comparison of teachers' and mothers' reports. *Am J Psychiatry* 154:532–535.

Sigman M, Mundy P (1989). Social attachments in autistic children. *J Am Acad Child Adolesc Psychiatry* 28:74–81.

Singer HS, Reiss AL, Brown JE, Aylward EH, Shih B, Chee E, Harris EL, Reader MJ, Chase GA, Bryan RN, Denckla MB (1993). Volumetric MRI changes in basal ganglia of children with Tourette's syndrome. *Neurology* 43:950–956.

Sowell ER, Levitt J, Thompson PM, Holmes CJ, Blanton RE, Kornsand DS, Caplan R, McCracken J, Asarnow R, Toga AW (2000). Brain abnormalities in early-onset schizophrenia spectrum disorder observed with statistical parametric mapping of structural magnetic resonance images. *Am J Psychiatry* 157:1475–1484.

Stamenkovic M, Schindler SD, Asenbaum S, Neumeister A, Willeit M, Willinger U, de Zwaan M, Riederer F, Aschauer HN, Kasper S (2001). No change in striatal dopamine reuptake site density in psychotropic drug naive and in currently treated Tourette's disorder patients: a [(123)I]-beta-CIT SPECT-study. *Eur Neuropsychopharmacol.* 11:69–74.

Steffenburg S, Gillberg C, Hellgren L, Andersson L, Gillberg IC, Jakobsson G, Bohman M (1989). A twin study of autism in Denmark, Finland, Iceland, Norway and Sweden. *J Child Psychol Psychiatry* 30:405–416.

Stromland K, Nordin V, Miller M, Akerstrom B, Gillberg C (1994). Autism in thalidomide embryopathy: A population study. *Dev Med Child Neurol* 36:351–356.

Suomi SJ (1973). Surrogate rehabilitation of monkeys reared in total social isolation. *J Child Psychol Psychiatry* 14:71–77.

Swedo SE, Leonard HL, Kruesi MJ, Rettew DC, Listwak SJ, Berrettini W, Stipetic M, Hamburger S, Gold PW, Potter WZ, Rapoport JL (1992a). Cerebrospinal fluid neurochemistry in children and adolescents with obsessive-compulsive disorder. *Arch Gen Psychiatry* 49:29–36.

Swedo SE, Pietrini P, Leonard HL, Schapiro MB, Rettew DC, Goldberger EL, Rapoport SI, Rapoport JL, Grady CL (1992b). Cerebral glucose metabolism in childhood-onset obsessive-compulsive disorder. Revisualization during pharmacotherapy. *Arch Gen Psychiatry* 49:690–694.

Szatmari P, Offord DR, Boyle MN (1989). Ontario Child Health Study: Prevalence of attention deficit disorder with hyperactivity. *J Child Psychol Psychiatry* 30:205–218.

Taylor E, Snadberg S, Thorley G, Giles S (1991). *The Epidemiology of Childhood Hyperactivity*. Institute of Psychiatry, Maudsley Monographs, Vol 33, Oxford University Press: Oxford, UK.

Taylor B, Miller E, Lingam R, Andrews N, Simmons A, Stowe J (2002). Measles, mumps, and rubella vaccination and bowel problems or developmental regression in children with autism: Population study. *BMJ* 324:393–396.

Tordjman S, Anderson GM, McBride PA, Hertzig ME, Snow ME, Hall LM, Thompson SM, Ferrari P, Cohen DJ (1997). Plasma beta-endorphin, adrenocorticotropin hormone, and cortisol in autism. *J Child Psychol Psychiatry* 38:705–715.

Ueno KI, Togashi H, Mori K, Matsumoto M, Ohashi S, Hoshino A, Fujita T, Saito H, Minami M, Yoshioka M (2002). Behavioural and pharmacological relevance of stroke-prone spontaneously hypertensive rats as an animal model of a developmental disorder. *Behav Pharmacol* 13:1–13.

Urban Z, Helms C, Fekete G, Csiszar K, Bonnet D, Munnich A, Donis-Keller H, Boyd CD (1996). 7q11.23 deletions in Williams syndrome arise as a consequence of unequal meiotic crossover. *Am J Hum Genet* 59:958–962.

Vaidya CJ, Austin G, Kirkorian G, Ridlehuber HW, Desmond JE, Glover GH, Gabrieli JD (1998). Selective effects of methylphenidate in attention deficit hyperactivity disorder: a functional magnetic resonance imaging study. *Proc Natl Acad Sci USA* 95: 14494–14499.

Valleni-Basile LA, Garrison CZ, Waller JL, Addy CL, McKeown RE, Jackson KL, Cuffe SP (1996). Incidence of obsessive-compulsive disorder in a community sample of young adolescents. *J Am Acad Child Adolesc Psychiatry* 35:898–906.

Van den Veyver IB, Zoghbi HY (2002). Genetic basis of Rett syndrome. *Ment Retard Dev Disabil Res Rev* 8:82–86.

Villemagne PM, Naidu S, Villemagne VL, Yaster M, Wagner HN, Jr., Harris JC, Moser HW, Johnston MV, Dannals RF, Wong DF (2002). Brain glucose metabolism in Rett Syndrome. *Pediatr Neurol* 27:117–122.

Volkmar FR, Tsatsanis KD (2002). Childhood schizophrenia. In Lewis M (ed). *Child and Adolescent Psychiatry. A Comprehensive Textbook*. Lippincott Williams & Wilkins: Philadelphia, pp. 745–754.

Weiler IJ, Irwin SA, Klintsova AY, Spencer CM, Brazelton AD, Miyashiro K, Comery TA, Patel B, Eberwine J, Greenough WT (1997). Fragile X mental retardation protein is translated near synapses in response to neurotransmitter activation. *Proc Natl Acad Sci U S A* 94:5395–400.

Werry JS (1996). Childhood schizophrenia. In Volkmar F (ed). *Psychoses and Pervasive Developmental Disorders in Childhood and Adolescence*. American Psychiatric Press: Washington, DC, pp. 1–48.

Wilens TE, Faraone SV, Biederman J, Gunawardene S (2003). Does stimulant therapy of Attention-Deficit/Hyperactivity Disorder beget later substance abuse? A meta-analytic review of the literature. *Pediatrics* 111:179–185.

Willemsen-Swinkels SH, Buitelaar JK, van Engeland H (1996). The effects of chronic naltrexone treatment in young autistic children: a double-blind placebo-controlled crossover study. *Biol Psychiatry* 39:1023–1031.

Wong DF, Singer HS, Brandt J, Shaya E, Chen C, Brown J, Kimball AW, Gjedde A, Dannals RF, Ravert HT, Wilson PD, Wagner HNJ (1997). D_2-like dopamine receptor density in Tourette syndrome measured by PET. *J Nucl Med* 38:1243–1247.

Yamashita Y, Matsuishi T, Ishibashi M, Kimura A, Onishi Y, Yonekura Y, Kato H (1998). Decrease in benzodiazepine receptor binding in the brains of adult patients with Rett syndrome. *J Neurol Sci* 154:146–150.

Zametkin AJ, Rapoport JL (1987). Neurobiology of attention deficit disorder with hyperactivity: Where have we come in 50 years? *J Am Acad Child Adolesc Psychiatry* 26: 676–686.

Zhang H, Leckman JF, Pauls DL, Tsai CP, Kidd KK, Campos MR (2002). Genomewide scan of hoarding in sib pairs in which both sibs have Gilles de la Tourette syndrome. *Am J Hum Genet* 70:896–904.

FURTHER READINGS

Barrett RP, Feinstein C, Hole WT (1989). Effects of naloxone on self-injury: A double-blind, placebo-controlled analysis. *Am J Ment Retard* 93:644–651.

Bass MP, Menold MM, Wolpert CM, Donnelly SL, Ravan SA, Hauser ER, Maddox LO, Vance JM, Abramson RK, Wright HH, Gilbert JR, Cuccaro ML, DeLong GR, Pericak-Vance MA (2000). Genetic studies in autistic disorder and chromosome 15. *Neurogenetics* 2: 219–226.

Bauman M, Kemper TL (1985). Histoanatomic observations of the brain in early infantile autism. *Neurology* 35:866–874.

Baxter LRJ, Phelps JM, Mazziotta JC, Guze BH, Schwartz JM (1987). Local cerebral glucose metabolic rates in obsessive-compulsive disorder: A comparison with rates in unipolar depression and normal controls. *Arch Gen Psychiatry* 44:211–218.

Benkelfat C, Nordahl TE, Semple WE, King AC, Murphy DL, Cohen RM (1990). Local cerebral glucose metabolic rates in obsessive-compulsive disorder. Patients treated with clomipramine. *Arch Gen Psychiatry* 47:840–848.

Berquin PC, Giedd JN, Jacobsen LK, Hamburger SD, Krain AL, Rapoport JL, Castellanos FX (1998). Cerebellum in attention-deficit hyperactivity disorder. A morphometric study. *Neurology* 50:1087–1093.

Berthier ML, Bayes A, Tolosa ES (1993). Magnetic resonance imaging in patients with concurrent Tourette's disorder and Asperger's syndrome. *J Am Acad Child Adolesc Psychiatry* 32:633–639.

Biederman J, Milberger S, Faraone SV, Kiely K, Guite J, Mick E, Ablon JS, Warburton R, Reed E (1995). Family-environment risk factors for attention-deficit hyperactivity disorder. *Arch Gen Psychiatry* 52:464–470.

Bird HR, Canino G, Rubio-Stipec M, Gould MS, Ribera J, Sesman M, Woodbury M, Huertas-Goldman S (1988). Estimates of the prevalence of childhood maladjustment in a community survey in Puerto Rico. *Arch Gen Psychiatry* 45:1120–1126.

Faraone SV, Biederman J, Weiffenbach B, Keith T, Chu MP, Weaver A, Spencer TJ, Wilens TE, Frazier J, Cleves M, Sakai J (1999). Dopamine D4 gene 7-repeat allele and attention deficit hyperactivity disorder. *Am J Psychiatry* 156:768–770.

Kates WR, Abrams MT, Kaufmann WE, Breiter SN, Reiss AL (1997). Reliability and validity of MRI measurement of the amygdala and hippocampus in children with fragile X syndrome. *Psychiatry Res: Neuroimaging* 75:31–48.

Malison RT, McDougle CJ, van Dyck CH, Scahill L, Baldwin RM, Seibyl JP, Price LH, Leckman JF, Innis LB (1995). [123I] Beta-CIT SPECT imaging demonstrates increased striatal dopamine transporter binding in Tourette's syndrome. *Am J Psychiatry* 152:1359–1361.

Meyer P, Bohnen NI, Minoshima S, Koeppe RA, Wernette K, Kilbourn MR, Kuhl DE, Frey KA, Albin RL (1999). Striatal presynaptic monoaminergic vesicles are not increased in Tourette's syndrome. *Neurology.* 53:371–374.

Young JG, Kavanagh ME, Anderson GM, Shaywitz BA, Cohen DJ (1982). Clinical neurochemistry of autism and associated disorders. *J Autism Dev Disord* 12:147–165.

Zilbovicius M, Garreau B, Samson Y, Remy P, Barthelemy C, Syrota A, Lelord G (1995). Delayed maturation of the frontal cortex in childhood autism. *Am J Psychiatry* 152:248–252.

15

AGING AND DEMENTIA

Mark T. Wright,[1] A. John McSweeny,[2] and Amy Kieswetter,[3]

Departments of Psychiatry[1,2,3] and Neurology[2], Medical College of Ohio, Toledo, Ohio

HISTORY

The concepts of aging-related cognitive changes and dementia have appeared in philosophical and scientific writings since ancient times. Starting in 7th century B.C. Greece, many intellectuals from Pythagoras to Galen weighed in with various opinions on the matter, but few suggested causes beyond speculations. Hippocrates, for example, thought that "paranoia," or aging-related mental decline, was caused by cooling and drying of the brain and was fatal (Berchtold and Cotman, 1998). In the latter part of the 17th century, a resurgence of interest in cadaveric dissection led to the examination of brains from elderly individuals in an attempt to understand changes related to aging. For instance, the English pathologist Matthew Baillie became the first to address the concept of brain atrophy with aging and dementia when he noted ventricular enlargement in the brains of some demented individuals. In the early 19th century, the conceptualization and treatment of the mentally ill were revolutionized by the work of the French physician Phillippe Pinel. Drawing on the writings of Galen, Cullen, and others in his work *A Treatise on Insanity*, Pinel (1806) suggested that mental illness was a disease that could be the subject of empirical study. Pinel also championed

Textbook of Biological Psychiatry, Edited by Jaak Panksepp
ISBN 0-471-43478-7   Copyright © 2004 John Wiley & Sons, Inc.

more humanitarian treatment of the mentally ill. He was the first to use the term *senile dementia* (leading to the use of the term *senility* as a medical diagnosis) and wrote that this was an inevitable part of aging. Pinel's student Pierre Esquirol differentiated developmental *amentia*, or *idiocy*, from *dementia*, which he thought resulted from disease. He also suggested several causes of dementia, including aging, and noted that multiple forms of psychopathology could be seen in demented individuals (Berchtold and Cotman, 1998).

In the late 19th century, advances in neuroscience gave rise to new understandings of the brain and of dementia. Morel (1860) and Wilks (1865) correlated a decrease in brain weight and an increase in sulcal size, respectively, with aging and cognitive decline. The revelation that neurosyphilis is associated with a decrease in vascular caliber in the brain preceded the seminal work of Alzheimer and Binswanger in the 1890s, which associated arteriosclerotic disease with brain atrophy and dementia (Roman, 1999). In 1892 Blocq and Marinesco first described cerebral plaques, and by 1907 Fischer wrote that plaques were a hallmark of dementia (Berchtold and Cotman, 1998). Simchowicz (1911) was the first to use the term *senile plaque* and held that plaque quantity correlated with disease severity. Following on Bielschowsky's description of neurofibrils, Alzheimer (1907) described his classic case (see below) and was the first to describe neurofibrillary tangles associated with neuronal degeneration. Given the relatively young age of his patient and the widespread tangles he noted, Alzheimer hypothesized that his patient had a previously undescribed disease that was distinct from senile dementia.

In *Textbook of Psychiatry*, Emil Kraepelin (1910) recognized and codified the use of the term *Alzheimer's disease* (AD). Kraepelin stopped short of stating that AD was distinct from senile dementia, though, and mentioned the possibility that it simply represented precocious senility. In discussing dementia in general, Kraepelin recognized its association with memory loss, language changes, personality changes, delusions, and depression as well as other forms of cognitive impairment and psychopathology.

In the mid-20th century, neuropathological studies led to increased confusion about the relationships between normal aging, AD, and senile dementia. Following on the work of Grunthal, Gellerstedt found that most normal elderly individuals had some brain plaques and tangles (Berchtold and Cotman, 1998). The nature of plaques was debated until the 1960s when electron microscopy showed plaques to be composed of an amyloid core with surrounding cellular elements, and tangles were shown to be composed of abnormal neurofilaments. In addition, clinical and neuropathological evidence suggested that AD was not distinct from senile dementia, and the two concepts were later unified (Halpert, 1983). The work of Blessed and colleagues (1968) clarified clinical criteria used to diagnose AD and showed a correlation between disease burden and illness.

Building on the work of these pioneers, modern investigators are intensively studying the cognitive and psychological changes associated with normal aging as well as AD and other causes of dementia. Numerous advances have been made in recent years in the nosology, epidemiology, genetics, clinical characteristics, and neuroanatomical and neurochemical changes of dementing illnesses, and these advances have led to increased diagnostic sophistication and new treatment approaches. The therapeutic nihilism that has dominated scientific and popular thought since the time of Hippocrates is today giving way to new hope for dementia sufferers and their families.

COGNITION AND MEMORY IN NORMAL AGING

Introduction

The intent of this chapter is to focus on abnormal cognitive functioning associated with aging, for example, dementia and mild cognitive impairment. However, it is useful to remind ourselves of the nature of normal functioning in the elderly in order to provide the context for abnormal conditions. Accordingly we will review briefly those changes in cognition and memory associated with successful aging.

Although we commonly think of aging as a matter of years, Mesulam (2000) and others have noted that is a simplistic point of view. Rather aging is best conceived as the interaction of time, genetics, and "stochastic encounters" with events that may compromise or enhance biological and/or psychological functioning (Mesulam, 2000). A multidimensional concept of aging helps explain the remarkable variability observed in aging in longitudinal studies such as the Nun Study[1] (Snowdon, 2001), which cast serious doubt on the idea that intellectual decline is inevitable in old age.

Changes in Brain Anatomy

It is now well established that there are observable changes in brain anatomy associated with aging. Indeed it is common for radiologists to report that a computed tomography (CT) or magnetic resonance imaging (MRI) scan of the brain shows "atrophy consistent with normal aging." Neuroanatomical studies indicate that by age 80, 15 percent of one's brain weight is lost overall, and there is an average 20 percent loss in the weight of temporal lobes, which are associated with memory functioning (Suhr, 2002). These data suggest that some changes in neurobehavioral functioning are likely in aging. However, the majority of elderly persons continue to manage their affairs competently.

General Changes in Cognitive Functioning

Early studies of age-related cognitive changes were quite pessimistic in that they demonstrated pervasive declines of cognitive functioning over the age span. These were typically cross-sectional group studies that suffered from two defects: (1) they

---

[1]In the Nun Study, a group of elderly American Roman Catholic nuns is being studied longitudinally in an attempt to discover factors that modify risk of developing AD and other neurological conditions. Detailed archival personal information gathered throughout the life of each study participant, data from yearly examinations, and neuropathological data from postmortem examinations are being synthesized.

confused cohort-education effects with developmental effects and (2) they did not control for the higher rate of serious illness, including dementing illnesses, in elderly populations, which impacted cognitive functioning. More recent studies continue to document cognitive declines with aging, especially in persons who are 75 years or older, but the changes are considerably more delimited than initially thought.

Sensory Changes

Changes in sensory abilities with aging, especially vision, are obvious. Those over the age of 40 are quite familiar with increasing difficulty in focusing on close stimuli, which often makes reading of small print laborious (Kosnik et al., 1988). Less obvious changes include diminished ability to see in dim light, decreased color discrimination, and increased visual processing time (Bieliauskas, 2001; Cavanaugh and Blanchard-Fields, 2002). Similar changes take place in auditory abilities and other senses, including somesthesia, balance, taste, and olfaction (Cavanaugh and Blanchard-Fields, 2002). There are also major declines in the ability of humans to identify odors after age 65 although women and nonsmokers retain the ability to identify odors better (Doty, 2001).

The implications of changes in sensory function for studies for dementia and cognitive changes in aging are twofold. First, the ability to perform cognitive tasks is dependent on the ability to receive, appreciate, and process basic sensory information accurately. One cannot be expected to perform a task involving spatial skills if one's vision is faulty, as documented in many studies (Cavanaugh and Blanchard-Fields, 2002). Second, in some cases sensory-perceptual functions include simple cognitive functions. Odor identification, for example, involves recall of information and matching of stimuli, in addition to basic sensation. Interestingly, a standardized odor identification test developed by Doty and colleagues has been found to be highly sensitive to AD and other dementias (Doty, 2001; McCaffery et al., 2000).

Specific Changes in Cognition with Aging

In a recent review on cognitive changes in aging, Bieliauskas (2001) noted that the "body of knowledge in cognition and aging is growing exponentially" and at times may seem confusing (page 104). However, some general trends from the literature do seem to be emerging. First, while there is a general trend for cognitive performance to decline with aging, the rate of decline can vary considerably among individuals (Bieliauskas, 2001; Benton et al., 1981). Second, not all cognitive functions decline at the same rate or to the same degree. In general, the changes in cognition and memory are more in terms of speed than power.

Functions Shown to Be Sensitive to Aging

The cognitive functions found to most consistently change with aging include speed of information processing, recall memory, working memory, complex attentional tasks, reasoning and executive tasks, and visuospatial processing (Bieliauskas, 2001).

Speed of information processing declines have been consistently demonstrated on reaction time tests and especially choice reaction time (Cavanaugh and Blanchard-Fields, 2002; Plude et al., 1996). Decreases in processing speed may account for a wide variety of age effects in studies of cognition (Salthouse, 1996), but some of these changes may reflect statistical and cognitive style artifacts (Bieliauskas, 2001; Cavanaugh and Blanchard-Fields, 2002). For example, Ratcliff et al. (2000), note that age-related declines in speed of processing may reflect preference for accuracy as compared to speed in the elderly.

Declines in memory performance are observed with aging, but primarily in recall, and particularly with speed of recall, rather than recognition. For example, using the Rey-Osterreith figures test, Fastenau et al. (2003) report considerable declines in recall between 30 and 70 years of age but very little change in recognition scores (see Fig. 15.1). As Hasher and Zacks (1988) have suggested, this differential decline may be secondary to the reduced efficiency of working memory and the inability to screen out irrelevant stimuli. This is supported by functional imaging studies indicating that the frontal lobes are recruited more in working memory tasks in the elderly than in younger individuals (Reuter-Lorenz et al., 2000). Older adults also perform less well on tests of source memory and are more susceptible to false memories (Cavanaugh and Blanchard-Fields, 2002).

Large-scale recent studies have confirmed a gradual decline in general memory performance after age 50, with more rapid drop in the 80s (Haaland et al., 2003). However, an interesting finding is that the primary change over the age span was in terms of the ability to recall information immediately after presentation, that is, immediate recall. The difference between immediate and delayed recall trials, as measured by percent retained over a 20- to 30-min interval, changed only slightly over the age span. In addition, the investigators also found little interaction between aging and recognition performance relative to immediate recall. Accordingly, the primary difference between young and older persons is with immediate recall. This finding indicates that the "aging effect" in memory is primarily due to differences in encoding rather than retention or retrieval. Other memory research suggests that encoding is related to executive functions. Specifically, older adults do not appear to "spontaneously organize incoming information or establish meaningful links to aid in recall as well or as often as younger adults" (Cavanaugh and Blanchard-Fields, 2002, page 220). Thus, the results of this large-scale study again imply age-related changes in frontal influences on memory, which may be more significant than changes in the temporal lobes.

Complex attentional tasks, including divided attention, selective attention, and vigilance, are sensitive to aging effects (Bieliauskas, 2001; Somberg and Salthouse, 1982). However, complexity is a key variable in these findings. Less complex attentional tasks show little change over the age span (Cavanaugh and Blanchard-Fields, 2002). Given the close relationship of working memory and complex attention, declines in these two areas of functioning may be related to common brain mechanisms, that is, the frontal lobes and associated subcortical circuits. Frontal/subcortical circuits and working memory are also implicated in the decline in performance that is commonly observed in tasks involving reasoning and executive functioning (Bieliauskas, 2001; Powell, 1994).

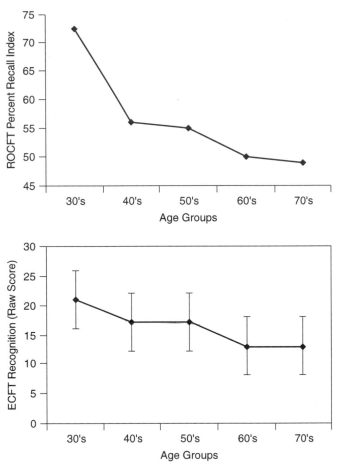

Figure 15.1. Recall versus recognition scores over the age span on the Complex Figure Task. (From Fastenau et al., 2003. Reproduced with permission.)

Visuospatial tasks are typically more sensitive to aging effects than verbal tasks. Why this is the case is not entirely clear, but novelty may contribute because verbal tasks are typically more familiar to subjects than visuospatial tasks. When younger and elderly persons are familiarized with visuospatial tasks, their performance becomes similar (Wadsworth-Denny and Pearce, 1994).

Other Functional Changes Associated with Aging

While verbal tests generally appear more resistant to aging than visuospatial tasks, aging may be associated with benign changes in language functions such as word-finding difficulties, comprehension problems, difficulties with naming, and reduced verbal fluency (although these findings could indicate prodromal dementia or be a function of limited education as well). Behavioral changes such as a decrease in drive, decreased novelty- and challenge-seeking, decreased goal setting, and a tendency to rely more strongly on first impressions in interpersonal situations also accompany normal aging (Cavanaugh and Blanchard-Fields, 2002). These changes may represent a more general example of the specific cognitive changes noted above, especially reduced speed of information processing and less proficient executive abilities.

Functions Showing Little Change with Aging

Fortunately, not all of the news regarding aging and cognition is bad. Several cognitive functions are relatively impervious to aging. Vocabulary, verbal comprehension, and recognition memory are preserved well into the later years (Bieliauskas, 2001; Kaufman, 1990). Accuracy of recall is more similar among older and younger persons than is speed of recall (Bieliauskas, 2001). In addition, elderly subjects do not show rapid forgetting when allowed to learn tasks to predetermined criteria (Rybarczyk et al., 1987), and they perform well on tests of implicit and autobiographical memory (Cavanaugh and Blanchard-Fields, 2002; Fleischman and Gabrelli, 1998). In addition, performance of familiar, that is, crystallized, tasks is better preserved than performance of novel or unfamiliar tasks. Simple attention is also typically well preserved in older adults (Cavanaugh and Blanchard-Fields, 2002). While some behavioral changes are common in aging, basic personality structures are quite stable over time (Cavanaugh and Blanchard-Fields, 2002). Finally, younger and older adults demonstrate equal ability at solving everyday life problems based on practical knowledge and experience, a skill described as "wisdom" (Baltes and Staudinger, 2000).

Implications for the Study of Dementia

The neuropsychological pictures of dementia and normal aging differ considerably and not simply as a matter of degree. AD patients show declines in most declarative memory functions, including recognition, as the disease progresses. Thus, the functions that best distinguish the young and elderly are not the same that best distinguish the normal elderly from those with dementia. Thus dementia is a group of diseases associated with aging and not a disease of accelerated aging.

MILD COGNITIVE IMPAIRMENT

Introduction

With the graying of America, the classification of memory difficulties has received increased attention. Commonly, clinicians encounter patients with memory and other cognitive problems, ranging from abundant memory slips to various other difficulties with routine living skills, but who do not meet the *Diagnostic and Statistical Manual of Mental Disorders*, Fourth Edition (DSM-IV) criteria for dementia. On formal neuropsychological evaluations they show mild deviations from normal capacities but do not show the striking memory deficits or problem-solving difficulties associated with AD and other forms of dementia.

However, it is critical to know when an abundance of such "senior moments" begins to reflect the development of a progressive neurodegenerative illness. The growing need to address such issues has led to the development of additional categories to classify cognitive impairments that do not meet diagnostic criteria for dementia.

Various terms have been suggested to describe these conditions, including age-associated memory impairment (AAMI), age-associated cognitive decline (AACD), and mild cognitive impairment (MCI). The first two terms imply that the cognitive changes are associated with aging per se rather than any disease process. Thus, they might lead clinicians and investigators away from other causes of cognitive impairment or decline. In addition, AAMI focuses exclusively on memory rather than cognition in general. As such, AAMI and AACD came under criticism, and MCI became the preferred term to describe persons who manifest changes in cognition and functioning that place them between normal individuals and those suffering from mild dementia (Petersen et al., 2001). Because MCI is believed to be a significant risk factor for the eventual development of dementia, and especially AD, the early identification of this syndrome as an entity separate from normal aging may be important for early intervention. Presently, its identification may also assist patients and their families with planning end-of-life issues. In the following section, definitions of MCI will be discussed, and the relationship of MCI to dementia and other conditions associated with aging will be reviewed.

Definition of MCI

Mild cognitive impairment is used to characterize individuals who do not meet criteria for dementia but are experiencing substantial difficulties with memory that do *not* interfere with routine daily functioning. In a report of the American Academy of Neurology (AAN), Petersen et al. (2001) defined MCI as the state of cognition and functional ability between normal aging and very mild dementia and provided the following diagnostic criteria: (1) A memory complaint, preferably corroborated by an informant, (2) objective memory impairment, (3) normal general cognitive function, (4) intact activities of daily living, and (5) the patient does not meet criteria for dementia.

It should be noted that this definition still focuses on memory impairment and assumes the preservation of other cognitive functions including executive functioning, visuospatial abilities, praxis, language, and recognition. Thus, this definition might be criticized as narrow in focus as was AAMI. However, others have suggested that declines may be evident in domains other than memory. According to this definition, MCI may represent a more heterogeneous disorder with various possible outcomes. In any case, despite the focus on memory in most definitions, the concept of MCI is relatively general and has not been associated with standardized diagnostic criteria (Hogan and McKeith, 2001). Further revisions in the concept are likely.

Etiology of MCI

Given the preliminary and general nature of the concept of MCI, a clear and concise list of possible etiologies is unlikely although systemic diseases likely account for some cases. Clearly, a significant percentage of the cases represent early stages of dementia, most commonly AD. Petersen et al. (2001) reviewed six longitudinal studies of patients who fit the general description of MCI and found that the annual rate of conversion to a diagnosis of dementia ranged from 6 to 25 percent, with the majority of the studies falling in the range of 12 to 15 percent. This is higher than the annual incidence of dementia, which ranges from 1.1 percent for 60 to 64 years of age to 8.7 percent for individuals who are 95 years or older (Bachman et al., 1993).

Some authors have theorized that the progression of MCI varies depending on the specific cognitive domains impaired at the time of initial presentation. Individuals with impairment in multiple cognitive domains may progress to AD or vascular dementia or show no progression. Purely amnestic MCI is believed to progress to AD. In contrast, MCI that presents with prominent deficits other than memory may develop into a frontotemporal dementia, dementia with Lewy bodies, primary progressive aphasia, Parkinson's dementia, or AD. In the case of dementia with Lewy bodies, an initial presentation of amnestic MCI may be less likely than nonamnestic MCI because individuals with diffuse Lewy body disease (DLBD) demonstrate relative preservation of the hippocampi in comparison to those with AD (Petersen et al., 2001).

Given the association between MCI and subsequent diagnosis of AD, or dementia in general, the AAN has recommended that persons who meet the basic criteria for MCI be monitored clinically. However, it should be emphasized that not all cases of MCI develop into dementia. Indeed, according to data reviewed by Hogan and McKeith (2001), the majority of persons identified with MCI do not convert to dementia within the first 2 to 3 years after identification (Ritchie et al., 2001).

There appear to be several causes of MCI in the elderly population other than preclinical dementia. The association between several systemic disease states common in the elderly and MCI is well known. For example, several studies have demonstrated that hypoxemic chronic obstructive pulmonary disease (COPD) results in cognitive dysfunction that is measurable with neuropsychological instruments and that the severity of the cognitive dysfunction is related to the severity of hypoxemia as well as quality of life (Grant et al., 1987; McSweeny and Labuhn, 1996). However, the nature of the cognitive dysfunction associated with hypoxemic COPD is different than that associated with AD and most other forms of progressive dementia. Rather than prominent memory deficits, individuals with chronic hypoxemia demonstrate impaired complex perceptual-motor learning and cognitive flexibility (Grant et al., 1987). Other studies have demonstrated associations between MCI and obstructive sleep apnea, nondementing cerebrovascular disorders, and other health problems (Brown et al., 1996; Rourke and Adams, 1996). In addition, depression, which is common in the elderly, is sometimes associated with memory difficulties, although this is by no means universally true, and depression-associated memory deficits appear to be quite different than those observed in AD (King and Caine, 1996).

In summary, while MCI is certainly associated with progressive dementia, it is not specific to dementia, and a diagnosis of MCI is a poor predictor of dementia risk over a 3-year period following initial identification (Ritchie et al., 2001). The fact that MCI is not specific to dementia has led to some controversy regarding the AAN identification and monitoring recommendation noted above. As Hogan and McKeith (2001) have pointed out, there are significant psychological and social problems associated with being labeled "at risk" for dementia, including personal distress and curtailment of driving privileges. Accordingly, more specific indicators of dementia risk and long-term studies of MCI as a risk factor are needed.

Mild Cognitive Impairment and Early Markers of Dementia

Some patients with MCI go on to develop the syndrome of dementia. Research with AD and other forms of dementia makes it clear that the cascade of events that eventually leads to dementia is well under way by the time clinical signs of a dementia are detected. This is most clearly the case with autosomal dominant conditions such as Huntington's disease. It is also apparent that in sporadic AD, the formation of abnormal beta amyloid and hyperphosphorylated tau precedes the development of clinical dementia, perhaps by several years (Cummings et al., 1998). Thus, it is likely that the most effective approach to treating AD and other forms of progressive dementia is early identification of persons known to be at risk.

Marilyn Albert and colleagues have conducted multiple studies of potential preclinical markers of AD (Albert and Moss, 2002). They collected data from normal elderly control subjects, persons with "questionable" AD who did not convert to a later diagnosis of AD, and persons with questionable AD who eventually converted to a diagnosis of probable AD. Although the authors did not use the term MCI in their studies, their definition of questionable AD, which is based on a score of 0.5 on the Clinical Dementia Rating Scale (CDR; Hughes et al., 1982), appears broadly comparable to MCI.

Employing data from multiple sources including neuropsychological tests, neuroimaging, and genetic assessments, multivariate analyses indicated that the best predictors of eventual conversion from MCI to AD included measures of learning and executive functioning, atrophy in the entorhinal cortex, superior temporal area, and caudal anterior cingluate as revealed by MRI, and hypoperfusion of the hippocampal-amygdaloid complex, portions of the anterior and posterior cingulate, and the anterior thalamus as revealed by single-photon emission computed tomography (SPECT) (Albert and Moss, 2002). Interestingly, knowledge of the apolipoprotein E (APOE) status did not enhance the prediction of later conversion to dementia beyond either neuropsychological testing or neuroimaging. In a related study, Lange et al. (2002) also found APOE status not to be a useful predictor of eventual AD, while impairment in verbal memory was useful.

Studies of other predictive approaches are also underway. For example, a Mayo Clinic group (Kantarci et al., 2002) is using magnetic resonance spectroscopy (MRS) to study brain metabolites as possible preclinical predictors. While not all measures have produced positive findings, the ratio of N-acetylaspartate to myoinositol (NAA/MI) may predict cognitive dysfunction in MCI as well as AD.

In summary, current studies suggest that a combination of neuropsychological and neuroimaging data are likely to provide the best prediction of which patients with MCI are likely to eventually develop the clinical syndrome of AD. Future studies of preventive treatment approaches might focus on those persons who have positive preclinical findings to determine if the pathological process of AD can be halted or even possibly reversed.

Possible MCI Therapies

Most attempts to treat MCI in the elderly focus on the possible conversion of MCI into AD. Multiple potential treatment alternatives are under investigation. Estrogen, modulators of glutamate receptors, nootropic agents, anti-inflammatory agents, antioxidant agents, monoaminergic enhancers, ergot alkaloids, neuropeptides, and cholinergic agents are some of the possible treatments being evaluated. Large trials are underway with cholinesterase inhibitors, COX-2 inhibitors, and vitamin E (Shah et al., 2000).

Using estrogen as a treatment for memory difficulties has been debated in the literature for a number of years. The hippocampus and basal forebrain possess estrogen and progestin receptors that are believed to play a role in memory. Basic science research has shown that estrogen increases the formation of dendritic spines and new synapses in the ventromedial hypothalamus and hippocampus. Estrogen may also facilitate the growth of cholinergic neurons by influencing nerve growth factor (NGF), which is synthesized by the hippocampus and transported to the basal forebrain where it promotes neuronal growth (Sherwin, 2000). Estrogen may also have a role in inhibiting lipid peroxidation, acting as a free radical scavenger and limiting the toxicity of beta-amyloid (Sramek et al., 2001).

Despite promising basic science research, estrogen has not consistently shown benefits in treating or preventing cognitive disorders. The data currently do not support the use of this agent for the treatment of AD. In one meta-analysis (LeBlanc et al., 2001) examining nine randomized controlled trials and eight cohort studies with respect to the role of estrogen and cognition, women with menopausal symptoms showed improvement in verbal memory, vigilance, reasoning, and motor speed but no benefit in other cognitive domains. Asymptomatic women did not improve. Likewise, clinical trials have failed to demonstrate benefits for coronary artery disease, cerebrovascular disease, osteoporosis, and cognition. Further, its long-term use may be contraindicated in women with intact uteruses due to the potential risk of endometrial hyperplasia, endometrial cancer, gallstones, and breast cancer.

Glutamate, a major excitatory amino acid (EAA) neurotransmitter in the mammalian brain, is also believed to affect cognition. The N-methyl-D-aspartate (NMDA) receptor, which binds glutamate and other neurotransmitters, is involved in learning, memory, and hippocampal synaptic plasticity. Studies in animals suggest that facilitating NMDA receptor functioning should improve cognition.

There are two EAA receptor agonists that have been used for memory enhancement: alpha-amino-3-hydroxy-5-methyl-4-isoxazolepropionate (AMPA) and NMDA.

Direct activation of NMDA receptors can lead to neurotoxicity; therefore, glycine-like agonists, which indirectly activate NMDA receptors, are deemed more promising. In one study of milacemide, mildly positive, but equivocal, results were observed, suggesting improvement in source memory (Schwartz et al., 1992).

Ginkgo biloba has received attention in the lay press and the medical literature. Initial reports appeared promising. However, more recent controlled studies have been negative when ginkgo was compared to placebo in the normal elderly, as well as persons with MCI or dementia (Solomon et al., 2002; van Dongen et al., 2000).

Vitamin E can ameliorate oxidative stress, and a primary event in AD pathology is believed to be oxidative stress involving the production of free radicals. Postmortem examinations of individuals with AD have revealed oxidative damage in neurofibrillary plaques and tangles as well as pyramidal neurons. Vitamin E is a lipid-soluble antioxidant that interacts with cell membranes, traps free radicals, and inhibits beta-amyloid-induced cell death. So far, trials have produced mixed results. One placebo-controlled study revealed benefits in treating moderately impaired AD patients with vitamin E (alpha-tocopherol) at 2000 IU/day: This yielded delays in functional decline, particularly in terms of the need for placement in long-term care facilities (Sano et al., 1997).

Cholinesterase inhibitors are being investigated in large multicenter trials for the treatment of MCI. Loss of neurons in the nucleus basalis of Meynert and other basal forebrain cholinergic nuclei is correlated with cognitive deficits in MCI and AD. Acetylcholinesterase inhibitors prevent the enzymatic breakdown of ACh, enhancing cholinergic transmission and thereby improving cognition. As discussed below, cholinesterase inhibitors are currently the only Food and Drug Administration (FDA)-approved medications for treating AD. Can cholinesterase inhibitors also benefit MCI patients and/or prevent their conversion to AD? These questions are currently under investigation in a large-scale, multisite study conducted by the National Institute on Aging comparing donepezil with vitamin E or placebo (Sramek et al., 2001).

Our understanding of MCI has increased greatly over the last decade, but implications for the early detection and prevention of dementia require further clarification. A comprehensive review of the current state of knowledge is available (Petersen, 2003).

DEFINITION OF DEMENTIA

Current scientific definitions of dementia focus on a loss of ability to comprehend information or one's environment as well as a lack of ability to act in a fashion that is appropriate to one's circumstances. In addition to incorporating the concept of a loss of cognitive functions from a presumably normal premorbid state due to a biological cause, most current definitions indicate that the affected subject retains relatively normal consciousness. In this respect, the definition offered by the International Neuropsychological Society dictionary (Loring, 1999), is typical: "Generalized loss of cognitive functions resulting from cerebral disease in clear consciousness (i.e., in the absence of confusional state)."

Consistent with the contemporary emphasis on quality of life in medical research and practice, many current definitions also note that the deterioration in mental functions disrupts the ability of the affected individual to carry out everyday life functions. Thus, according to Bondi et al. (1996, p. 165), dementia is "a syndrome of acquired intellectual impairment of sufficient severity to interfere with social or occupational functioning that is caused by brain dysfunction." Similarly Mesulam (2000, p. 444–445) defines dementia as "a chronic and usually progressive decline of intellect and/or comportment which causes a gradual restriction of customary daily living activities unrelated to changes of alertness, mobility, or sensorium." In contrast to dementia, MCI (see previous section) does not significantly affect everyday life functions. The most widely used definition of dementia in North American clinical practice is that offered by the American Psychiatric Association (2000) in the *Diagnostic and Statistical Manual-IV-TR*. The DSM-IV defines dementia as a syndrome characterized by multiple cognitive deficits including memory impairment (an inability to learn new material or a loss of previously learned material) and at least one of the following deficits: aphasia (a disturbance of language), apraxia (an inability to carry out learned movements despite intact sensorimotor functioning and comprehension of the task), agnosia (an inability to recognize something despite intact sensation), or executive dysfunction (problems with higher-order functions such as planning, initiation, sequencing, monitoring, stopping, and organizing). These cognitive deficits must be severe enough to cause significant impairment in occupational or social functioning and must represent a decline from a previously higher level of functioning. A diagnosis of dementia is not made if the cognitive deficits only appear during the course of a delirium. The DSM-IV requires that a dementia be related to a general medical condition or central nervous system (CNS)-active substance, and several etiologies of dementia are specified.

While widely used in clinical work and research, this definition of dementia is not without criticisms. A requirement of functional impairment decreases the sensitivity of the DSM-IV diagnosis of dementia. In highly functioning individuals, dementing illnesses often do not cause significant functional impairment early in their course, and even poorly functioning individuals in supported living situations may not show functional impairment until a dementing illness is severe. The DSM-IV requirement that memory impairment be present also decreases the sensitivity of the definition. Patients who do not develop obvious memory problems until late in the course of their illness (e.g., frontotemporal dementia patients) would not be regarded as demented in the early or middle stages of illness.

In an attempt to circumvent these problems, Cummings and Benson (1992) have put forth an alternative definition of dementia. They suggest that dementia is a syndrome characterized by acquired and persistent abnormalities in at least three of the following five domains: memory, language, visuospatial skills, personality or mood, and executive functioning. This definition of dementia does not require memory impairment, functional impairment, or a medical/neurological etiology and therefore has a higher level of sensitivity than the DSM-IV definition. A lower threshold for diagnosing early dementia may be important now because treatments are available that can slow the progression of some of the more common dementing illnesses discussed below.

DIAGNOSIS OF DEMENTIA

Once a patient is found to have the syndrome of dementia, it is necessary to identify the etiology. Numerous illnesses can cause dementia as broadly defined (see Table 15.1). Differentiation of these illnesses is important because some of them are reversible and some can be arrested. It is also important to identify the diseases that are neither reversible nor arrestable (e.g., neurodegenerative diseases) because some disease-specific symptomatic and neuroprotective treatments are now available and are discussed below.

Evaluation of a demented patient should always begin with a good history and examination. Histories of cognitive, neuropsychiatric, and functional impairment can be elicited from the patient, his or her caregivers, and medical records. Knowledge of patterns and timing of impairment greatly aids in establishing an etiology. Thorough

TABLE 15.1. Some Representative Causes of the Dementia Syndrome

Reversible Dementia without Persisting Deficits	Arrestable Dementia with Persisting Deficits	Progressive Dementia
Depression	Vascular dementia	Alzheimer's disease
Hypoxia (e.g., from anemia, decreased cardiac output, lung disease)	Alcoholic dementia	Frontotemporal dementias
Electrolyte imbalance (e.g., hyponatremia)	Trauma (e.g., dementia pugilistica)	Huntington's disease
Hepatic insufficiency	Syphilis (i.e., general paresis)	Parkinson's disease
Endocrine disease (e.g., hyperthyroidism, Addison's disease, Cushing's disease)	Some intoxications (e.g., lead)	Diffuse Lewy body disease
Some intoxications (e.g., therapeutic drugs)	B_{12} deficiency (e.g., long-standing)	Multiple sclerosis
B_{12} deficiency (e.g., of short duration)	Normal pressure hydrocephalus (e.g., long-standing)	Creutzfeldt-Jakob disease
Normal pressure hydrocephalus (e.g., of short duration)	Postencephalitic dementia	Human immunodeficiency virus dementia
	Anoxic dementia	Progressive supranuclear palsy Amyotrophic lateral sclerosis

Adapted from Wright and Cummings (1996).

cognitive, neurological, and general medical examinations give objective evidence of deficits and also greatly aid in diagnosis.

The history and examination should guide the choice of medical tests in patients with dementia. Medical testing can be helpful with (1) identification of any reversible or arrestable illnesses that may be causing or worsening the dementia, and (2) identification and staging of nonreversible/nonarrestable illnesses for the purpose of appropriate treatment selection.

Laboratory studies are mainly done to screen for reversible and arrestable causes of dementia. The AAN and the American Psychiatric Association (APA) have published dementia practice guidelines in which appropriate laboratory screening studies have been suggested (APA, 1997; Knopman et al., 2001b). Tests for uncommon causes of dementia such as heavy-metal intoxication are not recommended unless the patient's history or exam suggest that this should be done. Lumbar puncture (LP) for analysis of cerebrospinal fluid is likewise not routinely done but should be considered when indicated by the history or exam. Standard surface electroencephalography (EEG) is probably not useful as a screening tool in the evaluation of dementia but should be used in certain circumstances, for example, if the patient's history suggests seizures, or if the patient may have a disease with a characteristic EEG pattern such as Creutzfeldt-Jakob disease.

Structural neuroimaging using noncontrasted CT or MRI is a mainstay of the dementia evaluation. Structural imaging can reveal reversible and arrestable causes of dementia such as space-occupying lesions (hematomas, tumors, hydrocephalus, etc.). In patients with neurodegenerative diseases, structural imaging can sometimes reveal patterns of atrophy and other changes that can help with diagnosis. Functional neuroimaging using SPECT or positron emission tomography (PET) scanning measures cerebral blood flow and cerebral metabolic rate, respectively, and can reveal patterns of dysfunction characteristic of certain illnesses.

A formal neuropsychological evaluation can be used to delineate a patient's cognitive deficits and quantify their severity. A profile of relatively preserved and relatively impaired functions can be essential in differential diagnosis, particularly in the more borderline or difficult cases or when cognitive deficits are subtle or complex. Neuropsychological findings are also useful in addressing immediate practical needs, selecting treatments, and monitoring the patient's progress over the long-term. Table 15.2 summarizes the recommended procedures for a dementia evaluation.

SOME MAJOR CAUSES OF THE SYNDROME OF DEMENTIA

Introduction

As already noted, there are many brain diseases that can cause dementia. In this chapter we are primarily interested in the dementing diseases associated with aging and will focus on the four most common dementing diseases: Alzheimer's disease, frontotemporal dementia, vascular dementia, and dementia with Lewy bodies.

TABLE 15.2. The Dementia "Work-up"

Studies that should be done routinely in all patients	1. History and physical exam 2. Neurological exam 3. Mental status testing 4. B_{12} level 5. Thyroid function tests 6. Noncontrasted CT or MRI
Studies commonly done in clinical practice, but costs/benefits not established by research	1. Complete blood count 2. Basic chemistries (electrolytes, renal function tests, liver function tests) 3. Folate level 4. Sedimentation rate
Studies that can be helpful with differential diagnosis but may not be commonly available outside referral centers	1. Neuropsychological assessment 2. Functional neuroimaging (SPECT, etc.)
Studies that should be done only when suspicion for a specific illness is high	1. Syphilis tests 2. HIV test 3. Heavy-metal screening 4. Cerebrospinal fluid analysis (e.g., for 14-3-3 protein associated with Creutzfeldt-Jakob disease) 5. EEG (e.g., in patient with suspected seizures)
Studies mainly of interest in research/clinical usefulness has not been established by research	1. Genetic testing (e.g., APOE genotyping) 2. Cerebrospinal fluid analysis for AD-specific biomarkers (e.g., beta-amyloid and tau)

ALZHEIMER'S DISEASE

History

In 1907, Alois Alzheimer, a Munich neuropathologist and clinician, published a report of a woman in her 50s who died in a Frankfurt asylum after a $4\frac{1}{2}$-year illness. Alzheimer wrote that the patient's illness was characterized by progressive cognitive decline (memory and language dysfunction, getting lost) as well as neuropsychiatric symptoms (psychosis, screaming, carrying and hiding objects). On postmortem examination of the patient's brain, Alzheimer noted atrophy as well as large blood vessel arteriosclerosis. Using microscopy and the Bielschowsky silver stain, Alzheimer also found neuronal loss, plaques, glial proliferation, and neurofibrillary tangles, a previously unknown phenomenon. Given the relatively young age of his patient, the unusual clinical features, and the unique neuropathological findings, Alzheimer hypothesized that he had discovered a disease distinctive from senile dementia (Alzheimer, 1907).

TABLE 15.3. Fact Summary—Alzheimer's Disease

Typical age of onset	65–85 years
Sex ratio	Women ≥ men
Primary clinical/behavioral features	Progressive memory and cognitive deficits
Primary brain regions affected	Mesial temporal lobe, hippocampus, entorhinal areas
Neuropathology	Atrophy, neurofibrillary tangles, neuritic plaques
Neurochemistry	Loss of acetylcholine
Primary treatment	Cholinesterase inhibitors

By the 1960s and 1970s, the concepts of Alzheimer's disease (AD) and senile dementia had been unified as discussed above. Following this conceptual shift, clinical (McKhann et al., 1984) and pathological (Khachaturian, 1985; National Institute on Aging, 1997) criteria were established for the diagnosis of AD.

When studies of the neuropathology and neurochemistry of AD revealed cholinergic (e.g.,Whitehouse et al., 1981) and other abnormalities, the stage was set for the development of pharmacological treatments. Almost 100 years after Alzheimer's seminal case report, clinicians continue to be confronted with patients closely resembling the woman he described, and such patients and their family members eagerly await the results of extensive research being done on this devastating disease (see Table 15.3).

Age, Gender, and Epidemiology

The prevalence of AD increases with increasing age. AD is present in about 1 percent of individuals in the 60 to 65 year-old age group; this number increases to 40 percent in the 85 or older age group (von Strauss et al., 1999).

Most epidemiological studies have suggested a higher risk of AD for females. However, recent results from the Mayo Clinic Study of Older Americans indicates the risk for men and women is approximately equal (Edland et al., 2002.)

Epidemiological studies have consistently implicated AD as the most common form of dementia in the elderly. Findings from the Nun Study (Snowdon, 2001; Snowdon and Markesbery, 1999) suggest that approximately 43 percent of confirmed dementia cases are due to AD alone and another 34 percent are due to AD combined with vascular causes. Thus, AD may be implicated in the majority of dementia cases.

Etiology

Age is the most important risk factor for AD. While AD can be diagnosed in patients as young as 40, it is mostly a disease of the elderly. The prevalence of dementia doubles every 5 years after age 65 (Jorm et al., 1987), and some recent U.S. studies have similarly shown that the incidence of AD doubles every 4 to 5 years in the elderly (Kawas et al., 2000; Bachman et al., 1993). It is not clear whether rates continue to increase or level off in the oldest age groups. Some recent studies suggest an increase in the risk of developing AD into the mid-80s and a decrease in risk thereafter. Snowdon (2001), for example, reports that 40 percent of the autopsied brains of participants in the Nun Study who died between the ages of 85 and 89 showed marked Alzheimer's pathology whereas only 22 percent of brains from persons who reached at least 100 years before death showed such pathology.

Genetic predisposition plays a predominant role in cases of early-onset AD and interacts with environmental and life-history factors to produce late-onset cases. A number of dominantly inherited genetic mutations can cause early-onset AD, but such cases account for less than 1 percent of the total AD population. Mutations in the *presenilin 1* gene on chromosome 14, which codes for one of the secreteases that cleave the amyloid precursor protein (APP), account for 50 percent or more of the dominantly inherited, early-onset AD cases (Schellenberg et al., 1992). Most individuals with trisomy 21 (Down syndrome) develop cortical amyloid plaques consistent with AD by age 40 as a result of carrying an extra copy of the *APP* gene, which is found on chromosome 21. Patients without Down syndrome who have *APP* gene mutations can likewise develop AD and account for about 1 to 3 percent of the dominantly inherited, early-onset AD cases (Saint George-Hyslop et al., 1987). Mutations in the *presenilin 2* gene on chromosome 1, which code another secretase that cleaves APP, cause about 5 to 10 percent of the dominantly inherited, early-onset AD cases (Levy-Lihad et al., 1995). The apolipoprotein E (*APOE*) gene on chromosome 19 codes for apolipoprotein E (apoE), which plays a role in cholesterol transport and possibly in neuronal repair and neuroplasticity. There are three alleles of this gene: The E3 allele is by far the most common in all populations, and this is followed by the E4 and E2 alleles. It has been shown that the various *APOE* genotypes alter the risk of late-onset AD: The E2 allele seems to decrease risk, and the E4 allele seems to increase risk in a dose-dependent fashion. E4 gene dose is likewise inversely related to age of disease onset, with almost all E 4/4 homozygotes developing AD by age 80 (Corder et al., 1993; Mayeux et al., 1993; Pericak-Vance et al., 1991).

In recent years a *cognitive reserve hypothesis* has been developed that holds that individuals with greater premorbid intelligence, language abilities, and educational achievement can more effectively compensate for losses caused by AD than individuals with lesser abilities (Mesulam, 2000; Snowdon et al., 1996). Functional imaging studies have supported the reserve hypothesis by showing that, at a given level of dementia severity, patients with higher premorbid intelligence quotients (IQs) and levels of education have more severe deficits on imaging than patients with lesser abilities (Alexander et al., 1997; Stern et al., 1992). Studies examining brain size (which correlates positively with both IQ and education) have similarly found that increased premorbid brain mass may have a protective effect against the clinical manifestation of AD (Schofield, 1999).

Studies examining the relationship between head trauma and the subsequent development of AD have yielded conflicting results. Traumatic brain injuries could increase the risk of AD by decreasing brain reserve or by playing a facilitative role in the pathogenesis of AD. Brain trauma can cause an increase in the deposition of beta-amyloid, the main constituent of AD plaques, in the brain. An interaction between head trauma and *APOE* genotype has also been noted (Jordan, 1997; Mayeux et al.,

1995) wherein the *APOE* E4 gene dose correlates positively with the manifestation of AD after brain trauma.

Sapolsky and colleagues (McEwen and Sapolsky, 1995; Sapolsky, 1996) have demonstrated that stress and subsequent hyperactivity of the hypothalamic/pituitary/adrenal axis may lead to cell death in the hippocampus. While this process seems to occur in individuals with posttraumatic stress disorder (PTSD), traumatic stress victims have not been shown to be at increased risk for AD.

Recent large-scale studies conducted in Finland (Kivipelto et al., 2002) and the United States (Knopman et al., 2001a) suggest that many of the risk factors for cardiovascular disease and vascular dementia, including diabetes mellitus, high cholesterol, and hypertension, also increase the risk of developing AD. Indeed, the increase in risk for these factors, which are treatable, appears to be greater than the increase in risk provided by the *APOE* E4 allele (Kivipelto et al., 2002). These findings provide hope that medications commonly used in primary care may have a preventive effect with respect to AD. Initial results with statins appear promising and argue that control over risk factors for cardiovascular (CV) disease is one way to substantially reduce the risk for AD (Samuels and Davis, 2003).

Mesulam (2000) has integrated data regarding the etiology of AD into a "neuroplasticity failure" hypothesis that posits that the genetic, environmental, general health, and life-history risk factors compromise neuronal repair mechanisms that would otherwise inhibit or prevent the neuropathological cascade leading to AD. Accordingly, effective treatment and prevention of AD will involve reducing neuroplasticity burden and/or enhancing plasticity mechanisms.

Clinical Features

Cognitive

MEMORY. Multiple studies have documented that the most dramatic, consistent, and usually the earliest neuropsychological finding in AD is an anterograde amnesia characterized by problems in declarative memory (Bondi et al., 1996; Dunn et al., 2000). Episodic (event) memory difficulties may be apparent earliest but declines in semantic (information) memory soon follow (Dunn et al., 2000). Indeed most aspects of declarative memory are impaired in AD. Hallmarks of the memory deficit in AD include poor learning and retention as well as a rapid rate of information loss over time (Butters et al., 1995; Zec, 1993). Thus, a percent retention measure after a delay ranging from 5 to 30 min is often favored by clinicians in the assessment of patients with suspected AD. However, Dunn et al. (2000) found a Paired Associate Learning task to be particularly sensitive to AD.

Patients with AD seem relatively sensitive to interference effects and thus make numerous intrusion errors on multiple list-learning tasks. Although recognition may be preserved early, as the disease progresses AD patients show difficulties on both recognition and recall measures, indicating that the primary memory deficit in mid- to late-stage AD is one of storage failure and information loss rather than retrieval failure. This sets AD apart from some other dementias, especially frontotemporal dementia.

Encoding appears to be impaired as is performance on some tasks of implicit memory, with the exception that procedural memory, for example, skill learning, appears to remain relatively intact in AD, especially when compared to *subcortical dementias* such as those associated with Parkinson's disease or Huntington's disease (Butters et al., 1995). Working memory also appears to be relatively preserved in the early stages of AD, although subtle deficits may be discerned on formal neuropsychological measures.

Poor retrograde memory is also observed in AD, albeit usually later than deficits in anterograde memory. There appears to be a temporal gradient in recall in early stages of the disease such that recently learned information is recalled with more difficulty than remotely learned information. However, this gradient flattens as the disease progresses and AD patients eventually have general difficulty recalling events from all decades of their lives, including autobiographical information (Butters et al., 1995; Dunn et al., 2000). Stimuli with emotional content are generally recalled better than nonemotional stimuli. However, this effect appears to be absent or greatly reduced in AD patients (Hamman et al., 2000).

OTHER COGNITIVE ASPECTS OF AD. Other cognitive functions are also impaired relatively early in AD. Albert et al. (2001) found measures of executive functioning and cognitive flexibility to be the most sensitive to early AD, following memory measures. McPherson et al. (2002) report that this executive dysfunction is linked to the neuropsychiatric syndrome of apathy commonly observed in AD (see below). Helmes and Østbye (2002) found that tests of visuospatial function were most sensitive after memory tests. Thus, the AD patient typically will have trouble copying detailed figures. Families of patients may report that a patient has gotten lost in public, or even at home, in midstage AD.

Declines in language functions are also reported, especially categorical fluency and naming (Albert et al., 2001, Albert and Moss, 2002; Bondi et al., 1996; Nebes, 1997). In early to middle AD, patients often have "empty speech," full of vague generalities, or speech lacking in information content. Patients with AD may make paraphasic errors (i.e., substitute incorrect sounds or words for intended sounds or words) in speaking and in writing. With disease progression, AD patients develop comprehension difficulties. As the disease becomes severe, echolalia, palilalia, and eventually mutism are seen. The language deficit in AD appears to be primarily semantic, that is, related to the ability to comprehend and communicate meaning. Syntax, or grammar, is retained (Nebes, 1997). Simple attentional skills, including focusing and alertness, are usually retained early in the disease but more complex attentional tasks, such as divided attention, are impaired (Bondi et al., 1996; Nebes, 1997). In addition, problems with performing calculations are commonly seen early in the course of AD. While patients with AD have little trouble using concrete objects, they do demonstrate ideomotor apraxia, that is, they have trouble demonstrating actions when the appropriate object is not available ("show me how. . .") (Zec, 1993).

Zakzanis et al. (1999) have performed a meta-analysis of studies on the cognitive effects of AD and frontotemporal dementia. Their results, as adapted by Cullum et al.

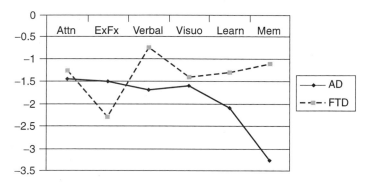

Figure 15.2. Profiles of neuropsychological findings in Alzheimer's disease and frontotemporal dementia. The results are displayed in terms of Z scores based on normal elderly norms. Attn = attention, ExFx = executive functioning, Verbal = verbal functioning, Visuo = visuospatial functioning, Learn = learning, Mem = memory. (Adapted with permission from Cullum et al., 2003, based on data from Zakzanis et al., 1999.)

(2003), which are displayed in Figure 15.2, allow the reader to contrast the cognitive profiles of the two diseases.

OLFACTORY DEFICITS AND AD. Although not typically considered a cognitive function by neuropsychologists, odor identification appears to be quite sensitive to AD (Doty, 2001). In addition, it has the advantage of being less confounded with education than most cognitive measures (McSweeny, 1992; McSweeny et al., 1991). Indeed, two studies suggest that a simple odor recognition test is equal to measures of memory in terms of sensitivity to AD (McCaffery et al., 2000; McSweeny et al., 1991). Even more impressive is a study by Morgan and Murphy (2002) that achieved perfect classification of elderly normals and AD patients using a combination of an odor identification test and olfactory event-related potentials. These studies buttress the utility of olfactory measures in the assessment of AD although, as noted below, other dementing disease can also result in anosmia.

Neuropsychiatric. Personality changes are commonly seen in patients with AD. Apathy, or a loss of interest and motivation, can be an early manifestation of AD. Disinhibition and social impropriety are often seen in the earlier stages of AD, and agitation and aggression can complicate the later stages (Mega et al., 1996).

Many AD patients with apathy are mistakenly thought to be depressed (Levy et al., 1998). Severe depression is actually unusual in AD. About 50 percent of AD patients can develop some depressive symptoms such as sadness and tearfulness; this rarely indicates profound depression, though. Suicide is very rare in AD (Cummings et al., 1987).

About 50 percent of AD patients will develop delusions. Delusional concerns about infidelity of the spouse and theft are common, as is the "phantom boarder" delusion (a belief that unwelcome individuals are living in the home) (Cummings and Victoroff, 1990).

Examination and Test Findings

An extended office or bedside cognitive examination will reveal difficulties with recent memory, language, visuospatial abilities, and calculations as discussed above. As AD progresses and the frontal lobes are affected, executive dysfunction will also be seen. The neurological examination in AD is normal until the disease becomes advanced. Parkinsonism can be seen in the later stages of the illness. In the late stages of AD, the posture becomes markedly flexed and the limbs rigid, leading to contractures.

Routine laboratory studies will reveal no abnormality specific for AD and are usually done only to rule out other causes of dementia. Measurement of cerebrospinal fluid levels of beta-amyloid, tau protein, and phosphorylated tau as well as other proteins may aid in the diagnosis of AD but is not yet done in routine clinical practice (Blennow and Vanmechelen, 1998). The issue of genetic testing for AD is complex. Tests for genes known to increase the risk of AD are available but are generally only clinically useful in families with early-onset, autosomal dominant disease. It is known that *APOE* genotype influences the risk of developing AD, but because this risk is in turn modified by many other factors, the predictive value of an individual's *APOE* genotype is unclear. For this reason, *APOE* genotyping should not be used in routine clinical practice at the present time (Post et al., 1997).

The standard EEG will often be normal in patients with early AD. In middle and later stages, quantitative EEG (QEEG) can demonstrate an increase in slow-wave activity (delta and theta power) that correlates with disease progression (Hegerl and Moller, 1997).

Structural imaging (e.g., MRI) usually reveals atrophy. Atrophy is particularly seen in the hippocampus and other medial temporal lobe structures. Medial temporal atrophy occurs early in the illness and can precede clinical signs and symptoms of dementia (Braak and Braak, 1991). Studies have shown that medial temporal atrophy can discriminate AD patients from those without AD (O'Brien, 1995), but because medial temporal atrophy can also be seen in other disease states, this finding can only be used to support a diagnosis of AD. Functional imaging (e.g., PET) usually demonstrates hypometabolism in the affected temporal, parietal, and posterior cingulate cortices. Because the sensitivity of PET in AD is high, it can be useful in detecting the illness at an early stage when treatments that slow the disease process may be most helpful. The specificity of the temporal/parietal pattern of hypometabolism is also high, making PET a useful adjunct in the differential diagnosis of dementia (Silverman et al., 1999). A PET study using a radiolabeled ligand that binds to plaques and tangles has shown that this technique can be used to localize and quantify disease burden in living patients with AD (Shoghi-Jadid et al., 2002). Imaging methods that more specifically demonstrate beta-amyloid are in development (Bacskai et al., 2002). When further refined, this approach could be helpful with the diagnosis of AD and could be used to monitor effects of treatments that interrupt the biochemical processes of AD.

Neuropsychological assessment will demonstrate the cognitive abnormalities discussed above and can quantify these abnormalities for the purpose of diagnosis, monitoring disease progression and/or monitoring effects of treatment.

Neuropathology. On gross examination, the brains of AD patients usually demonstrate atrophy (see Fig. 15.3). This is manifested as shrunken gyri, increased sulcal width, and ventriculomegaly (hydrocephalus ex vacuo). When viewed coronally, the brains of AD patients typically show an enlargement in the space between the hippocampus in the medial temporal lobe and the temporal horn of the lateral ventricle. AD preferentially affects the medial temporal structures (hippocampus) and temporal poles as well as the temporoparietal junction. Some frontal lobe involvement is also seen; involvement of the primary sensorimotor cortices and subcortical structures is limited, especially early in the disease.

The senile, or neuritic, plaque, which should be differentiated from the more diffuse beta-amyloid common in the brains of the elderly, is one of the hallmark histological lesions of AD. Plaques are aggregations of amyloid protein, dystrophic neurites (neuronal axons and dendrites), astrocytic cell processes, and microglia. As an early plaque matures, a dense core of amyloid surrounded by a halo of cells and cell processes forms. In AD, plaques characteristically form in the cortical association areas (e.g., the temporoparietal area) and in the cortical layers containing pyramidal neurons.

Neurofibrillary tangles (NFTs) are the other hallmark histological finding of AD, although they are also observed in other neurodegenerative diseases and to a lesser extent in normal aging (Wisniewski et al., 1979). NFTs are found in a wide variety of locations in AD including the cortex, medial temporal structures, substantia nigra, locus ceruleus, raphe nuclei, and nucleus basalis of Meynert. NFTs are aggregations of cytoskeletal proteins and are composed mainly of paired helical filaments. They are seen as intraneuronal inclusions until a neuron degenerates, and then they become

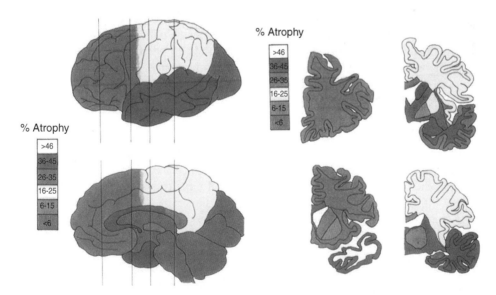

Figure 15.3. Morphometric analysis of regional brain atrophy in Alzheimer's disease. (From Mann et al., 1994. Reproduced with permission.) See ftp site for color image.

extraneuronal. The concentration of tangles provides an index of the regional synaptic loss and functional declines in the cortex due to AD. Braak and Braak (1996) have provided a staging system for characterizing the severity of NFT pathology as the disease progresses that is now commonly used by other investigators.

Neuronal loss in AD is most prominent in the frontal and temporal lobes and hippocampus. A decrease in the amount of synaptophysin, a protein associated with presynaptic nerve terminals, is noted in the frontal, temporal, and parietal lobes (Masliah et al., 1989). Neurons are also lost from subcortical structures including the nucleus basalis of Meynert, locus ceruleus, and raphe nuclei.

Other neuropathological changes characteristic of AD include reactive astrocytosis and microgliosis, granulovacuolar degeneration, Hirano bodies, amyloid angiopathy, and areas of white matter hypodensity and atrophy (Bronge, 2002). It should be noted that granulovacuolar degeneration, Hirano bodies, and amyloid angiopathy are, like plaques and tangles, seen in other disease processes as well as normal aging (Perl, 2000).

Neurochemistry. The fact that deposition of beta-amyloid precedes the formation of plaques and tangles as well as the development of microgliosis and astrocytosis suggests a central pathogenic role for this molecule. The chemical composition of senile plaques has been characterized. In addition to amyloid, AD plaques have been found to contain apolipoprotein E (apoE). The different isoforms of apoE bind amyloid with different affinities. Also associated with AD plaques are acetylcholinesterase, serotonin, neuropeptide Y, cholecystokinin, ubiquitin, substance P, and a number of other molecules.

Neurofibrillary tangles are associated with the proteins ubiquitin and tau. Tau is a microtubule-associated protein that plays a role in assembly and stabilization of microtubules. It is characteristically hyperphosphorylated in AD. The relationship between the formation of plaques and tangles is unclear (Mudher and Lovestone, 2002).

Loss of cells from the nucleus basalis of Meynert and other cholinergic basal forebrain nuclei results in a marked decrease in cholinergic input to the cortex (Whitehouse et al., 1981). Atrophy of the locus ceruleus, raphe nuclei, and substantia nigra result in decreased noradrenergic, serotonergic, and dopaminergic activity, respectively.

Natural History

The rate of progression of AD varies both within and between patients. AD shortens survival, particularly in men, patients over age 70, patients with more severe dementia, and patients with more severe functional impairment (Heyman et al., 1996). Patients with AD become bedridden in the late stages of the illness; death usually results from dehydration, malnutrition, and/or infection. Aspiration pneumonia is especially frequent.

Treatment

Recognition of the cholinergic deficit associated with AD has given rise to a number of medications that facilitate cholinergic neurotransmission. Benefits demonstrated by giving intravenous physostigmine, a short half-life inhibitor of acetylcholinesterase

(AChE), led to the development of longer half-life, orally administered AChE inhibitors (AChEI). These medications have been shown to significantly improve cognition when compared to placebo, and this effect can be maintained for years. AChEIs are also useful psychotropic drugs in patients with AD: Improvements in apathy, hallucinations, and other neuropsychiatric symptoms have been shown (Cummings, 2000).

Tacrine was the first AChEI to be widely used clinically. Tacrine is a nonselective AChEI; because it inhibits both AChE and butyrylcholinesterase, the cholinesterase predominant outside the central nervous system, tacrine is associated with significant cholinergic side effects including nausea, vomiting, and diarrhea. Another significant side effect of tacrine is hepatotoxicity; this necessitates discontinuation of the drug in some users, but users developing this side effect can be rechallenged with the drug. Significant side effects, four times a day dosing, and newer AChEIs have relegated tacrine to a secondary position among the AChEIs. Donepezil is a more selective inhibitor of AChE and can be taken once daily. Rivastigmine, a derivative of physostigmine, is also a more specific inhibitor of AChE. Cholinergic side effects necessitate slow titration (over weeks) when starting patients on rivastigmine. Rivastigmine is dosed twice daily. Galantamine is both an AChEI and an allosteric modulator of the cholinergic nicotinic receptor. Galantamine is given twice daily.

A number of pharmacological approaches to AD have focused on intervention in the disease process itself. In women, estrogen is probably a neurotrophin that facilitates synaptogenesis and learning. Studies have suggested that postmenopausal estrogen supplementation in women can decrease the risk of developing AD, but other factors present in the estrogen-using population confound these results. It is unclear if estrogen is helpful in women who have developed AD (Cholerton et al., 2002). Several epidemiological studies have likewise suggested that chronic use of nonsteroidal antiinflammatory drugs (NSAIDS) may decrease the risk of developing AD. However, clinical trials of corticosteroids and COX inhibitors have not supported this finding (Pasinetti, 2002). Lipoprotein oxidation and subsequent cellular membrane damage has been posited as a pathogenic mechanism in AD, and the use of oxygen-free radical scavengers such as vitamins E and C has been investigated. In a study of the effects of vitamin E, illness progression in AD patients was noted to be slowed (Sano, 1997). As research on the usefulness of estrogen, NSAIDS, and vitamins is still evolving, general recommendations regarding the use of these substances cannot be made at this time.

The potential utility of N-menthy-D-aspartate (NMDA) antagonists in the treatment of AD has been suggested by the finding of the overstimulation of NMDA receptors by glutamate in neurodegenerative disorders. One NMDA antagonist, memantine, has demonstrated significant clinical benefit in the treatment of moderate to severe AD (Reisberg et al., 2003) providing hope for treatment of the disease in its later stages.

FRONTOTEMPORAL DEMENTIA

History

From 1892 to 1906, Arnold Pick reported a series of cases in which patients developed cognitive and behavioral abnormalities in association with focal frontal and temporal

TABLE 15.4. Fact Summary—Frontotemporal Dementia

Typical age of onset	55–62 years
Sex ratio	Men = women
Primary clinical/behavioral features	Progressive disinhibition of behavior and loss of executive functioning
Primary brain regions affected	Frontal lobes and anterior temporal lobes
Neuropathology	1. Astrocytosis with or without Pick cells and Pick bodies 2. Microvacuolar pathology
Neurochemistry	Loss of serotonin
Primary treatment	Selective serotonin reuptake inhibitors (proposed)

lobe atrophy. In 1911, Alzheimer discovered argyrophilic intraneuronal inclusions in similar cases and named these structures Pick bodies. In 1926, Pick's students Onari and Spatz coined the term Pick's disease to describe patients with frontotemporal atrophy and Pick bodies.

Interest in this subject waned until the 1980s when groups in Manchester, England (Neary et al., 1986), and Lund, Sweden (Brun, 1987; Gustafson, 1987), rediscovered a dementia stemming from focal frontal atrophy. These groups found on microscopic examination that the characteristic changes of Alzheimer's disease were absent in their patients and that multiple histological pictures (including Pick bodies in a minority of patients) could be found in patients with frontal atrophy. The Lund and Manchester groups coined the term *frontotemporal dementia* (FTD) to describe the syndrome seen in these patients and developed clinical criteria for the diagnosis of this illness (Brun et al., 1994; revised by Neary et al., 1998).

Mesulam (1982) renewed interest in cases of focal left temporal lobe atrophy with his description of *primary progressive aphasia* (PPA), a dysfluent language disorder. Snowden et al. (1989) described a third frontotemporal syndrome, *semantic dementia* (SD), a fluent language disorder marked by a loss of ability to appreciate word meaning and primarily associated with temporal lobe atrophy. More detailed descriptions of these three syndromes are available in Snowden et al. (1996) (see Table 15.4).

Age, Gender, and Epidemiology

Unlike many other causes of dementia, FTD often manifests in middle age. The mean age of onset is 55 to 62 years and is significantly lower than the age of onset for AD (Grossman, 2002; Snowden et al., 1996). Most patients with FTD develop the illness between ages 45 and 65 with a range of 21 to 75 years.

Frontotemporal dementia in general and PPA specifically are seen in women as commonly as in men. SD is more common in women (Snowden et al., 1996).

Early clinical population-based studies (Neary et al., 1988) estimated that FTD accounts for about 20 percent of all cases of presenile dementia. Stevens et al. (1998) found a prevalence of 1.2 per million population in the 30 to 40-year-old age group and a prevalence 28 per million population in the 60 to 70-year-old age group. These findings show that FTD is not rare but it is much less common than AD.

Patients with SD make up about 15 percent of the FTD population. PPA comprises about 10 percent of the FTD population, and patients with primary progressive apraxia, another variant, account for about 2 percent of the population.

Etiology

It is believed that there is a strong familial component in about 40 percent of cases of FTD, and the pattern of inheritance appears to be autosomal dominant in 80 percent of familial FTD cases (Stevens et al., 1998).

A number of kindreds with autosomal dominant FTD have been shown to have abnormalities of the chromosome 17 gene coding for tau (Foster et al., 1997). These families show clinical heterogeneity: In addition to the characteristic findings of FTD, psychosis, amyotrophy (muscular wasting), and parkinsonism are variably present in patients with these tau gene mutations. This heterogeneity is thought to arise from the fact that different gene mutations affect tau processing and functioning differently.

Other lines of evidence suggest that tau mutations may be sufficient but not necessary for the appearance of an FTD syndrome. Some of the chromosome 17 kindreds do not seem to have a tau mutation, and one Danish kindred with an autosomal dominant FTD has been found to have an abnormality on chromosome 3 (Brown et al, 1995). FTD associated with motor neuron disease has been linked to chromosome 9 (Hosler et al., 2000).

The apolipoprotein E genotype does not appear to influence the risk for FTD. No social, occupational, geographical, or environmental factors have been found to correlate with FTD.

Clinical Features

Cognitive. The basic neuropsychological profile in FTD can be seen and contrasted with the AD profile in Figure 15.2. Diminished executive functions are a hallmark of the cognitive profile in patients with FTD. Difficulties with planning, organizing, and problem solving may be reported by a patient's caregivers. Speech output characteristically decreases with time, and FTD patients can demonstrate verbal perseveration and stereotypies, echolalia, and eventually mutism. Overall performance on neuropsychological tests may be diminished by slowing of response initiation as well as by relatively low effort. Calculations may be impaired secondary to general lack of effort as well as impaired problem-solving skills (Snowden et al., 1996).

Memory is often impaired in FTD. A typical frontal lobe pattern is evident in which the primary difficulty is one of retrieval rather than loss of information or a failure to form associations between stimuli as is the case in AD. Specifically, FTD patients are disorganized and inefficient in their retrieval strategies. Thus, FTD patients perform better on recognition than recall and improve on memory tests when given a hint or cue whereas AD patients do not benefit from cues, particularly in the mid- to late-disease stages. FTD patients also show less difference in performance on immediate and delayed recall tasks than is typical of AD patients (Snowden et al., 1996).

Visuospatial perception and constructional praxis are usually preserved until late in the illness, although the reproduction of complex figures may be disorganized and show perseverative elements (Snowden et al., 1996). Some FTD patients show remarkable preservation of spatial abilities and related artistic abilities. Drawings by FTD patients may be quite complex and detailed although usually not original or creative. Miller and colleagues (1998) have reported on three patients with FTD who continued to develop and apply their artistic skills even after they were institutionalized. This would be unheard of in AD and most other dementias.

The primary cognitive finding in the PPA variant of FTD (also known as *progressive nonfluent aphasia*) is a nonfluent expressive language disorder that includes agrammatisms, phonemic paraphasias, and anomia as the early and prominent signs (Grossman, 2002). Impaired word retrieval and repetition as well as reading paralexias have also been reported. Semantic fluency tests are reported to be better performed than those involving initial letter word generation. As might be expected, verbal memory is more impaired than nonverbal memory, and PPA patients have higher performance IQ than verbal IQ scores on the Wechsler intelligence scales. Snowden et al. (1996) report that PPA patients show better preserved executive skills early in the disease than most FTD patients. Like other FTD patients, PPA patients show preserved spatial abilities until quite late in the disease.

Patients with SD show a loss of ability to appreciate meaning, especially in language. Associative agnosia is common (Grossman, 2002). Speech is fluent with preserved syntax and phonology. However, it may lack meaning and be marked by semantic paraphasias. Unlike the case with PPA, initial word generation is superior to semantic category word generation (Snowden et al., 1996). SD patients demonstrate a unique pattern of memory deficits in which recent autobiographical memory is preserved but semantic memory is impaired. A *reversed temporal gradient* may be observed in which the patient is able to recall what happened the day before but is not able to recall major historical events from their earlier years (Snowden et al., 1996).

Like other FTD patients, SD patients show good visuoconstructive skills. They may be able to produce detailed and accurate reproductions of pictures but may not be able to describe what they have drawn (Snowden et al., 1996).

Neuropsychiatric. The most marked changes in patients with FTD are in the emotional/behavioral realm. Patients early in the course of an FTD can demonstrate anxiety, depression, and hypochondriasis. Personality changes are a hallmark of FTD. Passivity, inertia, and emotional blunting develop in patients with FTD. Problems with social interaction are frequently seen: FTD patients commonly lose social awareness and inhibitions and become tactless and intrusive. Aggression and antisocial behaviors as well as dramatic changes in personal, political, and religious beliefs are also reported leading to a suggestion that FTD is a disease that affects the concept of "self" (Miller et al., 2001; Mychack et al., 2001). There is some evidence that the changes in social behavior that are characteristic of FTD, and particularly Pick's dementia, are observed much more often in patients with greater deterioration in the right frontotemporal regions as compared to the left (Mychack et al., 2001).

Aberrant motor behaviors are also frequently seen in patients with FTD. Overactivity, pacing, and wandering are common as are perseverative, stereotyped, and compulsive behaviors. Utilization behavior, or the automatic manipulation of objects in the environment, can be seen in FTD patients. Hyperorality (a tendency to place nonfood objects in the mouth) can be seen in FTD patients, and death by asphyxiation has been described (Mendez and Foti, 1997). Dietary changes are also commonly seen in FTD patients: overeating, food "faddism" (an excessive focus on certain foods), and a preference for sweets can be noted. Excessive use of tobacco and alcohol can also be seen.

Examination and Test Findings

On cognitive examination, patients with FTD will characteristically show executive dysfunction. Various office or bedside tests will reveal perseveration, stimulus-boundedness, and problems with planning, sequencing, and organization. When asked to interpret proverbs, or when given pairs of objects and asked to find the objects' similarities and differences, FTD patients will show an impairment in abstraction abilities. Attentional impairment is also seen.

The neurological examination may reveal primitive reflexes, that is, frontal release signs. These reflexes include the snout, suck, root, palmomental (chin contraction to hand irritation), and grasp reflexes. Parkinsonism and signs consistent with motor neuron disease may also be seen. Asymmetry is sometimes noted in the physical findings in patients with FTD.

Basic laboratory studies and the EEG will be unrevealing. Structural neuroimaging (CT or MRI) can demonstrate atrophy of the frontal and/or temporal lobes. Functional neuroimaging will demonstrate hypoperfusion/hypometabolism in the frontal and/or temporal lobes. Asymmetry can be seen.

A neuropsychological evaluation can confirm the presence of cognitive dysfunction as noted above. The evaluation should include tests of executive function and cognitive flexibility as impairment in these areas is a key characteristic of FTD. Memory testing can clarify whether reported memory problems are characteristic of FTD or of the PPA or SD variants. In addition, language testing can be used to detect the nonfluent language disturbance in PPA or the fluent aphasia and loss of word meaning in SD. Finally, assessment of visuospatial skills can help differentiate FTD from AD and other dementing disorders in which these abilities decline.

Neuropathology. On gross anatomical examination, the brain of an FTD patient will characteristically show atrophy of the frontal lobes, anterior temporal lobes, and/or striatum (see Fig. 15.4). On microscopic examination, approximately 60 percent of FTD patients will be found to have microvacuolar-type pathology. In brains with microvacuolar pathology, loss of neurons and spongiform changes in the superficial

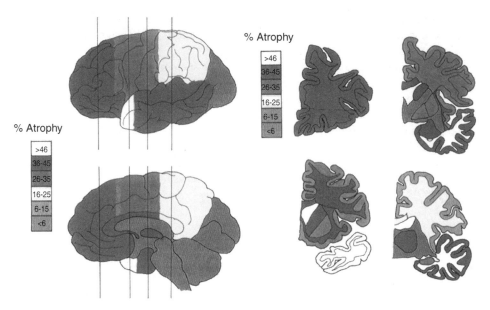

Figure 15.4. Morphometric analysis of regional brain atrophy in frontotemporal dementia. (From Mann et al., 1994. Reproduced with permission.) See ftp site for color image.

neuropil are noted. Of FTD patients 25 percent have the Pick type of FTD with loss of neurons, gliosis, and tau- and ubiquitin-positive inclusions in neurons. Other pathologies seen in FTD patients include Pick changes associated with motor neuron disease and progressive subcortical gliosis; cases of FTD not associated with clear pathological changes have also been recognized (Snowden et al., 2002).

The cognitive/behavioral picture seen in patients with FTD correlates with the anatomical pattern of disease. Patients with the disinhibited form of FTD usually have pathological changes in the orbitofrontal cortex and anterior temporal lobes. The apathetic form of FTD is usually associated with pathology in the dorsolateral frontal cortex. Patients with the stereotypic form of FTD usually have prominent disease in the striatum and temporal lobes. FTD patients with prominent changes in social behavior usually have a predominance of disease in the right hemisphere. Patients with the SD variant of FTD characteristically have temporal lobe disease. Patients with PPA have disease in the left-hemisphere language circuit, and patients with primary progressive apraxia characteristically have frontoparietal disease. While the clinical syndrome correlates with the anatomical pattern of disease in patients with FTD, it usually does not predict histological type (Snowden et al., 2002).

Neurochemistry. Abnormalities of the serotonergic system have been documented in FTD. A 40 percent decrease in the number of serotonergic neurons has been demonstrated in brainstem serotonergic nuclei (Yang and Schmitt, 2001). Decreased serotonin receptor binding has been demonstrated in the frontal and temporal cortices as well as the hypothalamus (Swartz et al., 1997). Impairment in the nigrostriatal dopaminergic system has been reported in FTD (Rinne et al., 2002). Excitatory amino acid AMPA receptors are decreased in number in the frontal and temporal cortices in FTD patients and may be differentially decreased in various pathological subtypes of FTD (Procter, 1999). Multiple studies of the cholinergic system in FTD have failed to demonstrate an abnormality of cholinergic functioning. The locus ceruleus is likewise spared in FTD.

Natural history

Frontotemporal dementia usually begins insidiously and progresses gradually. The mean duration of illness is about 8 years for all forms of FTD, with a range of 2 to 20 years (Snowden et al., 2002).

Treatment

Following on studies demonstrating serotonergic abnormalities in FTD, Miller and colleagues (Swartz et al., 1997) have demonstrated that selective serotonergic reuptake inhibitors (SSRIs) may be helpful in the treatment of these patients' psychopathology. In one small study, patients treated with paroxetine showed significant improvements in behavioral symptoms, reflected by a reduction of caregiver stress (Moretti et al, 2003).

As no abnormality of the cholinergic system has been demonstrated in FTD, there appears to be no role for cholinesterase inhibitors in the treatment of FTD at this time.

VASCULAR DEMENTIA

History

Expanding upon the work of Binswanger and Alzheimer, Kraepelin in 1896 differentiated arteriosclerotic from senile dementia (Berchtold and Cotman, 1998). Despite this, in the first half of the 20th century *hardening of the arteries* was considered to be the most common form of dementia, and AD was considered to be a rare illness of younger people. It was thought that hardening of the arteries led to decreased cerebral perfusion and that this led to the formation of cortical plaques and tangles. By 1970 it had been shown that the correlation between vascular pathology and plaque and tangle formation is weak and that plaque and tangle disease is much more common than arteriosclerotic disease (Tomlinson et al., 1970). Hachinski coined the term *multi-infarct dementia* and posited that actual brain tissue destruction and not hypoperfusion is necessary for the manifestation of dementia (Hachinski et al., 1974). Today, the term *vascular dementia* (VaD) has supplanted multi-infarct dementia in clinical usage in recognition of the fact that vascular syndromes other than multiple ischemic strokes (e.g., hemorrhagic strokes) can also cause cognitive and neuropsychiatric impairment (see Table 15.5).

TABLE 15.5. Fact Summary—Vascular Dementia

Typical age of onset	Over 50 years
Sex ratio	Men > women
Primary clinical/behavioral features	Stepwise cognitive impairment
Primary brain regions affected	Variable/multiple
Neuropathology	Multiple lacunar infarcts
Neurochemistry	Variable/multiple systems
Primary treatment	Treatment of stroke risk factors

Age, Gender, and Epidemiology

Vascular dementia is usually thought to be the second most common cause of dementia after AD. However, pure VaD may, in fact, be relatively uncommon. Knopman and Selnes (2003) concluded that pure VaD is less than half as common as comorbid VaD/AD. Findings from the Nun Study indicated that pure VaD was quite rare, accounting for only 2.5 percent of patients with dementia in that population compared to 34 percent of patients with concomitant VaD and AD (Snowdon, 2001; Snowdon and Markesbery, 1999). Because it is now known that risk factors for cerebrovascular disease also increase the risk of AD, and the presence of lacunar brain infarcts influences the manifestation of AD, "mixed" AD/VaD and the boundaries between these two diagnostic entities are receiving increasing attention (Roman, 2002). Indeed, some authors have suggested that the diagnosis of VaD may be outdated (Stewart, 2002) or should be discarded altogether (Bowler and Hachinski, 2000).

Etiology

Cerebrovascular disease is most prevalent in men over the age of 50, but it can present in others with vascular risk factors as outlined below. A number of risk factors are known to predispose individuals to cerebrovascular disease. Systemic conditions such as hypertension, hyperlipidemia, and diabetes mellitus are well-known vascular disease risk factors. Hypotensive events, for example, due to cardiac arrhythmia, can also lead to cerebral damage via hypoperfusion. Coronary artery disease and myocardial infarction also correlate with cerebrovascular disease. Atrial fibrillation and other risk factors for cerebral emboli can also lead to cerebral infarction. Nonatherosclerotic causes of cerebral blood vessel occlusion can also lead to infarction. Cerebral vasculitis due to infection or inflammatory disease can cause infarction. In recent years homocysteine elevation has been found to be a risk factor for cerebral infarction (Vermeer et al., 2002).

Drugs and toxins can also increase the risk of cerebral infarct. Cigarette smoking is a well-known risk factor for vascular disease. Oral contraceptives use can be associated with thrombotic and hemorrhagic stroke, especially in women over the age of 35, women with hypertension, and women who smoke.

Certain genetic syndromes are also associated with cerebrovascular disease. Cerebral autosomal dominant arteriopathy with subcortical ischemic leukoencephalopathy

(CADASIL) is a rare genetic illness in which affected individuals present with young adulthood-onset, severe white matter ischemic disease (Abe et al., 2002).

Clinical Features

Cognitive. In patients with VaD, cognitive impairment often begins abruptly and progresses in a stepwise fashion, as would be expected in an illness caused by discrete stroke events. Some VaD patients, though, have an insidious onset and a slow progression of their illness like patients with AD and other degenerative dementias.

Attempts to characterize the neuropsychological profile in VaD have been complicated by the fact that VaD is commonly comorbid with AD. In addition, the neuropsychological presentation of VaD in patients depends on the areas of the brain affected by vascular disease, which by its nature is quite variable from patient to patient. Thus, it is not possible to provide a cognitive description of VaD that is valid for the entire population of persons who present with this disease.

As would also be expected in an illness affecting discrete areas of the brain, the cognitive deficits of VaD patients are often referred to as "patchy." Comparisons of VaD with AD have often focused on deficient executive functioning and psychomotor slowing as being more typical of the former disease than the latter (Knopman and Selnes, 2003; Looi and Sachdev, 1999). A frontal-subcortical cognitive pattern is often reported with recognition memory being less affected than recall (Knopman and Selnes, 2003). Other cognitive deficits, including visuoconstructive and language problems have been reported but likely depend on the specific populations under study.

Neuropsychiatric. Several forms of psychopathology can accompany VaD. Personality changes ranging from lability to apathy are common. Depression is more common, more severe, and more persistent in VaD than in AD. Mania can also be caused by cerebrovascular disease but is rarer than depression. Psychosis can also be seen in VaD patients. Hallucinations are more common in VaD than in AD. Delusions are seen in 40 to 50 percent of VaD patients (Cummings et al., 1987). Affective blunting and pseudobulbar affective changes (disinhibited laughing and crying in the absence of, or out of proportion to, an emotional stimulus) can be noted in VaD patients; these facts should be kept in mind when evaluating VaD patients for mood disorders. The severity of neuropsychiatric symptoms in patients with VaD does not correlate with the severity of cognitive impairment (Sultzer et al., 1993).

Examination and Test Findings

Mental status assessment may reveal dysfunction in multiple cognitive domains. Executive dysfunction may be more prominent than dysfunction in other domains. The neurological examination will reveal cranial nerve dysfunction and focal pyramidal and extrapyramidal abnormalities. Gait and balance abnormalities are frequently seen. Urinary incontinence is also seen in many VaD patients.

No laboratory study can diagnose VaD. However, these patients often have laboratory abnormalities that reflect risk factors for VaD, such as elevated cholesterol or blood glucose levels.

The electroencephalogram is often more normal than it is in patients with AD. Focal infarcts can produce corresponding focal abnormalities on the EEG, and EEG abnormalities in VaD are usually more asymmetric than in AD. Subcortical infarcts are often electrically silent.

Structural neuroimaging (CT or MRI) reveals focal infarcts and/or extensive white matter ischemic changes in patients with VaD. Infarctions in the brain watershed areas (frontal/parietal) can be found after acute episodes of hypoperfusion. Functional neuroimaging usually reveals patchy areas of decreased blood flow or metabolism consistent with ischemia and/or infarcts. Abnormalities in the primary sensorimotor or visual cortices are usually due to cerebrovascular disease as these areas are relatively spared in AD.

Neuropsychological assessment may produce a patchy pattern of cognitive deficits with executive dysfunction and psychomotor slowing that can complicate the assessment of other functions. In patients with VaD there is usually a relative preservation of language abilities unless the language areas have been damaged by an infarct. However, as noted above, the neuropsychological presentation of VaD is quite variable.

Neuropathology. Pathological examination of the brains of VaD patients can reveal different types of cerebral infarcts. Emboli, arterial thrombosis, or other causes of arterial occlusion can cause infarcts in the territory distal to the obstruction. Small lacunar infarcts can be seen, and these are most often found in the basal ganglia and thalamus. Widespread lacunes can produce the vascular dementia syndrome known as the *lacunar state*. Infarctions of the white matter can also be seen; widespread white matter microinfarcts are sometimes referred to as *Binswanger's disease*. Lacunes and white matter infarcts are usually associated with fibrinoid necrosis of small arteries and arterioles. Episodes of decreased cerebral perfusion due to cardiac arrhythmia or other causes can cause watershed infarctions in the distal, overlapping areas between the major arterial distributions. Pathological examination can also reveal areas of incomplete ischemic injury as well as ischemia-induced atrophy (Olsson et al., 1996).

Areas of functionally abnormal tissue are frequently present and may not be detectable on routine pathological examination. Focal infarcts are often surrounded by a penumbra of dysfunctional tissue, and areas of the brain far-removed from an infarct can develop secondary functional impairment (diaschisis).

In rare cases, the syndrome of dementia can be caused by a single stroke located in a "strategic" area. For example, infarction of the angular gyrus can manifest as dementia (Benson et al., 1982).

Neurochemical Changes. Cerebrospinal fluid (CSF) levels of acetylcholine are reduced in patients with vascular dementia. CSF acetylcholine levels are higher in VaD than in AD, although the frequent comorbidity of these two diseases complicates the interpretation of these findings. The activity of choline acetyltransferase, acetylcholine's synthetic enzyme, is also reduced in VaD (Tohgi et al., 1996).

Abnormalities in the dopaminergic system have also been described in VaD. CSF dopamine levels are increased in VaD and correlate with disease progression. CSF levels of homovanillic acid (HVA), a dopamine metabolite, are decreased in VaD (Tohgi et al., 1992). Dopamine D_2 receptors in the caudate nuclei of VaD patients have a decreased binding affinity for dopamine when compared to receptors from control subjects. This difference in binding affinity does not seem to correlate with prior use of neuroleptic medication (Allard et al., 2002).

Different findings have been reported in studies of the serotonergic system in VaD. Measures of presynaptic and postsynaptic serotonergic cell density have been found to be equal in cases of VaD and controls (Hansson et al., 1996). Serotonin metabolism seems to be decreased, though, and CSF levels of 5-HIAA, a metabolite of serotonin, have been found to be decreased in VaD (Tohgi et al., 1992). Increased activity of the hypothalamic/pituitary/adrenal axis can be seen in VaD and may be a consequence of decreased serotonergic inhibition of this system (Gottfries et al., 1994).

Natural History

Vascular dementia usually progresses in a "stepwise" fashion over the course of 6 to 8 years. The cause of death in VaD patients is usually stroke or cardiovascular disease.

Treatment

Progression of cerebrovascular disease can be arrested or slowed via various approaches. *Primary prevention* focuses on control of risk factors for cerebrovascular disease such as hypertension, hyperlipidemia, diabetes mellitus, and smoking. *Secondary prevention* of cerebrovascular disease mainly focuses on the use of anticoagulant medications such as warfarin and antiplatelet agents to prevent cerebral infarction (Kaplan and Sacco, 2002). Limited evidence suggests that these preventive approaches can improve or stabilize patients with VaD. Elevated homocysteine levels are usually treated with folate supplementation.

Limited research has suggested a role for cholinesterase inhibitors in the treatment of VaD. In a small case series, Mendez and colleagues (1999) found that donepezil seemed to improve processing speed, arousal, and behavioral initiation in patients with VaD.

Psychopathology is a frequent accompaniment of VaD as outlined above and can be approached in much the same way that it is approached in other conditions. In using psychotropic medications in VaD patients, the fact that the patients may be susceptible to parkinsonism should be kept in mind.

DEMENTIA WITH LEWY BODIES

History

While known previously, the disease now referred to as Parkinson's disease (PD) was first systematically described by James Parkinson in 1817. Parkinson noted that

TABLE 15.6. Fact Summary—Dementia with Lewy Bodies

Typical age of onset	50–80 years
Sex ratio	Men > women
Primary clinical/behavioral features	1. Fluctuating cognition
	2. Visual hallucinations
	3. Parkinsonism
Primary brain regions affected	Cortex and subcortical nuclei
Neuropathology	Lewy bodies
Neurochemistry	Loss of acetylcholine
Primary Treatment	Cholinesterase inhibitors

the disease was associated with a resting tremor, truncal flexion, and a festinating (accelerating) gait. Parkinson thought that in this disease "the senses and intellect (are) uninjured" despite the fact that neuropsychiatric symptoms were present in the cases he reported (Adams and Victor, 1993). Charcot was among the first to note that patients with this illness develop increasing cognitive dysfunction as the illness progresses.

In 1912, Friedrich Lewy examined the brains of patients with PD and was the first to describe the neuronal inclusion bodies that now bear his name. It was not until 1961, though, that Okazaki and colleagues (1961) reported two cases of dementia associated with cortical Lewy bodies. Further cases of this illness appeared in the literature through the late 1980s, and by 1991 the first operational criteria for the diagnosis of what is now known as dementia with Lewy bodies (DLB) were published (Byrne et al., 1991). The concept of DLB was further refined by McKeith and colleagues (1992b), and a meeting of DLB researchers in 1995 resulted in consensus clinical criteria for the diagnosis of DLB (McKeith et al., 1996) (see Table 15.6).

Age, Gender, and Epidemiology

The onset of DLB is usually seen between ages 50 and 80 with a mean age of onset of 72 (Byrne et al., 1989). In neuropathologically confirmed case series, DLB is about 50 percent more common in males than females (Jellinger, 1996). The prevalence and incidence of DLB in the general population have not yet been determined. DLB accounts for approximately 20 percent of dementia cases referred for autopsy, and this number approximates those reported from clinical settings (Jellinger, 1996).

Etiology

Genetic factors may play a role in some patients with DLB. A few kindreds with DLB have been described (Galvin et al., 2002; Tsuang et al., 2002). Symptomatic and neuropathological variability has been noted both within and between families. The apolipoprotein E E4 allele frequency is increased in patients with DLB (Benjamin et al., 1994).

Clinical Features

Motor. In a study by Aarsland and colleagues (2001), parkinsonism was noted in 68 percent of a population of DLB patients with advanced disease. When compared to a community sample of PD patients, the DLB patients had more severe parkinsonism in general; no difference was noted in resting tremor. The parkinsonism of DLB is usually characterized by bradykinesia, limb rigidity, and gait disturbance. Other physical problems associated with DLB include syncopal spells and falling; these phenomena are seen in about one-third of DLB patients (McKeith, 2002).

Cognitive. Cognitive problems observed in DLB overlap to some extent with both PD and AD reflecting the combination of subcortical and cortical pathology in the disease. Slowed psychomotor skills and information processing are commonly reported as is visuospatial dysfunction (Knopman and Selnes, 2003). Attentional impairment is also a frequent and prominent accompaniment of DLB (Cullum et al., 2003) and may be related to the periods of transient unresponsiveness seen in DLB patients. The appearance of confusion is also prominent in patients with DLB, and the confusion and attentional impairment may lead to a misdiagnosis of delirium. Memory dysfunction is associated with DLB, although it appears to be less severe than in AD (Heyman et al., 1999). However, memory assessment is often complicated by disrupted attention and generally disorganized cognition. As is the case with PD, some studies have reported executive dysfunction and a reduction in verbal fluency (Knopman and Selenes, 2003).

Neuropsychiatric. Psychopathology is frequently seen in DLB patients. Approximately two-thirds of DLB patients have visual hallucinations at some point in their illness. The visual hallucinations of DLB are more persistent than those seen in other illnesses and are characteristically well formed and detailed. Patients often report hallucinations of people and animals that make no noise. Hallucinations in other sensory modalities can be seen in DLB, as can delusions. The delusions of DLB are often related to the content of the visual hallucinations and can be complex and bizarre. About 40 percent of DLB patients will have a major depressive episode; this rate is similar to that seen in patients with PD and is greater than that seen with AD (McKeith, 2002). Rapid eye movement (REM) sleep behavior disorders also occur in patients with DLB.

It is important to note that fluctuation is a hallmark of DLB. Fluctuation is noted in approximately 75 percent of DLB patients at some point in their illness. Symptom fluctuation coupled with attentional impairment and psychosis can lead to a misdiagnosis of delirium.

Examination and Test Findings

When examining a DLB patient, fluctuations in level of consciousness and attention may be seen. Tests of memory can be normal early in the disease. Prominent visuospatial problems and executive dysfunction are usually demonstrable in DLB patients. Other dysfunction consistent with a predominantly cortical dementing process such as language problems may also be present. The mental status examination may also reveal signs consistent with depression and/or psychosis in patients with DLB. The neurological examination will not always reveal parkinsonism in cases of DLB. DLB patients who are being treated with dopamine antagonist medications such as antipsychotics can demonstrate severe parkinsonism, and this is another feature of DLB as discussed below.

General laboratory studies are not helpful in the diagnosis of DLB. The EEG is almost always abnormal in DLB patients; generalized slowing and focal delta activity in the temporal areas can be seen (Briel et al., 1999).

Structural imaging studies of patients with "pure" DLB have shown an absence of medial temporal lobe atrophy; this can be helpful in differentiating DLB from AD (O'Brien et al., 1998). In DLB, the decrease in metabolic activity is greater than in AD patients (Higuchi et al., 1998). Functional imaging studies comparing DLB and AD suggest that frontal and parietal dysfunction can be seen with both DLB and AD, temporal dysfunction is seen exclusively with AD, and parietooccipital dysfunction is exclusively seen with DLB (Colloby et al., 2002).

A neuropsychological evaluation can demonstrate and quantify the cognitive abnormalities associated with DLB. Prominent problems with attention, visuospatial skills, slowed information processing speed, and executive dysfunction are common with DLB. However, because DLB patients vary considerably and overlap to a significant degree with both AD and PD patients in terms of cognitive deficits, differential diagnosis of DLB on the basis of neuropsychological tests alone is not possible.

Neuropathology. Both cortical and brainstem Lewy bodies are seen in the majority of cases. The cortical Lewy bodies of DLB stain poorly with routine staining and are best demonstrated with ubiquitin and alpha-synuclein immunocytochemistry. DLB is associated with loss of neurons in the substantia nigra and nucleus basalis of Meynert. In DLB, the degree of substantia nigra cell loss is intermediate between that of age-matched controls and PD patients, and the number of substantia nigra Lewy bodies in DLB is likewise intermediate between that of PD and AD patients. Patients with DLB can also have cortical AD pathology. Plaque formation can approximate that of AD patients, while neurofibrillary tangles are infrequent. Ubiquitin- and alpha synuclein-positive neurites are also seen in the cortex and subcortical nuclei of DLB patients (Gomez-Tortosa et al., 1999; McKeith, 2002).

Neurochemistry. Choline acetyltransferase (ChAT) is decreased in both the cortex and the striatum in patients with DLB (Langlais et al., 1993). This abnormality coupled with loss of neurons from the cholinergic basal forebrain results in a marked cholinergic deficit in patients with DLB. In response to this loss of presynaptic cholinergic input, postsynaptic muscarinic M_1 receptors are up-regulated in DLB (Perry et al., 1990b).

Loss of substantia nigra neurons results in decreased dopaminergic input to the striatum (Langlais, 1993). D_1, D_2, and D_3 receptors have been shown to be unchanged in DLB; no up-regulation of postsynaptic D_2 receptors takes place as might be predicted from the decrease in presynaptic dopaminergic activity (Perry et al., 1990a).

Natural History

Early studies of the survival of DLB patients suggested that they decline much more rapidly than AD patients. More recent evidence has suggested that the DLB outcome data are skewed by individuals with rapidly progressive disease and that the overall rate of decline may be similar to that of AD.

McKeith and colleagues (1992b) have attempted to describe the typical clinical course of DLB. The first stage lasts from 1 to 3 years before the patient's presentation and is characterized by memory lapses. The patient may have episodes of delirium with medical illnesses. In the second stage, patients commonly present to clinicians. Attentional impairment and other cognitive dysfunction, apathy, hallucinations, and sleep disturbances are noted as are bradykinesia and gait impairment. The clinical fluctuation characteristic of DLB is often noted in the second stage. In the third and final stage of DLB, patients progress to a severe dementia over months to years, and behavioral problems, especially disorganization, are prominent. Clinical fluctuation persists in the third stage, and some periods of relative lucidity can be seen. End-stage DLB patients experience severe flexion and immobility like PD and AD patients, and death is similarly due to cardiac or pulmonary disease.

Treatment

Given the marked cholinergic deficiency in DLB, it is not surprising that DLB patients can show marked improvement when treated with cholinesterase inhibitors. Improvements in hypersomnolence, attentional impairment, apathy, psychosis, and agitation have been noted in DLB patients treated with cholinesterase inhibitors (McKeith, 2002).

Because depression and psychosis are common in DLB, antidepressants and antipsychotic medications are often needed. In prescribing antipsychotic medications, physicians should keep in mind the marked neuroleptic sensitivity characteristic of DLB (McKeith et al., 1992a) and use minimal doses of agents with low affinity for D_2 receptors such as clozapine. Ondansetron, a 5HT-3 receptor antagonist, may be a valid alternative approach to the treatment of psychosis in DLB patients (Perry et al., 1993). Given their significant side effects, the usefulness of dopaminergic agents in the treatment of DLB is unclear. If these agents are used, they should be initiated in small doses, and the patient should be observed for confusion and psychosis.

CONCLUSIONS

While it can occur in younger individuals, dementia is mainly an affliction of the aged. Dementia is a syndrome characterized by acquired and significant impairment in multiple cognitive domains and is frequently accompanied by various forms of psychopathology. The syndrome of dementia can be produced by a variety of neurological, psychiatric, and medical illnesses as well as substances. Most cases of dementia are caused by idiopathic neurodegenerative changes that will require additional basic neurobiological research to understand their etiologies in detail and permit the development of more effective therapies. A thorough neuropsychiatric and medical evaluation can suggest the etiology of a patient's dementia. When the etiology, neuroanatomical, and neurochemical characteristics of a dementia are known, knowledge of these characteristics makes rational neuroprotective and symptomatic pharmacological treatment possible. Good dementia management requires monitoring and support of the patient's family members and other caregivers in addition to neuropsychiatric/medical management.

REFERENCES

Aarsland D, Ballard C, McKeith I, Perry RH, Larsen JP (2001). Comparison of extrapyramidal signs in dementia with Lewy bodies and Parkinson's disease. *J Neuropsychiatry Clin Neurosci* 13:374–379.

Abe Y, Muakami T, Matsubara E, Manabe Y, Nagano I, Shoji M (2002). Clinical Features of CADASIL. *Ann NY Acad Sci* 977:266–272.

Adams RD, Victor M (1993). *Principles of Neurology*, 5th ed. McGraw-Hill: New York.

Albert MS, Moss MB (2002). Neuropsychological approaches to preclinical identification of alzheimer's disease. In Squire LR, Schacter DL (eds). *Neuropsychology of Memory*, 3rd ed. Guilford Press: New York, pp. 248–262.

Albert MS, Moss MB, Tanzi R, Jones K (2001). Preclinical prediction of AD using neuropsychological tests. *J Int Neuropsychol Soc* 7:631–639.

Alexander GE, Furey ML, Grady CL, et al. (1997). Association of premorbid intellectual function with cerebral metabolism in Alzheimer's disease: Implications for the cognitive reserve hypothesis. *Am J Psychiatry* 154:165–172.

Allard P, Englund E, Marcusson J (2002). Caudate nucleus dopamine d(2) receptors in vascular dementia. *Dement Geriatr Cogn Disord* 14:22–25.

Alzheimer A (1907). Über eine eigenartige Erkrankung der Hirnrinde. *Allgemiene Zeitschrift für Psychiatrie und Psychisch-Gerichtlich Medizin* 64:146–148.

American Psychiatric Association (1997). Practice guideline for the treatment of patients with alzheimer's disease and other dementias of late life. *Am J Psychiatry* 154:S1–S39.

American Psychiatric Association (2000). *Diagnostic and Statistical Manual of Mental Disorders*, 4th ed., Text Revision. American Psychiatric Association: Washington, DC.

Bachman DL, Wolf PA, Linn RT, et al. (1993). Incidence of dementia and probable alzheimer's disease in a general population: The Framingham study. *Neurology* 43:515–519.

Bacskai BJ, Klunk WE, Mathis CA, Hyman BT (2002). Imaging amyloid-beta deposits in vivo. *J Cereb Blood Flow Metab* 22:1035–1041.

Baltes PM, Staudinger UM (2000). Wisdom: A metaheuristic (pragmatic) to orchestrate mind and virtue toward excellence. *Am Psychol* 55:122–126.

Benjamin R, Leake A, Edwardson JA, et al. (1994). Apolipoprotein E genes in Lewy body and Parkinson's disease. *Lancet* 343:1565.

Benson DF, Cummings JC, Tsai SI (1982). Angular gyrus syndrome simulating alzheimer's disease. *Arch Neurol* 39:616–620

Benton AL, Eslinger PJ, Damasio AR (1981). Normative observations on neuropsychological test performances in old age. *J Clin Neuropsych* 3:3–42.

Berchtold NC, Cotman CW (1998). Evolution in the conceptualization of dementia and alzheimer's disease: Greco-roman period to the 1960s. *Neurobiol Aging* 19:173–189.

Bieliauskas LA (2001). General cognitive changes with aging. In Leon-Carrion J, Giannini M (eds). *Behavioral Neurology in the Elderly*. CRC Press: Boca Raton, FL, pp. 85–108.

Blennow K, Vanmechelen E (1998). Combination of the different biological markers for increasing specificity of in vivo alzheimer's testing. *J Neural Transm Suppl* 53:223–235.

Blessed G, Tomlinson BE, Roth M (1968). The association between quantitative measures of dementia and of senile change in the cerebral grey matter of elderly subjects. *Br J Psychiatry* 114:797–811.

Bondi MW, Salmon DP, Kaszniak AW (1996). The neuropsychology of dementia. In Grant I, Adams KM (eds). *Neuropsychological Assessment of Neuropsychiatric Disorders*, 2nd ed. Oxford University Press: New York, pp. 164–199.

Bowler JV, Hachinski V (2000). Criteria for vascular dementia: Replacing dogma with data. *Arch Neurol* 57:170–171.

Braak H, Braak E (1991). Neuropathological staging of alzheimer related changes. *Acta Neuropathol* 82:239–259.

Braak H, Braak E (1996). Evolution of the neuropathology of alzheimer's disease. *Acta Neurol Scand Suppl* 165:3–12.

Briel RC, McKeith IG, Barker WA, et al. (1999). EEG findings in dementia with Lewy bodies and Alzheimer's disease. *J Neurol Neurosurg Psychiatry* 66:401–403.

Bronge L (2002). Magnetic resonance imaging in dementia: A study of brain white matter changes. *Acta Radiol Suppl* 428:1–32.

Brown GG, Baird AD, Shatz MW, Bornstein RA (1996). The effects of cerebral vascular disease on neuropsychological functioning. In Grant I, Adams KM (eds). *Neuropsychological Assessment of Neuropsychiatric Disorders*, 2nd ed. Oxford University Press: New York, pp. 342–378.

Brown J, Ashworth A, Gydesen S, et al. (1995). Familial non-specific dementia maps to chromosome 3. *Hum Mol Gen* 4:1625–1628.

Brun A (1987). Frontal lobe degeneration of non-Alzheimer's type I. Neuropathol. *Arch Gerontol Geriat* 6:209–233.

Brun A, Englund B, Gustafson L, et al. (1994). Clinical and neuropathological criteria for frontotemporal dementia. *J Neurol Neurosurg Psychiatry* 57:416–418.

Butters N, Delis DC, Lucas JA (1995). Clinical assessment of memory disorders in amnesia and dementia. *Ann Rev Psychol* 46:493–523.

Byrne EJ, Lennox G, Lowe J, Godwin-Austen RB (1989). Diffuse Lewy body disease: Clinical features in 15 cases. *J Neurol Neurosurg Psychiatry* 52:709–717.

Byrne EJ, Lennox G, Godwin-Austen RB, et al. (1991). Dementia associated with cortical Lewy bodies. Proposed diagnostic criteria. *Dementia* 2:283–284.

Cavanaugh JC, Blanchard-Fields F (2002). *Adult Development and Aging*, 4th ed. Wadworth: Belmont.

Cholerton B, Gleason CE, Baker LD, Asthana S (2002). Estrogen and Alzheimer's disease: The story so far. *Drugs Aging* 19:405–427.

Colloby SJ, Fenwick JD, Williams ED et al. (2002). A comparison of (99m)Tc-HMPAO SPET changes in dementia with Lewy bodies and Alzheimer's disease using statistical parametric mapping. *Eur J Nucl Med Mol Imaging* 29:615–622.

Corder EH, Saunders AM, Strittmatter WJ, et al. (1993). Gene dose of apolipoprotein E type 4 allele and the risk of alzheimer's disease in late onset families. *Science* 261:921–923.

Cullum CM, Paulman RG, Koss E, Chapman SB, Lacritz L (2003). Evaluation of cognitive functions. In Weiner MF, Lipton AM (eds). *The Dementias: Diagnosis, Treatment and Research*, 3rd ed. American Psychiatric Publishing: Washington, DC, pp. 285–320.

Cummings JL (2000). Cholinesterase inhibitors: A new class of psychotropic compounds. *Am J Psychiatry* 157:4–15.

Cummings JL, Benson DF (1992). Dementia: Definition, prevalence, classification and approach to diagnosis. In Cummings JL, Benson DF (eds). *Dementia: A clinical approach*. Butterworth-Heinemann: Boston.

Cummings JL, Victoroff JI (1990). Noncognitive neuropsychiatric syndromes in alzheimer's disease. *Neuropsych, Neuropsychol, Behav Neurol* 3:140–158.

Cummings JL, Miller B, Hill MA, Neshkes R (1987). Neuropsychiatric aspects of multi-infarct dementia and dementia of the Alzheimer's type. *Arch Neurol* 44:389–393.

Cummings JL, Vinters HV, Cole GM, Khachaturian ZS (1998). Alzheimer's disease: Etiologies, pathophysiology, cognitive reserve, and treatment opportunities. *Neurology* Suppl 51:S2–S17.

Doty RL (2001). Olfaction. *Annu Rev Psychol* 52:423–452.

Dunn B, Owen A, Shakian B (2000). Neuropsychological assessment of dementia. In O'Brien J, Ames D, Burns A (eds). *Dementia*, 2nd ed. Arnold: London, pp. 49–59.

Edland SD, Rocca WA, Petersen RC, Cha RH, Kokmen E (2002). Dementia and alzheimer disease incidence rates do not vary by sex in Rochester, Minn. *Arch Neurol* 59:1589–1593.

Fastenau PS, Denberg NL, Abeles N (2003). The ROCFT and the extended complex figure test: A lifespan perspective. In Knight JA, Kaplan E, Juettner BA (eds). *The Handbook of the Rey-Osterreith Complex Figure Test Usage: Clinical and Research Applications*. Psychological Assessment Resources: Odessa.

Fleischman DA, Gabrelli JDE (1998). Repetition priming in normal aging and alzheimer's disease: A review of findings and theories. *Psychol Aging* 13:88–119.

Foster NL, Wilhelmsen K, Sima AAF, et al. (1997). Frontotemporal dementia and parkinsonism linked to chromosome 17: A consensus conference. *Ann Neurol* 41:706–715.

Galvin JE, Lee SL, Perry A, Havlioglu N, McKeel DW Jr, Morris JC (2002). Familial dementia with Lewy bodies: Clinicopathologic analysis of two kindreds. *Neurology* 59:1079–1082.

Gomez-Tortosa E, Newell K, Irizarry MC, Albert M, Growdon JH, Hyman BT (1999). Clinical and quantitative pathologic correlates of dementia with Lewy bodies. *Neurology* 53:1284–1291.

Gottfries CG, Blennow K, Karlsson I, Wallin A (1994). The neurochemistry of vascular dementia. *Dementia* 5:163–167.

Grant I, Prigatano GP, Heaton RK, McSweeny AJ, Wright EC, Adams KM. (1987). Progressive neuropsychological impairment in relation to chronic obstructive pulmonary disease. *Arch Gen Psychiatry* 44:999–1006.

Grossman M (2002). Frontotemporal dementia: A review. *J Int Neuropsychol Soc* 8:566–583.

Gustafson L (1987). Frontal lobe degeneration of non-Alzheimer type. II. Clinical picture and differential diagnosis. *Arch Gerontol Geriatrics* 6:209–233.

Haaland KY, Price L, Larue A (2003). What does the WMS-III tell us about memory changes with normal aging? *J Int Neuropsychol Soc* 9:89–96.

Hachinski VC, Lassen NA, Marshall J (1974). Multi-infarct dementia: A cause of mental deterioration in the elderly. *Lanet* 2:207–210.

Halpert BP (1983). Development of the term "senility" as a medical diagnosis. *Minn Med* 66:421–424, 455.

Hamann SB, Monarch ES, Goldstein FC (2000). Memory enhancement for emotional stimuli is impaired in early alzheimer's disease. *Neuropsychology* 14:82–92.

Hansson G, Alafuzoff I, Winblad B, Marcusson J (1996). Intact brain serotonin system in vascular dementia. *Dementia* 7:196–200.

Hasher L, Zacks RT (1988). Working memory, comprehension & aging: A review and new view. In Bower GT (ed). *The Psychology of Learning and Motivation* (Vol. 22). Academic Press: New York, pp. 193–225.

Hegerl U, Moller H-J (1997). Electroencephalography as a diagnostic instrument in alzheimer's disease: Reviews and perspectives. *Int Psychogeriatr* 9(Supp 1):237–246.

Helmes E, Østbye T (2002). Beyond memory impairment: Cognitive changes in alzheimer's disease. *Arch Clin Neuropsychol* 17:179–194.

Heyman A, Peterson B, Fillenbaum G, Pieper C (1996). The consortium to establish a registry for Alzheimer's disease (CERAD). Part XIV: Demographic and clinical predictors of survival in patients with Alzheimer's disease. *Neurology* 46:656–660.

Heyman A, Fillenbaum GG, Welsh-Bohmer KA, et al. (1999). Comparison of Lewy body variant of alzheimer's disease with pure alzheimer's disease: Consortium to establish a registry for alzheimer's disease. Part XIX. *Neurology* 52:1839–1844.

Higuchi M, Arai H, Tashiro M, et al. (1998). Diagnostic assessment and neuropathological correlates of cerebral metabolic changes in dementia with Lewy bodies: PET and postmortem brain studies. *Neurobiol Aging* 4S:S205.

Hogan DB, McKeith IG (2001). Of MCI and dementia: Improving diagnosis and treatment. *Neurology* 56:1131–1132.

Hosler BA, Siddique T, Sapp PC, et al. (2000). Linkage of familial amyotrophic lateral sclerosis with frontotemporal dementia to chromosome 9q21-q22. *JAMA* 284:1664–1669.

Hughes CP, Berg L, Danziger WL, Cohen LA, Martin RL (1982). A new clinical scale for the staging of dementia. *Br J Psychiatry* 140:566–572.

Jellinger KA (1996). Structural basis of dementia in neurodegenerative disorders. *J Neural Transm* 47:1–29.

Jordan BD, Relkin NR, Ravdin LD, Jacobs AR, Bennett A, Gandy S (1997). Apolipoprotein E epsilon 4 associated with chronic traumatic brain injury in boxing. *JAMA* 278:136–140.

Jorm AF, Korten AE, Henderson AS (1987). The prevalence of dementia: A quantitative integration of the literature. *Acta Psychiatr Scand* 76:465–479.

Kantarci K, Smith GE, Ivnik RJ, et al. (2002). [1]H Magnetic resonance spectroscopy, cognitive function, and Apolipoprotein E genotype in normal aging, mild cognitive impairment and alzheimer's disease. *J Int Neuropsychol Soc* 8:934–942.

Kaplan ED, Sacco RL (2002). Use of antiplatelet therapy for stroke prevention. *Clin Geriatr* 10:55–62.

Kaufman AS (1990). *Assessing Adolescent and Adult Intelligence*. Allyn and Bacon: Boston.

Kawas C, Gray S, Brookmeyer R, Fozard J, Zonderman A (2000). Age-specific incidence rates of alzheimer's disease: The Baltimore longitudinal study of aging. *Neurology* 54:2072–2077.

Khachaturian ZS (1985). Diagnosis of alzheimer's disease. *Arch Neurol* 42:1097–1105.

King DA, Caine ED (1996). Cognitive impairment and major depression: Beyond the pseudo-dementia syndrome. In Grant I, Adams KM (eds). *Neuropsychological Assessment of Neuropsychiatric Disorders*, 2nd ed. Oxford University Press: New York, pp. 200–217.

Kivipelto M, Helkala E, Laakso MP, et al. (2002). Apolipoprotein e4 allele, elevated midlife total cholesterol level, and high midlife systolic blood pressure are independent risk factors for late-life alzheimer disease. *Ann Intern Med* 137:149–155.

Knopman D, Selnes O (2003). Neuropsychology of dementia. In Heilman KM, Valenstein E (eds). *Clinical Neuropsychology*, 4th ed. Oxford University Press: Oxford, pp. 574–616.

Knopman D, Boland LL, Mosley T, et al. (2001a). Cardiovascular risk factors and cognitive decline in middle-aged adults. *Neurology* 56:42–48.

Knopman DS, DeKosky ST, Cummings JL, et al. (2001b). Practice parameter: Diagnosis of dementia (an evidence-based review). Report of the Quality Standards Subcommittee of the American Academy of Neurology. *Neurology* 56:1143–1153.

Kosnik W, Winslow L, Kline DW, Rasinski R, Sekular R (1988). Visual changes in everyday life throughout adulthood. *J Gerontol* 43:63–70.

Kraepelin E (1910). *Psychiatrie: Ein Lehrbuch für Studierende und Ärzte*. Johann Ambrosius Barth: Leipzig.

Lange KL, Bondi MW, Salmon DP, et al. (2002). Decline in verbal memory during preclinical alzheimer's disease: Examination of the effect of APOE genotype. *J Int Neuropsychol Soc* 8:943–955.

Langlais PJ, Thal L, Hansen L, Galasko D, Alford M, Masliah E (1993). Neurotransmitters in basal ganglia and cortex of Alzheimer's disease with and without Lewy bodies. *Neurology* 43:1927–1934.

LeBlanc ES, Janowaky J, Chan BKS, Nelson H (2001). Hormone replacement therapy and cognition: Systemic review and meta-analysis. *JAMA* 285:1489–1499.

Levy ML, Cummings JL, Fairbanks LA, et al. (1998). Apathy is not depression. *J Neuropsychiatry Clinical Neurosci* 10:314–319.

Levy-Lahad E, Wijsman EM, Nemens E, et al. (1995). A familial alzheimer's disease locus on chromosome 1. *Science* 269:970–973.

Looi JC, Sachdev PS (1999). Differentiation of vascular dementia from AD on neuropsychological tests. *Neurology* 53:670–678.

Loring D (ed) (1999). *INS Dictionary of Neuropsychology*. Oxford University Press: New York.

Mann DMA, Neary D, Testa H (1994). *Color Atlas and Text of Adult Dementias*. Mosby-Wolfe: London.

Masliah E, Terry RD, DeTeresa RM, Hansen LA (1989). Immunohistochemical quantification of the synapse-related protein synaptophysin in alzheimer disease. *Neurosci Lett* 103:234–239.

Mayeux R, Stern Y, Ottman R, et al. (1993). The apolipoprotein E4 allele in patients with alzheimer's disease. *Ann Neurol* 34:752–754.

Mayeux R, Ottman R, Maestre G, et al. (1995). Synergistic effects of traumatic head injury and apolipoprotein-E4 in patients with Alzheimer's disease. *Neurology* 45:555–557.

McCaffery RJ, Duff K, Solomon GS (2000). Olfactory dysfunction discriminates probable alzheimer's dementia from major depression: A cross validation and extension. *J Neuropsychiatry Clin Neurosci* 12:29–33.

McEwen BS, Sapolsky RM (1995). Stress and cognitive function. *Cur Opin Neurobiol* 5:205–216.

McKeith IG (2002). Dementia with Lewy bodies. *Br J Psychiatry* 180:144–147.

McKeith I, Fairbairn A, Perry R, Thompson P, Perry E (1992a). Neuroleptic sensitivity in patients with senile dementia of Lewy body type. *Br Med J* 305: 673–678.

McKeith IG, Perry RH, Fairbairn AF, Jabeen S, Perry EK (1992b). Operational criteria for senile dementia of Lewy body type (SDLT). *Psychol Med* 22:911–922.

McKeith IG, Galasko D, Kosaka K, et al. (1996). Consensus guidelines for the clinical and pathologic diagnosis of dementia with Lewy bodies (DLB): Report of the consortium on DLB international workshop. *Neurology* 47:1113–1124.

McKhann G, Drachman D, Folstein M, Katzman R, Price D, Stadlan EM (1984). Clinical diagnosis of alzheimer's disease: Report of the NINCDS-ADRDA work group under the auspices of the Department of Health and Human Services Task Force on Alzheimer's disease. *Neurology* 34:939–944.

McPherson S, Fairbanks L, Tiken S, Cummings JL, Back-Madruga C (2002). Apathy and executive dysfunction in alzheimer's disease. *J Int Neuropsychol Soc* 8:373–381.

McSweeny AJ (1992). The utility of olfaction measures in the diagnosis of dementia. *Clin Neuropsychologist* 6:325.

McSweeny AJ, Labuhn KT (1996). The relationship of neuropsychological functioning to life quality in systemic medical disease: The example of chronic obstructive pulmonary disease. In Grant I, Adams KM (eds). *Neuropsychological Assessment of Neuropsychiatric Disorders*, 2nd ed. Oxford University Press: New York, pp. 577–602.

McSweeny AJ, Zilkoski M, McGreevey JF, Nathan H (1991). Evaluation of dementia rating scales in relation to olfaction and memory. *Clin Neuropsychologist* 5:258.

Mega MS, Cummings JL, Fiorello T, Gornbein J (1996). The spectrum of behavioral changes in alzheimer's disease. *Neurology* 46:130–135.

Mendez MF, Foti DJ (1997). Lethal hyperoral behaviour from the Kluver-Bucy syndrome. *J Neurol Neurosurg Psychiatry* 62:293–294.

Mendez MF, Younesi FL, Perryman KM (1999). Use of donepezil for vascular dementia: Preliminary clinical experience. *J Neuropsychiatry Clin Neurosci* 11:268–270.

Mesulam MM (1982). Slowly progressive aphasia without generalized dementia. *Ann Neurology* 11:592–598.

Mesulam MM (2000). *Principles of Behavioral and Cognitive Neurology*, 2nd ed. Oxford University Press: Oxford.

Miller BL, Cummings J, Mishkin F, et al. (1998). Emergence of artistic talent in frontotemporal dementia. *Neurology* 51:978–982.

Miller BL, Seeley WW, Mychack P, et al. (2001). Neuroanatomy of the self: Evidence from patients with frontotemporal dementia. *Neurology* 57:817–821.

Morel BA (1860). *Traité des maladies mentales*. Masson: Paris.

Moretti R, Torre P, Antonello RM, Cazzato G, Bava A (2003). Frontotemporal dementia: Paroxetine as a possible treatment of behavior symptoms. A randomized, controlled, open 14-month study. *Eur Neurol* 49:13–19.

Morgan CD, Murphy C (2002). Olfactory event-related potentials in Alzheimer's disease. *J Int Neuropsychol Soc* 8:753–763.

Mudher A, Lovestone S (2002). Alzheimer's disease—do tauists and baptists finally shake hands? *Trends Neurosci* 25:22–26.

Mychack P, Kramer JH, Boone KB, Miller BL (2001). The influence of right frontotemporal dysfunction on social behavior in frontotemporal dementia. *Neurology* 56(Supp 4): S11–S15.

National Institute on Aging (NIA)–Reagan Working Group (1997). Consensus recommendations for the postmortem diagnosis of alzheimer's disease. *Neurobiol Aging* 18:S1–S27.

Neary D, Snowden JS, Bowen DM, et al. (1986). Cerebral biopsy in the investigation of presenile dementia due to cerebral atrophy. *J Neurol Neurosurg Psychiatry* 49:157–162.

Neary D, Snowden JS, Northen B, Goulding P (1988). Dementia of frontal lobe type. *J Neurol Neurosurg Psychiatry* 51:353–361.

Neary D, Snowden JS, Gustafson L, et al. (1998). Frontotemporal lobar degeneration. A consensus on clinical diagnostic criteria. *Neurology* 51:1546–1554.

Nebes RD (1997). Alzheimer's disease: Cognitive neuropsychological aspects. In Feinberg TE, Farah MJ (eds). *Behavioral Neurology and Neuropsychology*. McGraw-Hill: New York, pp. 545–550.

O'Brien JT (1995). Is hippocampal atrophy on magnetic resonance imaging a marker for alzheimer's disease? *Int J Geriatr Psychiatry* 10:431–435.

O'Brien J, Harvey G, Hughes J, et al. (1998). Magnetic resonance imaging differences between dementia with Lewy bodies and Alzheimer's disease. *Neurobiol Aging* 4S:S205.

Okazaki H, Lipton LS, Aronson SM (1961). Diffuse intracytoplasmic ganglionic inclusions (Lewy type) associated with progressive dementia and quadraparesis in flexion. *J Neurol Neurosurg Psychiatry* 20:237–244.

Olsson Y, Brun A, Englund E (1996). Fundamental pathological lesions in vascular dementia. *Acta Neurol Scand* 168(Suppl):31–38.

Pasinetti GM (2002). From epidemiology to therapeutic trials with anti-inflammatory drugs in Alzheimer's disease: The role of NSAIDs and cyclooxygenase in beta-amyloidosis and clinical dementia. *J Alzheimers Dis* 4:435–445.

Pericak-Vance MA, Bebout JL, Gaskell PC, et al. (1991). Linkage studies in familial alzheimer disease: Evidence for chromosome 19 linkage. *Am J Hum Genet* 48:1034–1050.

Perl DP (2000). Neuropathology of alzheimer's disease and related disorders. *Neurology Clinics* 18:847–864.

Perry EK, Marshall E, Perry RH, et al. (1990a). Cholinergic and dopaminergic activities in senile dementia of Lewy body type. *Alzheimer Dis Assoc Disord* 4:87–95.

Perry EK, Smith CJ, Court JA, Perry RH (1990b). Cholinergic nicotinic and muscarinic receptors in dementia of Alzheimer, Parkinson, and Lewy body types. *J Neural Trans* 2:149–158.

Perry EK, Irvin D, Kerwin JM, et al. (1993). Cholinergic neurotransmitter and neurotrophic activities in Lewy body dementia. Similarity to Parkinson's and distinctions from Alzheimer's disease. *Alzheimer Dis Assoc Disord* 7:62–79.

Petersen RC (2003). *Mild Cognitive Impairment: Aging to Alzheimer's Disease*. Oxford University Press, Oxford.

Petersen RC, Stevens JC, Ganguli M, Tangalos EG, Cummings JL, DeKosky ST (2001). Practice parameter: Early detection of dementia: Mild cognitive impairment (an evidence-based review) Report of the Quality Standards of Subcommittee of the American Academy of Neurology. *Neurology* 56:1133–1142.

Pinel P (1806). *A Treatise on Insanity* (D. D. Davis, trans). Cadell & Davies: Sheffield.

Plude DJ, Schwartz LK, Murphy LJ (1996). Active selection and inhibition in the aging of attention. In Blanchard-Fields F, Hess TM (eds). *Perspectives on Cognitive Change in Adulthood and Aging*. McGraw-Hill: New York, pp. 165–189.

Post SG, Whitehouse PJ, Binstock RH, et al. (1997). The clinical introduction of genetic testing for Alzheimer disease. An ethical perspective. *JAMA* 277:832–836.

Powell DH (1994). *Profiles in Cognitive Aging*. Harvard University Press: Cambridge, MA.

Procter AW, Qurne M, Francis PT (1999). Neurochemical features of frontotemporal dementia. *Dement Geriatr Cogn Disord* 10(Supp 1):80–84.

Ratcliff R, Spieler D, McKoon G (2000). Explicitly modeling the effects on response time. *Psychonomic Bulletin and Review* 7:1–25.

Reisberg B, Doody R, Stöffler A, Schmitt F, Ferris S, Möbius J (2003). Management in moderate-to-sever Alzheimer's disease. *NEJM* 348:1333–1341.

Reuter-Lorenz, Stanczack L, Miller AC (2000). Neural recruitment and aging: Two hemispheres are better than one, especially as you age. *Psychol Sci* 10:494–500.

Rinne JO, Laine M, Kaasinen V, Norvasuo-Heila MK, Nagren K, Helenius H (2002). Striatal dopamine transporter and extrapyramidal symptoms in frontotemporal dementia. *Neurology* 58:1489–1493.

Ritchie K, Artero S, Touchon J (2001). Classification criteria for mild cognitive impairment: A population-based validation study. *Neurology* 56:37–42.

Roman GC (1999). A historical review of the concept of vascular dementia: Lessons from the past for the future. *Alzheimer Dis Assoc Disord* 13(Suppl 3):S4–S8.

Roman GC (2002). Vascular dementia may be the most common form of dementia in the elderly. *J Neurol Sci* 203–204:7–10.

Rourke SB, Adams KM (1996). The neuropsychological correlates of acute and chronic hypoxemia. In Grant I, Adams KM (eds). *Neuropsychological Assessment of Neuropsychiatric Disorders*, 2nd ed. Oxford University Press: New York, pp. 379–402.

Rybarczyk BD, Hart RP, Harkins SW (1987). Age and forgetting rate with pictorial stimuli. *Psychol Aging* 2:404–406.

Saint George-Hyslop PH, Tanzi RE, Polinsky RJ, et al. (1987). The genetic defect causing familial alzheimer's disease maps on chromosome 21. *Science* 235:885–890.

Salthouse TA (1996). The processing speed theory of adult age differences in cognition. *Psychol Rev* 103:403–428.

Samuels SC, Davis KL (2003). Advances in the treatment of alzheimer's disease. In Weiner MF, Lipton AM (eds). *The Dementias: Diagnosis, Treatment and Research*, 3rd ed. American Psychiatric Association: Washington, DC.

Sano M, Ernesto C, Thomas RG, et al. (1997). A controlled trial of selegiline, alpha-tocopherol, or both as treatment for alzheimer's disease: The alzheimer's disease cooperative study. *N Engl J Med* 336:1216–1222.

Sapolsky RM (1996). Why stress is bad for your brain. *Science* 273:749–750.

Schellenberg GD, Bird TD, Wijsman EM, et al. (1992). Genetic linkage evidence for a familial alzheimer disease locus on chromosome 14. *Science* 258:668–670.

Schofield P (1999). Alzheimer's disease and brain reserve. *Australas J Aging* 18:10–14.

Schwartz BL, Hastroudi S, Herting RL, et al. (1992). The effects of milacemide on item and source memory. *Clin Neuropharmacol* 15:114–119.

Shah Y, Tangalos EG, Petersen RC (2000). Mild cognitive impairment: When is it a precursor to Alzheimer's disease? *Geriatrics* 55:9–62.

Sherwin B (2000). Mild cognitive impairment: Potential pharmacological treatment options. *J Am Geriatr Soc* 48:431–441.

Shoghi-Jadid K, Small GW, Agdeppa ED, et al. (2002). Localization of neurofibrillary tangles and beta-amyloid plaques in the brains of living patients with Alzheimer disease. *Am J Geriatr Psychiatry* 10:24–35.

Silverman DHS, Small GW, Phelps ME (1999). Clinical value of neuroimaging in the diagnosis of dementia: Sensitivity and specificity of regional cerebral metabolic and other parameters for early identification of Alzheimer's disease. *Clinical Positron Imaging* 2:119–130.

Simchowicz T (1911). Histologische Studienüber die Senile Demenz. *Histologische und Histopathologischen Arbeiten über der Grosshirnrinde* 4:267–444.

Snowden JS, Goulding PJ, Neary D (1989). Semantic dementia: A form of circumscribed cerebral atrophy. *Behav Neurology* 2:167–182.

Snowden JS, Neary D, Mann DMA (1996). *Fronto-temporal Lobar Degeneration: Frontotemporal Dementia, Progressive Aphasia, Semantic Dementia.* Churchill Livingstone: New York.

Snowden JS, Neary D, Mann DMA (2002). Frontotemporal dementia. *Br J Psychiatry* 180:140–143.

Snowdon D (2001). *Aging with Grace.* Bantam Books: New York.

Snowdon DA, Kemper SJ, Mortimer JA, Greiner LH, Wekstein DR, Markesbery WR (1996). Linguistic ability in early life and cognitive function and Alzheimer's disease in late life. *JAMA* 275:528–532.

Snowdon DA, Markesbery WR (1999). The prevalence of neuropathologically confirmed vascular dementia: Findings from the nun study. *First International Congress on Vascular Dementia* 10:19–24.

Solomon PR, Adams F, Silver A, Zimmer J, DeVeaux R (2002). Ginkgo for memory enhancement: A randomized controlled trial. *JAMA* 288:835–840.

Somberg BL, Salthouse TA (1982). Divided attention abilities in young and old adults. *J Exp Psychol Hum Percept Perform* 8:651–663.

Sramek JJ, Veroff AE, Cutler NR (2001). The status of ongoing trials for mild cognitive impairment. *Expert Opinion Investigational Drugs* 10:741–752.

Stern Y, Alexander GE, Prohovnik I, Mayeux R (1992). Inverse relationship between education and parietotemporal perfusion deficit in Alzheimer's disease. *Ann Neuro* 32:371–375.

Stevens M, van Duijn CM, Kamphorst W, et al. (1998). Familial aggregation in frontotemporal dementia. *Neurology* 50:1541–1545.

Stewart R. (2002). Vascular dementia: A diagnosis running out of time. *Br J Psychiat* 180:152–156.

Suhr J (2002, March). Cognitive changes in aging: Clinical implications. Presentation made at the Medical College of Ohio Annual Conference on Geriatric Medicine, Toledo.

Sultzer DL, Levin HS, Mahler ME, High WM, Cummings JL (1993). A comparison of psychiatric symptoms in vascular dementia and Alzheimer's disease. *Am J Psychiatry* 150:1806–1812.

Swartz JR, Miller BL, Lesser IM, Darby AL (1997). Frontotemporal dementia: Treatment response to serotonin selective reuptake inhibitors. *J Clin Psychiatry* 58:212–216.

Tohgi H, Ueno M, Abe T, Takahashi S, Nozaki Y (1992). Concentrations of monoamines and their metabolites in the cerebrospinal fluid from patients with senile dementia of the Alzheimer type and vascular dementia of the Binswanger type. *J Neural Transm Park Dis Dement Sect* 4:69–77.

Tohgi H, Abe T, Kimura M, Saheki M, Takahashi S (1996). Cerebrospinal fluid acetylcholine and choline in vascular dementia of Binswanger and multiple small infarct types as compared with Alzheimer-type dementia. *J Neural Transm* 103:1211–1220.

Tomlinson BE, Blessed G, Roth M (1970). Observations on the brains of demented old people. *J Neurol Sci* 11:205–242.

Tsuang DW, Dalan AM, Eugenio CJ et al. (2002). Familial dementia with Lewy bodies: A clinical and neuropathological study of two families. *Arch Neurology* 59:1622–1630.

van Dongen MC, van Rossen G, Kessels AG, et al. (2000). The efficacy of ginkgo for elderly people with dementia and age-associated memory impairment: New results of a randomized clinical trial. *J Am Geriatr Soc* 48:1183–1194.

Vermeer SE, van Dijk EJ, Koudstaal PJ, et al. (2002). Homocysteine, silent brain infarcts, and white matter lesions: The Rotterdam Scan Study. *Ann Neurol* 51:285–289.

von Strauss EM, Viitanen D, De Ronchi D, et al. (1999). Aging and the occurrence of dementia. *Arch Neurol* 56:587–592.

Wadsworth-Denney N, Pearce KA (1994). Effects of practice on the matching familiar figures test: A comparison of young, middle-aged and elderly adults. *Aging and Cognition* 1:177–187.

Whitehouse PJ, Price DL, Clark AW, Coyle JT, DeLong MR (1981). Alzheimer's disease: Evidence for selective loss of cholinergic neurons in the nucleus basalis. *Ann Neurol* 10:122–126.

Wilks S (1865). Clinical notes on atrophy of the brain. *J Mental Sci* 10:381–392.

Wisniewski K, Jervis GA, Moretz RC, et al. (1979). Alzheimer neurofibrillary tangles in disease other than senile and presenile dementia. *Ann Neurol* 5:288–294.

Wright MT, Cummings JL (1996). Neuropsychiatric disturbances in Alzheimer's disease and other dementias: Recognition and management. *Neurologist* 2:207–218.

Yang Y, Schmitt HP (2001). Frontotemporal dementia: Evidence for impairment of ascending serotonergic but not noradrenergic innervation. Immunocytochemical and quantitative study using a graph method. *Acta Neuropathol (Berl)* 101:256–270.

Zakzanis KK, Leach L, Kaplan E (1999). *Neuropsychological Differential Diagnosis*. Swets & Zeitlinger: Lisse, Netherlands.

Zec RF (1993). Neuropsychological functioning in Alzheimer's disease. In Parks RW, Zec RF, Wilson RS (eds). *Neuropsychology of Alzheimer's Disease and Other Dementias*. Oxford University Press: New York, pp. 3–80.

Part III

FUTURE PROSPECTS

The future of psychiatry lies in our capacity to fathom the true sources of emotional distress in the human brain and in our capacity to prevent and to alleviate such distress with ever more effective interventions. Much of the essential knowledge for future progress is emerging from a detailed understanding of the evolved core emotional systems that evolution provided all mammals as tools for their animate existence. Many animal models are helping us decipher the neuroevolutionary psychobiology of brain emotional systems and the resulting nature of affective experiences. Perhaps the most important understanding at this level is to be achieved in the realm of neuro-chemistries. Those that help us characterize emotional learning processes and other forms of use-dependent brain plasticity allow us a glimpse into how organisms adapt to various environments and how they navigate the world when confronted by specific life challenges.

Studies in humans provide new strategies on how emotional responses can be regulated. Relevant brain systems can be manipulated directly by emerging technologies such as transcranial magnetic stimulation (TMS) and other somatic approaches. We can envision a day when there will be medicinal agents that will facilitate positive forms of use-dependent plasticities in the mental apparatus of the nervous system. However, these approaches will never replace the vast array of traditional human healing skills. In the future, there will probably be neurochemical interventions that are so emotionally specific that we may be amazed how many of them work best in specific socioemotional contexts. As such agents are developed, we may need to better understand the depths of

Textbook of Biological Psychiatry, Edited by Jaak Panksepp
ISBN 0-471-43478-7   Copyright © 2004 John Wiley & Sons, Inc.

the human psyche in order to provide optimal assistance for those who desire help with their emotional lives. It is from the combination of approaches that the most effective future tools will emerge. In dealing with the human brain/mind, we must recognize that there is no single path to an adequate understanding of the human mental apparatus. A healthy mind is as integral a part of a healthy body, as the body is an essential substrate for the mind. As Freud put it "The ego is first and foremost a body ego" (Sigmund Freud's essay on "The Ego and the Id" (1923) *Standard Edition*, Vol. 19, p. 18).

In accepting human complexities, we must increasingly recognize the importance of "meaning" in human lives. While science can give us some assurance about the "truth of fact" it has comparatively little to say about the "truth of meaning." The latter is a creation of how the basic evolved values of our nervous system interact with vast general-purpose cerebral spaces and world events that create mental realities out of human fantasies and imagination. It is only by combining the best of brain/mind science with those aspects of the humanities and social sciences that attempt to deal with human meanings, that adequate frameworks for dealing with human lives can emerge.

16

EMERGING NEUROSCIENCE OF FEAR AND ANXIETY: THERAPEUTIC PRACTICE AND CLINICAL IMPLICATIONS

Jaak Panksepp

J.P. Scott Center for Neuroscience, Mind and Behavior
Department of Psychology, Bowling Green State University, Bowling Green, Ohio

INTRODUCTION

There has been more research on the neurobiological nature of fear than any other emotional system of the brain. However, long before this cornucopia of findings, highly effective treatments for anxiety disorders became available because of the serendipidous discovery of the efficacy of benzodiazepines (BZs) in the early 1960s. Few major advances in anxiety therapeutics have emerged directly from modern neuroscience research, but there is vast promise in the study of neuropeptide systems (see Chapter 21).

The present chapter is an elaboration of themes considered in Panksepp (1998a, 2000), summarizing clinical and preclinical data related to generalized anxiety disorders. My subsidiary goal is to advance the debatable neurophilosophical position that affective

Textbook of Biological Psychiatry, Edited by Jaak Panksepp
ISBN 0-471-43478-7 Copyright © 2004 John Wiley & Sons, Inc.

processes can be studied in animals and that emotional feelings (albeit not related cognitions) arise largely from subcortical neural processes. Hence this chapter has been placed in this Future Prospects section. A sea change is occurring in the study of fear and anxiety, but there is presently little agreement as to the utility of affective concepts in understanding the mammalian brain.

Early in the past century it was common for theorists to assert that fear simply reflected the evaluative belief that certain aspects of the world are dangerous. Accordingly, many assumed we would clarify fear by asking people what made them scared and anxious. Although such cognitive appraisals are of obvious importance in understanding the external precipitants and temporal and cognitive elaboration of emotions, they are not adequate for a scientific understanding of the affective aspects. Indeed, the contingent, environmentally linked cognitive processes associated with experienced fears are bound to vary greatly among species, depending on the qualities of their cortico-cognitive apparatus. Humans are often scared of dark places, while rats prefer them. Rats fear the smell of cats; humans do not.

A general function of cognitions is to discriminate and parse environmental differences, while fearful feelings are evolutionarily more ancient and hence more similar among species, arising to a substantial degree from genetically homologous emotional circuits (or *affect programs* in psychological terms). This assertion can now be scientifically evaluated by the capacity to translate neurochemical discoveries in animals to the study of subjective responses in humans (Panksepp, 1999a,b, 2000, 2001). In short, the neural substrates of anxieties and fears can finally be analyzed with the tools of modern neuroscience [for a survey of an earlier generation of progress, see Burrows et al. (1990)]. Until we begin to fathom the natural emotional-kinds of the mammalian brain, progress in new drug development in biological psychiatry will continue to be slow.

Epistemological/Ontological Biases

One of the foremost basic-science issues in psychiatry that presently needs illumination is how the brain generates affective experience. Unfortunately, there continues to be a reluctance to explore such topics, partly as a hangover from the "behaviorist era" in animal research. To this day, the prevailing epistemological bias in behavioral neuroscience is to restrict scientific study and discussion to learned behavioral indices of fear and anxiety that can most readily be objectified, while avoiding discussions of potential affective experiences in animals where definitive data, and hence agreement, are more difficult to obtain. Thus, investigators of animal fear conditioning poignantly assert that they know "almost nothing... about anatomical circuits that mediate the experience of fear" (Davis, 1999, p. 472).

In line with the ongoing behavioristic traditions, most investigators who pursue animal brain research typically claim that subjective issues are beyond the grasp of rigorous scientific inquiry. Partly this dismissive position is advanced because an acceptance of animal feelings (even as a working hypothesis) has the potential to intensify socioscientific problems [i.e., troublesome animal rights and welfare issues, see Broom (2001) and Spruijt et al. (2001)], not to mention raising philosophical issues that are hard to resolve empirically (Zachar and Bartlett, 2001).

Many neurobehaviorists are content to neglect this important topic and to assume that the animals they study in the laboratory have no emotional feelings. Some suggest that human affective experiences arise largely from brain areas that are unique to humans—the expansive, higher working memory areas of the dorsolateral frontal cortex (e.g., LeDoux, 1996) or the symbolic re-representation functions, the linguistic capacities, of the human brain (Rolls, 1999). Yet others believe that the projections from "amygdaloid nuclei to the hippocampus and cortex are involved in the experience of fear" (Davis, 1999, p. 472). These perspectives remain without much empirical support.

My goal here is not to diminish the important work of those who choose to view their animals as unfeeling creatures, but to open intellectual space for the alternative view—that primitive forms of affective consciousness, including negative feelings of fearfulness, can be studied in animals, especially through various conditioned place avoidance (CPA) and emotional vocalization measures (Knutson et al., 2002; Panksepp et al., 2002). A credible working hypothesis is that such central emotional states are elaborated by ancient limbic mechanisms that have encoded "evolutionary learning" into genetically specialized neural systems that interact massively with higher cognitive structures (see Chapter 2). According to this view, learning does not create affect; evolution did. Fear learning allows animals to become anxiously aroused in anticipation of world events that have proved to be dangerous during the life span of individual organisms and thereby to use cognitive skills to navigate the vicissitudes of the world more effectively. Thus, explicit fear learning blends the conditioning of ancient *instinctual fear behaviors* such as freezing and flight, easy to study in animals, with various *cognitive* capacities that are difficult to resolve empirically in animals. The guiding thesis here is that the intrinsic nature of affect is more integrally linked to the former than the latter. If correct, it would seem that focusing on neural processes that are most likely to mediate affect (e.g., instinctual fear responses) deserve the most attention in biological psychiatry. The nature of related learning mechanisms is of secondary, albeit substantial, importance.

In conjunction with popular learning theory views, the emotional instincts have traditionally been envisioned as unconscious motor outputs of the nervous system. This is probably a flawed assumption. The core of affect generation is probably constituted from intrinsic aspects of the instinctual, subcortical, emotional operating systems of the brain in action. This perspective easily avoids the "re-representation dilemma" entailed in views that envision affect to require some type of re-coding of primitive instinctual "information" in higher cognitive regions, especially those unique to humans. This naturalistic viewpoint also provides a straightforward strategy for seeking new information about neurochemical systems for affective processes that can be culled from animal research. Neuroscientists can easily investigate the brain circuits that control instinctual actions such as separation distress cries, fighting, and fleeing, just to name a few; and they can use the emerging neurochemical knowledge to evaluate affective predictions in humans (Panksepp, 1998a). This strategy can be empirically evaluated and refined by standard experimental approaches, while the cortical re-representation views advanced by some are harder to disconfirm.

The rest of this chapter will summarize (i) an overall conceptualization of the experience of anxiety and the general nature of the FEAR system, followed by (ii) a brief summary of the accepted pharmacological treatment of anxiety disorders and new neuropetidergic possibilities, and closing with (iii) a synopsis of modern fear research as pursued in the context of behavioral learning theories. The aim is to share these themes in ways that may have practical clinical utility, although there is insufficient space to detail all the relevant data (e.g., see Charney et al., 1999; Charney and Bremner, 1999).

SUBCORTICAL FEAR SYSTEM OF THE MAMMALIAN BRAIN: THE "ROYAL ROAD" TO UNDERSTANDING THE NATURE OF ANGST

The central state of fear consists of an aversive state of mind—a pervasive nervousness and tension—accompanied by sustained, negatively valenced, apprehensive, worrying thoughts (often delusional), which inform organisms how their safety might have been threatened. Although accompanied by patterns of autonomic and behavioral arousal that surely contribute to the feeling state in a multitude of feedback and feedforward ways, the major driving force for the experiential tension appears to be a distinct, albeit widely ramifying, subcortical circuitry that induces animals to hide (freeze) in response to seemingly distant dangers and to escape (flee) when danger is more imminent. When such *states of being* become conditioned, by a diversity of aversive stimuli (e.g., foot shock) being temporally linked with affectively neutral environmental events, organisms begin to anticipate dangers and to protect themselves by generating adaptive emotional and cognitive responses in advance of the impending threats. However, there are many dangers in the world, and there may also be multiple, partially overlapping, systems that generate trepidation and distinct forms of negative affect as well. For instance, the system that generates social separation anxiety is substantially different than the FEAR system that will be the focus of discussion here. The convention of capitalizing FEAR and the names of other basic emotional systems of the mammalian brain is used to highlight the fact that the referents are specific neural systems (Panksepp, 1998a).

Review of the Brain Substrates of FEAR and Anxiety

The experiences of fear and anxiety reflect the actions of complex, poorly understood emotional systems of the brain, for which no common neural denominator—no generally accepted mechanistic explanation—yet exists. In order to make sense of how these substrates are functionally organized, we must currently simplify to a substantial extent. In any event, the capacity of organisms to respond effectively to threats to survival was such an important evolutionary issue that it was not simply left to individual learning. As already noted, the study of the evolved neurochemistries of these mechanisms provides an optimal strategy for yielding new, clinically useful information.

The trajectory of one major fear system (e.g., Fig. 16.1) courses between basolateral and central regions of the amygdala [and other higher brain zones such as the bed nucleus of the stria terminalis (BNST) and perhaps lateral septal area] and projects

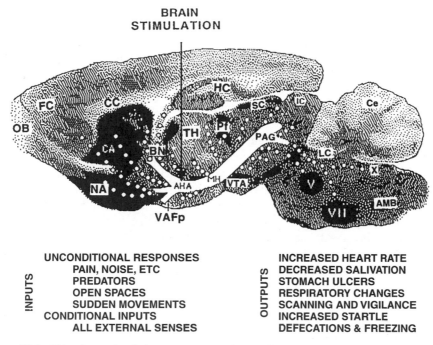

BRAIN STIMULATION

INPUTS	OUTPUTS
UNCONDITIONAL RESPONSES	INCREASED HEART RATE
PAIN, NOISE, ETC	DECREASED SALIVATION
PREDATORS	STOMACH ULCERS
OPEN SPACES	RESPIRATORY CHANGES
SUDDEN MOVEMENTS	SCANNING AND VIGILANCE
CONDITIONAL INPUTS	INCREASED STARTLE
ALL EXTERNAL SENSES	DEFECATIONS & FREEZING

Figure 16.1. This schematic of the FEAR system depicted on a sagittal section of the rat brain (the background of which highlights high-density acetylcholine esterase staining in black). This transhypothalamic executive system for FEAR orchestrates many cognitive, affective, behavioral, hormonal, and physiological changes that characterize various fearful states. The executive circuit is a two-way avenue of communication between the BNST and the central regions of the amygdala, which transmits information caudally primarily by the ventral amygdalofugal pathway and the mesencephalic periaqueductal or central gray (CG). This circuit courses through the anterior and medial hypothalamic areas of the diencephalon, where it is especially easy to elicit fearful behaviors (both freezing and flight) using ESB. There are multiple entry and exit points in this circuit (as depicted by the branching bubbles) that synchronize the many brain and bodily processes that must be concurrently influenced when an animal is threatened. Anatomical designations are as follows: AHA, anterior hypothalamic area; CA, caudate nucleus; Ce, cerebellum; CG, central gray; BN, bed nucleus of the stria terminalis; FC, frontal cortex, Hc, hippocampus; LC, locus coeruleus; MH, medial hypothalamus; NA, nucleus accumbens; Th, thalamus; V, motor nucleus of the trigeminal nerve; and VII, nucleus of the facial nerve. [This figure is reprinted from Panksepp (1998a), *Affective Neuroscience*, with the kind permission of Oxford University Press.]

downward through the anterior and medial hypothalamus to the periaqueductal gray (PAG) of the midbrain and adjacent tegmental fields. Henceforth, this neural trajectory will be called the FEAR system, to distinguish it from other, less well-understood, negative affective systems, including those that precipitate panic attacks, social disgust, and separation distress, to name a few. Electrical and chemical stimulation along the circuits generates fearful states along with many fear-related behaviors and auto-nomic changes in both experimental animals and humans (Depaulis and Bandler, 1991; Panksepp, 1985, 1998a, 2000).

It has long been known that one can arouse coherent freezing, flight, and other *defensive* responses, as well as associated autonomic changes, with electrical and chemical stimulation along this extended circuit. Animals readily learn to turn off this type of brain stimulation, even though under some testing conditions they do not exhibit efficient learned avoidance of such apparently aversive central states. This problem—the failure to obtain certain types of avoidance behavior—permitted inves-tigators to devalue affective issues, claiming that the striking emotional behaviors were sham emotions with no experiential contents. However, the failure of avoidance behavior to become manifest appears to have arisen from straightforward method-ological problems such as the failure to use sensitive measures (e.g., place avoidance paradigms), and perhaps from neural circuit "quirks" such as how exteroceptively driven learning processes interface with primitive emotional systems (Panksepp et al., 1991).

It is now clear that an enormous amount of learning can influence the FEAR sys-tem through higher limbic areas (most prominently various amygdaloid-hippocampal-temporal and frontal cortical regions). This conditioning can emerge, as described by LeDoux (1996, 2000), through short-loop sensory inputs such as those arising from tha-lamus (the so-called low road to fear conditioning) as well as higher sensory-perceptual processing (the so-called high road to fear). In addition there is an evolutionarily cre-ated royal road to understanding fear—a FEAR circuit that descends from amygdala, BNST and other telencephalic areas that converges on the PAG (Fig. 16.1 and 16.2) and coordinates the many evolved behavioral, physiological, and primitive affective aspects of fear (Panksepp, 1982, 1990). The importance of such primitive FEAR cir-cuitry in conceptualizing the nature of human anxiety has been affirmed by recent brain imaging studies (Chapter 2 and Damasio et al., 2000) and is gradually gaining acceptance in behavioral neuroscience (Rosen and Schulkin, 1998). Only the higher amygdalar reaches are currently well recognized in psychiatry (Charney et al., 1999; Johnson and Lydiard, 1995) and human experimental psychology (Öhman and Mineka, 2001). The full extent of the circuitry provides the optimal approach for detailing the underlying causes of anxiety and is a clarion call for psychiatry and other mind sciences to reinvest in animal brain research.

This parsimonious view—that affect is largely a subcortical brain function shared homologously with other mammals—which entails no need for cortical re-representation or readout of affect, may require a neural conceptualization of a primordial "core self" (Damasio, 1999; Panksepp, 1998 a,b). Many higher cortical regions of the brain are essential for regulating (e.g., sustaining, dampening, as well as restructuring) emotions, but, to the best of our knowledge, those higher brain regions do not have the intrinsic capacity to create the primal valenced quality of affective experience. Indeed, many of the higher regions, in their important regulatory roles, may actually dampen the affective features (e.g., consider that young children with immature cortical controls generally feel affect more intensely than adults, even though they do not yet have the

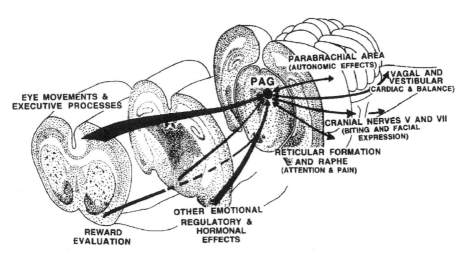

Figure 16.2. General overview of the anterograde and retrograde connectivities of the mesencephalic defense systems (FEAR and RAGE) as they converge on the periaqueductal gray (PAG) of the mesencephalon. The two emotions are so closely integrated that current anatomical techniques cannot easily discriminate between the two. Putative functional integrations are indicated. [This figure is reprinted from Panksepp (1998a), *Affective Neuroscience*, with the kind permission of Oxford University Press.]

cognitive capacities to sustain affective states through ruminations). In this context, it is noteworthy that there are rich anatomical connections from frontal cortical areas to the PAG (Holstege et al., 1996), and higher cognitive processes can regulate the arousal of these lower brain regions (Tracey et al., 2002). Such "mental" dampening and restructuring of emotional arousal is surely more refined in humans than any other species.

It may well be that most anxiety disorders arise from constitutional shifts in the sensitivity of these core systems as opposed to merely the sustained incoming impact from learned stimuli. In other words the FEAR system, like all emotional systems, may *sensitize* in response to chronic overarousal (Adamec and Young, 2000; Maren, 1999).

When the arousal of such systems becomes free floating, disconnected from external perceptions, various pathological states emerge, ranging from generalized anxiety to posttraumatic stress disorders (PTSD). During maturation, the genetically provided and learned aspects of fear become inextricably blended. The most useful new information for biological therapeutics will probably be derived from a better understanding of the unconditional neurochemical substrates of fear and a study of how such systems become sensitized, and overresponsive, rather than through a study of how unconscious fear reflexes are linked to neutral stimuli through classical conditioning. Such conditioning studies may be more germane to understanding the emergence of specific phobias, providing ideas on how therapists may be better able to de-condition acquired fears (Öhman and Mineka, 2001).

The FEAR system, as all other major emotional systems of the brain, is hierarchically arranged. Higher brain regions harvest perceptual/cognitive information (the periamygdaloid cortex of the temporal lobe); the middle hypothalamic zones control autonomic/hormonal responses that bias fear in reference to activities of homeostatic detectors that monitor bodily needs (e.g., animals will be less afraid of approaching resources in potentially dangerous situations if they are hungry); the critical lower zones in the PAG and surrounding midbrain orchestrate the integrated behavioral/bodily responses, with most of the individual response elements being situated in yet lower regions of the brainstem (Fig. 16.1). The more caudally such electrical stimulation of the brain (ESB) is imposed, the more rapid and intense is the evoked fear response and to all appearances (including human subjective reports) the resulting affective experiences. Responses evoked from higher brain areas (e.g., amygdala) are critically dependent on the integrity of the lower brain regions (e.g., PAG) but not vice versa (Panksepp, 1998a).

Of course, the arousal of this system has widespread consequences on the brain, partly through direct interactions with higher brain areas such as the frontal and temporal cortices. There are also indirect consequences through interactions with various general-purpose cholinergic and biogenic-amine (e.g., norepinephrine and serotonin) arousal/attention systems arising from the brain stem. These effects surely modulate the quality of the resulting subjective experiences. Anxious ruminations require those higher brain areas, but it is important to reemphasize that there is no evidence that neocortical tissue has the intrinsic capacity to generate affective states. The cortico-cognitive realms parse and re-represent primal feelings through their capacity to make finer and finer discriminations and distinctions. Thus, the position that affect is largely generated subcortically does not deny that primitive emotional dynamics can be used as tokens of information in the deliberative systems of the neocortex that regulate and fine-tune emotional arousal.

There will be many ways to regulate fears, but a reasonable working hypothesis is that the most powerful and clinically useful effects will be those that act directly on the specific neurochemistries of the FEAR system. Pharmacological dampening of this system facilitates calmness. So far this has been achieved with rather general modulators of brain gamma-aminobutyric acid (GABA), norepinephrine, and serotonin activities. It will soon be achieved through our increasing knowledge of more specific chemistries such as the neuropeptides (Chapter 21), as well as neurosteroids that can modulate GABA receptors (Heilig, 1995; Paul and Purdy, 1992) and new biogenic amine GABA facilitators (Skolnick et al., 2001).

Before proceeding to therapeutic issues, let us briefly consider the abundance of existing animal models for studying various types of anxiety. Parenthetically, the large variety of preclinical measures of anxiety may reflect the diversity of psychobiological states of trepidation that may exist within the brain. We might recall that the complex hierarchy of anxiety Freud advocated consisted of (i) fear of loss of object, (ii) fear of loss of love of the object, (iii) castration anxiety, and (iv) superego anxiety [as detailed in *Inhibitions, Symptoms and Anxiety* (volume 20) of the Standard Edition as well as in the *New Introductory Lectures* (volume 22)]. Such issues cannot be studied in animal research, and future taxonomies of anxiety should be based as much on neurobiological data as on more theoretical psychological perspectives.

Preclinical (Animal) Models for the Study of Fear

Many animal models of anxiety have been developed since the beginning of the biological psychiatry era. Indeed, most of the preclinical search for new antianxiety agents has been based on the systematic deployment of animal models. Regrettably, it is not clear how these models relate to the amygdala-hypothalamic-PAG FEAR system. Only a few investigators have been willing to invest in that brain-based model, while most continue to use behavior-only drug-challenge models, in the hope that it will be possible to relate psychiatric diagnostic categories of anxiety to animal models simply at the behavioral level. An alternative is to build a new conceptual foundation for psychiatry based on the nature of the critical underlying neural systems (Chapter 1). Thus, a great deal of basic neuroscience work on the reactivity of the FEAR and related negative affect systems remains to be done [but the abundant ongoing work in several Brazilian laboratories is especially noteworthy, e.g., Brandao et al. (1999) and Carobrez et al. (2001)]. Probably the best ways to monitor negative affective changes are via the study of instinctual escape and conditioned place avoidance responses and vocal indicators of negative affect such as 22-kHz ultrasonic calls in rodents (Knutson et al., 2002).

In general, the efficacies of potential new anxiolytic drugs identified in animal trials have not been impressive when taken to human trials (Cheetham and Heal, 2000). Either this means that there is a great deal of evolutionary divergence in the neurobiological substrates of anxiety in animals and humans or that optimal animal models have typically not been utilized. The sparse use of direct activation of the trajectory of the FEAR system with electrical and chemical stimulation suggests that the latter may be the case. At the same time, we must recognize that there are an enormous number of aversive states to be avoided by animals (ranging from pain to various types of hungers, thirsts, and other bodily needs), and only some are related to anxiety. It is likely that all of these affects have distinct neurobiological underpinnings.

Thus, better taxonomies of fearful states need to be developed. Fear can be evoked by (i) painful stimuli, (ii) by cues previously associated with aversive stimuli, (iii) by various nonpainful but potentially dangerous stimuli that have reflected the high probability of threat in the evolutionary history of a species (e.g., smell of cats for rats), and perhaps (iv) even certain frustrating events, such as the delay of expected rewards. These types of animal models, each of which may have distinct cognitive and motivational modulatory controls, are differentially sensitive to antianxiety drug manipulations. Because of the number of existing models, which parse the emotional dimension of fearfulness in different ways, the existing anxiety models in the behavioral literature often give the impression of being unintegrated, indeed, chaotic.

The available models can be systematically divided into those that use obviously painful/aversive procedures to evoke symptoms of anxiety (i.e., punishment procedures) and those that use no obvious punishments. These two approaches can be used in two distinct ways: those that measure the instinctual responses of animals, and those that primarily monitor changes in learned behaviors. This yields a 2 × 2 table of four general types of models as described elsewhere (Panksepp, 1998a, Table 11.1). Again, the approach that has probably received the least attention, at least on the Anglo-American research scene, is the one that uses direct stimulation of the FEAR system, especially at very low current levels that induce freezing behavior (Panksepp et al., 1991). Future research should also focus more on ecologically valid behavioral models of fear, such as various naturalistic ones where the defensive behaviors of animals can be systematically monitored (Blanchard et al., 2001). Such approaches are most likely to provide sufficiently rich patterns of behavioral change where subcomponents of instinctual defensive responses and associated cognitive strategies can be dissected (e.g., Blanchard et al., 1993; Sgoifo et al., 2001).

Most models are reasonably sensitive to modulation by minor tranquilizers, suggesting they do share common motivational features. However, a conceptual conundrum runs through the literature: Antianxiety effects are routinely *assumed* when drugs release punishment-inhibited behaviors. Thus, animals given shocks when they press levers for food (or are confronted by stimuli that predict shocks during such appetitive baseline behaviors), generally inhibit lever pressing, and it is typically assumed that drugs are exerting antianxiety effects when animals sustain higher lever-pressing rates under drug rather than placebo conditions. Alternative explanations are too rarely considered—for example, that such drugs simply made animals more disinhibited and hence impulsive (Soubrie, 1986). Also, at present there are no accepted guidelines to decide which fear-related behaviors, from the many available approaches, are optimal predictors for the various anxiety disorders and why, although some are trying to think through the issues (e.g., Sgoifo et al., 2001).

Most investigators would probably agree that the available models may be describing many distinct fears and/or different ways in which animals cognitively or behaviorally cope with a single type of fear. The most urgent task is to develop methodologies that are able to evaluate the affective properties of drugs as directly as possible. Some have advocated a direct study of instinctual emotional behaviors (Panksepp, 1998a), especially emotional vocalizations and conditional consequences, as one of the best strategies (Knutson et al., 2002; Panksepp et al., 2002). The utilization of social-isolation-induced distress vocalizations in animals, which was advocated as a measure of separation anxiety many years ago (Panksepp et al., 1980, 1985, 1988), is finally becoming an increasingly popular model for the evaluation of potential anxiolytic drugs (e.g., Kehne et al., 2000).

In closing this brief discussion of models, let us consider the relations between pain and fear. It is germane to consider how pain can be a source process in the genesis of anxiety, since painful stimuli such as foot shock have been traditionally used to produce fear conditioning in animals. Animals readily escape from and avoid places where they have been hurt. Pain and fear systems can be dissociated in the brain, even though they do strongly interact. For instance, fear states cannot be readily evoked with ESB of classical spino-thalamic pain systems. Only at midbrain levels, where classic pain systems project into PAG reticular fields (Fig. 16.1), will localized brain stimulation yield fear reactions such as freezing and flight. Conversely, although pain systems send inputs into FEAR circuits (especially at sites such as the PAG), ESB applied to the FEAR system does not routinely evoke sensations of pain, at least as indexed by pain-type vocalizations. Likewise, damage to brain areas that contain FEAR circuitry do not typically reduce pain thresholds in animals [for a summary, see Panksepp et al. (1991)].

However, arousal of FEAR systems does modify pain sensitivity. Whether these effects represent attentional shifts or true analgesic effects remains uncertain. Both animals and humans fail to attend to their bodily injuries when frightened, and fear-induced analgesia is partly due to arousal of pain inhibition circuits of the PAG, including serotonin and endogenous opioid components (Fanselow, 1991; Miczek et al., 1994). The interactions of FEAR with other emotional systems remain to be characterized.

TREATMENT OF ANXIETY IN CLINICAL PRACTICE

Symptoms of Anxiety

The *Diagnostic and Statistical Manual of Mental Disorders* (DSM-IV) of the American Psychiatric Association (1994) includes eight major types of anxiety disorders, most of which have been summarized in previous chapters, including PTSD (Chapter 11), panic attacks (Chapter 12), obsessive-compulsive disorders (Chapter 13), and various acute stress reactions (Chapter 4). Here we will be primarily concerned with generalized anxiety disorders, but the coverage is also relevant for specific phobias, including social phobias and agoraphobia. The most common clinical symptom of all these disorders is excessive worry and sustained feelings of mental anguish. Among the common symptoms of *generalized anxiety* there are a variety of psychological disturbances, such as uncontrollable apprehensive expectations, jumpiness, and a tendency for excessive vigilance and fidgeting. The accompanying autonomic symptoms commonly include gastrointestinal irritability, diarrhea, and frequent urination, as well as other visceral symptoms such as tachycardia, chronic dryness of the mouth, and increased but shallow respiration. Some are bothered more by the physical symptoms, while in others psychological distress is the prevailing concern. Practically all of these autonomic and psychological changes can be promoted by artificial activation of the FEAR system.

The specific phobias may reflect classical conditioning of specific fear responses. The social phobias may be based more on overactivity of yet other aversive brain systems such as the PANIC system, which mediates separation distress (Panksepp et al., 1988). Chronic, low-level arousal of separation feelings may tend to generate shyness and resulting attempts to sustain socioaffective homeostasis by restricting social activities to those with whom one is closely bonded (Schmidt and Schulkin, 1999). To some extent, distinct neurochemistries (e.g., neuropeptides) regulate these distinct types of anxiety (Chapter 21).

Historical Perspectives

Prior to the advent of modern biological psychiatry, there were no agents that selectively diminished feelings of anxiety. Until the development of the benzodiazepine (BZ) class of minor tranquilizers, the main drugs that could successfully control human anxiety were opioids, alcohol, barbiturates, and meprobamate (Gray, 1987). All of these had serious problems that precluded continuous long-term use, including most prominently pharmacological tolerance, poor safety margins, addictions, and the potential to be used for suicide. However, during the past few decades our neurobiological appreciation of the sources of anxiety (Goddard et al., 1999), from generalized anxiety disorders (Conner and Davidson, 1998) to social phobias (Stein, 1998), has been impressive. Although vigorous new drug development has proceeded in the area, major new payoffs have been modest, except for the emerging use of antidepressants to treat anxiety (Cheetham and Heal, 2000).

Benzodiazepines

The pharmacological treatment of anxiety was revolutionized when investigators at Hoffman-LaRoche discovered that chlordiazepoxide (CDP) could sedate laboratory rats and, subsequently, that it could calm wild zoo animals. The entry of that initial agent (trade name Librium) into routine clinical practice was rapid. CDP exhibited remarkable specificity; the safety margin was vastly superior to anything used before. CDP reduced anxiety dramatically at a miniscule fraction of the lethal dose. That was a spectacular improvement over all other agents that had ever been used, and the BZs rapidly supplanted other antianxiety drugs on the market. Soon, even more potent versions, from diazepam (Valium) to clonazepam (Klonopin), became available. These agents varied only in terms of onset of anxiolytic effect, the duration of action, and potency. These properties were used to parley other BZs toward alternative indications—for sleeping aids with rapid onset BZs (see Table 4.1) and the treatment of alcoholism with the longer-acting agents (Roy-Byrne and Cowley, 1991). Along the way, several additional medical uses were identified, including alleviation of muscular spasms and antiepileptic effects, especially for seizures emanating from the limbic system.

The mild nonspecific sedation commonly observed early in drug therapy exhibited rapid tolerance, while anxiolytic effects remained sustained, with comparatively little tolerance during long-term, intermittent use of low doses. The efficacies of BZs in dissolving anticipatory fearfulness, reducing anxiety neuroses, and, with some extremely potent agents, even panic attacks (e.g., clonazepam and alprazolam), have repeatedly been affirmed in many well-controlled clinical trials (Goddard et al., 1999; Nutt, 1990). There was comparatively little physical dependence during modest intermittent use; however, as long-term sustained use of high doses became common practice, dependence and a high-anxiety withdrawal syndrome resembling delirium tremens of alcohol detoxification became a major problem (Petursson, 1994). The substantial benefits of BZs in ameliorating alcohol withdrawal affirmed that alcohol and BZs act upon common brain substrates, which turned out to be the BZ-GABA receptor complex (Tallman and Gallagher, 1985).

Although a variety of BZs rapidly came to market, it was not until 1979 that BZ receptors were finally identified in the brain (Young and Kuhar, 1980). A different variant of the receptor was identified in the periphery that mediated antispasmodic effects of BZs. A variety of other BZs were eventually developed, and they found market niches as sleeping aids (Table 4.1) and alcohol-craving reducers. However, their basic modes of neuronal action all remained the same. The practice of using different agents for different disorders is not based on any fundamental difference in their mode of action, but rather on differences in potency and speed of entry into and exit from the brain. The search for less addictive BZs through the development of partial agonists for the BZ receptor have not been especially successful, despite promising results in preclinical trials (Cheetham and Heal, 2000).

Although BZs proved to be remarkably safe medicinals, the shortcomings revealed during ensuing years led to a reinvigorated search for alternative agents. Beside the aforementioned dependence syndrome during long-term use, the adverse side effects included disorientation and memory loss (especially in the elderly) and at times increases in appetite and the occasional release of aggressive tendencies, especially in passive-aggressive individuals. In routine clinical practice, the sedation resulting from BZs is typically of short duration, although it often persists among the elderly.

With careful use, the drawbacks of BZs are modest compared to many other psychopharmaceuticals, but care in monitoring side effects is advisable. Accidents that happen when clients are taking such agents may lead to troublesome legal claims in litigious societies. In this vein, Hoffman-LaRoche aborted the development of BZ receptor antagonists for the alleviation of the symptoms of drunkenness, only partly because of the potential liability if individuals taking such agents were to have accidents. In general, these antagonists do not increase anxiety symptoms unless individuals are already anxious. In sum, although BZs are remarkably effective antianxiety drugs, a concerted effort continues to identify additional and even more specific agents that have fewer shortcomings (Kunovac and Stahl, 1995).

Buspirone to Paxil

Even though there are many candidates in the wings to succeed BZs, the only major items that have reached the market are buspirone (Buspar) and selective serotonin reuptake inhibitors (SSRIs) such as paroxetine (Paxil), which have distinct profiles of action (Eison and Temple, 1986; Goddard et al., 1999). The therapeutic effect of these agents appears to be based on the ability of the serotonin [5-hydroxytryptamine (5-HT)] systems to modulate anxiety (Handley, 1995). Buspirone has the relatively selective effect of stimulating 5-HT_{1A} receptors, which are concentrated on serotonin cell bodies. At this site, buspirone reduces serotonin neuronal activity, and hence it acutely diminishes serotonin release in higher brain areas, which can lead to long-term up-regulation of postsynaptic serotonin receptors.

Although some investigators believe that buspirone alleviates anxiety by reducing 5-HT activity, the benefits may also be due to a compensatory functional elevation of brain serotonin activity. There are abundant postsynaptic 5-HT_{1A} receptors in the brain, and it presently remains possible that the postsynaptic effects of buspirone contribute as much to the antianxiety effects of this drug as binding to presynaptic sites. Thus, even though certain types of serotonin activity are anxiogenic [e.g., at the 5-HT_2 site (Charney et al., 1987)], the antianxiety effects of buspirone may largely be due to a long-term postsynaptic facilitation of serotonin sensitivity in the brain (Stahl et al., 1992). Indeed, SSRIs such as venlafaxine (Effexor) may facilitate buspirone effects (Davidson et al., 1999; Sramek et al., 2002).

In any event, the therapeutic benefits of buspirone tend to be milder than those obtained with BZs, but fewer side effects are encountered. Buspirone produces no sedation, nor does it have any problematic short-term psychological effects that might promote abuse. It produces no dependence or withdrawal upon discontinuation. It also has no abuse potential. Unfortunately, buspirone appears to exhibit comparatively little benefit in those individuals who have previously benefited from BZs (Schweizer et al., 1986), perhaps because patients have become dependent on the strong, rapid, and easily perceived psychological changes produced by BZs. Accordingly, current practice is that buspirone should be the initial treatment of choice at the onset of long-term pharmacotherapy, while BZs are used more in short-term situations because of the possibility of dependence. Unlike some of the newer BZs such as alprazolam, buspirone has no efficacy as an antipanic agent.

It has long been recognized by clinicians that many antidepressants, especially the SSRIs, often rapidly ameliorate anxiety symptoms. After all, telencephalic serotonin systems inhibit practically all emotional and motivational processes within the brain. One SSRI, namely paroxetine (Paxil), is currently approved for the treatment of generalized anxiety disorders (Rocca et al., 1997) and others, especially extended-release venlaflaxine, are bound to follow (Davidson, 2001; Gorman, 2002). This does not mean that many of the other SSRIs would not be equally useful. They simply have not undergone the necessary clinical evaluations to receive approval. Most of the older tricyclic antidepressants had some anxiolytic effects (Rickels et al., 1993). There is not sufficient comparative clinical research to specify the differences in the profile of SSRI and tricyclic actions on anxiety as compared to the BZs. One straightforward possibility is that SSRIs are more effective for anxiety feelings commonly associated with depression. It has long been known that anxiety symptoms are often present in depression (Bakish, 1999). Of course, unlike the BZs and buspirone, the SSRI antianxiety agents have the added benefit of often counteracting depressive symptoms (Ninan, 1999).

Drugs are also available for managing the undesired peripheral physiological symptoms of anxiety. Palpitations and sweating can be reduced with ß-noradrenergic blockers (e.g., propranolol). Such "beta-blockers" effectively control the outward symptoms of anxiety such as those that commonly accompany public speaking and musical performances. Within the brain, it is also clear that ß-noradrenergic synapses promote the consolidation of fear memories (Cahill and McGaugh, 1998).

Social Phobias

Practically all of the drugs discussed already have a potential role in the treatment of social phobias, the avoidance of social interactions that probably arises from emotional feelings of insecurity (Pots et al., 1996). Among the first to have demonstrated efficacy were monoamine oxidase (MAO) inhibitors such as phenelzine (Liebowitz, 1988). SSRIs (Mancini and Ameringen, 1996; Stein et al., 1998) and BZs (Davidson et al., 1994) are also quite effective. Likewise, tricyclic drugs such as imipramine, which was initially found to be an effective antipanic agent, is also remarkably useful for ameliorating the common childhood anxiety response leading to school phobias and enuresis (Gittelman and Klein, 1985). Such symptoms may arise substantially from overactive separation-anxiety systems of the brain.

Neurochemistry of Fear

Future anxiolytic drug development is dependent on further clarification of the neurochemical systems that control fearfulness in the brain (Davis, 1999; LeDoux, 2000; Panksepp, 1998a, 2000). The abundant BZ receptors that exist along the main "artery" of the FEAR circuit that courses between the amygdala and PAG (Fig. 16.1) provide a substrate whereby traditional minor tranquilizers (as well as alcohol and barbiturates) may inhibit anxiety (Haefely, 1990). The distinct GABA and BZ binding sites on this complex (as well as those that bind alcohol and barbiturates) synergistically facilitate neuronal inhibition (by promoting chloride flow into the cell). Thus, BZs quell anxiety by hyperpolarizing neurons that distribute fearful messages within the brain. Stimulants for BZ receptors not only directly reduce activity in the FEAR circuit, they may also directly suppress higher processing of related thoughts and appraisals through effects on abundant BZ receptors in the neocortex. BZ receptor antagonists (e.g., flumazenil) given alone are typically behaviorally inactive in nonanxious organisms, which suggests that endogenous anxiety molecules are generally absent at BZ receptor sites. However, these antagonists do block the effects of administered BZs as well as anxiety provoked by "inverse agonists" such as ß-carbolines (see below). Also, they increase the number of attacks in panic-prone individuals (Nutt et al., 1990).

A key question for understanding this system is: What endogenous molecules normally act on BZ receptors? A definitive answer remains elusive, but a perennial candidate has been the diazepam-binding inhibitor (DBI), an endogenous peptide that may promote anxiety when released onto BZ receptors (Ferrarese et al., 1993). DBI appears to be an "inverse agonist" at BZ receptors, actively increasing the arousability of the brain substrates for fearfulness by decreasing inhibition in the system. However, elevated DBI has not been evident in panic disorders (Payeur et al., 1992). In any event, inverse agonists such as various ß-carboline drugs exert neurophysiological effects opposite to those of BZs (i.e., actively inhibiting inflow of chloride into neurons) after interacting with the BZ-GABA complex, and the overall emotional effect is to promote anxiety. Thus, it seems reasonable that endogenous anxiogenic substances may facilitate fearful affect by blocking the activation of the BZ-GABA receptor complex.

Many other neurotransmitters are capable of promoting anxiety signals through the brain. For instance, norepinephrine (NE) and serotonin have long been touted as potential anxiogenic systems. Certain drugs that facilitate NE and serotonin activity [e.g., after the $alpha_2$-NE receptor antagonist, yohimbine, and the $5-HT_{2C}$ receptor agonist m-chlorophenylpiperazine (MCPP), respectively] do promote anxiety in humans (Charney et al., 1987). Some of these effects probably reflect modulation of general arousal rather than evocation of specific emotional responses. It is unlikely that biogenic amine systems contribute *specifically* to the experiences of anxiety. Rather, they do so by regulating ongoing brain activities (e.g., memory) that can prolong or shorten anxious rumination.

One fear transmitter is the simple excitatory amino acid glutamate. Intense fear responses are evoked by microinfusions of various glutamate agonists, such as kainic acid and N-methyl-D-aspartate (NMDA), into the lower ventricular system as well as various sites within the FEAR system (Carobrez et al., 2001). Such fearful episodes are counteracted by various glutamate receptor antagonists. Although one might assume that new antianxiety drugs could be created from these agents, such a strategy seems outwardly impractical because of the broad spectrum of brain functions, from sensory processes to memory, that are controlled by glutamatergic synapses. Undesirable side effects of the strong glutamate receptor antagonists are numerous, but mild glutamate antagonists have recently yielded some promising results in the treatment of depression (Skolnick et al., 2001). There is also some data that down-regulation of glutamatergic transmission with selective metabotropic glutamate agonists may provide therapeutically useful anxiolysis (Helton et al., 1998).

The number of drug targets among the neuropeptides is rapidly growing. In addition to DBI, the clarification of a large number of neuropeptides that modulate anxiety-like behaviors in animals has provided a cornucopia of promising candidates for further drug discovery. Most of these neuromodulators are enriched along the trajectory of the FEAR system, As detailed in Chapter 21, among the next generation of antianxiety drugs, we will certainly find corticotrophin-releasing hormone (CRH) receptor antagonists, since CRH is a major neuropeptide vector that promotes various, albeit still poorly defined, anxieties (Chalmers et al., 1996; Heilig et al., 1994, and see Chapter 4). Briefly, centrally administered CRH promotes agitated arousal and reduces all positively motivated behaviors from feeding to all sociosexual activities (Dunn and Berridge, 1990). Animals show conditioned freezing in environments where they previously experienced CRH, and CRH antagonists diminish freezing induced by normal stressors (Candor et al., 1992).

One form of anxiety that deserves special attention arises from separation distress systems in action. CRH is highly effective in promoting such instinctual responses (Panksepp and Bekkedal, 1997). The effectiveness of nonpeptide CRH antagonists on more routine animal models of anxiety has been sufficiently impressive (Chapter 4) that several are undergoing clinical evaluation. Separation anxiety should be a prime target of such therapies. Many other neuropeptides reduce separation anxiety behaviors following central administration, including opioids acting on *mu* receptors. Oxytocin and prolactin are very effective when centrally administered (Panksepp, 1991, 1998a).

Based on the fact that the neuropeptide α-melanocyte-stimulating hormone (α-MSH) facilitates camouflage-type color changes in reptiles (a physiological defense response), it should not be surprising that behaviorally clear freezing/hiding responses can be activated by central administration of α-MSH in organisms that no longer show those pigmentary effects (Panksepp and Abbott, 1990). Adrenocorticotrophic hormone (ACTH), derived from the same pro-opiomelanocortin (POMC) gene as α-MSH, evokes the same effects in birds, and high doses of the molecule into the PAG evoke vigorous flight in rats.

Anxiogenic peptides have also been found in the cholecystokinin (CCK) family, perhaps the most abundant peptide in the brain. Intravenous administration of certain

CCK fragments in humans can promote panic attacks and a variety of fearlike symptoms in animals (Harro et al., 1993). Unfortunately, preliminary human clinical trials with CCK antagonists have failed to demonstrate efficacy in the treatment of panic or general anxiety disorders, a characteristic that may be explained by their poor pharmacokinetic characteristics (Pande et al., 1999) or perhaps their mixed affective effects in different neural circuits (You et al., 1998).

The affective changes evoked by most such molecules remain to be monitored using appropriate behavioral paradigms (e.g., place avoidance and conditioned freezing paradigms), but if they prove effective in such tests, it would be predicted that antagonists for such neuropeptides may ameliorate fearful inhibitions in humans. Of course, in pursuing such interpretations, we might recall that a large number of negative affects can be elaborated in the mammalian brain. Hence, many psychological subtleties will have to be considered that require careful behavioral ethological studies in animals and psychoethological ones in humans (Panksepp, 1999a,b).

As elaborated in Chapter 21, some of the forthcoming neuropeptide modulator medicines may *not* have robust therapeutic effects on their own. Instead, they may provide an optimal affective bias for various other environmentally based therapies to work better. Such a concept will need to be studied first in animal models, to see whether certain types of antianxiety conditioning will proceed more effectively in the presence of specific neurochemical background activities that in themselves do not modify the intensity of an animal's response to threats. Although there is little relevant data of this sort, a didactic precedent is identification of experimental agents that promote social activities if they had been experienced in affectively positive environments, while reducing such activities if the drugs had previously been administered in aversive environments (Bekkedal et al., 1999).

A goal for future research is to specify, more precisely, how the emerging antianxiety chemistries mediate subcomponents of the overall affective process subsumed by the concept of anxiety. Do certain neuropeptides elaborate specific fears while others are more global modulators of FEAR and separation distress/PANIC responses (e.g., helping regulate the intensity and duration of emotional episodes, etc.)? Concurrent work with several animal models, hopefully using several species, may help tease apart the distinct functions of the increasing number of known neurochemistries that regulate anxiety within the mammalian brain. Also, considering that the broadcasting of information and affect in the nervous system is widespread [facilitated perhaps via ascending NE, 5-HT, and Acetylcholine (ACh) systems], the way in which learning as well as generalized arousal/attentional systems interact with specific affective processes needs to be further elucidated.

DISPERSION AND FUNCTIONS OF FEAR SYSTEMS IN THE BRAIN: CONTINUING STUDIES OF THE NEUROANATOMY OF FEAR

Modern neuroscience techniques can now estimate the widespread influences of fear within the brain. Immunocytochemical visualization of the genetic transcription and translation of growth-promoting oncogenes, such as *c-fos*, have allowed investigators to monitor the cerebral consequences of many fear-provoking stimuli, including foot shock (Beck and Fibiger, 1995), nonpainful threatening stimuli, such as environments that have been paired with aversive events (Silveira et al., 1993), as well as the effects of direct activation of FEAR circuits following brain stimulation (Silveira et al., 1995). Not only is there abundant arousal of brain areas from the PAG to the amygdala, there is typically massive cortical activation, especially if animals are tested while awake as opposed to anesthetized. Similar patterns of neuronal activation are evident in animals defeated during fighting (Kollack-Walker et al., 1997), during exposure to predators (Dielenberg et al., 2001), and even in animals simply exposed to the fearful 22-kHz distress squeals of conspecifics (Beckett et al., 1997). Such work is revealing neural details, both anatomical and neurochemical, that no human brain imaging yet approximates.

These widespread changes evident in animal brains can be contrasted with the relatively modest brain effects documented in humans in functional magnetic resonance imaging (fMRI) and positron emission tomography (PET). Such studies [for a full review, see Phan et al. (2002) and Zald (2003)], even when conducted on chronically anxious individuals, typically yield highly restricted regional arousals in areas such as the amygdala (Irwin et al., 1996; Rauch et al., 1995). In part, this is explained simply by the fact that the utilization of group statistics often masks the more widespread brain effects seen in individual subjects. The modest effects are also, in part, due to the use of comparatively weak cognitive-type fear stimuli (e.g., angry faces, etc.). Also, certain technologies (e.g., fMRI approaches) may not yet have the resolution to highlight many of the subcortical brain areas that are, in fact, aroused during fear using more sensitive tools (Damasio et al., 2000, and also see Chapter 2).

EXPERIENTIAL-AFFECTIVE ATTRIBUTES OF FEAR AND ANXIETY

Amygdala and Fear

If one is interested in the affective nature of fear and anxiety, one cannot help but have a love-hate affair with the amygdala. This brain area, more than any other, has become synonymous with the neural substrate of fear in both the popular and prevailing scientific imaginations (LeDoux, 1996). While there is abundant evidence that many sensory-perceptual streams (including olfaction, taste, vision, and sound) do converge on the amygdala to mediate an important cognitive link between emotional information and the bodily and affective responses of fear [for comprehensive summary, see Zald (2003)], evidence for an essential role of the amygdala in elaborating the affective valence of anxiety, or any other emotion, remains meager (Damasio, 1999; Adolphs et al., 2003).

We can be certain that the amygdala helps mediate the learned anticipatory processes related to fear (Davis, 1992, 1994, 1999; LeDoux, 2000), as well as many other emotions, including anger, drug craving, sexual behavior, and various motivational expectations related to taste and smell (Zald, 2003). Only learning from somatosensory cues does not require amygdalar participation. The range of cognitive functions that subregions of the amygdala subserve is large, including attentional modulation, conditioning, memory enhancement, and certain symptoms of emotionality, including the regulation of startle, freezing, flight, as well as coordinated hormonal and autonomic bodily changes. However, the activation of the amygdala to fearful and other emotional stimuli tends to be short-lived, habituating rapidly, which suggests that the amygdala is responsive to the initial informational input to emotional systems, rather than maintaining arousal, which should be the case if this area sustained affective states (Zald, 2003).

Only a minority of studies that have attempted to show correlations between amygdala activity and affective states have succeeded, and at times they have been in unexpected, inverse directions, while relations to the arousal of other brain areas are positive (Zald et al., 2002). Sometimes the correlations become stronger when subjects confronted by negative emotional visual stimuli are requested to maintain their affective responses (Schaefer et al., 2002). However, there is also evidence that when subjects make hedonic ratings to affectively valenced slides, as compared to simply viewing them, amygdala activation goes down (Phan et al., 2002). In sum, although it is certain that the amygdala helps process various cognitive inputs that can trigger fear (Bechara et al., 1995; Young et al., 1996), it is certainly not the exclusive or even major area of the brain that generates the affective experience of anxiety.

At the same time, human ESB studies affirm that stimulation of the amygdala can promote a large range of affective experiences, including anxiety (Gloor, 1997), but this would be quite consistent with the hypothesis that the amygdala is largely a neural interface between cognitive systems that parse potential emotional meaning from sensory inputs (which vary greatly among different species) and those more ancient systems, common to all animals, that generate coherent fearful responses with more intense affective attributes. If this is true, a distinction between cognitive and affective forms of consciousness is essential to make sense of how the brain is organized (Panksepp, 2001). The higher reaches of the brain that process knowledge concerning emotional stimuli, and the many fine-grained environmental differences that need to be distinguished, are not simply isomorphic with the brain systems that generate affective states.

This has important implications for what should be deemed conscious experience and unconscious neural processes. It is now quite clear that the amygdala can participate in the unconscious processing of cognitive information, but most of the studies that consider unconscious emotions have rarely attempted to properly evaluate affective issues. Indeed, recent work indicates that autonomic conditioning of fear, which may mark affectively experienced states, can still occur in humans even after higher limbic structures such as amygdala and hippocampus have been destroyed (Tranel and Damasio, 1990). It seems likely that a great deal of affective experience can still be generated by the FEAR system when its ability to harvest cognitive inputs is severely impaired (Adolphs et al., 2003). Although a consensus has emerged during the past dozen years that fear conditioning is mediated by amygdalar outputs onto such a neural system (Davis, 1994, 1999; LeDoux, 2000; Maren and Fanselow, 1996), there is practically no evidence that the amygdala is essential for the affective experiential aspects of fear. To sum up this troublesome and contentious area of research, I would also emphasize that "the human amygdala is neither necessary to consciously evaluate and report subjective emotional experiences, nor is it necessary for the more general subjective experience of affective states" (Zald, 2003, p. 113), a conclusion echoed by Anderson and Phelps (2002).

Subcortical FEAR System and Feelings of Anxiety

So, once again, which areas of the brain are most important for elaboration of the affective urgency of fearfulness? Although we cannot monitor animal or human affective experiences directly using any measurement procedure, potentially useful behavioral indices, including sensitive place avoidance measures, strongly suggest that an intensely negative internal state has been produced by artificial activation of the FEAR system. If given the chance, rats avoid environments in which they have received such ESB (Panksepp, 1996); if no opportunity for escape is provided, the animals freeze for long periods, as if they had been exposed to a frightful predator (Brandao et al., 1999; Panksepp et al., 1991). The ability of peptides such as substance P to evoke conditioned place aversion when placed into the PAG (Aguiar and Brandao, 1994) suggests the importance of very low level brain areas in the generation of affect. The future use of sensitive vocal expressions of negative emotions may be especially useful indices of affective changes emanating from subcortical emotional circuits in animals (Knutson et al., 2002; Panksepp et al., 1988, 2002).

Most importantly, since the 1950s there have been a sufficient number of observations on humans undergoing neurosurgery, who have verbally reported anxiety and foreboding during ESB of homologous subcortical brain sites (Gloor, 1997; Panksepp, 1985). Although it is possible that the affective experience is a result of indirect "action at a distance" whereby those lower-brain stimulation effects are "read out" in higher cortical regions that mediate cognitive forms of consciousness, that is a dubious and unparsimonious assumption. One merely needs consider the emotional vigor of animals that have been deprived of their higher neocortical reaches; such animals even play quite normally (e.g., Panksepp et al., 1994). In contrast, no one has generated acute affective states by stimulating cortical regions, even though such states are readily evoked from brain areas where ESB produces instinctual emotional responses in animals.

Until demonstrated otherwise, a reasonable working hypothesis is that the whole FEAR circuit is necessary for a fully elaborated anxiety response. It is important to reemphasize that such core emotional circuits can be sensitized by repeated activation with ESB or stressful life experiences (Adamec and Young, 2000). Once such "limbic permeabilities" are established (Maren, 1999), as may occur most dramatically in PTSD (van der Kolk, 1987), there are no robust ways to reverse them (Davidson, 1997), even though certain experimental agents (e.g., cholecystokinin receptor blockade) can provide prophylaxis against trauma effects in an animal model (Adamec and Young, 2000). We can also anticipate that rich social contact and sincere support after trauma might do the same (Ruis et al., 1999).

Learned Fears

Fear learning allows organisms to channel their behavioral resources so they can evaluate potential threats and seek safety effectively. While the FEAR system has various intrinsic sensitivities (e.g., being aroused by painful and predatory stimuli), it also has the ability to become fearfully responsive to new inputs that inform the organisms about environmental events that may predict dangers. Organisms are prepared to make fearful associations to certain stimuli but not others (Öhman and Mineka, 2001). Autonomic fear responses classically condition more rapidly when electric shock is paired with angry faces than when paired with smiling ones (Öhman et al., 1989). Thus, it seems likely that the neural systems that decode angry emotional expressions have evolutionarily privileged and/or environmentally "sensitized" inputs to FEAR circuitry (Adolphs et al., 1994).

There is bound to be enormous variety in such sensory-perceptual channels to the FEAR system among different species. While humans are prepared to develop fears to dark and high places, approaching mean-faced strangers, as well as spiders and snakes, rats are more prone to fear well-illuminated, open spaces, the smell of cats, and other predators. But neutral stimuli, as well as fantasies in humans, may also probably come to conditionally access the FEAR system. During the past decade, several investigators have unraveled how environmental conditioning proceeds in the amygdala as a function of specific learning mechanisms.

Neutral lights and tones paired with painful shock can access the headwater of FEAR circuitry fairly directly through low-road thalamic sensory analyzers as well as the more complex high-road perceptual analyzers of the neocortex. With regard to the low road, there are direct anatomical connections from the medial geniculate of the thalamus to the central nucleus of amygdala, and with regard to the high road less direct neocortical ones (Davis et al., 1995; LeDoux et al., 1990). If one combines both affective and cognitive measures in an animal fear-learning paradigm, one can demonstrate that manipulations that reduce the unconditional emotional indicators (e.g., freezing) can be dissociated from the cognitive choices animals make to avoid fear stimuli (Killcross et al., 1997; Nader and LeDoux, 1997). This issue is especially important at a human level, where one can obviously have a cognitive appreciation of what is dangerous without feeling much trepidation, and vice versa.

The intraamygdaloid synaptic mechanisms by which fear learning transpires is being detailed (LeDoux, 2000). Fear associations are heavily influenced by glutamatergic synapses (Schafe et al., 2001) as well as ß-adrenergic ones concentrated in the amygdala (Cahill et al., 1994). However, the FEAR system has multiple perceptual inputs. For instance, while the amygdalae primarily harvest information from discreet environmental cues, more complex spatial information is linked to contextual fear conditioning via the hippocampus (Fanselow et al., 1994; Phillips and Le Doux, 1992). Also, it remains likely that some conditioning can be elaborated at hypothalamic and mesencephalic levels of the FEAR circuit, but that work is in the preliminary stages (e.g., De Oca et al., 1998).

As investigators work out the details of the associative mechanisms, new ideas should emerge about how one might de-condition learned fears with the assistance of neurochemical interventions (Muller et al., 1997). For instance, the consolidation of fearful memories is controlled by a glutamate-dependent synaptic facilitation process, as are all memories (Schafe et al., 2001). Thus, it comes as no surprise that the extinction of conditioned fears, which is an active learning process, is also mediated by the same chemistries (Falls et al., 1992). This suggests that existing fears will need to be de-conditioned by an active form of new learning mediated by the same synaptic chemistries (glutamate) as the original learning, making global neurochemical interventions in glutamatergic systems unlikely interventions for helping erase fearful memories. Many of the neuropeptides discussed above are concentrated in these circuits, but little is presently known about how they participate in the elaboration of learning. The possibility that other manipulations of these associative networks, for instance, by the menagerie of anxiolytic neuropeptides such as opioids and neuropeptide Y (Chapter 21), might be able to specifically facilitate the diminution of fearful, but not other types of memories, continues to intrigue scientists who study fear learning.

Varieties of Anxiety Systems in the Brain

Of course, the neuronal complexities that we face as we seek a definitive understanding of anxiety within the mammalian brain remain vast. Surely, several forms of "trepidation" are elaborated by distinct emotional systems of the brain, and meaningful functional differentiations have been identified in a "single" complex brain zone such as the amygdala (Killcross et al., 1997). As briefly noted earlier, a discrete separation distress/PANIC system runs from the BNST and preoptic areas, through dorsomedial regions of the thalamus, down to the mesencephalic PAG (Panksepp et al., 1988). How any of the postulated anxiety or PANIC systems actually contribute to panic attacks remains a controversial issue (Chapter 12).

Clinically, an early differentiation between brain systems that contribute to panic attacks and those that generate anticipatory anxiety was based on the observation that first-generation BZ antianxiety agents (e.g., chlordiazepoxide and diazepam) were not as effective for controlling either panic attacks or separation anxiety as tricyclic antidepressants (e.g., imipramine and chlorimipramine). Although such tricyclics turned out to be excellent antipanic agents, they had comparatively modest effects on anticipatory anxiety (Klein and Rabkin, 1981). This pharmacological distinction no longer holds for the newer and more potent BZs. For instance, alprazolam and oxazepam are effective antipanic agents (Schweizer et al., 1993), but BZs are also effective inhibitors of separation distress in some species (Panksepp, 2003). It is not yet certain whether these effects are due to direct BZ receptor influences, or perhaps alternative paths such as the facilitation of serotonin transmission or reduced beta adrenoreceptor activity. Of course, the ability of some new antianxiety agents to reduce panic may also indicate that the fear and separation distress systems also share certain inhibitory influences. The massive interactions of highly overlapping emotional systems, (Panksepp, 1982) highlight difficulties we must confront in brain research as well as clinical practice. Since quite a bit is known about the brain localizations of the separation distress/PANIC and FEAR systems, such issues could be empirically disentangled.

Many anxiety-related disorders may actually be constituted of mixtures of several emotions. The sustained mood changes that accompany PTSD often include mixtures of anxiety and anger. PTSD symptoms can often be ameliorated with antiseizure medications, for instance, carbamazepine, a GABA facilitator that does not consistently benefit either anticipatory anxiety or panic attacks (Charney et al., 1993). Likewise, carbamazepine can block "kindling"—the seizure potentiation induced via once-a-day application of an ESB burst to seizure-prone areas of the temporal lobe such as hippocampus and amygdala, which has yielded an animal model for PTSD (Adamec and Young, 2000). Kindled animals often exhibit chronic emotional changes, including increased fearfulness, irritability, and at times heightened sexuality.

Many other psychiatric problems are accompanied by anxiety. Obsessive-compulsive rituals often represent attempts to ward off encroaching anxieties, but there is presently no evidence they are mediated by the systems discussed above. They may largely represent the higher ruminative representations of emotional systems in frontal cortical regions of the brain (Davis, 1999). However, it is worth reemphasizing that the serotonin uptake inhibitor chlorimipramine, which has long been the main treatment for obsessive-compulsive disorders, is also a reasonably effective antipanic agent (Altemus, 1995), as is imipramine (Klein and Rabkin, 1981).

In sum, it presently seems likely that brain systems that mediate generalized anxiety disorders and panic attacks, separation anxiety, and posttraumatic stress disorders can be neurally differentiated to some extent, but they also share some neurochemical controls. Indeed, all strong emotional states share some nonspecific alarm or alerting components. When any of a variety of threatening stimuli first appear on the psychological horizon, generalized cerebral arousal/attentional systems, arising partly from brain cholinergic and noradrenergic circuits, are recruited. Likewise, a diversity of negative affective states and forms of emotional arousal, are accompanied by pituitary-adrenal stress responses to help mobilize many brain and bodily resources to cope with stressors (for a review, see Chapter 4). It is a bit of a surprise that panic attacks are rarely accompanied by pituitary-adrenal arousal, but that may be explicated by the suffocation-alarm theory of panic (Klein, 1993), which recognizes how low in the brainstem some emotional systems may reside (also see Chapter 2).

CONCLUDING REMARKS

To understand the nature of fear and the other emotions, we must consider how affective experiences are constructed in the brain. Since subjective psychodynamic issues are so difficult to address with standardized empirical procedures, we typically must infer such processes indirectly from behavioral endpoints. Unfortunately, the details of the relevant brain mechanisms are typically inaccessible in human research. Hence, substantive progress on such questions will require investments in appropriate animal models in which the neurobiological details can be unraveled. It is still a debatable issue which behavioral measures are best for monitoring the various affective states, but novel inroads have been made on such issues (Knutson et al., 2002; Panksepp et al., 2002).

Also, brain imaging techniques may eventually be able to monitor emotional feelings directly from the human brain (e.g., see Chapter 2 and 7; Damasio et al., 2000), but validation of such issues may require the use of neurochemical and pharmacological challenges that have been derived from theoretically guided animal research.

   Although the issue of subjective emotional experiences in animals has been downplayed by modern neurobehaviorists (see LeDoux, 1996), it is not difficult to envision how affective states such as fear could facilitate adaptive behavioral strategies in the nervous system (Panksepp, 1999a,b). If other mammals do, in fact, experience subjective emotional states such as fear, then it may be possible to study the underlying brain mechanisms reasonably directly through an analysis of their instinctual emotional behaviors and arrive at credible working hypotheses concerning the evolutionary sources of basic human affective capacities. In other words, the only direct readout of evolutionarily engraved central networks of the brain are the natural behaviors that animals exhibit. If a study of those ancient instinctual operating systems of the animal brain is a major key to understanding how the human mind is emotionally organized, then an intensive study of those circuits should yield new neurochemical insights for psychiatric practice.

REFERENCES

Adamec RE, Young B (2000). Neuroplasticity in specific limbic system circuits may mediate specific kindling induced changes in animal affect—implications for understanding anxiety associated with epilepsy. *Neurosci Biobehav Revs* 24:705–723.

Adolphs R, Tranel D, Damasio H, Damasio A (1994). Impaired recognition of emotion in facial expressions following bilateral damage to the human amygdala. *Nature* 372:669–672.

Adolphs R, Tranel D, Damasio AR (2003). Dissociable neural systems for recognizing emotions. *Brain and Cognition*, in press.

Aguiar MS, Brandao, ML (1994). Conditioned place aversion produced by microinjections of substance P into the periaqueductal gray of rats. *Behav Pharmacol* 5:369–373.

Altemus M (1995). Neuroendocrinology of obsessive-compulsive disorder. In Panksepp J (ed). *Advances in Biological Psychiatry* Vol. 1. JAI Press: Greenwich, CT, pp. 215–233.

American Psychiatric Association (1994). *Diagnostic and Statistical Manual of Mental Disorders, DSM IV*. American Psychiatric Association: Washington, DC.

Anderson AK, Phelps EA (2002). Is the human amygdala critical for the subjective experience of emotion? Evidence of intact dispositional affect in patients with amygdala lesions. *J Cogn Neurosci* 14:709–720.

Bakish D (1999). The patient with comorbid depression and anxiety: The unmet need. *J Clin Psychiatry* 60:20–24.

Bechara A, Tranel D, Damasio H, Adolphs R, Rockland C, Damasio AR (1995). Double dissociation of conditioning and declarative knowledge relative to the amygdala and hippocampus in humans. *Science* 269:1115–1118.

Beck CHM, Fibiger HC (1995). Conditioned fear-induced changes in behavior and in the expression of the immediate early gene *c-fos*: With and without diazepam pretreatment. *J Neurosci* 15:113–121.

Beckett SRG, Duxon MS, Aspley S, Marsden CA (1997). Central *c-fos* expression following 20 kHz/ultrasound induced defence behaviour in the rat. *Brain Res Bull* 42:421–426.

Bekkedal MYV, Rossi III J, Panksepp J (1999). Fetal and neonatal exposure to trimethylol-propane phosphate alters rat social behavior and emotional responsivity. *Neurotoxicol Teratol* 21:435–43.

Blanchard RJ, Yudko EB, Rodgers RJ, Blanchard DC (1993). Defense system psychopharmacology: An ethological approach to the pharmacology of fear and anxiety. *Behav Brain Res* 58:155–156.

Blanchard DC, Griebel G, Blanchard RJ (2001). Mouse defensive behaviors: Pharmacological and behavioral assays for anxiety and panic. *Neurosci Biobehav Revs* 25:205–218.

Brandao ML, Anseloni VZ, Pandossio JE, De Araujo JE, Castilho VM (1999). Neurochemical mechanisms of the defensive behavior in the dorsal midbrain. *Neurosci Biobehav Revs* 23:863–875.

Broom DM (ed) (2001). *Coping with Challenge: Welfare in Animals Including Humans.* Dahlem Workshop Report 87, Dahlem University Press: Berlin.

Burrows GD, Roth M, Noyes R Jr (eds) (1990). *Handbook of Anxiety, Vol. 3, The Neurobiology of Anxiety.* Elsevier: Amsterdam.

Candor M, Ahmed SH, Koob GF, Le Moal M, Stinus L (1992). Corticotropin-releasing factor induces a place aversion independent of its neuroendocrine role. *Brain Res* 597:304–309.

Carobrez AP, Teixeira KV, Graeff FG (2001). Modulation of defensive behavior by periaqueductal gray NMDA/glycine-B receptor. *Neurosci Biobehav Revs* 25:697–709.

Cahill L, McGaugh JL (1998). Mechanisms of emotional arousal and lasting declarative memory. *Trends Neurosci* 21:294–299.

Cahill L, Prins B, Weber B, McGaugh JL (1994). ß-Adrenergic activation and memory for emotional events. *Nature* 371:702–704.

Chalmers DT, Lovenberg TW, Grigoriadis DE, Behan DP, De Souza EB (1996). Corticotrophin-releasing factor receptors: From molecular biology to drug design. *Trends Neurosci* 17:166–172.

Charney DS, Bremner JD (1999). The neurobiology of anxiety disorders. In Charney DS, Nestler EJ, Bunney BS (eds). *Neurobiology of Mental Illness.* Oxford University Press: New York, pp. 494–517.

Charney DS, Woods SW, Goodman WK, Heninger, GR (1987). Serotonin function in anxiety: II. Effects of the serotonin agonist MCPP in panic disorder patients and healthy subjects. *Psychopharmacol* 92:14–24.

Charney DS, Deutch AY, Krystal JH, Southwick SM, Davis M (1993). Psychobiologic mechanisms of posttraumatic stress disorder. *Arch Gen Psychiatry* 50:294–305.

Charney DS, Nestler EJ, Bunney BS (eds) (1999). *Neurobiology of Mental Illness.* Oxford University Press: New York.

Cheetham SC, Heal DJ (2000). Antidepressant and anxiolytic drugs. In Bittar EE, Bittar N (eds). *Biological Psychiatry.* JAI Press: Stamford, CT, pp. 511–567.

Conner KM and Davidson JRT (1998). Generalized anxiety disorders: Neurobiological and pharmaco-therapeutic perspectives. *Biol Psychiatry* 44:1286–1294.

Damasio AR (1999). *The Feeling of What Happens: Body and Emotion in the Making of Consciousness.* Harcourt Brace: New York.

Damasio AR, Grabowski TJ, Bechara A, Damasio H, Ponto LLB, Parvizi J, Hichwa RD (2000). Subcortical and cortical brain activity during the feeling of self-generated emotions. *Nature Neurosci* 3:1049–1056.

Davidson JR (2001). Pharmacotherapy of generalized anxiety disorder. *J Clin Psychiatry* 62(Suppl 11):46–50.

Davidson JRT (1997). Biological therapies for posttraumatic stress disorder: An overview. *J Clin Psychiatry* 58(Suppl):29–32.

Davidson JRT, Tupler LA, Potts NL (1994). Treatment of social phobia with benzodiazepines. *J Clin Psychiatry* 55(suppl):28–32.

Davidson JRT, DuPont RL, Hedges D, Haskins JT (1999). Efficacy, safety, and tolerability of venlafaxine extended release and buspirone in outpatients with generalized anxiety disorder. *J Clin Psychiatry* 60:528–535.

Davis M (1992). The role of the amygdala in fear and anxiety. *Ann Rev Psych* 43:353–375.

Davis M (1994). The role of the amygdala in emotional learning. *Internat Revs Neurobiol* 36:225–266.

Davis M (1999). Functional neuroanatomy of anxiety and fear: A focus on the amygdala. In Charney DS, Nestler EJ, Bunney BS (eds). *Neurobiology of Mental Illness*. Oxford University Press: New York, pp. 463–474.

Davis M, Campeau S, Kim M, Falls WA (1995). Neural systems of emotion: The amygdala's role in fear and anxiety. In McGaugh JL, Weinberger NM, and Lynch G (eds). *Brain and Memory: Modulation and Mediation of Neuroplasticity*. Oxford Univ. Press: New York, pp. 3–40.

De Oca BM, DeCola JP, Maren S, Fanselow MS (1988). Distinct regions of the periaqueductal gray are involved in the acquisition and expression of defensive responses. *J Neurosci* 18:3426–3432.

Depaulis A, Bandler R (eds) (1991). *The Midbrain Periaqueductal Gray Matter: Functional Anatomical and Neurochemical Organization*. Plenum Press: New York.

Dielenberg RA, Hunt GE, McGregor IS (2001). "When a rat smells a cat": The distribution of Fos immunoreactivity in rat brain following exposure to a predatory odor. *Neuroscience* 104:1085–1097.

Dunn AJ, Berridge C (1990). Physiological and behavioral responses to corticotropin-releasing factor administration: Is CRH a mediator of anxiety or stress responses? *Brain Res Revs* 15:71–100.

Eison AS, Temple DL (1986). Buspirone: Review of its pharmacology and current perspective on its mechanism of action. *Am J Med* 80 (Suppl. 3B):1–9.

Falls WA, Miserendino MJD, Davis M (1992). Extinction of fear-potentiated startle: Blockade by infusion of an NMDA antagonist into the amygdala. *J Neurosci* 12:854–863.

Fanselow MS (1991). Analgesia as a response to aversive Pavlovian conditional stimuli: cognitive and emotional mediators. In Denny MR (ed). *Fear, Avoidance and Phobias: A Fundamental Analysis*. Lawrence Erlbaum: Hillsdale, NJ, pp. 61–86.

Fanselow MS, Kim JJ, Yipp J, De Oca P (1994). Differential effects of the *N*-methyl-D-aspartate antagonist D,L-2-amino-5-phosphonovalerate on acquisition of fear of auditory and contextual cues. *Behav Neurosci* 108:235–240.

Ferrarese C, Appollonio I, Bianchi G, Frigo M, Marzorati C, Pecora N, Perego M, Pierpaoli C, Frattola L (1993). Benzodiazepine receptors and diazepam binding inhibitor: A possible link between stress, anxiety and the immune system. *Psychoneuroendocrinology* 18:3–22.

Gittelman R, Klein DF (1985). Childhood separation anxiety and adult agoraphobia. In Tuma AH, Maser J (eds). *Anxiety and the Anxiety Disorders*. Lawrence Erlbaum: Hillsdale, NJ, pp. 389–402.

Gloor P (1997). *The Temporal Lobe and Limbic System*, Oxford University Press: New York.

Goddard AW, Coplan JD, Gorman JM, Charney DS (1999). Principles of the pharmacotherapy of anxiety disorders. In Charney DS, Nestler EJ, Bunney BS (eds). *Neurobiology of Mental Illness*. Oxford University Press: New York, pp. 548–563.

Gorman JM (2002). Treatment of generalized anxiety disorder. *J Clin Psychiatry* 63:17–23.

Gray JA (1987). *The Psychology of Fear and Stress*, 2nd ed. Cambridge University Press: Cambridge, England.

Haefely WE (1990). The GABA-benzodiazepine receptor: Biology and pharmacology. In *Handbook of Anxiety, Vol. 3. The Neurobiology of Anxiety*. (Burrows GD, Roth M, Noyes R, Jr (eds). Elsevier: Amsterdam.

Handley SL (1995). 5-Hydroytryptamine pathways in anxiety and its treatment. *Pharmacol Ther* 66:103–148.

Harro J, Vasar E, Bradwejn J (1993). CCK in animal and human research on anxiety. *Trends Pharmac Sci* 14:244–249.

Heilig M (1995). Antisense inhibition of neuropeptide Y (NPY)-Y1 receptor expression blocks the anxiolytic-like action of NPY in amygdala and paradoxically increases feeding. *Regulatory Peptides* 59:201–205.

Heilig M, Koob GF, Ekman R, Britton KT (1994). Corticotropin-releasing factor and neuropeptide Y: Role in emotional integration. *Trends Neurosci* 17:80–85.

Helton DR, Tizzano JP, Monn JA, Schoepp DD, Kallman MJ (1998). Anxiolytic and side-effect profile of LY354740: A potent, highly selective, orally active agonist for group II metabotropic glutamate receptors. *J Pharmacol Exp Ther* 284:651–660.

Holstege G, Bandler R, Saper CB (ed) (1996). *The Emotional Motor Systems. Progress in Brain Research,* Vol. 107, Elsevier: Amsterdam.

Irwin W, Davidson RJ, Lowe MJ, Mock FJ, Sorenson JA, Turski PA (1996). Human amygdala activation detected with echo-planar functional magnetic resonance imaging. *NeuroReports* 7:1765–1769.

Johnson MR, Lydiard RB (1995). The neurobiology of anxiety disorders. *Psychiatric Clin N Am* 18:681–725.

Kehne JH, Coverdale S, McCloskey TC, Hoffman DC, Cassella JV (2000). Effects of the CRH1 receptor antagonists, CP 154,526, in the separation-induced vocalization anxiolytic test in rat pups. *Neuropharmacol* 39:1357–1367.

Killcross S, Robbins TW, Everitt BJ (1997). Different types of fear-conditioned behaviour mediated by separate nuclei within amygdala. *Nature* 388:377–380.

Klein DF (1993). False suffocations alarms, spontaneous panics, and related conditions. *Arch Gen Psychiatry* 50:306–317.

Klein DF, Rabkin, J (eds) (1981). *Anxiety: New Research and Changing Concepts*. Raven Press: New York.

Knutson B, Burgdorf J, Panksepp J (2002). Ultrasonic vocalizations as indices of affective states in rat. *Psych Bull* 128:961–977.

Kollack-Walker S, Watson SJ, Akil H (1997). Social stress in hamsters: Defeat activates specific neurocircuits within the brain. *J Neurosci* 17:8842–8855.

Kunovac JL, Stahl SM (1995). Future directions in anxiolytic pharmacotherapy. *Psychiatric Clin N Am.* 18:895–909.

LeDoux JE (1996). *The Emotional Brain.* Simon and Schuster: New York.

LeDoux JE (2000). Emotion circuits in the brain. *Ann Rev Neurosci* 23:155–184.

LeDoux JE, Cicchetti P, Xagoraris A, Romanski LM (1990). The lateral amygdaloid nucleus: Sensory interface of the amygdala in fear conditioning. *J Neurosci* 10:1062–1069.

Liebowitz MR (1988). Pharmacotherapy of personality disorders. In Clynes M, and Panksepp J (eds). *Emotions and Psychopathology* Plenum Press: New York, pp. 77–94.

Mancini C, Ameringen MV (1996). Paroxetine in social phobia. *J Clin Psychiatry* 57:519–522.

Maren S (1999). Long-term potentiation in the amygdala: A mechanism for emotional learning and memory. *Trends Neurosci* 22:561–567.

Maren S, Fanselow MS (1996). The amygdala and fear conditioning: Has the nut been cracked? *Neuron* 16:237–240.

Miczek K, Haney M, Tidey J, Vivian J, Weert E (1994). Neurochemistry and pharmacotherapeutic management of aggression and violence. In Reiss A, Miczek K, Roth J (eds). *Understanding and Preventing Violence. Vol. 2, Biobehavioral Influences*, National Academy Press: Washington, DC, pp. 245–514.

Muller J, Corodimas KP, Fridel Z, LeDoux JE (1997). Functional inactivation of the lateral and basal nuclei of the amygdala by muscimol infusion prevents fear conditioning to an explicit CS and to contextual stimuli. *Behav Neurosci* 111:683–691.

Nader K, LeDoux JE (1997). Is it time to invoke multiple fear learning systems in the amygdala. *Trends Cog Sci* 1:241–244.

Ninan PT (1999). The functional anatomy, neurochemistry, and pharmacology of anxiety. *J Clin Psychiatry* 60(Suppl 22):12–17.

Nutt DJ (1990). The pharmacology of human anxiety. *Pharmac Ther* 47:233–266.

Nutt DJ, Glue P, Lawon C, Wilson S (1990). Flumazenil provocation of panic attacks: Evidence for altered benzodiazepine receptor sensitivity in panic disorder. *Arch Gen Psychiat* 47:917–925.

Öhman A, Mineka S (2001). Fears, phobias, and preparedness: Toward an evolved module of fear and fear learning. *Psych Rev* 108:483–522.

Öhman A, Dimberg U, Esteves F (1989). Preattentive activation of aversive emotions. In (Archer T, Nilsson L-G (eds). *Aversion, Avoidance and Anxiety.* Lawrence Erlbaum: Hillsdale, NJ, pp. 169–193.

Pande AC, Greiner M, Adams JB, Lydiard RB, Pierce MW (1999). Placebo-controlled trial of the CCK-B antagonist, CI-988, in panic disorder. *Biol Psychiatry* 46:860–862.

Panksepp J (1982). Toward a general psychobiological theory of emotions. *Behav Brain Sci* 5:407–467.

Panksepp J (1985). Mood changes. In Vinken PJ, Buyn GW, Klawans HL (eds). *Handbook of Clinical Neurology, Revised Series, Vol. 1(45) Clinical Neuropsychology.* Elsevier: Amsterdam, pp. 271–285.

Panksepp J (1990). The psychoneurology of fear: Evolutionary perspectives and the role of animal models in understanding human anxiety. In Burrows GD, Roth M, Noyes R, Jr (eds). *Handbook of Anxiety, Vol. 3, The Neurobiology of Anxiety* Elsevier, Amsterdam, pp. 3–58.

Panksepp J (1991). Affective neuroscience: A conceptual framework for the neurobiological study of emotions. In Strongman KT (ed). *International Review of Studies on Emotion, Vol. 1* Wiley: Chichester, England, pp. 59–99.

Panksepp J (1993). Neurochemical control of moods and emotions: Amino acids to neuropeptides. In Lewis M, Haviland JM (eds). *Handbook of Emotions*, Guildford Press: New York, pp. 87–107.

Panksepp J (1996). Modern approaches to understanding fear: From laboratory to clinical practice. In Panksepp J (ed). *Advances in Biological Psychiatry*, Vol. 2. JAI Press: Greenwich, CT, pp. 209–230.

Panksepp J (1998a). *Affective Neuroscience: The Foundations of Human and Animal Emotions.* Oxford University Press: New York.

Panksepp J (1998b). The periconscious substrates of consciousness: Affective states and the evolutionary origins of the SELF. *J Consciousness Studies* 5:566–582.

Panksepp J (1999a). Emotions as viewed by psychoanalysis and neuroscience: An exercise in consilience, and accompanying commentaries. *NeuroPsychoanalysis.* 1:15–89.

Panksepp J (1999b). On preventing another century of misunderstanding: Toward a psychoethology of human experience and a psychoneurology of affect. *NeuroPsychoanalysis* 2:240–255.

Panksepp J (2000). Fear and anxiety mechanisms of the brain: Clinical implications. In Bittar EE, Bittar N (eds). *Biological Psychiatry*, JAI Press: Stamford, CT, pp. 155–177.

Panksepp J (2001). The neuro-evolutionary cusp between emotions and cognitions: Implications for understanding consciousness and the emergence of a unified mind science. *Evolut Cogn* 7:141–163.

Panksepp J (2003). Can anthropomorphic analyses of "separation cries" in other animals inform us about the emotional nature of social loss in humans? *Psych Rev*, 110:376–388.

Panksepp J, Abbott BB (1990). Modulation of separation distress by alpha-MSH. *Peptides* 11:647–653.

Panksepp J, Bekkedal M. (1997). Neuropeptides and the varieties of anxiety in the brain. *Italian J Psychopathology* 1:18–27.

Panksepp J, Herman BH, Villberg T, Bishop P, DeEskinazi FG (1980). Endogenous opioids and social behavior. *Neurosci Biobehav Revs* 4:473–487.

Panksepp J, Siviy SM, Normansell LA (1985). Brain opioids and social emotions. In Reite M, Fields T (eds). *The Psychobiology of Attachment and Separation.* Academic Press: New York, pp. 3–49.

Pankscpp J, Normansell L, Herman B, Bishop P, Crepeau L (1988). Neural and neurochemical control of the separation distress call. In Newman JD (ed). *The Physiological Control of Mammalian Vocalizations*. Plenum Press: New York, pp. 263–300.

Panksepp J, Sacks DS, Crepeau LJ, Abbott BB (1991). The psycho- and neurobiology of fear systems in the brain. In Denny MR (ed). *Fear, Avoidance, and Phobias*. Lawrence Erlbaum: Hillsdale, NJ, pp. 7–59.

Panksepp J, Normansell L, Cox J, Siviy S (1994). Effects of neonatal decortication on the social play of juvenile rats. *Physiology & Behavior* 56:429–443.

Panksepp J, Knutson B, Burgdorf J (2002). The role of brain emotional systems in addictions: A neuro-evolutionary perspective and new "self-report" animal model. *Addiction* 97:459–469.

Paul SM, Purdy RH (1992). Neuroactive steroids. *The FASEB J* 6:2311–2322.

Payeur R, Lydiard RB, Ballenger JC, Laraia MT, Fossey MD, Zealberg J (1992). CSF diazepam-binding inhibitor concentrations in panic disorder. *Biol Psychol* 32:712–716.

Petursson H (1994). The benzodiazepine withdrawal syndrome. *Addiction* 89:1455–1459.

Phan KL, Wager T, Taylor SF, Liberzon I (2002). Functional neuroanatomy of emotion: A meta-analysis of emotion activation studies in PET and fMRI. *NeuroImage* 16:331–348.

Phillips RG, Le Doux JE (1992). Differential contribution of amygdala and hippocampus to cued and contextual fear conditioning. *Behav Neurosci* 106:274–285.

Potts NL, Book S, Davidson JR (1996). The neurobiology of social phobia. *Int Clin Psychopharmacol* 11(Suppl. 3):43–48.

Rauch SL, Savage CR, Alpert NM, Miguel EC, Baer L, Breiter HC, Fischman AJ, Manzo PA, Moretti C, Jenike MA (1995). A positron emission tomographic study of simple phobic symptom provocation. *Arch Gen Psychiat* 52:20–28.

Rickels K, Downing R, Schweizer E, Hassman H (1993). Antidepressants for the treatment of generalized anxiety disorder. A placebo-controlled comparison of imipramine, traxodone and diazepam. *Arch Gen Psychiatry* 50:884–895.

Rocca P, Fonzo V, Scott M, Znalda E, Ravizza L (1997). Paroxetine efficacy in the treatment of generalized anxiety disorder. *Acta Psychiatr Scand* 95:444–450.

Rolls ET (1999). *The Brain and Emotion*. Oxford University Press: Oxford, UK.

Rosen JB, Schulkin J (1998). From normal fear to pathological anxiety. *Psych Rev* 105:325–350.

Roy-Byrne PP, Cowley DS (1991). *Benzodiazepines in Clinical Practice: Risks and Benefits*. American Psychiatric Press: Washington, DC.

Ruis MAW, te Brake JHA, Buwalda B, De Boer SF, Meerlo P, Korte SM, Blokhüis HJ, Koolhaas JM (1999). Housing familiar male wild-type rats together reduces the long-term adverse behavioral and physiological effects of social defeat. *Psychoneuroendocrinology* 24:285–300.

Schaefer SM, Jackson DC, Davidson RJ, Aguire GF, Kimberg SL (2002). Modulation of amygdalar activity by conscious regulation of negative emotion. *J Cogn Neurosci* 14:913–921.

Schafe GE, Nader K, Blair HT, LeDoux JE (2001). Memory consolidation of Pavlovian fear conditioning: A cellular and molecular perspective. *Trends in Neurosci* 24:540–546.

Schmidt LA, Schulkin J (1999). *Extreme Fear, Shyness, and Social Phobia*. Oxford University Press: New York.

Schweizer E, Rickels K, Lucki I (1986). Resistance to the anti-anxiety effect of buspirone in patients with a history of benzodiazepine use. *New Engl J Med* 314:719–720.

Schweizer E, Rickels K, Weiss S, Zavodnick S (1993). Maintenance drug treatment of panic disorder. I. Results of a prospective, placebo-controlled comparison of alprazolam and imipramine. *Arch Gen Psychiatry.* 50:51–60.

Sgoifo A, Koolhaas J, Alleva E, Musso E, Parmigiani S (eds) (2001). Social stress: Acute and long-term effects on physiology and behavior. *Physiol Behav* 73:253–449.

Silveira MCL, Sandner G, Graeff FG (1993). Induction of Fos immunoreactivity in the brain by exposure to the elevated plus maze. *Behav Brain Res* 56:115–118.

Silveira MCL, Sandner G, Di Scala G, Graeff FG (1995). C-fos immunoreactivity in the brain following electrical or chemical stimulation of the medial hypothalamus of freely moving rats. *Brain Res* 674:265–274.

Skolnick P, Legutko B, Li X, Bymaster FP (2001). Current perspectives on the development of non-biogenic amine-based antidepressants. *Pharmacol Res* 43:411–423.

Soubrie P (1986) Reconciling the role of central serotonin neurons in human and animal behavior. *Behav Brain Sci* 9:319–364.

Spruijt BM, van den Bos R, Pijlman F.TA (2001). A concept of welfare based on reward evaluating mechanism in the brain: Anticipatory behaviour as an indicator for the state of reward systems. *Appl Animal Behaviour Sci* 72:145–171.

Sramek JJ, Zarotsky V, Cutler NR (2002). Generalised anxiety disorder: Treatment options. *Drugs* 11:1635–1648.

Stahl SM, Gastpar M, Keppel Hesselink JM (eds) (1992). *Serotonin 1A Receptors in Depression and Anxiety*. Raven Press: New York.

Stein MB (1998). Neurobiological perspectives on social phobia: From affiliation to zoology. *Biol Psychiatry* 44:1277–1285.

Stein MB, Liebowitz MR, Lydiard RB, Pitts CD, Bushnell W, Gergel I (1998). Paroxetine treatment of generalized social phobia (social anxiety disorder). *J Am Med Assoc* 280:708–713.

Tallman JF, Gallagher DW (1985). The GABA-ergic system: A locus of benzodiazepine action. *Ann Rev Neurosci* 8:21–44.

Tracey I, Ploghaus A, Gati JS, Clare S, Smith S, Menon RS, Matthews PM (2002). Imaging attentional modulation of pain in the periaqueductal gray in humans. *J Neurosci* 22:2748–2752.

Tranel D, Damasio AR (1990). The covert learning of affective valence does not require structures in hippocampal system or amygdala. *J Cog Neurosci* 5:79–88.

van der Kolk BA (ed) (1987). *Psychological Trauma*. American Psychiatric Press: Washington, DC.

You ZB, Tzschentke TM, Brodin E, Wise RA (1998). Electrical stimulation of the prefrontal cortex increases cholecystokinin, glutamate, and dopamine release in the nucleus accumbens: an in vivo microdialysis study in freely moving rats. *J Neurosci* 18:6492–6500.

Young AW, Hellawell DHJ, van de Wal C, Johnson M (1996). Facial expression processing after amygdalotomy. *Neuropsychologia* 34:31–40.

Young WS, Kuhar MJ (1980). Radiohistochemical localization of benzodiazepine receptors in the rat brain. *J Pharmacol Exp Ther* 212:337–346.

Zachar P, Bartlett S (2001). Basic emotions and their biological substrates. A nominalist approach. *Consciousness and Emotion* 2:189–222.

Zald DH (2003). The human amygdala and the emotional evaluation of sensory stimuli. *Brain Res Revs* 41:88–123.

Zald DH, Mattson DL, Pardo JV (2002). Brain activity in ventromedial prefrontal cortex correlates with individual differences in negative affect. *Proc Natl Acad Sci* 99:2450–2454.

17

SOMATIC TREATMENTS IN PSYCHIATRY

Ziad Nahas, Jeffrey P. Lorberbaum, Frank A. Kozel, and Mark S. George

Medical University of South Carolina, Institute of Psychiatry, Charleston, South Carolina

INTRODUCTION

The use of somatic interventions to control or treat mental symptoms dates back to ancient times (Clower et al., 2002; Kalinowsky, 1986; Tourney, 1967). Evidence for burr holes drilled into the skull to "cure the demons" goes back to the Neolithic age. The notions that convulsions and fever may help mental disorders have been known since Hippocrates, while in medieval times, make-believe surgeries were performed to extract the "stone of madness."

In the 17th century, Descartes hypothesized that the ventricles were the reservoir of vital fluids and basis for the rational mind. This deemphasized the brain's role. Conversely, modern somatic treatments for mental illness are rooted in the conceptualization that neural tissue is responsible for behavior. This started in 1796, when Gall proposed that different brain regions were responsible for different functions, a system he called phrenology. Although this notion was revolutionary and would prove essential to our current understanding of brain function, he and his followers were later involved in pseudo-science and contributed little to the functional neuroanatomy of the mind (Critchley, 1965).

Textbook of Biological Psychiatry, Edited by Jaak Panksepp
ISBN 0-471-43478-7   Copyright © 2004 John Wiley & Sons, Inc.

Almost a decade later, modern scientific conceptualization of brain functions and localizations began to emerge from animal experiments, cadaver dissections, and clinical observations conducted by Broca (Broca, 1865), Jackson (Jackson, 1873), and others. Also, the notion of neuronal transmission based on electrochemical signals replaced the 19th-century hydraulic neuronal transmission model (Tourney, 1967). These ideas of regional brain functional localization and electrochemical neuronal transmission would later evolve into the contemporary neuronal network models that guide and inform much of the current applications of somatic treatments in disorders such as obsessive compulsive disorder and depression. As the biological underpinnings of the complexity of the mind are still being worked out, current somatic interventions are being used both for understanding the neurobiology of mental illness as well as for treating disease (George et al., 1999b).

This chapter will discuss the current applications of somatic interventions in neuropsychiatric diseases, beginning with the oldest form of treatment—electroconvulsive therapy (ECT)—as well as a new variant of ECT called magnetic seizure therapy (MST). We will then discuss in order of increasing invasiveness transcranial magnetic stimulation (TMS), vagus nerve stimulation (VNS), deep brain stimulation (DBS), and finally neurosurgery for psychiatric conditions.

ELECTROCONVULSIVE THERAPY

Between 1917 and 1937, four methods for producing physiological shock were discovered, tested, and used in psychiatric practice for treating psychosis: fever, insulin-induced coma, medication-induced convulsions, and electrically induced convulsions (electroconvulsive therapy). In the Western world, only electroconvulsive therapy remains as a standard and effective treatment for psychiatric conditions (APA, 1998). First, malaria-induced fever was used to treat neurosyphillitic paresis. Later, insulin-induced coma was used to treat schizophrenia. Also, von Meduna noticed a "biological antagonism" between epilepsy and schizophrenia. The theory postulated that individuals with epilepsy were not likely to develop schizophrenia. This concept was later disproved. To treat schizophrenia/psychosis, von Meduna experimented with different drugs until he was able to obtain reliable convulsions with intravenous injection of pentamethylenetetrazol (or METRAZOL, a circulatory and respiratory stimulant) (von Meduna, 1937; Fink, 1984b). The seizures ensued quickly and violently. They caused spine fractures in a great number of patients. Later Bennett combined METRAZOL with curare and scopolamine to paralyze and sedate the patients (Bennett, 1994). In 1937, Cerletti and Bini applied transcranial electroconvulsive shock therapy to induce seizures safely and reliably (Bini, 1995). It was received with great enthusiasm given the remarkable therapeutic effects (in patients who now would most likely be classified as psychotically depressed) and the technical ease of administration compared to insulin or METRAZOL shock. Since then, ECT became the method of choice for convulsive therapy.

Over 60 years of experience have significantly improved this technique with the use of muscle relaxants, anesthesia with short-acting agents following preoxygenation of the brain, use of electroencephalography (EEG) seizure monitoring, and studies on optimal electrical stimulation parameters. The death rate, due primarily to cardiac arrhythmia, decreased from 0.1 percent in the 1950 to less than 2 for 100,000 ECT treatments (Abrams, 1997; Shiwach et al., 2002). One of the primary concerns with ECT remains the cognitive side effects (Sackeim, 2002). Patients do experience a variable degree of postictal confusion and retrograde amnesia with the procedure. These have been linked to electrode placement, intensity and waveform of stimulus, frequency of treatments, and underlying medical conditions (Sackeim et al., 1993). Although cognitive impairment is generally confined to information learned in the weeks surrounding ECT treatment itself, cognitive impairment has sometimes been reported several months after treatment. The capacity to learn and retain new information may be affected over these several months. There is no objective evidence that ECT has any long-term effect on the autobiographical memory (Lisanby et al., 2002). Structural brain magnetic resonance imaging (MRI) studies before and after ECT have also failed to show abnormalities attributed to the treatments (Devanand et al., 1994), nor changes in the hippocampal N-acetylaspartate signals (an indirect measure of neuronal integrity) (Ende et al., 2002).

Unlike the other contemporary somatic interventions, the Food and Drug Administration (FDA) never approved ECT for clinical use since such regulations came into effect much later. The current indications, possible adverse effects, and recommendations for treatment procedures have been summarized in a task force report published by the American Psychiatric Association Committee on ECT (1990). ECT has a proven efficacy in a variety of neuropsychiatric conditions such as in depression (including psychotic depression), mania, schizophrenia and neuroleptic malignant syndrome.

The primary use for ECT is in treating depression when pharmacotherapy has failed or has not been tolerated. It has response rates reported in the range of 80 to 90 percent as a first-line treatment, and in the range of 50 to 60 percent for patients who have not responded to 1 or more trials of treatment with antidepressant drugs (Sackeim et al., 2002b). Right unilateral (UL) ECT has traditionally been thought to be less efficacious than bilateral (BL) ECT but with less cognitive side effects. In the last decade, however, high-intensity UL ECT [with 6 times (Sackeim et al., 2000) or 8 to 12 times (McCall et al., 2002) the initial seizure threshold] have proven to equal BL ECT with less cognitive side effects.

The FDA-approved devices in the United States are limited to 576 milliCoulombs (mC), which limits the clinical application of suprathreshold intensities. Higher intensities lead to higher rates of cognitive impairment. Researchers at Columbia University are investigating changing the electrical pulse being given with ECT. Namely, they are stimulating with ultrabrief waveforms, a closer pulse to brain physiology, which may help decrease cognitive side effects (Sackeim et al., 2002c).

Although an effective treatment for getting a person out of an acute depressive episode, Sackeim et al. (2002a) have demonstrated that most depressed subjects who respond to ECT will require some sort of maintenance therapy. Even with adequate pharmacotherapy, 39 percent of patients will relapse within 6 months. The use of intermittent ECT for continuation (C-ECT) or maintenance treatment may also be considered. Retrospective reports show noticeable functional and socioeconomic benefits with C-ECT. Prospective controlled studies are underway.

A limiting factor to clinical response with ECT, which now holds for most antidepressant therapies (including TMS and VNS), is a history of treatment resistance or the number of prior treatment failures (Sackeim et al., 1992). Comorbid personality disorders are associated with a limited response as is outpatient ECT treatment.

In addition to depression, ECT has also been applied successfully in mania (Milstein et al., 1987) and schizophrenia (Tharyan et al., 2002). The concomitant use of neuroleptics has been found beneficial in some cases. Some are investigating whether ECT plays a neuroprotective role and leads to better prognosis if applied early in the course of illness, but this is currently unclear.

Electroconvulsive therapy has also been administered to treat psychiatric sequelae of a number of neurological disorders including depression secondary to a cerebral vascular accident, Parkinson disease, epilepsy and status epilepticus, multiple sclerosis, Huntington disease, tardive dyskinesia, and a few others (McDonald et al., 2002). Of these other disorders, the American Psychiatric Association has approved ECT only for Parkinson's disease and epilepsy although the clinical effects may not be long lived.

The ECT mechanisms of action have not been fully worked out (see Chapter 8). It was initially believed that a seizure with adequate quality and duration (a minimum of 25 sec) would reach into the diencephalic brain structures and stimulate the hypothalamic-pituitary-adrenal (HPA) axis (Abrams et al., 1976). This in turn would release neuropeptides such as adreno-cortico-trophic hormone (ACTH), thyrotropin releasing hormone (TRH), prolactin, vasopressin, and oxytocin (Nemeroff et al., 1991; Nakajima et al., 1989; Mathe et al., 1991). Contrary to this theory, parietal lead placement does not treat depression despite a surge in prolactin and oxytocin. Another old theory is that postictal delirium correlates with efficacy. This theory has also been abandoned.

It is now apparent that site of origination of the seizure is important in ECT treatment. Temporo-parietal lead placement, for example, does not treat depression (Bailine et al., 2001). Targeting a functional mood-regulating network (in the case of antidepressant effect) appears crucial to the efficacy of the procedure. Bilateral (BL) and right unilateral (UL) frontal placements are now the norm. More recently, informed by imaging work implicating the lateral and medial prefrontal cortex in mood regulation, researchers have applied the electrodes medially (approximately on the forehead above each eye) in a procedure labeled bifrontal ECT (BF). BF ECT has shown equal efficacy to BL ECT (both given at 1.5 times the seizure threshold), with BF having a slight cognitive/memory advantage as the electric current may spare the temporal lobes where the hippocampus is located (Bailine et al., 2002).

Some researchers have pointed out that the seizure itself is important in ECT's antidepressant effect (Krystal, 1998) since a failure to induce one is nontherapeutic. However, as will be developed below, data from TMS and VNS may argue against this principle. One working theory of the importance of seizures in ECT's antidepressant effect focuses on the dynamic interplay between the ictal and postictal phases. The placement of electrodes for inducing of a seizure, the ictal duration, intensity (high-voltage spikes and waves), and coherence in ictal-EEG between right and left hemisphere are all important factors in ECT's efficacy (Fink et al., 1982; McCall et al., 1995). So are the stimulated compensatory mechanisms for stopping the seizure. A greater suppression of the postictal EEG has been shown to be a key factor. Fink and colleagues demonstrated a relationship between frontal delta activity and response to treatment (Fink, 1984a). Neuroimaging studies have also shed light on this dynamic interplay (Rosenberg et al., 1988; Nobler et al., 1999). Studies have shown an increase in cerebral blood flow (CBF) up to 300 percent of baseline values and in cerebral metabolic rate (CMR) up to 200 percent during the ictal period. In contrast, these measures decrease postictally (Nobler et al., 2001). In imaging studies, it has been found that the degree of prefrontal deactivation following ECT correlated with improvement. Even when imaged 2 months following ECT, the inverse correlation between frontal region low CBF and clinical improvement remains. This may appear counterintuitive as Nobler et al. (1999) showed that in a depressed untreated cohort, the CBF in anterior and deeper limbic regions is relatively lower than it is in healthy matched controls. This finding has now been replicated in many studies. The role of this shutdown effect in regulating mood remains to be determined.

Another theory by which ECT has been proposed to work is the anticonvulsant hypothesis (Post et al., 1986). It posits that enhanced transmission of inhibitory neurotransmitters [gamma-aminobutyric acid (GABA) and endogenous opioids] constitutes the essential elements of ECT's therapeutic effect in mood disorders. However, how the anticonvulsant properties of ECT relate to the mechanisms of action of antidepressant drugs is still unknown.

MAGNETIC SEIZURE THERAPY

If the axiom that a seizure is necessary to obtain antidepressant effects holds true, the current mode of seizure induction needs to improve. The retrograde/anterograde amnesia due to nonintended passage of electricity through the hippocampus limits the widespread use of ECT. ECT research has gone through many refinements including electrode placements, intensity of stimulation, and waveforms applied. Current research in brief and ultrabrief pulses is an effort to increase the efficacy and decrease the cognitive impairment (Sackeim et al., 2002c). Another line of research aimed at delivering ECT more focally and reducing cognitive side effects uses magnetic fields rather than electric fields to induce seizures. Control over intracerebral current density and its spatial distribution (although improved with anterior electrode placement to target prefrontal and closely related subcortical networks) can be achieved using high oscillating magnetic fields (Lisanby et al., 2001b). Unlike electricity, magnetic fields pass unimpeded through skull and soft tissue and can be applied more focally than electricity. Magnetic convulsive therapy may offer the possibility of fewer cognitive side effects and perhaps an equal therapeutic efficacy to ECT.

It took over 10 years for researchers at Columbia University to develop such a technology (Sackeim, personal communication, May 2001). Lisanby and Sackeim custom-designed a transcranial magnetic stimulator (TMS) that can deliver fast trains of four times the electromyographic threshold and succeeded in inducing generalized seizures in nonhuman primates. Commercially available TMS machines have shorter pulse width and lower charging capacity and were unsuccessful in reproducibly inducing seizures (George et al., 1999) [see TMS section for more technical details and the safety implication for repetitive TMS (rTMS)]. Lisanby and Sackeim proposed the following: "The enhanced control over dosage and focality achieved with rTMS may offer the capacity to focus seizure induction in the prefrontal cortex, thereby improving the efficacy and limiting the cognitive side effects due to medial temporal lobe stimulation."

Lisanby and colleagues, working with Dr. Thomas Schlaepfer in Berne, Switzerland, applied this technology to induce four separate magnetically induced seizures in a depressed patient under general anesthesia (Lisanby et al., 2001b). The trains of stimulation were delivered at 40 Hz, 100 percent of maximal stimulator output (40 percent greater than commercially available TMS), administered for 4 sec. Although the researchers reported an improvement in depressive symptoms, the role of this method as a potential treatment for various neuropsychiatric conditions (including depression) remains to be proven.

As a first step, and under special Investigational Device Exemption (IDE) from the FDA, the safety and side effects of MST are currently being tested. It will first be tried in depressed patients who are undergoing a regular course of ECT, and then it will be tested as a stand-alone procedure. Clinical trials will likely follow. Compared with ECT, MST has the theoretical ability to be more circuit-based in that the region of brain where the seizure initiates can be more focally activated. However, as a potential therapy, this technique still depends on causing a generalized seizure and requires repeated episodes of general anesthesia. The other forms of device-based therapies do not rely on seizures and are thus theoretically less toxic. Whether a generalized seizure is required for brain stimulation technology to have its antidepressant effect has been a matter of intense debate. As discussed in subsequent sections, data from TMS (Nahas et al., 2001a; McNamara et al., 2001) and perhaps VNS (Rush et al., 2000) suggest that some forms of neural stimulation can treat depression without invoking generalized seizures, which are required with ECT.

TRANSCRANIAL MAGNETIC STIMULATION

Transcranial magnetic stimulation is a technology that has been developed to noninvasively activate nerve cells through the scalp (Barker et al., 1985). For example, if a single TMS pulse is applied over the "thumb area" of the motor cortex, it will induce a movement in the contralateral thumb. A unique aspect of TMS is its relative safety, ease of application, and the awake and interactive state of the subject being stimulated (Nahas et al., 2000a). The major side effect is unwarranted seizures, which have been absent since the adoption in 1998 of the International Workshop in the safety of repetitive pulse of TMS (rTMS) guidelines (Wassermann, 1998). TMS has been used as a neuroscience tool to study brain localization, brain connectivity, and cortical excitability in relation to other parameters such as peripheral electromyogram (EMG), electroencephalogram (EEG), blood flow, neurotransmitters, or the modulating effects of central nervous system (CNS) drugs (Epstein et al., 1996; Edgley et al., 1990; Amassian, 1993; Grafman et al., 1999; George et al., 1996b; Pascual-Leone et al., 1996; Martin et al., 1997; Nedjat et al., 1998; Mosimann et al., 2000). TMS has also found use as a neurophysiologic diagnostic tool and as a potential therapy for neuropsychiatric conditions. Here, we will focus on TMS as a somatic intervention for therapeutic purposes. Investigators are now using rTMS over the prefrontal regions to treat depression and are exploring other neuropsychiatric applications (George et al., 1999a).

Transcranial magnetic stimulation is not a new idea. In 1896, the French engineer Arsenne d'Arsonval applied TMS over the retina and induced phosphenes. In 1910. Pollacsek and Beer filed a patent in Vienna to use magnetic stimulation for the treatment of depression. However, it wasn't until the 1990s that the technology became sufficiently developed to allow induced electromagnetic fields that caused cortical neuron depolarization. TMS relies on Faraday's law of electromagnetic induction (Bohning, 1999). The TMS capacitor discharges high-amplitude electric current in the TMS coil and in turn generates a magnetic field, up to 20,000 times that of the earth, which passes unimpeded and very focally through the scalp. The magnetic field then induces a secondary electric field in the brain. In effect, the magnetic field gets converted to the electrochemical energy that directly depolarizes superficial neurons (at a maximum depth of 2 mm) and indirectly influences pathways to which these neurons connect.

Thus, TMS can affect cells at some distance from the stimulation site through transynaptic connections, as demonstrated with functional imaging studies (Paus et al., 1997; Kimbrell et al., 1997; Bohning et al., 1998). Because the induced electric field is parallel to the scalp, myelinated axons with a bend at the junction between gray and white matter are the primary candidates for depolarization with TMS.

Currently, TMS coils follow one of 2 basic designs (Bohning, 1999). They can be either round and generate a diffuse ring of magnetic field or a Figure 8 coil in which the summation of the 2 round coils is greatest at the center. This latter design allows a more focal stimulation. Single TMS pulses can produce isolated excitatory and inhibitory events in nerve pathways such as the corticospinal system. Since TMS applied to the motor cortex can readily induce a contralateral thumb movement, the intensity needed to generate 5 movements out of 10 trials is defined as *motor threshold* (MT). TMS pulses can also be delivered in pairs, a few milliseconds apart (paired-pulse TMS), to probe cortical excitability by examining the influence of a first pulse onto the effect of a second pulse on motor evoked potentials (MEPs) (Ziemann et al., 2000). Finally, trains of repetitive TMS (or rTMS) are postulated to modulate the neuronal activity both distally and at the site of stimulation. TMS thus offers the advantage of noninvasively modulating a neuronal network without the limitations of drug interactions and side effects seen with psychotropic drugs nor the need for general anesthesia necessary in ECT and MST (George et al., 1996a).

In the early 1990s the first applications of rTMS to treat depression emerged independently in the United States, Austria, and Israel. The nearly simultaneous publications that resulted form these efforts reported the initial attempts at treating depression using nonfocal stimulation with a round TMS coil held over the vertex (Hoflich et al., 1993; Grisaru et al., 1994; Kolbinger et al., 1995). Results were promising but inconclusive. Based on functional imaging evidence that showed a predominance of hypofrontality in depression, as well as data that prefrontal changes in rCBF predicted ECT response, George and Wassermann proposed that dorsolateral prefrontal cortex (DLPFC) stimulation might have a more powerful antidepressant effect (George et al., 1994). It was their impression in pilot work that a session of left DLPFC TMS temporarily improved mood in depressed subjects, whereas right DLPFC made them dysphoric. They published their first attempt using an open design in 1995 (George et al., 1995). All of the TMS studies since then have followed that lead, utilizing prefrontal stimulation [both left (Pascual-Leone et al., 1994; Berman et al., 2000; Padberg et al., 1998; Loo et al., 1999; George et al., 2000, Nahas et al. 2003). and right (Klein et al., 1999)].

The method for prefrontal localization in the George et al. (1995) article was defined as 5 cm forward and in a parasagittal plane from the optimal spot for producing contralateral thumb movement. This later became the standard applied rule although more recently the stereotactic navigation system demonstrated the limitation of this general rule in targeting Brodmann area 9 or 46 in most subjects (Herwig et al., 2002). If focality and targeted stimulation of these two areas are necessary for the antidepressant effect of rTMS, then this rule may account for the limited response rates seen so far in some clinical trials.

Recently, there have been four independent meta-analyses with different statistical methods investigating the acute antidepressant effect of rTMS (Fig. 17.1). Three found a moderate effect and clear significance from sham treatment (Burt et al., 2002; McNamara et al., 2001; Holtzheimer et al., 2001), whereas one using the Cochrane

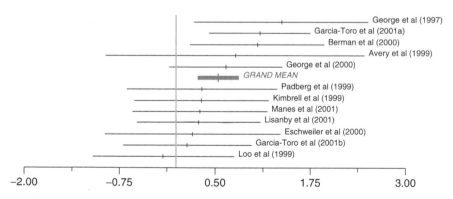

Figure 17.1. Forrest plot of Hedges' d effect size and 95% confidence intervals for left prefrontal rTMS treatment of depression. The 12 double-blind sham-controlled treatment trials of left prefrontal repetitive transcranial magnetic stimulation are graphed. The vertical line indicates the study's Hedges' d treatment effect size. The horizontal lines indicate the 95% confidence intervals of the treatment effect using nonparametrical variances. The grand mean effect is clearly significant with the confidence interval not including zero.

method concluded otherwise (Martin et al., 2002), even though researchers noticed positive effects after 2 weeks of fast left and slow right prefrontal TMS. Kozel and George (2002) identified and limited their meta-analysis to rTMS of left prefrontal cortex, first arms of randomization in sham-controlled studies of 2 weeks duration, and concluded that left prefrontal rTMS has an acute antidepressant treatment with clinically significant effects.

The large variance in placebo response across the sham-controlled TMS studies (the large variance in sham treatments was not explained at any point earlier) may be due to different cohorts across studies, only the subject (not the investigator) being blind to the treatment cell or variability in sham techniques. Concerning sham technique, some researchers hold the coil at a 45° or 90° angle with one lateral or anterior edge of the coil touching the scalp. This directs most of the magnetic field away from the brain, but it may still induce electric fields and possibly stimulate brain tissue (Lisanby et al., 1998; Loo et al., 2000). This shortcoming of current TMS research is being addressed with more sophisticated sham coils and more elaborate study designs in which TMS administrators remain masked to the randomization along with the patient. To date, four studies have shown no significant difference between TMS and sham treatment, two of these were designed with TMS as an add-on to a serotonin reuptake inhibitor treatment (Loo et al., 1999; Manes et al., 2001; Lisanby et al., 2001a; Garcia-Toro et al., 2001).

Because both TMS and ECT utilize electricity to induce electric currents in the brain, it has been tempting to compare them. There are now three published reports (Grunhaus et al., 2000, Janicak et al., 2002, Pridmore et al., 2000) that show equal efficacy for these techniques in the nonpsychotic depressed population. It is worthwhile to mention that these studies have mostly used TMS in longer trials (up to 20 days) than previously cited studies (maximum 10 days of treatment). This may well account for the higher response rate along with the possibility of a more homogenously studied population. Grunhaus et al. (2000) found that up to 4 weeks of daily fast left DLPFC rTMS among nonpsychotic patients was equivalent in efficacy to ECT, though ECT showed a better effect among psychotically depressed patients. The TMS cohort showed a 26 percent relapse rate, similar to ECT, in a naturalistic follow-up at 6 months (Dannon et al., 2002). (Note: Our group is, in fact, investigating TMS as maintenance treatment with either once per week session or 5 successive daily sessions per month.) In an investigation of combined treatments, Pridmore et al. (2000) studied 22 outpatients with either left unilateral ECT for 2 weeks or one ECT per week followed by 4 days of left prefrontal rTMS. At the end of 2 weeks, the two cohorts showed equal efficacy, with an average 75 percent drop in Hamilton Depression Rating Scale (HDRS). In this design, it appears that TMS may not interfere with ECT mechanisms and may be complimentary. Janicak et al. (2002) randomized 22 depressed adults to receive either 12 bilateral ECT treatments or 20 TMS sessions over 4 weeks, after which nonresponders were given the option to crossover to the other condition. Both groups showed equal efficacy (average drop of HAM-D was 65 percent), number of responders (about 67 percent of subjects with improvement greater then 50 percent), and time of antidepressant onset (between the second and third week). Reported subjective cognitive impairment was greater for the ECT groups than TMS.

These clinical studies administered stimulation intensity in the range of 80 to 110 percent of MT (the amount of TMS to generate thumb movement). As a group, they suggest that higher intensity stimulation may be more effective in treating depression, perhaps through maximizing energy delivery to the cortex. Blood flow changes induced by different TMS intensities over the prefrontal cortex in healthy subjects, using TMS interleaved with functional MRI (fMRI) support this notion (Nahas et al., 2000b). Left prefrontal stimulation at 100 percent and 120 percent MT produced a greater blood flow response under the coil than did 80 percent MT. At 120 percent MT, left prefrontal stimulation induces increased activity in ipsilateral insula. Bohning et al. (1998) showed similar findings over motor cortex with greater brain activity at 110 percent MT than 80 percent MT (Fig. 17.2).

A closer look at the data in depression trials suggests that a greater number of stimulation sessions is also indicative of greater response. All the ECT versus TMS studies have administered treatments for a period of greater than 2 weeks. Therefore,

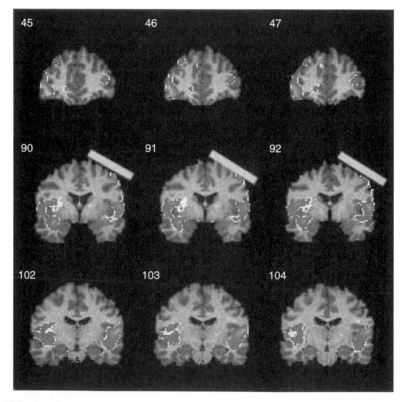

Figure 17.2. Probing of prefrontal/limbic connection using interleaved TMS/fMRI in five healthy adults. 1 Hz left prefrontal TMS (green bar) at 120% MT causes changes in left dorsolateral prefrontal cortex (site of stimulation), right orbitofrontal, bilateral auditory cortex, and right anterior temporal pole. See ftp site for color image.

the next generation of TMS studies is looking at maximizing both intensity and duration of treatment in order to increase effect size and enhance the clinical applicability of antidepressant effects. Additionally, our group has also shown that a greater distance from the skull to prefrontal cortex requires a higher stimulation intensity to produce an effect. Skull to prefrontal cortex distance increases with age at a greater ratio than distance to motor cortex so that using the MT to calculate prefrontal stimulation intensity, as is commonly done, may be faulty especially in the elderly (McConnell et al., 2001). Given the initial poor response in depressed elderly treated with TMS and the knowledge that the magnetic fields drop off logarithmically, Daryl Bohning in our group developed a formula to adjust the intensity of prefrontal delivered stimulation based on the motor threshold, distance from scalp to prefrontal cortex, and distance from scalp to motor cortex (Bohning, 1999)[1] By applying this customized delivery based on individual MRI scans, we have shown an improved depression response rate in the elderly.

The antidepressant mechanisms of action of TMS are still unknown. Nonfocal rTMS has been reported to induce ECT-like changes in rat brain monoamines, beta-adrenergic receptor-binding down-regulation, and astroglial gene expression up-regulation (Fleischmann et al., 1996; Ben-Sachar et al., 1997; Fujiki et al., 1997). More recently, Post and Keck (2001) have completed a series of studies using focal TMS in rat models. They modeled the TMS fields coupled to brain morphology to simulate comparable conditions in which focal TMS is applied in humans. They largely replicated earlier nonfocal TMS animal studies. There is now accumulating evidence that TMS also exerts a neuroprotective antioxidative effect and increases the intrahippocampal expression of brain-derived neurotrophic factor (BDNF) and cholecystokinin (CCK) (Post et al., 1999).

In humans, prefrontal rTMS can influence sleep by increasing rapid eyes movement (REM) latency and prolonging the non-REM-REM cycle (Cohrs et al., 1998). Left DLPFC TMS has been shown to increase peripheral thyroid stimulation hormone (TSH) levels in depressed subjects (Szuba et al., 1999; George et al., 1996b), as shown in mood induction studies, and healthy young adults, as shown in sleep studies (Cohrs et al., 1998). This finding raises the intriguing possibility that TMS may cause mood or antidepressant changes through effects of circulating hormones and the HPA axis. Functional neuroimaging studies before and after several left prefrontal TMS sessions administered to depressed subjects support the notion that left prefrontal stimulation shows local and distant effects, such as in the limbic system (mainly, the cingulate and amygdala) (Teneback et al., 1999; Nahas et al., 2001b; Paus, 2001).

To date, the one strong prognosticator of poor response is the degree of treatment resistance. Other potential prognosticators of response rate are late-onset depression

---

[1]Delivered intensity (percent MT) = MP($-0.36 \times d_{PC}$))/(exp($-0.36 \times d_{MC}$)) where d_{PC} is the measured MRI distance (in millimeters) from the scalp to the prefrontal cortex, and d_{MC} is the distance for motor cortex. This formula is based on Daryl Bohning's previous measurements of TMS magnetic fields with MRI phase maps. It assumes that the effective stimulation intensity is proportional to the magnetic field measured at the center of the coil and has the same rate of exponential decrease with distance (Bohning personall communication).

or vascular depression, baseline metabolic activity of prefrontal cortex (Speer et al., 1999), and lower or higher degree of cortical excitability (Maeda et al., 2002).

Although a number of clinical rTMS studies in depressed subjects have been published in the last 2 years with a modest but consistent effect size, fewer focused on schizophrenia. Geller et al. (1997) were perhaps the first to use TMS of the prefrontal cortex to study mood changes in schizophrenic patients and suggested that it could modulate schizophrenic symptoms. Slow and fast prefrontal rTMS has been tested for treatment of positive, negative, and/or mood symptoms with mixed results (Rollnik et al., 2000; Nahas et al., 1999). Hoffman et al. (2000) hypothesized that unlike the excitatory effect of fast stimulation, slow frequency rTMS would have inhibitory effects on brain activity. They demonstrated that slow temporal rTMS for 4 days significantly decreased auditory hallucinations compared to sham. These results were replicated in a group of nine subjects (d'Alfonso et al., 2002), although other labs have tried and have not been able to replicate these findings (K. Ebmeir, personal communication, Philadelphia, 5/22/02).

Obsessive-compulsive disorder (OCD) (Baxter, 1990) and Parkinson's disease have fairly well defined functional neurocircuitry. Yet, so far, TMS therapeutic investigations have yielded very limited and preliminary results (Greenberg et al., 1997). Potential uses of TMS to study and treat posttraumatic stress disorder (PTSD) and Tourette's disorder also warrant further research. All clinical investigations will benefit from improved sham applications to both investigator and study subject (Kosel et al., 2002).

VAGUS NERVE STIMULATION

The vagus nerve is classically described as the "wandering nerve." It sends signals from the central nervous system to control the peripheral cardiovascular, respiratory, and gastrointestinal systems. However 80 percent of its fibers are afferent, carrying information from the viscera back to the brain (Foley et al., 1937). The fibers first enter the midbrain at the nucleus tractus solitarius (NTS) level. From the midbrain, they either loop back out to the periphery in a reflex arc, connect to the reticular activating system, or reach the parabrachial nucleus (PB) and its connections to the NTS, raphe nucleus (RN), locus ceruleus (LC), the thalamus, paralimbic, limbic, and cortical regions. It is through this route that vagus nerve stimulation (VNS) modulates brain function. In this context it is noteworthy that yoga and deep breathing (primarily regulated by the 10th cranial nerve) are clearly associated with CNS effects (Loo et al., 1999). This neuroanatomy may be important in understanding how VNS treats epilepsy and potentially treats depression.

Over the past century, the peripheral modulation of the vagus showed changes in CNS neuronal activity (Maclean, 1990; Chase et al., 1966; Van Bockstaele et al., 1999). The contemporary history of VNS started in 1985, when Jake Zabara first experimented and later demonstrated the anticonvulsant action of VNS on experimental seizures in dogs during and after the stimulation periods (Zabara, 1992). These lasting beneficial effects meant that residual changes in neurotransmitters or perhaps a certain degree of neuronal plasticity was facilitated, which proved useful in controlling the seizures beyond the immediate stimulation. These observations led to the development of a NeuroCybernetic Prosthesis (NCP system) and an expanding amount of research, first in different types of seizure disorders (Penry et al., 1990) and later in other neuropsychiatric conditions such as depression (Rush et al., 2000).

The NCP is a pacemaker-like generator implanted in the anterior chest wall. It is linked to leads wrapped around the cervical portion of the left vagus nerve and is easily programmable with an external wand to deliver mild electrical stimulation at a preset intensity, duration, pulse width, and duty cycle. The battery life averages 8 to 10 years, making VNS an advantageous long-term treatment modality with 100 percent compliance. The most critical part of the one-hour-long implantation procedure is the dissection of the vagus nerve from the carotid artery. The surgical complications are more related to the risks of anesthesia than to rare infections or trauma to the vagus nerve and its branches. Vocal chord paralysis may occur if the recurrent laryngeal nerve is damaged. A few cases of arrythmias have been reported at the initial onset of the stimulation in the operating room without any long-term consequences. The American Academy of Neurology concluded that VNS for epilepsy is both "effective and safe" without significant gastrointestinal or cardiac side effects (Schachter et al., 1998a) based on studies in both children (Nagarajan et al., 2002) and adults (Schachter et al., 1998b). The most common side effect has been voice alteration or hoarseness, generally mild and related to the intensity of the output current. The mean overall decline of seizure frequency is about 25 to 30 percent, compared to baseline (Morris et al., 1999). Some patients (up to at least 10 percent) can be controlled solely with VNS with termination of all anticonvulsant medications, but the majority continues with concomitant pharmacotherapy, albeit often following a more simplified regimen.

The next phase of VNS therapy emerged when studies in epilepsy began to offer clinical and later prospective evidence that VNS improved mood independently from seizure control (Elger et al., 2000; Harden et al., 2000). Several additional factors led to the exploration of VNS for treating depression: the known neuroanatomy of the vagus, the role of anticonvulsants in treating mood disorders (Post, 1990), a positron emission tomography (PET) study by Henry et al. (1998) showing brain activity changes in limbic regions attributed to VNS, and studies showing that modulating the locus ceruleus neurotransmitters homeostasis played a crucial role in the therapeutic effects of this method (Walker et al., 1999). The first implant for this indication was performed in 1998, at the Medical University of South Carolina. This group of researchers joined by University of Texas Southwestern in Dallas, Columbia University in New York, and Baylor College of Medicine in Houston led an initial open-label pilot study of VNS in 60 adult outpatients with severe, nonpsychotic, treatment-resistant major depressive episode. This study reported a 30.5 percent response rate after 8 weeks of VNS therapy, with a 50 percent reduction in baseline HDRS 28-item. In this medication-resistant group, there was a 15.3 percent complete remission rate (exit HDRS28 <10) (Rush et al., 2000). A history of treatment resistance and the amount of concurrent antidepressant treatment during the acute VNS trial predicted a poorer VNS outcome (Sackeim et al., 2001). An open, naturalistic follow-up study (Marangell et al., 2002) with an additional 9 months of long-term VNS treatment and changes in psychotropic medications showed an improved response rate from 30.5 percent to 45 percent. The remission rate significantly increased to 29 percent at one year. This open-label study provided important evidence that VNS is both a feasible and safe procedure in depressed subjects. It revealed the antidepressant effect size needed to design larger double-blind pivotal studies. Based on these data, VNS has been approved as a treatment for depression in western Europe (except the United Kingdom) and in Canada but is still considered experimental by the U.S. FDA.

To overcome the limits of these open design studies, a multisite randomized, sham-controlled study was necessary. The logistics imposed by such design were unlike most pharmacological trials. VNS can cause voice alterations, which could give away the blind. Research teams were divided into blinded raters and unblinded programmers. At each site visit, subjects had to be seen by the programmer first, who would turn off the device before allowing the blinded rating group to interact with the subjects. These steps were quasi-choreographed and applied equally to both active and placebo phases to maximize the integrity of the blind. In sum, 235 subjects with moderate to severe refractory depressive episode were enrolled. They were held constant on their psychotropic medications 1 month prior to implant and for the duration of the initial acute phase. This initial phase was 12 weeks long, after which placebo nonresponders were crossed over to active stimulation. The initial report failed to show a statistically significant difference in 3 month response with active VNS (15 percent) compared to the sham group (10 percent). This may have been in part due to an underpowering of the study and a more severely ill enrolled cohort compared to what had been originally designed and expected. In addition, the average intensity of stimulation in this multicenter double-blind study is less than the one generally seen in epilepsy or initial depression study.

Like in epilepsy, the predictive factors for positive outcome or guidelines for stimulation parameters have not yet been established (Koo et al., 2001), but an effort is underway to maximally increase the intensity of stimulation in nonresponders. Despite the negative short-term results, the therapeutic role of VNS is still unfolding. As in the open study, a gradual and steady response is being noticed. By following the first 36 implanted subjects in an open-label fashion for an additional 9 months, where both pharmacological and parameter dosing changes have been made, their response rate has increased to 44 percent and appears to be sustained. Data at one year follow-up for all 235 subjects are not yet available. Clinical observations also suggest that some of the responders appear to stay in remission longer than they originally did with psychotropic medications alone. If this holds true, this will be a great departure from traditional antidepressant treatments (including ECT) and would greatly add to our knowledge of the pathophysiology of the illness.

The exact mechanisms of action of VNS are still unknown. Human cerebrospinal fluid (CSF) studies in epilepsy patients reveal an increase in 5-hydroxyindole acetic acid (5-HIAA), homovanillic acid (HVA) and GABA and a decrease in glutamate after 3 months of treatment (Ben-Menachem et al., 1995). VNS causes increases in HVA in depressed subjects and the increase in CSF norepinephrine may predict a better response to treatment. Patients with high corticotropin releasing factor (CRF) or low 5-HIAA did not show a strong antidepressant effect (Carpenter et al., 2002).

Sleep studies show a normalization of EEG rhythm patterns. Functional brain imaging studies demonstrate that VNS causes immediate and longer-term changes in brain regions with vagus innervations and implicated in neuropsychiatric disorders. These include the thalamus, cerebellum, orbitofrontal cortex, limbic system, hypothalamus, and medulla (Henry et al., 1998, 1999). Our group has succeeded in performing blood oxygen level dependent (BOLD) fMRI studies in depressed patients implanted with VNS generators (Bohning et al., 2001; Lomarev et al., 2002). The results show that VNS activates many anterior paralimbic regions, in a dose-dependent fashion, that changes over time. It appears as if the chronic stimulation dynamically and differentially modulates prefrontal/limbic circuitry. The net effect over 10 weeks of VNS treatment in depressed patients appears to be a gradual deactivation of the limbic regions (Nahas et al., 2002a). It is still unclear whether these changes are frequency or intensity dependent. Because of the ability to image the immediate effect of VNS on brain activity, the fMRI technique offers a unique opportunity to do sophisticated parametric studies and is likely to inform us about VNS dosing. Ultimately, VNS/fMRI may also be used to individually determine the best stimulation parameters to help a particular patient (Fig. 17.3).

Before its widespread use, and given the initial high cost of the implant and surgical procedure, efforts are underway to document whether VNS is both efficacious and cost effective in the long term for patients with depression. Other VNS open trials are underway in anxiety disorders (PTSD, panic disorder, and OCD), in the early stages of Alzheimer disease, rapid cycling bipolar disorder, and migraine headaches. In a related venue, subdiaphragmatic bilateral VNS is being tested in morbid obesity as it may modulate satiety signals.

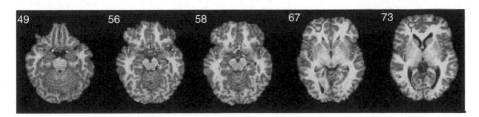

Figure 17.3. Vagus nerve stimulation (VNS)-induced regional cerebral activity by functional magnetic resonance imaging (fMRI). Nine subjects with depression who, on average, had the device implanted for 10.1 months. Immediately before the scan, the patient's VNS device was reprogrammed to a 7 sec on, 108 sec off stimulation cycle. The VNS frequency setting was 20 Hz, the pulse width was 500 ms, and the current settings, which were kept at the patient's treatment level setting, ranged from 0.5 to 1.25 mA (mean 0.54). Data were acquired at rest, with the VNS device on for 7 sec, acute VNS, for only 7 sec activated many brain regions including the orbitofrontal and parieto-occipital cortex bilaterally, the left temporal cortex, the hypothalamus, and the left amygdala. See ftp site for color image.

DEEP BRAIN STIMULATION

In 1948, Pool performed a neurosurgical implant of a silver electrode in the caudate nucleus in an attempt to treat a woman with depression and anorexia (Pool, 1954). In subsequent years, developments occurred in treating neurological disorders such as chronic pain, refractory movement disorder, and epilepsy. The technological advancements in stereotactic neurosurgery and the need for reversible targeted lesions facilitated the emergence of deep brain stimulation (DBS) as an alternative to surgical lesions in the treatment of various neurological disorders (see below). As opposed to epidural and subdural surface electrodes, DBS involves the placement of multicontact electrodes in subcortical regions such as the thalamus, basal ganglia, or white matter tracts (Rezai et al., 1999). The surgeon drills burr holes under local anesthesia and places the electrodes, guided by precise landmarking. The subject is typically awake during the surgery and is also instrumental in guiding the final positioning of the electrodes. For instance, in a case of essential tremor, where initial electrode guidance is via stereotactic coordinates and changes in neuronal firing patterns as probes are lowered, the true evidence that a subthalamic target is reached is when the electrodes are activated and the tremor stops. Typically in a second surgical phase, the surgeon places the pacemaker subdermally in the chest wall and connects it to the electrodes in the brain. An intracerebral hemorrhage is reported in 2 to 4 percent of the cases with a mortality rate up to 1.6 percent. Other complications include hematomas, infections, especially around the hardware, sometimes leading to permanent neurological sequelae.

The mechanisms of action of DBS are not known (Benazzouz et al., 2000; Ashby et al., 2000). One prevailing hypothesis stipulates that high-frequency stimulations (>100 Hz) create a depolarization blockade of neurons or axonal tracts. This continuous stimulation effectively mimics a lesion but is reversible, which makes this approach especially appealing since comparative studies with irreversible surgical lesions are quite favorable. Researchers have also found supportive evidence to suggest that DBS may act by reducing the activity of cells (and not block them), suggesting that the effect is mediated by stimulation of local GABAergic axon terminals. A third possibility may be re-establishing normal patterns of temporal activity and synchronization within the basal ganglia in movement disorders (Grill, 1999).

Deep brain stimulation is now routinely performed for refractory Parkinson's disease (PD), essential tremor, intention tremor and various chronic pain syndromes. There are three main targets used to treat PD: ventrolateral thalamus (VL), globus pallidus internus (GPi), and subthalamic nucleus (STN) (Limousin et al., 1998). The FDA has now clinically approved all three sites. The detailed knowledge of the motor circuitry and the pathophysiology of PD are an achievement for researchers in psychiatric disorders to emulate. Since their original descriptions by Alexander and DeLong in the mid-1980s, the cortico-basal-ganglio-thalamic loops have offered a framework for such endeavors (Alexander et al., 1986). In PD, there are two overlapping loops, the motor and the associative. The loss of dopaminergic input to the striatum due to substantia nigral degeneration results in dysregulation in basal ganglia functions. The net effect is excessive inhibitory influence of the GPi on the ventralis and ventralis anterior thalamic nuclei. Stimulating the STN or GPi with DBS results in a diminution of the inhibitory influence and restoration of fluid movement.

By comparison, the functional neuroanatomic circuits of the psychiatric illnesses are not as well understood. This makes the specific targeting of DBS problematic. Hence, one of the disorders more readily evaluated for such a treatment is OCD. The neuronal architecture of the disorder is based on functional imaging studies, clinical similarities and genetic linkages between OCD and movement disorders. It implies a dysregulation in the basal ganglia/limbic striatal circuits that modulate neuronal activity in and between the posterior portions of the orbitofrontal cortex (OFC) and the dorso-medial thalamic nuclei (Baxter, 1990). Obsessive-compulsive symptoms may be linked to a decreased activity in the striato-pallido-thalamic loop or an abnormally increased drive in the orbito-fronto-thalamic loop. A modulation of these loops by stimulating or inhibiting the appropriate region could possibly restore normal behavior and alleviate the negative emotional charge associated with producing the behavior.

Given the success rate of gamma-knife lesions of the anterior limb of the internal capsule in OCD patients, Nuttin et al. (1999) reported a case series of four patients with long-standing treatment-resistant OCD where chronic electrical stimulation of the internal capsule was performed instead of a bilateral capsulotomy. In three of the subjects beneficial effects were observed. Ongoing open studies at Brown University and Cleveland Clinic are testing DBS of the anterior limb of the internal capsule in OCD. Subjects seem to show slow but significant improvements in obsessive-compulsive symptoms and also positive mood effects. Given the limited numbers of patients enrolled in these studies and the long-term course for expected benefits to be observed, these findings must be deemed encouraging but preliminary (Greenberg, personal communication, November 2002).

Bejjani et al. (1999) have published a dramatic case report of mood induction with DBS in a subject without any prior history of depression. When the electrodes, implanted slightly below the STN, were activated, the subject experienced a severe dysphoria that remitted when stimulation was interrupted. Although not therapeutic, this case illustrates a modulation of a mood-regulating network. With a better understanding of the mechanisms of action of DBS, one can imagine that the reverse effect may be obtained. Our group is currently studying the role of GPi and STN DBS in treatment of depression in Parkinson's disease subjects. This study is coupled with fMRI to better understand the local and distributed effects of such stimulation and how this may correlate with clinical symptoms. This therapy is still very experimental and probably several years away from any clinical applications in mood disorders.

PSYCHIATRIC NEUROSURGERY

Of all the somatic therapies in psychiatric practice today, psychiatric neurosurgery requires the most knowledge about functional neuroanatomy since it is the most radical and irreversible of all interventions. It was only in the last years of the 19th century that rational approaches to psychosurgery were first tried, pursuant to well-publicized clinical cases like Phineas Gage whose frontal lobe lesion in a mining accident showed that frontal lesions could alter a person's personality. In 1894, a Swiss surgeon named Burkhardt performed an operation to selectively destroy the frontal lobes of several psychotic patients in an effort to control their symptoms. Subsequently, Fulton and Jackobsen reported that frontal ablation lessened anxiety in chimpanzees. From these observations, Moniz (1937) argued that by severing the connections between different brain regions, one could force impulses and thoughts to "re-channel" and in effect, coax the brain to "reorganize".

This provisional conclusion about brain organization in the late 1930s launched frontal lobotomy as a treatment for psychiatric disorders. Overcrowded mental asylums and the use of highly morbid convulsive therapy at the time also aided the popularity of lobotomy. Moniz (1937) and Lima's first lesion technique was to inject alcohol in the bilateral frontal lobes of asylum patients. They reported "improvement" in 14 out of 20 subjects. They later developed the leucotomy (a tool to interrupt white matter tracts) and described a rather large surgical target in the frontal lobes. Moniz was the first psychiatrist to receive the Nobel prize in 1949 for his contributions in treating psychosis with leucotomy.

Walter Freeman and James Watts introduced the procedure to the United States. They modified it so the disconnection was carried out through bilateral burr holes placed in the inferior frontal region at the level of the coronal suture. The leucotomy spatula was introduced blindly and swept back and forth. Freeman later devised the so-called ice-pick transorbital leucotomy, performed typically on patients who were postictal from ECT. He inserted a sharp blade under the eyelid through the thin bone into the orbitofrontal lobe. Many of the patients were reported to be improved although a great number of them were observed to have become amotivational and to have lost their capacity to be emotional (McLardy et al., 1949). This crude intervention was zealously promoted by Freeman himself and is likely the source of many of the controversies and stigma surrounding neurosurgery for psychiatric conditions.

Currently, the practice of psychiatric neurosurgery is much more restricted and regulated. Candidates are evaluated by multidisciplinary teams and must meet stringent criteria for severe resistance to conventional multimodal therapies. The majority has either refractory OCD, anxiety, or mood disorders. Treatment of schizophrenia with this modality has fallen out of favor. Current surgical procedures are much more refined and specific in their targets. There are four distinct stereotactic approaches that continue to be used: cingulotomy, subcaudate tracheotomy, limbic leucotomy, and anterior capsulotomy. They are generally performed bilaterally and share similar complication and risks profiles. These include minor symptoms such as headaches, low-grade fever, confusion, and isolated seizures. The most serious complication (intracranial hemorrhages) is rare (0.4 percent in some cases). Mortality directly related to any of the procedures is very rare. Lethargy, personality, cognitive, and behavioral changes are more specific to each intervention.

The aim of a cingulotomy is to lesion the cingulate fasiculus with thermocoagulation approximately 2 to 2.5 cm posterior to the tip of frontal horns, 7 mm lateral to the midline and 1 mm above the ventricular roof. It is the most reported neurosurgical procedure for psychiatric disease in North America and likely the safest. Studies show a range of 30 to 60 percent of significant improvement with affective disorders demonstrating the highest rate of response and OCD the lowest (Tippin et al., 1982).

The goal of a subcaudate tractotomy is to interrupt the fibers from the orbitofrontal cortex to the thalamus. This intervention was designed to minimize cognitive and personality impairments. The target is the substantia innominata (white matter beneath the head of the caudate). The lesion is created with radioactive rods with a half-life of 68 hr. The target area lies at the antero-posterior level of the planum spenoidale, extending from 6 to 18 mm from the midline, being 20 mm long in an antero-posterior direction. Studies have shown significant relief in up to 45 percent of severely ill subjects. Affective disorders are more likely to respond, although OCD symptoms also improve (Hodgkiss et al., 1995).

Limbic leucotomy is a combination of the two previous procedures. Three 6-mm lesions are placed in the posterior inferior medial quadrant of each frontal lobe, along with two lesions in each cingulated gyrus. Results in OCD have shown up to 89 percent improvement up to 16 months postoperatively with improvement in cognitive functions in some patients.

Finally, the aim of anterior capsulotomy is to disconnect fronto-thalamic fibers as they pass through the anterior limb of the internal capsule, between the head of the caudate and putamen. One of the earlier indications for this procedure was schizophrenia, but this has fallen out of favor. Recent reports indicate greatest responses in OCD and depression. Interestingly, a mean 10 percent weight gain is common (Lippitz et al., 1999).

Clinical improvement with all four interventions is progressive over several months. Unfortunately, given the limited use of standardized rating scales across different sites and the open nature of these reports, it is hard to compare results. A recent review (Cosgrove et al., 1995) used the "much improved" clinical outcome measure and found that in OCD capsulotomy was 67 percent effective followed by limbic leucotomy (61 percent), cingulotomy (56 percent), and subcaudate tractotomy (50 percent). In mood disorders, limbic leucotomy was 78 percent effective, subcaudate tractotomy was 68 percent effective, cingulotomy was 65percent effective and finally anterior capsulotomy was 55 percent effective. With the advent of deep brain stimulation, all these areas are potential candidates for neuromodulation with "reversible lesions." Theoretically, one could expect double-blind controlled studies with lead-in sham arms where the implanted wires are not activated.

FUTURE DIRECTIONS

Treating neuropsychiatric conditions with somatic nonpharmacological approaches is rooted in early 20th-century exploration of the mind as a complex interplay of neuronal networks. Recent advancements in neuroscience, neuroimaging, and better understanding of brain functions allow for more empirically based and precisely targeted neuromodulations. The 21st century is likely to witness a refinement of the interventions highlighted in this chapter, as well as many new therapies (Apuzzo et al., 2002). The introduction of genetic information or genetically modified cells for functional augmentation, restoration or ablation is becoming feasible (Anderson, 1998; Breeze et al., 1995; Thompson et al., 1999). The discovery of CNS neurotrophic agents and the perfection of delivery systems could lead to implantable pumps and novel drug delivery devices (Kaplitt et al., 2002). Even neuroprostheses are now conceivable (Cleland, 1998; Tanaka, 1994). We may gradually be entering a new land of psychiatric interventions where the mind and brain are treated as a unified but multifaceted entity.

Acknowledgments

The Brain Stimulation Laboratory acknowledges the support of NARSAD, Stanley Foundation, BPDRF, and NIH grants (DBS) and DARPA. The BSL has also received research support from Cyberonics and Neuronetics. The authors would also like to acknowledge the help of Drs Xingbao Li, Kaori Yamanaka, Alexander Mishory, Qiwen Mu, nurses Berry Anderson and Angela Walker for their valuable help in clinical and imaging related studies conducted, Ms Minnie Dobbins and Mr Shannon Smith for business support and Ms Carol Hanback for administrative support at the BSL.

REFERENCES

Abrams R (1997). The mortality rate with ECT. *Conv Ther* 13:125–117.

Abrams R, Taylor MA (1976). Diencephalic stimulation and the effects of ECT in endogenous depression. *Br J Psychiatry* 129:482–445.

Alexander GE, DeLong MR, Strick PL (1986). Parallel organization of functionally segregated circuits linking basal ganglia and cortex. *Annu Rev Neurosci* 9:357–381.

Amassian VE (1993). Unmasking human visual perception with the magnetic coil and its relationship to hemispheric asymmetry. *Brain Research* 605:312–316.

Anderson WF (1998). Human gene therapy. *Nature* 392:25–30.

APA (1990). APA announces development of guidelines for effective use of electroconvulsive therapy. *Hosp Community Psychiatry* 41:208–229.

Apuzzo ML, Liu CY (2002). Things to come. *Neurosurgery* 49(4):765–778.

Ashby P, Rothwell J (2000). Neurophysiologic aspects of deep brain stimulation. *Neurol* 55: s17–s20.

Bailine SH, Rifkin A, Kayne E, et al. (2001). Comparison of bifrontal and bitemporal ECT for major depression. *Am J Psych* 58:607–609.

Bailine SH, Rifkin A, Kayne E, et al. (2002). Comparison of bifrontal and bitemporal ECT for major depression. *Am J Psychiatry* 157(1):121–113.

Barker AT, Jalinous R, Freeston IL (1985). Non-invasive magnetic stimulation of the human motor cortex. *Lancet* 1:1106–1107.

Baxter LR (1990). Brain imaging as a tool in establishing a theory of brain pathology in obsessive compulsive disorder. *J Clin Psychiatry* 51(s):22–25.

Bejjani B-P, Damier P, Arnulf I, et al. (1999). Transient acute depression induced by high-frequency deep brain stimulation. *New Eng J Med* 340:1476–1480.

Benazzouz A, Hallett M (2000). Mechanism of action of deep brain stimulation. *Neurol* 55: S13–S16.

Ben-Menachem E, Hamberger A, Hedner T, et al. (1995). Effects of vagus nerve stimulation on amino acids and other metabolites in the CSF of patients with partial seizures. *Epilepsy Res* 20:221–227.

Bennett AE (1979). Historical development of somatic therapies in affective disorders. *Int Pharmacopsychiatry* 14:85–93.

Ben-Sachar D, Belmaker RH, Grisaru N, Klein E (1997). Transcranial magnetic stimulation induces alterations in brain monoamines. *J Neural Transm* 104:191–197.

Bennett AE (1994). Curare: A preventive of traumatic complications in convulsive shock therapy (including a preliminary report on a synthetic curare-like drug). 1941. *Am J Psychiatry* 151:248–258.

Berman RM, Narasimhan M, Sanascora G, et al. (2000). A randomized clinical trial of repetitive transcranial magnetic stimulation in the treatment of major depression. *Biol Psychiatry* 47(4):332–337.

Bini L (1995). Professor Bini's notes on the first electro-shock experiment. *Conv Ther* 11: 260–221.

Bohning DE (1999). Introduction and overview of TMS physics. In George MS, Belmaker RH. (eds). *Transcranial Magnetic Stimulation in Neuropsychiatry*, American Psychiatric Press: Washington, D.C., pp. 13–44.

Bohning DE, Pecheny AP, Epstein CM, Vincent DJ, Dannels WR, George MS (1997). Mapping transcranial magnetic stimulation (TMS) fields in vivo with MRI. *NeuroReport* 8: 2535–2538.

Bohning DE, Shastri A, Nahas Z, et al. (1998). Echoplanar BOLD fMRI of brain activation induced by concurrent transcranial magnetic stimulation (TMS). *Investigative Radiology* 33(6):336–340.

Bohning DE, Lomarev MP, Denslow S, Nahas Z, Shastri A, George MS (2001). Feasibility of vagus nerve stimulation-synchronized blood oxygenation level-dependent functional MRI. *Investigative Radiology* 36:470–479.

Breeze RE, Wells TH, Jr, Freed CR (1995). Implantation of fetal tissue for the management of Parkinson's disease: A technical note. *Neurosurgery* 36:1044–1047.

Broca P (1865). Sur le siege de la faculte du language articule. *Bull Anthropologie* 6:377.

Burt T, Lisanby SH, Sackeim HA (2002). Neuropsychiatric applications of transcranial magnetic stimulation. *Int J Neuropsychopharmacol* 5:73–103.

Carpenter L (2002). Vagus Nerve Stimulation in Treatment-Resistant Depression. *Biol Psychiatry* 51:8S–#447.

Chase MH, Sterman MB, Clemente CD (1966). Cortical and subcortical patterns of response to afferent vagal stimulation. *Exp Neurol* 16:36–49.

Cleland B (1998). Helping the blind to see. *Aust N Z J Ophthalmol* 26:193–114.

Clower WT, Finger S (2002). Discovering trepanation: The contribution of Paul Broca. *Neurosurgery* 2001 Dec;49(6):1417–25; discussion 1425-6, 49:1417–25; discuss.

Cohrs S, Tergau F, Riech S, et al. (1998). High-frequency repetitive transcranial magnetic stimulation delays rapid eye movement sleep. *NeuroReport* 26(9):3439–3443.

Cosgrove GR, Rauch SL (1995). Psychosurgery. *Neurosurg Clin N Am* 6:167–176.

Critchley M (1965). Neurology's debt to F. J. Gall (1758–1828). *Br Med J* 5465: 775–781.

d'Alfonso AA, Aleman A, Kessels RP, et al. (2002). Transcranial magnetic stimulation of left auditory cortex in patients with schizophrenia: effects on hallucinations and neurocognition. *J Neuropsychiatry Clin Neurosci* 14(1):77–79.

Dannon PN, Dolberg OT, Schreiber S, Grunhaus L (2002). Three and six-month outcome following courses of either ECT or rTMS in a population of severely depressed individuals—preliminary report. *Biol Psychiatry* 51:687–690.

Devanand DP, Dwork AJ, Hutchinson ER, Bolwig TG, Sackeim HA (1994). Does ECT alter brain structure? *Am J Psychiatry* 151:957–970.

Edgley SA, Eyre JA, Lemon RN, Miller S (1990). Excitation of the corticospinal tract by electromagnetic and electrical stimulation of the scalp in the macaque monkey. *J Physiol (Lond)* 425:301–320.

Elger G, Hoppe C, Falkai P, Rush AJ, Elger CE (2000). Vagus nerve stimulation is associated with mood improvements in epilepsy patients. *Epilepsy Res* 42:203–210.

Ende G, Braus DF, Walter S, Weber-Fahr W, Henn FA (2002). The hippocampus in patients treated with electroconvulsive therapy: A proton magnetic resonance spectroscopic imaging study. *Arch Gen Psychiatry* 57(10):937–943.

Epstein CM, Lah JJ, Meador K, Weissman JD, Gaitan LE, Dihenia B (1996). Optimum stimulus parameters for lateralized suppression of speech with magnetic brain stimulation. *Neurol* 47:1590–1593.

Fink M (1984a). Theories of the antidepressant efficacy of convulsive therapy (ECT). In Post RM, Ballenger JC (eds). *Neurobiology of Mood Disorders*, Williams and Wilkins: Baltimore, pp. 721–730.

Fink M (1984b). Meduna and the origins of convulsive therapy. *Am J Psychiatry* 141:1034–1141.

Fink M, Johnson L (1982). Monitoring the duration of electroconvulsive therapy seizures: 'Cuff' and EEG methods compared. *Arch Gen Psychiatry* 39:1189–1191.

Fleischmann A, Sternheim A, Etgen AM, Li C, Grisaru N, Belmaker RH (1996). Transcranial magnetic stimulation downregulates beta-adrenoreceptors in rat cortex. *J Neural Transm* 103:1361–1366.

Foley JO, DuBois F (1937). Quantitative studies of the vagus nerve in the cat. I. The ratio of sensory and motor studies. *J Comp Neurol* 67:49–67.

Fujiki M, Steward O (1997). High frequency transcranial magnetic stimulation mimics the effects of ECS in upregulating astroglial gene expression in the murine CNS. *Molecular Brain Res* 44:301–308.

Garcia-Toro M, Pascual-Leone A, Romera M, et al. (2001). Prefrontal repetitive transcranial magnetic stimulation as an add-on treatment in depression. *J Neurol, Neurosurg & Psych* 71: 546–548.

Geller V, Grisaru N, Abarbanel JM, Lemberg T, Belmaker RH (1997). Slow magnetic stimulation of prefrontal cortex in depression and schizophrenia. *Prog Neuropsychopharmacol Biol Psychiatry* 21:105–110.

George MS, Wassermann EM (1994). Rapid-rate transcranial magnetic stimulation (rTMS) and ECT. *Conv Ther* 10(4):251–253.

George MS, Wassermann EM, Williams WA, et al. (1995). Daily repetitive transcranial magnetic stimulation (rTMS) improves mood in depression. *NeuroReport* 6:1853–1856.

George MS, Wassermann EM, Post RM (1996a). Transcranial magnetic stimulation: A neuropsychiatric tool for the 21st century. *J Neuropsychiatry Clin Neurosci* 8:373–382.

George MS, Wassermann EM, Williams W, et al. (1996b). Changes in mood and hormone levels after rapid-rate transcranial magnetic stimulation of the prefrontal cortex. *J Neuropsychiatry Clin Neurosci* 8:172–180.

George MS, Lisanby SH, Sackeim HA (1999a). Transcranial magnetic stimulation: Applications in neuropsychiatry. *Arch Gen Psychiatry* 56:300–311.

George MS, Nahas Z, Lomarev M, Bohning DE, Kellner CH (1999b). How knowledge of regional brain dysfunction in depression will enable new somatic treatments in the next millenium. *CNS Spectrums: Int J Neuropsychiatric Med* 4:53–61.

George MS, Nahas Z, Molloy M, et al. (2000). A controlled trial of daily transcranial magnetic stimulation (TMS) of the left prefrontal cortex for treating depression. *Biol Psychiatry* 48(10):962–970.

Grafman J, Wassermann E (1999). Transcranial magnetic stimulation can measure and modulate learning and memory. *Neuropshcologia* 37(2):159–167.

Greenberg BD, George MS, Dearing J, et al. (1997). Effect of prefrontal repetitive transcranial magnetic stimulation (rTMS) in obsessive-compulsive disorder: A preliminary study. *Am J Psych* 154:867–869.

Grill WM, Jr (1999). Modeling the effects of electric fields on nerve fibers: influence of tissue electrical properties. *IEEE Trans Biomed Eng* 46:918–928.

Grisaru N, Yarovslavsky U, Abarbanel J, Lamberg T, Belmaker RH (1994). Transcranial magnetic stimulation in depression and schizophrenia. *European Neuropsychopharmacol* 4: 287–288.

Grunhaus L, Dannon PN, Schreiber S, et al. (2000). Repetitive transcranial magnetic stimulation is as effective as electroconvulsive therapy in the treatment of nondelusional major depressive disorder: an open study. *Biol Psychiatry* (47)4:314–324.

Harden CL, Pulver MC, Ravdin LD, Nikolov B, Halper JP, Labar DR (2000). A pilot study of mood in epilepsy patients treated with vagus nerve stimulation. *Epilepsy Behav* 1:93–99.

Henry TR, Bakay RAE, Votaw JR, et al. (1998). Brain blood flow alterations induced by therapeutic vagus nerve stimulation in partial epilepsy: Acute effects at high and low levels of stimulation. *Epilepsia* 39:983–990.

Henry TR, Votaw JR, Pennell PB, et al. (1999). Acute blood flow changes and efficacy of vagus nerve stimulation in partial epilepsy. *Neurol* 52:1166–1173.

Herwig U, Padberg F, Unger J, Spitzer M, Schonfeldt-Lecuona C (2002). Transcranial magnetic stimulation in therapy studies: Examination of the reliability of "standard" coil positioning by neuronavigation. *Biol Psychiatry* 50(1):58–61.

Hodgkiss AD, Malizia AL, Bartlett JR, Bridges PK (1995). Outcome after the psychosurgical operation of stereotactic subcaudate tractotomy, 1979–1991. *J Neuropsychiatry Clin Neurosci* 7:230–4.

Hoffman RE, Boutros NN, Hu S, Berman RM, Krystal JH, Charney DS (2000). Transcranial magnetic stimulation and auditory hallucinations in schizophrenia. *Lancet* 355(9209): 1073–1075.

Hoflich G, Kasper S, Hufnagel A, Ruhrmann S, Moller HJ (1993). Application of transcranial magnetic stimulation in treatment of drug-resistant major depression—A report of two cases. *Human Psychopharmacology* 8:361–365.

Holtzheimer PE, Russo J, Avery D (2001). A meta-analysis of repetitive transcranial magnetic stimulation in the treatment of depression. *Psychopharmacol Bull* 35:149–169.

Jackson JH (1873). Observations on the localisation of movements in the cerebral hemispheres. *W Riding Lun Asylum Med Reports* 3:175–190.

Janicak PG, Dowd SM, Martis B, et al. (2002). Repetitive transcranial magnetic stimulation versus electroconvulsive therapy for major depression: Preliminary results of a randomized trial. *Biol Psychiatry* 51:659–667.

Kalinowsky LB (1986). History of convulsive therapy. *Ann N Y Acad Sci* 462:1–4.

Kaplitt MG, Lozano AM (2002). Surgical drug delivery for neurodegenerative diseases. *Clin Neurosurg* 48:127–144.

Kimbrell TA, George MS, Danielson AL, et al. (1997). Changes in cerebral metabolism during transcranial magnetic stimulation. *Biol Psychiatry* 41:108S–#374 (abstract).

Klein E, Kreinin I, Chistyakov A, et al. (1999). Therapeutic efficacy of right prefrontal slow repetitive transcranial magnetic stimulation in major depression: A double-blind controlled study. *Arch Gen Psychiatry* 56:315–320.

Kolbinger HM, Hoflich G, Hufnagel A, Moller H-J, Kasper S (1995). Transcranial magnetic stimulation (TMS) in the treatment of major depression—a pilot study. *Human Psychophar-macol* 10:305–310.

Koo B, Ham SD, Sood S, Tarver B (2001). Human vagus nerve electrophysiology: A guide to vagus nerve stimulation parameters. *J Clin Neurophysiol* 18:429–433.

Krystal AD (1998). The clinical utility of ictal EEG seizure adequacy models. *Psychiatric Ann* 28(1):30–35.

Limousin P, Krack P, Pollak P, et al. (1998). Electrical stimulation of the subthalamic nucleus in advanced Parkinson's Disease. *NEJM* 339:1105–1111.

Lippitz BE, Mindus P, Meyerson BA, Kihlstrom L, Lindquist C (1999). Lesion topography and outcome after thermocapsulotomy or gamma knife capsulotomy for obsessive-compulsive disorder: relevance of the right hemisphere. *Neurosurgery* 44:452–458; discussion 458–460.

Lisanby SH, Luber B, Schroeder C, et al. (1998). Intracerebral measurement of rTMS and ECS induced voltage in vivo. *Biol Psychiatry* 43:100s.

Lisanby SH, Pascual-Leone A, Sampson SM, et al. (2001a). Augmentation of sertraline antide-pressant treatment with transcranial magnetic stimulation. *Biol Psychiatry NR#283*; 49:81S (abst).

Lisanby SH, Schlaepfer TE, Fisch HU, Sackeim HA (2001b). Magnetic seizure therapy for major depression. *Arch Gen Psychiatry* 58:303–305.

Lisanby SH, Maddox JH, Prudic J, Devanand DP, Sackeim HA (2002). The effects of electro-convulsive therapy on memory of autobiographical and public events. *Arch Gen Psychiatry* 57(6):581–590.

Lomarev M, Denslow S, Nahas Z, Chae JH, George MS, Bohning DE (2002). Vagus nerve stimulation (VNS) synchronized BOLD fMRI suggests that VNS in depressed adults has frequency and/or dose dependent effects at rest and during a simple task. *J Psychiatry Res* 36:219–227.

Loo C, Mitchell P, Sachdev P, McDarmont B, Parker G, Gandevia S (1999). A double-blind controlled investigation of transcranial magnetic stimulation for the treatment of resistant major depression. *Am J Psychiatry* 156:946–948.

Loo CK, Taylor JL, Gandevia SC, McDarmont BN, Mitchell PB, Sachdev PS (2000). Transcra-nial magnetic stimulation (TMS) in controlled treatment studies: Are some "sham" forms active? *Biol Psychiatry* 47:325–331.

Maclean PD (1990) *The Triune Brain in Evolution: Role in Paleocerebral Functions*, Plenum Press: New York.

Maeda F, Keenan JP, Pascual-Leone A (2002). Interhemispheric asymmetry of motor cortical excitability in major depression as measured by transcranial magnetic stimulation. *Br J Psychiatry* 177:169–173.

Manes F, Jorge R, Morcuende M, et al. (2001). A controlled trial of repetitive transcranial magnetic stimulation as a treatment of depression in the elderly. A controlled trial of repetitive transcranial magnetic stimulation as a treatment of depression in the elderly. *Psychogeriatrics* 13:225–231.

Marangell LB, Rush AJ, George MS, et al. (2002). Vagus nerve stimulation (VNS) for major depressive episodes: Longer-term outcome. *Biol Psychiatry* 51:280–287.

Martin JD, George MS, Greenberg BD, et al. (1997). Mood effects of prefrontal repetitive high-frequency TMS in healthy volunteers. *CNS Spectrums: Int J Neuropsychiatric Medicine* 2:53–68.

Martin JLR, Barbanoj MJ, Schlaepfer TE, et al. (2002). Transcranial magnetic stimulation for treating depression (Cochrane Review). In Cochrane Library: Oxford,

Mathe AA, Potter WC, Stenfors C, Rudorfer MV, Manji HK, Theodorsson E (1991). Effects of electroconvulsive treatment (ECT) on CSF neuropeptides in depressed patients. *ACNP Abstracts* 116.

McCall WV, Farah A, Reboussin DM (1995). Can we teach psychiatric residents to rate seizure regularity? *Conv Ther* 11:248–252.

McCall WV, Reboussin DM, Weiner RD, Sackeim HA (2002). Titrated moderately suprathreshold vs fixed high-dose right unilateral electroconvulsive therapy: Acute antidepressant and cognitive effects. *Arch Gen Psychiatry 2000* 57:438–444.

McConnell KA, Nahas Z, Shastri A, et al. (2001). The transcranial magnetic stimulation motor threshold depends on the distance from coil to underlying cortex: A replication in healthy adults comparing two methods of assessing the distance to cortex. *Biol Psychiatry* 49(5):454–459.

McDonald WM, Greenberg BD (2002). Electroconvulsive therapy in the treatment of neuropsychiatric conditions and transcranial magnetic stimulation as a pathophysiological probe in neuropsychiatry. *Depress Anxiety* 12(3):135–143.

Mclardy T, Meyer A (1949). Anatomical correlates of improvement after leucotomy. *J Mental Sci* 95:182–192.

McNamara B, Ray JL, Arthurs OJ, Boniface S (2001). Transcranial magnetic stimulation for depression and other psychiatric disorders. *Psychol Med* 31:1141–1146.

Milstein V, Small JG, Klapper MH, Small IF, Miller MJ, Kellams JJ (1987). Uni-versus bilateral ECT in the treatment of mania. *Conv Ther* 3:1–9.

Morris GL, Mueller WM (1999). Long-term treatment with vagus nerve stimulation in patients with refractory epilepsy. The Vagus Nerve Stimulation Study Group E01-E05. *Neurology* 53:1731–1735.

Mosimann UP, Rihs TA, Engeler J, Fisch HU, Schlaepfer TE (2000). Mood effects of repetitive transcranial magnetic stimulation of left prefrontal cortex in healthy volunteers. *Psychiatr Res* 94(3):251–256.

Nagarajan L, Walsh P, Gregory P, Lee M (2002). VNS therapy in clinical practice in children with refractory epilepsy. *Acta Neurol Scand* 105(1):13–17.

Nahas Z, McConnell K, Collins S, et al. (1999). Could left prefrontal rTMS modify negative symptoms and attention in schizophrenia? *Biol Psychiatry* 45:37S#120 (abst).

Nahas Z, DeBrux C, Lorberbaum JP, et al. (2000a). Safety of rTMS: MRI scans before and after 2 weeks of daily left prefrontal rTMS for the treatment of depression. *J ECT* 16:380–390.

Nahas Z, Lomarev M, Roberts DR, et al. (2000b). Left prefrontal transcranial magnetic stimulation produces intensity dependent bilateral effects as measured with interleaved BOLD fMRI. *Human Brain Mapping* 11(5):520 (abst).

Nahas Z, Li X, Chae JH, et al. (2001a). Repetitive transcranial magnetic stimulation in depression. *Epilepsy Behav* 2:S21–S29.

Nahas Z, Teneback CT, Kozel AF, et al. (2001b). Brain effects of transcranial magnetic delivered over prefrontal cortex in depressed adults: The role of stimulation frequency and distance from coil to cortex. *J Neuropsychiatry Clin Neurosci* 13(4):459–470.

Nahas Z, Kozel FA, Li X, Anderson B, George MS (2003). Left prefrontal transcranial magnetic stimulation (TMS) treatment of depression in bipolar affective disorder: a pilot study of acute safety and efficacy. *Bipolar Disord* 5:40–47.

Nakajima T, Post RM, Weiss SRB, Pert A, Ketter T (1989). Perspectives on the mechanism of action of electroconvulsive therapy: Anticonvulsant, dopaminergic, and c-fos oncogene effects. *Conv Ther* 5:274–295.

Nedjat S, Folkerts HW, Michael ND, Arolt V (1998). Evaluation of the side effects after rapid-rate transcranial magnetic stimulation over the left prefrontal cortex in normal volunteers. *Clin Neurophysiol* 107:96.

Nemeroff CB, Bissette G, Akil H, Fink M (1991). Neuropeptide concentrations in the cerebrospinal fluid of depressed patients treated with electroconvulsive therapy. Corticotrophin-releasing factor, beta-endorphin and somatostatin. *Br J Psychiatry* 158:59–63.

Nobler MS, Teneback CC, Nahas Z, et al. (1999). Structural and functional neuroimaging of ECT and TMS. *Progress in Neuro-Psychopharmacol & Biol Psychiatry* 12:144–560.

Nobler MS, Oquendo MA, Kegeles LS, et al. (2001). Decreased regional brain metabolism after ECT. *Am J Psych* 158:305–308.

Nuttin B, Cosyns P, Demeulemeester H, Gybels J, Meyerson B (1999). Electrical stimulation in anterior limbs of internal capsules in patients with obsessive-compulsive disorder. *Lancet* 354:1526.

Padberg F, Haag C, Zwanzger P, et al. (1998). Rapid and slow transcranial magnetic stimulation are equally effective in medication-resistant depression: A placebo-controlled study. *CINP Abstracts* 21st Congress:103–st0306 (abst).

Pascual-Leone A, Hallett M (1994). Induction of errors in a delayed response task by repetitive transcranial magnetic stimulation of the dorsolateral prefrontal cortex. *NeuroReport* 5:2517–2520.

Pascual-Leone A, Catala MD, Pascual AP (1996). Lateralized effect of rapid-rate transcranial magnetic stimulation of the prefrontal cortex on mood. *Neurol* 46:499–502.

Paus T (2001). Integration of transcranial magnetic stimulation and brain imaging. *Biol Psychiatry* 49:6S-#21.

Paus T, Jech R, Thompson CJ, Comeau R, Peters T, Evans AC (1997). Transcranial magnetic stimulation during positron emission tomography: A new method for studying connectivity of the human cerebral cortex. *J Neurosci* 17:3178–3184.

Penry JK, Dean JC (1990). Prevention of intractable partial seizures by intermittent vagal stimulation in humans: Preliminary results. *Epilepsia* 31 Suppl 2:S40–S43.

Pool JL (1954). Psychosurgery of older people. *J Geriatr Assoc* 2:456–465.

Post A, Keck ME (2001). TMS as a therapeutic tool in psychiatry: What do we know about neurobiological mechanisms? *J Psychiatr Res* 35:193–215.

Post A, Muller MB, Engelmann M, Keck ME (1999). Repetitive transcranial magnetic stimulation in rats: evidence for a neuroprotective effect in vitro and in vivo. *Eur J Neurosci* 11:3247–3354.

Post RM (1990). ECT: The anticonvulsant connection. *Neuropsychopharmacol* 3:89–92.

Post RM, Putnam F, Uhde TW, Weiss SRB (1986). ECT as an anticonvulsant: Implications for its mechanism of action in affective illness. In Malitz S, Sackeim HA (eds). *Electroconvulsive Therapy: Clinical and Basic Research Issues. Annals of the New York Academy of Sciences, Vol. 462*, New York Academy of Sciences: New York, pp. 376–388.

Pridmore S (2000). Substitution of rapid transcranial magnetic stimulation treatments for electroconvulsive therapy treatments in a course of electroconvulsive therapy. *Depress Anxiety* 12(3):118–123.

Rezai AR, Hutchinson W, Lozano AM (1999). Chronic subthalamic nucleus stimulation for Parkinson's disease. In Rezai AR, Hutchinson W, Lozano AM (eds). *The Operative Neurosurgical Atlas*, Vol. 8. American Association of Neurosurgeons: Rollings, IL.

Rollnik JD, Huber TJ, Mogk H, et al. (2000). High frequency repetitive transcranial magnetic stimulation (rTMS) of the dorsolateral prefrontal cortex in schizophrenic patients. *NeuroReport* Dec 18:11(18):4013–4015.

Rosenberg R, Vorstrup S, Andersen A, Bolwig T (1988). Effect of ECT on cerebral blood flow assessed with SPECT. *Conv Ther* 4:62–73.

Rush AJ, George MS, Sackeim HA, et al. (2000). Vagus nerve stimulation (VNS) for treatment-resistant depressions: A multicenter study. *Biol Psychiatry* 47:276–286.

Sackeim HA (2002). Memory and ECT: From polarization to reconciliation. *J ECT* 16(2):87–96.

Sackeim HA, Devanand DP, Prudic J (1992). Medication resistance as a predictor of ECT outcome and relapse. *ACNP Abstracts of Panels and Posters* 51 (abst).

Sackeim HA, Prudic J, Devanand DP, et al. (1993). Effects of stimulus intensity and electrode placement on the efficacy and cognitive effects of electroconvulsive therapy. *N Engl J Med* 328:839–846.

Sackeim HA, Prudic J, Devanand DP, et al. (2000). A prospective, randomized, double-blind comparison of bilateral and right unilateral electroconvulsive therapy at different stimulus intensities. *Arch Gen Psychiatry* 57(5):425–434.

Sackeim HA, Rush AJ, George MS, et al. (2001). Vagus nerve stimulation (VNS) for treatment-resistant depression: Efficacy, side effects and predictors of outcome. *Neuropsychopharmacol* 25:713–728.

Sackeim HA, Haskett RF, Mulsant BH, et al. (2002a). Continuation pharmacotherapy in the prevention of relapse following electroconvulsive therapy: A randomized controlled trial. *JAMA* 285(10):1299–1307.

Sackeim HA, Prudic J, Devanand DP, et al. (2002b). A prospective, randomized, double-blind comparison of bilateral and right unilateral electroconvulsive therapy at different stimulus intensities. *Arch Gen Psychiatry* 57(5):425–434.

Sackeim HA, Prudic J, Nobler MS, Lisanby SH, Devanand DP, Peyser S (2002c). Ultrabrief pulse ECT and the affective and cognitive consequences of ECT. *J ECT*

Schachter SC, Saper CB (1998a). Vagus nerve stimulation (Progress in Epilepsy Research). *Epilepsia* 39:677–686.

Schachter SC, Saper CB (1998b). Vagus nerve stimulation. *Epilepsia* 39:677–686.

Shiwach RS, Reid WH, Carmody TJ (2002). An analysis of reported deaths following electroconvulsive therapy in Texas, 1993–1998. *Psychiatr Serv* 52(8):1095–1107.

Speer AM, Kimbrell TA, Wassermann EM, Willis MW, Post RM (1999). 20 Hz and 1 Hz rTMS for 2 weeks differentially affects absolute rCBF in depressed patients. *Biol Psychiatry* 45:S130 (abst).

Szuba MP, Rai A, Kastenberg J, et al. (1999). *Rapid mood and endocrine effects of TMS in major depression. Proceedings of the American Psychiatric Association Annual Meeting* 201 (abst).

Tanaka S (1994). Hypothetical joint-related coordinate systems in which populations of motor cortical neurons code direction of voluntary arm movements. *Neurosci Lett* 180:83–86.

Teneback CC, Nahas Z, Speer AM, et al. (1999). Two weeks of daily left prefrontal rTMS changes prefrontal cortex and paralimbic activity in depression. *J Neuropsychiatry Clin Neurosci* 11:426–435.

Tharyan P, Adams CE (2002). Electroconvulsive therapy for schizophrenia (Cochrane Review). *Cochrane Database Syst Rev (2): CD000076.*

thompson TP, Lunsford LD, Kondziolka D (1999). Restorative neurosurgery: Opportunities for restoration of function in acquired, degenerative, and idiopathic neurological diseases. *Neurosurgery* 45:741–752.

Tippin J, Henn FA (1982). Modified leukotomy in the treatment of intractable obsessional neurosis. *Am J Psychiatry* 139:1601–1603.

Tourney G (1967). A history of therapeutic fashions in psychiatry, 1800–1966. *Am J Psychiatry* 124:784–796.

Van Bockstaele EJ, Peoples J, Valentino RJ (1999). A.E. Bennett Research Award. Anatomic basis for differential regulation of the rostrolateral peri-locus coeruleus region by limbic afferents. *Biol Psychiatry* 46:1352–1363.

von Meduna L (1937) *Die Konvulsionstherapie der Schizophrenie*, Carl Marhold: Budapest.

Walker BR, Easton A, Gale K (1999). Regulation of limbic motor seizures by GABA and glutamate transmission in nucleus tractus solitarius. *Epilepsia* 40:1051–1107.

Wassermann EM (1998). Risk and safety of repetitive transcranial magnetic stimulation: Report and suggested guidelines from the International Workshop in the Safety of Repetitive Transcranial Magnetic Stimulation, June 5–7, 1996. *Electroencephalogr Clin Neurophysiol* 108: 1–16.

Zabara J (1992). Inhibition of experimental seizures in canines by repetitive vagal stimulation. *Epilepsia* 33:1005–1012.

Ziemann U, Hallett M (2000). Basic neurophysiological studies with TMS. In George MS, Belmaker RH. (eds). *Transcranial Magnetic Stimulation in Neuropsychiatry*, American Psychiatric Press: Washington, DC, pp. 45–98.

18

PSYCHOANALYSIS AND PSYCHOPHARMACOLOGY: ART AND SCIENCE OF COMBINING PARADIGMS

Marcia Kaplan

Cincinnati Center for Psychoanalysis, Cincinnati, Ohio

INTRODUCTION

Sigmund Freud, the founder of psychoanalysis, anticipated current theory about brain correlates of human psychology. What Freud called *instinctual drives* can be described in modern terms as the basic emotional operating systems that are mediated by subcortical structures. These are modulated in turn by *ego functions*, which can now be defined as cortical capacities such as intelligence, reasoning, logic, organizing skills, frustration tolerance, capacity to defer gratification, and the like. The psychoanalytic method was designed to enable patients to overcome symptoms that Freud saw as stemming from unresolved infantile conflicts: "Where id was, there ego shall be." (Freud, 1933, p. 80) The more developed our cortical capacities to modulate subcortical processes, the more control we have over our feelings, behavior, relationships, and productivity. Though never traditionally defined this way, psychoanalysis has always had as its

Textbook of Biological Psychiatry, Edited by Jaak Panksepp
ISBN 0-471-43478-7   Copyright © 2004 John Wiley & Sons, Inc.

goal the sculpting of subcortico-cortical functions via the relationship between analyst and patient.

In his earliest efforts to formulate a psychology, Freud postulated a quantitative factor, which, in *Project for a Scientific Psychology* (Freud, 1895) he designated Q. This quantitative factor may be roughly translated as a physical energic factor. It has been compared to the SEEKING system theorized by Panksepp (Panksepp, 1998; Shevrin, 2001). Freud persisted to the very end with the notion of a quantitative factor in his subsequently elaborated metapsychology. In the *New Introductory Lectures on Psychoanalysis*, Freud referred to the constitutional factor that in 1933 could not be approached directly:

> Our analytic experience that [neurotic phenomena] can be extensively influenced, if the historical precipitating causes and accidental auxiliary factors of the illness can be dealt with, has led us to neglect the constitutional factor in our therapeutic practice, and in any case we can do nothing about it; but in theory we ought always to bear it in mind. (Freud 1933b, pp. 153–154)

Later, in his posthumously published *Outline of Psychoanalysis*, Freud spoke of the probability that definitive treatment of mental illness would be achieved by medication—not along with psychoanalysis but presumably instead of it.

> But here we are concerned with therapy only in so far as it works by psychological means; and for the time being we have no other. The future may teach us to exercise a direct influence, by means of particular chemical substances, on the amounts of energy and their distribution in the mental apparatus. (Freud, 1938, p. 195)

Freud treated patients with a wide range of pathology, some with severe mental illnesses. Since no effective somatic or pharmacological treatments were available to him (beyond an early brief infatuation and disillusionment with cocaine), it is not surprising that Freud questioned the effectiveness of the psychoanalytic method in these cases and looked to future advances in psychobiology to address their needs. He did not anticipate that psychoanalysis and its derivatives might someday be used together with medication treatment, but one suspects that he would have championed this combined approach.

DEFINITION OF PSYCHOANALYTIC CONCEPTS

Psychoanalysis is a theory of human psychology and a treatment method based on several basic principles, including: The dynamic unconscious, that is, the existence of mental contents that we are not aware of due to the process of repression, or the keeping of certain mental contents out of awareness. Freud emphasized the conflict between id (instinctual wishes pressing for gratification) and superego (the result of the oedipal conflict in which the young child accepts the superior strength and power of the same-sex parent and begins to identify with parental prohibitions) as the pathway to development of ego, the reasonable, adaptable, reality-oriented part of the self. Later theorists (Hartmann, Anna Freud, and others) felt that humans are endowed with ego functions from birth and that some of these functions are primary and autonomous (locomotion, ability to manipulate tools, capacity for language, capacity for relatedness to other humans, appreciation of humor, curiosity, reflectiveness, and others) rather than developed out of the id-superego struggle.

The process of repression of prohibited mental material is accompanied by the development of the ego mechanisms of defense (Freud, 1966), various observable behaviors that serve to keep objectionable ideas out of awareness. The defense mechanisms are linked to developmental levels from immature to mature, and range in their demand for distorting versus acknowledging reality (from psychotic to healthy). The analytic process is based on the concept of transference, or the development of intense feelings appropriate to important people from the individual's past that are experienced toward people in the present, in this case, the analyst. Transference feelings develop in all human interactions; for example, feelings about one's supervisor may have more to do with how one experienced one's father than the specific characteristics of the supervisor. These feelings become observable in the analytic situation in which patient and analyst meet several times per week, and through the use of free association, the requirement that the patient say whatever comes to mind during the session, also known as the fundamental rule of psychoanalysis. By analyzing transference feelings, unconscious mental contents become recognizable and the patient gains conviction about their existence.

Repetition compulsion refers to the predictability with which humans repeat certain painful situations without recognizing their part in bringing these situations about: For example, a woman with an alcoholic father marries a man who is an alcoholic. The phenomenon of repetition compulsion reflects the impact of the past on current behavior through the unconscious. If unconscious wishes become conscious through the analytic process, individuals may be able to make healthier choices in life.

Resistance is another important concept: Inevitably, despite the best intentions of the individual to cooperate with the analyst by saying whatever comes to mind, he/she comes to resist the process. This represents the individual's defensive efforts to avoid painful awareness of unacceptable wishes and fantasies. Analysis of resistance is a key part of analytic technique; the therapeutic alliance between analyst and patient enables the analyst to help the patient see how "perfectly reasonable" behavior may serve resistance. As an example, a woman in her third year of analysis, coming into greater awareness of the full impact of her competitive and hateful feelings toward the analyst, reflecting similar feelings toward her mother, interviews for a job in another city since she sees a number of reasons why her present job may become undesirable. She was unaware of the implicit meaning, specifically, that she is planning to undermine and leave the analyst, until the analyst brings it to her attention for further investigation.

Determining which psychotherapeutic technique will benefit which patient is unfortunately neither an art nor a science; the decision is most often based on the therapist's theoretical persuasion and preference for a particular form of treatment. Analyzable (see below) patients are also suitable for psychoanalytic psychotherapy, which is typically conducted up to three times weekly with the patient sitting up and face to face with the therapist. Psychoanalytic psychotherapy may utilize similar techniques such as analysis of transference and resistance but may also focus more on current life events and utilize greater amounts of support and advice. In modern practice, many patients seen in psychotherapy are treated with medications for anxiety and depression, and when medication is effective, many benefit from less intensive treatment processes. Since psychoanalysis is typically conducted four to five times per week, money and time factor into the decision about the intensity of treatment.

Analyzability, though difficult to define objectively, refers to the set of characteristics of individuals thought likely to benefit from psychoanalysis. [It is important to note that analyzability is impossible to predict, and that outcome studies over the past 50 years have shown that benefit from analytic treatment is always greater than is analyzability; i.e., even "unanalyzable" patients make considerable gains with analysis and psychoanalytic psychotherapy. These gains are largely achieved through the more supportive aspects of treatment (Wallerstein, 1996).] This list typically includes: average or high intelligence, capacity for self-observation, ability to verbalize one's feelings and thoughts, capacity for ongoing human relationships, motivation to engage in a lengthy therapeutic process, a sense of hopefulness about the future, capacity to defer gratification, adequate employment or adequate means to pay for treatment (as money and payment have many important meanings), and the lack of any serious psychiatric illness. This last is an obvious source of controversy since there is complete overlap between the symptoms of depression in patients with psychological conflicts that are amenable to analysis and in patients with depression who are not analyzable: "*in patients who are analyzable*, such things as sleep disturbances, loss of appetite, despondency, and so on, come and go and are part and parcel of what I am analyzing rather than being a function of physiological imbalances that I have to attend to with different means" (Nersessian, 1992). While depressed patients who are either not analyzable or not in analytic treatment are typically treated with antidepressants, patients in analytic treatment with symptoms of depression that do not respond to analytic investigation may also require medication.

CHALLENGE OF COMBINING PARADIGMS

Contemporary psychoanalysis and biological psychiatry have traditionally had different goals. Biological psychiatry has focused on developing accurate nosology and effective medication treatments for relief of the symptoms of mental disorders; functional improvement is the goal and permanent psychic change is not expected. The goal of psychoanalysis is not mood and behavior change, but rather the uncovering of unconscious mental contents, leading to new self-understanding, psychological autonomy and mental freedom. Change in mood and behavior may result from these new capacities but is not the goal at the outset.

Thus the polarization of biological psychiatry and psychoanalysis is understandable, but it has ill served both patients and trainees in various mental health fields.

Biological psychiatry, abetted by the managed-care industry, has made possible "relationshipless psychiatry" (Gardner, 2001) in which patients are "managed" by non-psychiatric (lower-cost) therapists and given prescriptions by psychiatrists who, at times, barely know them. Proponents of traditional psychoanalysis have maintained that mental states have a psychological background that, if analyzed, can lead to symptom remission but have largely failed to embrace the use of standard nosologic diagnosis, or to openly sanction the use of medication in alleviating symptoms. The combining of medication and psychotherapy by practitioners who understand both depth psychology and psychopharmacology represents a significant advance in the evolution of psychiatric practice. Since this approach falls between two very different paradigms, it calls for the willingness to adapt our psychoanalytic traditions and biological knowledge to the real needs of our patients.

Given the lack of controlled studies of psychoanalytic psychotherapies, (Gabbard et al., 2002), this practice must proceed on the basis of well-informed clinical judgment rather than results of definitive multicenter trials. Therapeutic thinking that bridges traditional paradigms will be illustrated in this chapter with descriptions of psychoanalytic cases.

Psychoanalysis, Medication, or Both?

Psychoanalysis is indicated for patients with adequate ego strengths who experience recurrent problems in relationships and/or work that are related to neurotic conflict rather than to significant psychiatric illness. The analyst strives to avoid the typical "medical" role of authoritative healer in an effort to optimally maintain the patient's ego autonomy over the course of a long and intensive relationship. In traditional psychoanalytic practice, the use of medication (or any other form of symptom relief such education, advice, or support) has been considered a parameter, or a deviation, from standard analytic process necessary to maintain the therapeutic environment, and to be dispensed with as soon as it is possible to return to the analysis of transference (Eissler, 1953). This viewpoint derives from experience with unambiguously analyzable patients who present with symptoms of depression or anxiety. In such cases, symptoms may arise in the context of deep conflicts stirred by the transference. Further psychoanalytic work, in theory, should lead to a resolution of the conflict and the remission of these symptoms without use of medication.

On the other hand, despite heroic efforts made in the mid-20th century to apply psychoanalysis to severe disorders such as pedophilia, alcoholism, and psychosis (Stone, 1954), mainstream analysts have come to terms with the limitations of the analytic method for these disorders, and analyzability guidelines typically recommend excluding patients with serious psychiatric illnesses (Weinshel, 1990). Nonetheless, patients with severe mental illnesses treated with intensive psychoanalytic psychotherapy did derive significant improvement (Wallerstein, 1986) even if they did not meet the usual analyzability criteria or achieve the usual goals of psychoanalysis. For example, some of these patients would today meet criteria for schizoaffective disorder (a mixture of mood and psychotic symptoms), obsessive-compulsive disorder, and manic depression, all diagnoses now treated primarily with medications.

The enormous range of pathology among patients seeking psychiatric treatment demands a flexible approach and willingness to use a multitude of techniques to enable patients to achieve optimal improvement. In fact, psychoanalysts now routinely treat psychiatrically ill patients (Doidge et al., 1994) and are prescribing medications for them. (Donovan and Roose, 1995). The availability of effective and tolerable psychotropic medication has made the situation even more complicated: How do we tell what symptoms are neurotic in origin and treatable with psychotherapy and which demand pharmacological intervention?

Even without definitive proof that psychotherapy is efficacious for the treatment of specific mental disorders (Roth and Fonagy, 1996), there is widespread use of various forms of psychotherapy for typical problems presenting to mental health professionals, whether or not medication is prescribed. Based on expert consensus, the American Psychiatric Association has recommended a combination of psychotherapy and pharmacotherapy for the treatment of major depression, eating disorders, bipolar affective disorder, and borderline personality disorders (American Psychiatric Association, 2000a, 2000b, 2001, 2002). A recent randomized, controlled trial demonstrated that the combination of pharmacotherapy and a form of cognitive behavioral therapy was significantly more efficacious for chronic depression that either treatment alone (Keller et al., 2000). While supportive therapies combined with medication may be adequate for many patients, some individuals require psychoanalytic psychotherapy or analysis for definitive treatment of their problems.

Case Example: Medication and Psychoanalysis Can Work Synergistically.
Dr. A, a 28-year-old male medical resident, entered psychoanalysis for long-standing difficulty maintaining intimate relationships with women and confusion about his future career direction. He was the older of two sons. His father was a successful attorney who had divorced his mother when he was a teenager. His chronically depressed mother had gotten some benefit from a selective serotonin reuptake inhibitor (SSRI) antidepressant. Dr. A requested and was given an SSRI antidepressant, which improved his mood somewhat. Despite the antidepressant and analytic sessions, he gradually worsened. He became unable to concentrate or sleep, ruminated continually about being worthless, and had trouble leaving his apartment; he began missing work, and contemplated dropping out of his training program. At that point, Dr. A was referred to a psychopharmacologist for evaluation, who suggested he increase the dose of SSRI, add a second antidepressant, bupropion, and eventually, an atypical antipsychotic, quetiapine.

With this medication regimen, Dr. A was able to sleep, could concentrate better, and was able to get back to work. He stopped the quetiapine and SSRI within 6 months, but remained on bupropion for the subsequent $2\frac{1}{2}$ years, and made significant progress in analysis toward understanding the severe depression he had experienced. In part, depression was his biological inheritance as grandmother and mother both had severe bouts of depression. In addition, he had long struggled with enormous anger and resentment toward his father for leaving his mother, and guilt about leaving his mother behind himself, as he had been her confidant both before and after his father's defection. He paid for the satisfaction he derived from his promising career with depression that kept him psychologically close to his mother. Even getting treatment made him feel that he was a defector like his father, and came to be understood as a reason for his initial negative response to analysis.

Dr. A came to better terms with his fantasies regarding his role in his parents' lives and dealt with his fear that leaving the female analyst would be experienced by her, as by his mother, as a defection, resulting in her emotional withdrawal from him in retaliation. He developed a mutually satisfying relationship with a woman physician in another training program at the hospital and got married prior to ending his analysis. He accepted a postgraduate fellowship in another city. He and the analyst agreed he should continue bupropion, and Dr. A planned to consult a psychiatrist once he moved regarding the question of ongoing need for medication.

Dr. A derived dramatic benefit from medication, which in turn made it possible for him to use analytic treatment more fully. He had a family history of depression in several maternal relatives, as is common in patients presenting with symptoms of major depression. While it is now universally agreed that schizophrenia is a heritable brain disorder rather than the result of faulty mothering, there are many diagnostic categories, like the depression Dr. A suffered, that remain to be so clearly defined. Willick (2001) has addressed the outmoded psychoanalytic explanation for schizophrenia as a cautionary tale; what we feel sure of can engender confirmatory "data" from the consulting room that provides the "proof" for erroneous theory and practice. The assumption that Dr. A's neurotic conflicts were the sole origin of the symptoms of depression and thus would respond to psychoanalytic treatment alone, might have exposed him to unnecessary morbidity, and even mortality.

Essentially, there is a two-part process for the analytic practitioner: a diagnostic evaluation that determines the absence or presence of significant psychiatric illness and a treatment plan that may include medication for that illness; and concurrently, an assessment of analyzability. A patient presenting with a severe depression may be analyzable once treated effectively with medication. While some patients presenting with severe depression are analyzable and might have resolution of their symptoms with analysis alone, the standard of care in psychiatry would hold that psychoanalysis is not a treatment for major depression, bipolar affective disorder, schizophrenia, and other Axis I disorders. The analyst would be well advised to inform the patient about all available treatments for the diagnosed disorder, and to obtain informed consent to use analysis without medication, if medication treatment is the standard of care for that disorder.

Does Medication Interfere with Motivation for Psychodynamic Treatment?

Some analysts express concern that medication treatment will eliminate the symptoms that motivate patients to enter and continue psychotherapy. There is no question that psychic pain motivates patients to seek treatment, and relief of that pain will eliminate the motivation to attend psychotherapy sessions for some patients. Fifty years ago, in the heyday of psychoanalysis, and in the absence of effective alternatives, many patients pursued psychoanalytic treatment for anxiety and depressive disorders. It is not clear how often analysis was the indicated, or ideal, treatment, or how often it was effective for these symptoms. For many patients, combined medication and supportive therapy is quite effective, and sometimes a preferable alternative to depth psychotherapy. Sometimes very concrete individuals show a new capacity for insight once symptoms are effectively treated but may never need extensive psychotherapeutic investigation to maintain optimal functioning.

While introspection and self-understanding have unquestionably been deemphasized and devalued in modern culture, in the author's experience, patients who are so inclined do not lose interest in pursuing psychological understanding when they are successfully treated with medicine. Patients who are interested in self-exploration engage in psychotherapy whether they are given medication or not. Many patients taking medication express the wish to learn about and master the conflicts that caused symptoms in hopes of making medication unnecessary in the future. Patients attempting to minimize awareness of dependency needs are able to keep those needs out of awareness when they are given medication that relieves symptoms. Not every patient has the capacity for or interest in achieving self-understanding, and medication makes it possible for many to function at their highest level. It is the responsibility of the analyst prescribing medication to maintain a reflective, analytic stance, and to make clear the benefits of psychoanalysis beyond the gains from medication; analyzable patients who feel well with medication and no longer want psychotherapy will be more likely to return for further work if they feel the analyst does not need them to stay and does not disapprove of their decision.

Must Medication Be Discontinued for Psychoanalysis to Be Successful?

If medication is to be used with patients in analysis, must medication be stopped in order to demonstrate analytic success? While effective analysis leads to greater capacity for self-understanding and emotional modulation (see below) it remains unclear whether this protects from the recurrence of Axis I disorders. Patients with obsessive-compulsive disorder gain relief of symptoms with medication but typically relapse once medication is stopped. Most evidence suggests that psychodynamic therapies are not helpful for obsessive-compulsive disorder, although there is evidence for benefit from cognitive-behavioral strategies (Foa and Franklin, 2000). Patients who have had more than one episode of major depression have a risk of recurrence in excess of 80 percent, and medication treatment generally prevents recurrences. The benefits of psychoanalysis or analytic psychotherapy might confer protection against such recurrences, but there is no data as yet to support this theory. No studies have been carried out using long-term depth psychotherapy or psychoanalysis in patients with depression or obsessive-compulsive disorder. A definitive answer to the question could come from use of standardized diagnosis, and prospectively collected long-term outcome data regarding whether successfully analyzed patients with a history of major depression or obsessive-compulsive disorder have a lower risk for recurrence compared with a control group of unanalyzed patients with the same diagnoses.

Benefits of Psychoanalysis Compared with Benefits of Medication

Medication and psychoanalysis are indicated for different aspects of mental disorders. Psychoanalysis and psychoanalytically oriented psychotherapy help individuals identify the sources of psychic pain, become familiar with their own life histories, and grieve the loss of previously sustaining fantasies that also predispose them to repetitive failures in relationships and productivity. In psychoanalysis this is accomplished largely through the development and analysis of the transference relationship, while in psychoanalytic psychotherapy, there is less emphasis on the transference and more use of defense-building strategies, education, and support.

Medication restores basic functions such as sleep, appetite, concentration, and energy, stabilizes mood, and relieves anxiety or psychosis. Thus, benefits of medication are quite different in nature from the benefits of analytic treatment. Medications reduce current turmoil but do not address the underlying etiology of that turmoil, or the maladaptive defenses that predispose to symptoms. Psychoanalysis leads to greater awareness and tolerance of ideas and affects, and analysands gain better emotional and behavioral adaptability. Early on in treatment, however, analysands may become more symptomatic as they become aware of material that had been avoided or repressed.

Emotional modulation is an important benefit of psychoanalytic therapy. Emotional modulation may be defined as the capacity to identify one's preconscious emotional reactions and make appropriate adjustments to maintain mood, energy, and motivation. Psychologically healthy (or successfully analyzed) individuals are able to tolerate inevitable adverse life events by using reflection, self-analysis, sublimation, and other mature coping skills. Some of this capacity is learned through contact with the analyst, who models a calm reflective stance, and while it is not acquired through use of medication, can probably be enhanced by antidepressant, antianxiety, and mood-stabilizing medications.

Example. Ms. A learns that she has not been invited to a party given by a friend and notes a change from a light-hearted mood to a somber one, followed by reflection about the last several interactions with the friend, and how to cope with having been excluded. She thinks over whether to talk to her friend about it, ignore it, or exclude the friend from her own future guest lists, and she eventually regains a neutral mood. Ms. B, an individual with significant narcissistic vulnerability, experiences the same news by becoming overtly depressed and suicidal after ruminating for some time about being unlovable and worthless and engaging in fantasies of revenge. She did not make a connection between the depressive reaction and the experience of rejection. At her next session, Ms. B reports to her psychiatrist feeling more depressed without identifying any precipitant for the worsening; the psychiatrist might then assume that the medication is not working, and prescribe another medication to better suppress the negative affects, rather than talk with Ms. B about strategies for coping with rejection.

Medications work through a variety of mechanisms affecting mood, anxiety, and vegetative functions such as sleep, energy, and appetite for food and sex. Serotonergic facilitation, via SSRIs such as fluoxetine, sertraline, paroxetine, and others promote relaxation and sleepiness, while suppressing all the basic emotional systems and motivations; general improvement in mood and decrease in anxiety may promote pleasurable relating to others, though sexual functioning is often diminished. Play is diminished in animals (Panksepp, 1998) and it is not unusual for patients taking SSRI medications to report that they feel emotionally blunted, unable to either laugh or cry (Hoehn-Saric et al., 1991; Garland and Baerg, 2001). Selective serotonergic-noradrenergic reuptake inhibitors (SNRIs) such as venlafaxine, nefazodone, and mirtazapine are designed to overcome this blunting effect by increasing available adrenaline as well as serotonin.

The anticipation of rewards as well as the experience of some forms of pleasure in humans and other mammals is mediated in part by dopamine neurons in the ventral striatum (including the nucleus accumbens), which can be stimulated physiologically by eating, sex, or exercise and by substances such as nicotine, alcohol, or cocaine. (Ikemoto and Panksepp, 1999) [Serotonin is involved in the pleasurable effects of methylenedioxymethamphetamine, also known as Ecstasy or MDMA, a popular drug of abuse among young adults at raves or marathon dance parties; MDMA causes release of serotonin and dopamine stores and blocks serotonin reuptake, all of which contribute to the rewarding effects of this drug; users report an oceanic feeling of closeness to others and increased interest in being with the social group but diminished sexual interest or responsiveness. There is evidence for long-term neurotoxic effects of MDMA in humans.] Serotonergic facilitators used in psychiatric practice do not lead to stimulation of these reward- and pleasure-related brain areas and may in fact reduce the desire for various rewards. Thus many patients treated with SSRI antidepressants report lack of energy, enthusiasm, and motivation. The antidepressants venlafaxine (Effexor), nefazodone (Serzone), and mirtazapine (Remeron) are all referred to as selective norepinephrine and serotonin reuptake inhibitors, or SNRIs, and are designed to increase brain norepinephrine as well as serotonin transmission, with the objective of overcoming this blunting effect of the SSRIs. The only currently marketed antidepressant thought to increase dopamine levels is bupropion (Wellbutrin); due to its lack of serotonergic effect, bupropion does not quiet anxiety to the same extent as the SSRIs or SNRIs, so must be used in patients without severe anxiety, or adjunctively with other serotonergic medications.

Also note that through antagonism of one of the serotonin receptors (5-HT$_{2A}$), the atypical antipsychotics and some of the antidepressants (such as nefazodone and mirtazapine) may also increase dopamine transmission, contributing to their positive effects on mood.

Who Prescribes, Analyst or Psychopharmacologist?

The psychotropic armamentarium has been greatly expanded in the past few decades and will expand further with the addition of medicines targeting the hypothalamic-pituitary-adrenal axis, glutamate receptors, neuropeptides such as substance P and somatostatin, cytokines, and other approaches that move beyond the traditional monoamine hypothesis of depression. The serotonergic antidepressants, mood stabilizing anticonvulsants, atypical antipsychotics, dopamine agonists, stimulants, and opiates are now more commonly used than the still-effective tricyclics, monoamine oxidase inhibitors, and conventional neuroleptics due to their superior safety and side effect profiles.

The analyst should be familiar with these medications and the conditions they are used to treat, or recognize the indication for referral to a psychopharmacologist. This decision is straightforward for nonmedical analysts who feel their patients require medication but remains controversial among medical analysts. Since psychopharmacologists use many of these medications "off-label," that is, for indications other than the Food and Drug Administration (FDA)-approved ones, lack of extensive personal experience with psychotropic medications can lead to inadequate psychopharmacologic strategies and deprive analysts of the conviction that patients can really benefit from medications. This may perpetuate the conviction that medications are unnecessary or not helpful. Some (Wylie and Wylie, 1995) argue for sending the patient in analysis for consultation with a psychopharmacologist in order to preserve an analytic stance and avoid contamination of the transference. Some (Stern and Roose, 1995) argue for sending the patient to a psychopharmacologist to avoid inadequate medication treatment since inquiring directly about the effects of medication and side effects, and answering patient questions about medications leads to a disruption of the analytic process and an abandonment of technical neutrality. Still others prefer to prescribe and have found that the discussion about medications and the symptomatic changes can become a positive part of the complex fabric of the analytic relationship (Ostow, 1990). The decision is less controversial in the case of psychoanalytic psychotherapy, though some continue to assert that medication always corrupts the process of psychotherapy (Breggin, 1997). When the analyst does prescribe medication, the termination process must include discussion of how medication prescribing will be handled after termination.

Medication as Part of a Treatment Relationship. Patients given medication in the absence of a supportive therapeutic relationship with the prescribing doctor may get less benefit from it than expected. The same medication that fails when given without a stable treatment alliance may work well in the context of a trusting relationship. And conversely, medication that has maintained symptom relief may fail when the relationship with the prescribing psychiatrist is disrupted.

Example: Reaction to Separation from the Therapist. Dr. B, a single college professor, was treated with lithium for a childhood onset bipolar illness. Repeated attempts to stop the lithium led to episodes of hypomania and depression, so he and his psychiatrist agreed to continue it indefinitely. Traumatized by a sadistic, explosively angry father and furious with the loving but ineffective mother who could not defend him against his father's rage, Mr. B could not tolerate exploration into feelings about his past and demanded that the psychiatrist allow him to control the topics addressed in sessions. Though quite impaired in interpersonal relationships, Dr. B managed fairly well professionally as long as he had a session with his psychiatrist every month, where he discussed current issues concerning his sexual performance with women and anger with his department chair. When the psychiatrist left for a 3-month maternity leave,

Dr. B developed severe depression and a blood sugar of over 850 mg/dL that required transient insulin treatment and psychiatric hospitalization. Once his psychiatrist was back in her office and available to see him regularly, his blood sugar returned to normal, where it remained for the next 8 years without need for oral hypoglycemics or insulin, and the lithium again worked to control his mood cycling.

Dreams and Medication

Dreams occupy a privileged position among the various types of mental contents reported by patients in analysis, as they frequently illuminate ideas that are actively defended against in waking life. Traumatized patients often present with recurrent nightmares about the traumatic situation, and depressed patients often report troubling dreams. In some patients with chronic anxiety and depression, the presence or absence of nightmares parallels their state of distress. Ostow (2002) suggests using dreams to help identify subtle changes in mood that may not be reported, as a guide to benefits of medication or need for additional intervention. A patient who is unaware of distinct mood improvement with medication may report dreams that reflect a lowered level of anxiety and distress; alternatively, the recurrence of nightmares may herald a relapse of depression or anxiety requiring attention. It is important to note that several of the SSRI and SNRI antidepressants (primarily fluoxetine, sertraline, and venlafaxine) reduce slow-wave sleep and may have other effects on the dreaming mechanism. Patients on these medications frequently report that their dreams are much more bizarre, vivid, and "real" than before.

One must be aware of the meaning of the symptom (as with Dr. A) that can interfere with response to medication. There are many determinants of the failure to respond to medication, including noncompliance due to the fear of medication causing loss of control or intolerable side effects, covert use of alcohol or other drugs, and ongoing use of problematic defense mechanisms that lead to ongoing dysfunction and depression. Some patients may cling to their symptoms as a means of thwarting the doctor's efforts to treat symptoms, as a resistance, or as a reenactment of an important relationship from the patient's past. All such possible reasons for poor medication response are essential to explore with analytic patients and can lead to important new understanding, just as would discussion of any other interactions between analyst and analysand (e.g., reactions to fee increases or vacation schedules).

Clinical Presentations

Some patients want only symptom relief and have no intrinsic interest in self-understanding. They are best treated with a straightforward psychopharmacologic approach that includes education to improve adherence. Others, aware that painful affects have important psychic determinants, can be engaged in psychotherapy but develop resistance to deepening the process, especially once symptoms are under control. Some enter psychotherapy or analysis already on medication for severe symptoms, and others develop problematic symptoms in the course of psychotherapy or analysis that require treatment. The following cases will illustrate some issues involved in each situation.

Case Example: Combined Psychotherapy and Medication Treatment as a Prelude to Psychoanalysis. Dr. R, a 33-year-old mathematician newly appointed to a university faculty, was referred to a medical analyst by a social worker he had consulted for treatment of a lifelong depression. He had been treated with a number of antidepressant medication regimens prescribed by internists and general psychiatrists over the previous 10 years, with widely varying success. He felt subject to uncontrollable changes in his mood that sometimes left him literally unable to function. Medications that seemed to work for a few months could suddenly have no effect, and he descended into a deep depression from which it took months to emerge. His superior intelligence and capacity for bursts of sustained effort had made it possible for him to finish his doctorate, and he had been married to a devoted and loving wife for 6 years. They were reluctant to have children because of his precarious emotional states. He had never engaged in intensive psychotherapy but had seen a number of social workers for brief supportive therapy.

Dr. R was the youngest of five children born to parents who accumulated considerable wealth through the father's ruthless business acumen. As a child Dr. R had been the object of much sadistic emotional and physical abuse not only at his father's hands, but also by his older brothers who were unsupervised by their alcoholic mother. He does not remember sexual improprieties, but is troubled by a recurrent dream of being penetrated from behind by an older man who means to trick him and ridicule him. Among his siblings only Dr. R was able to leave the family emotionally to a substantial extent. He had essentially ended contact with his father and had only brief, painful contacts with mother who was usually inebriated and always highly self-absorbed. Family visits left him in a depressed, overwhelmed state.

Over the course of several years of weekly and twice-weekly sessions, Dr R developed a strong alliance with his analyst who helped him begin tolerating more awareness of the impact of his childhood and the relevance of childhood patterns to current relationships. At one point the analyst raised discussion of converting the treatment to analysis, but Dr. R declined. The analyst felt Dr. R might be instinctively protecting himself from the awareness of negative transference, which he couldn't afford. He needed to maintain a positive transference to the good maternal figure he had found in the analyst but also began bringing in dreams and attempting to make connections between childhood events and reactions in his current life.

After several more mood cycles that seemed unresponsive to the effects of psychotropic medications, Dr. R and the analyst came to understand his bursts of high energy as the equivalent of a manic phase of manic-depressive illness, a condition likely affecting other family members. With the addition of valproate and olanzapine to an SSRI and a stimulant, Dr. R had a brief period of stability that was interrupted by the development of an inability to finish a paper that threatened his chances for promotion. This inhibition was clearly related to earlier conflicts about success and competition. At this point Dr. R understood fully the limits of medication treatment and the risk of losing his job due to unresolved psychological conflicts; he asked about entering psychoanalysis. It was agreed that the long history of supportive treatment with the prescribing analyst would make it difficult to switch to an analytic format. He was given a referral to another analyst for analytic treatment so that the prescribing analyst could maintain the medication treatment.

This case illustrates the common presentation of depression complicating underlying neurotic conflict and the sequelae of childhood trauma. Dr. R was quite fragile and initially resistant to pursuing psychotherapy. He had hoped to gain control of his symptoms with medication. He had no history of euphoria or overtly manic behavior, but as a result of regular contact with his analyst, it became apparent that he cycled between depression, mild hypomania, and mixtures of the two that may have been made worse by antidepressant and stimulant treatment. (A common but frequently unrecognized point is that one or both of Dr. R's parents may also have bipolar mood instability, with concomitant negative influences on their capacity to parent. Thus, both nature and nurture factors play a role.) With time, he came to feel safe enough with the analyst to touch on painful memories he had long avoided and became convinced of the power of these memories as his dreams kept pace in illustrating the issues discussed in sessions.

In the analyst's opinion, Dr. R was not initially prepared to deal with the full force of transference given the nature of his childhood experience and the bipolar mood disorder that was difficult to control. The combination of medication and psychoanalytic psychotherapy gave him both the necessary mood stability and the conviction that it would be safe for him to investigate his mental life more fully in analysis.

The effectiveness of medication is always a function of the context of the patient's emotional life. The same medication that maintains euthymia under ordinary life circumstances may no longer work when the patient is under extreme stress. There is also the issue of setting realistic goals for medication: maintaining adequate sleep, energy, concentration, and appetite are reasonable expectations, but medication does not teach individuals how to recognize what they are feeling or how to modulate their emotional responses to the world. In the case of Dr. R, he had looked to medication to keep his mood stable and his energy level high while avoiding awareness of the impact of childhood trauma (and ongoing derivatives in adult transference relationships) that pervaded his life. His reactions to hostilities from a senior faculty member attempting to block his promotion made clear the childhood roots of his "escaping into depression" as a response to his father's vicious emotional abuse and his mother's alcoholic incapacity to protect him. Previous psychiatrists had overlooked the impact of childhood history and its effects on his adult functioning. Closer contact with the analyst raised the possibility of bipolar mood fluctuation and led to improvement in the pharmacologic treatment approach, while also creating the opportunity for Dr. R to investigate the past that haunted him.

Case Example: Beginning Medication after Starting Psychoanalysis.
Ms. M, a middle-aged married woman with two teenagers, sought treatment for lifelong depression that interfered with her capacity for pleasure and intimacy. She was evaluated by a biologic psychiatrist who found that she did not meet criteria for any Diagnostic and Statistical Manual (DSM) disorders and referred her to an analyst for psychotherapy. The analyst found that Ms. M had serious impairment in relations with

her husband and children and that her narcissistic vulnerability had tragically limited her capacity to realize her considerable potential. She was subject to bouts of gastrointestinal distress and felt miserable much of the time but denied problems with sleep, appetite, or energy level.

Ms. M entered analysis with only vague awareness of the impact of her considerable history of neglect and abuse in childhood. The opening phase was marked by a struggle to free associate (say whatever was on her mind) and the bringing in of photographs and scrapbooks as a means of telling the analyst the story of her painful history. As memories of sexual abuse by her grandfather came into focus, she developed severe abdominal pain, suicidal preoccupation, and hopelessness that all served to enrage her. Just as she had felt toward the mother who neglected her, Ms. M felt the analyst was sadistically subjecting her to these humiliating feelings that interfered with her ability to maintain the little bit of equilibrium she had gained in life. Efforts by the analyst to work interpretively with the intense negative transference did not quiet the symptoms that threatened to end the therapy, and antidepressant treatment was offered. This led to enough mood stability that Ms. M could continue the analysis, which was eventually quite helpful to her.

Like Dr. R, significant childhood trauma leading to symptoms of depression and complex posttraumatic stress disorder, contributed to Ms. M's presentation, and led her to consultation with a biologic psychiatrist in an effort to remain unaware of the full force of childhood history. Although Ms. M would be considered analyzable by most standards, the effects of childhood trauma limited her capacity to use traditional analytic treatment. Traumatized patients have difficulty maintaining the "as-if" quality of the treatment relationship and may need pharmacologic help in managing the negative aspects of the transference. This is essentially a parameter, used to help the patient regain effective ego strength. Ostow (1990) has noted the "surprising rigidity" shown by patients who require medication, but feels that nonetheless, the procedure often has benefits.

Many reviewers have concluded that even if a patient is judged analyzable, the outcome is unpredictable (Wallerstein, 1996). Some "good neurotics" like Ms. M cannot tolerate the rigors of traditional analytic treatment, while many severely ill patients have benefited greatly from psychoanalytic psychotherapy. Considerable differences exist in analysts' beliefs regarding which symptoms can be addressed with psychotherapeutic means and which require medication. Medication treatment does not confer the capacity for emotional modulation, though by eliminating overwhelming depression and anxiety it might make it possible for an individual to enter the therapy that would lead to the development of this capacity.

Case Example: Starting Psychoanalysis with a Patient Already on Medication. Mr. J, a 50-year-old married computer scientist, came for treatment of depression and insomnia that developed after the death of his mother. Despite lifelong alcohol dependence, he had had a successful career, but his marriage and other relationships were impaired by sadistic impulses that he made little attempt to disguise. He was now in a major depressive episode, with suicidal thoughts, sadness, poor concentration, loss of appetite, and intense dysphoria exacerbated by the drinking that once soothed him. Treatment with nefazodone, a sedating antidepressant, helped a little, and he was able to abstain from alcohol, but eventually venlafaxine, a more stimulating antidepressant, was added, leading to distinct improvement and cessation of the suicidal preoccupation. Mr. J entered analysis after 15 weekly sessions spent adjusting medication and investigating his history and current problems.

Mr. J worked well with dreams, which evolved over the course of the analysis from essentially mechanical landscapes devoid of people to interactions among people. For the first time in his life he could begin to identify feeling states in others. The analysis enabled him to successfully deal with hostilities in his work environment and enabled him to accept the limitations of his marriage and his part in creating them. He was able to deal straightforwardly with his father's death some years later. He has remained on antidepressant medication, prescribed now by his internist.

Specific Psychopharmacologic Considerations

The art of matching medications to individual patients requires experience with the agents themselves, ideally gained through prescribing them for nonanalytic patients, along with careful attention to the nuances of the patient's symptoms compared to side effects. In starting psychoactive medications, there is a high likelihood of unwanted side effects, and these may permanently affect the patient's willingness to use medication in the future. Therefore, the basic rule is to use the smallest available initial dose, very slow titration, and to encourage the patient to raise any questions or concerns rather than discontinue the medication.

Many of the antidepressants will have side effects that become troublesome at some specific dose for each patient. Early in the course of treatment, sleep disturbances and nausea are common, and later emotional blunting, loss of libido, and various gastrointestinal effects may emerge. For this reason, combining two medications at small to moderate doses may be more tolerable and effective than using a single medication at high dose. SSRIs may be combined with SNRIs, tricyclic antidepressants TCAs, bupropion, mood stabilizers, antipsychotics, and benzodiazepines. The decision to start a second drug is usually made when there is not full remission and limiting side effects are encountered with the first drug.

Antidepressants that affect noradrenergic and/or dopaminergic transmission [such as bupropion, venlafaxine (at doses above 75 mg), nefazodone, mirtazapine, tricyclics, and monoamine oxidase inhibitors MAOIs] may counteract the sedation and blunting caused by SSRI medications. Many patients feel more energy and motivation when these medications are used alone or in combination with the SSRIs. In some cases, the stimulant medications such as methylphenidate (Ritalin, Concerta, Focalin, Metadate, and others), and amphetamine (Adderall, Dexedrine, Dextrostat, and others) are necessary to overcome the lack of motivation, apathy, and fatigue caused by either the underlying depression or the serotonergic medications used to treat it. Direct dopamine agonists such as pramipexole (Mirapex) have also been advocated as an augmentation strategy for depression (Izumi et al., 2000, Sporn et al., 2000, DeBattista et al., 2000).

The mood stabilizers and atypical antipsychotics are extremely useful as augmenting medications added to an adequate antidepressant dose that is not fully effective. Patients need not be psychotic or manic to benefit from the addition of these agents. The atypical antipsychotics are quite useful for nonpsychotic patients in severe depressive and anxiety states, with insomnia and agitation that do not immediately respond to antidepressants (Kaplan, 2000). These medications carry a much smaller risk of extrapyramidal motor system side effects or tardive dyskinesia than do the conventional antipsychotics since they occupy the dopamine receptors only transiently. The risk of tardive dyskinesia is estimated to be approximately 0.3 percent for these atypical agents.

Sedation can be a significant initial side effect of quetiapine or olanzapine, though patients frequently develop tolerance to this effect. Weight gain occurs in most patients given olanzapine or mirtazapine, which can precipitate insulin resistance and type II diabetes. These side effects can be used to advantage with patients with insomnia, agitation, or anorexia. Ostow (2002) has reported successful treatment of anorexia with olanzapine.

Case Example: Use of Atypical Antipsychotic to Augment an Antidepressant for Anxiety and Agitation.

Mr. D is a 30-year-old accountant who began treatment for depression in childhood and who has been in psychotherapy for most of his life. He has been in once-weekly treatment with the same analyst who prescribes antidepressant medication for 12 years. Both parents are chronically depressed and his mother experienced a severe post-partum depression after his birth, heralding a childhood of considerable emotional deprivation. Despite superior intelligence, Mr. D had inadequate social skills and high levels of generalized anxiety even as a young child; his interpersonal difficulties at school interfered with his ability to derive satisfaction from his studies, and later from his work. He experiences such severe generalized anxiety that he now smokes 3 packs of cigarettes per day in order to manage it. This anxiety becomes nearly overwhelming when he is faced with interpersonal conflicts. He has tried using benzodiazepine tranquilizers added to the tricyclic antidepressant that has been most effective for his depression but becomes too sleepy to work and worries about becoming addicted. Quetiapine 25 mg at bedtime was added to his antidepressant leading to marked relief from his constant anxiety level. Eventually a total dose of 75 mg at bedtime was necessary to maintain this benefit.

Mood-stabilizing medications work (in theory) by modulation of excitatory and inhibitory amino acids via ion channels. Lithium and carbamazepine are well-proven antimanic agents; both require monitoring of blood levels, blood count, liver and renal functions, and thyroid status. While these medications stabilize mood changes, they do not function as antidepressants. Valproate, lamotrigine, and some of the atypical antipsychotics seem to have intrinsic antidepressant effects. In this regard, these mood stabilizers are better choices for patients with depression complicated by significant agitation and aggressiveness, a history of problems with impulse control, or hypomania induced by the use of antidepressants. Topiramate has been somewhat helpful with mania, depression and posttraumatic stress symptoms in various small case series and has the significant advantage of weight loss as a side effect.

Case Example: Appropriate Medication Treatment for Bipolar Affective Disorder Presenting as Depression. Dr. L, a married female internist, had experienced lifelong insomnia, agitation, and moodiness that were exacerbated by hormonal interventions associated with attempts at in vitro fertilization. She had a history of serious childhood emotional and physical trauma, with aspects of both neglect and abuse at the hands of her self-absorbed mother. Dr. L had coped with this history by devoting herself to her studies/work, by entering into sadomasochistic relations with others that reflected the relationship with her mother, and via her fantasies of giving birth to and raising her own children in a healthy, loving environment. The infertility and lack of success with in vitro fertilization led to a serious suicide attempt using overdoses of the two antidepressants she had been prescribed.

From this vantage point, it became clear that her difficulties were not only the result of an untreated depression, but that her agitation, insomnia, and moodiness reflected a bipolar mood disorder. (Again, her mother's emotional instability, previously conceptualized as borderline personality disorder, may have been in part untreated bipolar affective disorder.) Dr. L had been seen at least twice weekly and had a trusting relationship with her therapist, yet even increasing the frequency of sessions did not stabilize the depression. The antidepressants were discontinued and Dr. L was started on carbamazepine, which enabled her to sleep regularly for the first time in years. She noted relief from the agitation but eventually required lamotrigine and quetiapine added to the carbamazepine for ongoing depression.

Concomitantly with the medication treatment, Dr L was encouraged to pursue adoption, something she and her husband had previously ruled out. Within a year they adopted a baby girl, which led to further improvement and stability in Dr L's mood. She was able to return to full-time practice, take part in social activities, and deal with her daughter's needs effectively, even as her responsibilities required a decrease in the number of sessions to once every 2 weeks.

FUTURE PROSPECTS

The controversy regarding the use of medication with psychoanalysis or psychodynamic psychotherapies may someday seem quaint and misguided, much like the concept of the "refrigerator mother" causing schizophrenia in her child. Psychotropic medications are both an enormous boon to those of us who strive to relieve suffering and distressingly nonspecific in their capacity to manipulate psychological processes even as we come to understand these processes at neurochemical and neurophysiological levels of analysis. New medications are constantly being introduced and the monoamine theory will be supplanted with more sophisticated approaches over time. Our understanding of pharmacodynamics (the specific ways that drugs interact at receptor sites in individuals) and pharmacogenomics (the genetic patterns that affect how individuals respond to drugs) will eventually make prescribing medication for a given individual a far more accurate procedure. Genetic engineering (the insertion of genetic material necessary to cure a disorder) may someday make drug treatment unnecessary for certain illnesses, but given the huge complexity of psychiatric disorders that involve mood, affect, cognition, and behavior, specific genetic causes for most psychiatric illnesses will be difficult to identify. The role of life events in the etiology and progression of psychiatric disturbances must not be minimized.

The SSRIs opened the way to a new conceptualization of depression as a medical illness that can be treated much like diabetes can be treated with insulin, but psychodynamically oriented psychopharmacologists know this is far from either a simple or adequate solution. In fact, whether treating depression or diabetes, the relationship with the doctor is primary and remains a key to optimal therapeutic practice. Medications often have variable effectiveness; it is the medication plus the relationship that sustains well-being. Psychoanalysts understand and accept this principle, and those who are interested in working with medications (whether prescribed by themselves or others) while remaining open-minded about theory are commonly the most effective. Psychoanalysis has much to gain from investigation of growing knowledge from the neurosciences about brain function, and psychoanalytic theory can continue to evolve to take account of these advances (Solms and Turnbull, 2002).

CONCLUSIONS

Patients with straightforward neurotic problems should not require medication treatment through the course of an analysis, but many analysts will be assessing patients with a wide range of psychopathology who may need a variety of treatment approaches. The use of standard nosologic diagnosis (DSM-IV) in addition to psychoanalytic diagnosis helps clarify the possible treatment options, and the use of appropriate medication treatment will increase the range of patients who can make use of psychoanalytic psychotherapy and psychoanalysis (Gray, 1996).

The medical psychoanalyst interested in learning to use medication is encouraged to use standard antidepressant, antianxiety, and mood-stabilizing medications with patients who are not in analysis to gain experience and confidence in prescribing. Some patients will require medication in order to engage in analysis, and the medical psychoanalyst must determine his/her level of comfort in prescribing for patients in analysis. The author recommends dealing with medication use as one would with any other piece of data in analytic treatment: Strive to clarify and address the patient's view of the use of medicine, fears and concerns about taking medication, and the transference meaning of medication. Like physicians in primary care and general psychiatry, the analyst may experience considerable relief and even gratification in seeing patients get better with medication. For the internist or general psychiatrist, the relief from symptoms means the goal has been achieved; for the analyst, the work is just beginning.

REFERENCES

American Psychiatric Association (2000a). Practice guidelines for the treatment of patients with eating disorders. *Am J Psychiatry* 157(Suppl):1–39.

American Psychiatric Association (2000b). Practice guidelines for the treatment of patients with major depression. *Am J Psychiatry* 157(Suppl):1–45.

American Psychiatric Association (2001a). Practice guidelines for the treatment of patients with borderline personality disorder. *Am J Psychiatry* 158(Suppl):1–52.

American Psychiatric Association (2002). Practice guidelines for the treatment of patients with bipolar disorder (revision). *Am J Psychiatry* 159(Suppl):1–50.

Breggin PR (1997). Psychotherapy in emotional crises without resort to psychiatric medications. *Humanistic Psychologist* 25:2–14.

DeBattista C, Solvason HB, Breen H, et al. (2000). Pramipexole augmentation of a selective serotonin reuptake inhibitor in the treatment of depression. *J Clin Psychiatry* 20:274–275.

Doidge N, Simon B, Gillies LA, Ruskin R (1994). Characteristics of psychoanalytic patients under a nationalized health plan: DSM-III-R diagnoses, previous treatment, and childhood trauma. *Am J Psychiatry* 151:586–590.

Donovan SJ, Roose SP (1995). Medication use during psychoanalysis: A survey. *J Clin Psychiatry* 56:177–178.

Eissler KR (1953). The effect of the structure of the ego on psychoanalytic technique. *J Amer Psychoanalytic Assn* 1:104–143.

Foa EB, Franklin ME (2000). Psychotherapies for obsessive-compulsive disorder: A review. In Maj M, Sartorius N, Okasha A, et al. (eds). *Obsessive-Compulsive Disorder*, Vol. 4, Wiley: Chichester, England, pp. 93–115.

Freud A (1966). *The Ego Mechanisms of Defense*. International Universities Press: New York.

Freud S (1895). *Project for a Scientific Psychology*. Standard Edition. Hogarth Press: London, Vol. 1, pp. 283–391.

Freud S (1933). Lecture 31, *The Dissection of the Psychical Personality*. Standard Edition. Hogarth Press: London, Vol. 22, p. 80.

Freud S (1933). Lecture 34, *Explanations, Applications, and Orientations*. Standard Edition. Hogarth Press: London, pp. 153–154.

Freud S (1937). *An Outline of Psychoanalysis*. Standard Edition. Hogarth Press: London, Vol. 23, p. 195.

Freud S (1937–39): *An Outline of Psychoanalysis*. Standard Edition. Hogarth Press: London, Vol. 23, p. 182.

Gabbard GO, Gunderson JG, Fonagy P (2002). The place of psychoanalytic treatments within psychiatry. *Arch Gen Psychiatry* 59:505–510.

Garland EJ, Baerg EA (2001). Amotivational syndrome associated with selective serotonin reuptake inhibitors in children and adolescents. *J Child Adol Psychopharmacol* 11:181–186.

Gardner R (2001). Evolutionary perspectives on stress and affective disorder. *Sem Clin Neuropsychiatry* 6:32–42.

Gray SH (1996). Developing practice guidelines for psychoanalysis. *J Psychotherapy Practice Res* 5:213–227.

Hartmann H (1951). Technical implications of ego psychology. *Psychoanalytic Quart* 20:31–43.

Hoehn-Saric R, Harris GJ, Pearlson GD, Cox CS (1991). A fluoxetine-induced frontal lobe syndrome in an obsessive compulsive patient. *J Clin Psychiatry* 52:131–133.

Ikemoto S, Panksepp J (1999). The role of nucleus accumbens dopamine in motivated behavior: A unifying interpretation with special reference to reward-seeking. *Brain Res Rev* 31:6–41.

Izumi T, Inoue T, Kitagawa N, et al. (2000). Open pergolide treatment of tricyclic and heterocyclic antidepressant-resistant depression. *J Affective Disorders* 61:127–132.

Kaplan MJ (2000). Atypical antipsychotics for mixed depression and anxiety. *J Clin Psychiatry* 61:388–389.

Keller MB, McCullough JP, Klein DN, et al. (2000). A comparison of nefazodone, the cognitive behavioral-analysis system of psychotherapy, and their combination for the treatment of chronic depression. *New Engl J Med* 342:1462–1470.

Nersessian E (1992). The use of medication in patients who are in analysis. *J Clin Psychoanalysis* 1:41–45.

Ostow M (1990). On beginning with patients who require medication. In Rothstein A (ed). *On Beginning an Analysis*. International Universities Press: Madison, CT, pp. 201–227.

Ostow M (1993). How does psychiatric drug therapy work? In Schachter M (ed). *Psychotherapy and Medication: A Dynamic Integration*. Jason Aronson: Northvale, NJ, p. 133.

Ostow M (2002). Use of dreams by psychopharmacologists (letter). *Am J Psychiatry* 159:319–320.

Panksepp J (1998). *Affective Neuroscience: The Foundations of Human and Animal Emotions*. Oxford University Press: New York.

Roth A, Fonagy P (1996). *What Works for Whom? A Critical Review of Psychotherapy Research*. Guilford Press: New York.

Shevrin H (2001). Drug dreams: An introduction. *JAPA* 49:27–56.

Solms M, Turnbull O (2002). The brain and the inner world: An introduction to the neuroscience of subjective experience. Other Press: New York.

Sporn J, Ghaemi SN, Sambur MR, et al. (2000). Pramipexole augmentation in the treatment of unipolar and bipolar depression. *Annals Clin Psychiatry* 12:137–140.

Stern RH, Roose SP (1995). Medication use in training cases: A survey. *JAPA* 43:163–170.

Stone L (1954). The widening scope of indications for psychoanalysis. *JAPA* 2:567–594.

Wallerstein RS (1986). *Forty-Two Lives in Treatment*. Guilford Press: New York.

Wallerstein RS (1996). Outcomes of psychoanalysis and psychotherapy at termination and at follow-up. In Nersessian R, Kopff RG (eds). *Textbook of Psychoanalysis*. American Psychiatric Press: Washington, DC.

Weinshel EM (1990). How wide is the widening scope of psychoanalysis and how solid is its structural model? Some concerns and observations. *JAPA* 38:275–296.

Willick MS (2001). Psychoanalysis and schizophrenia: A cautionary tale. *JAPA* 49:69–73.

Wylie H, Wylie M (1995). Resistances and obstructions: Their distinction in psychoanalytic treatment. *J Clinical Psychoanalysis* 4:185–207.

19

DEPTH PSYCHOLOGICAL CONSEQUENCES OF BRAIN DAMAGE

Oliver H. Turnbull[1] and Mark Solms[2]

[1] *School of Psychology, University of Wales, Bangor, United Kingdom*
[2] *Department of Psychology, University College, London, United Kingdom, Department of Psychology, University of Cape Town, South Africa*

INTRODUCTION

It is clear that a wide variety of psychiatric changes can occur after brain damage or disease, including mood and anxiety disorders, apathy, psychotic symptoms, as well as a range of cognitive and behavioral disorders. It has also become increasingly clear that classifying together such disorders under the broad umbrella of *organic* does no justice to the diverse causes of psychological changes that occur after brain damage and disease.[1] The personality changes seen after frontal lesions, for example, differ dramatically from those seen after right convexity lesions. Indeed, the changes seen

---

[1] The clearest example of this was the category called Organic Mental Syndrome described in DSM-III-R (American Psychiatric Association, 1987), which referred to disorders due to "transient or permanent dysfunction of the brain" (1987, p. 98). This category included disorders as diverse as delirium, dementia, and the amnesic syndrome—but, of course, not disorders such as schizophrenia and bipolar mood disorder.

Textbook of Biological Psychiatry, Edited by Jaak Panksepp
ISBN 0-471-43478-7   Copyright © 2004 John Wiley & Sons, Inc.

after lesions to different regions *within* the frontal lobe (between, say, the medial, orbital, and dorsolateral surfaces) can themselves be vast. Moreover, there is often diversity in the clinical presentation within one class of lesion site. For example, in this chapter we will discuss the various ways in which damage of the right convexity may present either as an *unawareness* of deficit (anosognosia) or an obsessive *interest* in deficit coupled with a hatred of the paretic, or affected/disabled, limb (misoplegia). Closer investigation of the cause of the psychological changes in such patients has demonstrated that deficits are often more complex than they first appear and that a depth psychological investigation of such patients can greatly facilitate our understanding of the underlying nature of the neuropsychological deficit.

What has led to this increased understanding of the psychological consequences of brain damage? In part, it has followed from developments in basic neuropsychology. The past several decades have seen an increasingly sophisticated understanding of the diversity of psychological deficits in neurological patients, in domains as diverse as language, perception, and executive function. This growth in interest in neuropsychology began in the 1970s (Hecaen and Albert, 1978; Luria, 1973; Walsh, 1978), steadily increased through the 1980s (Ellis and Young, 1988; Heilman and Valenstein, 1985; Shallice, 1988), and appears to have continued its expansion through the 1990s (Banich, 1997; Bradshaw and Mattingley, 1995; Cytowic, 1997; Kolb and Wishaw, 1990; McCarthy and Warrington, 1990; Parkin, 1996; Martin, 1998). We now know an enormous amount about the way in which psychological function, especially *cognitive* function, is disrupted by damage to the brain. Indeed, part of this progress is a direct result of models of psychological function developed by cognitive psychology in the 1960s and 1970s, which led to the rapid growth of the field of cognitive *neuro*psychology beginning in the 1980s (e.g., Ellis and Young, 1988, and several others, as cited above). However, while these developments have been highly informative about the way in which cognitive abilities are organized within the brain, they have not been enormously helpful in explaining the neural organization of the psychological functions of greatest interest to psychiatry. One exception has been the recent development of a so-called cognitive neuropsychiatry, which has attempted to tackle issues of psychiatric interest (see Halligan and David, 2001). However, it might well be argued that a cognitive neuropsychiatry will always make limited progress in understanding psychiatric problems, if it continues to ignore the domain of emotion (see Turnbull, 2001, for more on this issue).

The second cause of change has been more recent, dating only to the early 1990s (see Solms and Turnbull, 2002). Following the gradual decline of behaviorism, the advent of functional brain imaging technology, and the emergence of a molecular neurobiology, topics such as emotion, motivation, and personality have suddenly

This intellectual sleight of hand would have implied that schizophrenia, for example, had no organic basis—an obviously untenable position—leading to the acknowledgment that "all psychological processes ... depend on brain function" (1987, p. 78). The double standard that neurological disorders might be organic, and psychiatric disorders *functional* was always doomed to failure—and the DSM IV (American Psychiatric Association, 2000) now renames that chapter Delirium, Dementia, and Amnestic and other Cognitive Disorders' (2000, p. 135).

emerged from the shadows and assumed center stage in many leading neuroscientific laboratories around the world (Damasio, 1994, 2000; Le Doux, 1996; Panksepp, 1998; Rolls, 1999). Not surprisingly, this has produced an explosion of new insights into the natural laws that govern our inner life. Because these issues are of central concern to psychiatry, and also because major psychiatric symptoms (including delusions and hallucinations) involve disturbances of core emotional systems (Panksepp, 1985, 1998), developments in neuropsychology have had the greatest impact on psychiatry over the past decade.

After a brief review of methodology, this chapter will address the "surface" (cognitive) neuropsychology issues surrounding the consequences of brain disease and damage, beginning with a review of the prevalence of psychiatric changes in the overall population of neurological patients. There follows a review of the range of "classic" neuropsychological deficits of greatest interest to psychiatry: the several disorders of executive function seen after frontal lesions and the typical changes seen after lesions to the right and left convexity. In each case we review the basic neuropsychological features of the problem, that is, the cognitive deficits commonly associated with the disorder, and cognitive models of the "psychiatric" disorder itself.

Thereafter, we review the depth neuropsychology[2] features of each disorder, with a brief discussion of individual case histories. By *depth* psychology, using the terminology of Freud (1915, p. 173), we refer to a part of the mental apparatus that is central for generating motivations and emotions, but that often lies outside of conscious awareness. In investigating these psychological functions, therefore, we are attempting to bring the observational techniques of psychoanalysis to bear on matters of prime concern to cognitive neuroscience. A detailed account of the way in which this might be done is beyond the scope of this chapter (though see Kaplan-Solms and Solms, 2000, for detail; or Solms and Turnbull, 2002, for a review). However, a brief account of this method is described below.

DEPTH NEUROPSYCHOLOGY AND ISSUES OF METHODOLOGY

In order to properly conduct a depth neuropsychological investigation, a *method* must be developed/utilized to allow one and the same thing to be simultaneously studied from both the psychoanalytic and the neuroscientific perspectives, so that the two sets of observations and the resultant theoretical accounts refer to the same reality. Only this enables us to link the *subjective* and *objective* approaches in mind/brain realities rather than merely semantic constructs. One suitable approach is the well-established clinico-anatomical method, familiar to those with experience of the theoretical underpinnings of internal medicine in general, and clinical neurology in particular. This method was explicitly introduced into neuroscience some 150 years ago, by Jean-Martin Charcot, the world's first professor of neurology, famous for his work at the

---

[2]The term *depth neuropsychology* has also come to be used interchangeably with the term *neuropsychoanalysis*.

Salpêtrière Hospital in Paris. The method involves systematic clinical correlation of compromised mental functions with anatomical damage to particular areas of the brain. The goal is to establish lawful, clinico-anatomical correlations between the different mental functions and the different parts of the brain. This approach has been the central method in neuropsychology for many years, uncovering the basic neurobiological correlates of psychological functions as diverse as language, memory, and executive functions.

What is required, for the purposes of a *depth* neuropsychology, is the simple extension of this method to psychological functions beyond cognition. In many respects, this is a simple extrapolation. People who suffer brain tumors, strokes, and other injuries are still people, with well-developed personalities, complex histories, and rich internal worlds. Since these things are the stuff of psychoanalysis, such patients can be studied psychoanalytically as can anyone else. In this way, basic clinico-anatomical correlations can be drawn, directly linking psychoanalytical concepts with neurological ones and thereby integrating them with each other on a valid empirical, rather than speculative, basis. By taking neurological patients into psychoanalytical assessment and therapy, one can determine whether, and in what way, a particular function of the mental apparatus has been affected by a brain lesion. A therapist with appropriate training can simultaneously help them come to terms with what has happened to them. Observed changes can then be correlated with the brain area that has been damaged. This reveals the contribution that the part of the brain in question made to the organization of that mental function. If, for example, we observe that patients with ventromesial frontal lobe damage suffer a near-total breakdown of what psychoanalysis would call *secondary process inhibition* (a process that one might describe in neuroscientific terminology as that of executive regulation of emotion), we may reasonably hypothesize that this psychoanalytical function is co-extensive with the neuropsychological functions of the ventromesial frontal region (see Fig. 19.1).

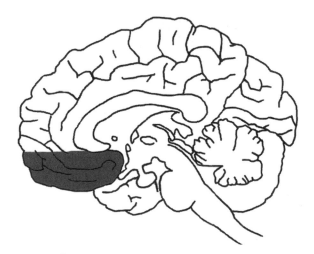

Figure 19.1. Ventromesial frontal lobes.

This assumes that the correlation between the observed lesion and the observed mental change was not simply a coincidence. That assumption is tested by checking one's observations in the individual case against analogous observations in as many similar cases as possible. In this respect neuropsychoanalytic research is no different from any other branch of neuropsychological research. By investigating small groups of patients, it is possible to discern reliable patterns of association between brain regions and mental functions of psychoanalytic interest. Kaplan-Solms and Solms (2000) describe three small groups of this sort, for three separate brain regions. The results appear to be quite reliable, but this research tradition is still in its infancy (see Solms and Turnbull, 2002).

PREVALENCE OF PSYCHOLOGICAL CHANGES IN NEUROLOGICAL PATIENTS

Psychological function can be altered in diverse ways after brain damage or disease. Here we will focus on several studies that discuss the incidence of such psychological changes. *Psychiatric* changes are common after focal brain disease and brain injury. For example, a number of studies have investigated the consequences of traumatic brain injury, where depression appears to be the most prevalent *psychiatric* outcome. Recent studies have estimated that clinical depression affects a majority of traumatic brain injury sufferers in the period immediately after their brain injury (e.g., Deb et al., 2000; Silver et al., 1991; see Hales and Yudofsky, 1997, for review). At 12 months postinjury clinical depression was still prevalent in some 20 percent of patients (Deb et al., 2000; Fedoroff et al., 1992), frequently persisting beyond 24 months (Rao and Lyketsos, 2000). Similarly, anxiety disorders, including posttraumatic stress disorder and obsessive-compulsive disorder, are common after traumatic brain injury (Jorge, 1993; Kant et al., 1996; Van Reekum et al., 2000), as are a range of psychotic disorders (Hales and Yudofsky, 1997, pp. 532–533). Indeed, a conflation of the effects of traumatic brain injury and psychosis has led to some confusion in the literature, so that studies have demonstrated disorders classified as psychosis, schizophrenia, and schizoaffective disorder in patients whose major explicit problem has been traumatic brain injury (e.g., Wilcox and Nasrallah, 1987; see Hales and Yudofsky, 1997, for further cases). Unfortunately, such studies focus more on epidemiology than neuropsychology, so that traumatic brain injury (to take one instance of pathology) is viewed as a unitary pathological category. In practice, several brain regions are routinely damaged in closed-head injury: the orbital frontal lobes, the anterior temporal lobes, and the upper brainstem all may be involved. In addition, there are frequent lesions to regions that are quite inconsistent across cases, making this pathology notoriously unreliable for the purposes of clinical-anatomical correlation (Kertesz, 1983). *Epidemiological* studies typically fail to investigate the consequences of lesion to specific brain regions, much less the particular psychological *mechanisms*, which contribute to the psychiatric changes in each case.

Such studies do little justice to our current understanding of the way in which psychological functions are organized within the brain. Why are these patients depressed, anxious, and psychotic after their brain injury? Is it a simple consequence of well-understood *cognitive* deficits sustained in the accident? For example, are they depressed because they are now amnesic or aphasic? Could it even be a consequence of *peripheral* (i.e., nonbrain) injuries to the body, as anyone might become depressed following a brachial plexus lesion or facial scarring after a motor vehicle accident? When one systematically investigates the effects of focal brain lesions, it becomes clear that *specific* sorts of psychological change reliably follow from particular lesion sites. For those working in cognitive neuropsychology (and cognitive neuropsychiatry) it is of no consequence whether the lesion is caused by stroke, head injury, or tumour—providing it disrupts the brain region or psychological function of interest. Matters of epidemiology are also of no great concern, with scientists showing a clear preference for striking, or exceptionally pure, cases. As a result, the field has been dominated by single-case investigations or the multiple single-case approach (Caramazza, 1986; Shallice, 1988). It is from this tradition that the work in this chapter derives.

In our first example of depth neuropsychological changes, we briefly discuss one class of lesion site, that of disorders to the lateral surface of the left convexity, where patients suffer *substantial* cognitive deficits—primarily in the domain of language, though also extending to the domains of voluntary action and some classes of visuospatial ability. Such patients quite commonly also suffer a right hemiparesis. Their psychological response to such losses is of great interest. As one might expect from a situation in which individuals have lost a range of important abilities, they are often overcome with feelings of loss and are frequently depressed. However, they cope with these problems in precisely the same way that neurologically normal individuals would cope with them: that is, they gradually come to terms with their loss through a period of mourning. In the course of this process, they begin to rebuild a life that takes account of their new circumstances.

We discuss some cases of this sort at the beginning of this chapter because such reactions to brain damage or disease are not universally found in neurological patients, as will become clear in the later parts of this chapter, where one sees (for example) a denial of deficit, with the patient adopting a distorted view of his or her explicit circumstances (i.e., of reality). Such changes in the very fabric of the person appear to follow from lesion to parts of the brain that lie closer to the *core* of the personality—probably because they impinge on systems centrally involved in the regulation of emotion and motivation (Solms and Turnbull, 2002).

LESIONS TO THE LEFT CONVEXITY

Patient Who Loses Her Thoughts[3]

Mrs. M was a patient who sustained a hemorrhage in the midtemporal area of the left hemisphere. Initially, when Mrs. M awoke in hospital, she showed the classic features

---

[3]See Kaplan-Solms and Solms (2000, pp. 90–115) for a detailed description of this case, or Turnbull et al. (in press a) more a quantitative investigation of the emotional state of this patient.

of a Wernicke's aphasia[4]: feeling as though everyone was speaking a strange, unfamiliar language that she could not understand, where in fact she had a deficit of language comprehension ability. The cognitive basis of such disorders is comprehensively covered in any basic neuropsychology text (e.g., Kolb and Wishaw, 1990; McCarthy and Warrington, 1990). In essence it appears to involve a disruption to the system that differentiates the perception of phonemes (e.g., *p* vs *b*) from each other. This ability forms the basic foundation of all (auditory) language comprehension; its loss makes familiar speech sound as unintelligible as a foreign language.

Mrs. M momentarily feared that she might be in heaven, especially as she began to recall what had happened to her. However, she rapidly made better sense of her environment. Although she could not understand what anyone said to her, it was evident from the appearance and behavior of the people around her (nurses, doctors, and other patients) that she was in a hospital. Mrs. M's phonemic hearing soon recovered, and she began to comprehend what was said to her, so long as people spoke in short sentences. She was now suffering from a residual disorder of audio-verbal short-term memory, causing, in Luria's (1973) terminology, an acoustico-mnestic aphasia (again, for more detail see the short-term memory sections of any basic neuropsychology text). As a result, she was unable to hold in mind anything that people said to her for more than a brief moment.

This was associated with a curious subjective state. Mrs. M kept "losing" her thoughts. A thought would occur to her, but before she was able to do anything with it, it was gone. Just as she was unable to hold on to what other people said to her, so too she was unable to retain what she "said" to herself. It was as if her memorial consciousness had become a sieve. The same thing happened when she tried to converse with other people. She would formulate the words that she wanted to say, but before she could utter them they had vanished, leaving her speechless and confused.

The severity of this condition fluctuated. Occasionally, Mrs. M noticed that her whole mind had gone "blank"—all her thoughts were lost—not just those related to things she had heard or wanted to say. This state of mind, in which she could not think consciously of anything, was understandably frightening and embarrassing. She responded by retiring to bed and waiting for her thoughts to "come back", which they typically did after several weeks and months. When Mrs. M was at home during weekends, she would frequently withdraw from social interactions and sit privately in her bedroom, waiting for her "mind to come back," as she put it.

In cognitive terms it is understandable that her thoughts would disappear in this way. This patient sustained damage to the midtemporal region of the left hemisphere—a region responsible for holding strings of words (or other audio-verbal sounds) in short-term (or immediate) memory. Damage to this system not only affects the ability to hold in mind the words that one hears but also the words that one generates in one's own consciousness. This is because the same audio-verbal "buffer" is used for words that are generated internally as for words that are externally perceived. Since

---

[4]For those unfamiliar with neuroanatomical and neuropsychological terminology, a glossary is available in Turnbull (2002).

the patient's audio-verbal system could not retain her internally generated thoughts in working memory, these thoughts would disappear. In passing, it is of some note that this seems to confirm Freud's proposal (and that of many others) that we communicate our thoughts to our conscious selves by clothing them in words.

What of Mrs. M's psychiatric status? Did she develop a set of psychotic delusions? As suggested above, she did not. There is abundant evidence that her ego functions were fundamentally intact: Despite her difficulties, her behavior continued to be governed by rational and reality-based thinking. For example, she tested her (momentary) delusional belief that she was in heaven against the evidence of her external perception, and this mental work resulted in the subordination of her fantasies to realistic perceptions. Similarly, when she lost her thoughts, she was rational enough to retire to her bedroom, waiting for her mind to return—a perfectly sensible solution to the problem. Clearly, this patient had not really lost her mind; all she had lost was the capacity to *represent* (or retain) her thoughts in extended consciousness. Her mind (her ego, and superego, see Kaplan-Solms and Solms, 2000) continued to exist and continued to govern her behavior *unconsciously*. She had lost only a highly specific aspect of ego functioning that lies far from the core of personality.

Patient Who Cannot Express His Thoughts in Words[5]

Although he was only in his 20s, Mr. J suffered a stroke (caused by bacterial endocarditis), affecting Broca's area and surrounding regions. As a result, his speech lacked fluency, he spoke in a *telegrammatic* fashion, and he could say very few words (i.e., a Broca's aphasia). The disorder suffered by Mr. J (which is now thought to represent a range of underlying language deficits; again see basic neuropsychology texts) disrupts systems that control language output at the phoneme, phrase, and sentence level. His disability, which also included hemiparesis (i.e., paralysis of the right side of his body), had dramatically affected his life, as one would expect. He lost his job, his romantic partner, and most of his friends. He understandably feared that he had no future prospects. All that he had previously taken for granted in life was slipping away. It was a tragic situation, and Mr. J was filled with anger, sadness, and loss.

When he was offered psychotherapy, he eagerly grasped the opportunity. There was much that he wanted to discuss, even though he no longer had the words to do so. One of the many things he wanted to tell his therapist was that he now felt like "half a man." He communicated this by drawing a stick figure of a man, bisecting it vertically, and saying "man . . . halfie . . . halfie." This communication was pregnant with meaning. It conveyed the essence of his emotional situation, and it simultaneously linked them symbolically with his neurological (hemiparetic) condition. He had lost his masculinity and the self-esteem that was attendant upon it. However, he worked extremely hard in his psychotherapy to come to terms with these losses, and ultimately he was able to construct a new, viable life for himself, built on revised premises and priorities.

---

[5]For more detail, see Kaplan-Solms and Solms, 2000, pp. 75–86, or Turnbull et al. (2002) more a quantitative investigation of the emotional state of this patient.

In short, this was a patient who was almost literally wordless; and yet he was able to make productive use of psychoanalytical therapy—the so-called talking cure—to negotiate the painful process of mourning and gain new insights about himself that enabled him to endure, with great courage, circumstances that would defeat many people with perfectly intact brains. We may conclude, as a provisional hypothesis, that the core of the personality of such patients, that is, systems involved in the generation and regulation of emotion/motivation, remain intact, at least to a first approximation. The same is not true for neurological patients with lesions to other brain areas.

VENTROMESIAL FRONTAL LOBES

The celebrated case of Phineas Gage illustrates the prototypical example of personality change after lesion to the frontal lobe. In the 1840s Gage was employed, in a supervisory and highly responsible role, laying railway tracks in the midwestern United States. He was pressing down a charge of dynamite into a rock formation, using a tamping rod, when the charge exploded, causing the rod to shoot through his head, from underneath his cheek into the frontal lobe of his brain and out the top of his skull. Partly because the rod passed through so rapidly, probably cauterizing the tissue on its way, the damage to Gage's brain was not widespread; only a relatively small area of frontal tissue was affected.[6] Gage did not even lose consciousness, and he made a rapid physical recovery.

His physician, however, observed some interesting changes when he reported the case in a local medical journal a few years after the incident. Despite the good physical recovery and relatively small extent of the brain injury, Dr. Harlow noted that his patient was radically changed as an individual: His personality was changed. Before the accident Gage had been the foreman of his team—a position of some responsibility—he was regarded as a reliable character, and he was highly valued by his employers. However, this is what Harlow said about Gage after the accident:

> His physical health is good, and I am inclined to say that he has recovered ... [but] the equilibrium or balance, so to speak, between his intellectual faculties and animal propensities, seems to have been destroyed. He is fitful, irreverent, indulging at times in the grossest profanity (which was not previously his custom), manifesting but little deference for his fellows, impatient of restraint or advice when it conflicts with his desires, at times pertinaciously obstinate, yet capricious and vacillating, devising many plans of future operation, which are no sooner arranged than they are abandoned ... In this regard his mind was radically changed, so decidedly that his friends and acquaintances said that he was "no longer Gage" (Harlow, 1868, p. 327).

Disregarding the now quaint language, the message of this physician's description still comes through clearly: As a result of his brain damage, Gage was "no longer Gage." The inescapable conclusion is that Gage's personality—his very identity—was

---

[6]See Damasio et al. (1994) for a precise description of the extent of the brain injury in this case.

somehow dependent upon the few cubic centimeters of brain tissue that were damaged in his accident. Today we know, from observing countless similar cases, that damage to this brain tissue almost always produces the very same type of personality change as it did in Gage. There is some variability, depending above all on the premorbid personality, but these patients are typically "fitful and irreverent, showing little deference for others, impatient of advice, especially if it conflicts with their desires," and so on. These are some of the cardinal features of what is now known as the *frontal lobe personality*. Practicing neuropsychologists have encountered literally hundreds of Phineas Gages, all with damage to the same part of the brain. This suggests that there is a predictable relationship between specific brain events and specific aspects of who we are. If any one of us were to suffer the same lesion in that specific area, we would be changed in much the same way that Gage was; and we, too, would no longer be *ourselves*.

Emotion-Based Learning

Neurological patients such as Phineas Gage had long been a puzzle to the neuropsychological community. The disorder is most commonly seen in cases of closed-head injury. Such patients often show relatively normal intelligence, and near-normal performance on a range of tasks specifically designed to test frontal lobe function. However, in spite of this, they choose unsuitable friends, enter inadvisable relationships, and engage in inappropriate activities (Bechara et al., 2000). This behavior typically leads to financial losses, career termination, and loss of affection of family and friends. The role of emotion, and especially emotion-based learning, has recently changed our understanding of the behavior of such patients. It appears that their poor judgment and decision-making abilities follow from an incapacity to use emotion-based learning systems, which provide information about the likely outcome of future decisions (see Damasio, 1994, 1996). Consistent with this claim, participants perform poorly if the task does not have direct emotional consequences for them (Turnbull et al., 2003).

This literature has suggested a biological basis for the substantial role of emotion in cognition, and this aspect of mental life can now be reliably assessed using the Iowa Gambling Task (Bechara et al., 1994). In this task the subject is faced with four decks of cards and asked to choose any deck, in any sequence. The subject wins or loses money with each turn and should learn to choose the decks that offer the best financial return. Some decks have frequent high gains but also occasional substantial losses. Sustained playing of these decks leads to overall financial loss. Other decks have more modest payouts but lead only to small and infrequent loses, so that sustained playing of the decks leads to small but consistent gains. The game is complex, and participants do not appear, subjectively, to understand the contingencies of the game. Nevertheless, participants quite rapidly develop a "feeling" about which decks are good or bad. This probably derives from small activations of emotion in the seconds preceding the choice of a high-risk "bad" deck—when the participant is contemplating which deck to choose (see Damasio, 1994, 1996). Activation of the autonomic nervous system is the physiological correlate of this emotional experience and can be directly measured using changes in skin conductance (see Damasio, 1994, 1996). In other words, participants receive "advance warning" of the consequences of their actions, coded in terms of emotion, allowing them to avoid negative consequences (Bechara et al., 1994).

Participants typically favor the risky decks in the early stages of the game, but neurologically normal participants (even those who regard themselves as "gamblers") rapidly shift to decks where they will accrue the smaller amounts of money over longer periods. Neurological patients with lesions to the ventromesial frontal lobes also show a strong skin conductance response after a bad choice has been made (showing that they still feel emotion), but have no ability to develop the advance warning effect that could alert them of a potentially poor-outcome choice. As a result they do not develop an avoidance of bad choices, and consistently lose money (Bechara et al., 1994). This inability to predict the likely emotional outcome of their actions is probably the cause of their many difficulties in everyday life.

Acquired Sociopathy

There have also been, in the last few years, some interesting suggestions about the role of the ventromesial frontal lobes in childhood. This work is based on patients injured in serious falls or car accidents—where the injury occurred under 2 years of age (Anderson et al., 1999). Unsurprisingly, because of lesions to their ventromesial frontal lobes, these individuals behave much like the adult patients described above. Thus, they consistently do badly in relationships, their general social interactions are poor, and their career progression is far from normal. This aspect of their presentation comes as no real surprise to us.

However, an *additional* factor appears in these neurological patients in that they fail to develop other core psychological abilities. In particular, they seem to lack empathy, and on formal tests of social and moral judgment and reasoning they do very badly. The claim has been made that these represent instances of "acquired sociopathy." Anderson et al. (1999) discuss the case of a young woman who had been run over by a vehicle at the age of 15 months. From the age of 3 she was noted to be "largely unresponsive to verbal or physical punishment" (p. 1032). By her teenage years she would have met many of the criteria for a diagnosis of conduct disorder and was stealing from her family and peers, had a conspicuous lack of friends, lied chronically, and had a history of multiple arrests. She had frequent unprotected sex and gave birth to a child, but "there was no evidence that she experienced empathy, and her maternal behavior was marked by a dangerous insensitivity to the infant's needs" (p. 1032). As in other cases of this type, the patient becomes sociopathic not by virtue of poor environmental circumstances or the nonoptimal attachment relationships that sometimes occur in dysfunctional families (see Schore, 1994, for more on the importance of the ventromesial frontal lobes for affect regulation). Rather, their behavior seems to result from an absence of the biological structures that underpin empathy. This conclusion is bolstered by functional imaging work investigating the size of the frontal lobes in psychopaths/sociopaths, which suggests that they have smaller than average frontal lobe volume (Raine et al., 2000). We should not conclude from these data that all cases of sociopathy result from brain damage or disease, but this developing literature points to the biological basis of this class of psychiatric disorder.

CONFABULATION AND THE NEUROBIOLOGY OF EMOTION SYSTEMS

Adults who have no history of psychiatric disorder show a range of features closely resembling those of psychosis when highly specific brain regions are damaged (e.g., Burgess and McNeil, 1999; Conway and Tacchi, 1996; Solms, 1997, 1998; Villiers et al., 1996). These patients are typically described as showing confabulation. Localization is not well-established (see Benson et al., 1996), but the patients typically have lesions to the ventral and/or medial frontal lobes and associated subcortical structures. The breakdown of *reality monitoring* becomes a typical symptom (Feinberg, 1997; Solms, 1997, 1998). That is, thoughts are interpreted as real perceptions, relatives are thought to be impostors (Capgras delusion, see Hirstein and Ramachandran, 1997), and dreams are mistaken for real experiences. This remarkable phenomenon (and localization of its associated lesion site) has been described in isolated neuropsychological reports for a number of years (Tallard, 1961; Whitty and Lewin, 1957; see Berrios, 1998, for historical review). Recent investigations suggest that simple "executive system" accounts may not fully explain the nature of the disorder (e.g., Burgess and McNeil, 1999) and that motivation/emotion systems may shape the nature of the false belief in such patients (e.g., Conway and Tacchi, 1996; Fotopoulou et al., under review; Villiers et al., 1996). The importance of this brain region in false beliefs is also consistent with the effect of anticholinergics, such as scopalomine, which can produce hallucinatory states (Perry and Perry, 1995), and the paranoid delusions that are part of a dopamine-modifying stimulant psychosis (Mendelson and Mello, 1996).

Recent studies have investigated a small group of these patients in psychoanalytic psychotherapy (Kaplan-Solms and Solms, 2000; Solms, 1998) and has produced a range of evidence favoring a emotion-based explanation of confabulation. In the language of cognitive neuroscience, the false beliefs in these patients were caused by the excessive influence of emotion and motivational systems over cognitive processes (see Fotopoulou et al., under review; Turnbull et al., in press). However, the account has also been cast in psychoanalytic terms, as the excessive influence of the system unconscious (Kaplan-Solms and Solms, 2000).

Freud outlined four principal properties of the system unconscious in his study "The Unconscious." These are: the replacement of external by psychical reality, exemption from mutual contradiction, mobility of cathexis (or primary process thinking), and timelessness (Freud, 1915, p. 187). Several of these principles (timelessness and exemption from mutual contradiction) are self-evident. Mobility of cathexis is best understood using the transference concept by which the attitudes and feelings associated with one person can be directed toward another. The replacement of external by psychical reality can reasonably be understood as arguing that these patients accept views of external reality that are congruent with affective states. In the basic scenario, they are likely to accept versions of reality that lead to positive affective consequences and reject views of external reality that lead to negative affective consequences. The clinical series of Kaplan-Solms and Solms (2000) appeared to present with false beliefs that met all the criteria described by Freud (1915), and these are briefly discussed below.

Exemption from Mutual Contradiction

One patient was an English gentleman in a neurological rehabilitation unit who had lived abroad for some years. Like all the other cases described in this section, he had bilateral medial frontal lesions (see Kaplan-Solms and Solms 2000, pp. 200–242). A close friend of his had died some 20 or 30 years previously, while they were both living in Kenya. One day he excitedly informed the staff that he had met a friend of his in the hospital. "Can you believe it," he said, "Phil Adams[7] is here in the same unit as me. You know the chap I told you about who died in Kenya 20 years ago; it's wonderful to see him again." When questioned as to how Phil Adams could be in the hospital if he had died in Africa 20 years before, the patient stopped for a moment and said: "Yes, that must cause interesting legal problems—being dead in one country and alive in another." He was quite capable of accepting two mutually exclusive facts as being simultaneously true. In relation to an emotion-based account of confabulation, there are clear affective advantages to meeting old friends (even dead ones) when you are in hospital.

Timelessness

A second patient (a woman who suffered from damage in the same brain region) had experienced several instances of medical difficulties prior to the stroke for which she had been admitted on this occasion. One was a deep vein thrombosis (in her leg), another a hysterectomy. To this woman, her current hospitalization was one and the same as the others. She would speak as if she was in the neurological ward for the purposes of a hysterectomy, but in virtually the next sentence she would suggest that her admission was due to a deep vein thrombosis, and then again, also, for a stroke. Indeed, she even seemed to think she was hospitalized at all the locations of the previous admissions simultaneously—so that she was in King's College Hospital, the Royal Free Hospital, and the Royal London Hospital, all at the same time. A series of separate temporal events had thus become merged into a single experience.

Timelessness of a different kind was displayed by the gentleman with the dead friend, described above. His wife always came to visit him at 5 p.m., which was visiting time. No doubt in the hope that his wife would soon arrive, the patient was constantly of the opinion that it was 5 p.m.—even straight after breakfast or before lunch. During one lunchtime, when his error was being corrected by a staff member for the umpteenth time, he noticed a No Smoking sign on the wall, which took the form of a red circle with a diagonal line through it. Mistaking this sign for a clock, he retorted: "Look ... it *is* 5 o'clock!" As in the example mentioned above, hospital visiting hours offer the patient certain affective advantages.

---

[7]Not his real name. All subsequent names are also changed, to protect the identity of the patients concerned.

Replacement of External Reality by Psychical Reality

In these cases, the demands of the internal world of the drives take precedence over the constraints of external reality, and inner wishes displace outer perceptions. An example of this kind of error is the above-mentioned case where the No Smoking sign became a clock showing 5 p.m., because this accorded with the patient's wishes. His inner reality dominated over his external perception in a way that we do not normally allow. In the same way, his wish to meet his dead friend (or to be among friends) distorted his perception of a stranger in the hospital (someone whose features probably reminded him of his friend). Even when he recalled the fact of his friend's death, the external evidence could be put to one side in the service of maintaining the wish.

Primary Process (Mobility of Cathexis)

Situations in which feelings invested in one object are transferred to others are apparent in the example where the patient conflates a stranger with his long-dead friend. However, a better example comes from another patient, who clearly recognized her husband when he visited her in hospital and treated him as such. Yet, when he was not there, she regularly referred to the man in the bed next to hers as being her husband and behaved accordingly toward him. Again, the wish-fulfilling properties of such conflations are clear. She wanted her husband to be there. When he was, that was fine; but when he wasn't, it was not at all difficult to ignore or modify her conception of reality to fit with her requirements.

In these cases, then, it appears that the false beliefs seen in neurological patients can, at least in part, be explained by an emotion-based model. Additional studies (e.g., Fotopoulou et al., under review; Turnbull et al., in press) that have investigated patients of this sort in a more systematic and quantitative way are entirely consistent with this emotion-based account (though they have revealed a range of issues that merit further investigation). For example, the false beliefs of these patients almost invariably transform their current situation into a more affectively pleasant one, in which family and old friends come to visit, or the hospital ward is perceived as a hotel, or is now directly attached to the living room of their home.

An emotion-based account of confabulation is of direct relevance to issues within psychiatry. For example, such an account offers some interesting insights into the possible neurobiological foundations of false beliefs—especially the suggestion that the excessive influence of core emotion systems over cognition might account for patently incorrect opinions about the world being held in the face of reasoned argument. It is of no small interest to psychiatry that the brain regions implicated in neurological patients with false beliefs are the same medial frontal sites as those implicated in schizophrenia. Indeed, the link between the two conditions becomes even clearer at the pharmacological level because poor regulation of a dopamine-based emotion system may lie at the core of false beliefs in both schizophrenia (e.g., Grace, 1991; Moore et al., 1999; Weinberger and Lipska, 1995) and other classes of false belief phenomena, such as dreams (Solms, 1997, 2000). More extensive discussion of this issue is beyond the scope of this chapter (see Solms and Turnbull, 2002, Chapters 4 and 6 for more detail).

LESIONS TO THE RIGHT CONVEXITY

The right hemisphere is conventionally said to be specialized for spatial cognition (De Renzi, 1982). Where damage to association cortex in the left hemisphere produces disorders of various aspects of language, damage to the equivalent parts of the right hemisphere produces disorders of a range of spatial, or visuo-spatial, abilities. These patients cannot draw a bicycle without misaligning the component parts; they cannot copy a simple construction made with children's blocks; and they cannot learn the route from their bed to the toilet [for a detailed review see DeRenzi (1982) or for more general coverage see basic neuropsychology text]. However, some right-hemisphere functions do not sit easily under the heading of spatial cognition. This is readily apparent from the syndrome that most typically occurs with right parietal lobe damage. This pattern of signs and symptoms, often described as the *right-hemisphere syndrome*, has three cardinal components. One of the components comprises the unequivocally spatial deficits just described (such as constructional apraxia and topographical disorientation), but the two other components of the syndrome are more complex. These go by the names *neglect* (or hemispatial neglect, or hemineglect) and *anosognosia*.

Neglect

Patients with this condition neglect, that is, ignore, the left-hand side of space (see Robertson and Marshall, 1993, for a review). If, for example, you stand to the right of such a patient and ask "how are you today Mrs. Jones?" she is likely to reply "fine, thank you." If you stand to her left and ask the same question, she is likely to simply ignore you. This is not because she fails to see or hear you. We have known for some time (see De Renzi, 1982, for historical review) that neglect is a disorder of attention rather than perception—for example, because such patients *can* see objects on their left side, providing that they are sufficiently salient (i.e., bright, flashing, moving, etc.). This problem affects not only objects in external space but even the left half of the patient's own body. Such patients frequently shave only the right hand side of the face, dress only the right-sided limbs, and eat only the food on the right-hand side of the plate.

Anosognosia

Anosognosia means unawareness of illness. When Mrs. Jones says she is "fine, thank you" she really means it; even though, as a patient with a substantial right-hemisphere lesion, she is actually paralyzed down the left side of her body. Although they cannot walk and need to use a wheelchair to get around, these patients claim to be fine and insist that there is nothing wrong with them. Their lack of awareness of their incapacities and their rationalizations concerning their problems extends to the point of delusion (see Ramachandran, 1994; Ramachandran and Blakslee, 1998; and Turnbull, 1997, for detailed examples). If, for example, you question a patient who claims that she is able to run why she is in a wheelchair, she might respond, "there was nowhere else to sit."

When you ask her why she is not moving her left arm, she might say: "I exercised it a lot earlier today, so I'm resting it." These patients seem prepared to believe anything, so long as it excludes admitting they are ill. Not uncommonly these patients make bizarre claims about their paralyzed limbs, such as denying that the paralyzed arm belongs to them, and saying that it belongs to someone else, a syndrome called somatopara-phrenia. They also frequently express intense dislike and hatred toward the paralyzed limb, beg surgeons to amputate it, and may even physically assault the limb themselves (misoplegia). Milder cases suffer from anosodiaphoria, where patients do not frankly deny that they are ill but seem indifferent or unconcerned about it. They acknowledge their deficits intellectually but seem unaware of the emotional implications.

Understanding the Right-Hemisphere Syndrome

The range of symptoms just described cannot be reduced to disorders of spatial cognition. Although there is a spatial component to these symptoms, some aspects of the right-hemisphere syndrome could just as well be described as disorders of *emotional* cognition. The emotional functions of the right hemisphere are now generally recognized, and many aspects of the problem have been comprehensively studied. The same applies to the *attentional* functions of the right hemisphere.

Various theories have been advanced in recent years that attempt to account for the nonspatial aspects of the right-hemisphere syndrome. The first of these is the *attention arousal hypothesis* (see Heilman and Valenstein, 1997; Ramachandran, 1994; Ramachandran and Blakslee, 1998). According to this theory, the right hemisphere attends to both the left and the right sides of space; whereas the left hemisphere only attends to the right side. Accordingly, when the left hemisphere is damaged, bilateral attention is preserved, but when the right hemisphere is damaged only unilateral attention remains. This model accounts for neglect and the attentional aspects of anosognosia but explains little else about the syndrome (see Kaplan-Solms and Solms, 2000, or Turnbull, 1997, for some of these arguments).

A second theory attempts to account for the emotional aspects of the syndrome but ignores the spatial aspects. This might be called the *negative emotion hypothesis* (Davidson and Irwin, 1999). According to this theory, the right hemisphere is specialized for negative emotions whereas the left is specialized for positive emotions. Damage to the left hemisphere thus reduces the capacity for positive emotion, causing depression and so-called catastrophic reactions (sudden onset of crying, moments of pretearfulness, etc.), which are more common with left- than right-hemisphere lesions. Damage to the right hemisphere has the opposite effect: The patient is inappropriately happy. Although this simple dichotomy between positive and negative emotions may seem rather oversimplified (cf. Solms and Turnbull, 2002, Chapter 4) it has been seen as offering a reasonable account of the basis of anosognosia.

Damasio (1994) has proposed a third theory, the *somatic monitoring hypothesis* (see also Heilman et al., 1998). This theory is based on the idea that the right hemisphere is specialized for somatic awareness, that is, awareness of the body as a "thing." Since, emotion is generated—in part—by awareness of one's bodily state, right-hemisphere damage impairs emotional awareness. This theory is more sophisticated than the previous two, and it appears to accommodate all the major features of the right-hemisphere syndrome (spatial, emotional, and attentional), but we shall soon see that it offers at least one major difficulty.

It is interesting to note the simple reasoning behind all these theories. Initially, investigators observed that right-hemisphere lesions cause defects of spatial cognition, so they hypothesized that the right-hemisphere might be specialized for spatial cognition. Then they observed that right-hemisphere lesions also cause defects of attention, so they added that the right hemisphere might be specialized for attention arousal. Then they noticed that right-hemisphere patients are inappropriately unconcerned about their deficits, so they added that the right hemisphere may be specialized for negative emotions. Then, in order to account for the fact that right-hemisphere patients are unaware of the state of their own bodies, they hypothesized that the right hemisphere is specialized for somatic monitoring. All of these hypotheses are fairly simplistic from a *psychological* point of view. The underlying reasoning is typical of the clinico-anatomical method (see Solms and Turnbull, 2002, Chapter 2): If something is clinically deficient due to brain damage, then the damaged tissue must have been specialized for producing that now-deficient function.

Psychoanalysts have learned to mistrust this type of reasoning when it is applied to the emotional life of human beings, which is viewed as a dynamic process/system of complex interactions. Psychoanalysts are therefore not surprised to find that the underlying mechanism of a disorder often turns out to be the very opposite of what it appears to be. A patient might appear to be inappropriately happy, not because he cannot generate negative emotions but because he cannot *tolerate* them.

Psychoanalytic Perspective

The observation that right-hemisphere patients are inappropriately unconcerned is not based on deep psychological investigations. It is based on simple bedside evaluations of mood or psychometric pencil-and-paper tests such as the Minnesota Multiphasic Personality Inventory (MMPI) or Beck Depression Inventory, which rely on the patient's own assessment of his or her mood. Our group has carried out an investigation that bypasses such explicit approaches. A series of five patients with damage to the perisylvian convexity of the right hemisphere were investigated in psychoanalytic psychotherapy [see Kaplan-Solms and Solms (2000), Chapter 8, for details, or Turnbull et al., 2002 for a quantitative analysis of the emotional life of these patients].

The first two patients exhibited typical features of the right-hemisphere syndrome—they were incompletely aware of their (substantial) cognitive and physical deficits and they neglected the left-hand side of space (including the left side of their own bodies). They also displayed classical emotional indifference to their disabilities. However, this "indifference" was quickly observed to be a highly fragile state. In their psychotherapy sessions, both patients burst into tears for brief moments during which they seemed to be overwhelmed by emotions of the very kind that are normally conspicuous by their absence. This gave the impression of suppressed sadness, grief, dependency fears, and the like rather than a true absence of such feelings.

For example, one of these patients—Mrs. M—found herself suddenly bursting into uncontrollable tears while reading a book (see Kaplan-Solms and Solms, 2000, pp. 167–172). She then regained her composure and continued reading. When asked the next day by her therapist what she had been reading when she started to cry, she couldn't remember. All that she could recall was that it had something to do with a court case. On further investigation, it turned out that she had been reading about a court case involving parents who were fighting for compensation for a thalidomide child. Mrs. M, who had suffered a severe stroke during childbirth and lost the use of her left arm and leg, had clearly identified her own disability with that of the thalidomide child. However, she was completely unaware of this connection. Mrs. M also (who was of Eastern European, Jewish descent) burst into tears repeatedly while watching the film *Fiddler on the Roof*. It would clearly be erroneous to claim that this patient could not experience negative emotions; more accurate would be to say that she could not tolerate them, particularly feelings of loss.

The second case was a man (Mr. C; see Kaplan-Solms and Solms, 2000, pp. 160–167). He too was paralyzed by a right-hemisphere stroke but "unaware" of his deficit. Accordingly, his physiotherapist was unable to enlist his cooperation in trying to teach him how to walk again. He seemed oblivious of his deficit and totally unconcerned about it. When recounting the relevant events to his psychotherapist the next day, however, he suddenly burst into tears. When she probed the underlying feelings, Mr. C blurted out: "but *look* at my arm, what am I going to do if it doesn't recover, how am I ever going to work again." He then regained his composure and reverted to his typical "indifferent" state. This behavior is not consistent with the somatic monitoring hypothesis. Mr. C was not unaware of the state of his body. Rather, he had suppressed conscious awareness of the state of his body. Attention is not an emotionally neutral function. As with Mrs. M, such occurrences were common with this patient. They were also not very difficult to understand. Both of these cases were intolerant of the depressive feelings associated with their loss (which they were certainly unconsciously aware of), and they were therefore unable to work through these feelings by the normal process of mourning.

Failures in the process of mourning take many forms. In the well known "Mourning and Melancholia," Freud (1917) contrasted the normal process of mourning with the pathology of melancholia (i.e., clinical depression). He argued that, in mourning, a person gradually comes to terms with loss by giving up (separating from) the lost love object, whereas in depression this cannot happen because the patient denies the loss. You cannot come to terms with a loss if you do not acknowledge its existence. Freud argued that this was particularly apt to happen if the original attachment to the lost object had been a narcissistic one, in which the separateness of the love object is not recognized but rather treated as if it were part of the self—in contrast to *object love*, a more mature form of attachment, where the independence of the love object is acknowledged. Freud argued that in melancholia the patient denies the loss of the love object by identifying himself with it, by literally becoming that object in fantasy. The depression itself then results from the internalization of the feelings of resentment toward the object that has been abandoned (so that the narcissist attacks the internalized object with all the ruthless vengefulness of a lover scorned).

This explanation also seems to fit the third case of right-hemisphere syndrome that was investigated psychoanalytically. This case, Mrs. A (see Kaplan-Solms and Solms, 2000, pp. 173–179), suffered severe spatial deficits, neglect, and anosognosia but, at the same time, she was profoundly depressed. This is unusual for right-hemisphere patients, producing a paradoxical situation in which the patient was unaware of a loss (anosognosia) and yet simultaneously displaying severe depressive reactions to it. She was constantly in tears, lamenting the fact that she was such a burden to the medical and nursing staff, whose generous attention she did not deserve since she was not fit to live, and so on. The psychoanalytic investigation revealed that Mrs. A was in fact, unconsciously very much aware of her loss, but she was denying it by means of the introjective process described above. Unconsciously, Mrs. A did have an internalized image of her damaged, crippled self, and she attacked that image to the point of twice attempting to kill herself. In this case, the patient was overwhelmed by feelings of the same type that the previous two patients managed (for the most part) to successfully suppress. In the final two cases, the situation was more complicated still.

A further patient, Mr. D (see Kaplan-Solms and Solms, 2000, pp. 187–197), was anything but unconcerned and indifferent about his deficits. He was absolutely obsessed by them and displayed a symptom mentioned earlier: *misoplegia* (hatred of the paretic limb). Mr. D had only a mild paresis of the left hand, and he would have been able to use it if he had tried. However, he refused to use the hand and actually demanded that the surgeon cut it off because he loathed it so much. This patient once became so enraged at his hand that he smashed it against a radiator, claiming that he was going to break it to pieces and post the bits of flesh in an envelope to the neurosurgeon who had operated on him. This reaction conveys vividly the emotional state of these patients.

It is interesting that the same lesion site can produce such opposite emotional reactions: unawareness of a limb and denial of its deficits versus obsessive hatred of a limb and its imperfections. This state of affairs almost demands a psychodynamic (or at least some other form of dynamic) explanation. The psychoanalyst who treated these two patients came to the conclusion that their underlying psychodynamics were very similar to those of Mrs. A; they too attacked their internal awareness of their loss, but rather than attempt to kill themselves (like Mrs. A), they reacted by trying to literally detach the hated (damaged) image of themselves—or parts of themselves—from the rest, in order to preserve their intact selves.

No doubt, other permutations are possible.[8] What all of these cases have in common is a failure of the process of mourning. Underlying the range of clinical presentations was this common dynamic mechanism: These patients could not tolerate the difficult feelings associated with coming to terms with loss. The superficial differences

---

[8]Moss and Turnbull (1996) described a 10-year-old child, with the classic right-hemisphere syndrome, who alternated between a state of denial (anosognosia) and hatred (misoplegia) in relation to his left hand. During the period when he hated it, he said that he wanted to have that arm surgically removed and replaced with the left arm of his mother.

between the patients is attributable to the fact that they defended themselves against this intolerable situation in various ways.

A Reinterpretation

We are now in a position to integrate some of the findings described above. In strictly cognitive terms, it is well known that the right perisylvian convexity is specialized for spatial cognition. In psychoanalytic terms, it appears that damage to this area undermines the patients' ability to represent the relationship between self and objects accurately (a function that is, of course, a form of spatial cognition). This may in turn undermine object relationships in the psychoanalytic sense: Object love (based on a realistic conception of the separateness between self and object) collapses, and the patients' object relationships regress to the level of narcissism. This results in narcissistic defenses against object loss, rendering these patients incapable of normal mourning. They deny their loss and all the feelings, including external perceptions associated with it, using a variety of defenses to shore up this denial whenever the intolerable reality threatens to break through.

The psychoanalytic argument relating to anosognosia, presented in the previous section, was initially developed in the context of the standard psychoanalytic method. However, there has recently been a series of quantitative investigations of the behavior of anosognosics (Turnbull et al., 2002), and these attempts thus far are quite consistent with the original claim. For example, the data suggest that patients with anosognosia appear to have some form of implicit awareness of their deficit, and also that anosognosics appear to be overcome with one class of emotion—feelings of separation and loss (Turnbull et al., 2002). These data are entirely compatible with the psychoanalytic claim that an inability to come to terms with loss forms the basis of the disorder. Whether this is the sole basis of the denial of deficit in these patients will clearly require further research.

CONCLUSION

Psychoanalytic investigation of the inner life of neurological patients clearly has much to offer us. In each instance described above, it has been able to throw important light on a number of syndromes that neurocognitive theories cannot fully explain due to their failure to accommodate the psychological complexities of human emotional life. However, psychoanalytic hypotheses are no less prone to error than cognitive ones and therefore need to be subjected to the same rigorous empirical tests. Though detailed discussion of such investigations has been beyond the scope of this chapter, some progress has recently been made in investigating the various classes of disorder reported above with greater empirical rigor than is possible in the context of the conventional psychoanalytic setting. Where appropriate investigations have been performed, it appears that the data from the more highly controlled studies are consistent with the earlier, purely clinical, investigations (Turnbull, 2003; Turnbull et al., 2002; in press c).

It also seems appropriate to point out that our research has focused only on a few of the many psychiatric disorders that may follow from brain damage. To take the narrowest of examples, we have described the confabulatory states that are seen after bilateral medial frontal lesions. However, the depth psychological issues that follow from lesions in other frontal sites (such as disinhibition or adynamia) require far closer scrutiny than we have been able to offer thus far. On a broader scale, there are a range of disorders that follow from lesions (and excitatory states) involving limbic regions that clearly require further investigation. These include the personality changes seen after the viral encephalopathies (such as herpes simplex encephalitis) that target the medial temporal lobes. Similarly, there are fascinating issues related to the preictal experiences of those with epilepsies (especially complex partial epilepsy), not to mention modifications of interictal personality in those whose seizures are not fully controlled. A range of interesting changes to personality also occur after lesions to the diencephalon, not only in Korsakoff's syndrome, but also after disruption to the various hypothalamic emotion and motivation systems. We could easily extend this list of brain regions of interest to a depth psychology. Indeed, it is becoming apparent that an extraordinarily wide range of brain regions (perhaps even the majority) play some role in motivation, emotion, and personality.[9]

It is clear that we stand at the dawn of an exciting new era in psychological science. All sorts of possibilities are opening up. We appear, at last, to have within our grasp the possibility of studying the biological basis of a range of psychological and psychiatric phenomena that were poorly understood even a decade or two ago. In understanding the way in which focal brain disease/damage affects the mental apparatus, we appear to be gaining a much clearer understanding of the "psychiatric" presentation of many neurological patients. In addition, we now also appear to better understand how mental disorders in general arise. Perhaps the clearest example would be the fact that the confabulatory states of patients with ventromesial frontal lesions might be similar to those of traditionally psychiatric individuals with psychosis. With a better understanding of the biological basis of psychiatric disorder, we will be able to target our therapies to those who can benefit most, and in the ways that work best. We may even extend our clinical reach in previously undreamt of directions.

REFERENCES

American Psychiatric Association (1987). *Diagnostic and Statistical Manual of Mental Disorders*, 3rd ed.-Revised, APA: Washington, DC.

American Psychiatric Association (2000). *Diagnostic and Statistical Manual of Mental Disorders*, 4th ed. APA: Washington, DC.

Anderson SW, Bechara A, Damasio H, Tranel D, Damasio A (1999). Impairment of social and moral behavior related to early damage in human prefrontal cortex. *Nature Neurosci* 2:1032–1037.

---

[9]Davidson (2000) suggests that "there are no parts of the brain dedicated exclusively to cognition and others to emotion ... [such that] the duality between reason and emotion that has been perpetuated through the ages is a distinction that is not honored by the architecture of the brain" (p. 91).

Banich MT (1997). *Neuropsychology: The Neural Basis of Mental Functioning*. Houghton Mifflin: Boston.

Bechara A, Damasio AR, Damasio H, Anderson SW (1994). Insensitivity to future consequences following damage to human prefrontal cortex. *Cognition* 50:7–15.

Bechara A, Damasio H, Damasio AR (2000). Emotion, decision making and the orbitofrontal cortex. *Cerebral Cortex* 10:295–307.

Berrios GE (1998). Confabulations: A conceptual history. *J History Neurosci* 7:225–241.

Benson DF, Djenderedjian A, Miller MD et al. (1996). Neural basis of confabulation. *Neurology* 46:1239–1243.

Bradshaw JL, Mattingley JB (1995). *Clinical Neuropsychology: Behavioral and Brain Science*. Academic Press: San Deigo.

Burgess PW, McNeil JE (1999). Content-specific confabulation. *Cortex* 35:163–182.

Caramazza A (1986). On drawing inferences about the structure of normal cognitive systems from the analysis of patterns of impaired performance: The case for single-patient studies. *Brain and Cognition* 5:41–66.

Conway MA, Tacchi PC (1996). Motivated confabulation. *Neurocase* 2:325–338.

Damasio A (1994). *Descartes' Error*. Grosset/Putnam: New York.

Damasio AR (1996). The somatic marker hypothesis and the possible functions of the prefrontal cortex. *Phil Trans Roy Soc London (Biology)* 351:1413–1420.

Damasio A (2000). *The Feeling of What Happens*. William Heinemann: London.

Damasio H, Grabowski T, Frank R, Galaburda A, Damasio A (1994). The return of Phineas Gage: The skull of a famous patient yields clues about the brain. *Science* 264:1102–1105.

Davidson RJ (2000). Cognitive neuroscience needs affective neuroscience (and vice versa). *Brain and Cognition* 42:89–92.

Davidson RJ, Irwin W (1999). The functional neuroanatomy of emotion and affective style. *Trends Cognitive Scie* 3:11–21.

Deb S, Lyons I, Koutzoukis C (2000). Neurobehavioral symptoms one year after head injury. *British J Psychiatry* 58:360–365.

De Renzi E (1982). *Disorders of Space Exploration and Cognition*. Wiley: Chichester.

Ellis AW, Young AW (1988). *Human Cognitive Neuropsychology*. Lawrence Earlbaum: Hove, Sussex, UK.

Fedoroff JP, Starkstein SE, Forrester AW (1992). Depression in patients with acute traumatic injury. *Am. J Psychiatry* 149:918–923.

Feinberg TE (1997). Anosognosia and confabulation. In Feinberg TE, Farah MJ (eds). *Behavioral Neurology and Neuropsychology*. McGraw Hill: New York, pp. 369–390.

Fotopoulou A, Solms M, Turnbull OH (under review). *Wishful Reality Distortions in Confabulation*.

Freud S (1915). The unconscious. *SE* 14:166–215.

Freud S (1917). Mourning and melancholia. *SE* 14:239.

Grace AA (1991). Phasic versus tonic dopamine release and the modulation of dopamine system responsivity: A hypothesis for the etiology of schizophrenia. *Neuroscience* 41:1–24.

Guillain, G (1959). *J-M Charcot: His life, His work*. London: Pitman Medkar Publishing Company.

Halligan PW, David AS (2001). Cognitive neuropsychiatry: Towards a scientific psychopathology. *Nature Neuro* 2:209–215.

Harlow J (1868). Recovery from passage of an iron bar through the head. *Mass Med Soc Publ* 2:327–347.

Hecaen H, Albert ML (1978). *Human Neuropsychology*. Wiley: New York.

Heilman KM, Valenstein E (1995). *Clinical Neuropsychology*. Oxford University Press: Oxford.

Heilman KM, Valenstein E (1997). *Clinical Neuropsychology*. Oxford University Press: Oxford.

Heilman KM, Barrett AM, Adair JC (1998). Possible mechanisms of anosognosia: A deficit in self-awareness. *Phil Trans Roy Soc London (Series B: Biology)* 353:1903–1909.

Hales RE, Yudofsky SC (1997). *Textbook of Neuropsychiatry*, 3rd ed. American Psychiatric Press: New York.

Hirstein W, Ramachandran VS (1997). Capgras syndrome: A novel probe for understanding the neural representation of the identity and familiarity of persons. *Proc Roy Soc London* 264:437–444.

Jorge RE (1993). Comparison between acute and delayed-onset of depression following traumatic brain injury. *J Neuropsychiatry Clin Neurosci* 5:43–49.

Kant R, Smith P, Seemiller L, Duffy JD (1996). Obsessive compulsive disorder after closed head injury: Review of the literature and report of four cases. *Brain Injury* 10:65–73.

Kaplan-Solms K, Solms M (2000). *Clinical Studies in Neuro-Psychoanalysis*. Karnac Books: London.

Kertesz A (1983). *Localisation in Neuropsychology*. Academic Press: New York.

Kolb B, Wishaw IP (1990). *Fundamentals of Human Neuropsychology*. Freeman & Co: New York.

Le Doux J (1996). *The Emotional Brain*. Touchstone: New York.

Luria AR (1973). *The Working Brain* Basic Books: New York.

McCarthy RA, Warrington EK (1990). *Cognitive Neuropsychology: A Clinical Introduction*. Academic Press: New York.

Martin GN (1998). *Human Neuropsychology*. Prentice Hall: London.

Mendelson JH, Mello NK (1996). Management of cocaine abuse and dependence. *New Engl J Med* 334:965–972.

Moore H, West AR, Grace AA (1999). The regulation of forebrain dopamine transmission: Relevance to the pathophysiology and psychopathology of schizophrenia. *Biological Psychiatry* 46:40–55.

Moss AD, Turnbull OH (1996). Hatred of the hemiparetic limbs (misoplegia) in a 10 year-old child. *J Neurol Neurosurgery Psychiatry* 61(2):210–211.

Parkin AJ (1996). *Explorations in Cognitive Neuropsychology*. Blackwell: Cambridge, MA.

Panksepp J (1985). Mood changes. In Vinken P, Bruyn G, Klawans H (eds). *Handbook of Clinical Neurology*, Vol. 45. Elsevier: Amsterdam, pp. 271–285.

Panksepp J (1998). *Affective Neuroscience: The Foundations of Human and Animal Emotions*. Oxford University Press: New York.

Perry E, Perry R (1995). Acetylcholine and hallucinations: Disease-related, compared to drug-induced, alterations in human consciousness. *Brain and Cognition* 28:240–258.

Ramachandran VS (1994). Phantom limbs, neglect syndromes, repressed memories, and Freudian Psychology. *Int Rev Neurobiol* 37:291–333.

Ramachandran VS, Blakslee S (1998). *Phantoms in the Brain: Human Nature and the Architecture of the Mind.* Fourth Estate: London.

Rao V, Lyketsos C (2000). Neuropsychiatric sequelae of traumatic brain injury. *Psychosomatics* 41:95–102.

Raine A, Lencz T, Bihrle S, LaCasse L, Colletti P (2000). Reduced prefrontal grey matter volume and reduced autonomic activity in antisocial personality disorder. *Arch Gen Psychiatry* 57:119–127.

Robertson IH, Marshall JC (1993). *Unilateral Neglect: Clinical and Experimental Studies.* Lawrence Earlbaum Associates: Hove, Sussex, United Kingdom.

Rolls ET (1999). *The Brain and Emotion.* Oxford University Press, Oxford, United Kingdom.

Schore A (1994). *Affect Regulation and the Origin of the Self.* Lawrence Erlbaum Associates: Mahwah, NJ.

Shallice T (1988). *From Neuropsychology to Mental Structure.* Cambridge University Press, Cambridge.

Silver JM, Yudofsky SC, Hales RE (1991). Depression in traumatic brain injury. *Neuropsychiatry, Neuropsychology and Behavioral Neurology* 4:12–23.

Solms M (1997). *The Neuropsychology of Dreams* Lawrence Earlbaum Associates: Mahwah, NJ.

Solms M (1998). Psychoanalytic observations on four cases on ventromesial frontal lobe damage. *Psyche-Zeitschrift Fur Psychoanalyse Und Ihre Anwendungen* 52:919–962.

Solms M (2000). Dreaming and REM sleep are controlled by different brain mechanisms. *Behav Brain Sci* 23:843–850.

Solms M, Turnbull OH (2002) *The Brain and The Inner World: An Introduction to the Neuroscience of Subjective Experience.* Other Press/Karnac Books: London.

Tallard GA (1961). Confabulation in the Wernicke-Korsakoff syndrome. *J Nervous and Mental Dis* 132:361–381.

Turnbull OH (1997). Neglect: Mirror mirror, on the wall—is the left side there at all? *Curr Biol* 7:709–711.

Turnbull OH (2001). Cognitive neuropsychology comes of age. *Cortex* 37:445–450.

Turnbull OH (2002). Notes on neuroscientific terminology. In Kaplan-Solms K, Solms M (eds). *Clinical Studies in Neuro-Psychoanalysis: Introduction to a Depth Neuropsychology,* 2nd ed. Karnac Books/Other Press: New York, pp. 285–296.

Turnbull OH (2003). Emotion, false beliefs, and the neurobiology of intuition. In: Corrigall J, Wilkinson H (eds). *Revolutionary Connections: Psychotherapy and Neuroscience.* Karnac Press: New York, pp. 133–160.

Turnbull OH, Jones K, Reed-Screen J (2002). Implicit awareness of deficit in anosognosia: An emotion-based account of denial of deficit. *Neuropsychoanalysis* 4:69–86.

Turnbull OH, Berry H, Bowman CH (2003). Direct versus indirect emotional consequences on the Iowa Gambling Task. *Brain & Cognition.*

Turnbull OH, Jenkins S, Rowley ML (in press). The pleasantness of false beliefs: An emotion-based account of confabulation. *Neuropsychoanalysis.*

Van Reekum R, Cohen T, Wong J (2000). Can traumatic brain injury cause psychiatric disorders. *J Neuropsychiatry Clin Neurosci* 12:316–327.

Villiers CD, Zent R, Eastman RW, Swingler D (1996). A flight of fantasy: False memories in frontal lobe disease. *J Neurology, Neurosurgery and Psychiatry* 61:652–653.

Weinberger DR, Lipska BK (1995). Cortical maldevelopment, anti-psychotic drugs, and schizophrenia: A search for common ground. *Schizophrenia Res* 16:87–110.

Walsh KW (1978). *Neuropsychology: A Clinical Approach.* Churchill Livingstone: Singapore.

Whitty C, Lewin W (1957). Vivid day-dreaming: An unusual form of confusion following anterior cingulectomy. *Brain* 80:72–76.

Wilcox JA, Nasrallah NA (1987). Childhood head trauma and psychosis. *Psychiatry Res* 21:303–307.

20

SOCIOPHYSIOLOGY AND EVOLUTIONARY ASPECTS OF PSYCHIATRY

Russell Gardner, Jr.[1] and Daniel R. Wilson[2]

[1] *University of Wisconsin Medical School & Medical College of Wisconsin, Madison, Wisconsin, 214 DuRose Terrace Madison, WI 53705*
[2] *Creighton University School of Medicine, Omaha, Nebraska*

"[D]iseases are not entities but rather . . . represent the course of physiological phenomena under altered circumstances." Daniel X. Freedman, 1982, when President of the American Psychiatric Association, about psychiatric disorders (agreeing with Rudolf Virchow who stated the same about medical disorders more generally).

INTRODUCTION

When examined closely, psychiatric disorders fundamentally entail social communication problems for those afflicted. Sociophysiology represents a useful concept that refers to normal functional brain-body system actions, ranging from autonomic to affective to cognitive components that become disordered in psychiatric illnesses (Gardner, 1997). An excellent example from animal studies would be the severe effects of social defeat

Textbook of Biological Psychiatry, Edited by Jaak Panksepp
ISBN 0-471-43478-7 Copyright © 2004 John Wiley & Sons, Inc.

on the physiology of the laboratory rat, including loss of body weight, testicular involution, adrenal hypertrophy, and chronic fearfulness. In adult animals such effects can often be reversed dramatically by the availability of friendly social contacts (e.g., Ruis et al., 1999). One could anticipate that positive social interventions soon after traumatic events could do much to block the long-term negative consequences of similar stressors in humans.

Even though stress-induced disorders reduce health and well-being, their high epigenetic prevalence suggest these brain, bodily, and behavioral changes were adaptive in the past (for a summary of stress physiology, see Chapter 4). Using this as a jump-off point, we examine psychiatric disorders from the perspective of the normative evolutionary order from which they depart. Our analysis invokes the work of Charles Darwin (1859) who initiated much of our present understanding as to how living forms attained their characteristics, including various behavioral attributes.

This chapter emphasizes how psychiatric disorders arise from the sociophysiological aberrations of evolved communication repertoires among conspecifics (members of a same species). Evolutionary biology studies how behavior has developed in animal species by making across-species contrasts and comparisons and making inferences about ancestral species. An evolutionary focus on behavior takes a central position in this view of biological psychiatry that expands beyond cellular and molecular mechanisms underlying beneficial drug actions. The chapter (1) briefly surveys relevant evolutionary concepts, (2) reviews general sociobiological factors of ultimate causation, (3) examines psychiatric pathogenesis in terms of communicational biology, (4) examines research that models sociophysiology in substance abuse and social rank hierarchy, and (5) finally considers preliminary treatment implications of a "social brain" paradigm.

RELEVANT EVOLUTIONARY CONCEPTS

Charles Darwin distrusted the word *evolution* because in his time it implied a preordained goal of perfection, like an unfolding flower, or some kind of heavenly design. By contrast, although Darwin (1859) used the word *selection*, he moved the focus away from a designing God. He borrowed the term *selection* from breeders of domesticated plants and animals but applied it to his new ideas on how life forms had descended, emphasizing "natural" selection to indicate biological adaptation to environments. It explained many phenomena previously given religious rationale. Evolution, the term ultimately adopted, no longer connotes unfolding perfection because Darwin's meaning has now gained full scientific acceptance. Despite scientific acceptance, however, the old and perhaps lingering first meaning of evolution may contribute to a general lack of perception that psychiatric disorders may be, in part, products of evolutionary mechanisms. How can something have "evolved" that gives such pain, distress, and reduced life quality for patients and relatives?

Calvin (1987) described natural selection in its core features as a general process ("the Darwin machine") with six parts: (1) an extant pattern (2) that possesses a copying mechanism (3) with some variant copies (4) that cannot infinitely coexist in (5) a multifaceted environment that influences the competitive outcome with differential variant survival (selection). (6) The process repeats in closed repeating loops for variation and selection. An individual must survive long enough to reproduce in order to be "fit" in the sense that genes bequeathed survive in the next generation and beyond. Helping one's progeny beyond birth increases such "fitness" when they themselves thereby have more or healthier offspring. Some short-term gains ultimately reduce fitness, for example, adrenocortical hyperactivity helps resist transient "stressors" but may cost the overall system if the reaction pattern persists, thereby fostering illness and reducing offspring numbers of chronically stressed individuals. However, if progeny issue forth despite such problems, and if those progeny themselves in turn produce fruitful offspring, then fitness does not decline. This contrasts to the common sense use of the term *fitness* to imply good individual health. McGuire and Troisi's textbook (1998) on Darwinian psychiatry hinges on the evolutionary principle that individual variations act at the center of evolutionary change, yielding genetic mechanisms that can help produce, under various social pressures, phenotypes sufficiently unusual as to be deemed atypical. The end result is that many major psychiatric problems emerge at an approximate rate of 1 to 10 per 100 as opposed to 1 to 4 per 10,000 of population, which is true of most neurogenetic illnesses (Wilson, 1993).

The human brain evolved from precursor animals as the Darwin machine drove nervous system evolution and formation. Yet most of the human brain's sociophysiological functions cannot be completely preprogrammed as there are too few genes. Rather, structures are built from a phylogenetic template that ontogenically reorganizes itself via growth factors and pruning processes in responding constantly to use patterns. Apoptosis (pruning) is cell shrinkage and disappearance without inflammation. Both Calvin and Gerald Edelman (1987) have suggested that selection pressures operate in neuron formation in a process Edelman called *neural Darwinism*. McGlashan and Hoffman (2000) noted that cell parts or neurites (e.g., dendrites and synapses) might also require pruning to increase cognitive capacity, accuracy, efficiency, and speed of learning at the expense of flexibility. They suggest schizophrenia might in part result from insufficient pruning (of course, many other variables also likely operate in this illness as discussed in Chapter 9). In any event, operation of the Darwin machine in the brain phylogeny and ontogeny helps explain the large number of neurons and patterns generated despite the many fewer genes in the human genome.

The gene idea helped formalize Darwin's concept of variability. After the rediscovery of Mendel's experimental demonstration of inheritance factors, variability could be examined as a function of specific forms. This concept—new as the 20th century began and concretized by the then new term *gene*—fostered modern genetic theory extending presently to the major genome projects. Indeed, scientific genetics focuses on individual differences. Modern molecular biology provides a major foundation for body metabolism in how deoxyribonucleic acid (DNA), ribonucleic acid (RNA), and protein structures dynamically function.

Genomic "basic plans" are evident as the neuroaxis reflects, in part, stages of sociophysiological evolutionary selection, for instance, as various genetically ingrained socioemotional functions of the brain and body. Indeed, much of the human genome is derived from ancestral species. Hence many similar genomic traits persist and function in higher animals and some in even all life forms. Moreover, all organisms share a number of genes, as dramatically evidenced by homologs across multiple genomes presently being decoded and compared. Current estimates show that some 10 percent of human genes clearly relate to particular genes in the fly and the worm, ranging from the antennapedia to the cognate human central nervous system (Pääbo, 2001). Thus, human bodies derive from evolved basic plans not unique to our species though displaying recent, uniquely human features. For example, skin protects the body from the environment for many species, but humans apply grooming and cosmetics to it in culturally determined *ways* to enhance status and mating opportunities.

The Mouse Genome Project represents a useful exemplar of human-nonhuman continuity. Although this genome is about 14 percent smaller than the human, over 90 percent of it and human genes, can be partitioned into corresponding regions of conserved synteny, reflecting segments in which the gene order in the most recent common ancestor has been conserved in both species (Mouse Genome Sequencing Consortium, 2002). Not surprisingly, diverse genome projects have begun to alter earlier theories of behavior. That core genomic features stem from ancestral forms to all living species is a fact of modern sociobiology. Sarah Hrdy (1999, page xi), a specialist on evolutionary biology as it pertains to reproduction, states, "I see the world through a different lens than most people. My depth of field is millions of years longer, and the subjects in my viewfinders have the curious habit of spontaneously taking on the attributes of other species: chimps, platypuses, australopithecines." Nobel Laureate David Baltimore (2000) suggests "our genes look much like those of fruit-flies, worms and even plants ... genes that encode the basic functions of life—for people, flies, worms and even bacteria—are only a few hundred to a few thousand." In contrast, however, the human brain outweighs that of the chimpanzee by a factor of 3 despite near identity of the two genomes.

As a part of this, signal-system codes stem from phylogenetic precursors. Vertebrate brains, in registering signals from conspecifics, rely on a basic plan apparatus already phylogenetically old before the chordate split from invertebrates. Subsequent mammalian and primate evolution greatly elaborated this apparatus. Changes came to overlay and modify but not replace earlier features that organize experience and relationships (Stevens and Price, 1996, 2000). Evolutionary processes act more like tinkerers than engineers, "tweaking" extant structures to take on new functions. The tongue first evolved for tasting and eating, not its more recent role in speech.

The Research Committee of the Group for the Advancement of Psychiatry (GAP; Bakker et al., 2002, p. 219) suggests: "Brains, including human brains, derive from ancient adaptations to diverse environments and are themselves repositories of phylogenetic adaptations. In addition, individual experiences shape the brain through epigenesis, *i.e.*, the expression of genes is shaped by environmental influences." Illustrating this, Panksepp (1998) notes that present-day rapid eye movement (REM) dream experience may give insight to ancient modes of awareness, inferring this from the brainstem location for REM generators. He suggests, that what is now the REM state was the original form of waking consciousness in early brain evolution, an ancient form that may have had to be suppressed actively for higher brain evolution to proceed efficiently. If true, then all humans (and nearly all other mammalians) retain this primitive consciousness in each night's sleep as most people experience vivid dreams characteristic of the REM brain state. Even further down in the brain stem (and presumably even more anciently derived), medulla oblongata neural centers pace body systems such as respiration and vomiting. Though ancient and fundamental, these functions also command respect in present conscious experience as they function in concert with more recently elaborated frontal cortices but likewise illustrate residual adaptations that first arose in deep time. In a striking example of this, panic attacks appear to be strongly influenced by ancient brainstem suffocation alarm mechanisms (Klein, 1993).

Paul MacLean (1990) pioneered study of the brain and its complex functions through the lens of evolutionary history, deriving his conclusions from ancient sources as well as earlier work by Broca and Papez. He posited a triune brain. In succession above the vegetative base he described (i) the R-complex (R referring to "reptilian"), including prominently the basal ganglia, (ii) the paleolimbic system, and (iii) then the neolimbic/neocortex. Major elements of reptilian and early mammalian sociophysiology are conserved in human brains, notably the R-complex. MacLean also demonstrated that humans retain many communicational features evolved in earlier vertebrate selection. Human communicational repertoires such as courtship and mating or more general social rank hierarchical signals exemplify ancient programs evident in his classical studies of reptilian behavior. Such communicational propensity states retain vast neuromental assemblages from much earlier animal evolution with complex connections and modifications that extend between these structures and those more recently evolved such as the cerebral cortex (Mega and Cummings, 1999).

Symptoms of some psychiatric disorders stem from disinhibition of R-complex communications. The 19th century neurologist, J. Hughlings Jackson, used clinical evidence to deduce that the brain evolved in a hierarchical sequence. He noted dissolution of abilities after organ damage that perhaps echoed a phylogenetic history (discussed in Taylor, 1958). As any medical student knows, clinical signs of frontal lobe impairment feature the "unmasking" of ancient plans for behavior after cortical injury (e.g., infantile grasping and suckling reflexes; Salloway et al., 2001). Apparently these represent ancient patterns embedded in the genome that are usually active in subtle ways that fit smoothly into conversations and other communicational settings. But when frontal cortical damage occurs, many "reptilian" communications such as slavish imitative responses to another individual's posture involuntarily occur (echopraxia) or behaviors may be repeated (perseveration), similar to patterns seen in present day lizards, as in courtship. Another symptom, echolalia, repeating another person's words in obligatory fashion, demonstrates co-option of cortical language functions for the dictates of the ancient response formula. Fibers project downstream from frontal cortex to the caudate nucleus, and lesions there may also produce parallel reptilian stereotypies. Obsessive-compulsive symptoms and appetitive syndromes experienced by patients with streptococcal induced autoantibody damage to the basal ganglia may result from similar pathogenesis. (Rapaport and Fiske, 1998; Sokol, et al., 2002).

The limbic system underlies familial and other affiliative functions. MacLean (1990) highlighted a level of organization evolutionarily subsequent to the R-complex, focusing on Broca's "limbic system." In the 19th century Broca named the complex for its rimlike location but did not speculate on function. MacLean, following earlier theory by Papez, suggested emotions serving social life achieved a new organization in early mammals in the form of familial attachments. Insects, birds, and fish also care for families as likely did some late dinosaurs, so MacLean's early mammals probably did not completely "originate" or "reinvent" limbic structures. Ancestral reptiles and mammalians endowed humans with much of the same communicational sociophysiology. Siegel (1999) points out that for humans, attachment is based on collaborative communication and that secure attachment involves contingent communication, in which the signals of one person are directly responded to by the other.

Most of these major affective systems reside in precortical levels. Panksepp (1998) notes that many of the ancient evolutionarily derived brain systems all mammals share still serve as the foundations for the deeply experienced affective proclivities of the human mind. Such ancient brain functions evolved long before the emergence of the human neocortex with its vast cognitive skills. Deliberately using vernacular terms, Panksepp labels: (1) an appetitive, motivational SEEKING system that fosters energetic search and goal-directed behaviors, (2) a RAGE system aroused by thwarting experiences correlated with frustration, (3) a FEAR system that minimizes bodily destruction, (4) a PANIC apparatus with separation distress to enhance bonding, (5) LUST systems, somewhat different for males and females, that subsume mating and reproduction, (6) a maternal CARE system for nurturing infants, and (7) a roughhousing PLAY system to provide youngsters with skill-honing opportunities. In the human species each of these involves interactions with other people so that emotions can be viewed as communicational states. Moreover, neural circuits crucial to motivational communications arose considerably earlier than did the telencephalic amygdala typically implicated in fear conditioning.

In the current research environment, emotions are studied for their brain features but not for their communicative value. For example, Ekman and Davidson (1994, p. 4) state in a critical update of emotion research that, "the only question omitted . . . involved the expression of emotion . . . because there are, regrettably, only a few scientists working on the many remaining questions about expression." Salsen (2001) noted that most theoretical and research treatments of emotions simply ignore the communicative value, despite the implicit assumption that messages are important. His frustration-conflict theory suggests emotions result from thwarted action states in the brain and body as negative emotions correlate with frustrated anticipation and positive ones with its relief. The message for biological psychiatry suggests that many emotional concerns that people deal with may clarify if communicative issues receive additional emphasis. For instance, most marital problems and satisfactions may boil down to the extent that couples tend to impact each other's autonomic-emotional responses negatively or positively (Gottman et al., 2002). If so, effective therapeutic maneuvers may attend to sociophysiological dimensions that promote autonomic nervous system harmony via corticofugal regulation of lower brain emotional systems.

The size and accessibility of the six-layered isocortex greatly expanded in later mammaloprimates. The famous "split-brain" experiments of (Gazzaniga and Sperry, 1967) showed the two hemispheres operate in a coordinated but different fashion. Moreover, the cortex serves many distinctively advanced—even human—capacities such as analytic, perceptual, organizing, and planning executive operations, but these systems can also regulate lower autonomic reaches of the brain.

Many impulses that originate in ways not controlled by the rational self seem correlated with damage to these massive structures. When frontal lobe damage occurs, impulsivity with sexual or aggressive displays often results to the frequent consternation of other people. Some people excessively use their cortical functions for acquiring drugs that affect mood such as caffeine, nicotine, and numerous illicit agents that act in various brain sites, but notably in medial basal ganglia. Thus, even though certain emotional aspects of addictions gel in subcortical areas, such as in dopamine circuitry, the accompanying strategic aspects are related more to higher cortical functions.

That the human brain is much larger than that of the other primates, even in terms of relative body size, may relate in large part to increasingly complex human sociality (Dunbar, 1996). Although other great apes kiss, hug, and connect with powerfully communicative interindividual bonds, Dunbar calculated a correlation between primate group size and the ratio of neocortex to the total brain size and found that it accounts for 40 percent of the variance. Group size refers to bonded individuals—conspecifics friendly to one another and indeed genetically related to some degree. Allman (1999) confirmed the finding, even after adding the previously omitted, less gregarious, orangutan to his analysis. Dunbar suggested that "gossip"—meaning bonding small-talk in which humans extensively participate—largely replaced interindividual grooming typical of nonhuman primates; he suggests that such verbal-auditory communication provides greater efficiency of bonding because more individuals can interact per session.

Others agree sociality figured strongly in human cerebral cortical evolution. Mithen (1996) suggests that language first evolved to handle social information, and that it remained exclusively 'a social language'. He further notes that intellectual success is correlated with social success, and if social success means high biological fitness, then any heritable trait which increases the ability of an individual to outwit his fellows will soon spread throughout the gene pool. In another work on the origin of human symbolic abilities, Deacon (1997) notes that our intelligence triumphed over the unique demands of reproductive competition and cooperation. . . . Two and a half million years of sustained selection maintained by unprecedented communicational and cognitive tricks have taken humans far from their beginnings both in the physical changes in the brain that resulted and in the mental and cultural world that co-evolved with it. He suggests human groups "should not exist," such as they are in complexity and scale given predictions that the evolution of communication of other animals would imply. That they nevertheless do exist stems in part from the development of linguistically based and increasingly socially "ritualized"—cultural stories dramatically retained over many thousands of generations in a mode that fostered protocultural and cultural accumulation of explanation and, eventually, wisdom sufficient to allow the rise of complex societies and economies.

In summary, the human genome has been sculpted for millions of years and has given rise to the human brain as an organ of layered neuromental assemblages. Many communicative functions reflect deep and ancient genetic plans that allow the higher reaches of the brains of highly social organisms to bring their ancestral skills to bear epigenetically and uniquely upon its multifaceted encounters with the world. Now, we turn to sociobiology, population genetics, and factors of ultimate evolutionary causation.

SOCIOBIOLOGICAL FACTORS OF ULTIMATE CAUSATION

Evolutionary biologists distinguish between *proximate* and *ultimate* or *evolutionary* factors in understanding inherited traits at two levels of evolutionary causality. Proximate research deals extensively with immediate details of a mechanism (i.e., physical structure including the molecules involved, or on whole organism levels, specific circumstances that elicit behavior). Ultimate research addresses adaptive features deduced from intergenerational and genomic mechanisms. Both levels of causation are indispensable sides of a same coin, but, thus far, evolutionary psychology/psychiatry has largely taken up issues of ultimate causation.

The relatively new field of sociobiology (Wilson, 1975) concerns itself with biobehavioral processes from ultimate causation to proximal expression. It is deeply rooted in the behavior genetics, developmental psychobiology, and sociobiology that preceded it (e.g., Bowlby, 1969; Scott and Fuller, 1965). The impact of Wilson's contributions was tempered by wide controversy including a rebuke from Gould and Lewontin (1979) that evolutionary "just so" stories were unsupported by research data and should be avoided. Segerstrale (2000) comprehensively reviewed the sociobiology field and concluded that by deploying scientific rules of evidence, sociobiological research has resulted in a solid body of data, earning it legitimacy as it moves beyond the rather political considerations of early critics.

Ethology is a related approach. Ethologists examine animal behavior via Tinbergen's four perspectives: (1) mechanistic—neural, physiological, or psychological elements underlie expression and registration, (2) ontogenetic—development in an individual's life, (3) functional—how a given trait helps survival and reproduction, and (4) phylogenetic—how ancestral and contemporary features overlap or diverge. Ethology and sociobiology complement one another and are also compatible with psychiatry. They may assist the pathophysiological formulation of its conditions. The emergent field of evolutionary psychology has focused on selected features of this intellectual arena, reflecting how ultimate evolutionary theoretical framings and more proximal empirical analyses can cross fertilize each other.

Much work labeled as evolutionary psychology centers on altruistic behavior and inclusive fitness. Reciprocal altruism refers to exchange mechanisms ("I do for you and in return you will do for me") and does not represent altruism in the sense of losing or risking something for seemingly little gain (like losing one's life to rescue another person). Social insects present the outward paradox that nonreproducing members of the colony (e.g., helper ants, worker bees) work hard for the group, yet their individual genes do not directly descend to subsequent generations. Puzzled about how such insects evolved, evolutionary geneticist William Hamilton (1964) recognized that gene frequencies in relatives resemble each other proportionately more than do those of less related individuals (relatives share "the same genes") and, hence, indirect reproduction was possible via selection within an inclusive kinship.

Dawkins (1976, 1989) popularized Hamilton's ideas using the "selfish gene" metaphor—an organism transiently embodies an immortal gene that never dies so long as the reproductive line perseveres or until mutation occurs. Hamilton's formula hinges on genetic relatedness and reads: $C < Br$ [where C represents the costs to a giver, which must be less than the fitness benefits (B) obtained by helping an individual whose degree of relatedness is indicated by value r].

Hamilton's reasoning and formulas have been applied widely in evolutionary psychology to explain altruism in many species, including humans, and at various physiological levels ranging from germ cell to kin lineages. Daly and Wilson (1988) predicted that benefit and hostility to others would occur in proportion to kinship, and they documented that closer genetic relatives display greater benevolence and less deadly hostility toward each other with respect to familial violence. Spouses, in-laws, and step-children die more often in family violence by a factor of 10, compared to parents, siblings, and genetically related children. Moore et al. (2002) invoked similar Hamiltonian thinking for their findings on sperm behavior of European deer mice. Some sperm "paved the way" for others in the same ejaculate so that the latter gain more rapid access to the ovum. This "teamwork" allowed the first ejaculator to out-race sperm from other males mating near the same time. Since the helper sperm lost their capacity to bind to the zona pellucida and fertilize, they displayed altruistic behavior from an inclusive fitness perspective.

Darwin's (1871) proposals on *sexual selection* likewise remain central to evolutionary thinking with renewed interest in male-male competition on one hand and female selectivity on the other. Females possess greater investment from the greater time and body resources (e.g., ovulation, lactation) devoted to offspring, as well as a lower level of possible fecundity. This contrasts with males who sometimes invest only ejaculate with no ensuing parental concerns. Due to somatic constraints, fathers can never invest as much affiliation as mothers. This dichotomy of *parental investment* (Trivers, 1972) explains why females often demonstrate choosiness about prospective mates—estimating which candidate will produce better quality offspring, examining, for instance, fighting ability, cleverness, and health (lack of anemia may be assessed through red skin or appendages). The peahen illustrates another estimation of health, for example, when she evaluates the "ornament" of the peacock's tail. If fancy tails indicate male healthiness (he can afford such "luxury"), the better her offspring would be with his genes. It has been suggested that human estimations of "beauty" link to such fitness detection concerns (Miller, 2000).

Likewise, numerous authors (see Hrdy, 1999) note infanticide in many species practiced by a male newly consorting with the mother. He does this so that, in ultimate causation terms, his own genes sooner have access to the female's reproductive efforts and also to help assure that his own effort is not "cuckolded." In many species females quickly become fertile upon no longer nurturing the young of the previous father. Also, maternal infanticide can result from a mother's estimation of poor resources. For example, a woman early in life may kill her children, but later if married well, typically displays model maternal attachments. Some human cultures have sanctioned the culling of infants that may not thrive. Proximate mechanisms sometimes overcome ultimate gain. Hrdy (1999) points out that efficient proximate mechanisms sometimes eclipse the optimal relational, inclusive-fitness calculations of Hamilton, Trivers, and others. For instance, humans and other primates exhibit one such phenomenon prominently in the form of *allomothering*—infant care by other females ("aunties") or by adoptive parents.

Trivers (1974) suggested parents and offspring feel different values according to their roles, which explains many sibling and parent-child conflicts. For example, siblings commonly compete even though parents typically urge that they not; each sibling wishes to gather as many resources as possible, but the parents wish to apportion these equally, given that each child carries on an equal number of parental genes. Deriving from this tradition, Haig (1996) noted some genes even within a body might compete with others, as with eye color. Alleles with a gene from each parent express only one (dominant versus recessive). Examining imprinted genes conferred separately from mother and father, Haig investigated facets of pregnancy and fetal growth and concluded that certain of the father's genes seem to exploit the mother maximally for as many offspring as possible while hers work to conserve her resources to do a better job on fewer. Even body tissue may derive from one parent instead of the other; for instance, the elements of cerebral cortex may derive more from maternally imprinted genes, while development of subcortical areas (in mice) are influenced more by paternal ones (Keverne et al., 1996). Since subcortical areas facilitate emotional sociophysiology while cortical tissues foster more cognitive distinctions, it may be that paternal genes influence the more instinctual-emotional aspects of reproductive skills while maternal genes are more important for cognitive-economic decisions.

The scientific paradigm that "selfish motives" operate in organisms and their subparts (e.g., genes) via robustly neoDarwinian selection originally arose to counter earlier ideas that individuals perform altruistically for the "good of the group." This elicited powerful rebuttals reliant on precise application of Hamilton's kinship selection formulas. But in recent point-counterpoint contributions, commentators suggest models by which tightly bonded groups can indeed be considered "organisms" or adaptive units, wherein altruism operates at the level of group selection (as distinct from the direct consanguinity ratios that drive kinship selection); therefore self-sacrifice and altruism may merit more complex explanations (D.S. Wilson, 2002).

All humans are related to one other in the sense of sharing comparable genes, but this does not prevent formation of conspecific subgroups, alien and antagonistic to one another (Wrangham and Peterson, 1996). For example, human laughter facilitates in- and out-group operation: Bonding laughter cements in-group relations, but mocking laughter emphasizes the rejection of alien individuals (Eibl-Eibesfeldt, 1989). Obviously, scorn, shunning, and shame powerfully act in human emotional homeostasis and sociophysiological cascades that can promote mental distress.

LeCroy and Moller (2000) summarize evolutionary psychological perspectives from the human vantage point, whereas Wrangham and Peterson (1996) use a comparative primate perspective in a book provocatively titled *Demonic Males*. Chimpanzees and humans display similar male-bonding and warfare strategies, for instance, that dramatically contrast to bonobos, where females are far more influential perhaps in part as this allows them greater social time dedicated to sexual communication with less hostile aggression.

Psychiatric symptoms can sometimes represent proximate sociocommunicative mechanisms imprecisely deployed. Evolutionary psychiatrists have speculated that, if an individual's communicational mechanisms are stimulated at a time and place other than that which spawned its ultimate "design," then the person may develop a disorder. This relates closely to mismatch theory, which holds that mechanisms evolved for life in previous eras may not suit the present time (Bailey, 1989). In technical terms, this may reflect an aspect of genomic phenotypic elasticity. Along with Hamiltonian and selfish gene ideas, Glantz and Pearce (1989) utilized mismatch theory to formulate guidelines for an approach they called *Evolutionary psychotherapy*.

Darwinian game theory represents another powerful heuristic, particularly as population geneticist Maynard Smith (1982) specified evolutionary stable strategies (ESS) to analyze how individuals compete for heightened reproductive fitness in each generation. For example, a K-reproductive strategy entails much attention to the well-being of offspring, whereas another, r-reproductive strategy, entails fertilizing as many females as possible but investing little or nothing in those produced so that quantity gains emphasis over quality. Mealey (2000) elaborated how sex differences represent different developmental and evolutionary strategies. One of the most striking examples is male sociopathy with its characteristic selfishness and exploitation.

Over a century ago, Robertson (1890) suggested the symptoms of disease need to be traced to the functions of health, and that both need to be carried back to their origin in evolution. The next section deals with how this suggestion results in pathogenetic formulations for psychiatry. How has psychiatric disorder deviated from usual sociophysiological order?

PSYCHIATRIC PATHOGENESIS AS COMMUNICATIONAL DISORDER

The GAP Research Committee (Bakker et al., 2002, p. 219) suggested that the concept of the brain as an organ that manages social life provides significant power for psychiatry's basic science. This committee defined the social brain by its function, namely,

> ... the brain is a body organ that mediates social interactions while also serving as the repository of those interactions ... between brain physiology and the individual's environment. The brain is the organ most influenced on the cellular level by social factors across development; in turn, the expression of brain function determines and structures an

individual's personal and social experience. The social brain framework . . . helps organize and explain all psychopathology. A single gene-based disorder like Huntington disease is expressed to a large extent as social dysfunction. Conversely, traumatic stress has structural impact on the brain as does the socially interactive process of psychotherapy.

The group further suggested that burgeoning developments in neural and genetic areas put added demands on the conceptual structures of psychiatry, and that findings from such work must be juxtaposed and correlated with the behavioral and experiential facets of psychiatry to give it a firm biological foundation. Psychiatry's full and unified entry into the realm of theory-driven and data-based medical science has been overdue, but the social brain concept allows psychiatry to utilize pathogenesis in a manner parallel to practice in other specialties. The social brain concept

ultimately offers to

- unify the biological, psychological and social factors in psychiatric illness,
- dissect components of illness into meaningful functional subsets that deviate in definable ways from normal physiology,
- improve diagnostic validity by generating testable clinical formulations from brain-based social processes.

This section first defines the broad nature of human communication and then notes that psychiatric disorders display problems in social interactions from observational-ethological viewpoints. We suggest that pathogenesis formulations unfurl from sociophysiological considerations. A core method for understanding psychiatric pathogenesis entails across-species contrasts and comparisons. When humans and other animals exhibit homologous similarities, a common ancestor can be inferred with genomic and body elements inherited in common. When on the other hand, humans contrast with other animals, the observer can infer that the origins occurred in the unique evolution of humans from precursor primates. Examining communicational propensities as features that humans share with other species helps establish their antiquity in deep time; indeed, animal models of disorder become possible when mechanisms are shared (Gardner and McKinney, 2001). Contrariwise, when structures and mechanisms contrast between humans and other animals, as with verbal language and broadened human alliance formation, animal models provide less relevance.

The brain mediates many functions, but conspecific communication accounts for a large proportion of its activity. This can be appreciated by considering, for example, the amount of cerebral cortex devoted to verbal and nonverbal communication including pattern recognitions and pattern generation required for writing, as well as facial recognition, planning behaviors, and suppression of impulses originating from lower centers. Verbal communication of course reflects an extraordinary human capability critical to using detailed stories for informing, planning, bonding, gossip, and entertainment.

Neurology frequently terms aphasias and other language disruptions as "communicational" disturbances, but such linguistic impairments represent only a subset of communicational disorders. Social interactions entail much more than words alone and long preceded language in the phylogeny of mating signals and other interindividual exchanges. Humans share many of the communicational abnormalities evident in psychiatry with other animals so that ancient roots can be inferred. On the other hand, humans as a highly gregarious species provide help to their fellow conspecifics and contrast to other animals by exhibiting more connectedness and helpfulness to others, frequently strangers. Indeed, this may represent a core ingredient of psychotherapy (Wampold, 2001), further developed in the last section of this chapter.

Communication is an intrinsic function of the social brain that occurs when an individual emits signals so that at least one other conspecific might register, interpret, and act upon the contents of the message. Posture, context behavior, tone, volume, emotional, and other nonverbal signals may augment or replace vocalization (Smith, 1977). Burgoon et al. (1994) assert that no one exists in a vacuum, and that "Everyone belongs to a spiraling hierarchy of interpersonal bonds, family, groups, and organizations. The pervasiveness of communication in this hierarchy is but one indication of the importance of this process in our lives." Animals link with each other not only for reproduction and offspring nurturance but for joint foraging, warmth, and protection from predators. Broadly construed, individuals use signals to space themselves most appropriately from one another. Solitary species exist that are as disparate as the monotreme spiny anteaters (echidnas) and primate orangutans, but of course members of both link for mating.

Communication among conspecifics is so important an attribute of animate life that basic and ancient genomic programs encode it. Earliest genomic elements probably originated with the master control genes (hox, homeobox, or homeotic), the sequences that organize body plan templates common to vertebrates and nonvertebrates (Gehring, 1998). Signal systems encoded in the genome and, developing over millions of years, have influenced the social organizational patterns of many descendant species. For instance, the promotor region of the vasopressin receptor gene influences the degree of sociality that field mice exhibit and genetic engineering of this region increases social responsivity in mice with asocial temperaments (Young et al., 1999).

To summarize, communication pervades human experience and virtually all psychopathology entails aberrant social signals. Our research and clinical challenge hinges on understanding what causes aberrancies to occur and how they can be mended. Patients exhibit the imperative nature of some communicational propensity states (delusions, mania, depression, obsessions, and compulsions). An emphasis on propensity stems from the observation that while no certain signal can be predicted when an individual experiences such a state, the general nature of the signal can; thus, charismatic leaders and manics tend to push an agenda of controlling others, normally appeasing and depressed people signal relative worthlessness, and members of discriminated-against-minority groups and patients with persecutory delusions feel suspicious and fearful of harm from enemies. Consistency of delusional details may vary even in the same patient during an illness, but the force of conviction and pressured feelings do not vary until the condition eases. This may stem from the lower brain location of neurons (more anciently evolved) that brought about or perpetuate the aberrant condition. Information from psychopharmacology has amply demonstrated that the actions of many drugs that affect psychiatric status also influence biogenic amine availability or function at synapses. Also, these moieties—that function as neurotransmitter and neuromodulator agents—have been studied using across-species contrasts and comparisons methodology.

Communicational propensity states typify many psychiatric disorders in that these states resemble normal signal patterns but may be expressed at the wrong time or place, or are expressed too strongly, or stem from incorrect social assessment or other idiosyncrasy. Of course, some people who deservedly or adaptively feel and express low self-esteem in fact express appeasement or submission in a way that helps survival and welfare. For an across-species comparison, dogs may get along better when they behave submissively and if they feel guilty for transgressions. In addition to producing uncomfortable experience, such guilt and shame responses possess adaptive functions, allowing competing individuals to coexist more peaceably. Examples follow of psychiatric disorders that may also represent communicational disorders.

Distorted suspicions held with great tenacity characterize persecutory delusions. A pathogenetic formulation suggests that patients feel the object of out-group hostility that would be rational were they in the territory of enemies. Wrangham and Peterson (1996) note xenophobia or hatred of out-group individuals characterizes both human and chimpanzee populations. If an individual belongs to a hated out-group and shows up in the wrong territory, he or she would do well to display what a person with persecutory delusions experiences: fear, expectation of persecution, great wariness, and great resistance to reassurance. Hence, a defining characteristic of psychosis, fixity of belief, might preserve life if stimulated at the right time and location. Antipsychotic medications counter these attitudes in the psychiatric setting where the feelings outweigh the reality. They dampen dopamine receptors and operate on both very ancient and more recently evolved receptor types.

When depressed patients are observed, they exhibit undue submissiveness and self-derogation. This can be characterized as appeasement displays that would be adaptive should a punishing authority in fact be in charge (Price, 1967; Price et al., 2003). This underlines the observation that affects contribute powerfully to social communications. Submission displays characterize group living throughout the animal world.

Undue efforts to dominate and influence other people typify mania (Gardner, 1982) as well as antisocial personality disordered patients. Intrusive and aggressive behaviors cause the diagnosis of conduct disorders of children and sociopathy in adults. Of course, taking an aggressive or leadership role may be highly adaptive given propitious circumstances, as may persistence in its pursuit. That these conditions are more freely encountered with frontal cortical brain damage hints that human evolution provided suppressive factors for such expression, an idea also enhanced by high concentrations of the inhibitory gamma-aminobutyric acid (GABA) in the cerebral cortex, the most prevalent neurotransmitter in this brain region.

Disinhibited sexual and aggressive behaviors characterize both alcohol intoxication and mania with some similarities in clinical presentation. This similarity helps derive pathogenetic models and methods of investigating sociophysiological pathogenesis some of which are detailed below. Pedophilia entails undue sexual attraction to children, and the term *rape* labels inappropriate sexual advances. Both entail forced mating. Of course, mating behaviors entail extremely ancient conspecific communications.

Other communicational features can also be seen in psychiatry. For instance, social distancing represents a feature of schizophrenia, schizoid personality disorder, and autistic disorders. Of course, at times, being alone can benefit the person, as with creative artists (Storr, 1988). People with schizotypal personality disorders and early schizophrenia tell of experiences that are quite "odd" or atypical experiences vis a vis social norms. Yet at times such experiences have high social value as they may be prized by other group members, who consider them to reveal religious insights. A missing 'theory of the other person's mind' seems to characterize autistic patients—the patient can't feel, think, or act as another person does and therefore lacks empathy.

Undue attention to desirable appearance represents a partial factor in restrictive eating disorders as well as in tightly held convictions about body features in body dysmorphic disorder. Persons with dependent and borderline personality disorders work to elicit nurturance but accomplish it in a discordant way that typically alienates others, causing them to be regarded as "problem patients." Moreover, borderline patients often tell of troubled familial backgrounds with the communicational problems of boundary violations, abuse, and ambivalent nurturance. The idea of psychiatric syndromes as communicational pathology seems clearest when maladaptive social signaling persists despite the punishing results of alienation from others, hospitalization, incarceration, disability, and even the risk of death, as from suicide. Social anxiety obviously entails conspecific communications. Abnormal fears as in this and other anxiety disorders often calm if a friend (often family) is nearby. Solace of this kind seems to characterize social animals, certainly humans.

In summary, viewed pathophysiologically, psychiatric patients emit verbal and nonverbal communications that evolved to be adaptive, but timing, circumstance, and persistence may make them maladaptive. Regarding conspecific competition, Price and Sloman (1987) suggested escalating and deescalating strategies that accompanied winning or losing, respectively, and that these relate to affective spectrum expressions such as mania and depression. Indeed, affective or mood disorders can also be viewed as communicational disorders (Gardner, 1988) in the course of which patients signal excessive social dominance or submission to others. This does not trivialize the feelings involved because social rank issues obviously generate powerful affects, such as those that accompany defeat, submission, and loss on the one hand and victory and triumph on the other. Communications expressed by patients can be adaptive in certain contexts, but not in the context in which the psychiatric disorder has emerged.

In the following, research findings illustrate neurophysiological and neurochemical attributes of various levels of the social brain. They anticipate research formulations that may elaborate sociophysiological pathogenesis. For example, D.R. Wilson (2002) notes that the effects of cocaine illustrate the stimulation of Price's manic/escalation and depressive/deescalation strategic social rank hierarchy competitive behaviors. That is, cocaine actions in the brain mimic both manic and depressive symptoms. Acute administration increases synaptic dopamine that then escalates mood and activity. Yet chronic overstimulation of D_2 receptors eventually induces down-regulated physical dependence (Barr et al., 2002). Similarly, abrupt cessation of cocaine depletes dopamine and induces acute agitated depression. A succeeding chronic syndrome of anhedonia, dysphoria, lethargy, somnolence, and apathy may last a year or more.

Emerging cellular-molecular research on the origins of neuromodulators and neurotransmitters relates to communicational biology relevant both to the action of psychiatric drugs on the one hand and to across-species contrasts and comparisons core to sociophysiological pathogenesis on the other hand. The major classes of neurotransmitters originated remarkably early as intracellular messengers of unicellular organisms (D.R. Wilson, 2002; Smith, 2002). Biogenic amines seem to have functioned first as intracellular signals and then acquired capacities for intercellular communication and hormonal action as well—still retaining intracellular roles. Protozoans and nearly all metazoans exhibit their use. Even prokaryotes show a catecholamine-catabolizing enzyme, monoamine oxidase. Catecholamine receptors developed from primordial muscarinic acetylcholine receptors before arthropod and chordate lineages diverged. Dopamine probably emerged as the first but with functions limited to metabolic activity because all chordates exhibit its presence; but it probably was last to extend to neurotransmission given its location in neuronal groups higher in the neuroaxis than either norepinephrine or epinephrine. Serotonin may have originated in chordate gut tissue (indeed, 90 percent of human serotonin resides in the gut), but cyclostome (lamprey) brain tissue shows its presence thereby establishing its neural role at about the chordate-vertebrate interface.

With vertebrate evolution, further neurotransmitter and receptor variations evolved to mediate basic sociophysiological repertoires, such as fear (clinically described as anxiety). These appear to have elaborated further to serve conspecific relations, as they vary with social rank hierarchies. Serotonin and dopamine co-evolved in the course of brain as they mediated increasingly complex neuropharmacological pathways of social rank hierarchy regulation. Owens and Risch (1995) depict molecular analytic techniques that allowed recent fuller appreciation of how dopamine and serotonin work in an orchestrated fashion, often with seeming reciprocity. As these subsystems play important roles for psychoactive drugs, their normal metabolism provides conceptual models for how drugs act, and equally importantly for the central thesis of this chapter, furnishes empirical inroads for the underpinnings for how psychiatric disorders may represent aberrations of normal sociophysiology.

In addition to pathogenesis, sociophysiology also provides apt metaphors for illness/treatment explanations, in themselves important components of doctor and patient decision making, as will be developed below. Interestingly, among Sigmund Freud's enduring conceptual legacies, that of transference and countertransference, is intrinsically one of social communication. Next we turn to research efforts that model sociophysiological research integrating whole organism biology (behavior) with cell biological data.

RESEARCH ON SUBSTANCE ABUSE AND SOCIAL RANK HIERARCHY

A major problem for psychiatry's basic sciences is a clear need for a comprehensive integration of proximal to ultimate phenomena—from organ and cell levels on through to the level of individual and group behavior. Research efforts often assume that clinical phenomena "empirically" are best studied in individual subjects—as though they existed in isolation. This has worked against pathophysiological formulations. Addiction research has recently provided encouraging data, however. It studies the human propensity to seek and use reinforcing drugs with consequent drug craving. Society finds drug addiction pervasively troubling. Behaviorally, addicts go to great lengths to acquire drugs. While a "communicational problem" may seem counterintuitive because the person seems to act out a "personal need," drugs stimulate feelings that relate to social roles, such as enhanced sense of power after imbibing alcohol (Newlin, 2002). Twelve-step and other social programs play integral roles in reversing maladaptive drinking and other drug use, suggesting social processes are innately involved in the tendency to develop addictions. More specific evolved sociophysiological foundations may underlie the epigenetic risk of substance abuse (Wilson, 1988). The "abuse" may have arisen not as addiction per se but from adaptive qualities (Nesse and Berridge, 1997). Addiction ubiquitously requires culture for its realization, although its mechanisms predate culture. Therefore, addicts may have latent but important genomically selected sociophysiological attributes. This aspect of addiction may repay careful proximate investigations.

A variety of neuropharmacological systems subserve this sociophysiology. For example, opiates operate in the central nervous system by stimulating endogenous opiate receptors to effect subjective well-being, and alcohol facilitates GABA receptor activity as do benzodiazepines and hypnotic-sedatives (though alcohol, uniquely among sedative-hypnotics, also blocks a glutamate receptor thereby causing greater intoxication). Cocaine increases synaptic levels of dopamine, serotonin, and norepinephrine via inhibition of presynaptic reuptake transporters to induce arousal while amphetamine action is primarily via direct cell entry that causes monoamine release and synaptic availability. Nestler (1999) unites these diverse receptor actions within an overarching model as the pathways extend up the neuroaxis from the pontine brainstem to include hypothalamic nuclei and converge on the mesolimbic dopamine system with resultant reinforcement for continued drug usage.

In addition to the more accepted dopamine systems, Newlin (2002) implicates the pontine locus coeruleus in addiction mechanisms. He suggests addicts evolutionarily pursue a self-perceived survival fitness strategy. Acute intoxication causes the person to feel psychologically engaged with the world but fosters chronic psychopathology as it both habituates and sensitizes a neural system vulnerable to temporary, artificial activation by drugs of abuse.

Electrostimulation of this system causes individuals to seek restimulation. In some rodent models the switch is self-activated many times per second. Panksepp (1998) has argued that this should not be labeled "reward" as earlier investigators did because the reward in fact involves the appetitive arc of an appetite-satiation cycle. As this appetitive engagement process differs considerably from the reward associated with sexual or food satisfaction, he labeled the overall neurophysiological system as SEEKING and emphasized how it enhances individual interest in and exploration and mastery of the environment.

Additional complimentary data stems from substance abuse research. Morgan et al. (2002) linked dopamine systems to social rank hierarchy. Using positron emission tomography (PET) investigators evaluated the self-administration of cocaine on D_2 receptor occupancy in Rhesus monkeys with different ranks of social dominance. High dominance produced evidence of heightened dopamine activity in the basal ganglia compared to when the same animals were socially isolated or in contrast to subordinate status. Indeed, dominant animals (top rankers in groups of four) showed no interest in cocaine (for them it had no reinforcement value). This was not true of the lowest-ranking subordinates, however, who universally showed great interest. The negative correlation for drug use and status accounted for 55 percent of the variance.

Human social rank hierarchies can be examined by the manifest behaviors of other psychiatric conditions, for example, mood disorder. Mania seems to caricature charismatic leadership. On the other hand, normal leaders exemplify "alpha" behavior, presumably via a phylogenetically sustained apparatus of social rank modulation. President Lyndon Johnson, though not functionally nor technically "manic," displayed core characteristics of mania—extraordinary energy, sociability, planning behavior, strong humor, and a dominating manner (Caro, 2002). In this he reflected activation of an alpha communicational propensity state keyed to effective leadership. The neuroregulatory apparatus can become dysmodulated, however, particularly as to threshold, rate, and reversal factors that influence triggering, exhibition, and/or undue social persistence (Gardner, 1982). Thus, clinical presentation can be recast into syndromal and subsyndromal components that may lend greater understanding to clinical problems as well as naturally adaptive features.

A related study compared manic patients and normals (Gardner, 1998) according to features of their communicational propensity state. That is, acutely ill manic patients were assessed using an "alpha scale" derived from the core social dominance characteristics of mania as listed in the form of a 13-item checklist in a training manual for the *Diagnostic and Statistical Manual. Third Edition* (DSM-III). Their scores did not differ statistically from those of healthy community leaders matched for age and sex; the two groups did differ, however, from two other matched groups: healthy low-profile community citizens and bipolar patients euthymic from lithium treatment. Members of the two latter groups did not differ from each other on the alpha scale nor from a large introductory psychology class. This can be understood as reflecting a system for alpha communications (human dominance). Dominants in most animal groups have more mating privileges. This and related phenomena are often seen in high-ranking humans, as well (Wrangham and Peterson, 1996). Such propensities evolved initially to mediate proximal competition for mating and other resources, only later influencing other functions, such as parenting in mammals, and ultimately in humans, such roles as teaching and political positions.

To date, commentators have poorly appreciated the biology of social rank hierarchies. Some male fish, for example, change sex in response to social subordination. From the standpoint of evolutionary genetics, "her" genes may then be transmitted to progeny after "she" mates with the dominant male (Keenleyside, 1979). Social insect drones, naked mole rats, and New World monkeys also directly suppress sexual reproductive physiology when occupying subordinate positions in the social structure (Abbott et al., 1989). Sapolsky (1990) distinguished between dominant and subordinate baboons by measuring stress hormones linked to the pathophysiology of affective and anxiety disorders. Biological profiles of subordinates differ from those of more dominant animals in many species (Sapolsky, 1993). Moreover, hormone levels in both dominant and subordinate animals vary as a function of group stability, but social rank instability affects individuals differently, both with respect to directional trends in rank (going up versus down) as well as basic temperament (Sapolsky, 1994). Sociophysiological feedback in the natural environment largely determines dominance-subordination relationships. Moreover, pharmacological probes emphasize differences between dominant and subordinate animals. For example, rhesus monkeys given amphetamine react according to rank. Dominants show augmented threat, chase, and attack behaviors, but subordinates increased submissive behaviors, for example, fear grimaces and turning away (D.R. Wilson, 2002). A female rhesus monkey given amphetamine showed marked differences as she moved from one group to another. A low ranker in the first group, she behaved in an isolated fearful way; and amphetamine dramatically accentuated this. But when in the new group, where the alpha male favored her thereby elevating her status, she changed behavior accordingly and under the influence of amphetamine she threatened even more effectively and repeatedly.

In caged vervet monkey colonies of both sexes, serotonin levels reflect rank in males (Raleigh et al., 1984). Serotonin blood levels persistently measure twice higher in dominants compared to their subordinates (the same effect exists in humans but less dramatically, perhaps because human social rank represents a more complicated state). When removed from the cage and alone, the alpha vervet's serotonin blood levels fell over time while that of one of the subordinates remaining behind rises, as he newly assumes alpha status. Restoration of the formerly dominant male to the colony results in renewed increase in serotonin levels correlated with his renewed stature as dominant (this doesn't happen with a sufficiently delayed reunion, which diminishes rank continuity). Use of the serotonin reuptake inhibitor, fluoxetine, caused subordinates to achieve elevated alpha status (Raleigh et al., 1991).

Interestingly, discussions of basal ganglia physiology characteristically focus on movement disorders from the untoward effects of neuroleptic drugs. Yet such discussions may benefit from MacLean's focus (1990) on these structures that function in part to mediate ancient communicational repertoires that developed in deep time as part of the R-complex. Postural effects with communicational impact stem from increased dopamine in the basal ganglia; thus, the precursor molecule levodopa used as a treatment for parkinsonism may produce an expanded posture when the dose exceeds therapeutic levels (Crane and Gardner, 1969). Ethological observations in many species show that dominance correlates with the animal exhibiting larger posture and submissive yielding with a smaller pose. The levodopa-induced arms-torso extension resulting in a body expansion resembles that assumed by a person exerting dominance. In contrast, people with parkinsonism exhibit abnormally low levels of dopamine in these structures and typically show a flexed shrunken posture similar to a person submitting. Of course, these social rank postures are normally deployed in more distinct, socially communciative forms, that is, throwing the shoulders back and raising the arms when showing authority versus bowing and kneeling when submitting or supplicating.

Sex hormones also reflect social context and rank, in many species including humans. Androgen levels in both men and women vary depending on their degree of social competition or cooperation and also with success in competitive games (Kemper, 1984). Increases occur in even nonphysical competition such as chess. Thus neurotransmitter and endocrine parameters not only reflect features of social status, affect, and mood but link directly to reproductive biology itself.

D.R. Wilson (2002) integrates social dominance research within the triune hierarchy in a review that summarizes current knowledge of the phylo-ontogeny of neuromentation and neurotransmission. Notably, atavistic reptilian algorithms for dominance and submission remain active amid more affable mammalian complexes such as thermoregulation, motherhood, parenting, pair bonding, support of kin, play, and eusocial affiliation (MacLean, 1990). Vertebrate brains, notably those of humans, seem able to integrate a sense of self-esteem from various sources. Illustrating a theme underlined elsewhere in this chapter, self-esteem not unsurprisingly rises and falls on the basis of reciprocated signals (Eibl-Eibesfeldt, 1989), self-esteem being linked to the rank the individual possesses in the eyes of conspecifics. Expression and registration of such signals originate from phylogenetically old, deeply canalized sociophysiological systems bequeathed to any individual from inherited genomic elements that organize behavior. Subsequent mammalian and primate evolution greatly elaborate these sociophysiological repertoires; novel elements overlay but do not wholly replace more primitive features. Retentions themselves often modify and integrate rising primato-mammalian sociophysiology, for example, later limbic, cortical, neocortical tissues (and neuroendocrine innovations) intermesh with simpler functions that arose earlier.

Despite the tyranny sometimes of ancient forms, however, the human capacity for experiencing communicational states can be quite plastic. Thus, if one deliberately chooses to be subordinate, then interestingly one becomes "in charge" of that new position so that it can be assumed "conflict free." This can be distinguished from "resentful" submission, for instance, that may represent cognitive appreciation of the necessity to submit, but another level still holds out for winning. This, of course, is hardly unique to humans (e.g., dogs seem very satisfied with subordinate roles, though they also exert control over masters). And of course, the use of language in fostering more comfortable submissive states demonstrates part of the power of this human "invention."

Table 20.1 illustrates how MacLean's (1990) demonstration of the triune hierarchy of brain levels helps organize much complex sociophysiology. Simply rendering these three levels in matrix form across the two social modes (modeled by game

T A B L E 20.1. Evolutionary Sociophysiology: "Hawk" and "Dove" Game Theory Models at Three Brain Levels

Three Brain Levels, Social Mode, and Repertoires and Cognitive-Behavioral and Neurobiological Aspects	Two Social Modes	
Neomammalian Cortex SAHP Sociotropic–Cognitive/SAHP Cognition ≫ affect $S_1 > S_1 \sim D_3, 4 > D_1$ Advanced neurohormones & peptides	*"Hawk" Attractive* Optimistic charmer Manic sociopathy $S_2, D_3, 4$, and NE high	*"Dove" Avoidant* Pessimistic and shamed Depressed and obsessive S_2 low $D_3, 4$ and NE?
Paleomammalian Submissive Acquisative–emotive/RHP Affect > cognition $S_1 > S_2, D_2, 3, 4 > D_1$ Primitive neurohormones and peptides	*Limbic RHP* Roused winner Aggressive and sadistic $S_1, D_3, 4$ and NE high	*Dominant* Downcast loser Morbid and masochistic $S_1, D_3, 4$ and NE low
Reptilian Midbrain RAB Territorial–instinctive/RAB Instinct ≫ affect ≫ cognition $S_1 \gg S_2 \ll D_1 \gg D_2, 3, 4$ Few neurohormones and peptides	*Fighting* Strident and strong Violent and solipsist D_1 and NE high S?	*Fleeing* Cowering and weak Frightful, abulic D_1 and NE low S?

Hawk = evolutionarily stable strategy (ESS) sociophysiological repertoires—dominant.
Dove = evolutionarily stable strategy (ESS) sociophysiological repertoires—submissive.
RAB = ritualized agonistic behavior.
RHP = resource holding potential.
SAHP = social attention holding potential.
S = serotonin subreceptors (by numbered type, if applicable).
D = dopamine subreceptors (by numbered type, if applicable).
NE = norepinephrine subreceptors (by numbered type, if applicable).

theory) yields an illustrative template in which a variety of neurobiological, cognitive-behavioral, and other sociophysiological information can be correlated. For example, the three levels each display a different evolutionarily stable strategy that entails varying ratios of instinctive, emotive, and rational behavioral repertoires that may be presumed to have evolved in serial assemblages. These begin with the more primitive ritualized agonistic behavior (RAB) of the reptilian midbrain, resource holding potential (RHP) in the paleomammalian paleolimbic system and social-attention holding potential (SAHP) in the eusocial neomammalian, neolimbic, and neocortical regions (Gilbert, 1992). Likewise, as a working hypothesis based on an array of existing data, the three levels may exhibit unique variations—phylogenies really—of peptidergic and neurotransmitter receptor subtypes, normative and pathological expressions, and other heuristics for evolutionary selective attainment (Wilson, 2002a). Moreover, these serial levels each modulate sociophysiological communications in a bimodal fashion with characteristic expressions of phylogenetic repertoires for dominance and submission and associated neurobiological or behavioral markers and clinical phenomenology.

The above summarizes research illustrating how levels of analysis can be sociophysiologically integrated. Of course, the field of neuroscience labels so vast an arena that it almost defies coherent conceptual modeling. But a precisely focused basic science rubric for psychiatry may foster research creativity and levels of integration. In particular, the application of evolutionary science with its basic tools of Darwinian analysis should promote a comprehensive genomics beyond the current inductive program of "micro-Mendelism," and additionally, lend foundational depth and comprehensive breadth to human behavioral capacities and dysfunctions.

PRELIMINARY TREATMENT IMPLICATIONS

Since all psychiatric disorders reflect disturbances in communications, and both the brain and body devote much metabolic action to mediating social behaviors (aberrant features of which correlate with psychiatric illness), the study of communicational sociophysiology will foster more illuminating across-species comparisons. Such studies will generate robust evolutionary inferences, particularly on the operation of conserved versus emergent features of brain-behavioral systems in specific clinical problems.

All psychiatric treatments hinge on communication. Of course, this is the prime *métier* of psychotherapy, but psychopharmacology also requires effective communication in that patients must disclose syndromic phenomena and physicians must elicit cooperation via informed consent. In addition, pharmacological agents impact communicational propensity states, functions, and attributes. Also, akin to psychotherapy, placebo effects represent the benefits of interpersonal communication and cultural expectation: The patient expecting to be helped feels helped and indeed often is, for reasons other than the intended effects of the agent in question (Brown, 1998).

Scott (1989) has suggested that conspecifics regulate each other in that physiology can be affected more or less directly by factors in the ecosystem and in social systems. An individual's behavior can also affect a social system or ecosystem, but effects are usually much more evident in the reverse direction, from the higher levels down. Communicational behaviors grounded in the body influence the bodies of other conspecifics, for example, the stress-producing effects of a hostile put-down on the one hand, or the restorative effects of a mother on a distressed child on the other. Hofer (1984) working with rat pups and their mothers noted that the mother regulates infant homeostasis. Both Harlow (McKinney, 1988) and Bowlby (1988) documented the importance of attachment for primate infants. The salutary effects of people on one another extends well beyond childhood; attachment enhances health and reduces effects of stressors throughout life (Wolf and Bruhn, 1993).

MacLean (1990) also documents how the cortex itself may have arisen and increased its size as a neuroendocrine communicational device because its oldest component—the thalamocingulate gyrus—mediated the mother-offspring distress call that emerged at some indeterminate point around the reptilian-mammalian transition. D.R. Wilson (2002) emphasizes how the molecules that enhance bonding, and indeed all neurotransmission, originated in deep time and persist into the present with phylogenetic lineages of revealingly specific derivation. Via chemicals of parenting and motherhood such as oxytocin and arginine-vasopressin, babies express themselves exquisitely to elicit parental attention and attachment (Hrdy, 1999; Harris, 1995; Siegel, 1999). Panksepp (1998) considers the operation of these neurochemical systems in his emotion studies of nonprimate mammals, showing them to work in more primitive brain regions (and to have arisen earlier) than many human researchers assume.

Humans continue the capacity for eliciting help into adult life, indeed lifelong, and in many forms; they likely accomplish this by neoteny, that is, the retention of youthful traits into maturity. Part of this involves humor, as expressed in playful communications, such as comedy. Panksepp and Burgdorf (2000) highlighted that play too represents an ancient system among the emotions; for instance, even rat pups not only play but when vigorously touched (tickled) they utter ultrasonic "laughter." Indeed, Panksepp (1998) also suggests that, in part, attention deficit and hyperactivity disorder is not so much a disease as a strategy for learning via increased play. That it seems a disorder may stem from strictures on activity in present-day educational settings.

Humans expect to help as well as to be helped. Hrdy (1999) describes allomothers, mother-aides, or substitutes, who help care for infants or who adopt them, a role that exists throughout primates. In humans, help is sought and proffered throughout the life span. Beyond motherhood and parenthood, humans institutionalize helping other conspecifics in the form of education, medical care, retail services, and innumerable other service professions and roles—positions that are occupied less formally and extensively in other species.

Using controlled methods, researchers have extensively investigated psychotherapy over the last half of the 20th century (Wampold, 2001). Results document effectiveness with benefits that stem from general communication operating across various forms of treatment—psychodynamic, cognitive-behavioral, interpersonal, and many others. This suggests that each type of therapy reflects the ally-seeking capacity that humans possess to a high degree, seemingly from their relatively large cerebral cortex. Such capacities need to be considered during psychopharmacology treatment too, of course. Drugs impact brain systems that are essential to the production of communicational attributes and propensity states; but they (and surgery as well) can also promote placebo effects that may also reflect affiliation-seeking processes. Placebo means "to please," so the very word emphasizes positive components of the clinical relationship.

Circuits connecting frontal lobes to subcortical systems critically function to organize, plan, display empathy, maintain relatively steady mood and concentration, and respond appropriately to social cues (Mega and Cummings, 2001). More posterior structures decode faces and organize the person in space using primary senses singly and in combination, creating gestalts and allowing written language use. Luria (1972) presented the illuminating case study of a war veteran brain-damaged in the posterior cortical areas; he had great difficulty in the language decoding tasks involved in writing his story as Luria requested, but he persisted and succeeded. The patient's intact frontal lobes determined his energetic and resourceful completion of the task over many years that resulted from the therapeutic instruction and later appreciation of the accomplishment, including how Luria supported him and later arranged for publication.

Story use summarizes how human cortical functions shape communication. People avidly tell and listen to stories using verbal language, and they shape their lives according to stories learned when young that then modify as life goes on. Encompassing ones can be restated as cultural mores, belief systems, national or ethnic customs, as well as legal, political and religious systems. They modify ancient communicational propensity states that provide impetus and meaning. But the motivating urges stemming from deep time become triggered according to personal and interactive story lines that typify recently evolved levels. The individual typically assesses his or her attributes, circumstances, and ambitions in adolescence and adulthood and comes up with an individual story line that is then lived out, with modifications and adjustments, but with the story realized in dramatic and verbal forms (Donald, 1991). Alpha and audience communicational propensity states promote story using in a variety of ways; for example, people choose to become audiences at concerts, political rallies, lectures, or poetry readings. Complex negotiations with variations on rival story lines allows conflict resolution between warring parties, transforming action-focused combat, for instance, to more optimal outcomes that work according to mutually constructed and consensually agreed-on plans. In this way primitive communicational propensities may be overcome as human allies communicate via their complex system of language interaction.

CONCLUSIONS

In closing, we agree with the GAP Research Committee (Bakker et al., 2002) in their conclusion:

> [T]the concept of the brain as an organ that manages social life provides significant power for psychiatry's basic science. Burgeoning developments in neural and genetic areas put added demands on the conceptual structures of psychiatry. Findings from such work must be juxtaposed and correlated with the behavioral and experiential facets of psychiatry to give it a firm biological foundation. Psychiatry's full and unified entry into the realm of theory-driven and data-based medical science has been overdue. The social brain concept allows psychiatry to utilize pathogenesis in a manner parallel·to practice in other specialties.

REFERENCES

Abbott DH, Barrette J, Faulkes CG, George A (1989). Social contraception in naked moles rats and marmoset monkeys. *J Zoology* 219:703–710.

Allman JM (1999). *Evolving Brains*, Scientific American Library: New York.

Bailey K (1987). *Human Paleopsychology: Applications to Aggression and Pathological Processes.* Erlbaum, Hillsdale, NJ.

Bakker C, Gardner R, Koliatsos V, et al. (2002). The social brain: A unifying foundation for psychiatry. *Academic Psychiatry* 26:219.

Baltimore D (2000). 50,000 genes and we know them all (almost). *The New York Times*, June 25, p. 17.

Barr AM, Markou A, Phillips AG (2002). A "crash" course on psychostimulant withdrawal as a model of depression. *Trends Pharmacol Sci* 23:475–482.

Bowlby J (1969). *Attachment and Loss: Volume 1. Attachment.* New York, NY: Basic Books.

Bowlby J (1988). Developmental psychiatry comes of age. *Am J Psychiatry* 145:1–10.

Brown WA (1998). The placebo effect. *Scientific* Am January, 90–95.

Burgoon M, Hunsaker FG, Dawson EJ (1994). *Human Communication*, 3rd ed. Sage Publications: Thousand Oaks, CA.

Calvin WH (1987). The brain as a Darwin machine. *Nature* 330:33–34.

Caro R (2002). *The Years of Lyndon Johnson: Master of the Senate.* Alfred A. Knopf: New York.

Crane GC, Gardner R (eds) (1969). *Psychotropic Drugs and Dysfunctions of The Basal Ganglia: A Multidisciplinary Workshop.* Public Health Service, Publication #1938: Washington DC.

Daly M, Wilson M (1988). *Homicide.* Aldine de Gruyter: New York.

Darwin C (1859). *The Origin of Species: by Means of Natural Selection or the Preservation of Favored Races in the Stuggle for Life.* Modern Library: New York.

Darwin C (1871). *The Descent of Man, and Selection in Relation to Sex.* Princeton University Press: Princeton, NJ.

Dawkins R (1976, 1989). *The Selfish Gene.* New Edition. Oxford University Press: New York.

Deacon T (1997). *The Symbolic Species: The Co-Evolution of Language and the Brain.* Norton: New York.

Donald M (1991). *Origins of the Modern Mind: Three Stages in the Evolution of Culture and Cognition.* Harvard University Press: Cambridge, MA.

Dunbar RIM (1996). *Grooming, Gossip, and the Evolution of Language.* Harvard University Press: Cambridge, MA.

Edelman GM (1987). *Neural Darwinism: The Theory of Neuronal Group Selection.* Basic Books: New York.

Eibl-Eibesfeldt I (1989). *Human Ethology.* Aldine de Gruyter: New York.

Ekman P, Davidson RJ (eds) (1994). *The Nature of Emotions: Fundamental Questions.* Oxford University Press: New York.

Freedman DX (1982). Presidential address: Science in the service of the ill. *Am J Psychiat* 139:1087–1101.

Gardner R (1982). Mechanisms in manic-depressive disorder: An evolutionary model. *Arch Gen Psychiat* 39:1436–1441.

Gardner R (1988). Psychiatric syndromes as infrastructure for intraspecific communication. In Chance MRA (ed). *Social Fabrics of the Mind.* Erlbaum: Hove, England, pp. 197–226.

Gardner R (1997). Sociophysiology as the basic science of psychiatry. *Theoretical Medicine* 18:335–356.

Gardner R (1998). The brain and communication are basic for clinical human sciences. *British Journal of Medical Psychology* 71:493–508.

Gardner R, McKinney WT (2001). Ethology and the use of animal models. In Henn F, Sartorius N, Helmchen H, Lauter H (eds). *Contemporary Psychiatry Volume I. Foundations of Psychiatry.* (English version). Springer: Heidelberg, Germany, pp. 300–307.

Gazzaniga MS, Sperry RW (1967). Language after section of the cerebral commissures. *Brain* 90:131–48.

Gehring WJ (1998). *Master Control Genes in Development and Evolution: The Homeobox Story.* Yale University Press: New Haven, CT.

Gilbert P (1992). *Depression: The Evolution of Powerlessness.* Guilford Press: New York.

Glantz K, Pearce JK (1989). *Exiles from Eden: Psychotherapy from an Evolutionary Perspective.* Norton: New York.

Gottman JM, Murray JD, Swanson CC, Tyson R, Swanson KR (2002). *The Mathematics of Marriage: Dynamic Nonlinear Approach.* MIT Press: Cambridge, Mass.

Gould SJ, Lewontin RC (1979). The spandrels of San Marco and the Panglossian paradigm: A critique of the adaptationist programme. *Proceedings of the Royal Academy of London B* 205:581–598.

Haig DM (1996). Altercations of generations: Genetic conflicts of pregnancy. *Am J Reproductive Immunol* 35:226–232.

Hamilton WD (1964). The genetical evolution of social behavior. *J Theoret Biol* 7:1–52.

Harris JC (1995). *Developmental Neuropsychiatry. Volume I. Fundamentals.* Oxford University Press: New York.

Hofer MA (1984). Relationships as regulators: A psychobiologic perspective on bereavement. *Psychosomatic Med* 46:183–197.

Hrdy SB (1999). *Mother Nature: A History of Mothers, Infants, and Natural Selection.* Pantheon Books: New York.

Keenleyside MHA (1979). *Diversity and Adaptation in Fish Behavior.* Springer: Berlin.

Kemper TD (1984). Power, status and emotions: A sociobiological contribution to a psychological domain. In Scherer K, Ekman P (eds). *Approaches to Emotion* Erlbaum: Hillsdale, NJ.

Keverne EB, Fundele R, Narasimha M, Barton SC, Surani MA (1996). Genomic imprinting and the differential roles of parental genomes in brain development. *Dev Brain Res* 92:91–100.

Klein DF (1993). False suffocation alarms, spontaneous panics, and related conditions. *Arch Gen Psychiatry* 50:306–317.

LeCroy D, Moller P (eds) (2000). Evolutionary Perspectives on Human Reproductive Behavior. *Annals of the New York Academy of Sciences*: New York, Vol. 907.

Luria AR (trans Solotaroff L) (1972). *The Man with a Shattered World: The History of a Brain Wound.* Harvard University Press: Cambridge, MA.

MacLean PD (1990). *The Triune Brain in Evolution: Role of Paleocerebral Function.* Plenum: New York.

McGlashan TH, Hoffman RE (2000). Schizophrenia as a disorder of developmentally reduced synaptic connectivity. *Arch Gen Psychiat* 57:637–648.

McGuffin P, Riley B, Plomin R (2001). Toward behavioral genetics. *Science* 291: 1232–1249.

McGuire MT, Troisi A (1998). *Darwinian Psychiatry.* Oxford University Press: New York.

McKinney WT (1988). *Models of Mental Disorders: A New Comparative Psychiatry.* Plenum: New York.

Mealey L (2000). *Sex Differences: Developmental and Evolutionary Strategies.* Academic Press: New York.

Mega MS, Cummings JL (2001). *Frontal subcortical circuits: Anatomy and function.* In Salloway SP, Malloy PF, Duffy JD, (eds) *The Frontal Lobes and Neuropsychiatry Illness* APPI: Washington, D.C. pp. 15–32.

Miller G (2000). *The Mating Mind: How Sexual Choice Shaped the Evolution of Human Nature.* Anchor Books: New York.

Mithen S (1996). *Prehistory of the Mind.* Thames and Hudson: London.

Moore H, Dvoráková K, Jenkins N, Breed W (2002). Exceptional sperm cooperation in the wood mouse. *Nature* 418:174–177.

Morgan D, Grant KA, Gage HD, Mach RH, Kaplan JR, Prioleau O, Nader SH, Buchheimer N, Ehrenkaufer RL, Nader MA (2002). Social dominance in monkeys: Dopamine D_2 receptors and cocaine self-administration. *Nature Neurosci* 5:169–174.

Mouse Genome Sequencing Consortium (2002). Initial sequencing and comparative analysis of the mouse genome. *Nature* 420:520–562.

Nesse RM, Berridge KC (1997). Psychoactive drug use in evolutionary perspective. *Science* 278:63–66.

Nestler EJ (1999). Special challenges in the investigation of mental illness. In Charney DS, Nestler EJ, Bunney B (eds). *Neurobiology of Mental Illness.* Oxford University Press: New York, pp. 578–590.

Newlin DB (2002). The self-perceived survival ability and reproductive fitness (SPFit) theory of substance abuse disorders. *Addiction* 97:427–445.

Owens MJ, Risch SC (1995). In Schatzberg AF, Nemeroff C (eds). *Atypical Antipsychotics, in Psychopharmacology*, APPA: Washington, DC.

Pääbo S (2001). The human genome and ourselves. *Science* 291:1219–1220.

Panksepp J (1998). *Affective Neuroscience: The Foundations of Human and Animal Emotions.* Oxford University Press: New York.

Panksepp J, Burgdorf J (2000). 50 kHz chirping (laughter?) in response to conditioned and unconditioned tickle-induced reward in rats: Effects of social housing and genetic variable. *Behav Brain Res* 115:25–38.

Price JS (1967). Hypothesis: The dominance hierarchy and the evolution of mental illness. *Lancet* 2:243–246.

Price J, Sloman L (1987). Depression as yielding behaviour: An animal model based upon Schjelderup-Ebbe's pecking order. *Ethology and Sociobiology* 8S:309–335.

Price J, Sloman L, Gardner R, Gilbert P, Rohde P (1994). The social competition hypothesis of depression. *Br J Psychiatry* 164:309–315.

Price JS, Gardner R, Erickson M (2003). Depression, anxiety and somatization as appeasement displays. *J Affective Disorders*, in press.

Raleigh M, McGuire M, Brammer G, Yuwiler A (1984). Social status and whole blood serotonin in vervets. *Arch Gen Psychiatry* 41:405–410.

Raleigh M, McGuire M, Brammer G, Yuwiler A (1991). Serotonergic mechanisms promote dominance acquisition in adult male vervet monkeys. *Brain Res* 559:181–190.

Rapaport JL, Fiske A (1998). The new biology of obsessive-compulsive disorder: implications for evolutionary psychology. *Perspectives in Biology and Medicine* 41:159–175.

Robertson GM (1890). Melancholia, from the physiological and evolutionary points of view. *J Mental Sci* 36:53–67.

Ruis MAW, te Brake JHA, Buwalda B, De Boer SF, Meerlo P, Korte SM, Blokhuis HJ, Koolhaas JM (1999). Housing familiar male wild-type rats together reduces the long-term adverse behavioral and physiological effects of social defeat. *Psychoneuroendocrinology* 24:285–300.

Sadek JR, Hammeke TA (2002). Functional neuroimaging in neurology and psychiatry. *CNS Spectrums* 7:276–299.

Salloway SP, Malloy PF, Duffy JD (eds) (2001). *The Frontal Lobes and Neuropsychiatric Illness*. APPI: Washington DC.

Salsen E (2001). A century of emotion theories—proliferation without progress? *History & Philosophy of Psychol* 3:56–75.

Sapolsky RM (1990). Adrenocortial function, social rank and personality among wild baboons. *Biol Psychiatry* 28:862–878.

Sapolsky RM (1993). Endocrine alfresco: Psychoendocrine studies of wild baboons. *Recent Progress in Hormone Res* 48:437–468.

Sapolsky RM (1994). Individual differences in the stress response. *Sem Neurosci* 6:261–269.

Scott JP (1989). *The Evolution of Social Systems*. Gordon and Breach: New York.

Scott JP, Fuller JL (1965). *Genetics and the Social Behavior of the Dog*. University of Chicago Press: Chicago.

Segerstrale U (2000). *Defenders of the Truth: The Battle for Science in the Sociobiology Debate and Beyond*. Oxford University Press: New York.

Siegel DJ (1999). *The Developing Mind: Toward a Neurobiology of Interpersonal Experience*. Guilford Press: New York.

Smith WJ (1977). *The Behavior of Communicating: An Ethological Approach*. Harvard University Press: Cambridge, MA.

Smith JM (1982). *Evolution and the Theory of Games*. Cambridge University Press: Cambridge, UK.

Smith CUM (2002). Deep time and the brain: the message of the molecules. In Cory GA, Gardner, R (Editors): *The Neuroethology of Paul MacLean: Convergences and Frontiers*. Westport, CT: Praeger, pp. 31–44.

Sokol MS, Ward PE, Tamiya H, Kondo DG, Houston D, Zabriskie JB (2002). D8/17 expression on B lymphocytes in anorexia nervosa. *Am J Psychiatry* 159(8):1430–1432.

Stevens A, Price J (1996, 2000). *Evolutionary Psychiatry: A New Beginning*. Routledge: New York.

Storr A (1988). *Solitude: A Return to the Self*. Free Press: New York.

Sutton E (1988). *An Introduction to Human Genetics*, 4th ed. Harcourt Brace Jovanovich: New York.

Taylor J (ed) (1958). *Selected Writings of John Hughlings Jackson. Volume 2. Evolution and Dissociation of the Nervous System. Speech. Various papers, addresses and lectures*. Staples Press: London.

Trivers RL (1972). Parental investment and sexual selection. In *Sexual Selection and the Descent of Man 1871–1971*. Campbell B (ed). Aldine: Chicago, pp. 136–179.

Trivers RL (1974). Parent-offspring conflict. *Am Zoologist* 14:249–264.

Wampold B (2001). *The Great Psychotherapy Debate: Models, Methods, and Findings*. Erlbaum: Mahwah, NJ.

Wilson EO (1975). *Sociobiology: The New Synthesis*. Cambridge, MA: Harvard University Press.

Wilson DR (1988). Evolutionary epidemiology. Selected abstracts of the first meeting of the Human Evolution and Behavior Society. *Human Nature Rev (http://human-nature.com* ISSN 1476-1084).

Wilson DR (1993). Evolutionary epidemiology: Darwinian theory in the service of medicine and psychiatry. *Acta Biotheoretica* 41:205–218.

Wilson DR (2002). Neuroethologic, game mathematic & evolutionary epidemiologic analyses. In Cory G, Gardner R (eds). *The Neuroethology of Paul MacLean*. Greenwood-Praeger: New York.

Wilson DS (2002) *Darwin's Cathedral: Evolution, Religion, and the Nature of Society*. University of Chicago Press: Chicago.

Wolf S, Bruhn JG (1993). *The Power of Clan: The Influence of Human Relationships on Heart Disease*. Transaction Publishers: New Brunswick, NJ.

Wrangham R, Peterson D (1996). *Demonic Males: Apes and the Origins of Human Violence*. Houghton-Mifflin: New York.

Young LJ, Nilsen R, Waymire KG, MacGregor GR, Insel TR (1999). Increased affiliative response to vasopressin in mice expressing the V1a receptor from a monogamous vole. *Nature* 400:766–768.

21

FUTURE OF NEUROPEPTIDES IN BIOLOGICAL PSYCHIATRY AND EMOTIONAL PSYCHOPHARMACOLOGY: GOALS AND STRATEGIES

Jaak Panksepp[1] and Jaanus Harro[2]

[1] *J.P. Scott Center for Neuroscience Mind & Behavior, Department of Psychology, Bowling Green State University, Bowling Green, Ohio*
[2] *Department of Psychology, Center of Behavioral and Health Sciences, University of Tartu, Tartu, Estonia*

INTRODUCTION

The biological psychiatry revolution that started in the middle of the 20th century transformed a discipline devoted mostly to psychodynamic principles into one based on biologic and psychopharmacologic factors (see Chapter 1). The discovery and clarification of brain dopamine (DA), norepinephrine (NE), serotonin or 5-hydroxytryptamine (5-HT), acetylcholine (ACh), and gamma-aminobutyric acid (GABA) functions

Textbook of Biological Psychiatry, Edited by Jaak Panksepp
ISBN 0-471-43478-7   Copyright © 2004 John Wiley & Sons, Inc.

promoted the appreciation that specific neurochemical imbalances contributed substantially to major psychiatric conditions. A characterization of the intervening psychological processes was gradually deemed to be less important for successful treatment than clear diagnostic categories that could lead to specific prescriptions.

As the linking of objective behavioral symptoms to psychiatric disorders was increasingly institutionalized in successive revisions of the *Diagnostic and Statistical Manual of Mental Disorders* (DSMs), standard drug prescription practices were facilitated. However, too much drug discovery initiative became devoted to modification of reasonably well-established themes, coupled with an excessive reliance on diagnostic tools that may have insufficient biological validity. Preclinical research relied excessively on the use of automated behavioristic learning tasks that may not adequately discriminate distinct emotional systems in action. The focus of this chapter will be on the nature of basic mammalian affective processes as revealed by the study of the natural emotional behaviors of organisms. Basic neuroaffective issues must be brought to the forefront of new drug discovery initiatives, which, for a generation, have not been optimally deployed because of the prevailing assumption that psychiatric disorders largely reflect global neurochemical imbalances as opposed to imbalanced activities of specific emotional systems.

Although it is now generally accepted that consensus-defined psychiatric disorders are associated in some way with imbalances among brain neurochemical systems, few believe that current diagnostics are causally related to any singular neurochemical correlates. However, as psychiatric practice has been streamlined into an efficient medical model, the importance of emotional lives, both of clients and practitioners, have diminished as a source of insight for the administration and development of new types of psychopharmacological assistance. Concurrently, visions of how socioemotional environments may impact psychopharmacological practices have diminished (however, see Chapter 18 for one important strategy that remains centered on client's lives).

Although the robustness and specificity of existing pharmacoclinical relations continue to be debated (e.g., Valenstein, 1998; Valenstein and Charney, 2000), the acceptance of symptom-driven prescription practices has changed the face of psychiatry in unmistakable ways, often for the better (i.e., greater diagnostic/prescription agreements) but also at times for the worse (e.g., the disregard of important individual differences in ongoing research). For instance, many drug trials may fail because biologically heterogeneous populations exist under one diagnostic category (e.g., autism). Therapeutic effects may be better identified by preselecting apparent drug responders and then studying that subset using double-blind procedures. Also, certain drugs and associated therapies may only work optimally if the right psychosocial conditions are enhanced. Two childhood disorders, autism and attention deficit hyperactivity disorders (ADHD), will be considered later from this vantage. This concept, in need of further systematic investigation, highlights the reasonably well-accepted view that biological interventions tend to work best when combined with psychosocial interventions. As Wyatt et al. (1996) asserted, even for the severest disorders such a schizophrenia: "future biological treatments and preventions will also involve appropriate nonbiological considerations" (p. 357).

A key ingredient in this transformation could be the wider recognition that there is, in fact, substantial chemical coding of emotional processes in the brain and that these chemical processes are also responsive to environmental events. This viewpoint has been more widely accepted in mainland European than Anglo-American scientific circles. Among the latter, conceptions of the mind as a *tabula rasa* and the resulting massive focus on learning associationism in the mind sciences continues to prevail (Pinker, 2002). Even in behavioral neuroscience, the idea that there is neurochemical coding for various evolved psychobehavioral processes of the brain diminished in the 1970s following an initial phase of optimism. For instance, the biogenic amine chemistries that initiated the first phase of the biological psychiatry revolution (Figure 1.1), were eventually found to modulate essentially all emotional and motivational processes in rather widespread and often nonspecific ways (Myers, 1974). But now, the vast array of neuropeptides—short chains of amino acids—concentrated in specific brain circuits (Tohyama and Takatsuji, 1998) are beginning to offer an unprecedented degree of functional specificity.

The emergence of the neuropeptide revolution in the 1970s has yet to yield many clinically useful drugs to modify brain activities in psychiatrically beneficial ways, but there are many novel possibilities [for summaries of some of the possibilities, see Hökfelt et al. (2000), Panksepp (1993), and Snyder and Ferris (2000)]. The neuropeptide concept (de Wied, 1999) has provided the impetus for the discovery of many agents that specifically affect a diversity of brain and bodily functions (Strand, 1999). The general neuroanatomies of four major neuropeptide systems are depicted in Figure 21.1. These systems probably operate in global ways to establish new homogeneous states of the nervous system such as in the arousal of certain emotions and motivations.

Although the amount of work on emotional issues has been minuscule compared to easily monitored behavioral measures such as activity, feeding, grooming, learning, and memory (e.g., Kovacs and de Wied, 1994; McLay et al., 2001), the abundance of peptides in the limbic system that can modify the instinctual emotional actions of organisms coaxes us to also consider that many of these agents do modulate distinct affective/emotional state-control processes within the brain (Panksepp, 1993, 1998a).

Although neuropeptides are present in the brain at several orders of magnitude lower concentrations than the classic neurotransmitters, their molecular scarcity is compensated for by their high affinity for receptors, as well as the fact that they are released in the brain in activity-dependent ways—as they are dynamically called upon to regulate mind, body, and behavior. As emphasized throughout this chapter, the existence of such specific agents may also pose new and substantial challenges for therapeutic practice. One aim of this chapter is to promote the needed discussions.

The practical problems range from the need to develop new modes of administration of substances that do not readily cross intestinal-blood and blood-brain barriers (Kastin et al., 1999). This may require the use of intranasal and sublingual routes of administration (Fehm et al., 2000) and continued development of nonpeptide congeners (Hruby, 2002) that can access the relevant receptive fields in the brain (Tohyama and Takatsuji, 1998). Techniques to facilitate access of peptides into the brain are emerging (Rubio-Aliaga and Daniel, 2002). Also, the receptive fields for neuropeptides

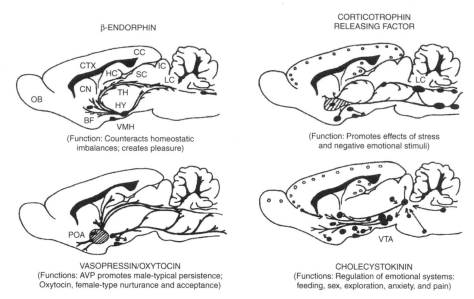

β-ENDORPHIN

(Function: Counteracts homeostatic
imbalances; creates pleasure)

CORTICOTROPHIN
RELEASING FACTOR

(Function: Promotes effects of stress
and negative emotional stimuli)

VASOPRESSIN/OXYTOCIN
(Functions: AVP promotes male-typical persistence;
Oxytocin, female-type nurturance and acceptance)

CHOLECYSTOKININ
(Functions: Regulation of emotional systems:
feeding, sex, exploration, anxiety, and pain)

Figure 21.1. Parasagittal depiction of the dispersion of four major neuropeptide systems. LC, locus coeruleus; DB, dorsal NE bundle; VB, ventral NE bundle; CC, corpus callosum; CN, caudate nucleus; AC, anterior commissure; OB, olfactory bulb; CTX, cortex; BG, basal forebrain; HC, hippocampus; TH, thalamus; SC, superior colliculus; IC, inferior colliculus; HY, hypothalamus; VTA, ventral tegmental area. Small circles in the cortex indicate the presence of local interneurones for CRH (also commonly known as CRF or corticotropin-releasing factor). [This figure is reprinted from Panksepp (1998a), *Affective Neuroscience*, with the kind permission of Oxford University Press.]

are remarkably dynamic. The relevant genetic mechanisms are called upon only at certain times developmentally. Some are activated by stress (Hökfelt et al., 2000), while others fluctuate with changing motivations, as in steroid-mediated sociosexual receptivity (Carter et al., 1999; Insel, 1997).

Since few clinical applications for neuropeptide therapies presently exist, we will here attempt to look into the crystal ball for future possibilities. We will first organize our coverage around some of the demonstrated neuropeptide changes in major psychiatric disorders, and then on the basis of neuropeptides that have been implicated in the regulation of emotional and motivational processes. But first, let us focus on agents that have come close to entering clinical practice.

NEUROPEPTIDE MEDICINES: STILL WAITING IN THE WINGS

The ultimate proof of concept for neuropeptide approaches in psychiatry lies in emergence of clinically effective drugs. There is only one definitive example to date, and that is the family of opioidergic compounds. These drugs that mimic the effects of endogenous opioids are the most potent, generally effective analgesics. It is quite probable that opioid agonists could have other beneficial clinical effects related to emotional circuits (see below), but the use of these drugs is restricted by their high abuse potential, which in itself reflects the emotional value of the endogenous opioidergic systems.

At present, the only neuropeptidergic drugs that are approved for treating psychiatrically significant living problems are those that antagonize opioid receptors, for instance, naloxone and naltrexone. Their first approved use was in the treatment of narcotic overdoses as well as maintenance of opiate abstinence. Subsequent work indicated significant efficacy in the treatment of alcohol craving (O'Malley et al., 2002), which may reflect a general reduction in reward craving (de Wit et al., 1999) that extends even to gambling urges (Kim and Grant, 2001) and perhaps binge eating as well (Marrazzi et al., 1995). However, as we will discuss toward the end of this chapter, there have also been some off-label uses, such as for the treatment of self-injurious behaviors as well as certain symptoms of early childhood autism (Aman and Langworthy, 2000; Chabane et al., 2000). One can envision many additional indications, perhaps the most extreme being as a treatment for maladaptive social-addictive problems that lead to pedophilia, if we are correct in assuming that difficult-to-treat behavior arises, in part, from maladaptive patterns of opioid reward urges in the brain. Aside from such opioid-modulating drugs, no neuropeptide modulators have yet been accepted for routine psychiatric use.

The clinical opportunities for targeting precise psychiatric/emotional symptoms in this emerging field are more vast than commonly recognized, and there are currently increasing numbers of ongoing clinical initiatives. One of the more promising ones involves early work on the antidepressant effects of the proline-lycine-glycine (PLG) tripeptide that constitutes the "tail" of oxytocin (de Wied and van Ree, 1989). This work has been translated into a new generations of related neuropeptide agents, such as netamiftide (4,F-Phe-4-OH-Pro-Arg-Gly-Trp-NH_2), which is reported to have a novel profile of antidepressant activity, including rapid onset (Feighner et al., 2001). The recognition that the Tyr-PLG (or Tyr-MIF-1) system, an endogenous opioid-modulating peptide system still searching for a function (Kastin et al., 2001), which may modulate brain reward (Nores et al., 1999), providing one potentially coherent account for the antidepressant effects. After all, opioids were recognized to have *acute* antidepressant effects long before the advent of modern psychiatry. At present, netamiftide remains on the fast track for development (being in Phase III trials), even though the last hurdle is often the greatest.

Among the most prominent three "near hits" so far have been (1) the use of Adrenocorticotropic Hormone (ACTH) fragments, such as Organon-2766, in the treatment of many neurological problems, including attentional/cognitive disorders in developmentally impaired children (as detailed below); (2) a substance P neurokinin$_1$ (NK_1) receptor antagonists for depression (Kramer et al., 1998), which was placed on the back burner because it could not compete credibly with strong placebo effects in double-blind trials (Enserink, 1999); and (3) there also continues to be widespread enthusiasm for the eventual use of corticotropin-releasing hormone (CRH) antagonists for the treatment of stress and anxiety (Reul and Holsboer, 2002), even though the initial agent used had problematic liver toxicity effects despite being otherwise well toler-ated (Holsboer, 2001a,b). Then there are an enormous number of items that remain largely in the conceptual realm, ranging from the use of cholecystokinin (CCK) recep-tor blockers in the treatment of schizophrenia (Vanderhaeghen and Crawley, 1985) to the working hypothesis that vasopressin-related vectors may be beneficial in the treat-ment of depression (Scott and Dinan, 2002). Such emerging hypotheses will receive the most attention in this chapter.

If one were currently to select a single neuropeptide that has had the most promis-ing and most widely evaluated track record in humans, it would be the first item in the above list (i.e., Org-2766). This peptide emerged gradually from David de Wied's work on memory enhancing ACTH-related peptides (Kovacs and de Wied, 1994). It also proved to have various interesting neuroprotective effects after peripheral nerve injury as well as following damage to certain central systems such as DA pathways (Strand, 1999). Subsequent work on structure activity relations led to localization of activity in the ACTH-(4–10) fragment and to the synthesis of an array of orally active synthetic peptides, the most promising of which was called Organon-2766 [H-Met(O(2))-Glu-His-Phen-D-Lys-Phe-OH]. This orally available, artificial peptide is about a thousand times as potent as the parent compound (ACTH 4–9), and has now been widely studied as a neuroprotective agent (e.g., van Rijzingen et al., 1996), and it has been reported to promote attentional-cognitive processes and in the treatment of autistic children, potentially by modulating opioid dynamics (Buitelaar et al., 1992). However, as is so common in the field, more recent studies have been less compelling than the ear-lier ones (Buitelaar et al., 1996). The commercial failure of this exceedingly safe and well tolerated peptide highlights the difficulties of taking agents that have been highly effective in preclinical studies to human applications. It is not clear why this is so, but perhaps future research will reveal that Org-2766 will prove to be more effective dur-ing the early rather than the later phases of certain disorders (e.g., for strokes, ADHD, and the prophylactic treatment of impending cognitive decline; Nyakas et al., 1995).

EMOTIONAL FOUNDATIONS OF PSYCHIATRIC DISORDERS

Before discussing neuropeptide drug discovery initiatives, we will briefly summarize the two intellectual trends that are now opening up new vistas in medicinal devel-opments for the regulation of discrete emotional problems. The first is the approach known as *affective neuroscience*, which aspires to conceptualize the evolved emo-tional operating systems of the mammalian brain (Panksepp, 1998a). The second is *social neuroscience*, which recognizes the importance of evolved social-emotional circuitries in generating affective experiences (also see Chapter 20). Both are yielding new evolutionary vistas for a psychiatry that is based on a scientific understanding, in equal measure, of the emotional aspects of mind, brain, and behavior.

Emergence of Affective Neuroscience

The unraveling of the neurochemistries of basic emotional, motivational, and attentional processes of the mammalian brain (Panksepp, 1998a) is providing many novel brain targets for psychiatric drug development (McLay et al., 2001; Panksepp, 1993). Our belief is that a neuroethological analysis of the natural (instinctual) emotional behaviors of animals provides the best overall strategy for decoding how emotional feelings are organized in the brain (e.g., Knutson et al., 2002; Panksepp, 1998a). There is robust evidence for the working hypothesis that affective consciousness emerges from subcortical neurodynamics for instinctual emotional tendencies that mediate "intentions in action" (Panksepp, 2000, 2003a). Affective consciousness appears to be built fundamentally on the primitive neural systems of the brain that mediate homeostatic and emotional adjustments (Damasio et al., 2000; Panksepp, 1998a, 2000, 2003a). By drawing predictive relationships between the neurobiological vectors that regulate such emotional behaviors in our animal models and comparable feeling states in humans (Panksepp, 1999), the primal sources of human emotional feelings can be abstracted from and validated against the evidence emerging from preclinical work on other animals.

Emergence of Social and Emotional Neuropeptides

Modern functional neuroscience also continues to coax us to accept that certain social-emotional processes are intrinsic, evolved components of the mammalian brain/mind (Insel, 1997; Panksepp et al., 2002b). Many of these systems provide novel ways of thinking about the neurobiological aspects of psychiatric problems (see Chapters 1, 2, and 16) as well as the sociophysiology of evolved emotional systems (Chapter 20).

As we begin to accept that the mammalian brain is a social organ, with neuro-chemistries that promote various interactive social activities and respond in distinct ways to the quality of those interactions (Carter et al., 1999), we should also be less surprised that placebos (Mayberg et al., 2002) and various psychotherapies have demonstrable therapeutic effects on the brain (Baxter et al., 1992; Furmark et al., 2002; Schwartz et al., 1996). Indeed, certain effective psychopharmaceuticals have neural effects similar to placebo effects, with both recruiting social support systems of the brain (Petrovic et al., 2002), which are in part opioid based (Panksepp, 1998a). As we recognize how brain chemical systems change as a function of social experiences (Insel, 1997; Young, 2002), it becomes especially important to consider how distinct environments and therapeutic contexts might provide background support for the emotion-specific chemistries to operate optimally. For instance, social isolation reduces brain serotonin activity, which promotes irritability, while friendly interactions can change brain chemistries in ways resembling selective serotonin reuptake inhibitor (SSRI) antidepressants (see Chapter 5).

Such findings affirm that benefits of many psychotherapies may be related as much to the affective qualities of therapeutic relationships as the nonsocial aspects of specific interventions. This phenomenon has long been recognized in psychotherapeutic practice (Beutler et al., 1994) and may help account for the emerging neurophysiology of placebo effects (Mayberg et al., 2002), which may be related to opioid dynamics in the brain (Petrovic et al., 2002). Changes in neuropeptide and steroid dynamics that mediate social feelings are highly responsive to the quality of animal interactions (e.g.,

Carter, 1998; Insel, 1997; Meaney, 2001). This kind of knowledge should find a prominent place in the biological psychiatry of the future. Indeed, recent work is highlighting how rapidly and effectively adrenal steroids can modulate depressive episodes (Gold et al., 2002).

The clinical opportunities for highly targeted therapeutics in this emerging field are vast. However, the bottom line will be that therapeutic targets need to be selected on the basis of two major criteria: (1) the correct analysis of the normal neurophysiological and neuropsychological functions of the various neuropeptides in normal brain/mind functions, and (2) the analysis of how peptide systems might be imbalanced in better-defined psychiatric disorders. The end result of such analyses should be to identify and develop therapeutic peptide targets (often with nonpeptide medicines), which may help reestablish affective homeostasis perhaps in conjunction with appropriate psychosocial interventions.

NEUROPEPTIDES IN PSYCHIATRIC DISORDERS

Similarly to the classic neurotransmitters, mounting evidence is available about changes in neuropeptide expression and processing in several psychiatric disorders. Neuropeptides are present in brain tissue as well as in cerebrospinal fluid (CSF). Although the neurotransmitter function of neuropeptides is associated with their synthesis in situ in brain and anatomical distribution via neuropeptidergic fiber systems, their abundant presence in the CSF may be primarily due to simple drainage into the CSF, and may serve as a useful indirect marker of neuropeptide function and metabolism. Alternatively, neuropeptides functioning as neurohormones may be actively delivered into the CSF from central or peripheral sources and employ the pathways of CSF circulation as avenues of transport (Burbach, 1982). CSF levels of neuropeptides may help establish global functional states in the nervous system (e.g., affective states), and they may achieve this by orchestrating activities in many other neurochemical systems (Rothman et al., 2002). Thus CSF peptide titers may have an active regulatory role in relation to central nervous system (CNS) functions and behaviors, such as pain and anxiety symptoms, as well as a function of therapeutic doses of psychoactive drugs (Post et al., 1982).

So far neuropeptide studies in many psychiatric conditions have produced some variable results. A major possible problem is heterogeneity in subject populations, as well as various technical obstacles in obtaining comparable samples, especially of post-mortem material. Regarding the CSF studies, the use of neuropeptide titers for studying in vivo alterations in central neuronal activities is enhanced by a knowledge of CSF physiology and pathology. Degradation of CSF constituents during collection, storage, and analysis may introduce errors in quantification (Wood, 1980). Ventriculospinal concentration gradients, circadian rhythms, physical activity, stress, medications, concomitant illness, obstructed CSF circulation, age, and sex alter the baseline neurochemical composition of CSF. For example, many studies on CRH levels in the CSF may be biased because of insufficient control for stress caused by sampling (Mitchell, 1998).

Among the better explored connections is the role of CRH in stress-related disorders, including depression (Holsboer, 2001a,b; Harro and Oreland, 2001; De Souza and Grigoriadis, 2002). Levels of CRH in the CSF have been found to be higher and CRH receptor densities lower in some populations of depressed patients, and the number of CRH-expressing neurons in the hypothalamic paraventricular nucleus is higher. Recurrence of depression can be fairly well predicted on the basis of enhanced cortisol response to CRH after dexamethasone-induced feedback inhibition of anterior pituitary (Reul and Holsboer, 2002). Several nonpeptide antagonists of the CRH_1 receptor subtype have recently been developed. There is preliminary evidence that such drugs may be efficient against anxiety and depression (Zobel et al., 2000).

While CRH is used by several neuronal populations in the CNS and peripheral nervous system, a recent discovery of orexins (also called hypocretins) has provided an example of a highly localized neuropeptide system that is unequivocally associated with at least one disorder of the CNS. Orexins are expressed in neurons of dorsolateral hypothalamus and regulate arousal states and feeding but also appear to be causally related to the sleep disorder narcolepsy (Sutcliffe and de Lecea, 2002). In humans, narcolepsy is caused by the loss of orexin neurons probably because of an autoimmune attack or by mutation of the orexin-2 receptor (Willie et al., 2001). Studies of this novel neuropeptide family have greatly enhanced our understanding of the biochemistry, physiology, and anatomy of switching between waking and sleeping, which in turn provides clues as to how better therapies may be developed to facilitate optimal arousal states. The excessive daytime sleepiness of narcoleptics is currently treated with DA-potentiating psychostimulants, but evidence that orexins can stimulate the DA neurons in the ventral tegmental area (Korotkova et al., 2003) suggests that orexin facilitators (e.g., receptor agonists) may promote arousal with a wider safety margin.

Following the idea that neurotensin may be strongly related to the pathogenesis of schizophrenia (see below), the density of neurotensin receptors was studied in the intermediate and caudal entorhinal cortex and hippocampal formation of subjects with schizophrenia or affective disorder and in control subjects (Hamid et al., 2002). Not only schizophrenic but also affective disorder subjects had decreased neurotensin receptor density in the entorhinal cortex. These findings highlight regional changes in neurotensin receptor binding levels in the mesial temporal lobe in psychopathology. However, since there was no clear diagnostic specificity for these changes, being evident to varying degrees in both schizophrenia and affective disorders, neurotensin may be related to some functional brain mechanism these diagnostic groups have in common.

In some instances, an absence of a major change in a neuropeptide in the presence of other neurotransmitter changes could also be a pathogenic mechanism, as suggested for galanin, a neuropeptide with multiple inhibitory actions on the circuitries of learning and memory. In Alzheimer's disease, levels of many neurotransmitters decrease, but the expression of galanin progressively increases (Counts et al., 2001). In these conditions, galanin may inhibit the activity of remaining cholinergic neurons and thus worsen the compensatory abilities of the declining brain. Recent studies that demonstrate that galanin overexpressing transgenic mice have reduced numbers of cholinergic neurons and performance deficits in memory tests (Steiner et al., 2001) suggest that galanin may be even more closely linked to the primary pathological process. Furthermore, the ability of galanin to increase the autoinhibition of the locus coeruleus (Hökfelt et al., 1999) has been proposed as one pathogenetic contributory factor to the development of depression (Harro and Oreland, 2001). In both instances, galanin receptor antagonists could be anticipated to be reasonable treatment options.

As already noted, nonpeptide antagonists of the NK_1 receptor have been added to the list of potential drugs to treat depression. In subjects with major depressive disorder there is decreased binding to NK_1 receptors across all layers of rostral orbitofrontal cortex (Brodmann's area 47) (Stockmeier et al., 2002). The pathophysiology of depression and the reported therapeutic benefit of NK_1 receptor antagonists may thus involve NK_1 receptors in prefrontal cortex. The ability of NK_2 antagonists to show anxiolytic-like properties in ethological tests, while being inactive in classic measures sensitive to benzodiazepines (see Chapter 16), has spurred interest in investigation of these compounds in anxiety disorders involving unavoidable traumatic stress, particularly posttraumatic stress disorder (PTSD) (Kent et al., 2002).

In conclusion, many changes in neuropeptides can be found in psychiatric disorders. However, it is not clear whether these are most fruitfully interpreted as pertinent to specific diagnostic entities or rather to distinct psychobiological domains (i.e., psychological endophenotypes) that contribute to different disorders (van Praag, 2000).

AFFECTIVE FOUNDATIONS OF PSYCHIATRIC DISORDERS AND THE NEUROCHEMICAL CODING OF EMOTIONS

An overview of core brain areas and neuropeptides that are especially important for the various basic emotional systems that appear to exist in the mammalian brain are summarized in Table 21.1. A host of neuropeptides are concentrated in these brain areas (Tohyama and Takatsuji, 1998), and many offer a precision of regulatory control in these systems that cannot be achieved with drugs that affect the biogenic amine, acetylcholine, GABA, and glutamate systems. It is fairly well accepted that the biogenic amines provide general state-control functions in the brain that have rather direct impact on all of the fundamental behavioral processes of the brain (Panksepp, 1986, 1998a). Although the massive receptor polymorphism in these systems continues to be a popular area for drug development (with 15 receptors existing for serotonin alone), it is unlikely that much will emerge that is conceptually new as opposed to being variants of reasonably well-established themes.

Likewise, GABA and glutamate, the most prolific inhibitory and excitatory transmitters, also participate in the regulation of every basic function of the brain. Of course, agents that have highly restricted and mild effects on such receptor subtypes may find practical uses, such as ampakines, which act upon amino-3-hydroxy-5-methyl-4-isoxesolepropionic acid (AMPA) glutamate receptors and memantine, a glycine agonist, to promote cognitive and memory functions (Doraiswamy, 2002; Wilcock et al.,

TABLE 21.1. Summary of Key Neuroanatomical and Neurochemical Factors That Contribute to Construction of Basic Emotions within the Mammalian Brain[a]

Basic Emotional Systems	Key Brain Areas	Key Neuromodulators
General Pos. Motivation **SEEKING**/Expectancy System	Nucleus Accumbens—VTA Mesolimbic and mesocortical outputs Lateral hypothalamus—**PAG**	Dopamine (+), glutamate (+), opioids (+), **neurotensin** (+); many other neuropeptides
RAGE/Anger	Medial amygdala to bed Nucleus of stria Terminalis (BNST). Medial and perifornical hypothalamic zones to **PAG**	**Substance P (+)**, ACh (+), glutamate (+)
FEAR/Anxiety	Central and lateral amygdala to medial hypothalamus and dorsal **PAG**	Glutamate (+), **DBI, CRH, CCK**, alpha-**MSH, NPY**
LUST/Sexuality	Cortico-medial amygdala, bed nucleus stria terminalis (BNST) Preoptic hypothalamus, VMH, **PAG**	Steroids (+), **vasopressin**, and **oxytocin, LH-RH, CCK**
CARE/Nurturance	Anterior cingulate, BNST Preoptic area, VTA, **PAG**	**Oxytocin (+), prolactin (+)** dopamine (+), **opioids (+/−)**
PANIC/Separation Distress	Anterior cingulate, BNST and preoptic area Dorsomedial thalamus, **PAG**	**Opioids(−), oxytocin (−) prolactin (−) CRF (+)** glutamate (+)
PLAY/Joy	Dorso-medial diencephalons Parafascicular area, **PAG**	**Opioids (+/−)**, glutamate (+) Ach (+), **TRH?**

[a]The monoamines serotonin, NE, and DA are typically not indicated as they participate to some extent in all emotions. Also, the higher cortical zones devoted to emotionality, for which there is modest preclinical data (albeit considerable human data), mostly in frontal, temporal, and insular cortices are not indicated. Index: ACh, acetylcholine; BNST, bed nucleus of the stria terminalis; CCK, cholecystokinin; CRH, corticotrophic-releasing hormone, DBI, diazepam-binding inhibitor; LH-RH, leutenizing hormone-releasing hormone; alpha-MSH, alpha-melanocyte stimulating hormone; NPY, neuropeptide Y; PAG, periaqueductal gray; VTA, ventral tegmental area; minus signs indicate inhibition of a process, and plus signs activations. Data derived largely from Panksepp 1998a.

2002). A promising avenue is the exploitation of different subunit compositions of several neurotransmitter-gated ion channels, as the behavioral function may be determined by a specific subunit (Möhler et al., 2002). Aside from such new twists, it is unlikely there will be many opportunities for developing psychologically specific agents from the classical neurotransmitters that have served as an impetus for the first two generations of psychopharmacological developments in biological psychiatry (see Figure 1.1).

In contrast, the opportunities among the neuropeptide systems remain vast. What is not as widely appreciated are the large number of working hypotheses that are already supported by existing preclinical work. Considering that all of the neuropeptide systems that we will discuss are very ancient in brain evolution, with remarkable conservation of functions across diverse species, we can utilize preclinical data for making robust predictions concerning the types of clinical effects that we may anticipate in future human studies. At the same time, there will be many details, from single-nucleotide polymorphisms (SNPs) to posttranslational and environmentally sensitive processing of relevant proteins, that may foil drug development initiatives. In the following section, we will select at least one promising exemplar for each of the emotional-motivational processes listed in Table 21.1 and briefly highlight how new drug development may proceed. Since each of these brain systems operates within a sea of additional complexities, we will also highlight dilemmas that can be anticipated with the use of some of these agents.

The overall problems to be faced are perhaps best exemplified by the enormous number of peptides that have been implicated in energy balance control. There is great optimism that this knowledge will usher in a new generation of appetite control agents (Dhillo and Bloom, 2001; Smith, 1999; Woods et al., 2000), but it remains dubious whether drugs developed for a single neuropeptidergic target will be sufficient to achieve sustained appetite control (Wikberg, 1999). However, each of these systems may be recruited effectively into a broader scale therapeutic and behavioral management program. Also, work on appetite control highlights one of the difficulties of translating information from animal models to human practice. It is easy to reduce food intake in animals in ways that have little to do with the simulation of normal satiety processes (e.g., stress, malaise, nausea). Once again, this points out the need to utilize many sensitive behavioral tests to evaluate the affective status of laboratory animals (e.g., Knutson et al., 2002).

For the field of energy balance regulation, the proposal has been put forward that social behaviors such as rough-and-tumble play may serve as a measure of normal satiety. It is known that hungry animals do not play much, and a single satisfying meal is sufficient to restore the urge to play. Thus, neuropeptides that truly simulate normal satiety, should also have some efficacy in reversing hunger-diminished urges to play (Siviy and Panksepp, 1985). Again, we must understand many affective processes before we really appreciate how various neuropeptides regulate behaviors.

Expectancy/SEEKING System

The classical transhypothalamic "reward" system that is facilitated by DA circuits arising from the ventral tegmental area (VTA) has been more accurately conceptualized as the functional network that evokes appetitive/anticipatory eagerness rather than the pleasure of consummatory sensations (Ikemoto and Panksepp, 1999; Robinson and Berridge, 1993; Panksepp, 1981). Overactivity of brain DA has long been implicated in the genesis of schizophrenia, while diminished DA activity is depressogenic. Although there are many neuropeptides that converge on DA neurons, the most impressive, so far, is the tridecapeptide neurotensin, which can both facilitate and inhibit brain DA arousal. Aside from opioids, neurotensin is the only peptide that has so far been found to yield 'reward' effects when placed directly onto VTA cell bodies (Rompre, 1995). The possibility that both neurotensin agonists as well as antagonists might be beneficial in the treatment of schizophrenia continues to be debated (Berod and Rostene, 2002; Kinkead and Nemeroff, 2002). With the recent development of peripherally effective neurotensin agonists (Fredrickson et al., 2003), such issues can be empirically resolved. These agents may effectively ameliorate certain schizophrenic symptoms as well as addictive urges.

Since brain DA activation is a common ingredient in practically all forms of drug addiction (Wise, 2002), investigators will need to worry whether neurotensin agonists may also be addictive. However, considering the anticipated mild effect that neurotensin agonists will probably have on this appetitive system, including complex mixtures of antagonistic and agonistic effects at the terminal fields in the nucleus accumbens and indirect agonistic effects at the DA cell bodies (Legault et al., 2002), neurotensin agonists may help to stabilize psychomotor arousal and sensitization in such a way as to reduce addictive urges at least in the presence of a therapeutic environment (Berod and Rostene, 2002). Also, considering the importance of DA for sustaining psychic "energy," neurotensin receptor stimulants may help counteract mild depressive episodes and low energy without promoting addictive urges.

Another peptide that deserves attention as a putative modulator of the dopaminergic SEEKING system is CCK. CCK is colocalized in a population of dopaminergic neurons (Hökfelt et al., 1980), and its release appears to have a bidirectional influence via two distinct receptor subtypes (Wunderlich et al., 2000). Thus, CCK_1 antagonists can strongly reduce the locomotor stimulant effects of amphetamine and antagonize the sensitization to amphetamine. In contrast, CCK_2 antagonists enhance both acute stimulation of locomotor activity and sensitization to amphetamine. These bidirectional effects, which may be further influenced by experiential environments, suggest complex regulatory mechanisms, some of which are controlled by environmental factors (Ladurelle et al., 1995).

FEAR/Anxiety Systems

For an extensive discussion of this emotional system, see Chapter 16. Here we will focus on specific neuropeptide modulators. Of all emotional systems, probably more neuropeptides have been implicated in the facilitation of fear and anxiety than any other emotional tendency. They include, most prominently, CRH, neuropeptideY (NPY), CCK, alpha-melanocyte stimulating hormone/adrenocorticotropic hormone (α-MSH/ACTH), diazepam-binding inhibitor (DBI), but also several others, and thus several neuropeptide systems have been considered as primary molecular targets in the treatment of anxiety (Kent et al., 2002).

Corticotropin-releasing hormone antagonisms is everyone's greatest hope for the immediate future. This peptide is thought to serve as the prime coordinator of physiological as well as behavioral stress responses. CRH-related peptides and CRH receptor subtypes are relatively widely distributed in the brain and can serve as targets for drug development for various purposes (Sarnyai et al., 2001). Noradrenergic projections of the locus coeruleus can mediate the role of CRH in general central nervous system stress response (Harro and Oreland, 2001), and the fear response to CRH may be more specifically associated with the central amygdala, which receives noradrenergic projections largely from other noradrenergic nuclei (Sarnyai et al., 2001).

The CRH antagonists are silent in many anxiety tests but are anxiolytic when animals are being stressed (Holsboer, 2001a,b). This suggests that CRH is released upon demand, supporting the general idea that neuropeptides are released only in case of increased neural activation (Hökfelt et al., 2000). This should facilitate their use as prophylactic compounds with limited side effects. One potential problem on the horizon is that there are two types of CRH receptors in the brain that may have opposing effects. Fortunately, each is preferentially activated by different molecules, the first by CRH and the second by urocortins (Reul and Holsboer, 2002). However, in avian models, both of these peptides dramatically facilitate separation distress vocalizations (Panksepp and Bekkedal, 1997).

Another thorny issue lies in the fact that CRH release is clearly a normal homeostatic mechanism (Dunn and Berridge, 1990) and is activated by stimuli that are stressful in a bodily sense but do not provoke unpleasant emotions. CRH obviously exerts many adaptive effects, and blocking the system may exacerbate certain bodily problems—for instance, inflammation responses, such as those accompanying irritable bowel syndrome, that are normally suppressed by circulating cortisol (Monnikes et al., 2001). There may also be undesirable psychobiological side effects of CRH antagonists—for instance, CRH-deficient mice consume twice as much ethanol as wild-type mice (Olive et al., 2003). Thus, CRH may be important in counteracting drugs of abuse and may be potentially helpful for the treatment of compulsive drug use. Of course, the affectively negative side effects may limit the use of such agents.

There may be something critically different in CRH-mediated neurotransmission in eustress and in emotional disorders. One relevant view is Nemeroff's stress-diathesis theory: Evidence mainly from preclinical studies suggests that stress early in life results in persistent central CRH hyperactivity and increased stress reactivity in adulthood. Genetic disposition coupled with early stress in critical phases of development may result in a phenotype that is neurobiologically vulnerable to stress and may lower an individual's threshold for developing depression and anxiety upon further stress exposure (Heim and Nemeroff, 1999). Thus, CRH antagonists deserve to be evaluated in specific anxiety disorders ranging from generalized anxiety disorder (GAD) to PTSD (See Chapters 11–13, and 16).

Other prominent peptides in the orchestra of anxiety are to be found among the posttranslational processing of CCK, already introduced in the context of SEEKING urges. Short fragments of CCK, CCK-4 and CCK-5 (pentagastrin) that selectively stimulate CCK_2 receptors elicit the full panic attack, patients with the disorder reacting to lower doses (Bourin et al., 1996). Regarding generalized anxiety, there is limited evidence. Animal studies using routine anxiety tests (see Chapter 16) have shown that anxiety-like responses can be induced by CCK, but these effects seem to depend upon environmental context (Harro et al., 1993). The brain regions involved remain to be described, albeit amygdala has been implicated. CCK receptor antagonists have anxiolytic-like properties in some but not all experimental paradigms. These drugs can prevent CCK-induced panic, but it has not yet been possible to demonstrate their clinical efficacy in any anxiety disorder. However, the effects of CCK_2 antagonists in animal experiments strongly depend on dose, having an inverted U-shaped dose-response curve (Harro et al., 1993), and thus it is quite possible that the doses and achieved brain levels of the drug have been suboptimal. In addition, one should consider the theoretical possibility that in the variety of neural circuits involved in anxiety disorders, CCK is very selectively involved in the neurobiology of panic disorder, which would make it a PANIC peptide rather than a FEAR peptide.

NeuropeptideY is an evolutionarily highly conserved peptide well known for its major role in feeding. Even though there is no unequivocal evidence of the role of NPY in anxiety from human studies, this peptide has been well described in animal models as an endogenous antianxiety compound (Kask et al., 2002). Studies have demonstrated that NPY administered intracerebroventricularly (icv) or intraamygdala elicits an anxiolytic response probably by stimulating the Y_1 receptor subtype (Heilig et al., 1994), and these have more recently been complemented with experiments using nonpeptide antagonists selective for the Y_1 receptor subtype, with anxiogenic-like properties (Kask et al., 1996). These studies highlight that endogenous NPY is released in novel or challenging environments to suppress the fear response, possibly being one of the mechanisms balancing the action of CRH release (Kask et al., 2002). Interestingly, while exogenous NPY is anxiolytic in several brain regions (e.g., amygdala, lateral septum, and locus coeruleus), endogenous NPY, as revealed in studies with Y_1 receptor antagonists, has so far been found anxiolytic only in the dorsal periaqueductal gray matter, a caudal part of the fear circuit (see Chapter 16).

NeuropeptideY is even better known for its orexigenic effects, which appear to be mediated through at least two receptor subtypes, Y_1 and Y_5 (Kask et al., 1998). Interestingly, in the quoted study it was found that diazepam eliminated the blocking effect of a Y_1 receptor antagonist on NPY-elicited feeding. It is tempting to suggest that Y_1 receptor activation is an additional measure in NPY-induced feeding (which involves several receptor subtypes) in part by reducing arousal. Thus NPY and Y_1 receptor could be conceptualized as a link with an ancient foraging system, promoting appetite (especially for food high in carbohydrates), facilitating DA-mediated locomotion, and reducing fear of novel places and foods at the same time.

There are other neuropeptide systems that have remained less well characterized due to limited understanding of their biology and a shortage of adequate tools but continue to be suspected as important mediators of some types of anxiety. Diazepam binding inhibitor is a peptide that together with some of its processing products, behaves as an inverse agonist of benzodiazepine receptors and an anxiogenic-like compound. It has been found to be increased in the CSF of patients with severe anxiety (Guidotti, 1991). Although DBI is preferentially concentrated in steroidogenic tissues and cells, where it may serve as a metabolic enhancer in stressful conditions, its messenger ribonucleic acid (mRNA) expression is enhanced in rats by conditioned emotional stimuli but not by restraint stress (Katsura et al., 2002). Alpha-MSH and ACTH, peptides of propiomelanocortin origin, elicit vigorous freezing response or flight when injected intracerebrally, at least in some species (Panksepp and Abbott, 1990; Panksepp and Normansell, 1990). A recent study in which brain-derived neurotrophic factor was conditionally knocked-out, demonstrated that mice with increased levels of propiomelanocortin were hyperactive after exposure to stressors and preferred dark compartments more strongly than wild-type controls (Rios et al., 2001). Most recently, a novel nonpeptide melanocortin-4-receptor antagonist was found to attenuate the α-MSH-increased cyclic adenosine monophosphate (cAMP) formation and to possess anxiolytic- and antidepressant-like properties in animal models (Chaki et al., 2003).

In sum, it is unlikely that evolution shaped a single "anxiety peptide" that universally elicits fear. Rather there exist distinct peptide-mediated responses to specific environmental challenges, which can function improperly, for example, by turning on at the wrong time or remaining unbalanced by the failure of endogenous antianxiety mechanisms. How such peptides regulate internal affective states, perhaps in conjunction with cognitive elaborations, should eventually tell us much about the varieties of anxiety (Chapter 16).

RAGE/Anger System

Ever since it became unpopular to consider the possibility that the brain contained intrinsic systems that promoted aggression (the politically correct view being that aggression is mostly induced by social injustice), the amount of substantive work on the rage/anger systems of the brain diminished substantially (for overview, see Panksepp, 1998a). However, continuing work on such systems in the cat brain has yielded clear evidence that opioid peptides reduce aggressive arousal (Gregg and Siegel, 2001). Since such antianger agents exhibit substantial pharmacological tolerance, addiction, and drug-withdrawal irritability, they will probably have little role in the routine management of aggression except perhaps, acutely. On the other hand, this work has also demonstrated that substance P, operating through NK receptors, is a robust facilitator of activity in basic anger promoting systems within the medial hypothalamus, making receptor antagonists for that system a prime target for evaluation.

This is now eminently possible because many nonpeptide NK receptor antagonists have already been developed and evaluated for safety for the management of pain and depression (Hill, 2000; Kramer et al., 1998). Although there is a current trend to conceptualize the substance P/tachykinin system simply as a "stress" or "anxiogenic" system, there is also clear data that anger-type biting responses are diminished in animal models by receptor antagonists (Griebel et al., 2001). Although various sensitive emotional measures for such drugs are available, such as stress-induced foot thumping in gerbils (Ballard et al., 2001), it will be important to empirically define whether such responses better reflect anger/irritability or fear/anxiety types of responses and which of the receptor subtypes influence which affective behaviors most intensely (Griebel et al., 2001). When it comes to the eventual evaluation of NK (substance P) receptor antagonists in human anger management, it may be wise to utilize specific testing strategies, such as provocations that evoke irritability (e.g., frustrative-aggressive tendencies that accompany reward reduction).

LUST/Sexuality Systems

Perhaps in this "Age of Viagra" new sexuality-facilitating agents are no longer needed. However, one could argue that beside the "mechanical aid" offered by such nitric oxide facilitating, erection-sustaining substances, there is still a substantial need for agents that facilitate the psychological side of eroticism. Based on preclinical work in animals, it is to be anticipated that certain neuropeptides and steroids may be harnessed to facilitate such ends. An abundance of neuropeptides and steroids have been identified within the fundamental sexual circuits concentrated in subcortical regions of the mammalian brain (Pfaff, 1999). For some time, it has been evident that testosterone supplementation can strengthen sexual urges in both males and females (Crenshaw and Goldberg, 1996).

The neuropeptide that has received the most attention is leutenizing hormone release hormone (LHRH). However, despite very promising animal results, human trials have been largely disappointing (Moss and Dudley, 1984). Whether this is simply due to the fact that this molecule does not penetrate to the right parts of the human brain or whether it requires the support of other psychosocial stimuli is unknown. However, nonpeptide congeners for this peptide receptor system could be developed and evaluated more systematically in psychological contexts that support erotic urges, perhaps in combination with mild facilitation of other systems such as the opioids, which figure heavily in various forms of pleasure as well as social confidence (Panksepp et al., 1985; van den Berg et al., 2000).

The most prominent additional neuropeptide systems implicated in sociosexual feelings and desires are the brain systems that utilize the posterior-pituitary nonapeptides oxytocin (OXY) and arginine-vasopressin (AVP). Oxytocinergic activity within the brain is substantially facilitated by the more female-specific adult sex hormones, estrogen and progesterone, while AVP systems are promoted by the more male-specific adult sex hormone testosterone. In animal models, OXY promotes female sexual behavior, but it is also compatible with male sexual urges, perhaps because the molecule is not only a general social hormone within the brain (Insel, 1997) but is released markedly by pleasurable somatosensory stimulation and at orgasm (Carter, 1998; Uvnäs-Moberg, 1998). Thus, it would be anticipated that under the right contextual conditions (i.e., those that support eroticism), oxytocinergics that get to the right regions of the brain, perhaps even via intranasal routes, would tend to increase intimacy and the quality of sociosexual interactions. On the other hand, AVP diminishes female sexual behavior, while promoting male sexual urges (Södersten et al., 1983). If it turns out that this latter effect is reflected largely in appetitive craving as opposed to erotic affects, AVP systems may *not* be a desirable target for drug development. Of course, peripherally active agents for both types of neuropeptide agonists may yield potentially troublesome antidiuretic and smooth-muscle stimulatory effects.

On the other hand, based on preclinical data, an AVP antagonist might serve as a drug for treatment of sexual aggression, including that seen in the context of sexual jealousy. In mice, this peptide has been found to mediate the attachments that males develop to females with whom they have copulated. Indeed, placement of AVP into the brains of male mice in the presence of females helps establish social preferences so strong that they subsequently exhibit intense aggression toward intruding males (Winslow et al., 1993). From an affective perspective, this may reflect a jealousy type of psychological response. Considering the amount of human aggression that arises in the context of sexual jealousy, it is worth considering whether antagonists for the human AVP system might diminish such obsessive, irritable feelings.

CARE/Nurturance and Social Bonding

Although there are other chemistries to be found, the most powerful peptides so far that regulate maternal behavior and social bonding are oxytocin, opioids, and prolactin (Carter, 1998; Nelson and Panksepp, 1998; Uvnäs-Moberg, 1998). Whether medicines can be developed to facilitate the arousability of these brain care-taking systems, and whether such agents could find a place in psychiatric practice, remains open for discussion and inquiry. It would seem that when mothers exhibit difficulty attaching emotionally to their infants, and vice versa, it might be worth considering interventions that have the potential to gently facilitate the process of mother-infant bonding. Of course, the amount of difficult clinical human work that would need to be done on such issues, and the variety of ethical concerns that would need to be addressed (see end of this chapter), makes it unlikely that such agents will be available in the foreseeable future.

Another realm of human distress management where such chemistries might find a place is in marriage therapy. A cogent answer has recently been provided for the age-old question "What makes some marriages happy, but others miserable?" The most powerful answer is to be found at an affective level; those couples who have the social-emotional skills to make each other feel better tend to thrive whereas those who facilitate negative feelings get themselves into self-sustaining cycles of misery (Gottman et al., 2002). This immediately raises the issue of how social-skills learning might be utilized in conjunction with agents designed to facilitate the affective endpoints they desire. For instance, oxytocin can facilitate the intensity of natural social reward (Panksepp et al., 1999). Might such stimulants for social-neuropeptide systems be able to facilitate psychotherapeutic interventions that aspire to promote social skills to help solidify affectively positive interactions, and thereby diminish psychological effects that sustain negative affective cycles (Gottman et al., 2002)?

In short, many converging lines of evidence have implicated oxytocin in the beneficial effects of social support on both mental and physical health. Oxytocin is released by prosocial activities and can counteract separation anxiety and stress in general, and thereby promotes development of social contacts and attachments (for a recent overview, see Taylor et al., 2002). One foreseeable problem is the uncertainty whether the relevant steroid-sensitive receptive fields are present in the brains of individuals who might be helped most by such interventions.

PANIC/Separation Distress, Grief, and Social Bonding

Among the most common and powerful human feelings are those related to "pain" of loss, especially the grief of social loss. This emotional process has been modeled by the study of the neurochemistries that are able to specifically reduce separation distress in young animals isolated from their social support systems (Panksepp, 2003b). The resistance of this emotional system to most psychotropic drugs has been a surprise, with only antidepressants such as imipramine and in some species benzodiazepines having modest effects (Panksepp et al., 1988). The neuropeptides that have yielded very robust and specific effects on animal crying are, in order of efficacy, oxytocin, opioid peptides that activate *mu* receptors, and prolactin (Panksepp, 1998a).

It is probably common knowledge among psychiatrists involved in hospice care that opiates, even at low doses, can powerfully counteract feelings of social loss and despair. However, this trade secret must be used cautiously because of potential drug tolerance and addictive potentials that can backfire in the long-run (intensifying negative feelings during withdrawal periods). Even more beneficial may be nonpeptide oxytocinergics in the regulation of emotions related to social loss, since molecule for molecule oxytocin is the most powerful way to reduce separation distress in various animal models (Panksepp, 1992). Also, the potential opioid antitolerance effects of oxytocin could be recruited to help sustain efficacy and minimize withdrawal (Kovacs et al., 1998). Likewise, the ability of CRH to promote separation distress (Panksepp et al., 1988; Panksepp and Bekkedal, 1997), and CRH antagonists to reduce such emotional responses (Kehne et al., 2000) suggests that the latter agents may effectively help control excessive separation anxiety. Furthermore, some of the peptides that have been implicated in FEAR mechanisms, for instance CCK, may actually be more important for modulating PANIC responses. Future work needs to contrast several animal anxiety models against each other more systematically.

We will cover the last emotional system in Table 21.1, playfulness, in the next section, as we consider two of the most controversial childhood psychiatric problems of our times, autism and attention deficit hyperactivity disorder (ADHD). The first has no adequate, generally accepted medications (although many psychotropics provide relief of specific symptoms), while the other has many "adequate" medicines, but professionals who prescribe them express little appreciation of the potential long-term brain/mind changes that can be provoked in animals with psychostimulants such as methylphenidate and amphetamines (Moll et al., 2001; Nocjar and Panksepp, 2002).

TWO CHILDHOOD DISORDERS: DEBATABLE EXAMPLES OF NEUROPEPTIDE AND NEUROBEHAVIORAL APPROACHES

The first theoretically driven hypothesis concerning a neuropeptidergic imbalance in a major psychiatric disorder was the opioid-excess theory of early childhood autism (Panksepp, 1979). This idea, although now evaluated many times, remains neither well confirmed nor adequately disconfirmed. The second, ADHD, the most prevalent childhood problem of our times, can be well-managed pharmacologically, but there is inadequate discussion of the many associated issues that should concern us with such therapies. Let us consider them from the perspectives advanced in this chapter.

Naltrexone and the Treatment of Autism

A paradigmatic example of a potentially useful neuropeptidergic intervention strategy (as well as the attending conceptual and pragmatic problems) can be highlighted by summarizing past attempts to utilize opiate antagonists in the treatment of autism. As already noted, the opioid linkage to autism was initially based on the striking similarities between classic autistic symptoms and those produced by injection of opioid drugs—including decreased separation distress, decreased gregariousness, decreased pain sensitivity, and increased stereotypies and rough-and-tumble play (Panksepp and Sahley, 1987).

After an initial flurry of small but promising open trials, the subsequent double-blind, placebo-controlled trials have provided mixed evidence with the broad-spectrum opiate receptor antagonist naltrexone. Some have yielded modest benefits (e.g., Kolmen et al., 1997; Panksepp et al., 1991), especially on self-injurious behaviors and overactivity (Campbell and Harris, 1996). Subsequent trials, using rather high doses of naltrexone, yielded no benefits (Willemsen-Swinkels et al., 1996), but some have advocated the use of quite low doses infrequently (e.g., 0.25 mg/kg orally every other day) and have claimed that the quality of psychosocial contexts may be essential to support the social-motivational changes produced by naltrexone (Panksepp et al., 1991). Considering the biochemical evidence for abnormal opioid dynamics in the autistic brain and body (Bouvard et al., 1995; Gillberg, 1995) and the fact that subgroups of individuals with the most severe imbalances remain to be separately studied, clearly more research is needed not only with naltrexone, but also the more specific antagonists for the other opioid receptors. The pros and cons of evaluating every child with naltrexone have been aired, and there is only general agreement that the drug does reduce overactivity symptoms (Campbell and Harris, 1996).

In sum, the subset of children that do benefit remains hard to specify, but presumably those that exhibit an initial negative affective response, which may reflect an acute opioid withdrawal phenomenon, may be most likely to benefit with careful selection of doses (Panksepp et al., 1991). It should also be noted that dietary maneuvers (i.e., low-casein, low-gluten diets that can be sources of dietary opioids) that may have benefits by reducing opioid titers remain active areas of inquiry (Knivsberg et al., 2001, 2002).

There are a host of methodological concerns that need to be considered in future trials. First, autism is not a single brain disorder, and only a subset of children might respond to naltrexone. Thus, one should first aspire to identify drug responders and then to conduct double-blind studies on them to maximize the characterization of therapeutic trends. Further, since opiate antagonists can increase social motivation, the suggestion has been made that increased provisioning of socially sensitive and responsive environments may be important for obtaining optimal therapeutic effects. For naltrexone to work beneficially, caretakers may need to exhibit increased levels of social concern and reciprocity (Panksepp et al., 1991). If this proves to be the case in larger studies, it may highlight a new general principle of therapeutic efficacy alluded to above: Namely, certain neuropeptidergic agents that modulate specific emotional processes may need conjoint optimization of social-environmental and/or psychotherapeutic supports for maximal efficacy. So far, no neuropeptide modulator has been evaluated with such a principle in mind. Of course, the large number of therapeutic claims in the literature, especially in an area where placebo effects seem to be substantial, makes it difficult to sift substantive findings from type 1 errors (Hunsinger et al., 2000).

Playfulness and ADHD

No peptide facilitator of playfulness has yet been discovered except for the capacity of low doses of opioids to promote rough-and-tumble play and social dominance in rats (Panksepp et al., 1985). Considering that this social process of the mammalian brain may be a fundamental source of joy, the search for other brain transmitters and neuromodulators that promote play, perhaps through modern molecular biological techniques, may lead to molecules that promote such positive affective states in humans. Their potential uses in the treatment of depression would be enticing (Panksepp et al., 2002b), since most current medications do not actively promote positive affect.

Another relationship of the play urges of the brain to psychiatric issues has been in attempts to conceptualize at least some of the impulsive and hyperactive symptoms of ADHD as unsatisfied play urges that need to be expressed, as is evident in animal models (Panksepp, 1998b). The utility of play therapy in an animal model of ADHD has been demonstrated (Panksepp et al., 2003). Considering that drugs used to treat ADHD are uniformly ones that reduce play urges, and which may sensitize reward and drug-seeking systems of the brain (Nocjar and Panksepp, 2002; Panksepp et al., 2002a), the issue of what natural play does for the developing brain/mind becomes an urgent neuropsychiatric question. Preliminary evidence suggests that in addition to well-accepted, but poorly demonstrated, psychological developmental effects, play may also promote neurotrophin gene expression that may have beneficial long-term effects for the brain (Gordon et al., 2003). These issues should coax us to consider some very troublesome issues in the use of antiplay drugs in child psychiatry, as well as the emerging role for neurotrophins in the genesis and treatment of psychiatric disorders.

NEUROTROPHINS AND PSYCHIATRIC DISORDERS

Neurotrophic factors are known to play a crucial role in growth, differentiation, and function in a variety of brain neurons during development and in adult life. Neurite outgrowth, synaptic plasticity, and the selection of functional neuronal connections depend upon the function of neurotrophic factors, particularly nerve growth factor (NGF) and brain-derived neurotrophic factor (BDNF). Animal studies suggest that these neurotrophic factors strongly influence the structure and function of developing, as well as adult, brain. Recent postmortem studies have provided evidence that pathogenesis of the most prominent psychiatric disorders such as schizophrenia and major depression may be associated with disturbances in neurotrophic factors.

The hypothesis that neurotrophins contribute to some neural developmental aspects of schizophrenia is based on findings indicating that the constitutive levels of NGF and BDNF are affected in schizophrenic patients (Aloe et al., 2000). For example, a significant increase in BDNF concentrations in cortical areas and a significant decrease of this neurotrophin in hippocampus of patients was observed when compared with controls (Durany et al., 2001), whereas neurotrophin-3 concentrations of frontal and parietal cortical areas were significantly lower in patients than in controls. Thus, alterations in expression of neurotrophic factors could be responsible for neural maldevelopment and disturbed neural plasticity. This may be an important event in the etiopathogenesis of schizophrenic psychoses.

Other recent postmortem studies on the molecular and cellular level suggest the involvement of neurotrophic factors in the pathogenesis of depression. The neurotrophins and monoamine neurotransmitters appear to play related roles in stress, depression, and therapies for treating depression (Rajkowska, 2000). Expression of BDNF is enhanced by increased serotonin and NE mediated neurotransmission. This, in turn, induces the sprouting of serotonergic axons in the neocortex. The expression of BDNF mRNA in the rat is particularly sensitive to monoaminergic activation in the cortical layers corresponding to those in which the most significant reductions in neuronal density and size (layers II/III) and most significant reductions in glia (layer V) were observed in clinical depression. On the basis of animal studies that have described effects of stress and chronic antidepressant treatments on specific neurotrophin-related target genes in the CNS, it has been proposed that in individuals genetically predisposed to depression, vulnerable neurons and glia may undergo atrophy or damage in conditions where the neurotrophic factors are not sufficiently active (Duman et al., 1997). Indeed, exogenously administered neurotrophins have antidepressant-like behavioral effects; even more interestingly, known antidepressants (which can increase BDNF mRNA levels after chronic treatment) do not elicit these effects in heterozygous BDNF knockout (BDNF$^{+/-}$) mice or in transgenic mice with reduced activation of trk B, the receptor of BDNF (Saarelainen et al., 2003).

Increasing evidence suggests that the expression of neurotrophic factors themselves is strongly modifiable and dynamic. Environmental changes, aggressive behavior, and anxiety-like responses alter both circulating and brain basal NGF levels (Aloe et al., 2000). Thus, it is conceivable that therapeutic effects of psychoactive drugs are in part associated with their ability to promote neurotrophin-dependent formation and stabilization of synaptic connectivity. Consideration of the nature-nurture interaction is probably highly important in neurotrophin research. Findings that stress can damage the hippocampus in animal experiments have led to theories as to how this relates to reduced brain area volumes in psychiatric conditions (with the smaller hippocampal volume in PTSD patients being a representative case—see Chapter 11). Recent evidence that smaller hippocampal volume rather predicts PTSD than is elicited by psychological trauma (Gilbertson et al., 2002) resonates well with animal research demonstrating that inherited variations in hippocampal size can influence neuroendocrine responses to stress (Lyons et al., 2001).

Understanding the microstructural changes that occur in the CNS in most if not all psychiatric conditions is blurring the distinction between "organic" and "functional" disorders. Because of such brain changes, the application of neurotrophic factors has become a seriously considered approach not only for the classic neurodegenerative diseases such as Alzheimer's, Parkinson's, and Huntington's disease, but for such placebo-sensitive disorders as depression as well. Clinical trials with neurotrophic factors in neurodegenerative diseases have not been as successful as originally expected but have taught us that the methods need to be refined and the treatment started as early as possible (Thoenen and Sendtner, 2002). Improvements in regulation of neurotrophin expression in situ, stimulation of synthesis of endogenous neurotrophins, as well as stimulating their receptors with nonpeptide small molecule ligands or modulation relevant intracellular signal transductions are all possible novel approaches.

With the molecular biology revolution and the clarification of the genomes of humans and various laboratory animals, the opportunities for novel drug developments are increasing. Also, some classic approaches may gradually be coming to fruition. For instance, from libraries of monoclonal antibodies (MAbs) to hippocampal tissues, along with behavioral screening procedures, have yielded candidate antibodies that recognize interesting target sites in the brain. After identifying the active sites of one such antibody, families of small peptides have been synthesized that have the neurobiological effects of the original Mabs, which may be active in the treatment of strokes, cognitive impairments, and neuropathic pain (Moskal et al., 2001). Through a large variety of such novel molecular approaches, pursued in combination with parallel behavioral studies, insights can be derived into the evolved regulatory systems of the brain that can cut across species barriers. As summarized in Panksepp et al. (2002b) "with the advent of tools for the analysis of gene expression, especially microarray technology, one can now go from the analysis of gene activation patterns in the brain to the identification of molecular targets for therapeutics interventions in psychiatry" (p. 112).

CONCLUSIONS

The emerging neurochemical understanding of the basic psychobehavioral processes of the mammalian brain is providing a remarkable number of novel brain targets for psychiatric drug development. If emotional principles of brain organization, derived mostly from animal studies, also apply to humans, then neurochemical modulation of neuropeptide systems should provide remarkable opportunities to promote and dampen the many distinct affective capacities of the human brain/mind. However, optimal development in this area may require more investigators to seriously consider the evolved emotional-affective nature of the brain and to better evaluate such central processes using behavioral procedures in sensitive animal models.

Compelling concepts have been emerging from basic animal research for some time. However, because of the success of the previous generation of agents (based largely on an understanding of biogenic amine systems), the development and implementation of neuropeptide related concepts in biological psychiatry has lagged far behind the preclinical evidence. As already discussed, neuropeptide concepts have also been notoriously difficult to translate into clinical practice. Partly this is because of species differences in pharmacokinetics and dynamics (Appendix A), but there are also a sufficient number of other relevant differences, including SNPs in the genetic coding regions for the relevant receptors to make simple translations from animal models to human uses problematic. Also, it is now clear that the social environmental variables impact gene expressions in the brain (e.g., Meaney, 2001; Bester-Meredith and Marler, 2001). Such neurochemical background effects may have important consequences on how other neurochemical factors operate.

Despite the rapid development of nonpeptide analogs, many prominent pharmacologists still do not believe that peptides are good targets for drug development. What they commonly overlook is the possibility that these agents may be used prophylactically, since many neuropeptides are only released in response to stress and other kinds of emotional arousal. The general principle here might be that such comparatively mild medicinals may need socioenvironmental supports for optimal efficacy. If so, such agents may also find wider usage for everyday emotional problems, as in the controversial concept of "cosmetic" psychopharmacology introduced by Kramer (1993). Indeed, neuropeptide modulators may have psychological effects that may help hone theoretical concepts in psychiatry to a finer edge.

With the clarification of the human genome, and the revelation of remarkable relations to those of other animals, we stand at the threshold of new drug discoveries that will emerge from the analysis of gene expression patterns in different environments (Panksepp et al., 2002b), some of which may be distinct for different individuals. As Florian Holsboer put it (2001a, p. 62): "We are awaiting a wealth of new information from functional genomics and proteomics, and it is most important that psychiatrists, psychologists, biologists and other professions involved in the process of... drug discovery find quickly a common platform suited to exploit this new research for the benefit of our... patients. While the prospect that... drug therapy will become personalized according to an individual's genotype may sound futuristic, I predict that a concerted interdisciplinary exploitation of biotechnology leads to knowledge so powerful that clinicians and patients will wonder how they ever got along without it."

Of course, if this comes to pass, we will be confronted by a host of ethical dilemmas. As Victor Hruby (2002, p. 856) remarked "It is often suggested that ethical considerations are not appropriate in a scientific discussion. In the case of drug design, this seems irresponsible at best.... Certainly, the desire to relieve human pain and disease is noble, but increasingly, scientists and the institutions in which they work ignore their ethical responsibilities. Just a few brief examples highlight some problems: first, the responsibility to put new knowledge in the public domain and make it widely accessible; second, the honest and rapid revelation of side effects of drugs; third, modification of human behavior—who decides what behaviors to modify? Who will profit? Who will benefit? And fourth, "pollution" of the human and other genomes—who can predict the long-term consequences?" Surely these concerns should remain of foremost importance as we come to develop new agents that have the potential to alter the normal and abnormal emotional dynamics of the human mind.

REFERENCES

Aloe L, Iannitelli A, Angelucci F, Bersani G, Fiore M (2000). Studies in animal models and humans suggesting a role of nerve growth factor in schizophrenia-like disorders. *Behav Pharmacol* 11:235–242.

Aman MG, Langworthy KS (2000). Pharmacotherapy for hyperactivity in children with autism and other pervasive developmental disorders. *J Autism Devel Dis* 30:451–459.

Ballard TM, Sanger S, Higgins GA (2001). Inhibition of shock-induced foot tapping behaviour in the gerbil by a tachykinin NK_1 receptor antagonist. *Eur J Pharmacol* 412:255–264.

Baxter LR, Jr, Schwartz JM, Bergman KS, et al. (1992). Caudate glucose metabolic rate changes with both drug and behavior therapy for obsessive-compulsive disorder. *Arch Gen Psychiatry* 49:681–689.

Berod A, Rostene W (2002). Neurotensin: An endogenous psychostimulant? Commentary. *Curr Opinion Pharmacol* 2:93–98.

Bester-Meredith JK, Marler CA (2001). Vasopressin and aggression in cross-fostered California mice (*Peromyscus californicus*) and white-fotted mice (*Peromyscus leucopus*). *Horm Behav* 40:51–64.

Beutler LE, Machado PPP, Neufeldt SA (1994). Therapist variables. In Bergin AE, Garfield SL (eds). *Handbook of Psychotherapy and Behavioral Change*. Wiley: New York, pp. 229–269.

Bourin M, Malinge M, Vasar E, Bradwejn J (1996). Two faces of cholecystokinin: Anxiety and schizophrenia. *Fundam Clin Pharmacol* 10:116–126.

Bouvard MP, Leboyer M, Launay J-M, et al. (1995). Low-dose naltrexone effects on plasma chemistries and clinical symptoms in autism: A double-blind, placebo-controlled study. *Psychiatry Res* 58:191–201.

Buitelaar JK, van Engeland H, de Kogel KH, de Vries H, van Hooff JA, van Ree JM (1992). The use of Adrenocorticotropic hormone (4–9) analog ORG 2766 in autistic children: Effects on the organization of behavior. *Biol Psychiatry* 31:1119–1129.

Buitelaar JK, Dekker ME, van Ree JM, van Engeland H (1996). A controlled trial with ORG 2766, an ACTH-(4–9) analog, in 50 relatively able children with autism. *Eur Neuropsychopharmacol* 6:13–19.

Burbach JP (1982). Neuropeptides and cerebrospinal fluid. *Ann Clin Biochem* 19:269–277.

Campbell M, Harris JC (1996). Resolved: Autistic children should have a trial of naltrexone. *J Am Acad Child Adolesc Psychiatry* 35:246–251.

Carter CS (1998). The neuroendocrinology of social attachment and love. *Psychoneuroendocrinology* 23:779–818.

Carter CS, Lederhendler I, Kirkpatrick B (eds) (1999). *The Integrative Neurobiology of Affiliation*, MIT Press: Cambridge, MA.

Chabane N, Leboyer M, Mouren-Simeoni MC (2000). Opiate antagonists in children and adolescents. *Eur J Child Adolesc Psychiatry* 9(Suppl 1):144–150.

Chaki S, Hirota S, Funakoshi T, et al. (2003). Anxiolytic-like and antidepressant-like activities of MCL0129 (1-[(*S*)-2-(4-fluorophenyl)-2-(4-isopropylpiperadin-1-yl)ethyl]-4-[4-(2-meth oxynaphthalen-1-yl)butyl]piperazine), a novel and potent nonpeptide antagonist of the melanocortin-4 receptor. *J Pharmacol Exp Ther* 304:818–826.

Counts SE, Perez SE, Kahl U, et al. (2001). Galanin: Neurobiologic mechanisms and therapeutic potential for Alzheimer's disease. *CNS Drug Rev* 7:445–470.

Crenshaw T, Goldberg JP (1996). *Sexual Pharmacology: Drugs That Affect Sexual Functioning*. Norton: New York.

Damasio AR, Grabowski TJ, Bechara A, et al. (2000). Subcortical and cortical brain activity during the feeling of self-generated emotions. *Nature Neurosci* 3:1049–1056.

De Souza EB, Grigoriadis DE (2002). Corticotropin-releasing factor: Physiology, pharmacology, and role in central nervous system disorders. In Davis KL, Charney D, Coyle JT, Nemeroff C (eds). *Neuropsychopharmacology: The Fifth Generation of Progress*. Lippincott Williams & Wilkins: Philadelphia, pp. 91–107.

de Wied D (1999). Behavioral pharmacology of neuropeptides related to melanocortins and the neurohypophyseal hormones. *Eur J Pharmacol* 375:1–11.

de Wied D, van Ree JM (1989). Neuropeptides: Animal behaviour and human psychopathology. *Eur Arch Psychiat Neurol Sci* 238:323–331.

de Wit H, Svenson J, York A (1999). Non-specific effect of naltrexone on ethanol consumption in social drinkers. *Psychopharmacology* 146:33–41.

Dhillo WS, Bloom SR (2001). Hypothalamic peptides as drug targets for obesity. *Curr Opinion Pharmacol* 1:651–655.

Doraiswamy PM (2002). Non-cholinergic strategies for treating and preventing Alzheimer's disease. *CNS Drugs* 16:811–824.

Duman RS, Heninger GR, Nestler EJ (1997). A molecular and cellular theory of depression. *Arch Gen Psychiatry* 54:597–606.

Dunn AJ, Berridge CW (1990). Physiological and behavioral responses to corticotropin-releasing factor: Is CRF a mediator of anxiety or stress responses? *Brain Res Rev* 15:71–100.

Durany N, Michel T, Zochling R, et al. (2001). Brain-derived neurotrophic factor and neurotrophin 3 in schizophrenic psychoses. *Schizophr Res* 52:79–86.

Enserink M (1999). Can the placebo be the cure? *Science* 284:238–240.

Fehm HL, Perras B, Smolnik R, Kern W, Born J (2000). Manipulating neuropeptidergic pathways in humans: A novel approach to neuropharmacology? *Eur J Pharmacol* 405:43–54.

Feighner JP, Ehrensing RH, Kastin AJ, et al. (2001). Double-blind, placebo-controlled study of INN 00835 (netamiftide) in the treatment of outpatients with major depression. *Int Clin Psychopharmacol* 16:345–352.

Fredrickson P, Boules M, Yerbury S, Richelson E (2003). Blockade of nicotine-induced locomotor sensitization by a novel neurotensin analog in rats. *Eur J Pharmacol* 458:111–118.

Furmark T, Tillfors M, Marteinsdottir I, et al. (2002). Common changes in cerebral blood flow in patients with social phobia treated with citalopram or cognitive-behavioral therapy. *Arch Gen Psychiatry* 59:425–433.

Gilbertson MW, Shenton ME, Ciszewski A, et al. (2002). Smaller hippocampal volume predicts pathologic vulnerability to psychological trauma. *Nature Neurosci* 5:1242–1247.

Gillberg C (1995). Endogeneous opioids and opiate antagonists in autism: Brief review of empirical findings and implications for clinicians. *Dev Med Child Neurol* 37:239–245.

Gold PW, Drevets WC, Charney DS (2002). New insights into the role of cortisol and the glucocorticoid receptor in severe depression. *Biol Psychiatry* 52:381–385.

Gordon NS, Burke S, Akil H, Watson J, Panksepp J (2003). Socially induced brain fertilization: Play promotes brain derived neurotrophic factor expression. *Neurosci Lett* 341:17–20.

Gottman JM, Murray JD, Swanson CC, Tyson R, Swanson KR (2002). *The Mathematics of Marriage: Dynamic Nonlinear Approach*. MIT Press: Cambridge, MA.

Gregg TR, Siegel A (2001). Brain structures and neurotransmitters regulating aggression in cats: Implications for human aggression. *Prog Neuro Psychopharmacol Biol Psychiatry* 25:91–140.

Griebel G, Moindrot N, Aliaga C, Simiand J, Soubrie P (2001). Characterization of the profile of neurokinin-2 and neurotensin receptor antagonists in the mouse defense test battery. *Neurosci Biobehav Rev* 25:619–626.

Guidotti A (1991). Role of DBI in brain and its posttranslational processing products in normal and abnormal behavior. *Neuropharmacology* 30:1425–1433.

Hamid EH, Hyde TM, Egan MF, et al. (2002). Neurotensin receptor binding abnormalities in the entorhinal cortex in schizophrenia and affective disorders. *Biol Psychiatry* 51:795–800.

Harro J, Oreland L (2001). Depression as a spreading adjustment disorder of monoaminergic neurons: A case for primary implication of the locus coeruleus. *Brain Res Rev* 38:79–128.

Harro J, Vasar E, Bradwejn J (1993). Cholecystokinin in animal and human research on anxiety. *Trends Pharmacol Sci* 14:244–249.

Heilig M, Koob GF, Ekman R, Britton KT (1994). Corticotropin-releasing factor and neuropeptide Y: Role in emotional integration. *Trends Neurosci* 17:80–85.

Heim C, Nemeroff CB (1999). The impact of early adverse experiences on brain systems involved in the pathophysiology of anxiety and affective disorders. *Biol Psychiatry* 46:1509–1522.

Hill RG (2000). NK_1 (substance P) receptor antagonists—why are they not analgesic in humans. *Trends Pharmacol Sci* 21:244–246.

Hökfelt T, Rehfeld JF, Skirboll L, Ivemark B, Goldstein M, Markey K (1980). Evidence for coexistence of dopamine and CCK in meso-limbic neurones. *Nature* 285:476–478.

Hökfelt T, Broberger C, Diez M, et al. (1999). Galanin and NPY, two peptides with multiple putative roles in the nervous system. *Horm Metab Res* 31:330–334.

Hökfelt T, Broberger C, Xu Z-QD, Sergeyev V, Ubink R, Diez M (2000). Neuropeptides—an overview. *Neuropharmacology* 39:1337–1356.

Holsboer F (2001a). Prospects for antidepressant drug discovery. *Biol Psychol* 57:47–65.

Holsboer F (2001b). The rationale for corticotropin-releasing hormone receptor (CRH-R) antagonists to treat depression and anxiety. *J Psychiat Res* 33:181–214.

Hruby VJ (2002). Designing peptide receptor agonists and antagonists. *Nature Rev* 1:847–858.

Hunsinger DM, Nguyen T, Zebraski S, Raffa RB (2000). Is there a basis for novel pharmacotherapy of autism? *Life Sci* 67:1667–1682.

Ikemoto S, Panksepp J (1999). The role of nucleus accumbens dopamine in motivated behavior: A unifying interpretation with special reference to reward-seeking. *Brain Res Rev* 31:6–41.

Insel TR (1997). A neurobiological basis of social attachment. *Am J Psychiatry* 154:726–735.

Kask A, Rägo L, Harro J (1996). Anxiogenic-like effect of the neuropeptide Y Y_1 receptor antagonist BIBP3226: Antagonism with diazepam. *Eur J Pharmacol* 317:R3–4.

Kask A, Rägo L, Harro J (1998). Evidence for involvement of neuropeptide Y receptors in the regulation of food intake: Studies with Y_1-selective antagonist BIBP3226. *Br J Pharmacol* 124:1507–1515.

Kask A, Harro J, von Hörsten S, Redrobe P, Dumont Y, Quirion R (2002). The neurocircuitry and receptor subtypes mediating anxiolytic-like effects of neuropeptide Y. *Neurosci Biobehav Rev* 26:259–283.

Kastin AJ, Pan W, Maness LM, Banks WA (1999). Peptides crossing the blood-brain barrier: Some unusual observations. *Brain Res* 848:96–100.

Kastin AJ, Fasold MB, Smith RR, Horner KA, Zadina JE (2001). Saturable brain-to-blood transport of endomorphins. *Exp Brain Res* 139:70–75.

Katsura M, Mohri Y, Shuto K, Tsujimura A, Ukai M, Ohkuma S (2002). Psychological stress, but not physical stress, causes increase in diazepam binding inhibitor (DBI) mRNA expression in brains. *Mol Brain Res* 104:103–109.

Kehne JH, Coverdale S, McCloskey TC, Hoffman DC, Cassella JV (2000). Effects of the CRF receptor antagonist, CP 154,523, in the separation-induced vocalization anxiolytic test in rat pups. *Neuropharmacology* 39:1357–1367.

Kent JM, Mathew SJ, Gorman JM (2002). Molecular targets in the treatment of anxiety. *Biol Psychiatry* 52:1008–1030.

Kim SW, Grant JE (2001). An open naltrexone treatment study in pathological gambling disorder. *Int Clin Psychopharmacol* 16:285–289.

Kinkead B, Nemeroff CB (2002). Neurotensin: An endogenous antipsychotic? Commentary. *Curr Opinion Pharmacol* 2:99–103.

Knivsberg AM, Reichelt KL, Nodland M (2001). Reports on dietary intervention in autistic disorders. *Nutr Neurosci* 4:25–37.

Knivsberg AM, Reichelt KL, Hoien T, Nodland M (2002). A randomised, controlled study of dietary intervention in autistic syndromes. *Nutr Neurosci* 5:251–261.

Knutson B, Burgdorf J, Panksepp J (2002). Ultrasonic vocalizations as indices of affective states in rat. *Psych Bull* 128:961–977.

Kolmen BK, Feldman HM, Handen BL, Janosky JE (1997). Naltrexone in young autistic children: Replication study and learning measures. *J Am Acad Child Adolesc Psychiatry* 36:1570–1578.

Korotkova TM, Sergeeva OA, Eriksson KS, Haas, HL, Brown RE (2003). Excitation of ventral tegmental area dopaminergic and non dopaminergic neurons by orexins/hypocretins. *J Neurosci* 23:7–11.

Kovacs GL, de Wied, D (1994). Peptidergic modulation of learning and memory processes. *Pharmacol Rev* 46:269–291.

Kovacs GL, Sarnyai Z, Szabo G (1998). Oxytocin and addiction: A review. *Psychoneuroendicronol* 23:945–962.

Kramer P (1993). *Listening to Prozac*. Viking: New York.

Kramer MS, Cutler N, Feighner J, et al. (1998). Distinct mechanism for antidepressant activity by blockade of central substance P receptors. *Science* 281:1640–1645.

Ladurelle N, Roques BP, Dauge V (1995). The transfer of rats from a familiar to a novel environment prolongs the increase of extracellular dopamine efflux induced by CCK8 in the poseterior nucleus accumbens. *J Neurosci* 15:3118–3127.

Legault M, Congar P, Miche FJ, Trudeau L-E (2002). Presynaptic action of neurotensin on cultured ventral tegmental area dopaminergic neurones. *Neuroscience* 111:177–187.

Lyons DM, Yang C, Sawyer-Glover AM, Moseley ME, Schatzberg AF (2001). Early life stress and inherited variation in monkey hippocampal volumes. *Arch Gen Psychiatry* 58:1145–1151.

Marrazzi MA, Bacon JP, Kinzie J, Luby ED (1995). Naltrexone use in the treatment of anorexia nervosa and bulimia nervosa. *Int Clin Psychopharmacol* 10:163–172.

Mayberg HS, Silva JA, Brannan SK, et al. (2002). The functional neuroanatomy of the placebo effect. *Am J Psychiatry* 159:728–737.

McLay RN, Pan W, Kastin AJ (2001). Effects of peptides on animal and human behavior: A review of studies published in the first twenty years of the journal *Peptides*. *Peptides* 22:2181–2255.

Meaney MJ (2001). Maternal care, gene expression, and the transmission of individual differences in stress reactivity across generation. *Ann Rev Neurosci* 24:1161–192.

Mitchell AJ (1998). The role of corticotropin releasing factor in depressive illness: A critical review. *Neurosci Biobehav Rev* 22:635–651.

Möhler H, Fritschy JM, Rudolph U (2002). A new benzodiazepine pharmacology. *J Pharmacol Exp Ther* 300:2–8.

Moll GH, Hause S, Ruther E, Rothenberger A, Huether G (2001). Early methylphenidate administration to young rats causes a persistent reduction in the density of striatal dopamine transporters. *J Child Adolesc Psychopharmac* 11:15–24.

Monnikes H, Tebbe JJ, Hildebrandt M, et al. (2001). Role of stress in functional gastrointestinal disorders. Evidence for stress-induced alterations in gastrointestinal motility and sensitivity. *Dig Dis* 19:201–211.

Moskal JR, Yamamoto H, Cooley PA (2001). The use of antibody engineering to create novel drugs that target *N*-methyl-D-aspartate receptors. *Current Drug Targets* 2:331–345.

Moss RL, Dudley CA (1984). The challenge of studying the behavioral effects of neuropeptides. In Iversen LL, Iversen SD, Snyder SH (eds). *Handbook of Psychopharmacology*, Vol. 18. Plenum: New York, pp. 397–354.

Myers RD (1974). *Handbook of Drug and Chemical Stimulation of the Brain*. Van Nostrand Reinhold: New York.

Nelson EE, Panksepp J (1998). Brain substrates of infant-mother attachment: Contributions of opioids, oxytocin, and norepinephrine. *Neurosci Biobehav Rev* 22:437–452.

Nocjar C, Panksepp J (2002). Chronic intermittent amphetamine pretreatment enhances future appetitive behavior for drug- and natural-reward: Interaction with environmental variables. *Behav Brain Res* 128:189–203.

Nores WL, Olson RD, Olson GA, et al. (1999). Tyr-W-MIF-1 induced conditioned place preference. *Peptides* 20:479–484.

Nyakas C, Felszeghy K, Bohus B, Luiten PG (1997). Permanent upregulation of hippocampal mineralocorticoid receptors after neonatal administration of ACTH-(4–9) analog ORG 2766 in rats. *Devel Brain Res* 99:142–147.

Olive MF, Mehmert KK, Koenig HN, et al. (2003). A role for corticotropin releasing factor (CRF) in ethanol consumption, sensitivity, and reward as revealed by CRF-deficient mice. *Psychopharmacology* 165:181–187.

O'Malley SS, Krishnan-Sarin S, Farren C, Sinha R, Kreek J (2002). Naltrexone decreases craving and alcohol self-administration in alcohol-dependent subjects and activates the hypothalamo-pituitary-adrenocortical axis. *Psychopharmacology* 160:19–29.

Panksepp J (1979). A neurochemical theory of autism. *Trends Neurosci* 2:174–177.

Panksepp J (1981). Hypothalamic integration of behavior: Rewards, punishments, and related psychobiological process. In Morgane PJ, Panksepp J (eds). *Handbook of the Hypothalamus*,

Vol. 3, Part A. Behavioral Studies of the Hypothalamus. Marcel Dekker: New York, pp. 289–487.

Panksepp J (1986). The neurochemistry of behavior. *Annu Rev Psychol* 37:77–107.

Panksepp J (1992). Oxytocin effects on emotional processes: Separation distress, social bonding, and relationships to psychiatric disorders. In Pdersen CA, Caldwell JD, Jiorikowski GF, Insel TR (eds). *Oxytocin in Maternal, Sexual and Social Behavior. Annals of NY Acad Sci, Vol. 652*, pp. 243–252.

Panksepp J (1993). Neurochemical control of moods and emotions: Amino acids to neuropeptides. In Lewis M, Haviland J (eds). *Handbook of Emotions.* Guilford Press: New York, pp. 87–107.

Panksepp J (1998a). *Affective Neuroscience, The Foundations of Human and Animal Emotion.* Oxford University Press: New York.

Panksepp J (1998b). Attention deficit hyperactivity disorders, psychostimulants and intolerance of childhood playfulness: A tragedy in the making? *Curr Directions Psychol Sci* 7:91–98.

Panksepp J (1999). Emotions as viewed by psychoanalysis and neuroscience. An exercise in consilience. *Neuro-Psychoanalysis* 1:15–38.

Panksepp J (2000). The neuro-evolutionary cusp between emotions and cognitions, implications for understand consciousness and the emergence of a unified mind science. *Consciousness Emotion* 1:17–56.

Panksepp J (2003a). At the interface of affective, behavioral and cognitive neurosciences. Decoding the emotional feelings of the brain. *Brain Cognition* 52:4–14.

Panksepp J (2003b). Can anthropomorphic analyses of "separation cries" in other animals inform us about the emotional nature of social loss in humans? *Psychol Rev* 110:376–388.

Panksepp J, Abbott BB (1990). Modulation of separation distress by alpha-MSH. *Peptides* 11:647–653.

Panksepp J, Bekkedal M (1997). Neuropeptides and the varieties of anxiety in the brain. *Italian J Psychopath* 1:18–27.

Panksepp J, Normansell L (1990). Effects of ACTH(1-24) and ACTH/MSH(4-10) on isolation-induced distress vocalization in domestic chicks. *Peptides* 11:915–919.

Panksepp J, Sahley T (1987). Possible brain opioid involvement in disrupted social intent and language development of autism. In Schopler E, Mesibov G (eds). *Neurobiological Issues in Autism.* Plenum: New York, pp. 357–382.

Panksepp J, Herman BH, Villberg T, Bishop P, DeEskinazi FG (1980). Endogenous opioids and social behavior. *Neurosci Biobehav Rev* 4:473–487.

Panksepp, J, Jalowiec J, DeEskinazi FG, Bishop P (1985). Opiates and play dominance in juvenile rats. *Behav Neurosci* 99:441–453.

Panksepp J, Normansell LA, Herman B, Bishop P, Crepeau L (1988).Neural and neurochemical control of the separation-distress call. In Newman JD (ed). *The Physiological Control of Mammalian Vocalization.* Plenum: New York, pp. 263–299.

Panksepp J, Lensing P, Leboyer M, Bouvard MP (1991). Naltrexone and other potential new pharmacological treatments of autism. *Brain Dysfunction* 4:281–300.

Panksepp J, Nelson E, Bekkedal M (1999). Brain systems for the mediation of social separation distress and social-reward: Evolutionary antecedents and neuropeptide intermediaries. In Carter CS, Lederhendler II, Kirkpatrick B (eds). *The Integrative Neurobiology of Affiliation.* MIT Press: Cambridge, MA, pp. 221–244.

Panksepp J, Burgdorf J, Gordon N, Turner C (2002a). Treatment of ADHD with methylphenidate may sensitize brain substrates of desire. Implications for changes in drug abuse potential from an animal model. *Consciousness Emotion* 3:7–19.

Panksepp J, Moskal JR, Panksepp JB, Kroes RA (2002b). Comparative approaches in evolutionary psychology: Molecular neuroscience meets the mind. *Neuroendocrinol Lett* 23:105–15.

Panksepp J, Burgdorf J, Turner C, Gordon N (2003). Modeling ADHD-type arousal with unilateral frontal cortex damage in rats and beneficial effects of play therapy. *Brain Cognition* 52:97–105.

Petrovic P, Kalso E, Petersson KM, Ingvar M (2002). Placebo and opioid analgesia: Imaging a shared neuronal network. *Science* 295:1737–1740.

Pfaff DW (1999). *Drive, Neurobiological and Molecular Mechanisms of Sexual Motivation.* MIT Press: Cambridge, MA.

Pinker S (2002). *Blank Slate: The Modern Denial of Human Nature.* Viking: New York.

Post RM, Gold P, Rubinow DR, Ballenger JC, Bunney WE Jr, Goodwin FK (1982). Peptides in the cerebrospinal fluid of neuropsychiatric patients: An approach to central nervous system peptide function. *Life Sci* 5:1–15.

Rajkowska G (2000). Histopathology of the prefrontal cortex in major depression: What does it tell us about dysfunctional monoaminergic circuits? *Prog Brain Res* 126:397–412.

Reul JMHM, Holsboer F (2002). Corticotropin-releasing factor receptors 1 and 2 in anxiety and depression. *Curr Opinion Pharmacol* 2:23–33.

Rios M, Fan G, Fekete C, et al. (2001). Conditional deletion of brain-derived neurotrophic factor in the postnatal brain leads to obesity and hyperactivity. *Mol Endocrinol* 15:1748–1757.

Robinson TE, Berridge KC (1993). The neural basis of drug craving: An incentive-sensitization theory of addiction. *Brain Res Rev* 18:247–291.

Rompre PP (1995). Psychostimulant-like effect of central microinjection of neurotensin on brain stimulation reward. *Peptides* 16:1417–1420.

Rothman RB, Vu N, Xu H, Baumann MH, Lu Y-F (2002). Endogenous corticotropin releasing factor regulates adrenergic and opioid receptors. *Peptides* 23:2177–2180.

Rubio-Aliaga I, Daniel H (2002). Mammalian peptide transporters as targets for drug discovery. *Trends Pharmacol Sci* 23:434–440.

Saarelainen T, Hendolin P, Lucas G, et al. (2003). Activation of the trkB neurotrophin receptor is induced by antidepressant drugs and is required for antidepressant-induced behavioral effects. *J Neurosci* 23:349–357.

Sarnyai Z, Dhaham Y, Heinrichs SC (2001). The role of corticotropin-releasing factor in drug addiction. *Pharmacol Rev* 53:209–243.

Schwartz JM, Stoessel PW, Baxter LR, Jr., Martin KM, Phelps ME (1996). Systematic changes in cerebral glucose metabolic rate after successful behavior modification treatment of obsessive-compulsive disorder. *Arch Gen Psychiatry* 53:109–13.

Scott LV, Dinan TG (2002). Vasopressin as a target for antidepressant development: An assessment of the available evidence. *J Affect Disord* 72:113–124.

Siviy SM, Panksepp J (1985). Energy balance and play in juvenile rats. *Physiol Behav* 35:435–441.

Smith GP (1999). Introduction to the review on peptides and the control of food intake and body weight. *Neuropeptides* 33:323–328.

Snyder SH, Ferris CD (2000). Novel neurotransmitters and their neuropsychiatric relevance. *Am J Psychiatry* 157:1738–1751.

Södersten P, Henning M, Melin P, Ludin S (1983). Vasopressin alters female sexual behaviour by acting on the brain independently of alteration in blood pressure. *Nature* 301:608–610.

Steiner RA, Hohmann JG, Holmes A, et al. (2001). Galanin transgenic mice display cognitive and neurochemical deficits characteristic of Alzheimer's disease. *Proc Natl Acad Sci USA* 98:4184–4189.

Stockmeier CA, Shi X, Konick L, et al. (2002). Neurokinin-1 receptors are decreased in major depressive disorder. *Neuroreport* 13:1223–1227.

Strand FL (1999). *Neuropeptides, Regulators of Physiological Processes.* MIT Press: Cambridge, MA.

Sutcliffe JG, de Lecea L (2002). The hypocretins: Setting the arousal threshold. *Nature Rev Neurosci* 3:339–349.

Taylor SE, Dickerson SS, Klein LC (2002). Toward a biology of social support In Snyder CR, Lopez SJ (eds). *Handbook of Positive Psychology.* Oxford University Press: London.

Thoenen H, Sendtner M (2002). Neurotrophins: From enthusiastic expectations through sobering experiences to rational therapeutic approaches. *Nature Neurosci* 5:1046–1050.

Tohyama M, Takatsuji K (1998). *Atlas of Neuroactive Substances and Their Receptors in the Rat.* Oxford University Press: Oxford, UK.

Uvnäs-Moberg K (1998). Oxytocin may mediate the benefits of positive social interaction and emotions. *Psychoneuroendocrinology* 23:819–835.

Valenstein, E (1998). *Blaming the Brain: The Truth about Drugs and Mental Health.* Free Press: New York.

Valenstein E, Charney D (2000). Are we "blaming" brain chemistry for mental illness. *Cerebrum* 2:87–114.

van den Berg CL, Van Ree JM, Spruijt BM (2000). Morphine attenuates the effects of juvenile isolation in rats. *Neuropharmacology* 39:969–976.

Vanderhaeghen JJ, Crawley JN (eds) (1985). *Neuronal Cholecystokinin. Annals of the New York Academy of Sciences*, Vol. 448. New York Academy of Sciences: New York.

van Praag HM (2000). Nosologomania: A disorder of psychiatry. *World J Biol Psychiatry* 1:151–158.

van Rijzingen IM, Gispen WH, Spruijt BM (1996). The ACTH (4–9) analog ORG 2766 and recovery after brain damage in animal models—a review. *Behav Brain Res* 74:1–15.

Wikberg JE (1999). Melanocortin receptors: Perspectives for novel drugs. *Eur J Pharmacol* 375:295–310.

Wilcock G, Mobius HJ, Stoffler A, MMM 500 group (2002). A double-blind, placebo-controlled multicentre study of memantine in mild to moderate vascular dementia (MMM500). *Int J Clin Psychopharmacol* 17:297–305.

Willie JT, Chemelli RM, Sinton CM, Yanagisawa M (2001). To eat or to sleep? Orexin in the regulation of feeding and wakefulness. *Annu Rev Neurosci* 24:429–458.

Willemsen-Swinkels SH, Buitelaar JK, van Engeland H (1996). The effects of chronic naltrexone treatment in young autistic children: A double-blind placebo-controlled crossover study. *Biol Psychiatry* 39:1023–1031.

Winslow JT, Hastings N, Carter CS, Harbaugh CR, Insel TR (1993). A role for central vasopressin in pair-bonding in monogamous prairie voles. *Nature* 365:544–548.

Wise RA (2002). Brain reward circuitry: Insights from unsensed incentives. *Neuron* 36:229–240.

Wood JH (1980). Neurochemical analysis of cerebrospinal fluid. *Neurology* 30:645–651.

Woods SC, Schwartz MW, Baskin DG, Seeley RJ (2000). Food intake and the regulation of body weight. *Ann Rev Psychol* 51:255–277.

Wunderlich GR, DeSousa NJ, Vaccarino FJ (2000). Cholecystokinin modulates both the development and the expression of behavioral sensitization to amphetamine in the rat. *Psychopharmacology* 151:283–290.

Wyatt RJ, Apud JA, Potkin S (1996). New directions in the prevention and treatment of schizophrenia: A biological perspective. *Psychiatry* 59:357–370.

Young LJ (2002). The neurobiology of social recognition, approach, and avoidance. *Biol Psychiatry* 51:18–26.

Zobel AW, Nickel T, Künzel HE, et al. (2000). Effects of the high-affinity corticotropin-releasing hormone receptor 1 antagonist R121919 in major depression: The first 20 patients treated. *J Psychiat Res* 34:171–181.

Appendix A

PHARMACODYNAMICS AND PHARMACOKINETICS

Department of Psychology, Center of Behavioral and Health Sciences, University of Tartu, Tartu, Estonia

INTRODUCTION

Much of what we know about the biological foundations of psychiatric disorders comes from pharmacological studies. Pharmacology deals with all aspects of the interaction of chemicals with biological systems, and psychopharmacology refers to the interactions of drugs that are used primarily because of their effects on the central nervous system (CNS).

Pharmacologists often divide their science into two main parts: pharmacokinetics and pharmacodynamics. In the simplest terms, pharmacokinetics attempts to describe what the body does to the drug, and pharmacodynamics describes what the drug does to the body. In studies of mental illnesses, pharmacodynamics reveals the molecular substrates of drugs that influence mental states, and hence molecular and cellular contributors to particular mental conditions. After examining the basic principles of pharmacodynamics, we shall, nevertheless, turn to the basic principles of the seemingly more abstract and boring pharmacokinetics, details of which frequently are the place

Textbook of Biological Psychiatry, Edited by Jaak Panksepp
ISBN 0-471-43478-7   Copyright © 2004 John Wiley & Sons, Inc.

where the devil rests. Given the scope of this book, the examples are taken from drugs acting on the CNS, and the focus of the discussion is set in consideration of relevance to pharmacotherapy of mental disorders and related research.

PHARMACODYNAMICS: WHAT CAN THE DRUG DO TO THE BODY?

Receptors and the Binding of Drug Molecules

The specificity and apparently high potency of certain chemicals, which makes it possible to use them as drugs, is provided by the existence of specific endogenous molecules on which the drugs can bind. These molecules, termed receptors, are proteins, and binding of a drug to a regulatory protein depends upon the structural conformity of both molecules. (There are a few exceptions from the protein rule: Some drugs act via binding to deoxyribonucleic acid (DNA) or lipid molecules.) Drugs are usually much smaller molecules than the regulatory proteins with which they interact. Ligands, a term referring to small molecules binding to a specific receptor, can be endogenous or exogenous: Morphine is an exogenous ligand for opioid receptors, whereas endorphins and enkephalins are the endogenous ligands. Figure A.1 demonstrates the specific binding of a drug to receptors, which can be quantified using radioactive isotopes. One can note that increasing the concentration of the drug increases its binding until saturation occurs because the number of available receptors is limited.

The term receptor is used liberally in physiology and pharmacology. In physiology receptor can mean a whole cell, in reference to detectors of sensory signals.

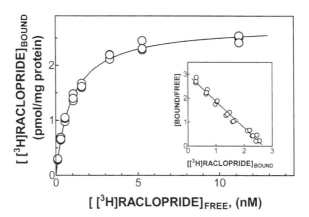

Figure A.1. Binding of drugs to specific receptors explains their potent physiological effects. This experiment demonstrates the binding of tritium-labeled raclopride to D_2 dopamine receptors in cell membranes prepared from the corpus striatum of the rat. On abscissa, concentration of free radiolabeled raclopride in the assay medium. On ordinate, amount of radiolabeled raclopride specifically bound to the receptors. On inset: Scatchard plot (often used for evaluation of the maximal available number of receptors). (Courtesy of Dr. Ago Rinken, Department of Organic and Bioorganic Chemistry, Tartu University.)

The most common meaning of the word, and the most universally accepted one by pharmacologists, is a protein molecule that recognizes endogenous signal molecules and mediates their effect to intracellular executive mechanisms. Such an example is provided in Fig. A.1, where binding of a drug to receptors that physiologically mediate the effect of the neurotransmitter dopamine is presented. Yet in pharmacology any molecule serving as a drug target, even an enzyme or transporter, can be termed a drug receptor. Furthermore, sometimes pharmacologists speak of silent receptors or acceptors, which are in essence any molecules binding a drug molecule without any resultant immediate physiological effect, such as serum proteins.

In the case of the so-called drug receptors, some drugs form covalent bonds with the receptive substance. First-generation monoamine oxidase inhibitors such as iproniazide serve as an example of this type of a drug-receptor interaction. Because covalent bonds are usually irreversible at body temperature, the enzyme in our example becomes nonfunctional permanently, and the effect of the drug lasts until a sufficient amount of a new enzyme protein is synthesized. Most drug-receptor complexes make use of noncovalent bonds, which support reversible interactions. The reversibility of ligand binding first presented in Fig. A.1 is shown in Fig. A.2: Various substances, including dopamine, the endogenous ligand, are able to compete with the radiolabeled drug and displace it from the receptors depending upon their concentration. Noncovalent bonds that establish reversible binding include ionic bonds, hydrogen bonds, van der Waals bonds, and spatial arrangements of hydrophobic groups of receptors and drugs. These bonds are relatively weak and require close approximation of surfaces for formation of a ligand-receptor complex. This makes the three-dimensional structure

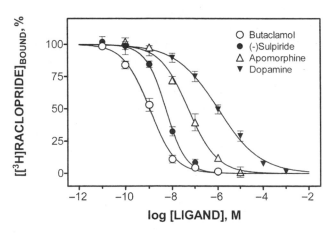

Figure A.2. In the case of reversible binding, drugs compete for the binding sites. This experiment demonstrates inhibition of [^{3}H]raclopride binding to D_2 dopamine receptors in rat striatal membranes by three synthetic drugs and dopamine, the endogenous ligand. On abscissa, concentration of competing substances added to the assay. On ordinate, the proportion of maximal specific binding of raclopride to the receptors. (Courtesy of Dr. Ago Rinken, Department of Organic and Bioorganic Chemistry, Tartu University.)

of receptors and drug molecules extremely important for any functional interaction. As a consequence, the structure-activity relationship, which forms one cornerstone in pharmacology, appears puzzling to a novice: Chemical structures that seem very similar may have very different receptor binding profiles, whereas structures with fairly different appearances may share enough three-dimensional similarity to interact with a common receptor. Thus, a drug-receptor complex is formed when the spatial arrangements of their respective molecules fit like a key in the lock, but not all aspects of the three-dimensional structures are critical for such a fit.

An important aspect in the key and lock concept of spatial compatibility is the conclusion that there must be stereospecificity in the action of drugs. Indeed, many drug molecules contain an asymmetrical carbon atom, which makes it possible to have two different molecules as mirror images of each other, termed stereoisomers. Unlike actual mirror images that we can easily recognize as the original faces, receptors do not recognize mirror images of drugs, which renders them biologically inactive. As a matter of fact, the mechanism of action of psychopharmacological drugs is often studied by comparing the effect of active drugs with their stereoisomers. Stereospecificity of effect—which means that only one of the mirror image molecules is biologically active—is suggestive of a receptor-mediated action.

Dose-Response Relationship

A simple rule of pharmacodynamics is that the size of the effect an agonist (or inverse agonist) elicits is dependent upon the dose of the drug (or, more precisely, its concentration at receptors). When the size of the effect is plotted against the dose, one can notice that the increase in the effect slows down and finally stops when the maximal obtainable response has been achieved (Fig. A.3). It is assumed that the occupancy of receptors and the effect size are proportional, and hence the maximal effect corresponds to the situation when all receptors are already occupied. (However, in many real situations, the maximal effect occurs when many receptors remain unoccupied. Such receptors are referred to as "spare receptors" or "receptor reserve.") Dose-response curves are frequently drawn on a semilogarithmic scale, as in Fig. A.3. Thus, a drug has a dose range in which its concentration logarithm and the size of the effect are linearly proportional, and within this range the predictions made about the dose-effect relationship are most reliable.

In behavioral pharmacology, when drugs are given systemically, we frequently obtain a less clear picture regarding dose dependency. For example, selective serotonin reuptake inhibitors show limited dose dependency in their clinical efficacy, and many antagonists of neuropeptide receptors produce inverted U-shape dose-response curves in animal experiments. The reasons are not always clear, but a biological psychiatrist must bear in mind that after systemic administration, a drug has multiple targets in different brain regions, and thus divergent actions can interfere with each other and shape the dose-response curve.

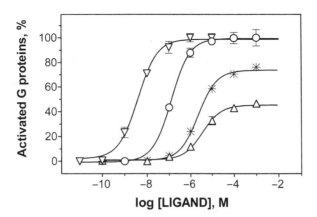

Figure A.3. Dose dependency of the effect of four different drugs. This experiment character-ized the activation of D_2 dopamine receptor-coupled G proteins, as measured by the acceleration of $[^{35}S]GTP\gamma S$ binding to membranes of CHO cells. Receptors were activated by different con-centrations of apomorphine (∇), quinpirole ($\bigcirc$), 5-methoxytryptamine ($*$), and 8-OH-DPAT ($\triangle$). On abscissa, concentration of competing substances added to the assay. On ordinate, percent of maximal effect. (Courtesy of Dr. Ago Rinken, Department of Organic and Bioorganic Chemistry, Tartu University.)

Receptor Affinity

The fraction of all receptors that bind drug molecules is determined by the concentra-tion of the drug in the vicinity of the receptor and by the dissociation constant of the drug-receptor complex. (The dissociation constant expresses the relationship between the rates of dissociation from and binding to the receptors, being essentially the ratio of the off-and-on rates of drug receptor complex formation. It depends, most impor-tantly, upon the chemical nature of the molecules involved in the interaction.) When we compare the dose-response curves of two drugs, apomorphine and quinpirole, on Fig. A.3, it is obvious that these drugs produce the same maximal effect. Nevertheless, for any given degree of response, a higher concentration of quinpirole is required if compared to apomorphine. If we assume that the size of the effect of a drug depends upon the proportion of receptors it occupies, we must conclude that quinpirole occu-pies fewer receptors at any given concentration. The measure that characterizes the ability of a drug in a given concentration to occupy respective receptors is affinity. Affinity can also be said to express the probability with which drug molecules (at a certain concentration) interact with receptors to form the drug-receptor complexes. A drug with a higher affinity is more capable of occupying receptors than one with a lower affinity, and in case their concentrations are equal the one with higher affinity outcompetes the other at the receptors. In our example, apomorphine has a higher affinity than quinpirole for their target (D_2 dopamine receptor), and hence lower doses of apomorphine are likely to elicit maximal (or, e.g., half-maximal) effect mediated via these receptors.

Efficacy or Intrinsic Activity

In the preceding discussion, we assumed that receptor occupancy is the sole determinant of the size of the effect a drug would elicit. Thus, all drugs acting on a certain type of receptor should have a similar maximal effect, and only the dose required to achieve this would vary. This is true only when comparing certain drugs. Otherwise, one can easily notice that drugs binding to a common receptor may have very different maximal effects. Compare the effects of drugs in Fig. A.3: With some drugs that have a specific receptor-mediated effect, the maximal achievable effect remains much lower than with others. Therefore we have to add to the concept of affinity another basic feature of drugs: efficacy or intrinsic activity. Intrinsic activity is a measure of the biological effectiveness of a drug-receptor complex to elicit further cellular changes of physiological importance. For illustrative purposes, one can imagine efficacy to depend upon how closely the drug molecule and the receptor binding site fit together.

Agonists, Antagonists, Mixed Agonist-Antagonists, Partial Agonists, Inverse Agonists

An agonist is a drug that elicits a physiological response by means of formation of drug-receptor complexes. If a drug is capable of producing the maximal possible response, it can be considered a full agonist. This term refers to the concept of intrinsic activity of drugs or drug-receptor complexes. Morphine and heroin are full agonists at opioid receptors, but many other drugs are partial agonists at these receptors. Partial agonists are drugs that are not capable of eliciting maximal response, even if all available receptors were occupied. In Fig. A.3, apomorphine and quinpirole behave as full agonists and 5-methoxytryptamine and 8-hydroxy-2-(di-n-propylamino)tetralin (8-OH-DPAT) as partial agonists. Because of the lower efficacy of partial agonists, it is conceivable that a partial agonist that mimics the effect of an agonist can actually reduce the effect of a full agonist by successfully competing for the same receptors. For this reason, partial agonists have previously been referred to as mixed agonists-antagonists. To understand this complicated issue, examine Fig. A.4. As demonstrated in Fig. A.3, 8-OH-DPAT is a partial agonist at D_2 dopamine receptors. When the cell culture used for assay does not contain any dopamine (the physiological or endogenous stimulator of D_2 receptors), or when dopamine levels are low, 8-OH-DPAT behaves like an agonist, albeit weak. At higher dopamine concentrations, the effect of this endogenous ligand becomes observable. However, now it is also evident that 8-OH-DPAT reduces the effect of dopamine. This is because 8-OH-DPAT has a weaker intrinsic efficacy at D_2 receptors than dopamine with which it competes for the binding sites.

A drug can have zero intrinsic activity yet still bind to a receptor with high affinity. Such drugs are antagonists and can be useful when endogenous signal transmission must be reduced or the patient has ingested a specific drug in an excessive dose. An

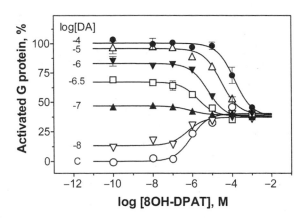

Figure A.4. Behavior of a partial agonist as either an agonist or antagonist in the same assay. This experiment characterized the activation of D_2 dopamine receptor-coupled G proteins, as measured by the acceleration of $[^{35}S]GTP\gamma S$ binding to membranes of CHO cells. On abscissa, logarithm of the molar concentration of 8-OH-DPAT added to the assay. On ordinate, percent of maximal effect. Each curve demonstrates the concentration-dependent effect of 8-OH-DPAT at a specific concentration of dopamine. C refers to no dopamine in assay. (Courtesy of Dr. Ago Rinken, Department of Organic and Bioorganic Chemistry, Tartu University.)

example of the former case is easily found in pharmacotherapy for schizophrenia. A common feature of antipsychotic drugs is their competitive antagonism at D_2 dopamine receptors. Benzodiazepine receptor antagonists such as flumazenil have little effect on mood but can rapidly eliminate the symptoms of benzodiazepine overdose when given in a sufficient dose to displace the tranquillizer molecules from the benzodiazepine receptors. An antagonist reduces the effect of a given concentration of an agonist. This can be visualized using dose-response curves, as in Fig. A.5. Pharmacologists say that antagonists shift the dose-response curve of an agonist to the right. The higher the concentration (or dose) of an antagonist, the larger the shift.

Some drugs are termed inverse agonists. An inverse agonist differs from an antagonist of the same receptor by eliciting a physiological or behavioral response. But an inverse agonist also differs from an agonist because the effect is in the opposite direction. Thus, benzodiazepine inverse agonists elicit anxiety, fear, and at higher doses seizures. All these effects can be eliminated by administering either agonists or antagonists of benzodiazepine receptors. In recent years, it has become apparent that inverse agonism is a fairly common phenomenon in pharmacology.

Side Effects

It should be noted, however, that even though drugs are designed to be relatively specific toward their molecular substrates, and such molecular specificity or specificity for a physiological effect is often emphasized in drug promotion, it would be unrealistic to expect absolute specificity from any drug. Specificity rather means that a drug should

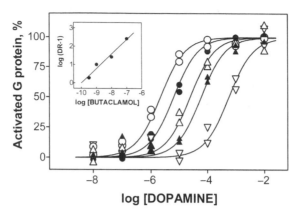

Figure A.5. A competitive antagonist shifts the dose-response curve of an agonist to the right. This experiment describes the inhibition of dopamine stimulation of [^{35}S]GTPγS binding by (+)butaclamol, a D_2 receptor antagonist. Binding of [^{35}S]GTPγS to rat striatal membranes was measured at the indicated concentration of dopamine in the absence (O) and in the presence of increasing concentrations (1 to 1000 nM) of (+)butaclamol. On abscissa, concentration of dopamine added to the assay. On ordinate, percent of maximal effect. On inset: Schild plot, a pharmacological tool to measure whether the antagonism at receptors is truly competitive. (Courtesy of Dr Ago Rinken, Department of Organic and Bioorganic Chemistry, Tartu University.)

act on other physiological substrates at much higher concentrations than to its target receptors. There are several sources of limitations to the specificity a drug can have in its action. The fact that living organisms generally use basic biochemical mechanisms in different settings makes it inevitable that drugs in general have either a plethora of physiological effects or at least a few. For example, endogenous opioids serve as messengers in the antinociceptive circuits in the brain and spinal cord, but in the enteric nervous system they also control gastroenteral secretions and motility, and in immune system, opioids modulate the inflammatory response, affecting, for example, phagocytic activity and responses to various chemoattractant molecules. Limitations to specificity for drug targets, due to the partial overlaps in spatial conformation, increases the potential for undesirable side effects. An example can be found in the present chapter: Fig. A.3 and A.4 feature 8-OH-DPAT as a partial agonist at D_2 dopamine receptors, but those familiar with experimental manipulations of serotonin know this drug as a full agonist at 5-HT$_{1A}$ receptors. Thus, there is a vast potential for side effects with any drug, but usually only a few of these occur frequently in most individuals.

Dose

Because all effects of drugs are quantitative by nature, the dose of a drug is a central theme in pharmacology. Dose is the quantity of a drug in units of mass that is, or should be, used to elicit an expected effect. In experimental pharmacology, one often refers to concentrations rather than doses, but in many in vivo conditions, and especially in treatment of patients, one has to rely on quantities. Nevertheless, drug levels in body fluids are expressed in concentration units. These depend on the dose, but also a number of principles of pharmacokinetics.

Both the main, desired effects and the side effects of drugs depend upon the dose. Drug development aims at drugs that would not elicit side effects at the doses used for treatment purposes, but this has not always been possible. Thus, with some drugs, therapeutic doses elicit unwanted effects as well, at least in a significant fraction of treated subjects. With other drugs, side effects usually occur at higher doses. When side effects occur, it is thus frequently possible to reduce the dose but continue the treatment. This is not always the case, however, especially when allergic reactions are involved.

Because every drug is capable of producing multiple effects, selectivity refers to the degree to which a drug acts upon a given site relative to all possible sites of action. In experimental pharmacology, this can be expressed in terms of concentration measures, but in a clinical setting where the health of a patient is at stake, one needs a simple indicator of the drug's safety. Basic textbooks suggest the therapeutic index as a simple means to provide a quantitative assessment of a drug's relative benefits and risks. This is customarily calculated by dividing the dose that produces toxic effects by the dose that produces the desired therapeutic effect in 50 percent of the treated population. A drug with a higher therapeutic index would appear a safer drug. Unfortunately, calculation of a therapeutic index is more complicated than that, and therefore even though textbooks suggest its use, they do not provide a table of values of therapeutic index for a series of drugs. The easiest way to explain the infeasibility of a single therapeutic index for any given drug is to recall that drugs have multiple therapeutic effects and multiple toxic effects. Nevertheless, there are safer drugs and more dangerous drugs. Therefore, thinking in terms of ratios between toxic and therapeutic doses is useful even if we fail to put it into precise calculations.

Potency and Efficacy of a Drug in Intact Organism

When speaking in clinical terms, the efficacy of a drug refers to its ability to produce a desired therapeutic effect, and potency can be expressed as the quantity of drug per kilogram of body weight that can produce a given therapeutic effect. Most of the basic principles of drug action have been discovered and refined using tissue preparations or cell cultures. Such techniques reveal quantitative relationships important in understanding the nature of drug action, but these relationships cannot always be directly translated into clinical efficacy or prediction of side effects. Sometimes the dose-effect curves of drugs in isolated systems and in intact organisms are very similar, but due to pharmacokinetic variables and interactions with multiple target molecules, this is not always the case. The drug may be poorly absorbed from the gastrointestinal tract, or it may be broken down too quickly. It is therefore important to consider the different aspects of pharmacokinetics in evaluating the efficacy and potency of drugs.

PHARMACOKINETICS: WHAT CAN HAPPEN TO A DRUG IN THE BODY?

Drug Absorption

Any drug must reach its target molecules before it can exert any effect. The first obstacle lies in the tissues that the drug molecules must penetrate in order to reach blood, which can carry them to the target. Drug absorption is this process whereby a drug reaches the bloodstream from the locus where it is applied to the body. Not all of the drug reaches the blood. Bioavailability, the term that reflects the extent to which a drug is absorbed, refers to the proportion of drug administered that actually reaches blood. (It may seem more desirable to know the concentration of the drug at the site of action, but such measurements would in most cases be impractical or even impossible.) Bioavailability depends upon the drug, the drug formula, the route of administration, and the physiological conditions in the organism. For example, drugs with high solubility in lipids are more easily absorbed, and the lipid solubility of many drugs is influenced by the pH levels in the immediate aquous media because acidity influences ionization of the drug molecules, and drugs in an ionized state are less soluble in lipids. On the other hand, the influence of physicochemical factors on drug absorption depends upon which tissue the drug is applied: Lipid solubility is critical for drugs administered orally or on the skin, but in the vicinity of the peripheral capillary beds (like after administration into the muscle), a drug is absorbed well regardless of its ionization level. An example of the intentional manipulation of absorption rates is the modern pharmaceutical industry's ability to tailor drug formulas to release the active ingredient either faster or more slowly, as in depot preparations of antipsychotics, where the slow hydrolysis of ester bonds supports prolonged release of the drug over a period of weeks at a constant rate.

Methods of Administration

Drugs can be given orally or rectally, injected into muscle or vein, or inhaled. The route of administration may have a profound effect upon the speed and efficiency of action and also on any adverse effects of the drug. There is rationale behind each route of administration, but no one method is best for all occasions. Table A.1 lists the main routes of applications, mentioning their stronger and weaker sides.

Oral administration is the most common approach. In this instance, the drug must be soluble and resistant to low pH in the stomach and to enzymes in the digestive tract. Relative ease is a major advantage of this route of administration, and all major psychiatric drugs are most frequently given in this way. The drawbacks include a relatively slow onset of action, which can be disturbing in case of, for example, antianxiety and sedative-hypnotic drugs. Figure A.6 shows that half an hour after oral administration, drug levels in the blood have not yet reached their peak, which is observable 1 to 2 hr after drug taking. There is also large interindividual variability in bioavailability. Gastrointestinal absorption is affected by gastrointestinal motility, blood flow, and the physicochemical characteristics of the specific drug formula. Many physiological states and chemical substances reduce or increase gastrointestinal motility and thus

T A B L E A.1. Main Routes of Drug Administration: Benefits and Limitations

Route	Utility	Limitations
Parenteral		
By injection	Precise dosing, fast action	Inconvenient to the patient, infection risks
Intravenous	Bioavailability 100%, absorption circumvented	Higher overdose risk, no manipulation with absorption
	Fastest action, valuable in emergency	Risk of fast and strong allergic reactions, air embolism
	Large volumes can be administrated over time	Requires skill, slow injecting, not suitable for poorly soluble substances
Intramuscular	Gastrointestinal tract circumvented	Volume moderate, some substances are too irritating
	Depot preparations: slow and sustained release	Hazardous during anticoagulant therapy
Subcutaneous	As intramuscular; suitable for some poorly soluble suspensions and solid pellets	Small volumes
		Local irritation to necrosis
By inhalation	Fast onset of action	Gaseous or aerosol formula necessary
Through skin	Slow-release formulas	Limited bioavailability
Enteral		
Oral	Simple, minimal effect of infection	Bioavailability variable
	Optimal for many drugs	Hepatic first-pass effect, slow onset on action
Sublingual	Hepatic first-pass avoided	Absorption depends on drug
	Relatively fast onset of action	
Rectal	Hepatic first-pass reduced	Local irritation, some drugs are not absorbed
	Applicable when patient is unable to take drug	

drug absorption, and not all drug formulas are equivalent with regard to the proportion of the active compound that reaches the blood.

When a drug is placed in the mouth and absorbed through the mucosa of the oral cavity, the route of administration is called sublingual (or buccal). This method of administration differs from oral administration principally because the hepatic first-pass effect (see below) is avoided. Other mucous membranes may be used for drug application, such as nasal or vaginal. Cocaine is frequently administered to nasal mucosa, and nicotine preparations exist for applying to the nasal or oral cavities. In psychiatry, this route of administration is not frequently used because even though bioavailability can be enhanced that way, the blood levels of the drug so achieved are highly variable. Nevertheless, in case an efficient peptide drug is discovered, this route of administration will be of choice until nonpeptide analogs will have been developed. Drug absorption

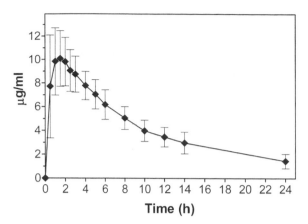

Figure A.6. Plasma levels (mean ± SEM) of a drug after administration of a single oral dose (500 mg) in 18 volunteers. On abscissa, time after administration. On ordinate, plasma levels of the drug. (Courtesy of Dr. Rein Pähkla, Department of Pharmacology, Tartu University.)

through mucous membranes is more efficient than through skin, but drug formulas exist for being applied to skin as well. These are intended for maintaining stable blood levels for extended periods of time (as in the case of nicotine patches to reduce tobacco cravings) and are not suitable for the rapid achievement of high drug levels in the site of action.

Some problems with oral administration can be avoided by administering the drug rectally. Certain drugs have better bioavailability when applied rectally, and this route of administration is suitable for vomiting or unconscious patients. Hepatic first-pass applies only to absorption from the superior rectal vein area. Many drugs, unfortunately, irritate the rectal mucosa, and absorption can be unpredictable.

Inhalation is a powerful route of drug administration. The rate of absorption is high in the lungs, and high levels in the brain can be achieved rapidly, which can be critical to the mode of action. In the arena of substance abuse, this is believed to serve as the basis of accelerated development of cocaine addiction among crack users. However, there is no evidence that such an enhancement of efficacy could be feasible for drugs used in clinical practice. Inhaled drugs must be in the form of gas or aerosol. Due to close contact between alveolar cell lining and blood vessels in the lungs, as well as extensive vascularization, absorption of drugs is prompt. Inhalation of such aerosols as are produced by burning substances (as occurs in tobacco or marijuana smoking) carries significant risks due to untoward effects of tars and other ingredients of smoke noxious to the sensitive tissue.

When a rapidly occurring effect of a precisely determined amount of a drug is important, injection can be selected. Drugs can be given subcutaneously or, more commonly nowadays, intramuscularly or intravenously. The latter option yields complete bioavailability and is the fastest. In Fig. A.7 one can see that half an hour after intravenous administration, drug levels in a peripheral tissue are already nearly

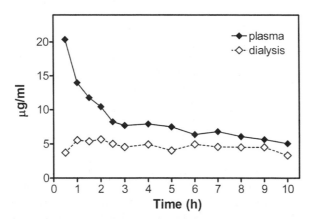

Figure A.7. Plasma levels (continuous line) of a drug after administration of a single intravenous dose (500 mg) in a volunteer. The dashed line indicates drug levels in tissue as measured with subcutaneously placed microdialysis probe. On abscissa, time after administration. On ordinate, plasma levels of the drug. (Courtesy of Dr. Rein Pähkla, Department of Pharmacology, Tartu University.)

maximal. Also note that even though the doses used orally (Fig. A.6) and intravenously (Fig. A.7) are equal, plasma levels achieved by intravenous administration are considerably higher. However, the faster a drug enters the bloodstream, the less one can do to reduce adverse effects, if these emerge. Administration by injection is also inconvenient to the patient, and bears the risks of disseminating viruses and bacteria that can cause serious infectious conditions such as acquired immunodeficiency syndrome (AIDS), hepatitis or bacterial endocarditis. On some occasions, intravenous administration is used because the drug is too irritating to muscle or subcutaneous tissue, but the possibility of injury of the veins must also be considered. Intraarterial administration is technically more demanding and its use is restricted to specific procedures.

Subcutaneous and intramuscular injection bypass the problems related to enteral routes. Nevertheless, in contrast to the intravenous route, absorption is an issue and its rate and efficiency depend on the drug. The magnitude of effect and time of onset may be favorable compared to oral administration when using these parenteral routes of administration, but the opposite may also be true (as in the case of benzodiazepines). Blood flow in the area of injection is a major factor in the rate of absorption, and the technique of injecting may contribute to variability.

Injections have been used extensively for administration of several psychiatric drugs, but because drug formulas for enteral use are more easy and safe to administer, and there is no clear evidence for any enhancement of efficacy by injecting the drug in long-term treatment, these parenteral routes of administration have been reserved for the necessity of fast action (e.g., to achieve an immediate calming effect by an intramuscular dose of lorazepam), or for giving the depot preparations of antipsychotics.

Distribution

Absorbed drugs are distributed throughout bodily tissues. Most of even the psychoactive drugs will linger in areas other than the brain, and this contributes to unwanted side effects. Nevertheless, the total amount of the drug absorbed determines the size and the duration of its effects because there is a balance between drug concentrations in the brain, blood, and other tissues. Factors influencing distribution, that is, how much of the absorbed drug is taken up by a particular organ or tissue, and how fast the drug gets there, depend upon the chemical characteristics of the drug, vascularization of the tissue, and the existence of specific barriers.

An important factor to consider is the degree to which unspecific binding to blood plasma proteins occurs. Many drug molecules bind to blood-borne proteins such as albumin, and an equilibrium develops between bound and free fractions of the drug in the blood. Protein-bound drug cannot leave the blood vessels and thus is neither eliciting any action nor being cleared from the body. Protein-bound drug thus constitutes a reservoir from which the drug is released dependent upon the speed with which the free drug leaves the bloodstream by entering into tissues. Some psychoactive drugs have very high proportions of the bound fraction. For example, approximately 19 out of 20 molecules of diazepam in the blood are bound to plasma proteins at a given time.

Drugs must pass cell membranes in order to be absorbed or to enter tissues. Cell membranes consist of complex lipid molecules, called phospholipids, that form a bilayer with their hydrophilic parts forming the surfaces of the membrane. This phospholipid bilayer contains protein molecules of varying size. Some of these form channels, others can act as transporters through the cell membrane. Because of the lipid nature of cell membranes, drugs that are well soluble in lipids penetrate these membranes easily by simple diffusion and distribute in accordance with the concentration gradient, that is, toward tissues and body parts where the concentration of the drug is lower.

Blood-Brain Barrier

In most tissues, blood capillaries have pores in their walls that consist of a single layer of cells large enough to permit the passage of most drug molecules not bound to plasma proteins. Because of these pores, the entry of drugs into tissue extracellular fluid is not influenced by the lipid solubility of the drug, but rather by the rate of blood flow through the given tissue. This situation is different in the brain, where the capillary walls contain no pores and are further surrounded by the basement membrane, a type of extracellular matrix, and sheaths formed by the processes of astrocytes, star-shaped glia cells. Thus, access to the neurons is strongly associated with lipid solubility of the drug, and therefore psychoactive drugs must be lipid soluble.

Placental "Barrier"

The fetus of a pregnant woman receives biologically important substances, including nutrients, and excretes metabolic waste products through the placenta. Substances can move from maternal blood to fetal blood and vice versa by passing cell membranes. This places restrictions on the distribution of some chemicals, but in general the permeability of this "barrier" is determined by lipid solubility of the drug. Placental permeability to drugs is lower than in the liver or kidney but approximately equal to muscle tissue. Therefore psychoactive drugs, both clinically used and recreational, readily cross the placenta, and many of them are known to affect fetal growth and development. It is also well recognized that drugs capable of producing physical dependence in their users, such as opiates, induce symptoms of drug withdrawal in infants born to addicted mothers. Effects of many psychoactive substances on the fetus have not been studied to a sufficient degree, and the decision to use a drug during pregnancy must be made after careful weighing the possible benefits to the mother and risks to the fetus.

Structural abnormalities can be induced by drugs during the critical periods of fetal development. The most exemplary case of such an effect, called teratogenesis, is the drug catastrophy associated with the use of thalidomide. Thalidomide was marketed and used as a tranquillizer in the early 1960s. It was discovered too late that this drug, when consumed during the fifth through seventh weeks of pregnancy, greatly enhances the risk for abnormal limb growth in the fetus. The thalidomide case was, in fact, pivotal in the implementation of major safety measures in drug development that are currently in effect.

Later in pregnancy, drugs cannot elicit major structural abnormalities but can still have a negative impact, for example, by inducing fetal hypoxia. Because psychoactive drugs readily cross the placenta, it is not appropriate to speak of a placental barrier when focusing on psychopharmacology.

Drug Redistribution

Even though the termination of drug action is mainly accomplished by the processes of drug elimination that will be discussed below, temporal changes in the direction of distribution may contribute to the reduction of a drug's action. For example, highly lipid-soluble barbiturates such as thiopental rapidly cause anaesthesia after intravenous administration because the brain is also receiving a good supply of blood. Subsequently, thiopental enters other lipid-rich tissues that are poorly vascularized and perfused such as subcutaneus fat. The reduction of thiopental blood levels will favor the passage of the drug from the brain back to the blood. Thus the action of a single dose of thiopental is short-lasting.

Drug Elimination: Metabolism/Biotransformation and Excretion

Some effects of psychoactive drugs persist longer than the molecules that brought them about—such as the long-term effects of hallucinogens. Obviously, changes elicited in normal neurochemical balances can continue without the immediate influence of a drug. Nevertheless, as a rule, drugs cease to cause their specific physiological effects when they are structurally altered so that this renders them inactive or when they have been excreted from the body. Together these processes are called elimination, and the main elimination pathway for many drugs is their metabolic biotransformation in the liver and renal excretion of the water-soluble metabolites so produced. Nevertheless, there are exceptions to this rule. For example, active metabolites are sometimes formed in the liver.

The liver is mainly responsible for transforming biologically active molecules into harmless substances. Biotransformation is exerted through a host of chemical reactions catalyzed by enzyme systems in the liver cells, which are specialized for the efficient modification of substances belonging to various classes of chemicals. Thus an important concept in pharmacokinetics is the hepatic first-pass. When the major portion of a drug dose passes through the liver without first being distributed throughout the body, much of it can be metabolized before ever having the chance to reach its site of action. This occurs when the drug is administered orally, because drugs absorbed from the small intestine enter the hepatic portal circulation, and the inactivation of some drugs is of such proportion that an alternative route of administration is required.

Certain drugs have active metabolites. For example, oxazepam is itself an active metabolite of diazepam, and thus has a shorter duration of action. The possibility of active metabolites should always be considered with new drugs in the experimental phase.

Drugs and their metabolites can leave the body through the kidneys in urine, by exhalation via the lungs, excretion in bile into the intestine, or in sweat or saliva. For psychoactive drugs, the first route is the one to consider. In addition, one should acknowledge that in breastfeeding women, psychoactive drugs are present in milk, and this can have an deleterious effect on the infant.

Three processes that occur in the kidneys are important for drug excretion. The first of these is glomerular filtration, which refers to the formation of ultrafiltrate of blood plasma in the kidney subunits. This primary urine is free of plasma proteins, and thus protein-bound drugs remain in the blood. Most of this fluid and its ingredients are reabsorbed. Thus, reabsorption is the second important step. As in other diffusion processes involving cell membranes, substances that are lipid soluble can pass these semipermeable barriers easily. Psychoactive drugs, as emphasized above, are lipid soluble, and thus prone to be reabsorbed. The biotransforming action of the liver, which leads to the formation of more water-soluble molecules, is thus important for the excretion of these substances. The third process in urine formation, active excretion of certain substances, has less significance in psychopharmacology.

Drug Half-Life

Figures A.6 to A.8 demonstrate how drug levels in plasma go down after administration of a single dose. An important indicator of the duration of a drug's effects is the time required for its concentration in blood to decline by half. This is frequently a constant interval independent of the actual concentration at a given moment. Immediately after absorption, plasma levels of a drug decline faster because the drug is distributed into tissues. Thereafter elimination processes are responsible for the slower reduction

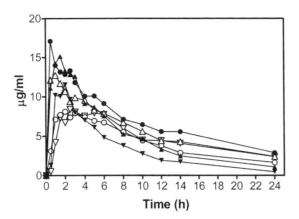

Figure A.8. Plasma levels of a drug after administration of a single oral dose (500 mg) in six volunteers. On abscissa, time after administration. On ordinate, plasma levels of the drug. (Courtesy of Dr. Rein Pähkla, Department of Pharmacology, Tartu University.)

in plasma levels. Because we need to be able to predict how long a drug effect will last and when the organism will be free of the substance, elimination half-life is one of the most important variables in pharmacology.

If a drug has short elimination half-life, it must be taken several times per day, which diminishes the apparent ease of oral administration and reduces patient compliance. Such drugs may be formulated into sustained- or slow-release tablets or capsules (e.g., venlafaxine or bupropion).

Accumulation and Steady-State Concentration

Sometimes drugs are taken just once, for example, to relieve anxiety caused by an exasperating event. Often it is necessary, however, to have the drug present in the brain for prolonged periods of time. It is usually assumed beneficial to maintain steady concentrations, and the drug administration regime must support this aim. The drug must be administered repeatedly according to a schedule. In the beginning of repeated administration, drug levels will increase with each dose taken because it is normally important to take a new dose before the concentration in the blood has fallen to zero. Thus the drug accumulates in the body. The aim is to achieve a persistent, or steady-state, concentration in the blood (and at the site of action) with only limited fluctuations. Drug half-life is again an important measure. For example, if the second dose of a drug is given when one half-life of the drug has passed, the concentration of the drug will increase to 150 percent of what was observed after the first dose. Continuing the same treatment schedule would, however, cause a further increase, which becomes ever slower until the steady state (in our example, 200 percent of the initial peak level) is achieved. Knowing the drug half-life, it is possible to design a treatment schedule with minimal fluctuations in plasma levels.

Variability and Therapeutic Drug Monitoring

It is important to note that the many variables involved in a drug's effectivity create an enormous potential for interindividual variability in their clinical potency. For example, drug half-life may be a constant in a given individual in a given situation, but absorption and elimination rates vary to a great extent between individuals. Absorption was illustrated in Fig. A.6, presenting the mean values in a group of 18 volunteers. In Fig. A.8, data are presented from a few selected individuals in the same experiment. Note the variability in peak plasma levels, in the time when this peak level occurs, and in plasma levels several hours after administration of the drug. To give another example, benzodiazepines such as diazepam may have unexpectedly large and long-lasting sedative effects in the elderly because the drug's half-life can extend to days due to remarkably reduced biotransformation in some individuals. It is easy to understand that repeated dosing under such circumstances leads to accumulation of the drug that can exceed safe levels. On the other hand, drug levels should not drop below the minimum necessary for a therapeutic effect. Since it is important to maintain adequate drug levels despite the problems created by interindividual variability, plasma levels of the drug are sometimes monitored in therapeutic settings. The major presumption in therapeutic drug monitoring is that plasma levels correlate reasonably well with potency, which, fortunately, is often the case. The variation in drug sensitivity within a population is largely genetic in origin, and a new science of pharmacogenetics has recently emerged to address the many questions that arise in this area.

DRUG INTERACTIONS, TOLERANCE, AND DEPENDENCE

Drug Interactions

It should be evident from the preceding discussions of processes studied in pharmacokinetics and pharmacodynamics that vast potential exists for one drug to affect the action of another, if they are both in the body at the same time. Drugs can alter absorption, distribution, biotransformation and excretion of other drugs. Furthermore, antagonistic, additive, and synergistic interactions can occur on the level of molecular targets of the drugs, or because of functional interactions in affected physiological systems. Interactions occur not only between prescribed psychoactive drugs but also with such socially accepted drugs as alcohol, nicotine, and caffeine, not to speak of illicit psychoactive drugs. Many drug interactions go unnoticed because of their minor significance to well-being and the inability of the subject to ascribe the symptoms to drug interaction. Others are potentially life-threatening, such as the additive effect of central nervous system (CNS) depressants, such as alcohol and benzodiazepine anxiolytics.

An additive effect refers to a simple summation of the effects of two drugs. A synergistic effect is greater than would have been predicted from the effects of the drugs in isolation. One classic example is the infamous "cheese effect": When both monoamine oxidase (MAO) isoenzymes are inhibited (as is the case with first-generation MAO inhibitors), release of noradrenaline elicited by the amino acid tyramine can lead to a fatal increase in blood pressure. (The amino acid was named after *tyros*, the Greek word for cheese, because this foodstuff is rich in it. Eating cheese and certain other foods while taking first-generation MAO inhibitors can therefore elicit headache, hypertensive crisis, and stroke. Thus this example serves also to emphasize that interactions can occur between medicines and food.) Pharmacological antagonism as a competition at the receptor sites was discussed above. In practice, physiological antagonism is much more common: A drug reduces other drug's effect because of opposing actions arising at distinct sites.

Tolerance

When a given drug dose fails to elicit an effect of the expected magnitude after repeated administration, tolerance toward the drug has developed. Tolerance may be physiological or behavioral. There are several potential mechanisms for physiological changes that reduce the potency of a drug. With repeated administration many psychoactive drugs can increase the efficacy of the hepatic enzyme systems that metabolize them. This process, called enzyme induction, can increase the speed of elimination of these drugs. Barbiturates serve as a classic example of this type of tolerance induction.

To overcome tolerance, the dose must be increased or drug administration must be stopped for a period of time. Doctors working with opiate addicts say that occasionally their patients volunteer for treatment not in order to become completely free from their habit, but to reduce the tolerance and the amount of drug they need because the financial burden has become unbearable. Other pharmacokinetic mechanisms for tolerance development include a reduction in absorption of the drug and an increase in the number of drug acceptor sites that bind the physiologically active molecules. From the side of pharmacodynamic mechanisms, tolerance may develop because of a down-regulation of the number of receptors, decrease in efficiency of the intracellular signal transduction, or recruitment of functionally antagonistic physiological mechanisms, which can be a fairly complex phenomenon.

Cross tolerance refers to the fact that tolerance induced by a drug may generalize to the efficacy of other, related drugs. For example, opiates elicit cross tolerance. Cross tolerance can also occur because of the enzyme induction in the liver since the relatively low specificity of the hepatic enzyme systems means that an increase in the catalytic activity or in the expression of a given enzyme caused by a drug will enhance the biotransformation of several drugs that are inactivated via similar chemical reactions. When tolerance develops rapidly—as when a single dose severely weakens any forthcoming drug responses—it is called tachyphylaxia. Tachyphylaxia occurs with such drugs that deplete the endogenous resources recruited in their mechanisms of action, for example, causing an extensive release of a neurotransmitter.

In psychopharmacology, behavioral tolerance plays a role, but remains difficult to explain in physiological terms. It is manifested as a reduction of the potency of the drug in familiar circumstances and can include volitional control that the subject has learned to exert over behavior. For example, a subject may acquire a degree of control over the inebriant effects of alcohol or cannabis, creating the impression of being in a sober state.

Drug Dependence

Drug dependence can be physical or psychological. The latter refers to addiction to a specific class of drugs. The former is more common and reflects the situation in which the exogenous compound has become a part of the homeostasis of the organism. The hallmark of physical dependence is the appearance of a withdrawal reaction some time after the repeatedly administered drug has been withheld. Symptoms of drug withdrawal can be fairly unspecific, but readministering the drug promptly terminates their presence. Antagonists of the target receptors of the drug do not offer relief but rather can be used to precipitate a withdrawal reaction.

Note on the Placebo Effect

Psychopharmacological studies also observe effects of treatments that cannot be characterized by the rules of pharmacodynamics and pharmacokinetics. Studies of drug efficacy typically include placebo groups, and these reveal that a remarkable proportion of subjects experience desirable changes and "side effects" when given a placebo, the biologically inactive substitute for the drug. The very existence of the placebo effect and its high prevalence even in serious persistent disorders such as depression reminds us that manipulations of brain chemistry by means of drugs are subject to interactions with other environmental and intrinsic factors that channel their effects through the same neural circuits in the brain.

FOR FURTHER READING

Benet LZ, Kroetz DL, Sheiner LB (1996). Pharmacokinetics: The dynamics of drug absorption, distribution, and elimination. In Hardman JG, Limbird LE, Molinoff PB, Ruddon RW, Gilman AG (eds). *Goodman & Gilman's The Pharmacological Basis of Therapeutics*, 9th ed. McGraw-Hill: New York, pp. 3–27.

DeVane CL (1998). Principles of pharmacokinetics and pharmacodynamics. In Schatzberg AF, Nemeroff CB (eds). *Textbook of Psychopharmacology*, 2nd ed. American Psychiatric Press: Washington, DC, pp. 155–169.

Feldman RS, Meyer JS, Quenzer LF (1997). *Principles of Neuropsychopharmacology*. Sinauer Associates: Sunderland, pp. 1–25.

Julien RM (1995). *A Primer of Drug Action*, 7th ed. WH Freeman: New York, pp. 6–51.

Kostyniak PJ (1995). Pharmacokinetics. In Smith CM, Reynard AM (eds). *Essentials of Pharmacology*. WB Saunders: Philadelphia, pp. 37–45.

Page CP, Curtis MJ, Sutter MC, Walker MJA, Hoffman BB (1997). *Integrated Pharmacology*. Mosby: London, pp. 17–90.

Rang HP, Dale MM, Ritter JM (1999). *Pharmacology*, 4th ed. Churchill Livingstone: New York, pp. 3–97 and 785–816.

Ross EM (1996). Pharmacodynamics: Mechanisms of drug action and the relationship between drug concentration and effect. In Hardman JG, Limbird LE, Molinoff PB, Ruddon RW, Gilman AG (eds). *Goodman & Gilman's The Pharmacological Basis of Therapeutics*, 9th ed. McGraw-Hill: New York, pp. 29–41.

Roth JA (1995). Drug metabolism. In Smith CM, Reynard AM (eds). *Essentials of Pharmacology*. WB Saunders: Philadelphia, pp. 25–36.

Salzman C, Satlin A, Burrows AB (1998). Geriatric psychopharmacology. In Schatzberg AF, Nemeroff CB (eds). *Textbook of Psychopharmacology*, 2nd ed. American Psychiatric Press: Washington, DC, pp. 961–977.

Stowe ZN, Strader JR, Nemeroff CB (1998). Psychopharmacology during pregnancy and lactation. In Schatzberg AF, Nemeroff CB (eds). *Textbook of Psychopharmacology*, 2nd ed. American Psychiatric Press: Washington, DC, pp. 979–996.

Winter JC (1995). Introduction to pharmacology: Receptors; dose-effect relationships, interactions, and therapeutic index; drug absorption, and termination of action. In Smith CM, Reynard AM (eds). *Essentials of Pharmacology*. WB Saunders: Philadelphia, pp. 1–17.

Winter JC (1995). Routes of administration. In Smith CM, Reynard AM (eds). *Essentials of Pharmacology*. WB Saunders: Philadelphia, pp. 18–21.

INDEX

Textbook of Biological Psychiatry, Edited by Jaak Panksepp
ISBN 0-471-43478-7   Copyright © 2004 John Wiley & Sons, Inc.

683